MW00629541

Captive Seawater Fishes

Captive Seawater Fishes
Science and Technology

STEPHEN SPOTTE
Sea Research Foundation and Marine Sciences Institute
The University of Connecticut
Noank, Connecticut

A WILEY-INTERSCIENCE PUBLICATION
John Wiley & Sons, Inc.
NEW YORK / CHICHESTER / BRISBANE / TORONTO / SINGAPORE

Library of Congress Cataloging in Publication Data:

Spotte, Stephen
Captive seawater fishes : science and technology / Stephen Spotte.
p. cm.

"A Wiley-Interscience publication."
Includes bibliographical references and index.
ISBN 0-471-54554-6
1. Marine aquariums, Public. 2. Marine aquarium fishes.
I. Title.
QL78.5.S66 1991
639.3'42—dc20 91-19348
CIP

ISBN 0-471-54554-6

Printed in the United States of America

10 9 8 7 6 5 4 3 2 1

To my parents
Helen H. and Adler E. Spotte

Preface

The setting is a modern public aquarium, although in some situations an aquaculture facility might be a suitable substitute. The protagonists are captive seawater fishes. We marvel at their staggering diversity and sympathize as they battle the dark forces of poor water quality, inadequate nutrition, and disease. A tortuous plot requires the reader to cross deep gorges choked with the wild, forbidding waters of science and technology. Anyone expecting a handy reference volume faces disappointment: this book is organized to be read, not consulted. Captive fishes demand an intellectual tithe from those who curate them.

Technical books take many forms, but those that are truly original radiate both a purpose and a point of view. The ideas presented are alive and vibrant, suspended in a force field between the poles of imagination and scholarship. The writing is clear and bold and without fear of solecisms. Authors who opt for originality risk criticism from conservative peers, but such risks are worthwhile when the alternative is a featureless landscape unmarred by curiosity.

My purpose was to write an original book, one of depth and richness. As to point of view, I believe strongly that curatorial practices should be based on understanding the biological requirements of captive fishes, not on the application of technology. In qualitative terms it matters little whether the container is an aquarium exhibit or an aquaculture raceway. The approach to solving problems requires a common gestalt.

I decided against peppering the text with literature citations and technical digressions in an effort to keep the primary information unencumbered. Supporting material—often expanded discussions of important text statements—has been relegated to a separate section, but linked with the text by numerical superscripts. Vladimir Nabokov's novel *Pale Fire* is arranged similarly. Nabokov's recommended solution to the annoyance of constant page-turning was to buy an extra copy of his book and cut it apart.

Science alone has little practical application, and works dealing strictly with technology omit information necessary to foster understanding. Aspects of both science and technology have therefore been included. Discussions of controversial topics are balanced and occasionally placed in historical context.

The first outline called for a modest account of captive seawater environments. As the years passed (eight years to be exact), other subjects were added. It became clear that to understand how captive fishes adapt would require a renaissance approach, and I eventually wrote chapters on physiology, sensory perception, behavior, space, nutrition, and health. The results sometimes depart radically from standard treatments of these subjects offered elsewhere.

The literature grew vast and intimidating as the focus broadened. I read everything I could find and tried to understand it all, no doubt a losing proposition. Only fools wade knowingly into the restless flood of science. Those who argue that one person cannot cover every subject adequately forget that the same applies to single subjects. The author's objective should be the acquisition of knowledge, not perfection, and the fun is lost in not attempting the impossible. As Albert Szent-Györgyi said, "It is much more exciting not to catch a big fish than not to catch a little fish."

The writing of a complex book is an odyssey through uncharted terrain. It is, in a real sense, a rite of passage, requiring the continuous lifting of horizons as new knowledge is gained and wisdom emerges. In tracking the protean changes of my own thinking through the final draft I was startled to see how much of the early writing remained. It seems to have aged gracefully with the newer material like a blend of old and new wines. I left it alone. The work you are about to read is iconoclastic in places and eclectic overall, but no matter; science thrives on skepticism. The tale of my journey is about to unfold, and the experience has been exhilarating. I hope you feel it too.

STEPHEN SPOTTE

Noank, Connecticut
August 1991

Acknowledgments

The following people read parts of the manuscript and offered many valuable criticisms and suggestions: Gary Adams, Thames Valley State Technical College and Sea Research Foundation; James W. Atz, American Museum of Natural History; Patricia M. Bubucis, Sea Research Foundation; Lee C. Eagleton, Pennsylvania State University; David H. Evans, University of Florida; Joseph S. Levine, formerly of Boston College; Robin M. Overstreet, Gulf Coast Research Laboratory; and C. Lavett Smith, American Museum of Natural History. Colleagues around the world graciously offered the use of illustrative and tabular material. In this regard, I particularly thank George C. Blasiola, Wardley Corporation; Paul J. Cheung, New York Aquarium and Osborn Laboratories of Marine Science; Barbara Ann Collins, Marine Biological Laboratory; Roy R. Manstan, Naval Underwater Systems Center; and Richard E. Wolke, University of Rhode Island. Joseph T. O'Neill prepared the graphics, and Anne Barrière typed the manuscript. Pauline Goyette helped check references and wrote to authors and publishers for permission to reproduce copyrighted material. As always, the library staff of the Marine Biological Laboratory (Woods Hole) honored my requests for obscure references in good humor.

S. S.

Contents

CHAPTER 1 CHEMICAL PROCESSES / 1

Science / 1

Solutes and Solutions / 1

MATTER / 1
WATER AS A SOLVENT / 2
SOLUBILITY / 2
SEAWATER / 2

Measurement of Seawater Solutes / 6

SALINITY / 6
DENSITY / 7
SPECIFIC GRAVITY / 7

pH and Alkalinity / 9

pH / 9
ALKALINITY / 10
FACTORS THAT AFFECT ALKALINITY / 11
PROCESSES THAT AFFECT ALKALINITY / 12
CARBONATE ROCKS AND MATERIALS / 13
CARBONATE MINERALS IN THE OCEANS / 14
CARBONATE MINERALS IN AQUARIUMS / 19

Technology / 24

Method 1.1 Thermometer Calibration / 24

Method 1.2 Specific Gravity and Salinity Determinations / 26

SPECIFIC GRAVITY / 26
SALINITY / 31
PRACTICAL APPLICATIONS / 33

Method 1.3 pH Determination / 35

STANDARDIZATION AND CALIBRATION OF pH METERS / 36
RULES OF CALIBRATION / 38

Method 1.4 Alkalinity Determination / 41

HIGH PRECISION METHOD / 41
LOW PRECISION METHOD / 43

Method 1.5 Preparation of New Carbonate Mineral Filtrants / 44
Method 1.6 Maintenance of pH / 45
Method 1.7 Artificial Seawater—GP2 Maintenance Solution / 46
GP2 MAINTENANCE SOLUTION / 47
MIXING GP2 MAINTENANCE SOLUTION / 48
ADDING BRINE / 51
SPECIFIC GRAVITY—BRINE / 52

CHAPTER 2 BIOLOGICAL PROCESSES / 53

Science / 55
Mineralization / 55
PHOSPHORUS / 56
CARBON / 58
NITROGEN / 62
Nitrification / 64
Efficiency of Bacteriological Filters / 67
SURFACE AREA / 67
TOXIC SUBSTANCES / 69
DISSOLVED OXYGEN, TEMPERATURE, pH, SALINITY / 72
Dissimilation / 74
CARBON SOURCE / 75
DISSOLVED OXYGEN / 77
TEMPERATURE AND pH / 78
Assimilation / 78

Technology / 79
Method 2.1 Conditioning Bacteriological Filters / 79
Method 2.2 Carrying Capacity / 83
HIRAYAMA'S METHOD / 84
HALF-DEPTH METHOD / 86
Method 2.3 Design of Filter Beds / 91
Method 2.4 Maintenance of Bacteriological Filters / 94
Method 2.5 Design of Denitrification Systems / 94
COLUMAR DENTRIFICATION METHOD / 94
ANOXIC SEDIMENT METHOD / 95
Method 2.6 Design and Maintenance of Seaweed Filters / 97
Method 2.7 Reduction of Dissolved Organic Carbon with Granular Activated Carbon / 99
ADSORPTION / 100
ACTIVATED CARBON / 100
ADSORPTION EFFICIENCY / 102

GAC CONTACTORS / 105
DISPOSAL VERSUS REACTIVATION / 107

Method 2.8 Orthophosphate Determination (as total PO_4-P) / 108

Method 2.9 Total Ammonia Nitrogen (total NH_4-N) Determination / 110

INDOPHENOL BLUE METHOD / 110
SPECIFIC ION ELECTRODE METHOD / 115

Method 2.10 Estimation of the Allowable Upper Limit of Total NH_4-N / 117

Method 2.11 Nitrite Nitrogen (NO_2-N) Determination / 122

Method 2.12 Nitrate Nitrogen (NO_3-N) Determination—Low Concentrations / 128

Method 2.13 Nitrate Nitrogen (NO_3-N) Determination—High Concentrations / 133

CHAPTER 3 PHYSICAL PROCESSES / 136

Science / 137

Particle Separation / 137

GRANULAR MEDIA FILTERS / 137
CAPTURE MECHANISMS / 140
FILTRATION MODE VARIABLES / 142
BACKWASH MODE VARIABLES / 144

Seawater Supplies / 147

SURFACE SUPPLIES / 147
SUBSURFACE FILTRATION / 147
COARSE SAND FILTRATION / 147

Gas Supersaturation / 148

BASIS OF GAS SUPERSATURATION / 149
CAUSES OF GAS SUPERSATURATION / 151

Gas Transfer, Aeration, Circulation / 153

GAS TRANSFER / 153
AERATION / 154
CIRCULATION / 157

Foam Fractionation / 163

MECHANISMS / 164
LIMITING FACTORS / 164

Temperature Control / 168

Technology / 169

Method 3.1 Concrete Tanks / 169

Method 3.2 Preparation of Concrete Surfaces for Painting / 170

Method 3.3 Steel Filter Vessels / 171
Method 3.4 Process Design for High Rate Filters / 174
FILTRANT SELECTION AND DEPTH / 175
UNDERDRAINS AND SUPPORT MEDIA / 177
BACKWASH DESIGN FACTORS / 179
Method 3.5 Removal of Supersaturated Gases / 185
PACKED COLUMN DEGASSING / 185
TURBULENT FLOW DEGASSING / 185
VACUUM DEGASSING / 187
Method 3.6 Flow Rate Calculations for Airlift Pumps / 188
Method 3.7 Design and Operation of Foam Fractionators / 192
Method 3.8 Calculation of Cooling and Heating Requirements / 195
COOLING / 196
HEATING / 198
Method 3.9 Cleaning Old Painted Surfaces / 200

CHAPTER 4 PHYSIOLOGY / 201

The Gill / 201
Osmotic and Ionic Regulation / 203
PASSIVE AND ACTIVE TRANSPORT / 203
WATER AND ION BALANCE / 205
REGULATION OF ION FLUX / 206
FUNCTIONAL BENEFITS / 209
Respiration and Acid–Base Regulation / 210
GASES / 210
WATER AND BLOOD FLOW / 211
GAS MOVEMENTS ACROSS SECONDARY LAMELLAE / 212
MAINTENANCE OF NORMAL ACID–BASE BALANCE / 213
REGULATORY MECHANISMS / 214
EFFECTS OF ENVIRONMENTAL TEMPERATURE CHANGES / 214
EFFECTS OF ENVIRONMENTAL HYPERCAPNIA / 217
EFFECTS OF ENVIRONMENTAL HYPEROXIA / 218
EFFECTS OF ENVIRONMENTAL HYPOXIA / 221
Stress / 224
THE STRESS RESPONSE / 225
EXERCISE STRESS / 227
HANDLING STRESS / 228
ENVIRONMENTAL STRESS FACTORS / 229

CHAPTER 5 SENSORY PERCEPTION / 232

Science / 232

Vision / 232

THE EYE / 232
VISUAL ACUITY / 236

The Photic Environment / 242

PREDATION—THE "QUIET PERIOD" / 242
PREDATION AND LOW-LIGHT PHOTIC ENVIRONMENTS / 242

Coloration / 246

CHROMATIC FISHES / 246
SILVERY FISHES / 248
DIEL CHANGES IN COLORATION AND PATTERN / 250
CRYPTIC COLORATION / 253

Hearing / 256

SOUND / 256
NEAR-FIELD AND FAR-FIELD EFFECTS / 258
MECHANORECEPTION / 261
THE LABYRINTH / 263
SOUND PRODUCTION / 267
LOCALIZATION OF FAR-FIELD SOUND / 268

Electroreception / 269

Technology / 272

Method 5.1 Reduction of Predation—Photic Considerations / 272

CHAPTER 6 BEHAVIOR / 274

Science / 275

Fish Assemblages / 275

SHOALS, SCHOOLS, MILLS / 275
MECHANISMS OF COHESION / 276
EXTRANEOUS FACTORS / 278
SURVIVAL VALUE / 282

Dominance / 285

TYPES OF DOMINANCE / 287
TERRITORIAL DOMINANCE / 289
FITNESS AND TERRITORIAL DOMINANCE / 290
FOOD SUPPLIES AND TERRITORIAL DOMINANCE / 291
REPRODUCTION AND TERRITORIAL DOMINANCE / 293
"OPTIMAL" TERRITORY SIZE / 295
FITNESS AND INDIVIDUAL DOMINANCE / 298

Symbiosis / 303

PROTECTIVE ASSOCIATIONS / 304
REFUGE ASSOCIATIONS / 306
CLEANING ASSOCIATIONS / 309
FEEDING ASSOCIATIONS / 312

Technology / 312

Method 6.1 Exhibition of Schooling Fishes / 312

RECTANGULAR AQUARIUMS / 314
CYLINDRICAL AND CIRCULAR VERSUS FIGURE-EIGHT DESIGNS / 314

Method 6.2 Burrowing and Mound-Building Fishes / 315

CHAPTER 7 SPACE / 319

Science / 319

Resource Partitioning Models / 321

Coral Reefs / 323

DISTRIBUTION / 323
CLASSIFICATION / 326
VERTICAL ZONATION / 326
PATCH REEFS / 332

Biotopes and Habitats / 334

BIOTOPES / 334
HABITATS / 341

Technology / 351

Method 7.1 Shelter Space Allocation in Community Exhibits / 351

Method 7.2 Procedure for Adding a Known Mass of Fishes to an Aquarium Exhibit / 355

Method 7.3 Shelter Spaces for Fishes During Acclimation / 356

CHAPTER 8 NUTRITION / 357

Science / 358

Nutrients / 358

PROTEINS / 360
LIPIDS / 361
CARBOHYDRATES / 365

Vitamins / 366

Carotenoid Pigments / 366

Digestion Rate and Digestibility / 371

Energy / 371

PHYSIOLOGICAL FUEL VALUES / 372
METABOLISM / 372
PARTITIONING OF ENERGY / 372
ENERGY REQUIREMENTS / 373

Natural Foods / 374

LEAFY GREEN VEGETABLES / 374
FISH AND INVERTEBRATE FLESH / 375
FREEZE-DRIED FOODS / 375

Moist Feeds / 377

PROTEINS / 383
LIPIDS / 388
CARBOHYDRATES / 388
VITAMINS / 388
CAROTENOIDS / 388
BINDERS / 389
LEACHING / 390
STORAGE AND HANDLING / 391

Live Foods—Brine Shrimp / 391

FOOD VALUE / 393
FACTORS AFFECTING HATCH / 394

Live Foods—Rotifers / 397

REPRODUCTION / 397
FACTORS AFFECTING SURVIVAL AND REPRODUCTION / 398

Technology / 399

Method 8.1 Alginate- and Gelatin-Bound Moist Feeds / 399

Method 8.2 Hatch Procedures for Brine Shrimp Cysts / 406

GENERAL PROCEDURES / 406
HATCH VESSELS / 407

Method 8.3 Decapsulation of Brine Shrimp Cysts / 411

Method 8.4 Rearing Brine Shrimp on Dead Foods and Feeds / 413

Method 8.5 Rearing Brine Shrimp on Live Phytoplankton / 415

Method 8.6 Breeding Brine Shrimp / 417

Method 8.7 Rotifer Culture Procedures / 418

Method 8.8 Artificial Seawater—Culture Solutions / 421

GP2 CULTURE SOLUTION / 422
MIXING GP2 CULTURE SOLUTION / 423
MIXING GP2 LOW-SALINITY CULTURE SOLUTION / 428

Method 8.9 Phytoplankton Culture—The Culture Room / 430

Method 8.10 Preparation of Glassware and GP2 Culture Solution / 434
Method 8.11 Contamination Check / 436
SERIAL DILUTION / 437
ANTIBIOTIC TREATMENT / 438
Method 8.12 Inoculation and Incubation of Stock Cultures / 438
PRIMARY STOCK CULTURES / 438
SECONDARY STOCK CULTURES / 440
TERTIARY STOCK CULTURES / 441
CARBOY CULTURE / 442
Method 8.13 Enumeration / 443
SAMPLE COLLECTION AND FIXATION / 443
COUNTING / 443
LOADING THE COUNTING CHAMBER / 443

CHAPTER 9 HEALTH / 446

Science / 446
Infection and Disease / 446
Resistance to Disease / 447
PHYSICAL BARRIERS / 447
NATURAL RESISTANCE / 448
IMMUNITY / 449
VIRULENCE / 451
Clinical Signs and Pathological Effects / 452
INFLAMMATION / 452
CELLULAR DEGENERATION / 453
ABNORMAL CELL GROWTH / 453
Predisposition to Disease / 454
FASTING / 454
INJURY / 455
CROWDING / 456
HANDLING / 456
ENVIRONMENTAL QUALITY / 456
Transmission of Parasites / 456
EPIZOOTIOLOGY / 456
EPIZOOTIC AND ENZOOTIC DISEASES / 457
MODES OF TRANSMISSION / 457
Chemotherapy, Sterilization, Disinfection / 457
Chemotherapeutic Agents / 458
SELECTIVITY AND SENSITIVITY / 458
METHODS OF APPLICATION / 459
LIMITATIONS OF IMMERSION TREATMENTS / 459
FORMULATED PRODUCTS / 461

Sterilizing Agents / 461
UV RADIATION / 461
OZONE / 466
Disinfectants and Antiseptics / 467
OZONE-PRODUCED OXIDANTS / 468
COPPER / 469

Technology / 471
Quarantine / 473
Lymphocystis Disease / 474
SYNONYMS / 474
ETIOLOGY / 474
EPIZOOTIOLOGY / 474
CLINICAL SIGNS AND PATHOLOGICAL EFFECTS / 475
PROPHYLAXIS AND TREATMENT / 475
Mycobacteriosis / 476
SYNONYMS / 476
ETIOLOGY / 476
EPIZOOTIOLOGY / 476
CLINICAL SIGNS AND PATHOLOGICAL EFFECTS / 477
PROPHYLAXIS AND TREATMENT / 478
ZOONOSIS / 478
Vibriosis / 479
SYNONYMS / 479
ETIOLOGY / 479
EPIZOOTIOLOGY / 480
CLINICAL SIGNS AND PATHOLOGICAL EFFECTS / 480
PROPHYLAXIS AND TREATMENT / 482
ZOONOSIS / 484
Fin Rot / 486
SYNONYMS / 486
ETIOLOGY / 486
EPIZOOTIOLOGY / 486
CLINICAL SIGNS AND PATHOLOGICAL EFFECTS / 487
PROPHYLAXIS AND TREATMENT / 488
Amyloodinium Disease / 488
SYNONYMS / 488
ETIOLOGY / 488
EPIZOOTIOLOGY / 489
CLINICAL SIGNS AND PATHOLOGICAL EFFECTS / 491
PROPHYLAXIS AND TREATMENT / 491
Cryptocaryoniasis / 492
SYNONYMS / 492
ETIOLOGY / 493
EPIZOOTIOLOGY / 493
CLINICAL SIGNS AND PATHOLOGICAL EFFECTS / 495
PROPHYLAXIS AND TREATMENT / 496

Uronema Disease / 496
SYNONYMS / 496
ETIOLOGY / 496
EPIZOOTIOLOGY / 497
CLINICAL SIGNS AND PATHOLOGICAL EFFECTS / 497
PROPHYLAXIS AND TREATMENT / 498
Ichthyophonus Disease / 498
SYNONYMS / 498
ETIOLOGY / 500
EPIZOOTIOLOGY / 500
CLINICAL SIGNS AND PATHOLOGICAL EFFECTS / 503
PROPHYLAXIS AND TREATMENT / 504
Exophiala Disease / 505
SYNONYMS / 505
ETIOLOGY / 505
EPIZOOTIOLOGY / 505
CLINICAL SIGNS AND PATHOLOGICAL EFFECTS / 505
PROPHYLAXIS AND TREATMENT / 505
Tang Turbellarian Disease / 505
SYNONYMS / 505
ETIOLOGY / 505
EPIZOOTIOLOGY / 507
CLINICAL SIGNS AND PATHOLOGICAL EFFECTS / 508
PROPHYLAXIS AND TREATMENT / 508
Monogenetic Trematode Infestations / 509
SYNONYMS / 509
ETIOLOGY / 509
EPIZOOTIOLOGY / 509
CLINICAL SIGNS AND PATHOLOGICAL EFFECTS / 511
PROPHYLAXIS AND TREATMENT / 512
Crustacean Infestations / 512
SYNONYMS / 512
ETIOLOGY / 512
EPIZOOTIOLOGY / 512
CLINICAL SIGNS AND PATHOLOGICAL EFFECTS / 514
PROPHYLAXIS AND TREATMENT / 514
Gas-Bubble Trauma / 515
SYNONYMS / 515
ETIOLOGY / 515
EPIZOOTIOLOGY / 515
CLINICAL SIGNS AND PATHOLOGICAL EFFECTS / 515
PROPHYLAXIS AND TREATMENT / 516
Goiter Disease / 516
SYNONYMS / 516
ETIOLOGY / 516

EPIZOOTIOLOGY / 517
CLINICAL SIGNS AND PATHOLOGICAL EFFECTS / 518
PROPHYLAXIS AND TREATMENT / 518
Treatment Abstracts / 519
BACTERIA / 520
MONOGENETIC TREMATODES / 524

CHAPTER 10 EXHIBITION / 528

Science / 528
Light / 528
COLOR / 530
LIGHT ABOVE THE OCEAN / 532
SUBMARINE LIGHT / 532
Artificial Illumination / 536
THE NATURE OF ARTIFICIAL ILLUMINATION / 537
LAMPS / 538
INCANDESCENT LAMPS / 539
FLUORESCENT LAMPS / 539
Illumination and Background Coloration / 541
NATURALISTIC ILLUMINATION / 541
BACKGROUND COLORATION / 542
In Vitro *Photography of Fishes* / 544
CAMERAS / 544
FILTERS / 544
Undersea Photography of Fishes / 548
CAMERAS / 548
ELECTRONIC STROBES / 550
WATERTIGHT HOUSINGS / 552
FILMS / 555
The Philosophy of Exhibiting a Fish / 555
Layout of Exhibits / 556
EXHIBIT AQUARIUM SHAPES / 556
LAYOUT AND VISITOR MOVEMENT / 557

Technology / 559
Method 10.1 Aquarium Optics / 559
Method 10.2 Selection of Background Colors / 563
Method 10.3 Demonstration of Light Reflection by Silvery Fishes / 565
Method 10.4 Polarized Light Exhibits / 565
Method 10.5 Species Label Photography / 566
Method 10.6 In Vitro *Fish Photography* / 570

Method 10.7 Undersea Photography of Fishes / 572
Method 10.8 Fiberglass-Reinforced Plastic Decorations / 574
Method 10.9 Moving Water Exhibits / 582
SURGE ACTION / 582
WAVE ACTION / 584
Method 10.10 Angled Viewing Window Exhibits / 586
Method 10.11 Bioassay with Fertilized Sea Urchin Gametes / 586

NOTES AND REFERENCES / 589
APPENDIX I / 797
LITERATURE CITED / 813
INDEX / 893
CREDITS / 939

Captive Seawater Fishes

CHAPTER

1 Chemical Processes

Chemical processes are fitting subjects with which to begin a book about captive fishes. In a broad context, fishes themselves are complex solutions suspended in a thinner solution called seawater. The two are linked ineluctably: to assess the needs of a captive fish requires paying homage to the medium in which it lives. In the Science section salinity, density, specific gravity, pH, and alkalinity are treated critically as operational constructs. I juxtaposed their functions in aquarium seawater with the more distant role played by each in the chemistry of the oceans.

The Technology section describes methods of measurement and control, including sample problems. A procedure for mixing large volumes of artificial seawater is also provided. The relationship between hydrometer readings and specific gravity values will be difficult for most readers; it was not easy to write.

SCIENCE

Solutes and Solutions

MATTER Everything in the universe is made of *matter*. In its simplest form, matter is composed of *elements*. *Atoms* are the smallest particles of elements that combine to form *molecules*. For example, two atoms of hydrogen and one of oxygen combine to produce a molecule of water, H_2O. *Ions* are atoms or groups of atoms that are electrically charged. Those with positive charges are *cations*, and negatively charged atoms are *anions*. *Salts* yield ions when they dissolve. The different ions and their concentrations distinguish seawater from freshwater.

WATER AS A SOLVENT A *solvent* dissolves another substance called a *solute*. Together they make a *solution*. In any solution the concentration of the solvent is always greater than that of the solute. Water is an excellent solvent because of its structure. Its hydrogen atoms lie slightly off-center, producing a net positive charge where they are positioned closest together (Fig. 1-1). The side opposite the hydrogen atoms has a net negative charge. This configuration results in uneven distribution of electrical charges or *polarization*, causing each water molecule to behave as an electric *dipole* (a pair of equal and opposite electrical charges). Polarization causes water to be strongly attracted to itself and to any nearby ions. Salts that dissolve readily do so because dipoles of water are attracted to the ions they contain. If the ion is positively charged, water molecules orient with their negative (oxygen) side facing inward; if the ion is negatively charged, water demonstrates the reverse orientation and turns the side with hydrogen atoms inward (Fig. 1-2). The effect, called *hydration*, is to surround ions and prevent them from recombining.

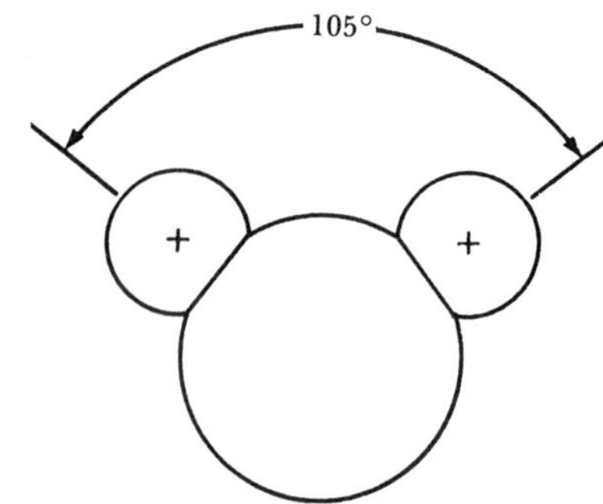

Figure 1-1 *The dipole arrangement of hydrogen and oxygen atoms in a water molecule.* Source: Stephen Spotte, drawn from various sources.

SOLUBILITY Table salt (sodium chloride, NaCl) is composed of sodium (Na^+, a cation) and chloride (Cl^-, an anion). If table salt is poured into a beaker of water, some of it dissolves. Sodium chloride, a solid, *dissociates* or breaks down into its individual ions which then become hydrated. The process by which solids dissolve is *dissolution*. Eventually, the water can no longer hold additional Na^+ and Cl^-, a condition known as *saturation* (Fig. 1-3). A saturated system is in *equilibrium*, and the solution and solid lose and gain ions at an equal rate.[1] *Precipitation* is the reverse of dissolution: ions leave solution and are redeposited on the surface of the solid.[2]

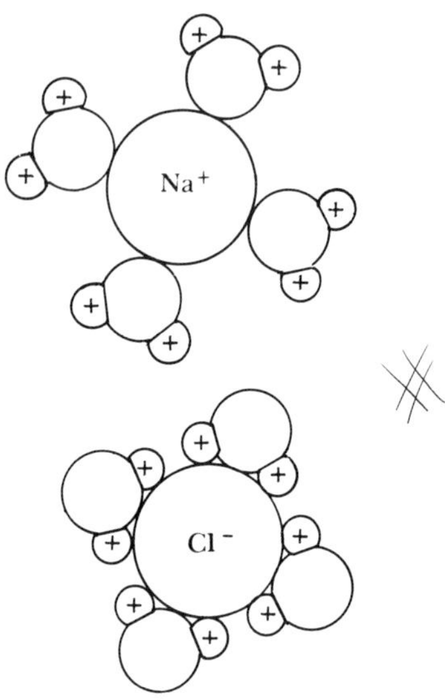

Figure 1-2 *Hydration of a positive and a negative ion. Note the different orientations of the water molecules.* Source: Stephen Spotte, drawn from various sources.

SEAWATER Probably every element on earth is dissolved in the oceans (Table 1-1),* but few are present in large concentrations. Despite its "saltiness," water is still the most abundant constituent of seawater, ~96.5%** by mass.† Seawater is distinguished from freshwater by having a greater mass of elements, which are classified as *major* or *minor*, depending on con-

*Very large and very small numbers often are expressed in "scientific notation" for convenience. Conversions are given in Table 1-2.

**The symbol ~ means "approximately."

†The quantity of matter in an object is its *mass;* the *weight* of the same object is a measure of the force of gravity on it. A man weighing 150 pounds on Earth would weigh only 30 pounds on the moon where gravity is less. His mass would be the same on both planets. In everyday usage we often say weight when we mean mass, and the two have come to mean the same thing.

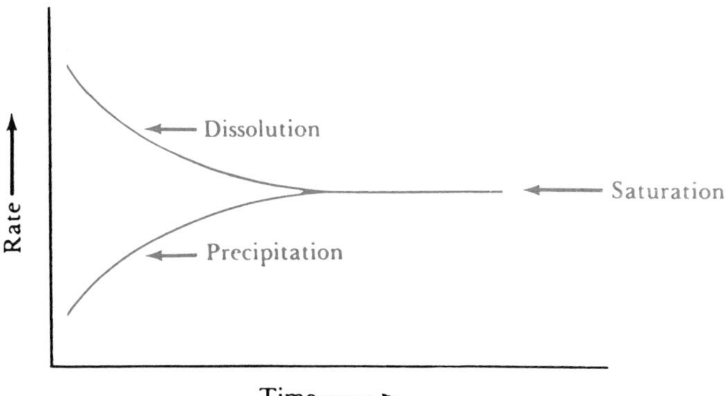

Figure 1-3 Relationship among dissolution, precipitation, and saturation. Source: Stephen Spotte.

TABLE 1-1 The inorganic composition of seawater: c_i = molar scale (mol/L of solution), m_i = molal scale (mol/kg of water), k_i = mokal scale (mol/kg of seawater).

Element	Species	mg/L	c_i	m_i	k_i
H	H_2O	108,000	$1.07 \cdot 10^{2}$	$1.09 \cdot 10^{2}$	$1.05 \cdot 10^{2}$
O	H_2O, O_2	857,000	$5.36 \cdot 10^{1}$	$5.42 \cdot 10^{1}$	$5.23 \cdot 10^{1}$
Cl	Cl^-	19,000	$5.36 \cdot 10^{-1}$	$5.43 \cdot 10^{-1}$	$5.24 \cdot 10^{-1}$
Na	Na^+	10,500	$4.57 \cdot 10^{-1}$	$4.63 \cdot 10^{-1}$	$4.46 \cdot 10^{-1}$
Mg	Mg^{2+}	1,350	$5.55 \cdot 10^{-2}$	$5.62 \cdot 10^{-2}$	$5.43 \cdot 10^{-2}$
S	SO_4^{2-}, $NaSO_4^-$	885	$2.76 \cdot 10^{-2}$	$2.80 \cdot 10^{-2}$	$2.70 \cdot 10^{-2}$
Ca	Ca^{2+}	400	$9.98 \cdot 10^{-3}$	$1.01 \cdot 10^{-2}$	$9.75 \cdot 10^{-3}$
K	K^+	380	$9.72 \cdot 10^{-3}$	$9.84 \cdot 10^{-3}$	$9.50 \cdot 10^{-3}$
C	HCO_3^-, CO_3^{2-}, CO_2	28	$2.33 \cdot 10^{-3}$	$2.36 \cdot 10^{-3}$	$2.28 \cdot 10^{-3}$
N	N_2, NO_3^-, NO_2^-, NH_4^+, NH_3	15	$1.07 \cdot 10^{-3}$	$1.08 \cdot 10^{-3}$	$1.05 \cdot 10^{-3}$
Br	Br^-	65	$8.14 \cdot 10^{-4}$	$8.24 \cdot 10^{-4}$	$7.95 \cdot 10^{-4}$
B	$B(OH)_3$, $B(OH)_4^-$	4.6	$4.26 \cdot 10^{-4}$	$4.31 \cdot 10^{-4}$	$4.16 \cdot 10^{-4}$
Si	$Si(OH)_4$	3.0	$1.07 \cdot 10^{-4}$	$1.08 \cdot 10^{-4}$	$1.04 \cdot 10^{-4}$
Sr	Sr^{2+}	8.0	$9.13 \cdot 10^{-5}$	$9.25 \cdot 10^{-5}$	$8.92 \cdot 10^{-5}$
F	F^-, MgF^+	1.2	$6.32 \cdot 10^{-5}$	$6.40 \cdot 10^{-5}$	$6.17 \cdot 10^{-5}$
Li	Li^+	0.17	$2.45 \cdot 10^{-5}$	$2.48 \cdot 10^{-5}$	$2.39 \cdot 10^{-5}$
P	HPO_4^{2-}, PO_4^{3-}, $H_2PO_4^-$	0.07	$2.26 \cdot 10^{-6}$	$2.29 \cdot 10^{-6}$	$2.21 \cdot 10^{-6}$
Rb	Rb^+	0.12	$1.40 \cdot 10^{-6}$	$1.42 \cdot 10^{-6}$	$1.37 \cdot 10^{-6}$
I	IO_3^-, I^-	0.06	$4.73 \cdot 10^{-7}$	$4.79 \cdot 10^{-7}$	$4.62 \cdot 10^{-7}$
Al	$Al(OH)_4^-$	0.01	$3.71 \cdot 10^{-7}$	$3.75 \cdot 10^{-7}$	$3.62 \cdot 10^{-7}$
Ba	Ba^{2+}	0.03	$2.18 \cdot 10^{-7}$	$2.21 \cdot 10^{-7}$	$2.13 \cdot 10^{-7}$
Fe	$Fe(OH)_2^+$, $Fe(OH)_4^-$	0.01	$1.79 \cdot 10^{-7}$	$1.81 \cdot 10^{-7}$	$1.75 \cdot 10^{-7}$
Zn	$ZnOH^+$, Zn^{2+}, $ZnCO_3^0$	0.01	$1.53 \cdot 10^{-7}$	$1.55 \cdot 10^{-7}$	$1.49 \cdot 10^{-7}$
Ni	Ni^{2+}	0.007	$1.19 \cdot 10^{-7}$	$1.21 \cdot 10^{-7}$	$1.17 \cdot 10^{-7}$
Mo	MoO_4^{2-}	0.01	$1.04 \cdot 10^{-7}$	$1.06 \cdot 10^{-7}$	$1.02 \cdot 10^{-7}$
Cu	$CuCO_3^0$, $CuOH^+$	0.003	$4.72 \cdot 10^{-8}$	$4.78 \cdot 10^{-8}$	$4.61 \cdot 10^{-8}$
As	$HAsO_4^{2-}$, $H_2AsO_4^-$	0.003	$4.00 \cdot 10^{-8}$	$4.05 \cdot 10^{-8}$	$3.91 \cdot 10^{-8}$
V	$H_2VO_4^-$, HVO_4^{2-}	0.002	$3.93 \cdot 10^{-8}$	$3.98 \cdot 10^{-8}$	$3.84 \cdot 10^{-8}$

TABLE 1-1 (*Continued*)

Element	Species	mg/L	c_i	m_i	k_i
Mn	Mn^{2+}, $MnCl^+$	0.002	$3.64\cdot10^{-8}$	$3.69\cdot10^{-8}$	$3.56\cdot10^{-8}$
Ti	$Ti(OH)_4^0$	0.001	$2.09\cdot10^{-8}$	$2.11\cdot10^{-8}$	$2.04\cdot10^{-8}$
U	$UO_2(CO_3)_2^{4-}$	0.003	$1.26\cdot10^{-8}$	$1.28\cdot10^{-8}$	$1.23\cdot10^{-8}$
Co	Co^{2+}	0.0004	$6.79\cdot10^{-9}$	$6.87\cdot10^{-9}$	$6.63\cdot10^{-9}$
Sn	$SnO(OH)_3^-$	0.0008	$6.74\cdot10^{-9}$	$6.83\cdot10^{-9}$	$6.59\cdot10^{-9}$
Ne	Ne(gas)	0.0001	$4.96\cdot10^{-9}$	$5.02\cdot10^{-9}$	$4.84\cdot10^{-9}$
Ag	$AgCl_2^-$	0.0003	$2.78\cdot10^{-9}$	$2.82\cdot10^{-9}$	$2.72\cdot10^{-9}$
Sb	$Sb(OH)_6^-$	0.0003	$2.46\cdot10^{-9}$	$2.50\cdot10^{-9}$	$2.41\cdot10^{-9}$
Kr	Kr(gas)	0.0002	$2.39\cdot10^{-9}$	$2.42\cdot10^{-9}$	$2.33\cdot10^{-9}$
Cs	Cs^+	0.0003	$2.26\cdot10^{-9}$	$2.29\cdot10^{-9}$	$2.21\cdot10^{-9}$
He	He(gas)	0.000007	$1.75\cdot10^{-9}$	$1.77\cdot10^{-9}$	$1.71\cdot10^{-9}$
Se	SeO_3^{2-}	0.00009	$1.14\cdot10^{-9}$	$1.15\cdot10^{-9}$	$1.11\cdot10^{-9}$
Hg	$HgCl_4^{2-}$, $HgCl_2^0$	0.0002	$9.97\cdot10^{-10}$	$1.01\cdot10^{-9}$	$9.74\cdot10^{-10}$
Cd	$CdCl_2^0$	0.00011	$9.79\cdot10^{-10}$	$9.91\cdot10^{-10}$	$9.56\cdot10^{-10}$
Cr	$Cr(OH)_3$, CrO_4^{2-}	0.00005	$9.62\cdot10^{-10}$	$9.74\cdot10^{-10}$	$9.40\cdot10^{-10}$
Sc	$Sc(OH)_3^0$	<0.00004	$8.90\cdot10^{-10}$	$9.01\cdot10^{-10}$	$8.69\cdot10^{-10}$
Ge	$Ge(OH)_4$	0.00006	$8.27\cdot10^{-10}$	$8.37\cdot10^{-10}$	$8.08\cdot10^{-10}$
W	WO_4^{2-}	0.0001	$5.44\cdot10^{-10}$	$5.51\cdot10^{-10}$	$5.31\cdot10^{-10}$
Ga	$Ga(OH)_4^-$	0.00003	$4.30\cdot10^{-10}$	$4.36\cdot10^{-10}$	$4.20\cdot10^{-10}$
Xe	Xe(gas)	0.00005	$3.81\cdot10^{-10}$	$3.86\cdot10^{-10}$	$3.72\cdot10^{-10}$
Zr	$Zr(OH)_4^0$	0.00002	$2.19\cdot10^{-10}$	$2.22\cdot10^{-10}$	$2.14\cdot10^{-10}$
Pb	$PbCO_3^0$, $Pb(CO_3)_2^{2-}$	0.00003	$1.45\cdot10^{-10}$	$1.47\cdot10^{-10}$	$1.41\cdot10^{-10}$
Y	$Y(OH)_3^0$	0.00001	$1.12\cdot10^{-10}$	$1.14\cdot10^{-10}$	$1.10\cdot10^{-10}$
Nb		0.00001	$1.08\cdot10^{-10}$	$1.09\cdot10^{-10}$	$1.05\cdot10^{-10}$
Bi	BiO^+, $Bi(OH)_2^+$	0.00002	$9.57\cdot10^{-11}$	$9.69\cdot10^{-11}$	$9.35\cdot10^{-11}$
La	$La(OH)_3^0$	$1.2\cdot10^{-5}$	$8.64\cdot10^{-11}$	$8.75\cdot10^{-11}$	$8.44\cdot10^{-11}$
Be	$BeOH^+$	0.0000006	$6.66\cdot10^{-11}$	$6.74\cdot10^{-11}$	$6.50\cdot10^{-11}$
Nd	$Nd(OH_3)^0$	$9.2\cdot10^{-6}$	$6.38\cdot10^{-11}$	$6.46\cdot10^{-11}$	$6.23\cdot10^{-11}$
Au	$AuCl_2^-$	0.00001	$5.08\cdot10^{-11}$	$5.14\cdot10^{-11}$	$4.96\cdot10^{-11}$
Tl	Tl^+	<0.00001	$4.89\cdot10^{-11}$	$4.95\cdot10^{-11}$	$4.78\cdot10^{-11}$
Re	ReO^-	0.0000084	$4.51\cdot10^{-11}$	$4.57\cdot10^{-11}$	$4.41\cdot10^{-11}$
Hf		<0.000008	$4.48\cdot10^{-11}$	$4.54\cdot10^{-11}$	$4.38\cdot10^{-11}$
Ce	$Ce(OH)_3^0$	$5.2\cdot10^{-6}$	$3.71\cdot10^{-11}$	$3.76\cdot10^{-11}$	$3.63\cdot10^{-11}$
In	$In(OH)_2^+$	0.000004	$3.48\cdot10^{-11}$	$3.53\cdot10^{-11}$	$3.40\cdot10^{-11}$
Pr	$Pr(OH)_3^0$	$2.6\cdot10^{-6}$	$1.85\cdot10^{-11}$	$1.87\cdot10^{-11}$	$1.80\cdot10^{-11}$
Dy	$Dy(OH)_3^0$	$2.9\cdot10^{-6}$	$1.78\cdot10^{-11}$	$1.81\cdot10^{-11}$	$1.74\cdot10^{-11}$
Ta		<0.000003	$1.66\cdot10^{-11}$	$1.68\cdot10^{-11}$	$1.62\cdot10^{-11}$
Gd	$Gd(OH)_3^0$	$2.4\cdot10^{-6}$	$1.53\cdot10^{-11}$	$1.55\cdot10^{-11}$	$1.49\cdot10^{-11}$
Er	$Er(OH)_3^0$	$2.4\cdot10^{-6}$	$1.43\cdot10^{-11}$	$1.45\cdot10^{-11}$	$1.40\cdot10^{-11}$
Yb	$Yb(OH)_3^0$	$2.0\cdot10^{-6}$	$1.16\cdot10^{-11}$	$1.17\cdot10^{-11}$	$1.13\cdot10^{-11}$
Sm	$Sm(OH)_3^0$	$1.7\cdot10^{-6}$	$1.13\cdot10^{-11}$	$1.14\cdot10^{-11}$	$1.10\cdot10^{-11}$
Ru		0.0000007	$6.93\cdot10^{-12}$	$7.01\cdot10^{-12}$	$6.77\cdot10^{-12}$
Ho	$Ho(OH)_3^0$	$8.8\cdot10^{-7}$	$5.34\cdot10^{-12}$	$5.40\cdot10^{-12}$	$5.21\cdot10^{-12}$

TABLE 1-1 (*Continued*)

Element	Species	mg/L	c_i	m_i	k_i
Th	$Th(OH)_4^0$	0.000001	$4.31 \cdot 10^{-12}$	$4.36 \cdot 10^{-12}$	$4.21 \cdot 10^{-12}$
Tm	$Tm(OH)_3^0$	$5.2 \cdot 10^{-7}$	$3.08 \cdot 10^{-12}$	$3.12 \cdot 10^{-12}$	$3.01 \cdot 10^{-12}$
Eu	$Eu(OH)_3^0$	$4.6 \cdot 10^{-7}$	$3.03 \cdot 10^{-12}$	$3.07 \cdot 10^{-12}$	$2.96 \cdot 10^{-12}$
Lu	$Lu(OH)_3^0$	$4.8 \cdot 10^{-7}$	$2.74 \cdot 10^{-12}$	$2.78 \cdot 10^{-12}$	$2.68 \cdot 10^{-12}$
Pa		$2.0 \cdot 10^{-9}$	$8.66 \cdot 10^{-15}$	$8.77 \cdot 10^{-15}$	$8.46 \cdot 10^{-15}$
Ra	Ra^{2+}	$1.0 \cdot 10^{-10}$	$4.42 \cdot 10^{-16}$	$4.48 \cdot 10^{-16}$	$4.32 \cdot 10^{-16}$
Rn	Rn(gas)	$0.6 \cdot 10^{-15}$	$2.70 \cdot 10^{-21}$	$2.74 \cdot 10^{-21}$	$2.64 \cdot 10^{-21}$

Source: Bidwell and Spotte (1985), recalculated according to MacIntyre (1976) from the elemental composition of Goldberg (1980) and the species composition of Brewer (1975).

TABLE 1-2 Expression of numbers in scientific notation.

Numbers >1	Scientific notation		Numbers <1
1.0	1.0×10^0	1.0×10^0	1.0
10.0	1.0×10^1	1.0×10^{-1}	0.1
100.0	1.0×10^2	1.0×10^{-2}	0.01
1,000.0	1.0×10^3	1.0×10^{-3}	0.001
10,000.0	1.0×10^4	1.0×10^{-4}	0.0001
100,000.0	1.0×10^5	1.0×10^{-5}	0.00001
1,000,000.0	1.0×10^6	1.0×10^{-6}	0.000001
10,000,000.0	1.0×10^7	1.0×10^{-7}	0.0000001
100,000,000.0	1.0×10^8	1.0×10^{-8}	0.00000001
1,000,000,000.0	1.0×10^9	1.0×10^{-9}	0.000000001

Source: Stephen Spotte.

centration. The major elements are those that make a substantial contribution to the measured salinity (i.e., have concentrations greater than 1 mg/kg* of seawater). *Salinity* is defined as the total mass of solutes dissolved in 1 kg of seawater.[3] The sum of these solutes is expressed in grams, and salinity is therefore expressed in g/kg. Because there are 1000 g in 1 kg, g/kg is the same as parts per thousand, the symbol for which is ‰. The symbol for salinity is *S*. A salinity reading of 35‰, the value typical of surface seawater, is a measure of all the dissolved solids, but mainly the major elements.[4] Eleven species (excluding hydrogen, oxygen, and nitrogen) account for 99.9% by mass of the total solutes in the oceans. Most exist as hydrated free ions, but they also can occur in other forms. Small concentrations of the major species form *ion pairs*, because the attraction between highly charged ions (*electrostatic attraction*) can over-

*The symbol for milligram is mg, and 1 mg is 1/1000 of a gram, g. A kilogram, kg, is 1000 g.

come the attraction of water dipoles. This is particularly true of chemical species that carry more than one charge (e.g., Mg^{2+}, Sr^{2+}, SO_4^{2-}). Sulfate, SO_4^{2-}, for example, carries a double negative charge, making it so attractive to highly charged cations (e.g., Mg^{2+}, Ca^{2+}) that only about 50% of the sulfate in seawater exists in a free state. Any reference to "salts" in seawater is only partly correct. Salts exist as precipitated solids, whereas the solutes in seawater are mainly ions.

The relative proportions, or ratios, of the major ions in seawater are remarkably similar the world around. Rainfall and surface evaporation, which dilute and concentrate seawater, have no overall effect. This was first reported in 1819 by Alexander Marcet. The observation later became known as the *rule of constant proportions*, or *Marcet's principle*, which states that regardless of how salinity varies locally, the ratios of the major ions in open ocean water are nearly constant.[5] Marcet's principle generally holds true for major ions both at the surface and in the deep oceans, but becomes unreliable at salinity values of $<30‰$.* At no depth is it valid for *nutrients* (carbon, phosphorus, nitrogen, and silicon) and other trace elements that are actively removed by plants and returned to solution through the decomposition of organic matter. Sections of the ocean may be depleted temporarily of nutrient elements or contain an abundance of them, depending on the intensity of biological activity. Trace elements do not affect the measured salinity because their concentrations are too low.

Measurement of Seawater Solutes

SALINITY The term "salinity" originally meant the total inorganic ion content of a specific mass of seawater.[6] However, it is impossible to distill or evaporate seawater and recover all the ions that originally were present because some of the volatile species are lost to the atmosphere or decompose on evaporation.[7] In practice, salinity refers to the concentration of major ions. Salinity is a mass ratio (g/kg). As such, it has no units of expression and is unaffected by temperature. A reading of $S = 35‰$ obtained at 0°C will be the same at 35°C. The "salinity" of seawater is commonly determined with *conductivity meters* (also called *salinometers*), which measure electrical conductivity, or with *refractometers*, which measure the *refractive index* of the water (the ratio of the speed of light in a vacuum to its speed in seawater).

Conductivity meters work only because seawater is a weak

*The symbol $<$ means "less than"; $>$ is "greater than."

conductor of electricity. Pure water is a poor conductor, but solutions of ions from the dissolution of salts are capable of conducting an electric current (Fig. 1-4). When ions perform this function they are called *electrolytes*. Substances such as sugar do not dissociate into ions and do not conduct a current. They are *nonelectrolytes*.[8]

DENSITY *Density* is stated in grams per cubic centimetre (g/cm^3). As a mass per volume relationship it is affected by temperature. Like other liquids, the mass per volume of water changes with changes in temperature. When heated, water expands. Its molecules disperse (increasing the amount of empty space among them), and its mass per volume decreases. On cooling, water contracts. Its molecules squeeze together, and the mass of a given volume increases. One gram of *pure water* (water devoid of solutes) has a volume assumed to be 1.000 g/cm^3 at 4°C (Table 1-3).

Cold seawater has more ions and molecules of solute and more water molecules than an equal volume of warm seawater, and it has a greater mass. This is illustrated in Figure 1-5. Density is a difficult measurement to make because the effects of temperature and salinity must be considered both separately and in combination. A rise in salinity, for example, increases the mass of a fixed volume of seawater, which increases its density.[9]

SPECIFIC GRAVITY The easiest way to determine the total solute concentration of seawater is with a *hydrometer*.[10] Such a measurement is an approximation only, but accurate enough for husbandry purposes. *Specific gravity* is the ratio of the dens-

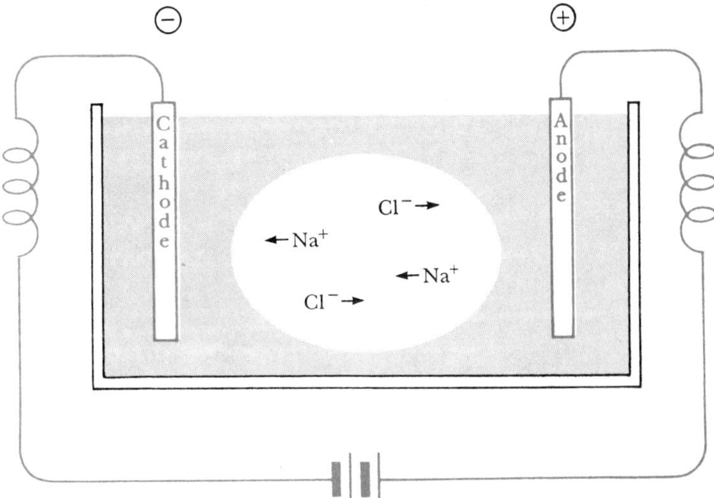

Figure 1-4 Conduction in electrolyte solutions. Also see Note 8. Source: Stephen Spotte.

TABLE 1-3 Density (g/cm^3) of pure water at different temperatures.

°C	Density	°C	Density
0	0.9998679	15.56	0.9990389
1	0.9999267	16	0.9989701
2	0.9999679	17	0.9988022
3	0.9999922	18	0.9986232
4	1.0000000	19	0.9984331
5	0.9999919	20	0.9982323
6	0.9999681	21	0.9980210
7	0.9999295	22	0.9977993
8	0.9998762	23	0.9975674
9	0.9998088	24	0.9973256
10	0.9997277	25	0.9970739
11	0.9996328	26	0.9968128
12	0.9995247	27	0.9965421
13	0.9994040	28	0.9962623
14	0.9992712	29	0.9959735
15	0.9991265	30	0.9956756

Source: Boyd (1979) with 15.56°C interpolated; original source unknown.

ities of seawater at the reference temperature (or corrected to the reference temperature) to distilled water at the standard temperature. *Standard temperature* is the temperature of the distilled water. The *reference temperature* is the temperature at which a particular hydrometer can be used without correction, typically 15.56°C (60°F). The *sample temperature* is the temperature at which the hydrometer reading is made and can differ from the reference temperature. Like salinity, specific gravity is a dimensionless ratio and has no units of expression. Unlike salin-

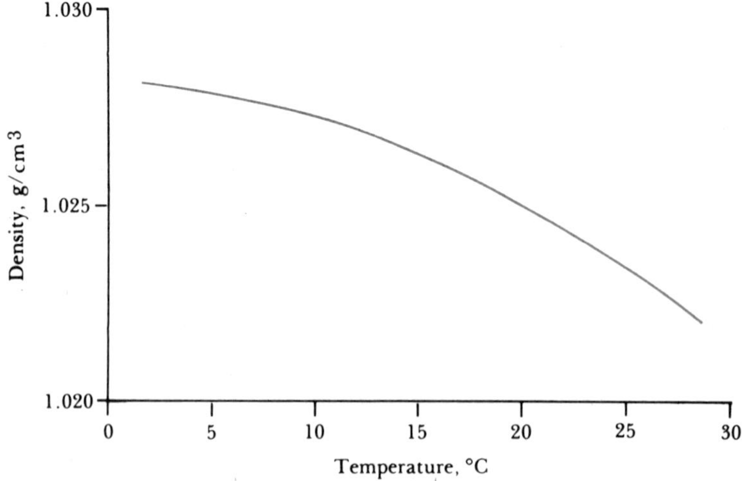

Figure 1-5 *Effect of temperature on the density of seawater.* Source: Anikouchine and Sternberg (1981).

ity, it is a ratio of densities and consequently affected by temperature. The only true specific gravity measurements are ones in which the sample and reference temperatures are identical. Anything else is a *hydrometer reading* at a stated temperature and must be converted to specific gravity (see Technology section).

pH and Alkalinity

Most aquarists have some notion of what pH and alkalinity mean, and I shall discuss these concepts in a general way before introducing them specifically in subsections that follow. The maintenance of stable pH values is important in seawater aquarium keeping because many chemical reactions that affect the living tissues of fishes are pH-dependent, although exact limits of tolerance are still poorly understood. In the absence of information that might define these limits it seems prudent to maintain aquarium seawater at pH 8.2, the typical value of clean ocean water. The stability of the pH is a function of the alkalinity. If alkalinity is depleted the pH may fall below the desired threshold. A rudimentary understanding of the chemical nature of pH and alkalinity obviously is a prerequisite to performing manipulative procedures necessary for their control. The general belief that carbonate minerals used as filtrants (e.g., crushed coral, oyster shell, and carbonate rocks) perform these tasks automatically within operational limits appears to be unfounded. The subsections below start with a theoretical framework for the concepts of pH and alkalinity and end with a discussion of the behavior of carbonate minerals in aquarium seawater.

pH The *pH* of a solution is the relative measure of its acidity or basicity. An acid or base added to water shifts disproportionately to relinquish ions of hydrogen, H^+, or hydroxyl, OH^-. If the shift favors production of an excess of H^+ the resulting solution is acidic. If OH^- is formed in greater proportion the solution is basic. The pH is measured on a scale of 1 to 14, with a value of 7 being exactly neutral. At neutrality the concentrations of H^+ and OH^- are identical.[11] Changes in pH are logarithmic, and the concentrations of H^+ and OH^- increase or decrease by a factor of 10 with each pH change of one unit. At pH 8 there are 10 times more OH^- ions than at pH 7. Similarly, water at pH 6 has 10 times more H^+ than at neutrality and 100 times more than water of pH 8, as depicted in Figure 1-6. Seawater of pH 8.2 is slightly basic.

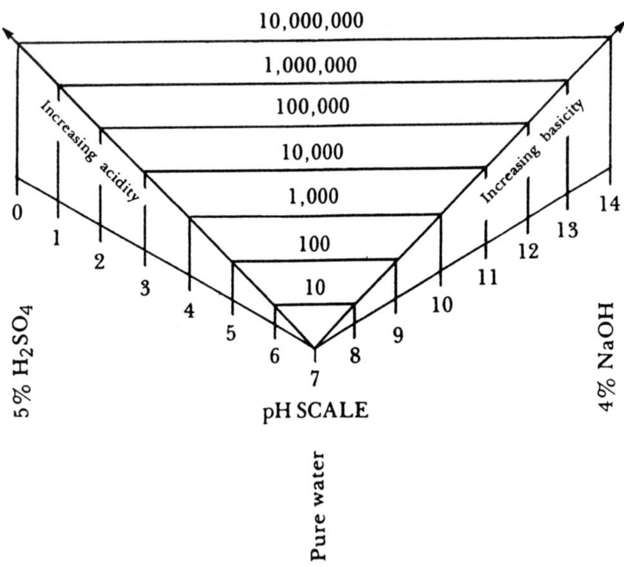

Figure 1-6 Logarithmic relationship of the pH scale. Pure water is neutral; 5% sulfuric acid is strongly acidic, and 4% sodium hydroxide is strongly basic. Source: Wescott (1978).

ALKALINITY The chemical interactions of dissolved CO_2, water, and the anions bicarbonate, HCO_3^-, and carbonate, CO_3^{2-}, control the pH of seawater through the equilibrium reactions[12]

$$CO_2 + H_2O \rightleftharpoons H_2CO_3 \rightleftharpoons H^+ + HCO_3^- \rightleftharpoons 2H^+ + CO_3^{2-} \quad (1.1)$$

Free or gaseous CO_2 from the atmosphere reacts with water (i.e., is hydrated) to form carbonic acid, H_2CO_3, which in turn dissociates into H^+ and HCO_3^-. Seawater contains CO_3^{2-}, and hydrogen ions released during dissociation of HCO_3^- react with CO_3^{2-} to produce more HCO_3^-. In the equilibrium reactions 1.1 the pH increases with forward shifts (top arrows) and decreases with reverse shifts (bottom arrows). At a given pH only one species predominates; at seawater pH values the overwhelming proportion exists as HCO_3^- (Fig. 1-7). *Alkalinity* is defined as the net negative charge of all anions that interact with H^+, with a value of 2.5 mEq/L*[13] being typical for seawater. On nongeologic time scales (i.e., those not measured in millions of years) the only anions of importance in seawater are bicarbonate, carbonate, and borate, $B(OH)_4^-$.[14] The contribution of borate is minor (Fig. 1-7), and alkalinity can be defined in practical terms as the sum of HCO_3^- and CO_3^{2-}. Any factor that causes these species to diminish in concentration also initiates a decline in

* mEq represents milliequivalents or 10^{-3} equivalents, Eq.

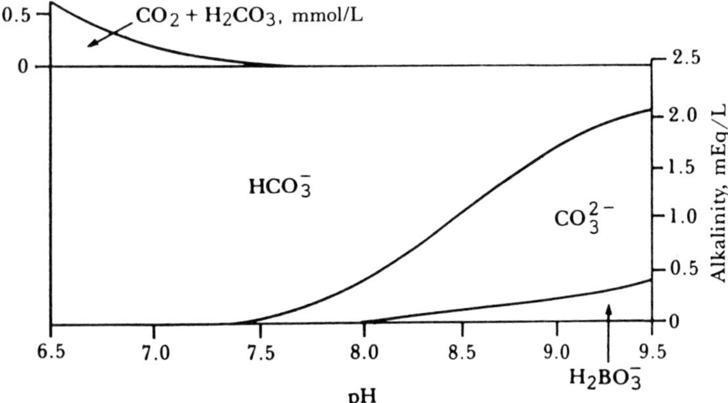

Figure 1-7 *Variation in the alkalinity components of seawater with changes in pH.* Source: Bathurst (1971).

pH. Thus long-term pH control is predicated on factors that affect alkalinity.

FACTORS THAT AFFECT ALKALINITY *Total CO_2* (ΣCO_2, the sum of all forms of CO_2 expressed in reactions 1.1) can be changed only if carbonate as H_2CO_3, HCO_3^-, or CO_3^{2-} is added or subtracted from seawater. Look at Figure 1-8 and assume that point *A* represents the alkalinity of seawater. If free CO_2 is added, ΣCO_2 will increase by the amount of the addition. However, CO_2 does not carry an electrical charge, and the alkalinity remains unchanged. Addition or removal of CO_2 causes point *A* to be shifted to the right or to the left, but because alkalinity neither increases nor decreases the point does not move up or down.

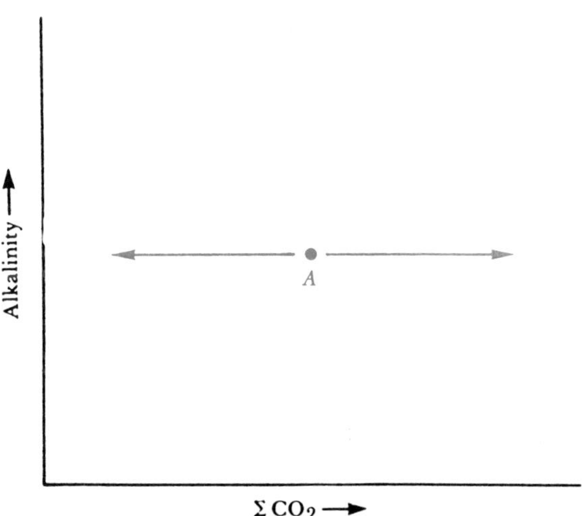

Figure 1-8 *Removal or addition of free CO_2 and the effect on alkalinity.* Source: Weyl (1970).

Addition of HCO_3^- poses a different situation (Fig. 1-9). If 1 mEq of HCO_3^- is added to 1 L of seawater, ΣCO_2 is increased by 1 mEq. Point *A* is shifted one unit to the right and one unit up, or upward at an angle of 45°. Removal of 1 mEq has the opposite effect. As the figure illustrates, the alkalinity increases or decreases according to whether HCO_3^- is added or removed.

If 1 mEq of CO_3^{2-} is added to 1 L of seawater, ΣCO_3 is increased by 1 mEq. However, because carbonate ion carries two negative charges, alkalinity will be changed by 2 mEq (Fig. 1-10). Point *A* is displaced one unit to the right and two units upward, or upward at an angle of 63.4°. Precipitation of CO_3^{2-} has the opposite effect.

If a strong acid such as hydrochloric acid, HCl, is added to seawater, H^+ combines with HCO_3^- to form H_2CO_3. The result is a decrease in alkalinity, although ΣCO_2 is unchanged (Fig. 1-11). This is illustrated by the vertical line. Addition of a base (e.g., sodium hydroxide, NaOH) raises the alkalinity but does not affect ΣCO_2. As a result, point *A* is shifted directly upward. In summary, addition or removal of HCO_3^- and CO_3^{2-} affects both ΣCO_2 and alkalinity. Addition or removal of free CO_2 affects ΣCO_2 but not alkalinity, and addition or removal of an acid or base changes the alkalinity but not ΣCO_2.

PROCESSES THAT AFFECT ALKALINITY The alkalinity of seawater is affected by several chemical reactions (Table 1-4). Reaction 1a in the table confirms the model in Figure 1-8 (i.e., addition of CO_2 to seawater results in no net change in alkalinity). Reaction 1b demonstrates that assimilation of nitrate ion, NO_3^-, by plants during photosynthesis increases the alkalinity; conversely, assimilation of ammonium ion, NH_4^+, results in a

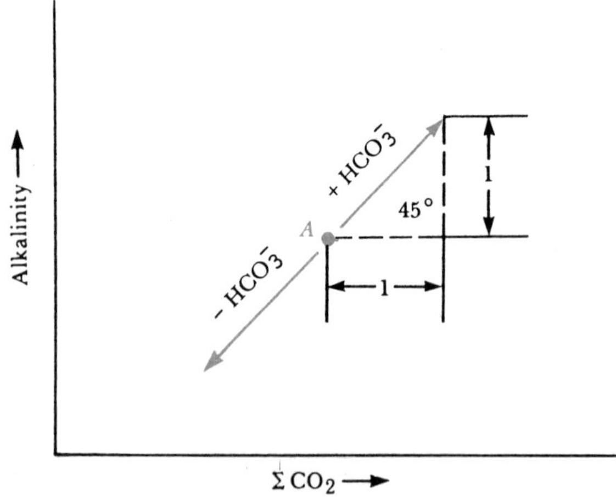

Figure 1-9 *Removal or addition of bicarbonate ion and the effect on alkalinity.* Source: Weyl (1970).

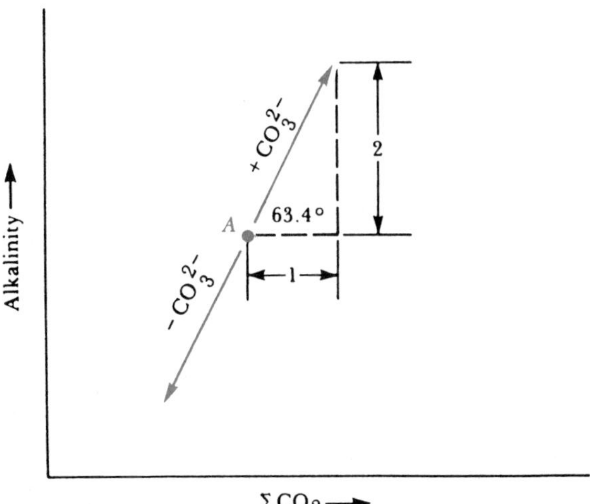

Figure 1-10 *Removal or addition of carbonate ion and the effect on alkalinity.* Source: Weyl (1970).

net decrease (reaction 1c). Nitrification reduces the alkalinity (reaction 2). Denitrification (reaction 3), often the terminal reaction in dissimilation (Chapter 2), results in a net increase in alkalinity. Sulfide oxidation and sulfate reduction (reactions 4a, 4b, and 5) decrease and increase the alkalinity. The last reaction, $CaCO_3$ dissolution, produces a net increase in alkalinity.

CARBONATE ROCKS AND MINERALS Geologists ordinarily define *carbonate rocks* as those containing >50% carbonate minerals.[15] *Carbonate minerals* are defined as *calcite* and *aragonite*, $CaCO_3$, and *dolomite*.[16] The chemical formula for dolomite,

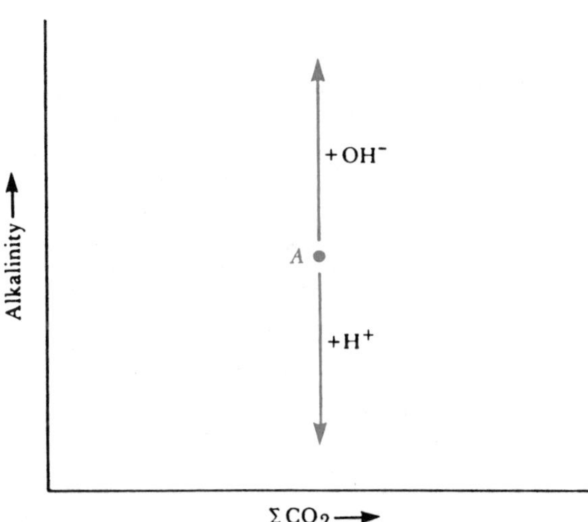

Figure 1-11 *Addition of an acid or base and the effect on alkalinity.* Source: Weyl (1970).

TABLE 1-4 Processes affecting alkalinity. Forward reactions of 1a to 1c represent photosynthesis; reverse reactions represent respiration.

Process	Alkalinity change for forward reaction
Photosynthesis and respiration	
(1a) $nCO_2 + nH_2O \rightleftharpoons (CH_2O)_n + nO_2$	No change
(1b) $106CO_2 + 16NO_3^- + HPO_4^{2-} + 122H_2O + 18\,H^+ \rightleftharpoons (C_{106}H_{263}O_{110}N_{16}P_1) + 138O_2$	Increase
(1c) $106CO_2 + 16NH_4^+ + HPO_4^{2-} + 108H_2O \rightleftharpoons (C_{106}H_{263}O_{110}N_{16}P_1) + 107O_2 + 14H^+$	Decrease
Nitrification	
(2) $NH_4^+ + 2O_2 \rightarrow NO_3^- + H_2O + 2H^+$	Decrease
Denitrification	
(3) $5CH_2O + 4NO_3^- + 4H^+ \rightarrow 5CO_2 + 2N_2 + 7H_2O$	Increase
Sulfide oxidation	
(4a) $HS^- + 2O_2 \rightarrow SO_4^{2-} + H^+$	Decrease
(4b) $FeS_{2(s)} + \frac{15}{4}O_2 + 3\frac{1}{2}H_2O \rightarrow Fe(OH)_{3(s)} + 4H^+ + 2SO_4^{2-}$	Decrease
Sulfate reduction	
(5) $SO_4^{2-} + 2CH_2O + H^+ \rightarrow 2CO_2 + HS^- + H_2O$	Increase
$CaCO_3$ dissolution	
(6) $CaCO_3 + CO_2 + H_2O \rightleftharpoons Ca^{2+} + 2HCO_3^-$	Increase

Source: Stumm and Morgan (1981).

$CaMg(CO_3)_2$, shows that it contains $CaCO_3$ and $MgCO_3$ (calcium carbonate and magnesium carbonate) in equal proportions. Magnesium is the principal cation in *magnesite*. Calcite and aragonite are *polymorphs* of $CaCO_3$ (i.e., they have the same chemical formula but different ionic structures).[17] Vaterite, the third polymorph of $CaCO_3$, is of minor importance and will not be discussed. A number of other carbonate rocks exist with intermediate compositions of calcite and dolomite (Table 1-5). The terminology used to classify them is widely disputed, and the table should be considered representative. Pure calcites (e.g., Iceland spar) are rare, and most contain some magnesium. It is customary to refer to carbonate minerals that contain magnesium as *magnesian calcites*.[18] Dolomite is the exception; it is known simply as dolomite.

CARBONATE MINERALS IN THE OCEANS To understand how carbonate minerals react with aquarium seawater it is use-

TABLE 1-5 Classification of rocks intermediate in composition between pure limestones and dolomites.

	Content, %	
Rock name	Calcite	Dolomite
Limestone	>95	<5
Magnesian limestone	90–95	5–10
Dolomite limestone	50–90	10–50
Calcite dolomite	10–50	50–90
Dolomite	<10	>90

Source: Bissell and Chilingar (1967).

ful to know something about their behavior in the oceans. Carbonate sediments abound beneath the ocean floors and as integral parts of the continents. Their origin in shallow seas is predominately *biogenic* (i.e., of biological origin), representing the accumulated skeletal debris of countless calcareous organisms (Fig. 1-12). Inorganic precipitation or *diagenesis* also produces carbonate sediments, but probably accounts for no more than 10% of the total. Temperate and tropical surface seawaters

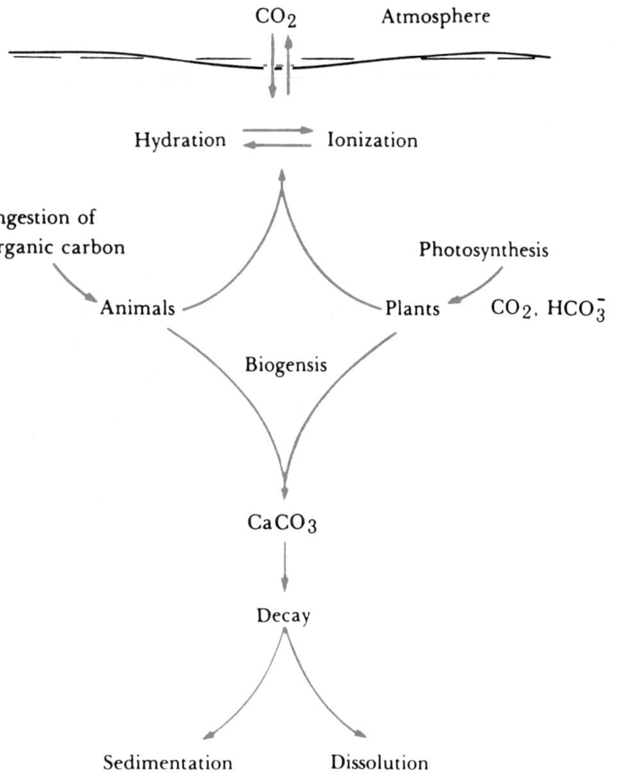

Figure 1-12 *Flux of carbon dioxide into the oceans. Free CO_2 from the atmosphere is hydrated and ionized (equilibrium reactions 1.1). Some is used by plants for photosynthesis. Animals ingest organic carbon. Respiration by both plants and animals produces CO_2. Some of the carbon assimilated into living tissue is eventually precipitated biogenically. The $CaCO_3$ released by decay enters the sediments or dissolves.* Source: Stephen Spotte.

ordinarily are *supersaturated* with $CaCO_3$,[19] but the deep oceans are *undersaturated* (Fig. 1-13). In other words, these environments exist at states that exceed and are less than the value at saturation. Such conditions are a result of biogenic production of CO_2 near the surface and the greater solubility of $CaCO_3$ in the deep oceans, which is caused by increased pressure.

Carbonate minerals become more soluble as CO_2 and salinity increase and temperature decreases. A sequence of equilibrium reactions defines the dissolution or precipitation of $CaCO_3$ in terms of influx or efflux of CO_2. The first involves transport of gaseous CO_2 from the atmosphere and its hydration:

$$CO_2 + H_2O \rightleftharpoons H_2CO_3 \quad (1.2)$$

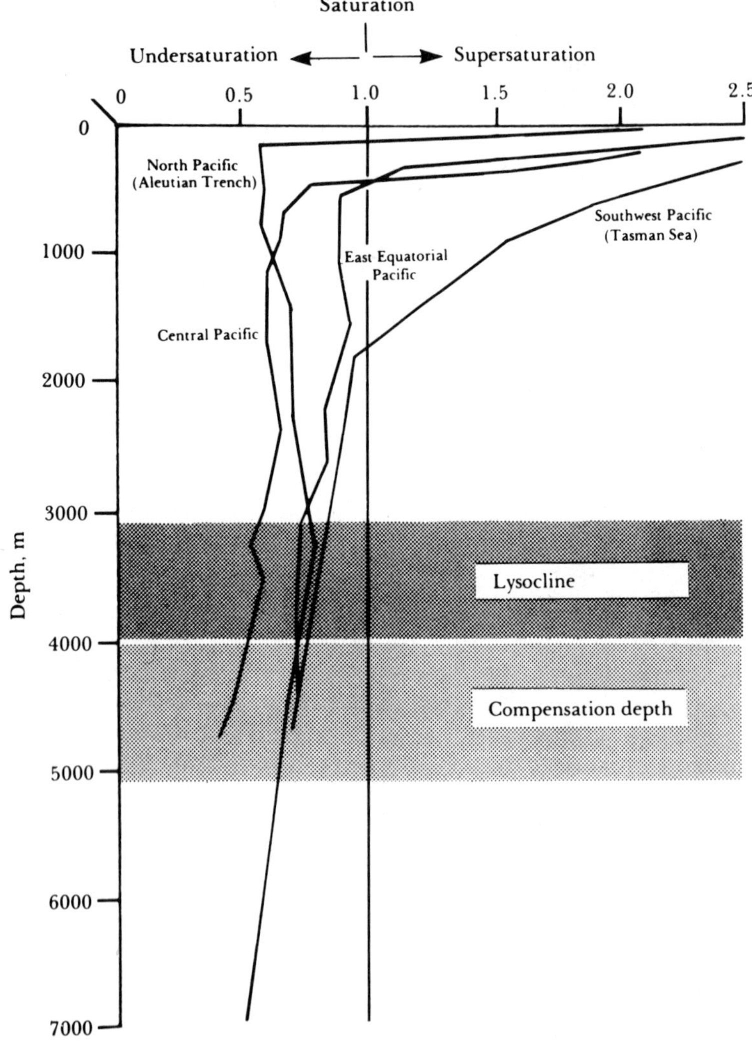

Figure 1-13 *Degree of saturation of one $CaCO_3$ polymorph (calcite) versus depth at four representative stations in the Pacific Ocean. Saturation is indicated by $\Omega = 1.0$ on the abscissa (x or horizontal axis); the descending vertical line from this value is the* crossover point *from supersaturation on the right side of the figure ($\Omega > 1.0$) to undersaturation on the left side ($\Omega < 1.0$). The* lysocline *is the depth at which the first signs of dissolution appear. The* compensation depth *is the depth at which dissolution results in a sudden decrease in $CaCO_3$ and below which $CaCO_3$ is essentially absent from the sediments. The saturation and compensation depths do not occur at the same point, indicating that much suspended $CaCO_3$ evidently persists in undersaturated water. Thus dissolution must be slow above the compensation depth, relative to the rate of precipitation.* Source: Berner (1974).

Hydrated CO_2, or H_2CO_3, then dissociates to form H^+ and HCO_3^-:

$$H_2CO_3 \rightleftharpoons H^+ + HCO_3^- \tag{1.3}$$

If carbonate ions are present the hydrogen ions released react with them to generate more HCO_3^-:

$$HCO_3^- \rightleftharpoons H^+ + CO_3^{2-} \tag{1.4}$$

The condition at equilibrium at the interface between a carbonate mineral and seawater is described by

$$CaCO_3 \rightleftharpoons Ca^{2+} + CO_3^{2-} \tag{1.5}$$

The hydration of CO_2 is represented by reactions 1.2 through 1.4; reaction 1.5 represents the dissociation of $CaCO_3$. If these reactions shift forward, both CO_2 and $CaCO_3$ are dissolved. If they shift in reverse as a result of evaporation or photosynthesis by algae, CO_2 is removed and $CaCO_3$ precipitates. The net reaction from summing the four reactions above can be written as

$$CO_2 + H_2O + CaCO_3 \rightleftharpoons Ca^{2+} + 2HCO_3^- \tag{1.6}$$

Reaction 1.6 illustrates the dissolution of $CaCO_3$ by CO_2 from respiration and the supersaturation of $CaCO_3$ from photosynthesis.

The pH of seawater depends on reactions 1.3 through 1.5. These control the quantities of H^+, HCO_3^-,and CO_3^{2-}. Free CO_2 can enter seawater from the atmosphere and as a metabolic by-product (Chapter 4). As shown by the reactions presented, a certain percentage of this new CO_2 reacts with water to produce H^+ and HCO_3^-, but some—a considerable proportion—forms undissociated H_2CO_3. A final fraction is retained ultimately as CO_3^{2-}.[20]

The solubilities of carbonate minerals are not easily predicted because their surfaces are altered by contact with seawater. Three situations are possible: (*1*) the mineral dissolves and loses Mg^{2+}, Ca^{2+}, or both to the seawater (in addition to CO_3^{2-}); (*2*) neither the mineral nor the seawater gains or loses ions; and (*3*) the mineral gains ions by precipitation of electrolytes from the seawater. The first possibility requires that the seawater be undersaturated with respect to the surfaces of the mineral. The second describes equilibrium, the condition whereby ions are gained and lost at an equal rate. The third can occur only if the seawater is supersaturated with respect to the surfaces of the mineral.[21]

Logically, carbonate minerals should precipitate spontaneously from supersaturated surface seawater, but this is not what happens. Inorganic ions—principally phosphate[22] and magnesium—and organic molecules[23] delay the process beyond predictable times. Magnesium ions appear to exert the greatest control over precipitation of $CaCO_3$ in open ocean waters.[24] Their influence is so pronounced that only biogenic removal ordinarily is possible.[25] Magnesium is a major constituent of seawater (Table 1.1), and enough is always present to react with the surfaces of carbonate minerals. A carbonate mineral placed in supersaturated seawater or artificial seawater containing the normal concentration of magnesium immediately acquires a surface precipitate or *overgrowth* of magnesian calcite (Fig. 1-14). The overgrowth alters the surface composition of the mineral and consequently its solubility. The change in solubility occurs as magnesium ions incorporated into the overgrowth approach equilibrium with those in the surrounding seawater. The effect is temporarily to increase the solubility of the surface of the mineral (Fig. 1-15) regardless of its original composition. By this I mean the *new* surface, because the original surface is no longer in contact with the solution. Thus the composition attained by the overgrowth is determined by the concentration of magne-

(a)

(b)

Figure 1-14 *Scanning electron photomicrographs of magnesian calcite overgrowths on pure calcite in artificial seawater of pH 8.40 supersaturated with* $CaCO_3$. (a) *Pure calcite crystals at the start of the experiment. 7875x.* (b) *Magnesian calcite overgrowths on pure calcite crystals after 10 to 50 h. 8250x.* Source: Berner (1975).

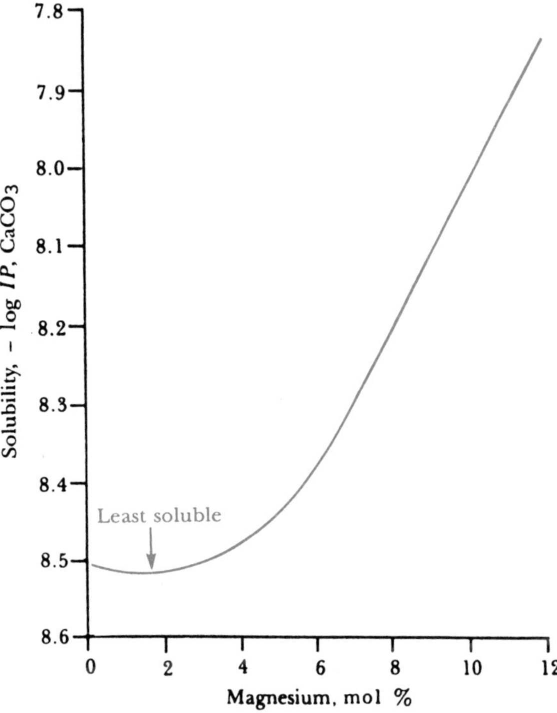

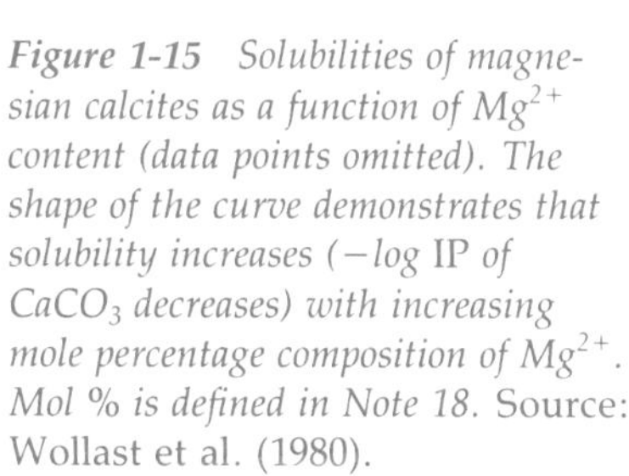

Figure 1-15 *Solubilities of magnesian calcites as a function of Mg^{2+} content (data points omitted). The shape of the curve demonstrates that solubility increases (−log* IP *of $CaCO_3$ decreases) with increasing mole percentage composition of Mg^{2+}. Mol % is defined in Note 18.* Source: Wollast et al. (1980).

sium in the seawater; the original composition of the mineral itself is less important.[26] In addition, a mineral's original composition affects the extent to which Mg^{2+} ions are incorporated into its surface layers. Those with high percentage compositions of magnesium adsorb the most Mg^{2+}.[27]

Carbonate minerals represent solid phases[21,26] that under certain conditions contribute ions to the surrounding liquid phase; similarly, components of the seawater can shift to the solid phase by precipitating. The belief that such phase changes occur to the benefit of aquarists under typical aquarium conditions has little basis in fact, an argument I develop more fully in the next subsection.

CARBONATE MINERALS IN AQUARIUMS For a carbonate mineral to control declining pH it obviously must dissolve and contribute anions to the seawater; in other words, it must produce HCO_3^- and CO_3^{2-} to react with H^+ generated by the increasing acidity of the surrounding solution caused by biological activity. Aquarium seawater often becomes more acidic with age.[28] Whether a carbonate mineral dissolves or precipitates depends to some extent on its original composition, but more importantly on the composition of the surrounding solution. The second factor is affected to some extent by the type of water system. In *open systems* fresh seawater is pumped through continuously, and ion depletion of the water does not occur. Suppose, for example, that calcite filtrants, which contain low concentrations of Mg^{2+}, are placed in an open-system aquarium. Assume also that the influent seawater is supersaturated with respect to $CaCO_3$. As illustrated in Figure 1-16, the first layer of precipitate formed on the surfaces of the filtrants is composed almost entirely of $CaCO_3$, along with a small amount of Mg^{2+}. Succeeding layers contain increasingly greater amounts of Mg^{2+}, which occupy sites in the overgrowth above both Ca^{2+} and Mg^{2+}. Each layer precipitated is accompanied by an increase in solubility, and the Mg^{2+} content increases with the square root of the thickness of the layer (Fig. 1-17). The layers of precipitate grow at an ever decreasing rate. The solubility of the overgrowth decreases as the growth rate approaches zero.

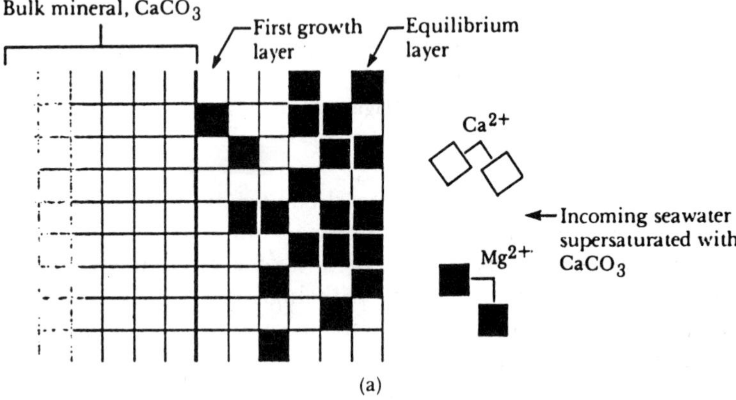

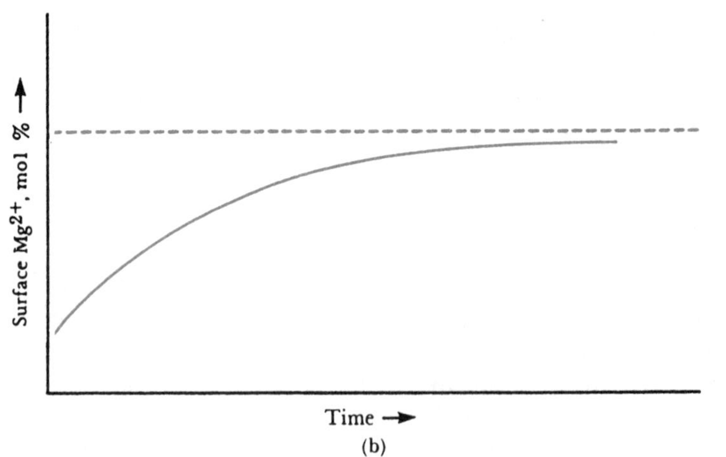

Figure 1-16 (a) *Diagrammatic illustration showing the formation of a magnesian calcite overgrowth on the surface of calcite in an open seawater system. The incoming seawater is supersaturated with respect to* $CaCO_3$. (b) *Graphic representation of part* (a) *showing* Mg^{2+} *precipitation on the surface of calcite as a function of time (units are dimensionless). Calcium is never depleted because the supply of seawater is unlimited. The broken line represents calcite with the minimum solubility for the particular seawater used.* Source: Stephen Spotte, drawn from data in Wollast et al. (1980).

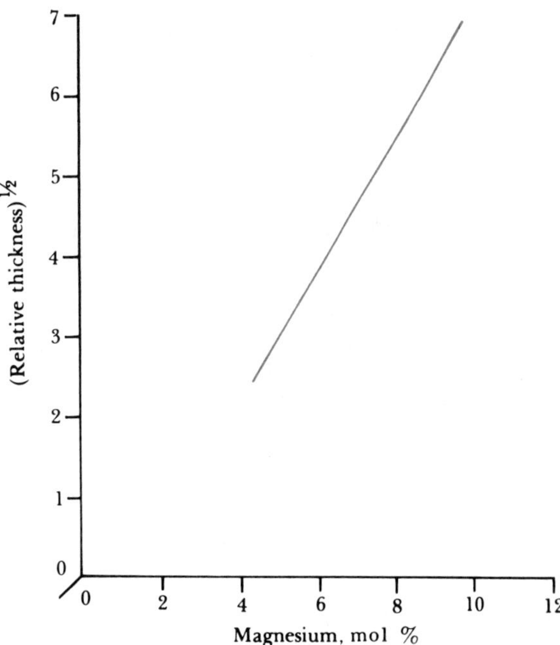

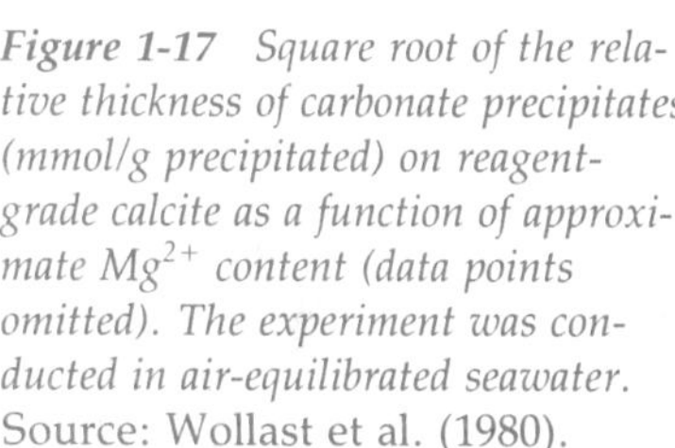
Figure 1-17 *Square root of the relative thickness of carbonate precipitates (mmol/g precipitated) on reagent-grade calcite as a function of approximate* Mg^{2+} *content (data points omitted). The experiment was conducted in air-equilibrated seawater.* Source: Wollast et al. (1980).

The overgrowth then recrystallizes, in the process rejecting Mg^{2+} and decreasing in solubility.[29]

Suppose next that calcite filtrants are added to a *closed-system* aquarium, by definition one containing a limited influx of new seawater. The water is recirculated continuously through a filter composed of crushed carbonate minerals. Such a system is subject to ion depletion. As before, assume that the seawater is supersaturated with respect to $CaCO_3$. If a large amount of calcite is placed in a small volume of seawater the first layer of precipitate is thick with a high Mg^{2+} concentration. This precipitate, like the one formed on calcite in open systems, rejects Mg^{2+} and continues to grow. Unlike the situation in excess seawater, however, the overgrowth contains successively less Mg^{2+} after each recrystallization. Eventually, a calcite is formed with a Mg^{2+} content that is most stable (i.e., least soluble) for the Ca^{2+} and CO_3^{2-} concentrations of that particular seawater (Fig. 1-18).

If much larger amounts of calcite are added to limited volumes of seawater the formation of the first layer of precipitate rapidly lowers the supersaturation of $CaCO_3$, resulting in an overgrowth that is thin and contains a low Mg^{2+} content. The overgrowth grows at an ever decreasing rate as it loses Mg^{2+} to the surrounding seawater and purifies. In the end it is again the calcite containing a Mg^{2+} content that provides the mini-

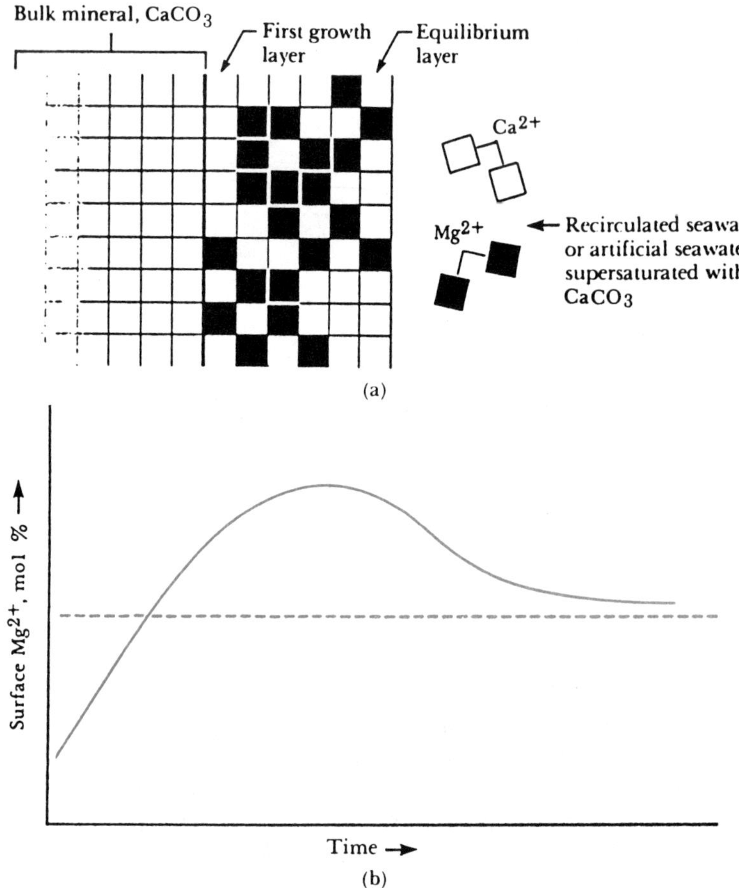

Figure 1-18 (a) *Diagrammatic illustration showing the formation of a magnesian calcite overgrowth on the surface of calcite in a closed seawater system. The seawater or artificial seawater is supersaturated with respect to* $CaCO_3$. (b) *Graphic representation of part* (a) *showing* Mg^{2+} *precipitation on the surface of calcite as a function of time (units are dimensionless). The supply of seawater is limited. The typical* Mg^{2+}/Ca^{2+} *ratio is 5. Calcium ion is depleted first, causing the concentration of magnesium ion in the precipitate to increase. Eventually, magnesium is depleted as well. The broken line represents calcite with the minimum solubility for the particular seawater used.* Source: Stephen Spotte, drawn from data in Wollast et al. (1980).

mum solubility. In both situations (i.e., open and closed systems), only the outermost layer of the magnesian calcite overgrowth appears to participate in exchange reactions with the seawater, and this layer is not thicker than the diameters of the molecules involved.[30]

Whether a carbonate mineral dissolves or precipitates is controlled by the degree of saturation of the surrounding seawater, but the *rate* at which either process occurs is limited by reactions at the mineral surfaces. These depend mainly on the composition and nature of the mineral. Consequently, the rates at which ions are gained and lost by a carbonate mineral can be altered substantially by even minor changes in the surface configuration and chemistry. As mentioned in the previous subsection, adsorption of contaminant ions from solution—notably magnesium, phosphate, and dissolved organic molecules—delays the precipitation of carbonate minerals by blocking appropriate surface sites. But the presence of these substances also retards their dissolution.[31]

What this means from a practical standpoint is simply that the *bulk minerals* themselves (i.e., the minerals minus their overgrowths of magnesian calcite) do not dissolve appreciably except at pH values below the tolerance limits of seawater fishes. In fact, at typical seawater pH values the opposite happens: the filtrants grow larger as magnesium carbonate precipitates on their surfaces, not shrink from dissolution. What dissolves, if anything, is the surface overgrowth, which is derived from the surrounding seawater. The gain of ions by carbonate minerals, in other words, causes equal molar losses of these ions from the solution. As a result, the concentration of anions contributed to the seawater by dissolution of the overgrowth cannot exceed the concentration removed initially; consequently, the net contribution to the alkalinity is essentially zero.

In the short term, carbonate minerals placed in seawater or artificial seawater rapidly lower the alkalinity and pH (Fig. 1-19),

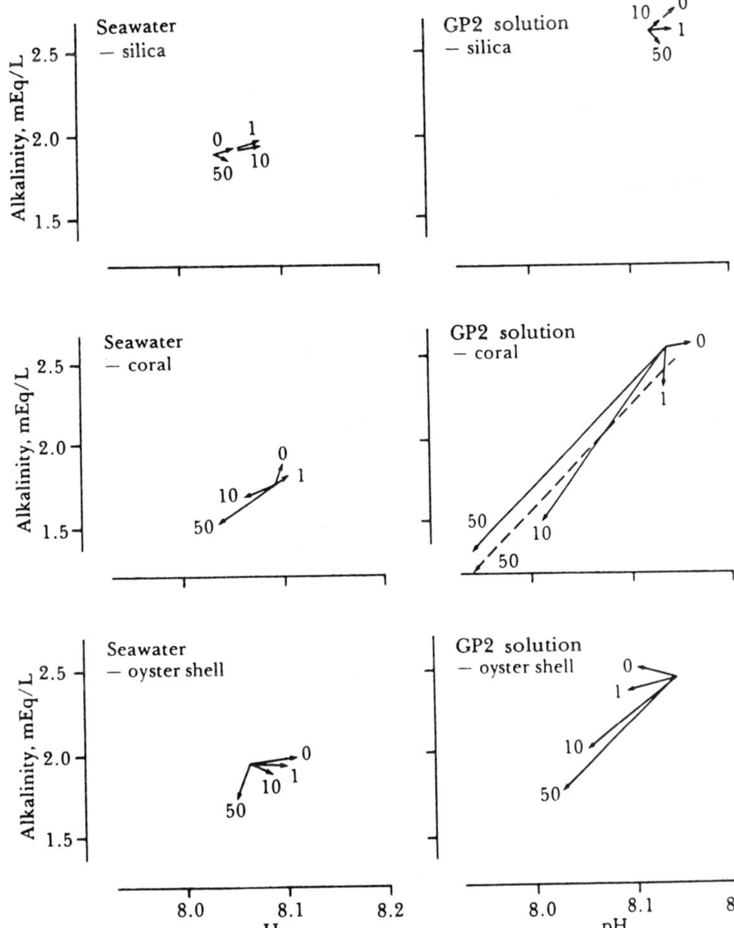

Figure 1-19 *Plot of alkalinity and pH of seawater and artificial seawater (GP2 solution) 24 h after addition of crushed filtrants (silica sand, coral, oyster shell). Arrowheads indicate conditions after 24 h. Numbers represent the volume of a filtrant in millilitres added to 500 mL of seawater or artificial seawater. Coral disturbs the carbonate system chemistry the most, and silica disturbs it the least.* Source: Adams and Spotte (1985).

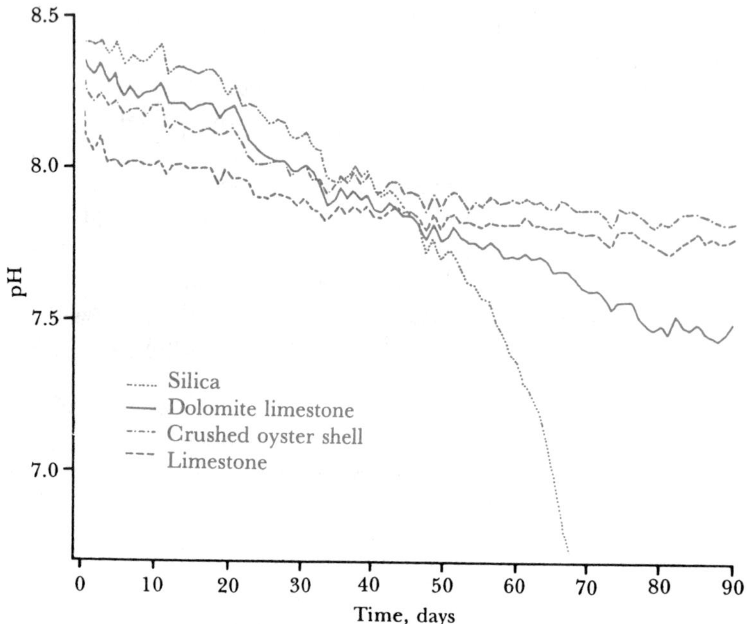

Figure 1-20 *Changes in pH in closed-system aquariums containing artificial seawater and different filtrants.* Source: Bower et al. (1981).

and the effect is enhanced as the ratio of the volume of mineral to volume of seawater is reduced.[32] In the long term, carbonate minerals are somewhat useful because they prevent the pH from falling below ~7.5 (Fig. 1-20).[33]

Any controversy that still exists among aquarists over which carbonate minerals are most soluble is irrelevant for two reasons. First, the solubility of a carbonate mineral depends on its surface composition. As just demonstrated, the acquisition of magnesian calcite overgrowths by all carbonate minerals quickly renders them indistinguishable in terms of solubility. Second, if overgrowths did not occur, selection of the most soluble mineral would require detailed analysis of its composition and the composition of the liquid phase. ''Standard'' carbonate minerals and ''standard'' seawaters do not exist. Peter K. Weyl wrote: ''The difficulty arises from asking the wrong question of nature. One should not ask 'What is the solubility of calcite in sea water?' until it has been established that there exists a unique solubility for the particular solution-solid system.''[34] For every sample of seawater there exists somewhere a carbonate mineral that when placed in it dissolves, precipitates, or does neither.

TECHNOLOGY

Method 1.1 Thermometer Calibration

Accurate temperature measurements are an essential part of husbandry, and even expensive thermometers must be calibrated before laboratory use. The following procedure should be done before any of the analytical methods that follow are attempted.

How to Calibrate Thermometers at Sea Level

1 Place the thermometer in a beaker of crushed ice until the temperature equilibrates (~15 min). Record the value.

2 Place the thermometer in the steam just at the surface of a beaker of boiling water until the temperature equilibrates (~5 min). Record the value.

3 On a sheet of metric graph paper (10 squares per centimetre) draw a straight, horizontal line. Mark intervals of 10°C. This is the reference line and forms the *abscissa* (x or horizontal axis).

4 Plot to +3 and −3°C on the *ordinate* (y or vertical axis) in increments of 1°C. Use an expanded scale as shown in Figure 1.21 (i.e., each 1°C is equivalent to 10°C on the abscissa). An expanded scale is necessary because of the small error (ordinarily <3% or <3°C).

5 Plot corrections of the two points obtained in the tests (cooling and heating) and connect them. Figure 1-21 illustrates how three thermometers were calibrated. Thermometer 1 read 0°C at freezing and 101°C at boiling. There was no cor-

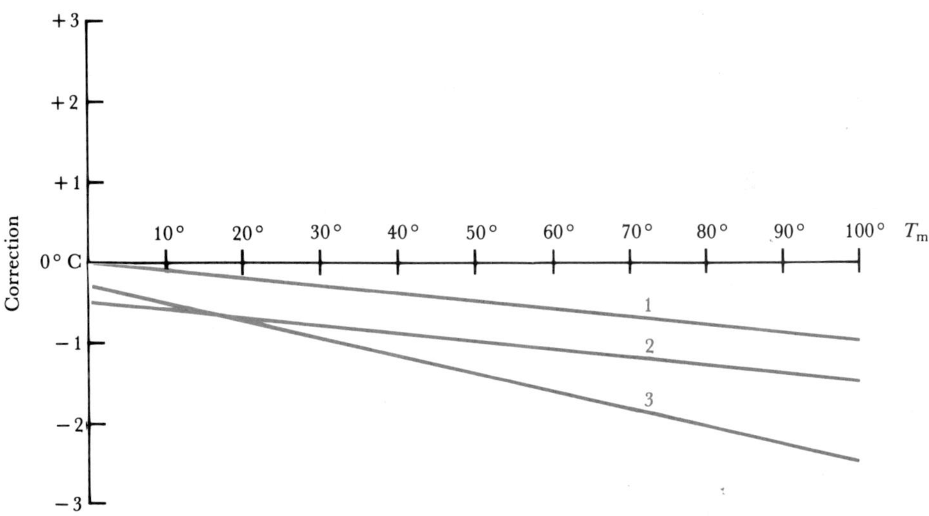

Figure 1-21 Calibration plot for three thermometers. Source: Patricia M. Bubucis, Sea Research Foundation.

rection at 0°C and −1°C at 100°C. When a measured temperature, T_m, of 20°C was obtained, the correction was −0.2°C, and the actual or corrected temperature, T_c, became 19.8°C. Thermometer 2 read 0.5°C at freezing and 101.5°C at boiling. Corrections were −0.5°C at freezing and −1.5°C at 100°C. The T_m of 20°C required a correction of −0.7°C, making T_c 19.3°C. Thermometer 3 read 0.3°C at freezing and 102.5°C at boiling. Corrections were −0.3°C at 0°C and −2.5°C at 100°C. A T_m of 20°C required a correction of −0.75°C, making T_c 19.2°C.

6 When corrections have been determined, write them in indelible ink on a label with adhesive backing, and stick the label to the top of the thermometer.

Method 1.2 Specific Gravity and Salinity Determinations

SPECIFIC GRAVITY The procedures below allow salinity to be determined from either hydrometer readings or specific gravity values. However, an intermediate step is required: the density of pure water at a reference temperature of 15.56°C must be obtained. Afterward, salinity at any temperature can be calculated. Alternatively, salinity can be read from Table 1-6 directly if the sample temperature and hydrometer reading are known.

It is important to recognize that a hydrometer reading varies in only two significant digits, and an error is introduced when the last digit is rounded to the nearest 0.001. In a reading of 1.025, for example, only the 2 and the 5 can vary; 1 and 0 remain constant. The possible error is 1 in 25, or 4%. This inherent error is perpetuated if the value derived is then converted to salinity. Greater measures of accuracy require reading to three effective significant digits and involve a series of hydrometers, each covering a narrow range. Such a procedure is unnecessary in routine husbandry.

The standard temperature used to calibrate most hydrometers meant for testing water is 15.56°C (60°F), but it can be any temperature. If the standard temperature is not 15.56°C the formula is

$$SG = \frac{\rho H}{\rho_K} \tag{1.7}$$

where SG = specific gravity corrected to the reference temperature, ρ or rho = the density of pure water at the reference temperature, ρ_K = a constant (the density of pure water at the

TABLE 1-6 Salinity (0.5 to 40‰) as a function of sample temperature (0 to 38°C) and hydrometer readings, *H*, for hydrometers calibrated at reference and standard temperatures of 15.56°C.

	Temperature, °C												
H	0	1	2	3	4	5	6	7	8	9	10	11	12
1.000	—	—	—	—	—	—	—	—	—	—	—	—	—
1.001	—	—	—	—	—	—	—	—	—	—	—	0.5	0.6
1.002	1.4	1.4	1.4	1.4	1.4	1.4	1.4	1.4	1.5	1.6	1.7	1.8	1.9
1.003	2.6	2.6	2.6	2.6	2.6	2.6	2.6	2.7	2.7	2.8	2.9	3.1	3.2
1.004	3.9	3.9	3.9	3.9	3.9	3.9	3.9	3.9	4.0	4.1	4.2	4.4	4.5
1.005	5.1	5.1	5.1	5.1	5.1	5.1	5.1	5.2	5.3	5.4	5.5	5.6	5.8
1.006	6.3	6.3	6.3	6.3	6.3	6.3	6.4	6.5	6.5	6.7	6.8	6.9	7.1
1.007	7.6	7.6	7.6	7.6	7.6	7.6	7.6	7.7	7.8	7.9	8.1	8.2	8.4
1.008	8.8	8.8	8.8	8.8	8.8	8.9	8.9	9.0	9.1	9.2	9.4	9.5	9.7
1.009	10.1	10.1	10.1	10.1	10.1	10.1	10.2	10.3	10.4	10.5	10.7	10.8	11.0
1.010	11.3	11.3	11.3	11.3	11.3	11.4	11.5	11.6	11.7	11.8	11.9	12.1	12.3
1.011	12.6	12.6	12.6	12.6	12.6	12.7	12.7	12.8	13.0	13.1	13.2	13.4	13.6
1.012	13.8	13.8	13.8	13.8	13.9	13.9	14.0	14.1	14.2	14.4	14.5	14.7	14.9
1.013	15.0	15.0	15.0	15.1	15.1	15.2	15.3	15.4	15.5	15.6	15.8	16.0	16.2
1.014	16.3	16.3	16.3	16.3	16.4	16.5	16.6	16.7	16.8	16.9	17.1	17.3	17.5
1.015	17.5	17.5	17.5	17.6	17.6	17.7	17.8	17.9	18.1	18.2	18.4	18.6	18.8
1.016	18.8	18.8	18.8	18.8	18.9	19.0	19.1	19.2	19.3	19.5	19.7	19.8	20.0
1.017	20.0	20.0	20.0	20.1	20.2	20.3	20.4	20.5	20.6	20.8	20.9	21.1	21.3
1.018	21.2	21.3	21.3	21.3	21.4	21.5	21.6	21.8	21.9	22.1	22.2	22.4	22.6
1.019	22.5	22.5	22.5	22.6	22.7	22.8	22.9	23.0	23.2	23.3	23.5	23.7	23.9
1.020	23.7	23.7	23.8	23.9	23.9	24.0	24.2	24.3	24.5	24.6	24.8	25.0	25.2
1.021	25.0	25.0	25.0	25.1	25.2	25.3	25.4	25.6	25.7	25.9	26.1	26.3	26.5
1.022	26.2	26.2	26.3	26.4	26.5	26.6	26.7	26.8	27.0	27.2	27.4	27.6	27.8
1.023	27.4	27.5	27.5	27.6	27.7	27.8	28.0	28.1	28.3	28.5	28.7	28.9	29.1
1.024	28.7	28.7	28.8	28.9	29.0	29.1	29.2	29.4	29.6	29.7	29.9	30.1	30.4
1.025	29.9	30.0	30.0	30.1	30.2	30.4	30.5	30.7	30.8	31.0	31.2	31.4	31.7
1.026	31.1	31.2	31.3	31.4	31.5	31.6	31.8	31.9	32.1	32.3	32.5	32.7	33.0
1.027	32.4	32.5	32.5	32.6	32.8	32.9	33.0	33.2	33.4	33.6	33.8	34.0	34.2
1.028	33.6	33.7	33.8	33.9	34.0	34.1	34.3	34.5	34.6	34.8	35.1	35.3	35.5
1.029	34.9	34.9	35.0	35.1	35.3	35.4	35.6	35.7	35.9	36.1	36.3	36.6	36.8
1.030	36.1	36.2	36.3	36.4	36.5	36.7	36.8	37.0	37.2	37.4	37.6	37.8	38.1
1.031	37.3	37.4	37.5	37.6	37.8	37.9	38.1	38.3	38.5	38.7	38.9	39.1	39.4
1.032	38.6	38.7	38.8	38.9	39.0	39.2	39.3	39.5	39.7	39.9	—	—	—

	Temperature, °C												
H	13	14	15	16	17	18	19	20	21	22	23	24	25
1.000	—	—	—	—	—	0.6	0.8	1.0	1.3	1.6	1.9	2.3	2.6
1.001	0.8	1.0	1.2	1.4	1.6	1.8	2.1	2.4	2.6	2.9	3.3	3.6	3.9
1.002	2.1	2.3	2.5	2.7	2.9	3.1	3.4	3.7	4.0	4.3	4.6	4.9	5.3
1.003	3.4	3.6	3.8	4.0	4.2	4.5	4.7	5.0	5.3	5.6	5.9	6.2	6.6
1.004	4.7	4.9	5.1	5.3	5.5	5.8	6.0	6.3	6.6	6.9	7.2	7.6	7.9
1.005	6.0	6.2	6.4	6.6	6.8	7.1	7.4	7.6	7.9	8.3	8.6	8.9	9.3
1.006	7.3	7.5	7.7	7.9	8.2	8.4	8.7	9.0	9.3	9.6	9.9	10.3	10.6
1.007	8.6	8.8	9.0	9.2	9.5	9.7	10.0	10.3	10.6	10.9	11.2	11.6	12.0

TABLE 1-6 *(Continued)*

	Temperature, °C												
H	13	14	15	16	17	18	19	20	21	22	23	24	25
1.008	9.9	10.1	10.3	10.5	10.8	11.0	11.3	11.6	11.9	12.2	12.6	12.9	13.3
1.009	11.2	11.4	11.6	11.8	12.1	12.4	12.6	12.9	13.2	13.6	13.9	14.3	14.6
1.010	12.5	12.7	12.9	13.2	13.4	13.7	14.0	14.3	14.6	14.9	15.2	15.6	16.0
1.011	13.8	14.0	14.2	14.5	14.7	15.0	15.3	15.6	15.9	16.2	16.6	16.9	17.3
1.012	15.1	15.3	15.5	15.8	16.0	16.3	16.6	16.9	17.2	17.5	17.9	18.2	18.6
1.013	16.4	16.6	16.8	17.1	17.3	17.6	17.9	18.2	18.5	18.9	19.2	19.6	19.9
1.014	17.7	17.9	18.1	18.4	18.6	18.9	19.2	19.5	19.9	20.2	20.5	20.9	21.3
1.015	19.0	19.2	19.4	19.7	20.0	20.2	20.5	20.9	21.2	21.5	21.9	22.2	22.6
1.016	20.3	20.5	20.7	21.0	21.3	21.6	21.9	22.2	22.5	22.8	23.2	23.6	23.9
1.017	21.6	21.8	22.0	22.3	22.6	22.9	23.2	23.5	23.8	24.2	24.5	24.9	25.3
1.018	22.9	23.1	23.3	23.6	23.9	24.2	24.5	24.8	25.1	25.5	25.8	26.2	26.6
1.019	24.1	24.4	24.6	24.9	25.2	25.5	25.8	26.1	26.5	26.8	27.2	27.5	27.9
1.020	25.4	25.7	25.9	26.2	26.5	26.8	27.1	27.4	27.8	28.1	28.5	28.9	29.2
1.021	26.7	27.0	27.2	27.5	27.8	28.1	28.4	28.8	29.1	29.4	29.8	30.2	30.6
1.022	28.0	28.3	28.5	28.8	29.1	29.4	29.7	30.1	30.4	30.8	31.1	31.5	31.9
1.023	29.3	29.6	29.8	30.1	30.4	30.7	31.0	31.4	31.7	32.1	32.4	32.8	33.2
1.024	30.6	30.9	31.1	31.4	31.7	32.0	32.4	32.7	33.0	33.4	33.8	34.2	34.5
1.025	31.9	32.2	32.4	32.7	33.0	33.3	33.7	34.0	34.3	34.7	35.1	35.5	35.9
1.026	33.2	33.5	33.7	34.0	34.3	34.6	35.0	35.3	35.7	36.0	36.4	36.8	37.2
1.027	34.5	34.8	35.0	35.3	35.6	35.9	36.3	36.6	37.0	37.3	37.7	38.1	38.5
1.028	35.8	36.0	36.3	36.6	36.9	37.2	37.6	37.9	38.3	38.7	39.0	39.4	39.8
1.029	37.1	37.3	37.6	37.9	38.2	38.6	38.9	39.2	39.6	40.0	—	—	—
1.030	38.4	38.6	38.9	39.2	39.5	39.9	—	—	—	—	—	—	—
1.031	39.6	39.9	—	—	—	—	—	—	—	—	—	—	—

	Temperature, °C												
H	26	27	28	29	30	31	32	33	34	35	36	37	38
1.000	3.0	3.3	3.7	4.1	4.5	4.9	5.3	5.8	6.2	6.7	7.2	7.7	8.2
1.001	4.3	4.7	5.0	5.4	5.8	6.3	6.7	7.1	7.6	8.1	8.6	9.1	9.6
1.002	5.6	6.0	6.4	6.8	7.2	7.6	8.1	8.5	9.0	9.4	9.9	10.4	10.9
1.003	7.0	7.3	7.7	8.1	8.6	9.0	9.4	9.9	10.3	10.8	11.3	11.8	12.3
1.004	8.3	8.7	9.1	9.5	9.9	10.3	10.8	11.2	11.7	12.2	12.6	13.1	13.6
1.005	9.6	10.0	10.4	10.8	11.2	11.7	12.1	12.6	13.0	13.5	14.0	14.5	15.0
1.006	11.0	11.4	11.8	12.2	12.6	13.0	13.5	13.9	14.4	14.9	15.4	15.9	16.4
1.007	12.3	12.7	13.1	13.5	13.9	14.4	14.8	15.3	15.7	16.2	16.7	17.2	17.7
1.008	13.7	14.0	14.4	14.9	15.3	15.7	16.2	16.6	17.1	17.6	18.1	18.6	19.1
1.009	15.0	15.4	15.8	16.2	16.6	17.1	17.5	18.0	18.4	18.9	19.4	19.9	20.4
1.010	16.3	16.7	17.1	17.5	18.0	18.4	18.9	19.3	19.8	20.3	20.8	21.3	21.8
1.011	17.7	18.1	18.5	18.9	19.3	19.7	20.2	20.7	21.1	21.6	22.1	22.6	23.1
1.012	19.0	19.4	19.8	20.2	20.7	21.1	21.5	22.0	22.5	23.0	23.5	24.0	24.5
1.013	20.3	20.7	21.1	21.6	22.0	22.4	22.9	23.4	23.8	24.3	24.8	25.3	25.9
1.014	21.7	22.1	22.5	22.9	23.3	23.8	24.2	24.7	25.2	25.7	26.2	26.7	27.2
1.015	23.0	23.4	23.8	24.2	24.7	25.1	25.6	26.1	26.5	27.0	27.5	28.0	28.6
1.016	24.3	24.7	25.1	25.6	26.0	26.5	26.9	27.4	27.9	28.4	28.9	29.4	29.9
1.017	25.7	26.1	26.5	26.9	27.4	27.8	28.3	28.7	29.2	29.7	30.2	30.7	31.3

TABLE 1-6 *(Continued)*

	Temperature, °C												
H	26	27	28	29	30	31	32	33	34	35	36	37	38
1.018	27.0	27.4	27.8	28.2	28.7	29.1	29.6	30.1	30.6	31.1	31.6	32.1	32.6
1.019	28.3	28.7	29.2	29.6	30.0	30.5	30.9	31.4	31.9	32.4	32.9	33.4	34.0
1.020	29.6	30.1	30.5	30.9	31.4	31.8	32.3	32.8	33.3	33.8	34.3	34.8	35.3
1.021	31.0	31.4	31.8	32.2	32.7	33.2	33.6	34.1	34.6	35.1	35.6	36.1	36.7
1.022	32.3	32.7	33.1	33.6	34.0	34.5	35.0	35.4	35.9	36.4	36.9	37.5	38.0
1.023	33.6	34.0	34.5	34.9	35.4	35.8	36.3	36.8	37.3	37.8	38.3	38.8	39.3
1.024	35.0	35.4	35.8	36.2	36.7	37.2	37.6	38.1	38.6	39.1	39.6	—	—
1.025	36.3	36.7	37.1	37.6	38.0	38.5	39.0	39.5	39.9	—	—	—	—
1.026	37.6	38.0	38.5	38.9	39.4	39.8	—	—	—	—	—	—	—
1.027	38.9	39.3	39.8	—	—	—	—	—	—	—	—	—	—

Source: Gary Adams, Sea Research Foundation, calculated from a 1-atm equation of state for seawater (Millero and Poisson 1981); also see Fofonoff (1985).

standard temperature, 0.9990389 g/cm^3 at 15.56°C), and H = the hydrometer reading of the sample. The use of this equation nonetheless requires that the hydrometer reading be made at the reference temperature. The density of pure water at different temperatures is shown in Table 1-3. Hydrometers approved by ASTM (American Society for Testing and Materials) display reference and standard temperatures. Standard temperature is given second. If the sample temperature differs from the reference temperature (15.56°C in this case) a correction must be made in the hydrometer reading, as explained in the procedures below. Scales on hydrometers used for seawater analysis should cover the range 1.000 to 1.050 in increments of 0.001. Readings to this degree of accuracy are possible if the instrument has a narrow stem (Fig. 1-22). The specific gravity of seawater typically falls about midway between 1.020 and 1.030.

Three rules to remember are (*1*) a correction is necessary when the reference and sample temperatures are different; (*2*) reference, standard, and sample temperatures must always be stated when expressing the hydrometer reading, *H*; and (*3*) the fact that pure water has a density of unity at 4°C has no operational significance, because at the reference temperature of the hydrometer the specific gravity of pure water is *always* unity.[35]

I recommend that reference and standard temperatures be expressed first and second, respectively, a convention consistent with that used by most manufacturers of good hydrometers. A typical hydrometer reading before determining the density of pure water at the reference temperature might be expressed "*H* (15.56°C/15.56°C) = 1.025 at 10°C," meaning that a sample of seawater measured 1.025 at 10°C (hydrometer reading, H) when a hydrometer calibrated at reference and standard temperatures of 15.56°C was used. Density would be expressed as $\rho = 1.024$ g/cm^3 (see procedures below). Only the value of SG matters; H is unimportant except as a means of obtaining SG.

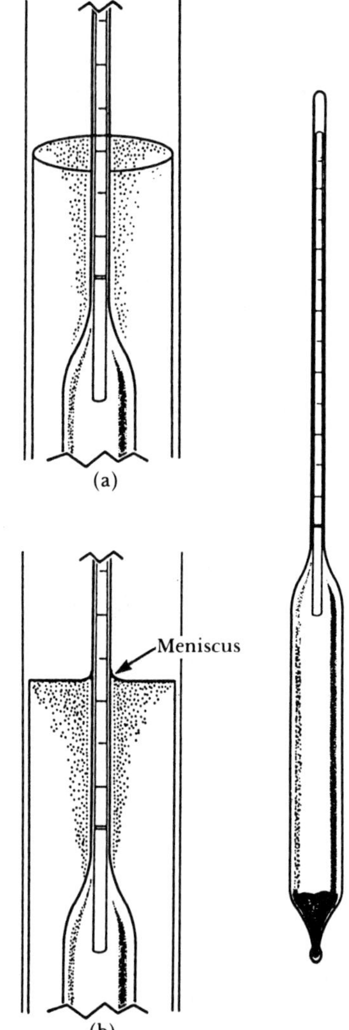

Figure 1-22 *A typical hydrometer used to measure the specific gravity of seawater is shown on the right. The correct way to read a hydrometer is to* (a) *focus your eyes slightly below the plane of the surface of the water, then* (b) *raise your eyes slowly until the surface changes from an ellipse to a straight line.* Source: Stephen Spotte, drawn partly from information in Peffer and Blair (1949).

How to Use a Hydrometer

1 Wash the hydrometer in freshwater to remove salts, then dry it.
2 Measure the temperature of the sample solution.
3 Collect a seawater sample in a smooth, clear glass container of sufficient depth to allow the hydrometer to float freely and large enough in circumference to prevent it from adhering to the sides. A 500-mL graduated cylinder is adequate. Opaque containers are unacceptable because the scale of the hydrometer cannot be seen at the level of the water line (see step 6).
4 Let the hydrometer remain in the sample solution for a few minutes. A difference in temperature between the instrument and sample can result in a false reading.
5 Immerse the hydrometer slowly and completely in the sample (push it all the way under the surface), then allow it to float freely.
6 After the instrument has come to rest, read the scale by focusing your eyes slightly below the plane of the surface of the liquid, then raising your eyes slowly until the surface (seen as an ellipse) becomes a straight line. Where this line cuts across the scale is the point at which the reading should be taken (Fig. 1-22).
7 Record the value and correct for temperature using the next procedure.

How to Determine Specific Gravity

1 Figure 1-23 shows the correction term that must be added to the hydrometer reading to obtain specific gravity. It is valid only for hydrometers calibrated at reference and standard temperatures of 15.56°C.[36]
2 Look in the far left or right column of the figure and find the range of H that brackets the value recorded in step 7 of the previous procedure. Follow this range across to the temperature of the sample and note the appropriate correction term (range −1 to +3).
3 Suppose H (15.56/15.56°C) = 1.023 at 23°C. At this sample temperature the correction term is either +1 or +2 (+0.001

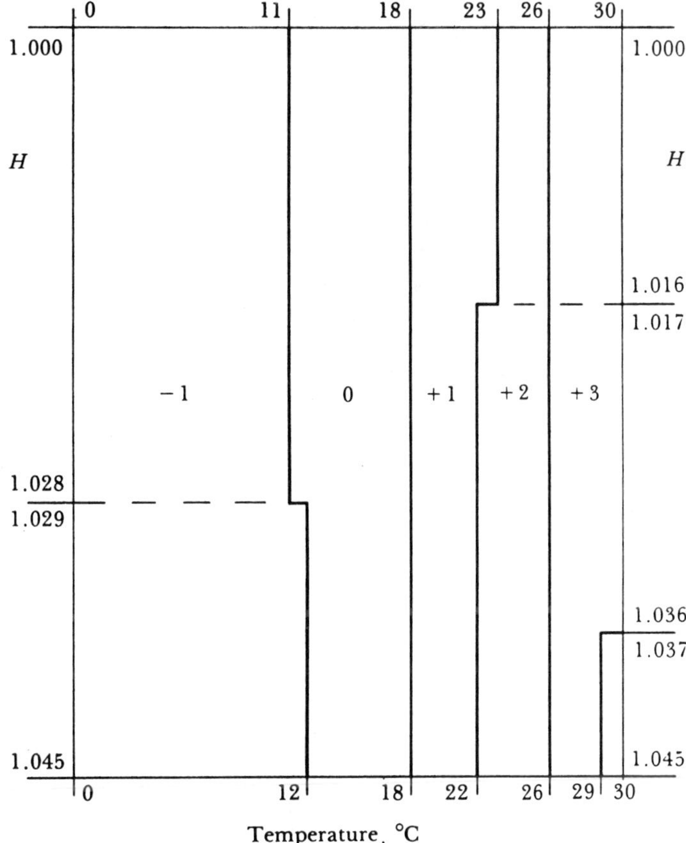

Figure 1-23 Correction terms (the numbers that convert H to give SG at each hydrometer reading and sample temperature). The figure is valid only for hydrometers calibrated at reference and standard temperatures of 15.56°C. The procedure for use of the figure is given in the text. The correction term is added to the third decimal place of H. Source: Gary Adams, Sea Research Foundation.

or +0.002), depending on whether H is ≤ 1.016 or ≥ 1.017.* Because 1.023 is >1.017 the correction term is +2 (i.e., +0.002), and SG = 1.025.

SALINITY The salinity of seawater can be measured with a salinometer or refractometer,[38] converted from SG, or estimated from SG to ±0.5‰ by the empirical equation

$$S = 1.1 + 1300(SG - 0.999) \tag{1.8}$$

The equation[39] is valid at S = 20 to 40‰. An example of a handheld refractometer is shown in Figure 1-24. When such an instrument is received, check the calibration using deionized water by the procedure below. Instructions for recalibration should be provided by the manufacturer.

*The symbol ≤ means "less than or equal to"; ≥ means "greater than or equal to."

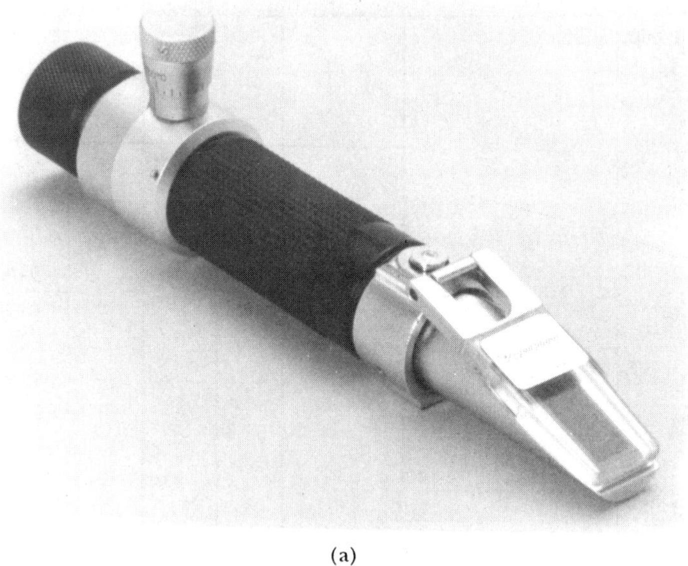

(a)

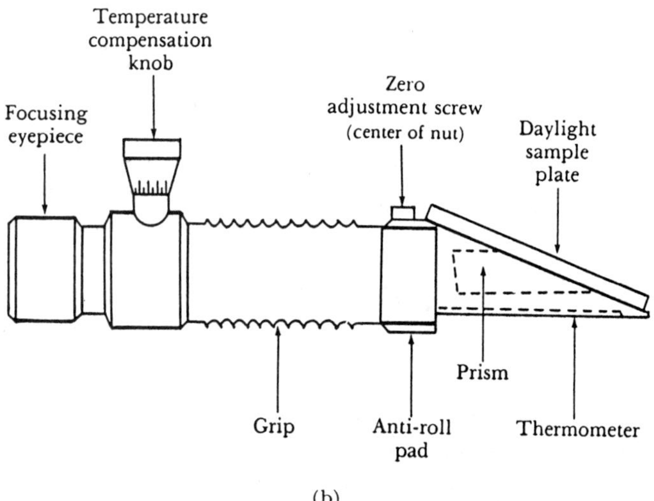

(b)

Figure 1-24 (a) *A hand-held refractometer for measuring the salinity of seawater and* (b) *its working parts.* Source: Aquafauna Bio-Marine, Inc., P.O. Box 5, Hawthorne CA 90250.

How to Measure Salinity with a Hand-held Refractometer

1 Turn the instrument over. On the bottom is a thermometer. Read the temperature of the sample seawater and adjust the temperature compensation knob to match it. Hold the refractometer by the black grip. Holding it elsewhere imparts body heat, causing a faulty temperature compensation.

2 Lift the sample plate. Examine the prism to be sure it is free of fingerprints and dirt. Wipe it clean if necessary.

3 Place several drops of sample water on the surface of the prism. Use enough to cover the prism completely, then carefully lower the sample plate so that no air bubbles are trapped underneath.

4 Point the prism end toward a light. Focus the eyepiece until the scale is clearly visible.

5 A horizontal boundary line will appear, separating the blue background from a brighter area underneath. Read the value at the line (the instrument shown in Fig. 1-24 gives both salinity and specific gravity values). If the line is diffuse repeat steps 3 and 4. The cause ordinarily is a dirty prism or insufficient sample volume on the prism.

PRACTICAL APPLICATIONS To maintain consistent use of units, equations 1.9 to 1.11 incorporate density, ρ, and not specific gravity, *SG*. This is necessary because volume multiplied by specific gravity does not yield mass. However, density in Standard International or SI units (e.g., g/cm^3) is numerically close to specific gravity at 15.56°C; where the symbol ρ appears a specific gravity value can be substituted. The difference in the results of computations using ρ and *SG* is generally less than one part in a thousand.

In a volume of seawater the mass of solutes can be expressed by

$$m = V\rho S \tag{1.9}$$

where m = mass (g), V = volume (L), S = salinity (‰), and ρ = density (g/cm^3). If freshwater evaporates or is added, the mass of solutes is considered to remain constant. Thus

$$V\rho_1 S_1 = (V - X)\rho_2 S_2 \tag{1.10}$$

where X is the amount of water lost by evaporation, and the subscripts 1 and 2 for S and ρ are values before and after evaporation. Solving for X gives

$$X = V\left(1 - \frac{\rho_1 S_1}{\rho_2 S_2}\right) \tag{1.11}$$

How to Reduce Salinity

1 An aquarium contains 500 L of seawater; H (15.56°C/15.56°C) = 1.029 at 10°C. How much seawater would have to be replaced with freshwater to attain S = 30‰?

2 First determine the original salinity using Figure 1-23 and Table 1-7. The correction term applied to H at 10°C is −1,

TABLE 1-7 Specific gravity, SG, at 15.56°C (i.e., hydrometer reading, H, with correction term in Fig. 1-23 added to the third decimal place) versus salinity, S.

SG	S, ‰	SG	S, ‰
1.000	1.0	1.017	22.2
1.001	1.3	1.018	23.5
1.002	2.6	1.019	24.8
1.003	3.9	1.020	26.1
1.004	5.2	1.021	27.4
1.005	6.5	1.022	28.7
1.006	7.8	1.023	30.0
1.007	9.1	1.024	31.3
1.008	10.4	1.025	32.6
1.009	11.7	1.026	33.9
1.010	13.0	1.027	35.2
1.011	14.4	1.028	36.5
1.012	15.7	1.029	37.8
1.013	17.0	1.030	39.1
1.014	18.3	1.031	40.4
1.015	19.6	1.032	41.7
1.016	20.9	1.033	42.9

Source: Gary Adams and Stephen Spotte, Sea Research Foundation, calculated from a 1-atm equation of state for seawater (Millero and Poisson 1981).

and SG is therefore 1.029 − 0.001 or 1.028. According to Table 1-7 this is equivalent to a salinity of 36.5‰.

3 What is the solute mass at 36.5‰? From equation 1.9,

$$(500)(1.028)(36.5) = 1.88 \times 10^4 \text{ g solute}$$

4 What is the solute mass at 30‰? A salinity of 30‰ is equivalent to SG = 1.023 (Table 1-7). Therefore,

$$(500)(1.023)(30) = 1.53 \times 10^4 \text{ g solute}$$

The amount of solute that must be discarded is the difference, or

$$1.88 \times 10^4 \text{ g} - 1.53 \times 10^4 \text{ g} = 3.5 \times 10^3 \text{ g solute}$$

5 The seawater to be discarded is SG = 1.028 and S = 36.5‰; therefore the volume containing 3.5×10^3 g of solute is

$$(V)(1.028)(36.5) = 3.5 \times 10^3$$

$$V = \frac{(3.5)\,(10^3)}{(1.028)(36.5)} = 93.3$$

6 The amount that must be replaced with freshwater is 93.3 L, or ~19% of the original volume.

How to Compensate for Evaporative Loss Based on Salinity

1 In an aquarium that originally contained 2000 L of seawater at $S = \sim 35‰$, evaporation has occurred and the salinity is now ~39‰. How much freshwater must be added?

2 Note that temperature is irrelevant, and any temperature could be used in this example. The amount of freshwater required is calculated as follows: $V = 2000$ L, $SG_1 = 1.027$, $S_1 = 35.2‰$, $SG_2 = 1.030$, and $S_2 = 39.1‰$. Values of SG and S are from Table 1-7. Substitution of values into equation 1.11 gives

$$X = 2000\left[1 - \frac{(1.027)(35.2)}{(1.030)(39.1)}\right] = 204.7$$

3 The amount of freshwater to be added is 204.7 L.

How to Compensate for Evaporative Loss Based on Specific Gravity

1 In an aquarium that originally contained 1500 L of seawater at $SG = 1.028$, evaporation has occurred and the specific gravity is now 1.030. How much freshwater must be added?

2 Because temperature is irrelevant in this example, density can be used in place of specific gravity. The amount of freshwater required is calculated as follows: $V = 1500$ L, $SG_1 = 1.028$, and $SG_2 = 1.030$. From Table 1-7, $S_1 = 36.5‰$ and $S_2 = 39.1‰$. Substitution of values into equation 1.11 gives

$$X = 1500\left[1 - \frac{(1.028)\ (36.5)}{(1.030)\ (39.1)}\right] = 102.5$$

3 The amount of freshwater to be added is 102.5 L.

Method 1.3 pH Determination

The measurement of pH requires, at minimum, a direct-reading pH meter[40] (i.e., a deflector-type electronic voltmeter) with an expanded scale (Fig. 1-25). Two electrodes also are needed: a *glass pH electrode* and a *reference electrode*. A *combination electrode* combines these; an *electrode pair* consists of two separate electrodes (Fig. 1-26).

The function of the electrode component is to measure the difference in hydrogen ion activity, f'_{H^+},[40] across a H^+-selective

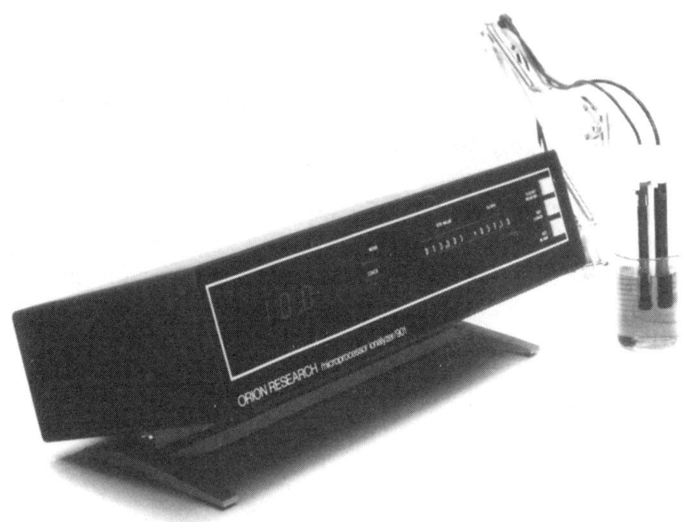

Figure 1-25 A direct reading pH meter suitable for measuring the pH of seawater. Source: Orion Research Incorporated, 840 Memorial Drive, Cambridge MA 02139.

membrane (i.e., a ''pH-sensitive'' membrane).[41] The measurement of pH is based on assumptions that (*1*) the membrane is perfectly permeable to H^+ at all measured f'_{H^+}, and (*2*) the potential difference across the glass membrane depends only on the difference in f'_{H^+} in the two phases separated by the membrane. The reference electrode is independent of the activities of all chemical species in the sample solution, and its function is to complete the circuit.

Combination electrodes have several advantages: (*1*) convenience (only one electrode must be handled); (*2*) availability of different sizes; (*3*) stability (the reference junction is located next to the glass bulb, which reduces noise and the subsequent erratic readings it causes); (*4*) a choice of glass or epoxy bodies; and (*5*) a choice of refillable or gel-filled bodies. An electrode pair offers the singular advantage of a choice of reference electrodes that are compatible with different sample types (e.g., determination of pH in waters of high or low ionic strength). For precision work in seawater an electrode pair is recommended. The reference electrode can be either single or double junction; the precision is comparable. A double junction type is recommended because the filling solution can be changed. This flexibility is sometimes useful when a contamination or interference problem is encountered, or when it is necessary to keep the sample solution out of contact with the internal element, which contains silver chloride, AgCl.

STANDARDIZATION AND CALIBRATION OF pH METERS

The pH meter assembly (meter plus electrode pair) is designed

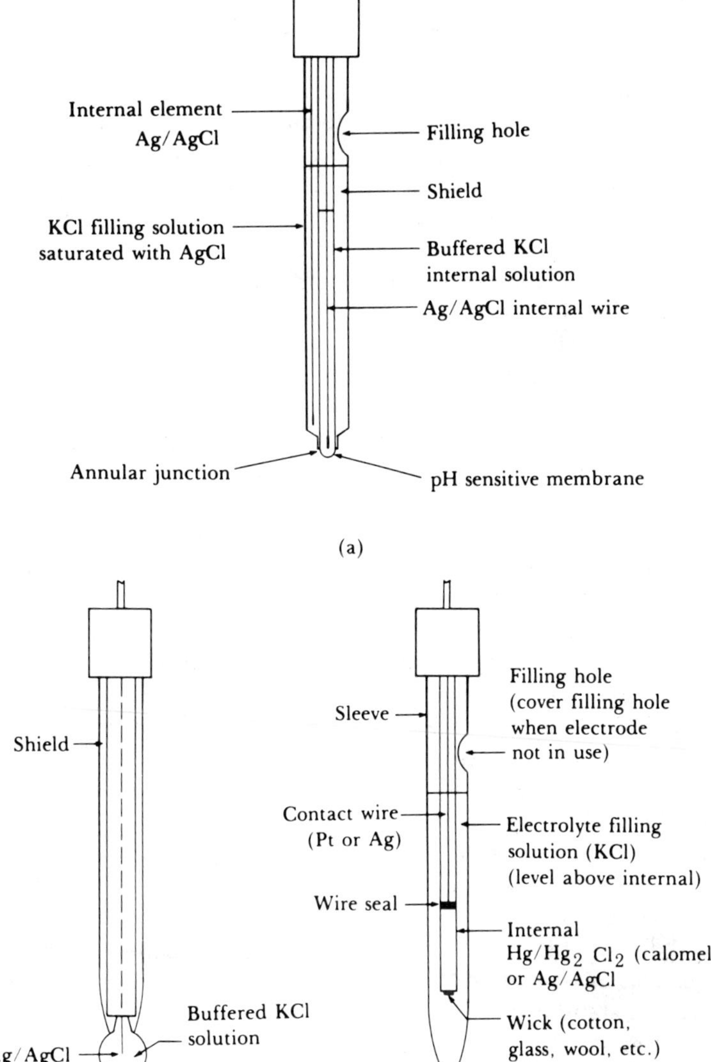

Figure 1-26 *The two types of pH electrodes:* (a) *combination and* (b) *electrode pair. The electrode pair consists of a pH glass electrode (left) and a reference electrode (right).* Source: Anonymous (1982).

to show a difference between the pH values of a standard buffer and an unknown (a sample of seawater) at the same temperature. The accuracy of the instrument is demonstrated after standardization and calibration by measuring the pH of a second standard solution. The two standards should bracket the pH of the sample. Errors caused by fluctuating temperature and the residual liquid junction potential are lessened by standardizing at pH values close to that of the sample. Standards of pH 7.0 and 10.0 are adequate for measuring the pH of seawater.[42] In alkalinity measurements (see Method 1.4), standard solutions of pH 4 and 7 are used.

The most accurate pH measurements are made by aligning the meter and electrode with the pH values of two standard solutions, then measuring the pH of the sample. The first standard buffer solution corrects for one type of nonideal behavior; the second buffer adjusts for another (see below). Compensation is performed in two steps, standardization and calibration.

When an ideal pH-electrode pair is immersed in a solution of pH 7.00, the theoretical output is 0.0 mV.* Electrodes, however, are seldom ideal, and the discrepancy must be corrected in the standardization circuitry. After manipulation, the meter reports a voltage of 0.0 mV. *Standardization* (synonyms are *offset adjustment* and *buffer adjustment*), as this procedure is called, is performed with a standard buffer solution of the same temperature as the sample.

Standardization alone is sufficient only if the pH of the buffer solution and test sample are identical (pH 7.00). Values other than perfect neutrality will be in error because the response of the glass membrane varies with pH in a non-Nernstian manner.[41] Standardization must be checked with a second standard buffer solution of known but different pH, a procedure called *calibration* (synonyms are *span*, *slope*, and *sensitivity adjustment*).

Calibration is necessary because the second source of nonideal behavior mentioned previously is the imperfect permeability of the glass membrane to H^+. This results in voltages different from those predicted by the Nernst equation.[41] The discrepancy is accounted for by calibration. The calibration procedure involves a series of steps.

Adjustment of the pH meter is accomplished with the ''slope'' or ''calibrate'' knob, which is different from the knob used in standardization. The calibration knob compensates for the nonideal behavior of the membrane's H^+ permeability by adjusting the meter to express the known pH value of the second buffer solution.

RULES OF CALIBRATION[43]

1 Calibration is performed after standardization (i.e., the first step in calibration is standardization).

2 Calibration is always performed with two buffers of the same temperature. The buffers selected should bracket the antic-

* mV represents millivolt or 10^{-3} V.

ipated pH of the samples. Because seawater has a pH of ~8.2, standard buffer solutions of 7.00 and 10.00 are recommended. *Fresh buffer solutions should be made each day.*

3 The temperature setting of the pH meter must correspond with the temperatures of the buffers, or an automatic temperature compensator can be used.

4 The first buffer solution must correspond with a specific value called the *isopotential point* of the pH meter. This is the pH shown when the amplifier output is set at 0.0 mV, ordinarily at pH 7.00.

5 After calibration, do not disturb the standardization point. The design of the meter retains the isopotential point (0.0 mV) when amplification is adjusted during calibration.

A pH meter is standardized by adjusting the isopotential point. Afterward, the pH displayed is in fact the isopotential point, typically established during manufacture at pH 7.00. After standardization, changing the standardization control knob to another isopotential point and then turning the temperature or calibration (slope) control knob alters the pH displayed. However, turning the calibration or temperature control knob without disturbing the knob that controls standardization has no comparable effect. Operationally, standardization is accomplished by (*1*) placing the electrode pair in pH 7.00 standard buffer solution, (*2*) adjusting the pH meter to the relative millivolt mode, (*3*) setting the reading at 0.0 mV with the standardization control knob, and (*4*) switching the meter to the pH mode.

In pH meters with expanded scales, calibration ''expands'' the response of the electrode to match the scale on the meter. Expanding one part of the scale expands the entire scale. Only the isopotential point remains constant. If the first buffer solution (i.e., the one used in standardization) corresponds to the isopotential point of the meter, adjustment of the second buffer does not influence how the meter interprets the first. However, standardization is negated if the first buffer does not correspond to the isopotential point because it will change when the meter is adjusted to the pH of the second buffer.

If the isopotential point is different from the isothermal point of the electrode (see below), pH readings taken at temperatures other than the temperature of the buffers will be incorrect, no matter how carefully the temperature control knob has been adjusted. The Nernst equation predicts that at a given pH, a change in temperature of the sample alters the output voltage of the electrodes. For example, an ideal electrode placed in a solution of pH 6.0 at 20°C has an output of 58.15 mV (Table

TABLE 1-8 Change in electrode response with temperature.

Temperature, °C	Change in mV per unit change in pH
15	57.15
20	58.15
25	59.16
30	60.16
35	61.17
40	62.17

Source: Rothstein and Fisher (1985).

1-8); at 30°C the output is 60.16 mV. The *isothermal point* is the pH at which the electrode output is unaffected by changes in temperature. In most electrodes this is pH ~7 (Fig. 1-27). The following procedure applies to Orion's Model 701A Digital Ionalyzer.

How to Standardize and Calibrate a pH Meter

1 Set the slope at 100%.
2 Set the temperature.
3 Place the electrode pair in the first buffer (4 or 7).
4 Turn the meter to "pH" and allow the output to stabilize.
5 Set the reading for 4.000 or 7.000 with the calibration knob.
6 Switch to "standby" and rinse the electrode pair with distilled water.
7 Place the electrode pair in the second buffer solution (7 or 10).

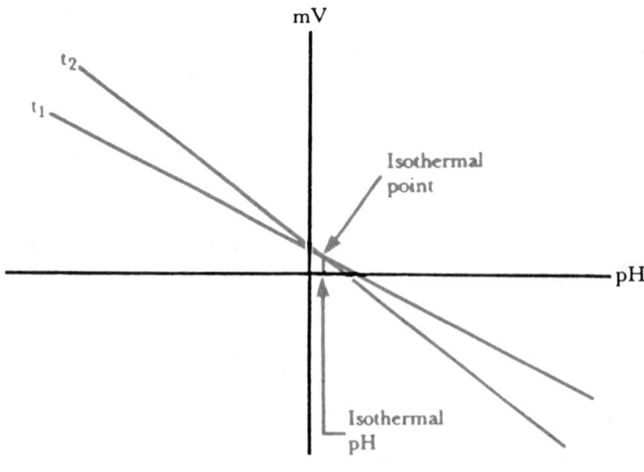

Figure 1-27 Isothermal point. Source: Rothstein and Fisher (1985).

8 Turn the meter to ''pH'' and allow the output to stabilize.
9 Adjust the temperature control until the meter reads 7.000 or 10.000.
10 Turn the slope control until the correct temperature is indicated.
11 If the slope is <90%, recalibrate with fresh buffer solutions. If the final slope is still <90%, check the instruction manual.

Method 1.4 Alkalinity Determination

HIGH PRECISION METHOD[44] The only instrument required for the high precision method of alkalinity determination is a pH meter with an electrode pair. A table and graph of empirical activity coefficients, f'_{H^+}, for the specific electrode pair used in the analysis must be prepared before alkalinity values can be calculated. A sample of seawater is acidified with HCl of known molarity to pH ~3.5, and the volume of HCl is then recorded with precision. Alkalinity is calculated from the difference between the amount of HCl added and the amount remaining in excess. Excess HCl is quantified by the equation

$$f'_{H^+} = \frac{(V_o + V_{HCl})10^{-pH}}{(V_{HCl} - V_2)M_{HCl}} \tag{1.12}$$

where V_o = volume of the seawater sample (mL), V_{HCl} = the volume of HCl titrant added (mL), 10^{-pH} = pH after acidification, V_2 = the second equivalence point of the titration (volume of HCl in millilitres), and M_{HCl} = the molarity of the titrant. Once f'_{H^+} is known, alkalinity in milliequivalents per litre is derived by

$$A = 1000\left[\frac{(V_{HCl})(M_{HCl})}{(V_o + V_{HCl})} - \frac{10^{-pH}}{f'_{H^+}}\right] \tag{1.13}$$

using a plot similar to Figure 1-28 to obtain f'_{H^+}. A series of f'_{H^+} values must be determined with the electrode pair to be used before any analyses can be performed. The procedure is tedious but unavoidable.

How to Obtain f'_{H^+} Values

The f'_{H^+} values, which are dimensionless, must be obtained once and then again if the performance of the electrodes changes.

1 Standardize the electrode pair with NBS buffers of pH 4 and 7.

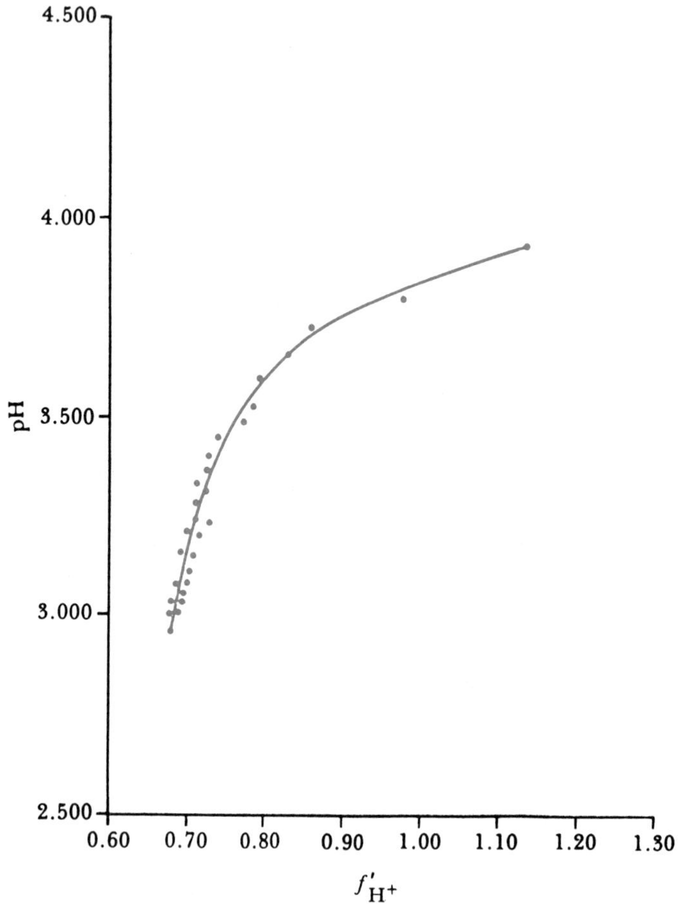

Figure 1-28 *Sample plot of* f'_{H^+} *versus pH in which* f'_{H^+} *is calculated from equation 1.12. A similar plot must be made for each electrode pair when the high precision alkalinity method is used.* Source: Patricia M. Bubucis, Sea Research Foundation.

2 Titrate 200-mL samples of seawater of different salinities with 0.1 mol/L HCl prepared from a commercial ampoule.

3 Make small incremental additions of acid (e.g., 0.1 mL) in the region of the second equivalence point, V_2, and continue to ~3 mL beyond.

4 Measure pH precisely after each acid addition.

5 For each addition record the total volume of HCl added (V_{HCl}), change in volume (ΔV_{HCl}),* pH, change in pH (ΔpH), and V_{HCl}/ΔpH. A plot of ΔpH$/\Delta V_{HCl}$ versus V_{HCl} will show a peak at V_2 (i.e., V_2 = maximum ΔpH$/\Delta V_{HCl}$).

6 For each titration point above V_2, calculate a value for f'_{H^+} using equation 1.12. Graph the data for pH versus f'_{H^+}.

*The symbol Δ represents "change in."

Reagents

0.025 mol/L HCl solution Prepare by diluting commercial standard 0.1 mol/L HCl.

pH 4 and 7 standard buffer solutions Prepare pH 4 and 7 buffer solutions using NBS buffers, either tablets or commercial solutions.

Analysis

1. Standardize the electrode pair with NBS buffers of pH 4 and 7.
2. To a 50-mL sample of seawater, add 5.0 mL of 0.025 mol/L HCl and mix.
3. Allow the temperature to equilibrate at 20 to 25°C and measure pH precisely.
4. Calculate alkalinity in milliequivalents per litre from equation 1.13.

LOW PRECISION METHOD[45] Values obtained using the low precision method ordinarily are within ~10% of the high precision method.

Reagents

0.01 mol/L HCl solution Start with commercial standard 0.1 mol/L HCl and dilute to 0.01 mol/L with distilled water. Add NaCl until the salinity is approximately equal to the salinity of the sample seawater.

pH 4 and 7 buffer solutions Same as the high precision method.

Analysis

1. Set up the pH meter assembly and a 25-mL burette so that the pH can be measured while the sample is being titrated and stirred.
2. Calibrate the pH meter with pH 4 and 7 buffer solutions and allow the sample to reach room temperature.
3. Pipette 50 mL of sample into a beaker.
4. Place the beaker on a magnetic stirrer (use low speed and a small stir bar). Record the starting pH. Also record the starting level of the HCl solution in the burette.
5. Titrate rapidly until the pH of the sample is reduced to 4.8. Record the difference between the starting level of HCl so-

lution in the burette and the level after titration (total amount of titrant used).

6 Perform the above steps in triplicate for each sample and average the final values.

7 Calculate alkalinity in milliequivalents per litre by the following equation, where V = the average volume of titrant, and M = the molarity of the acid:

$$A = \frac{(V)(M)(1000)}{50} \tag{1.14}$$

Method 1.5 Preparation of New Carbonate Mineral Filtrants

Rocks and minerals used as filtrants have two functions. They serve as attachment sites for bacteria that assist in maintenance of water quality (Chapter 2) and aid in removing suspended particulate matter that causes turbidity (Chapter 3). As discussed in the Science section, it is doubtful whether any filtrant contributes sufficient carbonate ions to offset declining alkalinity and pH, conditions characteristic of old, closed-system aquariums. The composition of a filtrant appears to be of low priority. When new carbonate filtrants are placed in contact with seawater and artificial seawater alkalinity is lost rapidly (Fig. 1-19), pH declines to <8.0 (Figs. 1-20 and 1-29), and the concentrations of calcium and magnesium are reduced.[32] To help minimize these changes new filtrants should be soaked in seawater or artificial seawater for at least 24 h prior to use.[46] Afterward, discard the soaking solution. Subsequent additions of sodium bicarbonate effectively counteract the loss of alkalinity, but do not prevent an initial loss of cations. Despite this shortcoming, carbonate mineral filtrants are desirable in certain ex-

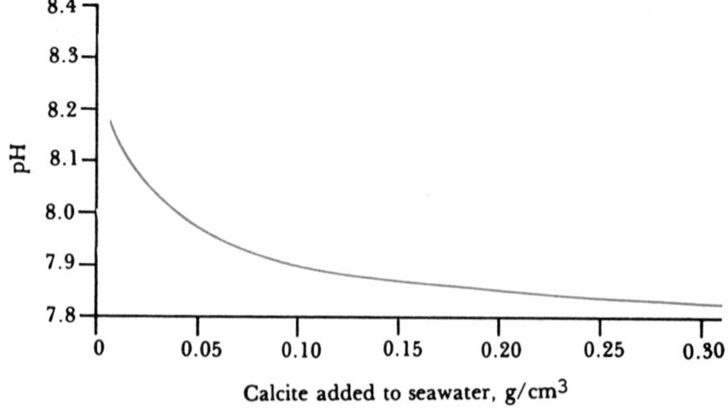

Figure 1-29 Effect of incremental additions of reagent-grade calcite on pH in air-equilibrated seawater (data points omitted). Length of time, although not specified, was <24 h. Atmospheric and dissolved CO_2 were first brought to equilibrium by bubbling with air until no pH change could be detected. The final pH was 7.84. Source: Wollast et al. (1980).

hibit situations (e.g., coral reef displays) for esthetic reasons and to prevent the pH from falling below ~7.5. The following procedure describes how new carbonate minerals intended as filtrants should be treated before use.

How to Prepare New Carbonate Mineral Filtrants

1. Obtain the filtrant material already crushed and graded to the proper size; otherwise, crush it and put it through a double sieve.
2. Wash the material thoroughly with tap water to remove surface dust.
3. Soak in seawater or artificial seawater for at least 24 h. This can be accomplished directly in the aquarium. Presoaking allows magnesian calcite to precipitate as an overgrowth on the filtrant surfaces. Use a volume ratio of ~3 (i.e., ~3/1, solution to filtrant).
4. Discard the water and fill the aquarium with new seawater or artificial seawater.

Method 1.6 Maintenance of pH

The pH value of aquarium seawater should be ~8.2. If an aquarium is aerated vigorously and continuously (i.e., atmospheric and dissolved CO_2 are maintained near equilibrium), any gradual decline in pH ordinarily is attributable to loss of alkalinity from a typical starting value of ~2.5 mEq/L. The most effective means of pH maintenance is to add sodium bicarbonate periodically.

How to Adjust pH[47]

1. An aquarium contains 110 L of seawater. Temperature and pH are 15°C and 7.9, respectively. How much sodium bicarbonate, $NaHCO_3$, is required to bring the pH to 8.2?
2. Measure pH and alkalinity.
3. Estimate the amount of sodium bicarbonate that must be added according to data in Table 1-9. The same data are depicted graphically in Figure 1-30.
4. As seen in Table 1-9, the correct amount is 0.085 g/L or (0.085)(110) = 9.35 g.
5. Dissolve the $NaHCO_3$ in seawater or artificial seawater of ambient temperature and pour the solution into the aquarium.
6. Circulate overnight, then determine the pH and alkalinity again.

TABLE 1-9 Amount of sodium bicarbonate (g/L) needed to attain pH 8.2 at different temperatures in full-strength seawater or artificial seawater.

	Temperature °C			
Initial pH	10	15	20	25
7.5	0.144	0.133	0.127	0.117
7.6	0.135	0.125	0.119	0.110
7.7	0.124	0.115	0.110	0.101
7.8	0.110	0.102	0.0974	0.0986
7.9	0.0917	0.0854	0.0815	0.0751
8.0	0.0685	0.0640	0.0611	0.0562
8.1	0.0385	0.0363	0.0346	0.0317

Source: Spotte (1979b).

Method 1.7 Artificial Seawater—GP2 Maintenance Solution

The function of a *maintenance solution* is to maintain an organism in its existing state. Ionic strength and major ion concentrations of many maintenance formulas are similar to seawater. Minor ions are not purposely added; they are present only as contaminants in major salts. Despite poor chemical definition, such formulas are suitable for keeping adult fishes. This suggests that background concentrations of trace ions essential for normal

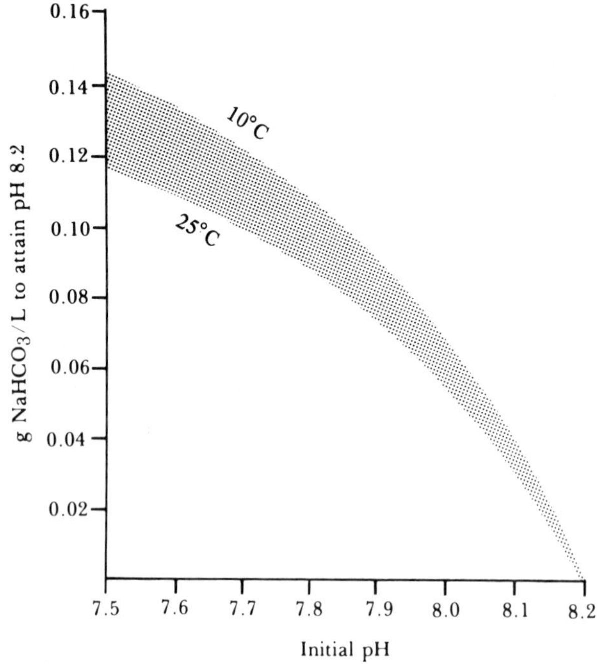

Figure 1-30 *Amount of $NaHCO_3$ required to raise the pH of aquarium seawater to 8.2. Curves were plotted from the data used to prepare Table 1-8.* Source: Spotte (1979b).

TABLE 1-10 Ionic species concentrations in GP2 maintenance solution.

Species	mol/L	μg/L
Cl^-	5.45×10^{-1}	1.92×10^{7}
Na^+	4.68×10^{-1}	1.08×10^{7}
Mg^{2+}	5.32×10^{-2}	1.29×10^{6}
S	2.82×10^{-2}	9.05×10^{5}
Ca^{2+}	1.02×10^{-2}	4.12×10^{5}
K^+	1.02×10^{-2}	4.11×10^{5}
C	1.40×10^{-3}	2.80×10^{4}
Br^-	8.40×10^{-4}	6.70×10^{4}
B	4.08×10^{-4}	4.44×10^{3}
Sr^{2+}	9.10×10^{-5}	8.00×10^{3}

Source: Spotte et al. (1984).

metabolic functions can be supplied consistently from sources other than the water. Fishes eat plants and other animals, ingesting essential nutrients in the process. They also swallow seawater continuously and exchange minor ions with the environment through the gills and skin (Chapter 4). Whether these last-mentioned processes benefit a well-nourished fish is uncertain. Tentative evidence suggests that absence of particular ions adversely affects growth and metamorphosis of fish larvae,[48] but this may simply reflect omission of an essential dietary component.

GP2 MAINTENANCE SOLUTION Maintenance solutions can be mixed from any of several recipes.[49] The one presented in Tables 1-10 and 1-11 is GP2 maintenance solution.[50] The letters GP stand for "general purpose" because the same concentra-

TABLE 1-11 Component concentrations in GP2 maintenance solution (S = 34‰). Use technical-grade materials except as indicated.

Solution	salt	Formula	mol/L	g/L
A	Sodium chloride	$NaCl$	3.92×10^{-1}	2.29×10^{1}
	Sodium sulfate	Na_2SO_4	2.67×10^{-2}	3.79×10^{0}
	Potassium chloride	KCl	9.05×10^{-3}	6.75×10^{-1}
	Sodium bicarbonate	$NaHCO_3$	2.19×10^{-3}	1.84×10^{-1}
	Potassium bromide	KBr	8.40×10^{-4}	1.00×10^{-1}
	Disodium borate	$Na_2B_4O_7 \cdot 10H_2O$	1.02×10^{-4}	3.90×10^{-2}
B	Magnesium chloride	$MgCl_2 \cdot 6H_2O$	5.07×10^{-2}	1.03×10^{1}
	Calcium chloride[1]	$CaCl_2 \cdot 2H_2O$	9.93×10^{-3}	1.46×10^{0}
	Strontium chloride[1]	$SrCl_2 \cdot 6H_2O$	9.08×10^{-5}	2.42×10^{-2}

Source: Spotte et al. (1984). *Note:* reagent-grade.[1]

tions of major ions form the basis of GP2 culture solution (Chapter 8). The basic formula is therefore suitable for both animals and plants. Seven of the nine salts listed in Table 1-11 can be technical-grade. Industrial-grade salts are unacceptable, as are rock salts, evaporated sea salts, and other notably impure materials. The two remaining salts should be reagent-grade, particularly calcium chloride, $CaCl_2$.[51] All components can be dissolved in tap water, and sterilization before use by microfiltration or autoclaving is not necessary for this or any other maintenance solution.

MIXING GP2 MAINTENANCE SOLUTION GP2 maintenance solution is mixed in one step by weighing individual salts and dissolving them sequentially in a mixing container. The solutions are allowed to flow into a large storage vat below (Fig. 1-31). Dissolving time is quicker if the tap water is ~30°C. The solution can be used as soon as it is brought to volume, the pH stabilizes at 8.0 to 8.3, and the temperature equilibrates with that of the room. When augmented by heavy aeration to circulate the water, complete mixing and pH and temperature

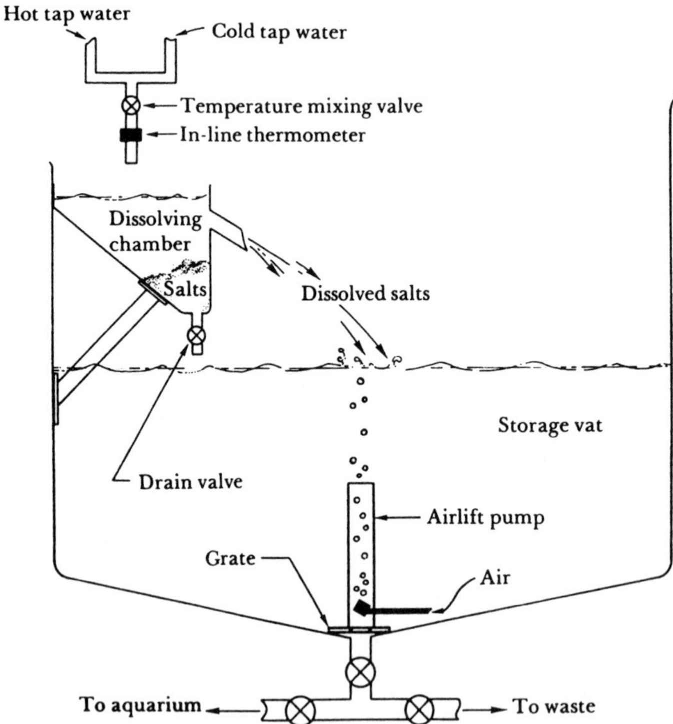

Figure 1-31 *Apparatus for mixing and storing large volumes of artificial seawater.* Sources: Spotte (1979a, 1979b).

equilibration can occur overnight. The arrangement illustrated shows the mixing container, storage vat underneath, and airlift pump for circulation. The dissolving container should have hot and cold tap water located nearby, preferably discharging through a common valve. An in-line thermometer placed after the mixing valve is useful for regulating the temperature of the influent water. The airlift can be made from a straight length of polyvinyl chloride (PVC) pipe (10-cm diameter or larger) with a hole drilled near one end. The size of the hole should just accommodate flexible airline tubing (0.95-cm diameter works well). The airlift can be fixed in place over the lowest part of the vat where undissolved salts accumulate.

How to Mix GP2 Maintenance Solution

1. Clean the storage vat by scrubbing the walls and floor with stiff brushes and a solution of sodium bicarbonate in warm water. Rinse thoroughly with tap water.
2. Turn on the airlift pump and close the drain valve.
3. Turn on the tap water to the dissolving container and adjust the temperature to $\sim 30°C$. Wait until water at the bottom of the vat is ~ 30 cm deep before proceeding.
4. Check the specific gravity of the brine-maker effluent and determine how much is needed from Table 1-12 (see procedures below).
5. Weigh the correct amounts of component salts for solution A (Table 1-11). Start with sodium sulfate. When all solution A components have been added, begin with those constituting solution B. Sodium chloride (as brine) should be added last.
6. Add the salts to the dissolving container in sequence while the tap water is running. Wait until each batch dissolves before adding more. Use this procedure:

   Fill the dissolving chamber half full with a component salt.

   Refill the container half full and repeat the above step until all salts have dissolved.

   Count the empty bags and containers as a check to be sure no components have been omitted.
7. Fill the storage vat to approximately 50% of its final volume. (After the correct level in a vat has been found the first time, the water levels at 50 and 100% should be marked permanently.)
8. Pump in the correct amount of brine and dilute to final volume with tap water.

TABLE 1-12 Specific gravity of brine versus salt concentration at 15.56°C.

SG	NaCl, g/L	*SG*	NaCl, g/L
1.000	0.00×10^0	1.054	7.77
1.002	2.64	1.056	8.06
1.004	5.28	1.058	8.36
1.006	7.94	1.060	8.65
1.008	1.06×10^1	1.062	8.95
1.010	1.33	1.064	9.25
1.011	1.60	1.066	9.54
1.013	1.87	1.068	9.84
1.015	2.14	1.070	1.01×10^2
1.017	2.41	1.072	1.04
1.019	2.68	1.074	1.07
1.021	2.96	1.076	1.10
1.023	3.23	1.078	1.14
1.025	3.51	1.080	1.17
1.027	3.79	1.082	1.20
1.029	4.06	1.084	1.23
1.031	4.34	1.086	1.26
1.032	4.62	1.088	1.29
1.034	4.90	1.090	1.32
1.036	5.19	1.092	1.35
1.038	5.47	1.094	1.38
1.040	5.75	1.096	1.41
1.042	6.04	1.098	1.44
1.044	6.33	1.100	1.48
1.046	6.61	1.102	1.51
1.048	6.90	1.104	1.54
1.050	7.19	1.106	1.57
1.052	7.48	1.108	1.60
1.110	1.64	1.160	2.44
1.112	1.67	1.162	2.48
1.114	1.70	1.164	2.51
1.116	1.73	1.167	2.55
1.118	1.77	1.169	2.59
1.120	1.80	1.171	2.62
1.122	1.83	1.173	2.66
1.124	1.86	1.175	2.69
1.126	1.90	1.177	2.73
1.128	1.93	1.178	2.74
1.130	1.96	1.180	2.76
1.132	2.00	1.182	2.80
1.134	2.03	1.184	2.84
1.137	2.07	1.186	2.87
1.139	2.10	1.188	2.91
1.141	2.13	1.191	2.95
1.143	2.17	1.193	2.99
1.145	2.20	1.195	3.02

TABLE 1-12 *(Continued)*

SG	NaCl, g/L	*SG*	NaCl, g/L
1.147	2.24	1.197	3.06
1.149	2.27	1.199	3.10
1.151	2.30	1.202	3.13
1.154	2.34	1.203	3.15
1.156	2.37	1.204	3.17
1.158	2.41		

Source: Stephen Spotte and Patricia M. Bubucis, Sea Research Foundation, calculated from data in International Salt Company (1972).

ADDING BRINE[52] It is convenient to add NaCl as concentrated brine instead of in crystalline form. This can be done with automatic dissolving equipment like the Sterling Brinomat® (Fig. 1-32). Bagged salt is awkward to handle in large amounts and requires considerable storage space. Bulk salt is cheaper and takes less space to store. Concentrated brine can be pumped easily to storage vats, and its addition in this form is quicker and more accurate than the procedure of emptying bagged NaCl into the dissolving container. Bulk salt is stored in the hopper of the Brinomat®. The hopper is refilled pneumatically through a connecting stainless steel pipe leading outside to a truck load-

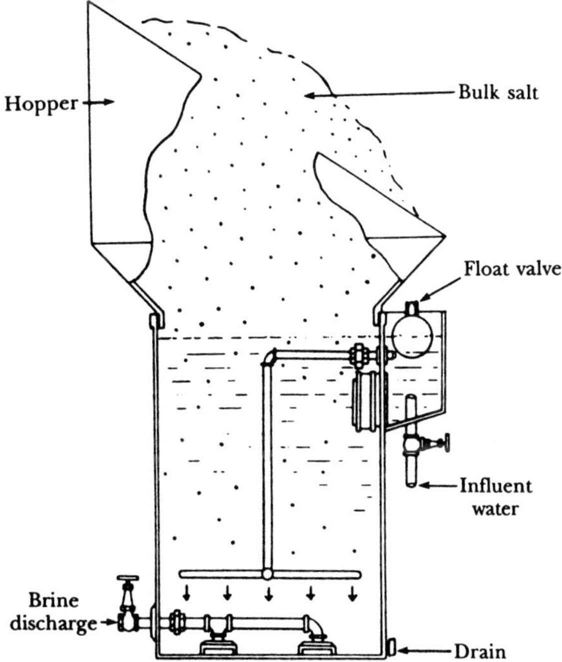

Figure 1-32 The Sterling Brinomat®, an apparatus for dissolving technical-grade NaCl to make concentrated brine. Source: International Salt Company, Clarks Summit PA 18411.

ing ramp. Tap water entering the Brinomat® flows vertically through the salt bed, regulated by a solenoid valve. As water moves downward a brine of increasing concentration is formed. Just above the bottom the brine reaches full strength, so long as the hopper is kept full. Dissolved salt is replaced automatically by dry salt from the hopper. Note that the brine becomes saturated *before* reaching the bottom of the Brinomat®. The lower portion of the salt bed never dissolves but acts as a mechanical filter to remove insoluble impurities before they enter the effluent. As brine is drawn from the unit and transferred to the storage vat, a float valve opens the solenoid and brine making continues automatically. A Brinomat® must be equipped with an accurate flow meter to measure the volume of brine entering the storage vat. Plastic or stainless steel pumps are recommended for pumping brine and seawater.

SPECIFIC GRAVITY—BRINE Sodium chloride ordinarily is at or near saturation when added to artificial seawater. Saturated brine is ~10 times the strength of seawater in terms of total solute concentration. Salinity measurements of brine are impractical because most refractometers read only to 100‰, and saturated brine is much more concentrated (Table 1-12). To measure the salinity would require at least fourfold dilution of the sample, which introduces a possible error. However, specific gravity is easily determined with a hydrometer calibrated for use in high saline waters.

How to Measure the Specific Gravity of Brine

1 Collect ~600 mL of brine in a clean glass bottle and place a thermometer in it.
2 Place the bottle in a water bath adjusted to 15.56°C until the temperature equilibrates.
3 Transfer the sample to a 500-mL glass graduated cylinder and determine specific gravity immediately.
4 Calculate the amount of brine to be added to the artificial seawater solution from Table 1-12. A temperature correction is not necessary because the reference and standard temperatures are the same.

CHAPTER

2 Biological Processes

Living organisms alter the composition of the water in which they live, and the resultant changes are sometimes harmful. The aquarist's task is to recognize these changes and attempt to control them, while realizing that no technology or combination of technologies has emerged as demonstrably superior for managing captive seawater. Unfortunately, empiricism is sometimes neglected in the rush to adapt processes developed for wastewater treatment. For example, it has not yet been shown by rigorous experimentation that rotating, trickling, and "dry-wet" filters are improvements over conventional subgravel filters. The pollutant load of aquarium waters is orders of magnitude less than the cleanest wastewater. Nor is there reason to believe that plastic packing is an improvement over sand and gravel as attachment sites for nitrifying bacteria, as I demonstrate in the Technology section.

Much of the following material on biological filtration has been taken from a previous publication,[1] in some instances with only minor changes. New information is included, but my thoughts on the subject have changed little in the intervening decade.

The production of organic matter is a biological process, and its removal in static adsorption configurations (e.g., activated carbon contactors) may depend partly on the presence of attached microorganisms. Activated carbon adsorption is therefore included in the Technology section of this chapter. Foam fractionation, which is dynamic, is discussed in Chapter 3.

Seawater aquariums tend to become *eutrophic* (high in nutrients, mainly carbon, phosphorus, and nitrogen). The nutrients produced by the metabolism of animals, plants, and bacteria provide substrates for still more biological growth. Some compounds containing nutrient elements—notably ammonia—are directly toxic.

The discussion of nitrogen toxicity has been relegated to the chapter notes, a decision some may find curious. I did this because emphasis should properly be placed on the mechanisms by which nitrogen is produced in aquarium water and then removed. The knowledge that ammonia is sometimes toxic even at micromolar concentrations is useful in a qualitative sense, but inadequate for quantitative purposes beyond the establishment of reasonable upper thresholds. The toxicity of any compound depends on many factors, including its environmental chemistry and the species, age, and health of the organism. As such, toxic thresholds are always conditional and inevitably ambiguous. This situation is compounded in public aquarium exhibits, which may contain dozens of species of unknown age and health status.

The processes that occur when living organisms either remove nitrogen from solution or convert it to less objectionable states are mineralization, nitrification, dissimilation, and assimilation. These terms are defined later, but it is useful to introduce them here (Fig. 2-1). The first three are functions carried out primarily by bacteria; the last is limited in this chapter to processes associated with seaweeds or macroalgae. Both mineralization and nitrification alter the chemical forms of nitrogenous compounds that are present, but do not remove nitrogen from the water. This is accomplished through assimilation and dissimilation.

Biological filtration results from the sum of the activities of bacteria (bacteriological filtration) and macroalgae (seaweed filtration). I define *biological filtration* as the series of steps in which nitrogenous organic compounds are mineralized, converted to inorganic nitrogen of successively higher oxidation states, and

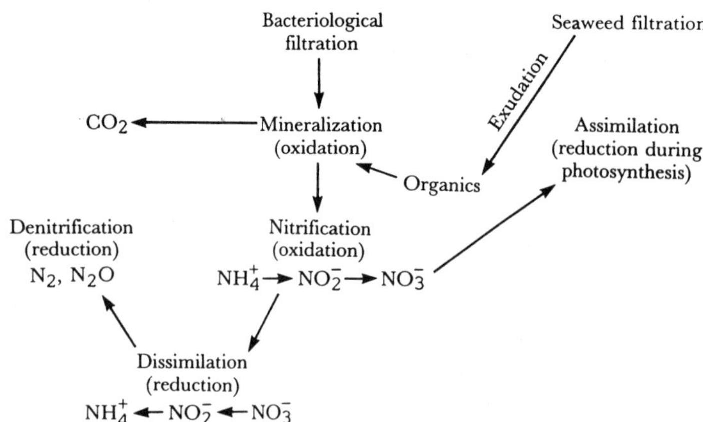

Figure 2-1 The principal processes in biological filtration. Source: Stephen Spotte.

finally removed from solution by complete biochemical reduction and subsequent loss to the atmosphere, or by partial reduction followed by assimilation into algal tissues.[2]

The conversion of nitrogen requires energy. Photosynthetic organisms such as algae use light to initiate metabolic functions. Most bacteria are nonphotosynthetic and rely on other forms of energy, mainly chemical. Chemical energy is released from organic or inorganic compounds through chemical reactions. Organisms that use organic substances as principal energy sources are *heterotrophic*; *autotrophic* organisms use mostly inorganic compounds. When a chemical compound is the energy source, the process involves an oxidation-reduction or ''redox'' reaction. As the name suggests, many redox reactions include oxygen, but the true basis is a transfer of electrons. The oxidized substance is the energy source in any redox reaction; the electron acceptor is not, although it still is required for completion of the reaction. After the electron donor has been oxidized it is generally no longer a source of energy.

Oxygen is the most common electron acceptor in redox reactions. Aerobic respiration is one biochemical process in which oxygen becomes an electron acceptor. The bacteria responsible for mineralization and nitrification are aerobic, requiring oxygen for respiration. During mineralization, organic compounds are oxidized and used as energy sources. In autotrophic oxidation processes such as nitrification, the energy source and the electron donor are the same. Some organisms can carry out respiration in the absence of O_2 by *anaerobic respiration*. Dissimilatory nitrate reduction is often accomplished by anaerobic means when one compound used in the reaction is inorganic and the other organic.

The main subject of this chapter is the conversion and ultimate removal of nutrient compounds from aquarium seawater by biological oxidation and reduction. The first sections discuss scientific aspects of the processes just described; the removal methods presented later are an overview of applicable technology.

SCIENCE

Mineralization

Mineralization refers to the degradation of organic compounds to their inorganic constituents. As I use the term, mineralization applies only to the biochemical activities of bacteria. The bulk of mineralization and other microbial processes occurs in the filter bed, where bacteria are concentrated. A conventional

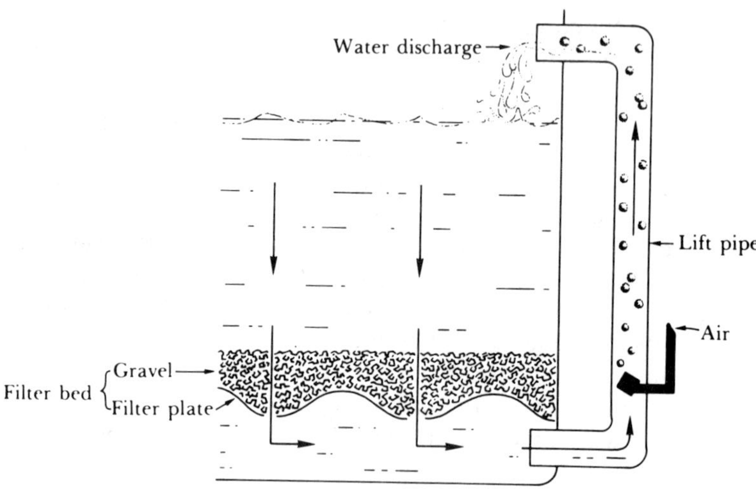

Figure 2-2 Conventional bacteriological or subgravel filter. The filter bed is composed of the gravel layer and supporting filter plate. Water circulates through the gravel and perforations in the filter plate, collects in the plenum underneath, and is recycled to the surface by airlift pumping. Sources: Spotte (1979a, 1979b).

bacteriological filter consists of a submerged gravel layer supported on a perforated plate (Fig. 2-2). The plate is raised above the bottom of the aquarium, leaving a space or plenum. The gravel and plate together make up the *filter bed*. Water circulating through the filter bed delivers oxygen to aerobic organisms attached to the gravel surfaces. Filtered water is drawn from beneath the filter bed and returned to the surface by airlift or mechanical pumps. The mechanics of airlift pumping are described in Chapter 3.

PHOSPHORUS[3] Phosphorus exists in seawater in three states: dissolved inorganic phosphorus, DIP, (also called orthophosphate, reactive phosphate, and phosphate), dissolved organic phosphorus, DOP, and particulate organic phosphorus, POP. This last form is associated with floating detritus and the suspended cells of microorganisms. Orthophosphate is the most important form of phosphorus in nature, and the same is probably true in seawater aquariums. In seawater of pH 8.0, 1% of the orthophosphate is present as $H_2PO_4^-$, 87% as HPO_4^{2-}, and 12% as PO_4^{3-}.[4]

In nature, the enormous mass of primary producers (phytoplankton in particular) and primary and secondary consumers (zooplankton) accounts for most of the phosphorus cycling. The onset of a phytoplankton bloom triggers a rise in all forms of phosphorus. The roles of planktonic organisms in the phosphorus cycling in seawater aquariums are insignificant. Phosphorus enters aquarium waters in four ways: (*1*) excretion by seaweeds, (*2*) excretion by fishes, (*3*) *autolysis* (the destruction of cells by enzymatic action) and release from damaged cells, and (4) lysis of dead cells and mineralization of DOC and POC. When cells *lyse*, they rupture and release their contents into the environment.

The phosphorus cycle as I envision it to occur in seawater aquariums is depicted in Figure 2-3. Seaweeds excrete DOP. A portion is reused during growth; the rest is mineralized to DIP by heterotrophic bacteria. In addition, seaweeds excrete a certain amount of DIP. Both DOP and DIP are reassimilated.[5] Lysed cells of animals, bacteria, and algae release DOP, some of which is mineralized by heterotrophs. Fishes excrete some phosphorus in the inorganic state; the remainder appears in feces as POP. Some of the phosphorus in fecal material sinks to the bottom of the aquarium and is adsorbed onto detritus. When part of the detritus is mineralized, inorganic phosphorus is liberated. Excess inorganic phosphorus released by fishes and seaweeds, and from mineralization of POP by heterotrophic bacteria, appears collectively as orthophosphate when measured in the laboratory (see Technology section).

Some of the excess phosphorus produced in a seawater aquarium perhaps precipitates as inorganic salts on the surfaces of gravel grains in the filter bed, although the existence of such a mechanism has not been demonstrated.[6] Two other processes are more plausible, and aeration is the force that drives them.

It has been suggested that orthophosphate becomes bound to organic molecules in solution and then adsorbed onto air

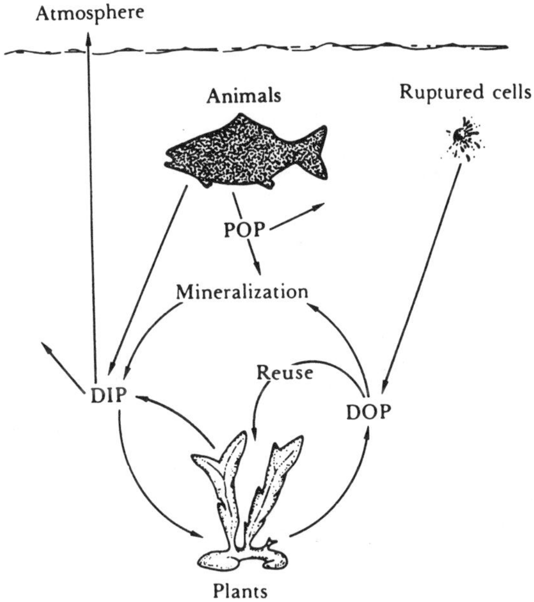

Figure 2-3 Proposed phosphorus cycle in seawater aquariums illustrating the cycling of dissolved inorganic phosphorus (DIP), dissolved organic phosphorus (DOP), and particulate organic phosphorus (POP). Source: Stephen Spotte after Spotte (1979b).

bubbles.[7] In one experiment, seawater aerated with a home aquarium-type air compressor removed >90% of the orthophosphate in 24 h.[7] The logarithm of the orthophosphate concentration remaining was a linear function of time. The relationship was straightforward: orthophosphate was removed from the aerated seawater at a rate proportional to its concentration. No biological involvement was detected, and the disappearance of orthophosphate was strictly a physicochemical phenomenon. During aeration, orthophosphate became bound to dissolved organic matter that in turn was adsorbed onto the rising air bubbles. When the bubbles burst at the surface, fine aerosol droplets were formed that included orthophosphate. In this way, much of it was lost from solution directly to the atmosphere, and analysis of the aerosol showed a higher total phosphorus concentration than the water over which the aerosol was collected. The possible mechanism is illustrated in Figure 2-4.

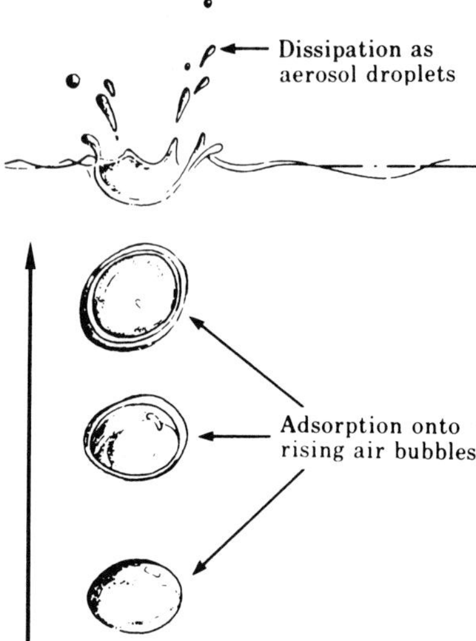

Figure 2-4 *Possible mechanism for removal of orthophosphate from seawater by aeration (see text). Orthophosphate is adsorbed onto the surfaces of rising air bubbles and dissipated as aerosol droplets when the bubbles burst at the surface.* Source: Stephen Spotte after Spotte (1979b).

Orthophosphate is probably lost from aerated seawater by still a second mechanism. Some of the organic molecules onto which phosphorus is adsorbed are highly surface active. *Surface activity* results from a change in the interfacial tension between two phases (e.g., air and water), which often lowers the tension. Substances collecting on rising bubbles produce monomolecular films that aggregate as insoluble organic particles.[8]

CARBON Carbon compounds that affect the alkalinity and pH of seawater are inorganic, derived from the atmosphere and sediments containing carbonate minerals (Chapter 1). Carbon originating from the cells of animals and plants is organic. Thousands of organic carbon compounds exist in the oceans. Here it is sufficient to classify them as particulate and dissolved, which are known to oceanographers as particulate organic carbon, POC, and dissolved organic carbon, DOC. Their sum is total organic carbon, TOC.[9]

A carbon cycle proposed for seawater aquariums is illustrated in Figure 2-5. Some organic carbon originating in food fed to fishes enters the environment in the form of urine and feces. Another fraction of metabolized food is respired as CO_2. Seaweeds release DOC (Table 2-1), which is mineralized by heterotrophic bacteria to produce more CO_2. The death of bacterial cells provides additional sources of organic carbon that are degraded to various degrees by bacteria in the filter bed. All respired CO_2, regardless of origin, is assimilated ultimately into reactions 1.1 (Chapter 1) from which the excess diffuses into the atmosphere.

Organic matter dissolved in aquarium seawater can be classed as *labile* (easily mineralized) or *refractory* (resistant to

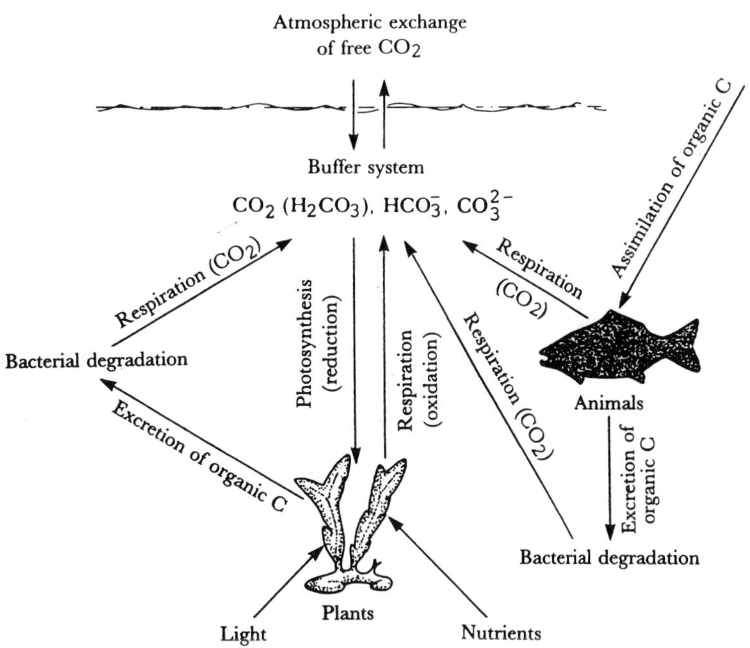

Figure 2-5 Proposed carbon cycle in seawater aquariums. Free (gaseous) CO_2 enters the water from the atmosphere. The respiration of plants and animals provides additional sources of free CO_2; still other sources are the mineralization of organic carbon by heterotrophic bacteria and bacterial respiration. Animals excrete organic carbon, and seaweeds leak part of the organic carbon assimilated and fixed during photosynthesis. Excess CO_2 diffuses into the atmosphere. Source: Spotte (1979b).

either biological or chemical degradation and therefore difficult to mineralize). Eventually, the concentrations of many labile compounds in captive seawater reach *steady state,* the point at which the rates of production and removal are similar. In contrast, refractory compounds increase in concentration (Fig. 2-6). The main refractory component consists of *humus,* a portion of which imparts the yellow coloration to old aquarium seawater. Synonyms are *yellow substance, yellow humus, uncharacterized fraction,* and the German term *Gelbstoff.* Humus is not a specific compound but a class of complex brown or yellow *polymers* (compounds made up of molecules of high molecular weight).[10]

Humus accounts for ~10 to 50% of the TOC in ocean water[11] and perhaps a larger percentage in aquarium seawater.[12] The main constituents are humic and fulvic acids.[10] The formation of humus or *humification* in nature begins when cellular constituents and exudates of plants are released into the environment. These substances react with proteinaceous and carbohydrate materials to produce humus (proteins and carbohydrates are described in Chapter 8). Many humic compounds in nature are so highly refractory that they exist unchanged for thousands of years.[13] The cellular contents and exudates of algae are the main sources of humus in the oceans.[14] The brown seaweeds (Phaeophyceae) contain phenolic compounds (Table 2-2). Under certain conditions some of these substances are toxic.[15]

TABLE 2-1 Exudation rates of dissolved organic carbon, DOC, by seaweeds under normal conditions of photoperiod, salinity, and temperature (values rounded). Units are mg C/(h·g) of wet tissue. Dashes indicate no data.

	Light	Dark	Location
Chlorophyceae (green algae)			
Cladophora sp.[2]	1.80[4]	—	Black Sea
Cladophora utriculosa[2]	1.25[4]	0.00[4]	Black Sea
Dictoyota dichotoma[1]	0.04	0.01	Caribbean
Ulva lactuca[3]	0.21	—	North Atlantic
Phaeophyceae (brown algae)			
Ascophyllum nodosum[2]	1.75[5]	—	Barents Sea
Ascophyllum nodosum[3]	0.31	—	North Atlantic
Fucis serratus[2]	2.70[5]	—	Barents Sea
Fucus vesiculosus[2]	2.55	—	Barents Sea
Fucus vesiculosus[3]	0.42	—	North Atlantic
Laminaria saccharina[2]	1.30[5]	—	Barents Sea
Laminaria agardhii[3]	0.38	—	North Atlantic
Laminaria digitata[3]	0.45	—	North Atlantic
Padina pavonia[2]	2.05	0.00	Black Sea
Sargassum natans[1]	0.01	0.00	Caribbean
Rhodophyceae (red algae)			
Acanthophora specifera[1]	2.91	8.84	Caribbean
Callithaminion corymbosum[2]	6.10[4]	0.75[4]	Black Sea
Chondria dasyphylla[1]	0.04	0.00	Caribbean
Chondrus crispus[3]	0.04	—	North Atlantic
Dasya elegans[2]	1.55[4]	0.25[4]	Black Sea
Polysiphonia harveyii[3]	0.00	—	North Atlantic
Polysiphonia sublifera[2]	2.85	1.85	Black Sea
Rhodimenia palmata[2]	6.35[5]	—	Barents Sea

Sources: Brylinsky (1977),[1] Khailov and Burkalova (1969),[2] Sieburth (1969).[3]
Notes: Data from good growth periods,[4] values averaged for winter and summer.[5]

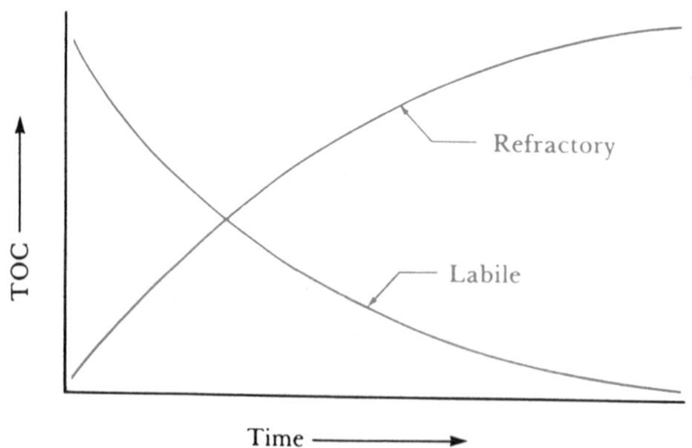

Figure 2-6 *The labile fraction of the total organic carbon (TOC) diminishes with time as a result of mineralization, eventually reaching steady state. The refractory component, in contrast, is resistant to degradation and continues to increase.* Source: Stephen Spotte.

TABLE 2-2 **Phenolic compounds in Adriatic brown seaweeds.**

Species	Dry mass, %	Phenolic compounds, % of dry mass
Colpomenia sinuosa	9	1.6
Cystoseira barbata	17	0.7–1.8
Cystoseira fimbriata	15	1.2–2.0
Dictyota dichotoma	14	0.1–1.0
Dilophus fasciola	14	0.3
Fucus virsoides	24	2.4–3.3
Halopteris scoparia	12	0.6
Scytosiphon lomentaria	11	1.1–1.3
Taonia atomaria	14	1.4

Source: Zavodnik (1981).

Captive seawater yellows with age even when algae are absent, which suggests that humification in aquariums may relate somehow to the large numbers of filter bed bacteria, but this is speculation. Two pathways are possible (Fig. 2-7), or perhaps a combination of the two.[16] The first begins when bacterial cells lyse. The lysed components may be specific compounds or cellular debris, but in either case the next step is *polymerization* (the

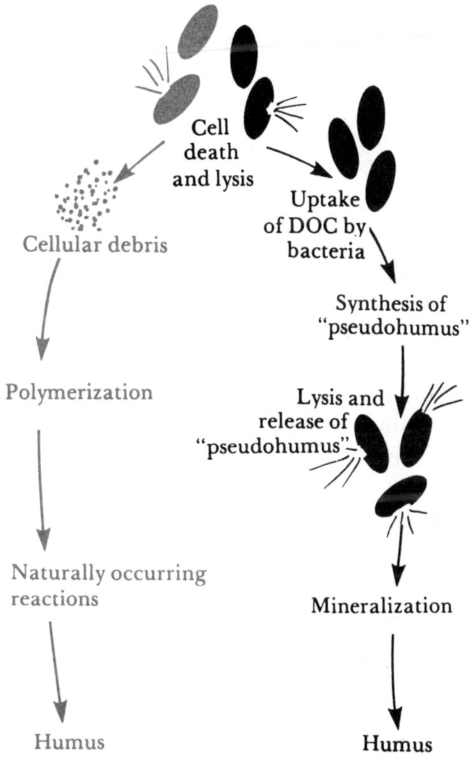

Figure 2-7 Proposed sequences by which humus originates from the lysing cells of filter bed bacteria. Source: Stephen Spotte, drawn from a discussion in Schnitzer and Khan (1972).

formation of polymers). Humus forms later as a result of naturally occurring chemical reactions. The second pathway defines a larger role for bacteria in presuming that products released during lysis are used to synthesize humuslike substances. At cellular death this "pseudohumus" is released into the environment and later mineralized to humus by bacteriological activity.

NITROGEN[17] Labile, nitrogenous organic compounds are the precursors of inorganic nitrogen—ammonia, nitrite, and nitrate—although ammonia is released directly by most aquatic animals as an end product of protein metabolism (Chapter 4). Of these three compounds, ammonia is by far the most toxic.[18] Even at high concentrations, nitrite and nitrate are apparently tolerated by adult seawater fishes without ill effects.[19]

The mineralization of nitrogenous compounds such as proteins and amino acids is an important biochemical process in seawater aquariums. When amino acids (Chapter 8) are used as carbon sources by living organisms, the first step in their transformation is usually removal of the amino group to form an organic acid. A common process among microorganisms is *transamination*, in which the amino group is exchanged for a keto group of a keto acid (Fig. 2-8). A second process is *dehydrogenation*, in which nitrogen in the amino acid is converted to ammonia instead of remaining bound in another amino acid, as is the case during transamination. A third process is *decarboxylation*: a carboxyl group is converted to CO_2 and the amino acid to an amine. During *deamination*, the fourth process, the amino group is removed, leaving an organic acid plus ammonia. Each method requires a specific set of enzymes. Consequently, different organisms may use one process preferentially, although many can use two or more.

The ammonia produced by deamination has three sources: (*1*) extracellular nitrogenous organic compounds derived from dead tissue and algal exudates,[20] (*2*) living bacteria during respiration, and (*3*) lysed cells.[21] Ammonia is released when the organic constituents of the nitrogenous compound are oxidized and used as energy sources. Ordinarily, the portions assimilated are hydroxy and keto acids.[21] Endogenous metabolism, the second mechanism listed above, produces ammonia from internal precursors during respiration. The rate of degradation of organics under these conditions depends on such factors as concentration of the specific compounds within the cell and the nutritional state of the bacteria. Bacterial cells become smaller as they respire and oxidize their own internal contents. Living cells have finite life spans, leading to the third mechanism.

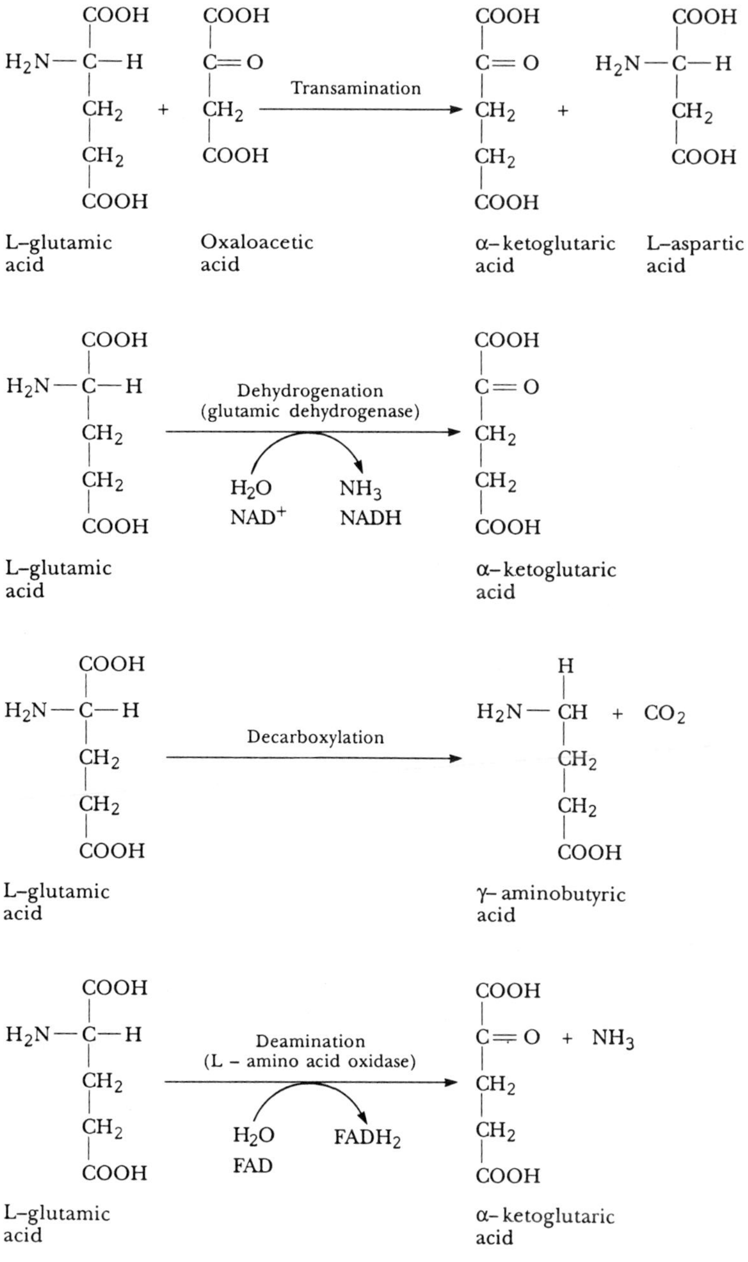

$$HOOC-CH(NH_2)-CH_2-CH_2-COOH + HOOC-C(=O)-CH_2-COOH \xrightarrow{\text{Transamination}} HOOC-C(=O)-CH_2-CH_2-COOH + HOOC-CH(NH_2)-CH_2-COOH$$

L-glutamic acid + Oxaloacetic acid → α-ketoglutaric acid + L-aspartic acid

$$HOOC-CH(NH_2)-CH_2-CH_2-COOH \xrightarrow[H_2O,\ NAD^+ \ \rightarrow\ NH_3,\ NADH]{\text{Dehydrogenation (glutamic dehydrogenase)}} HOOC-C(=O)-CH_2-CH_2-COOH$$

L-glutamic acid → α-ketoglutaric acid

$$HOOC-CH(NH_2)-CH_2-CH_2-COOH \xrightarrow{\text{Decarboxylation}} H_2N-CH_2-CH_2-CH_2-COOH + CO_2$$

L-glutamic acid → γ-aminobutyric acid

$$HOOC-CH(NH_2)-CH_2-CH_2-COOH \xrightarrow[H_2O,\ FAD\ \rightarrow\ FADH_2]{\text{Deamination (L - amino acid oxidase)}} HOOC-C(=O)-CH_2-CH_2-COOH + NH_3$$

L-glutamic acid → α-ketoglutaric acid

Figure 2-8 *Amino acid transformations.* Source: Spotte (1979b) after Brock (1970).

Eventually, any cell becomes unthrifty and dies. The sequential process of lysis and death results in rupture of the cell membrane and release of the cellular contents into the environment. One constituent is ammonia; others include nitrogenous organic compounds, which provide energy sources for oxidation by heterotrophic bacteria.

After mineralization has taken place, inorganic nitrogen ordinarily is converted to higher oxidation states by autotrophic bacteria. In some cases, heterotrophs also use inorganic nitrogen as an energy source.[22] Evidently, the choice of substrates by heterotrophic bacteria is less stereotyped than is sometimes thought, and it would be incorrect to think of these organisms only in terms of their capacity to oxidize organic matter.

Nitrification[23]

Mineralization is the first step in bacteriological filtration, and nitrification is the second. To aquarists, the importance of nitrification is the conversion of ammonia to compounds that are less toxic. During *nitrification*, ammonia is oxidized sequentially to nitrite and nitrate by

$$NH_4^+ + \tfrac{3}{2}O_2 \rightleftharpoons NO_2^- + H_2O + 2H^+ \tag{2.1}$$

$$NO_2^- + \tfrac{1}{2}O_2 \rightleftharpoons NO_3^- + 2H^+ \tag{2.2}$$

These reactions are carried out primarily by two groups of autotrophic bacteria.[24] The principal genus of ammonia oxidizers is *Nitrosomonas* (Fig. 2-9), of which one species (*N. europaea*) is recognized.[25] *Nitrosococcus oceanus* is important in the oceans and *N. mobilis* in brackish waters.[25] Nitrite oxidation in saline environments is accomplished mainly by *Nitrobacter winogradski*, *Nitrococcus mobilis*, and *Nitrospina gracilis*.[25]

Nitrifying bacteria obtain energy from the oxidation of reduced forms of inorganic nitrogen and derive most of their cellular carbon by fixing CO_2. Still, they are not obligate autotrophs. By definition such organisms are *photoautotrophic* or *chemoautotrophic*, and nitrifiers do not fit conveniently into either category.[26] The former are unable to grow in the absence of light; the latter cannot grow except in the presence of their specific nitrogen sources, ammonia or nitrite.[27] The capacity to assimilate organic compounds makes nitrifying bacteria facultative autotrophs. Under certain conditions, nitrifiers can use a substantial amount of organic carbon in the environment, both as a source of cellular carbon and as an energy source during respiration.[28]

Nitrogen enters aquarium seawater through (*1*) diffusion from the atmosphere and subsurface air bubbles, (*2*) excretion by seaweeds, (*3*) excretion by fishes, (*4*) oxidation processes of heterotrophic bacteria, and (*5*) lysis of bacterial cells. Some dinitrogen, N_2, may enter from the atmosphere by diffusing through the surface and from air bubbles injected into airlift pumps. The amount of N_2 present at a given time depends on

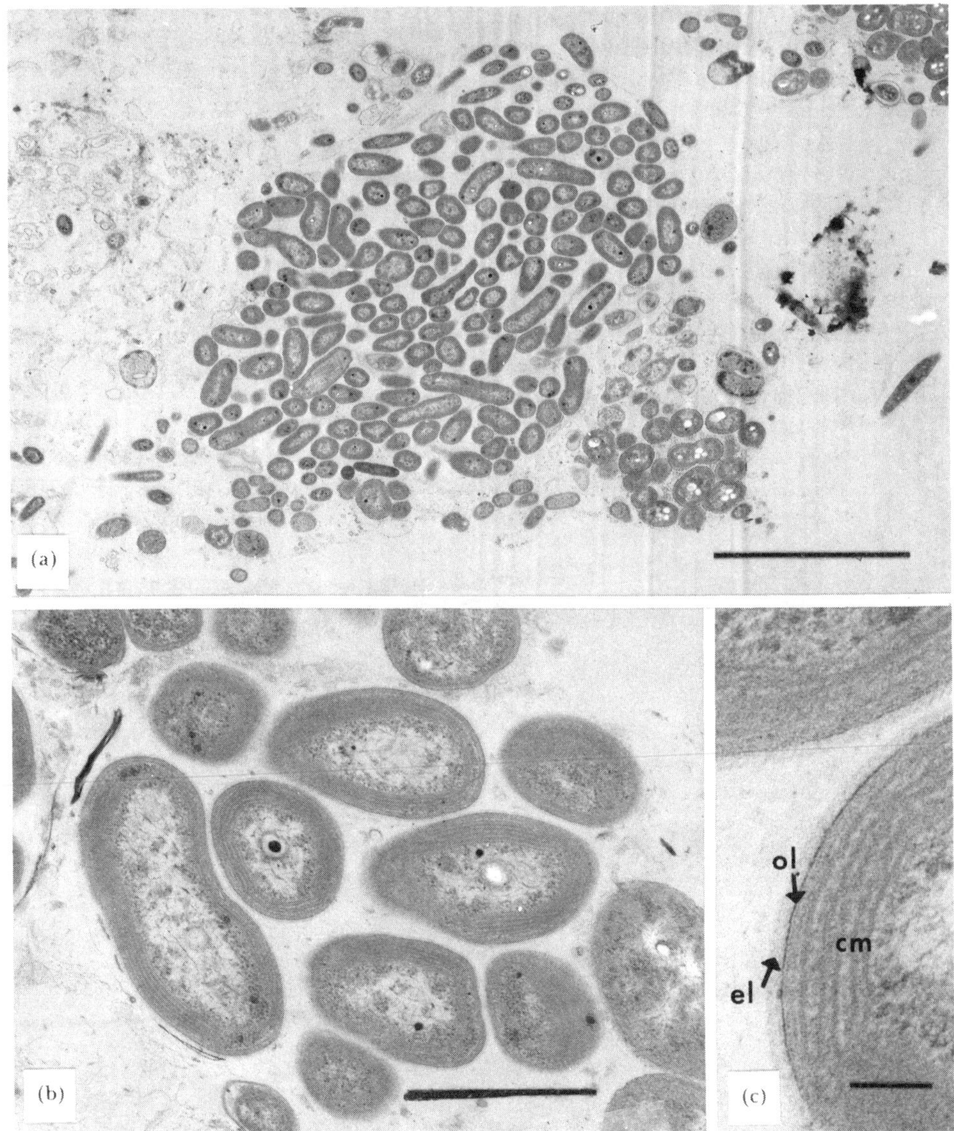

Figure 2-9 Scanning electron photomicrographs of seawater nitrifying-like bacteria from an aquarium containing striped bass (Morone saxatilis). (a) *A zoogloeal-type colony from the film on the wall of the aquarium (cells are not embedded in a polysaccharide-like matrix). Scale bar = 5 μm.* (b) *Typical rod-shaped marine bacterium with peripheral cytomembranes characteristic of* Nitrosomonas. *Scale bar = 1 μm.* (c) *Higher magnification showing the cytomembranes* (cm), *outer wall layers* (ol), *and the extra cell wall layer* (el) *commonly found in seawater species of* Nitrosomonas. *Scale bar = 0.1 μm.* Source: Johnson and Sieburth (1976).

differences in the partial pressure of nitrogen gas in the atmosphere, compared with the water. Few nitrogen-fixing microorganisms exist in conventional bacteriological filters, and N_2 is only of passing interest.

The cycling of nitrogen (Fig. 2-10) starts with release of nitrogen into the environment by animals and plants. Seaweeds release amino acids and peptides, but these substances represent a small fraction of the total extracellular material liberated. Most nitrogenous material in aquarium seawater originates from animals. Nitrogen, mostly as proteins and amino acids, is simplified into a variety of end products by animals during metabolism. The forms in which these compounds are excreted vary by species. In addition to CO_2 and water, the three primary end

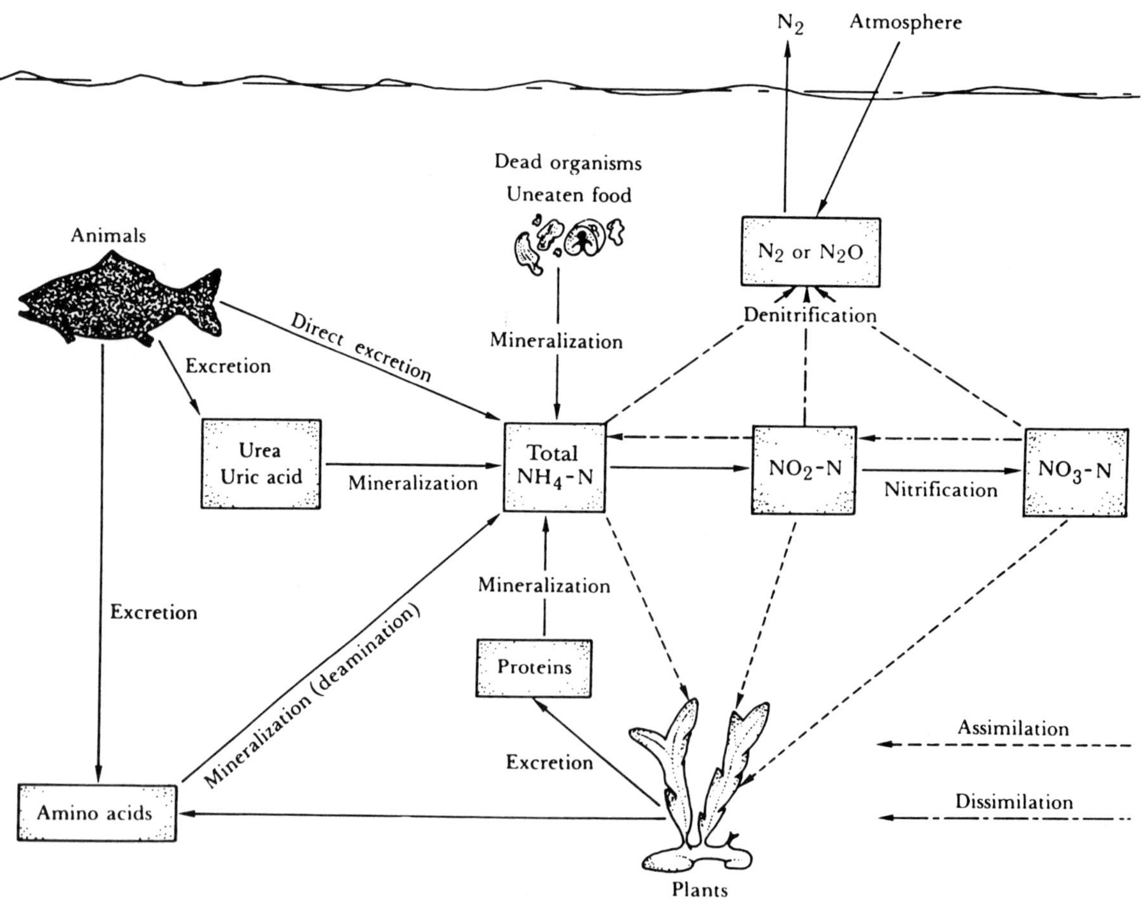

Figure 2-10 Proposed nitrogen cycle in seawater aquariums. Source: Spotte (1979b).

products of nitrogen breakdown are ammonia, urea (CH_4OH_2), and uric acid ($C_5H_4O_3N_4$).

The nitrogenous components of animal and plant excretory products are attacked quickly by bacteria. Urea, uric acid, and the extracellular nitrogenous products of algae are mineralized by heterotrophs. The ammonia produced by mineralization and dissimilation, or excreted directly into the environment by animals, is oxidized to nitrate by nitrifying bacteria. Nitrification results in accumulation of nitrate, because oxidation processes in the filter bed predominate. The reduction of nitrate to nitrite and ammonia through dissimilatory processes is accomplished to a limited extent by aerobic bacteria, although the assimilatory processes of seaweeds are far more efficient. Presumably, excess dinitrogen is lost to the atmosphere by diffusion, but whether this occurs to any significant extent has not been demonstrated.

Efficiency of Bacteriological Filters[29]

The efficiency of mineralization and nitrification in filter beds is affected by factors that limit the proliferation of nitrifying bacteria, or inhibit their biochemical activities. Among the most important are (*1*) surface area available for the attachment of bacteria, (*2*) the presence of toxic substances in the water, (*3*) the concentration of dissolved oxygen, (*4*) temperature, (*5*) pH, and (*6*) salinity. The last three factors allow little latitude from a management standpoint because they must be adjusted to requirements of the fishes.

SURFACE AREA Mineralization and nitrification are enhanced in the presence of POC suspended in the water or aggregated and trapped as detritus in the filter bed. The increased surface area offered by such material affects bacteriological growth, mainly by providing extra attachment sites.[30] In addition, adsorption of nutrients onto detritus and suspended POC encourages increased bacteriological activity by concentrating energy sources at locations where bacteria become attached. Surface area is therefore a two-dimensional factor. Its function at the first level is indirect and purely physical: more surfaces mean increased conversion by allowing larger populations to exist. At the second level, chemical attraction of microorganisms to an attachment site increases activity directly because energy sources are concentrated.

Surface area in mineralization is important at both levels; in nitrification, only the physical presence of added attachment sites is important. It is thought that heterotrophic bacteria do not degrade and assimilate DOC until after it has been adsorbed onto a particulate surface.[31] Chemical attraction to the attachment site evidently is not a factor in nitrification.[32]

Heterotrophic and autotrophic bacteria are not attached to gravel grains as individual cells, but exist as colonies within self-secreted layers of *biological films* (also called *matrices, slimes,* and simply *films*) that coat the grains. Biological films are produced by bacteria inhabiting them, and most consist of polysaccharides and gums. The thickness of biological films is limited by the nutrient load and dissolved oxygen concentration in the environment. The concentration of nutrients in the water at a given time is influenced by the animal density. To some extent, the ultimate population of filter bed bacteria depends on the surface area available for attachment (i.e., the number, size, and shape of the gravel grains). Once attached, however, the viability of the organisms depends on how efficiently dissolved gases and nutrients can penetrate the gelatinous matrix to living cells inside. The filter beds of aquaculture installations, with their heavy animal loads, perhaps contain thicker films than do the filter beds of public aquariums.[33]

Gravel grains in the filter bed offer the greatest amount of surface area for film formation. At first the direction of growth is lateral, but as all available surfaces become coated further expansion is outward, and the film thickens. Nutrients required by filter bed bacteria diffuse from the water into the film, along with dissolved oxygen. Waste products diffuse outward. As the film becomes thicker, diffusion of oxygen and nutrients toward the basal layer is impeded, and deeper portions of the film turn anaerobic. Without oxygen, aerobes near the base die. The cells lyse and relinquish their contents to heterotrophic anaerobes. As time passes and the film thickens, the flow of nutrients to deeper regions is restricted. Now the anaerobes die, lyse, and destroy the attachment point of the matrix to its surface. The film breaks apart, and the original surface becomes available for recolonization. In the growth and demise of a biological film, first oxygen becomes limiting, then the supply of nutrients.[34]

In biological films that are not metabolism-limited, nutrient concentration inside the film reaches a minimum value of N_i, at which time metabolism stops (Fig. 2-11). This is the case with deep films common in wastewater treatment plants. In situations in which the film is kept thin by the shearing force of rushing water, or by frequent breaking apart as a result of biochemical activities, metabolism of the nutrient material may occur throughout the entire layer. The deep film at which $N_c = N_i$ is the *effective depth*, L_e, and it contains organisms that are actively metabolizing the nutrient substratum.

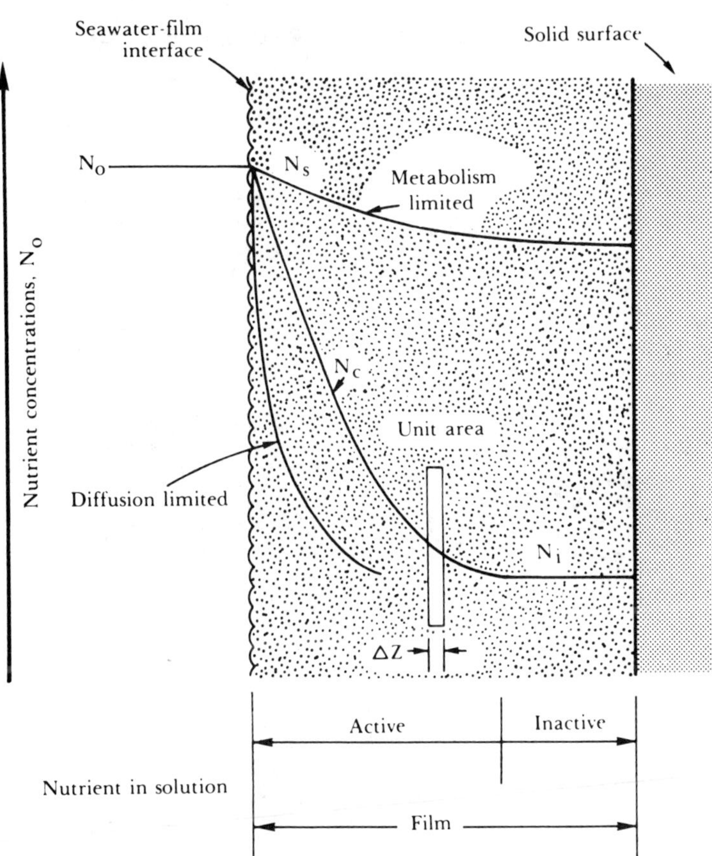

Figure 2-11 *Proposed profile of a biological film. Nutrient concentrations are represented by* N_o *in the water,* N_s *at the film surface,* N_c *inside the film, and* N_i *deep within the film as a constant limiting value. The gradient of* N_c *at* $Z = 0(\Delta N_c/\Delta Z)$ *is intermediate between low (metabolism limited) and high (diffusion limited) activity.* Source: Spotte (1979b) after Williamson and McCarty (1976).

Biological film formation in wastewater treatment systems follows a predictable pattern,[35] and the same features may also hold true in filter beds of seawater aquariums. Where biological activity is concerned, a newly formed film is thin and not limited by lack of oxygen. Nutrient uptake is rapid and efficient. Eventually, nutrient removal declines abruptly. In the life of a film this is the point of limiting thickness; in other words, outward growth has caused the underlying layers to become anaerobic. After a period of adjustment, activity rates again increase and become comparable with the initial rates. Changes in the population of aerobic and anaerobic organisms within a maturing film are shown in Figure 2-12. The life of a biological film is short. It matures quickly, is sloughed off, and a new one forms in a matter of days.[36]

TOXIC SUBSTANCES Several published studies describe the effects of different compounds on nitrification, but most of the information is of little value to aquarists. The majority of sub-

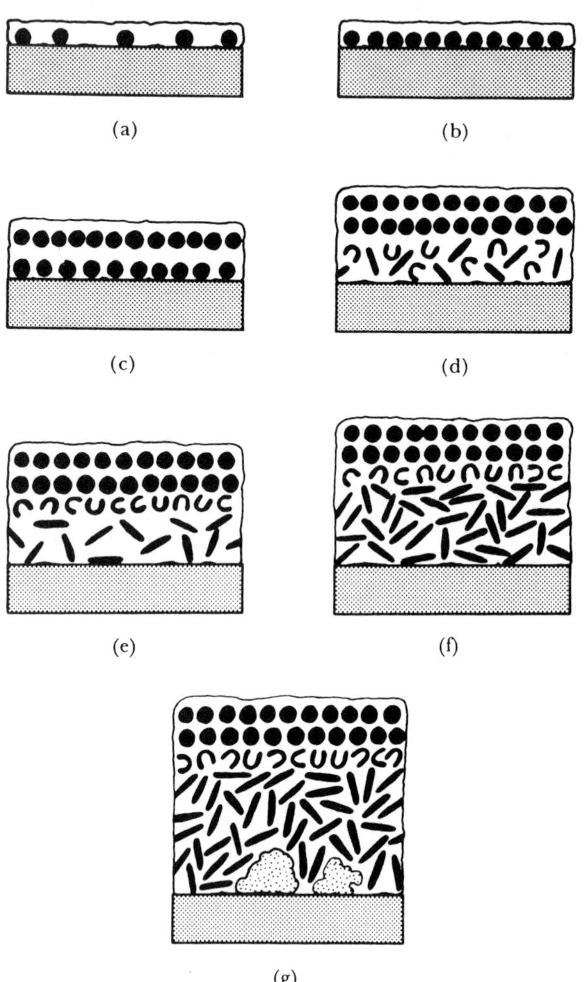

Figure 2-12 Proposed relationship of biological film density and thickness with the proposed film developmental stages (Fig. 2-11) shown in the appropriate regions. Abundant oxygen and nutrients (a) result in rapid growth (b and c). Aerobes start to die (d) as oxygen becomes limiting in the deeper regions, and anaerobic bacteria appear. Lysing aerobes furnish nutrients, and the overall bacterial population declines. At (e) the anaerobes adjust to the changing conditions. They proliferate, and the population begins to stabilize. At (f) the number of organisms attains steady state, which continues until nutrient supplies near the base are depleted, at which time the film disintegrates. Source: Spotte (1979b) after Hoehn and Ray (1973).

stances mentioned in the literature as being inhibitory have been tested using nitrifying bacteria isolated from soil or activated sludge. The species may be the same, but environmental conditions in aquariums are different, and the data seldom have direct application. Furthermore, most compounds tested have been industrial wastes and other pollutants rarely encountered in aquarium water. Aquarists are concerned mainly with the effects of two groups of substances: (*1*) ammonia, sulfide, and other metabolites; and (*2*) medications added for treatment of diseased fishes.

Early investigators sometimes did not distinguish between inhibition of growth and inhibition of activity (i.e., the capacity to oxidize substrates). Any compound that inhibits the oxidation of ammonia or nitrite by nitrifying bacteria must similarly inhibit their growth.[37] The reverse is not always true, however, and compounds that inhibit growth do not always inhibit ammonia or nitrite oxidation.[38]

Nitrite sometimes persists at higher than expected concentrations long after it should have disappeared and been replaced by nitrate. The cause may be dissimilatory activities by other bacteria (described below) or incomplete nitrification, a condition brought about by the inhibition of nitrite oxidation. Their own substrates are two of the substances most inhibitory to nitrifiers. The sequential rise and fall of ammonia and nitrite in aquarium water are caused partly by this self-inhibitory mechanism.[39]

It has been suggested that free ammonia, NH_3, and free nitrous acid, HNO_3, inhibit nitrification, at least in freshwater.[40] Accordingly, NH_3 at high concentrations may inhibit activities of both ammonia and nitrite oxidizers. As the concentration diminishes, NH_3 becomes less inhibitory to ammonia oxidizers than to nitrite oxidizers. Nitrification is an acid-forming process, and nitrite exists in equilibrium with HNO_2, as shown by

$$HNO_2 \rightleftharpoons H^+ + NO_2^- \tag{2.3}$$

The reaction shifts forward with declining pH. Ammonia inhibition is tempered by two factors. First, the pH declines as a result of nitrification, and the percentage of NH_3-N (free ammonia nitrogen) relative to the concentration of total NH_4-N (total ammonia nitrogen, the sum of the nitrogen in NH_4^+ plus NH_3) becomes smaller. Second, total NH_4-N declines as some of it is oxidized to nitrite. Both processes lessen the severity of ammonia inhibition to nitrite oxidizers.

Low levels of nitrite persist in some situations, although the ammonia concentration is small. In freshwater this has been attributed to inhibition of nitrification by HNO_2.[40] At certain concentrations HNO_2 inhibits the activities of both ammonia and nitrite oxidizers (Fig. 2-13). Delineations between zones shown in the figure are not sharp because of tempering factors (e.g., differences in the acclimation rate of the bacteria to environmental conditions, numbers of bacteria, temperature effects on reaction rates).[40]

Sulfide production in anaerobic sections of a filter bed inhibits nitrification.[41] Nitrifying bacteria demonstrate wide-ranging responses to natural organic compounds in the environment, including no effect, stimulation, and repressed growth and activity. In some cases, toxicity is concentration dependent.[42]

Many antibacterial agents and parasiticides used in the treatment of fish diseases apparently are harmless to nitrifying bac-

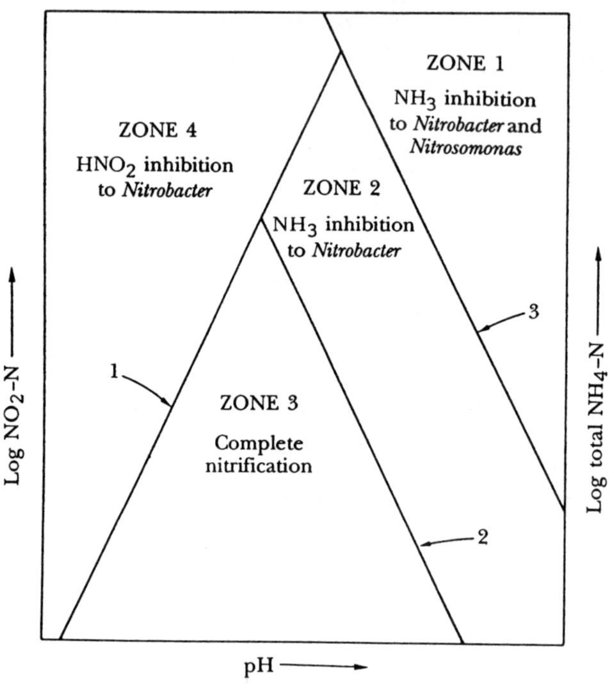

Figure 2-13 *Proposed relationships of free ammonia (NH_3), free nitrous acid (HNO_2), and inhibition to ammonia and nitrite oxidizers.* Zone 1: *The high concentration of NH_3 inhibits activities of both nitrifiers.* Zone 2: *The concentration of NH_3 is lower (ammonia oxidizers can function, but nitrite oxidizers are still inhibited).* Zone 3: *The concentration of NH_3 is small enough that both nitrifiers can carry out normal activities.* Zone 4: *Complete nitrification is possible if HNO_2 is absent. Boundaries are noted at* 1, 2, *and* 3. Source: Spotte (1979b) after Anthonisen et al. (1976).

teria, but others are toxic (Table 2-3).[43] There is little doubt that erythromycin, chlorotetracycline, methylene blue, and sulfanilamide inhibit nitrification in freshwater aquariums. Methylene blue was the most toxic substance tested. Mixed results have been obtained with chloramphenicol and potassium permanganate.

DISSOLVED OXYGEN, TEMPERATURE, pH, SALINITY

Maintaining proper conditions for nitrification is not difficult. In general, nitrifying bacteria function within wider ranges of dissolved oxygen, temperature, pH, and salinity than can be tolerated by most seawater fishes. Only dissolved oxygen is sometimes troublesome because the deeper sections of old, neglected filter beds tend to become anaerobic (see Technology section). Oxidation of ammonia and nitrite is most efficient when conditions are aerobic, and low concentrations of dissolved oxygen appear to affect ammonia oxidizers more adversely than nitrite oxidizers (Table 2-4).[44] The lowest nitrate value in the table was measured in the aquarium with the lowest dissolved oxygen concentration. This indicates dissimilation (i.e., anaerobic conditions), described in the next section.

Nitrification is most efficient between 20 and 35°C and proceeds slowly at 5°C and lower.[45] Nitrifying bacteria are active across a wide pH range.[46] In freshwaters the optimal pH for

TABLE 2-3 Effects of common antibacterial agents and parasiticides on the activities of nitrifying bacteria in freshwater (FW), seawater (SW), and artificial seawater (ASW). Some of the data cannot be compared directly because of differences in experimental protocols. Positive effect (inhibition) = +, <25% inhibition of nitrification = 0.

Compound	Concentration, mg/L	Water	Effect
Chloramphenicol[1,6]	13.3	ASW	+
Chloramphenicol[3]	50	FW	0
Chloramphenicol[5]	50	FW	+
Chlorotetracycline[5]	10	FW	+
Cupric sulfate[1]	1.2	ASW	+
Cupric sulfate[2]	1	FW	0
Cupric sulfate[4]	0.2–0.8	SW	+
Cupric sulfate[5]	5	FW	0
Erythromycin[2]	50	FW	+
Formalin[2,7]	25	FW	0
Formalin[5]	15	FW	+
Formalin + malachite green[2]	25 + 0.1	FW	0
Gentamycin sulfate[1]	5.3	ASW	0
Malachite green[2]	0.1	FW	0
Methylene blue[1]	8.0[6]	ASW	+
Methylene blue[2]	5	FW	+
Methylene blue[5]	1	FW	+
Neomycin sulfate[1]	66.7	ASW	+
Nifurpirinol[1]	0.1	ASW	0
Nifurpirinol[3]	1	ASW	0
Nifurpirinol[5]	4	FW	0
Oxytetracycline[2]	50	FW	0
Potassium permanganate[2]	4	FW	0
Potassium permanganate[5]	1	FW	+
Quinacrine hydrochloride[1]	12.0	ASW	0
Sulfamerazine[3]	50	FW	0
Sulfanilamide[5]	25	FW	+

Sources: Bower and Turner (1982),[1] Collins et al. (1975),[2] Collins et al. (1976),[3] Kabasawa and Yamada (1971),[4] Levine and Meade (1976).[5]

Notes: Ammonia oxidation only,[6] equivalent to 10 mg/L formaldehyde solution.[7]

TABLE 2-4 Inorganic nitrogen balance in seawater aquariums with different oxygen tensions after 3 months.

	Oxygen tension, % saturation		
Inorganic nitrogen	89	34	6
Ammonia, mg total NH_4-N/L	0.609	0.465	173.6
Nitrite, mg NO_2-N/L	0.017	0.023	0.018
Nitrate, mg NO_3-N/L	248.0	126.0	0.559

Source: Kawai et al. (1971).

ammonia oxidation (i.e., the pH that results in the highest rate of oxidation) decreases with increasing total NH_4-N (Fig. 2-14). Seawater nitrifiers appear to perform best at the salinities to which they have been acclimated, and activities tend to decline as the salinity varies in either direction from the acclimation value.[47]

Dissimilation[48]

During *dissimilation* or ''nitrate respiration,'' nitrate ions act as alternative hydrogen acceptors to oxygen, and reactions 2.1 and 2.2 shift in reverse. Under anaerobic conditions, in other words, the primary removal mechanism for nitrate is through respiratory action, rather than by assimilation.[49] In dissimilation, which can be carried out by a number of different bacteria,[50] the actual nitrogenous end product depends on the species of bacterium and can be nitrite, ammonia, nitric oxide (NO), ni-

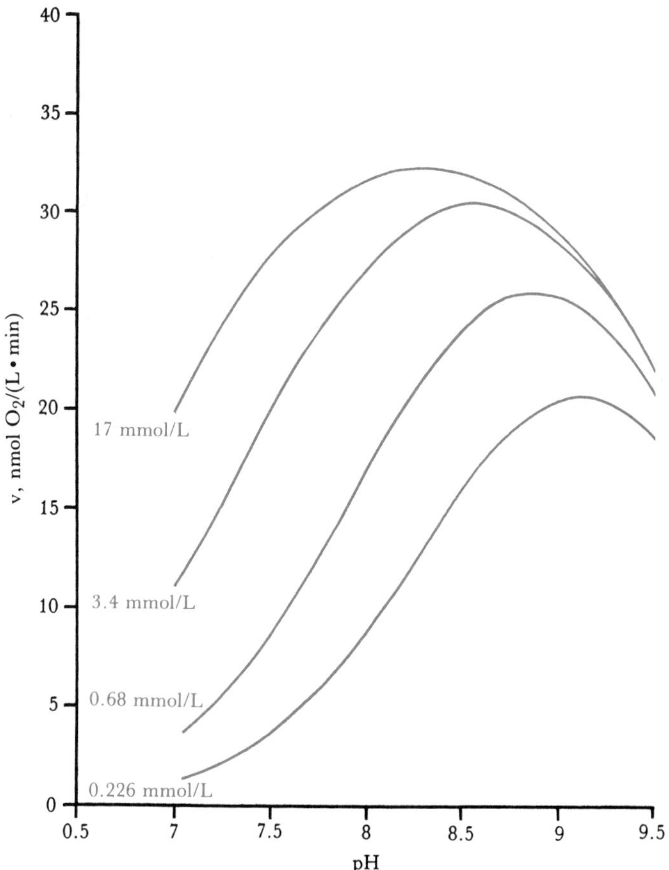

Figure 2-14 *The pH dependence of the rate of ammonia oxidation by* Nitrosomonas europaea *in freshwater, where* v *on the ordinate (y or vertical axis) is the observed rate of oxidation (data points omitted). The optimal pH decreases with increasing total NH_4-N.* Source: Quinlan (1984).

trous oxide (N_2O), or dinitrogen (N_2).[21] *Denitrification* is the dissimilatory reduction of nitrate and nitrite by essentially aerobic bacteria to the gaseous oxides (NO, N_2O), which in turn are reduced to N_2.[51] Many heterotrophic bacteria are denitrifiers under certain conditions (Table 2-5). Nitrogen in any of the above forms ultimately is removed from solution when its partial pressure in the water exceeds that in the atmosphere.

Many authors take denitrification to mean bacteriological nitrate reduction processes of all kinds. This is incorrect. Bacteria that reduce nitrate to nitrite or ammonia and stop there are not denitrifiers.[52] Denitrification, by definition, reduces inorganic nitrogen completely, and only bacteria capable of complete reduction can be called denitrifiers. Thus all denitrification is dissimilation, but the reverse is not true (Fig. 2-10). Denitrification is an important dissimilatory process, and specific reference will be made to it when possible.

The factors affecting dissimilation generally, and denitrification specifically, are (*1*) carbon source, (*2*) concentration of dissolved oxygen, (*3*) temperature, and (*4*) pH. Of these, oxygen may be the most limiting.

CARBON SOURCE Most dissimilatory bacteria are heterotrophic, and shifts in the species composition of a filter bed population can be expected if the carbon source changes.[53] Denitrification cannot occur without an available source of DOC. The amount of DOC ordinarily present in wastewater and aquarium waters is inadequate for efficient dissimilation. A two-stage system is commonly used to remove nitrate from wastewater.[54] Nitrification is carried out in the first stage under aerobic conditions. In the second stage the system is made anaerobic, and a carbon source is added to stimulate denitrification. Methanol is the most commonly used compound, and oxygen is removed from a denitrification column by addition of more methanol than required to complete denitrification by the proposed reaction[55]

$$O_2 + \tfrac{2}{3}\,CH_3OH \rightleftharpoons \tfrac{2}{3}\,CO_2 + \tfrac{4}{3}\,H_2O \qquad (2.4)$$

Other carbon sources that have been used include molasses,[56] ethanol,[56] glucose,[56] citrate,[57] acetate,[58] and malate.[59]

When methanol is used, denitrification is accomplished by the proposed reactions[55]

$$NO_3^- + \tfrac{1}{3}\,CH_3OH \rightleftharpoons NO_2^- + \tfrac{1}{3}\,CO_2 + \tfrac{2}{3}\,H_2O \qquad (2.5)$$

$$NO_2^- + \tfrac{1}{2}\,CH_3OH \rightleftharpoons \tfrac{1}{2}\,N_2 + \tfrac{1}{2}\,CO_2 + \tfrac{1}{2}\,H_2O + OH^- \qquad (2.6)$$

TABLE 2-5 Heterotrophic bacteria in water and soils known to be denitrifiers under certain conditions.

Alcaligenes (= *Achromobacter*)
A. cycloclastes
A. radiobacter
A. tumefaciens
A. faecalis
A. eutrophus
A. denitrificans
A. odorans
Azospirillum brasilense (= *Spirillum lipoferum*)
Bacillus
B. azotoformans
B. licheniformis
Chromobacterium violaceum
Cornebacterium nephridii
Flavobacterium spp.
Halobacterium marismortui
Kingella denitrificans
Neissera
N. sicca
N. flavescens
N. mucosa
Paracoccus (= *Microccus*) *denitrificans*
Propionibacterium
P. pentosaceum
P. acidi-propionici
Pseudomonas
P. aerogenes
P. aureofaciens
P. caryophilli
P. chlororaphis
P. fluorescens
P. lemoignei
P. mallei
P. mendocina
P. perfectomarinus
P. picketti
P. pseudoalcaligenes
P. pseudomallei
P. solonacearum
P. stutzeri
Spirillum psychrophilum
Thiobacillus denitrificans
Vibrio succinogenes (?)
Xanthomonas spp. (?)

Source: Knowles (1982).

The overall reaction[55] is

$$NO_3^- + \tfrac{5}{6}\,CH_3OH \rightleftharpoons \tfrac{1}{2}\,N_2 + \tfrac{5}{6}\,CO_2 + \tfrac{7}{6}\,H_2O + OH^- \quad (2.7)$$

Denitrification is not typical of anaerobic reactions; instead, it is similar to aerobic oxidation, except that O_2 is replaced by NO_3^- as the electron acceptor. In the process, nitrate is reduced. Methanol, as the electron donor, serves as the energy source and is oxidized. From reactions 2.5 to 2.7 it can be seen that 1 mol/L NO_3^- requires at least $\frac{5}{6}$ mol/L methanol for total denitrification (i.e., 1.90 mg/L methanol must be present for every mg NO_3^-/L). The shift of electrons is illustrated graphically in Figure 2-15. Methanol, the electron donor, is oxidized and becomes the energy source. Nitrate ion, the electron acceptor, is reduced to NO_2^- and cannot serve as a source of energy.

DISSOLVED OXYGEN The enzymes responsible for denitrification (i.e., the nitrogen oxide reductases) are, in general, suppressed by O_2.[60] Dissimilatory bacteria are unusually sensitive to environmental factors, in part because alternative respiration pathways exist.[57] Many bacteria that reduce nitrate ion are truly anaerobic; others use O_2 in preference to NO_3^- and switch only if the environment becomes anoxic.[49] These latter organisms are facultative because electrons are transferred opportunistically to the available electron acceptor.

Because dissimilation is primarily an anaerobic process (although carried out mainly by aerobic bacteria), optimal conditions for it to function are contrary to conditions that promote nitrification.[61] The presence of O_2, the more powerful electron acceptor, suppresses the use of NO_3^- in biological conversions

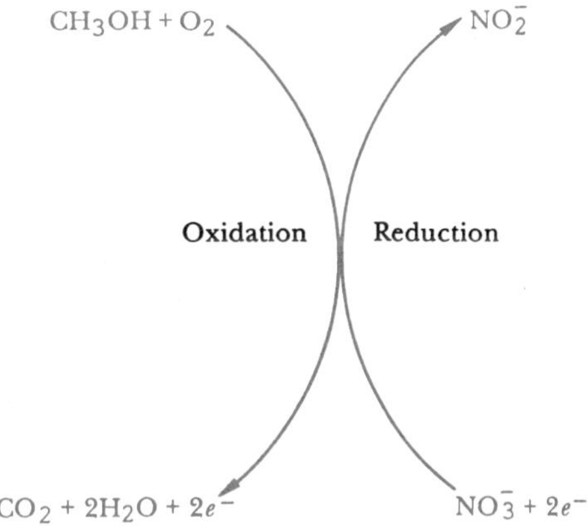

Figure 2-15 Nitrate reduction with methanol. Methanol (electron donor) is oxidized. Nitrate (electron acceptor) is reduced. Source: Spotte (1979b).

involving DOC. Moreover, mineralizaton, which is also an oxidative process, removes DOC compounds that could serve as potential electron donors in dissimilation.[61] Dissimilation probably takes place in seawater aquariums even when the filter bed environment is predominantly aerobic.[62]

TEMPERATURE AND pH Denitrification is probably effective within the same temperature range as nitrification.[63] Not much has been published on the effect of pH on denitrification in either freshwater or seawater. Denitrifying bacteria apparently can function throughout a wide pH range.[64]

Assimilation[65]

Considered superficially, seaweed filters appear to offer only advantages. Seaweeds take up[66] inorganic nitrogen, phosphorus, urea, and many other compounds from water and assimilate them into their tissues during growth.[67] Some species have marked preferences (Table 2-6). To eliminate these substances from the captive environment the aquarist has only to harvest some of the seaweed periodically and discard it. This sounds too good to be true, and it is. Living seaweeds are not adsorbent pads, removing unwanted substances selectively and returning nothing in the process. In fact, algae release numerous compounds into the water during respiration and photosynthesis (Tables 2-1 and 2-2). Whether seaweed filters, on balance, improve aquarium seawater is equivocal.[68]

Seaweeds add dissolved solids such as vitamins and amino acids, which may benefit bacteria and fishes, but mostly it is what they remove from water that makes their culture potentially useful. Seaweeds take up ammonia, but nitrification may be a more efficient means of ammonia control. The principal advantage of seaweed filters appears to be nitrate removal, although nitrate is not notably toxic to fishes.

Seaweed filters have some disadvantages. Healthy, unstressed seaweeds leak 1 to 5% of the net organic carbon fixed during photosynthesis back into the environment.[69] The result is accelerated eutrophication, even while other nutrients (nitrogen and phosphorus) are being removed. The increased quantities of DOC provide additional substrates for mineralization, leading to increased heterotrophic activity in the bacteriological filter. Seaweeds stressed by desiccation, elevated temperatures, or injury leak even more organic carbon, perhaps 40% of the net amount fixed.[70]

TABLE 2-6 Nitrogen preferences for growth in seaweeds. Multiple entries indicate no preference.

Species	Total NH_4-N	NO_3-N	Urea
Asterocystis ramosa[4]	x	x	
Chondrus crispus	x	x	
Codium fragile	x	x	x
Chordaria fragelliformis	x		
Enteromorpha linza	x	x	x
Fucus spiralis	x	x	
Fucus vesiculosus	x	x	
Gelidiella acerosa[4]	x	x	
Gelidium amansii		x	
Gonotrichum elegans		x	
Gracilaria tikvahiae	x		
Gracilaria foliifera[3]	x		
Gracilaria sp.[2]	x		
Gracilaria verrucosa[1]	x		
Nemalion multifidum		x	
Neoagardhiella baileyi	x		
Palmaria palmata		x	
Porphyra tenera[5]	x	x	x
Porphyra yezoensis[3]	x		
Pterocladia capillacea			x
Rhodosorus marinus[4]	x	x	
Ulva fasciata			x

Sources: References in Hanisak (1983) except where indicated; Chao-yuan et al. (1984),[1] Harlin et al. (1978),[2] Ryther (1976).[3]

Notes: Stated as "inorganic nitrogen,"[4] prefers NO_3^- at higher concentrations or may grow equally well on inorganic nitrogen and urea.[5]

TECHNOLOGY

Method 2.1 Conditioning Bacteriological Filters[71]

In *conditioned* filter beds the species and numbers of bacteria are stable enough that formation and removal of metabolic products are approximately at steady state.[72] Nitrification is often used as a measure of conditioning.[72] Three aspects of conditioning of interest to aquarists are (*1*) the nature of the time lags that delay new seawater aquariums from becoming suitable environments for animals, (*2*) how time lags can be reduced by accelerating the conditioning process, and (*3*) *carrying capacity* or the animal load that a conditioned filter bed can support.

Initially, cultures of nitrifying bacteria grow slowly, and the number of cells per unit of energy converted is low.[73] The heterotrophic population, in contrast, increases rapidly, but the different groups of organisms do not stabilize until much later (Fig. 2-16).[74] Nitrifying bacteria, unlike heterotrophs, are not present in large numbers at first, and their populations build slowly. Ammonia oxidizers attain maximum population density after a month or so in warm water; nitrite oxidizers require ~2 months.[75] Nitrification is sequential (Fig. 2-17). Nitrite oxidation does not proceed until ammonia conversion is well established. The result is a "peaking" of ammonia and nitrite concentrations as the populations and activities of the different species of nitrifiers reach steady state with their energy sources.[76]

In my opinion, the time lags in newly established filter beds are caused as much by the need of nitrifiers to acclimate to aquarium conditions as to the initial absence of nitrifying bacteria. Two facts support this argument: (*1*) nitrifiers in culture demonstrate extended lag periods that are not caused by an absence of organisms, and (*2*) time lags in filter beds can be reduced considerably by addition of bacteria already acclimated to aquarium conditions.

Heterotrophic and autotrophic bacteria capable of carrying

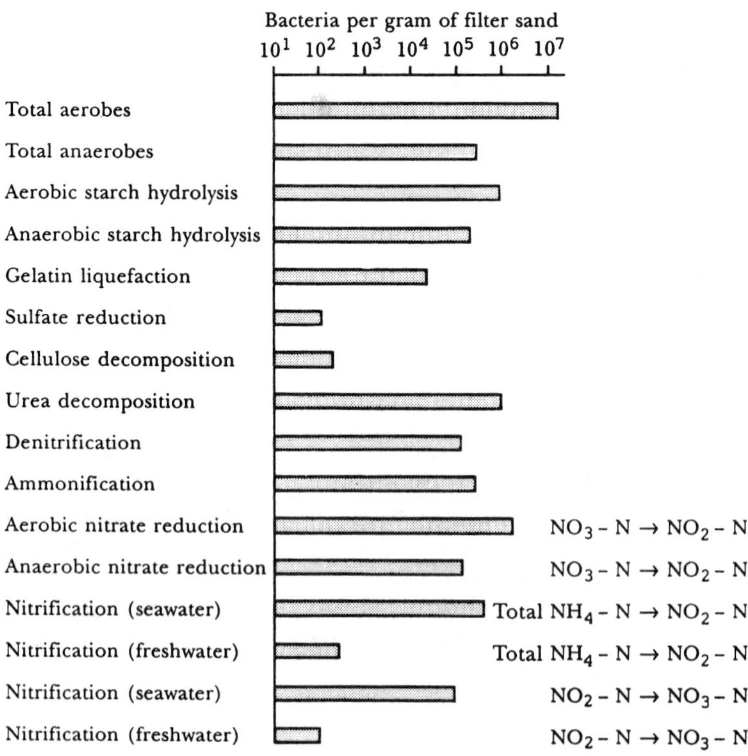

Figure 2-16 *Population of filter bed bacteria in small freshwater and seawater aquariums after 134 d. The filter sand was 20 cm deep and small grained (0.297 mm or 50 mesh). Protein decomposers or "gelatin liquefiers" increased markedly when the animals were fed foods high in nitrogen, such as raw fish. From a beginning population of 10^3/g of sand, protein decomposers increased a hundredfold after a month. The population declined to ~ 10^4/g of sand after 3 months and stabilized. In contrast, starch decomposers were scarce at the start and declined still further to 1/100th of the total population at the end of 3 months.* Sources: Spotte (1979a, 1979b) after Kawai et al. (1964).

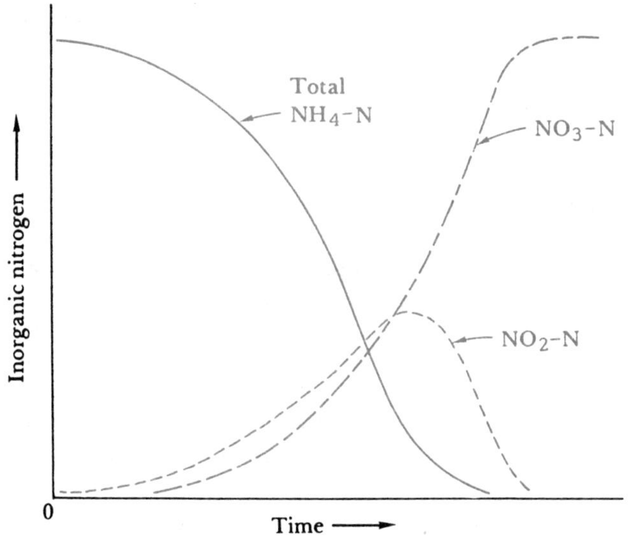

Figure 2-17 *Stylized nitrification curves showing the sequential rise and fall of ammonia and nitrite and the rise of nitrate as typically occurs in closed-system aquariums.* Source: Spotte (1979b) after Anthonisen et al. (1976).

out nitrification are nearly ubiquitous, and a sterile filter bed established with artificial seawater many miles inland soon acquires bacteria that can function in a saline environment. Nonetheless, environmental factors that affect nitrification—toxic substances, temperature, pH, dissolved oxygen, and salinity—are important considerations if conditioning is to be accelerated. Nitrifying bacteria cultured in the laboratory are sometimes difficult to establish in new aquariums unless the new and old environments are similar. For example, it does little good to culture nitrifiers in low saline conditions and then add them to full-strength seawater. The same holds true for disparate conditions of pH and dissolved oxygen. The most important factor is probably temperature. Bacteria cultured at 22°C cannot be expected to function at normal activity levels when added to aquarium water of 10°C. The organisms will survive, but the ensuing time lag makes their addition no more efficient than waiting for nitrification to become established naturally.[77]

How to Accelerate Bacteriological Filtration by "Seeding"[78]

New filter beds have too few bacteria to conduct bacteriological filtration efficiently. Once the different groups of bacteria have become established, still more time is needed before biochemical activities attain steady state. Conditioning can be accelerated by (*1*) inoculating the filter bed, or (*2*) spiking the water with nutrients (see the next subsection). Again it must be emphasized that the distinction between heterotrophic and autotrophic bacteria is not always clear from the standpoint of nutrient metabolism. The initial inorganic nitrogen excreted by animals as ammonia may be oxidized to some extent by heterotrophs. Conversely, some organics are taken up readily by autotrophs—nitrifiers, for example. Once established, a population of filter bed bacteria probably does not fluctuate much, although activity levels may vary.[79]

Inoculants of nitrifying bacteria for addition to newly established filter beds can be obtained from (*1*) pure or mostly pure laboratory cultures, (*2*) commercial suppliers (ordinarily in a freeze-dried state), and (*3*) conditioned filter beds of similar temperature and salinity. The first choice offers no advantages. Nitrifying bacteria are difficult to culture. In addition, laboratory cultures still require time to adapt to aquarium conditions. The simplicity of opening a packet of freeze-dried nitrifiers and emptying the contents into the water is appealing, but the results have proved inconsistent.[80] The easiest way to accelerate conditioning is to add a handful of old gravel from a conditioned filter bed (Fig. 2-18).[81] This ''dirty'' method has the ad-

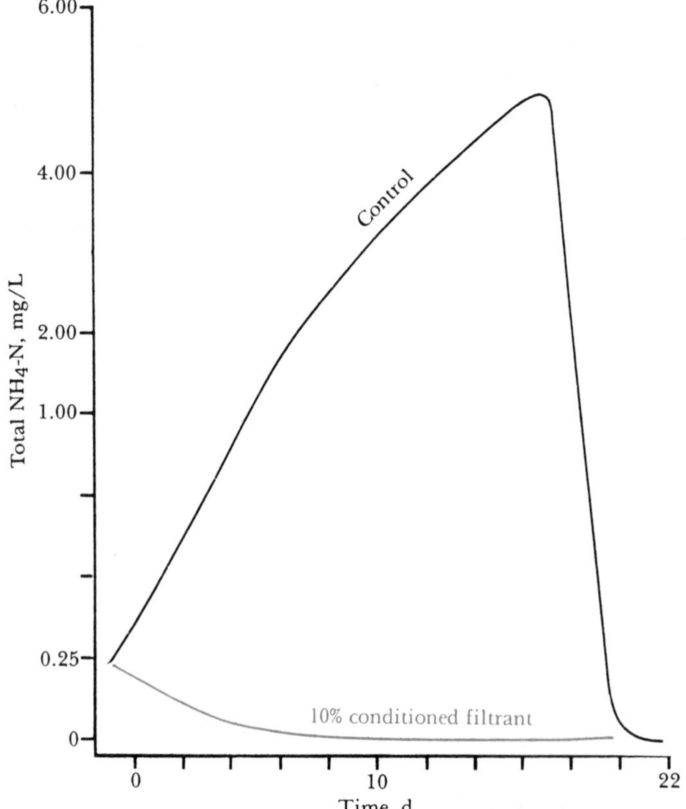

Figure 2-18 *Comparative changes in total NH_4-N in the seawater of small aquariums (data points omitted). Control aquariums had filter beds with new filtrant; experimental aquariums contained 90% new filtrant and 10% wet filtrant from a conditioned filter bed.* Source: Bower and Turner (1981).

vantage of supplying heterotrophic bacteria along with the nitrifiers. Even the addition of detritus is useful. The dirty method works best when conditions in the new aquarium are similar.

How to Accelerate Nitrification by Preconditioning[82]

Nitrification can also be accelerated by daily addition of measured amounts of ammonium salts, either ammonium chloride, NH_4Cl, or ammonium sulfate, $(NH_4)_2SO_4$. This procedure, called *preconditioning*, allows the aquarist to wait until ammonia and nitrite have been oxidized before adding animals. Preconditioning with ammonium salts may not be entirely satisfactory because mineralization processes require organic compounds. For this reason, preconditioning is especially effective if carried out after adding old aquarium gravel to the filter bed.

Before preconditioning a new filter bed, the daily ammonia input by the animals to be added should be estimated. Unless this is done, the filter bed might be preconditioned to a nutrient level that is too low, resulting in *ammonia breakthrough* (i.e., a sudden increase in the concentration of total NH_4-N). The formula used for estimating the daily ammonia input by salmonids is[83]

$$R_F \times \text{biomass} \times N_L \times N_U \times N_E = \text{total NH}_4\text{-N/24 h} \quad (2.8)$$

where R_F = food added per 24 h as a percentage of total animal biomass, N_L = percentage of dietary protein nitrogen, N_U = protein use factor, and N_E = percentage of total nitrogen excreted as ammonia (i.e., total NH_4-N). Assume that the daily food input is 2% of the animal biomass, animal biomass is 10 kg, dietary protein is 20% (3.2% nitrogen), protein use is 40%, and the amount of nitrogen excreted as total NH_4-N is 90%. I have assumed that most proteins average 16% nitrogen. Therefore

$$\begin{aligned} &0.02 \times 10 \text{ kg} \times 0.032 \times 0.4 \times 0.9 \\ &\quad = 2.3 \times 10^{-3} \text{ kg total NH}_4\text{-N/24 h} \end{aligned}$$

Based on this estimate, the filter bed should receive additions of 7.7 g NH_4Cl or 19.03 g $(NH_4)_2SO_4$ every 24 h until the nitrite concentration peaks. Information on protein content of foods is provided in Chapter 8.

Method 2.2 Carrying Capacity

Carrying capacity was defined previously as the biomass an aquarium can support. Carrying capacity ordinarily is considered in terms of nitrogen cycling. At least seven factors are important: (*1*) concentration of nitrogen generated in the water system, (*2*) rate of nitrogen excretion by the animals, (*3*) rate of nitrogen conversion by filter bed bacteria, (*4*) size of the filter bed, (*5*) grain size of the filtrant, (*6*) flow rate of water through the filter bed, and (*7*) effects of important environmental variables (temperature, pH, dissolved oxygen, salinity) on the first three factors.

Estimating the carrying capacity of a large exhibit aquarium with its relatively low biomass of animals and plants is an interesting but essentially pointless exercise. Even under the simplest experimental conditions the formation, excretion, and conversion of nitrogen are difficult to follow. The factors listed in the preceding paragraph can never be known precisely, and any calculation of carrying capacity is only an estimate.

HIRAYAMA'S METHOD The following discussion is based on Hirayama's formulas[84] with examples published previously.[85]

Hirayama's formula for calculating the carrying capacity of seawater aquariums is

$$\sum_{i=1}^{p} \frac{10W_i}{\dfrac{0.70}{V_i} + \dfrac{0.95 \times 10^3}{G_i D_i}} \geqq \sum_{j=i}^{q} (B_j^{0.544} \times 10^{-2}) + 0.051F \qquad (2.9)$$

The left-hand expression represents the oxidizing capacity of the filter bed or "oxygen consumed during filtration," OCF, measured as milligrams of oxygen consumed per minute (equivalent to biological oxygen demand or BOD/min), where W = surface area of the filter bed (m^2), V = flow rate through the filter bed (cm/min), D = filtrant depth (cm), and p = the number of filters serving the aquarium. In the above formula (actually an inequality), G represents the size coefficients of the filtrant grains determined by

$$G = \frac{1}{R_1} X_1 + \frac{1}{R_2} X_2 + \frac{1}{R_3} X_3 + \ldots + \frac{1}{R_n} X_n$$

$$(X_1 + X_2 + X_3 + \ldots + X_n = 100) \qquad (2.10)$$

where R = mean grain size of each partition of filtrant (diameter in mm), and X = the percentage mass of each partition.

The right-hand expression of the inequality (equation 2.9) represents the rate of "pollution" by the animals (oxygen demand excreted per minute). Like the left-hand expression, its units are mg O_2/min. In the expression under discussion now,

B = body masses of individual animals (g), F = amount of food entering the system daily (g), and q = the number of animals maintained.

As the formula illustrates, the oxidizing capacity of the filter bed must exceed or equal the rate of "pollution" by the animals. Also note that *as the masses of the individual animals decrease, the carrying capacity of the filter bed decreases*. In other words, carrying capacity according to Hirayama's formula is not simply a function of the total mass of animals. An aquarium that can support a single 100-g fish cannot necessarily support 10 fishes each weighing 10 g. Assume, for example, that in a hypothetical aquarium $W = 0.35\ \text{m}^2$, $V = 10.5$ cm/min, and $D = 36$ cm. If the filtrant is all of the same grade and $R =$ 4 mm, then from equation 2.10, $G = 0.25 \times 100 = 25$. Substitution of these values into the left-hand expression of equation 2.9 gives the OCF value:

$$\frac{10(0.35)}{\dfrac{0.70}{10.5} + \dfrac{0.95 \times 10^3}{25(36)}} = \frac{3.5}{0.067 \times \dfrac{950}{900}}$$

$$= \frac{3.5}{0.067 + 1.055} = \frac{3.5}{1.122} = 3.1\ \text{mg O}_2/\text{min}$$

Assume further that fishes of 200 g each are being maintained, and that they are fed at 5% of their individual body masses daily. From the right-hand expression of equation 2.9, x represents OCF; therefore

$$x = \sum_{j=1}^{q} (B_j^{0.544} \times 10^{-2}) + 0.051F \tag{2.11}$$

Table 2-7 shows the value of x for one fish as a function of mass in grams and feeding rate as percentage of body mass per day. From the table, feeding a 200-g fish 5% of its body mass each day corresponds to a "pollution load" of 0.69 mg O_2/min. The aquarium has an oxidizing capacity of 3.1 mg O_2/min. A 200-g fish and its food generate a "pollution load" of 0.69 mg O_2/min. Consequently, 4.5 fishes can be maintained (i.e., 3.1/0.69).

As a second example, determine if the same aquarium could support 10 50-g fishes and one that weighs 600 g, all of which are fed 5% of their individual body masses daily. As seen in Table 2-7, the "pollution load" is 10(0.21) + 1(1.85) + 1100(0.05)(0.051) = 6.75 mg O_2/min. The answer is no, because the "pollution load" exceeds carrying capacity, which is 3.1 mg O_2/min.

TABLE 2-7 "Pollution load" (oxygen demand in mg O_2/min) as a function of the mass of a fish and its feeding rate. Calculated from the right-hand expression of equation 2.9.

Body mass, g	Feeding rate, percentage of body mass per day 0.0%	2.5%	5.0%	7.5%	10.0%
30	0.06	0.10	0.14	0.18	0.22
40	0.07	0.13	0.18	0.23	0.28
50	0.08	0.15	0.21	0.28	0.34
60	0.09	0.17	0.25	0.32	0.40
80	0.11	0.21	0.31	0.41	0.52
100	0.12	0.25	0.38	0.50	0.63
150	0.15	0.34	0.54	0.73	0.92
200	0.18	0.43	0.69	0.94	1.20
250	0.20	0.52	0.84	1.16	1.48
300	0.22	0.61	0.99	1.37	1.75
400	0.26	0.77	1.28	1.79	2.30
500	0.29	0.93	1.57	2.21	2.84
600	0.32	1.09	1.85	2.62	3.38
800	0.38	1.40	2.42	3.44	4.46
1000	0.43	1.70	2.97	4.25	5.53
1500	0.53	2.45	4.36	6.27	8.18
2000	0.62	3.17	5.72	8.27	10.80
3000	0.78	4.60	8.43	12.30	16.10
4000	0.91	6.01	11.10	16.20	21.30
5000	1.03	7.40	13.80	20.20	26.50
6000	1.14	8.79	16.40	24.10	31.70
8000	1.33	11.50	21.70	31.90	42.10
10,000	1.50	14.20	27.00	39.70	52.50
20,000	2.19	27.70	53.20	78.70	104.10
30,000	2.72	40.90	79.20	117.50	155.70
40,000	3.19	54.20	105.20	156.19	207.20

Sources: Spotte (1979a, 1979b).

HALF-DEPTH METHOD[86] Experienced aquarists have intuitive knowledge of how much biomass an aquarium can support based on the amount of food added each day. *Half-depth* is the depth of a filter bed at which one-half the ammonia derived from the food is removed in a single pass (i.e., at each recirculation time). From this value the design depth can be obtained. The method has not been tested.

What I have termed the half-depth method is a conservative model in the assumption that (*1*) all nitrogen is excreted by the fishes with none retained in the tissues, and (*2*) nitrogen is excreted at a constant rate, regardless of how often the fishes are fed. The linear flow rate through the filter bed has been fixed at 6.8×10^{-4} m/s or 1 gal/(min·ft^2). In the following example the filter bed and aquarium have the same area (i.e., an internal subgravel filter is used). Design variables are listed in Table 2-8. *Void fraction* or *porosity* (the fraction of a filter bed that is empty space) is discussed in Chapter 3. In general, small filtrants have small void fractions and large specific surface areas. Plastic packing is an exception (see below). By plastic packing I mean commercially produced hollow cylinders and other shapes (e.g., spheres and saddles; Chapter 3). A dilution effect constant, ln(2) = 0.69, is necessary if the water is recirculated because the ammonia in a portion of it will have been diluted after passing through the bacteriological filter.

TABLE 2-8 Design variables and unknown information needed to calculate carrying capacity by the half-depth method.

Factor	Units
Design variables	
Area of the filter bed	m^2
Volume of the aquarium	m^3
Water temperature	°C
Linear flow rate of water through the filter bed, F	6.8×10^{-4} m/s
Amount of food fed daily	g
Ammonia content of the food	%
Mass of total NH_4-N added per recirculation time, r	g
Added concentration of total NH_4-N per volume per recirculation time, c	g/m^3 or mg/L
Allowable upper limit of total NH_4-N, U (see Technology section, Method 2.10)	mg/L or mol/L
Specific surface area of the filtrant, SSA (Fig. 2-19)	m^2/m^3 or ft^2/ft^3
Void fraction or porosity of the filtrant, P (Fig. 2-19)	None
Unknown information	
Recirculation time, T (time required for one pass through the filter) $= \frac{\text{depth}}{F}$	s
Ammonia reduction ratio, $R = \frac{[\text{total NH}_4-\text{N}] - U}{U \times \ln(2)}$	None
Half-depth, H	m
Temperature correction factor (Fig. 2-20)	None
Half-depth corrected for temperature, H_c	m
Design depth, $D = (H_c)(R)$	m

Source: Gary Adams and Stephen Spotte, Sea Research Foundation.

Compute the design depth of a subgravel filter with 0.49-mm sand for an aquarium maintained at 16°C. The aquarium is rectangular (3 m long × 2 m wide × 2 m high); volume = 12 m^3 and area = 6 m^2. Recirculation time, T, is calculated by

$$T = \frac{\text{depth of the aquarium}}{F} \tag{2.12}$$

$$= \frac{2 \text{ m}}{6.8 \times 10^{-4} \text{ m/s}}$$

$$= 2.9 \times 10^3 \text{ s}$$

If the linear flow rate, F, is not 6.8×10^{-4} m/s it can be found by

$$F = \frac{V}{\text{volume flow rate}} \tag{2.13}$$

where V = volume of the aquarium (m^3) and volume flow rate = flow rate through filter bed (m^3/s).

Each day the aquarium in this example receives 1000 g of food, of which 3.2% is total NH_4-N. The mass of ammonia in a volume of water passed once through the filter bed (i.e., the mass of total NH_4-N added per recirculation time, r) is calculated by

$$r = \text{feeding rate} \times \text{ammonia content of the food} \times \text{recirculation time} \tag{2.14}$$

$$= 1000 \frac{\text{g}}{\text{d}} \times 3.2\% \times 2.9 \times 10^3 \text{ s} \left(\frac{1 \text{ min}}{60 \text{ s}}\right)\left(\frac{1 \text{ h}}{60 \text{ min}}\right)\left(\frac{1 \text{ d}}{24 \text{ h}}\right)\left(\frac{1}{100\%}\right)$$

$$= 1.07 \text{ g}$$

The concentration, c, of total NH_4-N per recirculation time is

$$c = \frac{r}{V} \tag{2.15}$$

$$= \frac{1.07 \text{ g}}{12 \text{ m}^3}$$

$$= 0.09 \text{ g/m}^3 \text{ in SI units (or mg/L in metric units)}$$

In this example, establish a stringent allowable upper limit of 0.015 mg total NH_4-N/L (see Method 2.10), represented by U. Calculate the ammonia reduction ratio by

$$R = \frac{c - U}{U \times \ln(2)} \tag{2.16}$$

$$= \frac{0.09 - 0.015}{(0.015)(0.69)}$$

$$= 7.25$$

Find the depth of the filter bed at which one-half the total NH_4-N will be removed (half-depth, H) at 16°C. For 0.49-mm sand, SSA = 12,000 m^2/m^3, and P = 0.40 (Table 2-8 and Fig. 2-19). From Figure 2-19, H = 0.01 m.

Multiply half-depth, H, by the temperature correction factor (Fig. 2-20) to obtain corrected half-depth, H_c. From the figure, the temperature correction factor = 1.5 at 16°C, and H_c = 0.015 m. The design depth, D, is given by

$$D = (H_c)(R) \tag{2.17}$$

$$= 0.11 \text{ m}$$

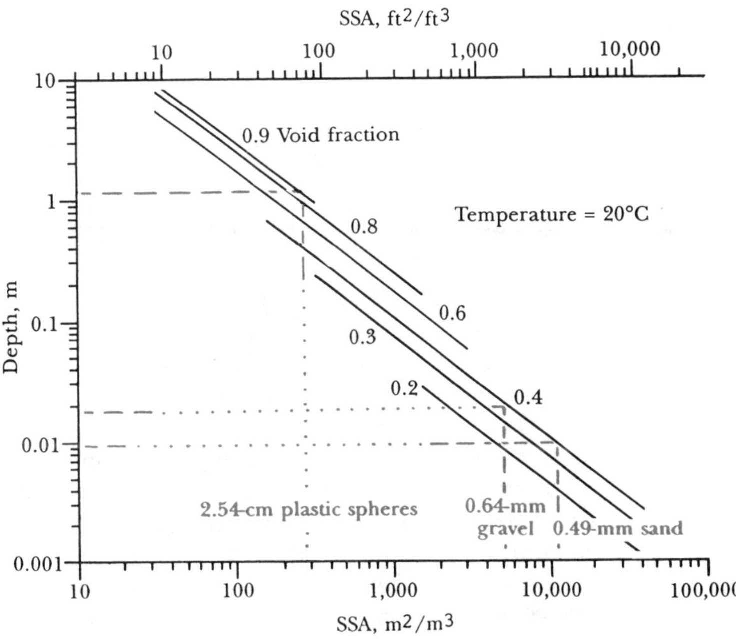

Figure 2-19 *Void fractions of filtrants as a function of filter bed depth and specific surface area, SSA.* Source: Gary Adams, Sea Research Foundation; drawn from various sources.

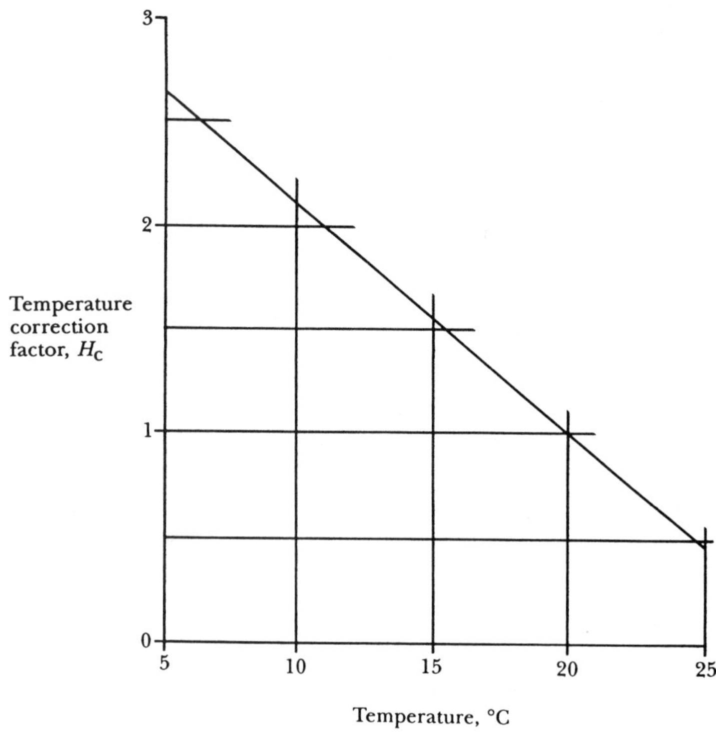

Figure 2-20 *Temperature correction factor needed to obtain corrected half-depth.* Source: Gary Adams, Sea Research Foundation; drawn from data in Haug and McCarty (1972).

The filter bed must be 0.11 m deep to maintain the concentration of total NH_4-N below the allowable upper limit of 0.015 mg/L.

As shown in Figure 2-19, the same procedure can be used to verify that a filter bed composed of 0.64-mm gravel ($\frac{1}{4}$-in., SSA = 52 m^2/m^3, P = 0.27) must be approximately twice as deep (0.20 m); a bed of 2.54-cm plastic packing of the type shown in Figure 3-44b (1-in., SSA = 280 m^2/m^3, P = 0.96) would have to be 13 m deep, or six times the depth of the aquarium.

Clearly, no advantage is gained by substituting plastic packing for sand and gravel. Switching from large to small plastic packing of the same design increases the specific surface area, but void fraction stays the same. Adequate removal of ammonia results not from any perceived superiority of the packing, but simply because aquarium seawater contains relatively low concentrations of ammonia. The rate at which water moves through a filter bed is controlled by the void fraction of the filtrant (Chapter 3). The low linear flow rate through aquarium filter beds can be sustained easily with sand and gravel.

Method 2.3 Design of Filter Beds[87]

The three most important design criteria for bacteriological filters are that (*1*) minimum depth of the filter bed should be 7 cm, no matter how small the aquarium; (*2*) surface area of the filter bed should equal that of the aquarium; and (*3*) flow rate through the filter bed should not be less than 6.8×10^{-4} m/s. All are simply rules of thumb and pertain to aquariums with subgravel filters. The publications of Hirayama and Hess (see the preceding subsections) demonstrate that shallow filter beds with large surfaces and small filtrant materials work best. In filter beds with small filtrants and low flow rates, the efficiency of nutrient conversions falls off rapidly with depth (Fig. 2-21).[88]

Filter plates of subgravel bacteriological filters should cover the entire bottom of the aquarium, as mentioned previously, and be sealed around the edges to keep gravel from accumulating underneath. Filter plates for large aquariums can be made of any material that is sturdy, porous, and inert in seawater. Fiberglass-reinforced plastic roofing panels (Fig. 2-22) and fiberglass-reinforced epoxy industrial grating* are two such materials. Roofing panels are available at lumber yards and hardware stores.

When roofing panels are used, slits should be cut into them crossways (at right angles to the ribs) using a table saw equipped with a blade for cutting plastic. Make the slits approximately 1 mm wide, 2.5 cm long, and 5 cm apart. Place the panels *slits down* in the aquarium, and seal them where the edges meet the walls. The best sealant is fiberglass tape (5 cm wide) embedded in silicone (Dow Corning RTV 795** or equivalent). A rib or two on the leading edges of adjacent panels can be overlapped if necessary and sealed together with silicone. After the silicone hardens, gravel can be added to the desired depth and spread evenly over the plate.

Saw fiberglass-reinforced epoxy grate to the required dimensions, then lay plastic fly screen on top (Fig. 2-23). Tie the screen in place with monofilament fishing line. Afterward, seal the edges of the grate where it meets the walls of the aquarium. Both roofing panels and grates must be supported above the bottom of the aquarium with spacers. Any material can be used, so long as it is inert and sturdy. Half circles of PVC pipe work well. The water must be able to circulate freely around the spacers.

*Joseph T. Ryerson and Sons, Inc., P. O. Box 484, Jersey City NJ 07303.

**Dow Chemical U.S.A., Midland City MI 48640.

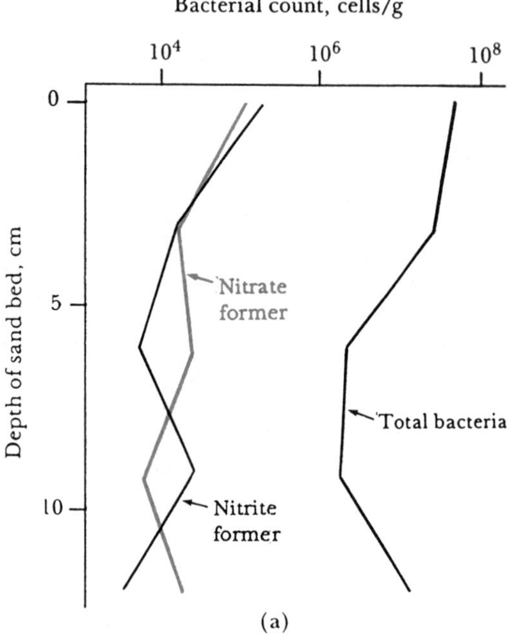

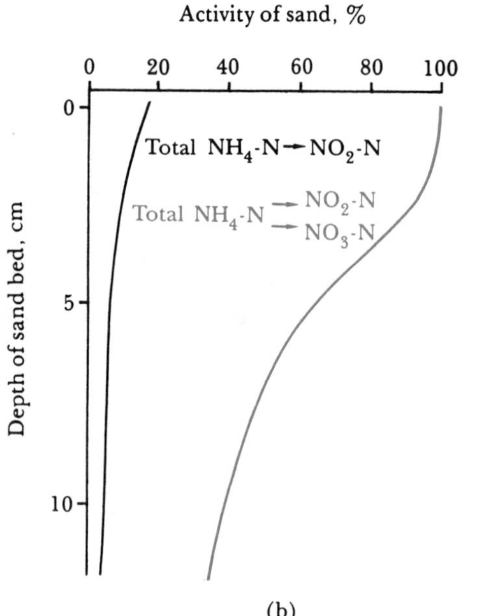

Figure 2-21 *Nitrifying bacteria at different depths in the filter bed of a seawater aquarium.* (a) *Populations.* (b) *Activities.* Source: Spotte (1979b) after Yoshida (1967).

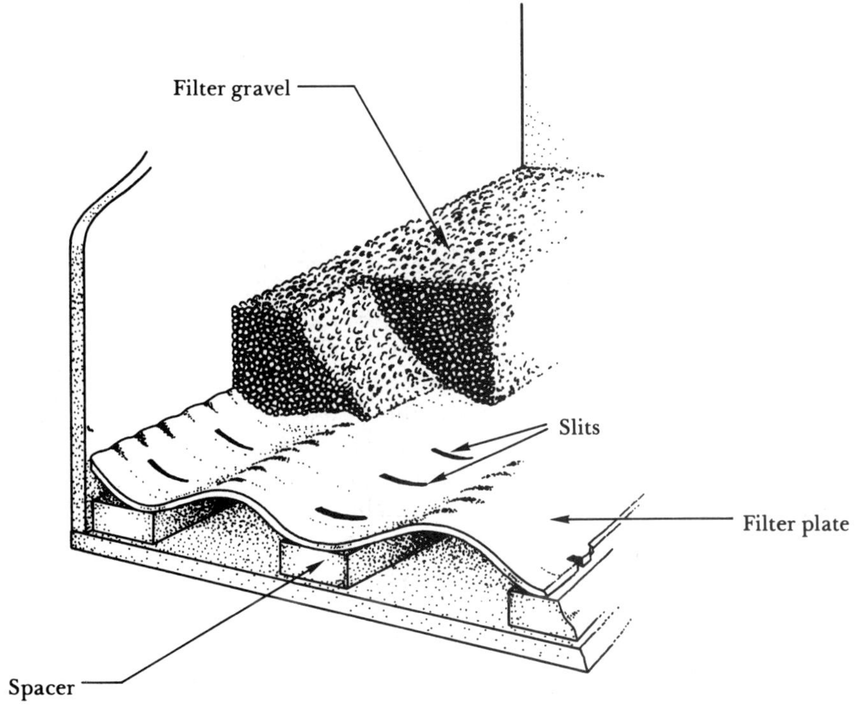

Figure 2-22 *Cutaway section of an aquarium with subgravel filter showing a filter plate made of fiberglass-reinforced plastic roofing material.* Sources: Spotte (1979a, 1979b) after Anonymous (1971).

Figure 2-23 *Fiberglass-reinforced plastic grate with overlying plastic fly screen.* Source: Spotte (1979b).

Method 2.4 Maintenance of Bacteriological Filters[89]

Every 2 weeks, change 10% of the water in closed-system aquariums. At the same time, remove some of the excess detritus that has accumulated since the last partial water change. Both procedures are accomplished easily with a siphon hose. The removal of old aquarium seawater may temporarily alter the biological and chemical balance of the system, particularly if large amounts of detritus are removed. Detritus, equivalent in particle size to silt, is a primary attachment site of filter bed bacteria because of its large surface area (Table 2-9). Stir the gravel gently. During partial water changes, some of the filter bed bacteria are removed along with excess detritus; the population is further reduced when biological film that has broken loose is siphoned out.[90] The effect is seldom noticeable in aquariums with low animal densities. If the aquarium supports an unusually large biomass there is sometimes a detectable time lag in nutrient conversion immediately after a water change.

Method 2.5 Design of Denitrification Systems

Denitrification of aquarium seawater can be achieved either actively or passively. The *active* method—columnar denitrification—incorporates process technology adapted from wastewater treatment and relies on sustaining a delicate carbon-nitrogen balance in both the influent and treated effluent waters. The *passive* or *anoxic sediment* method requires no technology. It relies simply on the diffusion of inorganic nitrogen and organic carbon through a layer of sediment devoid of oxygen, either at the bottom of the aquarium or in a contiguous vessel.

COLUMNAR DENITRIFICATION METHOD The design of active denitrification systems is fraught with problems because

TABLE 2-9 Surface areas of particles of different sizes. Note that the smaller the particle diameter the greater its surface area per unit of mass.

Particle	Diameter, μm	Surface area, cm^2/g
Fine gravel	2000–1000	11.3
Coarse sand	1000–500	22.7
Medium sand	500–250	25.4
Fine sand	250–100	90.7
Very fine sand	100–50	227
Silt	50–2	454
Clay	<2	11,300

Source: Brock (1966).

the controlling processes are dynamic and not self-regulating. During nitrification, the sequential reaction products are increasingly less toxic. As stated previously, waters from municipal wastes, aquaculture installations, and public aquariums are carbon limited from the standpoint of denitrification.[91] Exogenous sources of carbon (e.g., methanol) must be added to attain optimal C/N ratios. The introduction of exogenous carbon raises the risk of breakthrough into the treated effluent. Some carbon sources are toxic. Methanol, for example, inhibits the bacterial oxidation of ammonia at 48 mg/L,[92] but even harmless carbon results in a rise in DOC and heightened heterotrophic activity.

The risk of breakthrough is very real. Effluent quality in denitrification columns varies considerably, particularly during startup.[93] To sustain a properly balanced C/N ratio in both the influent and effluent waters requires continuous monitoring and adjustment. This is especially true if columnar denitrification is combined with seaweed filtration (Method 2.6). Primary productivity causes diel fluctuations in nitrate,[68] introducing a dangerous element of unpredictability. Even when conditioned columns are operated in the absence of seaweed filters the result is often dissimilation without complete denitrification.[94] In such situations, nitrate in the influent water represents potential ammonia in the effluent. Incomplete reduction culminates in worsening water quality as the concentrations of ammonia, nitrite, and DOC increase. Excess DOC is residual exogenous carbon pumped into the column (i.e., the amount remaining after complete nitrate reduction). Typically, DOC in the treated effluent rises when the C/N ratio is high; nitrite and ammonia increase at low C/N ratios.[94] A ratio between 1.5 to 2.5 may be necessary to completely preclude ammonia from the treated effluent, but increases in DOC are inevitable.[94] A C/N ratio of 1.0 is a suitable starting place.[95]

A denitrification column is illustrated diagrammatically in Figure 2-24. The packing material should be fine (e.g., 0.49-mm filter sand) to provide as much surface area as possible. I recommend tapering the top of the column to concentrate gases and improve blowoff efficiency. *Contact time*—the interval between introduction of the effluent and emergence of the treated effluent—should be 1 h.[94] Prolonged retention reduces the risk of breakthrough. Inorganic nitrogen can be monitored conveniently (Methods 2.9 through 2.13), but accurate measurement of DOC is labor intensive and expensive.

ANOXIC SEDIMENT METHOD[96] What I have termed the anoxic sediment method of denitrification relies on diffusion of solutes into a layer of bottom sediment (presumably fine sand)

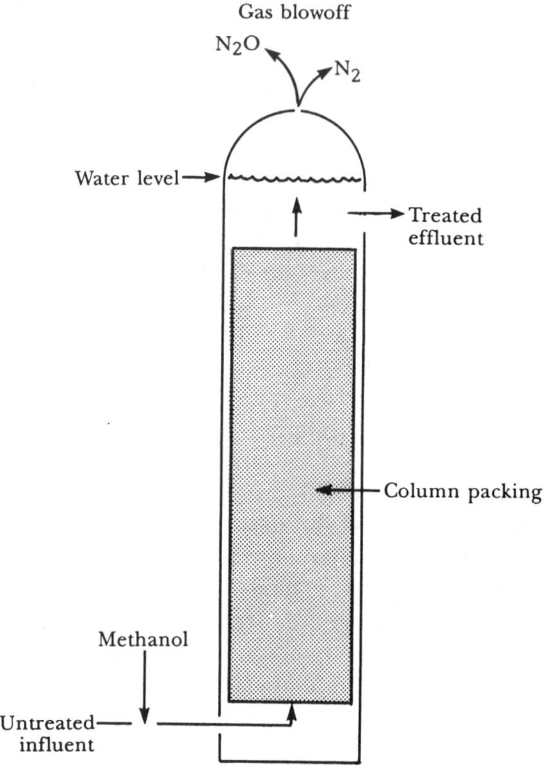

Figure 2-24 Denitrification column with methanol as the exogenous carbon source. The preferred column packing is small grained (e.g., 0.49-mm filter sand). The tapered top enhances gas blowoff. Contact time should be 1 h at a C/N ratio of 1. Source: Stephen Spotte.

and their subsequent transformation to less objectionable states by an undescribed, heterogeneous population of organisms. One study reported that after 10 months the nitrate concentration (expressed as NO_3^-) was 0.013 mg/L, compared with 110.0 mg/L in a comparable seawater aquarium equipped with a subgravel filter.

In principle, oxygen in the sediment diminishes along a vertical gradient (Fig. 2-25). The sediment layer is separated from the bottom of the aquarium by a plenum filled with stagnant water. Aerobic organisms inhabiting the surface layers carry out oxidation processes; reduction presumably occurs in the anoxic bottom layers. Reaction products evidently diffuse into both water masses. The bottom layers of sediment and water in the plenum appear to interact as a sort of closed system, although gaseous nitrogen must somehow reach the surface. The upper sediment layer is in contact with the primary bulk fluid of the aquarium and, by extension, with the atmosphere. This allows for the efflux of completely reduced nitrogen and its eventual loss from the system. At present, claims purporting to describe these processes are without an empirical basis.

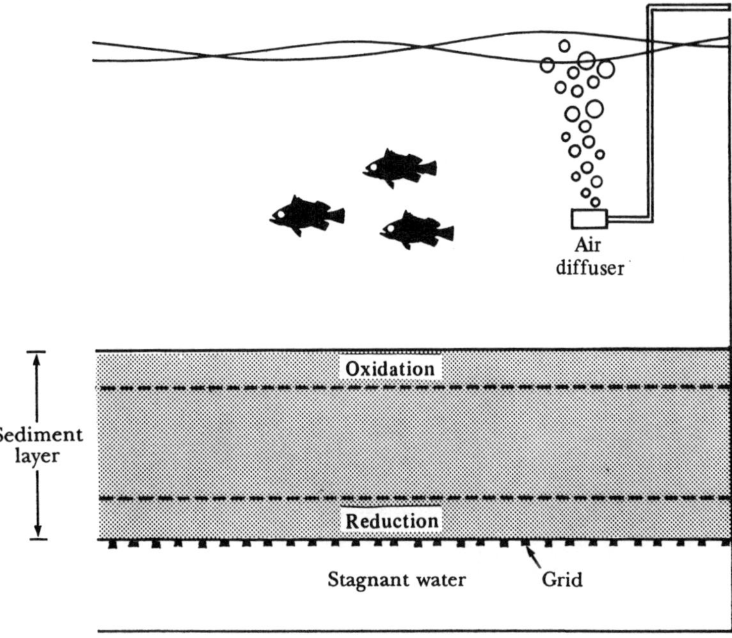

Figure 2-25 *Anoxic sediment denitrification illustrating a vertical gradation from aerobic to anaerobic. Solutes presumably diffuse into the different layers of sediment and are transformed by resident microorganisms; reaction products diffuse outward to the stagnant water or bulk seawater of the aquarium.* Source: Stephen Spotte after Jaubert (1989).

Method 2.6 Design and Maintenance of Seaweed Filters[97]

If estimation of carrying capacity seems vague, consider that factors impinging on the design of seaweed filters are even more difficult to quantify. The only approach is trial and error.[98] One thing to keep in mind is that seaweeds are leaky and exude organic acids, phenolic compounds, and other substances into the water. This is especially true of injured organisms.[70] Injury is difficult to avoid when part of the crop must be harvested at regular intervals. An active seaweed filter is likely to accelerate eutrophication and increase demands on the physical adsorption system (Method 2.7). In addition, an actively growing seaweed culture may raise the pH to dangerous levels unless this factor is monitored constantly.

Basic design criteria are that (*1*) maximum depth of the tray in which seaweeds are cultured should not exceed 30 cm; (*2*) the surface area should be as large as possible; (*3*) photoperiod can be constant, but not less than 16 h of light per 24 h; and (*4*) light intensity should be adequate for the species cultured.

Light levels necessary to saturate the photosynthetic pigments of mature seaweeds (Fig. 2-26) exceed those of most phytoplankton.[99] This suggests that light intensities suitable for phytoplankton culture (Chapter 8, Method 8.9) may be inadequate for seaweed filters. In general, photoperiod and light intensity are more important in algal culture (both phytoplankton

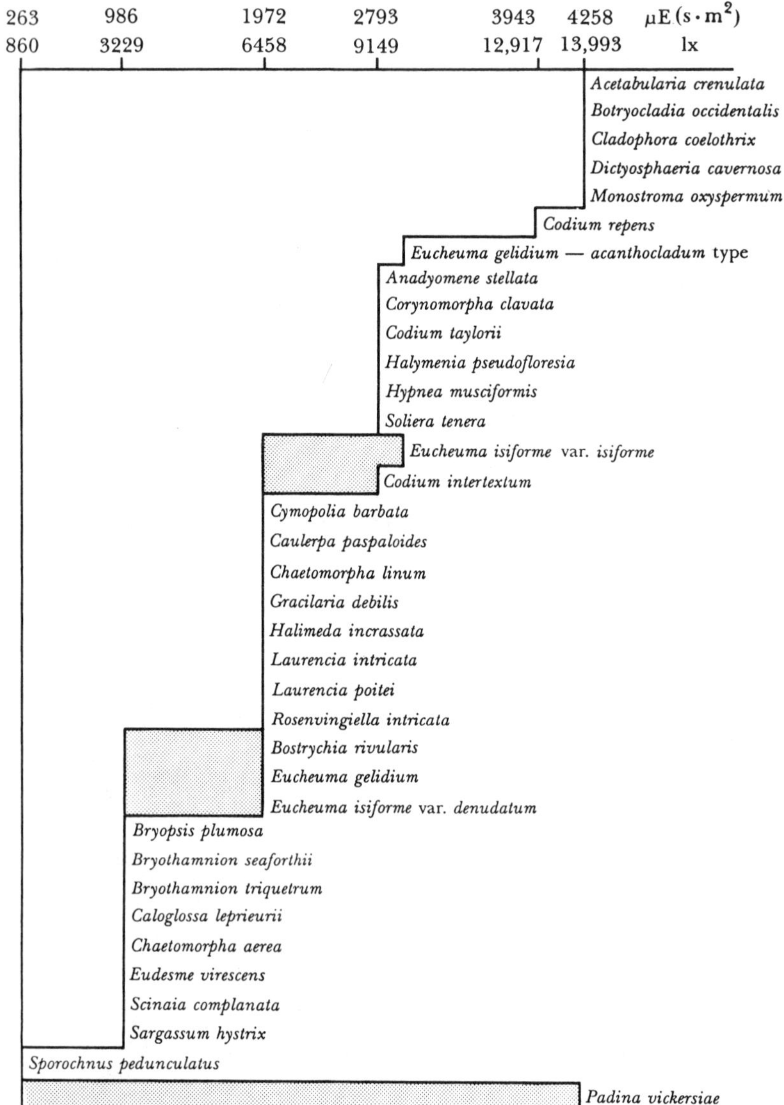

Figure 2-26 *Summary of optimal light intensities for 36 species of Florida seaweeds at 20°C. The statistically equivalent photosynthetic responses at higher intensities are shaded. μE = micro-einsteins; 1 lx = 10.76 footcandles.* Source: Mathieson and Dawes (1986).

and seaweed) than the spectral curves of the lamps used. Most seaweeds grow well under cool-white fluorescent light.[100] However, some species—particularly the chlorophytes—absorb light heavily into the red end of the spectrum, and some incandescent lighting to supplement the main fluorescent source often improves growth.[101] One recommendation is to use 10 W of incandescent light for each 100 W of fluorescent.[100] General lighting specifications are provided in Table 2-10.

Benthic seaweeds grow attached to objects on the bottom.

TABLE 2-10 General lighting specifications for seaweeds using cool white fluorescent lamps. 1 lux (lx) = 10.76 footcandles.

Algal group	Intensity, lx
Green, tropical	13,000–16,200
Green, temperate	7560–10,800
Brown	7560–10,800
Red	2160–8640

Source: Spotte (1979b).

Cobbles are a suitable substratum.[101] The floor of the tray should be sloped for easy draining (Fig. 2-27). If the species cultured has wide fronds, wipe them periodically to remove epiphytic growths; crop excess plants when the biomass exceeds that needed to keep nitrate at the expected concentration. The best position for a seaweed filter is after the bacteriological filter but before physical adsorption processes (see Method 2.7).

Method 2.7 Reduction of Dissolved Organic Carbon with Granular Activated Carbon

The metabolic processes of heterotrophic bacteria exert a heavy demand on eutrophic waters. Uneaten food and algal exudates

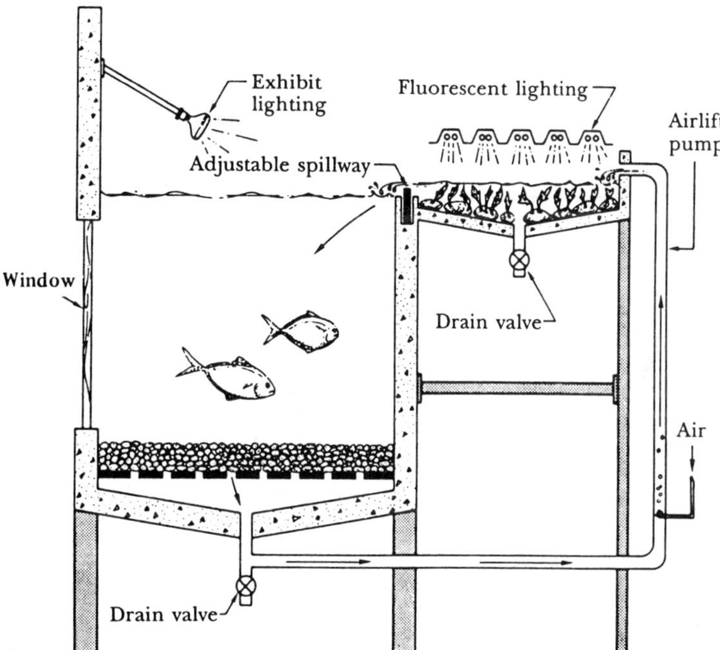

Figure 2-27 Seaweed culture tray illustrating the cycling of water between the tray and the aquarium. Source: Spotte (1979b).

contribute to the overall biomass of a water system by supporting an unnecessarily large population of heterotrophs. A substantial portion of the DOC can be removed by physical adsorption onto activated carbon.

Theoretically, DOC can be removed from seawater by the application of a strong oxidant such as ozone, O_3. Ozone splits many organic molecules on contact (Fig. 2-28). Ultimately, DOC is rendered to more basic components, and the carbon portion is driven from solution into the atmosphere as free (gaseous) CO_2. Such is the theory. In practice this rarely happens, and oxidation is not a useful method of reducing the concentration of DOC in aquarium seawater.[102] The alternative is to adsorb the material onto a suitable substratum, which is later discarded.

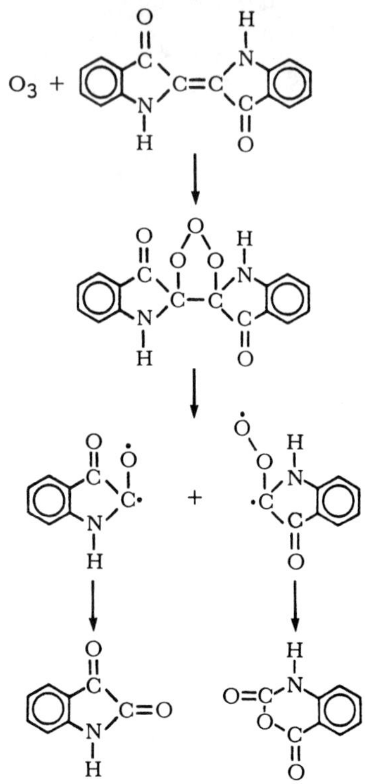

ADSORPTION Portions of both the labile and refractory constituents of DOC in aquarium seawater are removable by *adsorption*, defined as the collection of a substance from one phase onto another across an interface (Fig. 2-29). An *interface* is the boundary between two phases, one being seawater. The second in this case is the surface of the solid or *adsorbent*. During adsorption the substance collected (the *adsorbate*) leaves the water and becomes bound to the surface of the adsorbent. If the bond is strong the adsorption process is irreversible, and *chemical adsorption* has occurred. If the bonds are weak—a more likely situation in aquarium applications—the process is one of *physical adsorption*. A weak bond indicates that adsorption is reversible, often as a result of a change in adsorbate concentration. During *desorption*, the reverse process, adsorbates leave the adsorbent, pass back across the interface, and reenter the water. The result can be breakthrough of the adsorbate. The bulk of the adsorbate removed from aquarium seawater is DOC, but some consists of small aggregates constituting part of the POC.

ACTIVATED CARBON The most effective adsorbent for reduction of TOC in water is activated carbon, produced mainly from the source materials listed in Table 2-11. Activated carbon is manufactured in three steps: (*1*) dehydration, (*2*) carbonization, and (*3*) activation. Some authors do not distinguish between the first two. The source material is dehydrated by drying it at temperatures up to 170°C, sometimes in the presence of a dehydrating agent (e.g., zinc chloride, $ZnCl_2$, or phosphoric acid, H_3PO_3). Dehydration continues until no water remains. Carbonization then converts the dehydrated source materials to primary carbon, a mixture of ash (inert inorganic compounds),

Isatin

Isatoic anhydride

Figure 2-28 Mechanism of the ozone-indigo reaction and formation of the reaction products isatin and isatoic anhydride. Application of O_3 to an aqueous solution of indigo results in rapid decolorization of the water. Source: Grosjean et al. (1988).

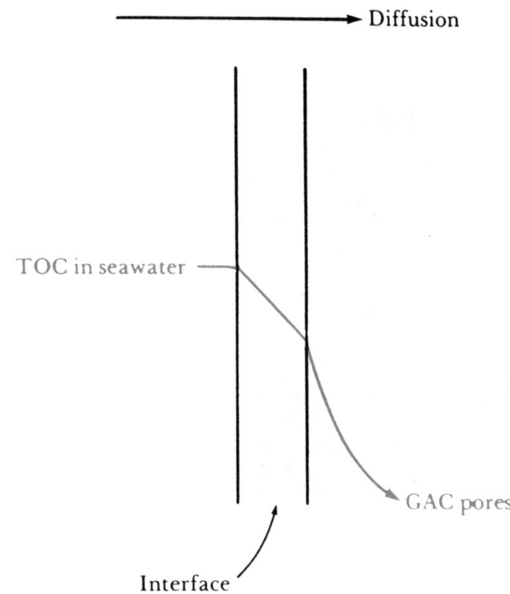

Figure 2-29 *Removal of TOC in a two-phase system across an interface. In this graphic the adsorbent is granular activated carbon (GAC).* Source: Stephen Spotte.

tars, and different chemical forms of amorphous and crystalline carbon. This ordinarily is accomplished at three successively higher temperatures (Fig. 2-30).

Carbonization is carried out in the near absence of air to prevent combustion. It begins when the temperature is raised above 170°C, which causes some of the organic matter to degrade and form carbon monoxide (CO), carbon dioxide, and acetic acid ($HC_2H_3O_2$). The temperature is then raised to 270 to 280°C and further decomposition occurs, resulting in formation of large amounts of tar, methanol (CH_3OH), and other by-products. Carbonization is completed at 400 to 600°C with a yield of ~80% primary carbon.

TABLE 2-11 Source materials for activated carbon.

Animal bones
Coal
Nutshells
Peat
Petroleum residues
Sawdust
Sugar cane pulp (bagasse)
Wastewater sludges
Wood

Source: Stephen Spotte.

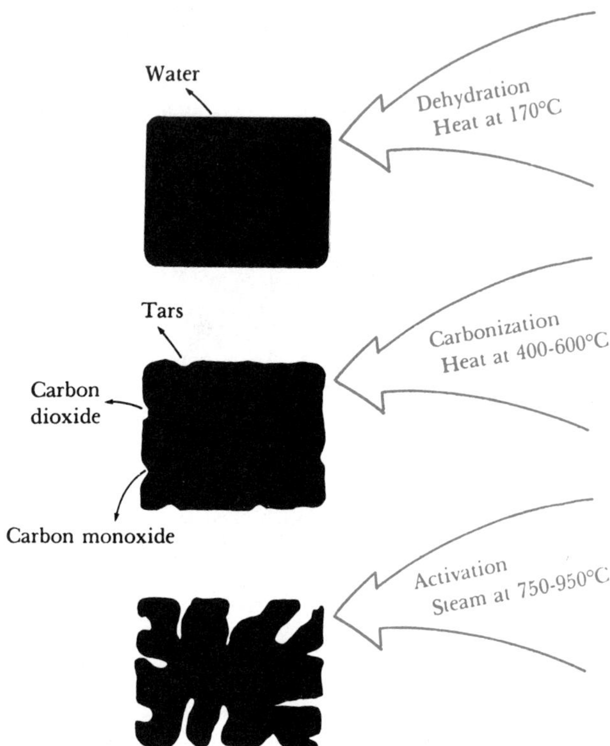

Figure 2-30 *Steps in the production of activated carbon: dehydration, carbonization, and activation.* Source: Stephen Spotte.

During *activation* the carbonized product is treated with an activating agent (e.g., CO_2, steam). Steam is used most commonly. Steam at 750 to 950°C opens millions of pores in the material by burning off the remaining decomposition products. The molecular structures of activated carbon (i.e., the structure of the pore walls) and pure graphite are similar. Graphite crystals are made up of fused hexagons arranged in layers (Fig. 2-31). The microcrystalline structure of activated carbon differs in being composed of parallel, unordered stacks of graphite planes.[103] The pores are of three sizes: macropores have diameters of 5 to 10 nm;* micropores, which are <0.2 nm; and transitional pores, which are intermediate in size. Activated carbons are classed as powdered (*powdered activated carbon*, PAC) or granular (*granular activated carbon*, GAC). Only granular types are suitable for aquarium use (Fig. 2-32). They have grain sizes >0.1 mm.[104]

ADSORPTION EFFICIENCY *Adsorption efficiency* refers to the rate at which adsorbates are collected from water (*adsorption rate*)

*1 nm (nanometre) = 10^{-9} m.

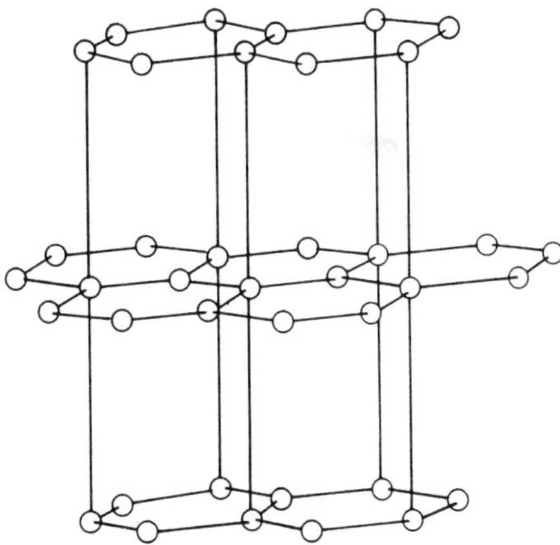

Figure 2-31 *Arrangement of carbon atoms in a graphite crystal.* Source: Walker (1962).

and the *adsorption capacity* of the adsorbent (i.e., the quantity of adsorbates that can be removed before the adsorbent is saturated or exhausted). Adsorption efficiency in the case of GAC depends to some extent on the source material and manufacturing process; otherwise, it is a function of the four properties listed in Table 2-12, which are presented in decreasing order of importance.

Adsorption is primarily a surface phenomenon, and the larger the surface area of a given type of activated carbon the greater its adsorption efficiency, within certain limits. Nearly all the surface area is contained in the extensive system of pores. The pore structure is formed by fissures between graphitic planes, and the extensive surface area is provided by the walls of these pores. Most activated carbons have surface areas of 500 to 1500 m^2/g, but a few contain as much as 2500 m^2/g. Beyond ~ 1500 m^2/g the pore sizes required to increase the surface area are so tiny that only the smallest organic molecules can be adsorbed. In addition, molecules that are similar in size to the pore openings diffuse into the interior of the activated carbon very slowly. The most effective activated carbons contain pores of several sizes.[105]

The presence of surface *oxides* (compounds containing oxygen) reduces adsorption capacity. Adsorption of organic mole-

Grain diameter, mm

4.70
3.33
2.36
1.65
1.40
1.17
0.991
0.833
0.701
0.589
0.495
0.417
0.351
0.295
0.246
0.175

Figure 2-32 *Granular activated carbons illustrated as actual grain sizes.* Source: Barnebey and Sutcliffe Corp., P.O. Box 2526, Columbus OH 43216.

TABLE 2-12 Characteristics of activated carbon that influence adsorption efficiency.

Surface area
Pore structure
Surface polarity
Grain size

Source: McGuire and Suffet (1978).

cules occurs on the walls of the pores at the carbon surface, which in new (unused) material are *nonpolar* (i.e., the molecules are arranged symmetrically and do not behave as dipoles). Nonpolarity has advantages in seawater applications because the affinity of the pore walls for inorganic electrolytes is greatly diminished, leaving them available for organic substances.

Surface oxides are formed when new activated carbon is placed in contact with oxidizing compounds such as oxygen, ozone, chlorine (Cl_2), and permanganate (MnO_4^-). Such exposure renders the pore walls highly polar, culminating in restrictions and ultimate blockage of the openings. Reducing the grain size of an activated carbon increases the adsorption rate temporarily but has little effect on adsorption capacity, considering that the surface area of a given mass of material remains almost unchanged. This is because >99% of the total surface area is internal. It would seem that GACs of small pore size—and therefore large internal surface area—would be preferable. Actually, GACs of uniformly small pore size perform poorly in water treatment applications. This is attributable in part to the restricted size range of molecules that can be adsorbed, and because exhaustion is approached more quickly. GACs of small pore size are characterized by reduced pore volume.[106]

Adsorption efficiency is affected by the temperature and pH of the water[107] and by contact time, in this case the amount of time that water containing the adsorbate is in contact with the adsorbent. Neither temperature nor pH is particularly important. Even if they were these factors cannot be altered merely to make adsorption more efficient. Both must be controlled within narrow limits for the welfare of captive fishes. Contact time occurs in three stages: (*1*) diffusion of the adsorbate across the interface, (*2*) adsorption onto the surface of the activated carbon, and (*3*) diffusion into the pore structure (Fig. 2-29). The first two steps are faster than the third. The last step therefore is *rate limiting* (i.e., the step that determines the overall rate of removal). Ideally, contact time should be slow enough to accommodate the third step. Specific contact time data obtained using aquarium seawater are not available, but a reasonable starting flow rate is 2.5 m/h.

Films that form on GAC in wastewater measurably enhance TOC reduction.[108] The proposed mechanism is the large surface area of GAC for the attachment and growth of bacteria,[109] although some experimental work has discounted the importance of microorganisms.[110] In only one of these studies has aquarium water been used.[111] Results indicated that the comparative effectiveness of the materials evaluated could be attributed almost entirely to physical adsorption, with little or no biological enhancement (Figs. 2-33 through 2-36).

Figure 2-33 *Scanning electron photomicrograph (SEM) of new (unused) hardwood GAC. Loose material is surface "fines." 525x.* Source: Spotte and Adams (1984).

GAC CONTACTORS Activated carbon is brought into contact with seawater inside a *contactor*. This is simply a container or chamber through which water from the aquarium is cycled continuously. Contactors can be arranged as single units, in series, or in parallel (Fig. 2-37). In ordinary circumstances single units suffice. A GAC contactor can be nearly any type of inert container. A length of PVC pipe capped at each end makes an efficient contactor. The unit can be plumbed underneath an aquarium for easy removal when it becomes necessary to replace the activated carbon.

Figure 2-34 *SEM of the surface of hardwood GAC after 40 d in the artificial seawater of a working aquarium. 520x.* Source: Spotte and Adams (1984).

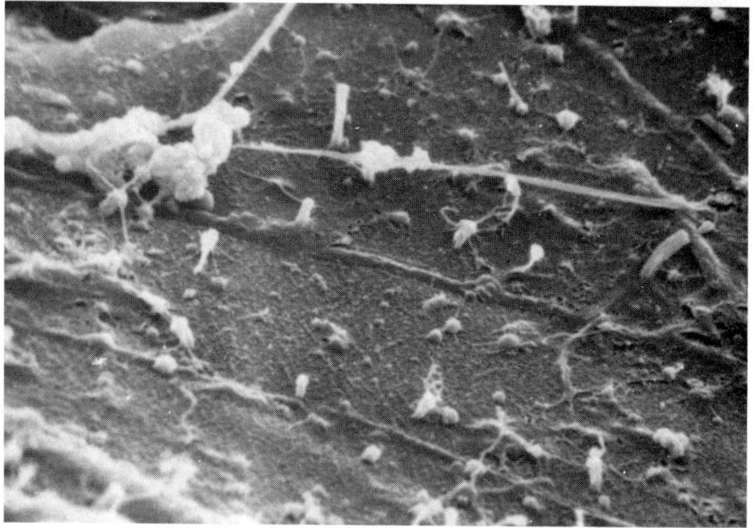

Figure 2-35 *SEM of the surface of used hardwood GAC after 78 d in the artificial seawater of a working aquarium. Visible microorganisms include cocci, rods, and stalked bacteria* (Caulobacter-*like), some appearing to be embedded in extracellular material or attached by it. Not visible in this photomicrograph but seen in others were choanoflagellates and small testate amoebas, which probably consume bacteria. 2350x.* Source: Spotte and Adams (1984).

How to Handle Activated Carbon

1 Purchase activated carbons that have been stored in sealed plastic bags or in jars with tight-fitting lids. Remove only the amount needed, then reseal the container. Activated carbons are efficient adsorbents of cigarette smoke, insecticides, and other airborne contaminants. Activated carbons vary considerably in their capacities to remove DOC from aquarium seawater (Fig. 2-38).

2 Use 1 g/L of water in the aquarium. Pay no attention to the grain size of the material because most of the surface area

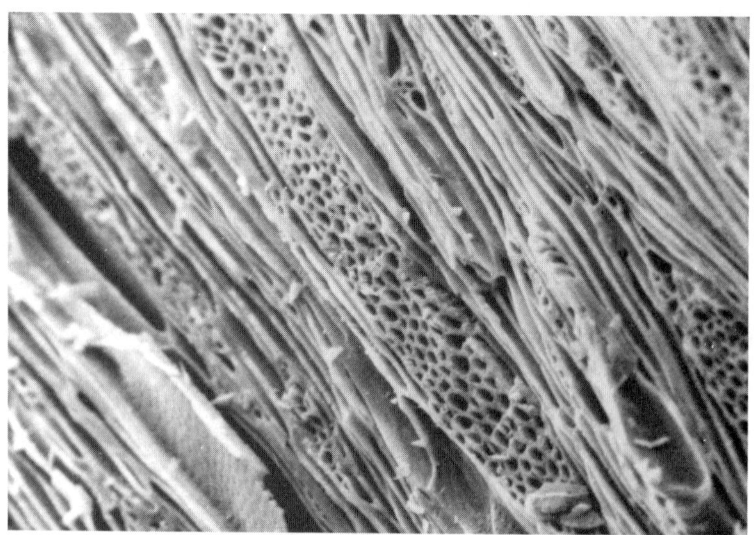

Figure 2-36 *SEM of the interior of used hardwood GAC after 78 d in the artificial seawater of a working aquarium. Note that the pores are clean and devoid of microorganisms, indicating that colonization occurs primarily on the external surfaces. 223x.* Source: Spotte and Adams (1984).

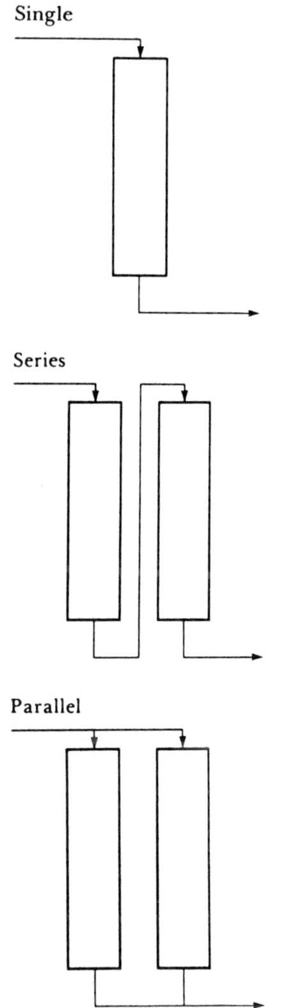

Figure 2-37 Contactors containing GAC can be connected to aquariums as single units, in series, or in parallel. Source: Stephen Spotte.

available for adsorption is inside the pores. Finely crushed materials offer no distinct advantage.

3 Rinse the activated carbon in distilled water or clean saline water to remove surface dust. This can be done by placing the material on a piece of plastic fly screen. Do not use tap water because chlorine is an oxidizing agent, and the effectiveness of the activated carbon will be reduced even before it is used.

4 Set the flow rate through the contactor. The rate selected is arbitrary.[112] The recommended rate is 2.5 m/h.

5 Discard old material and replace it every 4 weeks.

DISPOSAL VERSUS REACTIVATION Eventually, adsorption capacity is reached. Available adsorption sites are occupied, and the removal of adsorbates ceases. The GAC is exhausted. Reactivation is carried out routinely, but only on an industrial scale.[113] Onsite reactivation is not economically feasible until GAC usage approaches 4000 kg/day. Aquarists have no choice except to discard exhausted GAC and replace it. Contrary to what many think, reactivation cannot be accomplished effectively in the kitchen oven.

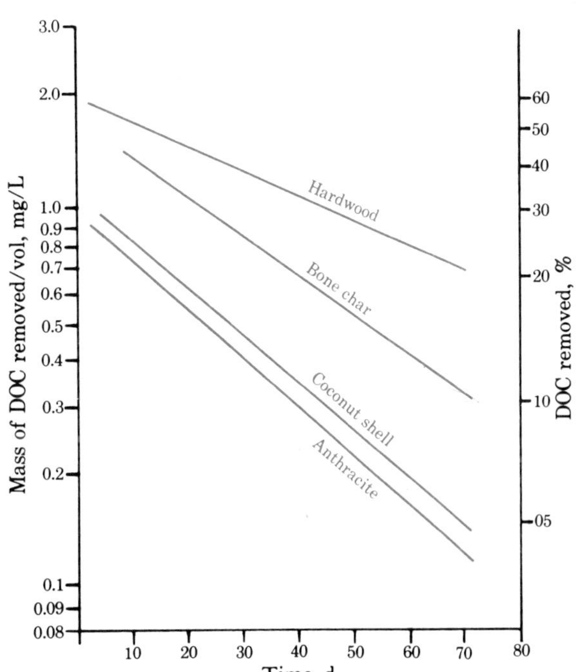

Figure 2-38 Activated carbons differ in their capacity to adsorb DOC. In this evaluation, GAC manufactured from hardwood was clearly superior to the other three. Source: Stephen Spotte, drawn from data in Spotte and Adams (1984).

Method 2.8 Orthophosphate Determination (as total PO_4-P)[114]

Principle All methods of measuring inorganic phosphorus are based on the reaction of phosphate ions with acidified molybdate to yield a phosphomolybdate complex, which is then reduced to an intense blue compound.[115] Detection limits vary according to modifications of the test. The method offered here easily exceeds the sensitivity required in most husbandry situations. Inorganic or orthophosphate in aquarium seawater ordinarily ranges from ~0.5 to 6 mg PO_4-P/L.[116]

Interferences Minimal in seawater determinations.

Chemicals (Reagent-grade)

Ammonium molybdate, $(NH_4)_6Mo_7O_{24} \cdot 4H_2O$

Anhydrous potassium dihydrogen phosphate, KH_2PO_4

Chloroform, $CHCl_3$

Concentrated sulfuric acid, H_2SO_4 (96%, specific gravity 1.84)

L-Ascorbic acid

Potassium antimonyl tartrate hemihydrate, $K(SbO)C_4H_4O_6 \cdot \frac{1}{2}H_2O$

Dedicated Glassware All glassware should be phosphate-free borosilicate. Prepare as below. Store in an acid bath between uses (0.1% H_2SO_4; 1 g concentrated H_2SO_4/L of distilled water, dH_2O).

1	1-L volumetric flask
1	500-mL volumetric flask
~12	50-mL volumetric flasks
~12	250-mL Erlenmeyer flasks
2	100-mL graduated cylinders
1	50-mL graduated cylinder
2	1-L amber glass bottles
1	100-mL amber glass bottle
3	500-mL clear glass bottles
3	10-mL glass pipettes
2	5-mL glass pipettes
1	1-mL glass pipette

Equipment and Supplies
(equivalent products can be substituted)

Aluminum foil

Phosphate-free, 0.45-μm membrane filters (47-mm Durapore® HVLP 047 00, Millipore® Corp., 80 Ashby Road, Bedford MA 01730)

Millipore® filter apparatus (Millipore Corp.)
Spectrophotometer or colorimeter with 880-nm filter

Preparation of Glassware

1 Start with new glassware.
2 Add 8 mL of mixed reagent (see Reagents) for each 100 mL of volume and swirl to coat the walls of the glassware.
3 Let stand for 20 min.
4 Discard used mixed reagent and rinse each container thoroughly with dH_2O. Glassware so treated is "phosphate free."
5 Store glassware in the sulfuric acid bath.
6 Glassware can be used again without repeating steps 1 through 4, provided it has not been washed in detergent between tests.

Reagents

Sulfuric acid solution (5 N) Add 70 mL concentrated H_2SO_4 to ~400 mL dH_2O in a 500-mL volumetric flask and dilute to volume. *Be careful.* Store in a clear glass bottle.

Ammonium molybdate solution Dissolve 40 g ammonium molybdate in ~900 mL dH_2O in a 1-L volumetric flask and dilute to volume. Transfer to an amber glass bottle. Store in the dark. Stable indefinitely, so long as it remains clear.

Potassium antimonyl tartrate solution Dissolve 1.4 g potassium antimonyl tartrate hemihydrate in dH_2O in a 500-mL volumetric flask and dilute to volume. Store in a clear glass bottle. Stable for many months, so long as it remains clear.

L-*Ascorbic acid solution* Dissolve 1.3 g L-ascorbic acid in 75 mL dH_2O. Refrigerate in an amber glass bottle at $<4°C$. Stable for no longer than 1 month.

Mixed reagent Transfer 125 mL of sulfuric acid solution to a 250-mL Erlenmeyer flask and add 12.5 mL of potassium antimonyl tartrate solution. Mix thoroughly. Add 37.5 mL of ammonium molybdate solution and mix thoroughly. Add 75 mL of L-ascorbic acid solution and mix again. Transfer to a clear glass bottle. Stable for ~24 h.

Phosphate stock solution Dissolve 0.439 g anhydrous (oven-dried at 105°C for 3 h) potassium dihydrogen phosphate in dH_2O in a 1-L volumetric flask and dilute to volume. Mix thoroughly. Concentration: 100 mg PO_4-P/L. Add a few drops of chloroform to retard the growth of bacteria and store refrigerated in an amber glass bottle. Stable for many months.

Phosphate standard solution Add 10 mL of phosphate stock solution to a 1-L volumetric flask and dilute to volume with dH_2O. Concentration: 1 mg PO_4-P/L. Prepare daily.

Analysis

1 Collect samples in labeled 250-mL Erlenmeyer flasks and cover immediately with new aluminium foil. Analyze within 2 h.[117] Warm the samples to room temperature (~20°C), then filter through a 0.45-μm membrane filter.

2 Pipette a volume of sample likely to contain 0.1 mg PO_4-P into a 50-mL volumetric flask,[118] add 8 mL of mixed reagent, dilute to volume with dH_2O, and mix.

3 To prepare a reagent blank, add 8 mL of mixed reagent to a 50-mL volumetric flask, dilute to volume with dH_2O, and mix.

4 Pipette 10 mL of phosphate standard solution (10 μg PO_4-P) into a 50-mL volumetric flask, add 8 mL of mixed reagent, dilute to volume with dH_2O, and mix.

5 Set absorbance to 0.00 at a wavelength of 880 nm using the reagent blank and a cell with a 1- or 5-cm path length.

6 After 10 min but before 30 min, read and record the absorbance of the standard.

7 Read and record the absorbance of the sample.

8 If the absorbance is greater than 1, prepare a new solution (step 2) using a smaller volume. If the absorbance is below 0.2, use a larger volume. Also prepare a new blank, but not a new standard.

9 Calculate PO_4-P concentration (which is proportional to absorbance) by

$$c_u = \frac{c_s V_s A_u}{V_u A_s} \tag{2.18}$$

where c_u = concentration of the sample (mg PO_4-P/L), c_s = concentration of the standard (mg PO_4-P/L), A_u = absorbance of the sample, A_s = absorbance of the standard, V_u = volume of the sample pipetted (L), and V_s = volume of the standard pipetted (L).

Method 2.9 Total Ammonia Nitrogen (total NH_4-N) Determination

INDOPHENOL BLUE METHOD[119] Ammonia is measured as the sum of NH_4^+ and NH_3, expressed as total NH_4-N (total ammonia nitrogen). The value obtained is converted to an operational factor from procedures in Method 2.10. Several ammonia tests are available.[120] This subsection describes an indophenol blue method modified for standard additions.

Principle[121] Ammonia reacts in an alkaline citrate solution with hypochlorite to form monochloramine. In the presence of phenol, a blue color is generated by catalytic amounts of potassium ferrocyanide and excess hypochlorite. Absorbance is measured at 640 nm (Fig. 2-39). The effective range is ~0.1(?) to 2.8 mg total NH_4-N/L in undiluted samples. The reaction mechanism is complex and still undescribed. Results are reproducible in waters of any salinity.

Interferences Development of the indophenol blue color is suppressed at low temperature, and cold samples should be placed in a water bath and warmed rapidly to room temperature (~20°C) before analysis (Fig. 2-40). Nitrite causes interference, resulting in falsely low values (Fig. 2-41).[122]

Chemicals (Reagent-grade)

Ammonium sulfate, $(NH_4)_2SO_4$
Chloroform, $CHCl_3$
Ethanol (95% v/v, not denatured)
Phenol

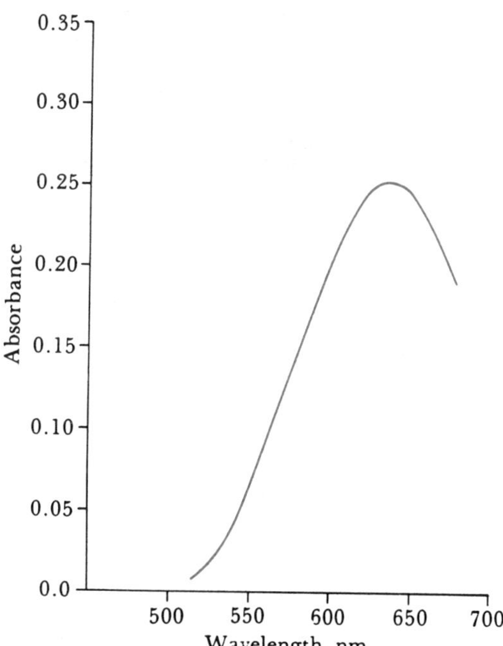

Figure 2-39 Absorption spectrum of indophenol blue at room temperature and 0.2 mg total NH_4-N/L (data points omitted). Source: Zadorojny et al. (1973).

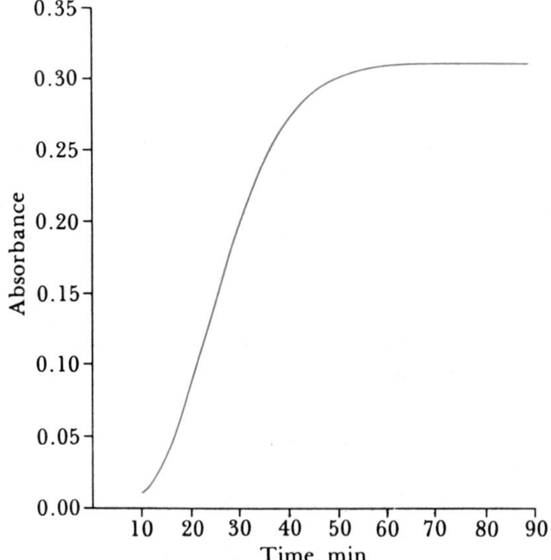

Figure 2-40 Color development of indophenol blue at room temperature as a function of time (data points omitted). Source: Zadorojny et al. (1973).

Potassium ferrocyanide, $K_4Fe(CN)_6 \cdot 6H_2O$
Sodium dichloroisocyanurate, $NaC_3N_3O_3Cl_2$
Sodium hydroxide, NaOH
Trisodium citrate, $Na_3C_6H_5O_7 \cdot 2H_2O$

Glassware Wash thoroughly in Alconox®, rinse in distilled-deionized water (ddH_2O), soak in an acid bath (1 *N* HCl) for at least 2 h, rinse again in ddH_2O, and air-dry before use.

3 250-mL beakers
2 25-mL beakers
1 1-L volumetric flask

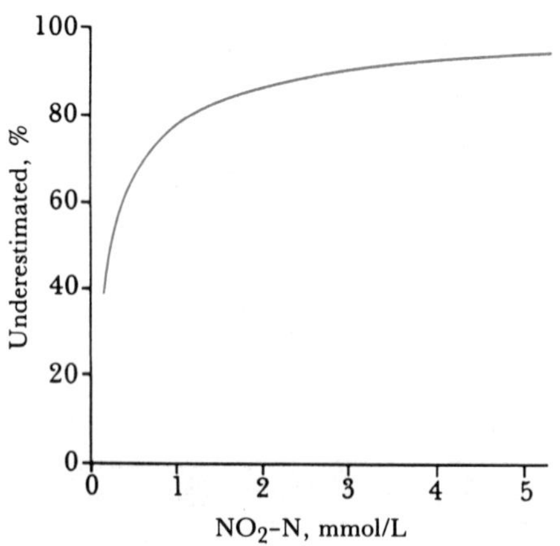

Figure 2-41 Percentage of total NH_4-N underestimated by the indophenol blue method in relation to the concentration of NO_2-N in the sample (data points omitted). Source: Helder and de Vries (1979).

1	100-mL volumetric flask
1	100-mL graduated cylinder
~12	125-mL Erlenmeyer flasks (two per sample)
2	250-mL clear glass bottles
1	250-mL amber glass bottle
1	25-mL beaker
1	1-L polypropylene bottle with screw cap

Equipment and Supplies
(equivalent products can be substituted)

Pipettor calibrated to 50 μL (Finnpipette, Labsystems Oy, Pulttitie 9-11, 00810, Helsinki 81, Finland); disposable tips (Cat. No. 11802, Markson Scientific Inc., Box 767, Del Mar CA 92014)

Pipettor adjustable to 2 and 5 mL (VWR 5 mL—831, Cat. No. 53499-605, VWR, P. O. Box 232, Boston MA 02101); disposable macrotips (Cat. No. 53517-997, VWR)

0.3-μm filters (47-mm Glass Fiber Filter Type A-E, Gelman Sciences, Inc., Ann Arbor MI 48106)

Millipore® filter apparatus (Millipore Corp., 80 Ashby Road, Bedford MA 01730)

Ultraviolet lamp (General Electric 15TB BLB Blacklight) in a high humidity-resistant fixture (Issue No. 459714, Lithonia Lighting, Cochran GA 31014).

Roll of Parafilm® (American Can Company, Greenwich CT 06380)

Cardboard box lined with aluminum foil; must fit over ultraviolet lamp

Magnetic stirrers

Magnetic stir bars

Water bath

Spectrophotometer or colorimeter with 640-nm filter

Reagents

Oxidizing reagent Mix the oxidizing reagent in five steps:

Add 0.2 g sodium dichloroisocyanurate to a dry, 100-mL volumetric flask.

Dissolve 1.6 g sodium hydroxide in 40 mL ddH_2O in a 250-mL beaker. Weigh the material in a 25-mL beaker, not on weighing paper. Dissolve partially in ddH_2O and transfer to the 250-mL beaker.

Dissolve 20 g trisodium citrate in 40 mL ddH_2O in another 250-mL beaker.

Place the beakers on magnetic stirrers. When the solutes in the two beakers have dissolved completely, combine in one of the beakers and transfer to the volumetric flask.

Mix to dissolve the sodium dichloroisocyanurate and dilute to 100 mL with ddH_2O used as rinse water from the two 250-mL beakers. Transfer to a clear glass bottle. Prepare daily.

Catalyst Dissolve 0.5 g potassium ferrocyanide in 100 mL ddH_2O in a 250-mL beaker. Transfer to an amber glass bottle. Prepare daily.

Phenol-alcohol reagent Dissolve 10.0 g phenol in 100 mL ethanol. Weigh the phenol in a 25-mL beaker, not on weighing paper. Transfer to an amber glass bottle and refrigerate at <4°C. Stable for many months.

Ammonium sulfate standard solution Dissolve 471.86 mg ammonium sulfate in a little ddH_2O in a 1-L volumetric flask and dilute to volume. Transfer to a 1-L polypropylene bottle with a screw cap. Add a few drops of chloroform to retard the growth of bacteria and store refrigerated. Concentration: 100 mg total NH_4-N/L. Stable for many months.

Analysis

1 Collect duplicate 50-mL samples in labeled, 125-mL Erlenmeyer flasks. Process within 1 h or refrigerate at 2°C and process as soon as possible.[123]

2 Filter the samples through 0.3-μm glass fiber filters.

3 To one sample of each pair add 50 μL of ammonium sulfate standard solution with the pipettor. Mix well. This is the standard addition.

4 Add to every flask, in order, 2 mL of phenol-alcohol reagent, 5 mL of oxidizing reagent, and 2 mL of catalyst. Use the 5-mL pipettor for all additions and swirl after each.

5 Cover the flasks with Parafilm® and place next to the ultraviolet lamp. Cover with the cardboard box. Allow color to develop for 40 min at room temperature.

6 Read and record the absorbance at 640 nm against a dH_2O blank in a cell with a 1-cm path length.

7 Calculate total NH_4-N concentration of the unspiked samples from

$$c_u = \frac{c_s V_s A_u}{A_{su}(V_u + V_s) - A_u V_u} \tag{2.19}$$

If V_s is small relative to V_u the formula can be simplified to

$$c_u = \frac{c_s V_s A_u}{V_u (A_{su} - A_u)} \tag{2.20}$$

where c_u = concentration of the sample (mg total NH_4-N/L), c_s = concentration of the ammonium sulfate standard (100 mg total NH_4-N/L), A_u = absorbance of the unspiked sample, A_{su} = absorbance of the spiked sample, V_u = volume of the sample (L), and V_s = volume of the ammonium sulfate standard (L).

8 If $A_s < A_u$, make new reagents and repeat. If A_s and A_u are very close, repeat with a larger spiked amount.

SPECIFIC ION ELECTRODE METHOD[124] Specific ion electrodes or ''ammonia probes'' are manufactured by several companies. Spectrophotometric procedures such as the preceding method are faster when large numbers of samples must be processed. Analysis of a single sample by the following procedure takes 5 min. A pH meter with an expanded scale is required. Orion Research Incorporated's* Model 901 Digital Ionalyzer is suitable because it features a scale that reads concentration directly when standard additions methods are used. The range of detection is 0.01 to 1.4×10^4 mg total NH_4-N/L.

Principle All ammonia is converted to NH_3 by raising the pH above 11 with sodium hydroxide. The hydrophobic gas-permeable membrane of the electrode then allows measurement of the partial pressure of ammonia gas (i.e., free ammonia) in the solution, which is related to the dissolved ammonia concentration by Henry's law.

Interferences Sample solutions with osmotic strengths greater than 1 mol/L must be diluted; alternatively, adjust the filling solution of the electrode according to the manufacturer's instructions. Temperature and stirring rates must be constant throughout the analysis.

Chemicals (Reagent-grade)

Ammonium chloride, NH_4OH
Sodium hydroxide, NaOH

Glassware

2 100-mL volumetric flasks
1 125-mL glass beaker

*Orion Research Incorporated, 840 Memorial Drive, Cambridge MA 02139.

1 50-mL glass pipette
1 1-mL glass pipette

Equipment and Supplies

Water bath
pH meter with expanded scale
Magnetic stirrer
Magnetic stir bar
One-hole stopper to fit a 125-mL beaker

Reagents

Sodium hydroxide solution Add 40 g NaOH to 80 mL distilled water, dH_2O, in a 100-mL volumetric flask. Dissolve and dilute to volume. Concentration: 10 mol/L.

Ammonium chloride standard solution Add 0.382 g NH_4Cl to 50 mL dH_2O in a 100-mL volumetric flask. Dissolve and dilute to volume. Concentration: 1000 mg total NH_4-N/L.

Analysis

1 Determine the slope of the electrode according to the manufacturer's instructions.
2 Rinse a 50-mL pipette with sample seawater.
3 Pipette 50 mL of sample into a 125-mL glass beaker and bring to 25°C (±0.05°C) in a water bath.
4 Add 1 mL of sodium hydroxide solution.
5 Place the electrode in the solution and stir slowly using a magnetic stirrer. Be certain to submerge the electrode the same distance in each sample and to stir all samples at the identical stirring rate. After 1 min, or when the potential has stabilized to ±0.1 mV, record the millivolt reading. Some ammonia can be lost to the atmosphere, depending on differences in partial pressure across the air-water interface. The beakers should be sealed with rubber stoppers that have holes drilled in the centers for insertion of the electrode. Stirring should be done with minimum turbulence.
6 Pipette into the beaker 5 mL of dilute ammonium chloride standard solution having ~10 times the anticipated ammonia concentration of the sample.[125]
7 Record the second potential after the electrode has stabilized at the new sample concentration and calculate the potential difference before and after addition of the standard.

8 The concentration of total NH_4-N is given by

$$c_u = \frac{c_s V_s}{(V_s + V_u)10^{\Delta E/S} - V_u} \tag{2.21}$$

where c_u = concentration of the sample (mg total NH_4-N/L), c_s = concentration of added standard (mg total NH_4-N/L), V_s = volume of added standard (L), V_u = volume of the sample (L), ΔE = potential difference, and S = the slope of the electrode.

Electrode Drift[126] Drifting potentials can be caused by inadequate temperature equilibration, improper stirring methods, membrane failure, and an unstable solution concentration. Temperature equilibration is critical and involves a stable sample temperature, in addition to stable temperature gradients in parts of the electrode not immersed in the sample. Membrane failure ordinarily is the cause of electrode drift if temperature is maintained and a millivolt versus time curve does not show an exponential approach to a constant ± 0.1 mV value in a 0.1 mol/L NH_4Cl solution.

Method 2.10 Estimation of the Allowable Upper Limit of Total NH_4-N[127]

Ammonium ion dissociates in water according to

$$NH_4^+ + H_2O \rightleftharpoons NH_3 + H_3O^+ \tag{2.22}$$

The equilibrium is affected by pH, temperature, and ionic strength, with pH exerting the greatest effect and ionic strength the least.[128] The reaction is of interest because NH_3 is believed to be far more toxic than NH_4^+, although this is equivocal to some extent.[129] Water quality criteria based on fixed allowable limits of NH_3-N are of little use unless the mediating chemical and physical factors that affect reaction 2.22 are considered. In addition, only total NH_4-N can be measured conveniently; the relative concentration of NH_3-N is a calculated value based on measurements of other factors that affect ammonium ion dissociation. Under normal circumstances, NH_3-N constitutes $<10\%$ of the total NH_4-N in seawater (Tables 2-13 through 2-16). For example, NH_3-N at pH 8.3, 25°C, and a salinity range of 32 to 40‰ is 8.18% of the total NH_4-N.[130]

If NH_3 is the ammonia species of greatest concern, proper husbandry procedures should require that an *allowable upper*

TABLE 2-13 Percentage NH_3-N of total NH_4-N in seawater (S = 18 to 22‰) at various temperatures and pH values; pK_a^s = the overall acid hydrolysis constants of NH_4^+ in seawater.[1]

		pH										
°C	pK_a^s	7.5	7.6	7.7	7.8	7.9	8.0	8.1	8.2	8.3	8.4	8.5
0	10.10	0.251	0.315	0.397	0.499	0.627	0.788	0.990	1.24	1.56	1.96	2.45
1	10.07	0.270	0.340	0.427	0.537	0.675	0.849	1.07	1.34	1.68	2.11	2.64
2	10.04	0.291	0.366	0.460	0.578	0.727	0.914	1.15	1.44	1.81	2.26	2.83
3	10.00	0.313	0.394	0.495	0.623	0.783	0.984	1.24	1.55	1.94	2.44	3.05
4	9.97	0.337	0.424	0.534	0.671	0.843	1.06	1.33	1.67	2.09	2.62	3.27
5	9.94	0.363	0.457	0.575	0.723	0.908	1.14	1.43	1.80	2.25	2.82	3.52
6	9.91	0.391	0.492	0.619	0.778	0.978	1.23	1.54	1.93	2.42	3.03	3.78
7	9.87	0.422	0.530	0.667	0.838	1.05	1.32	1.66	2.08	2.60	3.25	4.06
8	9.84	0.454	0.571	0.718	0.902	1.13	1.42	1.78	2.24	2.80	3.50	4.36
9	9.81	0.489	0.615	0.773	0.971	1.22	1.53	1.92	2.41	3.01	3.76	4.69
10	9.78	0.527	0.662	0.832	1.05	1.31	1.65	2.07	2.59	3.23	4.04	5.03
11	9.74	0.567	0.713	0.896	1.13	1.41	1.77	2.22	2.78	3.48	4.34	5.40
12	9.71	0.611	0.768	0.965	1.21	1.52	1.91	2.39	2.99	3.74	4.66	5.79
13	9.68	0.658	0.827	1.04	1.31	1.64	2.05	2.57	3.21	4.01	5.00	6.21
14	9.65	0.709	0.891	1.12	1.40	1.76	2.21	2.76	3.45	4.31	5.37	6.66
15	9.61	0.763	0.959	1.20	1.51	1.90	2.37	2.97	3.71	4.63	5.76	7.14
16	9.58	0.822	1.03	1.30	1.63	2.04	2.55	3.19	3.99	4.97	6.18	7.65
17	9.55	0.885	1.11	1.40	1.75	2.19	2.75	3.43	4.28	5.33	6.62	8.20
18	9.52	0.953	1.20	1.50	1.88	2.36	2.95	3.69	4.60	5.72	7.10	8.78
19	9.48	1.03	1.29	1.62	2.03	2.54	3.17	3.96	4.94	6.14	7.61	9.39
20	9.45	1.11	1.39	1.74	2.18	2.73	3.41	4.26	5.30	6.58	8.15	10.0
21	9.42	1.19	1.49	1.87	2.35	2.93	3.67	4.57	5.69	7.06	8.73	10.7
22	9.39	1.28	1.61	2.01	2.52	3.15	3.94	4.91	6.10	7.56	9.34	11.5
23	9.35	1.38	1.73	2.17	2.71	3.39	4.23	5.27	6.54	8.10	9.99	12.3
24	9.32	1.48	1.86	2.33	2.92	3.64	4.54	5.65	7.02	8.67	10.7	13.1
25	9.29	1.60	2.00	2.51	3.14	3.91	4.88	6.07	7.52	9.28	11.4	14.0

Source: Bower and Bidwell (1978).

Note: Whitfield (1974).[1]

limit of total NH_4-N be established. This is the concentration that if exceeded causes NH_3-N to reach levels considered to be dangerously toxic. I shall call this concentration the *arbitrary limit of NH_3-N*; as the term implies, it can be established arbitrarily. The alternative is to choose a concentration on the basis of experimentation. However, no experimental work has been published that assesses the effects of different ammonia concentrations on the species of seawater fishes most often kept in aquariums. Until such data are obtained, I recommend that the arbitrary limit be set at a concentration no greater than 0.01 mg NH_3-N/L.[131]

The NH_3-N concentration is not measurable directly, as mentioned previously, and must be calculated. The allowable upper limit method compares the measured concentration of total

TABLE 2-14 **Percentage NH_3-N of total NH_4-N in seawater (S = 23 to 27‰) at various temperatures and pH values; pK_a^s = the overall acid hydrolysis constants of NH_4^+ in seawater.**[1]

		pH										
°C	pK_a^s	7.5	7.6	7.7	7.8	7.9	8.0	8.1	8.2	8.3	8.4	8.5
0	10.13	0.234	0.294	0.370	0.466	0.585	0.736	0.925	1.16	1.46	1.83	2.29
1	10.10	0.252	0.317	0.399	0.501	0.630	0.792	0.996	1.25	1.57	1.97	2.46
2	10.07	0.271	0.341	0.429	0.540	0.679	0.853	1.07	1.35	1.69	2.12	2.65
3	10.03	0.292	0.368	0.463	0.582	0.731	0.919	1.15	1.45	1.82	2.28	2.85
4	10.00	0.315	0.396	0.498	0.626	0.787	0.989	1.24	1.56	1.95	2.45	3.06
5	9.97	0.339	0.427	0.537	0.675	0.848	1.07	1.34	1.68	2.10	2.63	3.29
6	9.94	0.365	0.460	0.578	0.726	0.913	1.15	1.44	1.81	2.26	2.83	3.54
7	9.90	0.394	0.495	0.622	0.782	0.983	1.23	1.55	1.94	2.43	3.04	3.80
8	9.87	0.424	0.533	0.670	0.842	1.06	1.33	1.67	2.09	2.62	3.27	4.08
9	9.84	0.457	0.574	0.722	0.907	1.14	1.43	1.79	2.25	2.81	3.52	4.39
10	9.81	0.492	0.618	0.777	0.977	1.23	1.54	1.93	2.43	3.03	3.78	4.71
11	9.77	0.530	0.666	0.837	1.05	1.32	1.66	2.08	2.60	3.25	4.06	5.06
12	9.74	0.571	0.717	0.901	1.13	1.42	1.78	2.23	2.80	3.49	4.36	5.43
13	9.71	0.615	0.772	0.970	1.22	1.53	1.92	2.40	3.01	3.76	4.68	5.82
14	9.68	0.662	0.832	1.05	1.31	1.65	2.06	2.58	3.23	4.03	5.03	6.25
15	9.64	0.713	0.896	1.13	1.41	1.77	2.22	2.78	3.47	4.33	5.39	6.70
16	9.61	0.767	0.964	1.21	1.52	1.91	2.39	2.99	3.73	4.65	5.79	7.18
17	9.58	0.826	1.04	1.30	1.64	2.05	2.57	3.21	4.01	5.00	6.21	7.69
18	9.55	0.890	1.12	1.40	1.76	2.21	2.76	3.45	4.31	5.36	6.66	8.24
19	9.51	0.958	1.20	1.51	1.89	2.37	2.97	3.71	4.62	5.75	7.14	8.82
20	9.48	1.03	1.30	1.63	2.04	2.55	3.19	3.98	4.97	6.17	7.65	9.44
21	9.45	1.11	1.39	1.75	2.19	2.74	3.43	4.28	5.33	6.62	8.19	10.1
22	9.42	1.20	1.50	1.88	2.36	2.95	3.69	4.60	5.72	7.09	8.77	10.8
23	9.38	1.29	1.62	2.03	2.54	3.17	3.96	4.93	6.13	7.60	9.38	11.5
24	9.35	1.39	1.74	2.18	2.73	3.41	4.25	5.30	6.58	8.14	10.0	12.3
25	9.32	1.49	1.87	2.34	2.93	3.66	4.57	5.68	7.05	8.72	10.7	13.1

Source: Bower and Bidwell (1978).
Note: Whitfield (1974).[1]

NH_4-N at known pH, temperature, and salinity with the arbitrary limit of NH_3-N. This permits a decision on whether to administer a partial water change and how much of the water to replace if the allowable upper limit of total NH_4-N has been exceeded. Information to complete this computation is given in Figure 2-42 and Tables 2-17 through 2-20.[132]

How to Use Figure 2-42 and Tables 2-17 through 2-20

1 Establish an arbitrary limit of NH_3-N. In this example the arbitrary limit is 0.01 mg NH_3-N/L.

2 Measure temperature, salinity, pH, and concentration of total NH_4-N. Suppose the values obtained are 20°C, 35‰, 8.2,

TABLE 2-15 Percentage NH_3-N of total NH_4-N in seawater (S = 28 to 31‰) at various temperatures and pH values; pK_a^s = the overall acid hydrolysis constants of NH_4^+ in seawater.[1]

		pH										
°C	pK_a^s	7.5	7.6	7.7	7.8	7.9	8.0	8.1	8.2	8.3	8.4	8.5
0	10.14	0.229	0.288	0.362	0.455	0.572	0.719	0.904	1.14	1.43	1.79	2.24
1	10.11	0.246	0.310	0.390	0.490	0.616	0.775	0.973	1.22	1.53	1.92	2.41
2	10.08	0.265	0.334	0.420	0.528	0.664	0.834	1.05	1.32	1.65	2.07	2.59
3	10.04	0.285	0.359	0.452	0.568	0.715	0.898	1.13	1.42	1.78	2.23	2.79
4	10.01	0.308	0.387	0.487	0.612	0.770	0.967	1.21	1.52	1.91	2.39	3.00
5	9.98	0.332	0.417	0.524	0.659	0.829	1.04	1.31	1.64	2.06	2.57	3.22
6	9.95	0.357	0.449	0.565	0.710	0.892	1.12	1.41	1.77	2.21	2.77	3.46
7	9.91	0.385	0.484	0.608	0.765	0.961	1.21	1.51	1.90	2.38	2.98	3.72
8	9.88	0.414	0.521	0.655	0.823	1.03	1.30	1.63	2.04	2.56	3.20	4.00
9	9.85	0.446	0.561	0.706	0.887	1.11	1.40	1.75	2.20	2.75	3.44	4.29
10	9.82	0.481	0.604	0.760	0.955	1.20	1.51	1.89	2.36	2.96	3.70	4.61
11	9.78	0.518	0.651	0.818	1.03	1.29	1.62	2.03	2.54	3.18	3.97	4.95
12	9.75	0.558	0.701	0.881	1.11	1.39	1.74	2.18	2.73	3.42	4.27	5.31
13	9.72	0.601	0.755	0.949	1.19	1.50	1.88	2.35	2.94	3.67	4.58	5.70
14	9.69	0.647	0.813	1.02	1.28	1.61	2.02	2.53	3.16	3.95	4.92	6.11
15	9.65	0.697	0.875	1.10	1.38	1.73	2.17	2.72	3.40	4.24	5.28	6.56
16	9.62	0.750	0.943	1.18	1.49	1.86	2.33	2.92	3.65	4.55	5.66	7.03
17	9.59	0.808	1.02	1.27	1.60	2.01	2.51	3.14	3.92	4.89	6.08	7.53
18	9.56	0.870	1.06	1.37	1.72	2.16	2.70	3.38	4.21	5.25	6.52	8.07
19	9.52	0.937	1.18	1.48	1.85	2.32	2.90	3.63	4.52	5.63	6.99	8.64
20	9.49	1.01	1.27	1.59	1.99	2.50	3.12	3.90	4.86	6.04	7.49	9.24
21	9.46	1.09	1.36	1.71	2.14	2.68	3.35	4.19	5.21	6.48	8.02	9.89
22	9.43	1.17	1.47	1.84	2.31	2.89	3.61	4.50	5.60	6.94	8.59	10.6
23	9.39	1.26	1.58	1.98	2.48	3.10	3.87	4.83	6.00	7.44	9.19	11.3
24	9.36	1.35	1.70	2.13	2.67	3.33	4.16	5.18	6.44	7.97	9.83	12.1
25	9.33	1.46	1.83	2.29	2.87	3.58	4.47	5.56	6.90	8.54	10.5	12.9

Source: Bower and Bidwell (1978).
Note: Whitfield (1974).[1]

and 0.28 mg total NH_4-N/L. From Figure 2-42 estimate whether the allowable upper limit of total NH_4-N has been exceeded (i.e., whether the concentration of total NH_4-N at the measured pH, temperature, and salinity produces a concentration of NH_3-N that exceeds 0.01 mg/L).

3 Look at the ordinate (y axis) of the figure, which depicts temperature. Find 20°C and move horizontally to the right. Locate the curve under pH 8.2 representing S = 35‰. From the point of intersection follow an imaginary line straight down to the abscissa (x axis), which depicts the ratio of total NH_4-N/NH_3-N. The ratio is dimensionless, and units can be milligrams per litre or millimoles per litre. The number on the abscissa is ~22.

TABLE 2-16 Percentage NH_3-N of total NH_4-N in seawater (S = 32 to 40‰) at various temperatures and pH values; pK_a^s = the overall acid hydrolysis constants of NH_4^+ in seawater.[1]

		pH										
°C	pK_a^s	7.5	7.6	7.7	7.8	7.9	8.0	8.1	8.2	8.3	8.4	8.5
0	10.16	0.218	0.275	0.346	0.435	0.547	0.687	0.863	1.09	1.36	1.71	2.14
1	10.13	0.235	0.296	0.372	0.468	0.589	0.740	0.930	1.17	1.47	1.84	2.30
2	10.10	0.253	0.319	0.401	0.504	0.634	0.797	1.00	1.26	1.58	1.98	2.48
3	10.06	0.273	0.343	0.432	0.543	0.683	0.858	1.08	1.35	1.70	2.13	2.66
4	10.03	0.294	0.370	0.465	0.585	0.735	0.924	1.16	1.46	1.83	2.29	2.86
5	10.00	0.317	0.398	0.501	0.630	0.792	0.995	1.25	1.57	1.97	2.46	3.08
6	9.97	0.341	0.429	0.540	0.678	0.852	1.07	1.34	1.69	2.11	2.65	3.31
7	9.93	0.367	0.462	0.581	0.730	0.918	1.15	1.45	1.82	2.27	2.85	3.56
8	9.90	0.396	0.498	0.626	0.787	0.988	1.24	1.56	1.95	2.45	3.06	3.82
9	9.87	0.426	0.536	0.674	0.847	1.06	1.34	1.68	2.10	2.63	3.29	4.11
10	9.84	0.459	0.577	0.726	0.912	1.15	1.44	1.80	2.26	2.83	3.54	4.41
11	9.80	0.495	0.622	0.782	0.982	1.23	1.55	1.94	2.43	3.04	3.80	4.74
12	9.77	0.533	0.670	0.842	1.06	1.33	1.67	2.09	2.61	3.27	4.08	5.08
13	9.74	0.574	0.721	0.906	1.14	1.43	1.79	2.25	2.81	3.51	4.38	5.46
14	9.71	0.618	0.777	0.976	1.23	1.54	1.93	2.42	3.02	3.78	4.71	5.85
15	9.67	0.665	0.836	1.05	1.32	1.66	2.07	2.60	3.25	4.06	5.05	6.28
16	9.64	0.717	0.900	1.13	1.42	1.78	2.23	2.79	3.49	4.36	5.42	6.73
17	9.61	0.772	0.970	1.22	1.53	1.92	2.40	3.00	3.75	4.68	5.82	7.22
18	9.58	0.831	1.04	1.31	1.64	2.06	2.58	3.23	4.03	5.02	6.24	7.73
19	9.54	0.895	1.12	1.41	1.77	2.22	2.78	3.47	4.33	5.39	6.69	8.28
20	9.51	0.963	1.21	1.52	1.90	2.39	2.98	3.73	4.65	5.78	7.17	8.87
21	9.48	1.04	1.30	1.63	2.05	2.57	3.21	4.01	4.99	6.20	7.69	9.49
22	9.45	1.12	1.40	1.76	2.20	2.76	3.45	4.30	5.36	6.65	8.23	10.1
23	9.41	1.20	1.51	1.89	2.37	2.97	3.71	4.62	5.75	7.13	8.81	10.8
24	9.38	1.29	1.62	2.04	2.55	3.19	3.98	4.96	6.17	7.64	9.43	11.6
25	9.35	1.39	1.75	2.19	2.74	3.43	4.28	5.32	6.61	8.18	10.1	12.4

Source: Bower and Bidwell (1978).
Note: Whitfield (1974).[1]

4 To obtain the concentration of total NH_4-N at which NH_3-N equals the arbitrary limit (i.e., the allowable upper limit), multiply the number just obtained (which is 22) by 0.01. The result is 0.22 mg total NH_4-N/L. At concentrations greater than this the arbitrary limit of NH_3-N has been exceeded, and a partial water change is required.

5 In this example the measured concentration of ammonia (0.28 mg total NH_4-N/L) is 27% greater than the maximum allowed (0.22 mg/L). At least 27% of the water must be discarded and replaced with new seawater of the same pH, temperature, and salinity.

6 The concentration of total NH_4-N at which NH_3-N equals 0.01 mg/L can be determined more precisely from the tables

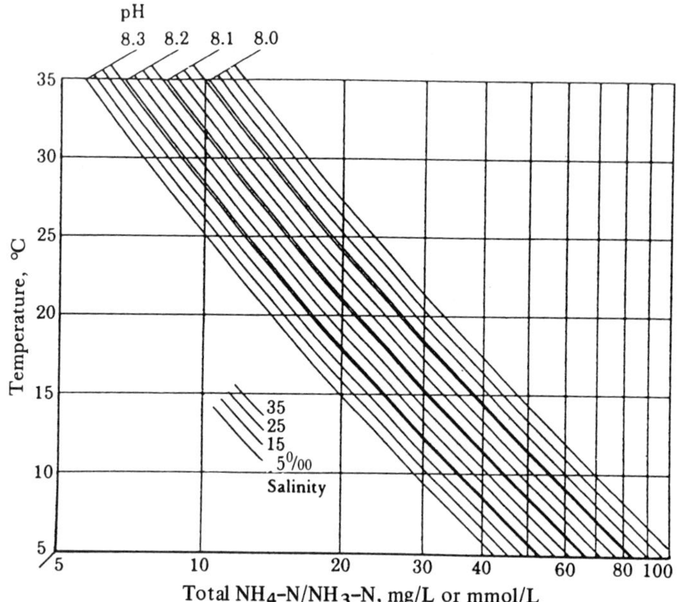

Figure 2-42 *Ratio of total NH_4-N to NH_3-N in saline waters as a function of pH, temperature, and salinity.* Source: Spotte and Adams (1983).

(the figure gives only an estimated concentration). Again, the ratio is dimensionless. Choose the table based on measured pH. Intermediate salinity values can be interpolated.

7 As seen in Table 2-19, the value of total NH_4-N/NH_3-N is 21.5 at 20°C and S = 35‰. The product of 21.5 × 0.01 is 0.215 mg total NH_4-N/L.

Method 2.11 Nitrite Nitrogen (NO_2-N) Determination[133]

Principle Nitrite is diazotized with sulfanilamide and coupled with *N*-(1-naphthyl)ethylenediamine to form an intensely colored azo dye. Absorbance is measured at 540 nm. The applicable range of detection is 5 to 50 μg NO_2-N/L when a cell light path of 5 cm is used and up to 180 μg NO_2-N/L in a cell with a 1-cm light path.

Interferences Not applicable in seawater analysis.

Chemicals (Reagent-grade)

Chloroform, $CHCl_3$

Concentrated hydrochloric acid, HCl

N-(1-naphthyl)ethylenediamine dihydrochloride, NED, $C_{12}H_{14}N_2 \cdot 2HCl$

Nitrite-free water

TABLE 2-17 **Ratio of total NH_4-N to NH_3-N at pH 8.0 and varying temperature and salinity.**

	Salinity, ‰						
°C	5	10	15	20	25	30	35
5	84.5	87.6	90.8	94.1	97.6	101.3	105.1
6	78.0	80.8	83.8	86.8	90.1	93.4	97.0
7	72.1	74.7	77.4	80.2	83.1	86.3	89.5
8	66.6	69.0	71.5	74.1	76.8	79.7	82.7
9	61.6	63.8	66.1	68.5	71.0	73.7	76.4
10	57.0	59.0	61.2	63.4	65.7	68.1	70.7
11	52.8	54.7	56.6	58.7	60.8	63.0	65.4
12	48.9	50.7	52.5	54.3	56.3	58.4	60.6
13	45.4	47.0	48.6	50.4	52.2	54.1	56.1
14	42.1	43.6	45.1	46.7	48.4	50.2	52.0
15	39.1	40.5	41.9	43.4	44.9	46.6	48.3
16	36.3	37.6	38.9	40.3	41.7	43.2	44.8
17	33.8	34.9	36.2	37.4	38.8	40.2	41.6
18	31.4	32.5	33.6	34.8	36.0	37.3	38.7
19	29.2	30.2	31.3	32.4	33.5	34.7	36.0
20	27.2	28.2	29.1	30.2	31.2	32.3	33.5
21	25.4	26.3	27.2	28.1	29.1	30.1	31.2
22	23.7	24.5	25.3	26.2	27.1	28.1	29.1
23	22.1	22.9	23.6	24.4	25.3	26.2	27.1
24	20.7	21.3	22.1	22.8	23.6	24.4	25.3
25	19.3	19.9	20.6	21.3	22.0	22.8	23.6
26	18.1	18.7	19.3	19.9	20.6	21.3	22.1
27	16.9	17.5	18.0	18.6	19.3	19.9	20.6
28	15.8	16.4	16.9	17.5	18.0	18.7	19.3
29	14.8	15.3	15.8	16.3	16.9	17.5	18.1
30	13.9	14.4	14.8	15.3	15.8	16.4	16.9
31	13.1	13.5	13.9	14.4	14.9	15.4	15.9
32	12.3	12.7	13.1	13.5	13.9	14.4	14.9
33	11.5	11.9	12.3	12.7	13.1	13.5	14.0
34	10.9	11.2	11.6	11.9	12.3	12.7	13.1
35	10.2	10.5	10.9	11.2	11.6	12.0	12.3

Source: Spotte and Adams (1983).

Sodium nitrite, $NaNO_2$
Sulfanilamide, $C_6H_8N_2O_2S$

Glassware Wash thoroughly in Alconox®, rinse in distilled-deionized water (ddH_2O), soak in an acid bath (1 *N* HCl) for at least 2 h, rinse again in ddH_2O, and air-dry before use.

~12	125-mL Erlenmeyer flasks
2	1-L volumetric flasks

1	500-mL volumetric flask
~12	50-mL volumetric flasks
2	100-mL graduated cylinders
1	5-mL pipette
3	2-mL pipettes
1	1-mL pipette
1	Rinse bottle filled with ddH_2O
1	1-L clear glass bottle
1	1-L amber glass bottle
2	500-mL amber glass bottles

TABLE 2-18 Ratio of total NH_4-N to NH_3-N at pH 8.1 and varying temperature and salinity.

	Salinity, ‰						
°C	5	10	15	20	25	30	35
5	67.4	69.8	72.3	75.0	77.7	80.7	83.7
6	62.2	64.4	66.7	69.2	71.7	74.4	77.2
7	57.5	59.5	61.7	63.9	66.3	68.7	71.3
8	53.1	55.0	57.0	59.1	61.2	63.5	65.9
9	49.1	50.9	52.7	54.6	56.6	58.7	60.9
10	45.5	47.1	48.8	50.5	52.4	54.3	56.3
11	42.2	43.6	45.2	46.8	48.5	50.3	52.2
12	39.1	40.4	41.9	43.4	44.9	46.6	48.3
13	36.2	37.5	38.8	40.2	41.7	43.2	44.8
14	33.7	34.8	36.0	37.3	38.7	40.1	41.5
15	31.3	32.3	33.5	34.7	35.9	37.2	38.5
16	29.1	30.1	31.1	32.2	33.3	34.5	35.8
17	27.0	28.0	28.9	29.9	31.0	32.1	33.3
18	25.2	26.0	26.9	27.9	28.8	29.9	30.9
19	23.4	24.2	25.1	25.9	26.8	27.8	28.8
20	21.8	22.6	23.4	24.2	25.0	25.9	26.8
21	20.4	21.1	21.8	22.5	23.3	24.1	25.0
22	19.0	19.7	20.3	21.0	21.7	22.5	23.3
23	17.8	18.4	19.0	19.6	20.3	21.0	21.7
24	16.6	17.2	17.7	18.3	19.0	19.6	20.3
25	15.5	16.1	16.6	17.1	17.7	18.3	19.0
26	14.6	15.0	15.5	16.0	16.6	17.1	17.7
27	13.6	14.1	14.5	15.0	15.5	16.0	16.6
28	12.8	13.2	13.6	14.1	14.5	15.0	15.5
29	12.0	12.4	12.8	13.2	13.6	14.1	14.6
30	11.3	11.6	12.0	12.4	12.8	13.2	13.7
31	10.6	10.9	11.3	11.6	12.0	12.4	12.8
32	10.0	10.3	10.6	10.9	11.3	11.6	12.0
33	9.4	9.7	10.0	10.3	10.6	11.0	11.3
34	8.8	9.1	9.4	9.7	10.0	10.3	10.6
35	8.3	8.6	8.8	9.1	9.4	9.7	10.0

Source: Spotte and Adams (1983).

TABLE 2-19 Ratio of total NH_4-N to NH_3-N at pH 8.2 and varying temperature and salinity.

	Salinity, ‰						
°C	5	10	15	20	25	30	35
5	53.7	55.6	57.6	59.7	62.0	64.3	66.9
6	49.6	51.4	53.2	55.2	57.2	59.3	61.6
7	45.8	47.5	49.2	51.0	52.8	54.8	56.8
8	42.4	43.9	45.5	47.1	48.8	50.6	52.5
9	39.2	40.6	42.1	43.6	45.2	46.8	48.6
10	36.3	37.6	39.0	40.4	41.8	43.4	45.0
11	33.7	34.9	36.1	37.4	38.7	40.1	41.6
12	31.2	32.3	33.5	34.7	35.9	37.2	38.6
13	29.0	30.0	31.1	32.2	33.3	34.5	35.8
14	26.9	27.9	28.8	29.8	30.9	32.0	33.2
15	25.0	25.9	26.8	27.7	28.7	29.7	30.8
16	23.3	24.1	24.9	25.8	26.7	27.6	28.6
17	21.7	22.4	23.2	24.0	24.8	25.7	26.6
18	20.2	20.9	21.6	22.3	23.1	23.9	24.8
19	18.8	19.5	20.1	20.8	21.5	22.3	23.1
20	17.6	18.1	18.8	19.4	20.1	20.8	21.5
21	16.4	16.9	17.5	18.1	18.7	19.4	20.0
22	15.3	15.8	16.3	16.9	17.5	18.1	18.7
23	14.3	14.8	15.3	15.8	16.3	16.9	17.5
24	13.4	13.8	14.3	14.8	15.3	15.8	16.3
25	12.6	13.0	13.4	13.8	14.3	14.8	15.3
26	11.8	12.1	12.5	12.9	13.4	13.8	14.3
27	11.0	11.4	11.7	12.1	12.5	12.9	13.4
28	10.4	10.7	11.0	11.4	11.8	12.1	12.5
29	9.7	10.0	10.4	10.7	11.0	11.4	11.8
30	9.2	9.4	9.7	10.0	10.4	10.7	11.1
31	8.6	8.9	9.2	9.4	9.7	10.1	10.4
32	8.1	8.4	8.6	8.9	9.2	9.5	9.8
33	7.7	7.9	8.1	8.4	8.6	8.9	9.2
34	7.2	7.4	7.7	7.9	8.1	8.4	8.7
35	6.8	7.0	7.2	7.4	7.7	7.9	8.2

Source: Spotte and Adams (1983).

Equipment and Supplies (equivalent products can be substituted)

0.3-μm filters (47-mm Glass Fiber Filter Type A-E, Gelman Sciences, Inc., Ann Arbor MI 48106)

Millipore® filter apparatus (Millipore Corp., 80 Ashby Road, Bedford MA 01730)

Spectrophotometer or colorimeter with 540-nm filter

TABLE 2-20 Ratio of total NH_4-N to NH_3-N at pH 8.3 and varying temperature and salinity.

	Salinity, ‰						
°C	5	10	15	20	25	30	35
5	42.9	44.4	46.0	47.7	49.4	51.3	53.2
6	39.6	41.0	42.5	44.0	45.6	47.3	49.1
7	36.6	37.9	39.3	40.7	42.2	43.7	45.4
8	33.9	35.1	36.3	37.6	39.0	40.4	41.9
9	31.4	32.5	33.6	34.8	36.1	37.4	38.8
10	29.1	30.1	31.1	32.3	33.4	34.6	35.9
11	27.0	27.9	28.9	29.9	31.0	32.1	33.3
12	25.0	25.9	26.8	27.7	28.7	29.8	30.9
13	23.2	24.0	24.9	25.7	26.7	27.6	28.6
14	21.6	22.3	23.1	23.9	24.8	25.6	26.6
15	20.1	20.8	21.5	22.2	23.0	23.8	24.7
16	18.7	19.3	20.0	20.7	21.4	22.2	23.0
17	17.4	18.0	18.6	19.3	19.9	20.6	21.4
18	16.2	16.8	17.3	17.9	18.6	19.2	19.9
19	15.2	15.7	16.2	16.7	17.3	17.9	18.5
20	14.2	14.6	15.1	15.6	16.1	16.7	17.3
21	13.2	13.7	14.1	14.6	15.1	15.6	16.1
22	12.4	12.8	13.2	13.6	14.1	14.6	15.1
23	11.6	12.0	12.3	12.7	13.2	13.6	14.1
24	10.9	11.2	11.6	11.9	12.3	12.7	13.2
25	10.2	10.5	10.8	11.2	11.5	11.9	12.3
26	9.6	9.8	10.2	10.5	10.8	11.2	11.6
27	9.0	9.2	9.5	9.8	10.2	10.5	10.8
28	8.4	8.7	9.0	9.2	9.5	9.8	10.2
29	7.9	8.2	8.4	8.7	9.0	9.3	9.6
30	7.5	7.7	7.9	8.2	8.4	8.7	9.0
31	7.1	7.3	7.5	7.7	7.9	8.2	8.5
32	6.7	6.8	7.1	7.3	7.5	7.7	8.0
33	6.3	6.5	6.7	6.9	7.1	7.3	7.5
34	5.9	6.1	6.3	6.5	6.7	6.9	7.1
35	5.6	5.8	5.9	6.1	6.3	6.5	6.7

Source: Spotte and Adams (1983).

Reagents

Sulfanilamide reagent Dissolve 5.0 g sulfanilamide in a solution of 50 mL concentrated HCl and 300 mL ddH_2O in a 500-mL volumetric flask[118] and dilute to volume. Store in an amber glass bottle. Stable for many months.

N-(1-naphthyl)ethylenediamine dihydrochloride (NED) reagent Dissolve 500 mg NED in ddH_2O in a 500-mL volumetric flask and dilute to volume. Store refrigerated in an amber glass bottle. Replace monthly or when a brown color develops.

Nitrite stock solution Dry anhydrous $NaNO_2$ at 110°C for 1 h and store in a desiccator. Dissolve 0.493 g in ddH_2O in a 1-L volumetric flask and dilute to volume. Concentration: 100 mg NO_2-N/L. Add a few drops of chloroform to retard the growth of bacteria and store refrigerated in an amber glass bottle. Stable for no longer than 2 months.

Working standard nitrite solution Dilute 10.0 mL of nitrite stock solution to 1 L with nitrite-free ddH_2O in a volumetric flask. Transfer to a clear glass bottle. Concentration: 1 mg NO_2-N/L. Prepare daily.

Nitrite-free water Properly prepared ddH_2O should be nitrite free. If not, to 1 L ddH_2O add a small crystal each of potassium permanganate, $KMnO_4$, and either barium hydroxide, $Ba(OH)_2$, or calcium hydroxide, $Ca(OH)_2$. Redistill in an all-borosilicate glass still and discard the first 50 mL of distillate. Collect the permanganate-free fraction (a red color with DPD reagent indicates the presence of permanganate).[134]

Analysis

1 Collect samples (at least 50 mL) in labeled, 125-mL Erlenmeyer flasks. Process within 1 h or refrigerate at 2°C and process as soon as possible.[123]

2 Filter the samples through 0.3-μm glass fiber filters.

3 Transfer 40 mL of each sample (four samples in this example) to labeled, 50-mL volumetric flasks.

4 *Standard* Prepare a standard by adding 1, 2, or 5 mL of working standard nitrite solution to a fifth 50-mL volumetric flask containing 40 mL ddH_2O. Final concentrations: 0.020 mg NO_2-N/L (1 mL), 0.040 mg NO_2-N/L (2 mL), and 0.100 mg NO_2-N/L (5 mL). Select the concentration closest to the expected NO_2-N concentration of the samples. If in doubt, prepare all three.

5 *Reagent blank* Prepare a reagent blank by adding 40 mL ddH_2O to a sixth 50-mL volumetric flask.

6 Add 1.0 mL of sulfanilamide reagent to all flasks. Mix and let stand for 2 min but not longer than 8 min.

7 Add 1.0 mL of NED reagent to all flasks and mix.

8 Dilute all flasks to volume with ddH_2O and mix.

9 After 10 min but within 2 h read the absorbance at 540 nm against the reagent blank in a cell with a 1-cm path length.

10 Record absorbance values and calculate the concentration (which is proportional to absorbance) by

$$c_u = c_s \left(\frac{A_u}{A_s}\right) \times 1.25 \tag{2.23}$$

where c_u = concentration of the sample (mg NO_2-N/L), c_s = concentration of the standard (mg NO_2-N/L), and A_u and A_s are the respective absorbances of the sample and standard. Multiplying by 1.25 corrects for the sample volume of 40 mL.

Method 2.12 Nitrate Nitrogen (NO_3-N) Determination—Low Concentrations[135]

Principle Nitrate is reduced nearly quantitatively to nitrite in the presence of cadmium, Cd. Because this method measures the sum of NO_3-N and NO_2-N, samples must also be analyzed for NO_2-N (see Method 2.11); the difference between the results of the two analyses is NO_3-N. The sensitivity is <0.1 mg NO_3-N/L, and the applicable range is 0.01 to 1.0 mg NO_3-N/L without dilution of the sample.

Interferences Not applicable in seawater analysis, with the exception of POC interference, which can be eliminated by prefiltering turbid water samples through glass fiber or membrane filters.

Chemicals (Reagent-grade)

Ammonium chloride, NH_4Cl
Ammonium hydroxide, NH_4OH
Cadmium granules, ~250 g, 40 to 60 mesh (Cat. No. 16110-3, VWR, P.O. Box 232, Boston MA 02101)
Chloroform, $CHCl_3$
Concentrated hydrochloric acid, HCl
Cupric sulfate pentahydrate, $CuSO_4 \cdot 5H_2O$
N-(1-naphthyl)ethylenediamine dihydrochloride, NED, $C_{12}H_{14}N_2 \cdot 2HCl$
Nitrate-free water
pH buffer standards of 4, 7, and 10
Potassium nitrate, KNO_3
Sulfanilamide, $C_6H_8N_2O_2S$

Glassware Wash thoroughly in Alconox®, rinse in distilled-deionized water (ddH_2O), soak in an acid bath (1 *N* HCl) for at least 2 h, rinse again in ddH_2O, and air-dry before use.

1	250-mL Erlenmeyer flask
~12	125-mL Erlenmeyer flasks
8	100-mL graduated cylinders
1	2-mL pipette
2	1-L volumetric flasks
1	500-mL volumetric flask
1	1-L polypropylene beaker
1	3-L polypropylene bottle
2	1-L amber glass bottles
1	1-L clear glass bottle
2	500-mL amber glass bottles
1	100-mL clear glass bottle

Equipment and Supplies
(equivalent products can be substituted)

Pasteur pipettes with amber pipette bulbs

Glass reductor (Cadmium Reduction Column, Cat. No. S-72228, Sargent-Welch Scientific Co., 7300 N. Linder Avenue, Skokie IL 60077) with Tygon® tubing and pinch clamps

Ring stand to hold the reductor

Jars for waste effluent from the reductor

Fine glass wool

Drierite®

0.3-μm filters (47-mm Glass Fiber Filter Type A-E, Gelman Sciences, Inc., Ann Arbor MI 48106)

Millipore® filter apparatus (Millipore Corp., 80 Ashby Road, Bedford MA 01730)

Magnetic stirrer

Magnetic stir bars

Spectrophotometer or colorimeter with 540-nm filter

Reagents

Ammonium chloride buffer Dissolve 10.0 g NH_4Cl in 900 mL ddH_2O in a 1-L polypropylene beaker and stir at a high rate on a magnetic stirrer. Add concentrated NH_4OH in drops from a Pasteur pipette to pH 8.5. This requires ~1.5 mL. Dilute to 1 L in a volumetric flask. Repeat the above steps twice for a total of 3 L of buffer. Store in a polypropylene bottle. Stable for many months.

Sulfanilamide reagent Dissolve 5.0 g sulfanilamide in a solution of 50 mL concentrated HCl and 300 mL ddH_2O in a 500-mL volumetric flask and dilute to volume. Store in an amber glass bottle. Stable for many months.

N-(1-naphthyl)ethylenediamine dihydrochloride (NED) reagent Dissolve 500 mg NED in ddH_2O in a 500-mL volumetric flask and dilute to volume. Store refrigerated in an amber glass bottle. Replace monthly or when a brown color develops.

Cupric sulfate solution Dissolve 10.0 g cupric sulfate pentahydrate in 500 mL ddH_2O in a 1-L volumetric flask and dilute to volume. The concentration is not critical. Store in a clear glass bottle. Stable for many months.

Nitrate stock solution Dry potassium nitrate in a drying oven overnight at 105°C and store excess material in a desiccator with Drierite®. Dissolve 0.7218 g in a little ddH_2O in a 1-L volumetric flask and dilute to volume. Concentration: 100 mg NO_3-N/L. Add a few drops of chloroform to retard the growth of bacteria and store refrigerated in an amber glass bottle. Stable for ~6 months.

Working standard nitrate solution Add 5.0 mL of nitrate stock solution to a 500-mL volumetric flask and dilute to volume with ddH_2O. Concentration: 1.0 mg NO_3-N/L. Prepare daily.

Nitrate-free water Distilled-deionized water.

Hydrochloric acid (2 N) Add 20 mL concentrated HCl to ddH_2O in a 100-mL volumetric flask and dilute to volume. Store in a clear glass bottle. Stable for many months.

Analysis 1—Preparation of a Cadmium Column

1 Assemble the reductor on a ring stand. By definitions used here, the *reductor* is the entire apparatus (glass cylinder, ring stand, Tygon® tubing, and pinch clamp). The *column* is the portion filled with cadmium granules.

2 Place a plug of glass wool in the bottom tip of the column and tamp it in place with a glass rod.

3 Empty ~25 g of cadmium granules into a 250-mL Erlenmeyer flask. Pour several millilitres of 2 *N* HCl over the granules to remove oxides. Swirl several times.

4 After ~3 min decant the HCl and replace it with ~100 mL of cupric sulfate solution. Shake the flask vigorously for 3 min. The blue color will fade, indicating adsorption of copper onto the cadmium granules. If necessary, decant and re-

peat this step with fresh cupric sulfate solution until a brown colloidal precipitate appears.

5 Wash the copper-treated cadmium granules with ~12 changes of ddH_2O, or until all turbidity (colloidal copper) disappears. The first rinses may be clear already, indicating a surfeit of copper, but later ones ordinarily are turbid. The rinsing process should therefore continue long enough to induce the appearance and subsequent disappearance of turbidity.

6 Empty the granules into the reductor. Use a spatula and rinse bottle filled with ddH_2O. Fill only the column portion. Tap the side of the column with a pencil or plastic rod to ensure a full pack.

7 Activate the reductor by passing through it ~100 mL of a solution consisting of 75 mL of ammonium chloride buffer plus 25 mL of working standard nitrate solution. Aspirate the unit by attaching a 60-cm syringe to the ends of the Tygon® tubing and drawing out the combined solution. Be sure the cadmium granules stay submerged. Aspiration removes all air from the column and ensures even percolation of the fluid. *Do not aspirate the granules to dryness.* Discard the liquid collected in the syringe. This step should be repeated if the reductor is not used for several days. Keep the reductor filled with ammonium chloride buffer when it is not in use.

8 Place a Petri dish cover over the reductor between analyses and when it is not in use.

9 Process the samples (see Analysis 2).

Analysis 2—Processing of Samples

1 Collect samples (at least 50 mL) in labeled, 125-mL Erlenmeyer flasks. Process within 1 h or refrigerate at 2°C and process as soon as possible.[123]

2 Filter the samples through 0.3-μm glass fiber filters.

3 Remove the Petri dish cover from the reductor and set it aside. Drain the ammonium chloride buffer used to wet the column between analyses into a waste jar. Leave only enough solution to barely cover the column.

4 Label a 125-mL Erlenmeyer flask and a 100-mL graduated cylinder. A pair (one flask, one graduated cylinder) is required for each reductor if more than one has been set up.

5 Add to a labeled flask 30 mL of a filtered seawater sample (or a portion diluted to 30 mL with ddH_2O) and 30 mL of ammonium chloride buffer and swirl.

6 In the labeled flask, mix 30 mL of working standard nitrate solution with 30 mL of ammonium chloride buffer and swirl. A series of dilutions is not prepared, nor is a standard calibration curve plotted.

7 Process at least one reagent blank with each batch of reagents or ddH_2O. The blank consists of 30 mL of ammonium chloride buffer and 30 mL ddH_2O.

8 Pour 30 mL of the sample, the standard, or the blank into the reductor, open the pinch clamp, and allow the solution to drain into the waste jar. The flow rate should be 7 to 10 mL/min. Close the pinch clamps when enough solution is left barely to cover the cadmium granules.

9 Add the remaining solution to the reductor, open the pinch clamp, and collect 25 mL in a labeled graduated cylinder.

10 After the last sample has been processed, pass a volume of ammonium chloride buffer equal to that of the column through the reductor. Leave enough solution to submerge the column (i.e., the granules) completely. Close the pinch clamp and place the Petri dish cover over the reductor. Try not to expose the granules to air, but if this should happen flood the reductor with ammonium chloride buffer immediately and draw out the air with the syringe before continuing.

11 Within 15 min after reduction add 1.0 mL of sulfanilamide reagent. Swirl and let stand for 2 min but not longer than 8 min.

12 Add 1.0 mL of NED reagent and swirl.

13 After 10 min but within 2 h read the absorbance at 540 nm against the reagent blank in a cell with a 1-cm path length.

14 Read and record the absorbance values and calculate the concentration (which is proportional to absorbance) by[136]

$$c_u = c_s \left(\frac{A_u}{A_s}\right) - 0.95c_n \qquad (2.24)$$

where c_u = concentration of the sample (mg NO_3-N/L), c_s = concentration of the standard (mg NO_3-N/L), c_n = concentration of NO_2-N as determined using Method 2.11, and A_u and A_s are the respective absorbances of the sample and standard. A correction factor of 0.95 accounts for the capacity of an effective cadmium column to reduce 95% of the nitrate in a sample.

Method 2.13 Nitrate Nitrogen (NO_3-N) Determination—High Concentrations[137]

Principle High concentrations of NO_3-N (>1.0 mg/L) can be measured by a hydrazine reduction method. Nitrate is reduced to nitrite with hydrazine catalyzed by copper in a solution buffered to pH 9.6. Nitrite nitrogen is then determined by diazotizing with sulfanilamide and coupling with *N*-(1-naphthyl)ethylenediamine to form an intensely colored azo dye. Absorbance is measured at 540 nm. The effective range is 4 to 60 mg NO_3-N/L. Samples must also be analyzed for NO_2-N (see Method 2.11). The difference between results of the two analyses is NO_3-N.

Interferences Same as Method 2.12.

Chemicals (Reagent-grade)

Acetone
Chloroform, $CHCl_3$
Cupric sulfate pentahydrate, $CuSO_4 \cdot 5H_2O$
Hydrazine sulfate, $(NH_2)_2 \cdot H_2SO_4$
N-(1-naphthyl)ethylenediamine dihydrochloride, NED, $C_{12}H_{14}N_2 \cdot 2HCl$
Phenol
Potassium nitrate, KNO_3
Sodium hydroxide, NaOH
Sulfanilamide, $C_6H_8N_2O_2S$

Glassware

~12	125-mL Erlenmeyer flasks
1	2-L volumetric flask
2	1-L volumetric flasks
4	500-mL volumetric flasks
1	200-mL volumetric flask
~12	50-mL volumetric flasks
2	50-mL graduated cylinders
1	2-L polyethylene bottle
1	1-L clear glass bottle
3	500-mL amber glass bottles
1	1-L amber glass bottle
1	250-mL glass-stoppered bottle
3	2-mL glass pipettes (pipettor is preferable)
4	1-mL glass pipettes (pipettor is preferable)
2	0.5-mL glass pipettes (pipettor is preferable)

Equipment and Supplies
(equivalent products can be substituted)

0.3-μm filters (47-mm Glass Fiber Filter Type A-E, Gelman Sciences, Inc., Ann Arbor MI 48106)

Millipore® filter apparatus (Millipore Corp., 80 Ashby Road, Bedford MA 01730)

Stoppers for 50-mL volumetric flasks

Water bath

Spectrophotometer or colorimeter with 540-nm filter

Reagents (Reagent-grade)

Cupric sulfate solution Dissolve 100 mg cupric sulfate pentahydrate in 500 mL ddH_2O in a 1-L volumetric flask and dilute to volume. Store in a clear glass bottle. Stable for many months.

Hydrazine sulfate reagent Dissolve 3.625 g hydrazine sulfate in ddH_2O in a 500-mL volumetric flask and dilute to volume. Store in an amber glass bottle. Stable for ~2 months.

Phenol solution Dissolve 9.2 g phenol in ddH_2O in a 200-mL volumetric flask and dilute to volume. Store in a glass-stoppered bottle in a dark, cool location. Stable for ~2 months.

Sodium hydroxide solution Dissolve 29.0 g NaOH in ddH_2O in a 2-L volumetric flask. Cool and dilute to volume. Store in a tightly sealed polyethylene bottle. Stable for ~6 months.

N-(1-naphthyl)ethylenediamine dihydrochloride (NED) reagent Same as Method 2.12.

Sulfanilamide reagent Same as Method 2.12.

Buffer reagent Mix 20 mL of sodium hydroxide solution with 20 mL of phenol solution and use within 1 h.

Reducer reagent Mix 20 mL of cupric sulfate solution with 20 mL of hydrazine sulfate reagent and use within 1 h.

Nitrate stock solution Same as Method 2.12.

Working standard nitrate solution Same as Method 2.12.

Analysis

1 Collect samples as in Methods 2.11 and 2.12. Filter turbid samples through 0.3-μm glass fiber filters. Collect large enough sample volumes to also analyze for NO_2-N.

2 Add 0.5 mL of sample (a larger volume for samples with lower NO_3-N concentrations) to a 50-mL volumetric flask.

Add 40 mL ddH_2O, 2 mL of buffer reagent, and 1 mL of reducer reagent.

3 Prepare standards by pipetting into 50-mL volumetric flasks 0.5, 1, and 2 mL of working standard nitrate solution. Use ddH_2O to prepare a reagent blank.

4 Add 40 mL ddH_2O, 2 mL of buffer reagent, and 1 mL of reducer reagent to the standards and blank.

5 Place all flasks in a water bath at 23°C for 20 h. Stopper the flasks loosely and shield from light.

6 After 20 h, add 2 mL acetone and mix. Wait 2 min.

7 Add 1 mL of sulfanilamide reagent. Mix and let stand for 2 min but not longer than 8 min.

8 Add 1 mL of NED reagent and mix.

9 Dilute all flasks to volume with ddH_2O and mix.

10 After 10 min but before 2 h read and record absorbances against the reagent blank at 540 nm in a cell with a 1-cm path length.

11 Plot milligrams of NO_3-N versus absorbance for the standards and read milligrams of NO_3-N from the curve. Divide this value by the sample volume in litres (divide by 0.0005 for a 0.5 mL sample) to obtain milligrams of NO_3-N + NO_2-N per litre.

12 Subtract the NO_2-N concentrations from the concentrations obtained in step 11 to get mg NO_3-N/L.

CHAPTER

3 Physical Processes

Captive fishes are affected by more than the chemistry and biology of the external environment. Processes of a physical nature also impinge on their lives. In modern public aquariums the important physical processes are particle separation, gas transfer, and heat exchange. Their technological analogs are filtration, aeration, and temperature control.

Seawater pumped straight from the ocean is turbid. The suspended particles that cause turbidity are seldom harmful, but impart a vaguely unhealthy appearance to the water, rendering it unfit for exhibition purposes. New seawater may also be the wrong temperature and contain dissolved gases at under- or supersaturated states. Similar problems can occur in facilities using recirculated artificial seawaters.

Few would disagree that aquarium water should be clear, be the correct temperature, and contain a balanced complement of dissolved gases. The dilemma arises when these basic truths must be reconciled with design engineering. Not uncommonly, the rich panoply of science is pushed aside in favor of equipment selection. In the end, the aquarium is poorer for it.

The majority of my biologist friends find the physical processes tedious. By inference, the proof lies in what these people are: had their interest in such subjects flowered, they would have been engineers. The point is well taken, and I kept it in mind while writing this chapter. Information presented is concise and no more rigorous than necessary. The Science section covers theoretical aspects of processes mentioned at the start, in addition to flow rates in airlift pumps and the removal of dissolved and particulate organic carbon by foam fractionation. The Technology section explains the applied or engineering aspects.

I think the physical processes are interesting. The principles of particle separation possess a stoic beauty. Upon seeing a high rate filter I envision an endless, patterned array of invisible streamlines. Gas transfer, although a thermodynamic maze, is still precise and orderly with few of the confounding variables that haunt the biological disciplines. And how could any biologist find heat exchange boring after hearing of the marvelous countercurrent heat exchangers possessed by tunas?

SCIENCE

Particle Separation

Particle separation during *granular media filtration* lowers turbidity[1] by capturing and retaining particulate organic carbon (POC) in a deep, porous bed of *granular media filtrant*: sand, anthracite, garnet or ilmenite, or some combination of these.

GRANULAR MEDIA FILTERS The mechanisms by which particles are separated from water and retained in a filter are complex and incompletely documented. The filtration process is generally considered to involve transport and attachment. Particles carried to the filtrant by the *transport fluid* (seawater in this case) are trapped by any of several physical and chemical mechanisms. The transport and attachment steps involve capture mechanisms and process variables (see below).

Classification of modern granular media filters is based on two criteria: (*1*) whether the filter unit is a pressure or vacuum type, and (2) size and specific gravity of the filtrants. The pressure inside *pressure filters* exceeds atmospheric conditions. The pump is located between the source of unfiltered water and the filter unit, and water is forced through the filtrant under pressure. This requires a closed vessel, and steel tanks typically are used (Fig. 3-1), although large vessels made of fiberglass-reinforced plastic are also available. *Vacuum filters* (less accurately called *gravity filters*) are operated at less than atmospheric pressure (Fig. 3-2). The pump is located on the effluent side of the filter unit. Water is drawn through the filtrant, creating a partial vacuum. Vacuum filters ordinarily are limited to a pressure differential of 1 atm.

Classification of granular media filters based on the type of filtrant used is shown in Table 3-1. The gravel underneath the filtrant is the *support medium*. *Rapid sand filters* are those in which fine or coarse sand is the only filtrant (Fig. 3-3a). The filtration rate is $\sim 1.4 \times 10^{-3}$ m/s. *Fine sand filters* use sand with a grain

Figure 3-1 Pressure granular media filters. Source: Crane Cochrane Environmental Systems, 800 Third Avenue, King of Prussia PA 19406.

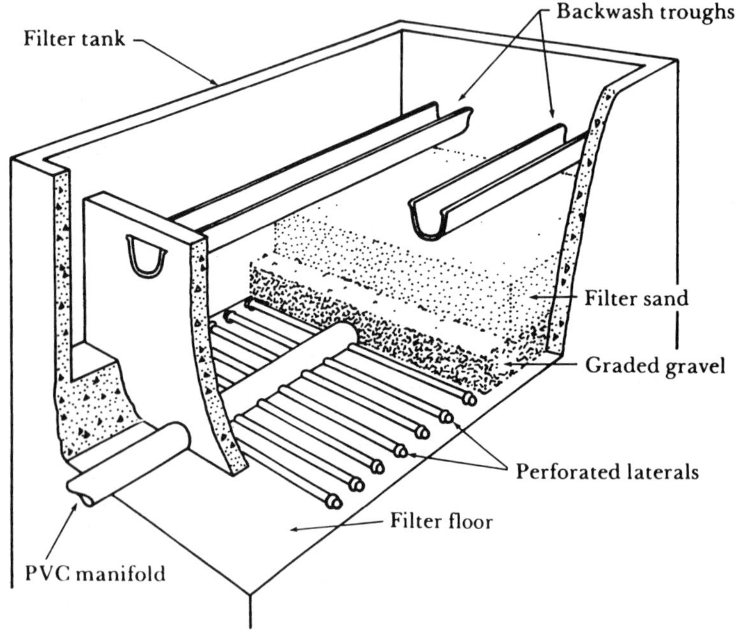

Figure 3-2 Vacuum granular media filter. Source: Rich (1973).

TABLE 3-1 Types of granular media filters based on filtrant grain size or composition of the media.

Rapid sand filters	
Fine sand	<0.5 mm grain size
Coarse sand	>0.5 mm grain size
High rate filters	
Dual media	Anthracite, sand
Multimedia	Anthracite, sand, garnet, or ilmenite

Source: Stephen Spotte.

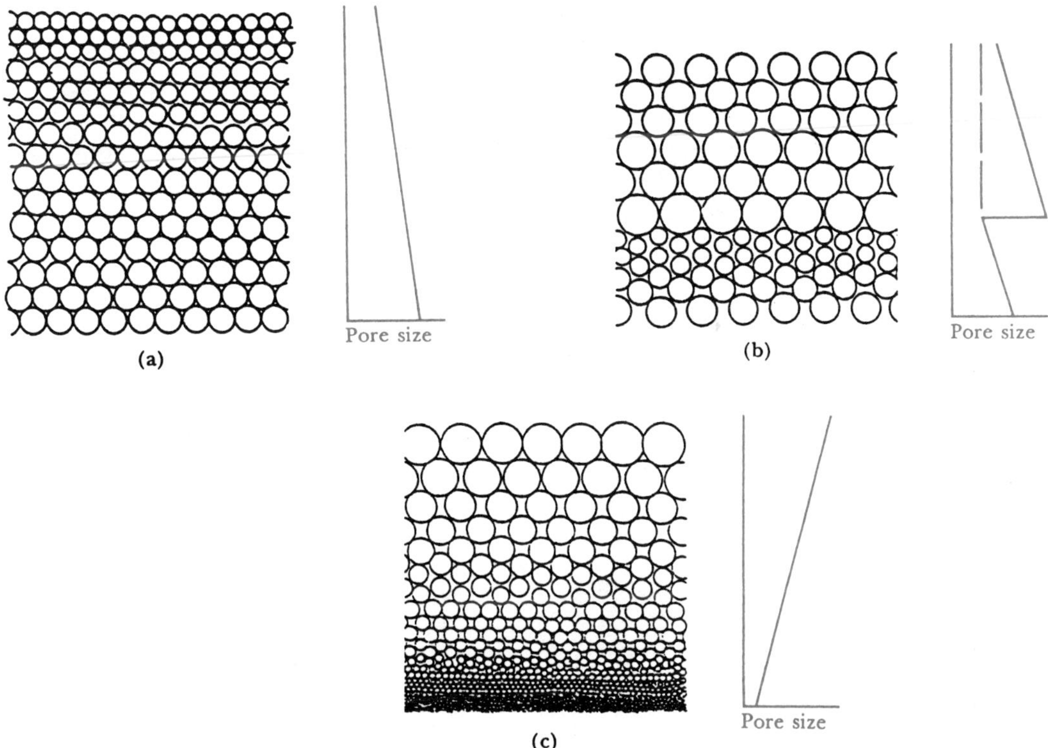

Figure 3-3 Filter media placement designs in cross section. (a) *Single media (e.g., rapid sand).* (b) *Dual media.* (c) *Multimedia.* Source: Neptune Microfloc, Inc., P.O. Box 612, Corvallis OR 97330.

diameter of <0.5 mm; *coarse sand filters* operate with larger grain sizes (0.7 to nearly 4 mm). *High rate filtration* can assume either of two configurations. *Dual media filters* use fine sand under a layer of crushed anthracite; in *multimedia filters* (also called *mixed media*), sand is sandwiched between a layer of anthracite on top and garnet or ilmenite underneath. Dual media (Fig. 3-3b) and multimedia (Fig. 3-3c) filter beds, with their coarse-to-fine placement, approach the ideal configuration (Fig. 3-4). Deeper penetration of POC into the filter bed is achieved with the coarsest medium on top and the finest at the bottom. This improves efficiency by allowing the filter to be operated longer between backwashes. Placement of the filtrants depends on their grain sizes and specific gravity values (see Technology section); the comparative distribution of filtrants by grain size and percentage composition (both factors as a function of depth) is illustrated in Figures 3-4 and 3-5. High rate filters are operated at 0.7 to 5.4×10^{-3} m/s, but typically 3.4×10^{-3} m/s.

CAPTURE MECHANISMS[2] Particulate organic carbon must first be transported into the filter; afterward, the mechanisms by which individual particles are captured and retained depend mainly on their size.[3] Particles with diameters of <1 μm attach to filtrant grains by surface phenomena that include chemical bonding and electrochemical forces. Particles between 1 and 30 μm are affected by both surface phenomena and mechanical

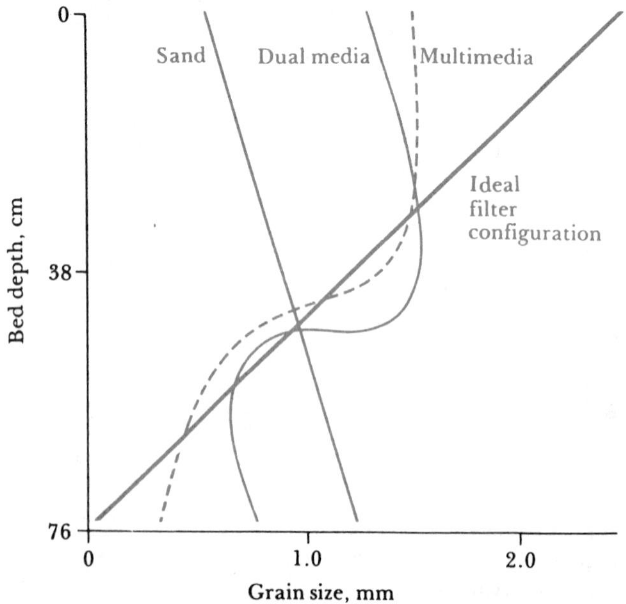

Figure 3-4 Comparison of single, dual, and multimedia by depth with the ideal filtrant configuration. Source: Neptune Microfloc, Inc., P.O. Box 612, Corvallis OR 97330.

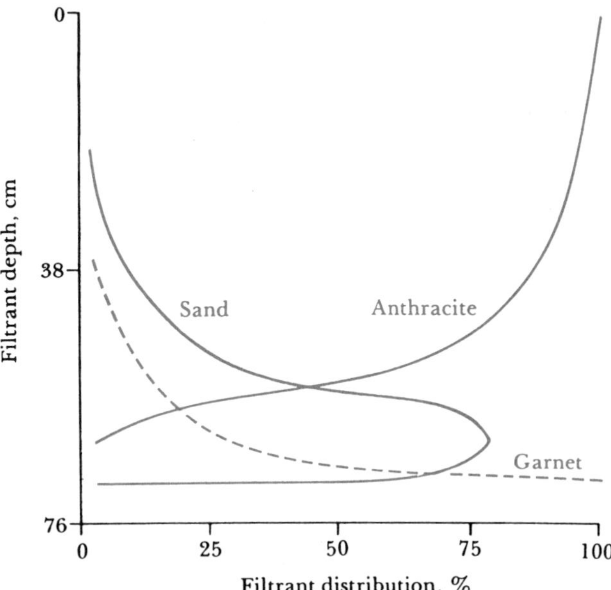

Figure 3-5 *Filtrant distribution by depth and percentage size in a multimedia filter bed.* Source: Neptune Microfloc, Inc., P.O. Box 612, Corvallis OR 97330.

forces. Particles >30 μm are captured and retained primarily by four mechanical processes. The most important of these is *straining*, in which a particle becomes trapped in the interstices of two or more filtrant grains and because of its size is unable to pass through. Sometimes more than one particle is trapped in the same interstice. Consider a triangular constriction formed by three adjacent, spherical filtrant grains (Fig. 3-6). The diameter of the constriction limits how deep one or more particles can penetrate. This limitation for a single particle is defined by $d/d_g = 0.154$, where d and d_g represent mean particle and filtrant grain diameter. Straining of three particles in the same interstice is limited by $d/d_g = 0.10$; for four particles by $d/d_g = 0.082$.

Particles in a filter follow *streamlines* or lines of water flow. Streamlines strongly influence the effectiveness of other capture mechanisms. A particle is unable to follow every twist and turn of a streamline. It ultimately collides with a filtrant grain, which stops its progress, and capture takes place by *interception*. This happens even if the particle and the seawater are the same density. Contact occurs if the streamline a particle is following comes nearer than $d/2$ from the surface of a filtrant grain, which can happen either in constrictions (i.e., interstices) or when bypassing the surface of a filtrant grain (Fig. 3-7). The fraction of POC that comes in contact with a static surface such as a filtrant grain is proportional to $(d/r_c)^2$, where r_c represents the constriction radius.

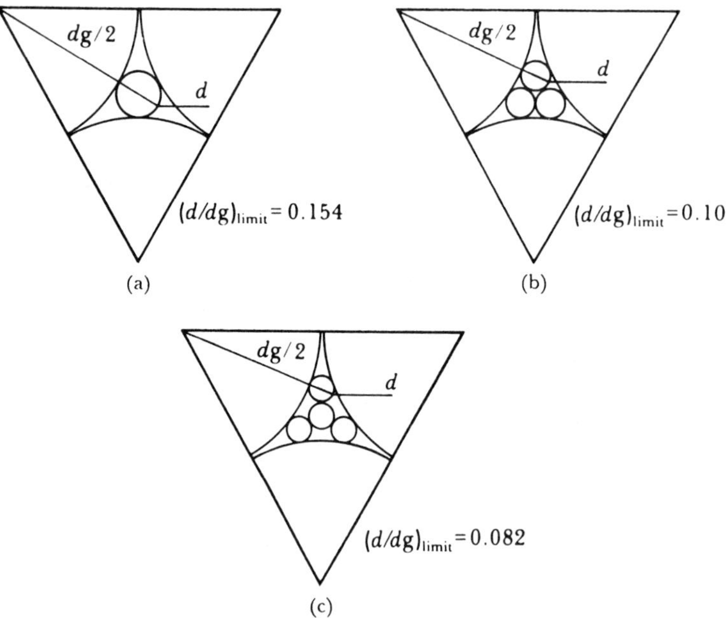

Figure 3-6 *Removal of a particle of POC by straining.* (a) *Capture of a single particle in a constriction formed by three adjacent filtrant grains. Penetration of the particle is limited by the diameter of the constriction. This limitation is defined by* $d/d_g = 0.154$ *where* d *and* d_g *represent mean particle and filtrant grain diameter.* (b) *Capture of three particles in the same interstice.* (c) *Capture of four particles in the same interstice.* Source: Herzig et al. (1970).

Particles with densities different from that of seawater are subject to gravitational forces. Their velocities are not the same as the velocity of the streamline, and they collide with filtrant grains by *sedimentation* (Fig. 3-8a). Particles that differ in density from the transport fluid cannot follow the same trajectory as the streamline. Any deviation brings them into sudden contact with filtrant grains, to which they attach by *inertial impaction* (Fig. 3-8b).

FILTRATION MODE VARIABLES Factors controlled by the design engineer and plant operator are *process variables*. These are hydraulic and mechanical characteristics of a filter determined by its mode. During the *filtration mode* influent seawater flows through the filter media, and POC is removed by capture mechanisms described above. The filter is in a *fixed bed configu-*

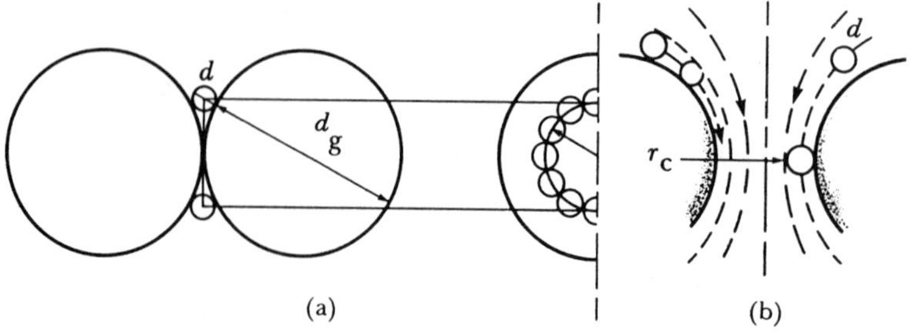

Figure 3-7 *Removal of a particle of POC by interception.* (a) *Contact occurs when the particle approaches within a distance of* < d/2 *from the filtrant grain.* (b) *The fraction of POC that comes in contact with a filtrant grain is proportional to* $(d/r_c)^2$, *where* r_c = *the radius of the constriction.* Source: Herzig et al. (1970).

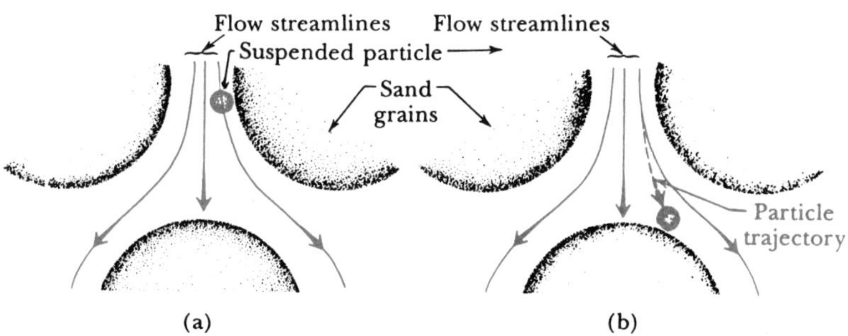

Figure 3-8 *Removal of a particle of POC by* (a) *sedimentation and* (b) *inertial impaction.* Source: Spotte (1973) after George Tchobanoglous (personal communication 1972).

ration, meaning that all filtrant grains are fixed in place. Important filtration mode variables are listed in Table 3-2. Of greatest importance is chemical treatment of the influent seawater before it reaches the filter. The purpose is to coagulate POC. This variable, called *flocculation,* is critical in drinking water and wastewater treatment. Two common flocculants are hydrated aluminum sulfate or alum, $Al_2(SO_4)_3 \cdot 18H_2O$, and a class of synthetic, water-soluble organic polymers known as *polyelectrolytes.* Neither is notably toxic, and some polyelectrolytes have been approved by the U.S. Environmental Protection Agency for drinking water treatment. However, the lack of bioassay data makes it hard to justify using any flocculant to treat aquarium seawater, which relegates POC removal to the other process variables listed in Table 3-2.[4]

Filtration rate, or the rate at which water is pumped through a filter, is a process variable of some importance, although its actual significance is sometimes overstated. Noticeable improvement of filtrate quality (i.e., POC removal) seldom is attained by altering the filtration rate (Fig. 3-9).

Interstices among filtrant grains constitute a considerable amount of empty space known as the *void fraction* or *porosity.* Void fraction during the filtration mode is typically ~0.4. In other words, ~40% of a filter consists of empty space.[5] Because water moves through a granular media filter by following

TABLE 3-2 Process variables for design and operation of filters used to remove POC from seawater supplies.

Filtration mode	Backwash mode
Filter bed depth	Auxiliary cleaning
Filtrant grain size	Backwash rate
Filtration rate	Backwash water viscosity
Flocculation	Filtrant grain size
Headloss	Support media
Void fraction or porosity	Underdrain system

Source: Stephen Spotte.

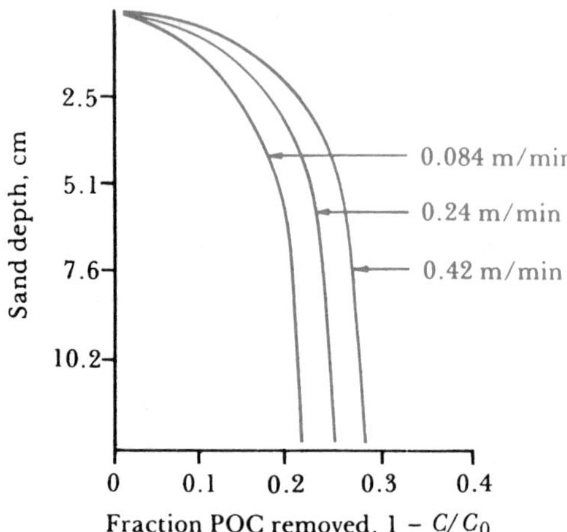

Figure 3-9 *Effect of filtration rate (3.64×10^{-3} m/s) on fraction of POC removed in a rapid sand filter in which sand size = 0.68 mm. The fraction removed increases with decreasing sand size and is $1 - C/C_0$ where C and C_0 represent the concentration of POC after and before filtration.* Source: Stephen Spotte after Tchobanoglous (1970).

streamlines, filtration rate is a function of void fraction. As POC becomes trapped in interstices and attached to filtrant grains, the void fraction diminishes. Entrapment of POC during continuous filtration causes a steady decline in void fraction until *terminal headloss* is reached, at which point water ceases to flow evenly through the bed because the filter is clogged. The most efficient filters trap the most POC with the lowest resultant headloss. As stated previously, an ideal filter bed has an average void fraction that decreases gradually with coarse to fine filtrants in the direction of water flow (Figs. 3-3 and 3-4). This permits more POC to be stored throughout the vertical depth of the bed, resulting in smaller headlosses. Because void fraction is a direct function of filtrant grain size, ideal configurations are arrangements in which larger grains are positioned on top of smaller ones, and the smallest are located deep in the bed. This description fits only high rate filters. In rapid sand filters, which use a single filtrant, the void fraction is uniform throughout. Most POC (~75 to 90%) is removed in the top few centimetres (Fig. 3-10), and rapid sand filters are less efficient than high rate filters.

BACKWASH MODE VARIABLES To be cleaned, a granular media filter is first taken out of the filtration mode by opening and closing a series of valves. A *backwash mode* is established by reversing the flow so that water rises upward through the filtrant and out an overflow port to waste. The wastewater carries with it most of the POC that has been captured and retained. When a filter is placed in the backwash mode its hydraulic and mechanical properties change abruptly. The bed is no longer fixed. Filtrant grains are lifted and separated, which expands the filter and briefly increases its void fraction by *fluidization*.

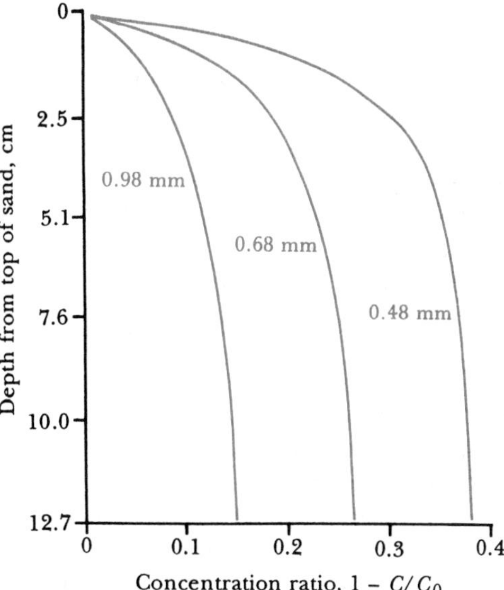

Figure 3-10 Effect of sand size on removal efficiency in a rapid sand filter. Filtration rate = 3.5×10^{-3} *m/s. Most of the POC is removed in the top few centimetres.* Source: Stephen Spotte after Tchobanoglous (1970).

Backwash rate is an important process variable (Table 3-2) because it affects the degree of fluidization and therefore the void fraction. A filter unit ordinarily is fluidized for 3 to 10 min, after which the flow of water is again returned to the filtration mode. Gauges show a decline in headloss because the filtrant has been restored to a nearly clean condition. During backwash the entire filter bed expands, which loosens POC and allows it to be separated hydraulically from interstices among filtrant grains.

Most rapid sand and high rate filters require at least one layer of graded support medium between the last layer of filtrant and the *underdrain*, a system of either plenums or perforated pipes. Filter underdrains serve two functions: (*1*) to collect seawater evenly from all parts of the bed when a system is in the filtration mode, and (*2*) to provide uniform dispersion of backwash water during the backwash mode. Fine sand and high rate filters require three or four graded layers of support media, depending on the design of the underdrain. Because of the large filtrant grain size, coarse sand filters are operated without support media, and filtrant and underdrain are in direct contact. The function of a support medium is to prevent the finer filtrants from clogging openings in the underdrain system and to aid in dispersing backwash water.

Fluidization alone is often inadequate to clean granular media filters. This is because collisions between filtrant grains do not occur in expanded beds, abrasion of the grains is therefore negligible, and attached POC is removed solely by hydrodynamic shear forces exerted at the water-filtrant surfaces.[6] Cleaning is improved substantially by auxiliary air scour, surface wash, or both. During *air scour* air is injected into the base of the lowest filtrant through a separate underdrain system to prevent extensive intermixing of the support media with the filtrant. Coarse sand filters require no support medium, and a common underdrain suffices. Air is applied at a regulated volume flow for 3 to 5 min, then shut off. Fluidization commences immediately. Compacted filtrant grains are separated by the rising air, and fluidization is made more effective. Simultaneous air scour and *subfluidization* (fluidization at backwash rates that do not permit the filtrant to reach optimal expansion) is highly effective in coarse sand filters in which the density of the filtrant is sufficient to prevent its loss with the wash water. However, subfluidization causes substantial filtrant loss when applied to fine sand and high rate filters.

Surface wash requires installation of a piping arrangement with a separate pump just above the surface of the filter. Jets of water are directed at the top layer of filtrant after the filter has been drained (Fig. 3-11). Surface wash disrupts filtrant grains

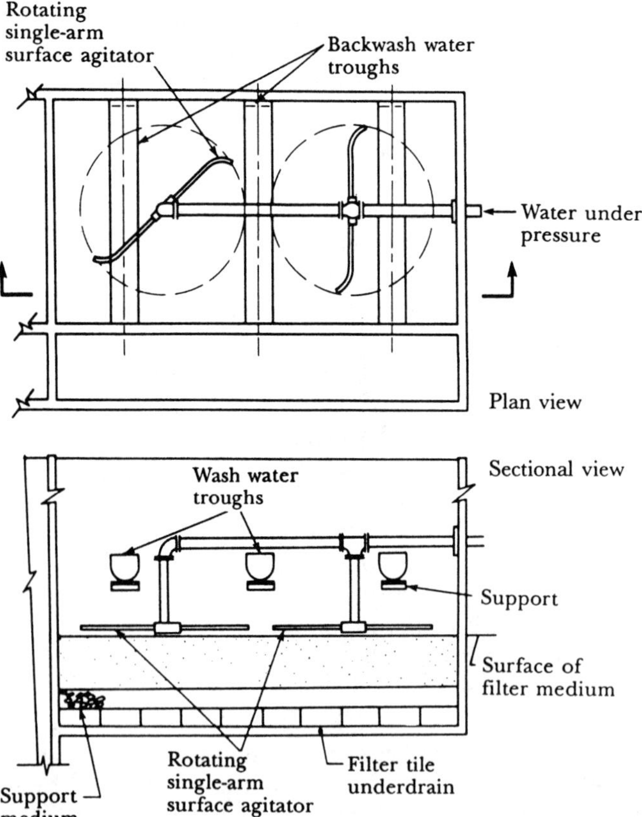

Figure 3-11 Surface wash in high rate filters. Source: Tchobanoglous and Schroeder (1985).

and makes fluidization more effective. In conventional designs the equipment is mounted in a fixed configuration, but some surface washers rotate and direct jets of water at the filtrant from different angles.

Seawater Supplies

In seaside installations seawater supplies can be pumped directly to holding tanks for later distribution. Good collection systems pump adequate volumes of clear seawater reliably and at reasonable cost. Low turbidity (i.e., a low POC concentration) is the most important criterion by which influent quality is judged.

SURFACE SUPPLIES Seawater supplies can be surface or subsurface. Surface supplies are obtained by pumping water through an open-ended pipe jutting into the ocean, a procedure that ordinarily must be followed by onshore filtration before the filtrate is fit to use. Surface supplies are subject to periodic increases in POC from plankton blooms, freshwater runoff, and increased turbidity from storms. *Biofouling* (the accumulation of mussels, barnacles, and other attached organisms) causes reduced flow and is a serious problem in the processing of surface seawater supplies. Typically, dual piping systems are installed. While one system is operating the other is shut down and allowed to become anoxic, or flushed with freshwater to kill fouling organisms. However, continuous high flow (>2.5 m/s) prevents fouling organisms from attaching.[7] Rapid-flow designs have the added advantage of reduced pipe diameters, which saves money and space.

SUBSURFACE FILTRATION Subsurface seawater supplies ordinarily are drawn through well points sunk in the ocean floor. The well points of modern systems are polyvinyl chloride (PVC) and placed in a sandy substratum below the low tide line (Fig. 3-12). Alternatively, seawater is obtained from large subsurface collectors such as the one illustrated in Figure 3-13. The use of any subsurface collector is limited to locations with surf and strong tidal flow. Continuous movement of the overlying sand is necessary to keep openings in the collection device free of silt. Subsurface collection ordinarily eliminates the need for additional processing because the water already has been strained through sand and gravel.

COARSE SAND FILTRATION Another option for offshore filtration is the coarse sand filter. The basic unit is a concrete case-

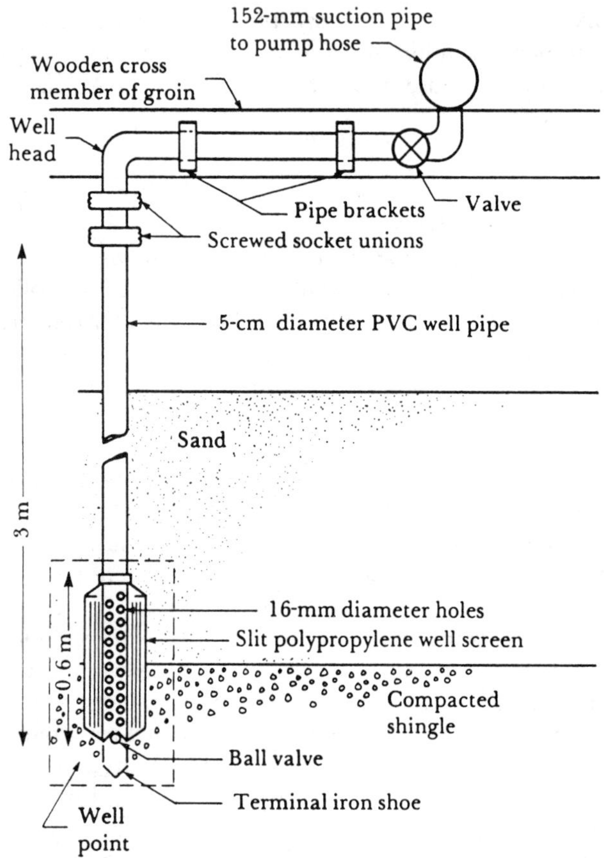

Figure 3-12 *Well point system used for collection of subsurface seawater supplies.* Source: Scholes (1980).

ment with an underdrain system placed on the ocean floor beyond the low tide line. Processed influent is transferred to holding tanks by means of an onshore pumping station (Fig. 3-14). As stated previously, coarse sand filters use filtrant material of a single grain size and no support medium. The filtrant rests directly on the underdrain. The grain size should be 0.7 to 4 mm. The bed should be at least 1 m deep.

Coarse sand filters are backwashed by reversing the direction of water flow at high tide, or by installing a header tank above grade and using previously filtered seawater to backwash the unit by gravity flow. Either method should be used in combination with air scour.

Gas Supersaturation

Under certain conditions (e.g., hot, sunny, windless days) surface seawater supplies can become supersaturated with gases. More commonly, gases in the influent supplies become super-

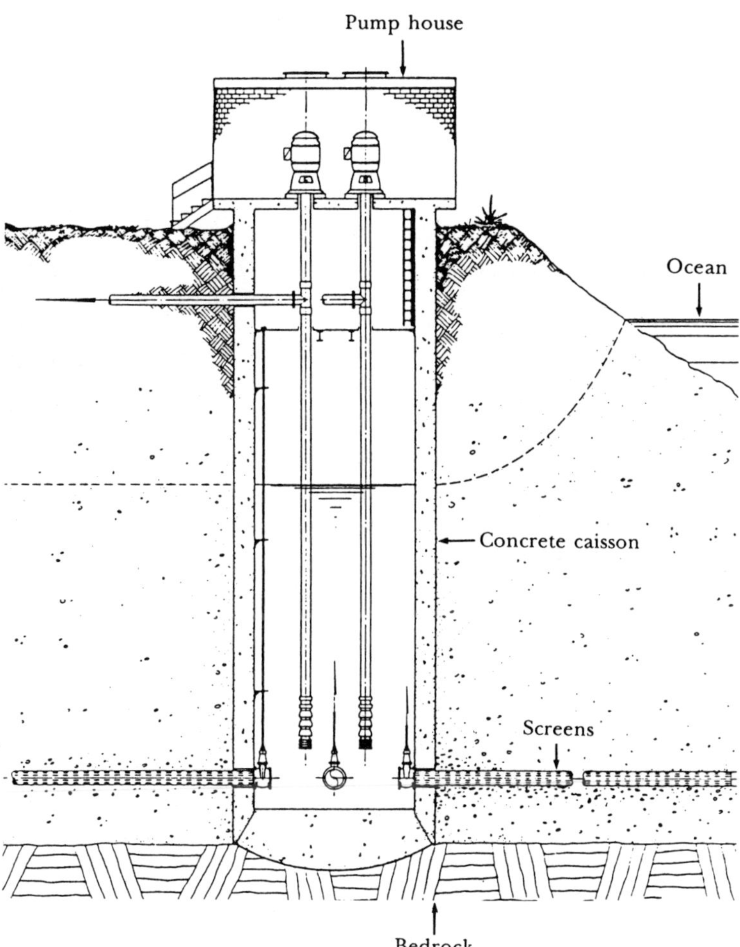

Figure 3-13 *Large collector for subsurface seawater supplies.* Source: The Ranney Company, P.O. Box 145, Westerville OH 43081.

saturated as a result of design flaws in the supply system, or from faulty maintenance (see below). In either case, fishes maintained in the receiving waters are susceptible to intermittent incidences of gas-bubble trauma (Chapter 9). Gases in excess of equilibrium concentrations can be removed near the source by packed column or vacuum degassing (see Technology section).

BASIS OF GAS SUPERSATURATION[8] Dry air is composed mainly of nitrogen (~78.1%) and oxygen (~20.9%). The partial pressure of a gas (assuming that it alone occupies a fixed volume) is described by

$$p = X\,(BP - p_w) \qquad (3.1)$$

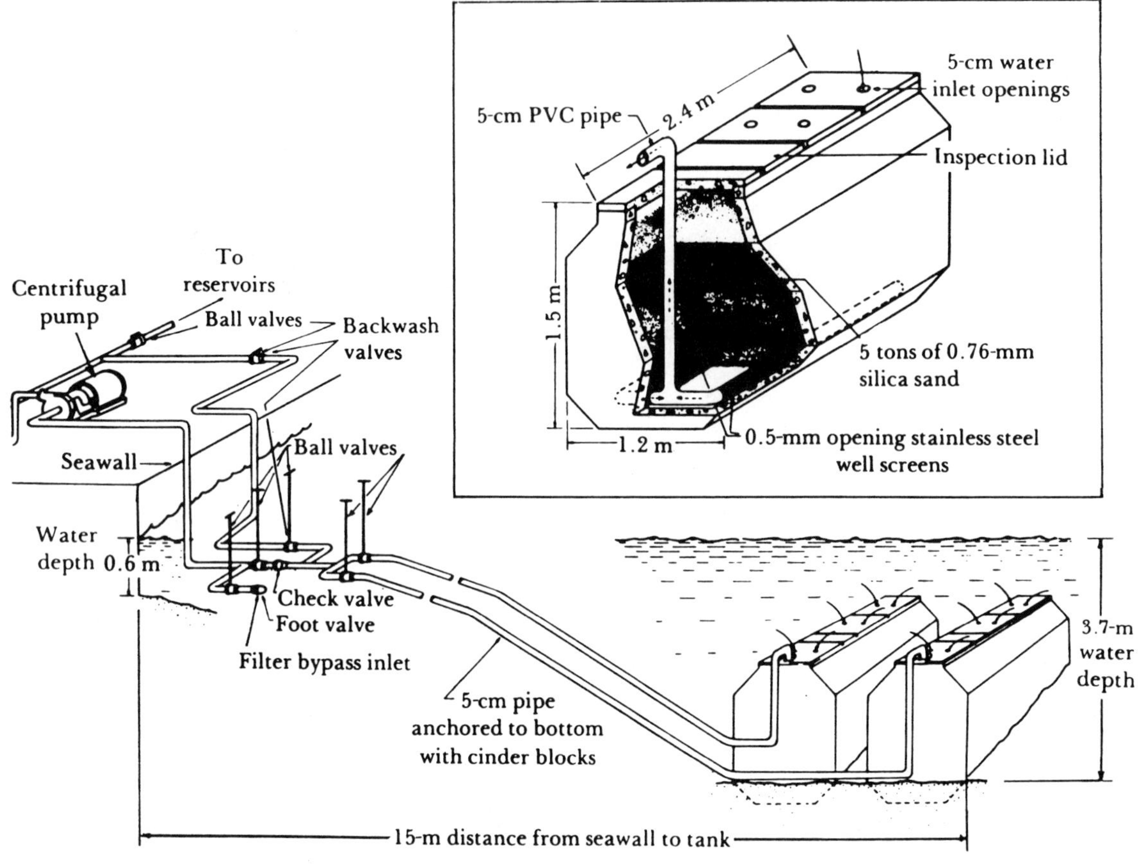

Figure 3-14 Coarse sand filter for collection of surface seawater. Source: Hettler (1971).

where p = partial pressure in the gas phase (mm Hg), X = mole fraction (dimensionless), BP = barometric pressure (mm Hg), and p_w = the vapor pressure of water (mm Hg). The partial pressure of a gas is affected slightly by temperature because p_w is a function of temperature. The partial pressure in water (i.e., the gas tension) is described by

$$P = \frac{c}{\beta} A \tag{3.2}$$

where c = the measured concentration of a gas in water (mg/L), β = Bunsen's coefficient in L/(L·atm), and A = the constant for the gas being measured. The partial pressure of a fixed concentration varies among gases, but at equilibrium the partial pressure of any gas is equal to its gas tension, shown by

$$P = p \tag{3.3}$$

A gas in solution can be in equilibrium ($P = p$), supersaturated ($P > p$), or undersaturated ($P < p$).

The supersaturation of just one gas may not induce gas-bubble trauma. For gas bubbles to form, the *total gas pressure, TGP*, must exceed the barometric pressure. The TGP = the sum of P of the five major gases (nitrogen, oxygen, argon, carbon dioxide, and water vapor); BP = the sum of p of the same gases. As before, three conditions are possible: $TGP = BP$ (equilibrium), $TGP > BP$ (supersaturation), and $TGP < BP$ (undersaturation). The difference between TGP and BP is the *differential hyperbaric gas pressure*, ΔP, a factor that can be measured directly by membrane-diffusion instrumentation. If $\Delta P < 0$, gas bubbles will not form if even one gas in solution is supersaturated.

CAUSES OF GAS SUPERSATURATION[8] Several conditions are known to produce gas supersaturation, but in the routine processing of seawater supplies for public aquariums only the heating of source water and entrainment of air in the piping system are worth considering. Gases become less soluble with increasing temperature (e.g., Table 3-3). At 10°C the solubility of dinitrogen, N_2, is 18.14 mg/L, but declines to 16.36 mg/L at 15°C. If N_2 at the lower temperature is in equilibrium with the atmosphere, then heated to 15°C without aeration or some other process to drive off the excess gas, $\Delta P = +64.5$ mm Hg (110.9% saturation; Fig. 3-15).

Conditions suitable for gas supersaturation are produced when air and water are in contact at pressures that exceed atmospheric conditions. Water falling over spillways drives air bubbles deep into the water column. The hydrostatic pressure is 73.4 mm Hg/m of vertical depth at 20°C.[9] The solubility of a gas is proportional to the total pressure, and the total gas solubility at 10.4 m is approximately twice that at the surface (i.e., $\Delta P = 1$ mm Hg). In addition to depth, the value of ΔP depends on the quantity of air entrained and the extent of mixing and turbulence. However, depth is the most important factor, and ΔP typically ranges from 18 to 44 mm Hg/m of bubble submergence.[10]

Gas supersaturation arises by the same mechanism if air is entrained into a pressurized water system through leaks on the suction side of the pump, or if the water intake device at the collection point is not completely submerged. Smaller air bub-

TABLE 3-3 Air solubility of oxygen (mg/L) in waters of various salinities.

	Salinity, ‰								
°C	0	5	10	15	20	25	30	35	40
0	14.621	14.120	13.636	13.167	12.714	12.277	11.854	11.445	11.051
1	14.216	13.733	13.266	12.815	12.378	11.956	11.548	11.154	10.773
2	13.829	13.364	12.914	12.478	12.057	11.650	11.256	10.875	10.507
3	13.460	13.011	12.577	12.156	11.750	11.356	10.976	10.608	10.252
4	13.107	12.674	12.255	11.849	11.456	11.076	10.708	10.352	10.008
5	12.770	12.352	11.947	11.554	11.175	10.807	10.451	10.107	9.774
6	12.447	12.043	11.652	11.272	10.905	10.550	10.206	9.872	9.550
7	12.139	11.748	11.369	11.002	10.647	10.303	9.970	9.647	9.335
8	11.843	11.465	11.098	10.743	10.399	10.066	9.744	9.431	9.128
9	11.559	11.194	10.839	10.495	10.162	9.839	9.526	9.223	8.930
10	11.288	10.933	10.590	10.257	9.934	9.621	9.318	9.024	8.739
11	11.027	10.684	10.351	10.028	9.715	9.412	9.117	8.832	8.556
12	10.777	10.444	10.121	9.808	9.505	9.210	8.925	8.648	8.379
13	10.537	10.214	9.901	9.597	9.302	9.017	8.739	8.470	8.210
14	10.306	9.993	9.689	9.394	9.108	8.830	8.561	8.300	8.046
15	10.084	9.780	9.485	9.198	8.921	8.651	8.389	8.135	7.888
16	9.870	9.575	9.289	9.010	8.740	8.478	8.223	7.976	7.737
17	9.665	9.378	9.099	8.829	8.566	8.311	8.064	7.823	7.590
18	9.467	9.188	8.917	8.654	8.399	8.151	7.910	7.676	7.449
19	9.276	9.005	8.742	8.486	8.237	7.995	7.761	7.533	7.312
20	9.092	8.828	8.572	8.323	8.081	7.846	7.617	7.395	7.180
21	8.914	8.658	8.408	8.166	7.930	7.701	7.479	7.262	7.052
22	8.743	8.493	8.250	8.014	7.785	7.561	7.344	7.134	6.929
23	8.578	8.334	8.098	7.867	7.644	7.426	7.214	7.009	6.809
24	8.418	8.181	7.950	7.725	7.507	7.295	7.089	6.888	6.693
25	8.263	8.032	7.807	7.588	7.375	7.168	6.967	6.771	6.581
26	8.113	7.888	7.668	7.455	7.247	7.045	6.849	6.658	6.472
27	7.968	7.748	7.534	7.326	7.123	6.926	6.734	6.548	6.366
28	7.827	7.613	7.404	7.201	7.003	6.810	6.623	6.441	6.263
29	7.691	7.482	7.278	7.079	6.886	6.698	6.515	6.337	6.164
30	7.558	7.354	7.155	6.961	6.772	6.589	6.410	6.236	6.066
31	7.430	7.230	7.036	6.846	6.662	6.483	6.308	6.137	5.972
32	7.305	7.110	6.920	6.735	6.555	6.379	6.208	6.042	5.880
33	7.183	6.993	6.807	6.626	6.450	6.278	6.111	5.948	5.790
34	7.065	6.879	6.697	6.520	6.348	6.180	6.017	5.857	5.702
35	6.949	6.767	6.590	6.417	6.248	6.084	5.924	5.768	5.617
36	6.837	6.659	6.485	6.316	6.151	5.991	5.834	5.681	5.533
37	6.727	6.553	6.383	6.218	6.056	5.899	5.746	5.597	5.451
38	6.619	6.449	6.283	6.121	5.963	5.810	5.660	5.513	5.371
39	6.514	6.348	6.186	6.027	5.873	5.722	5.575	5.432	5.292
40	6.412	6.249	6.090	5.935	5.783	5.636	5.492	5.352	5.215

Source: John Colt (personal communication 1990), calculated from data in Benson and Krause (1984).

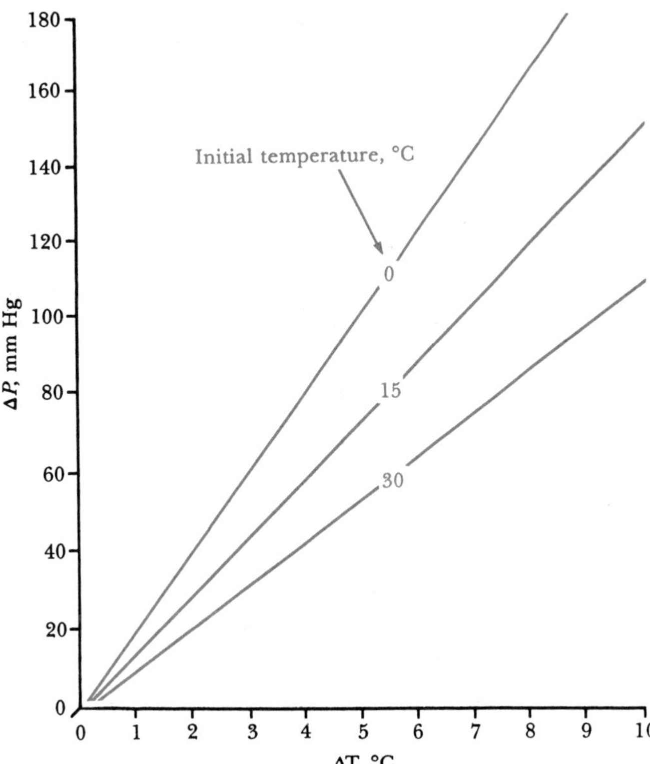

Figure 3-15 *Effects of heating on* P *assuming no gas transfer. For a given temperature increase the resulting* ΔP *is greater at a lower initial temperature.* Source: Colt (1984).

bles form in seawater than in freshwaters because the greater ionic strength raises the surface tension. Consequently, the dissolution rate of air in seawater is ~10 times greater.[11] Small leaks in seawater systems are often more difficult to detect because the bubbles may not be visible.

Gas Transfer, Aeration, Circulation

Newly mixed artificial seawater and filtered seawater recently collected from the ocean require aeration to ensure adequate concentrations of oxygen and equilibration of pH. *Aeration* is the physical process of injecting air into water under pressure. The main purpose is to promote gas exchange.

GAS TRANSFER Gas transfer between air and water is a function of the differences in partial pressure of a gas in the atmosphere, versus in the water, and the thickness of a surface film located at the air-water interface or around a rising bubble. This film, formed by surface tension, is the *laminar layer*. The laminar layer can be envisioned as a thin skin that is permeable to gas molecules. The laminar layer at the surface of the ocean

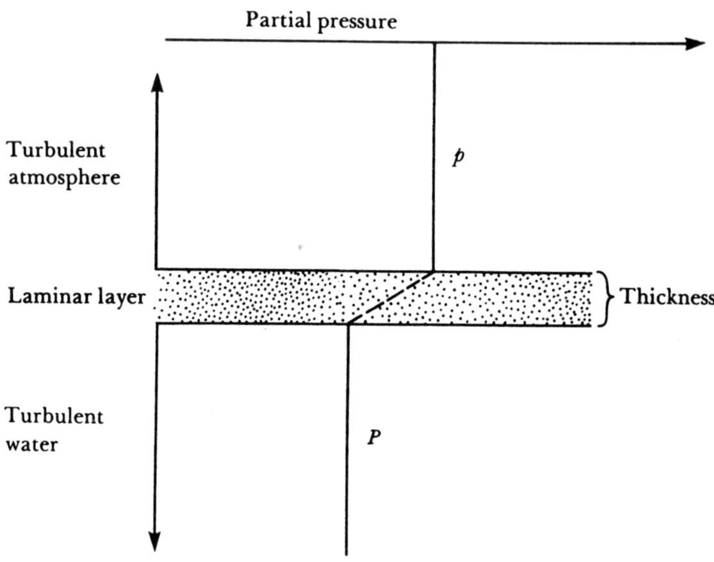

Figure 3-16 *Diagrammatic illustration of the laminar layer model for gas exchange at the sea surface.* Source: Kester (1975).

varies from 0.002 to 0.020 cm, with thinner spots resulting from stirring of the underlying water (Fig. 3-16).[12] The shape of a rising air bubble is altered by turbulence, causing the laminar layer to vary in thickness (Fig. 3-17). The laminar layer controls the rate of diffusion of a gas from air into water, and diffusion is faster if the laminar layer is thin.

The movement or *flux* of a gas through the laminar layer depends on differences in partial pressure between air and water and also on *diffusivity*, the rate of diffusion of the gas in question, shown by

$$\text{flux} = \frac{\text{concentration} \times \text{diffusivity}}{\text{thickness}} \tag{3.4}$$

where concentration is the partial pressure times solubility.[13] Oxygen and nitrogen, the most common gases in the atmosphere, have similar diffusivities ($\sim 2 \times 10^{-5}$ cm/s at 20°C). However, the concentration of any gas equals the pressure it exerts times its solubility, and solubilities of gases differ considerably. If nitrogen, oxygen, and carbon dioxide are compared the ratio is ~1/2/70 (i.e., at a given partial pressure the flux of different gases varies according to their solubilities).[14]

AERATION[15] New seawater supplies can be aerated at a location separate from the exhibits, in which case the aeration tank should be designed to provide maximum gas transfer. The efficiency of aeration is determined by the *oxygen transfer rate*,

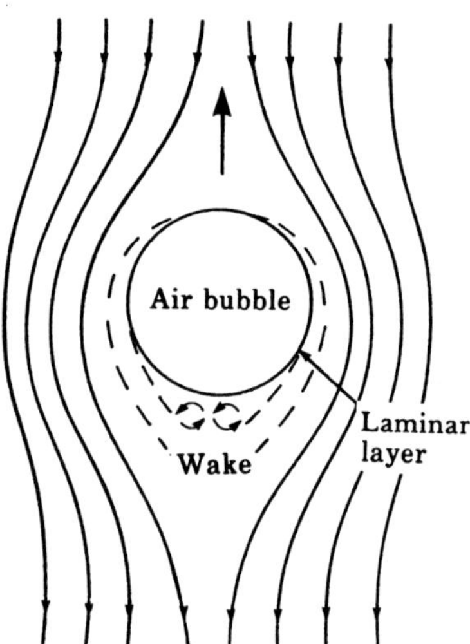

Figure 3-17 *Turbulence around a rising air bubble.* Source: Stephen Spotte after Rich (1973).

the time necessary for the dissolved oxygen concentration to approach saturation. The diffusion of oxygen from air bubbles into water is controlled by (*1*) initial surface areas of the bubbles, (*2*) initial concentration of dissolved oxygen, and (*3*) contact time between the bubbles and the water (i.e., the interval between the time they are released and when they reach the surface). Aeration is accomplished by injecting air through a system of static aerators, coarse-bubble diffusers (Fig. 3-18), or a manifold of polyvinyl chloride (PVC) pipe perforated at regular intervals by drill holes (Fig. 3-19).

A rising column of air and water has a lower specific gravity than the surrounding water, and the more buoyant air-water

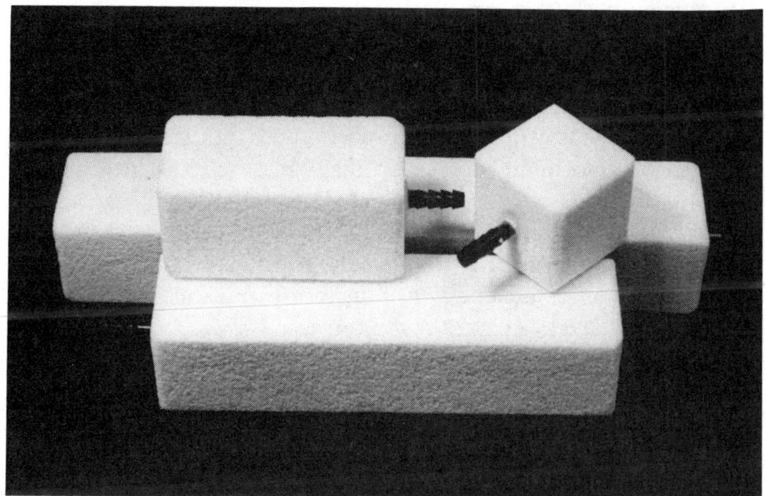

Figure 3-18 *Coarse-bubble diffusers.* Source: Stephen Spotte.

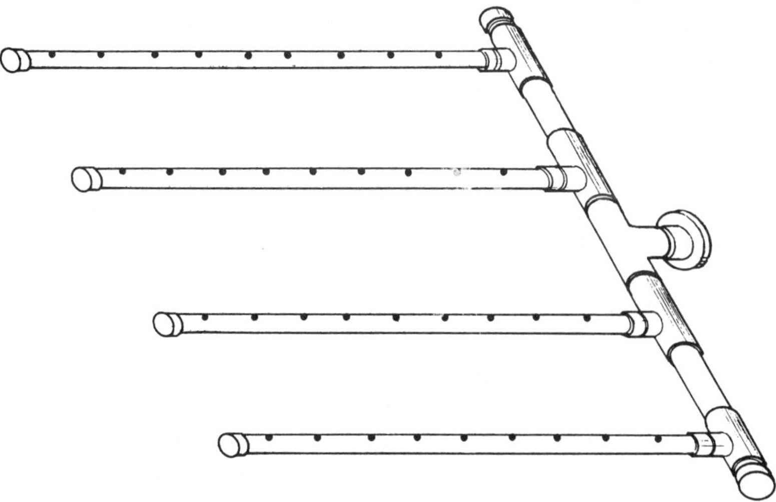

Figure 3-19 *Manifold of PVC pipe with drill holes.* Source: Stephen Spotte.

mixture is displaced upward by the denser water underneath. The principle is the same as that of an airlift pump (see the next subsection). Rising air expands as the hydrostatic pressure decreases, causing the volume of water displaced to be greater near the surface. This results in more intensive agitation at the surface of the water column than at the bottom. Consequently, surface turbulence bears little relationship to either the oxygen transfer rate or mixing conditions.

From a design standpoint, oxygen transfer rate depends on (*1*) depth of the aeration tank, (*2*) volume flow of air, and (*3*) mixing pattern. Deep aeration tanks are preferable because the bubbles take longer to ascend, and contact time is increased. Shallow tanks with large surface areas are more difficult to aerate efficiently. In general, the oxygen transfer rate increases with the volume flow of air. The mixing pattern resulting from aeration is determined by placement of the diffusers or manifold and by the distance between the aeration devices and the tank walls. Increasing the volume flow of air without changing the pattern of placement increases turbulence but has little effect on the mixing pattern.

Diffusers or manifolds of PVC pipe ordinarily are arranged in either axial or cross patterns, which differ in efficiency. An *axial pattern* is established in a rectangular tank by adjacent walls. The result is a single or double spiral flow. A single spiral forms when the diffuser or header is placed along one wall (Fig. 3-20a); a double spiral results from placing the air source longitudinally down the center of the tank (Fig. 3-20b). The double spiral is more efficient, and the disparity in the effectiveness of the two designs increases with depth. An axial pattern with a single spiral is the least efficient of axial and cross pattern arrangements (see below).

When an air-water mixture reaches the surface it spreads outward until coming in contact with a vertical wall or the horizontal flow from another column of rising air bubbles. A wall deflects the mixture downward at lower velocity.[16] A *stilling effect* (i.e., loss of momentum) occurs if the point of air release is immediately adjacent to a wall (Fig. 3-21a) because there can be no downward deflection. Similarly, when the flows of two columns collide at the surface there is loss of momentum and little downward flow (Fig. 3-21b).

A *cross pattern* is established by positioning adjacent air-water columns to reduce wall effects. In rectangular tanks the diffusers or manifolds are oriented parallel with the width of the tank (Fig. 3-22). A ''mixing cell'' forms around each rising column. The expected loss of momentum takes place when the outward radial flows of the columns collide at the surface, but much of

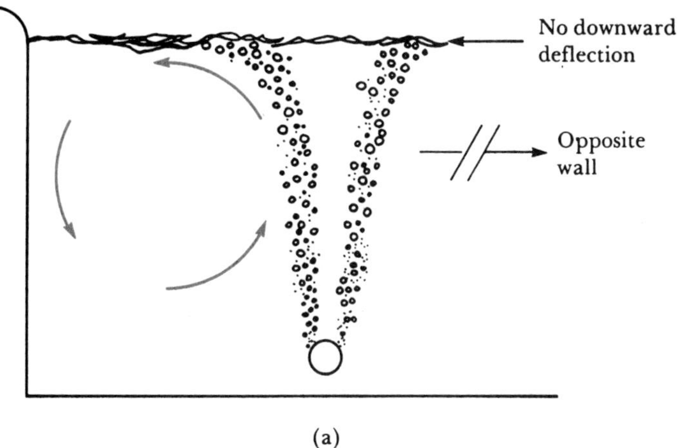

(a)

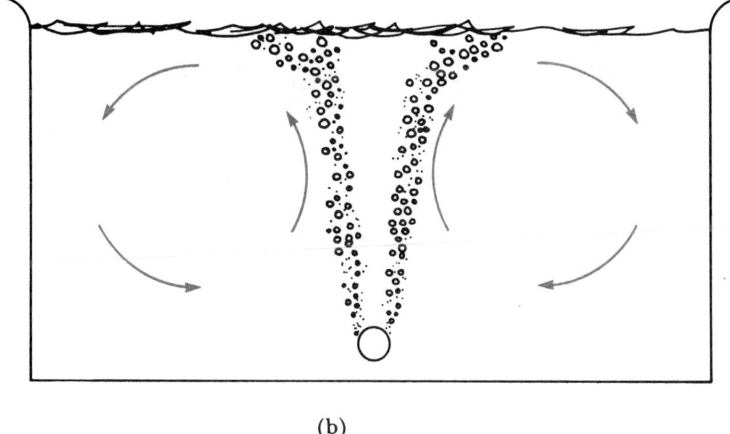

(b)

Figure 3-20 (a) *Single axial flow pattern established by downward deflection of an air-water mixture from a nearby wall. The surface flow on the right dissipates with no nearby wall.* (b) *Double axial flow pattern established by positioning the diffuser midway between two walls so that both serve as deflectors of the air-water mixture. The double axial pattern is markedly superior in terms of oxygen transfer rate.* Source: Stephen Spotte, drawn from information in Rooney and Huibregtse (1980).

the energy is absorbed in formation of vortices that draw bubbles downward, often to one-half the tank depth. The effect is to increase contact time and improve the oxygen transfer rate. Without wall effects spiral patterns are minimized, and replacement water is recruited from between the columns. As might be expected, the geometry of the tank is unimportant in aeration, and oxygen transfer rates in rectangular and cylindrical tanks are the same. The cross pattern is the most efficient design.

CIRCULATION The most commonly used devices for recirculating and aerating aquarium water are *airlift pumps* (also called *bubble columns* and *airlifts*). The airlift pump concept dates back perhaps 200 years.[17] Airlifts are classified by how the air is injected. Two of the commonest designs are the *central air line*

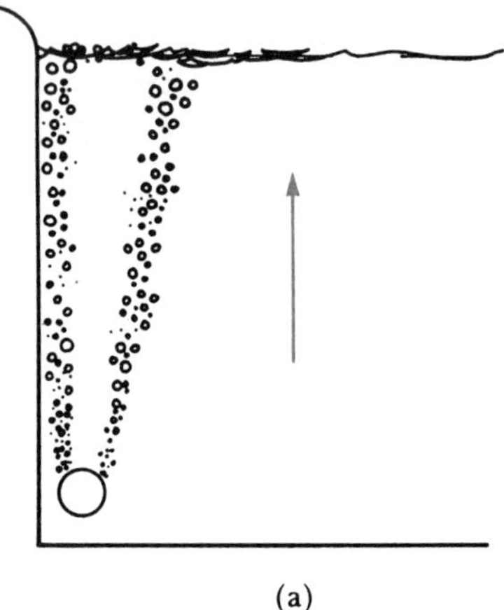

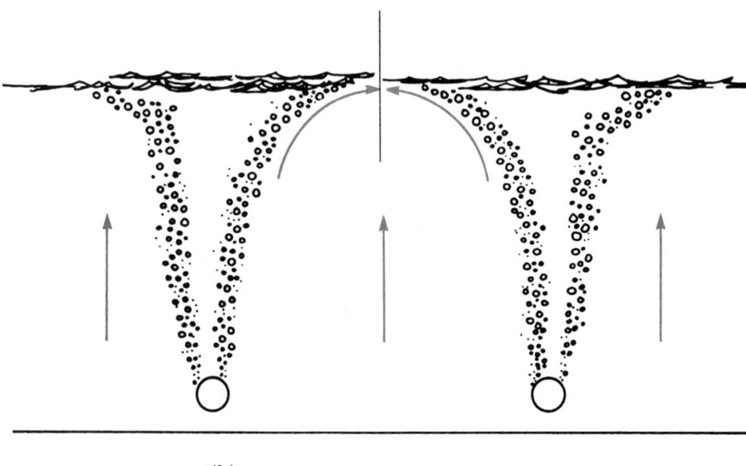

Figure 3-21 *Arranging diffusers incorrectly causes a stilling effect in a rising mixture of air and water.* (a) *Placing a diffuser too close to a wall reduces the wall's usefulness as a deflecting surface, and little of the air-water mixture is directed downward.* (b) *Positioning diffusers so that spreading surface flows collide also limits downward deflection, except in cross-pattern arrangements (Fig. 3-22).* Source: Stephen Spotte, drawn from information in Rooney and Huibregtse (1980).

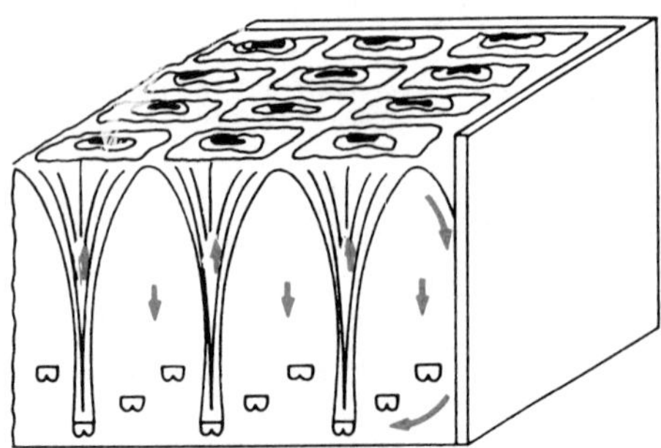

Figure 3-22 *The oxygen transfer rate is most effective when a cross pattern of diffuser or manifold placement is used. Surface discharges from individual "mixing cells" flow at right angles toward the next diffuser or manifold. Loss of momentum at interfaces between surface flows is more than compensated by small vortices that form. These draw air bubbles downward and increase contact time.* Source: Rooney and Huibregtse (1980).

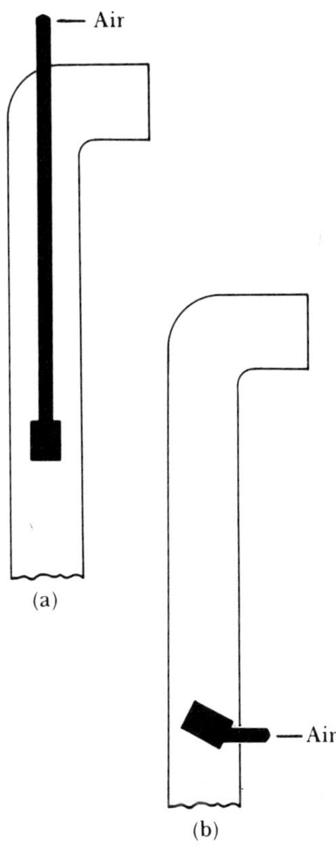

Figure 3-23 *Two common airlift pump designs.* (a) *Central air line.* (b) *Pohlé or side air inlet.* Source: Stephen Spotte.

and *Pohlé* or *side air inlet* (Fig. 3-23). The Pohlé design gives slightly better performance (greater volume flow on less energy), but the improvement is seldom noticeable, and either design is acceptable.

A typical airlift consists of two parts, an *eduction* or *lift pipe* and a *footpiece*. The footpiece couples the air source to the eduction pipe. Footpieces used in large aquariums are sometimes designed as jackets to provide a space or plenum that collects the injected air for even distribution into the eduction pipe (Fig. 3-24).

Mechanical pumps use electrical energy; airlift pumps operate on energy supplied by compressed air released as bubbles. The driving force, which causes the pump to operate continuously, is the unbalanced hydrostatic pressure in the eduction pipe resulting from a mixed column of water and air of lower specific gravity than the rest of the water in the aquarium. Water is not actually "lifted," but displaced upward as it mixes with the air.

The performance of an airlift improves as an increasing fraction of its total length is submerged. The relationship between performance and water depth can be considered in terms of *lift, total lift, submergence,* and *submergence ratio* (Fig. 3-25).

The two most important considerations in the design and operation of airlift pumps are gas transfer and pumping rate (Table 3-4).[18] Both are affected by the flow pattern of air bubbles inside the eduction pipe (Fig. 3-26) and in turn affect the contact time of air bubbles with the water. Contact time is described by

$$t = \frac{Z}{V_l} \tag{3.5}$$

where Z = length of the eduction pipe (cm) and V_l = the average liquid velocity in the lift pipe expressed as

$$V_l = \frac{Q_g}{A(1 - \epsilon)} \text{ (m/s)} \tag{3.6}$$

where Q_g = volumetric gas flow rate (m^3/s); A = the cross sectional area of the eduction pipe, $\frac{\pi D^2}{4}$, in m^2; and ϵ = average gas concentration in the eduction pipe (dimensionless).

A *bubble flow* pattern (Fig. 3-26) develops when the bubble size is substantially smaller than the diameter of the eduction pipe and the gas/void ratio is low. This is because the bubbles are distributed in a relatively even pattern. The gas must be dispersed through an air diffuser to achieve small bubbles. Bub-

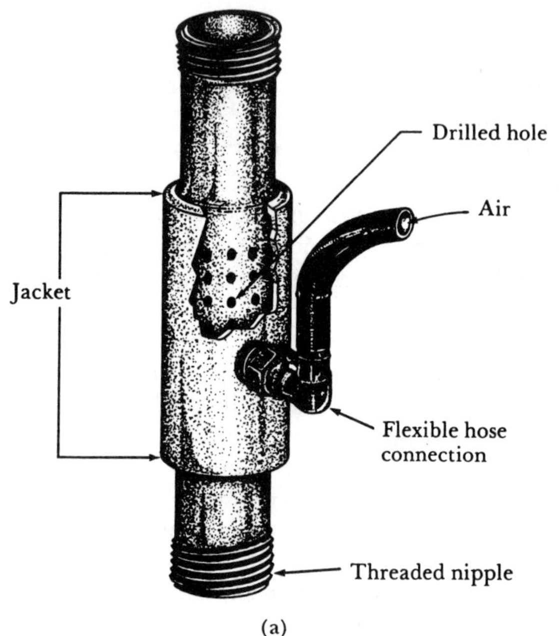

(a)

(b)

Figure 3-24 Airlift pump with plenum. (a) *Design.* (b) *Operational unit.* Sources: (a) Spotte (1979b); (b) Stephen Spotte.

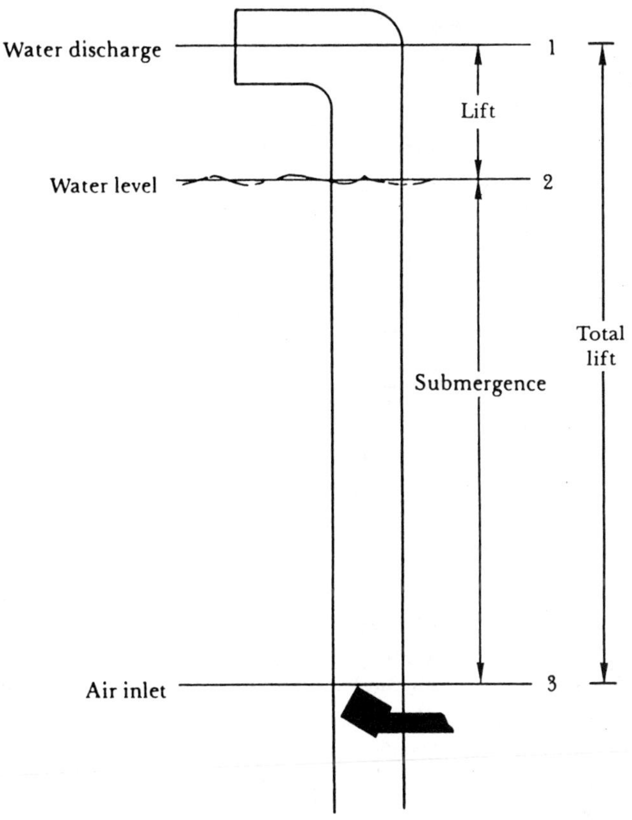

Figure 3-25 *Operating principles of the airlift pump.* Lift *is the distance between the surface of the water and the discharge point (1 to 2) or the vertical distance the water must be moved above the surface.* Total lift *is the distance between the air injection and water discharge points (1 to 3) or the total vertical distance the water must be moved.* Submergence *is the distance between the water level and the air injection point (2 to 3).* Submergence ratio *(not shown) is the ratio of the distance between the air injection point and the surface of the water (3 to 2) to total lift.* Sources: Stephen Spotte after Spotte (1979a, 1979b).

bles in the eduction pipe coalesce to form *gas slugs* or *Taylor bubbles* if the gas void is greater than ~25%. The resultant flow pattern (*slug flow*) is uneven, and water emerges from the end of the eduction pipe in spurts. Slug flow is characteristic of eduction pipes of small diameter (less than ~20 mm). A third flow pattern is *bubbly slug flow,* in which small bubbles are suspended between gas slugs. Bubble flow is the most efficient pattern, followed by bubbly slug flow. Slug flow will not be con-

TABLE 3-4 Design of airlift pumps.

Design factor	Design criteria	Performance factor affected
Flow pattern	Bubble flow	Gas transfer, pumping rate
Submergence ratio	>0.85	Gas transfer, pumping rate
Length/diameter ratio of eduction pipe	>50	Pumping rate

Source: Stephen Spotte, compiled from information in Reinemann and Timmons (1989).

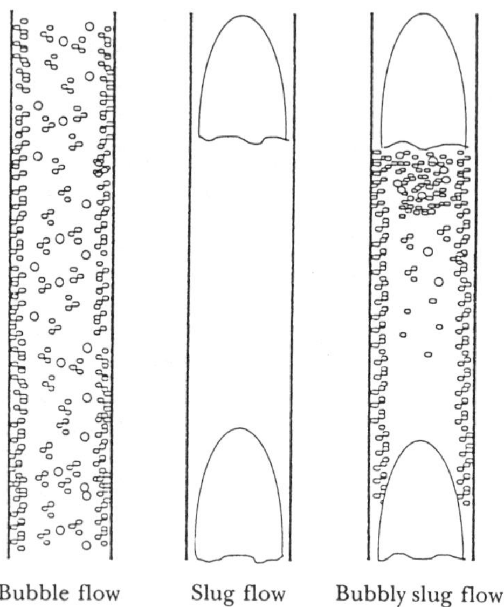

Figure 3-26 *Flow patterns in airlift pump operation.* Source: Reinemann and Timmons (1989).

sidered further except to state that it occurs when the air is not dispersed at the injection point.

The gas-to-liquid surface area is less in bubbly slug flow than in the bubble flow pattern. Consequently, the rate of gas transfer is reduced. The greater turbulence of bubbly slug flow patterns, however, tends to increase the gas transfer rate. The performance of an airlift is shown in Figure 3-27. The transition

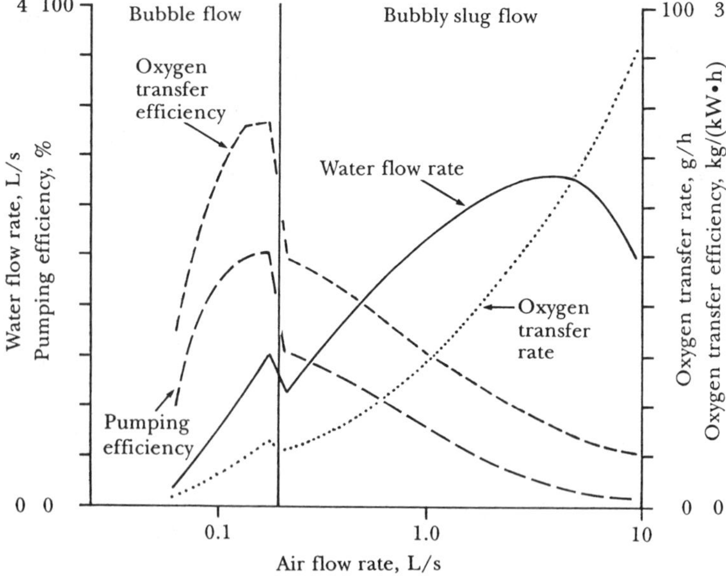

Figure 3-27 *Airlift pumping and aeration performance: eduction pipe diameter = 0.05 m, submergence ratio = 0.9, pipe length = 2.5 m, water temperature = 15°C, input oxygen concentration = 5 mg/L, compressor efficiency = 0.60.* Source: Reinemann and Timmons (1989).

from bubble flow to bubbly slug flow depends on the concentration of air in the eduction pipe. This in turn depends on the submergence ratio and the flow rate of the injected air. In addition, the maximum pumping efficiency decreases steeply as the length/diameter ratio of the eduction pipe declines below ~50 (Fig. 3-28). In well designed and operated airlifts, maximum pumping efficiency equals or exceeds that of centrifugal pumps.

Maximum gas transfer and pumping efficiency occur when the bubble flow patterns just described are controlled, but this can be achieved only at submergence ratios >0.85, low air flow rates, and with air dispersion at the injection point. Maximum oxygen transfer is comparable with fine-bubble diffusion, and the flow rate of effluent water is greatest at the submergence ratio of 1.0 (Fig. 3-29).

Foam Fractionation[19]

Foam fractionation removes DOC from solution by adsorbing it onto surfaces of air bubbles rising in a closed column. Accumulated organic matter is later discarded with the foam that is produced. The substances removed are called *surfactants* because they are surface active, a characteristic of some organic compounds to be discussed shortly. The term *foam fractionation* describes the removal of dissolved surface-active substances from solution (Fig. 3-30). An accurate synonym is foam separation; less accurate ones are airstripping and protein skimming. *Froth flotation* refers to removal of surface-active particulate organics from water. To simplify the following discussion

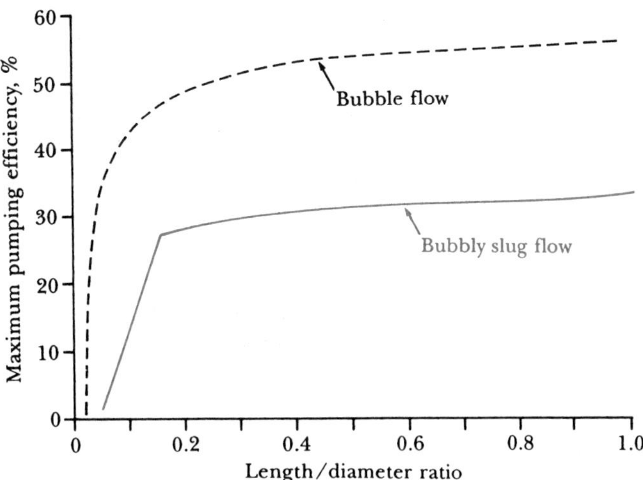

Figure 3-28 *Decrease in pumping efficiency versus length/diameter ratio.* Source: Reinemann and Timmons (1989).

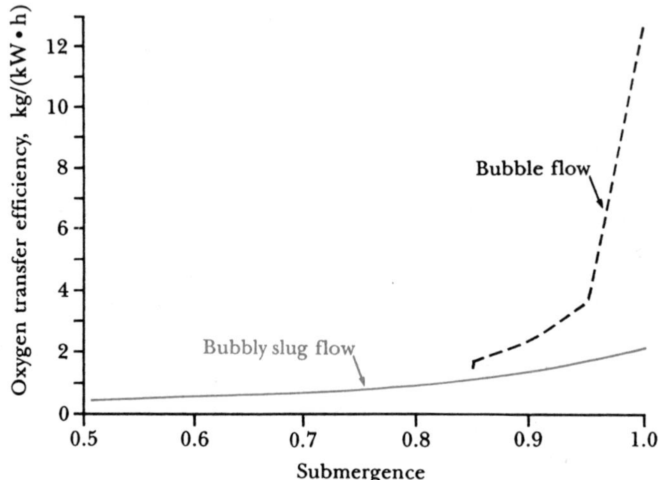

Figure 3-29 *Maximum oxygen transfer efficiency versus submergence ratio: eduction pipe diameter = 0.05 m, pipe length = 2.5 m, water temperature = 15°C, input oxygen concentration = 5 mg/L, compressor efficiency = 0.60.* Source: Reinemann and Timmons (1989).

this process is considered together with foam fractionation, with the idea that both are at work in aquarium water.

MECHANISMS A surfactant molecule in water is polar at one end and nonpolar at the other. The polar end, if attracted to water molecules around it, becomes hydrophilic, whereas the nonpolar portion is not attracted to water molecules and is hydrophobic. As the name suggests, surface-active molecules tend to congregate near the surface with their hydrophobic parts in contact with the air. This characteristic allows them to be concentrated at the air-water interface for rapid removal.

To be effective, the foam fractionation process requires a contact column in which air and water containing the surfactants can interact. Air-liquid interfaces are provided by supplying air bubbles to the contact column and allowing them to mix with water and flow to the top. The hydrophobic groups are dissolved; particulate surfactants migrate to the bubble-water interfaces, while the hydrophilic ends of the same molecules remain in the water (Fig. 3-31). The rising bubbles thus acquire ''skins'' of surface-active material. At the top of the contact column the skins burst and form layers of foam. If the foam is stable the surface-active portion accumulates, but the *residue* (water containing nonsurface-active substances) drains away. By removing the foam layer, surfactants—both dissolved and particulate—can be separated from seawater and discarded. Foam fractionation serves to reduce the levels of DOC and POC in one step.

LIMITING FACTORS Successful foam fractionation depends on the nature of the foam. Two important properties are drain-

(a)

(b)

Figure 3-30 *Foam formation is a natural process in high-energy coastal areas.* (a) *Pine Cay, Turks and Caicos Islands, British West Indies.* (b) *St. Paul Island, Pribilof Islands, Alaska.* Sources: (a) Patricia M. Bubucis, Sea Research Foundation; (b) Stephen Spotte.

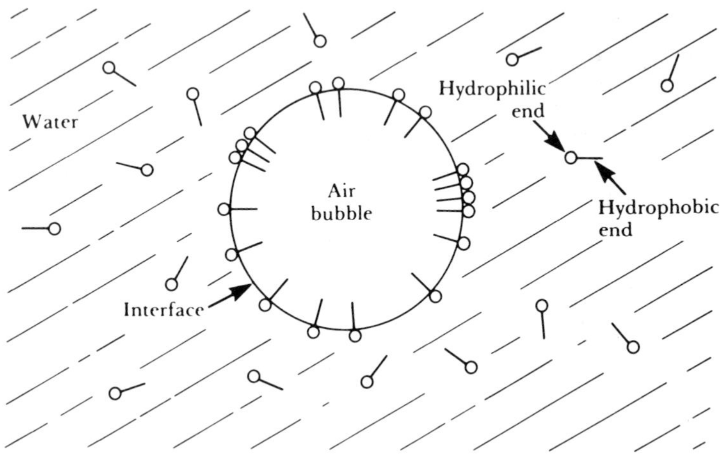

Figure 3-31 Diagrammatic illustration of an air bubble adsorbing the surface-active ends of DOC molecules. Sources: Spotte (1979a, 1979b) after Ng and Mueller (1975).

ability and stability. *Foam drainability* is the property that allows the residue to flow away from the newly formed foam by gravity. In foams that drain poorly, pressure exerted by water flowing downward is enough to rupture the bubbles before they can be removed. Foam drainability is affected by foam bubble size, viscosity (defined in Chapter 8, Note 33), and surface tension.[20]

Foam stability is the property that enables foam bubbles to withstand drainage without rupturing.[21] Unless a foam is somewhat stable it will not last long enough to be removed. Foam stability requires that (*1*) the film concentration of the surface layer be different from that of the water, and (*2*) the surface layer be of high viscosity. Other important factors affecting foam stability are the concentration of surface-active materials, pH, temperature, and size of the air bubbles injected into the contact column. Small bubbles are more effective than larger ones because of their greater surface area for DOC adsorption. Optimal values of all these factors provide a surface film concentration different from the bulk liquid (seawater in this case), and which create a high viscosity in the surface layer.[20]

With one exception, all factors listed in the preceding paragraphs are beyond the control of aquarists. The two primary factors affecting foam stability—differences in the composition and viscosity of the surface layer—are properties inherent in any liquid containing surfactants. Temperature and pH must be adjusted to meet the immediate physiological needs of animals and plants, rather than foam production. Surfactant concentration results from excretion of organic compounds by living organisms. Aquarists cannot control the rate at which these substances appear any more than they can control foam composition. Only bubble size can be manipulated, and there are problems even with this.

The most critical factor affecting bubble size is the pressure drop across the air diffuser.[22] Pressure drop is a function of air flow rate and pore size of the diffuser. The first bubbles will emerge from the largest pores because less work is required than to force bubbles through small pores. Smaller bubbles appear as the pressure increases. Other factors affecting bubble size include such properties of the seawater as surface tension, viscosity, and density. In seawater that contains large amounts of surface-active material, the bubbles will be of smaller average size than in water with low concentrations of surfactants, because of the effect of surfactant concentration on the surface tension around bubbles. Smaller bubbles also are produced when either the viscosity or the density of the water increases.

Small bubbles have greater surface areas on which to adsorb surfactants than large bubbles. In addition, small bubbles are influenced to a greater extent by fluid friction and rise more slowly. This increases their contact time with water in the column. Reducing the bubble diameter increases the efficiency of surfactant adsorption, unless the bubbles become too small to break the surface tension at the air-water interface. Foam cannot be produced unless the surface of the water is broken.

Bubble diameter is a difficult factor to gauge because the controlling processes are dynamic. The physical characteristics of rising bubbles change continuously from the moment they enter a contact column until they break the surface. Furthermore, uniform bubbles seldom are emitted in sequence from the same pore of an air diffuser. Often a stationary bubble is formed at a pore and remains attached there. New air enters and forces its way through the top of the original bubble. These secondary bubbles are smaller. If the pressure is increased, the stationary bubble is released and a new one forms. As any bubble rises it expands as a result of the drop in hydrostatic pressure. Moreover, few bubbles remain spherical as they rise. Many become pear-shaped or elliptical from colliding with other bubbles or the walls of the contact column.

Bubbles sometimes join together between the release point and the surface of the water, especially when released in close proximity. Small bubbles gather gravitational energy as they coalesce, often gaining enough during ascent to break the surface.[23] Small bubbles tend to coalesce for the following reason.[23] If two bubbles of radius r meet and form a single bubble of radius R, the surface energy of the two separate bubbles will be $2\gamma \times 4\pi r^2$, where $\gamma = 8 \times 10^{-4}$ N/cm in pure water.* The surface energy of the single bubble will be $\gamma 4\pi R^2$. Total volume,

*N represents newtons.

however, remains unchanged. Therefore

$$2 \times \tfrac{4}{3}\pi r^3 = \tfrac{4}{3}\pi R^3 \tag{3.7}$$

and

$$R = r \times 2^{1/3} \tag{3.8}$$

The surface energy of the large bubble will be $\gamma \times \pi r^2 \times 2^{2/3}$, or less than the surface energy of the two small bubbles.

Temperature Control[24]

The same equations can be used for calculating the amount of cooling or heating needed in an aquarium. When calculating refrigeration requirements the factor determined is the capacity of the chilling unit in horsepower, hp. In heated aquariums wattage, W, of the heater is determined. In either case, heat flow in or out of the aquarium is computed on the basis of overall heat transfer coefficients. The heat transfer coefficients, U, of some common construction materials, in addition to the value of U at the water surface, are given in Table 3-13 in the Technology section. Heat flow is calculated by multiplying each heat transfer area, A, in cm^2 by its respective overall heat transfer coefficient and summing the terms. This value is then multiplied by the overall temperature difference, ΔT. Heat flow, Q, in cal/s is given by

$$Q = (A_1U_1 + A_2U_2 + \ldots)\,\Delta T \tag{3.9}$$

Convert to Btu/h by multiplying the result by 14.3. Dividing by 12,000 converts the answer to tons of refrigeration, which is a close approximation of horsepower requirements. In the case of a heated aquarium, the heat flow in Btu/h is multiplied by 3.41 to obtain the continuous wattage needed to maintain the desired temperature.

The essential features of a vapor compression refrigeration cycle are shown diagrammatically in Figure 3-32. A typical refrigeration unit consists of a high pressure side and a low pressure side. A compressor driven by an electric motor cycles a refrigerant (usually freon, CCl_2F_2) throughout the system. The refrigerant changes states from liquid to gas and back again under varying pressure. In doing so, heat is removed from aquarium water at the evaporator and dissipated into the room at the condenser.

A typical vapor compression refrigeration cycle will now be traced starting at the point between the high and low pressure

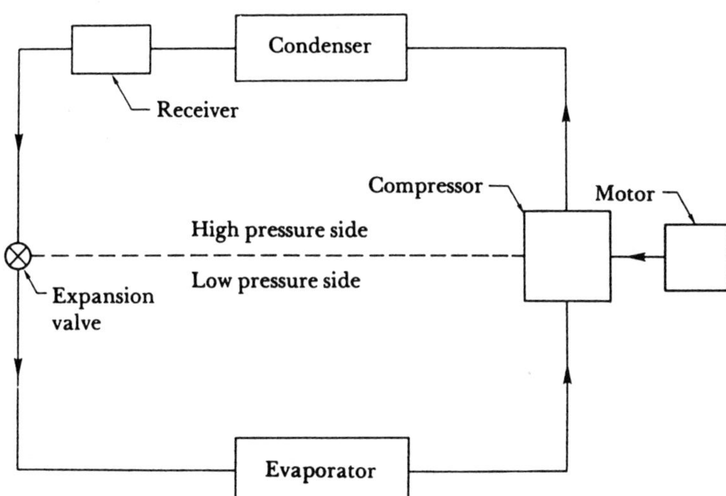

Figure 3-32 *Equipment diagram of a basic vapor compression refrigeration cycle.* Source: Spotte (1979b).

sides of the system. As liquid refrigerant leaves the expansion valve and enters the evaporator coils immersed in the water some of it changes instantly into gas because of the reduced pressure. In the process it removes heat from the remaining liquid refrigerant. The liquid (now cold) absorbs heat from the aquarium water circulating past the evaporator coils. As the cold liquid refrigerant gains heat it changes to a cold gas.

The cold gas refrigerant flows from the evaporator coils to the compressor and enters the high pressure side of the system. At the compressor it is compressed to a high pressure and temperature. The temperature of the gas in the refrigeration system is now higher than the temperature of the room air. Hot gas leaves the compressor and enters the condenser, where its heat is absorbed by the cooler air of the room. As heat is lost the gas condenses to a hot liquid and passes to the receiver. The receiver stores the hot liquid refrigerant until it can be cycled through the expansion valve and metered again into the evaporator coils to continue the cycle.

TECHNOLOGY

Method 3.1 Concrete Tanks[25]

Vacuum filters should be designed with walls to withstand hydrostatic pressure in two directions. They must also be watertight. Minimum wall thickness should be 22.5 to 30.5 cm. The design of concrete vacuum filters, concrete tanks, and holding tanks cannot be left entirely to contractors, architects, or engineers inexperienced in such matters. Mistakes in design and construction that result in leaks or deterioration of the concrete from exposure to seawater can be avoided if the following recommendations are followed.

1 If possible, do not use plastic water stops between pours of concrete. Such joints encourage leaks as time passes, rather than preventing them.
2 Concrete units should never be constructed as an integral part of a load-bearing wall. Shifting of the building will cause stress cracks.
3 There should be a minimum number of concrete pours during construction, and the material must be vibrated to assure uniform density. With careful preparation it is sometimes possible to form all walls in a single pour.
4 Use only high density, salt-resistant concrete and work it to a steel-troweled finish. Pockmarks in untroweled concrete are difficult to fill with paint and other surface protection systems. Broom finishes are rough, collect dirt, and not recommended.
5 If PVC pipe is used, it must be rough-sanded where it is expected to bond with concrete. Even then, leaks often form around a pipe inserted through a new concrete wall unless the area around the pipe on each side of the wall is chipped out and filled with Bondex®* or equivalent.

Method 3.2 Preparation of Concrete Surfaces for Painting[26]

The concrete of a filter housing, aquarium, or aeration tank must be protected from seawater, rather than the other way around. The small additions of inorganic ions to the seawater from leaching concrete are minor problems compared with the damage seawater can inflict on new concrete surfaces. The application of three coats of high-quality epoxy paint (one prime and two finish) ordinarily is adequate protection. But unless the concrete has been properly aged and prepared, only superficial bonding will take place.

How to Prepare Concrete for Painting

1 Allow new concrete to age for a minimum of 30 d.
2 Before painting, wash all surfaces with a dilute solution of trisodium phosphate or Taskmaster®** #1 diluted to a ratio

*Bondex International, Inc., Brunswick OH 44121.

**Detroit Graphite, 200 Sayre Street, Rockford IL 61101.

of 6. Afterward, acid-etch all surfaces with dilute muriatic acid or Taskmaster®* #4 diluted to a ratio of 3. Rinse with tap water.

3 When the concrete has dried, test for moisture with a moisture detector. Do not apply the surface protection system until the concrete has dried completely.

4 If epoxy paint is used, touch up all exposed metal surfaces with one coat of zinc-rich epoxy primer.

5 Apply one coat of clear epoxy primer to all concrete surfaces by airless spray; overlap onto metal or PVC surfaces if necessary. There is no reason to mask them.

6 Apply the first coat of finish epoxy paint, mixed and aged according to the manufacturer's specifications. Apply by airless spray. Rolling or brushing is not recommended. Epoxy is viscous and adheres easily to brushes or rollers, which makes filling pockmarks on vertical surfaces difficult. It is imperative that all pockmarks be filled, no matter how small. Dry thickness of the first finish coat must be 2.5 mil.**

7 After 6 h but before 24 h apply the second finish coat of epoxy. Use airless spray and apply to a dry film thickness of 2.5 mil.

8 All finish coats, unless decorative, should be high gloss for easier cleaning. Never use epoxy paints when the air temperature is below 18°C.

Method 3.3 Steel Filter Vessels[27]

Pressure vessels made of fiberglass-reinforced plastic are preferred. The conventional steel pressure vessels used in wastewater applications are unsuited for filtering seawater without modification. This entails (*1*) proper surface coating of any metal in contact with seawater, and (*2*) cathodic protection of the metal. Either measure alone is inadequate to quell the corrosive action of seawater. The way in which cathodic protection works is illustrated diagrammatically in Figure 3-33. As shown, the use of a sacrificial metal reduces corrosion of the underlying surface metal. The use of sacrificial zinc blocks in steel filter vessels protects the steel from seawater corrosion by the same mechanism. To minimize corrosion the following steps should be taken at the factory.

*Detroit Graphite, 200 Sayre Street, Rockford IL 61101.

**1 mil = 2.54×10^{-5} m.

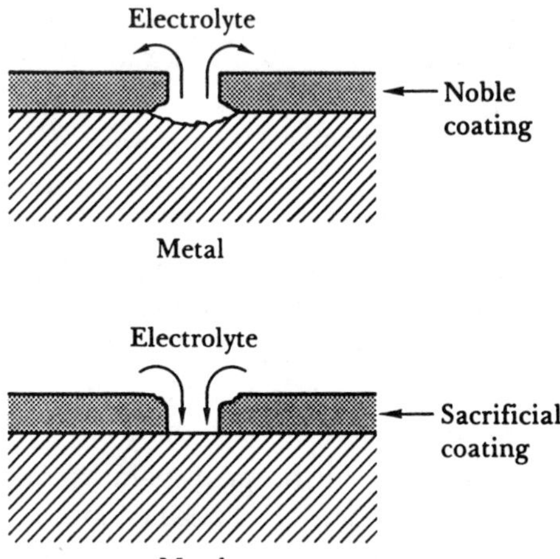

Figure 3-33 *Protection of steel by sacrificial coatings.* Source: Uhlig (1971).

How to Protect Steel Pressure Vessels from Galvanic Corrosion

1. Sandblast all interior vessel surfaces to near-white metal (Steel Structures Painting Council SP-10-63, or National Association of Corrosion Engineers No. 2 specification).
2. Apply one primer coat of coal tar epoxy to a dry film thickness of 8 mil. Use Carboline* Carbomastic® No. 3 or equivalent according to the manufacturer's specifications.
3. Apply a top coat of coal tar epoxy to a dry film thickness of 8 mil (16 mil total). Use Carboline Carbomastic® No. 12 or equivalent.
4. Test the fully cured coating with a holiday detector suitable for locating pinholes and voids in thin film coatings. The Tinker and Rasor Model M1/AC Holiday Detector** is acceptable. Repair any coating faults with coal tar epoxy (Carbomastic® No. 12 or equivalent) and retest after curing.
5. Install a ring of zinc ribbon around the inside circumference of the filter vessel (Fig. 3-34). One ring should be near the bottom and the other near the top. In addition, there should be four vertical strips of zinc ribbon spaced evenly apart and spanning the distance between the top and bottom rings. The material is installed by exposing ~7.6 cm of the steel core wire and spot-welding it to the walls of the vessel. Use ASARCO Diamond Line® Zinc Anode Ribbon† (0.09 kg/cm) or equivalent.

* Carboline, 350 Hanley Industrial Court, St. Louis MO 63144.

** Tinker and Rasor, 417 Agostino Road, San Gabriel CA 91778.

† ASARCO, Totowa NJ 07511.

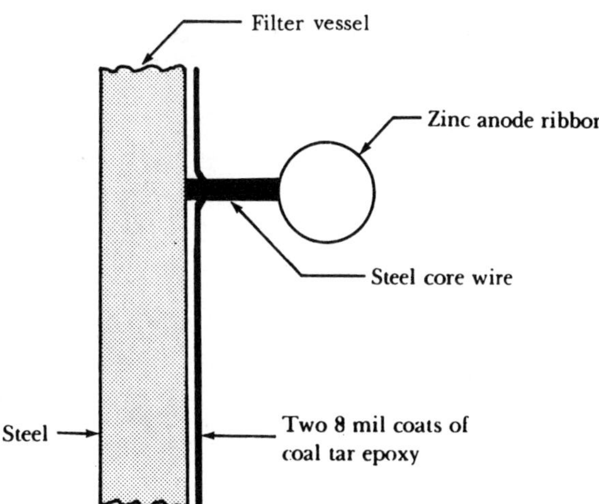

Figure 3-34 Installation of zinc anode ribbon for cathodic protection of steel pressure vessels. Source: Stephen Spotte.

6 Coat the exposed weld areas of the steel core wire at the ribbon connections with two coats of coal tar epoxy (Carbomastic® No. 12 or equivalent). *Do not coat the zinc.*

7 Sandblast and coat each manhole cover and install a length of zinc ribbon on the seawater side.

8 Inspect the ribbons and coal tar epoxy coating every 6 months.

All flanges, suction diffusers, blowoff nipples, and so forth must be nonmetallic or austenitic, low-carbon stainless steel (e.g., 304L or 316L). If only steel parts and fittings can be obtained they must be coated with coal tar epoxy.

Steel filter vessels should be placed on concrete pads at least 20 cm thick to prevent spilled seawater from corroding the legs. Some manufacturers recommend that the interior bottom sections of the vessels (the part below the underdrain assembly) be filled with concrete to eliminate anoxic conditions in the bottom layers of support gravel. This is a bad procedure, particularly if seawater is involved. The section of the vessel covered by concrete is inaccessible for maintenance. Anoxic areas are far less serious than the corrosion that occurs on the walls adjacent to the concrete. Only support media (gravel or cobbles) should be used in the bottoms of filter vessels.

Many conventional steel pressure vessels provide a small manhole at the top as the only means of entry. This makes changing the filter media or zinc ribbons difficult and prolongs the time a filter is down for servicing. Steel pressure vessels can be modified to alleviate this shortcoming (Fig. 3-35). A circular opening 91.5 cm in diameter is cut into the side of each filter

Figure 3-35 *Hatch installed in the side of a conventional steel pressure filter for easy removal of filtrants and support media.* Source: Spotte (1979b).

vessel (183 cm diameter). Afterward, a hatch made of boiler plate 0.64 cm thick is welded over each hole. Steel faceplates of 1.9-cm boiler plate with 0.64-cm rubber gaskets are bolted over the hatches. The parts of the hatch and faceplate have a section of 0.64-cm-thick boiler plate welded to them at a right angle, each with a hole drilled in the center to hold a chainfall hook. The faceplate itself is held in place against the hatch with 24 high-tension, 1.27-cm steel bolts. When a filter vessel must be serviced it is drained, the faceplate is unbolted and lifted out of the way with a chainfall, and the filtrant is shoveled quickly through the opening. Afterward, the coal tar epoxy coating is checked, zinc ribbons are replaced and coated at the weld sites with coal tar epoxy, and the unit is refilled with new filter media. Downtime is short. The hatch and face plate assemblies can be made to specifications at a local machine shop.

Method 3.4 Process Design for High Rate Filters

Preliminary planning for design of systems used in onshore filtration involves four decisions, the first being whether to use dual or multimedia (rapid sand filtration is not a viable alternative). Experimental work shows that effluent quality is comparable,[28] and I therefore recommend dual media. In addition, the high price of crushed, graded garnet or ilmenite required in multimedia filtration adds to the initial cost. Multimedia design information is included here for those who reject these arguments. Second, a decision must be made about whether to use pressure or vacuum units. Pressure units require less floor space but often more maintenance, especially if made of steel. Vacuum units ordinarily are made of concrete and need little maintenance. Third, surface wash is an important factor if backwash effectiveness is otherwise limited (i.e., if the seawater supply contains consistently high concentrations of POC). Surface wash is unnecessary if the incoming water has been prefiltered offshore. The fourth decision involves selection of the underdrain system.

FILTRANT SELECTION AND DEPTH[29] Total filter bed depth for high rate filters should be 76 cm for relatively clean seawater supplies and 91 cm if the influent is consistently turbid. The depth of each layer of filtrant is provided in Table 3-5. Deeper beds are unnecessary. Filtrants are selected in part by grain size and uniformity of grain size. *Effective size*, d_e, is the grain diameter in millimetres at which 10% of the grains by weight are smaller. The 10% factor corresponds closely to the median size by actual count of grains in a random sample.[30] The limits of effective size are defined by a *uniformity coefficient*, *uc*, which is the ratio of grain diameter, *d*, containing 60% material finer than itself (by grain count) to the size with 10% finer than itself (effective size), or d_{60}/d_{10}. This ratio covers the size range of one-half the grains of a single type of filtrant. Typical effective size and uniformity coefficient values for graded anthracites are given in Table 3-6.

Filtrants when in the filtration mode are kept in place by gravity, and only their grain sizes and uniformity coefficients matter. These factors are unimportant during fluidization. What matters instead are the settling velocities, representative sizes, and specific gravities of the different filtrants. The *settling velocity* of a filtrant grain is the rate at which it sinks in still water. *Representative size* is defined by $d_e \times uc$, which corresponds to 60% size by weight, or simply *60% size*. Anthracite has a specific gravity of ~1.6 and is the least dense. Garnet and ilmenite, with values of ~4.2, are densest. Sand is intermediate, averaging ~2.65. The settling velocities of all filtrants must be identical for a filter bed to fluidize properly, and this results in the large disparity in grain size. Thus anthracite must be larger than

TABLE 3-5 Depth of filter media in high rate filters for waters of varying turbidity; FTUs = formazin turbidity units.

	Dual media		Multimedia	
Filter media	76-cm bed[3] (<10 FTUs)	91-cm bed[1] (>10 FTUs)	76-cm bed[4] (<10 FTUs)	91-cm bed[2] (>10 FTUs)
Anthracite	51	64	45	61
Sand	25	27	23	22
Garnet	—	—	8	8

Sources: Culp (1977),[1] Culp and Culp (1974),[2] unknown,[3] Culp et al. (1978).[4]

TABLE 3-6 Effective size, d_e, and uniformity coefficient, uc, of crushed, graded anthracite. Units are millimetres.

d_e[1]	uc[1]	d_e[2]	uc[2]
0.60–0.69	1.7	0.60–0.80	< 1.7
0.60–0.79	1.7	0.60–0.80	1.6
0.70–0.79	1.7	0.85–0.95	1.7
0.80–0.89	1.7	0.80–1.00	1.6
0.80–0.89	1.5	0.80–1.00	1.5
0.90–0.99	1.7	1.00–1.20	1.5
0.90–0.99	1.5	1.00–1.20	1.4
1.00–1.10	1.7	1.20–1.40	1.5
1.00–1.10	1.5	1.40–1.60	1.5
1.20–1.50	1.7	1.60–1.80	1.5

Sources: Reading Anthracite Coal Company, 200 Mahantongo Street, Pottsville PA 17901;[1] Unifilt Corporation, P.O. Box 97, Zelienople PA 16063.[2]

sand, and sand must be larger than both garnet and ilmenite. Ignoring these factors results in (*1*) inadequate backwash, which leaves filters dirty (i.e., headloss is not decreased appreciably); (*2*) excessive intermixing of filtrants during backwash; and (*3*) loss of filtrants with the wash water during backwash. The first two rules in Table 3-7 describe how high rate filter media should be selected.

How to Size Media for High Rate Filters

1 Neither garnet or ilmenite is used in dual media filters, the subject of this example. Therefore, start with the sand. Obtain d_e and uc.

2 Select a sand of small grain size and low uc (<1.6 mm). If d_e is stated as a range (e.g., 0.38 to 0.45 mm), determine the mean (0.42 mm in this case).

TABLE 3-7 Rules for selecting media for high rate filters on the basis of grain size.

Rule 1 The settling velocities of all media in a filter bed must be the same for the bed to fluidize properly.

Rule 2 To have equal settling velocities the ratios of grain size (60% size) for garnet (or ilmenite), sand, and anthracite must be 2/3/6.

Rule 3 Based on the first two rules the backwash rate (in metres per minute) for garnet or ilmenite is 1.5 times grain size in millimetres (60% size). For sand, backwash rate numerically equals 60% size. For anthracite, backwash rate is one-half 60% size.

Source: Spotte (1979b).

3 Multiply d_e (or mean of the stated range) by *uc* to obtain 60% size. In this example, 0.42 mm × 1.5 mm = 0.63 mm.

4 Select the anthracite next (Table 3-6). Choose one with a low *uc* (1.5 mm or less) and a 60% size twice that of the sand (in this case ~1.20 mm).

UNDERDRAINS AND SUPPORT MEDIA[31] Three commercially available underdrains are the Leopold filter bottom, Wheeler filter bottom, and pipe lateral. The first two can be used only in vacuum filters; the third is suited for use in either vacuum or pressure units. The Leopold filter bottom (Fig. 3-36) consists of fitted, high density polyethylene blocks measuring 91 × 30 × 28 cm and weighing 6.6 kg. The blocks are corrosion proof and durable. Precision molding allows them to be assembled quickly in modular fashion. Filtered seawater passes downward through orifices in the tops of the blocks. The orifices are spaced 5 cm on centers. The interior of a block consists of adjacent triangles, each forming a plenum. The outside triangles are collection sites for water from the top orifices. The common walls where the three triangles meet contain orifices to regulate water flow. Filtered water flows from the outside triangles into the center triangle, and from there to a common header that serves as a collection point for the entire filter. During backwash, the flow is reversed. Water is forced into the center triangle, then into the outside triangles, and finally

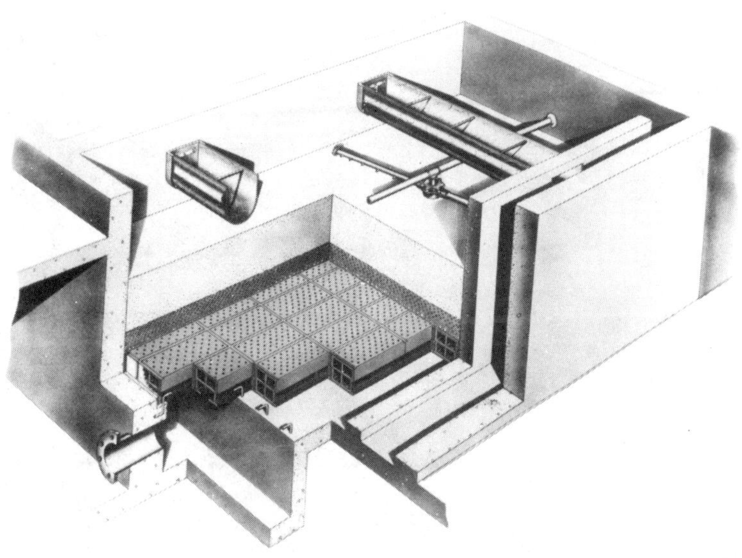

Figure 3-36 Leopold filter bottom. Source: The F. B. Leopold Co., Inc., 227 South Division Street, Zelienople PA 16063.

through the top orifices for upward distribution into the support media.

The Wheeler filter bottom (Fig. 3-37) consists of a series of pyramidal depressions on 30.5-cm centers. A porcelain thimble with an orifice opening of 1.9 cm is located at the bottom of each depression. Within each inverted pyramid are five porcelain spheres with diameters of 2.9 and 7.6 cm. The spheres are arranged to dissipate water from the orifice with minimum disturbance of the support media.

A pipe lateral underdrain is illustrated in Figure 3-38 and also Figures 3-1 and 3-2. Unlike Leopold and Wheeler bottoms, which actually cover the entire floors of vacuum filter units and form false bottoms, pipe laterals are buried in the last layer of support medium. The pipes must be PVC to resist the corrosive effects of seawater. Perforations in the pipes should be located on the undersides so that backwash water dissipates against the bottom of the filter unit to prevent upsetting the support media. Orifice diameters are 0.6 to 1.3 cm and spaced 7.6 to 20.3 cm apart. Design specifications are given in Table 3-8.

Uniformity of grain size is less important for support media than for the filtrants. Grain sizes ordinarily are expressed as screen size (either U.S. or Tyler), or as grain diameter in millimetres. Table 3-9 shows how these units of expression are related. Two numbers are required when either screen size con-

Figure 3-37 *Wheeler filter bottom.* Source: BIF, P.O. Box 217, West Warwick RI 02893.

Figure 3-38 Pipe lateral underdrain for a pressure filter. Source: Leem Filtration Products, Inc., 124 Christie Avenue, Mahwah NJ 07430.

vention is used. The first is the diameter of the screen opening on which the gravel is retained; the second is the size through which the gravel passes. Gravel of Tyler screen size 25 × 35 means that this material passes through a sieve with openings of ~0.7 mm but is retained on a second screen having openings of ~0.5 mm. Gravels larger than 4.7 mm cannot be expressed by U.S. or Tyler screen sizes. Grain sizes and depths of support media for each type of underdrain are given in Table 3-10.[32]

BACKWASH DESIGN FACTORS[33] The backwash rate must be strong enough to permit POC (which is less dense than any of the filtrants) to be carried away with the effluent, but not so powerful that filtrant grains are shifted substantial vertical distances. Some intermixing of filtrants in high rate filters is un-

TABLE 3-8 Guide for designing pipe lateral underdrain systems.

Ratio of orifice area to bed served = 150
Ratio of lateral area to area of orifices served = 2–4
Ratio of manifold area to area of laterals served = 1.5–3
Diameter of orifices = 0.6–1.9 cm
Spacing of orifices = 7.6–30.5 cm on centers
Spacing of laterals should be about the same as spacing of orifices

Source: Fair et al. (1971).

TABLE 3-9 Granular filtrants with grain size expressed three ways.

U.S. screen size	Tyler screen size	Grain diameter, mm
4	4	4.70
6	6	3.33
8	8	2.36
10	12	1.65
12	14	1.40
14	16	1.17
16	18	0.991
20	20	0.833
24	25	0.701
28	30	0.589
32	35	0.495
35	40	0.417
42	45	0.351
48	50	0.295
60	60	0.246
80	80	0.175
100	100	0.147
150	140	0.104

Source: Stephen Spotte, compiled from various sources.

TABLE 3-10 Grain size and depth of support media required for high rate filters using different underdrain systems.

Grain size, mm	Depth (top to bottom), cm
Leopold filter bottom	
3.2 × 6.4	12.6
6.4 × 12.7	5.0
12.7 × 19.0	5.0
Wheeler filter bottom	
4.8 × 9.5	15.2
9.5 × 15.9	7.6
15.9 × 25.4	7.6
25.4 × 31.8	To cover underdrain
Pipe lateral underdrain	
3.2 × 6.4	17.8
6.4 × 12.7	7.6
12.7 × 19.0	7.6
19.0 × 25.4	10 cm above wash-water outlet

Source: Spotte (1979b) after Culp et al. (1978).

avoidable. Headloss development and filtrate quality usually are not affected adversely, and the result is positive instead of negative. The tendency for intermixing is greatest at an interface (garnet-sand and sand-anthracite). This results in homogeneous zones in which the void fraction of the upper layer of filtrant is diminished but increased in the layer beneath. The void fraction of the intermixed zone has fixed bed hydraulic characteristics that are intermediate (Fig. 3-39). Thus the trend is in the desired direction of coarse-to-fine filtration. However, this is possible only because the filtrants differ substantially in specific gravity and 60% size.

Complete intermixing is undesirable because the bed is then homogeneous from top to bottom. The point at which complete intermixing occurs is described by the backwash rate (e.g., velocity of water flow) and bulk density of a cross section of the bed during fluidization. *Bulk density* is the combined densities of the backwash water and a filtrant at stated fluidization. Any filtrant is denser than water. Bulk density thus decreases with an increase in backwash rate because the void fraction of the bed becomes greater (i.e., the water/filtrant ratio increases), as shown in Figure 3-40.

High rate filters should be backwashed at a fixed rate between 0.5 and 0.85 m/min, ordinarily nearer 0.5 because the velocity is a function of filtrant grain size (see below). During backwash the bed is expanded 20 to 50%, which increases the fixed-bed void fraction from ~0.4 to between ~0.48 and ~0.6. The high backwash rates used in wastewater filtration (>0.85

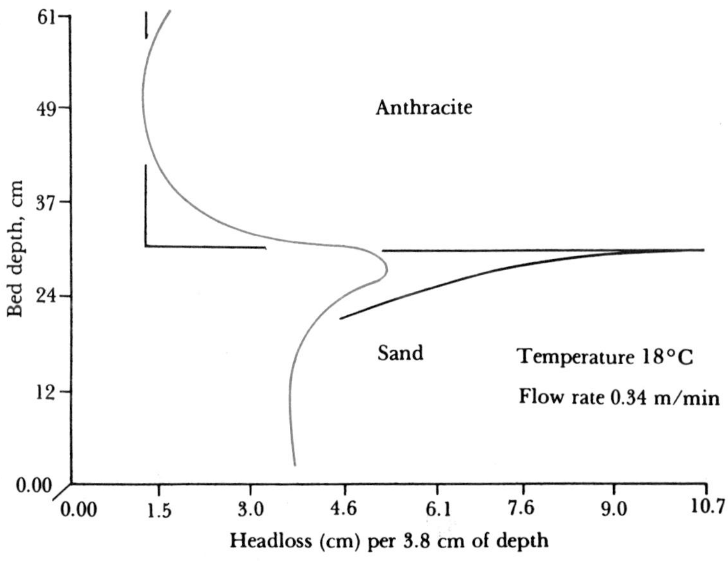

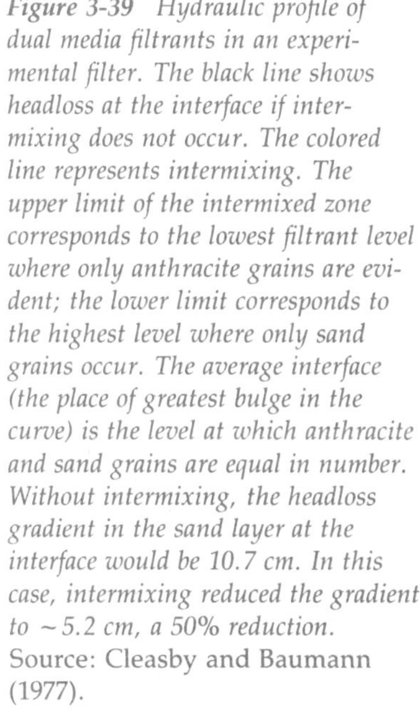

Figure 3-39 *Hydraulic profile of dual media filtrants in an experimental filter. The black line shows headloss at the interface if intermixing does not occur. The colored line represents intermixing. The upper limit of the intermixed zone corresponds to the lowest filtrant level where only anthracite grains are evident; the lower limit corresponds to the highest level where only sand grains occur. The average interface (the place of greatest bulge in the curve) is the level at which anthracite and sand grains are equal in number. Without intermixing, the headloss gradient in the sand layer at the interface would be 10.7 cm. In this case, intermixing reduced the gradient to ~5.2 cm, a 50% reduction.* Source: Cleasby and Baumann (1977).

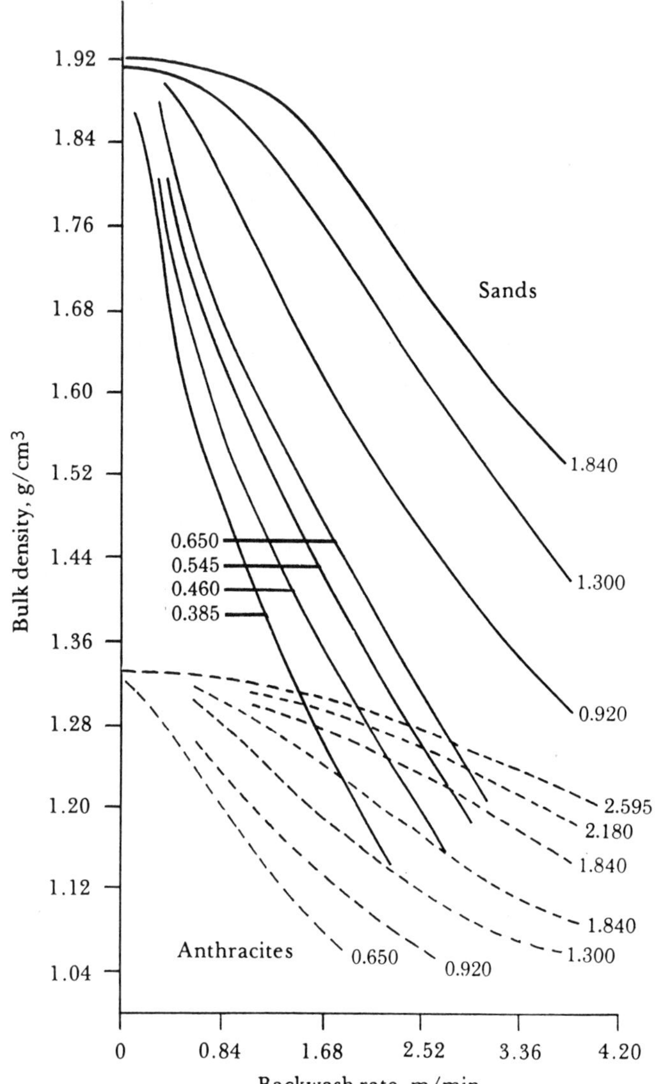

Figure 3-40 Bulk density versus backwash rate for several grades of anthracite and silica sands. The bulk density of every material decreases with increasing backwash rate. Complete intermixing of a particular anthracite-sand combination occurs when the bulk densities of the two materials are identical at the same backwash rate (i.e., where the curves intersect). Source: Stephen Spotte after Cleasby and Baumann (1977).

m/min) are unnecessary when processing seawater supplies. Even the dirtiest seawater is clean compared with wastewater. Design characteristics are therefore not comparable.

State and federal regulations often prohibit direct discharge of saline backwash water into sanitary sewers. The sudden influx of a large volume of saline water can disrupt biological processes in the filters of small sewage treatment plants. Regulatory authorities may require the backwash effluent to be emptied into a suitable tank made of steel or concrete, then metered slowly into the sewer system. The backwash tank must be large enough to hold the effluent volume from at least one backwash.

The transport of large amounts of garnet or anthracite to the surface of a filter bed is evidence that the backwash rate is too high. Rule 3 of Table 3-7 explains how to determine the backwash rate. Quite simply, it is the numerical equivalent (in metres per minute) of the 60% sand size, which in high rate filters is ~0.5 mm. If garnet (or ilmenite) and anthracite have not yet been sized, their 60% sizes can be estimated from Figure 3-41. Assume in this example that the 60% size of the sand is 0.5 mm. The backwash rate is therefore 0.5 m/min. The insert shows how to determine 60% sizes of garnet (or ilmenite) and anthracite based on a known value for sand. In this example they are ~0.3 and 1 mm.

Optimal backwash rate depends on water temperature because bed expansion varies inversely with viscosity of the back-

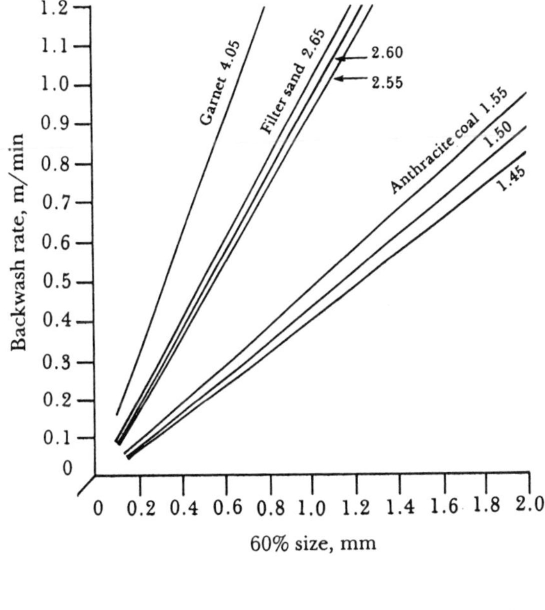

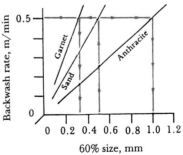

Figure 3-41 Backwash rate of rapid sand and high rate filters at 20°C. Numbers on the curves represent specific gravity. Source: Spotte (1979b) after Kawamura (1975a).

wash water. Tap water should be used to backwash filters that process temperate seawater supplies; otherwise, the temperature cannot be controlled. The calculated backwash rate must be altered slightly for temperatures other than 20°C. This is done by using Figure 3-42. For example, if the water temperature is 5°C the multiplier is 0.87, and the corrected backwash rate is 0.5 m/min × 0.87 = 0.44 m/min. If the temperature is 27°C the correction factor is 1.05, and the adjusted backwash rate becomes 0.53 m/min.

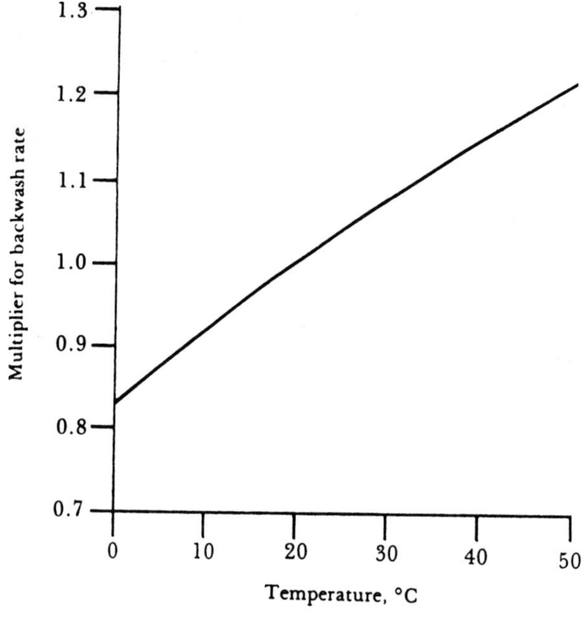

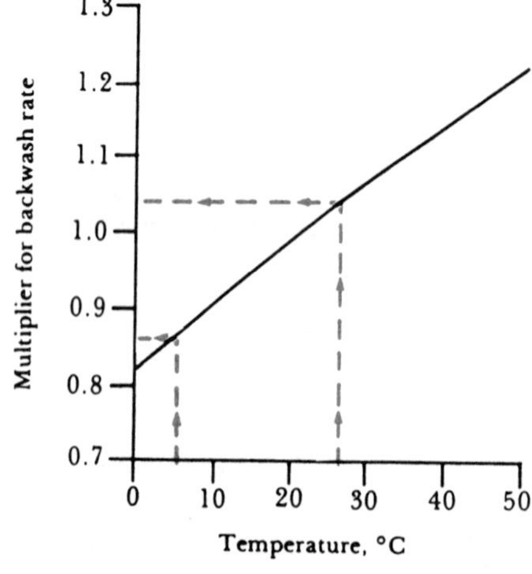

Figure 3-42 Backwash temperature correction factor. Source: Spotte (1979b) after Kawamura (1975b).

Method 3.5 Removal of Supersaturated Gases

PACKED COLUMN DEGASSING[34] Gases in excess of saturated values can be stripped from solution by *packed column degassing*. A somewhat misleading synonym is deaeration. Water in a continuous stream is injected at the top of a vertical column; the treated effluent is removed at the bottom (Fig. 3-43). The column is packed with spherical or cylindrical plastic objects (plastic packing) to increase the internal surface area (Fig. 3-44). As water cascades over the packing material its surface tension is broken, and excess gases are released. Packed columns are efficient and less expensive to operate than vacuum degassers because they require no mechanical pumping (see below). The most important design factors are (*1*) column packing height, (*2*) packing material size, (*3*) flow rate, and (*4*) ΔP of the seawater supply. Column packing height affects other factors (e.g., contact time, surface area of the packing material). In freshwaters the value of ΔP diminishes rapidly until a packed column height of ~120 cm (Fig. 3-45).[35] Specific design criteria are given in Table 3-11.

TURBULENT FLOW DEGASSING[36] Water can be degassed by turbulent flow in a depressurized vessel open to the atmosphere, but the process is less efficient than packed column or vacuum degassing (see below). I call this method *turbulent flow*

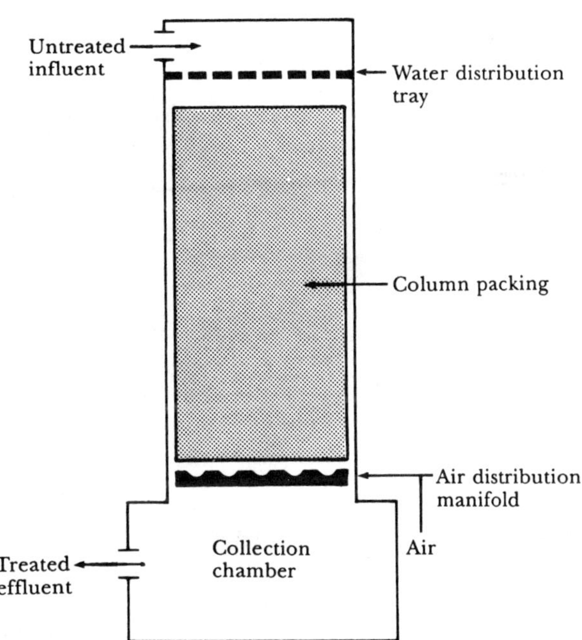

Figure 3-43 Packed column degasser. Source: Stephen Spotte.

(a)

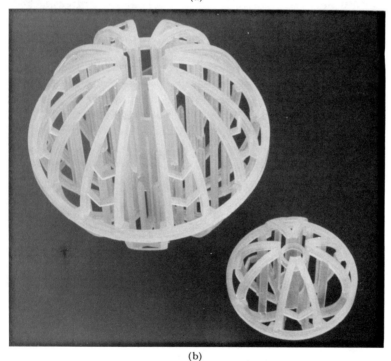

(b)

Figure 3-44 *Plastic packing of the type typically used in packed column degassers. Materials with diameters of 2.54 cm have proved effective.* (a) *Cylinders.* (b) *Spheres.* Sources: (a) Norton Chemical Process Products, P.O. Box 350, Akron OH 44309; (b) Jaeger Products, Inc., P.O. Box 1563, Spring TX 77383.

degassing. The degassers in Figure 3-46 are made of thin-walled PVC pipes 1.9 m long (0.304 m inside diameter) capped at the ends, with longitudinal saw cuts for exposing influent seawater to the air. The area of each saw cut is 0.304 m^2. The units depicted are mounted in raised wood frames 1.12 m above the

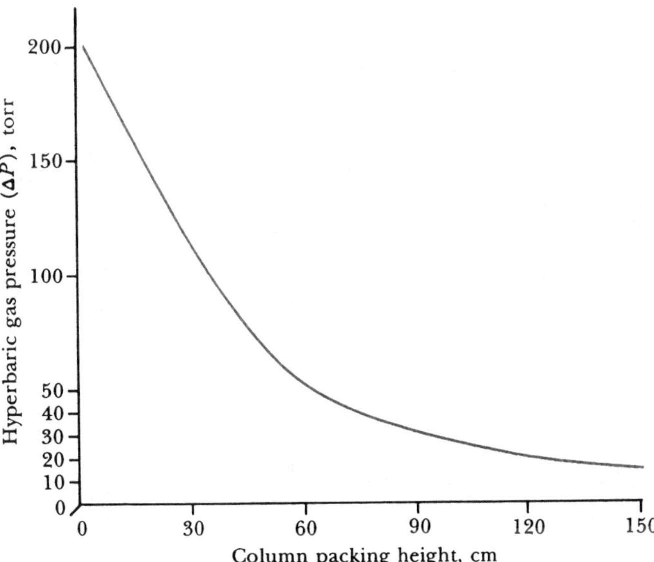

Figure 3-45 Effect of column packing height on degassing (data points omitted). Source: Bouck et al. (1984).

seawater tables of a marine laboratory; one degasser serves two tables. The stream of water entering a degasser is dispersed through a perforated pipe 1.12 m long (0.041-m inside diameter) to reduce impingement velocities. Supersaturated gases are brought rapidly to steady state, after which the water is discharged by surface overflow to the seawater tables below through vertical feed pipes 0.178 m long (0.0127-m inside diameter). The minimum velocity through the rapid-flow seawater supply system is 2.7 m/s.

VACUUM DEGASSING A *vacuum degasser* that has been tested with good results in freshwater is illustrated in Figure 3-47. Most of the column is filled with plastic packing. A diffuser made of a piece of capped pipe drilled with 3-mm holes is connected to the inlet. The vacuum is sustained by a rotating vane pump ($\frac{1}{6}$-hp) with a free air capacity of 37 L/min and minimum continuous operating pressure of 33 kPa* absolute (with

*kPa = kilo-pascals.

TABLE 3-11 Design criteria for a packed column degasser.

Packed column height	120 cm
Flow rate	1 L/(min·cm^2)
Plastic packing size	2.54 cm

Source: Stephen Spotte, compiled from information in Bouck et al. (1984).

Figure 3-46 *Turbulent flow degassers installed above the water tables in the University of Connecticut's marine laboratory at Noank.* Source: Caolo and Spotte (1990).

respect to a standard atmosphere of 101 kPa absolute). The vacuum level is maintained by manual positioning of a bleeder value open to the atmosphere. Because the unit is under vacuum, treated water must be pumped out. The pump has a power of 1.5 hp and is capable of providing 330 L/min at a head of 12.8 m. The water level in the column is maintained manually with the aid of a sight glass. The unit performs well in both cold (6.4 to 7.7°C) and warm (22 to 24.6°C) influent waters.

Method 3.6 Flow Rate Calculations for Airlift Pumps[37]

There still is no widely accepted equation for the design of airlift pumps. If the Német correlation[38] is adapted to airlifts used for pumping water, the result is

$$Q = (0.504\, s^{1.5} L^{0.33} - 0.0752) D^{2.5} \qquad (3.10)$$

where Q = the maximum flow rate of water when air flow is optimal (L/min), s = the submergence ratio, L = eduction pipe length (cm), and D = eduction pipe diameter (cm). Equation 3.11[39] is a more recent derivative:

$$Q = (0.758\, s^{1.5}\, L^{0.33} + 0.012)\, D^{2.2} \qquad (3.11)$$

Castro's data,[40] used by Lee C. Eagleton to derive equation 3.11, covered a range of diameters from 1.7 to 7.8 cm, lengths

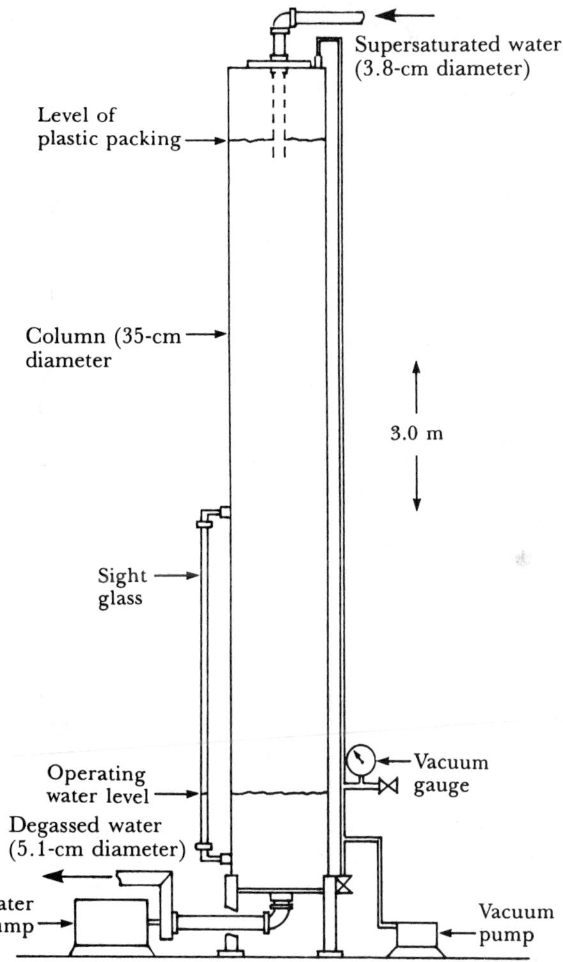

Figure 3-47 *Vacuum degasser designed for continuous operation. The column is filled with plastic packing (<4-cm diameter, void fraction = 0.9, specific surface area = 140 m^2/m^3, packing density = 13,772 pieces/m^3).* Source: Fuss (1983).

from 60 to 300 cm, and submergence ratios of 0.6 to 1.0. However, the minimum acceptable submergence ratio for the operation of aquarium airlifts is 0.8.[41] The Castro data were obtained for a range of variables of likely interest to aquarists, whereas Németˌ used data from many sources, including those describing oil flow from wells. As such, the Castro data and equation 3.11 are recommended. Table 3-12 gives the flow rate obtained (assuming that air flow rate is optimal) for a number of different airlift configurations using equation 3.11. Repeating the calculations presented in the tables using equation 3.10 shows that the Német correlation gives lower flow rates than found by Castro for eduction pipe diameters of 1 to 2 cm, and larger flow rates for pipes 6 to 8 cm in diameter. The equations give similar results for pipe diameters of 3 to 4 cm.

TABLE 3-12 Flow rate, Q, (L/min) for airlift pumps as a function of eduction pipe length, L, and diameter, D, using equation 3.11 at submergence ratios, s, of 0.8, 0.9, and 1.0.

		D, cm					
L, cm	s	1.0	2.0	3.0	4.0	6.0	8.0
30	0.8	1.7	7.7	18.7	35.3	86.1	162.1
	0.9	2.0	9.2	22.4	42.2	102.9	193.7
	1.0	2.4	10.9	26.5	50.0	122.0	230.0
50	0.8	2.0	9.1	22.2	41.9	102.2	192.4
	0.9	2.4	10.9	26.6	50.0	122.1	229.8
	1.0	2.8	12.9	31.4	59.2	144.0	272.0
75	0.8	2.3	10.4	25.5	48.0	117.0	220.4
	0.9	2.7	12.5	30.4	57.3	139.8	263.2
	1.0	3.2	14.7	36.0	67.7	165.0	311.0
100	0.8	2.5	11.5	28.1	52.8	128.9	242.7
	0.9	3.0	13.7	33.5	63.1	153.9	289.8
	1.0	3.5	16.2	39.6	74.5	182.0	342.0
150	0.8	2.9	13.2	32.1	60.5	147.6	277.9
	0.9	3.4	15.7	38.4	72.2	176.2	277.9
	1.0	4.0	18.6	45.3	85.3	208.0	331.9
200	0.8	3.2	14.5	35.4	66.6	162.5	306.0
	0.9	3.8	17.3	42.2	79.5	194.0	365.0
	1.0	4.4	20.4	49.8	93.8	299.0	431.0
300	0.8	3.6	16.6	40.5	76.3	186.1	350.4
	0.9	4.3	19.8	48.4	91.0	222.2	418.3
	1.0	5.1	23.4	57.0	107.4	262.0	493.0

Sources: Spotte (1979a, 1979b) after Lee C. Eagleton, Department of Chemical Engineering, Pennsylvania State University (personal communication 1978), and Gary Adams, Sea Research Foundation (personal communication 1978).

A safety factor of 25% is recommended when using equation 3.11 for airlift pump design.[42] In other words, values for submergence ratio, length, and diameter should be selected to give a calculated flow rate that is 25% larger than needed. This factor guards against problems related to obtaining the optimal flow rate and also provides a margin to cover minor restrictions to maximum flow, either at the bottom or the top of the pipe. A sample airlift design problem follows. It involves the use of Figure 3-48, a graph of dimensionless ratios depicting the volume of water that can be moved per volume of air at specified length/diameter ratios and submergence ratios. For example, if an airlift pump consists of an eduction pipe 90 cm long and 2.5 cm in diameter, the length/diameter ratio is 36. At a submergence ratio of 0.8 this yields a value of 0.5, or 1 L of water moved for every 2 L of air. The ratio becomes even more efficient at a submergence ratio of 0.9, with 0.75 L of water moved for every

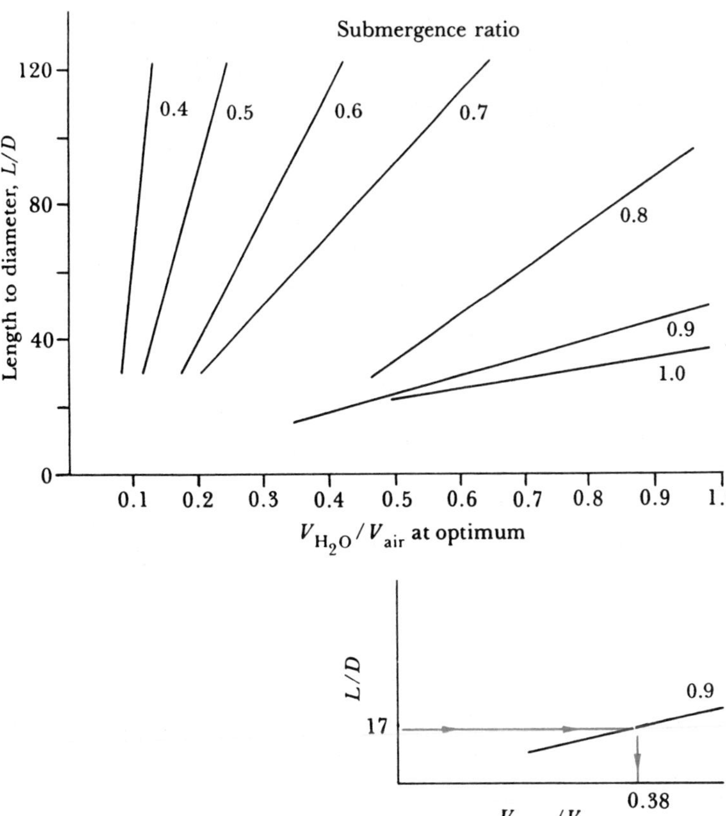

Figure 3-48 Dimensionless graph showing length/diameter ratios of eduction pipes versus water flow to air flow volume ratios when air flow is optimal. Sources: Spotte (1979a, 1979b), drawn from data in Castro et al. (1975).

1 L of air. Maximum efficiency is reached at the submergence ratio of 1.0 when the air is moving more water than its own volume. Ordinarily, less water is moved for the same amount of air as the length/diameter ratio diminishes. It appears as if the minimum acceptable ratio based on one set of data[43] would be approximately 20.

How to Calculate the Flow Rate of Airlift Pumps

1 The problem is to design an airlift pump for an aquarium 90 cm deep with a surface area of 3 m^2.

2 Determine the water flow rate following the rule that each m^2 of surface area requires 40 L/min of flow rate (equivalent to 0.7×10^{-3} m/s). Therefore

$$[3\ \text{m}^2][40\ \text{L}(\text{min}\cdot\text{m}^2)] = 120\ \text{L/min}$$

$$\text{plus } 25\% = 150\ \text{L/min}$$

3 Choose a submergence ratio (e.g., 0.9). From Table 3-12 find the eduction pipe diameter needed for the flow rate determined in the first step. Thus s = 0.9 and L = depth/submergence ratio = 900.9 = 100 cm, and D = 6 cm. Equation 3.11 can be solved for D (equation 3.12) and D can be calculated directly, but ordinarily this is not necessary:

$$D = \left[\frac{150}{0.758\ (0.9)^{1.5}(90)^{0.33} + 0.012}\right]^{0.45} = \sim 6 \text{ cm} \quad (3.12)$$

4 Calculate the length/diameter ratio (100/6 = 17). Using Figure 3-48, read the volume ratio (water/air) from the 0.9 submergence ratio line, as shown by the inset.

5 Because the volume of water, V_{H_2O}, equals 150 L, then V_{air} = 150/0.38 = ~400 L/min.

Method 3.7 Design and Operation of Foam Fractionators[44]

The design of effective foam fractionation devices is more art than science, mainly because the thermodynamics of the process are obscure.[45] From an engineering standpoint the important factors to consider are the air/water ratio, bubble diameter, liquid height, foam height, and contact time between air bubbles and water in the contact column.[20] Liquid height can be eliminated from consideration because the foam fractionation devices normally used in aquariums operate on the airlift principle. The liquid height in the contact column and in the aquarium are nearly the same. In such designs foam drains away by gravity. The return of the residue to the water is also by gravity. Foam height depends on the nature and concentration of the surfactants and on air flow rate. Proper foam height and the methods of controlling it will be discussed shortly.

Bubble size and air flow rate are the most important design factors because they control the two processes that are potentially rate limiting in foam fractionation: (*1*) transfer of surfactants from the dissolved to the adsorbed state (mass transfer), and (2) transport of adsorbed surfactants to the top of the contact column (solute throughput). *Solute throughput* is the amount of adsorbed surfactant transported per unit cross-sectional area of contact column per unit time. The rate of mass transfer depends on three factors: the diffusion coefficient of the solute molecule, the degree of turbulence in the liquid column, and the amount of surface per unit volume to which the surfactant molecules can move.[22] An ideal air/water ratio is obtained at a gas flow of 1.8 cm/(s·cm^2) of contact column cross sectional area; an ideal bubble size is 0.8 mm.[46]

As mentioned previously, small bubbles rise slowly in contact columns because of increased friction exerted on their surfaces by the water. Contact time can be increased by reducing the size of the bubbles. Another way is to design columns so that the bubbles must travel farther and be in contact with the water longer. One design technique is the *countercurrent* method in which the air and water move past each other in opposite directions. This increases friction and drag on the bubbles and reduces their rate of ascent. In the *cocurrent* or static method, water and bubbles rise together, as in an airlift pump. The two methods are illustrated in Figures 3-49 and 3-50.

In the cocurrent design (Fig. 3-49), air is injected through a diffuser (2). As the bubbles rise (*1*) they mix with the water. The surface-active fraction of DOC is adsorbed onto the bubble surfaces, producing a foam at the air-water interface (*3*). As foam accumulates it spills into a collection chamber (*5*). The col-

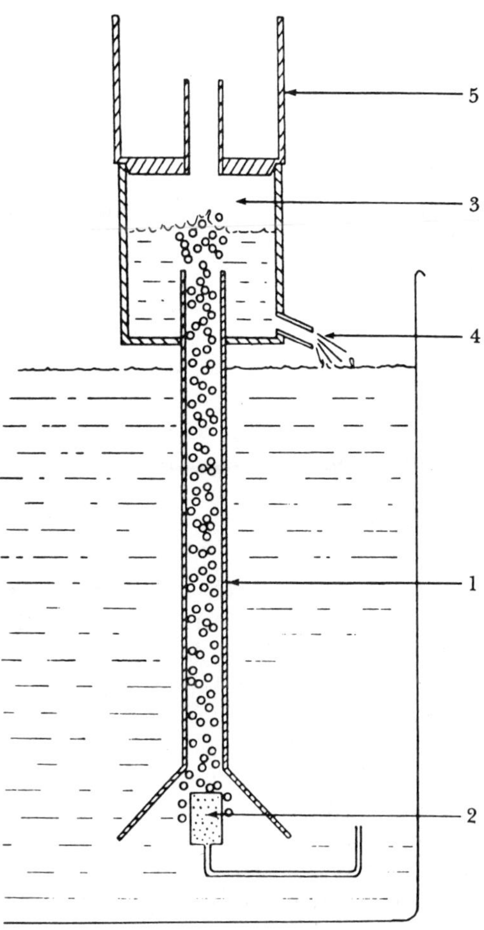

Figure 3-49 *Cocurrent foam fractionator. Numbers are explained in the text.* Sources: Spotte (1979a, 1979b) after Sander (1967).

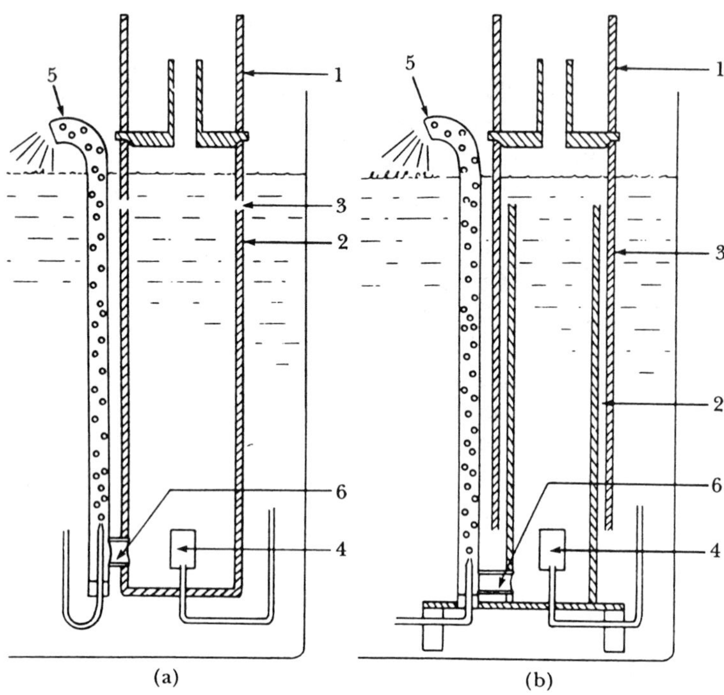

Figure 3-50 *Countercurrent foam fractionators. Numbers are explained in the text.* Sources: Spotte (1979a, 1979b) after Sander (1967).

lection chamber can be removed and cleaned. Treated water is returned to the aquarium at (*4*).

In the countercurrent design (Fig. 3-50), water moves downward against a stream of rising air bubbles. In Figure 3-50a, air moves through a diffuser (*4*) and into the contact column (*2*). Untreated water enters the column near the top (*3*). The top of the column also serves as a separation chamber, and excess foam passes into a collection chamber (*1*), which can be removed for cleaning. Unlike the cocurrent design, treated water is expelled beneath instead of above the surface. Water passes from a connecting tube (*6*) near the bottom of the column and is airlifted back to the aquarium (*5*). The mechanism is similar in Figure 3-50b except that the contact column (*2*) is fitted with a larger outside column (*3*) that forms a sheath. The advantage is that untreated water cannot be driven back to the aquarium by injected air, as it can be at (*3*) in Figure 3-50a. This makes the design of Figure 3-50b slightly more efficient.

Contact columns should be smooth inside, with no breaks or joints between the air injection point and the water surface.[47] As mentioned previously, the air diffuser should be of known average pore size; it should also be made of stainless steel or fritted glass. The diameter of the column should be large enough to allow the bubble stream to rise without touching the

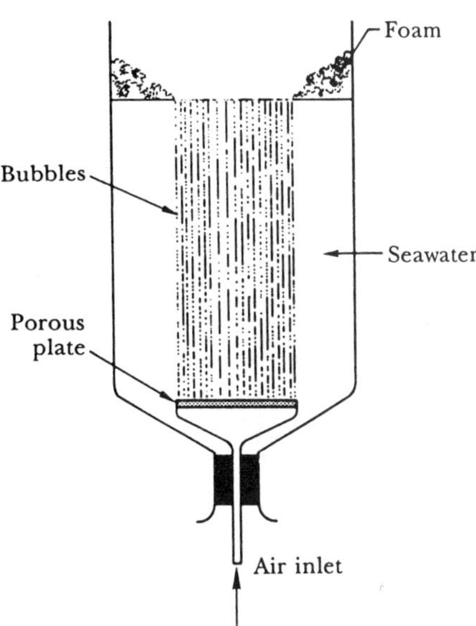

Figure 3-51 *Top of a properly designed contact column. The bubble stream rises without touching the walls.* Source: Spotte (1979b) after Sebba (1962).

walls (Fig. 3-51), which eliminates turbulence caused when bubbles reflect off the inside walls of the column.[48] This design also allows foam fractionation to take place at the center of a circle at the top of the contact column. The foam is forced to the edges where it can be collected and drained off.[49]

Foam height is controlled by the air flow rate. If the rate is in perfect adjustment there is no excessive turbulence, the foam does not collapse before it can be removed, and surfactants do not reenter the water with the residue. The air flow rate should be adjusted so that it barely exceeds the rate of foam collapse. If the rate is increased beyond this level, the removal rate of surfactants decreases rapidly.[50] Foam stability diminishes with decreasing surfactant concentration in the water, making it necessary to adjust the air flow rate upward.

Method 3.8 Calculation of Cooling and Heating Requirements[24]

Ordinarily, the evaporator coils in seawater aquarium applications are titanium, copper, or plastic (e.g., polypropylene). Copper coils must be coated to protect aquarium inhabitants from copper poisoning. Typical coatings are Teflon®, vinyl, polypropylene, neoprene, and epoxy. The evaporator coils can be placed in the water system wherever adequate circulation is available to augment heat exchange. A modern unit for cooling and heating aquarium seawater is shown in Figure 3-52.

(a)

(b)

Figure 3-52 *Titanium unit capable of heating or cooling seawater.* Source: Acry-Tec, 7352 Trade Street, San Diego CA 92121.

COOLING Heat transfer coefficients for some common materials are given in Table 3-13. Refrigeration requirements can be calculated by the following example. An aquarium made of concrete with double glass (two panes of glass separated by an air space or vacuum) is shown in Figure 3-53. It has an overall ΔT requirement of 11°C; that is, refrigeration temperature will be 11°C below ambient. The problem is to compute the horsepower needed to chill the water.

TABLE 3-13 Overall heat transfer coefficients, *U*, for common construction materials.

Material	U, cal(s·cm^2·°C)
Single plate glass	0.63×10^{-4}
Double glass with air space	0.34×10^{-4}
5-cm concrete	0.57×10^{-4}
15-cm concrete	0.47×10^{-4}
1-cm fiberglass-reinforced plastic	0.54×10^{-4}
1-cm fiberglass-reinforced plastic plus wet (soaked) 2-cm plywood	0.21×10^{-4}
2-cm dry epoxy coated plywood	0.48×10^{-4}
Water surface	0.65×10^{-4}

Source: Spotte (1979b).

Note: Values were derived empirically and represent surfaces with gently moving water on one side and gently moving air on the other, and are higher than natural convection coefficients.

According to the dimensions in the figure, heat transfer will occur at the places indicated in Table 3-14. The dimensions of each location, the material from which the aquarium is made, and values for U and AU are also given in Table 3-14. From

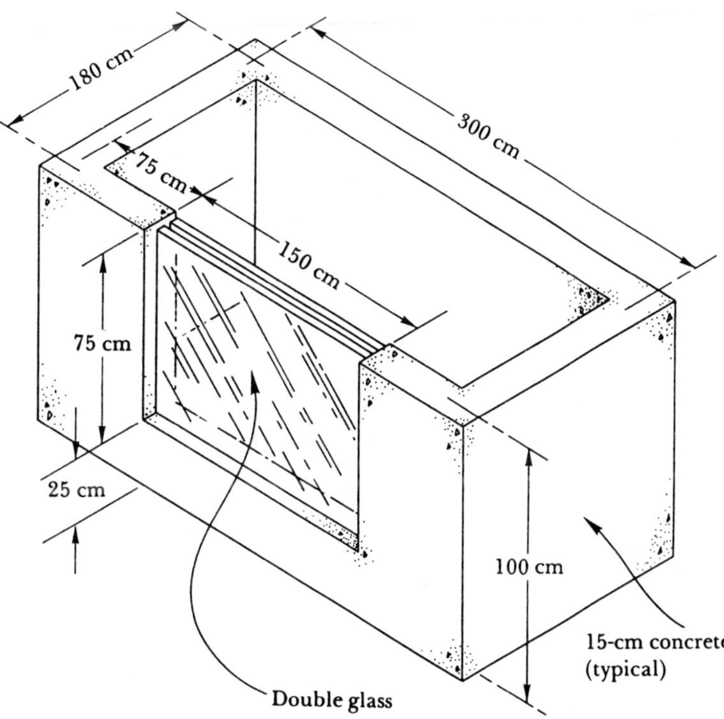

Figure 3-53 Aquarium made of concrete and containing double glass. See sample problems in text. Source: Spotte (1979b).

TABLE 3-14 Locations where heat transfer will take place in the aquarium illustrated in Fig. 3-53.

Location	Area, cm^2	Material	U, cal(s·cm^2·°C)	$A \times U$
Ends	3.60×10^4	15-cm concrete	0.45×10^{-4}	1.62
Back	3.00×10^4	15-cm concrete	0.45×10^{-4}	1.35
Front	1.88×10^4	15-cm concrete	0.45×10^{-4}	0.85
Bottom	5.40×10^4	15-cm concrete	0.45×10^{-4}	2.43
Glass	1.13×10^4	Double glass with airspace	0.34×10^{-4}	0.38
Water surface	4.70×10^4	—	0.65×10^{-4}	3.05

Source: Spotte (1979b).

equation 3.9 stated previously,

$$Q = (\Sigma AU)\ \Delta T = 9.69 \times 11$$
$$= 106.6 \text{ cal/s}$$

To use the equation if values for AU are not known,

$$Q = [3.6(0.45) + 3(0.45) + 1.9(0.45) + 5.4(0.45) + 4.7(0.65) + 1.13(0.34)]\ 11$$
$$= 106.6 \text{ cal/s}$$

To convert to Btu/h,

$$106.6 \text{ cal/s} \left(\frac{1 \text{ kg/cal}}{1000 \text{ cal}}\right)\left(\frac{3.97 \text{ Btu}}{1 \text{ kg/cal}}\right)\left(\frac{3600 \text{ s}}{1 \text{ h}}\right)$$
$$= 1523.5 \text{ Btu/h}$$

and

$$\text{hp} = 1523.5 \text{ Btu/h} \left(\frac{1 \text{ hp}}{12{,}000 \text{ Btu/h}}\right)$$
$$= 0.13$$

HEATING The subject here is limited to heating seawater with immersion heaters (Fig. 3-54). The immersible portion of a unit can be made of any material that has reasonable heat transfer properties and is inert in seawater. Common materials are quartz, impervious carbon, Teflon®, and the metals titanium

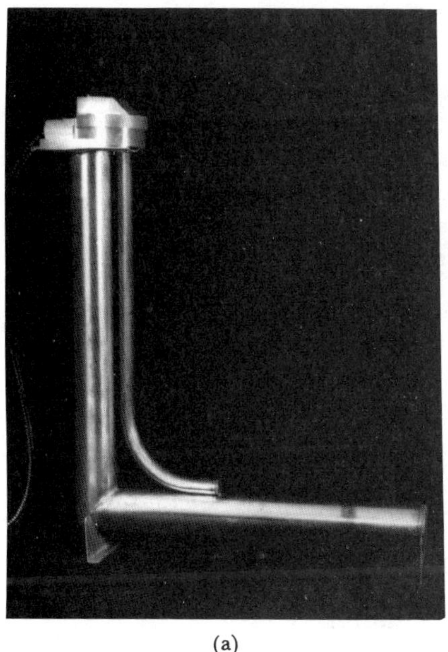

(a)

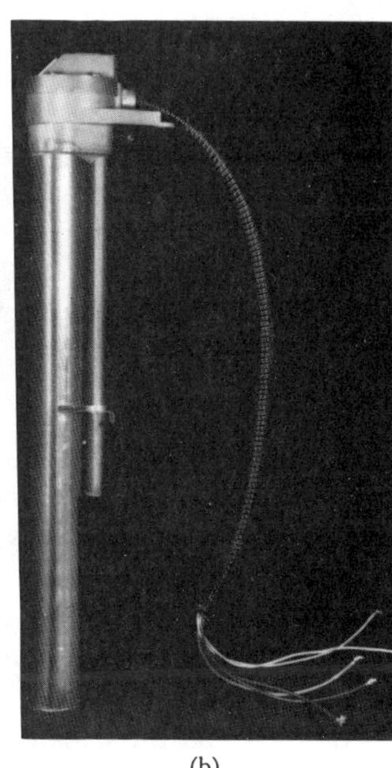

(b)

Figure 3-54 *Immersion heaters in two shapes made of titanium for use in seawater. The units are manufactured in sizes up to 6000 W and can be assembled in triplicate.* (a) *L-type.* (b) *Bayonet.* Source: Argent Chemical Laboratories, 8702 152nd Avenue NE, Redmond WA 98052.

and 316L stainless steel. Immersion heaters must be grounded properly or they are potential safety hazards, particularly the larger units requiring more than 120 V for normal operation. In addition, no immersion heater should be operated without a thermostat to control temperature.

Among the best designed and most reliable immersion heaters are those manufactured for the chemical industry. Many of the models available are sturdy, safe, and reliable units that work well in seawater. Some units are available in sizes up to 36,000 W (480 V) in stainless steel or titanium; smaller quartz heaters are also available.

If the aquarium described in the previous example is to be heated and maintained at 4°C above ambient, the wattage requirement can be found from equation 3.9:

$$Q = [3.6(0.45) + 3(0.45) + 1.9(0.45) + 5.4(0.45) + 4.7(0.65) + 1.13(0.34)]4$$

$$= 38.8 \text{ cal/s}$$

$$38.8 \text{ cal/s} \left(\frac{14.3 \text{ Btu}}{1 \text{ cal/s}}\right) = 555 \text{ Btu/h heat flow}$$

$$555 \text{ Btu/h} \left(\frac{1 \text{ W}}{3.41 \text{ Btu/h}}\right) = 163 \text{ W}$$

Method 3.9 Cleaning Old Painted Surfaces

Epoxy paints become stained and discolored after prolonged immersion in seawater. New paint cannot be applied until the surface has been cleaned. The solution described below removes stains instantly with no scrubbing required.

How to Mix the Cleaning Solution

1. Dissolve 98 g of ferrous ammonium sulfate, $Fe(NH_4)_2 \cdot 6H_2O$, in 1 L of tap water. The water should be at room temperature.
2. Add 200 mL of concentrated (93 to 98%) sulfuric acid, H_2SO_4. The resulting reaction generates heat; therefore, add acid to water and not the other way around.
3. Dilute to 10 L with tap water. The surface area covered is 40 m^2/L of cleaning solution.

How to Apply the Cleaning Solution

1. Apply the solution directly to the old painted surface with a large, long-handled brush. Wear rubber gloves and safety goggles. Use only in areas with adequate ventilation. If the solution comes in contact with skin or eyes, flush thoroughly with cold tap water.
2. Rinse the old surfaces immediately with liberal amounts of tap water. No additional preparation is required. Allow the surface to dry completely and apply the new paint.

C H A P T E R

4 Physiology

Nothing is more critical to the successful keeping of fishes than understanding their physiology. In comparison, everything else is superfluous, mere trappings. All aquarium procedures should have one ultimate purpose: to assist in maintaining captive fishes in a normal physiological state. The principles of physiology are difficult. Most aquarists ignore them, preferring to concentrate on technology in the vague hope that better equipment will somehow compensate. This is wishful thinking. Applications of technology properly come *after* the needs of the organism have been identified; they are never a substitute. For example, which design is more important, that of a fish gill or an air diffuser? If every known factor affecting gas exchange across the gills is not controlled to the fish's advantage, replacing old air diffusers with more efficient models is pointless. Similarly, knowing how to process seawater is of limited value if factors that impinge on the capacity of captive fishes to assimilate and excrete inorganic ions and maintain internal acid-base status are disregarded. In my opinion, all other aspects of fish keeping—monitoring the environment, providing adequate nutrition, and controlling diseases—are like the gropings of blind men describing an elephant. Not to appreciate physiology is to withhold the elephant.

The purpose of this chapter is to show the elephant's silhouette by painting its salient features. Many excellent reviews are available on the subject of fish physiology. My purpose is not to compete with them, but rather to provide an overview of those aspects that pertain directly to keeping seawater fishes in captivity: the nature of the gill, osmotic and ionic regulation, respiration and acid-base regulation, and stress. A Technology section is not included. Suitable practices in aquarium management are those that minimize stress.

The Gill

The basic structure of a *teleost* (advanced bony fish) gill is illustrated in Figure 4-1.[1] Prominant features are the *gill arches* made

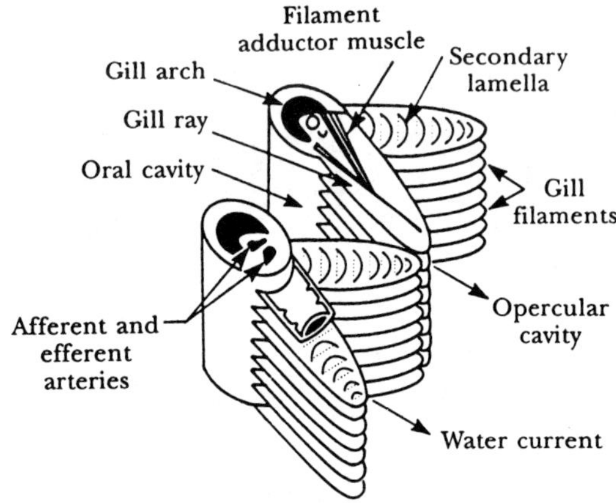

Figure 4-1 *Diagrammatic structure of a teleost gill. Arrows indicate direction of water flow.* Source: Hughes (1961).

of resilient, flexible cartilage. Most teleosts have eight, four on a side. Each gill is traversed internally by blood vessels and supports a pair of *gill filaments*. Gases and inorganic ions are exchanged between the blood and external environment through *secondary lamellae,* which branch laterally from the gill filaments. The delicate surfaces of the secondary lamellae are protected from particulate matter by *gill rakers*.[2]

A fish *ventilates* its gills or "breathes" in the following manner (Fig. 4-2). First the *opercula* (bony gill covers) shut in unison against the body. The gill arches then bulge outward causing water to enter the mouth and flow into the *oral cavity* (also called the *buccal cavity*). The *oral valve* near the mouth closes, the gill arches contract, the opercula lift outward simultaneously, and water is forced over the gill filaments and into the *opercular cavity*.[3] In the brief interval between cycles the tips of each pair of gill filaments fan out until they touch the tips of the adjacent pair on either side, forming a loose curtain between the oral and opercular cavities (Fig. 4-1). Gases and inorganic ions are ex-

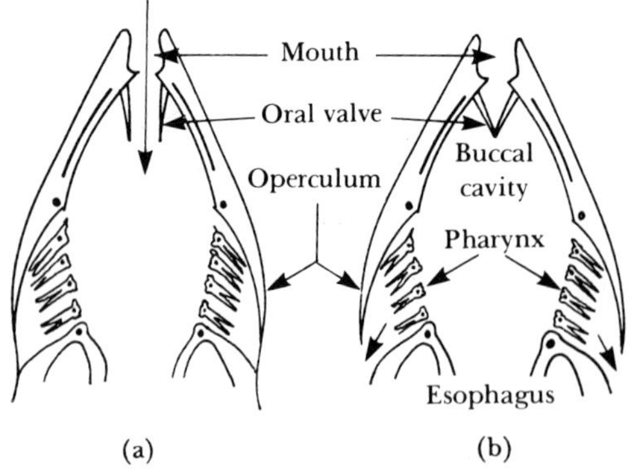

Figure 4-2 *Ventilatory mechanisms of a teleost.* (a) *During inspiration the opercula close, the oral valve opens, the oral cavity dilates with expansion of the gill arches, and water enters.* (b) *During expiration the oral valve closes, the gill arches contract, the opercula open, and water is forced over the gill filaments into the opercular cavity.* Source: Storer and Usinger (1957).

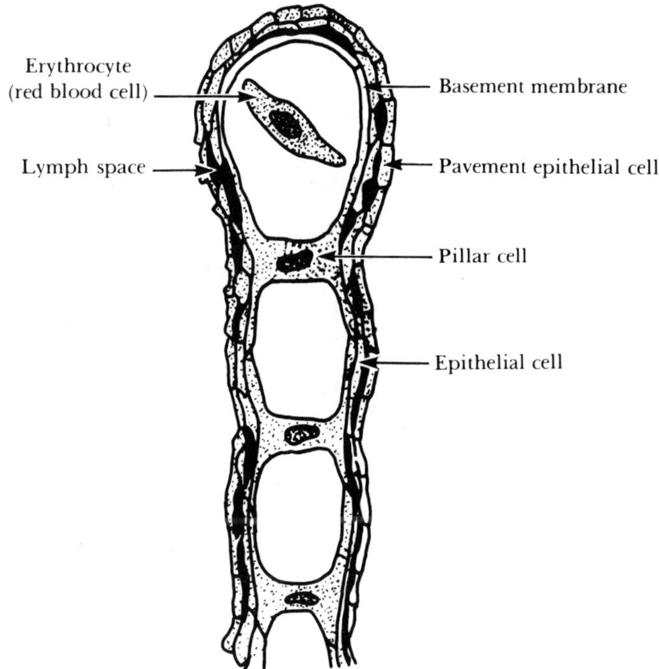

Figure 4-3 *Section through a secondary lamella of a teleost. The illustration is approximately to scale for a rainbow trout* (Oncorhynchus mykiss). Source: Randall (1982).

changed between the blood and the water through thin,[4] pleated surfaces of epithelium overlying networks of blood vessels (Fig. 4-3). The term *epithelium* denotes a layer or layers of cells covering the surface or lining of a cavity.

Osmotic and Ionic Regulation

Osmotic regulation (also called *osmoregulation*) is the general term used to describe the process by which aquatic animals regulate the water content of their tissues and body fluids. *Ionic regulation* is the control of the ionic composition of the tissues and fluids.

PASSIVE AND ACTIVE TRANSPORT[5] *Diffusion* is the random distribution of substances throughout the space available. It occurs because molecules are in constant motion, and the direction in which they move is random. Increases in temperature stimulate molecular activity and subsequently the diffusion rate. *Osmosis* is the diffusion of water.

Many membranes of living organisms are *semipermeable*, meaning that certain molecules pass through them easily, others more slowly, and still others not at all (Fig. 4-4). Living membranes are all essentially permeable to water, but their

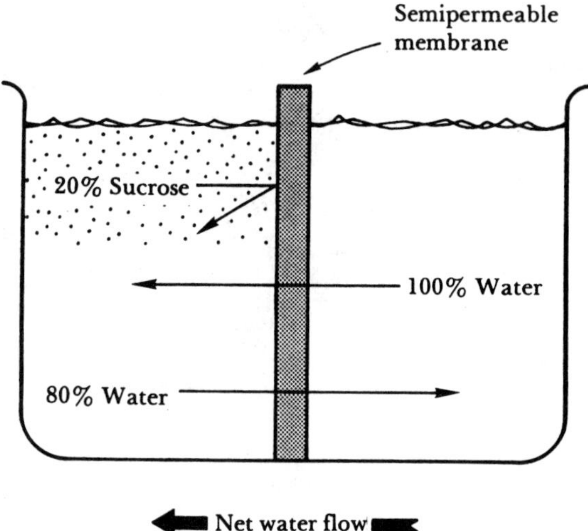

Figure 4-4 *The membrane depicted is not permeable to sucrose ($C_{12}H_{22}O_{11}$) molecules but is easily penetrated by molecules of water, which are much smaller. Sucrose molecules are reflected back when they strike the membrane, whereas water passes through. If the same number of molecules strikes the membrane from each side more will penetrate it and pass from right to left, and the net flow of water will be toward the left side of the container.* Source: Cockrum and McCauley (1965).

permeability to solutes is more variable. When a solute causes water to flow differentially through a semipermeable membrane it is said to exert *osmotic pressure*. The level of osmotic pressure applied to a membrane is directly proportional to the *numbers* of molecules or particles of solute, not to their composition.[6] The distinction is important because it allows some seawater organisms to regulate water and solute balance by using their own metabolic products, as will be explained later.

Diffusion does not require an expenditure of energy by living cells and thus is a form of *passive transport* (Fig. 4-5). Some

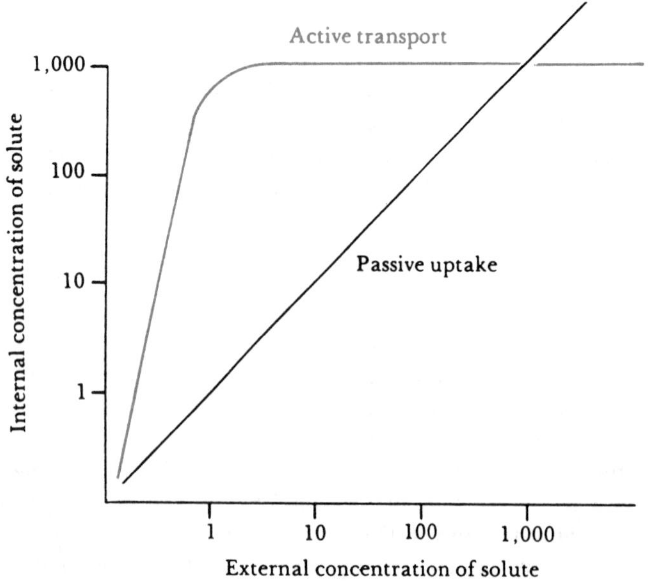

Figure 4-5 *Relationship between external and internal solute concentrations in active transport and passive transport (i.e., diffusion). The external and internal concentrations are identical in passive transport. In active transport the internal concentration is greater than the external concentration, but becomes saturated at high external concentrations.* Source: Spotte (1979) after Brock (1970).

membranes can pump substances through themselves, often against a greater concentration. This ability, called *active transport* (Fig. 4-5), uses energy generated by cells. Many organisms concentrate specific solutes from seawater by active transport. Often these substances are needed to carry out metabolic functions, but active transport can also aid in the elimination of excess solutes.

WATER AND ION BALANCE Two solutions are *isosmotic* if their total solute concentrations are the same.[7] A *hyposmotic solution* is more dilute, and one that is *hyperosmotic* more concentrated, than the comparison solution. Teleosts face a problem of maintaining hyposmotic or hyperosmotic body fluids depending on whether they live in seawater or freshwater.

Freshwater teleosts are hyperosmotic; that is, their fluids contain greater concentrations of ions than the surrounding water. They face a net diffusional loss of ions and *osmotic loading* (a net osmotic gain of water). Freshwater teleosts drink little, but the permeable structure of their gills and skin allows water to enter anyway.[8] Their internal fluids would become rapidly isosmotic in the absence of efficient ''physiological pumps'' to force excess water back into the environment. Water and ions are ingested passively with food and lost from the body by different pathways (Fig. 4-6a).

Seawater teleosts are hyposmotic. They face a net diffusional gain of ions (mainly sodium, Na^+, and chloride, Cl^-) and a net osmotic loss of water. Their main problems are thus *ionic loading* (accumulation of excess ions) and dehydration. Seawater teleosts drink continuously, and subsequent adsorption of monovalent ions such as Na^+, Cl^-, and potassium (K^+) in the gut is accompanied by the uptake of water (Fig. 4-6b). Most of the added ion load is transported by the blood to the gills and excreted. The urine is not a vehicle for removal of monovalent ions; it is isosmotic with the blood and excreted sparingly. The ions it contains are mostly multivalent species such as calcium (Ca^+), magnesium (Mg^{2+}), and sulfate (SO_4^{2-}).

Ionic and osmotic regulation in seawater *elasmobranchs* (sharks, skates, and rays) is depicted in Figure 4-6c. Both freshwater and seawater teleosts possess blood ion concentrations that are approximately one-third the strength of seawater,[9] as do seawater elasmobranchs.[10] However, the osmotic pressures of teleost body fluids are strictly functions of the inorganic ion concentration. The inorganic ion concentrations of elasmobranch body fluids are similar to those of teleosts, but their osmotic pressures equal or exceed the value for seawater. This apparent anomaly is explained by the presence of organic mol-

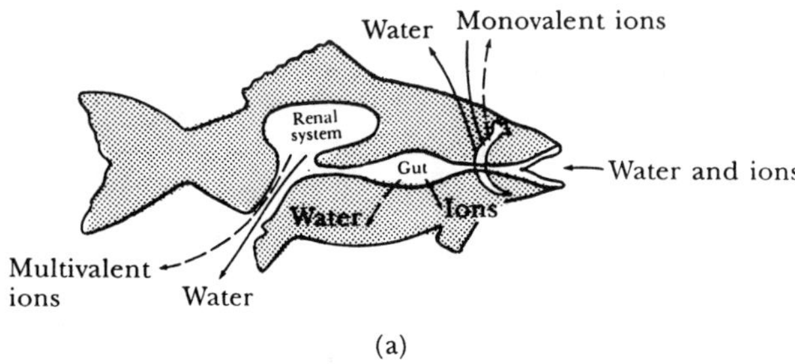

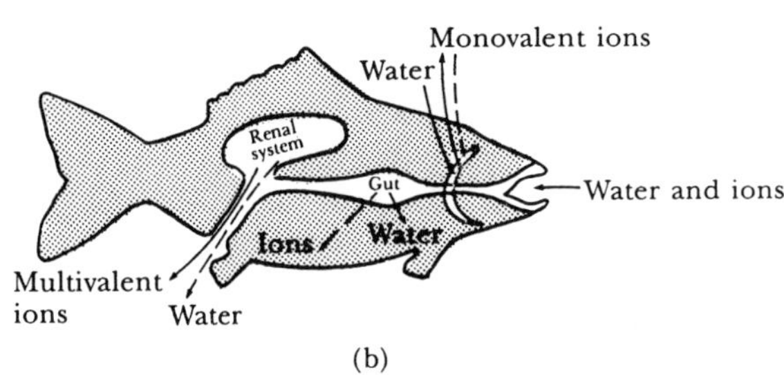

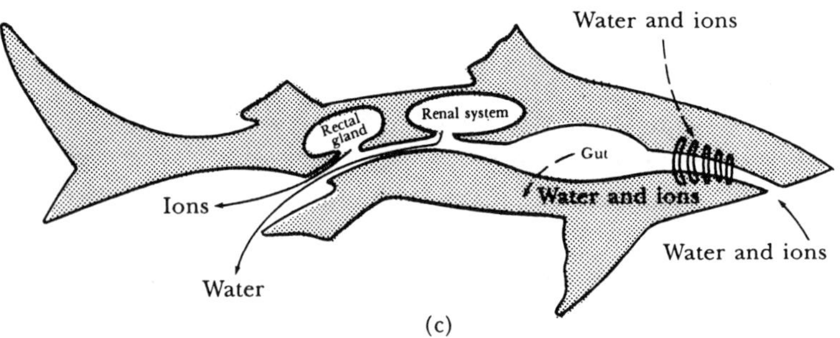

Figure 4-6 *Osmotic and ionic regulation in* (a) *freshwater teleosts,* (b) *seawater teleosts, and* (c) *seawater elasmobranchs. Solid and broken lines represent active and passive transport processes.* Source: Spotte (1979) after McCauley (1971).

ecules, mainly urea, CH_4N_2O, but also trimethylamine oxide, C_3H_9NO.[11] Thus even though the total concentration of ions *per se* is practically the same as in teleosts, elasmobranch body fluids contain more particles. The advantage of being isosmotic is that no severe loss of water can occur. Unlike seawater teleosts, elasmobranchs do not drink copious quantities of water[12] and therefore do not have a heavy intake of ions and the attendant problem of excreting them.

REGULATION OF ION FLUX As noted previously, freshwater teleosts must deal with the problems of ion depletion and osmotic loading. The study of ion flux in these species must necessarily concentrate on mechanisms by which ions are assimilated from the environment. It is known that Na^+ and Cl^- are taken up by the *branchial epithelium* (the thin tissue covering the gills) independently, and that most of the blood ammonium

(NH_4^+) and bicarbonate (HCO_3^-), ions are exchanged for environmental Na^+ and Cl^-, respectively.[13] This exchange process, or "coupling," usually is expressed as Na^+/NH_4^+ and Cl^-/HCO_3^-. A freshwater teleost depleted of either *counterion* (one of the ions in a coupled pair) compensates for the deficiency selectively if both are added to the water (i.e., the ion not needed is not assimilated). Basic features of this ion flux model in freshwater teleosts are illustrated in Figure 4-7. The gill is by

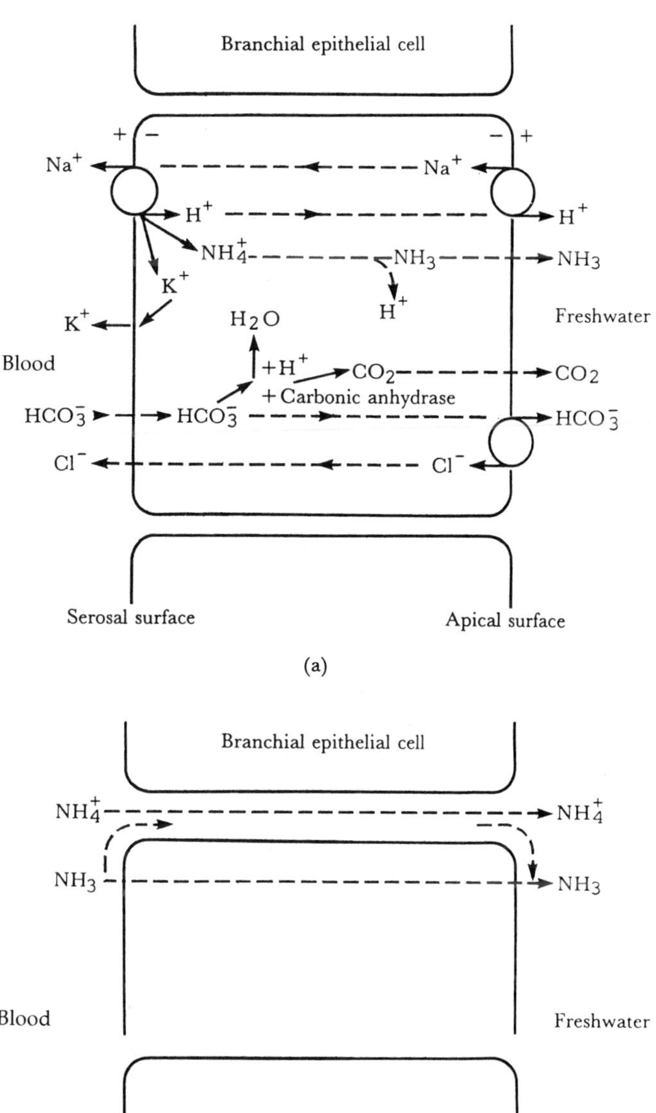

Figure 4-7 Ion flux model for gill epithelia of freshwater teleosts. Solid and broken lines represent active and passive transport processes. (a) *Transcellular flux.* (b) *Paracellular flux. Circles indicate carrier mediated processes.* Carriers *are compounds that facilitate the tandem transport of two ions of opposite electrochemical charge.* Sources: Evans (1982) and McDonald and Prior (1988).

far the most important site of ion flux in all teleosts, regardless of habitat, and I shall concentrate on its functions.

As the figure illustrates, in freshwater teleosts intracellular Na^+ may be actively exchanged for blood NH_4^+ at the *serosal* or *basolateral* cell surface (inner surface or blood side). The exchange also may involve active uptake of H^+ and K^+ from the blood. Potassium ions are recycled by passive transport; H^+ traverses the epithelial cell passively and is exchanged actively for Na^+ at the *apical* cell surface (*mucosal* or water side). Intracellular NH_4^+ moves by passive transport into the cell from the blood, where it may dissociate. Free ammonia, NH_3, can diffuse into the environment across the apical membrane,[14] but passive NH_4^+ excretion appears to be *paracellular* (between cells). Bicarbonate ions move passively into the cell from the blood where they dissociate to produce either water or H^+ plus CO_2. The latter reaction is catalyzed by the enzyme carbonic anhydrase. Some HCO_3^- moves passively through the cell and is actively exchanged at the apical surface for Cl^-. Chloride ions move passively across the cell and serosal surface and enter the blood. Other models have been proposed in which all outward movement of NH_4^+, HCO_3^-, Na^+, and Cl^- is paracellular.[15]

The mechanics of branchial ion flux in seawater teleosts are more equivocal.[16] As shown in Figure 4-8, a neutral carrier located on the serosal membrane couples active transport of Cl^- and passive movement of Na^+ from the blood into the epithelial

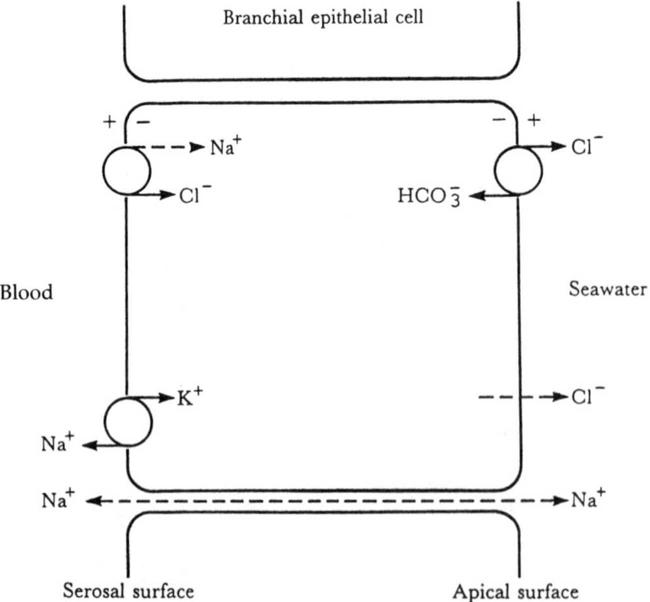

Figure 4-8 *Simplified ion flux model for gill epithelia of seawater teleosts. Solid and broken lines represent active and passive transport processes. Circles indicate carrier mediated processes.* Source: Evans (1982).

cell. Chloride diffuses passively outward from the cell. Sodium is in passive equilibrium through paracellular sites.[17] Active exchange at the serosal surface is controlled by Na^+ and K^+ and at the apical surface by HCO_3^- and Cl^-.

Compared with teleosts, ion flux in elasmobranchs has been incompletely described. A major site is the rectal gland (Fig. 4-6c). Teleosts do not have rectal glands. Ion exchange across the rectal gland epithelium closely resembles exchange processes across the branchial epithelium of seawater teleosts.[18] The serosal epithelium is traversed by active (Cl^-) and passive (Na^+) transport (Fig. 4-9). Active exchange of Na^+ for K^+ also takes place. Assimilated Cl^- traverses the cell and is excreted passively into the environment across the apical membrane.[19] The excretion of Na^+ apically evidently is passive and occurs through paracellular sites. Excretion of Na^+ and Cl^- by the gills appears to be substantial.[20]

FUNCTIONAL BENEFITS Assimilation of certain ions from the water in exchange for others in the blood has obvious advantages for animals living in hyposmotic environments.[21] To discover that identical processes exist in animals bathed in a hyperosmotic solution such as seawater is somewhat surprising. The added Na^+ and Cl^- taken up during excretion of NH_4^+ and HCO_3^- only worsens the problem of ion loading. The net gain of inorganic ions during ion exchange by seawater teleosts may be less important in maintenance of physiological stasis than the more immediate exigency of ridding the blood

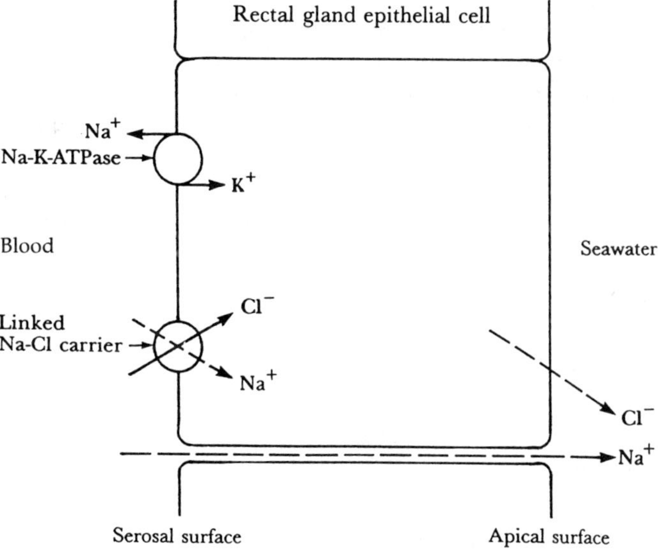

Figure 4-9 Ion flux model for rectal gland epithelia of seawater elasmobranchs illustrating Na^+ *and* Cl^- *transport. Solid and broken lines represent active and passive transport processes. Circles indicate carrier mediated processes.* Source: Silva et al. (1977b).

and tissues of potentially dangerous metabolic by-products (e.g., nitrogen, represented by ammonia, and acid as net H^+). Excretion of such compounds is mandatory for all fishes regardless of habitat.

Respiration and Acid-Base Regulation

GASES The three most important gases in physiology are oxygen, carbon dioxide, and nitrogen. They exist in the atmosphere in the proportions listed in Table 4-1. When dissolved in water each is in equilibrium with the partial pressure of its atmospheric complement, and a gas in solution is said to be under that particular *partial pressure*. Atmospheric pressure at sea level is 760 mm Hg, the approximate sum of the partial pressures shown in the table.[22] Nitrogen will not be considered further. Excretion of nitrogen as ammonia was discussed previously.[14]

Table 4-2 lists the abbreviations and symbols used in the text and accompanying chapter notes. The partial pressures of O_2 and CO_2 in water (PwO_2, $PwCO_2$) are controlled largely by biological activity. Assimilation of O_2 by plants and animals during respiration (defined below) lowers the PwO_2 in the immediate vicinity, and the concomitant production of CO_2 as a waste product of metabolism causes a rise in $PwCO_2$ in weakly buffered waters. Photosynthesis by plants removes CO_2 and results in a net input of O_2. Neither respiration nor photosynthesis causes PwO_2 and $PwCO_2$ to fluctuate substantially in the upper levels of the ocean, but marked deviations are not uncommon in small bodies of freshwater.

Changes in the concentrations of O_2 and CO_2 (CwO_2, $CwCO_2$) are caused by shifts in temperature and salinity, which affect the solubilities of both gases. The solubility of O_2 varies inversely with temperature and salinity (i.e., as temperature and salinity decrease the solubility of O_2 increases). Thus cold freshwaters can hold more O_2 than warm seawaters (Table 3-3). The $CwCO_2$ also is affected by temperature and salinity, but identical incremental changes in these factors do not alter the solubility of CO_2 in the same proportion as O_2.

TABLE 4-1 Composition of dry atmospheric air and partial pressures of the three major gases.

Gas	Composition %	Partial pressure, mm Hg
Oxygen	20.95	159.2
Carbon dioxide	0.03	0.2
Nitrogen	79.09	600.6

Source: Stephen Spotte, compiled from various sources.

TABLE 4-2 Symbols used in aquatic respiration physiology.

Symbol	Meaning
E_w	Oxygen extraction coefficient
p	Partial pressure of a gas in air
P	Partial pressure of a gas in water or blood
PwO_2	Partial pressure of O_2 in water
$PwCO_2$	Partial pressure of CO_2 in water
CwO_2	Concentration of O_2 in water
$CwCO_2$	Concentration of CO_2 in water
$[HCO_3^-]a$	Concentration of bicarbonate ion in arterial blood
$[HCO_3^-]w$	Concentration of bicarbonate ion in water
pHw	pH of water
pHi	pH of inspired water
pHe	pH of expired water
pHa	pH of arterial blood
PiO_2	Partial pressure of O_2 in inspired water
PeO_2	Partial pressure of CO_2 in expired water
$PiCO_2$	Partial pressure of CO_2 in inspired water
$PeCO_2$	Partial pressure of CO_2 in expired water
CiO_2	Concentration of O_2 in inspired water
CeO_2	Concentration of O_2 in expired water
$CiCO_2$	Concentration of CO_2 in inspired water
$CeCO_2$	Concentration of CO_2 in expired water
PaO_2	Partial pressure of arterial blood O_2
$PaCO_2$	Partial pressure of arterial blood CO_2
$PvCO_2$	Partial pressure of venous blood CO_2
V	Ventilatory flow rate
Vw	Water ventilation rate
$\dot{M}O_2$	Oxygen consumption
$Vw/\dot{M}O_2$	Ventilatory convection requirement (the volume of water a fish must breathe to extract a unit quantity of O_2)
βwCO_2	Capacitance coefficient or solubility of CO_2 in water ($\Delta CwCO_2/\Delta PwCO_2$ where Δ represents change)
NoNc	Normoxia-normcapnia
HoNc	Hyperoxia-normcapnia
NoHc	Normoxia-hypercapnia
HoHc	Hyperoxia-hypercapnia
α	Solubility coefficient

Source: Stephen Spotte, compiled from various sources.

WATER AND BLOOD FLOW[23] Gases, water, and ions are assimilated and excreted simultaneously from water as it flows between the secondary lamellae (Fig. 4-10). Water movement is sustained by the pumping action described previously and increased by raising the ventilation rate, *amplitude* (volume of water taken in with each ventilation cycle), or both. Residence time for water between the secondary lamellae is short, within

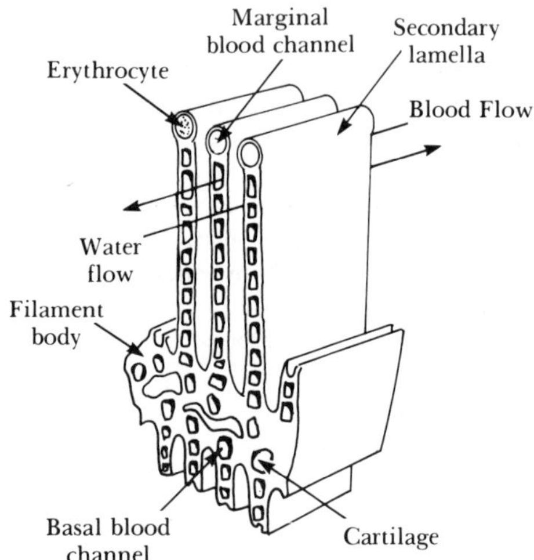

Figure 4-10 *Section through the secondary lamella of a teleost gill drawn approximately to scale.* Source: Randall (1982).

the range of 10 to 150 ms.* Blood driven by pumping action of the heart is directed first through the gills and afterward through the systemic circuit serving the rest of the body. Blood moves through the secondary lamellae around *pillar cells* (Fig. 4-3) that bind layers of epithelium together and separate the blood channels. Blood and water flow in opposite directions. The thickness of the layer of moving blood depends on blood pressure, but averages 9 to 10 μm. The secondary lamellae do not vary in height as a function of blood pressure; instead, thickness of the blood sheet increases with increasing pressure, causing the lamellae to expand laterally. Only ~60% of all secondary lamellae are perfused with blood when a fish is resting, and at such times the lower *basal lamellae* are perfused preferentially. Increases in blood pressure, which occur when a fish becomes active or the water is oxygen deficient, increase the percentage of secondary lamellae that are perfused (a process called *lamellar recruitment*).

GAS MOVEMENTS ACROSS SECONDARY LAMELLAE
Gases contain no electrical charges and therefore move by passive transport. The fish gill represents an ideal respiratory organ in having a large surface area with short diffusion distances. Both characteristics augment diffusion. Red blood cells or *erythrocytes* suspended in the plasma are the ultimate units of respiration (Fig. 4-11). These oval, flattened cells assimilate O_2 transported into the plasma from the external environment through epithelial layers of the secondary lamellae. At the same

*The abbreviation ms stands for millisecond, which is 10^{-3} s.

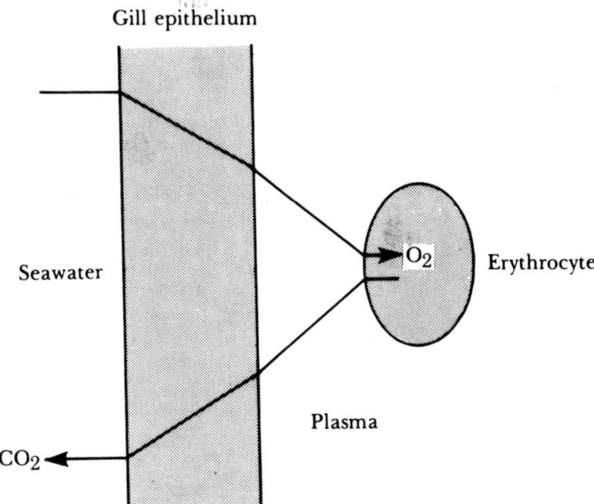

Figure 4-11 *Simple diffusion model for passive transport of O_2 and CO_2 from the interior of an erythrocyte across a sequence of tissue barriers. Hydration of CO_2 in the gill epithelium is not shown. The gases diffuse in opposite directions toward areas of lower partial pressure.* Source: Stephen Spotte.

time erythrocytes release CO_2 to be transported back across the secondary lamellar epithelium for excretion into the water. Both gases must diffuse across several boundaries before reaching their destinations. The surface of the outer layer of the secondary lamellar epithelium is in constant contact with a layer of water 5 to 8 μm thick. Molecules of O_2 must penetrate the water boundary, then move sequentially across a layer of mucus coating the outer surface of the secondary lamellar epithelium and through the inner epithelial cells before entering the blood. Blood O_2 is assimilated into erythrocytes and bound with *hemoglobin*, a respiratory pigment, for transport to oxygen-depleted tissues located along the systemic circuit downstream from the gills. Carbon dioxide traverses these boundaries in the opposite direction.

MAINTENANCE OF NORMAL ACID-BASE BALANCE Warm-blooded animals maintain constant blood pH (i.e., constant OH^-/H^+ ratios) precisely and independently of external factors in the environment. Cold-blooded animals are able to do this with far less precision. Blood pH typically varies from 7.4 to >7.8 in fishes, amphibians, and reptiles. The temperature of the environment exerts considerable influence over blood pH in these animals. Blood pH falls with rising temperature and increases with a decrease in temperature. Cold-blooded, air-breathing animals (e.g., amphibians and reptiles) regulate their blood pH by maintaining a *constant relative alkalinity* with changes in temperature, which is defined as a constant difference between the pH of the extracellular fluids (e.g., pH*a*) and the pH of pure water at neutrality (i.e., when values for the two factors are plotted against the temperature the lines are parallel). *Relative pH* is a more accurate term, considering that what is being regulated is the OH^-/H^+ ratio.[24] In fishes, blood pH falls with rising temperature, but constant relative pH is not maintained.[24]

In all fishes studied, $PaCO_2$ remains constant or increases as temperature rises, but the magnitude of any such change cannot be accounted for entirely by changes in pH*a*. The primary factor regulating pH*a* is $[HCO_3^-]a$.[25] In amphibians and reptiles, however, adjustments in pH*a* are solely the result of changes in $PaCO_2$.[26]

REGULATORY MECHANISMS[27] Acid-base balance is a function of the OH^-/H^+ ratio. Physiological mechanisms that regulate this ratio in fishes are (*1*) the presence of bicarbonate and nonbicarbonate blood buffers, (*2*) excretion of H^+, (*3*) excretion of NH_4^+, and (*4*) excretion of HCO_3^-. As mentioned previously, pH*a* in fishes is regulated loosely in comparison with warm-blood animals. Nonetheless, the OH^-/H^+ ratio is considered to exist in a steady state condition. Thus $PaCO_2$ remains in steady state as well. Changes in $PaCO_2$ affect the ratio of OH^-/H^+, but not because of any regulatory role. Instead, the status of $PaCO_2$ is predetermined primarily by the level of O_2 in the water, as described later.

Excretion of H^+ into the environment through the gills was discussed previously (also see Note 13). Its elimination from the internal fluids is part of the ion exchange process carried out continuously. Additional H^+ is eliminated at gill sites as ammonia. The chemical state of the ammonia released affects acid-base status. Excretion of NH_4^+ has the same physiological effect as releasing H^+. However, release of NH_3, which is a neutral molecule, does not alter the OH^-/H^+ ratio and has no effect on acid-base balance. Large amounts of HCO_3^- are produced internally when ammonia is ionized by the uptake of H^+. Much of the amount needed in excess of acid-base regulation is transported across the gill epithelium in exchange for Cl^- in the environment (also see Note 13). Experimental evidence suggests that HCO_3^- and not OH^- is the internal ion used in the exchange, although the actual ionic species exchanged are unimportant from the standpoint of acid-base balance, so long as the correct OH^-/H^+ ratio is preserved.[28]

EFFECTS OF ENVIRONMENTAL TEMPERATURE CHANGES[29] The effect on acid-base status of a sudden increase in water temperature of 10°C has been described in the larger spotted dogfish (*Scyliorhinus stellaris*), an elasmobranch. As indicated in Figure 4-12a, pH*a* drops instantly by 0.4 unit. This is attributable to a threefold increase in $PaCO_2$ (Fig. 4-12b). The $PaCO_2$

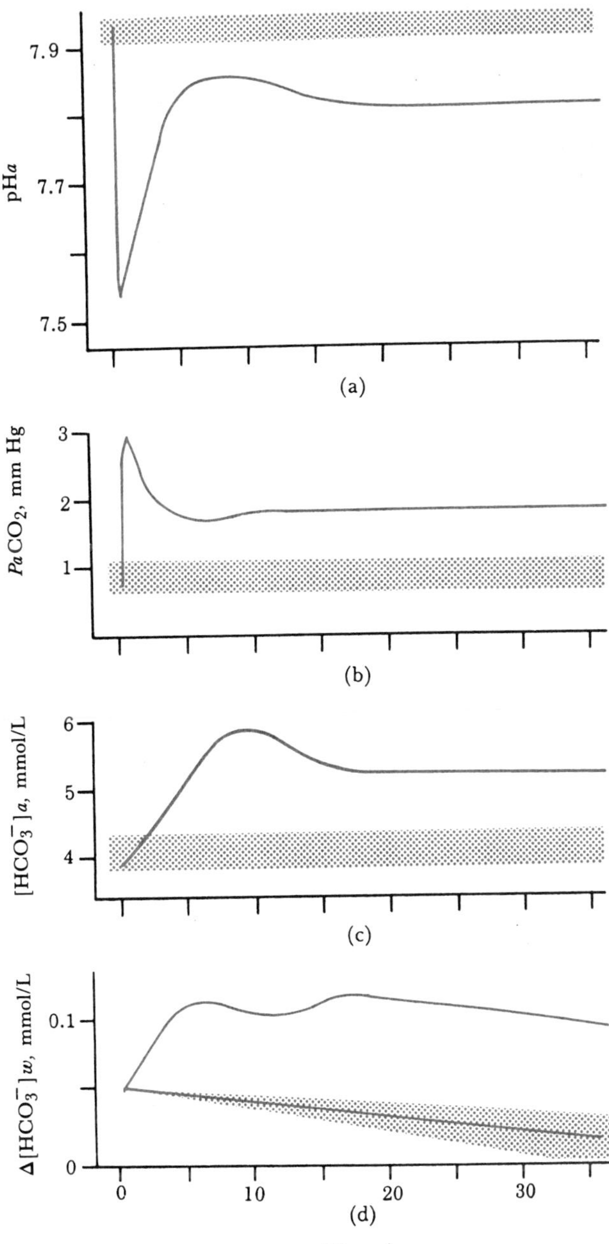

Figure 4-12 *Effect of factors controlling acid-base status in larger spotted dogfish* (Scyliorhinus stellaris) *subjected to a sudden increase in temperature from 10 to 20°C (data points omitted). Shaded areas are a range of ±2 standard errors of the mean of control values.* (a) *p*Ha, (b) $PaCO_2$, (c) $[HCO_3^-]$a, *and (d)* $\Delta[HCO_3^-]$w. *The line inside the shaded area represents* $[HCO_3^-]$a *of the controls.* Source: Heisler (1978).

rapidly reaches a value typical for acclimation at the higher temperature. After 5 h the pH*a* achieves steady state typical for acclimation to 20°C, recovery being based almost entirely on a rise in $[HCO_3^-]a$ (Fig. 4-12c), which is mobilized in the initial 15 h after the temperature change. At the same time, HCO_3^- is released into the surrounding seawater (Fig. 4-12d).

Changes in the acid-base status of larger spotted dogfish acclimated to 20°C and suddenly subjected to water of 10°C follow the patterns shown in Figure 4-13. Alterations in $[HCO_3^-]a$ and $[HCO_3^-]w$ (Figs. 4-13c and 4-13d) are almost inverted images of changes illustrated in Figure 4-12c and 4-12d, but the "overshoots" and "undershoots" of pH*a* and $PaCO_2$ (Figs. 4-13a and 4-13b) are comparatively less pronounced, as indicated by the shallower vertical variations of the lines.

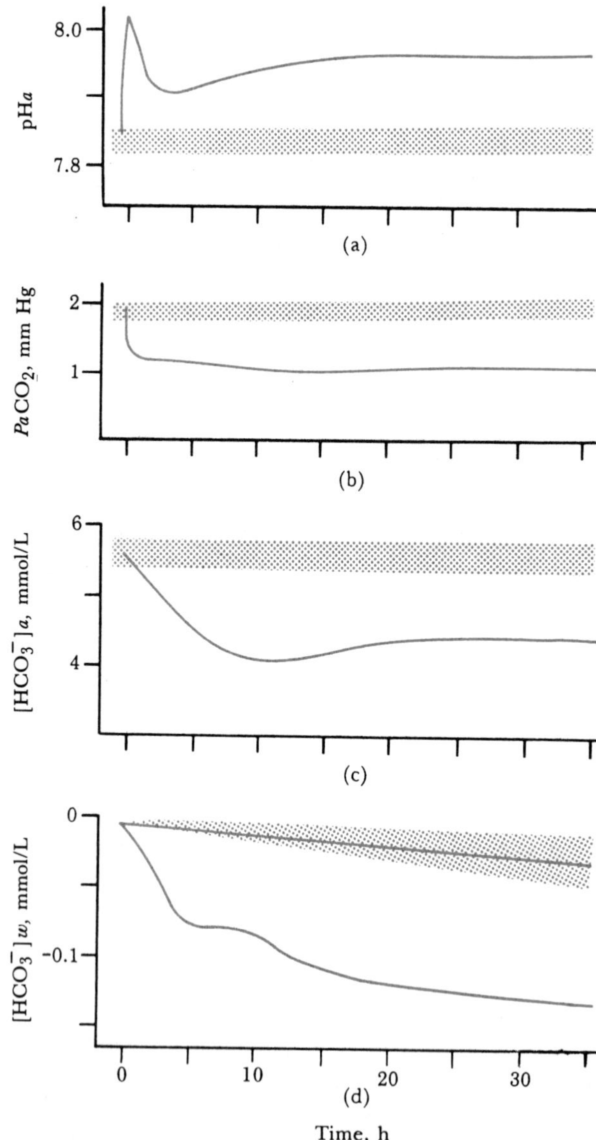

Figure 4-13 *Effect of factors controlling acid-base status in larger spotted dogfish subjected to a sudden temperature decrease of 20 to 10°C (data points omitted). Shaded areas are a range of ±2 standard errors of the mean of control values.* (a) pHa, (b) $PaCO_2$, (c) $[HCO_3^-]$a *and* (d) $\Delta[HCO_3^-]$w. *The line inside the shaded area represents* $[HCO_3^-]$a *of the controls.* Source: Heisler (1978).

Changes in pH*a* during the first hour, caused by a temperature shift in either direction, can be attributed almost entirely to shifts in $PaCO_2$. Subsequent changes are caused by variations in $[HCO_3^-]a$ resulting from exchange processes. These have two origins: (*1*) intracellular sites in the muscles and other tissues, and (*2*) the seawater in which the animal is immersed. Both locations serve as reservoirs of HCO_3^- that are mobilized following a depression in pH*a*. Changing the temperature from 10 to 20°C results in a substantial transfer of HCO_3^- from intracellular sites to the reservoir of $[HCO_3^-]a$, and from there to the seawater. These transfers are reversed when the temperature is lowered from 20 to 10°C. All exchange processes are nearly complete after 18 h. Transfer of HCO_3^- from intracellular sites to the blood is inadequate to account for the total buffering that occurs under these conditions, and a final adjustment must take place during transfer of HCO_3^- from seawater into the $[HCO_3^-]a$ pool.

EFFECTS OF ENVIRONMENTAL HYPERCAPNIA *Hypercapnia* is defined as abnormally high PCO_2. Hypercapnic conditions can exist either in the external environment (*environmental hypercapnia*, high $PwCO_2$) or in the body fluids of animals (*physiological hypercapnia*, high $PaCO_2$). The first situation induces the second and the consequences are (*1*) to increase $PaCO_2$, which lowers the diffusion gradient of CO_2 between the blood and the water ($PaCO_2/PwCO_2$ gradient); and (*2*) to reduce blood pH. The second effect is the direct result of an increase in inspired CO_2. As pH*a* falls, excess H^+ ions are produced, a condition termed *respiratory acidosis* that makes the blood more acidic. Physiological hypercapnia persists unless excess H^+ ions are buffered by a subsequent increase in $[HCO_3^-]a$, or excreted into the environment.

Exposing fishes to conditions of environmental hypercapnia induces similar responses in all species studied so far (e.g., Fig. 4-14). The initial decline in pH*a* is countered by increased branchial uptake of HCO_3^- from the water and mobilization of HCO_3^- from intracellular sites in the muscles.[30] Both movements involve active transport. In larger spotted dogfish the additional HCO_3^- is incorporated into the $[HCO_3^-]a$ pool and used to buffer excess $PaCO_2$ produced by the decline in pH*a*. Normal acid-base status is recovered rapidly even during sustained hypercapnia, but the time until complete recovery varies by species of fish and $[HCO_3^-]w$. Larger spotted dogfish require 8 h for pH*a* to return to within <0.1 unit of normal, whereas rainbow trout (*Oncorhynchus mykiss*) acclimated to freshwater require >50 h to achieve the same degree of compensation.[31]

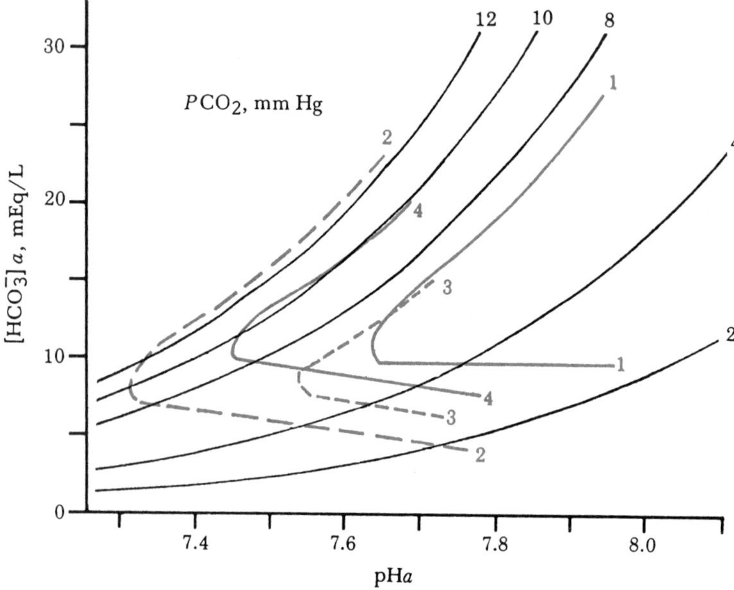

Figure 4-14 Compensatory changes in $[HCO_3^-]$a *after exposure to environmental hypercapnia in freshwater-acclimated rainbow trout (curves 1 and 2), freshwater channel catfish* (Ictalurus punctatus, *curve 3), and larger spotted dogfish (curve 4); data points omitted.* Source: Heisler (1980).

An increase in pH*w*, which raises $[HCO_3^-]w$, speeds up recovery of acid-base status considerably in larger spotted dogfish subjected to hypercapnic conditions; lowering the pH*w* slows recovery or prevents it (Fig. 4-15).

EFFECTS OF ENVIRONMENTAL HYPEROXIA In terms of O_2 concentration and partial pressure the external environment can be *normoxic* (normal), *hypoxic* (less than normal), or *hyperoxic* (greater than normal). Exposing a fish to water that is hyperoxic depresses its ventilation rate, which causes physiological hypercapnia. Hyperoxic conditions both in the oceans and in seawater aquariums are rare enough to warrant only passing attention, but conditions in which fishes transported in plastic bags filled with seawater and an overlying layer of gaseous O_2 are exceptional.[32]

The response of fishes to known conditions of O_2 (hypoxia, normoxia, hyperoxia) and CO_2 (normcapnia, hypercapnia) follows a predictable pattern.[33] As illustrated in Fig. 4-16a, exposure to water that is hyperoxic-normcapnic (HoNc) or hyperoxic-hypercapnic (HoHc) results in an increase in the partial pressure of O_2 in both inspired (PiO_2) and expired (PeO_2) gill water. The value of PeO_2 must always be the lower of the two because some O_2 is assimilated from water passing over the gills, but the fact that values for both factors increase is attributable to the substantial rise in PwO_2. The difference between PiO_2 and PeO_2 becomes less pronounced under conditions of

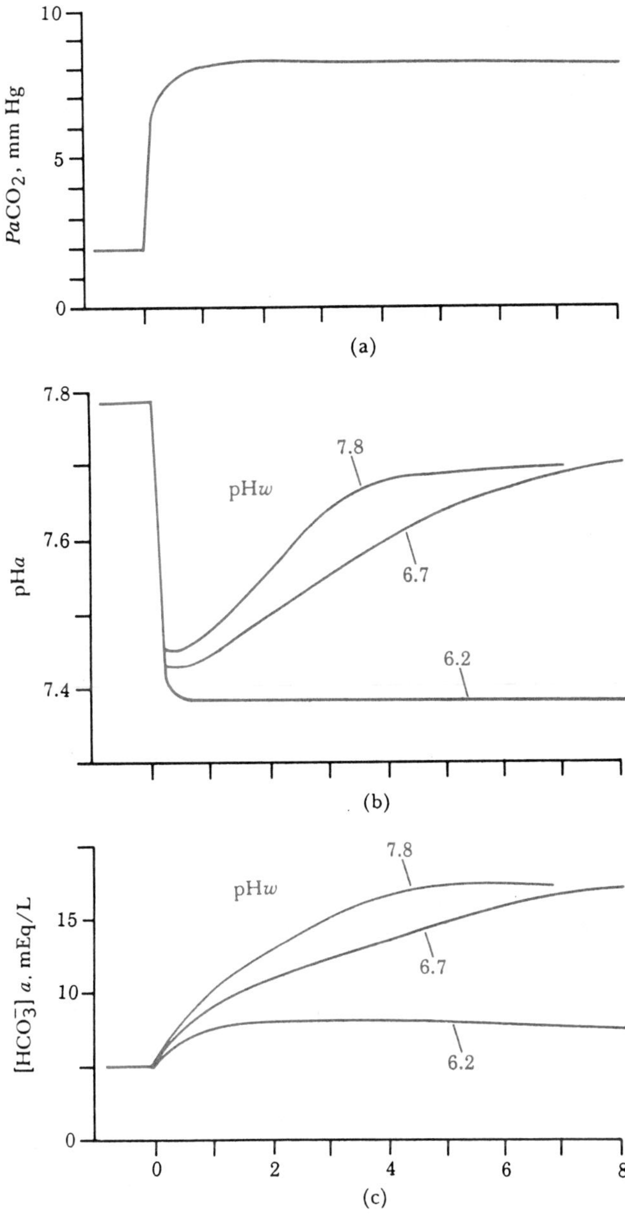

Figure 4-15 *Recovery of pHa and* [HCO_3^-]a *in larger spotted dogfish exposed to environmental hypercapnia as a function of pHw and time (data points omitted).* (a) *Environmental hypercapnia as a function of time.* (b) *Recovery of pHa as a function of pHw and time.* (c) *Recovery of* [HCO_3^-]a *as a function of pHw and time. Note that normal values of pHa and* [HCO_3^-]a *are not regained except at higher seawater pH values.* Source: Heisler (1980).

normoxia-hypercapnia (NoHc) and smaller still when the environment is returned to normal (NoNcR, where R represents return to normal conditions). However, the ratio of the amount of O_2 removed to the amount available decreases during hyperoxia, compared with the value at normoxia.[34] This is not shown in the figure but is consistent with the observation that

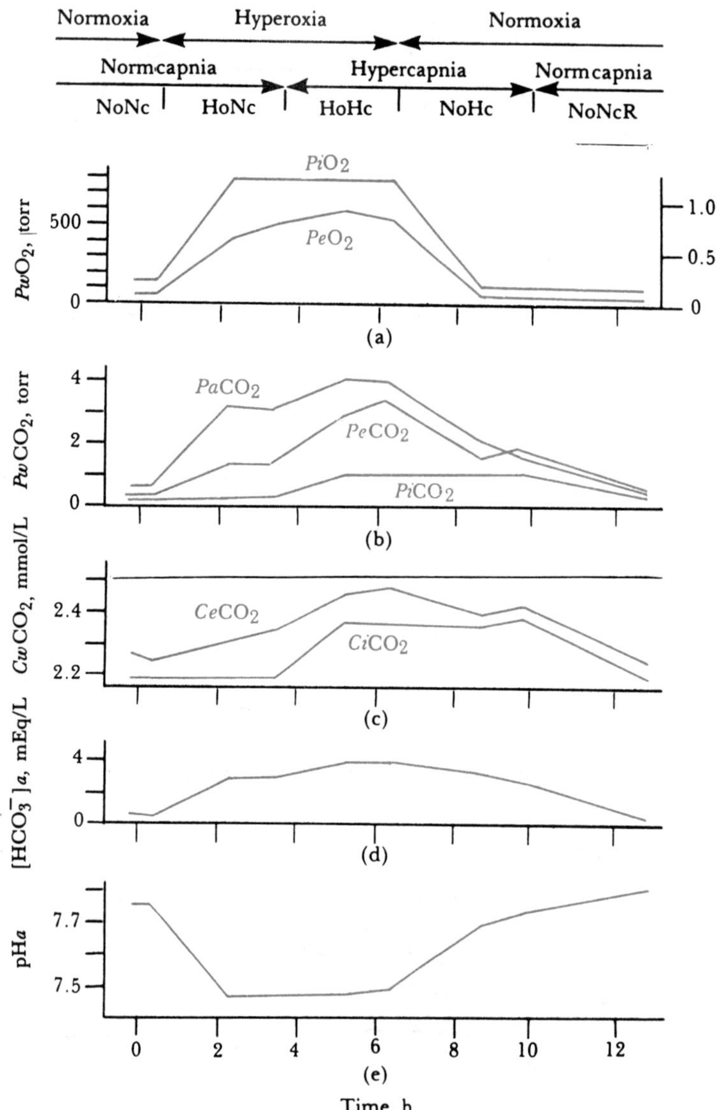

Figure 4-16 *Physiological profile (data points omitted) from a single, unanesthetized smaller spotted dogfish* (Scyliorhinus canicula) *under conditions of normoxia-normcapnia (NoNc), hyperoxia-normcapnia (HoNc), hyperoxia-hypercapnia (HoHc), normoxia-hypercapnia (NoHc), and return to normoxia-normcapnia (NoNcR).* (a) *Effect of seawater partial pressure and concentration of oxygen* (PwO_2, CwO_2) *on partial pressure of inspired and expired oxygen* (PiO_2, PeO_2). (b) *Effect of seawater* CO_2 *partial pressure* ($PwCO_2$) *on partial pressures of arterial blood* CO_2 ($PaCO_2$), expired CO_2 ($PeCO_2$), *and inspired* CO_2 ($PiCO_2$). (c) *Effect of seawater* CO_2 *concentration on concentrations of expired and inspired* CO_2 ($CeCO_2$, $CiCO_2$). (d) *Change in* $[HCO_3^-]a$ *as a function of experimental conditions.* (e) *Change in pHa as a function of experimental conditions. 1 torr = 1 mm Hg at 0°C.* Source: Truchot et al. (1980).

ventilation rate is depressed during hyperoxia (i.e., a fish is not forced to increase its ventilation rate because PwO_2 is substantially greater than during normoxia).

The partial pressure of arterial blood CO_2 ($PaCO_2$) increases as the seawater becomes HoHc (Fig. 4-16b), as do values for partial pressures $PeCO_2$ and $PiCO_2$. The value for $PeCO_2$ is greater because CO_2 is being released at the gills. The value for $PiCO_2$ remains unchanged during NoHc, whereas values for the other two factors decline. All three factors decline on return to NoNc.

As seen in Figure 4-16c, fluctuation in the CO_2 concentration difference between expired and inspired seawater ($CeCO_2 - CiCO_2$) varies similarly with the change in $CiO_2 - CeO_2$ (Fig. 4-16a, right ordinate), but is less pronounced. As indicated in Figure 4-16d, $[HCO_3^-]a$ increases to buffer the rise in $PaCO_2$. There is a concomitant decrease in pH*a* (Fig. 4-16e), which logically follows a rise in $PaCO_2$. Upon return to NoNc, values of $PaCO_2$ and $[HCO_3^-]a$ decline and pH*a* increases, indicating a return to normal.

The most remarkable lesson to be learned from how fishes respond to environmental hyperoxia is that oxygenation of the tissues overrides any requirement to rectify simultaneous disturbances in acid-base balance. In other words, a fish placed in a hyperoxic environment ''forgets'' to breathe because its tissue oxygen requirements are satisfied, even though the subsequent reduction in gill ventilation rate causes a rise in $PaCO_2$. The latter effect could be offset to some extent by hyperventilation, which would clear the opercular cavities and increase the $PaCO_2/PwCO_2$ diffusion gradient, but hyperventilation is an atypical response to hyperoxia. Ultimate restoration of the acid-base balance is left to adjustments in $[HCO_3^-]a$, a prolonged, extra-ventilatory mechanism.[35] The inability of fishes to ''recognize'' impending physiological hypercapnia during periods of hyperoxia has important implications when sealed plastic bags filled with seawater and gaseous O_2 are used in transport.[32] In particular, current shipping practices used with large sharks should be evaluated from the standpoint of their physiological implications. The continuous flooding of a shark's gills with seawater perfused with oxygen may induce long-lasting acid-base imbalances that perhaps account for later morality.

EFFECTS OF ENVIRONMENTAL HYPOXIA Fishes respond physically to environmental hypoxia by an increase in ventilation rate,[36] illustrated graphically in Figure 4-17.[37] Several physiological responses have been isolated, not all of them considered here. As the environment becomes hypoxic, *brachycardia* (a decline in heart rate) ensues, but the output of blood by the heart is maintained by a simultaneous increase in *stroke volume* (i.e., more blood is pumped with each heartbeat).[38] The combination of brachycardia and increased stroke volume causes a rise in blood pressure.[38] Increased blood pressure promotes lamellar recruitment and ensures even distribution of blood flow within the secondary lamellae. In addition, the secondary lamellae become more rigid, which is thought to augment gas transfer across the lamellar epithelium. The assimilation of oxygen by the gills of a quiescent fish is *perfusion limited* (i.e., lim-

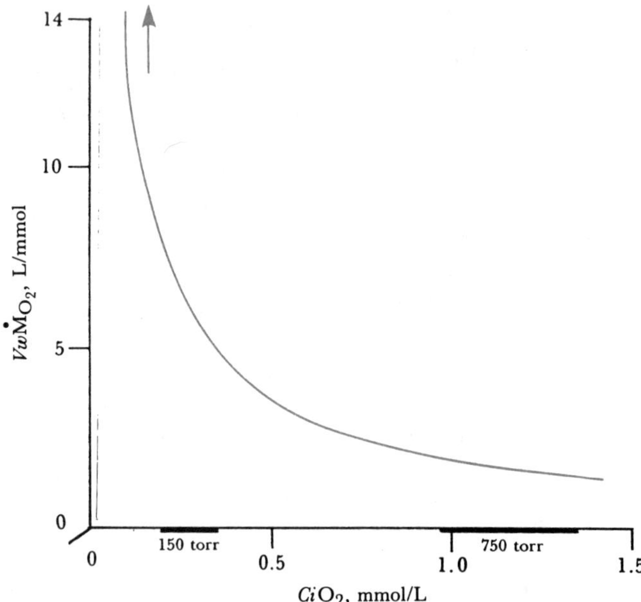

Figure 4-17 *Ventilatory convection requirements* ($Vw/\dot{M}_{O_2}$) *of fishes and crustaceans as a function of* CiO_2 *(data points omitted). Darkened areas indicate normoxic (left) and hyperoxic (right) waters. At stated* PiO_2, CiO_2 *increases with decreasing temperature. The arrow on the upper end of the curve indicates that still higher values are possible (up to 40 L/mmol have been recorded in some aquatic animals).* Source: Dejours (1979).

ited by the rate of blood flow) during normoxic conditions. Thus uptake of O_2 and rate of blood flow are proportional. In this respect, fish gills resemble the lungs of mammals. During hypoxia the gills become diffusion limited,[39] and blood oxygen decreases.[40] The levels of organophosphates (ATP and related compounds) in the erythrocytes are reduced, resulting in a marked increase in the affinity of the hemoglobin for oxygen.[41] In effect, the hemoglobin becomes miserly with what little oxygen is available and subsequently binds it more tightly.[42] This ensures more efficient distribution to tissues downstream from the gills.

The reversible binding of O_2 to iron in the hemoglobin molecule is the most important oxygen transport property of blood. The simplified reaction is written

$$Hb + O_2 \rightleftharpoons HbO_2 \tag{4.1}$$

At high PaO_2 hemoglobin molecules, Hb, combine with oxygen to form oxyhemoglobin, HbO_2, and the reaction shifts forward. At low oxygen levels O_2 is released and the reaction shifts in reverse. Each iron atom in a hemoglobin molecule binds a molecule of O_2. At high PaO_2 all available sites are occupied, and the hemoglobin is saturated. At given PaO_2 a specific proportion exists between the amounts of hemoglobin and oxyhemoglobin. The relationship between PaO_2 and HbO_2 (i.e., the reaction above) can be shown graphically by plotting an oxygen dissociation curve. The exact shape of an oxygen dissociation curve is species dependent. For example, hemoglobins of the oyster toadfish, *Opsanus tau*, and Atlantic mackerel, *Scomber scombrus* (Fig. 4-18), are saturated (100% HbO_2), respectively, at about 17 and >40 mm Hg, indicating that oyster toadfish hemoglobin has the greater oxygen affinity. The positioning of an oxygen dissociation curve appears to depend to some extent on activity level. The Atlantic mackerel and striped marlin (*Tetrapturus audax*) are pelagic, fast-swimming fishes that live in well oxygenated surface waters. The low affinity of their hemoglobin for oxygen facilitates rapid delivery of O_2 to the tissues. If the water is well aerated, PaO_2 will be near 100% saturation. In contrast, the oyster toadfish is a sluggish, bottom-dwelling fish adapted to poorly oxygenated water. If we assume that life style partly determines the shape of a species' oxygen dissociation curve, then it evidently is more important for oyster toadfish hemoglobin to be more adept at assimilating oxygen from the environment than unloading it to the tissues.

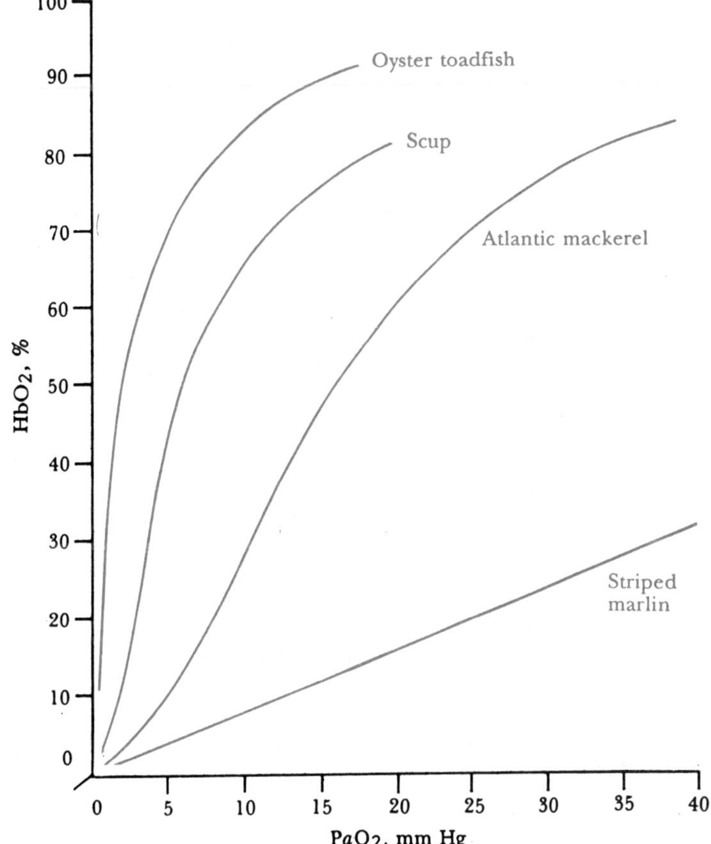

Figure 4-18 *Oxygen dissociation curves (data points omitted) for four seawater teleosts: oyster toadfish* (Opsanus tau), *scup* (Stenotomus chrysops), *Atlantic mackerel* (Scomber scombrus), *and striped marlin* (Tetrapturus audax). *The curves show that blood of the oyster toadfish is saturated (100%* HbO_2*) at ~17 mm Hg, whereas blood of the Atlantic mackerel still is not saturated at 40 mm Hg. Scup blood is intermediate. The position of the curve for oyster toadfish blood relative to Atlantic mackerel blood (i.e., farther to the left) indicates that toadfish hemoglobin has comparatively greater affinity for oxygen. Note the extreme position of the curve for the striped marlin.* Sources: Hall and McCutcheon (1938) for the oyster toadfish, scup, and Atlantic mackerel; Wells and Davie (1985) for the striped marlin.

Stress

I shall start this section by discussing what is meant by stress. Not to do so leads inevitably to confusion, considering that in biology the term can have numerous meanings. A. D. Pickering wrote: "All definitions of stress . . . share the common premise of a stimulus acting on a biological system and the subsequent reaction of the system." Thus a stress can be a stimulus, a response, or both.[43] When stress takes the form of a response it will be called a *stress response;* when a stimulus is involved it will be referred to as a *stress factor* (*stressor*, the prevalent synonym in the literature, seems stilted and vague).

To say that a fish is "stressed" when exposed to a stress factor is meaningful only if the stress response can be measured. Considered at a rudimentary level, all living organisms respond to stimuli. Stress responses—including those associated with "stress"—are therefore manifestations of adaptive evolution. This poses an obvious problem: if a stress response is considered to deviate from normal, what constitutes the normal response? Pickering observed that the definition of *normal response* is so fraught with problems that ". . . it is simpler to think of stress responses as extreme forms of a continuous series of adaptive responses."[43] Such an approach is certainly adequate for aquarists, simply because captivity often imposes situations in which stress factors are magnified.

The subheadings that follow are somewhat misleading in implying that various stress responses are stimulus specific. This clearly is not the case. Netting a fish, chasing it, or subjecting it to environmental hypercapnia or hypoxia all induce stress responses that, for the most part, are indistinguishable. Perhaps a better procedure would have been to categorize the responses themselves and minimize the importance of stimuli that induce them. I felt that a technique-oriented presentation was preferable. The accompanying chapter notes emphasize experimental methods that have been used by researchers to elicit stress responses. I included this information because the stimuli described (e.g., chasing fishes with a net) are also common aquarium practices (Table 4-3). My intention is to show that such practices induce physiological effects that are immediate and often profound. Keep in mind that aquarium practices are human artifacts and therefore amenable to change, but the stress responses they evoke in fishes are real and much less flexible. The task of aquarists is to reduce the magnitude of these responses by refining methods of capture, transport, and handling. But first a case must be made for the importance of stress in aquarium management.

TABLE 4-3 Stress factors that initiate the stress response in fishes.

Behavioral stress
Crowding
Intra- and interspecific aggression[1]
Handling stress
Capture
Struggling during capture
Confinement in a small space
Restriction of movement
Exercise stress
Prolonged forced swimming
Being chased with a net
Temperature stress
Transfer to higher temperature
Transfer to lower temperature
Salinity stress
Transfer to higher salinity
Transfer to lower salinity
Hypoxia stress
Removal from the water
Exposure to low environmental oxygen
Toxicity stress
Exposure to high environmental ammonia
Exposure to copper, formalin, chlorine, ozone[2]

Source: Stephen Spotte, compiled from various sources.
Notes: Chapter 6,[1] Chapter 9.[2]

THE STRESS RESPONSE The stress response of fishes can be seen as a series of sequential events starting with *neuroendocrine responses* (Fig. 4-19). These occur almost as soon as a stress factor is encountered and include physiological processes involving the nervous and *endocrine* (hormone-producing) systems. Such responses are primary effects of stress, and they lead quickly to metabolic and osmotic disturbances, which are secondary effects. In other words, when a fish is subjected to a stress factor its neuroendocrine system responds by releasing certain hormones into the blood, and the effects of elevated concentrations of these substances disturb physiological stasis. This is the *primary stress response*. The main hormones involved are *catecholamines* (adrenaline and noradrenaline) and *corticoste-*

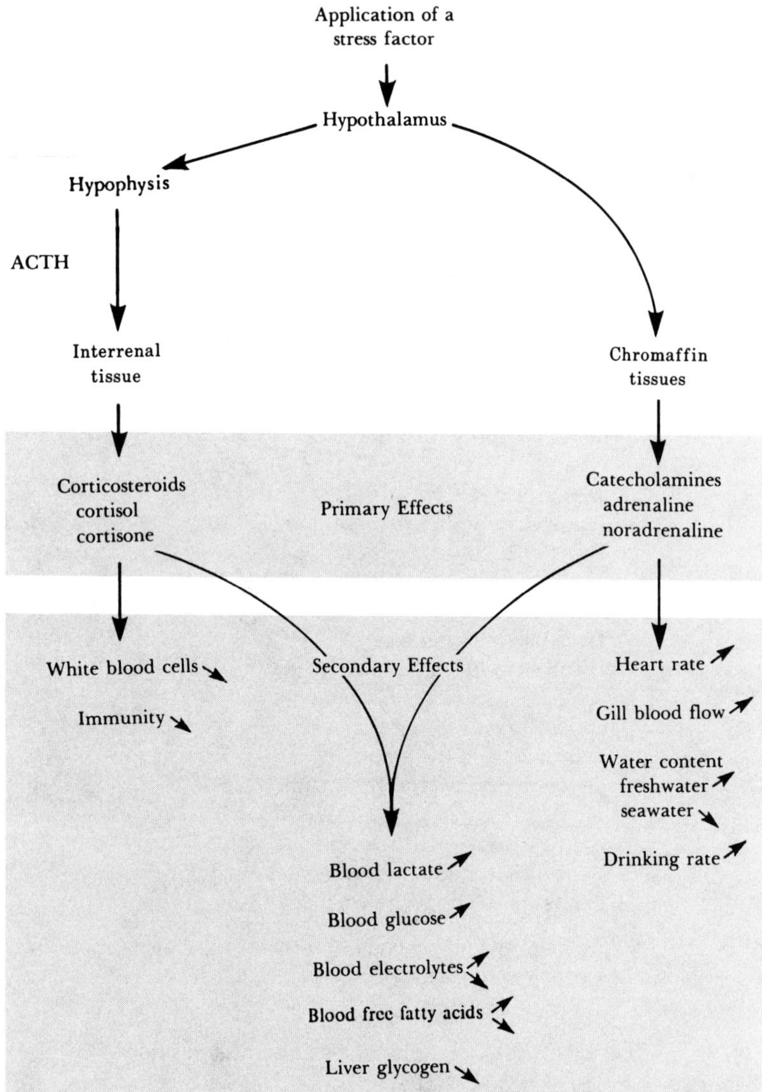

Figure 4-19 *Mobilization and eventual exhaustion of the stress response has five major components:* (1) *application of a stress factor;* (2) *activation of the hypophysis via the hypothalamus;* (3) *release of ACTH by the pituitary gland to the interrenal tissue;* (4) *release of corticosteroids and catecholamines into the blood by interrenal and chromaffin tissues, respectively; and* (5) *breakdown of excess corticosteroids and catecholamines and excretion of their elemental constituents into the environment.* Source: Mazeaud et al. (1977).

roids (cortisol and cortisone). Primary and secondary effects are measurable physiological factors, but not otherwise observable. Secondary stress effects resulting from the *secondary stress response* include osmoregulatory disturbances,[44] depletion of blood ascorbic acid (vitamin C),[45] changes in the oxygen-binding properties of the hemoglobin,[46] altered lactate metabolism,[47] altered lipid metabolism,[48] changes in blood chemistry and hematology,[49] and immune suppression resulting in predisposition to disease.[50] Prolonged, intermittent, or sometimes even brief exposure to a stress factor can induce long-lasting physiological disturbances. Factors known to induce primary and secondary stress responses include injury and disease;[51] anesthesia;[52] crowding and social conflict;[53] close confinement, restricted movement, or restraint;[54] confinement in shallow water;[55] confinement in constant darkness;[56] environmental hypoxia or struggling in air (physiological hypoxia);[57] thermal shock;[58] salinity shock;[59] chase, capture, handling, or transport;[60] environmental hypercapnia;[61] starvation;[62] and exposure to toxicants.[63]

Tertiary responses, the third and final stage of the sequence, are often the tangible evidence that a stress factor has been applied.[64] *Immune suppression* (suppression of the immune system, Chapter 9) is among the most important of these, because it results in decreased resistance to infectious microorganisms and the appearance of clinical and pathological signs of disease (Chapter 9).

The stress response is sequential because hormones that control it are released in sequence. Two pathways have been identified (Fig. 4-19).[65] One of these occurs along the hypothalamic-pituitary-interrenal axis (abbreviated as HPI axis), beginning with adrenocorticotropin, ACTH. The *hypothalamus* is situated on the underside of the brain, and just below it lies the *hypophysis* (also called the *pituitary gland*). Endocrine cells that make up the interrenal tissues occupy various positions either in direct contact with the kidneys or nearby.[66] Secretion of corticosteroids into the blood is controlled by ACTH. After the stress factor has been removed these substances are broken down by normal metabolic processes, and the constituents are extruded into the environment. The role of the hypothalamus (i.e., whether it controls production and release of ACTH by the hypophysis) is still in question, and the highest level in the sequence that can be accepted with assurance at this time is the hypophysis.[67] The second pathway involves activation of the chromaffin tissues (presumably by the hypothalamus) with subsequent release of catecholamines into the blood.[66]

EXERCISE STRESS Fishes forced to exercise strenuously[68] for only a few minutes suffer acid-base inbalances that can have fatal consequences hours or even days later. This phenomenon is known as *delayed post-exercise mortality*. Oxygen requirements rise sharply during exercise stress because bursts of swimming quickly deplete the tissue O_2 supply. The subsequent increased uptake of O_2 elevates the concentration of CO_2 produced by the tissues. The excess CO_2 enters the blood and causes respiratory acidosis (i.e., increased $PaCO_2$ or physiological hypercapnia). Metabolic activities in the muscles simultaneously generate organic acids and H^+, resulting in *metabolic acidosis*. The combined acidoses reduce affinity of the blood for oxygen and interfere with the unloading of O_2 at the tissues. The effects of respiratory acidosis are relatively brief,[69] and delayed post-exercise mortality appears to be caused by intracellular toxicity from organic acids produced metabolically but not released into the blood.[70] The chemical characteristics of these compounds are unknown. At one time lactic acid was believed to be a primary cause of delayed post-exercise mortality, but this now seems doubtful.[71] However, lactate undoubtedly contributes to the acidotic condition of fishes subjected to exercise stress (Fig. 4-20).[72] Other secondary effects of exercise stress include immediate increases in blood hematocrit and hemoglobin concentrations, the latter accompanied by a dramatic decrease in spleen mass as hemoglobin is mobilized and transferred to the blood.[73]

HANDLING STRESS The consequences of capture, handling, crowding, and confinement (combined here as *handling stress*) are universally overlooked by aquarists, probably because no cause-effect relationship is immediately apparent (i.e., stressed fishes frequently die later but not during application of the stress factor). These delayed mortalities can often be avoided by reducing the severity of the stresses and permitting fishes that have been recently captured or transported adequate time to recover.[74]

Blood corticosteroid and catecholamine concentrations become elevated within minutes after handling stress (Fig. 4-21), and secondary stress effects follow quickly. The magnitude and duration of both responses depends on numerous factors (e.g., species, reproductive state, intensity and nature of the stress factor, mediating environmental conditions). The primary stress effects can disappear within hours or persist for several days before subsiding to prestress levels.[75] Secondary stress effects include respiratory acidosis and *hyperglycemia* (elevated blood sugar or glucose).[76] A period of 1 to 4 d is required for the latter value to return to prestress concentrations.[77]

Water permeability increases with increased concentrations of blood catecholamines in teleosts subjected to handling or exercise stress.[78] In freshwater teleosts this is manifested by a net gain of water, dilution of blood components or *hemodilution*, and a transient increase in body mass.[79] Seawater teleosts experience the opposite effect: net loss of water, *hemoconcentration*, and a transient decrease in body mass.[79] In seawater fishes these effects are caused in part by a marked decline in drinking rate.[80]

ENVIRONMENTAL STRESS FACTORS The most important environmental stress factors appear to be exposure to sudden

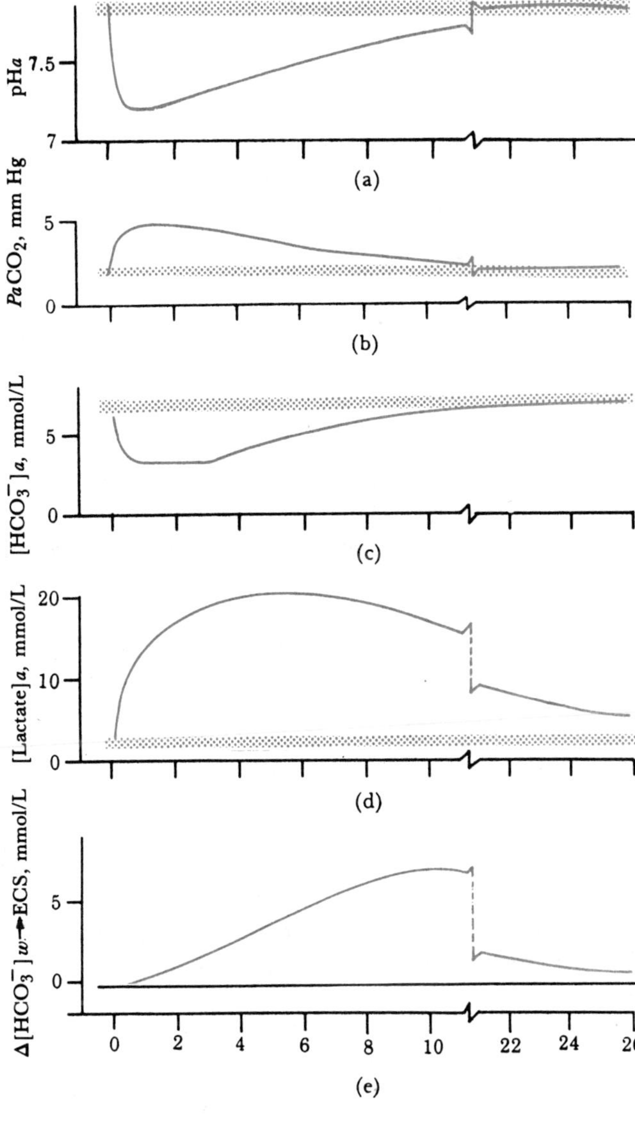

Figure 4-20 *Acid-base imbalance (secondary stress response) in larger spotted dogfish induced by 10 min of severe exercise (data points omitted). Responses of other species are similar but differ quantitatively. Shaded areas and straight horizontal line at* (e) *are prestress values.* (a) *The fall in pHa is accompanied by* (b) *a rise in $PaCO_2$ and* (c) *a subsequent decline in* $[HCO_3^-]$a. (d) *Lactate increases, and* (e) *bicarbonate is transferred to extracellular spaces, ECS. All factors have returned to normal 24 h after application of the stress.* Source: Holeton and Heisler (1983).

and substantial changes in temperature, water that is hypercapnic or hypoxic, and the presence of toxic substances. All induce primary and secondary stress responses. Salinity and acidity stresses are important considerations in maintenance of freshwater fishes. In nature, seawater fishes seldom encounter situations in which either factor varies enough to be stressful. During shipping or transport the pH of seawater can become

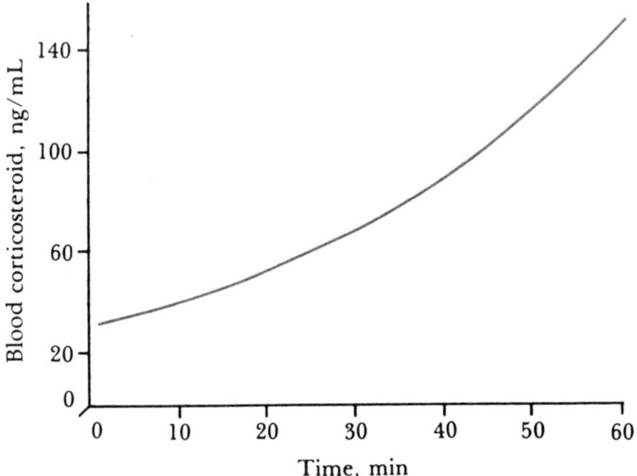

Figure 4-21 Increase in blood corticosteroid concentration in rainbow trout during the first hour of close confinement in a net (data points omitted). Source: Davis and Parker (1983).

truly acidic (<7.0) and not merely relatively so, unless preventive measures are taken.[32]

The pattern of acid-base imbalance induced by environmental hypercapnia has been described in an earlier section and is similar to that caused by exercise and handling stress (Fig. 4-20). A rise in $PaCO_2$ occurs almost instantly and is quickly accompanied by concomitant declines in $[HCO_3^-]a$ and pH*a*. The initial increase in lactate is minor and does not become important for several hours. Lactate peaks as $PaCO_2$ and $[HCO_3^-]a$ are returning to near-normal values. Thus the first acidosis is respiratory in origin, whereas the subsequent effect is attributable to metabolic factors. Thermal stress results immediately in primary and secondary stress responses,[81] as does exposure to hypoxic water.[82] An increase in the concentration of blood adrenaline apparently has adaptive significance during hypoxia stress by (*1*) promoting lamellar recruitment and thus enlarging the functional surface area of the gills, and (2) causing increased systemic blood flow and enhanced O_2 transfer between the blood and the environment.[83]

Ammonia is the most important toxic compound in aquarium seawater. As a by-product of nitrogen metabolism, it is generated by the tissues and extruded into the environment continuously.[84] Surprisingly little is known about the toxic mechanisms of ammonia, or even the chemical form and conditions under which it enters fishes at times of elevated total NH_4-N in the environment. The model illustrated in Figure 4-22 attempts to explain how environmental ammonia might enter freshwater teleosts across the gill epithelium. In seawater teleosts NH_4^+ conceivably could enter the gill epithelium during a reversal of the normal ion exchange process with Na^+. Experiments have shown that increased concentrations of NH_4^+ in

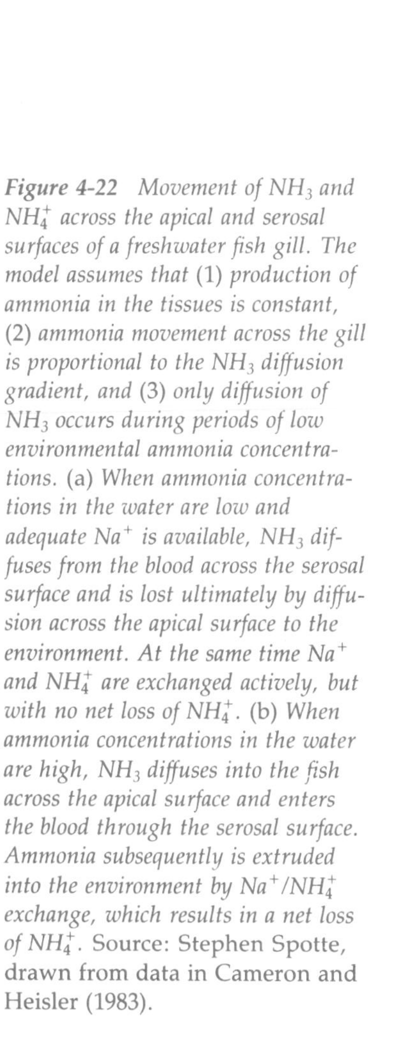

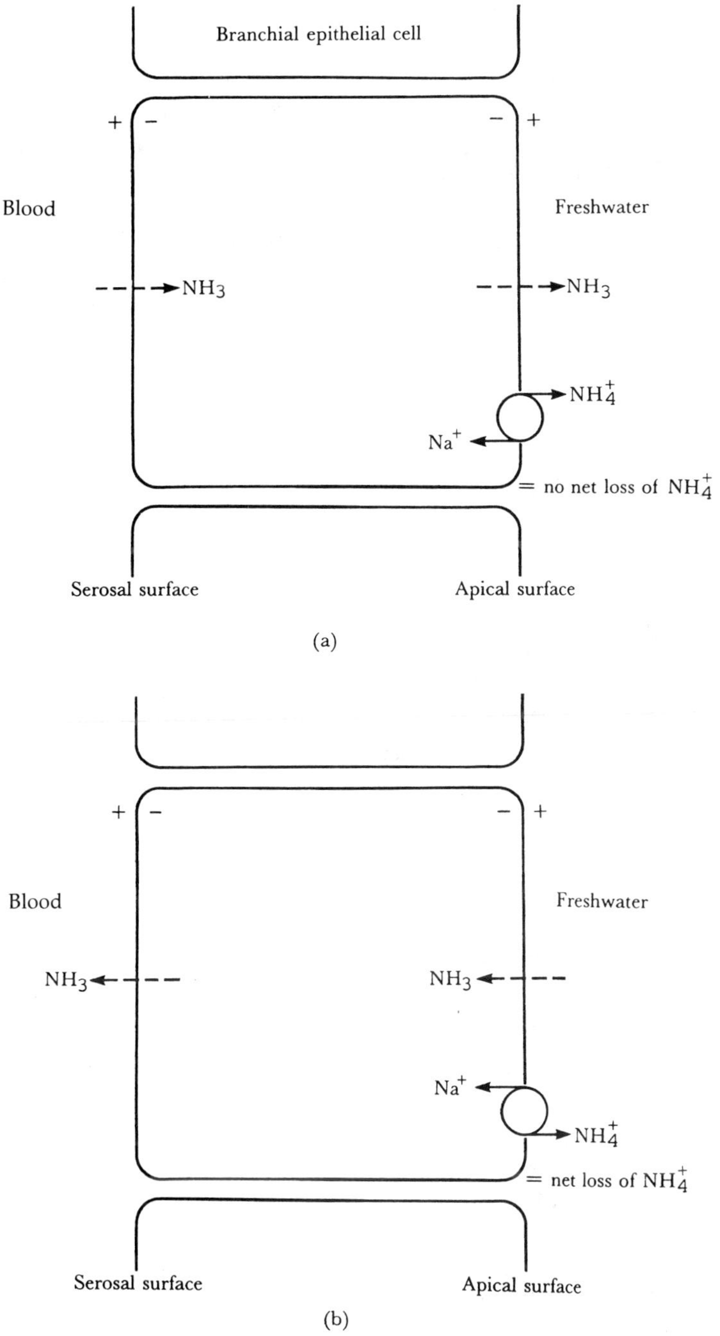

Figure 4-22 *Movement of NH_3 and NH_4^+ across the apical and serosal surfaces of a freshwater fish gill. The model assumes that* (1) *production of ammonia in the tissues is constant,* (2) *ammonia movement across the gill is proportional to the NH_3 diffusion gradient, and* (3) *only diffusion of NH_3 occurs during periods of low environmental ammonia concentrations.* (a) *When ammonia concentrations in the water are low and adequate Na^+ is available, NH_3 diffuses from the blood across the serosal surface and is lost ultimately by diffusion across the apical surface to the environment. At the same time Na^+ and NH_4^+ are exchanged actively, but with no net loss of NH_4^+.* (b) *When ammonia concentrations in the water are high, NH_3 diffuses into the fish across the apical surface and enters the blood through the serosal surface. Ammonia subsequently is extruded into the environment by Na^+/NH_4^+ exchange, which results in a net loss of NH_4^+.* Source: Stephen Spotte, drawn from data in Cameron and Heisler (1983).

the environment inhibit assimilation of Na^+, or actually reverse the Na^+/NH_4^+ exchange process causing Na^+ excretion to increase.[84]

CHAPTER

5 Sensory Perception

Sensory perception can be studied at both the anatomical and functional level. It would seem that after suitable evaluation the knowledge gained could be applied directly to the design of aquarium exhibits. Unfortunately, this is not the case. The sensory anatomy of fishes has been described in exquisite detail, but far less is known about how sensory information is received and processed. For example, we understand the lateral line's anatomy better than its functions. In this chapter I describe three sensory systems of fishes—vision, hearing, and electroreception—from both anatomical and functional perspectives.

SCIENCE

Vision

To appreciate fully the evolutionary adaptations of vision in fishes requires an understanding of how light behaves in water. Treatment of the subject here would be awkward, and readers unfamiliar with the properties of submarine light are asked to read the first part of Chapter 10 before continuing. I apologize for the inconvenience.

THE EYE[1] The high density of water (relative to air), in concert with substantial light loss caused by attenuation, markedly lowers *visual acuity* (i.e., resolving power or the capacity for seeing images clearly) of terrestrial vertebrates when they open their eyes underwater.[2] To enhance visual acuity in the submarine world, the eyes of fishes have evolved in ways that differ in important respects from the eyes of terrestrial vertebrates

(Fig. 5-1). Water's high density tends to cause extreme farsightedness or *hyperopic vision* in fishes. Light is gathered and focused on the retina to form an image, but not until being refracted through boundary layers consisting sequentially of the cornea, aqueous humor, and finally the lens. The extent to which refraction can occur depends on the curvature of the boundary between the two media (i.e., air or water and the boundary layers of the eye) and the difference in their refractive indices, which are density dependent. The boundary layers of greatest importance are where the external medium (air or water) touches the cornea and at the front and back of the lens where it meets the aqueous and vitreous humors (Fig. 5-1). Differences in the refractive indices of air and the aqueous humor are substantial, and for terrestrial vertebrates light gathering and focusing can be accomplished largely by a curved cornea that serves as a lens. Little additional refraction is required to form a clear image on the retina. Consequently, this can be achieved by an oval lens barely denser than the humors in which it functions. Such a lens is fluid and can be focused when

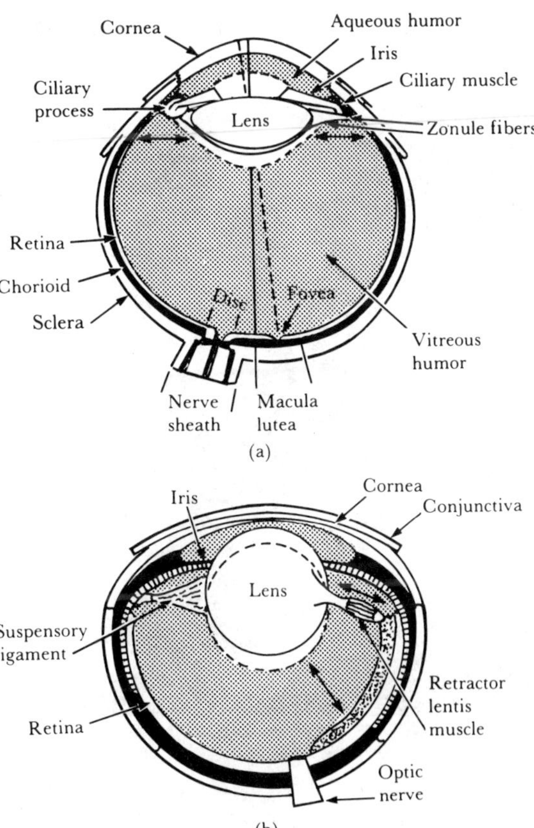

Figure 5-1 *Cross sections through the eyes of a terrestrial and aquatic vertebrate illustrating anatomical adaptations to air and water.* (a) *Eye of a human being. Note that the cornea is shaped like a lens. Note also the oval lens and ciliary muscles that alter the shape of the lens for focusing.* (b) *Eye of a teleost. Note the round, solid lens protruding almost to the cornea. Images are brought into focus as the lens is moved back and forth with respect to the retina.* Sources: Levine (1980) and Walls (1963).

its shape is altered by contraction and relaxation of a surrounding muscle ring (Fig. 5-1a).

The high density of water presents a problem for fishes, because water's refractive index is closer (compared with air) to that of the two humors. This diminishes the capacity of the cornea to refract light, leaving to the lens the burden of both gathering light and projecting it accurately onto the retina. Fishes have overcome the problem of hyperopia through the evolution of crystalline lenses of high density and exaggerated curvature that protrude through the pupil almost to the cornea. In the majority of fishes the pupil is fixed in a wide-open position and cannot be changed to accommodate different levels of illumination. Neither can the shape of a typical lens be altered appreciably, as it can be in terrestrial vertebrates, and light is focused by changing the position of the lens with respect to the retina through muscular and ligament action (Fig. 5-1b).

The evolutionary response to ambient light levels is evident in the appearance of the eye. The eyes of deepwater fishes ordinarily are enlarged, as are those of fishes that are *crepuscular* (active at dawn and dusk, both time periods called *twilight*) and nocturnal (Fig. 5-2a, Plate 1a). Diurnal species, which are active

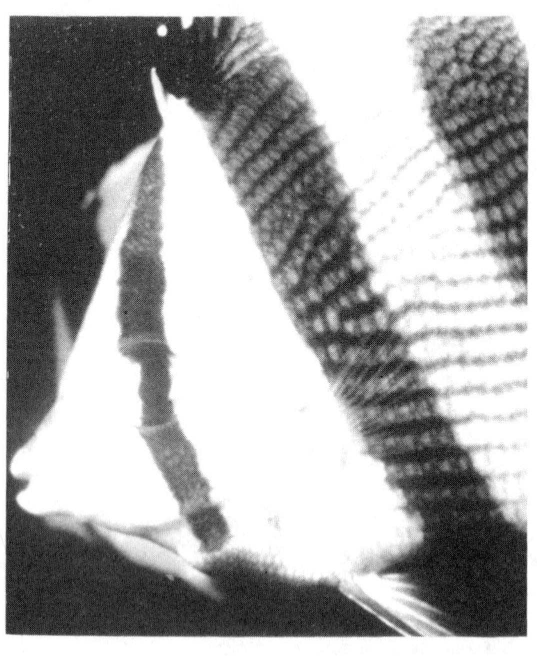

(a)

(b)

Figure 5-2 Size differences in the eyes of (a) *a diurnal fish* (Chaetodon striatus) *and* (b) *a nocturnal fish* (Holocentrus rufus). Source: Stephen Spotte.

in full daylight, ordinarily have eyes that are comparatively smaller (Fig. 5-2b, Plates 1b and 1c).

Variations in evolutionary adaptation to different light levels also are apparent in *visual cells* of the retina (sometimes called *retinal cells* and *photoreceptor cells*), of which there are two types (Fig. 5-3). *Rods* are low-light receptors and a system of high *photosensitivity* (i.e., sensitivity to the ambient level of illumination), making *scotopic* or night vision possible. The *cones* are high-light receptors and used in *photopic* or daytime vision. Thus scotopic and photopic elements of vision are rod and cone mediated, respectively. The visual cells in combination enable fishes to see at different levels of available light. In many species the cone mediated visual system makes possible wavelength discrimination, which is synonymous with *color vision*[3] or the capacity to distinguish hue (Chapter 10).

In diurnal fishes both the cones and rods are numerous and packed tightly (Fig. 5-4). Paired and single cones ordinarily are present, arranged in uniform, mosaic patterns (Fig. 5-5). Deepwater, crepuscular, and nocturnal species possess cones that are greatly enlarged in comparison (Fig. 5-6).[4] In addition, the mosaic expands, which opens spaces between cone cells. These

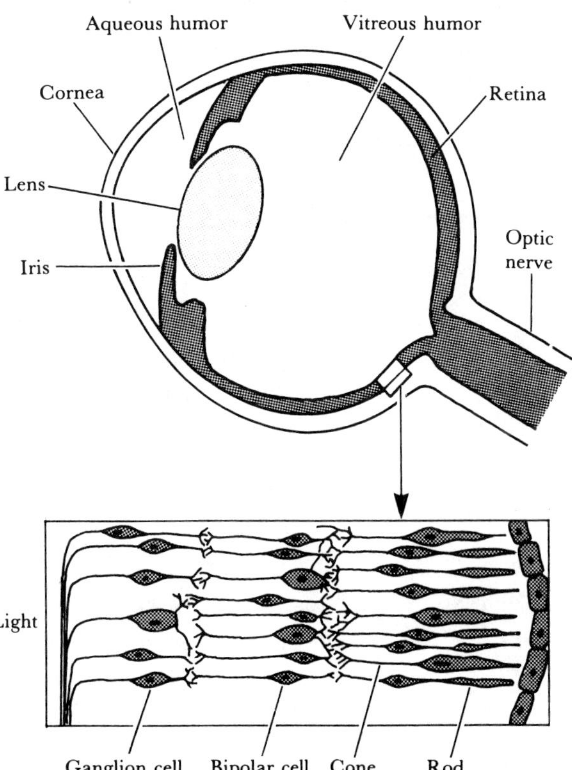

Figure 5-3 Diagrammatic illustration of the human eye. At least two other kinds of cells are found in the retina, in addition to visual cells. These are bipolar neurons *and* ganglion cells. *Light striking the photoreceptors generates nerve impulses to both types of cells. The nerve impulses are carried to the brain by the optic nerve. Each retina contains ~ 125 million photoreceptors.* Source: Ebert et al. (1973).

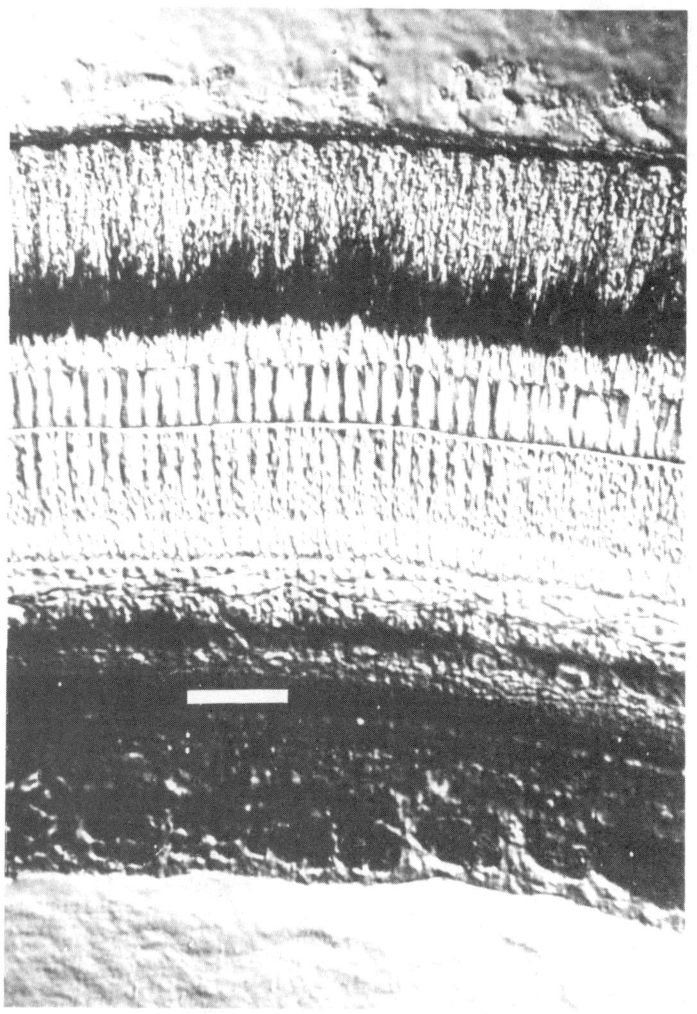

Figure 5-4 *Longitudinal section through the retina of a winter flounder* (Pseudopleuronectes americanus). *Sectional layers are* (1) *pigment epithelial layer,* (2) *visual cell layer,* (3) *external limiting membrane,* (4) *external nuclear layer,* (5) *external plexiform layer,* (6) *internal nuclear layer,* (7) *internal plexiform layer,* (8) *ganglion cell layer, and* (9) *internal limiting membrane. Note the densely packed cones and numerous rods immediately underneath in the external nuclear layer. Scale bar* = *50* *μm.* Source: Barbara Ann Collins, Laboratory of Sensory Physiology, Marine Biological Laboratory.

are occupied by numerous rods. Compared with cones, rods require fewer photons to "excite" or activate them into producing a neural signal. Moreover, the rods are connected in neural networks that combine and amplify signals from individual receptors. This summation effect produces a few larger signals from many smaller ones, but at the expense of reduced visual acuity.

VISUAL ACUITY[5] The degree of visual acuity possible underwater depends on two relative characteristics of the visual cells: (*1*) adeptness at gathering photons from the surrounding dimness and (2) capacity for distinguishing objects against the diffuse light of the background, called the *background spacelight*.

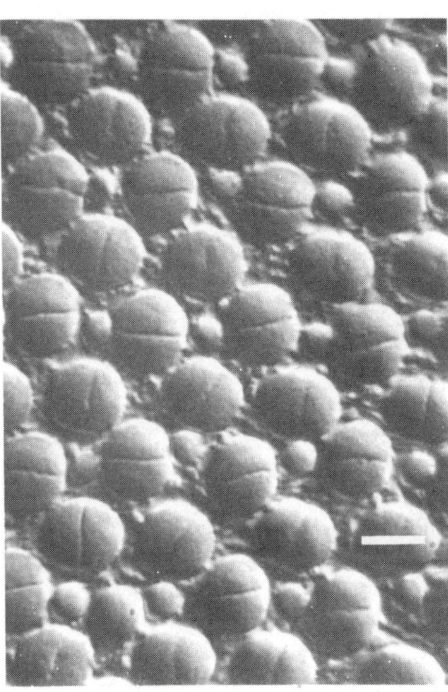

Figure 5-5 *Mosaic patterns in the retina of a sea raven* (Hemitripterus americanus). *Scale bar = 10 μm.* Source: Collins and MacNichol (1984).

These functions define the limits of photosensitivity and contrast perception, respectively. Both rely ultimately on the number of visual pigments present in the rods and cones and whether the wavelength of light that each pigment absorbs most effectively is the same or different from the dominant wavelength of the background spacelight. All vertebrates with vision have at least one visual pigment, and many possess several. In fishes, neither the number of pigments nor the wavelengths they match can be correlated on a phylogenetic basis. Closely related species often have visual pigments that differ markedly.

The visual cells are photosensitive because the visual pigments are *photolabile* or capable of being changed by light.[6] In fishes, the relationship between light (its color and intensity) and photosensitivity of the rods and cones to individual wavelengths is direct. Thus a demonstrable relationship exists between the optical properties of water—its distinct spectrum and overall transmittance—and the spectral characteristics of the visual pigments. Visual pigments are able to absorb light of most visible wavelengths, but each has an absorption maximum at which it is most effective (Fig. 5-7). In terms of photosensitivity, any disparity between the absorption maximum of a visual pigment and the color of the ambient light is potentially maladaptive.[7] Matched visual pigments are the most photosensitive because they absorb (i.e., spectrally match) the dominant

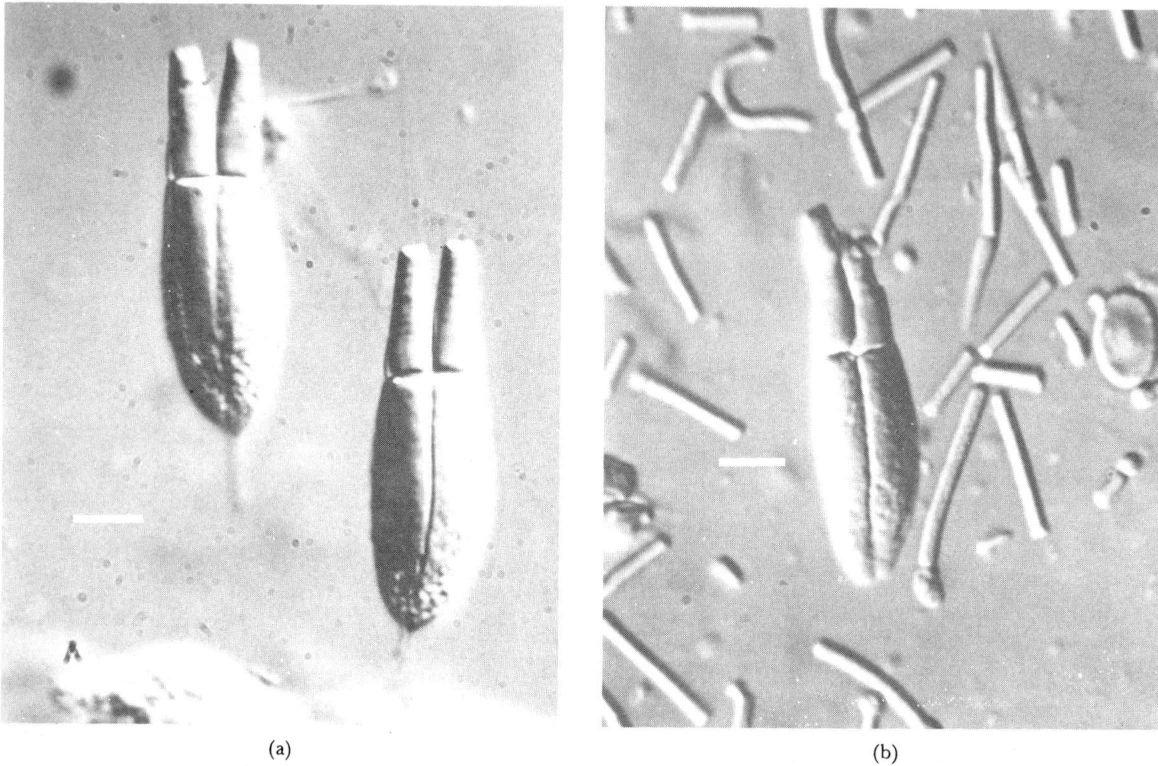

(a) (b)

Figure 5-6 *Paired cone cells of a sculpin (probably the longhorn sculpin,* Myoxocephalus octodecemspinosus). (a) *Two isolated paired cone cells.* (b) *A single isolated paired cone cell surrounded by rods. The elliptical object on the right is an erythrocyte. Scale bars = 10 μm.* Source: Barbara Ann Collins, Laboratory of Sensory Physiology, Marine Biological Laboratory.

wavelength of the background spacelight more efficiently than they absorb other wavelengths. Single, matched rod pigments are characteristic of fishes that are deepwater, crepuscular, nocturnal, and in some cases pelagic; in other words, species active at times or places when low levels of ambient light make photosensitivity more critical than contrast perception.

The retinas of diurnal fishes that inhabit shallow inshore waters and the upper or *epipelagic zone* of the open oceans are bathed in the broad spectrum of downwelling daylight. In addition, the intensity of available light is greater than it is in the deep oceans or at night. Light gathering is not as difficult, and photosensitivity is less a limiting factor in visual acuity.[8] The enhancement of contrast perception requires pigments that are mismatched or *offset* from the dominant wavelength of the background spacelight.[9] The capacity to see contrast is further

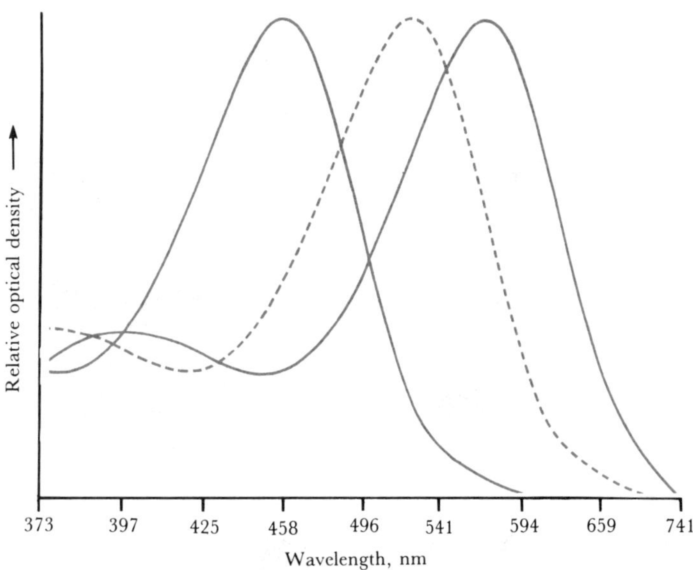

Figure 5-7 *Computer generated curves of the absorption spectra of three visual pigments with different absorption maxima, graphed as optical density (see Note 11) across the visible spectrum. The height of a curve at any point in the spectrum indicates the relative probability that light of that wavelength will be absorbed. Note that both curves have sharp peaks and fall off rapidly on the shorter and longer wavelengths to either side.* Source: Levine (1980).

improved in fishes that possess two or more cone visual pigments; in other words, in those species with color vision.[10]

A visual pigment with a wavelength of maximum absorbance, λ_{max},[11] that is offset from the λ_{max} of the background spacelight will absorb less visible energy from both the background spacelight and the object. As a result, the reflected light becomes brighter relative to the background and easier to see. An object that is darker than the background spacelight becomes less visible. The clarity with which an object can be detected depends on its *radiance* or degree of contrast. For detection of nearby bright objects the most effective visual pigment is one in which the λ_{max} value is offset from the wavelength of greatest water transparency; in other words, the wavelength for which the water is least opaque.[12] However, for all dark objects and distant bright ones the best visual pigments have a λ_{max} value that coincides approximately with the wavelength of maximum transparency of the water.[13]

The guidelines just described hold true generally for daylight conditions in clear seas, but the rapid attenuation of light even in the clearest water means that vertical depth must still be considered. A fish swimming in a horizontal plane sees more light of longer wavelengths when it looks up (Fig. 5-8). When it looks down the light flooding the retina is comparatively *monochromatic* (i.e., tending toward a single wavelength). The degree of contrast of an object against the background spacelight depends on the factors given previously (distance and degree of reflectivity), in addition to its direction and size. If these are

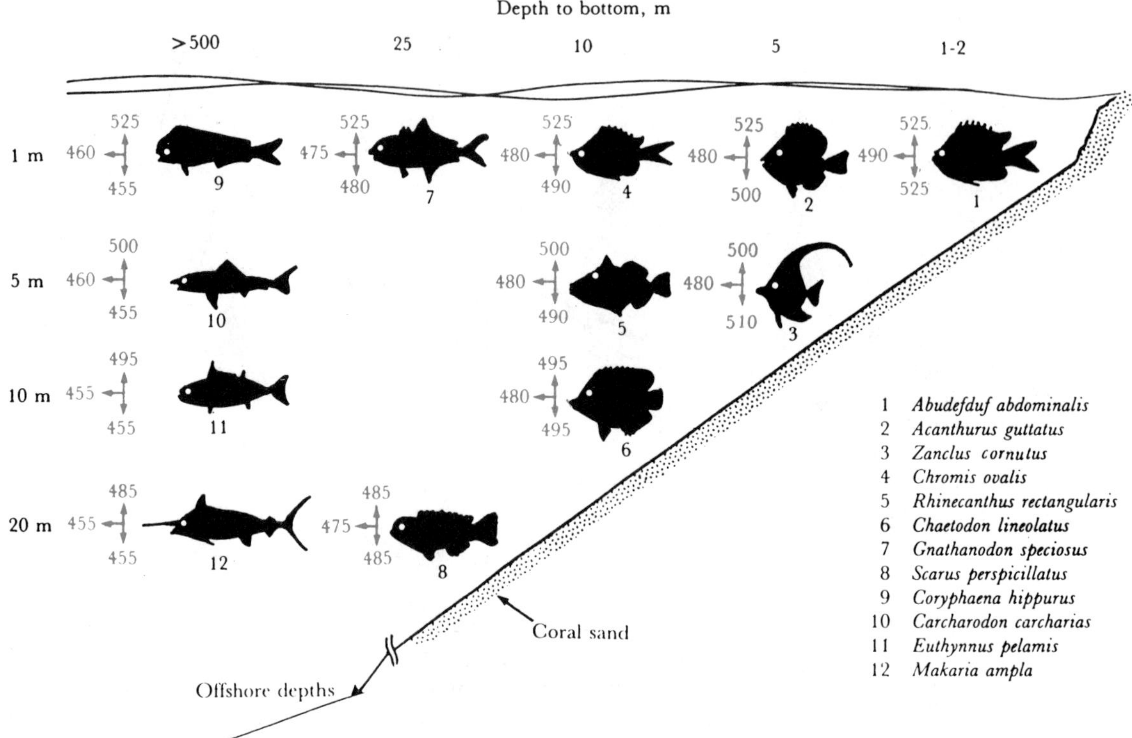

Figure 5-8 *Spectral properties of the background spacelight in clear, tropical oceans near coral reefs and more distantly in pelagic zones. Total depth in metres is shown at the water surface. Vertical depths at which light measurements were made are given on the left ordinate. At each location the median wavelength,* λP_{50} *(the wavelength that divides in half the number of photons present in the spectrum under consideration), is shown for three sight lines: upward, horizontal, and downward. In shallow water the reflective coral sand bottom affects the horizontal and downward light values. Fishes that inhabit these locations and adjacent pelagic regions are illustrated (not to scale); numbers beneath the illustrations encode species names in the lower right. The figure is based on light measurements made at Eniwetak Atoll and Hawaii.* Source: Munz and McFarland (1977).

kept constant it is possible to assess the effect of matched and offset visual pigments on degree of contrast for both bright and dark objects as a function of depth (Figs. 5-9 and 5-10).

It appears that a combination of matched and offset visual pigments is an adaptation particularly well suited for shallow-water, diurnal fishes. Matched pigments enhance photosensitivity; offset pigments enhance contrast perception. Color vision cannot occur in photic environments in which the light is monochromatic or absent.[10] Downwelling daylight in tropical

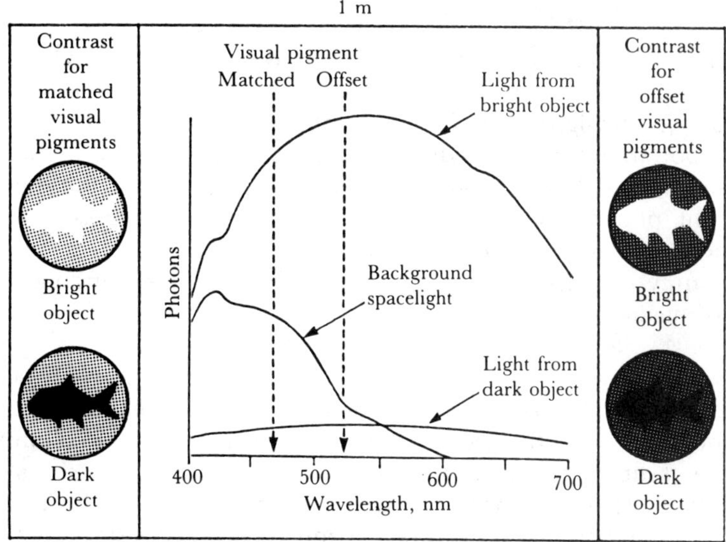

Figure 5-9 Comparison of the relative contrast of bright (reflective) and dark (nonreflective) objects viewed by a diurnal fish in a horizontal plane at a depth of 1 m. Assume that the visual pigments either match the background spacelight or are offset from it. Both bright and dark objects are assumed to be gray. Light reflected into the plane of vision includes sunlight reflected directly. Reflected light close to the bright objects is 50 to 100 times more intense than the background spacelight (scaling not indicated on the ordinate). The insets show the relative contrast that would be produced by each visual pigment. The matched pigment enhances the contrast of a dark object; the offset pigment improves the contrast of a bright object. Source: McFarland and Munz (1975b).

seas penetrates the surface in a broad, flat spectrum, and all known visual pigments of fishes found in these habitats are, despite their narrowness, matched pigments simply because they absorb within the available spectrum. Offset visual pigments have perhaps been selected for when the background spacelight approaches monochromaticity. This condition occurs at all depths in a horizontal plane and when looking downward.[14]

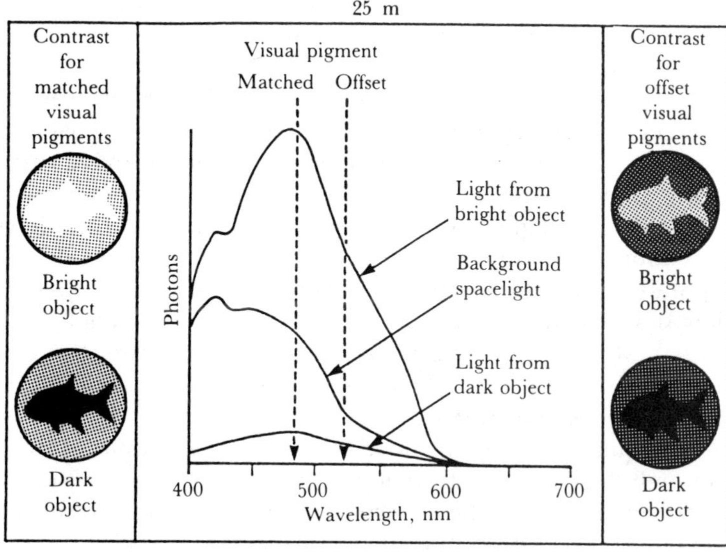

Figure 5-10 Comparison of the relative contrast of bright (reflective) and dark (nonreflective) objects viewed by a diurnal fish in a horizontal plane at a depth of 25 m. Assumptions are the same as in Figure 5-9. At the greater depth, reflections from bright objects are 20 to 40 times more intense than the background spacelight (scaling not indicated on the ordinate). The insets show the relative contrast that would be produced by each visual pigment. The matched pigment results in greater contrast than the offset pigment for both bright and dark objects. Source: McFarland and Munz (1975b).

The Photic Environment

The photic environment can be divided broadly into daylight, twilight, moonlight, and starlight. To aquarists the characteristics of daylight or the high-light photic environment are most important from the standpoint of exhibiting fishes. This section emphasizes how periods of low light intensity (i.e., the low-light photic environment) affect the natural interactions of predators and prey. It is my contention that predation in community exhibits can be reduced by a better understanding of fish visual systems.

PREDATION—THE ''QUIET PERIOD'' A startling event occurs on coral reefs at dusk: the myriad diurnal fishes disappear into crevices in the reef, and their places in the water column are assumed by nocturnal species. This changing of ''shifts'' (called *changeover*) has been well documented.[15] The most interesting behavioral feature encompasses what Edmund S. Hobson called the ''quiet period.''[16] As dusk descends, diurnal species begin an orderly transition from open areas to the reef below. Approximately 20 min are required for complete evacuation of the water column, and few diurnal fishes remain at 10 to 15 min after sunset. Their nocturnal replacements emerge suddenly, starting ~30 min after sunset. The overall activity level decreases at dusk, leaving a hiatus or ''quiet period'' of 20 min or so when the water column is occupied by crepuscular predators. Then the quiet period ends, and the space above the reef fills abruptly with nocturnal fishes (Fig. 5-11, Plates 1d and 2a). The same events occur in reverse order at dawn (Fig. 5-12). Predation is most intense just before and during the quiet period,[17] when crepuscular predators dominate the reef.

PREDATION AND LOW-LIGHT PHOTIC ENVIRONMENTS[18] Low-light photic environments are critical for scotopic vision in fishes. The scotopic visual pigments apparently provide maximum photosensitivity at twilight. Two features characterize twilight, moonlight, and starlight: (*1*) a reduction in the level of illumination and (*2*) a shift in the spectrum of downwelling light. The twilight spectrum undergoes a decrease in the yellow-orange wavelengths caused by attenuation of red light (Fig. 5-13a). Moonlight has a broader submarine spectrum than twilight (Fig. 5-13b). Starlight is less intense than moonlight but with a similar spectrum.

The quiet period corresponds with the final minutes of falling light associated with twilight, the time at which vision is suspended between the extinction of cone function and the onset of rod function. Neither visual system is performing at peak

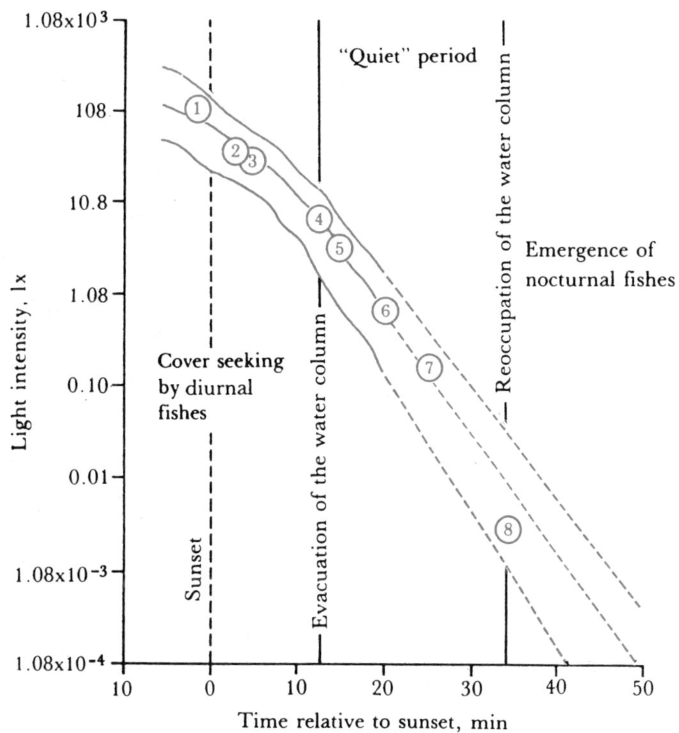

Figure 5-11 *Summary of events during evening changeover on a Hawaiian reef. Curves represent maximum and minimum light values of each minute relative to sunset (top and bottom, respectively), and mean values (middle). Numbers represent species and events:* (1) *when the last* Thalassoma duperrey *(Labridae) took shelter on five evenings;* (2) *when one* Labroides phthirophagus *(Labridae) took shelter on five evenings;* (3) *when the last* Chromis leucurus *(Pomacentridae) took shelter on three evenings;* (4) *abrupt vacating of the water column by diurnal fishes and start of the "quiet period" on 12 evenings;* (5) *when* Apogon snyderi *(Apogonidae) first left shelter on five evenings;* (6) *when* A. menesemus *first left shelter on five evenings;* (7) *when* Holocentrus sammara *(Holocentridae) first left shelter on four evenings;* (8) *when* Myripristis *spp. (Holocentridae) appeared abruptly in large numbers above the reef signaling the end of the "quiet period" on eight evenings.* Source: Hobson (1972).

effectiveness, and immediately before and during this period crepuscular predation is at maximum. Crepuscular predators gain a clear advantage at twilight,[19] but prey species take evasive measures. As dusk encroaches they shift downward out of the water column and move about near the reef. Predators active at twilight often strike from below when prey fishes are silhouetted against the remaining background spacelight, but disorganized movements of the prey make singling out an individual target more difficult. In addition, by shifting closer to the reef prey fishes reduce their contrast. Although the coral reef fishes studied to date—predators and prey alike—have rods with similar scotopic visual pigments, their cones differ in number and size. Those of diurnal fishes are small and densely packed, often 100,000/mm^2. Nocturnal fishes have fewer cones (e.g., 3000 to 9000/mm^2) of larger size. The cones of some crepuscular predators often are intermediate in density (e.g., 20,000 to 30,000/mm^2) but so large that the amount of light gathered is equal to that of diurnal species. These fishes have reduced photopic vision (i.e., lower visual acuity) compared with diurnal species, but the nature of their visual systems makes them successful predators at twilight.

Many diurnal fishes leave the safety of the reef on bright,

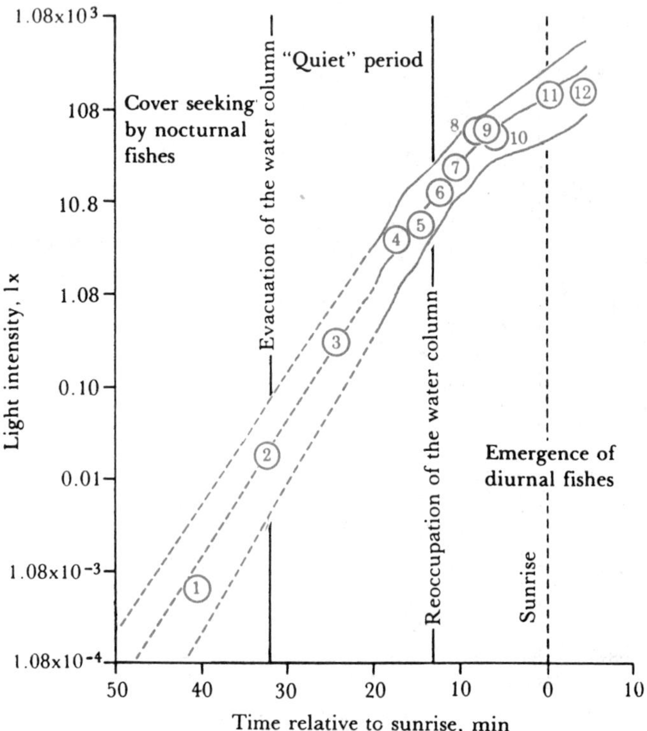

Figure 5-12 *Summary of events during the morning changeover on a Hawaiian reef. Curves and symbols are the same as in Figure 5-11:* (1) *when a specific school of* Priacanthus cruentatus *(Priacanthidae) returned to the reef on six mornings;* (2) *when the last* Myripristis *spp. took shelter in the reef;* (3) *when surgeonfishes (Acanthuridae) started to assemble in depressions in the reef on six mornings;* (4) *when an aggregation of* Dascyllus albisella *(Pomacentridae) in a specific location had moved away from shelter on five mornings;* (5) *when diurnal fishes first surged 1 to 2 m into the water column signaling the end of the "quiet period" on nine mornings;* (6) *when the first parrotfish (Scaridae) appeared away from shelter on nine mornings;* (7) *when the aggregation of* Dascyllus albisella *(number 4) had risen 3 m above the reef on five mornings;* (8) *when* Chromis leucurus *first left cover on nine mornings;* (9) *when* Labroides phthirophagus *first left cover on nine mornings;* (10) *when* Thalassoma duperrey *first left shelter on 16 mornings;* (11) *when* Acanthurus nigrofuscus *(Acanthuridae) first appeared in schools above the reef on three mornings;* (12) *when the aggregation of* Dascyllus albisella *(numbers 4 and 7) was 5 m above the reef on three mornings.* Source: Hobson (1972).

moonlit nights. These same species are absent from the water column on nights heavily overcast. The scotopic visual pigments of coral reef fishes do not match twilight perfectly. The λ_{max} values of most species range from 489 to 499 nm.* The submarine twilight spectrum suggests that λ_{max} values of 490 to 515 nm would provide a better match (Fig. 5-13a). It appears that the scotopic visual pigments of both diurnal and nocturnal fishes represent an evolutionary compromise between the slightly different visual requirements of twilight and moonlight. As described at the start of this subsection, starlight is less intense than moonlight but has a similar spectrum. A visual pigment, in other words, provides optimal vision in the photic environment of greatest use. However, the scotopic visual systems of fishes provide maximum photosensitivity at twilight, and the compromise (assuming there is one) has been tipped in that direction.

Moonlight and starlight strongly affect the behavior of nocturnal fishes that are vulnerable to predation by larger species. On coral reefs, the numbers of large nocturnal predators are

*1 nm (nanometer) = 10^{-9} m.

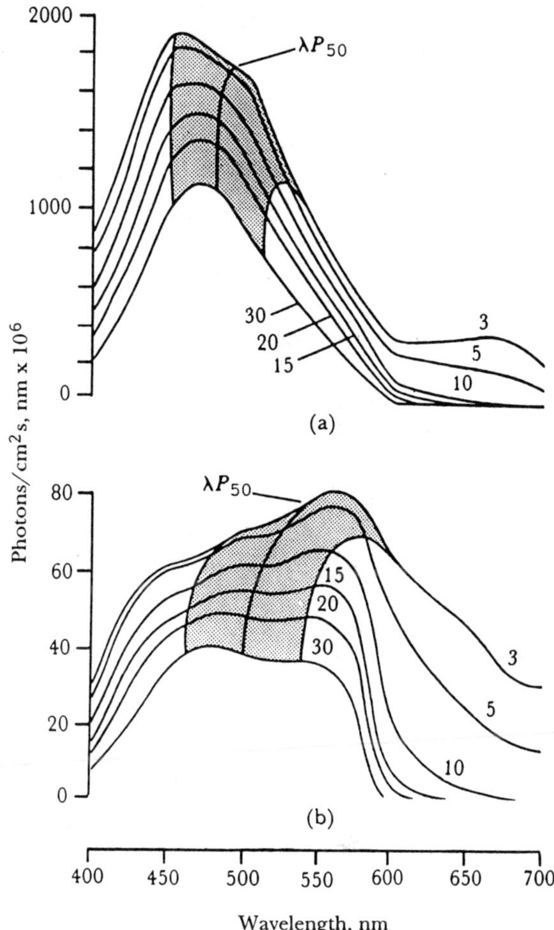

Figure 5-13 *Spectral distribution of downwelling light under conditions of* (a) *twilight and* (b) *moonlight. Numbers on the curves indicate depth in metres under the surface. Locations intersected by the midline in the shaded areas represent the median wavelength,* λP_{50}, *of the visible spectrum (400 to 700 nm). Width of the shaded area represents the* semiquartile range *or wavelengths for each curve that include the central 50% of total photons in the visible spectrum (i.e.,* $\lambda P_{75} - \lambda P_{25}$). *Shifts in* λP_{50} *and the mid-50% of photons result from greater attenuation of longer wavelengths. Spectral shifts for moonlight are greater than for twilight.* Source: Munz and McFarland (1973).

greatly reduced, compared with the numbers active in daylight and twilight. As a result, smaller nocturnal species venture farther from shelter on dark, overcast nights, and are increasingly dispersed. These same species stay closer together on clear nights when the surface of the sea is flooded by moonlight and starlight.[20]

The λ_{max} range of 489 to 499 nm is thought to have evolved as a result of two characteristics of twilight: (*1*) its spectral distribution and (2) the threat of impending predation that it poses. The spectral distribution of twilight in clear, tropical seas peaks broadly at 450 to 500 nm (Fig. 5-13a). A visual pigment with a λ_{max} value in this range would serve as an effective "trap" for twilight. For shallow-water fishes, the values given above should be adequate. However, fishes that frequent the slightly deeper reef (e.g., below ~20 m) possess scotopic visual pigments centered at 493 nm, although 475 to 485 nm would appear to be more effective. The difference between λ_{max} values of most diurnal fishes and those of the parrotfishes (Scaridae), which are centered at 484 nm, suggests a reason.

Parrotfishes possess greater amounts of blue-sensitive scotopic visual pigment than most diurnal species of coral reef fishes found at shallow and intermediate depths, but they are never seen on the night reef. A λ_{max} value of 484 nm would be appropriate for twilight vision, especially at slightly greater depth, because the spectral distribution of downwelling light changes little (Fig. 5-13a). Many parrotfishes even secrete mucous ''cocoons'' about themselves (Plate 2b), further indication that nocturnal activities are not part of the typical pattern. Wrasses (Labridae), which are related closely to parrotfishes, are exclusively diurnal and seldom observed even at twilight. Some species burrow partly or completely into the loose, sandy substratum in late afternoon and do not emerge until well after dawn. There is some question as to whether their rod visual pigments (λ_{max} >502 nm) are even functional.[21]

It has been suggested that the ''reason'' (in any evolutionary sense) why the scotopic visual pigments of most coral reef fishes peak near 493 nm instead of 485 nm or less depends on the degree of activity displayed during periods of moonlight. Possession of slightly lower λ_{max} values would increase photosensitivity at twilight but pose a liability in moonlight, the time when a λ_{max} value of 545 nm would be more effective at depths of ~3 m (Fig. 5-13b). Visual pigments in the λ_{max} range of 489 to 499 nm thus represent a compromise for species that are active both at twilight and on moonlit nights. Parrotfishes and wrasses, which are never active nocturnally, need not compromise. In summary, the scotopic visual systems of most coral reef fishes are oriented mainly to twilight. The photopic systems of crepuscular predators also have evolved for enhanced visual acuity at twilight.

Coloration

Coloration in fishes is remarkably varied. Some larvae are transparent and devoid of coloration. The subjects here are chromatic and silvery pigmentation, diel changes in coloration and pattern, and cryptic coloration.

CHROMATIC FISHES[22] *Chromatophores* are skin cells that impart true coloration, but also silvery and iridescent appearances. They contain pigment granules that selectively absorb and reflect light (Fig. 5-14). Chromatophores are distinguished

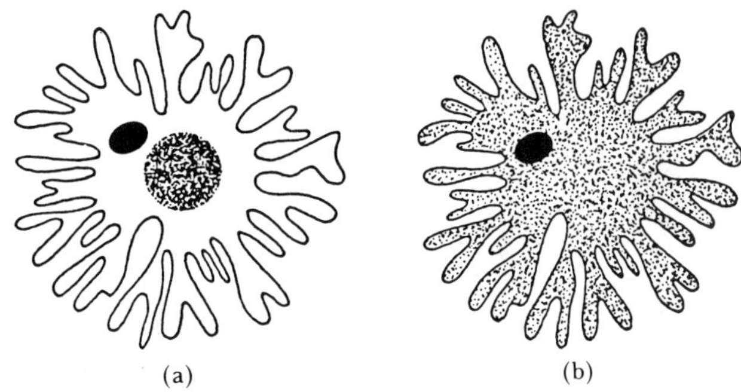

Figure 5-14 *The chromatophore of a fish is a multibranched cell containing pigment in its cytoplasm.* (a) *The fish is pale when the pigment granules are concentrated at the center of the cell.* (b) *When the granules are dispersed throughout the cell the fish appears dark. Some fish chromatophores contain several pigments, each capable of responding to a different stimulus.* Source: Wilson et al. (1978).

by the coloration of their pigment granules: *erythrophores* (red and orange), *xanthophores* (yellow), *melanophores* (black), *leucophores* (white), and *iridophores* (reflecting). Combinations of chromatophores with different pigment granules produce subdued hues and shades (Plates 2c, 2d, and 3a). The specific pigmentary organelles contained in chromatophores are termed *erythrosomes, xanthosomes, melanosomes, leucosomes,* and *iridosomes* (called *reflecting platelets* in the older literature). Green arises from a combination of black and yellow chromatophores; brown results from black plus yellow. The ability of many fishes to change coloration rapidly is made possible by the migration of pigment granules within the chromatophores.

The paling and darkening of fishes is controlled by both neural and hormonal mechanisms illustrated in the provisional sequences of Figure 5-15. Neurally mediated processes are rapid; processes that depend on hormone concentration are limited by the rate at which the hormone can be synthesized, distributed, and bound by appropriate receptors in target tissues.

Darkening occurs with the dispersion of the black pigment *melanin* throughout the melanophores. The process is controlled by *melanin dispersing hormone,* MDH, secreted by the *adenohypophysis* (i.e., the anterior lobe of the hypophysis or pituitary gland, Chapter 4). The function of MDH is to increase melanin synthesis within the melanophores and hasten its dispersion.

The hormone *melatonin* causes paling by inducing melanin to aggregate within the melanophores. Melatonin is manufactured by the pineal gland or *epiphysis.* The epiphysis is light stimulated, and melatonin production is controlled photoperiodically. Melatonin stimulated effects are slow (i.e., not neurally mediated) and probably occur on a diel cycle. They perhaps account for the nighttime darkening of many diurnal fishes and also the reverse effect in which nocturnal species become darker

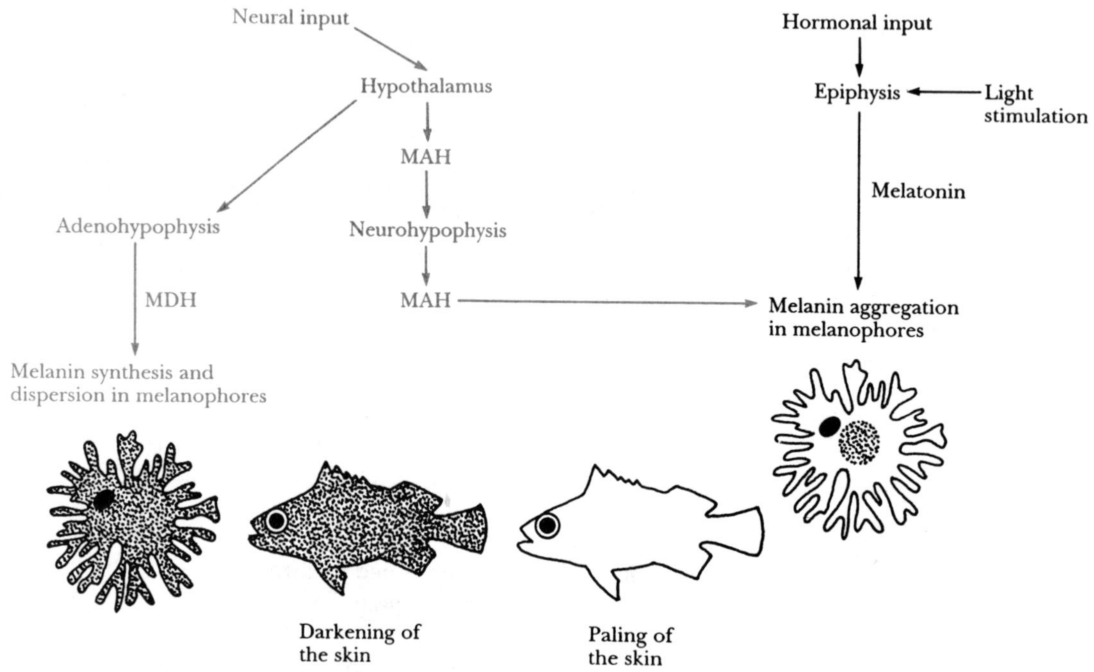

Figure 5-15 *Neural and hormonal control of melanophores. The processes depicted are provisional and may not be entirely correct. Melanin dispersing hormone, MDH, produced by the adenohypophysis causes melanin synthesis and dispersion and subsequent darkening of the skin. Melatonin produced by the epiphysis stimulates production of melanin aggregating hormone, MAH, resulting in melanin aggregation and lightening of the skin.* Source: Stephen Spotte.

during the day (see the subsection below on temporal changes in coloration and pattern). In addition, melatonin is responsible for integumental patterns. Rapid paling, in contrast, is controlled by the suppression of melanin dispersion during release of *melanin aggregating hormone,* MAH. This compound is thought to be synthesized by the hypothalamus, then stored by the *neurohypophysis* (posterior lobe of the hypophysis) and later released.[23]

SILVERY FISHES[24] Silvery fishes are silvery because they secrete the nitrogenous compounds guanine, $C_5H_5N_5O$, and hypoxanthine, $C_5H_4N_4O$, as thin crystals in the skin and scales. Arrays of these crystals reflect light like tiny mirrors. The crystals themselves are not highly reflective, but when sandwiched between alternating layers of cytoplasm their reflectivity is enhanced. This is caused by differences in the refractive indices of the two materials (1.8 for the crystals compared with 1.33 for

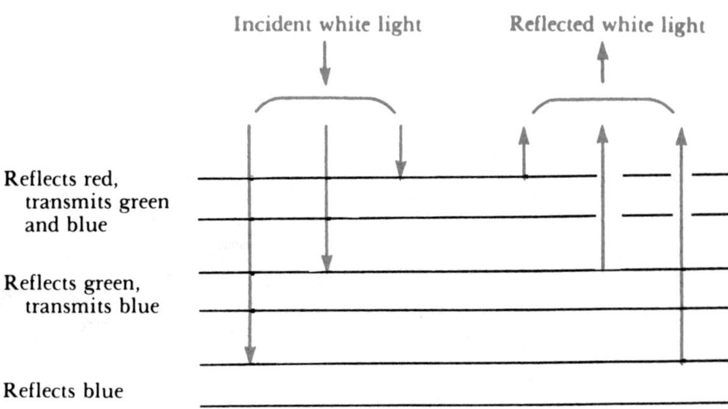

Figure 5-16 *Overlapping, reflecting crystals produce the bright sheen characteristic of silvery fishes. If the first layer* (left) *reflects "red" light (see Chapter 10, Note 12), the second green, and the third blue, the reflected increments* (right) *appear as a full spectrum of light (i.e., white light).* Source: Denton (1971).

cytoplasm). The light reflected is essentially colorless because the stacks of crystals and cytoplasm (i.e., iridosomes) overlap in several vertical layers. The colors of single iridosomes result from the interference of light and not its absorption. Consequently, a wave of light is reflected sequentially as it penetrates the stacks of iridosomes. The total reflection includes all wavelengths and appears silvery or "white" (Fig. 5-16).

The ability to reflect white light may serve a camouflage function and possess survival value. Attenuation causes submarine light to be diffuse and nearly constant in a horizontal plane. A silvery fish viewed in such a plane becomes invisible if the light it reflects is the same intensity as the background spacelight (Fig. 5-17). Reflectivity is observed when the foreground light

Figure 5-17 *White mullets* (Mugil curema) *over a bright sandy bottom. The photographic exposure was made at midday in ambient light. The fish cast pale shadows, but because the light reflected from their sides is equal in intensity to the background spacelight, they are nearly invisible. Bonaire, Netherlands Antilles, 3 m.* Source: Stephen Spotte.

Figure 5-18 *Individuals in a dense school of dwarf herrings* (Jenkensia lamprotaenia) *are clearly visible because the photographic exposure was made with an electronic strobe that illuminated the foreground, making it brighter than the background. The strobe was discharged as the fish swam past the camera in the same horizontal plane but at an angle of 90°, a situation that permitted maximum lateral reflection. Key Largo, Florida, 17 m.* Source: Stephen Spotte.

is more intense than the background spacelight (Fig. 5-18, Plate 3b). Thus the sides of a silvery fish will always reflect light equal in intensity to the ambient light (assuming that the sides are perfect reflectors). It is against the background spacelight that a silvery fish or any other submarine object must be detected. But a fish's sides are not the only mitigating factors; its dorsal and ventral surfaces also deserve consideration. For a fish to be camouflaged when viewed from above, its back cannot reflect light of greater intensity than the dim light scattered upward from below. Such a situation requires the back to be dark, which typically is the case. The ventral surface presents a different problem. When seen from below a fish is silhouetted against the brighter light streaming downward through the surface. This is offset to some extent by the tapering sides, which reduce the amount of exposed surface area. The *argenteum*—a layer of reflecting crystals—offers additional reflecting capacity. The sum of these features is sometimes augmented by orientation of the iridosomes (Fig. 5-19).

DIEL CHANGES IN COLORATION AND PATTERN Some species change coloration, pattern, or both when feeding. The blue tang (*Acanthurus coeruleus*), a diurnal species that inhabits West Indies coral reefs, ordinarily demonstrates only changes in coloration. The fish are pale blue when cruising in a group (Fig. 5-20a, Plate 3c). When the group pauses to feed on benthic algae, all individuals darken instantly (Fig. 5-20b, Plate 3d). Blue tangs also lead a solitary existence part of the time, and solitary fish are typically a variable but often intermediate shade of blue.

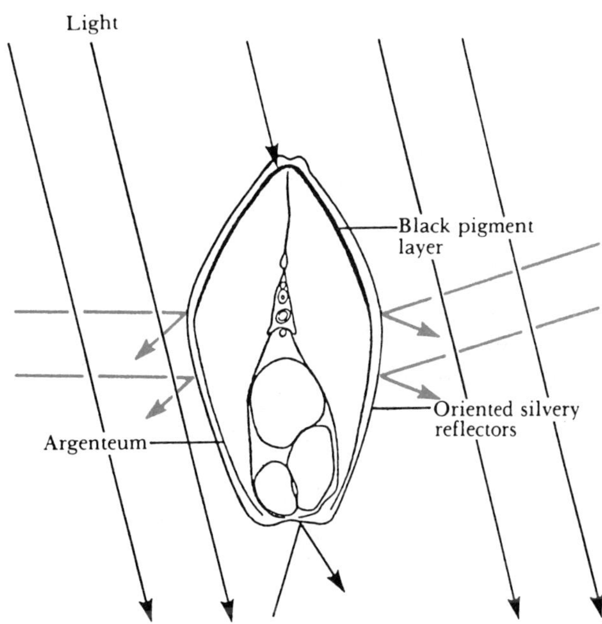

Figure 5-19 *Diagrammatic cross section of a scad or horse mackerel* (Trachurus trachurus). *The parallel arrangement of reflecting crystals appears to be advantageous. It allows the sides of the fish to reflect the maximum amount of light that strikes them in a horizontal plane. On the dorsal surface only the edges of the crystals face upward, causing descending light to be absorbed into the dark pigment below. The sides taper ventrally, which reduces the surface area exposed from beneath, and any light available to be reflected upward is enhanced by the argenteum.* Source: Denton (1971).

Other species display different patterns and coloration at night versus during the day. Blue tangs are patternless during daylight hours, but marked with vertical bars when resting at night in crevices in the reef (Plate 4a). Terminal males of the stoplight parrotfish (*Sparisoma viride*) assume dark, mottled patches at night (Plate 4b). The creole-fish (*Paranthias furcifer*) is a planktivorous sea bass indigenous to the West Indies. During the day creole-fish feed in large groups above the deep reefs, at which time they are patternless and their coloration is mauve (Fig. 5-21a, Plate 4c). At dusk the feeding groups disintegrate and each fish finds a separate crevice in the reef in which to pass the night. The background coloration of creole-fish at night is paler, interrupted by white spots and sometimes by dark, liver-colored patches in an irregular pattern (Fig. 5-21b, Plate 4d). Many of the grunts display conspicuous coloration and patterns during the day but are pale and patternless when feeding at night in eelgrass and rubble patches (Plates 10a and 10b). The nocturnal flamefish (*Apogon maculatus*) is distinctly red during the day, but pale and nearly translucent when emerging to feed at dusk. If trapped for a few seconds in a powerful underwater light, the fish regains its daytime coloration. Spotted goatfish (*Pseudopeneus maculatus*) display three conspicuous lateral spots during the day. When resting on open rubble patches at night the spots disappear, are retained, or are transformed into large blotches (Fig. 5-22). Finally, the coloration and pattern in some species does not vary between day and night (Plate 5a).

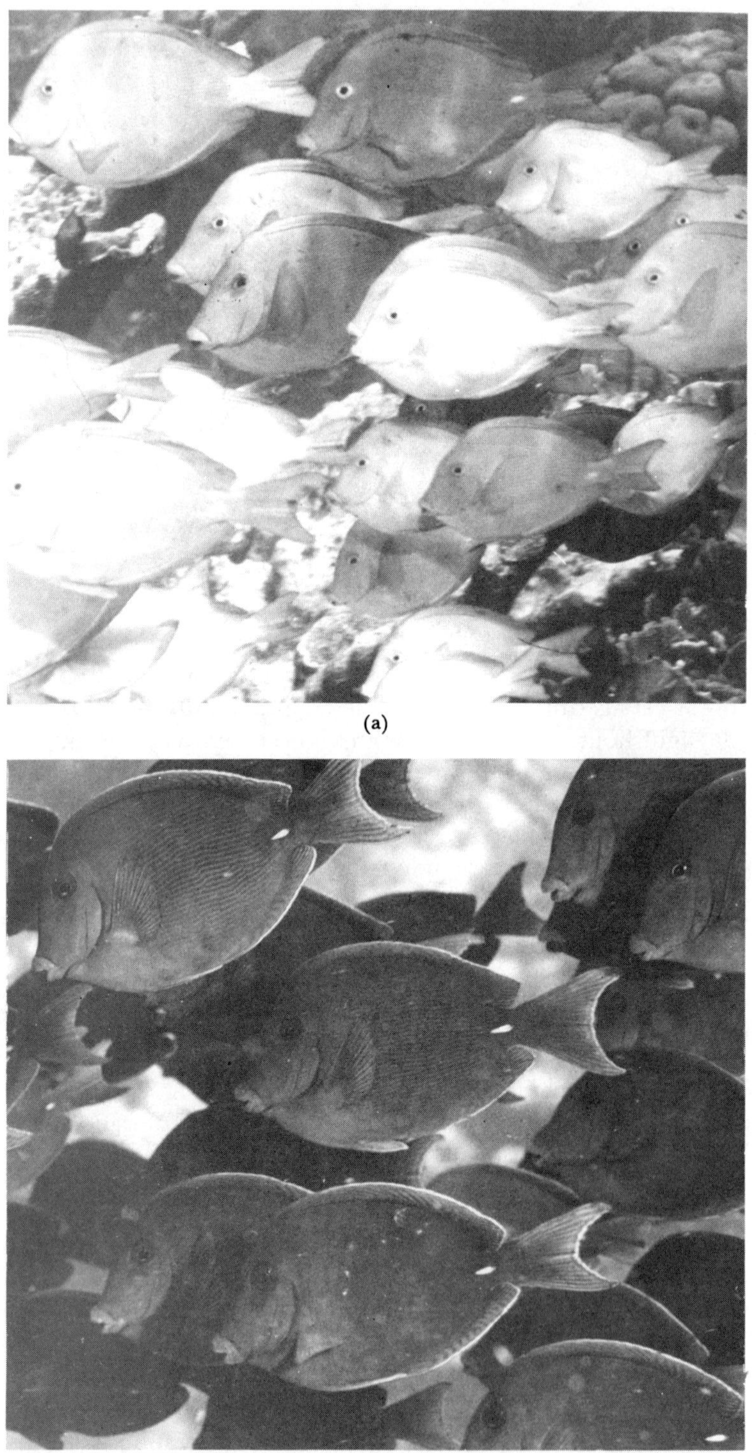

(a)

(b)

Figure 5-20 *Different coloration displayed by the blue tang* (Acanthurus coeruleus). (a) *Pale while cruising. Bonaire, Netherlands Antilles, 4 m.* (b) *Dark while feeding. Bonaire, Netherlands Antilles, 6 m. Photographs are of the same group of fish and were taken minutes apart.* Source: Stephen Spotte.

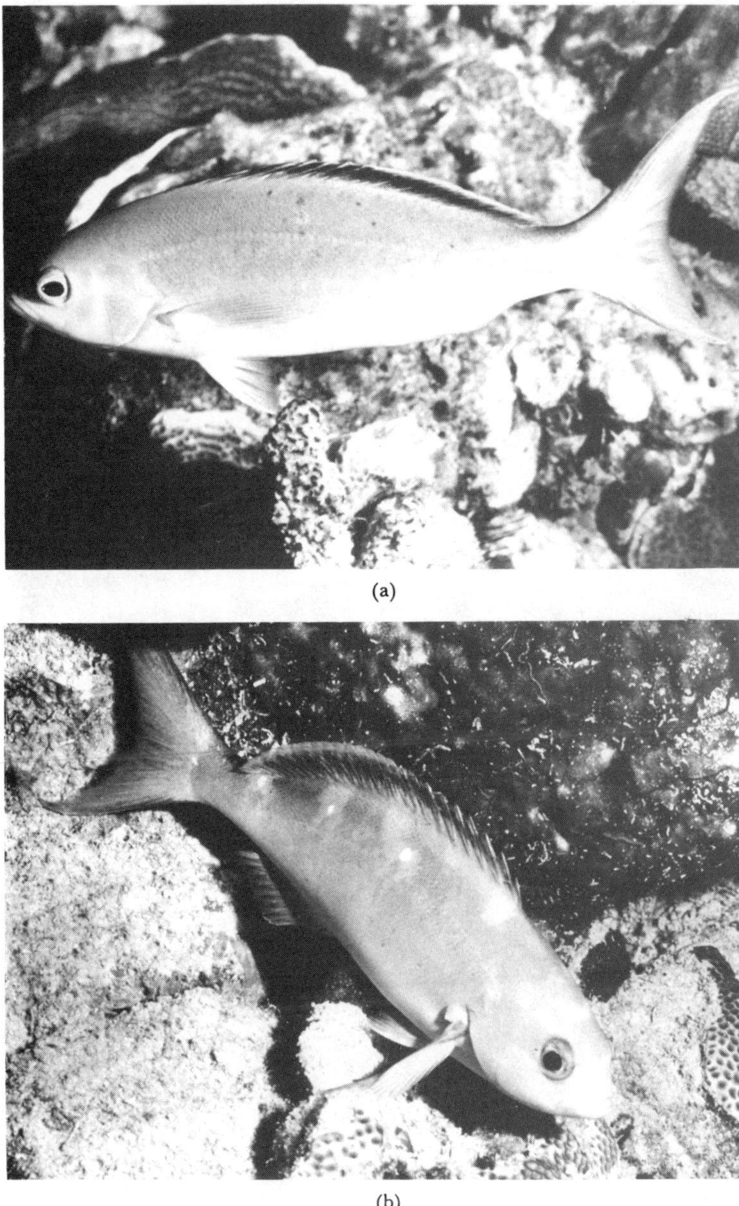

Figure 5-21 (a) *Creole-fish* (Paranthias furcifer) *feeding in the plankton above a deep reef during daylight hours are patternless. Bonaire, Netherlands Antilles, 20 m.* (b) *Individual creole-fish resting in crevices in the reef at night are spotted and often mottled. Bonaire, Netherlands Antilles, 30 m.* Source: Stephen Spotte.

CRYPTIC COLORATION Protective or *cryptic coloration* allows fishes to disappear discreetly into the background. The silvery coloration of many oceanic fishes is cryptic by representing a form of concealment in open water. Coloration and pattern are largely fixed in some species, but varied and facile in others. As described previously, many fishes can change from pale to

(a)

(b)

(c)

Figure 5-22 *Variation in pattern displayed by the spotted goatfish* (Pseudopeneus maculatus), *which is active both day and night.* (a) *Typical daytime pattern. Bonaire, Netherlands Antilles, 10 m. Individuals depicted in* (b) *and* (c) *were photographed in the same vicinity on a coral rubble bottom during the same night dive. Bonaire, Netherlands Antilles, 7 m.* Source: Stephen Spotte.

dark in an instant and return to a pale state just as quickly. Similarly, bars or stripes,can appear and disappear with speed and fluidity.

Passive elements in the environment often stimulate these changes, and the result is enhanced concealment. The trumpetfish (*Aulostomus maculatus*) often conceals itself in bushy gorgonians (Plates 5b and 5c). The slender filefish (*Monacanthus tuckeri*) is nearly always found in association with gorgonians (Plate 5d). Other species conceal themselves within the infrastructure of the reef (Plate 6a). The appearance of a fish at a given moment may depend on the coloration, pattern, and brightness of the background. Fishes that inhabit sandy or rubble-strewn substrates are often pale and dull (Fig. 5-23, Plates 6b and 6c). Still other species rely on venom for protection, but cryptic coloration for prey capture (Plates 6d and 7a).

Active stimuli (i.e., those inducing an immediate behavioral response) are also responsible for deviation from the normal

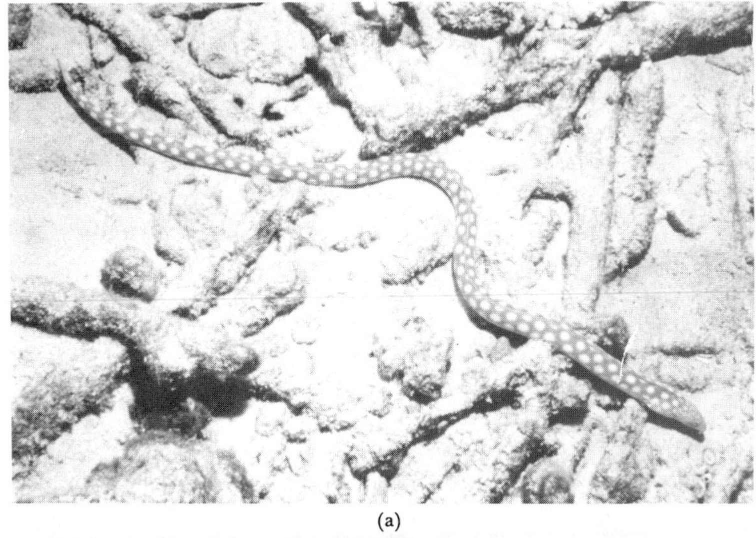

(a)

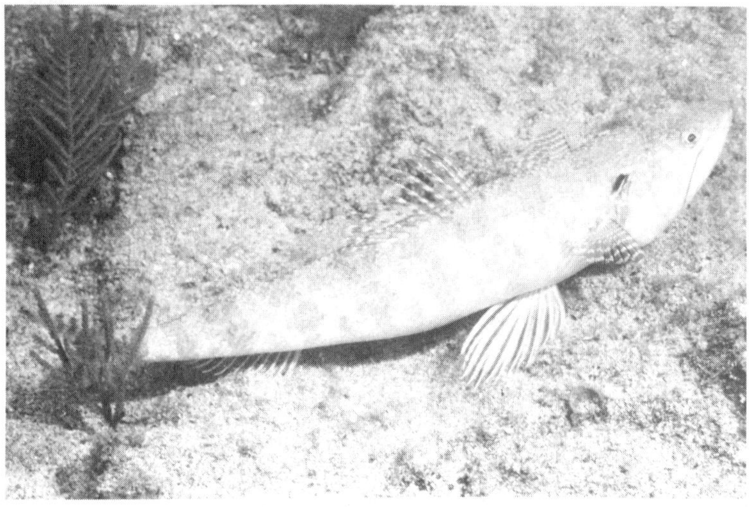

(b)

Figure 5-23 *Cryptic coloration in two West Indies teleosts.* (a) *The sharptail eel* (Myrichthys acuminatus) *lives on mixed sand and rubble bottoms. Bonaire, Netherlands Antilles, 17 m.* (b) *The sand diver* (Synodus intermedius) *inhabits sandy bottoms, but also areas of hard limestone, as illustrated here. Bonaire, Netherlands Antilles, 11 m.* Source: Stephen Spotte.

coloration and pattern, including cryptic features. Fishes often respond to active stimuli by acquiring or losing distinctive markings (e.g., bars, stripes), or by turning lighter or darker. Behaviors associated with such changes include abrupt school formation, courtship and spawning, predation, evasion of predators, and aggressive display.[24] Fishes waiting to be "cleaned" at "cleaning stations" sometimes acquire intense patterns and flush pale or dark. Even the mild anxiety caused by a slowly approaching scuba diver influences the appearance of some species (Plates 7b and 7c).

Hearing

The primary acoustic organs of fishes are the inner ear and lateral line. The inner ear is typical of vertebrates generally, but the lateral line is characteristic only of fishes and certain other aquatic vertebrates. It has no known counterpart among terrestrial animals. The purpose of this section is to provide a brief description of how elasmobranchs and teleosts generate and receive sounds, starting with the nature of underwater sound. As will be apparent, confusion over the mechanisms used by aquatic vertebrates to perceive acoustic stimuli can be traced directly to how "sound" and "hearing" have historically been defined.[25] Arguments favoring one definition or another have not always centered on mere "semantics," as some have claimed, because each term embodies essential features of a paradigm used to interpret a specific aspect of nature. The fact that more than one paradigm still exists is evidence of fundamental disagreements yet to be resolved.

SOUND[26] The term *sound* has two meanings. Subjectively, sound is what is received by the ears and "heard." Objectively, sound is a vibration or mechanical disturbance from equilibrium in an *elastic medium*, defined as a medium that resumes equilibrium after the disturbance has passed. Two such media are water and air. *Elasticity* is the tendency to resist deformation. No treatment of sound in the context presented here is complete unless both the biology and the physics are considered. The purpose of this subsection is to introduce aspects of the physics of sound that are relevant to biology—in other words, to sound reception.

A mechanical disturbance is propagated by a medium as a *sound wave*. The nature of the disturbance is defined by physical changes it induces in the medium. These include alterations in density, pressure, and particle displacement (defined below). Elasticity makes mechanical disturbances possible. Any such disturbance moves as a wave. When one part of a medium moves, motion is transmitted to adjacent parts at a definite speed. *Sound velocity*, or the speed at which sound travels, is a function of the density and compressibility of the medium. The *density* of a substance is its mass per unit volume; *compressibility* is a measure of how easily it can be squeezed into a smaller volume. The denser a medium and the more compressible it is, the slower the speed of sound through it. Water is ~1000 times denser than air but less compressible, and sound velocities in the two media are, respectively, ~1500 and 344 m/s (the latter at 20°C). Sound velocity in air is affected slightly by humidity, temperature, and barometric pressure. Temperature and pressure are independent variables in shallow waters; in deeper waters temperature is affected by pressure. Sound velocity increases with increasing salinity, and values in the oceans can attain 1540 m/s, which slightly exceeds the value for freshwaters. *Acoustics* is the discipline concerned with the generation, propagation, reception, and control of sound waves.

Sound is characterized in several ways. Most sounds are produced by vibration of a medium. In physics the term *vibration* denotes any sustained motion in which each particle (defined below) moves back and forth about an equilibrium position. In the simplest situation, such motion has a unique *periodic time* or *period*. The inverse of this quantity, the *frequency*, represents the number of complete back-and-forth excursions per unit time or period. The number of complete vibrations is the number of *cycles* (i.e., back-and-forth excursions) per second, expressed in hertz, Hz. Another means of characterization is by *excess pressure* (also called *acoustic pressure* and *sound pressure*) in a medium, compared with normal equilibrium pressure when the same medium is in an undisturbed state. Sound pressure ordinarily is measured in pascals, Pa.* In association with excess pressure is physical displacement of the medium from equilibrium, called *particle displacement* (or simply *displacement*). In physics a *particle* refers to a volume of gas or liquid of very small dimensions compared with the wavelength of a propagated sound wave, but large compared with molecules. Another important way of describing sound is by its *intensity*, defined as the average rate of energy per unit time across a unit area of the medium through which the wave is passing. Intensity is usually expressed logarithmically in decibels, dB.[27]

Sound in air is usually defined as periodic pressure waves that can be detected by the human ear. Human hearing is considered to range from 20 to 20,000 Hz. However, this definition

*1 Pa = 1 newton/m^2.

has little meaning when applied to underwater acoustics. Acoustic energy can exist in two forms: (*1*) distant pressure waves called *far-field effects* and (*2*) particle displacements known as *near-field effects*, which are detected by fishes at close range, ordinarily no farther than a few centimetres. In water, which is less compressible than air, sound propagation involves both.[28] The simultaneous occurrence of two forms of acoustic energy makes separating them extremely difficult and accounts largely for the difficulty in defining ''sound.''

NEAR-FIELD AND FAR-FIELD EFFECTS Sounds that fishes respond to (i.e., those that demonstrably affect their behavior) are complex and seldom stationary. Describing them is difficult. I shall attempt to do so for two reasons. First, the capacity of elasmobranchs and teleosts to locate the origin of far-field sounds has long been disputed. Second, it is questionable whether the distinction between near-field and far-field is realistic from the standpoint of either biology (sound reception) or physics (sound production). In the 1960s many held that only locations of near-field sounds could be detected by animals living in water.[29] Information gathered in the 1970s demonstrated clearly that some aquatic animals not only are able to perceive propagated pressure waves, but can localize their sources, a subject treated in a later subsection. The question of how they do this remains unanswered. The following discussion is simplistic and not entirely representative of real-life situations. The purpose is to describe the theoretical difficulties of far-field sound perception by using simple models for underwater sound propagation.

Perhaps the least complicated sound source is a small air bubble contracting and expanding (i.e., pulsating or vibrating) at a steady frequency (Fig. 5-24). The bubble has a radius A when contracted and a radius $A + \Delta$ when expanded. As the

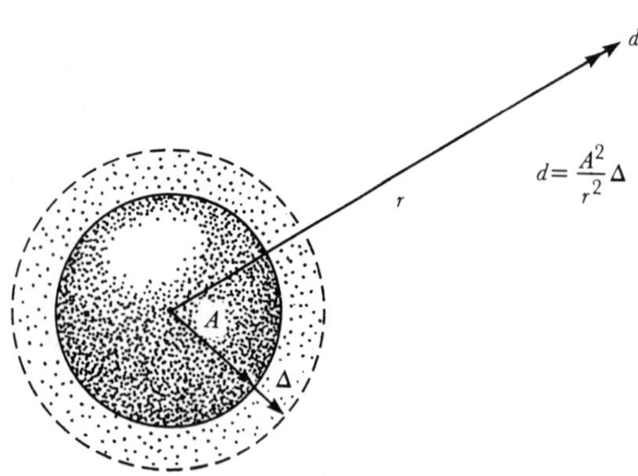

Figure 5-24 *Near-field of a pulsating air bubble. See text.* Sources: van Bergeijk (1964, 1967).

bubble expands it pushes away the surrounding water in a radial direction (i.e., outward from the center). Although water is an elastic medium, it also is relatively incompressible. The water being pushed away is therefore displaced. The displacement of water particles is passed on. Imagine, for example, concentric spheres radiating away from a propagating source. The displacement becomes smaller as the radius of one of the spheres increases, because the volume of water originally displaced is then distributed over a larger area. On a radiating sphere of radius r the displacement can be described as

$$d = \frac{A^2}{r^2\Delta} \tag{5.1}$$

The amplitude of d decreases as $1/r^2$. In addition, d is always displaced radially. In other words, the direction of displacement measured at any point is always located on a straight line outward in that direction.

The displacements described so far represent the bubble's near-field. If water demonstrated no elasticity, only a near-field effect would exist. But water is compressible to some extent, and a pulsating bubble also produces an elastic pressure wave that coexists with displacements in the near-field. Its amplitude, however, decreases as $1/r$. If measurements are made close to the bubble, displacement amplitudes of motions produced in the near-field are much greater than particle displacement amplitudes in a plane wave (i.e., a wave of one dimension) with the same pressure amplitude. As distance from the source, r, increases, the near-field displacement amplitude decreases as the first power of r. Thus at some distance the two amplitudes are equal. This distance can be defined as 1 wavelength/2π away from the source (Fig. 5-25). The wavelength, λ, is defined by the frequency at which the bubble is vibrating. Distances, r, that are smaller than this equal amplitude constitute the near-field; all others fall into the far-field. The far-field is a pure propagated (i.e., pressure) wave; the near-field is a blend of propagated waves and near-field displacements, the latter dominant. The pulsating bubble model described here is applicable only to conditions in which acoustic energy is not limited by geological features or other strictures (e.g., the mid-Pacific Ocean where the depth is >1000 m).[30]

A crucial point is that displacements have both direction and magnitude (i.e., amplitude) and can therefore be described by vectors. As shown in Figure 5-24, the length of the arrow illustrates magnitude, and its direction shows the direction of the displacement. Pressure waves cannot be represented by vec-

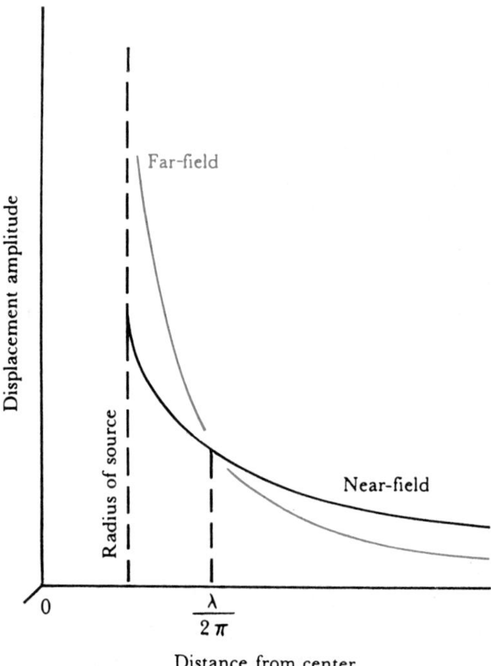

Figure 5-25 Displacement amplitude of near-field and far-field effects as a function of distance from the center of a pulsating, spherical sound source. The amplitudes are equal at a distance of $\lambda/2\pi$ from the center. Source: Gary Adams, Sea Research Foundation.

tors; their quantity is expressed only in magnitude. A single pressure measurement gives no information about the location of the sound source in relation to where a measurement is made. A near-field displacement measurement provides such information, but only for a pulsating bubble.

The last statement can be clarified by considering a slightly more complex source of sound, which is a vibrating, solid, sphere. As a model, a solid sphere comes closer to representing natural underwater sound sources generated by swimming animals. As the sphere moves forward it pushes water ahead (Fig. 5-26). Water is drawn into the space occupied previously and also is deflected along the surface of the sphere in the opposite direction. The displacement is proportional to $1/r^3$ and to $A^3\Delta$ (i.e., to the volume of the sphere times its amplitude). The motion can be described by a vector, most conveniently the vector sum of a radial and an angular displacement:

$$d_r = \frac{A^3}{r^3} \Delta \cos \theta \qquad (5.2)$$

$$d_\theta = \frac{A^3}{r^3} \Delta \frac{\sin \theta}{2} \qquad (5.3)$$

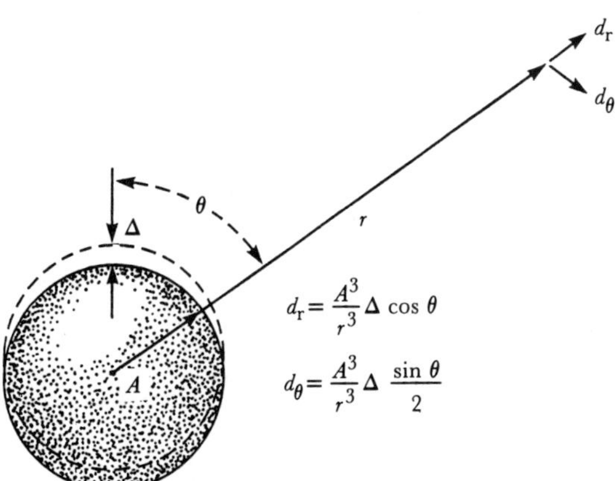

Figure 5-26 *Near-field of a vibrating, solid sphere. See text.* Sources: van Bergeijk (1964, 1967).

It is important to note that the direction of motion seen at one point in the near-field of a vibrating sphere gives no information about the exact position of the sphere with respect to the point at which measurements are made.[31] The angle θ must be known, which means that the sphere's location must be known as well. This represented one of two cornerstones of the 1960s model, that of physics. The other, considered from a biological perspective, stated that elasmobranchs and teleosts lack the necessary anatomical apparatus to localize sounds in the far-field. More will be said about both shortly.

MECHANORECEPTION The lateral line functions mechanically in the detection of nearby objects—primarily moving ones—by the near-field effects they produce in water, enabling fishes to locate moving objects with remarkable precision. Moreover, the size of an object, its velocity, and direction of movement can probably be distinguished as well.

Sensory organs of the lateral line that function in mechanical reception, called the *ordinary lateral line organs,* are distributed over the skin (Fig. 5-27). Although the obvious part of the ordinary lateral line system is the visible lateral streak from which the name is derived, the most elaborate development occurs on the head. The ordinary lateral line and inner ear have a common embryologic origin and similar innervation and morphology,[32] and they typically are considered together as the *acousticolateralis system*.

Near-field detection works in the following way (Fig. 5-28). Envision two fishes, one moving and the other stationary. When the moving fish glides past the stationary fish tangentially in a straight line and at constant speed, its near-field is controlled by equations describing a vibrating, solid sphere (Fig.

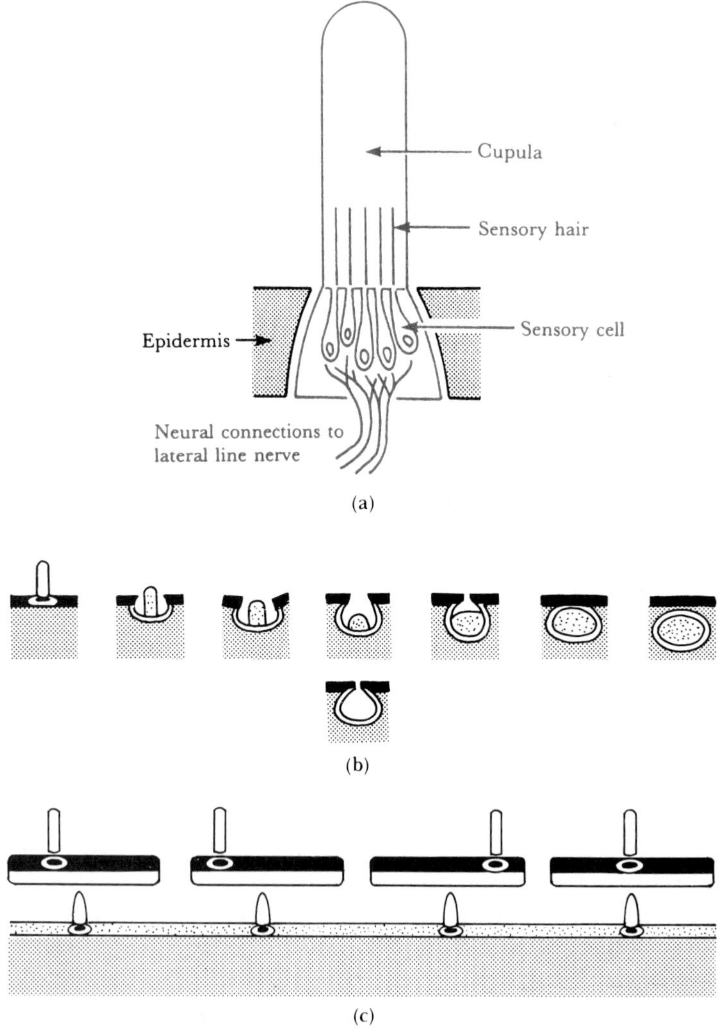

Figure 5-27 (a) *A single ordinary lateral line organ or* free neuromast *consists of a cluster of pear-shaped* sensory cells *surrounded by long, slender* supporting cells *(not shown).* Sensory hairs *on top of the sensory cells project into a gelatinous* cupula, *which is secreted by the free neuromast and projects into the water.* (b) *Some free neuromasts may be transformed into* canal organs, *illustrated here in successive stages of transformation. The cupula persists but is surrounded by a fluid, the* canal endolymph. *In both arrangements the cupulae are stiff but flexible and function in essentially the same way, although free neuromasts respond directly to external currents. The response of the canal organs is indirect after local displacement of the canal endolymph.* (c) *Hydrodynamic pressure bends the cupulae. This activates the lateral line system by causing deformation of the sensory hairs. Discharged impulses are transmitted through nerve fibers to a common center in the brain.* Source: Dijkgraaf (1952).

5-26). The displacement amplitude, in other words, decreases as the cube of the distance. Consequently, as the moving fish approaches the stationary fish the magnitude of the water displacement at the stationary fish's lateral line increases rapidly, then decreases at the same rate as the moving fish glides past. If the moving fish is undulating (i.e., swimming) instead of gliding, displacements caused by its actions are superimposed on the impulse, and the shape of the curve becomes ragged (broken lines of Fig. 5-28).

This explanation would appear adequate to account for mechanoreception by the ordinary lateral line organs (i.e., detection of near-field acoustic phenomena) were it not for the work

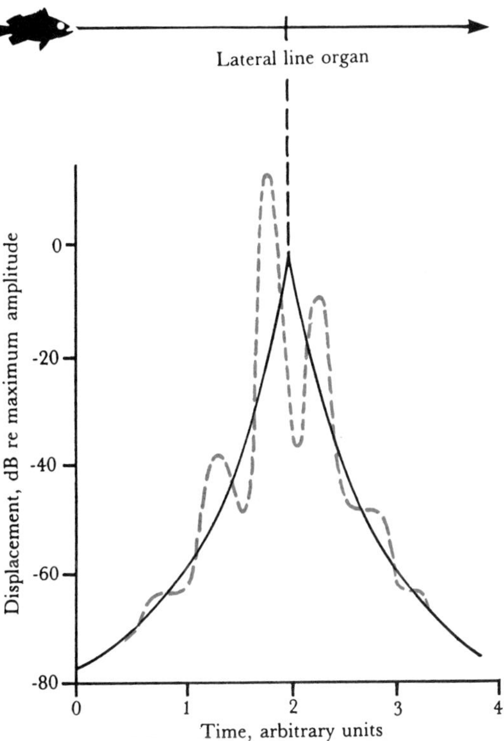

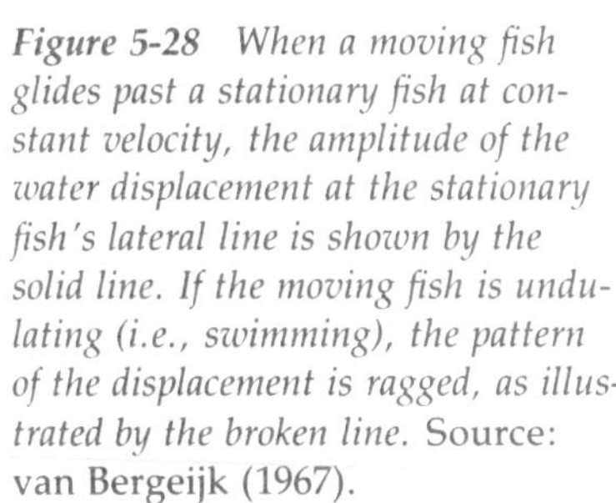
Figure 5-28 *When a moving fish glides past a stationary fish at constant velocity, the amplitude of the water displacement at the stationary fish's lateral line is shown by the solid line. If the moving fish is undulating (i.e., swimming), the pattern of the displacement is ragged, as illustrated by the broken line.* Source: van Bergeijk (1967).

of Sven Dijkgraaf, which purported to demonstrate a tactile function instead. Thus two incompatible models claim to explain the basic functions of the lateral line. What I shall call *Dijkgraaf's tactile modality model* was the earlier. Dijkgraaf referred to his proposed tactile function as *Ferntastsinn* or ''distant touch.'' The other—termed here *van Bergeijk's acoustic modality model*—considered the lateral line to function mechanically in detection of near-field acoustic phenomena. In my opinion, the second model is more nearly correct, but ''correct'' in this case must be tempered somewhat because both viewpoints hinge once again on how ''hearing'' and ''sound'' are defined.[33]

THE LABYRINTH[34] In elasmobranchs and teleosts, receptors of hearing and balance are concentrated in the ear, just as they are in all vertebrates. However, the elasmobranch or teleost ear is rudimentary compared with the ears of higher vertebrates. Only a *labyrinth* or *inner ear* is present. An eardrum and middle ear are absent, and the labyrinth lacks a cochlea. In the absence of an eardrum, vibrations received are conducted to the labyrinth through body tissues. The labyrinth represents an evolutionary submersion of the lateral line organs into the skull.

The labyrinth consists of two major sections (Fig. 5-29). The dorsal part or *pars superior* functions mainly as an equilibrium system and detector of gravity. It includes three *semicircular canals,* each with its ampulla. The *utriculus* with a *utricular otolith* or ear stone lies at the base of the pars superior. Ventral to the pars superior is the *pars inferior,* consisting of the *sacculus* and *lagena.* Both structures contain otoliths. The principal function of the pars inferior is sound detection. Sound impinging on a fish results in near-field effects, which in turn cause the entire fish to move back and forth. This can be visualized as ''fish displacement'' (Fig. 5-30). If the sound originates in the near-field, shifting of the otoliths lags behind displacements of the fish because the otoliths are denser than the tissues. The otoliths are suspended in fluid and surrounded by bundles of cilia originating from sensory hair cells. These cells make up the sensory epithelium or *macula* in each chamber of the pars infe-

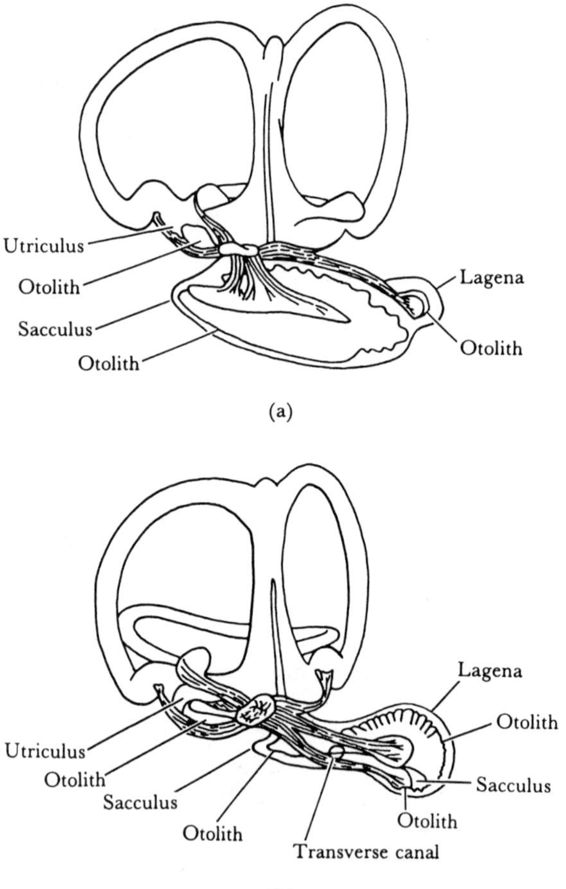

Figure 5-29 Medial view of the labyrinth. The fish species are (a) Lucioperca sandra *and* (b) Cyprinus idus. Source: Popper and Fay (1973).

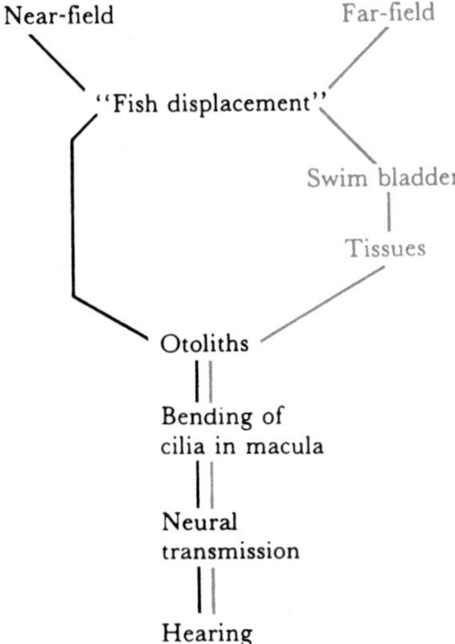

Figure 5-30 Diagrammatic illustration of the mechanics of hearing by aquatic vertebrates. Near-field displacement energy is transmitted directly to the otoliths. Energy received from the far-field is transformed first to displacement energy inside the swimbladder, which acts as a transducer. Source: Stephen Spotte.

rior. As the otoliths shift position in their fluid they bend the cilia. This results in deformation of sensitive hair cell membranes, stimulating nerve impulses to the brain that are interpreted as "hearing."

When sound is received from the far-field, the amplitude of "fish displacement" decreases: the whole fish vibrates to stimulate the otoliths, and the sound must be amplified. This requires a *transducer,* a mechanism that transforms energy but also can serve as both a source and receiver of sound. In this case far-field (pressure) energy is converted to near-field (displacement) energy before being transmitted to the labyrinths. To be effective the transducer must be composed of materials that differ in acoustic properties and density from the surrounding water. Air bubbles are efficient transducers. They are more compressible than water and pulsate when exposed to sound (Fig. 5-24). In some teleosts a transducing function is performed by the *swimbladder,* a gas-filled sac in the abdominal cavity between the spine and intestine. A swimbladder is essentially an air bubble and can be made to expand and contract if placed in an alternating pressure field. The swimbladder expands as pressure on its surfaces is reduced, and it contracts with increases in pressure. The pulsating surface of the swimbladder causes surrounding tissues to vibrate. The result is a considerable near-field displacement that provides energy necessary to stimulate the labyrinths (Fig. 5-31).

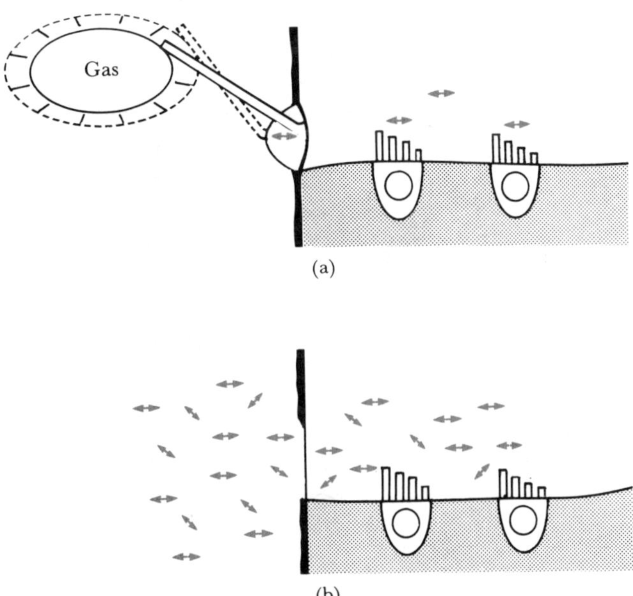

Figure 5-31 Diagrammatic illustration of the two basic types of vertebrate sound detectors: (a) with a transducer, and (b) without. In (a), gas inside the swimbladder changes volume in response to pressure. In the process, pressure energy is transformed to a displacement of the swimbladder surface. The resultant displacement energy is then transmitted to hair cells of the labyrinth. The hair cells respond indirectly to the pressure component of a sound, although the stimulus is not sensed directly. Elasmobranchs and teleosts without swimbladders use the mechanism in (b). Hair cells of the labyrinth respond directly to displacement in the environment. Source: Corwin (1981a).

As mentioned previously, pressure energy received from the far-field is converted to displacement energy before transmission to the labyrinths. When a swimbladder is subjected to far-field pressure waves it expands and contracts at the frequency of the pressure changes, becoming a secondary sound source from which a displacement field and a pressure field radiate.[35] In many species displacement energy is transmitted to the labyrinths by a series of linked bones, the *Weberian ossicles* (Fig. 5-32). Species that possess Weberian ossicles appear to have the best hearing (i.e., the lowest auditory thresholds and highest upper frequency limits). These are the ostariophysans, a large group of mostly freshwater teleosts that includes four families, the cyprinids, silurids, characinids, and gymnotids.

The labyrinth, like the ordinary lateral line organs, consists of displacement-sensitive receptors. As described above, the swimbladder behaves as a transducer. When far-field sounds are received a pressure-displacement energy transformation occurs, and only displacement energy is transmitted to the inner ear. Energy transmission occurs by means of specialized structures such as the Weberian ossicles. Elasmobranchs and many

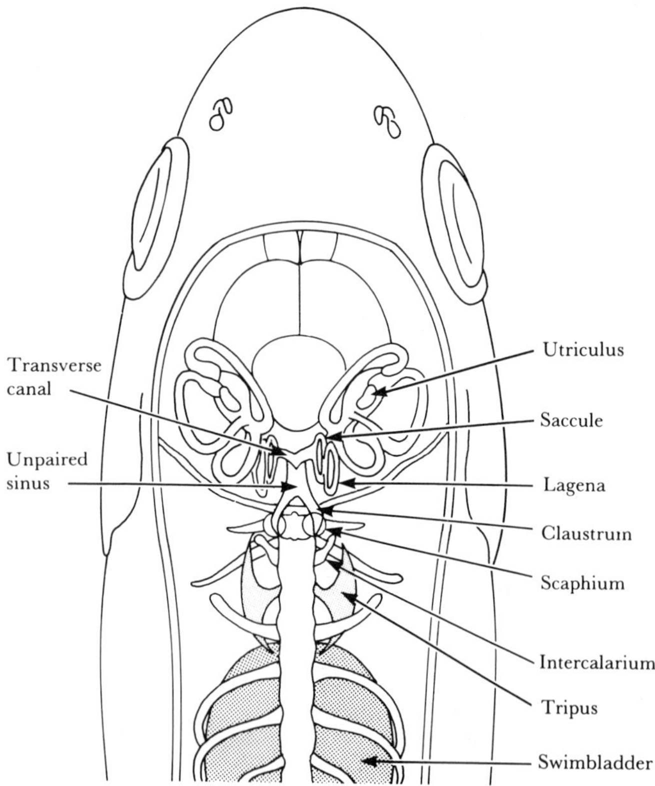

Figure 5-32 Weberian apparatus of a teleost. The Weberian ossicles occur in four pairs called the tripus, intercalarium, scaphium, *and* claustrum. *The tripus connects with the swimbladder. Pressure waves cause the swimbladder to expand and contract. The vibrations are transmitted sequentially by the ossicles to the unpaired sinus, transverse canal, and sacculus.* Source: von Frisch (1938).

teleosts lack swimbladders. The labyrinths of these species may be strictly displacement sensitive, suggesting that far-field acoustic stimuli are received and processed differently. How sources of acoustic stimuli are thought to be located and the subsequent behavioral responses are described in a later subsection. From a mechanistic standpoint, the species tested appear to respond only to displacement components of sound fields, and it is not known whether behavioral responses are elicited by stimulation of the labyrinth or the ordinary lateral line organs.[36]

SOUND PRODUCTION[37] Elasmobranchs are not known to produce sounds in a specialized sense, but teleosts generate them by several mechanisms. The most apparent is *stridulation*, defined as biological production of sound by the rubbing together of certain hard body parts. Stridulation is often accomplished by the grinding of opposing denticles in the pharynx. The resultant noises may be apparent during feeding, as a warning of encroachments into territories, during courtship, and as an element of the alarm response. Grunts (Haemulidae) are best known for producing stridulated sounds (Plate 7d). In these and some other teleosts the swimbladder acts as a sound "resonator." Still other species (e.g., the puffers, Tetraodontidae) stridulate by means of molariform teeth. Sea catfishes of the genera *Bagre* and *Arius* rub special fin rays and spines together to produce sounds, as do several freshwater catfishes. In anemonefishes (*Amphiprion* spp.), seahorses (*Hippocampus* spp.), and the chain pipefish (*Syngnathus louisianae*) the sonic mechanism is the rubbing of bones.

The swimbladder appears to be important in sound production by many teleosts. When it resonates, the swimbladder alters the character of the sound emitted. Several leatherjackets (Balistidae) are known to generate sounds by rubbing their pectoral fins against the sides of the body where lateral evaginations of the swimbladder are covered with skin. The swimbladder can also function as a "drum." The queen triggerfish (*Balistes vetula*) reportedly generates sounds by beating its pectoral fins against the portion of its body located directly above the swimbladder. Some sea basses (Serranidae) beat their opercula to produce sounds. As their name suggests, the drums (Sciaenidae) produce drumming noises by rapid movements of muscles that join the walls of the swimbladder (Plate 8a). In other teleosts the sonic mechanism consists of short muscles originating from the skull and attached to the ribs and tissues that form the anterior dorsal region of the swimbladder. Several sea basses, squirrelfishes (Holocentridae), and scorpionfishes (Scorpaenidae) use this arrangement to vibrate the swimbladder (Plates 6b, 6d, 7a, and 8b). Still other anatomical arrangements have been described, but in all cases the sound-producing mechanisms are similar. The frequency of the sound emitted directly reflects the frequency at which the sonic muscles contract, which in some species can reach 200/s. Muscle action produces volume and pressure changes in the swimbladder, causing its surface to pulsate. The pulses travel through the tissues to the outside environment with minimum loss.

LOCALIZATION OF FAR-FIELD SOUND Evidence presented so far demonstrates convincingly that all elasmobranchs and teleosts respond to acoustic near-fields. However, some also respond to sounds from the far-field and can locate the direction of the source. *Localization* is defined as a behavioral response in which the animal moves toward or away from the sound source. Implicit in this definition is a directional component in the response (i.e., directional hearing). Much of the early experimental work on far-field sound detection emphasized descriptions of acoustic stimuli that attract predators, especially sharks. The low-frequency, pulsed signals that predators find attractive presumably are similar to sounds generated hydrodynamically by other feeding predators or their prey. All species of sharks tested in nature are attracted to synthesized sounds of specific kinds, in addition to sounds of biological origin. Whether sharks are attracted to a sound depends on its quality, in particular the spectral content or frequency, repetition of pulse rate, and intensity. To elicit positive responses the frequency must be between 10 and 1000 Hz, with frequencies of 40 to 300 Hz being the most attractive. Frequencies >1000 Hz apparently are not detected. Pure tones of all frequencies fail to attract free-ranging sharks, as do continuous sounds, regardless of frequency. The most rapid positive responses are elicited by sounds that have irregular pulses.[38] The intensity must be sufficient to be heard above the ambient background noise. In both elasmobranchs and teleosts responsiveness typically diminishes when the intensity falls to ~15 to 25 dB above the intensity of ambient background noise. This obviously is of greatest importance when the source originates in the far-field.[39] The same pulsed, low-frequency sound used to attract sharks repels them when the intensity is increased abruptly.[40]

Most studies describing the behavioral responses of teleosts to synthesized sounds have been conducted for purposes of improving commercial fisheries or preventing fishes from being drawn into power plant intake pipes. Intermittent, low-frequency sounds generated synthetically attract certain predatory teleosts.[41] The few nonpredatory species tested are typically repelled.[42]

Unanswered questions remain in the case of elasmobranchs and even teleosts with swimbladders: how do they manage to localize acoustic stimuli generated in the far-field?[43] Do they localize on the basis of direction or displacement? Directional displacement cues exist in the near-field, but near-field signals attenuate rapidly with distance from the source. One explanation is what I shall call the *acoustic gradient hypothesis*. Presumably, when an elasmobranch or teleost detects a sound in the far-field it enters the near-field by exploratory swimming and then locates the source, in effect by responding to the increasing "concentration gradient" of the signal intensity.[44] The labyrinths obviously are important for locating far-field sounds, but the mechanism has not been identified. There is limited evidence that at least one shark (*Chiloscyllium griseum*) can discriminate between sounds on the basis of sound pressures alone and also distinguish displacement energy from pressure energy.[45]

Electroreception[46]

Weak currents from natural electric fields are received by specialized receptors in the lateral line. These organs are different from the mechanoreceptors described previously. Natural electric fields are of three types: (*1*) inanimate fields of physical and chemical origin (e.g., the earth's magnetism),[47] (*2*) bioelectric fields from electric organs such as those of "electric fishes," and (*3*) bioelectric fields from sources other than electric organs (i.e., the "incidental" fields of all plants and animals).[48] Detection of bioelectric fields is considered here.

The internal chemistry of a seawater elasmobranch or teleost differs from the chemistry of the surrounding solution, causing a discrepancy in the electrical potential across epithelial tissue of the boundary layer (Chapter 4, Note 15). As discussed in Chapter 4, active transport of inorganic ions produces local transepithelial potentials. As a result, steady currents generated in the tissues leave the animal and enter it at other places, and stray bioelectric fields are formed in the surrounding water. Many deep and superficial tissues contribute to the formation of bioelectric fields around aquatic animals, but the most steady currents are located at places where active transport is concentrated, such as the lining of the mouth, gills, anus, and skin. The strongest direct-current fields are in the area of the head. The strength of a field depends on the activity level of the animal and its condition.

Several organs adapted for electroreception have been identified in elasmobranchs and teleosts. All are modified lateral line organs. As electroreceptor systems they are classed as *active* or *passive*. The former detect signals of external origin; the latter are equipped with an internal energy source (i.e., an electric organ).[49] The actual electroreceptors are *specialized lateral line organs*. Physiologically (i.e., functionally), they are either *tonic* or *phasic*. Morphologically, tonic electroreceptors are *ampullary*, giving rhythmic, long-lasting (i.e., tonic) responses to low-frequency, direct-current stimuli. Each electroreceptor cavity is connected to the exterior by a canal (Fig. 5-33). Functionally, phasic receptors are sensitive to high frequencies and insensitive to sustained or direct-current stimuli. Morphologically, they are *tuberous* and possess no clearly evident canals to the outside environment. Apparently, the open connections are *paracellular* (between cells). All species known to possess tuberous (phasic) electroreceptors maintain continuous low-voltage electric fields around themselves by means of electric organs and are confined to tropical freshwaters. Phasic electroreceptors are absent in elasmobranchs and teleosts that live in seawater.[50]

Among the most intensely studied tonic electroreceptors are the *ampullae of Lorenzini*, located in or near the heads of elasmobranchs (Fig. 5-34).[51] Other organs of different structure but corresponding function have been described in a tropical seawater catfish (*Plotosus anguillaris*) and several groups of freshwater teleosts (Fig. 5-35).[52] In benthic elasmobranchs—perhaps all elasmobranchs—the ampullae of Lorenzini are used to locate prey. In some species, detection of bioelectric fields generated by living prey are developed to a high degree. The ray *Raja* (= *Raia*) *clavata* can detect electric gradients as low as 10^{-8} V/cm^2, enabling it to perceive weak currents generated by respiratory muscles of a resting plaice (*Pleuronectes platessa*) at distances of 5 to 10 cm.[53] It remains to be shown whether elasmobranchs

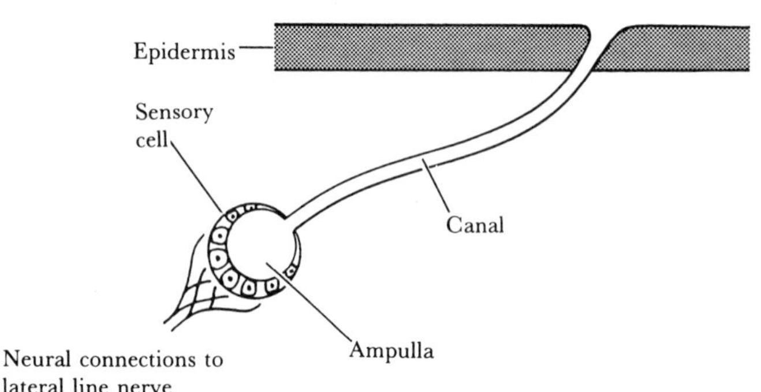

Figure 5-33 *Diagrammatic cross section through a specialized (ampullary) lateral line organ. Sensory hairs (kinocilia) are not shown but are thought to extend from sensory cells into the ampulla. The ampulla and canal connecting it to the opening in the epidermis is filled with a jellylike substance. The canal may be several millimetres or centimetres long. Canals in teleosts are shorter than in elasmobranchs, and ampullae are sometimes located over much of the body.* Source: Szabo (1974).

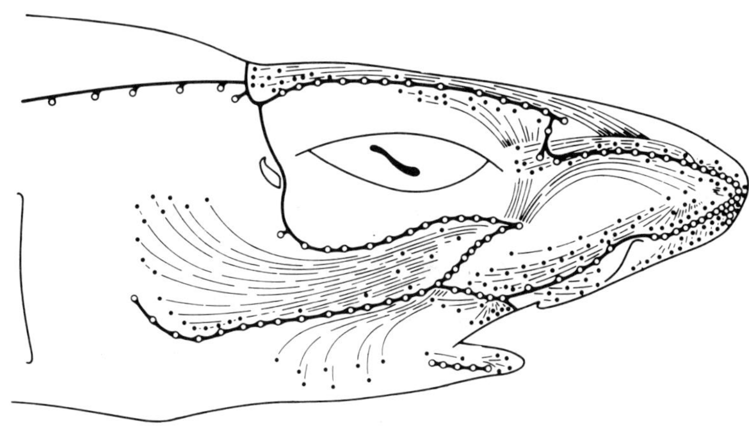

Figure 5-34 *Ampullae of Lorenzini in the head of the smaller spotted dogfish* (Scyliorhinus canicula). *Clusters of ampullae are shown in the snout, underneath the eye, and in the lower jaw. Solid circles represent electroreceptor pores on the surface. I assume—but am not certain—that the open circles connected by unbroken lines represent canals. The original German text is unclear on this point.* Source: Dijkgraaf and Kalmijn (1963).

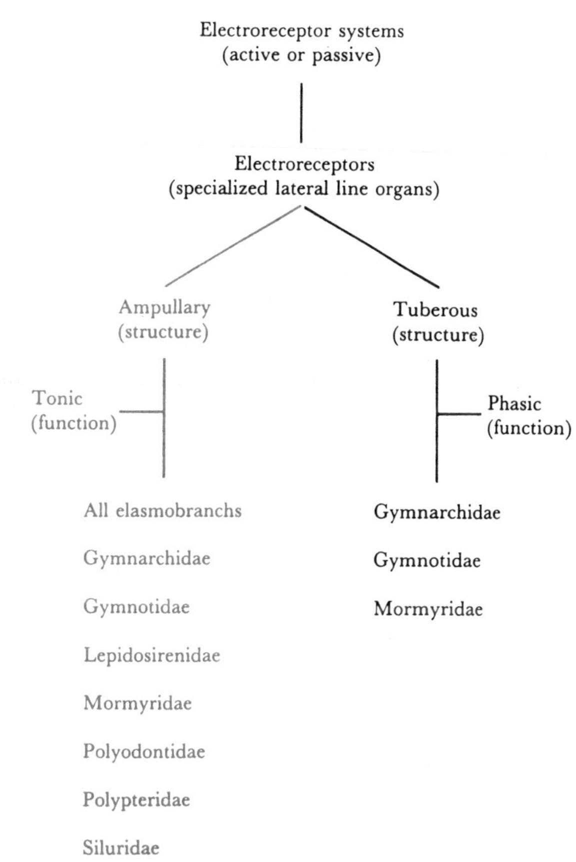

Figure 5-35 *Families of freshwater teleosts known to possess electroreceptors analogous to ampullae of Lorenzini.* Source: Stephen Spotte, drawn from information compiled by Szabo (1974).

can distinguish between different prey items on the basis of electroreception alone.[54]

TECHNOLOGY

Method 5.1 Reduction of Predation—Photic Considerations

Available evidence suggests that predation by fishes is primarily visual and mediated by photic conditions, mainly the intensity of available light. The heaviest periods of predatory activity occur at twilight, or the transition period between photopic and scotopic vision. During this brief interval the visual acuity of crepuscular predators exceeds that of their prey. I recognize that placing fishes in such neat categories as crepuscular, nocturnal, and diurnal is too patently convenient to have much ecological meaning. However, if the inhabitants of a community exhibit are considered categorically, it is reasonable to think that predation can be reduced by careful control of the photic environment. I hasten to add that such an assumption is my opinion. Nonetheless, it is common to observe a gradual depletion of wrasses, damselfishes, gobies, and other small species in community exhibits that also contain groupers, flounders, and similar predators. Most predation seems to occur at night, but this may be more an artifact of human—than fish—behavior. Aquarists typically perform their duties during the ''diurnal'' period, then leave and do not return until morning. They seldom know if predation occurs on a predictable, temporal basis, or haphazardly.

Few public aquarium exhibits are ever truly dark, even at night. Ordinarily, a few work lights are left on. The photic environment is thus dimmed considerably, but not blackened. I believe that much predatory activity occurs shortly after the exhibits lights have been turned off at the end of each working day. If the twilight vision of crepuscular predators is indeed superior, the advantage would be tipped undeniably in their favor. The practice in many institutions is to turn the exhibit lights off abruptly, leaving insufficient time for prey species to find cover. Diurnal fishes left stranded in the water column are vulnerable to crepuscular predators, especially species with questionable scotopic vision (e.g., parrotfishes and wrasses). All diurnal fishes that are potential prey need time to locate crevices in which to hide, or to bury themselves in the substratum.

What I propose is the implementation of an artificial ''quiet period'' in which the exhibit lights dim slowly to nocturnal conditions (i.e., simulated ''moonlight'') over a period of 1 h (Fig.

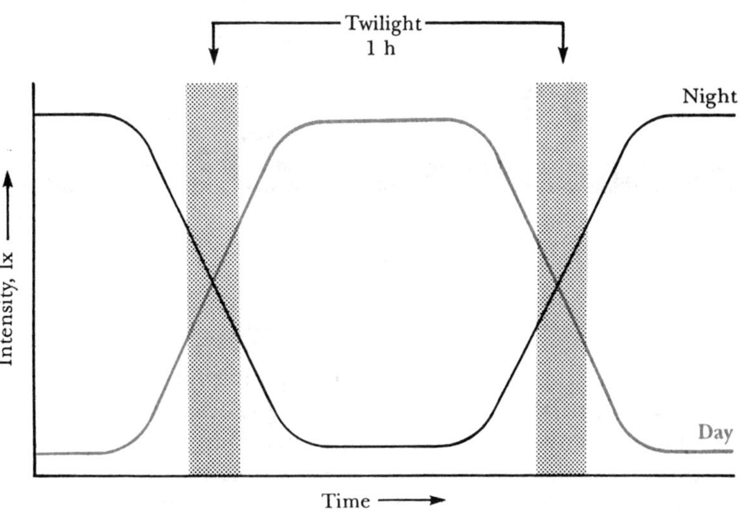

Figure 5-36 *Twilight periods at the beginning and end of each day may allow small diurnal and nocturnal fishes in community exhibits time to seek shelter, perhaps reducing the incidence of predation by larger crepuscular predators.* Source: Stephen Spotte.

5-36). In the morning the level of illumination should increase at the same rate, reaching full "daylight" intensity after 1 h. This procedure reproduces both dusk and dawn conditions. It is doubtful whether predation would be eliminated, but the objective is merely to reduce it. Prey species would at least be given a chance to survive within the context of their evolutionary adaptations.

CHAPTER

6 Behavior

Everyone would agree that a peaceful gathering of fishes (e.g., a school) is social. Given a choice, many species obviously prefer the company of others to being alone. Different behaviors—territorial dominance, for example—can only be viewed as antisocial, and I shall occasionally refer to them as such. The idea that social behavior has an antithesis is useful.

When researching the section on dominance I reviewed numerous descriptions of dominance behavior as witnessed in laboratory aquariums, thinking the results might be applicable in aquarium keeping. But the resemblance proved superficial, and I turned instead to reports describing ecological studies conducted primarily on coral reefs. It could be argued that any discussion of fish behavior in a book such as this should be restricted to laboratory data, because the protean behavior patterns seen in nature are either altered by captivity or cannot be expressed at all. Admittedly, coral reef exhibits and coral reefs are not ecological analogs, except to those who would also ignore the distinction between barnyards and tropical rainforests. However, laboratory situations seldom involve more than one species and a few specimens. The data are useful in a limited way and undeniably interesting, but a public display consisting of dozens of species has more in common with nature, or so it seems to me. To stock such an exhibit properly requires rudimentary knowledge of what behavior means in an ecological context.

I shall attempt to describe several kinds of social and antisocial behavior in fishes, with emphasis on species that inhabit coral reefs. Fishes behave in varied and complex ways, a fact that could not be known were it not for the fish behavior literature, which is equally varied and complex. The urge to drift away into this labryinth of endless corridors was difficult to resist. I attempted to stay on track by selecting aspects of behavior that I believe are most interesting from the standpoint of exhibiting fishes. I hope that aquarists will gain new insight and apply the information in the form of innovative exhibits and graphics. Much of the Science section is a critical overview. I feel this is warranted because many of the principles we have come to believe may not be entirely accurate. They needed to be dusted off and examined in new light. The numerous quotations in the chapter notes are there because behavior patterns often require subjective interpretation by the investigator who reports them. In such situations it seemed best to use the author's own words, rather than risk misrepresenting the findings.

SCIENCE

Fish Assemblages

Considered superficially, a school of fish is merely a metaphor for lost individuality. To the more imaginative observer, deeper inspection can reveal other dimensions, such as the frightening power of mindless evolution. After watching fishes school back and forth in an aquarium, novelist Virginia Woolf wrote: "Blue and silver armies, keeping a perfect distance for all their arrow-like quickness, shoot first this way, then that. The discipline is perfect, the control absolute; reason there is none. The most majestic of human evolutions seems feeble and fluctuating compared with theirs."[1]

To scientists the real danger is in assuming that such striking form must inevitably be imbued with function. Many species of fishes school at some time in their lives. Surely this is evidence of survival value. But is it? Schooling is thought to reduce predation on individuals, increase swimming efficiency, improve prey capture by predators, and make feeding and reproduction more efficient. These hypotheses, however appealing, are not bolstered by strong experimental evidence.[2] I shall examine some of them in the subsections that follow. For information purposes, an account of how fishes behave in groups is warranted if only to provide balanced conceptual material for the preparation of graphics. Reproductive efficiency is not discussed.

SHOALS, SCHOOLS, MILLS[3] What I shall call *assemblages*—shoals, schools, and mills—embody the most obvious expressions of social behavior in fishes. Consistent with any denouement of the subject is a mental image of mechanistic precision. Actually, the behavior of fishes in groups is varied and dynamic, defying rigid definition. The fixed patterns ordinarily associated with synchronous swimming describe only a single aspect, that of uniform orientation or *polarization*. Early definitions decreed that to constitute a ''school,'' all individuals must be oriented in the same direction. However, diurnal species often break ranks at night, and even the most dedicated schooling planktivores would find feeding and spawning impossible under conditions of permanent group polarity.[4] As explained below, a rigid definition of schooling has value, provided its usage is not in conflict with terms that clearly define ''nonschooling'' behavior.

Mandatory synchrony imposes a burden of inflexibility, and ''school'' has always been inadequate to describe nonpolarized elements of fish assemblages. To account properly for both polarized and nonpolarized behavior requires more than one definition. A *shoal* refers to an assemblage of fishes in which the individuals do not demonstrate uniform polarity. Individuals in a shoal can be of one species or several, so long as they remain together. In a loose sense a shoal of fishes is perhaps analogous to a ''flock'' of birds. The essential criterion of a *school* is movement in synchrony, which requires group polarity. Within limits, the individuals of a school all face in the same direction, swim at the same speed, and are separated by the same amount of space. A school can include more than one species, so long as synchronous movement is sustained. A *mill* is a stationary assemblage of one or more species swimming together in a circular or elliptical pattern, not necessarily in a polarized manner. The individuals move, but the assemblage remains in the same location. Mills occur when individuals at the front of a shoal or school turn back abruptly and intercept those behind. In captivity, milling is seen when the aquarium is too small or not designed to allow continuous forward movement. Although milling is occasionally seen in nature, I shall treat it as an artifact of captivity.[5]

As behaviors, shoaling and schooling are transformed in space and time and therefore dynamic; they do not exist as permanent entities. This is evident in the fluidity with which shoals merge into schools only to disintegrate into shoals once again (Fig. 6-1, Plates 8c and 8d). Reference to ''schooling species'' in the proper dynamic context means that at certain times and under certain conditions these fishes demonstrate behavior defined arbitrarily as ''schooling.''

MECHANISMS OF COHESION Shoaling, milling, and schooling involve swimming behavior of increasing precision. A discussion of cohesion obviously should address the most highly regimented of these, which is schooling. Fishes in a school must move forward, maintain polarity, and respond to

(a)

(b)

Figure 6-1 (a) *A shoal of planktivorous brown chromis* (Chromis multilineatus) *feeding in the water column above a West Indies coral reef. Note the absence of polarization.* (b) *Under threat of predation (in this case the presence of a scuba diver) the fish quickly form schools and swim to safety in the reef below. When the threat is removed the schools break apart into shoals so that feeding can continue. Bonaire, Netherlands Antilles:* (a) *33 m,* (b) *17 m.* Source: Stephen Spotte.

the split-second directional changes of their companions without bumping into them.[6] To execute these movements in synchrony the individuals all swim at the same speed, and each maintains a volume of space about itself known as *individual distance*.[7] As might be expected, individual distance varies less in schools than in shoals and mills.[8] Schools apparently are kept together by continuous sensory input, primarily visual.[9] Indirect evidence suggests that lateral line perception of near-field effects (Chapter 5) generated by the swimming motions of individual fishes may aid in mediating schooling, but confirmation is lacking.[10] At present, no case can be made for sound or olfactory stimuli.

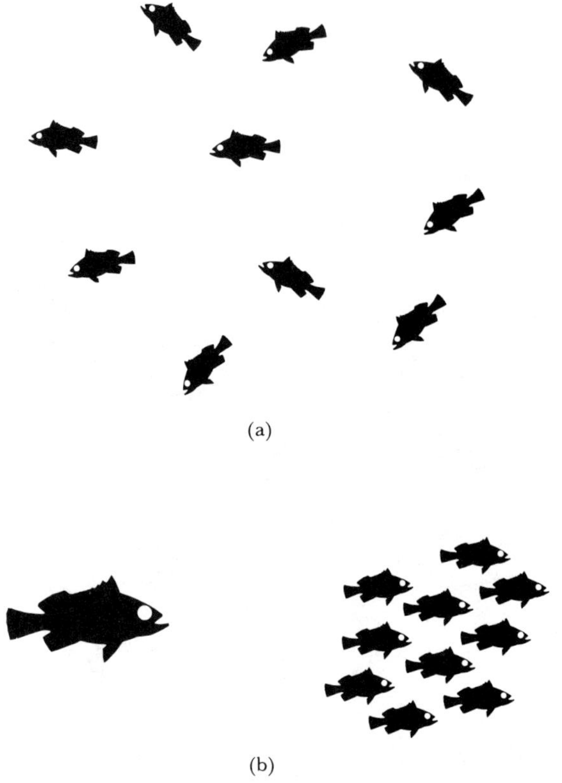

Figure 6-2 *Individual distance.* (a) *A shoal of prey fish feeds on plankton in mid-water. Orientation of the individual fish is nonpolar, and individual distances are variable, perhaps several body lengths.* (b) *A school quickly forms when a predator approaches, and individual distances often shrink to less than a body length.* Source: Stephen Spotte.

EXTRANEOUS FACTORS Shoaling fishes close ranks and school in response to extraneous factors, such as threat of predation (Fig. 6-2)[11] and even tidal flow (Fig. 6-3) or currents (Plate 9a). On a more predictable basis, schools form in response to rhythmic extraneous factors. Behaviors that occur regularly in every 24-h cycle of daylight and darkness are prompted by *diel rhythms*. In many fishes, schools form and disperse so rhythmically as to be predictable within minutes. Diel schooling is always associated with feeding, which encompasses the period of greatest activity.[12] Between times, many coral reef species assemble in languid, nonfeeding shoals (Fig. 6-4, Plate 7d). These can be *homotypic* (made up of a single species, Plate 9b) or *heterotypic* (two or more species). Some form only homotypic shoals, whereas others form either. Homotypic shoals are common in fishes that are nocturnal planktivores. In general, it can be stated that during the inactive part of the diel cycle the behavior of fishes relates mainly to their own security; during the active portion their behaviors are dominated by their own feeding.[13] Schools form on the way to and from the feeding site, which may be several metres or kilometres distant; the act of

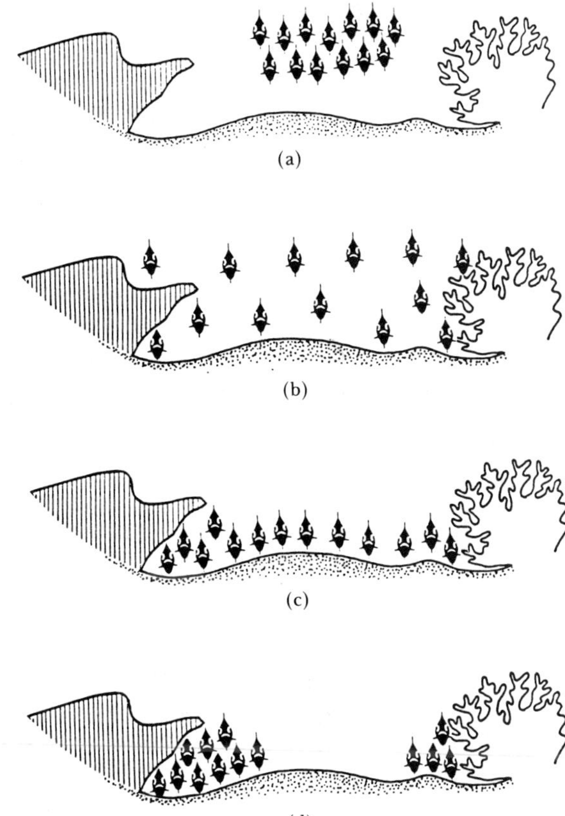

Figure 6-3 *Daily position shifts by a shoal of* Lutianus monostigma *with change in current speed at Aldabra in the Indian Ocean.* (a) *Slack tide.* (b) *Current speed ~1 km/h.* (c) *Current speed ~2 km/h.* (d) *Current speed ~3 km/h.* Source: Potts (1970).

Figure 6-4 *Hermatypic, nonfeeding shoal on a daytime coral reef. Key Largo, Florida, 10 m.* Source: Stephen Spotte.

feeding ordinarily requires breaking of ranks and is incompatible with schooling. Emphasis here is on diel rhythms of coral reef fishes.

Three categories of diel rhythms have been identified: (*1*) vertical movements in the water column, (*2*) movements within the reef structure, and (*3*) movements away from the reef.[14] Vertical movements are typical of planktivorous fishes that alternate between feeding in the water column and sheltering in the reef below.[15] Species involved are either diurnal or nocturnal, and there is no overlap in their movements.

Many species travel daily between resting places and feeding locations on a different part of the reef. Both the timing of these movements and the routes taken are often predictable. Fishes in this category include certain herbivores, such as the parrotfishes (Scaridae, Plate 9c) and surgeonfishes (Acanthuridae, Plates 3c and 3d). These and all other herbivorous coral reef fishes are diurnal.

The most extensive diel movements are seen in fishes that use the reef during inactive periods but move away from it to feed. All are nocturnal and predatory.[16] They include certain silversides (Atherinidae), grunts (Haemulidae), snappers (Lutjanidae), goatfishes (Mullidae), and herrings (Clupidae). The distance traveled is variable. Goatfishes, for example, remain close to the reef and disperse at night to feed; other fishes travel considerable distances (see below).

Sweepers (*Pempheris* spp.) remain hidden in homotypic shoals during the day (Fig. 6-5, Plate 9d). As dusk falls, individuals emerge and school back and forth along the vertical wall of the reef. With darkness the school, which has been large and compact, divides into smaller groups of 100 to 150 fish, which move away from the reef and into the water column to feed on zooplankton. The process is reversed just before dawn, and by daylight the whole group is back under its home ledge.[17]

A different pattern is illustrated by a silverside (*Pranesus pinguis*) in the Marshall Islands of the Indo-West Pacific.[18] During daylight, quiescent shoals of silversides are strung out along the shore in water 1 to 2 m deep. In late afternoon a shoal coalesces just beneath the surface over deeper water, and schooling commences with the approach of dusk. The fish are restless, and the school moves occasionally, only to return to its original location. Attacks from below by predators cause individuals to "explode" in all directions, but this also occurs for no apparent reason. Shortly after sunset the school moves out to feed in the open sea, sometimes 2 km from shore. At dawn the process is reversed, and positions on the diurnal shoaling site are resumed within a few minutes after sunrise.

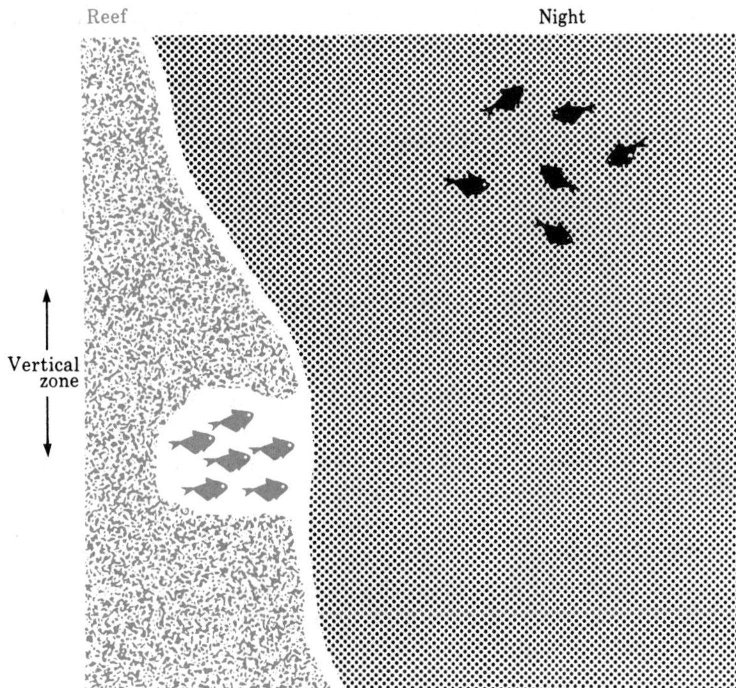

Figure 6-5 *Sweepers* (Pemphris *spp.*) *remain hidden in caves and crevices of the reef during the day. At night they emerge into the water column and disperse to feed on plankton.* Source: Stephen Spotte.

Grunts of the West Indies, Gulf of California, and other tropical and subtropical regions are nocturnal carnivores. They form inactive, heterotypic shoals during the day and at dusk migrate to sandy areas or grassbeds to feed on benthic invertebrates. These movements can occur over long distances.[19] In the West Indies, juveniles of several species are common on shallow patch reefs during the day; adults occur diurnally on both patch reefs and the main reefs farther from shore. Behavior of the French grunt (*Haemulon flavolineatum*, Plates 10a and 10b), and white grunt (*H. plumieri*) will be described briefly. Movement from the reefs to inshore grass beds begins ~10 min after sunset, and all individuals have left within 20 min. Return to the reef takes place from 20 to 30 min before sunrise. As dusk falls, the shoals of grunts disperse until each fish is a uniform distance above the bottom. Movement begins with increasing darkness. Separate heterotypic shoals stream along well-defined pathways just above the surface of the reef. Movement continues until the shoals are gathered at the inshore edge of the reef. A few individuals make brief forays into the grass beds, then return to the main shoal. Suddenly the entire shoal moves into the grass just as the last light disappears. Once in the grass beds the grunts disperse for a night of solitary feeding. Tag and recapture experiments have demonstrated that specific locations on the reef, grass bed, and the substratum linking them are familiar.[20]

SURVIVAL VALUE This subsection describes certain mechanisms of predation and predator avoidance that are thought to have survival value.[21] I advise reading it with the understanding that no single factor tips the balance permanently in favor of either the predator or the prey. A failed predator goes hungry, and unsuccessful prey are eaten, but such events apply only to individuals. From an evolutionary perspective they are fleeting and trivial. Both groups must succeed as species to remain extant. Peter H. Klopfer wrote: "The race between the adaptations of the predator for capturing the prey and those of the prey for escaping a predator may be viewed as a race whose finish line is constantly moved ahead of the contestants."[22] The focus here is on momentary shifts that appear to favor either predator or prey.

In my opinion, the survival aspects of schooling can be reduced to a sequence of concepts purporting to illustrate cause and effect (Fig. 6-6).[23] I started with the singular problem of all schooling fishes—no place to hide. Solitary bottom-dwelling species can burrow into the substratum, hide in seaweed, squeeze among corals and rocks, or simply remain motionless. Schooling fishes, in contrast, inhabit the water column, a three-dimensional void where vulnerability extends in all directions.

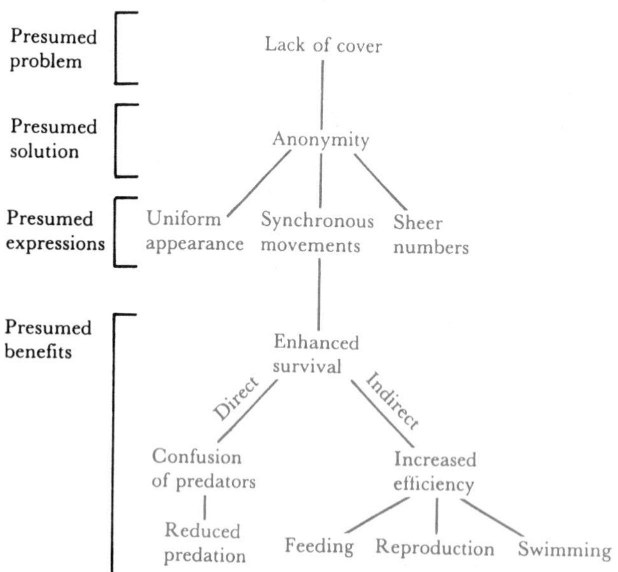

Figure 6-6 *Hypothetical direct and indirect benefits of schooling.* Source: Stephen Spotte.

The presumed solution to the problem of no cover is *anonymity*, defined in this context as seeking cover among companions.[24] The expressions of anonymity are uniform appearance, synchronous movements, and sheer numbers (Plate 10c). In sum, these supposedly enhance survival through two additional sequences, one immediate and direct, the other remote and indirect. The direct benefit may be ''confusion'' of predators and a lowered incidence of predation. The indirect benefit is increased efficiency, meaning the best results for the least expenditure of energy. Schooling is believed by some to make feeding, reproduction, and swimming more efficient.

Only homotypic schools contain individuals of uniform appearance.[25] Any survival value inherent in heterotypic schools must be predicated on other factors. The discussion here deals just with schools of single species. Synchronous movement apparently is an important reinforcing element of anonymity. Prey fish in a school that are wounded or heavily parasitized swim differently and appear to be more heavily preyed upon.[26] The presence of sheer numbers of schooling prey is thought to have a ''dilution effect,'' which reduces the risk of attack on an individual and also the success of an attack.[27] The result is manifested as enhanced survival of the individual.

To summarize, individuals in homotypic schools are uniform in appearance and therefore anonymous, by definition they move in synchrony, and the overall effect is enhanced by sheer numbers. A predator's response is thought to be ''confusion,'' although what this actually means is unclear.[28] Considering the context (i.e., successful escape of the prey), I shall define *confusion* as any delay or disruption in the predator's attack sequence of sufficient magnitude to permit the prey to escape. I shall next define the *attack sequence* as a series of closely linked behaviors starting with detection of the prey, followed by pursuit of it, and culminating in a *strike* or capture attempt. It remains to be determined how variable this simplified scheme actually is. For example, the predator may visually isolate an individual prey fish and then pursue it. Alternatively, what seems to be the end of an unsuccessful attack sequence—the scattering of a prey school by a predator without a capture—may actually be an intermediate stage, that of separating an individual for a strike by first disrupting the school.[29] The fish being pursued can avoid predation by jumping into the air, which momentarily removes it from the predator's field of vision (Fig. 6-7).

Some evidence exists that fish on the periphery of schools are more vulnerable to attack.[30] If true, the survival value of schooling to the individual may depend on how randomly it

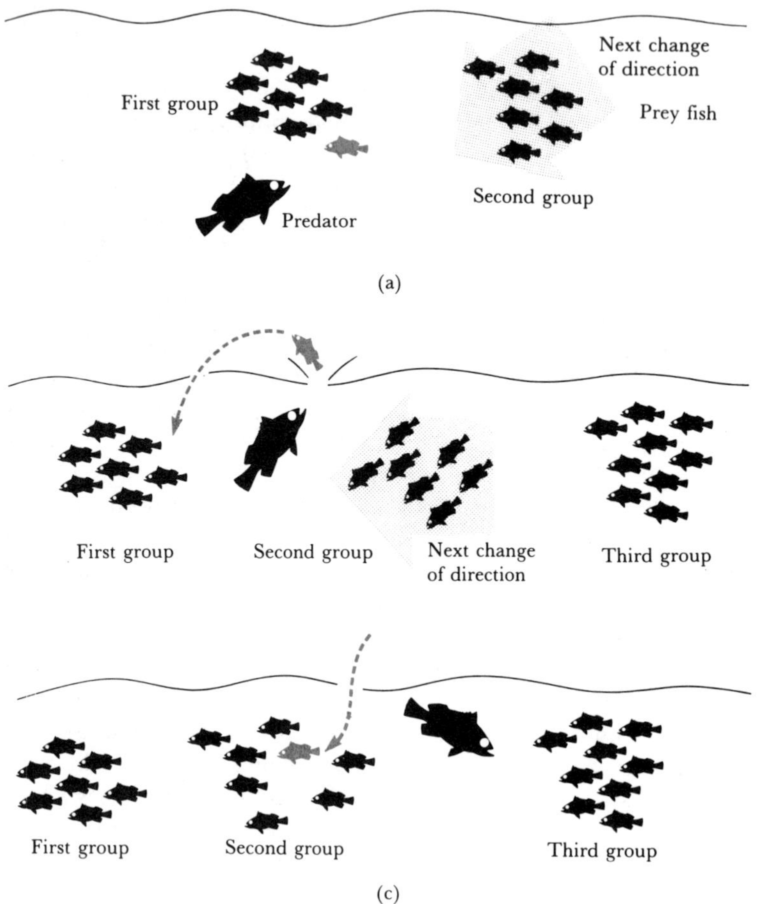

Figure 6-7 *Evasion of a predator by jumping. The sequence is hypothetical.* (a) *A prey fish in a moving school is singled out for attack.* (b) *The prey fish takes evasive action by jumping, which breaks the predator's visual contact. At the same time the school splits, forming a "halo" around the predator. The first group continues to move forward. Individuals in the second group change direction, then turn and follow the first group.* (c) *Upon entering the water the prey fish seeks cover within the second group, which has moved into the space just vacated by the first group, and is lost from view. Meanwhile, a third group comprising the rest of the school moves into view.* Source: Stephen Spotte, drawn from information in Major (1977).

changes positions. In other words, if position within a school is completely random the probability of long-term survival is the same for all members, although the probability of immediate survival is reduced for those swimming on the periphery. If individuals are positioned nonrandomly, those at the center stand a greater chance of surviving when the school is attacked. This increases long-term survival as well. Few studies have monitored how individuals interact with conspecifics while schooling, but the sparse data available indicate that position within a school may not be random.[31]

Schooling appears to offer no feeding advantages to planktivorous fishes,[32] but the same is apparently not true of piscivorous species, provided the prey also schools. Evidence interpreted as cooperative hunting has been observed in some species of jacks and tunas on both pelagic (Fig. 6-8) and inshore prey (Fig. 6-9).[33] The value of confusion as a defense mecha-

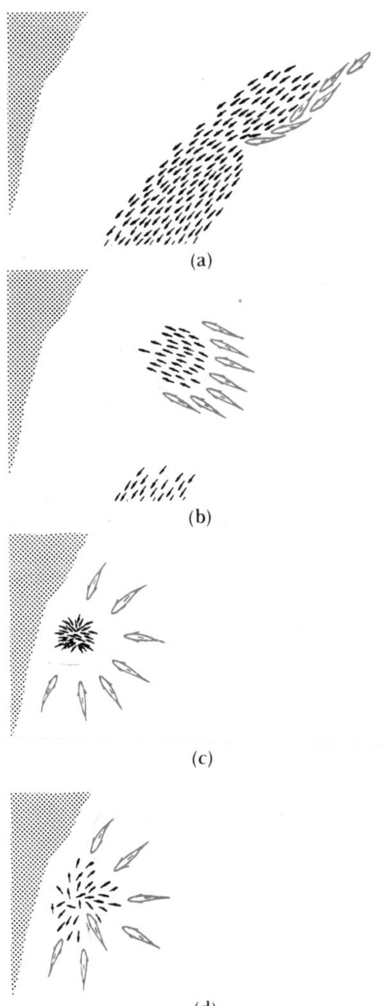

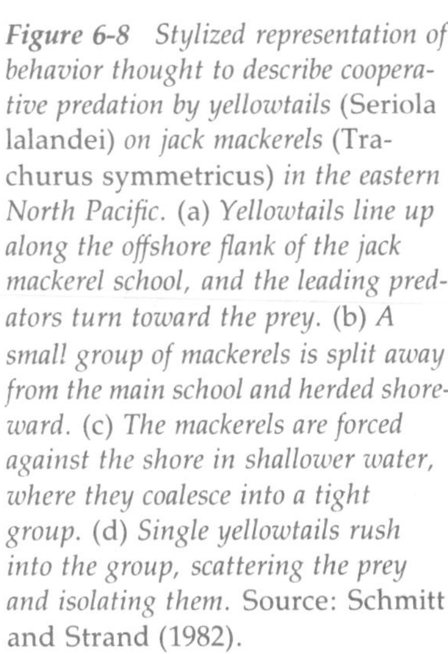

Figure 6-8 Stylized representation of behavior thought to describe cooperative predation by yellowtails (Seriola lalandei) *on jack mackerels* (Trachurus symmetricus) *in the eastern North Pacific.* (a) *Yellowtails line up along the offshore flank of the jack mackerel school, and the leading predators turn toward the prey.* (b) *A small group of mackerels is split away from the main school and herded shoreward.* (c) *The mackerels are forced against the shore in shallower water, where they coalesce into a tight group.* (d) *Single yellowtails rush into the group, scattering the prey and isolating them.* Source: Schmitt and Strand (1982).

nism by the prey is actually reversed when predators disrupt the integrity of the school. The effect is then to induce confusion where none existed. A few individuals are momentarily isolated, and the loss of anonymity leaves them vulnerable to a strike.[34] A few reports suggest that schooling increases swimming efficiency by minimizing hydrodynamic forces such as friction and drag, but conclusive evidence is lacking.[35]

Dominance

A striking and as yet unmentioned characteristic of fish assemblages is their egalitarianism. In a shoal, school, or mill no individual leads or follows, nor is a particular fish dominant or

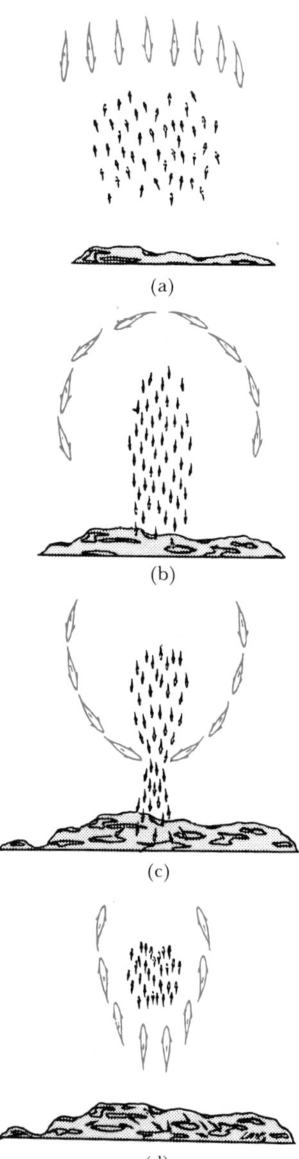

Figure 6-9 *Stylized representation of presumed cooperative predation by yellowtails on Cortez grunts* (Lythrulon flaviguttatum) *in the eastern North Pacific.* (a) *Yellowtails form a line perpendicular to a rocky reef and parallel with the shoreline (not shown) as they approach the prey.* (b) *The group of yellowtails splits into a semicircle as the grunts flee toward the reef.* (c) *The grunts are intercepted.* (d) *Part of the group is herded away from the safety of the reef into open water and attacked.* Source: Schmitt and Strand (1982).

subordinate. All occupy the same social rank. Social equality is maintained even when a school disintegrates during feeding. Competition in many nonschooling species is more obvious because of differences in the social status of competing individuals. Those that are dominant maintain their superiority in part by behaving aggressively or *agonistically* toward competitors.[36] In most fishes the agonistic response typically involves such behaviors as erecting the fins, chasing, posturing (sometimes with tail beating), and biting. Recognition of agonistic behavior and the factors that induce it can help lower the incidence of stress and injury resulting from antisocial strife in community exhibits.

Dominance is antisocial behavior defined as priority of access to resources for which individuals compete.[37] The key element is competition; without it, dominance relationships could not exist. Dominance can be considered from two perspectives. The first focuses on behavior, principally the number of individuals and their relationships. The second is concerned with ecological factors thought to make dominance behavior adaptive. Both are considered in this section.

TYPES OF DOMINANCE Several types of dominance have been identified, and sometimes the distinctions are vague. In fishes the best known is *territorial dominance,* the measurable component of space-related dominance behavior.[38] Some coral reef fishes are territorial as juveniles but not as adults, others the reverse, and still others maintain territories while in both phases. I shall deal only with adult fishes. In modern zoological usage a *territory* is a fixed portion of the home range that confers priority of access to one or more critical resources.[39] The excluded individuals have priority at another place or time. A *home range* is an area used regularly by an individual or group during ordinary diel activities,[40] and it can be occupied with or without implications of dominance. Many species share their home ranges peacefully. Others—notably some damselfishes (Pomacentridae)—defend all occupied space against intruders. In such cases home range and territory are operational synonyms.

When individuals dominate others but not in a space-related context they demonstrate *individual dominance.* Sometimes territorial and individual dominance exist simultaneously. As explained later, males of some fishes maintain harems. The male exerts individual dominance over all harem females, but within fixed territorial boundaries.

The simplest form of individual dominance is the *dominance hierarchy* or *rank order,* classically illustrated by the linear "peck order" of barnyard hens. One bird (the alpha hen) dominates the others, the one below her (the beta hen) dominates all except the alpha bird, and so forth to the omega hen at the bottom of the peck order, which dominates none. Linear dominance hierarchies are rare in large groups of animals; less permanent, triangular relationships tend to develop instead. *Monarchial systems* also can be formed: one individual dominates all others, and aggression practically ceases. Only a few coral reef fishes are known to form dominance hierarchies. In the West Indies some bicolor damselfish (*Stegastes partitus*) maintain individual territories (Plate 10d); other *S. partitus* and some other damselfishes live in colonies (Plate 11a). The latter are linear dominance hierarchies in which the degree of dominance is size dependent. Large individuals dominate smaller ones, and most aggressive interactions occur between fish of similar size (Fig. 6-10). Conversely, little aggression takes place between individuals of different size. Dominance hierarchies are predicated on mutual recognition of a dominant-subordinate relationship. When conditions are normal (e.g., adequate space is available for subordinates to escape), potential disputes are settled quickly and harmlessly. If conditions are abnormal, as they sometimes are in poorly planned community exhibits, the subordinate individual is stressed by continuous harassment, often injured, and occasionally killed. Dominance hierarchies involving coral reef fishes are uncommon in nature; in captivity they are often artifacts induced by space limitations and crowding.

Dominance of any kind can be *absolute* or *relative*. If absolute, it exists independently of time and location. If relative, it is reversible with changes of place and time, predictable, and without alteration of individual relationships. The societies of some species are organized into *absolute dominance hierarchies*, in which the rank order is the same wherever the group goes and in all circumstances. An absolute hierarchy changes only when individuals move up or down the ranks through interactions with rivals. Other species display *relative dominance hierarchies*, and even individuals with the highest rank defer to subordinates under certain conditions. Whether this form of behavior exists

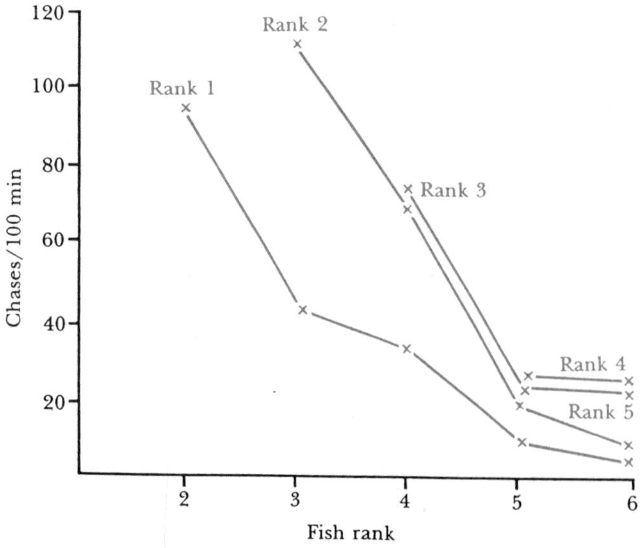

Figure 6-10 *Combined data from observations of seven groups of bicolor damselfish* (Stegastes partitus) *consisting of six to eight individuals. Each curve is a composite of chases directed by one rank at all subordinate ranks (e.g., rank 1 chased rank 2 a total of 96 times). A chase is defined as a rapid movement toward another individual that is moving away or starting to move away from the chaser. Symbols (x) indicate statistically significant differences between adjacent points; in other words, rank 1 chased rank 2 significantly more than it chased rank 3.* Source: Sadovy (1985).

in fishes is unclear. Some behaviorists consider relative hierarchies to be intermediate between absolute hierarchies and territorial dominance. Others maintain that individual and territorial dominance are, respectively, extreme expressions of absolute and relative dominance.

TERRITORIAL DOMINANCE Territories can be occupied by fishes individually and in pairs, groups, and leks (defined below).[41] Numerous damselfishes are individually territorial, but except for some surgeonfishes, butterflyfishes (Chaetodontidae), parrotfishes, and perhaps a few others, not many coral reef species can be included in this category. Not surprisingly, most research on individual territorial dominance has involved damselfishes. This is partly because they are easy to study and often territorial all year. Moreover, no group of fishes flaunts its repertoire of aggressive behaviors with more élan. Damselfish territories are mostly small (Table 6-1) and often crowded together (Fig. 6-11).

Pair territories are occupied solely by a breeding pair of fishes. At least one butterflyfish (*Chaetodon baronessa*) occupies pair territories, as does one wrasse (*Labroides dimidiatus*), although the latter also has a social structure based on harems. The damselfish *Acanthochromis polyacanthus* is temporarily pair territorial during the breeding season, and a few small, cryptic gobies (e.g., *Gobiodon* and *Paragobiodon*) occur frequently in pairs and are probably territorial. All damselfishes of the genus *Amphiprion* form permanent territorial pairs and live in association with single sea anemones. Territorial dominance based on breeding pairs may be uncommon in coral reef fishes because parental care of the young is rare. Of the fishes just listed, none except *A. polyacanthus* is known to provide parental care.

TABLE 6-1 Approximate territory sizes of permanently territorial damselfishes.

Species	Territory, m^2	Region
Dascyllus aruanus[7]	5	Indo-West Pacific
Hypsypops rubicundus[2]	10.7–14.7	Eastern North Pacific
H. rubicundus[4]	3.15	Eastern North Pacific
Pomacentrus flavicauda[5]	2	Indo-West Pacific
Stegastes dorsopunicans[1]	0.6	West Indies
Stagastes leucostictus[3]	0.3–3.5	West Indies
S. planifrons[6]	<2–>3	West Indies
S. planifrons[8]	1.4–3.6	West Indies

Sources: Bartels (1984),[1] Clarke (1970),[2] Ebersole (1977),[3] Foster (1972),[4] Low (1971),[5] Myrberg and Thresher (1974),[6] Sale (1971; occupies group territories),[7] Sammarco and Williams (1982).[8]

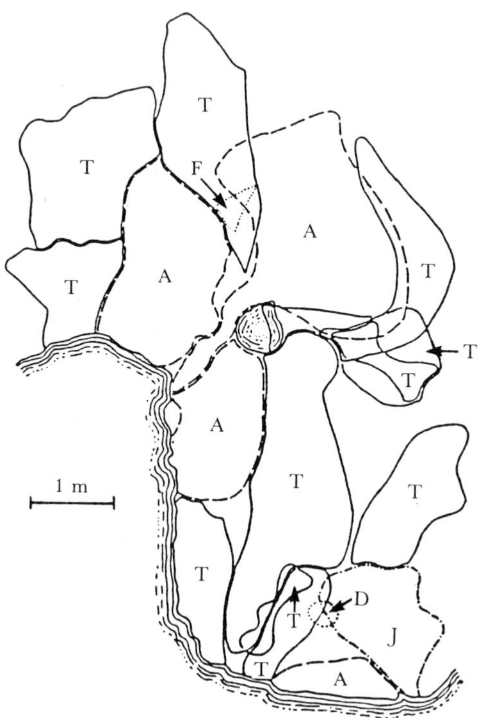

Figure 6-11 *Intra- and interspecific territorial relationships among damselfishes at Heron Island, Great Barrier Reef, Australia. Territories are held for extended periods—probably for life—and represent activity by both sexes. T =* Pomacentrus tripunctatus, *A =* P. apicalis, *J =* P. jenkinsi, *F =* P. flavicauda, *and D =* Abudefduf dickii. Source: Nursall (1974).

Among coral reef fishes only certain members of the damselfish genus *Dascyllus* (notably *D. aruanus*) definitely occupy territories in groups. Coral reef fishes that lek are more widespread. *Lekking* or *arena behavior* describes a type of polygamous mating system in which males are territorial only during spawning periods, when they gather at specific locations and compete for females that visit the sites. After mating, the females leave. Some of the damselfishes, surgeonfishes, wrasses, and parrotfishes demonstrate this behavior.[42]

FITNESS AND TERRITORIAL DOMINANCE The concept of territorial dominance can be considered from two perspectives. The first comprises functional aspects. Pertinent questions address whether success in gaining a territory increases *fitness* (i.e., reproductive capacity); in other words, whether territorial behavior is adaptive. Into the second category fall activities amenable to observation and measurement: distance from the territorial perimeter where intruders are repelled, number of nips at intruders per unit time, evidence of recognition (e.g., intra- versus interspecific aggression), and so forth. These are the ecologist's potsherds, identifiable artifacts that in sum and context represent windows on the infrastructures of animal societies.

Priority of access to resources, a key characteristic of dominance, must be achieved through interaction. A *resource* is defined as any commodity—tangible or intangible—that increases fitness. Some contemporary behavioral ecologists believe that territorial dominance represents a form of competition for resources in short supply. If *adaptations* are evolutionary mechanisms that increase fitness, then territorial dominance can be viewed as adaptive.[43] In the context of these definitions, a territorial species monopolizes or retains access to the resources it requires to remain fit. The principal ones involve food supplies, mates and nest sites, and shelter spaces. Considered together, they comprise a kaleidoscope of subtle, interlocking patterns. The relative importance of each is species dependent, and the challenge for behaviorists has been to identify adaptive features and filter out the behavioral "white noise." Of the three resources listed above, retention of shelter spaces probably has the least adaptive importance. Space as a resource (minus aspects related to dominance) is the subject of Chapter 7.

In every species only some individuals succeed in establishing territories, and the rest are excluded. If increased fitness correlates positively with territorial dominance, it follows that failure to gain and hold a territory diminishes fitness. Successful individuals possess certain characteristics that competitors—whether the same or other species—do not. At least three have been identified: (*1*) large size relative to competitors, (*2*) an aggressive nature, and (*3*) prior residence. I shall not discuss prior residence because information is lacking. The interactions of two West Indies damselfishes illustrate the importance of size.[44] The yellowtail damselfish (*Microspathodon chrysurus*) and dusky damselfish (*Stegastes dorsopunicans*) often occupy adjacent territories. Both are aggressive, but at maturity the yellowtail damselfish has a body mass that is six times greater. Nonetheless, a dusky damselfish can prevent encroachment provided the body mass of its larger neighbor is less than, equal to, or up to approximately twice its own mass (Fig. 6-12). If the body mass of the yellowtail damselfish is more than twice as great it can dominate the smaller fish and occupy its territory.

FOOD SUPPLIES AND TERRITORIAL DOMINANCE Many damselfishes are omnivores but feed heavily on attached seaweeds. An important aspect of maintaining territories appears to be defense of the algal food supply, and considerable time is spent patrolling territorial borders and excluding food competitors. The fact that both sexes are often territorial lends credence to this idea.[45]

Large, fleshy algae are not the primary producers on coral reefs. Most of the algal biomass takes the form of a fuzzy "turf"

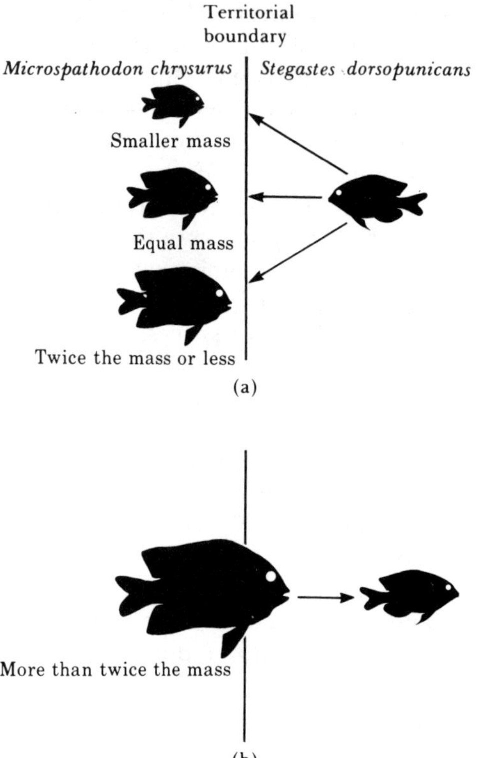

Figure 6-12 *Yellowtail damselfish* (Microspathodon chrysurus) *and dusky damselfish* (Stegastes dorsopunicans) *often occupy adjacent territories on West Indies coral reefs. The yellowtail damselfish at maturity has a body mass that is six times greater.* (a) *A smaller dusky damselfish can defend its territorial borders if its neighbor is smaller, equal in size, or not more than twice as large.* (b) *If the size disparity exceeds a factor of two, the yellowtail damselfish can invade and occupy the territory of the smaller fish.* Source: Stephen Spotte, drawn from information in Robertson and Lassig (1980).

<2 cm high that blankets the dead limestone substratum. Damselfishes of several species maintain *algal lawns* of preferred seaweeds within their territories, effectively "cultivating" private gardens. If success is measured in terms of standing algal biomass, the energy expended is worthwhile. Heavy grazing by nomadic parrotfishes and surgeonfishes in undefended locations of the reef results in domination by crustose coralline algae and low species diversity.[46] Within damselfish territories algal growth on otherwise identical substrates is lush and diverse, consisting principally of erect, filamentous forms.[47] At least one damselfish is carnivorous, and algal lawns are used differently. The garibaldi (*Hypsypops rubicundus*) is a cold-water damselfish indigenous to the eastern North Pacific. Adults feed on benthic invertebrates, primarily sponges and sea anemones. Most feeding occurs inside territorial boundaries. An algal lawn is cultivated, but only during the breeding season when it serves as a nest site.[48]

Damselfishes that cultivate algal lawns defend them against their own and other species. The intensity of the agonistic response and the location within the territory from which the response can be elicited varies with the identity of the intruder. In some species agonistic behavior is most intense and occurs closest to the territorial boundary when the intruder is a herbivore (Fig. 6-13).[49] Carnivores are often allowed inside. This has been interpreted as evidence that food competitors are recognized, and that territorial defense is not simply random aggression. In the West Indies the threespot damselfish (*Stegastes planifrons*, Plate 11b) also excludes from its territory an algal-feeding invertebrate, the longspine sea urchin (*Diadema antillarum*).[50]

Establishment and maintenance of algal lawns by damselfishes can adversely affect reef corals in two ways.[51] Territorial dominance behavior by *Hemiglyphiododon plagiometopon* and *Pomacentrus bankanensis* in the Indo-West Pacific results in reduced grazing pressure by food competitors, which accelerates bioerosion by boring invertebrates. The corals become fragile and less able to withstand shear stresses exerted by storm waves. An effect attributable directly to damselfish behavior has also been reported. In the West Indies, the threespot damselfish extends the perimeters of its algal lawn by nipping live corals, which removes tissue and eventually kills them (Fig. 6-14, Plate 11c).

REPRODUCTION AND TERRITORIAL DOMINANCE For simplicity I shall recognize three categories of territory holders: (*1*) permanent, (*2*) seasonal, and (*3*) part-time. Damselfishes provide the best examples of the first two categories. Permanently territorial species (Table 6-2) actively repel intruders

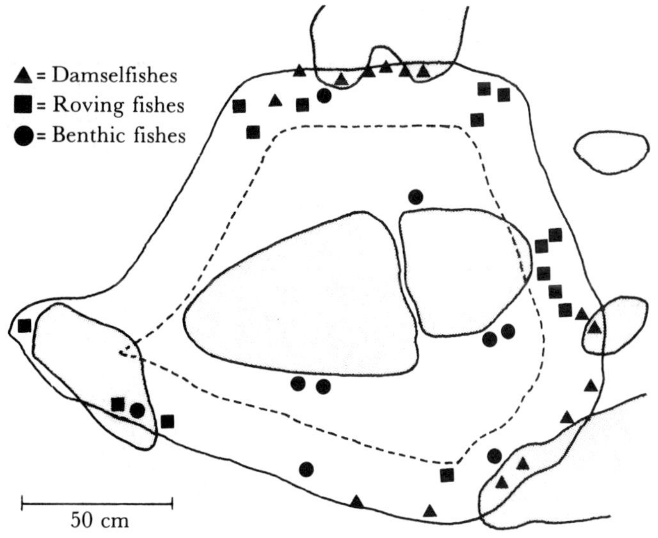

Figure 6-13 *Map of a territory maintained by damselfish* (Pomacentrus flavicauda) *near Heron Island, Great Barrier Reef, Australia. Irregularly shaped objects are dead coral boulders. The solid perimeter line encloses the outer part of the territory and the broken line the inner part. Symbols represent agonistic encounters: triangles = damselfishes (including conspecifics); squares = roving fishes, mainly herbivores and a few omnivores (e.g., parrotfishes, surgeonfishes, butterflyfishes, leatherjackets); and circles = benthic carnivores (e.g., blennies, gobies). Fishes in two categories (triangles and squares) were attacked at the border, but the others were ignored even when well inside the borders.* Pomacentrus flavicauda *reacted agonistically to 38 species belonging to 12 families. Of these, 35 species are herbivores or omnivores and potential food competitors. Sixteen species of six families—all carnivores—were ignored.* Source: Low (1971).

Figure 6-14 An algal lawn maintained by a single threespot damselfish (Stegastes planifrons) on a West Indies coral reef. The algae grows only on nonliving substrates. To prepare a surface suitable for algal growth the fish kills the living coral inside its territory by nipping it. Bonaire, Netherlands Antilles, 20 m. Source: Stephen Spotte.

TABLE 6-2 Duration of space-related dominance in damselfishes.

Permanently territorial	
Hypsypops rubicundus[2]	Eastern North Pacific
Parma victoriae[9]	Indo-West Pacific
Pomacentrus flavicauda[6]	Indo-West Pacific
Stagastes fasciolatus[3,5]	Indo-West Pacific
S. planifrons[8]	West Indies
Seasonally territorial	
Acanthochromis polyacanthus[10]	Indo-West Pacific
A. zonatus[4]	Indo-West Pacific
Chromis chromis[1]	Indo-West Pacific
C. multilineata[7]	West Indies
C. punctipinnis[12]	Eastern North Pacific
Dascyllus albisella[11]	Indo-West Pacific

Sources: Abel (1961),[1] Clarke (1970),[2] Hixon and Brostoff (1983),[3] Keenleyside (1972),[4] Losey (1982),[5] Low (1971),[6] Myrberg et al. (1967),[7] Myrberg and Thresher (1974),[8] Norman and Jones (1984),[9] Robertson (1973),[10] Stevenson (1963),[11] Turner and Ebert (1962).[12]

throughout the year, whether breeding or not. In these fishes control of the food supply may be important at all times. To my knowledge, all permanently territorial damselfishes breed seasonally and otherwise are sexually inactive. Agonistic behavior typically is most intense during the breeding season, but clearly evident all year.[52]

Seasonally territorial damselfishes maintain territories only briefly during the breeding season (Table 6-2) and abandon them afterward. Most are planktivores. Food is obtained from the water column, not the substratum. Males establish territories and defend them against intrusion by other males. Females are permitted inside to breed and lay eggs, and nests are guarded by the males until hatching (Fig. 6-15).

Many part-time territorial fishes that inhabit coral reefs breed throughout the year, sometimes every day. Territories are occupied briefly, often less than an hour or so. Larger males dominate smaller ones and mate more often, ordinarily by defense of specific locations where spawning occurs, or by maintenance of harems. Notable examples are certain wrasses and parrotfishes. Mating systems are diverse in these families, and the concept of territory, when applicable, assumes different dimensions (Table 6-3). Males of some species lek. Those of other species maintain permanent territories with harems of six or so adult females. In still others, males establish temporary territories for brief periods each day and spawn in pairs with visiting females. Some species of wrasses and parrotfishes spawn in groups consisting of a male and several females. In these situations adult males are dominant and exclude subordinate males, but are not territorial. The mating system of the West Indies creole wrasse (*Clepticus parrae*) is without any structure. Males and females simply pair off and spawn.

"OPTIMAL" TERRITORY SIZE[53] The sizes of territories and home ranges occupied by most animals vary greatly by location and over time. The mitigating factors are complex, puzzling, and hard to isolate and measure. Not surprisingly, they often appear unpredictable. Among these factors are degree of aggressiveness and other behavioral traits, sex, size, age, food abundance, population density, and season. Researchers have sometimes doubted whether "optimal" space is even a valid concept.[54] Generalizations obviously can be misleading, and the following comments warrant only loose interpretation.

The most common factor studied has been food abundance. Ordinarily, occupied space increases as food availability declines, and the reverse occurs when food is abundant. However, this principle is not universally true. Some ecologists con-

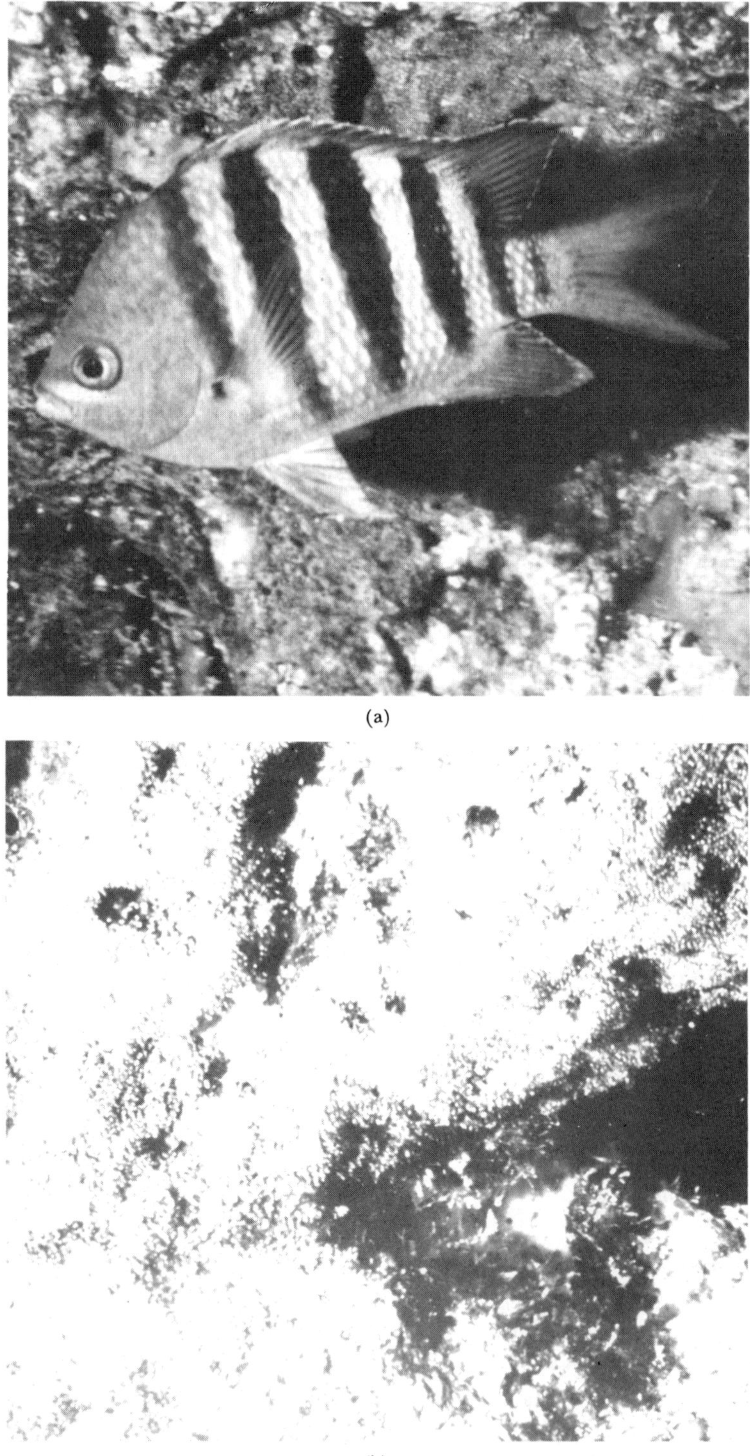

(a)

(b)

Figure 6-15 *Male sergeant majors* (Abudefduf saxatilis) *probably occupy territories only during the breeding season.* (a) *A male guarding its nest.* (b) *Eggs attached to the substratum. Bonaire, Netherland Antilles, 12 m.* Source: Stephen Spotte.

TABLE 6-3 Mating systems of West Indies wrasses and parrotfishes.

	Labridae—wrasses
Bodianus rufus	Males are not permanently territorial but maintain harems and probably pair-spawn
Clepticus parrae	Mating system unstructured
Halichoeres bivittatus	Males form temporary territories and pair- or group-spawn
H. garnoti	Mating system unknown
H. maculipinna	Males form temporary territories and pair- or group-spawn
H. pictus	Mating system unknown
H. poeyi	Males form temporary territories and pair-spawn
H. radiatus	Mating system unknown
Thalassoma bifasciatum	Spawning is in leks with group spawning also common
	Scaridae—parrotfishes
Cryptotomus roseus	Males form temporary territories and pair-spawn
Scarus iserti	Terminal males may be permanently territorial and pair-spawn in harems, but initial males are nonterritorial and group-spawn
S. taeniopterus	Males may be permanently territorial and pair-spawn in harems
S. vetula	Males are permanently territorial, maintain harems, and probably pair-spawn
Sparisoma atomarium	Males are permanently territorial and pair-spawn in harems
S. aurofrenatum	Males are permanently territorial and pair-spawn in harems
S. chrysopterum	Males are permanently territorial and pair-spawn
S. radians	Males form temporary territories, and spawning is in pairs and groups
S. rubripinne	Males form temporary territories and pair-spawn
S. viride	Males form temporary territories and pair-spawn

Source: Stephen Spotte, compiled from information in Robertson and Warner (1978) and Warner and Robertson (1978).

sider home-ranging and territorial animals as belonging to either of two categories. *Feeding-time maximizers* extend their occupied space when food is plentiful.[55] In these species reproductive success correlates with the daily net gain in energy. Conversely, *feeding-time minimizers* have fixed daily energy requirements and respond to changes in food availability in the conventional way.[55] Opposing hypotheses have attempted to explain the negative correlation between food abundance and the amount of occupied space, mainly in territorial species. The classic view holds that animals somehow ''assess'' food availability and adjust the sizes of their territories to include enough food resources to sustain fitness.[56] The second hypothesis proposes that animals acquire as much space as possible, with the sizes of their territories ultimately regulated by intraspecific competition; in other words, territory size is controlled by the energy expended to maintain it, not food abundance.[57]

Most studies showing that the amount of occupied space is influenced by food abundance have dealt with home ranging, nonaggressive species.[58] Presumably, home ranges can be expanded during times of food shortages. When a negative correlation between the size of the occupied space and the number of neighboring conspecifics has been demonstrated, the species have nearly always been territorial.[59]

FITNESS AND INDIVIDUAL DOMINANCE[60] Among the most interesting—and confusing—expressions of individual dominance in fishes occur in species that undergo sex reversal as adults (i.e., are *sequential hermaphrodites*). The change can be female to male (*protogyny*), or male to female (*protandry*). Protogyny is the more common.[61] Some of the best known examples are found in the wrasses and parrotfishes. Sex reversal appears to have adaptive value, suggesting that fitness is increased. If true, then evolution sometimes favors patterns of sexuality that differ from a changeless existence as male and female. Dominance regulates reproductive success in both protogynous and protandrous species. In protogynous fishes (but also many others that do not undergo sex reversal), females mate preferentially with larger, older males that gain dominance over lesser competitors. One result of strong sexual selection is *sexual dimorphism,* in which males and females at maturity are markedly different in size, specialized structures, coloration (including pattern), or a combination of these (Fig. 6-16, Plates 11d and 12a).

Apart from size, coloration is often the most obvious feature (Fig. 6-17). It is illustrated in the smallest adults as *initial coloration*. The largest adult males display *terminal coloration*. Im-

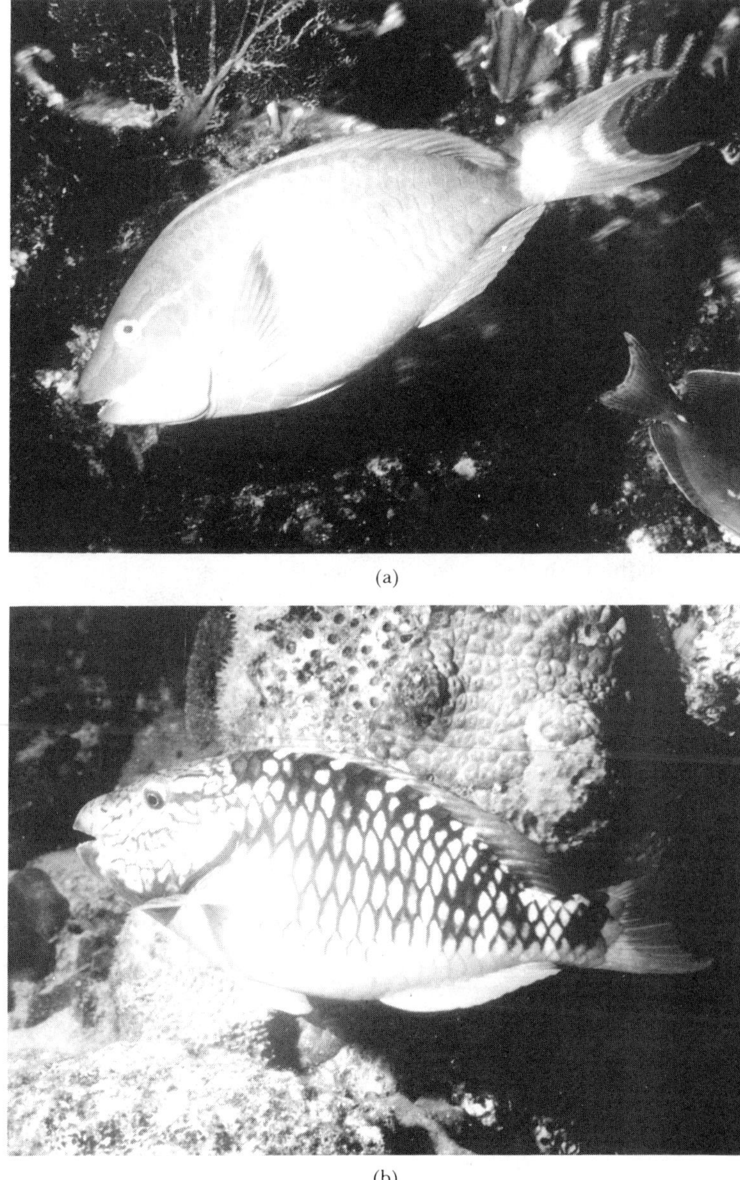

(a)

(b)

Figure 6-16 *Sexual dimorphism in the stoplight parrotfish* (Sparisoma viride). (a) *Terminal male, Key Largo, Florida, 13 m.* (b) *Adult, Bonaire, Netherlands Antilles, 20 m.* Source: Stephen Spotte.

mature specimens have *juvenile coloration*. The comparative coloration of adult males and females in *sexually dichromatic* species is distinctly different. In *sexually monochromatic* species the two sexes are indistinguishable as adults on the basis of coloration. Females of monochromatic species are capable of developing the same coloration (including patterns) as males, but in dichromatic species they cannot, and all individuals of a single

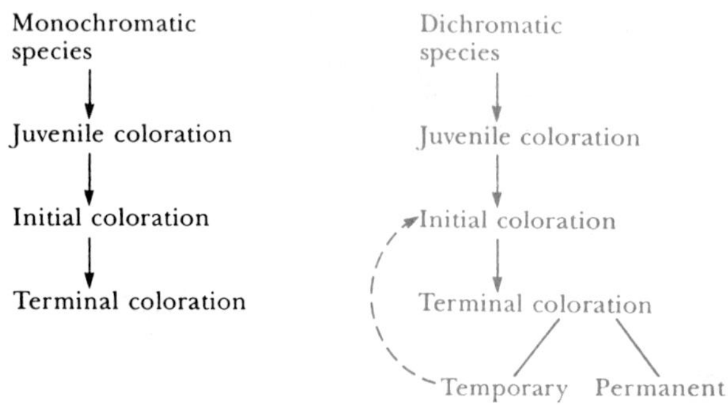

Figure 6-17 *Development of monochromatism and dichromatism in teleosts.* Source: Stephen Spotte, drawn from information in Warner and Robertson (1978).

color phase are males. Two types of dichromatic males, called *temporary* and *permanent*, are known. In one, terminal fishes can revert to the initial coloration; in the other they cannot (Fig. 6-17). In terms of sexuality, *primary males* are born as males, whereas *secondary males* are females that undergo sex reversal.[62] A species that has both primary and secondary males is *diandric*, and one with only secondary males is *monandric* (Table 6-4).

TABLE 6-4 Coloration (including pattern) and sexuality of West Indies wrasses and parrotfishes.

Fishes	Monochromatic	Dichromatic	Monandric	Diandric
		Labridae—wrasses		
Bodianus rufus	x		x	
Clepticus parrae		x	x	
Halichoeres bivittatus		x		x
H. garnoti		x[1]	x	
H. maculipinna		x		x
H. pictus		x		x
H. poeyi		x[2]		x
H. radiatus		x[3]	unknown	
Thalassoma bifasciatum		x		x
		Scaridae—parrotfishes		
Cryptotomus roseus		x	x	
Scarus iserti		x		x
S. taeniopterus		x	unknown	
S. vetula		x		x
Sparisoma atomarium		x	x	
S. aurofrenatum		x	x	
S. chrysopterum		x	x	
S. radians		x	x	
S. rubripinne		x	x	
S. viride		x	x	

Source: Stephen Spotte, compiled from information in Robertson and Warner (1978) and Warner and Robertson (1978).
Notes: Partly dichromatic,[1] slightly dichromatic,[2] partly dichromatic?[3]

The adaptive advantage of sex reversal is embodied in the *size advantage hypothesis*.[63] Its basic premise is simple. If fitness, measured as the number of eggs produced or fertilized, varies between the sexes as a function of size, individuals that change sex at the appropriate time will produce more offspring than conspecifics that do not. Two factors can cause fertility to vary by sex differences: (*1*) the comparative numbers of male and female *gametes* (eggs or sperm) produced and (*2*) the mating system of the species. The relevance of the first is circumstantial (Fig. 6-18). Male teleosts typically produce millions of gametes, but the capacity to produce or store eggs limits female fertility. From a female's standpoint the number of available males is irrelevant. A male's fertility is often limited by the number of females with which to mate, in addition to their fertility. In such situations the amount of sperm produced is irrelevant. The expected fertility of female fishes thus increases with body size, whereas male fertility is affected most by the mating system.

Reproductive success is a function of the mating system. In fishes that are sequential hermaphrodites, fitness depends on sex and size. Mating systems thus regulate the quantitative aspects of reproductive success and ultimately fitness. In most monogamous fishes, males and females are similar in size. The

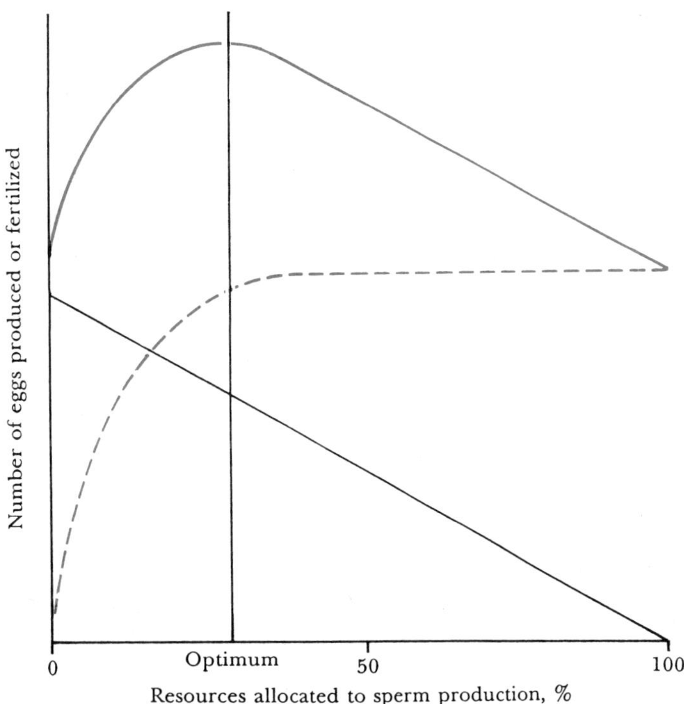

Figure 6-18 *Ordinarily, the number of eggs an individual produces is related directly to the energy devoted to their manufacture (black line). The situation with sperm cells is different because the relatively low production often results in maximum success (broken line). Thus a small amount of sperm can fertilize all of a mate's eggs, making additional investments superfluous. Individuals with the greatest overall reproductive rate that combines male and female functions are favored (solid colored line), and the optimal result in this situation is obtained when most of the energy is devoted to egg production.* Source: Warner (1984) after Fischer (1981).

fertility of both sexes also is similar, and sex reversal offers no advantage (Fig. 6-19a). In other monogamous species protandry is advantageous, and the female is larger than the male (e.g., anemonefishes, *Amphiprion* spp.) If the mating system consists of many individuals shedding gametes simultaneously (group spawning), male fertility is limited by the amount of sperm produced. In effect, the sperm cells compete, not the males. Sperm production increases with body size, as does egg production by females, and the potential fertility of males and females should be the same.

Mating systems of other species consist of larger males dominating subordinates and monopolizing the available females. Small, subordinate males might never mate, but small females have no such difficulty. Sex reversal would probably be adaptive. If a fish functioned as a female when small and later became a breeding-size male, it could theoretically produce more fertilized gametes—and by inference more offspring—over its life span than a fish that retained its original sex (Fig. 6-19b). Still other species reproduce by random pairing, a mating sys-

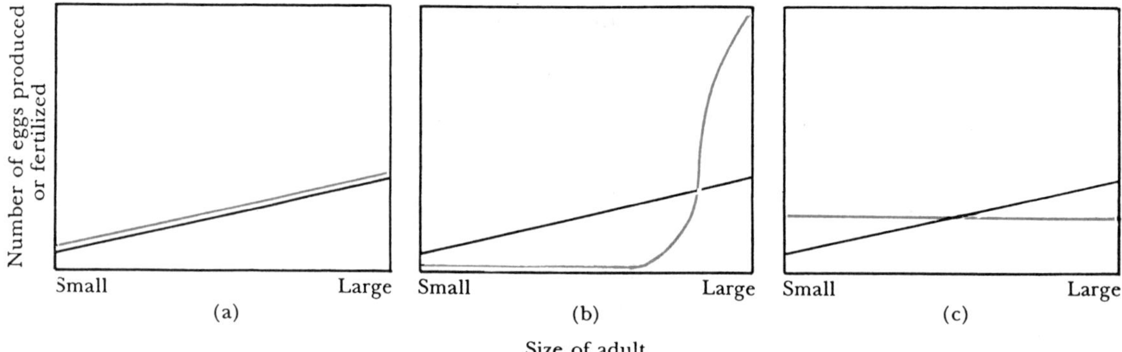

Figure 6-19 *Expected fertility of a female teleost (black line) is measured as the number of eggs produced and depends directly on size. Thus there is a steady increase with growth. A male's expected fertility (colored line), measured as the number of eggs fertilized, is a function of the mating system.* (a) *When males and females form monogamous pairs matched by size, or when males compete to fertilize eggs and thus to produce the most sperm, both sexes demonstrate a similar increase in fertility with size, and there is no natural selection for sex change.* (b) *When large males monopolize mating and exclude smaller males, male fertility rises markedly at a certain point in growth. A fish that stays female when small and becomes a male when attaining large size is favored selectively.* (c) *When mating consists of random pairing, an individual functions best as a male when small (with a chance of fertilizing a larger female) and as a female when large to capitalize on high capacity for egg production.* Source: Warner (1984) after Warner (1975).

tem that seems to favor protandry (Fig. 6-19c). Because gamete production in male teleosts typically exceeds that of females by a considerable margin, small males can fertilize females of any size. When the mating system is not dominated by large males, small size would be advantageous to males, considering the high probability of mating with females that are larger. Conversely, large size would favor females to capitalize on increased egg production.

Sex reversal in some coral reef fishes is controlled socially. *Labroides dimidiatus*, a protogynous Indo-West Pacific wrasse, lives in permanent groups consisting of a male and six or so females. The females constitute a harem, and the male mates with each one daily. If the male is removed the largest female changes sex and assumes the male's role. Sex reversal is rapid. Male behaviors are evident within hours, including spawning behavior. Active sperm cells are produced by 10 d.[64] Social control of sex reversal also is evident in some protandrous species. Anemonefishes live in association with large sea anemones. In some species (e.g., *Amphiprion bicinctus, A. clarkii*) one or more smaller juveniles can be present, in addition to an adult pair. Only individual adults of the breeding pair are sexually functional, and their presence represses growth and subsequent development of the juveniles. If the female of the pair is removed the male turns into a female. One of the juveniles then becomes a male, and a resident adult pair is assured.[65]

Symbiosis

Defined literally, *symbiosis* means living together. Without qualification, such a broad definition has little relevance. An infinite number of associations involving two or more living organisms can be called symbiotic. Coral reefs, for example, are complex associations of living plants and animals. Consequently, all coral reef fishes exist in symbiotic association with the living reef (Plate 12b). A reductionist approach obviously is necessary before any adaptive functions can be identified. A common technique is to partition symbiotic associations into a balance sheet of costs and benefits (Table 6-5). In *parasitism* the symbiont de-

TABLE 6-5 Costs and benefits of symbiosis.

	Host	Symbiont
Parasitism	Suffers	Benefits
Commensalism	No change	Benefits
Mutualism	Benefits	Benefits

Source: Stephen Spotte.

rives benefits at the expense of the host. *Commensalism* produces no change in the host's status, but benefits the symbiont. In *mutualism* both host and symbiont benefit. The costs and benefits of many symbiotic relationships are unknown. Future investigation of social arrangements now considered to be commensalism or mutualism may show that neither party benefits, leaving us with the literal meaning of symbiosis. Parasitism is discussed in Chapter 9. Examples of commensalism and mutualism are considered here.

PROTECTIVE ASSOCIATIONS A prominant example of protective symbiosis on Indo-West Pacific coral reefs is the association of certain damselfishes of the genera *Amphiprion*[66] and *Dascyllus* with several species of large and potentially lethal sea anemones (Plate 12c).[67] These associations are plastic and vary by species of fish and sea anemone (Table 6-6), and also by location. *Dascyllus* spp. are facultative symbionts, but all species of *Amphiprion* are thought to be obligate anemone dwellers (Fig. 6-20). In the most extensive field study yet conducted, no individual *Amphiprion* was ever seen without a symbiotic anemone.[68] Consequently, use of the colloquial term ''anemonefish'' is properly limited to this genus.

As a symbiont, the fish gains at least two benefits. One is protection from predators. Anemonefishes denied access to their host anemones in nature may be captured quickly by predatory fishes.[69] Anemones also serve as auxiliary food sources. Although anemonefishes are mainly planktivores and benthic omnivores, they feed opportunistically on the live tentacles, sloughing mucus, excretia, and even the captured food of their hosts.[70] Captive anemonefishes of certain species have been observed many times taking food to their hosts, leading to speculation that the anemones are being ''fed.'' This suggests a mutualistic association because the anemones would benefit. However, to my knowledge the behavior occurs rarely in nature. Other explanations seem more appropriate,[71] and I shall consider the relationship to be commensal (i.e., only the fish benefits, and the anemone is a passive partner).

Anemonefishes are territorial and repel intruders of their own and other species. The anemone is the focal point of the territory, and some anemonefishes defend the space around and above it for a metre or more.[72] Site attachment to the anemone is stronger than to its location.[73] If the anemone is moved, the fishes move with it. Anemonefishes kept in aquariums without anemones seldom display agonistic behavior, but territorial dominance is quickly evident after an anemone is introduced.[74]

Although anemonefishes live unharmed among the tentacles

TABLE 6-6 Known associations of sea anemones with Indo-West Pacific anemonefishes.

	Sea anemone species										
Fish species	*Cryptodendrum adhaesivum*	*Entacmaea quadricolor*	*Macrodactyla doreensis*	*Heteractis magnfica*	*Heteractis crispa*	*Heteractis aurora*	*Heteractis malu*	*Stichodactyla haddoni*	*Stichodactyla gigantea*	*Stichodactyla mertensii*	Total actinian associates
Premnas biaculeatus		x									1
Amphiprion ocellaris				x					x	x	3
Amphiprion percula				x	x				x		3
Amphiprion polymnus					x			x			2
Amphiprion sebae								x			1
Amphiprion latezonatus					x						1
Amphiprion akallopisos				x						x	2
Amphiprion nigripes				x							1
Amphiprion perideraion			x	x	x				x		4
Amphiprion sandaracinos										x	1
Amphiprion leucokranos				x	x						2
Amphiprion ephippium		x			x					(x)	2
Amphiprion frenatus		x									1
Amphiprion mccullochi		x									1
Amphiprion melanopus		x		x	x						3
Amphiprion rubrocinctus		x							x		2
Amphiprion clarkii	x	x	x		x	x	x	x	x	x	9
Amphiprion akindynos		x		x	x	x		x			5
Amphiprion allardi		x				x				x	3
Amphiprion bicinctus		x		x	x	x			x		5
Amphiprion chagosenis											?
Amphiprion chrysogaster						x		x		x	3
Amphiprion chrysopterus				x	x	x		x		x	5
Amphiprion fuscocaudatus										x	1
Amphiprion latifasciatus											?
Amphiprion tricinctus		x				x				x	3
Total number obligate fish associates	1	11	2	10	11	7	1	6	6	9	
Dascyllus trimaculatus		x	x	x	x	x		x	x	x	8
Dascyllus albisella							x				1

Source: Dunn (1981).

Figure 6-20 *The anemonefish* Amphiprion clarkii *among the tentacles of a sea anemone* (Heteractis crispa). *Madang, Papua-New Guinea, Micronesia.* Source: Gerald R. Allen, Western Australian Museum.

of their hosts, protection is neither absolute nor permanent. If separated from its anemone for a time, a fish is likely to be stung and killed when reintroduced, unless it goes through a sequence of activities called *acclimation*. During acclimation, physical contact with the tentacles is made cautiously, and full contact may not be attained for up to 3 h.[75] In addition, a certain degree of host specificity has been discovered, and protection against the stings of one species of anemone is no guarantee of protection against those of another, even if closely related.[76] The source of protection appears to be the outer mucous layer of the fish's skin, which is up to four times thicker than in fishes not known to associate with sea anemones.[77] The mucous layer serves as a chemically neutral, physical barrier;[77] if it is disturbed, the fish is vulnerable to being stung.

At least 30 fish species in the West Indies form symbiotic associations with sea anemones, mainly *Condylactis gigantea*, but the relationships are less well described than those of the Indo-West Pacific, and all appear to be facultative.[78] Some fishes associate with sea anemones as juveniles but not as adults. This group includes several wrasses (*Halichoeres garnoti, Hemipteronotus novacula*, and *Thalassoma bifasciatum*) and an unidentified parrotfish. Adult fishes include a clinid (*Starksia hassi*) and a goby (*Quisquilius hipoliti*). Several species appear to avoid the tentacles, although *S. hassi* is an exception.

REFUGE ASSOCIATIONS[79] Certain species of coral reef fishes take refuge inside large sessile invertebrates, ordinarily massive and tubular sponges (Table 6-7). The distinction between pro-

TABLE 6-7 Representative West Indies massive and tubular sponges and their commensal fishes.

Host sponge	Commensal fishes
Agelas confiera	*Gobiosoma horsti*
	G. louisae
	Phaeoptyx xenus
Callyspongia digitalis (?)	*Gobiosoma louisae*
	Phaeoptyx xenus
Callyspongia plicifera	*Gobiosoma horsti*
	Phaeoptyx xenus
Callyspongia vaginalis	*Apogon quadrisquamatus*
	Gobiosoma sp.
	G. louisae
	G. horsti
	Phaeoptyx xenus
Ianthella ianthella	*Gobiosoma louisae*
Ircinia strobilina	*Evermannichthys silus*
	Quisquilius hipoliti
	Risor ruber
	Starksia lepicoelia
Neofibularia n. *nolitangere*	*Gobiosoma* sp.
Spheciospongia vesparia	*Evermannichthys metzelaari*
	Gobiesox stumosus
	Pariah scotius
Spongia barbara	*Evermannichthys convictor*
Verongia archeri	*Gobiosoma chancei*
	G. louisae
	Phaeoptyx xenus
Verongia fistularis	*Gobiosoma chancei*
	G. louisae
	Phaeoptyx xenus
	Risor ruber
	Thalassoma bifasciatum
Verongia lacunosa	*Gobiosoma chancei*
	G. louisae
Veroniga sp.	*Gobiosoma louisae*
	G. horsti
Xestospongia muta	*Risor ruber*

Source: Stephen Spotte, compiled from information in Tyler and Böhlke (1972).

tective and refuge associations is arbitrary. However, sea anemones are potentially dangerous to predators of their symbiotic fishes, whereas sponges and most other invertebrates are not. Refuge associations are commensal and may be facultative or obligate. Several species of fishes that are facultative symbionts shelter in sponges during the inactive portion of their diel cycles, but also select crevices in the reef. In the West Indies the gobies *Evermannichthys metzelaari*, *Risor ruber*, *Gobiosoma chancei*, and *G. horsti* are never found except in association with sponges, nor is *Phaeoptyx xenus*, a cardinalfish (Apogonidae). The first two species always occur in massive sponges, whereas species of *Gobiosoma* and *Phaeoptyx* are more often commensal with tubular types.

Other fishes shelter with invertebrates (e.g., crustaceans) in coral crevices. The possible advantage gained by either animal is uncertain. Several such associations are known from the Indo-West Pacific. One involves the shrimp *Alpheus lottini* and *Paragobiodon lacunicola*, a goby. The fish remains in contact with one of the shrimp's antennae or its body, performing "shivering" movements every few minutes (Fig. 6-21a; also Plate 12d). This behavior apparently serves as a signal, but the nature of the message is unknown. Certain fishes and crabs form associations in the same colonies of coral. The crab is *Trapezia cymodoce*;

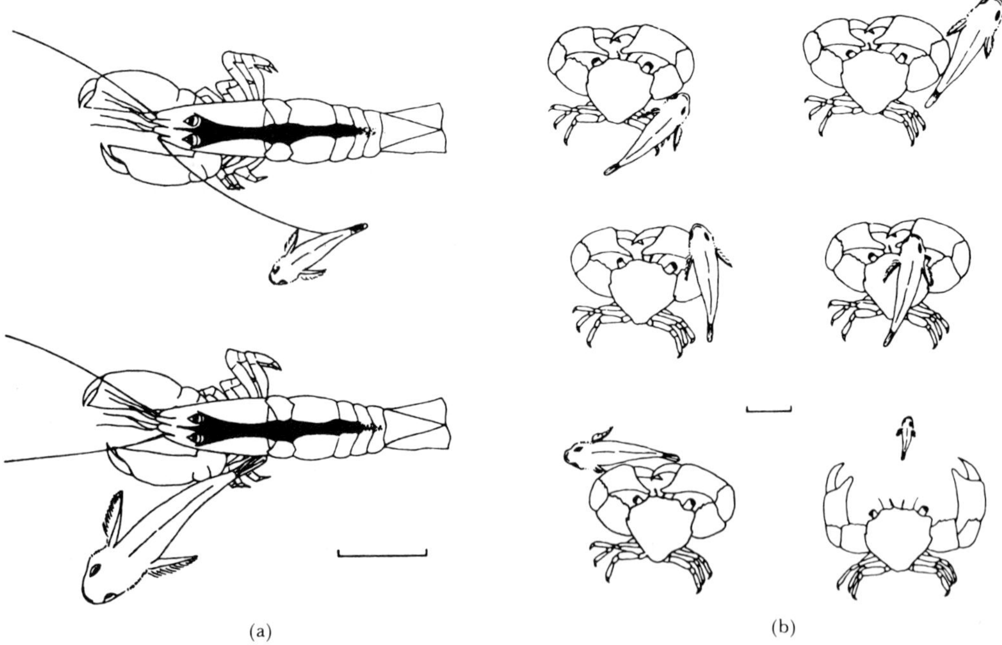

Figure 6-21 *Two symbiotic associations known to occur on the Great Barrier Reef.* (a) *Interactions between a shrimp* (Alpheus lottini) *and a fish* (Paragobiodon lacunicola). *Top and bottom illustrations show antennal and body contact. Scale bar = 1 cm.* (b) *Spatial relations between a crab* (Trapezia cymodoce) *and a fish* (Paragobiodon spp.). *The fish in the lower right illustration is a juvenile; all others are adults. Scale bar = 1 cm.* Source: Lassig (1977b).

the fishes are *Paragobiodon echinocephalus* and *P. lacunicola*. Each association involves one crab and one fish. A resident fish assumes several positions with respect to the crab (Fig. 6-21b) and occasionally performs ''shivering'' movements. The fish sometimes behaves agonistically toward the crab, but the crab either does not respond or moves a short distance away. Agonistic behavior by the crab has not been reported. Juvenile fishes are occasionally captured and eaten by resident crabs. It is thought that eventually a signal system develops, perhaps mediated through ''shivering'' movements of the fish, that allows peaceful coexistence.

CLEANING ASSOCIATIONS Some fishes demonstrate *cleaning behavior* by removing ectoparasites, scales, and mucus from the body surfaces, gill cavities, and mouths of host fishes,[80] ordinarily at specific places on the reef called *cleaning stations* (Fig. 6-22). The location of a cleaning station remains the same, although individual cleaners may change.[81] The ecological importance of cleaning stations (i.e., whether their presence has a positive effect on the health of host fishes that visit them) is controversial.[82]

A cleaning sequence apparently involves communication and some degree of mutual recognition between symbiont and host (Table 6-8). Host fishes typically approach a cleaning station and

Figure 6-22 *Cleaning station on a West Indies coral reef. Bonaire, Netherlands Antilles, 14 m.* Source: Stephen Spotte.

TABLE 6-8 Behaviors shown by cleaner fishes and their hosts and thought to represent communication based on mutual recognition.

Cleaners

Inspect: Swimming close to the host fish and appearing to explore its surfaces
Clean: Feeding on living or dead matter attached to the exterior surfaces of the host or its mouth or gill cavities
Dance: Rapid up and down body movements performed near the host

Hosts

Pose: Assuming a head-up or head-down position, often with mouth open and fins erect; sometimes accompanied by a change in coloration or pattern
Body jerk: Short, quick movement of the body or head
Attack: Quick movement toward the cleaner

Source: Losey (1971).

assume characteristic postures (e.g., head up, head down, mouth open, fins erect, or some combination of these) collectively called *posing* (Fig. 6-23). In some cases the host alters its coloration and pattern simultaneously. The cleaner swims close to the posing host and *inspects* it. Inspection—particularly in cleaner wrasses—may involve a *dance,* consisting of up and down swimming movements. Afterward, the symbiont *cleans* the surfaces of the host, in the process even entering its mouth and gill cavities. The host may occasionally *jerk* its body and either dash away and quickly return or simply move a few centimetres. This action occurs before or during cleaning and may or may not dislodge the symbiont. Sometimes the host moves rapidly toward the cleaner, appearing to *attack* it and causing it to retreat.

In some species these behaviors either do not occur or are less obvious. The cleaning goby (*Gobiosoma evelynae*) occupies cleaning stations on coral reefs throughout the West Indies. When not servicing clients it occupies heads of living coral (Fig. 6-24, Plate 13a). Host fishes are boarded by the gobies without fanfare (Fig. 6-23c). Often several gobies service a single host (Plate 13b).

Cleaning behavior is generally thought to be mutualistic because both parties presumably benefit. However, the importance of ectoparasites, scales, and mucus as dietary items is species dependent,[83] and clear evidence of benefits to the host have yet to be obtained.[84] Many facultative cleaners appear to ingest material from their hosts opportunistically. Some species are cleaners only as juveniles and abandon the practice as

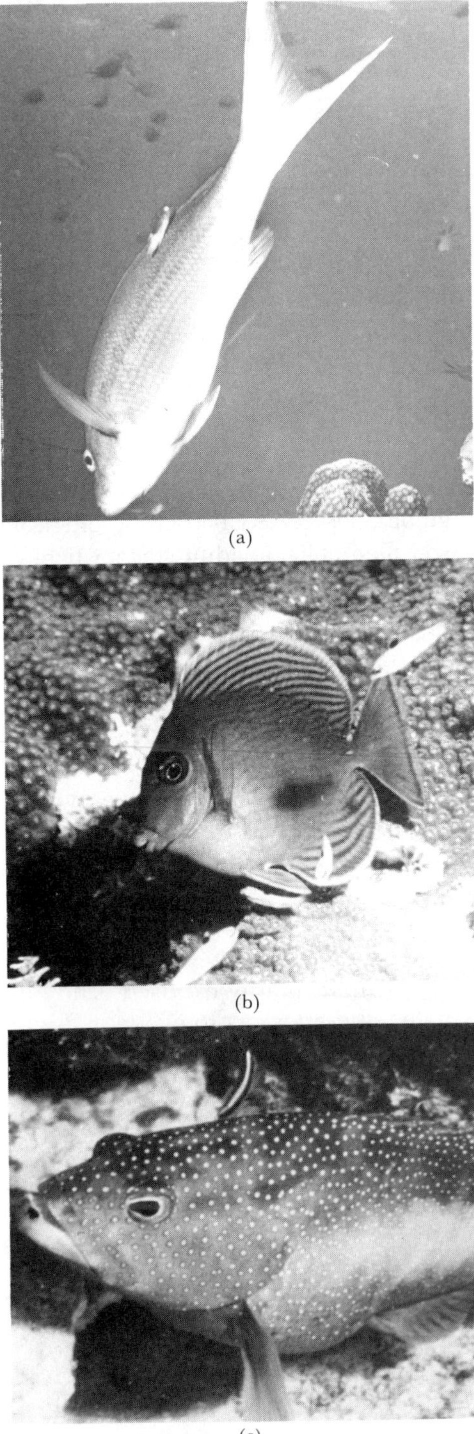

(a)

(b)

(c)

Figure 6-23 (a) *Yellowtail snapper* (Ocyurus chrysurus) *posing on its side and being cleaned by a juvenile Spanish hogfish* (Bodianus rufus). *Bonaire, Netherlands Antilles, 15 m.* (b) *Blue tang* (Acanthurus coeruleus) *with fins erect being cleaned by juvenile bluehead wrasses* (Thalassoma bifasciatum). *Key Largo, Florida, 6 m.* (c) *Coney* (Epinephelus fulvus) *being cleaned by a goby, probably the cleaning goby* (Gobiosoma evelynae). *Belize, Central America, 9 m.* Source: Stephen Spotte.

Figure 6-24 *Cleaning gobies* (Gobiosoma evelynae) *occupy heads of living coral when not cleaning host fishes. Pine Cay, Turks and Caicos Islands, British West Indies, 4 m.* Source: Stephen Spotte.

adults.[85] ''Obligate'' adult cleaners are uncommon, and use of the term should be relegated to a strictly ecological context. In other words, so-called obligate adult cleaner fishes usually are facultative cleaners in captivity and can survive without hosts.[86]

FEEDING ASSOCIATIONS The feeding associations described here are transient and involve two or more fishes, often of different species. The relationships all appear to be commensal. Few have been described in more than superficial terms. A common feeding association in the West Indies involves the trumpetfish (*Aulostomus maculatus*).[87] In a typical display a trumpetfish follows another fish closely for several minutes, even touching it (Fig. 6-25a). Common hosts are large parrotfishes of several species and the Spanish hogfish (*Bodianus rufus*). When the host bites into a piece of dead coral or a live sponge, the trumpetfish darts in quickly and seizes small fishes or shrimps that are momentarily exposed. The host often behaves as if irritated and attempts to evade its temporary symbiont by rapid and erratic swimming, scratching against the substratum (Fig. 6-25b), or ducking into crevices (Fig. 6-25c). Another common relationship involves the yellow goatfish (*Mulloidichthys martinicus*) and a number of other species attracted by the goatfish's excavation of the substratum (Fig. 6-26, Plate 13c).

TECHNOLOGY

Method 6.1 Exhibition of Schooling Fishes

''Shoal'' and ''school'' are terms that adequately describe the orientation of social groups of fishes in the wild. The spatial limits of conventional aquariums sometimes restrict schooling

(a)

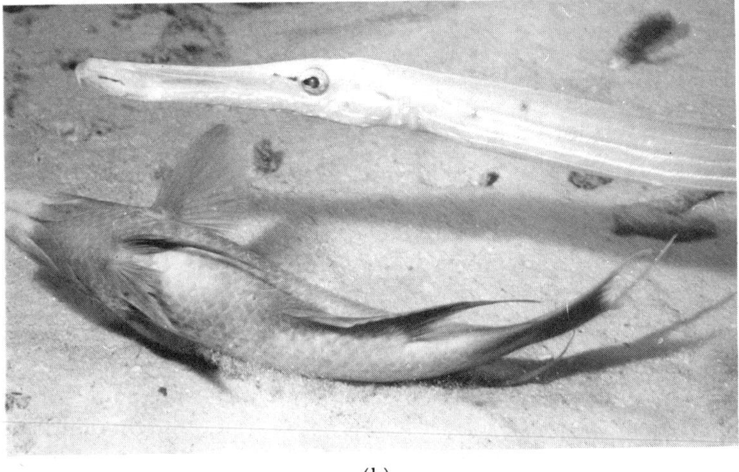

(b)

(c)

Figure 6-25 (a) *During some feeding associations the symbiont—in this case a trumpetfish* (Aulostomus maculatus)—*follows its temporary host closely, even to the point of touching it. The host depicted is an adult Spanish hogfish* (Bodianus rufus). (b) *In an apparent attempt to escape, the hogfish scratches against the bottom.* (c) *Finally it ducks under a ledge. Bonaire, Netherlands Antilles, 7 m.* Source: Stephen Spotte.

Figure 6-26 *The yellow goatfish* (Mulloidichthys martinicus, *far right) digs in the soft substratum in search of small invertebrates. Temporary feeding associations form when other species are attracted, in this case a schoolmaster* (Lutjanus apodus, *far left), trumpetfish* (Aulostomus maculatus), *and Spanish hogfish* (Bodianus rufus). *Bonaire, Netherlands Antilles, 8 m.* Source: Stephen Spotte.

by prohibiting continuous forward movement. To keep moving forward and simultaneously avoid the walls of the aquarium, the fish are forced to mill (i.e., swim in a circular or elliptical pattern). As will be shown, milling is not representative of schooling in its true sense, and public aquarium exhibits that purport to show schooling but restrict the forward movement of the fish are misleading. Demonstrations of schooling behavior ordinarily require aquariums designed for continuous forward swimming.

RECTANGULAR AQUARIUMS Schooling fishes mill if their forward movement is restricted. By definition, schooling requires each individual to be oriented in the same direction, to swim at the same speed, and to be separated by the same amount of space. These criteria cannot be met if the school or the individuals in it are large compared with the space available.[88] Rectangular aquariums are often unsuitable for exhibiting large schooling fishes.

CYLINDRICAL AND CIRCULAR VERSUS FIGURE-EIGHT DESIGNS Cylindrical designs have proved the most popular configurations for exhibiting large schooling fishes, but they too are flawed. Large fishes swimming continuously in cylindrical exhibits sometimes develop lesions from rubbing against the glass and walls. Fishes are hyperopic (Chapter 5) and may lack the capacity to detect gradually curving surfaces. Circular channels do not prevent the accumulation of curves along the swimming path. Some touching of the sides is perhaps unavoidable as the fishes ''anchor'' themselves to the curvature of the walls. Fishes in cylindrical aquariums and circular channels typically swim in the same direction for prolonged periods—sometimes months or years—evidently because anchoring to the curvature of the walls takes precedence over responses to shifts in the angle of light[89] (see below).

Perhaps the best shape for pelagic fish exhibits is a figure eight. Experimental work on a small scale shows promise for large exhibits of similar design. One experimental apparatus is shown in Figures 6-27 and 6-28. It offers two apparent advantages over other designs. First, the problem of accumulating curves is eliminated. Second, directional shifts can be controlled by changing the angle of light, which perhaps ameliorates stereotyped swimming patterns.[90] This in turn might promote such natural behaviors as breeding and reduce the formation of lesions caused by anchoring to the walls. Whether any of this is actually true remains to be demonstrated.

Method 6.2 Burrowing and Mound-Building Fishes

Some coral reef fishes excavate permanent or temporary burrows and require substrates of unusual depth, grain size, and void fraction. The material can be placed on top of subgravel filters or directly on the bottoms of bare aquariums. Fishes that

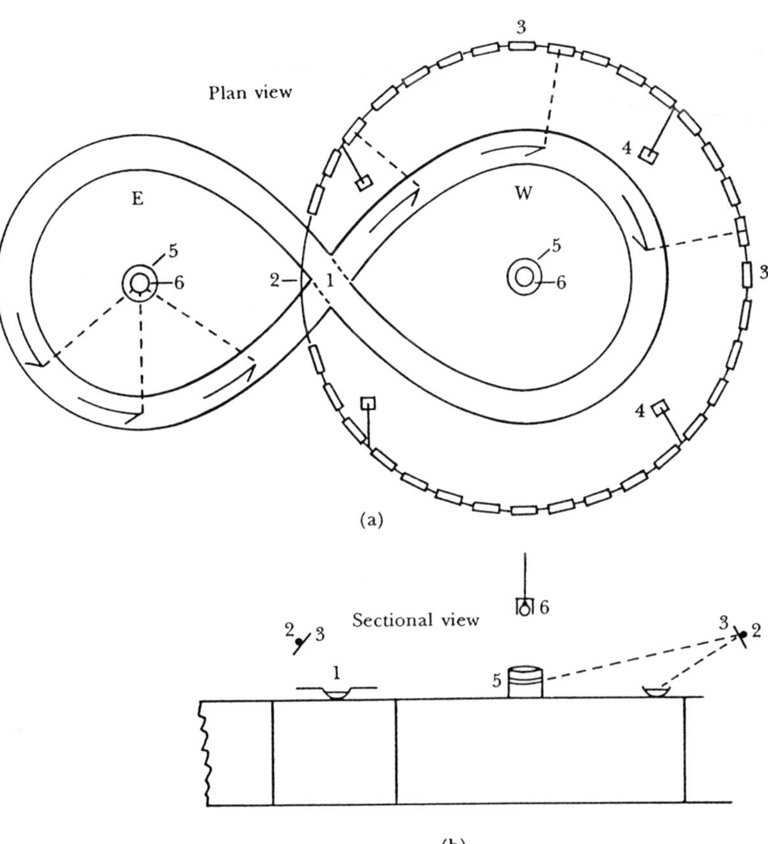

Figure 6-27 (a) *Plan and* (b) *sectional views through an experimental figure eight channel oriented east (E) and west (W). (1) Crossing point where one arm is submerged under the other (see Fig. 6-28). (2) Supporting ring for peripheral mirrors. (3) Mirrors. (4) Supporting base for the equipment ring. (5 and 6) Peripheral light source (a bulb enclosed in an opaque container and shining through a circular opening 1.7 cm wide). Other details omitted.* Source: Stephen Spotte after Levin et al. (1989).

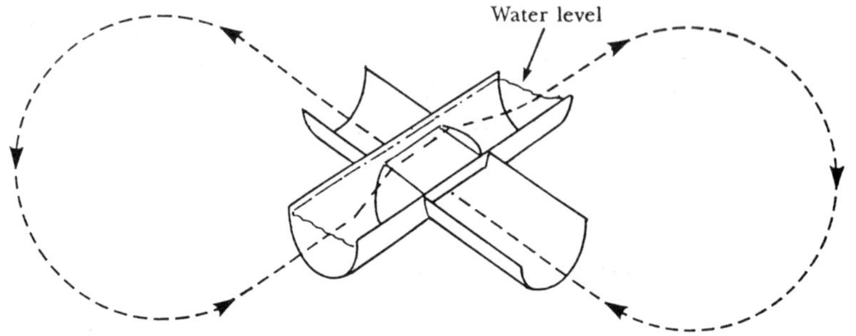

Figure 6-28 *Detail of the crossing point of the channel (Fig. 6-27). The platform at the center is transparent plastic. Arrows indicate swimming paths.* Source: Levin et al. (1989).

burrow include garden eels (Congridae), jawfishes (Opistognathidae), and some of the wrasses. Members of the first two families dig permanent burrows (Fig. 6-29, Plate 13d). Wrasses simply bury themselves for the night, but the substratum must be composed of low-density, small-grained materials that retain adequate void fraction (i.e., do not become compacted). Tilefishes (Malacanthidae) build mounds on top of the substratum from coral rubble shells and other items; alternatively, they excavate burrows underneath flat ledges of coral rock (Fig. 6-30).[91]

A suitable substratum for wrasses and many burrowing fishes consists of equal parts silica sand (0.49-mm filter sand) and low-density "algal sand" of the type excreted by certain green seaweeds (e.g., *Halimeda*). Algal sand is calcium carbonate. Filter sand provides a fine-grained substratum; algal sand, being larger and less dense, keeps the mixture porous. Used alone this mixture is sufficient to maintain garden eels and wrasses under simulated natural conditions. Garden eels glue sand grains to the walls of their burrows with mucopolysaccharides produced by a gland at the tip of the tail.[92] Jawfishes

Figure 6-29 *The yellowhead jawfish* (Opistognathus aurifrons) *excavates burrows in sand and rubble. Pine Cay, Turks and Caicos Islands, British West Indies, 4 m.* Source: Stephen Spotte.

Figure 6-30 *The sand tilefish* (Malacanthus plumieri) *builds mounds or excavates burrows under flat rocks (this photograph). Unlike the jawfish, which seldom ventures more than a few centimetres from its burrow, the home range of a sand tilefish often extends 10 m or more from the burrow entrance. Pine Cay, Turks and Caicos Islands, British West Indies, 16 m.* Source: Stephen Spotte.

require a third ingredient: an adequate quantity of crushed coral rock of assorted diameters and equivalent to pea gravel or smaller. Jawfishes line the walls of their burrows with pebbles.[93] At night the burrow is closed by pulling a pebble over the opening. The vertical tunnel is approximately the same length as the fish, but opens into a rounded chamber. Construction of a burrow requires ~8 h. If pebbles are not provided the walls collapse at the slightest disturbance, or cannot be constructed. In the latter situation, jawfishes attempt to dig burrows in the corners of the aquarium where two vertical surfaces are available. The excavated material is then piled in front (Fig. 6-31), resulting in an unnatural exhibit. In exhibits of garden eels, jawfishes, and wrasses the depth of the substratum should be a minimum of 1.5 times the length of the largest fish.

Unlike garden eels and jawfishes, which excavate vertical burrows, sand tilefish (*Malacanthus plumieri*) are mound builders. Mounds are constructed on sand and coral rubble bottoms near reefs, and each is built and occupied by one fish. Inside the mound is a horizontal tunnel with a single opening to the outside.[94] Captive sand tilefishes need an assortment of large,

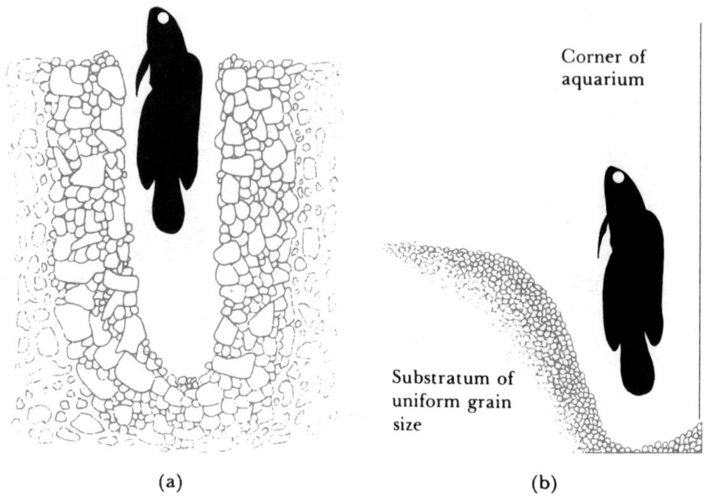

Figure 6-31 *Without a heterogeneous substratum, the burrows of captive jawfishes collapse.* (a) *Burrow constructed in a proper substratum.* (b) *Attempt at burrow construction in a homogeneous substratum, which is unstable. The fish is forced to use the corners of the aquarium as substitute walls.* Source: Stephen Spotte.

flat materials, much of it 2 cm or more in diameter. Equal parts broken clam or oyster shells and crushed coral rock form a suitable mixture. It can simply be scattered on the surface of a sandy substratum. Flat materials are necessary to build stable, interlocking ceilings over the burrows.

CHAPTER

7 Space

Fishes of tropical coral reefs are imposingly diverse,[1] and they exist where space and other resources seem too limited to support such diversity. Two or more species frequently occupy similar habitats (defined below). A few square metres of coral reef can be populated by dozens of different fishes.[2] How so many species can coexist has yet to be explained satisfactorily, but *resource partitioning* or the dividing up of resources by species present evidently is of great importance. A *resource* is again defined as any commodity—physical or social—that increases *fitness*, the capacity to reproduce. The two most important resources on coral reefs are space (Table 7-1) and food because they affect all individuals all the time. Lesser ones (i.e., those required periodically) include receptive mates and occasionally care-giving behavior by other individuals. An example of the last is a damselfish guarding its nest. Space partitioning exclusive of dominance behavior is the subject considered here.

My purpose in writing this chapter is to show that space is an important variable in the planning of fish exhibits. Space is worth the same consideration as water quality, nutrition, and other factors of greater familiarity.

SCIENCE

A *population* refers to the sum of individuals of a species occupying a habitat, and a *community* is the sum of the populations. In a social context, a community has been defined as a group of species in which the potential for interaction is greater than the potential for interacting with other species.[3] *Habitat* is defined as a structurally distinguishable place; a *niche* is a series—perhaps infinite—of multidimensional attributes of a species. The location of a community is its community habitat or *biotope*. This suggests that biotope, like habitat, connotes a distinguishable place, although to restrict its usage in this way—as I shall do—will probably be frowned on by ecologists. Biotope applies

TABLE 7-1 Representative published studies that describe some aspect of space partitioning by fishes, mostly exclusive of territorial requirements.

Eastern North Pacific	Barkley Sound, British Columbia[19]
	Southern California[52]
	La Jolla, California[12]
	Gulf of California[28, 37, 55]
Western North Pacific	Kuchierabu Island, Japan[26]
Indo-West Pacific	Hawaiian Islands[22, 29]
	Oahu, Hawaii[9]
	Kaneohe Bay, Hawaii[49]
	Marshall Islands[27]
	Eniwetak Atoll, Marshall Islands[21, 38]
	Cocos Lagoon, Guam[30]
	Fanning Island, Line Islands[10]
	Canton Atoll, Phoenix Islands[24]
	Takapoto Atoll[3]
	Great Barrier Reef[2, 56]
	One Tree Island, Great Barrier Reef[46, 53, 54]
	Coral Sea, Great Barrier Reef[59]
	Wistari Reef, Great Barrier Reef[8]
	Madagascar (west coast)[16]
	Tuléar, Madagascar[58]
	Tuamotu Islands, French Polynesia[5, 17, 18]
	Central Philippines[45]
Red Sea	Gulf of Aqaba[6, 7, 25]
	Port Sudan[15]
South Atlantic Bight[34]	
Western North Atlantic	Bermuda[4]
	Key Largo, Florida Keys[1, 31]
	Alligator Reef, Florida Keys[50, 51]
	Dry Tortugas[31]
West Indies	Bimini, Bahamas[11]
	Grand Bahama Island, Bahamas[14]
	Providencia, Bahamas[57]
	Little Cayman, Cayman Islands[40]
	Virgin Islands[41]
	St. Croix, U.S. Virgin Islands[20, 21, 32]
	St. John, U.S. Virgin Islands[39, 42, 47]
	Discovery Bay, Jamaica[13]
	Cuba[35, 36]
	Glovers Reef, Belize[13]
	Carrie Bow Cay, Belize[23]
	Curacao, Netherlands Antilles[33]
	Islas las Aves, Venezuela[1]
	Various locations[43, 48]
Theoretical considerations[44]	

Sources: Alevizon and Brooks (1975),[1] Anderson et al. (1981),[2] Bagnis et al. (1979),[3] Bardach (1959),[4] Bell and Galzin (1984),[5] Bouchon et al. (1981),[6] Bouchon-Navaro and Harmelin-Vivien (1981),[7] Bradbury and Goeden (1974),[8] Brock

TABLE 7-1 *(Continued)*

et al. (1979),[9] Chave and Eckert (1974),[10] Clarke (1977),[11] Clarke et al. (1967),[12] Colin (1974),[13] Colton and Alevizon (1981),[14] Edwards and Rosewell (1981),[15] Fourmanoir (1963),[16] Galzin (1987),[17] Galzin and Legendre (1987),[18] Gascon and Miller (1982),[19] Gladfelter and Gladfelter (1978),[20] Gladfelter et al. (1980),[21] Gosline (1965),[22] Greenfield and Greenfield (1982),[23] Grovhoug and Henderson (1978),[24] Gundermann and Popper (1975),[25] Gushima and Murakami (1976, 1979),[26] Hiatt and Strasburg (1960),[27] Hobson (1965, 1968),[28] Hobson (1972, 1974, 1984),[29] Jones and Chase (1975),[30] Jones and Thompson (1978),[31] Kaufman and Ebersole (1984),[32] Luckhurst and Luckhurst (1978a, 1978b, 1978c),[33] Miller and Richards (1980),[34] Mochek and Silva (1975),[35] Mochek and Valdes-Munoz (1984/1985),[36] Molles (1978),[37] Odum and Odum (1955),[38] Ogden and Ebersole (1981),[39] Potts (1980),[40] Randall (1963),[41] Risk (1972),[42] Robins (1971),[43] Roughgarden (1974),[44] Russ (1989),[45] Sale and Douglas (1984),[46] Smith and Tyler (1972),[47] Smith and Tyler (1973a, 1975),[48] Smith et al. (1973),[49] Starck (1968),[50] Starck and Davis (1966),[51] Stephens et al. (1970),[52] Talbot and Goldman (1972),[53] Talbot et al. (1978),[54] Thomson and Lehner (1976),[55] Tyler (1971),[56] Tyler and Böhlke (1972),[57] Vivien (1973),[58] Williams (1982).[59]

only to a community, and habitat only to single species.[4] The term *ecotope* encompasses all these concepts; that is, habitat, niche, and biotope (Fig. 7-1).

It is important to remember that by the above definitions the terms biotope and habitat describe only physical characteristics of the environment. Conceptually, they are one-dimensional. The term ecotope includes these same physical attributes in addition to intangible, strictly social and biological elements (e.g., niche). From a conceptual standpoint, ecotopes are multidimensional. Before a coral reef can properly be called an ecotope the social and biological requirements of the organisms living there must be satisfied. To say this another way, biotopes and habitats can theoretically exist in the absence of fishes, whereas ecotopes, fishes, and all other living organisms present define one another and are ecological synonyms. Under no circumstance are elements of an aquarium exhibit analogous to an ecotope, and ''aquarium ecology'' is oxymoronic.

Resource Partitioning Models

Opposing hypotheses have attempted to explain resource partitioning by coral reef fishes. The first holds that reef fishes are resource specialists.[5] Their requirements are different enough that interspecific competition is either negligible or not sufficiently important to preclude coexistence. Competition for limited resources determines both the number of species and the species composition on a coral reef. The classic niche concept of ecology is acknowledged, meaning that use of resources within a habitat is species specific. According to the resource specialist view, a community of coral reef fishes is orderly,

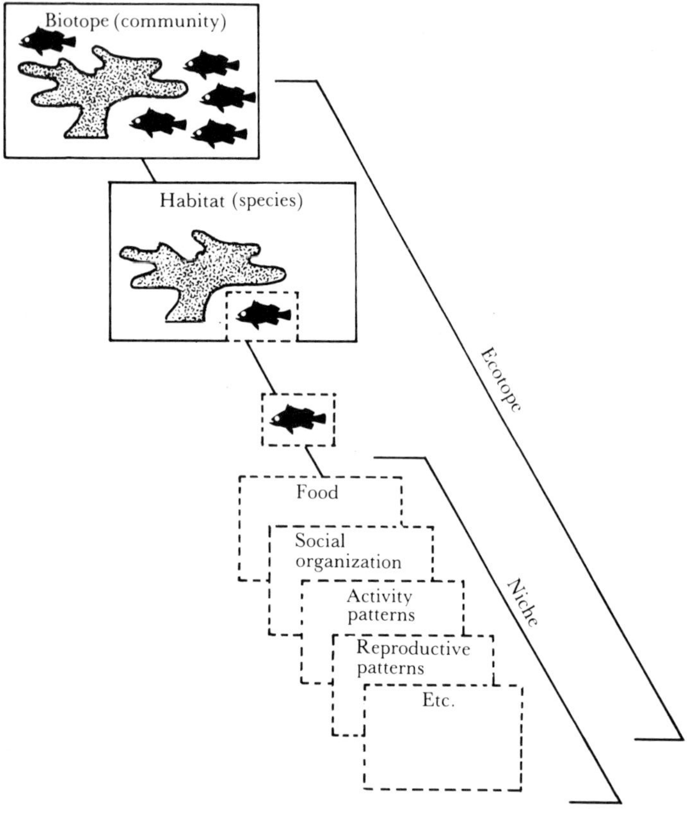

Figure 7-1 *Graphic representation of niche, habitat, biotope, and ecotope.* Source: Stephen Spotte.

structured, and from a conceptual standpoint, deterministic. Each population exists at steady state with its resources. This situation is maintained when resident fishes lost from disease, predation, and departure are replaced by newly metamorphosed larvae recruited from the plankton. Fluctuations in resident populations are attenuated by a population of larval conspecifics that always exceeds the number of vacant spaces on the reef at any time. The recruitment of planktonic larvae is impossible to ignore when modeling resource partitioning among coral reef fishes. Of the estimated 8000 species thought to inhabit coral reefs,[1] just one is known to produce larvae that are not planktonic at some point.[6]

The second hypothesis states that coral reef fishes are resource generalists.[7] More than one species can occupy a niche, resulting in a system of *guilds* (i.e., overlapping use of the same resources by more than one species).[8] Storms cause habitat alterations, and chance factors such as disease and predation regulate recruitment and keep a species from excluding others. Implicit in the second hypothesis are chaos and departure from steady state that stem from disruption of the physical environment and variable larval recruitment. From the resource generalist view, resource limitations have only a local, intermittent—and ultimately negligible—influence on population densities of resident fishes. In simple terms, site occupation as visualized in the second hypothesis is not a deterministic process as it is in the first; vacant space is potentially available to the species that happens along. Conceptually, the resource generalist hypothesis is stochastic.

Neither hypothesis has been tested extensively (i.e., few attempts have been made to falsify one or the other), and experimental work so far does not fully support either.[9] Surprisingly few coral reef ecologists have made serious attempts to integrate their findings with general principles long used to interpret the organizational structures of terrestrial vertebrates. An important question remains unanswered: are oceanic and terrestrial vertebrate communities governed by a common set of natural laws, or do the oceans impose conditions that require different solutions to similar problems of community organization?[10]

Coral Reefs

Nowhere are fish faunas so variable as on coral reefs; this variability stems largely from multiple structural features of the reefs themselves and the diverse array of algae and invertebrates they support. Coral reefs are predictable entities in terms of structure and morphology, but the unseen forces that produced them are less obvious. A coral reef is the product of many shaping influences, including geologic history, wind, tides, wave and surge activity, depth, prevailing currents, and composition of the indigenous reef building biota. The subsections below touch on three aspects of coral reefs as preludes to how fishes use them as biotopes and habitats: (*1*) coral reefs as global entities, (*2*) classification by structural formation, and (*3*) individual zones along vertical profiles. A fourth section deals specifically with patch reefs.

DISTRIBUTION Coral reefs occur in three major regions of the world: Indo-West Pacific, eastern Pacific, and Atlantic. The last includes the West Indies. I shall concentrate on the first and last. On a global scale, the central portion of the Indo-West Pacific contains the greatest number of fish species, with decreasing diversity outward (Fig. 7-2, Table 7-2). This feature also describes the diversity of living coral reef organisms in general (Fig. 7-3), including *hermatypic* or reef building corals (Fig. 7-4).

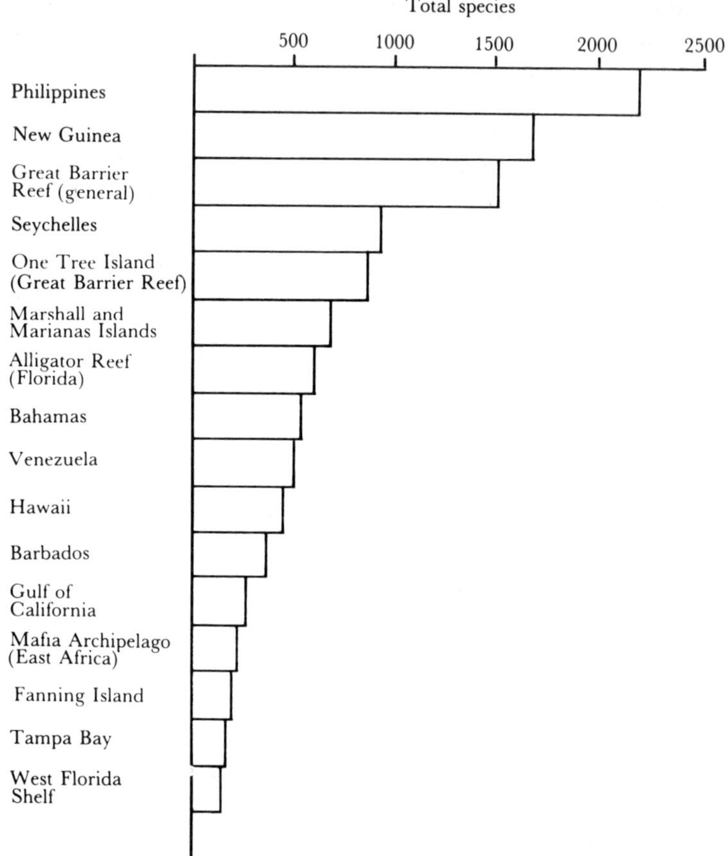

Figure 7-2 *Total species of coral reef fishes in 16 geographical regions.* Source: Sale (1980).

TABLE 7-2 Comparison of genera and species (genera/species) for representative families of teleosts in the West Indies and one location in the Indo-West Pacific.

Family	West Indies	Marshall Islands
Acanthuridae—surgeonfishes	1/4	4/22
Apogonidae—cardinalfishes	3/21	7/32
Blenniidae—combtooth blennies	6/15	15/35
Clinidae—clinids	14/16	2/6
Holocentridae—squirrelfishes	7/11	5/19
Labridae—wrasses	7/19	21/55
Pomacentridae—damselfishes	5/15	5/41

Source: Gilbert (1973).

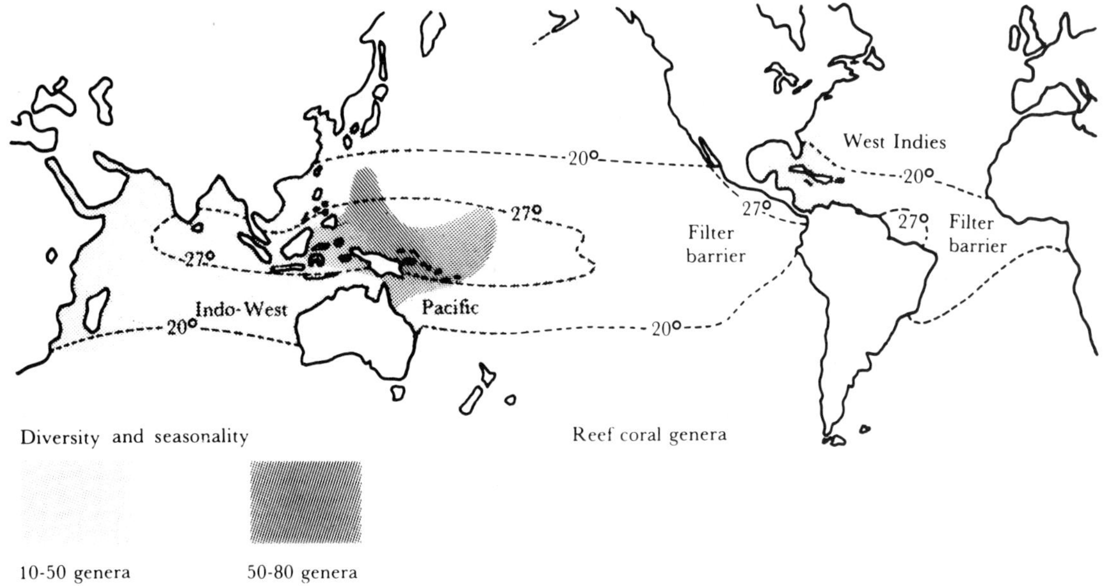

Figure 7-3 *Approximate limits of the Indo-West Pacific and West Indies ecotopes as defined by genera of reef corals compared with minimum average ocean temperatures* (i.e., isocrymes). *Approximate mean summer-winter temperature range along the 20°C isocryme is 6°C; along the 27°C isocryme it is 3°C. Filter barriers represent limits beyond which coral reef organisms (including fishes) seldom are in residence. Two reasons ordinarily are given: frigid currents and other physical factors that adversely influence the survival of planktonic larvae, and inability of new arrivals to compete with resident species.* Source: Newell (1971).

All hermatypic corals are *hard corals* (order Scleractinia). The West Indies claim ~60 species of hermatypic corals, compared with ~700 indigenous to the Indo-West Pacific.[11] Reef growth is still prolific in the West Indies because many coral species demonstrate variable morphology, enabling them to grow in a

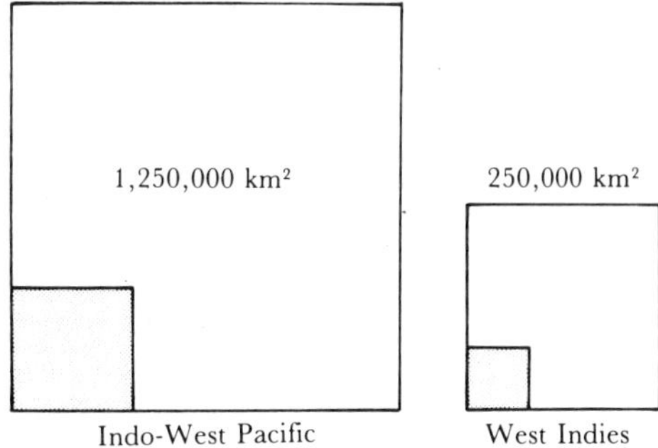

Figure 7-4 *Comparative areas occupied by coral reefs in the Indo-West Pacific and West Indies. Actual areas of living reef (shaded areas) are approximately 10% of the total in each region.* Source: Newell (1971).

variety of environments.[11] The dominant hard corals of shallow waters are essentially the same, but because fewer species exist in the West Indies the complex associations of corals typical of the Indo-West Pacific are seen less often.

CLASSIFICATION[12] Coral reefs fall loosely into one of three classifications (Fig. 7-5). *Fringing* or *shore reefs* border existing land. In tropical oceans, fringing reefs develop near all shores where conditions favor the growth of hermatypic corals. A hard substratum is one requirement, and the width of the reef that subsequently develops depends on the steepness of the near-shore submarine slope. Reefs are narrowest where slopes are steepest. The longest modern reef is of the fringing type and parallels the shores of the Red Sea. If its contours were straightened it would measure ~4000 km.

A *barrier reef* is separated from preexisting land by a lagoon. The Great Barrier Reef off Australia's northeast coast is the largest aggregation of reefs in the world, stretching for >1900 km. It varies in width from ~16 to ~300 km and envelopes an area of >207,000 km^2. Although referred to in the singular, the Great Barrier Reef actually is a composite of thousands of individual reefs. The second largest barrier reef is adjacent to New Caledonia (Indo-West Pacific) and is ~650 km long. The longest barrier reef in the Atlantic parallels the coast of Belize for ~240 km at a distance of 12 to 40 km offshore.

An *atoll* is a ring-shaped island or chain of islands enclosing a central lagoon and surrounded by open ocean. The lagoon contains no preexisting land. More than 300 atolls and extensive barrier reefs exist in the Indo-West Pacific, whereas ~10 atolls and two definite barrier reefs have been documented in the West Indies.[11] Several minor reef types have been identified, but I shall consider only *patch reefs*. These are formed at sea level and rise from submarine shelves or the floors of lagoons. Patch reefs are isolated from each other and from the larger reefs. As such, they are easily recognized as small, shallow, distinctly separate entities.

VERTIC, L ZONATION The structural features of a coral reef—including the abundance and diversity of hard corals—change more or less consistently along a vertical profile, and this is evident as *vertical zonation* (or simply *zonation*). Zonation patterns are the result of physical and biological factors operating in unison. Wave and surge action, geomorphology of the underlying substratum, tides, wind direction, depth, silt deposition, and temperature regulate the extent and diversity of

PLATE 1

(a) *The cardinalfish* (Archamia dispilus) *is active at night and shelters during the day within the infrastructure of the reef. Its eyes are enlarged, an adaptation believed to enhance vision in dim light.*
Sabang, Palawan (South China Sea), Philippines, 6 m. Source: *Stephen Spotte.*

(b) *The blenny* (Ecsenius bicolor) *is active during the day. Its eyes are of normal size.*
Sabang, Palawan (South China Sea), Philippines, 6 m. Source: *Stephen Spotte.*

(c) *The hawkfish* (Cirrhitichthys falco) *is also active during the day and possesses eyes of normal size.*
Tres Marias, Ulugan Bay, Palawan (South China Sea), Philippines, 14 m. Source: *Stephen Spotte.*

(d) *Blackbar soldierfish* (Myripristis jacobus) *are among the nocturnal fishes that appear above the reef after the ''quiet period.'' These specimens, already in pale, nighttime coloration, were photographed at dusk.*
Bonaire, Netherlands Antilles, 13 m. Source: *Stephen Spotte.*

PLATE 2

(a) *The pale cardinalfish* (Apogon planifrons) *hides within the infrastructure of the reef during the day, but emerges after dusk to feed on zooplankton.*
Pine Cay, Turks and Caicos Islands, British West Indies, 11 m. Source: *Stephen Spotte.*

(b) *Some parrotfishes secrete mucous cocoons about themselves at night. The fish shown is a terminal male queen parrotfish* (Scarus vetula).
Bonaire, Netherlands Antilles, 31 m. Source: *Stephen Spotte.*

(c) *The chromatophores of fishes are responsible for a vast array of patterns and stunning combinations of colors. These butter hamlets* (Hypoplectrus unicolor) *are barred with undertones of blue.*
Andros, Bahamas, 13 m. Source: *Stephen Spotte.*

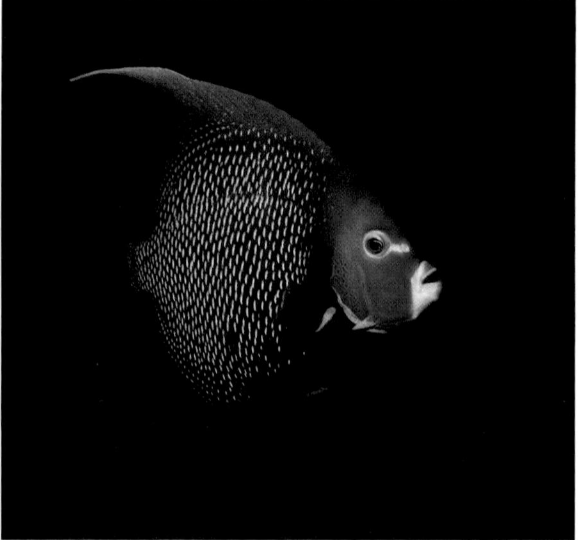

(d) *Chromatophores of the adult French angelfish* (Pomacanthus paru) *are responsible for yellow-edged scales on a background of black.*
Bonaire, Netherlands Antilles, 20 m. Source: *Stephen Spotte.*

PLATE 3

(a) *Chromatophores of the royal (or regal) angelfish* (Pygoplites diacanthus) *are responsible for still other color combinations: blues, yellows, and oranges.*
Tres Marias, Ulugan Bay, Palawan (South China Sea), Philippines, 20 m. Source: *Stephen Spotte.*

(b) *Silvery fishes are reflective if the intensity of the foreground light exceeds that of the background spacelight, as demonstrated by this school of horse-eye jacks* (Caranx latus).
Pine Cay, Turks and Caicos Islands, British West Indies, 11 m. Source: *Stephen Spotte.*

(c) *Blue tangs* (Acanthurus coeruleus) *are often pale when cruising.*
Anguilla Cay, Bahamas, 3 m. Source: *Stephen Spotte.*

(d) *Blue tangs* (Acanthurus coeruleus) *sometimes become dark when stopping to feed. This is the same school shown in Plate 3c, but photographed several minutes later.*
Anguilla Cay, Bahamas, 3 m. Source: *Stephen Spotte.*

(a) *Schools of blue tangs* (Acanthurus coeruleus) *disperse at night. Each fish finds its own resting place and assumes a barred pattern.*
Pine Cay, Turks and Caicos Islands, British West Indies, 16 m. Source: *Stephen Spotte.*

(b) *The terminal male stoplight parrotfish* (Sparisoma viride) *is evenly patterned while active during the day (Plate 12a), but mottled at night.*
Bonaire, Netherlands Antilles, 20 m. Source: *Stephen Spotte.*

(c) *The creole-fish* (Paranthias furcifer), *a planktivorous sea bass, is evenly colored when feeding during the day.*
Bonaire, Netherlands Antilles, 22 m. Source: *Stephen Spotte.*

(d) *The creole-fish* (Paranthias furcifer) *at night assumes a mottled appearance.*
Bonaire, Netherlands Antilles, 28 m. Source: *Stephen Spotte.*

PLATE 5

(a) *The pattern and coloration of the copper-banded butterflyfish* (Chelmon rostratus) *does not vary between day and night. This specimen was photographed at night.*
Coco Loco Island, Sulu Sea, Philippines, 6 m. Source: *Stephen Spotte.*

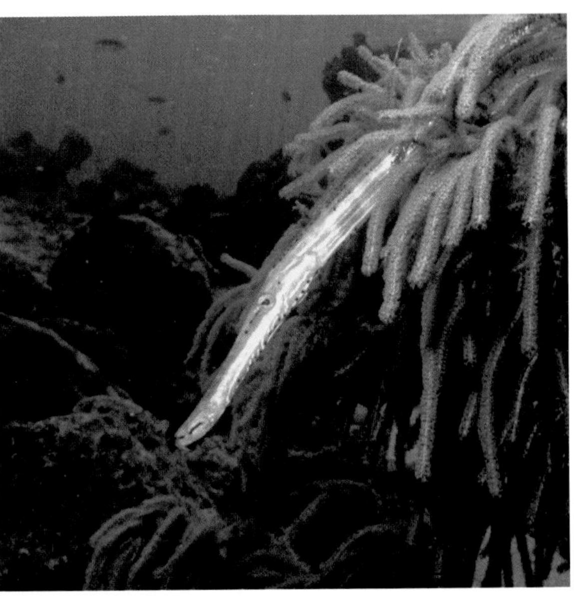

(b) *An adult trumpetfish* (Aulostomus maculatus) *hiding in a large specimen of the slimy sea plume* (Pseudopterogorgia americana).
Bonaire, Netherlands Antilles, 22 m. Source: *Stephen Spotte.*

(c) *A juvenile trumpetfish* (Aulostomus maculatus) *concealed on a slimy sea plume.*
Pine Cay, Turks and Caicos Islands, British West Indies, 10 m. Source: *Roy Manstan, Naval Underwater Systems Center.*

(d) *A slender filefish* (Monacanthus tuckeri) *concealed among the branches of a gorgonian, probably* Eunicea *sp.*
Pine Cay, Turks and Caicos Islands, British West Indies, 14 m. Source: *Stephen Spotte.*

PLATE 6

(a) *The tiger grouper* (Mycteroperca tigris) *conceals itself within the infrastructure of the reef. Its coloration and pattern vary with the surroundings.*
Ambergris Cay, Belize, Central America, 13 m. Source: *Stephen Spotte.*

(b) *The barbfish* (Scorpaena brasiliensis) *lies motionless on the bottom and assumes the mottled coloration and pattern of its surroundings.*
Key Largo, Florida, 11 m. Source: *Stephen Spotte.*

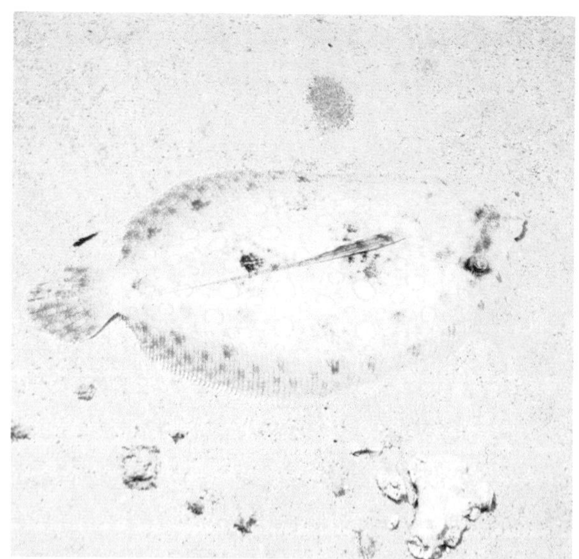

(c) *The peacock flounder* (Bothus lunatus) *is pale when resting on sandy bottoms.*
Bonaire, Netherlands Antilles, 4 m. Source: *Stephen Spotte.*

(d) *The venomous clearfin turkeyfish* (Pterois radiata) *is a diurnal predator. Cryptic coloration is perhaps less important at night, when this specimen was photographed.*
Coco Loco Island, Sulu Sea, Philippines, 8 m. Source: *Stephen Spotte.*

PLATE 7

(a) *The venomous turkeyfish* (Pterois volitans) *relies on stealth and cryptic coloration to capture prey. This specimen was observed feeding actively on small, benthic fishes in early afternoon.*
Tres Marias, Ulugan Bay, Palawan (South China Sea), Philippines, 15 m. Source: *Stephen Spotte.*

(b) *Despite its name, the whitespotted filefish* (Cantherhines macroceros) *is not always spotted, especially when undisturbed.*
Bonaire, Netherlands Antilles, 21 m. Source: *Stephen Spotte.*

(c) *The approach of a scuba diver often stimulates the appearance of white spots in the whitespotted filefish* (Cantherhines macroceros).
Pine Cay, Turks and Caicos Islands, British West Indies, 16 m. Source: *Stephen Spotte.*

(d) *Grunts produce stridulated sounds using the swimbladder as a resonator. Species shown are the cottonwick* (Haemulon melanurum, *upper) and bluestriped grunt* (H. sciurus, *lower*).
Key Largo, Florida, 10 m. Source: *Stephen Spotte.*

PLATE 8

(a) *The spotted drum* (Equetus punctatus) *is capable of making an audible drumming sound by rapid movements of muscles joining the walls of the swimbladder. The sea anemone is* Condylactis gigantea.
Rocher du Diamont, Martinique, French West Indies, 30 m. Source: *Stephen Spotte.*

(b) *Squirrelfishes produce sound by means of muscles that vibrate the swimbladder. The specimen shown is the squirrelfish* (Holocentrus rufus).
Key Largo, Florida, 13 m. Source: *Stephen Spotte.*

(c) *Shoal of planktivorous brown chromis* (Chromis multilineatus) *feeding over a deep reef.*
Bonaire, Netherlands Antilles, 33 m. Source: *Stephen Spotte.*

(d) *If a shoal of brown chromis* (Chromis multilineatus) *is threatened, the fish quickly form a school and swim to safety in the reef.*
Bonaire, Netherlands Antilles, 17 m. Source: *Stephen Spotte.*

PLATE 9

(a) *Mixed shoal of grunts* (Haemulidae) *and snappers* (Lutjanidae) *shielded from the prevailing current by a large sea fan* (Gorgonia *sp.*).
Bimini, Bahamas, 6 m. Source: *Roy Manstan, Naval Underwater Systems Center.*

(b) *When not feeding, the venomous catfish* (Plotosus lineatus) *forms homotypic shoals.*
Coco Loco Island, Sulu Sea, Philippines, 6 m. Source: *Stephen Spotte.*

(c) *Midnight parrotfish* (Scarus coelestinus) *cruising a shallow reef. Parrotfishes and all other herbivorous coral reef fishes are diurnal.*
Anguilla Cay, Bahamas, 7 m. Source: *Stephen Spotte.*

(d) *Homotypic, diurnal shoal of glassy sweepers* (Pempheris schomburgki) *sheltered in the reef.*
Key Largo, Florida, 10 m. Source: *Stephen Spotte.*

PLATE 10

(a) *Large shoals of French grunts* (Haemulon flavolineatum) *are common on daytime reefs of the West Indies. These specimens display the typical diurnal coloration and pattern.*
Key Largo, Florida, 9 m. Source: *Stephen Spotte.*

(b) *French grunts* (Haemulon flavolineatum) *disperse at dusk for a night of solitary feeding in beds of turtle grass or on rubble bottoms. The specimen shown has assumed its pale nocturnal coloration and pattern.*
Bonaire, Netherlands Antilles, 11 m. Source: *Stephen Spotte.*

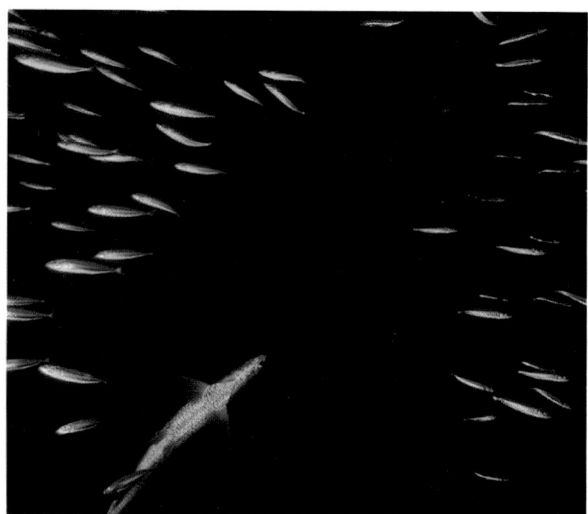

(c) *Nocturnal attack by a tarpon* (Megalops atlanticus) *on a large school of unidentified clupeids (probably* Harengula *sp.). The photograph was taken from below. Note how the prey fish have scattered in an outwardly radiating pattern.*
Bonaire, Netherlands Antilles, 11 m. Source: *Roy Manstan, Naval Underwater Systems Center.*

(d) *Territorial specimen of the bicolor damselfish* (Stegastes partitus). *The long, slender object in the foreground is a black coral colony* (Stichopathes *sp.*).
Bonaire, Netherlands Antilles, 34 m. Source: *Stephen Spotte.*

PLATE 11

(a) *The damselfish* (Dascyllus reticulatus) *lives peacefully in colonies.*
Sabang, Palawan (South China Sea), Philippines, 5 m. Source: *Stephen Spotte.*

(b) *Juvenile threespot damselfish* (Stegastes planifrons) *are yellow, but darken with maturity (Plate 11c).*
Key Largo, Florida, 15 m. Source: *Stephen Spotte.*

(c) *The adult threespot damselfish* (Stegastes planifrons) *in the upper part of the photograph has killed most of the coral* (Montastrea annularis) *inside its territory to cultivate an "algal lawn." All coral near the center of the territory has been killed; the fish is in the process of killing coral in the lower portion of the photograph.*
Bonaire, Netherlands Antilles, 28 m. Source: *Stephen Spotte.*

(d) *Adult stoplight parrotfish* (Sparisoma viride).
Ambergris Cay, Belize, Central America, 17 m. Source: *Stephen Spotte.*

PLATE 12

(a) *Terminal male stoplight parrotfish* (Sparisoma viride).
Anguilla Cay, Bahamas, 3 m. Source: *Stephen Spotte.*

(b) *Juvenile eight-banded butterflyfish* (Chaetodon octofasciatus) *seldom venture very far from their coral refuges. In a loose sense, all coral reef fishes exist in symbiotic association with the living reef.*
Coco Loco Island, Sulu Sea, Philippines, 5 m. Source: *Stephen Spotte.*

(c) *Anemonefish* (Amphiprion frenatus, *adult female*) *among the tentacles of a sea anemone* (Entacmaea quadricolor).
Tres Marias, Ulugan Bay, Palawan (South China Sea), Philippines, 18 m. Source: *Stephen Spotte.*

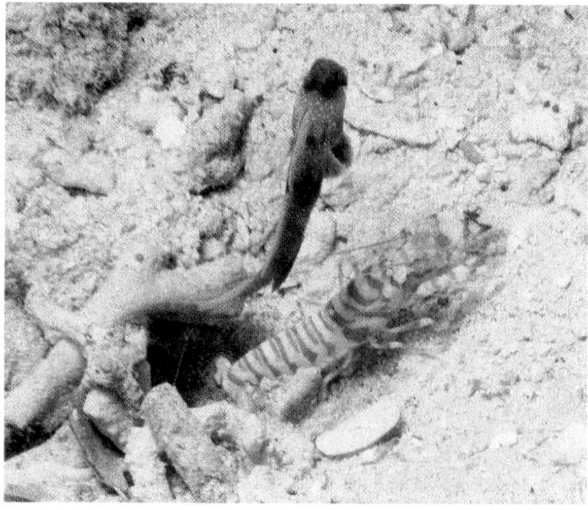

(d) *Several species of gobies share burrows with alpheid shrimps. The fish shown* (Cryptocentrus *sp.*) *shared its burrow with a pair of alpheids (one of the second shrimp's antennae is visible). The shrimp excavate the burrow and keep it clear of debris while the goby stands watch near the entrance. The goby evidently senses danger more efficiently than the shrimp, and one shrimp keeps its antennae in frequent contact with the fish to monitor its signals.*
Coco Loco Island, Sulu Sea, Philippines, 1.5 m. Source: *Stephen Spotte.*

PLATE 13

(a) *Cleaning gobies* (Gobiosoma evelynae) *establish cleaning stations on heads of live coral, in this case brain coral* (Diploria *sp.*).
Pine Cay, Turks and Caicos Islands, British West Indies, 3 m. Source: *Stephen Spotte.*

(b) *Cleaning gobies* (Gobiosoma evelynae) *on a Nassau Grouper* (Epinephelus striatus).
Pine Cay, Turks and Caicos Islands, British West Indies, 15 m. Source: *Stephen Spotte.*

(c) *A schoolmaster* (Lutjanus apodus, *far right*), *trumpetfish* (Aulostomus maculatus, *center right*), *and Spanish hogfish* (Bodianus rufus, *center left*) *attracted by the digging activity of a yellow goatfish* (Mulloidichthys martinicus, *far left*). *The four species formed a transient feeding association that lasted 6 min.*
Bonaire, Netherlands Antilles, 8 m. Source: *Stephen Spotte.*

(d) *Garden eels* (Nystactichthys halis) *live in colonies on a soft substratum. The burrows they dig are permanent. During the day, garden eels emerge partially to feed on drifting zooplankton.*
Bonaire, Netherlands Antilles, 30 m. Source: *Roy Manstan, Naval Underwater Systems Center.*

PLATE 14

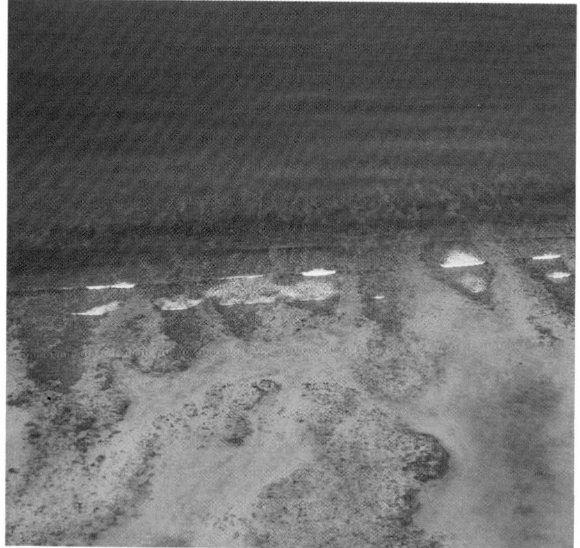

(a) *Aerial view of a fringing reef. Waves breaking over the reef crest form a white line. The lagoon is shown in the foreground. Faint, lighter streaks radiating seaward are grooves and spurs.*
Providenciales, Turks and Caicos Islands, British West Indies. Source: *Patricia M. Bubucis, Sea Research Foundation.*

(b) *Beginning of the reef front.*
Bonaire, Netherlands Antilles, 16 m. Source: *Stephen Spotte.*

(c) *Deeper section of the reef front. The fish are banded butterflyfish* (Chaetodon striatus).
Bonaire, Netherlands Antilles, 32 m. Source: *Stephen Spotte.*

(d) *In the West Indies, the surge zone just seaward of the reef crest is notable for stands of elkhorn coral* (Acropora *spp.*).
Bonaire, Netherlands Antilles, 2 m. Source: *Stephen Spotte.*

PLATE 15

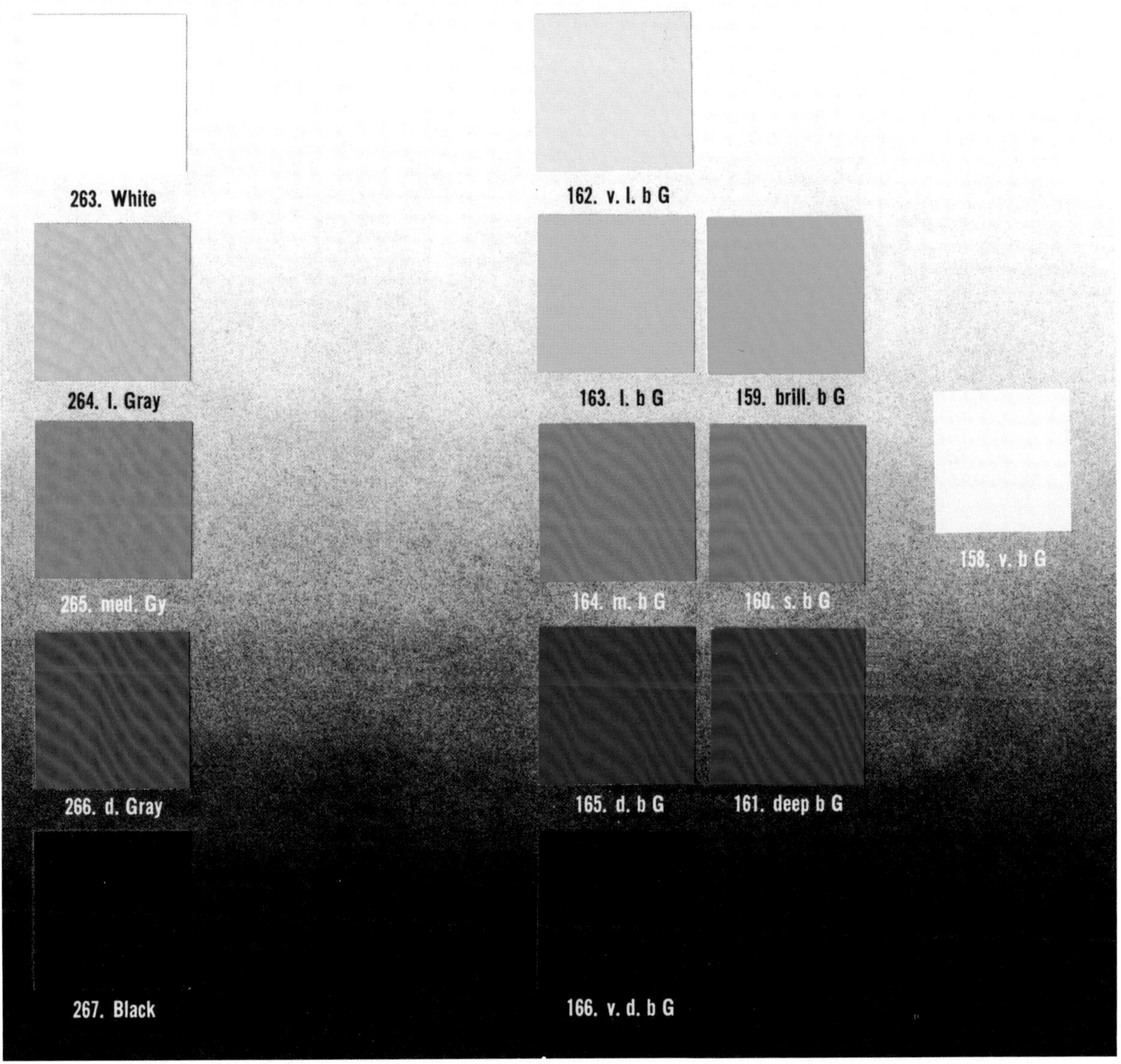

Bluish green from ISCC-NBS Color-Name Charts Illustrated with Centroid Colors. *Designations under each standard color are the abbreviated ISCC-NBS color names and corresponding centroid or color-name-block number. One color (158) could not be matched by conventional methods and was left blank by NBS scientists. The colors shown are reproductions and do not exactly match the original colored chips.*
Source: *National Bureau of Standards, Route 270 and Quince Orchard Road, Gaithersburg MD 20899.*

PLATE 16

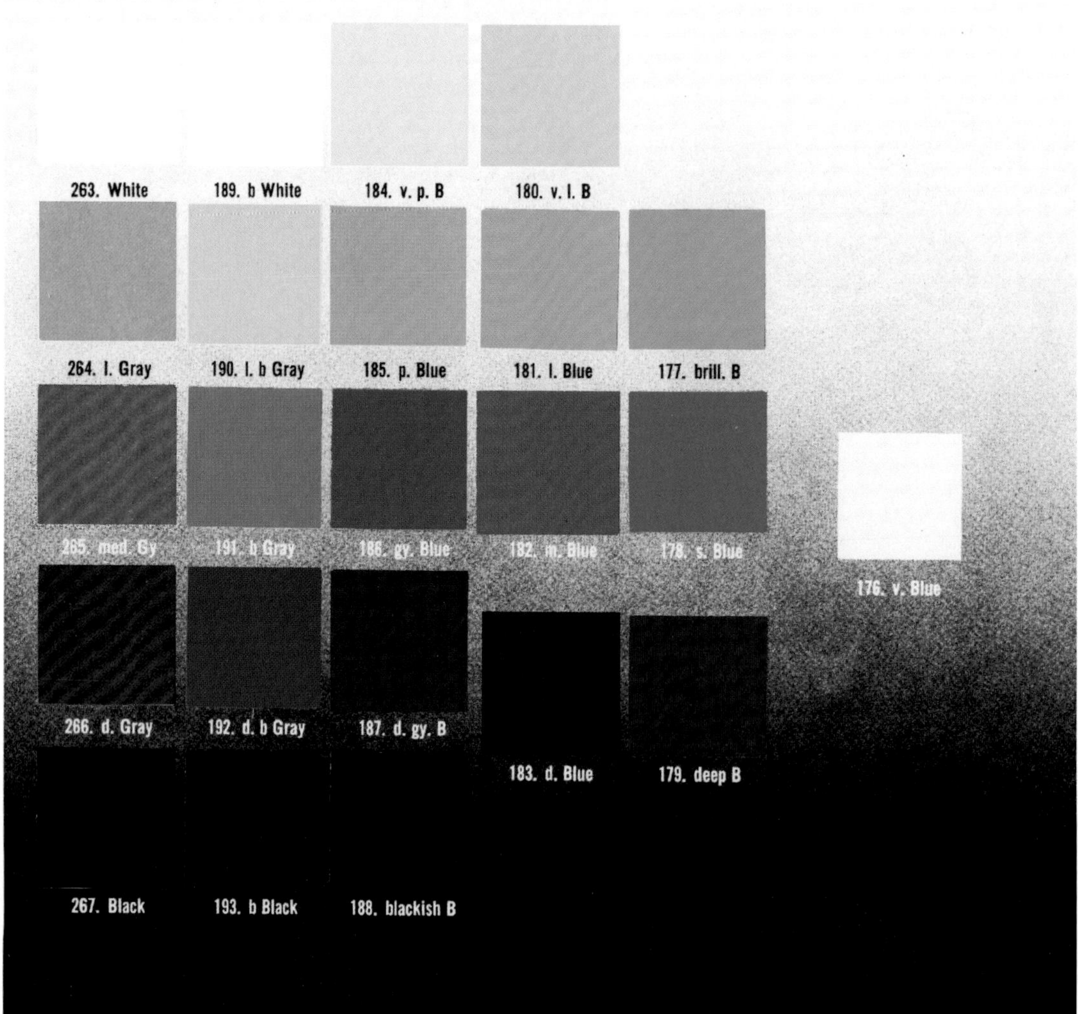

Blue from ISCC-NBS Color-Name Charts Illustrated with Centroid Colors. *Designations under each standard color are the abbreviated ISCC-NBS color names and corresponding centroid or color-name-block number. One color (176) could not be matched by conventional methods and was left blank by NBS scientists. The colors shown are reproductions and do not exactly match the original chips.*

Source: *National Bureau of Standards, Route 270 and Quince Orchard Road, Gaithersburg MD 20899.*

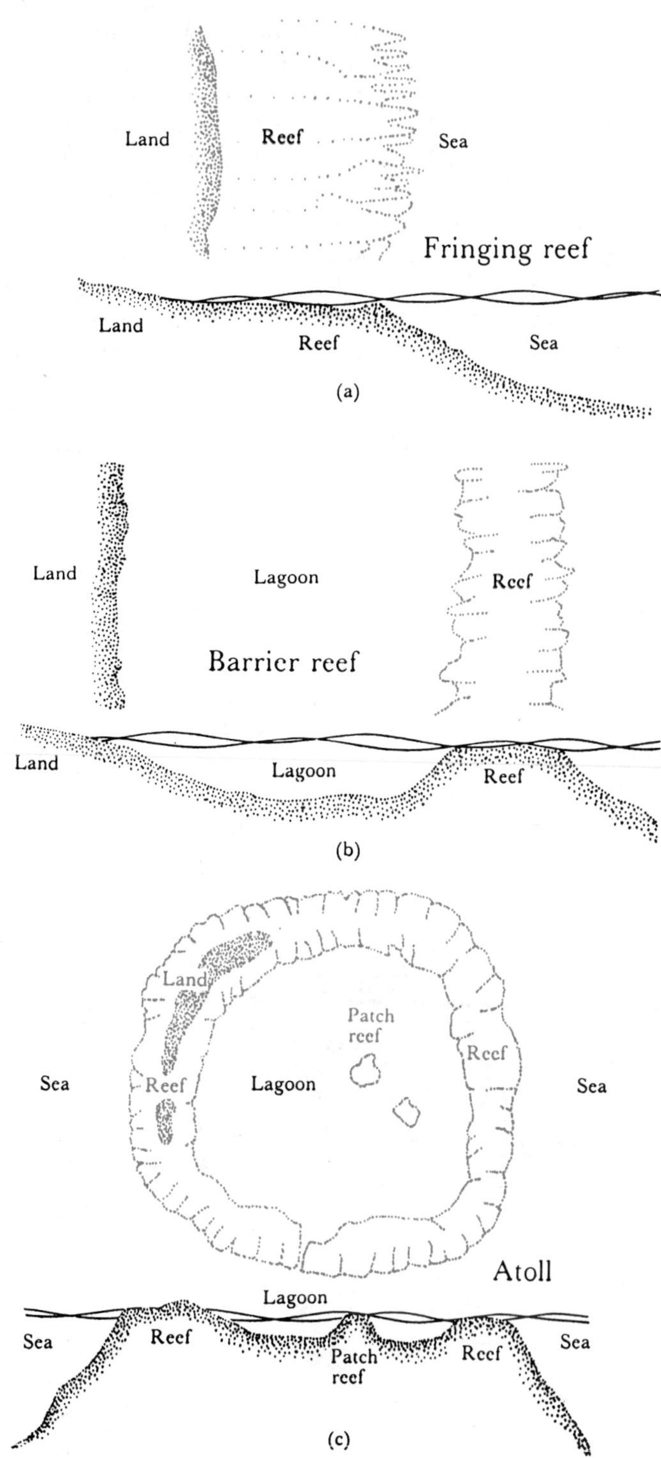

Figure 7-5 Fringing reefs, barrier reefs, and atolls. Source: Stephen Spotte, drawn from various sources.

coral growth. These in turn directly affect fish density and species diversity. Zones in the West Indies are delineated more clearly than in the Indo-West Pacific, apparently because the comparative paucity of hard corals enables one or a few species to dominate.[13] Terminology used to describe zonation patterns of coral reefs is inconsistent—perhaps necessarily so—and the following descriptions are less precise than I would have liked.[14]

Most of the components that define structural elements of an atoll also describe fringing and barrier reefs (Fig. 7-6). Some of the major features described here are visible in Plate 14a. The *outer seaward slope* on the windward side descends steeply from the point at which living coral and coralline algae become sparse. This typically is ~60 m in the Indo-West Pacific, but often twice that or more in the West Indies. Unlike fringing and barrier reefs, atolls are surrounded by open ocean and therefore have more than one outer seaward slope. In other words, all outward parts of an atoll face seaward, and the outer seaward slope is a component of both the windward and leeward reefs. The *reef front* defines the upper, seaward face (Plates 14b and 14c). It extends to the edge of the reef from above the point at which coral and coralline algal growths become sparse. The reef front often includes a *reef terrace* that slopes from 8 m to as deep as ~25 m. If large and clearly defined, the reef terrace can be considered a separate zone. On the seaward side, the reef front also includes the living, wave-breaking face of the reef, sometimes designated as an independent entity, the *surge zone* (not

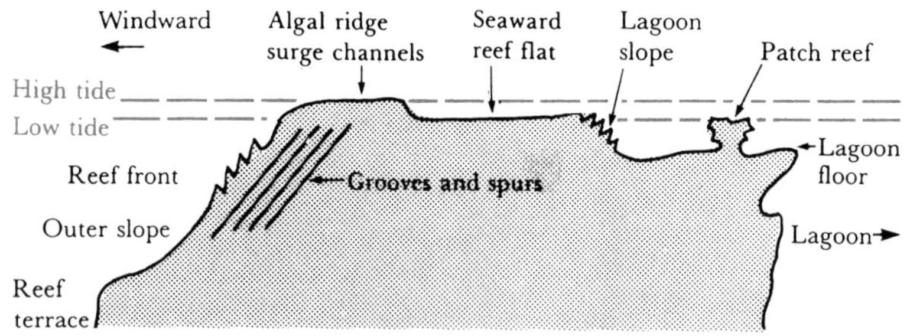

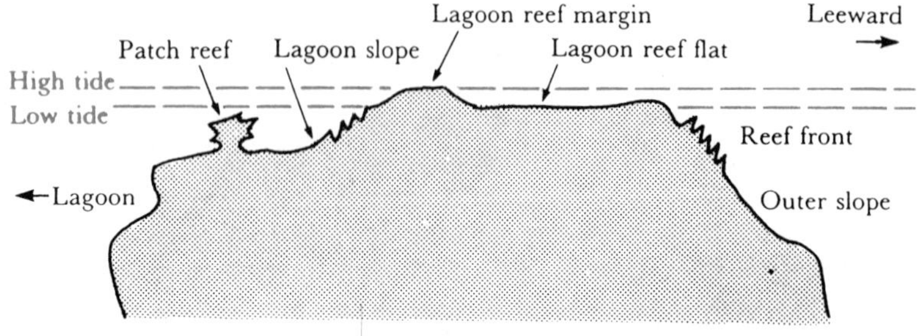

Figure 7-6 Diagrammatic cross section of an atoll illustrating vertical zonation. Most of the same features apply to fringing and barrier reefs. Sawtoothed places indicate dense growths of hard corals. Source: Stephen Spotte.

indicated specifically in the figure but illustrated in Plate 14d). The reef terrace may contain a combtooth arrangement of ridges several metres high and separated by open gulleys filled with coarse, calcareous sand or a finer mixture of sand and sediment. This is the *groove and spur* region or *buttress zone* (Figs. 7-7 and 7-8). The grooves are sometimes incorrectly referred to as surge channels (defined below). With every breaking wave, water piles up on the algal ridge (defined below), then rapidly drains away across the reef front. Gradually, sections of the reef front are eroded. Spurs are areas of actively growing hard corals; grooves are barren and devoid of coral growth. Groove and spur regions are common on seaward reef fronts where tides are strong, the reach of the swells is long, and wave and surge action are heavy. Spurs can be 10 m high. On Florida fringing reefs they vary in width from ~10 to 20 m, extending into the prevailing seas and swells for several hundred metres and rising vertically to ~30 m.[15]

The *seaward reef margin*—the seaward edge of the reef flat (see below)—is marked intermittently by an *algal ridge,* a shallow, high-energy area of intense algal growth permeated with *surge channels*. The latter represent landward extensions of the groove and spur system. Ordinarily, surge channels are a metre or so in width. The reef flat is submerged at high tide and partially emergent at low tide. The algal ridge is actually the upper crest

Figure 7-7 Groove and spur region of a fringing reef. Pine Cay, Turks and Caicos Islands, British West Indies, 15 m. Source: Stephen Spotte.

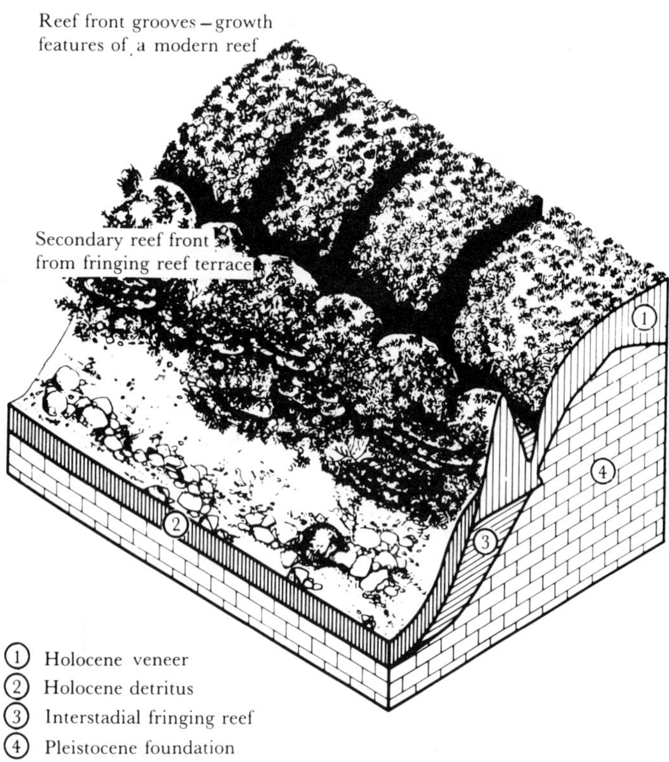

Figure 7-8 *Block diagram of a modern reef illustrating the reef front and the groove and spur system.* Source: Hopley (1982).

of the reef and sometimes called the *reef crest*. In areas of heavy surf this zone is reduced to a flat pavement of encrusting coralline algae, and *algal pavement* is still another synonym. The impingement of high wave energy characteristic of Indo-West Pacific reefs results in extensive algal ridge formations. Comparable development is rare in the West Indies,[16] where a zone of fire coral (*Millipora* spp.) may form instead (Fig. 7-9). *Millipora* is a hydrozoan and not a true coral. The upper, shoreward section of the reef is represented by the *seaward reef flat*, which is exposed or awash at low tide. It is protected from heavy surf by the algal ridge. The *seaward beach* (not shown) is the next recognizable zone. Behind it, on the leeward side of a slight rise, is the *lagoon beach* (not shown in Fig. 7-6). The *lagoon reef margin* is often difficult to identify and may even be absent. If well defined, a *lagoon reef front* and *lagoon reef terrace* may also be apparent (neither is shown in Fig. 7-6). The *lagoon slope* represents the border zone of the lagoon and slopes downward from the lagoon reef margin (or lagoon beach) to the *lagoon floor*, which is nearly level. The lagoon slope is sometimes called the *boulder tract* because it is frequently strewn with chunks of limestone substratum and pieces of dead coral.

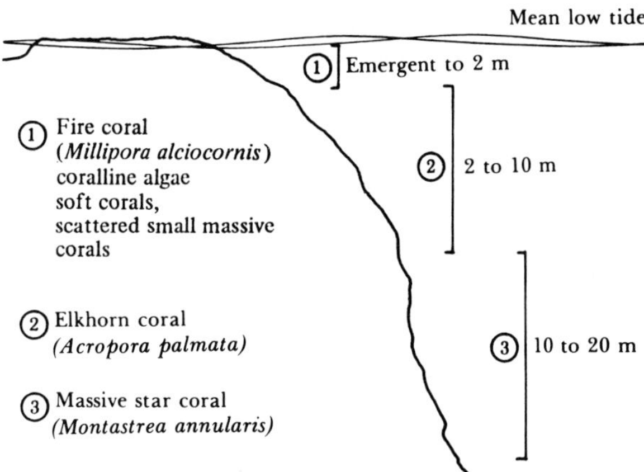

Figure 7-9 *High-energy zone of a typical coral reef in the West Indies.* Source: Stephen Spotte.

In summary, atolls have both a windward and leeward outer seaward slope and differ in this respect from fringing and barrier reefs (Fig. 7-5). Vertical zonation of Indo-West Pacific and West Indies reefs is similar but more sharply defined in the West Indies, probably because competitive exclusion is abetted by comparatively fewer corals. Two other differences are apparent (Fig. 7-10). Consistently greater impingement of wave energy on Indo-West Pacific reefs results in the formation of well developed algal ridges. Conversely, the outer seaward slope of Indo-West Pacific reefs is less extensive than its West Indies counterpart.

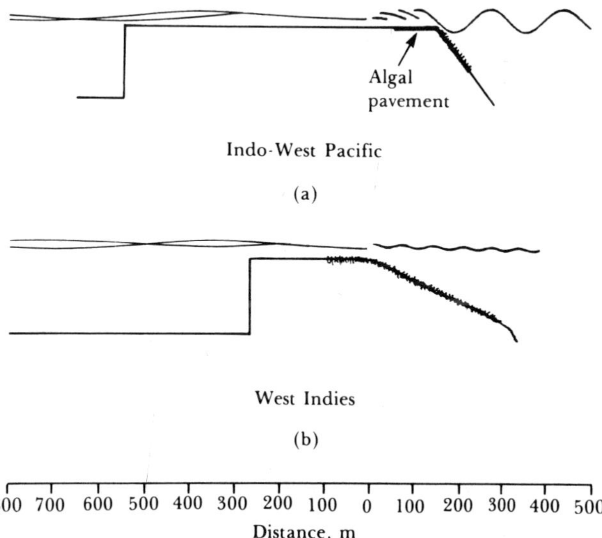

Figure 7-10 *Diagrammatic comparison of the seaward perimeters of typical Indo-West Pacific and West Indies reefs. The important differences are: (1) width of the perimeter, (2) an extensive algal pavement on the Indo-West Pacific reef, (3) the dominant outer seaward slope on the West Indies reef, and (4) impingement of higher wave energy on the Indo-West Pacific reef. Areas with straight lines are mainly sand and rubble.* Source: Kinsey (1981).

PATCH REEFS Portions of atoll lagoons and the leeward sides of fringing and barrier reefs are populated by patch reefs. Patch reef formation in the West Indies occurs sequentially: genesis, youth (early development), maturation, and senescence. In the Florida Keys,[17] genesis is apparent when *soft corals* (order Alcyonacea) invade and colonize an area of sea grass, mainly *Thalassia testidinum* and *Syringodium filiforme,* in water 2 to 6 m deep. Initially, the soft corals grow in unconsolidated calcareous sediments that overlie bedrock limestone. The first hard corals to arrive are brain corals (*Diploria* spp.) and siderastreans (*Siderastrea* spp.). Few early colonists of either the soft or hard coral group survive. Patch reef formation relies on the continuous death and subsequent falling over of both coral types to form a suitable substratum for later colonists. The next of these is a fire coral, *Millipora alcicornis*. In youth, patch reefs are distinguished by a diverse array of hard corals, some without common names: star corals (*Montastrea* spp.), brain corals, finger corals (*Porites* spp.), *Favia fragum,* lettuce coral (*Agaricia agarites*), *Mussa* spp., and *Dichocoenia stokesii*. The soft corals trap particulate organic carbon, which enlarges the area of substratum by increasing the rate of sedimentation. At maturity, patch reefs are 10 to 20 m in diameter and characterized by large, boulderlike coral heads, mainly star and brain corals positioned around the periphery with smaller siderastrean boulders located more toward the center. Because the water is shallow, many of the larger coral heads break off in storms. The process is hastened by activities of boring organisms, resulting in erosion of the coral heads at their bases (Fig. 7-11). Grazing by resident sea urchins and herbivorous fishes denudes the surrounding grass bed for several metres in all directions, creating a barren ''halo'' of coarse, calcareous sand. Overhanging coral heads formed by lateral growth at the periphery of the reef provide shelter for fishes and other animals. However, the steep angle of growth increases the incidence of falling. Senescence is indicated by startling changes that include cessation of growth by massive hard corals and formation of dense soft coral ''forests'' (Fig. 7-12).[18] The interval from genesis to senescence is estimated to take centuries.

The *dome patch reef* is another type characteristic of the West Indies.[19] The reef consists initially of a single large head of star coral (*Montastrea annularis,* Fig. 7-13). A typical head can reach 5 m in diameter and 3 m in height. Dome patch reefs ordinarily are formed in deeper water where low light intensity causes *M. annularis* to assume a domelike morphology. As the colony grows, the edges overhang the base, forming a thin lip around the circumference of the coral head. Subsequent erosion of the

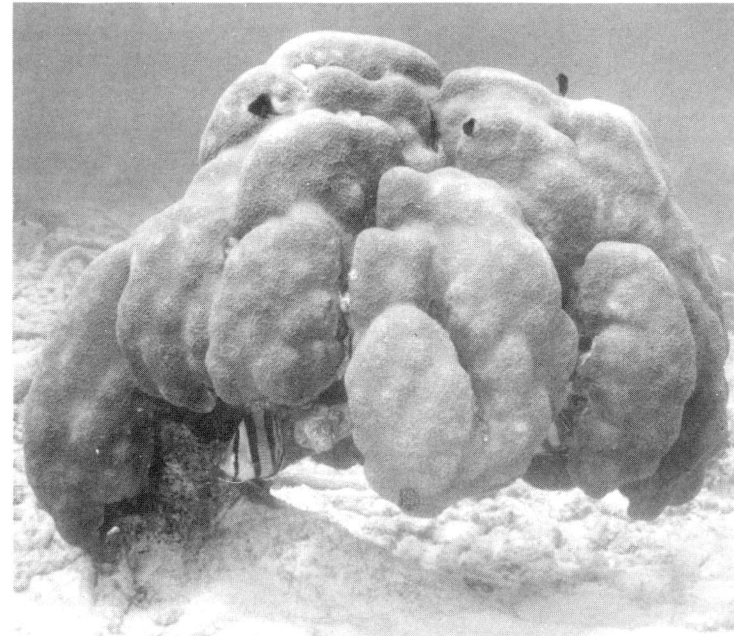

Figure 7-11 *Example of erosion at the base of a coral head. This specimen was not in the vicinity of a patch reef, but the photograph is an accurate portrayal of the erosion process. Bonaire, Netherlands Antilles, 10 m.* Source: Stephen Spotte.

underside beneath the lip produces channels to the interior. At a diameter of ~1 m the head consists of a hollow, domelike structure with numerous openings into a central cavity. By then other soft and hard corals will have colonized the dead areas (Fig. 7-14). The dome eventually collapses near the middle leav-

Figure 7-12 *West Indies patch reef at senescence. Note the extensive coverage by soft corals. Anguilla Cay, Bahamas, 4 m.* Source: Stephen Spotte.

Figure 7-13 *Diagrammatic illustration of the proposed formation of a dome patch reef in the West Indies. The interior of the star coral* (Montastrea annularis) *head has eroded, causing the upper structure to collapse. What remains is a limestone platform ringed with coral colonies that were attached near the base. These eventually spread and grow into a patch reef of greater complexity.* Source: Smith and Tyler (1975).

ing a lifeless area surrounded by a living ring of star coral. The dead portion is soon colonized by other organisms, rendering a mature patch reef reminiscent of the first type. According to some estimates, large dome patch reefs perhaps survive for 500 years.

Biotopes and Habitats

Physically, a reef is divisible into vertical zones riddled with spaces of different sizes and shapes. Each is a potential place for a fish to spend the inactive portion of its diel cycle. With admitted laxity I shall consider biotopes to be embodied within vertical zones, with the caveat that a single biotope may include overlapping zones. Thus zones are physical expressions of biotopes in terms of the living plants and animals found there (Fig. 7-15). From the standpoint of space partitioning, the term habitat will include space occupied by a species during both the active and inactive portions of its diel cycle.

BIOTOPES Superficial examination of a coral reef fish community leaves three impressions: (*1*) certain species seem more common in some zones than in others (Fig. 7-16, Tables 7-3 and 7-4); (*2*) species diversity and abundance appear directly related to the amount of available cover, including percentage of the substratum covered by live coral (Fig. 7-17, Tables 7-5 and 7-6); and (*3*) the extent to which vertical distribution occurs correlates positively with the degree of diversity within the community.[20] These impressions are correct only in a relative sense, for two reasons. First, the concept of species distribution by zones is subjective, and considerable overlap occurs. Second, because diel activity cycles vary by species, only a portion of

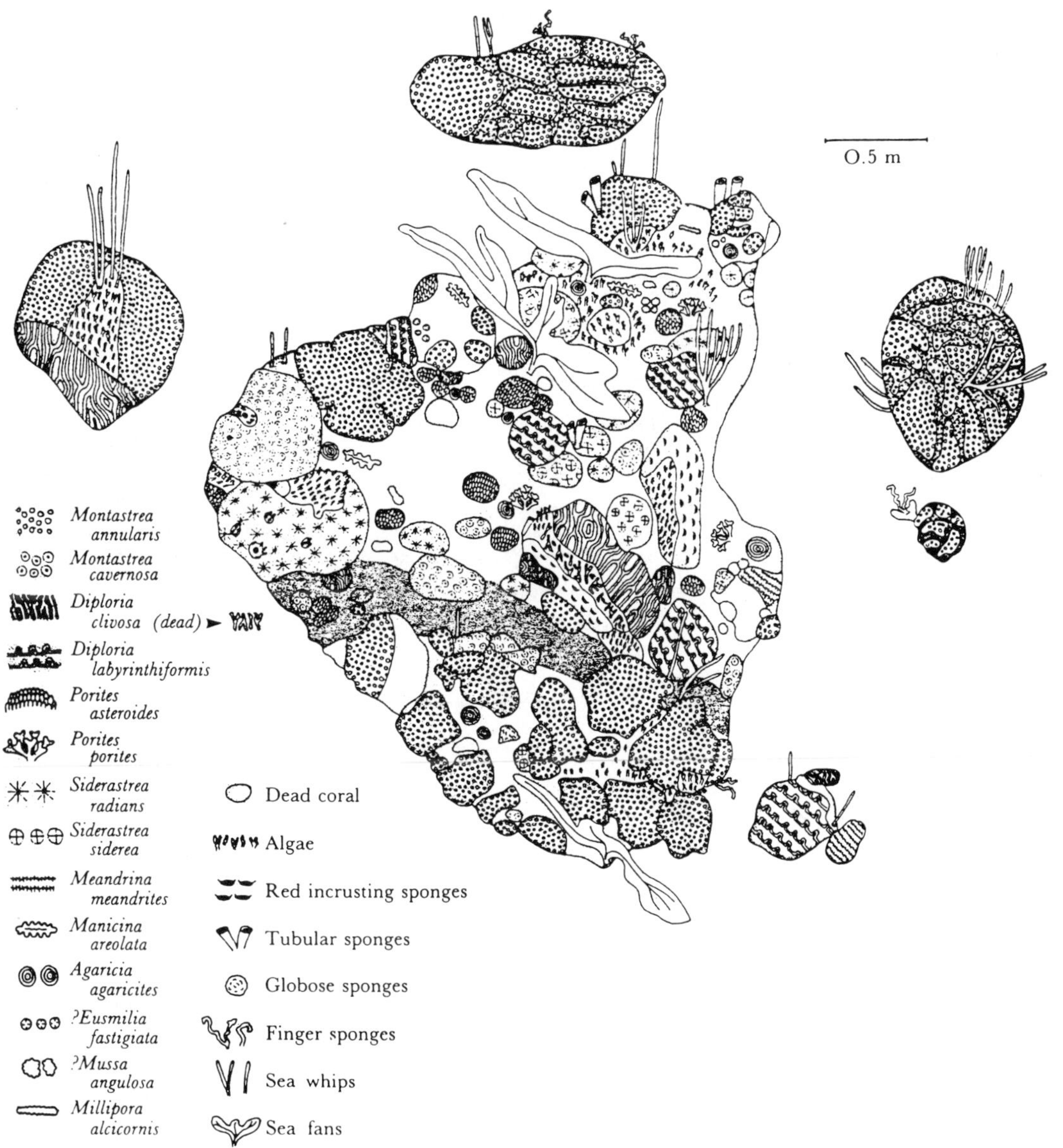

Figure 7-14 Sketch of the distribution of sessile invertebrates on a small West Indies patch reef and smaller satellite reefs. Source: Smith and Tyler (1972).

the fish community is visible at one time. During daylight hours, for example, the shallow, well illuminated areas of reef are dominated by herbivores that congregate to feed on attached algae, and all are diurnal. Inspection of the shallow zones at night reveals different species, none a herbivore.

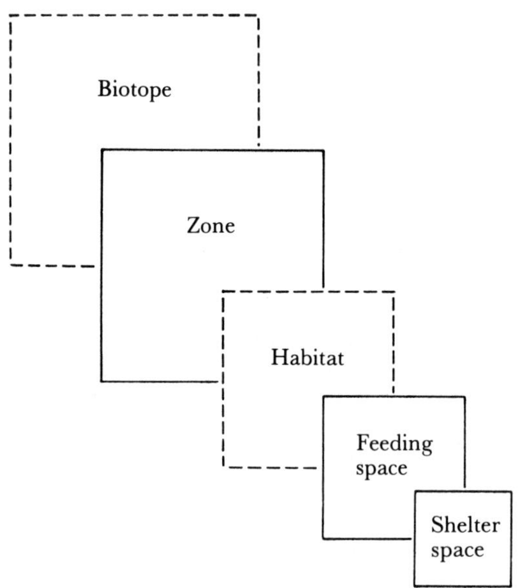

Figure 7-15 *Graphic representation of the relationship between (1) zones and biotopes and (2) shelter spaces, feeding spaces, and habitats. In terms of relative space, a biotope can include portions of overlapping zones. The space contained within a habitat is the sum of the shelter space and feeding space required by a species.* Source: Stephen Spotte.

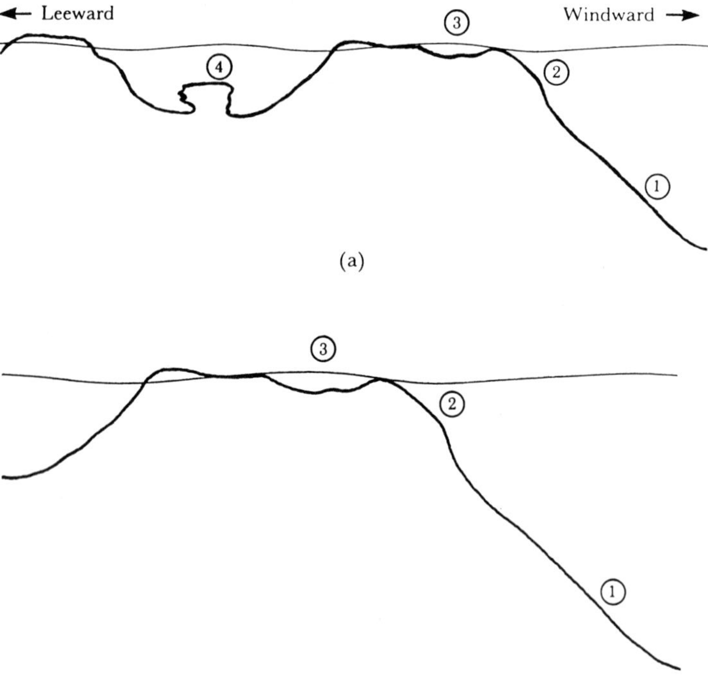

Figure 7-16 *Graphic to accompany Tables 7-3 and 7-4.* (a) *Outer seaward slope (1), upper reef front (2), reef flat (3), lagoon patch reefs and reef tops (4).* (b) *Outer seaward slope (1), upper reef front (2), reef flat (3).* Source: Stephen Spotte.

TABLE 7-3 Representative occupancy of coral reefs zones by Indo-West Pacific teleosts. Key to the numbers is shown in Figure 7-16a. Families and species are listed alphabetically. The table is a composite of representative species compiled for Fanning Island and the Hawaiian, Marshall, and Phoenix Islands; some do not occur at all four sites. Lagoon reef tops and lagoon patch reefs are considered here as a single "zone," and species listed as inhabiting them have been combined. Fish families and species are listed alphabetically.

Fishes	Zone
Acanthuridae—surgeonfishes	
Acanthurus achilles	1,2,3
A. aliala	2
A. glaucopareius	1,2,3
A. guttatus	2,3
A. leucopareius	1
A. lineatus	1,2,3
A. nigrofuscus	1,2,3
A. triostegus	1,2,3
A. xanthopterus	1,2,3,4
Ctenochaetus cyanoguttatus	3
C. striatus	1,3
C. strigosus	1,4
Naso brevirostris	1,4
N. hexacanthus	1
N. lituratus	2
N. unicornis	2
Zebrasoma flavescens	1,2
Z. rostratum	3
Z. scopas	1,4
Z. veliferum	2
Albulidae—bonefishes	
Albula vulpes	3
Apogonidae—cardinalfishes	
Apogon septemfasciatus	3
Cheilodipterus quinquelineataus	1
Aulostomidae—trumpetfishes	
Aulostomus chinensis	1
Balistidae—leatherjackets	
Balistapus undulatus	1,4
Melichthys niger	1,3
Rhinecanthus rectangulus	2,3
Sufflamen chrysopterus	1
Xanthichthys ringens	1
Belonidae—needlefishes	
Platybelone argala platyura	3

TABLE 7-3 *(Continued)*

Fishes	Zone
Blenniidae—combtooth blennies	
Aspidontus taeniatus	1
Cirripectus sebae	2
C. variolosus	1,2,3
Entomacrodus striatus	3
Istiblennius afilinuchalis	3
I. coronatus	3
I. lineatus	3
I. paulus	3
Rhabdoblennius rhabdotrachelus	3
Caracanthidae—orbicular velvetfishes	
Caracanthus maculatus	1,3
Carangidae—jacks	
Caranx melampygus	4
C. melanopterus[1]	1
Elagatis bipinnulata	1
Scomberoides sanctipetri	1
Chaetodontidae—butterflyfishes	
Chaetodon auriga	1,3,4
C. bennetti	1,4
C. ephippium	1
C. kelinii	1
C. lineolatus	1
C. lunula	1
C. meyeri	1
C. multicinctus	1
C. ornatissimus	1
C. punctatofasciatus	1
C. trifasciatus	1,4
C. ulietensis	1,4
Forcipiger longirostris	1
Heniochus acuminatus	1,4
H. monoceros	1
H. varius	1
Megaprotodon trifascialis	1
Chanidae—milkfish	
Chanos chanos	1,3
Cirrhitidae—hawkfishes	
Cirrhitichthys oxycephalus	1,3
Paracirrhites arcatus	1,2
P. forsteri	1,2,4
P. hemistictus	1
P. xanthus	4
Gobidae—gobies	
Bathygobius acutus	3
Hemiramphidae—halfbeaks	
Hyporhamphus acutus	3

TABLE 7-3 *(Continued)*

Fishes	Zone
Holocentridae—squirrelfishes	
Myripristis amaenus	4
M. kuntee	1
M. murdjan	1,4
Sargocentron caudimaculum	4
S. lacteoguttatum	2
S. spiniferum	1,4
Kuhliidae—aholeholes	
Kuhlia marginata	3
Kyphosidae—sea chubs	
Kyphosus cinerascens	1,2,3
Labridae—wrasses	
Bodinaus axillaris	1
B. diana	1
Cheilinus undulatus	1,3
Epibulus insidiator	1
Gomphosus varius	1,2,3,4
Halichoeres hortulanus	3
H. margaritaceus	2,3
H. trimaculatus	1,3
Hemigymnus fasciatus	1
Labroides bicolor	1
L. dimidiatus	1,3,4
L. rubrolabiatus	1,4
Pseudocheilinus evanidus	1
Stethojulis axillaris	3
S. balteata	2
S. linearus	3
Thalassoma amblycephalum	1,3,4
T. duperrey	1,2
T. fuscum	2
T. harwickii	3,4
T. lunare	1,3
T. lutescens	1
T. purpureum	3
T. umbrostygma	3
Lethrinidae—emperors	
Lethrinus xanthochilus	3
Gnathodentex aureolineatus	4
Monotaxis grandoculis	1
Lutjanidae—snappers	
Aprion virescens	1
Lutjanus bohar	1,4
L. fulyus	1,4
L. gibbus	2
L. kasmira	4
L. monostigma	1

TABLE 7-3 *(Continued)*

Fishes	Zone
Mullidae—goatfishes	
Mulloidichthys samoensis	3
Upeneus arge	3
Muraenidae—morays	
Gymnothorax flavimarginatus	1
G. pictus	3
Pempheridae—sweepers	
Pempheris oualensis	2
Pomacanthidae—angelfishes	
Centropyge bicolor	1
C. flavissimus	3,4
C. loriculus	1
C. potteri	1
Pomacanthus imperator	1
Pomacentridae—damselfishes	
Abudefduf abdominalis	1
A. imparipennis	1,2,3
A. leucopomus	3
A. lacrymatus	2
A. sordidus	2,3
Amphiprion chrysopterus	4
Chromis acares	1
C. caeruleus	1,4
C. lepidolepis	1
C. leucurus	1
C. margaritifer	1,4
C. vanderbilti	1,2
C. verater	1
Dascyllus trimaculatus	1
Glyphidodontops biocellatus	3
G. glaucus	3
G. leucopomus	3
Plectroglyphiododon dickii	4
P. imparipennis	1,2,3
P. lacrymatus	2
P. phoenixensis	2
P. johnstonianus	1
Pomacentrus coelestis	1,3,4
P. vaiuli	1,3
Stegastes albifasciatus	3
S. aureus	3
S. fasciolatus	1,2
S. nigricans	1,4
Pseudochromidae—dottybacks	
Pseudochromis nigricans	3
P. tapeinosoma	2

TABLE 7-3 (*Continued*)

Fishes	Zone
Scaridae—parrotfishes	
Scarus brevifillis	3
S. frenatus	1,3
S. ghobban	1,3,4
S. jonesi	3
S. oviceps	3,4
S. pectoralis	1,3
S. sordidus	1,4
Serranidae—sea basses	
Anyperodon leucogrammicus	4
Epinephelus argus	1
E. fuscoguttatus	1
E. hexagonatus	1
E. merra	1,2,3
E. microdon	1
E. spilotoceps	1,3
E. urodelus	1,4
Gracila albomarginata	1
Plectropomus leopardus	2
P. truncatus	2
Tripterygiidae—threefin blennies	
Tripterygion minutus	4
Zanclidae	
Zanclus cornutus	1

Source: Stephen Spotte, compiled from information in Chave and Eckert (1974), Grovhoug and Henderson (1978), Hiatt and Strasburg (1960), and Hobson (1974).

Notes: Could not be found in current listings;[1] names have been changed where appropriate to reflect current usage.

The composition of fish communities on large reefs shows reasonably close correlation when comparable zones in different places are compared (Tables 7-3 and 7-4). Correlation of reef structure and diversity with the diversity and abundance of fish species is relatively weaker for data collected in the Indo-West Pacific than in the West Indies, indicating that although mechanisms regulating the composition of fish communities are fundamentally the same in both regions, they differ quantitatively.[21]

HABITATS Fishes are most active when feeding and least active when not, but they occupy space in either situation. The habitat boundary of a species encompasses space beyond that required for feeding, reproduction, and other activities. *Shelter*

TABLE 7-4 Space partitioning by teleosts on Harvey Reef, Port Sudan, Red Sea. Key to the numbers is shown in Fig. 7-16b. The authors did not identify a fourth zone. They also considered the algal ridge and reef crest to represent separate zones. I combined their algal ridge, reef crest, and reef top and and called the composite Zone 3. Fish families and species are listed alphabetically.

Fishes	Zone
Acanthuridae—surgeonfishes	
Acanthurus nigrofuscus	3
A. sohal	3
Ctenochaetus striatus	3
Naso lituratus	1,2,3
Zebrasoma desjardinii (?)	1,2,3
Balistidae—leatherjackets	
Balistapus undulatus	1,2,3
Oxymonacanthus halli	2,3
Chaetodontidae—butterflyfishes	
Chaetodon auriga	3
C. austriacus	1,2,3
C. paucifasciatus	1
Heniochus intermedius	1
Labridae—wrasses	
Gomphosus caeruleus	1,2,3
Halichoeres hortulanus	3
H. scapularis	3
Pseudochelinus hexataenia	2,3
Stethojulis albovittata	3
Thalassoma klunzingeri	3
Mullidae—goatfishes	
Parupeneus forsskali	1,2,3
Pomacanthidae—angelfishes	
Pygoplites diacanthus	2,3
Pomacentridae—damselfishes	
Amblyglyphiododon flavilatus	1
A. leucogaster	2,3
Chromis caeruleus	2,3
C. dimidiata	2,3
C. ternatensis	2,3
Chrysiptera unimaculata	3
Dascyllus aruanus	1
Plectroglyphiododon lacrymatus	1
Pomacentrus sulfureus	2,3
P. trichourus	1
Stegastes nigricans	3
Pseudochromidae—false chromis	
Pseudochromis fridmani	1

TABLE 7-4 *(Continued)*

Fishes	Zone
Scaridae—parrotfishes	
Hipposcarus harid	1,2,3
Scarus ferrugineus	1,2,3
S. niger	1,2,3
S. sordidus	1,2,3
Serranidae—sea basses	
Anthias squamipinnis	1
Epinephelus argus	1,2,3
E. miniatus	1

Source: Edwards and Rosewell (1981).

Note: Names have been changed where appropriate to reflect current usage.

spaces are those portions of the habitat where fishes spend the inactive part of the diel cycle. They are smaller than feeding spaces, often discrete, and recognizable by the fishes using them. *Feeding spaces* are larger sections of the habitat where fishes spend the active portion of the diel cycle. They have boundaries that are less easily defined. The sum of all habitats of the species present is represented by the biotope, identifiable in this discussion as a vertical zone. Shelter spaces include sim-

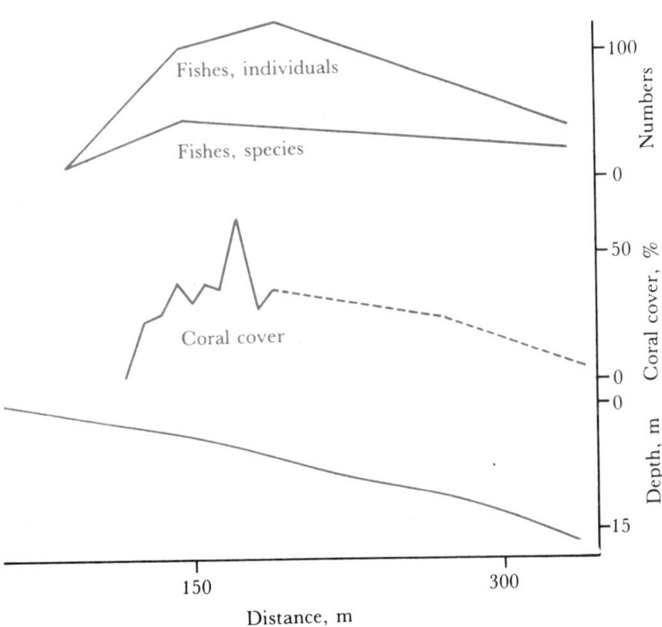

Figure 7-17 *Percentage of live coral cover on Tutia Reef, Kenya, in addition to fish standing crop density and number of species as estimated by collecting with explosives.* Source: Talbot (1965).

TABLE 7-5 Teleost species diversity and abundance in the Phoenix Islands, Indo-West Pacific, on a shallow, nearshore reef with live coral coverage >50%. Predominant corals: *Pocillopora, Montipora, Porites, Pavona, Halomitra,* and *Herpolitha*. Fish families and species are listed alphabetically.

Fishes	Number of individuals
Acanthuridae—surgeonfishes	
Acanthurus achilles	5
A. glaucopareius	4
A. lineatus	10
A. triostegus	50
A. xanthopterus	10
Acanthurus spp. (2)	>300
Ctenochaetus striatus	1
C. strigosus	>50
Naso brevirostris	>50
Zebrasoma scopas	3
Apogonidae—cardinalfishes	
Cheilodipterus quinquelineatus	8
Aulostomidae—trumpetfishes	
Aulostomus chinensis	1
Balistidae—leatherjackets	
Elagatis bipunnulatus	>50
Carangidae—jacks	
Caranx melampygus	6
Chaetodontidae—butterflyfishes	
Chaetodon auriga	5
C. bennetti	4
C. ephippium	3
C. kleini	>20
C. lunula	>30
C. meyeri	6
C. trifasciatus	>12
C. ulietensis	10
Forcipiger longirostris	3
Heniochus acuminatus	10
H. monoceros	>12
H. varius	3
Megaprotodon strigangulus	5
Cirrhitidae—hawkfishes	
Paracirrhites arcatus	10
P. forsteri	10
Holocentridae—squirrelfishes	
Myripristis spp. (3)	>100
Sargocentron spinifer	5
Kyphosidae—sea chubs	
Kyphosus cinerascens	>20
Labridae—wrasses	
Cheilinus undulatus	3
Gomphosus varius	6
Labridae spp. (3)	>1000

TABLE 7-5 *(Continued)*

Fishes	Number of individuals
Labroides dimidiatus	3
L. rubrolabiatus	2
Thalassoma amblycephalum	>1000
T. lunare	12
Lethrinidae—emperors	
Lethrinus sp.	5
Monotaxis grandoculis	>30
Lutjanidae—snappers	
Aprion virescens	6
Lutijanus bohar	>20
L. fulvus	>20
L. monostigma	>20
Mullidae—goatfishes	
Parupeneus spp.	>15
Muraenidae—morays	
Gymnothorax flavimarginatus	2
Pomacanthidae—angelfishes	
Centropyge bicolor	2
C. flavissimus	10
C. loriculus	10
Pomacentridae—damselfishes	
Chromis caeruleus	>200
C. margaritifer	>2000
Chromis sp.	>3000
Dascyllus trimaculatus	·5
Pomacentrus coelestis	>100
Stegastes nigricans	20
Scaridae—parrotfishes	
Scarus frenatus	5
S. ghobban	15
S. pectoralis	10
S. sordidus	>100
Scaridae spp. (3)	>300
Scombridae—mackerels	
Scomberoides lysan	4
Serranidae—sea basses	
Anyperodon leucogrammicus	3
Epinephelus argus	6
E. merra	10
E. microdon	5
E. urodelus	4
Gacilia albomarginatus	1
Serranidae spp. (3)	>100
Sphyraenidae—barracudas	
Sphyraenidae sp.	>30
Zanclidae	
Zanclus cornutus	5

Source: Grovhoug and Henderson (1978).

Note: Names have been changed where appropriate to reflect current usage.

TABLE 7-6 Teleost species diversity and abundance in the Phoenix Islands, Indo-West Pacific, on a shallow, nearshore reef with a coral rubble bottom. Live coral covered ~10 to 15% of the bottom. Predominant corals: *Pocillopora* and *Porites*. Fish families and species are listed alphabetically.

Fishes	Number of individuals
Acanthuridae—surgeonfishes	
Acanthurus lineatus	>100
A. olivaceus	2
Acanthurus spp. (2)	>150
Ctenochaetus strigosus	>500
Zebrasoma scopas	8
Balistidae—leatherjackets	
Melichthys vidua	1
Chaetodontidae—butterflyfishes	
Chaetodon auriga	2
C. ephippium	1
C. lunula	1
C. meyeri	2
C. ornatissimus	3
C. guardimaculatus	5
C. ulietensis	2
Forcipiger longirostris	1
Cirrhitidae—hawkfishes	
Paracirrhites xanthus	3
Labridae—wrasses	
Coris gaimard	2
Epibulus insidiator	3
Labridae spp. (2)	>100
Thalassoma amblycephalum	>1000
Lutjanidae—snappers	
Lutjanus bohar	13
L. fulvus	20
Mullidae—goatfishes	
Parupeneus barberinus	3
P. trifasciatus	1
Pomacanthidae—angelfishes	
Centropyge flavissimus	7
Pomacentridae—damselfishes	
Chromis caeruleus	46
C. margaritifer	>1000
Plectroglyphidodon dickii	40
Stegastes nigricans	>100
Pomacentrus sp. (yellow)	>10
Scaridae—parrotfishes	
Scarus spp. (2)	>25
Serranidae—sea basses	
Epinephelus argus	3
E. urodelus	8
E. microdon	3

TABLE 7-6 *(Continued)*

Fishes	Number of individuals
Zanclidae	
Zanclus cornutus	5

Source: Grovhoug and Henderson (1978).

Note: Names have been changed where appropriate to reflect current usage.

ple overhangs, crevices and caves within the reef's infrastructure, tubeworm holes, sponges, and even open areas of the reef near particular soft corals or other landmarks (Table 7-7).[22] Planktivores use crevices, caves, or overhangs when inactive, but emerge to feed in the water column. The distance between the two locations may be a few metres or several kilometres (Chapter 6). Still other planktivores feed in the vicinity of their shelter spaces, venturing only short distances (Fig. 7-18). A few species (e.g., those dwelling in tubeworm holes and sponges) conduct all activities within their shelter spaces and probably never leave. Benthic predators vacate shelter spaces to hunt along the substratum. The proximity of so many species may result in narrow habitat partitioning among coral reef fishes.

TABLE 7-7 Habitat partitioning by representative teleosts in Curacao, Netherlands Antilles.

Ledges	*Apogon townsendi*
	Gramma loreto
	Myripristis jacobus
	Priacanthus cruentatus
	Quisquilius hipoliti
Crevices and Caves	*Apogon lachneri*
	A. phenax
	Equetus punctatus
	Flameo marianus
	Liopropoma carmabi
	L. mowbrayi
	L. rubre
	Lipogramma trilineata
	Plectrypops retrospinis
Tubeworm holes	*Acanthemblemaria spinosa*
	A. greenfieldi
	Emblemariopsis bahamensis
Sponges	*Gobiosoma horsti*
	Starksia hassei

Sources: Primarily Luckhurst and Luckhurst (1978b), but also Greenfield and Greenfield (1982).

Note: Names have been changed where appropriate to reflect current usage.

Figure 7-18 *Garden eels* (Nystactichthys halis) *are diurnal planktivores, but feed without completely leaving their burrows. Bonaire, Netherlands Antilles, 30 m.* Source: Stephen Spotte.

Closely related species sometimes partition habitat space vertically and are distributed by depth (Fig. 7-19). In other cases the habitat requirements are similar whether or not the species are closely related (Fig. 7-20). Still another form of habitat partitioning is controlled by the tides. Some fishes occupy inshore areas at all times, but transients follow the deepening water column shoreward, then drift seaward as the tide falls (Fig. 7-21).

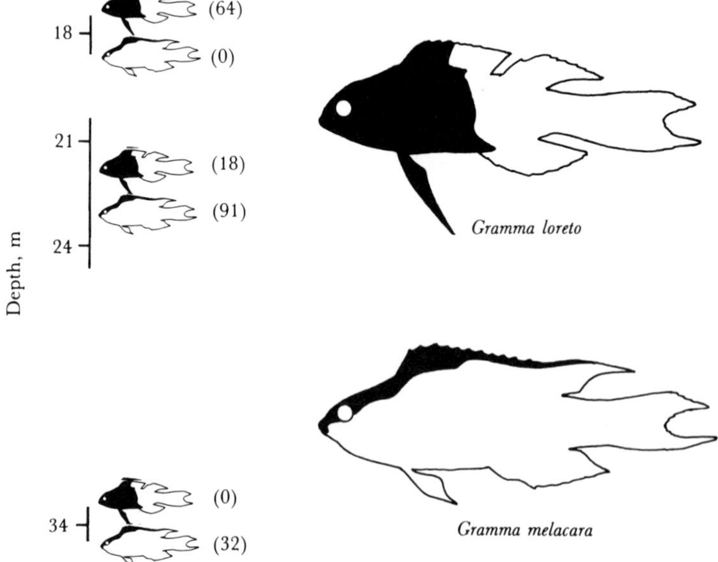

Figure 7-19 *Vertical distribution of two West Indies basslets,* Gramma loreto *and* G. melacara. Source: Stephen Spotte, drawn from information in Greenfield and Greenfield (1982).

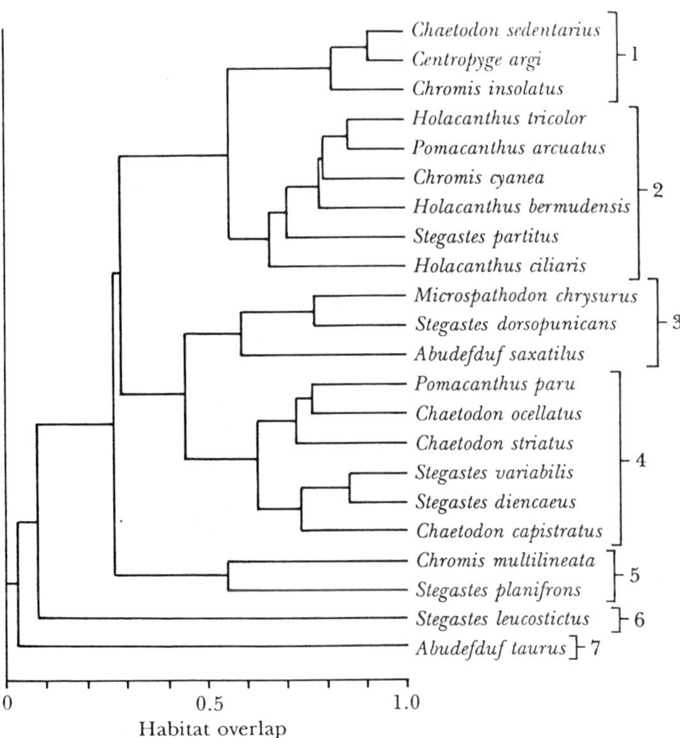

Figure 7-20 Dendrogram showing groupings of West Indies butterflyfishes and damselfishes by habitat overlap. The lower the junction (in this case the farther it is to the right) between two units, the closer the correlation (i.e., the greater the similarity). Names have been changed where appropriate to reflect current usage. Source: Clarke (1977).

The diversity of fish species (i.e., species richness) usually—but not always—correlates well with important structural features of the reef, notably surface area, surface and substratum complexity, and height.[23] Correlation is especially poor in the case of patch reefs,[24] perhaps because they are small and isolated. Somewhat surprisingly, the simple features defined by area and height evidently are more important than complexity, measured as the amount of coral cover and extent to which the substratum is perforated with holes and crevices.[24] In this respect, superficial impressions can be misleading, although surface area and substratum complexity—including the amount of live coral cover—is important (Fig. 7-17).[24] Places of sparse coral and little surface relief are uniformly low in both species richness and abundance (compare Tables 7-5 and 7-6). *Ramose* coral heads are traversed with labyrinths produced by erosion and boring organisms. The combination of an intricate tunnel system and a highly convoluted exterior make ramose corals ideal shelter sites. (Fig. 7-22a). *Glomerate* coral heads, smooth on the outside and solid on the inside, offer comparatively few shelter spaces (Fig. 7-22b).

The capacity of a biotope to support a fish community is reflected in the *standing crop density*, which is a crude measure of

High tide

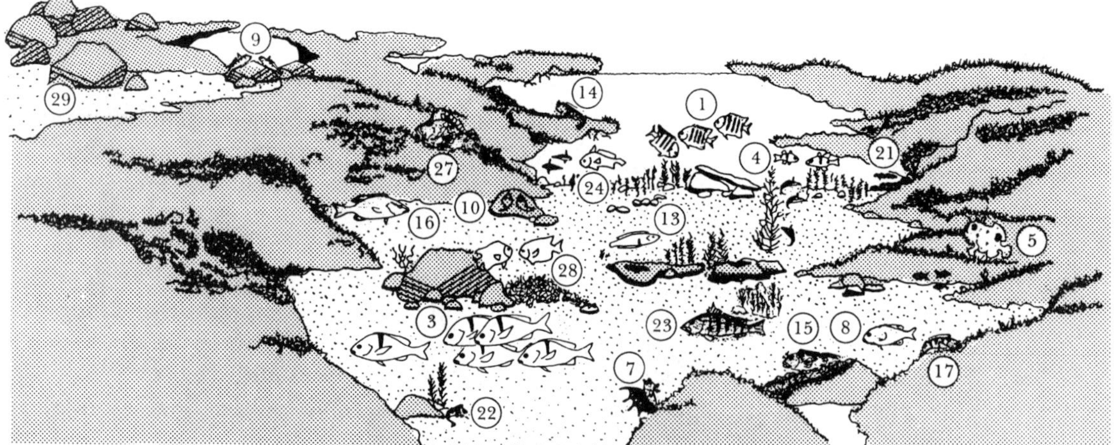

Low tide

Figure 7-21 Northern Gulf of California rocky shore fish community at high tide and low tide. (1) Abudefduf troschelii, *(2)* Anchoa helleri, *(3)* Anisotremus davidsoni, *(4)* Apogon retrosella, *(5)* Antennarius avalonis, *(6)* Balistes polyepis, *(7)* Emblemaria hypacanthus, *(8)* Girella simplicidens, *(9)* Gobiosoma chiquita, *(10)* Gobiesox pinniger, *(11)* Halichoeres dispilus, *(12)* Halichoeres nicholsi, *(13)* Halichoeres semicinctus, *(14)* Hypsoblennius gentilis, *(15)* Labrisomus xanti, *(16)* Lutjanus argentiventris, *(17)* Malacoctenus gigas, *(18)* Mugil cephalus, *(19)* Mycteroperca jordani, *(20)* Mycteroperca rosaea, *(21)* Ogilbia *sp.*, *(22)* Paraclinus sini, *(23)* Paralabrax maculatofasciatus, *(24)* Pareques viola, *(25)* Pomacanthus zonipectus, *(26)* Scomberomorus concolor, *(27)* Scorpaena mystes, *(28)* Stegastes rectifraenum, *(29)* Tomicodon humeralis. Source: Thomson and Lehner (1976).

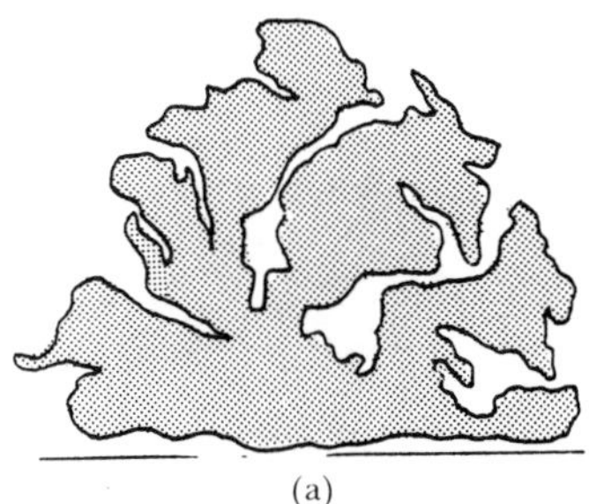

(a)

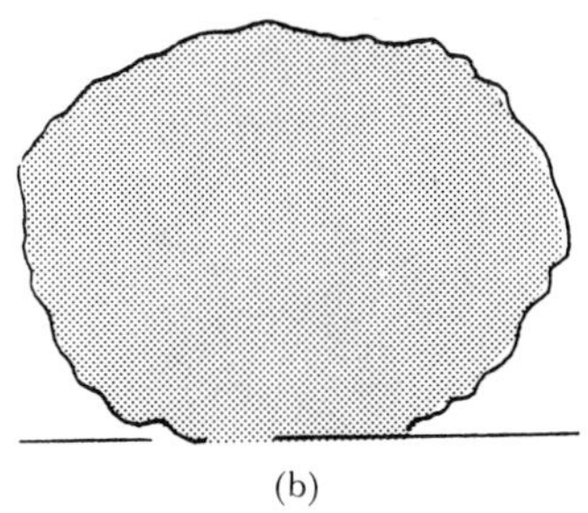

(b)

Figure 7-22 *Classification of coral heads by amount of shelter space.* (a) *Ramose.* (b) *Glomerate.* Source: Stephen Spotte.

TABLE 7-8 Numbers of fishes and standing crop density on representative coral reefs.

Region	Location	Fishes/m^2	Fishes, kg/m^2
West Indies	U.S. Virgin Islands[3]	2.25	0.16
	U.S. Virgin Islands[3]	4.895	0.158
Indo-West Pacific	Hawaii[2]	3.14	0.120
	Hawaii[2]	3.06	0.09
	Great Barrier Reef[1]	16.134	—
	Great Barrier Reef[4]	8.26	—

Sources: Bradbury and Goeden (1974),[1] Brock et al. (1979),[2] Randall (1963),[3] Sale and Douglas 1984).[4]

the total biomass of all fishes present. Only a few such measurements involving coral reef fishes have been published (Table 7-8). Standing crop density is determined by dividing a section of reef into transects, killing the fishes nonselectively with rotenone or explosives, and calculating the total wet mass of specimens recovered. Findings have generally supported the contention that standing crop density is greatest in parts of a reef that contain the most shelter spaces. It has been suggested that the maximum standing crop density of fishes in a coral reef biotope (i.e., all habitats combined) is ~2000 kg/hectare,[25] or 0.2 kg/m^2.

When fishes vacate shelter spaces to feed, these sites may be occupied by species active at other times (Figs. 7-23 and 7-24). Multiple use of space—both shelter and feeding space—is called *space sharing*.[26] Species shifts that occur during changeover (Chapter 5) allow the same spaces to be used by more than one species. Some individuals demonstrate strong attachment to a specific location and return regularly to the same shelter spaces.[27]

TECHNOLOGY

Method 7.1 Shelter Space Allocation in Community Exhibits

For purposes here, resources can be divided into two broad categories. *Intrinsic resources* are purely behavioral in origin. An example is care of the nest demonstrated by some benthic spawners. *Extrinsic resources* are provided by the environment. In the design and maintenance of aquarium exhibits, extrinsic resources are especially noteworthy because they are allocated by the aquarist. The two most important are food and space.

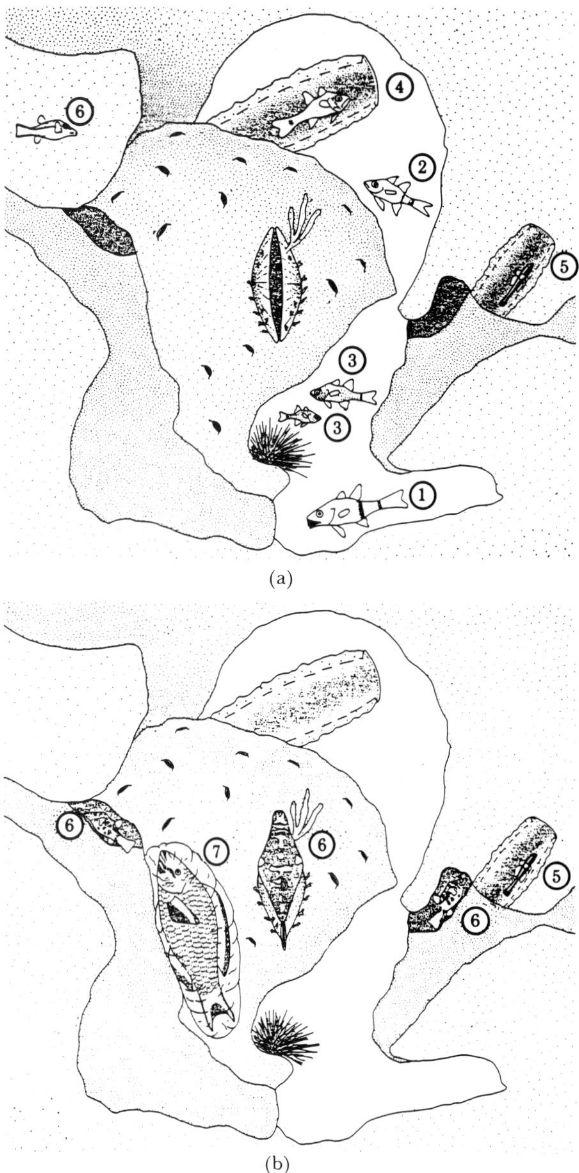

Figure 7-23 *Sharing of shelter space in a tunnel area of a reef in the U.S. Virgin Islands. The space has been compressed in the illustrations.* (a) *Day.* (b) *Night. Identification numbers and species names: (1)* Apogon binotatus, *(2)* A. townsendi, *(3)* Phaeoptyx pigmentaria, *(4)* P. xenus, *(5)* Gobiosoma horsti, *(6)* Canthigaster rostrata, *(7)* Scarus vetula. Source: Smith and Tyler (1972).

Food can be offered once daily or several times. Moreover, the amount of food, its particle size, and the length of time it is available can be controlled at each feeding. The feeding of fishes is therefore dynamic and potentially less limiting than space allocation. With minor exceptions (e.g., the digging of burrows by aquarium inhabitants), the latter occurs only once—when an exhibit is established.

The availability of shelter space is as important to coral reef

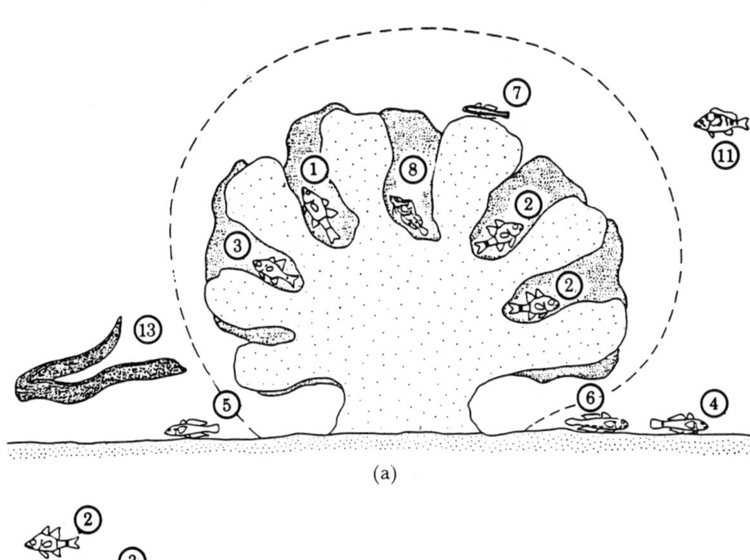

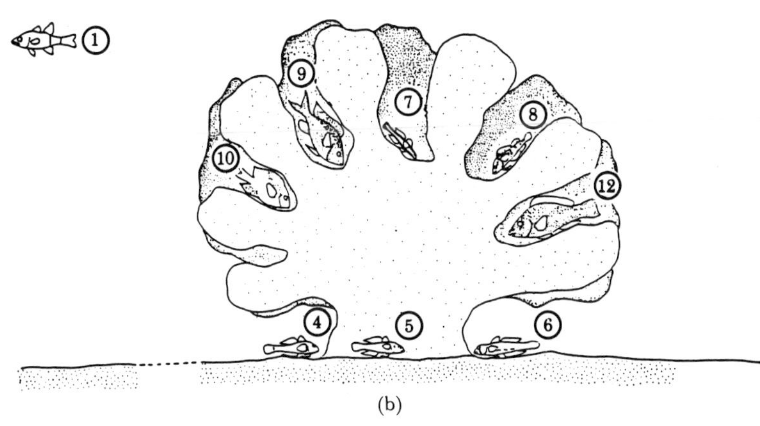

Figure 7-24 *Sharing of shelter space on a ramose head of* Montastrea annularis *in the U.S. Virgin Islands. Fishes are outsized in proportion to the coral head. Residents and visitors are inside and outside the broken line, respectively.* (a) *Day.* (b) *Night. Identification numbers and species names: (1)* Apogon binotatus, *(2)* A. townsendi, *(3)* Phaeoptyx conklini, *(4)* Coryphopterus eidolon, *(5)* C. glaucofraenum, *(6)* Gnatholepis thompsoni, *(7)* Gobiosoma evelynae, *(8)* Labrisomus haitiensis, *(9)* Chromis cyanea, *(10)* Stegastes partitus, *(11)* Hypoplectrus unicolor (= H. bicolor), *(12)* Sparisoma aurofrenatum, *(13)* Muraena miliaris. Source: Smith and Tyler (1972).

fishes as the internal dimensions of the aquarium. Of equal importance is the number and size of available holes and crevices. Without adequate shelter spaces, small fishes cannot hide from predators and dominant aquarium-mates. The result is increased mortality and socially induced stress.

Allocation of shelter space must be based on the requirements of the fishes displayed: their size, maturity, sex, type of social behavior (e.g., territorial, schooling, solitary nomads), and diel activity patterns (diurnal or nocturnal). An attempt must be made to reproduce essential physical features of the habitat. Representative habitats are given here (Table 7-9). Keep

TABLE 7-9 Shelter space preferences of representative coral reef teleosts. Some families contain species with different habitat preferences, and individuals of the same species are frequently found in more than one type of habitat. Families are listed alphabetically. Emphasis has been placed on the habitat type in which most species in a family spend the inactive portion of the diel cycle. *Key*: A: sand and coral rubble, B: ramose corals, C: ledges and caves, D: open places of mixed hard and soft corals with intermittent sand and rubble patches, and E: water column.

Family	A	B	C	D	E
Acanthuridae—surgeonfishes		x	x	x	
Albulidae—bonefishes	x				
Apogonidae—cardinalfishes		x	x		
Aulostomidae—trumpetfishes	x			x	
Balistidae—leatherjackets		x		x	x
Belonidae—needlefishes					x
Blenniidae—combtooth blennies		x	x		
Bothidae—lefteye flounders	x			x	
Caracanthidae—orbicular velvetfishes		x	x		
Chaetodontidae—butterflyfishes		x	x	x	
Chanidae—milkfish		x	x		
Cirrhitidae—hawkfishes		x	x		
Clinidae—clinids			x		
Clupeidae—herrings					x
Coryphaenidae—dolphins					x
Diodontidae—porcupinefishes			x	x	
Echeneidae—remoras					x
Ephippididae—spadefishes					x
Exocoetidae—flyingfishes					x
Fistulariidae—cornetfishes					x
Gerreidae—mojarras	x				
Gobidae—gobies		x	x	x	
Grammidae—basslets		x	x		
Haemulidae—grunts			x	x	
Hemiramphidae—halfbeaks					x
Holocentridae—squirrelfishes	x	x	x	x	
Inermiidae—bonnetmouths					x
Kyphosidae—sea chubbs					x
Labridae—wrasses	x	x	x		
Lutjanidae—snappers	x	x	x	x	
Malacanthidae—tilefishes	x				
Mullidae—goatfishes	x			x	
Muraenidae—morays		x	x		
Ogcocephalidae—batfishes				x	
Ophichthidae—snake eels	x				
Opistognathidae—jawfishes	x				
Ostraciidae—boxfishes			x	x	
Pempherididae—sweepers			x		
Pomacanthidae—angelfishes		x	x		
Pomacentridae—damselfishes	x	x	x		

TABLE 7-9 (*Continued*)

Family	A	B	C	D	E
Priacanthidae—bigeyes		x	x		
Scaridae—parrotfishes		x	x		
Sciaenidae—drums		x	x		
Scombridae—mackerels					x
Scorpaenidae—scorpionfishes	x	x	x	x	
Serranidae—sea basses		x	x		
Sparidae—porgies	x				
Sphyraenidae—barracudas					x
Synodontidae—lizardfishes	x				
Tetraodontidae—puffers		x	x		
Tripterygiidae—threefin blennies					

Source: Stephen Spotte, compiled from various sources, including personal observation.

in mind that considerable overlap occurs in some species, and that all species in a family seldom have the same requirements. The information presented is meant to be a general guide for establishing community exhibits. Techniques for making simulated living corals and other decorative objects from fiberglass-reinforced plastic are described in Chapter 10.

Method 7.2 Procedure for Adding a Known Mass of Fishes to an Aquarium Exhibit

The maximum standing crop density of fishes on coral reefs has been estimated at 0.2 kg/m^2.[25] This can be a starting point for addition of fishes to a community exhibit, although a smaller value (0.1 kg/m^2) might be safer, especially in exhibits with newly conditioned filter beds (Chapter 2). The procedure below describes how to arrive at a predetermined standing crop density. The necessary equipment consists of an accurate scale (either platform or hanging), a clean container, and a fine-mesh net. The procedure is offered with a number of disclaimers. Not considered are the carrying capacity of the filter bed, space requirements of individual species, number of individuals per total mass, and whether the species selected are socially compatible.

How to Add a Known Mass of Fishes to an Aquarium Exhibit

1 Compute the area of the aquarium in square metres.

2 Select a clean container, weigh it, and record the value (Fig. 7-25a).

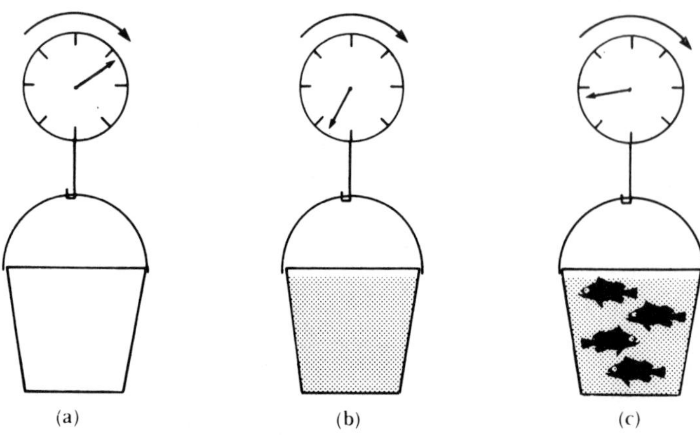

Figure 7-25 Procedure for obtaining a known mass of fishes: (a) weigh an empty container; (b) weigh the container after filling it with seawater, then subtract (a) from (b); and (c) add several fishes and subtract (b) from (c).

3 Fill the container to a mark with seawater from the exhibit and weigh it. Subtract the result from the value obtained in Step 2 (Fig. 7-25b). If the container is uncalibrated, mark the waterline with indelible ink.
4 Capture several fishes in a soft, fine-mesh net and quickly release them into the container.
5 Record the mass and subtract the result from the value obtained in step 3 (Fig. 7-25c). Also record the value obtained in this step.
6 Empty the container gently into the aquarium exhibit.
7 Repeat the procedure until the predetermined total mass of fishes has been added.

Method 7.3 Shelter Spaces for Fishes During Acclimation

Fishes that have been captured recently or received from a dealer must be acclimated before being placed in a community exhibit. Acclimation should include a minimum of 21 d in quarantine (Chapter 9). In my opinion, the social stresses experienced by unacclimated specimens are intensified when shelter spaces of the appropriate type and size are not provided. The use of shelter spaces in nature evidently is a fixed behavioral component of the diel cycle, not merely an option. Many species demonstrate strong site attachment, which is evidence that shelter spaces not only are recognized but that specific ones are preferred. A new fish has many adverse circumstances to overcome, including being homeless.

CHAPTER

8 Nutrition

In nature, fishes eat the foods necessary for sustenance, growth, and reproduction. Foraging, grazing, and predation consume most of the energy expended during times of greatest activity. Unfortunately for aquarists, fish nutritionists have concentrated on the needs of edible species. We know almost nothing about the requirements of exotic fishes. Aquarists therefore have two choices: they can continue to maintain exotic species and try to understand their nutritional needs, or keep only trout and a few other fishes for which adequate information is available. The decision is easy. A sautéed trout is delightful when artfully arranged with parsley, but a live trout viewed behind glass is rather mundane.

In the Science section, emphasis is on the nutritional requirements of fishes generally. This is prefaced by a loud disclaimer: the nutrient requirements of fishes vary by species, age, physiological status, water temperature, and many other factors. To state, for example, that all fishes must be fed proteins and lipids merely repeats a qualitative truth. A fish's *specific* requirements must be considered quantitatively, and it is here that the absence of information becomes restrictive. As will soon be apparent, "proteins" and "lipids" have limited dietary value unless they contain essential amino acids and fatty acids in the proper proportions and concentrations. These, of course, are unknown. I shall deal only with positive influences of nutrients.

The Technology section builds on the theoretical information presented in the Science section, emphasizing procedures for making moist feeds, using natural foods, and growing live foods. The presumed requirements displayed in a tabular format in the Science section are reinforced later by other tables of more immediate value. The purpose is to illustrate how the basic nutritional needs of fishes can be met by items of known composition. The Technology section is long, but necessarily so. In the absence of information, aquarists are forced to define adequate nutrition from the standpoint of variety.

The terms diet, feed, and food appear frequently. Nutritionists customarily use ''diet'' in reference to nutrient sources of relatively defined composition, including those that have been manufactured. In this context, ''feed'' and ''diet'' are synonyms, as in ''moist diets'' and ''dry diets'' for salmonids. I find this confusing and not particularly useful. As defined here, a *food* is any nutrient source that has not been altered appreciably. Examples are live foods (brine shrimp, rotifers) and natural foods (leafy green vegetables, fish flesh, freeze-dried brine shrimp). *Feed* will refer to manufactured nutrient sources (e.g., alginate- and gelatin-bound moist feeds, dry and moist pellets, flakes). Finally, *diet* is whatever a captive fish eats, ordinarily a combination of foods (live and natural) and feeds. In other words, a fish's *diet* is composed of its daily intake of nutrients and inert items, whatever they are. The foods ingested by coral reef fishes in nature are summarized in Figure 8-1 and Appendix I.

SCIENCE

The raw materials needed for life and growth are *nutrients*, and *nutrition* is the benefit that nutrients confer on living organisms. Plants synthesize the materials they require from inorganic compounds in soil, air, and water. Animals, however, need complex organic substances to conduct the vital functions of tissue maintenance, activity, and growth. These compounds cannot be synthesized and must be obtained secondhand from eating plants or other animals. Most fishes (~75%) are *carnivorous* and feed exclusively on invertebrates and other fishes (Table 8-1). Comparatively few are *herbivorous* and able to derive all their nutrient requirements from plants. More prevalent than the herbivores are the *omnivorous* species, which can use both plant and animal matter. From a practical standpoint there are no herbivorous fishes in captivity; that is, all seawater aquarium fishes known to feed exclusively on plant material in nature will accept animal matter.[1] Herbivores exist as such only in the oceans.

Nutrients

The cells of all plants and animals are composed of living *protoplasm*, a complex mixture of inorganic salts, water, and organic compounds. *Growth* is the synthesis of protoplasm. The organic constituents of protoplasm consist of carbon atoms bonded with hydrogen, oxygen, often nitrogen, and occasionally other elements. Protoplasm consists mainly of three types

	Hawaiian teleosts 107 Species										West Indies teleosts 201 Species									
Teleost species, % / Dietary volume, %	90-100	80-89	70-79	60-69	50-59	40-49	30-39	20-29	10-19	1-9	1-9	10-19	20-29	30-39	40-49	50-59	60-69	70-79	80-89	90-100
Chordata	5	1	1	3	4	1		1	4	22	16	4	4	2	2	2	2	1	2	13
Protochordata						2	2	3	1	11	8	2								
Hemichordata										1										
Echinodermata					1	2		1	3	17	8	5	5	1	1					
Chaetognatha							1	1		1										
Arthropoda	16	8	4	5	7	4	4	9	5	15	12	7	8	6	5	9	4	6	5	10
Annelida								2	6	19	17	10	2	2		1				
Echiuroidea											1									
Sipunculida									1	9	5	1								
Mollusca	1		1		1		3	4	6	20	25	10	6	2	1	1			1	
Nemertinea									1											
Bryozoa									1	3	1									
Ctenophora											1									
Cnidaria	4	2				2	2	1	2	11	10	1	2		1					
Porifera	1	1							2	9	2	1	1		1			1		1
Protozoa							1			2	1									
Protozoa & sand							1		1	2										
Non-algal plants											10	2								
Algae	4		1	1	1	2	2	3	5	19	6	1	1	1		1		1	2	8
Sand										3										
Detritus				1	1	2			2	3										
Unidentified animal matter					4	2	4	14	14	14	19	2	1		1					
Unidentified worms											2									
Unidentified eggs										3	6									

Figure 8-1 *Comparative dietary components of Hawaiian and West Indies coral reef fishes. Data represent numbers of teleost species. For example, 1 to 9% of the dietary volume (i.e., gut contents) was composed of mollusks in 25% of West Indies species examined.* Source: Stephen Spotte, Patricia M. Bubucis, and Gary Adams, Sea Research Foundation; drawn from data in Hobson (1974) and Randall (1967); see Appendix I.

of organic compounds: proteins, lipids, and carbohydrates. The vitamins, which constitute a fourth group, are found only in trace concentrations. The inorganic constituents of protoplasm are usually (and inappropriately) referred to as "minerals." The inorganics in foods and feeds are traditionally expressed as concentrations of individual elements, not as minerals or other precipitates.

TABLE 8-1 Feeding preference of some seawater fishes in captivity.

Carnivores	Omnivores
Basslets	Angelfishes
Bigeyes	Blennies
Brotulids	Butterflyfishes (some)
Butterflyfishes (some)	Cowfishes
Cardinalfishes	Damselfishes (most)
Conger eels	Filefishes
Cornetfishes	Gobies (some)
Croakers	Mullets
Damselfishes (some)	Parrotfishes
Drums	Puffers
Frogfishes	Surgeonfishes
Gobies (some)	Triggerfishes
Goatfishes	
Grunts	
Gunnels	
Hawkfishes	
Jawfishes	
Lizardfishes	
Moray eels	
Pipefishes	
Scorpionfishes	
Sea basses	
Snake eels	
Snappers	
Squirrelfishes	
Sweepers	
Trumpetfishes	
Wrasses	

Source: Stephen Spotte, compiled from information in Hiatt and Strasburg (1960) and Randall (1967); also see Appendix I.

PROTEINS Except for a small amount found in some vitamins, all nitrogen in living tissue is in the form of *proteins* and their basic constituents, the *amino acids*. Proteins contain 21 to 24 different amino acids, and variations in concentration and arrangement account for the nearly infinite variety of proteins found in nature. Proteins are required for tissue maintenance, for the synthesis of new tissue during growth, and as a source of energy. The nutrient requirement for proteins has two aspects: (*1*) the need for "total protein" (or total nitrogen)[2] and (*2*) the need for *essential amino acids*, EAAs, without which animals cannot live. No perfect protein exists; that is, no single protein is the ideal nutrient for a species of animal under all conditions. Amino acid requirements change as an animal grows, adds tissue, repairs or replaces tissue, or adapts its metabolic functions to physical and chemical pressures from the environment. For each such change there exists a particular ratio of amino acids that results in optimal use. Only some amino acids are required, and those that are not are the *nonessential amino acids*. The EAA requirements are known in quantitative terms for only four fishes: chinook salmon (*Oncorhynchus tshawytscha*), common carp (*Cyprinus carpio*), Japanese eel (*Anguilla japonica*), and channel catfish (*Ictalurus punctatus*).[3] All require the 10 amino acids listed in Table 8-2, but the amounts needed vary by species. A chinook salmon, for example, requires a diet consisting of 40 to 41% total protein, 6% of which must be arginine (i.e., 2.4% of the diet). The EAA requirements of seawater aquarium fishes are unknown.

LIPIDS When biological tissues are extracted with organic solvents such as ether, benzene, or chloroform, a portion dissolves. The soluble materials are *lipids*. Lipids are critical com-

TABLE 8-2 Protein and amino acid requirements of the four species of fishes for which complete requirements are known. Numbers in parentheses are percentage of diet. Combined methionine and cystine values are expressed on one line, with values for cystine alone on the line below. The same applies to phenylalanine and tyrosine.

	Chinook salmon	Common carp	Japanese eel	Channel catfish
	Total Dietary Protein, %			
	40–41	38.5	37.7	24
	Amino Acid, % of protein			
Arginine	6.0(2.4)	4.3(1.6)	4.5(1.7)	4.3(1.03)
Histidine	1.8(0.7)	2.1(0.8)	2.1(0.8)	1.5(0.37)
Threonine	2.2(0.9)	3.9(1.5)	4.0(1.5)	2.0(0.53)
Isoleucine	2.2(0.9)	2.5(0.9)	4.0(1.5)	2.6(0.62)
Leucine	3.9(1.6)	3.3(1.3)	5.3(2.0)	3.5(0.84)
Valine	3.2(1.3)	3.6(1.4)	4.0(1.5)	3.0(0.71)
Lysine	5.0(2.0)	5.7(2.2)	5.3(2.0)	5.1(1.23)
Methionine	4.0(1.6)	3.1(1.2)	3.2(1.2)	2.3(0.56)
Cystine	(1.0)	(0.0)	(0.0)	(0.0)
Phenylalanine	5.1(2.1)	6.5(2.5)	5.8(2.2)	5.0(1.20)
Tyrosine	(0.4)	(0.0)	(0.0)	(0.3)
Tryptophan	0.5(0.2)	1.1(0.4)	1.1(0.4)	0.5(0.12)

Source: Wilson (1985).

ponents of cell membranes, helping to keep them plastic and permeable. Lipids are required in the diets of all animals to provide stores of chemical energy, and to supply energy needed immediately for metabolic activities. The simplest lipids are the fats, oils, and waxes, and among their major structural components are the *fatty acids*. Fatty acids are composed of long, mostly even-numbered chains of carbon atoms, usually 14 to 22 (expressed C_{14} to C_{22}). Fatty acids, and lipids generally, are classed as *saturated* or *unsaturated*. Of concern here are fatty acids specifically. Later, when fish feeds are considered, the discussion will focus on the actual lipids, based on their fatty-acid compositions. This is because fats and oils are the materials added to fish feeds, not individual fatty acids.

Unsaturated fatty acids lack hydrogen atoms between two adjacent carbon atoms at one or more sites in the molecule, resulting in double bonds (Fig. 8-2). This distinguishes them from *saturated fatty acids*, which have a full complement of hydrogen atoms and contain only single bonds. *Polyunsaturated fatty acids*, PUFAs, which contain more than two molecular sites with double bonds, are more unsaturated than mono- and diunsaturated species. The actual quantitative estimate of unsaturation is expressed as an *iodine number*, (i.e., grams of iodine taken up by 100 g of lipid). Vegetable and fish oils are more unsaturated than solid animal fats, as indicated by their larger iodine numbers and greater number of double bonds (Table 8-3).

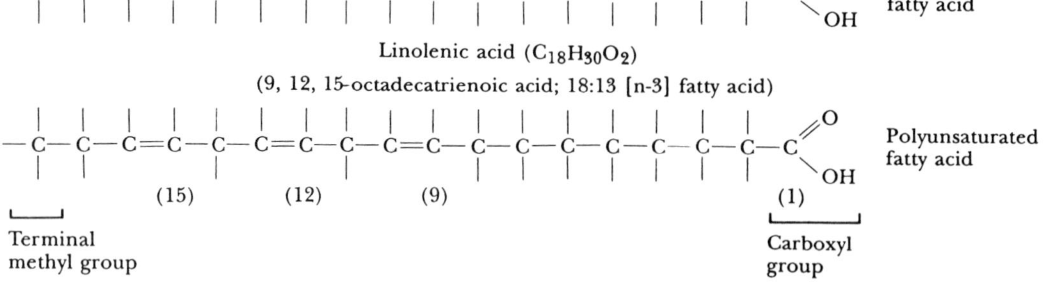

"Octadecane" ($C_{18}H_{38}$)

—C—C—C—C—C—C—C—C—C—C—C—C—C—C—C—C—C—C—

Saturated hydrocarbon

Stearic acid ($C_{18}H_{36}O_2$)

(octadecanoic acid; 18:0 fatty acid)

—C—C—C—C—C—C—C—C—C—C—C—C—C—C—C—C—C—C(=O)OH

Saturated fatty acid

Linolenic acid ($C_{18}H_{30}O_2$)

(9, 12, 15-octadecatrienoic acid; 18:13 [n-3] fatty acid)

—C—C—C=C—C—C=C—C—C=C—C—C—C—C—C—C—C—C(=O)OH

(15) (12) (9) (1)

Polyunsaturated fatty acid

Terminal methyl group

Carboxyl group

Figure 8-2 *Comparative chemical structures and nomenclatures of unsaturated and saturated fatty acids. Open-ended single bonds represent hydrogen bonds.* Source: Patricia M. Bubucis, Sea Research Foundation; drawn from various sources.

TABLE 8-3 Analytical values of representative lipids.

Lipid	Iodine number	Average number of double bonds per molecule
Coconut oil	6–10	0.2
Butter	22–38	0.9
Beef tallow	35–48	1.4
Lard	47–77	2.1
Human fat	57–73	2.2
Cottonseed oil	99–114	3.6
Soybean oil	120–141	4.5
Cod liver oil	137–166	5.6
Menhaden oil	140–185	5.6
Linseed oil	155–205	6.2

Source: Stephen Spotte, compiled from various sources.

Fatty acids are named systematically for the saturated hydrocarbon having the same number of carbons. The suffix -e of the hydrocarbon name is replaced with -oic for fatty acids. The stem of the name indicates the total numbers of carbons and double bonds joining carbons, and the prefix lists the positions of the double bonds, with carbons being numbered from the carboxyl group. For example, the systematic name fo linolenic acid is 9, 12,15-octadecatrienoic acid, indicating 18 (octadeca) carbons with three double bonds (triene) located after the 9th, 12th, and 15th carbons. Biochemists use a shorthand designation in which linolenic acid is written as 18:3(3), 18:3(n-3), or 18:3ω3 fatty acid. The first number (18) is the number of carbon atoms. After the colon is the number (3) of double bonds between carbon atoms, and the number (3) in parentheses or following the omega sign is the number of carbons from the last double bond to the terminal methyl group (Fig. 8-2). Linolenic acid has more than two double bonds and is a ω3-PUFA.

The chemical structures of fatty acids supplied in the diet determine their usefulness. Much of the total fatty acid consumed by a fish is deposited unchanged in the tissues of muscles and organs. The remainder is excreted with the feces or converted to fatty acids of different composition (see below). Whole-body analysis of a fish reveals both the form of the fatty acids it has recently ingested and its fatty-acid requirements. The second part of this statement is somewhat subjective by implying that a fish would not expend the energy to alter the structural compositions of fatty acids it consumes merely to deposit them in a different form, unless prompted by physiological necessity.

Biological membranes have been described as proteins floating in a sea of lipid. For membranes to be functional, the lipids must remain fluid. One characteristic of the aquatic environment is its relatively low and constant temperature. Lipids with high melting points (e.g., beef tallow) are sometimes thought to be poorly absorbed by fishes, particularly at low temperatures.[4] Fluidity (and hence melting point) of a lipid is determined largely by its degree of unsaturation. Long-chain (C_{20} to C_{22}) PUFAs are more fluid at low temperatures than those with shorter chains, and unsaturated fatty acids ordinarily have lower melting points than saturated types. Fishes generally—and seawater species particularly—require a high dietary percentage of long-chain PUFAs of the ω3 series, primarily 20:5ω3 and 22:6ω3. In all fishes ω3-PUFAs are referred to as *essential fatty acids*, EFAs, because they prevent fatty-acid deficiencies (Table 8-4). A high-quality lipid is therefore one that meets an animal's EFA requirements.

Freshwater fishes can use a greater percentage of ω6-PUFAs, perhaps because much of their food is of terrestrial origin.[5] Seawater organisms all the way up the food chain contain more ω3 fatty acids and fewer of the ω6 series, compared with terrestrial animals and plants. Consequently, freshwater fishes have greater tissue concentrations of ω6-PUFAs than do seawater species. In addition, their tissue lipids are higher in short-chain ω3-PUFAs (e.g., 18:3ω3). Fishes that feed on zooplankton can often desaturate short-chain fatty acids in their food, elongate them, and incorporate the long-chain species into their own tissues.[6] Only the large carnivores further up the food chain have natural diets in which 22:6ω3 is the main PUFA, and many are unable to desaturate short-chain fatty acids. In other words, the need to chain-elongate appears to be less pronounced with each step upward in the oceanic food chain. The point is that long-

TABLE 8-4 Essential fatty acid (EFA) requirements of fishes. Requirements range from 0.5 to 2.5% of the diet.

Common name	Scientific name	Requirement
Common carp	*Cyprinus carpio*	18:3ω6 and 18:3ω3
Japanese eel	*Anguilla japonica*	18:2ω6 and 18:3ω3
Tilapia	*Oreochromis zillii*	18:2ω6 or 20:4ω6
Tilapia	*Oreochromis nilotica*	18:2ω6
Ayu	*Plecoglossus altivelis*	18:3ω3 or 20:5ω3
Rainbow trout	*Oncorhynchus mykiss*	18:3ω3
Chum salmon	*Orcorhynchus keta*	18:2ω6 and 18:3ω3
Coho Salmon	*Orcorhynchus kisutch*	18:3ω3
Red seabream	*Chrysophrys major*	20:5ω3 or ω3-PUFAs
Turbot	*Scophthalmus maximus*	ω3-PUFAs

Source: Kanazawa (1985).

chain PUFAs must be supplied in the diet, particularly in the case of large carnivorous species.

CARBOHYDRATES The *carbohydrates* are organic compounds containing carbon, hydrogen, and oxygen, the latter two in a ratio of 2. On a mass basis, more carbohydrate material exists in the world than all other organic substances combined. This is because carbohydrates account for most of the organic structures of plants and are present to some extent in all animals. Carbohydrates sometimes are referred to as *saccharides*, from the Greek word *sakeharon*, meaning sugar. Forms such as glucose,[7] which cannot be hydrolyzed into simpler compounds, are called *monosaccharides* or "simple sugars." Others composed of two monosaccharide molecules (e.g., sucrose, lactose) are *disaccharides*. Those made up of more than two molecules of monosaccharide are *polysaccharides* (the prefix *poly* means many). Polysaccharides are "complex sugars." Typical examples are the starches, glycogen (see below), and *celluloses*. Cellulose, which has the same chemical formula as starch but is a much larger molecule, forms the walls of plant cells. It is relatively insoluble and can be digested by only a few animals. Much of the fiber excreted in the feces of herbivores and omnivores is undigested cellulose. All carbohydrate compounds can be hydrolyzed into their component monosaccharides by the action of specific enzymes.

Regardless of its form, once ingested by an animal every carbohydrate is converted eventually to glucose before being assimilated by the tissues. Glucose is the sugar of blood and other body fluids. Blood glucose serves many functions. The liver removes it, adds other monosaccharide molecules, and forms the polysaccharide *glycogen*, used ultimately as an energy source to sustain physiological activities. Glucose is oxidized preferentially to other physiologically combustible compounds to provide energy. Excess glucose (the amount remaining after energy requirements have been satisfied) is converted to lipids and stored in fatty tissues as reserve energy.

Omnivorous fishes can use carbohydrate effectively, but carnivorous species are more intolerant of it, particularly if the concentration is high.[8] Moreover, every species has its own carbohydrate tolerance level.[9] In many omnivores the ability to digest and use other nutrients (e.g., protein) is unaffected by the concentration of dietary carbohydrate. However, in many carnivores, increased dietary carbohydrate results in decreased efficiency of protein use. Addition of carbohydrate to the diets of carnivores has some *protein sparing effect* (i.e., protein is not used as a source of energy), but the feeding of lipid causes carbohydrate metabolism to decline in these species, and lipid is used as an energy source at an accelerated rate. The addition of both carbohydrate and lipid to the diets of carnivores maintained for exhibit purposes probably is not worthwhile, considering that lipid is used preferentially.[10]

Vitamins

The term *vitamin* refers to a group of organic compounds with similar general functions in metabolism, rather than to chemical compounds with biochemical similarities. Vitamins are sometimes considered nutrients, but unlike proteins, lipids, and carbohydrates they are not incorporated into the tissues. Their function is to catalyze specific biochemical reactions. As catalysts, vitamins regulate the rates of important reactions without being incorporated into the reaction products. Thiamin, for example, catalyzes the oxidation of sugars in the presence of oxygen to release energy to tissues. However, no thiamin is converted to energy in the process. Typically, only tiny concentrations of a substance are needed to perform any catalytic function, and dietary vitamins are not required in large amounts. In correct usage the term *vitamin* is reserved for a compound that an animal cannot synthesize and must acquire in food or as a by-product of the activities of intestinal bacteria, and has no relationship to specific physiological requirements. For example, thiamin probably is required by all animals, but it is vitamin B_1 only in species unable to synthesize it. When vitamin requirements are unknown, as they are in seawater aquarium fishes, it is preferable to use the generic name; however, this is sometimes awkward, and I shall refer to all compounds with ''vitaminlike'' (i.e., catalytic) activities simply as vitamins, with the understanding that some fishes may be able to synthesize one or more of them.

Vitamins ordinarily are separated into two groups, *water soluble* and *lipid soluble*. The physiological functions of water soluble vitamins are similar in all species. Lipid soluble vitamins are required by some groups of animals, but not all. Most fishes are thought to require 11 water soluble vitamins and four that are lipid soluble (Table 8-5). Negative functions caused by vitamin deficiencies are summarized in Table 8-6.

Carotenoid Pigments

Diminished skin coloration is a common occurrence in aquarium fishes, and diet is partly responsible. The foods consumed by fishes in nature contain pigments, some of which are de-

TABLE 8-5 Positive functions of vitamins in fishes.

	Water-soluble Vitamins
Thiamin	Required for good appetite, normal digestion, growth, fertility, normal functioning of nervous tissue
Riboflavin	Involved with pyridoxine in conversion of tryptophan to niacin; important in respiration of poorly vascularized tissues (e.g., cornea); involved in retinal pigmentation during light adaptation
Pyridoxine	Essential for tryptophan use and metabolism of amino acids generally; involved in synthesis of messenger RNA; important in protein metabolism, and stores are exhausted rapidly in carnivorous fishes
Pantothenic acid	Involved in synthesis of acetate, fatty acids, citrate, and in oxidation of pyruvate and acetaldehyde; essential for development of central nervous system; involved in adrenal function; coenzyme A is involved in intermediary metabolism of carbohydrates, lipids, proteins
Niacin	Transfer of H^+ or electrons to other coenzymes; involved in synthesis of high-energy phosphate bonds; involved in lipid, amino acid, protein metabolism
Biotin	Required for several carboxylation and decarboxylation reactions; involved in lipid synthesis generally and chain elongation of fatty acids; involved in conversion of unsaturated fatty acids to stable cis forms
Folic acid	Required for normal blood cell formation; involved in many single carbon metabolism systems (e.g., serine and glycine interconversion); involved in blood glucose regulation; improves cell membrane function and hatching of eggs
Ascorbic acid	Acts as a biological reducing agent for hydrogen transport; involved in many enzyme systems for hydroxylation; involved in detoxification of aromatic drugs; participates in production of adrenal steroids; necessary for formation of collagen and normal cartilage, teeth, and bone; necessary for bone repair and wound healing; acts synergistically with vitamin E in maintenance of intracellular antioxidants and free radical traps, and with vitamin E and selenium to maintain activity of glutathione peroxidase and superoxide dismutase; required for conversion of folic acid to folanic acid; involved in maturation of erythrocytes
Inositol	Structural component of cell membranes; lipotropic action prevents accumulation of cholesterol in one kind of fatty liver disease; involved with choline in homeostatis of lipid metabolism; serves as emer-

TABLE 8-5 *(Continued)*

	gency carbohydrate source in muscle; is a major component in phospholipid structures of animal tissues
Choline	Acts as a methyl donor for methylation of tissue intermediates; lipotropic and antihemorrhagic factor preventing development of fatty livers; involved in synthesis of phospholipids and fat transport; important component of phospholipids in cell membranes; essential for growth and good food conversion
	Fat-soluble Vitamins
A	Essential in maintenance of epithelial cells; promotes growth; stimulates new cell growth; aids in resistance to infectious diseases; essential (with retinene) for normal vision; required for regeneration of light-sensitive rhodopsin in retina
D	Vitamin D_3 functions as a precursor of 1,25-dihydrocholecalciferol, which stimulates calcium adsorption from the intestine; vitamin D maintains constant calcium and inorganic phosphate, is involved in alkaline phosphatase activity, promotes calcium adsorption, influences action of parathyroid hormone on bone
E	The tocopherols maintain homeostasis of cellular and plasma metabolites by acting as intra- and intercellular antioxidants, protect oxidizable vitamins and unsaturated fatty acids, and act as free radical traps to stop the chain reaction during peroxide formation and stabilize unsaturated carbon bonds of PUFAs; function with selenium and ascorbic acid to stop the chain reaction of PUFA peroxidation, help maintain permeability of capillaries and heart muscle, and may be involved in membrane permeability of fish eggs; involved with selenium and ascorbic acid in prevention of nutritional muscular dystrophy
K	Involved in messenger RNA synthesis and synthesis of blood clotting proteins; promotes rapid blood clotting; perhaps bacteriostatic; involved with vitamins A, E, and ascorbic acid in homeostatis of physiologically active vitamins A and E

Source: Stephen Spotte, compiled from information in Halver (1989).

posited in the skin, muscle, gonads, liver, and eyes.[11] In contrast, the foods and feeds offered to captive fishes are often deficient in pigment-producing compounds. The discussion here is limited to a single class, the carotenoid pigments.

The *carotenoids* are lipid soluble, yellow to orange-red pig-

TABLE 8-6 Negative functions (clinical signs and pathological effects) caused by vitamin deficiencies.

Vitamin	Signs
Thiamin	Poor appetite, muscle atrophy, convulsions, instability and loss of equilibrium, edema, poor growth
Riboflavin	Corneal vascularization, cloudy lens, hemorrhagic eyes, photophobia, dim vision, incoordination, abnormal pigmentation of iris, striated constrictions of abdominal wall, dark coloration, poor appetite, anemia, poor growth
Pyridoxine	Nervous disorders, epileptiform fits, hyperirritability, ataxia, anemia, anorexia, edema of peritoneal cavity, colorless serous fluid, rapid postmortem rigor mortis, rapid and gasping breathing, flexing of opercula
Pantothenic acid	Clubbed gills, prostration, anorexia, necrosis and scarring, cellular atrophy, gill exudate, sluggishness, poor growth
Niacin	Loss of appetite, lesions in colon, jerky or difficult motion, weakness, edema of stomach and colon, muscle spasms while resting, poor growth
Biotin	Anorexia, lesions in colon, muscle atrophy, spastic convulsions, fragmentation of erythrocytes, skin lesions, poor growth
Folic acid	Poor growth, lethargy, fragility of caudal fin, dark coloration, macrocytic anemia
Ascorbic acid	Scoliosis; lordosis; impaired collagen formation; altered cartilage; eye lesions; hemorrhagic skin, liver, kidney, intestine, muscle
*Myo*inositol	Poor growth, distended stomach, increased gastric emptying time, skin lesions
Choline	Poor growth; poor food conversion; hemorrhagic kidney, intestine
p-Aminobenzoic acid	No abnormal indication in growth, appetite, or mortality
Cyanocobalamin	Poor appetite, low hemoglobin, fragmentation of erythrocytes, macrocytic anemia
A	Impaired growth, exophthalmia, eye lens displacement, edema, ascites, depigmentation, corneal thinning and expansion, degeneration of retina
D	Poor growth, tetany of white skeletal muscle, impaired calcium homeostasis
E	Reduced survival, poor growth, anemia, ascites, immature erythrocytes, variable-sized erythrocytes, erythrocyte fragility and fragmentation, nutritional muscular dystrophy, elevated body water volume
K	Prolonged blood clotting, anemia, lipid peroxidation, reduced hematocrit

Source: Halver (1989).

ments responsible for the yellow, orange, and red coloration of fishes and other animals. Carotenoids accumulate through the food chain, starting with their manufacture by organisms capable of photosynthesis (in the sea, mainly algae plus certain photosynthetic bacteria and yeasts). Fishes and other animals are unable to synthesize carotenoids and can acquire them only by ingestion. Afterward, the original plant precursors (e.g., β-carotene) are often transformed into other carotenoids and intermediate compounds before being deposited. *Carotenoid pigmentation* is the biochemical process in which carotenoids are deposited by animals.[12] Two pathways are possible: (*1*) the pigment is ingested and later deposited in the same structural form, or (*2*) the ingested pigment is modified structurally to one or more different carotenoids before deposition.[13] The outcome depends on the form in which the pigment is ingested, requirements of the target tissue, and species of animal.[14] Canthaxanthin, astaxanthin, and zeaxanthin apparently are the prevalent end products of carotenoid metabolism in fishes.[14]

More than 400 carotenoids have been identified.[15] Of these, β-carotene, lutein, canthaxanthin, astaxanthin, tunaxanthin, and zeaxanthin occur either in fishes or in invertebrates consumed by fishes in nature. In the past, fishes have been classed by their capacity to use carotenoids,[16] but recent research has blurred these distinctions (Table 8-7). Class 1 fishes (''carp types'') can convert lutein (a yellow carotenoid), zeaxanthin, or intermediate compounds to astaxanthin, which is then depos-

TABLE 8-7 Classes of fishes by use of carotenoid pigments.

Class 1—''carp-type'' fishes
Convert lutein and zeaxanthin to astaxanthin; alternatively, do not deposit astaxanthin, but convert it to zeaxanthin
Do not convert β-carotene and canthaxanthin to astaxanthin
Lutein, zeaxanthin, or canthaxanthin must be supplied in the diet
Class 2—''red seabream-type'' fishes
Do not convert β-carotene, lutein, or canthaxanthin to astaxanthin
Directly deposit lutein, zeaxanthin, canthaxanthin, and astaxanthin
May convert astaxanthin to tunaxanthin via zeaxanthin, but deposit astaxanthin preferentially
Can convert zeaxanthin to astaxanthin
Canthaxanthin or astaxanthin must be supplied in the diet; in some species zeaxanthin can perhaps be substituted for astaxanthin

Source: Stephen Spotte, compiled from information in Katsuyama et al. (1987) and Meyers and Chen (1982).

ited. In other words, Class 1 fishes (principally herbivores and omnivores) can make direct use of carotenoids in plant material. Canthaxanthin and astaxanthin can also be ingested and deposited directly, but β-carotene is thought to be an inefficient precursor of astaxanthin. Lutein, zeaxanthin, or canthaxanthin must be supplied in the diet for normal pigmentation to be maintained.

Class 2 fishes (''red seabream types,'' including salmonids) are unable to convert β-carotene, lutein, or zeaxanthin to astaxanthin. Canthaxanthin and astaxanthin must be supplied in the diet for maintenance of normal pigmentation. Crustaceans can convert β-carotene to astaxanthin.

Digestion Rate and Digestibility

The food ingested by an animal has no nutrient value until it has been dissolved, or *digested*, and the simplified components rendered suitable for assimilation by the tissues. During digestion, proteins are reduced to amino acids, lipids to fatty acids, and carbohydrates to monosaccharides. Indigestible (i.e., inert) material is formed into feces and excreted. The time necessary for digestion to occur is affected by two factors: (*1*) water temperature and (*2*) the *digestibility*, or ease of dissolution, of the food. Ordinarily, an increase in temperature increases the digestion rate, regardless of a food's original composition. Digestibility depends on the composition of the food, in addition to the capacity of individual species to digest it. Omnivores produce more feces than carnivores because much of the plant material in their diets is indigestible. The comparatively fewer fecal materials produced by carnivores is the result of ingesting animal flesh, which is highly digestible. Carnivorous fishes that feed on animals closer to their own body size generally take longer to digest food than species that eat fishes and invertebrates much smaller than they are. Fishes that consume algae, detritus, and zooplankton have the fastest digestion rates. Algae are low in nutrients compared with animal flesh, and more must be ingested and processed over the same length of time before an equivalent nutritional benefit is gained.

Energy

Animals eat primarily to satisfy their energy requirements. All vital life processes require energy, and the origin of an animal's energy is contained in what it eats. After an animal has eaten and satisfied its immediate energy needs, excess dietary energy is stored or excreted. In fishes that are sedentary, stored energy is often lipid or glycogen deposited in the liver and other organs. Active fishes store the excess in muscle tissue, where it can be quickly mobilized to supply energy directly to muscles used in swimming.

PHYSIOLOGICAL FUEL VALUES Dietary energy is measured in calories, cal. A *calorie* is the amount of heat needed to raise the temperature of 1 g of water from 14.5 to 15.5°C. A *kilocalorie,* kcal, is 1000 calories. In older usage kilocalorie was synonymous with *Calorie,* written with a capital ''C,'' but many authors neglected to capitalize the term, which led to widespread confusion (the basic, or ''little calorie,'' is traditionally expressed with a lowercase ''c''). In this discussion, specific quantities of dietary energy are expressed in kilocalories, and the term calorie will be used when referring to energy in a general sense. In nutrition, protein and carbohydrate are assigned values of 4 kcal/g, and fat is considered to contain 9 kcal/g. Vitamins and minerals have no energy value and therefore contain no calories. The values just stated for protein, carbohydrate, and fat are the standard *physiological fuel values* used to compute the amount of energy in food.

METABOLISM *Metabolism* is the sum of all biochemical changes by which food is transformed for maintenance of the tissues, activity, and growth. However, before growth can occur, or excess energy ingested can be stored for later use, basic maintenance requirements must be satisfied. The minimum rate of energy expended is an animal's basal or *standard metabolism,* defined as the minimum energy required to sustain life. *Routine metabolism* refers to the energy requirements of an animal that is behaving normally and spontaneously, and ordinarily is twice the standard metabolic rate. *Active metabolism* describes the outer limits of an animal's endurance by representing the most energy that can be expended above the maximum level of sustained activity. Between routine and active metabolism is *feeding metabolism,* which is a measure of the inevitable increase in metabolic rate after an animal eats and often lasts for several days. Feeding metabolism is four times the standard metabolic rate.

PARTITIONING OF ENERGY Only a portion of the energy ingested by a fish or any other animal is used directly for tissue maintenance, activity, and growth (Table 8-8). Moreover, because maintenance and activity constitute an energy loss they are antagonistic with growth, which represents a gain in energy

TABLE 8-8 Percentage of energy partitioning in carnivorous and omnivorous fishes.

Feeding type	Metabolism	Growth	Excretion
Carnivore	44	29	
Omnivore	37	20	43

Source: Brett and Groves (1979).

through the addition of new tissue. Thus an increase in the metabolic rate depresses growth, especially if food is unavailable in sufficient quantities or is of such poor quality that the fish cannot compensate by increasing its food intake. Metabolic energy is derived from dietary calories, and the cost is considerable. In a typical carnivorous fish the relationship is expressed by

$$\text{Ingestion rate} = \text{Metabolic rate} + \text{Growth rate} + \text{Excretion rate} \quad (8.1)$$

For 100 kcal of *gross energy* ingested (the amount of energy determined in the laboratory with a bomb calorimeter), 20 kcal are excreted in the feces leaving 80 kcal as *digestible* (usable) *energy*. Of these, 7 kcal are excreted by the gills and kidneys (ammonia and urea combined), leaving 73 kcal of *metabolizable* (available) *energy*. A total of 14 kcal is expended during conversion of metabolizable energy to *net energy*, which is the energy remaining for maintenance, activity, and growth. Of these 59 kcal, 7 kcal are required for standard metabolism in an inactive, nonfeeding fish. The entire 59 kcal may be required by an active fish, leaving none for growth. In a growing fish, 29 kcal of the net energy can be used to synthesize new tissue.

ENERGY REQUIREMENTS The energy requirement of a fish depends on its activity level, temperature, and body size. The metabolism of nutrients produces heat. Fishes are *ectothermic* or ''cold blooded,'' and the heat produced is dissipated into the environment. In *endothermic* (''warm-blooded'') animals, metabolic heat is used to maintain stable body temperature. In fishes, an increase in water temperature of 10°C raises the standard metabolic rate by a factor of ~2.3. Size is another influential factor, and body size and energy requirements are inversely related; that is, smaller specimens have higher energy requirements than larger specimens of the same species. The minimum energy expenditures of fishes are poorly known, but a general guide is presented in Table 8-9. As shown, the stan-

TABLE 8-9 Effect of temperature on minimum energy expenditure by type of metabolism. Units are kcal/(h · kg).

Habitat	Temperature, °C	Standard	Routine	Feeding
Temperate seas	15	0.35	0.70	1.40
Tropical seas	26	0.50	1.00	1.50

Source: Brett and Groves (1979).

dard metabolic rates of tropical fishes are approximately 70% greater than those of temperate species.

Natural Foods

Natural foods are obtained fresh, frozen, or freeze-dried (*lyophilized*) and fed fresh, thawed, cooked, or freeze-dried. Typical natural foods are leafy green vegetables fed fresh or thawed after freezing, cooked or fresh fish and invertebrate flesh, and thawed or freeze-dried brine shrimp and other zooplankton. The nutrient composition of foods and feeds is expressed as *proximate composition*, determined in the laboratory by a series of tests that in sum are called *proximate analysis*. Proximate analysis provides a measure of energy (kcal/100 g) and also the amount of water, protein, lipid, carbohydrate, and ash (all in units of g/100 g). *Ash* is the inorganic residue remaining after the organic material has been combusted, and it shows how much of the food (as percentage dry mass) is undigestible. Fiber forms part of the proximate analysis if the food is plant material.

LEAFY GREEN VEGETABLES As shown by the proximate analyses in Tables 8-10 and 8-11, raw leafy green vegetables are

TABLE 8-10 Energy (kcal/100 g) and proximate composition (g/100 g) of fresh leafy green vegetables.

Vegetable	Energy	Water	Protein	Lipid	Carbohydrate	Ash	Fiber
Cabbage	24	92	1.4	0.2	5.3	0.8	1.0
Chard	21	92	1.4	0.2	4.4	2.2	0.9
Dandelion greens	44	86	2.7	0.7	8.8	2.0	1.8
Kale	40	87	3.9	0.6	7.2	1.7	1.2
Lettuce, headed	15	95	1.2	0.1	12.3	0.8	0.6
Mustard greens	22	92	2.3	0.3	4.0	1.2	0.8
Parsley	50	84	3.7	1.0	9.0	2.4	1.8
Spinach	20	93	2.3	0.3	3.2	1.5	0.6
Turnip greens	30	90	2.9	0.4	5.4	1.8	1.2
Watercress	18	94	1.7	0.3	3.3	1.1	0.5

Source: Albritton (1954).

TABLE 8-11 Concentrations of common vitamins (mg/100 g) in fresh leafy green vegetables.

Vegetable	β-carotene[1]	Ascorbic acid	Niacin	Riboflavin	Thiamin
Cabbage	0.05	50	0.3	0.05	0.06
Chard	1.68	38	0.4	0.07	0.06
Dandelion greens	8.19	36	0.8	0.14	0.19
Kale	4.52	115	2.0	0.26	0.10
Lettuce, headed	0.32	8	0.2	0.08	0.04
Mustard greens	3.88	102	0.8	0.20	0.09
Parsley	4.94	193	1.4	0.28	0.11
Spinach	5.65	59	0.6	0.20	0.11
Turnip greens	5.72	136	0.8	0.46	0.09
Watercress	2.83	77	0.8	0.16	0.08

Source: Albritton (1954).

Note: Vitamin A activity.[1]

composed mostly of water and are low in energy, protein, and lipid, but contain relatively high concentrations of carbohydrate, ash, fiber, and certain vitamins.

FISH AND INVERTEBRATE FLESH Captive fishes can be fed a variety of seafoods, either fresh, thawed, or cooked (boiled, steamed, or canned in water). Cooking does not alter the proximate composition much, and the energy content per gram actually increases because the percentage of tissue water is lowered (Table 8-12). Raw seafoods have been implicated in the transmission of certain infectious diseases to captive fishes (Chapter 9), and their use is not recommended. Compared with leafy green vegetables, the tissues of fishes and invertebrates contain less water, slightly less ash, and no fiber. They contain substantially more protein and lipid and less carbohydrate, although exceptions are the bivalve mollusks (clams, oysters, and mussels), which equal some of the leafy green vegetables in carbohydrate concentration. Do not use products canned in oil. Relevant data for other tissue constituents of raw commercial fishes and invertebrates are listed in Tables 8-13 through 8-17.

The tissues of some fishes and invertebrates contain *thiaminase*, an enzyme that catalyzes the breakdown of thiamin. Such species are *thiaminase positive* (Table 8-18). Exhibit fishes fed exclusively on the raw flesh of thiaminase-positive animals may become thiamin-deficient. The effect is neutralized by cooking: thiaminase and most other enzymes are destroyed by heat.

FREEZE-DRIED FOODS The process of *lyophilization* or *freeze-drying* has been known since the end of the last century, but was first introduced on a production scale during World War II

TABLE 8-12 Proximate composition of representative commercial fishes and invertebrates (muscle tissue unless otherwise indicated). Units are g/100 g except energy, which is kcal/100 g.

Common name	Scientific name	Water	Protein	Lipid	Ash	Carbohydrate	Energy
		Fishes					
Atlantic herring	*Clupea harengus harengus*	74.3	18.0	9.8	1.6	0.0	160
Pacific herring	*Clupea harengus pallasi*	72.8	18.3	8.5	1.3	0.0	150
Northern anchovy[1]	*Engraulis mordax*	71.2	13.8	10.7	3.8	0.0	152
Pacific anchovy[1]	*Engraulis japonicus*	70.3	16.6	4.8	5.2	3.1	122
Longjaw cisco	*Coregonus alpenae*	73.3	15.3	10.3	1.1	0.0	154
European pilchard	*Clupea pilchardus*	71.7	19.5	5.9	2.3	0.6	134
Spanish sardine[1]	*Sardinella aurita*	71.6	19.0	3.6	6.5	0.0	108
Rainbow smelt[1]	*Osmerus mordax*	79.9	15.5	4.0	2.3	0.0	98
Capelin	*Mallotus villosus*	81.8	15.0	3.1	0.6	0.0	88
Atlantic cod	*Gadus morhua*	80.9	16.9	0.6	1.7	0.0	73
Pacific cod	*Gadus macrocephalus*	82.1	16.7	0.7	1.0	0.0	70
Haddock	*Melanogrammus aeglefinus*	80.6	18.2	0.5	1.3	0.0	77
Pollock	*Pollachius virens*	78.9	19.2	0.8	1.4	0.0	84
Pacific hake	*Merluccius productus*	81.2	16.6	1.7	1.2	0.0	82
Silver hake	*Merluccius bilinearis*	80.3	16.6	1.3	1.2	7.2	107
Walleye pollock	*Theragra chalcogramma*	81.2	16.7	0.8	1.1	0.0	74
Starry flounder	*Platichthys stellatus*	80.2	17.1	1.8	1.1	0.0	85
Summer flounder	*Paralichthys dentatus*	78.8	20.0	0.4	1.1	0.0	84
Winter flounder	*Pseudopleuronectes americanus*	80.1	18.0	0.6	1.2	0.0	77
Witch flounder	*Glyptocephalus cynoglossus*	80.7	16.2	0.6	0.7	1.8	77
Atlantic halibut	*Hippoglossus hippoglossus*	77.7	18.0	2.7	1.1	0.5	98
Pacific halibut	*Hippoglossus stenolepis*	78.0	19.9	1.3	1.3	0.0	91
Atlantic mackerel	*Scomber scombrus*	61.6	19.6	9.6	1.5	8.2	198
Chub mackerel	*Scomber japonicus*	70.8	20.6	6.6	2.0	0.0	142
Albacore	*Thunnus alalunga*	67.6	25.2	6.3	1.4	0.0	158
Yellowfin tuna[2]	*Thunnus albacares*	70.6	23.4	4.1	1.7	0.2	131
Blue runner	*Caranx crysos*	75.2	21.5	2.2	1.5	0.0	96
Bluefish	*Pomatomus saltatrix*	75.0	20.6	3.8	1.5	0.0	96
Lingcod	*Ophiodon elongatus*	79.5	18.0	0.9	1.2	0.4	82
Striped mullet	*Mugil cephalus*	72.4	19.2	6.0	1.3	1.1	135
Redfish (ocean perch)	*Sebastes marinus*	77.7	18.4	3.1	1.2	0.0	102
Deepwater redfish	*Sebastes mentella*	75.8	18.5	4.8	1.1	0.0	117
Freshwater drum	*Aplodinotus grunniens*	76.7	17.4	5.5	1.1	0.0	119
		Invertebrates					
Blue crab	*Callinectes sapidus*	80.3	15.9	1.3	1.9	0.6	78
Dungeness crab	*Cancer magister*	80.0	17.3	1.3	1.5	0.0	81
King crab	*Paralithodes camtschatica*	81.9	15.2	0.8	1.5	0.6	70

TABLE 8-12 (*Continued*)

Common name	Scientific name	Water	Protein	Lipid	Ash	Carbohydrate	Energy
	Invertebrates (Continued)						
Snow crab	*Chinoectes bairdi*	79.7	18.4	1.3	1.2	0.0	85
Brown shrimp	*Penaeus aztecus*	76.2	21.8	0.8	1.6	0.0	94
Pink shrimp	*Penaeus duorarum*	77.9	20.2	0.7	1.7	0.0	87
White shrimp	*Penaeus setiferus*	78.9	19.4	0.3	1.4	0.0	80
Freshwater clam[1]	*Corbicula strata*	77.6	5.8	4.0	1.6	11.0	103
Bean clam[1]	*Donax radians*	85.2	8.8	1.7	2.2	5.1	74
Surf clam	*Spisula solidissema*	82.8	13.5	0.5	1.1	2.1	67
Razor clam[1]	*Solen siliqua*	80.5	11.1	1.8	2.0	2.0	71
Softshell clam[1]	*Mya arenaria*	84.6	10.7	1.2	1.4	2.1	62
Geoduck[1]	*Panope genirosa*	78.0	15.5	2.0	3.2	1.3	85
Quahog[1]	*Mercenaria mercenaria*	86.2	8.7	0.9	1.6	2.8	54
Blue mussel[1]	*Mytilus edulis*	80.0	11.6	1.7	2.2	4.5	80
Common oyster[1]	*Crassostrea edulis*	81.0	10.3	1.6	2.2	4.9	75
Eastern oyster[1]	*Crassostrea virginica*	84.0	7.9	1.7	1.6	4.8	72
Pacific oyster[1]	*Crassostrea gigas*	79.5	11.1	2.1	1.5	5.8	86
Bay scallop	*Aequipecten irradians*	80.2	14.8	0.6	1.5	2.9	76
Sea scallop	*Pecten magellanicus*	77.8	17.4	0.6	1.6	2.6	85
Longfinned squid	*Loligo pealei*	78.5	13.2	0.7	1.6	6.0	83
Pacific squid	*Loligo opalescens*	79.4	16.6	1.4	1.0	1.6	85

Source: Sidwell (1981).

Notes: Whole,[1] dark muscle tissue.[2]

for the preservation of blood plasma and manufacture of penicillin, the first mass-produced antibacterial compound derived from a microorganism.[17] Freeze-drying involves three steps: (*1*) freezing the material to be preserved, (*2*) drying by direct extraction of the ice as water vapor under high vacuum (a procedure called *sublimation*), and (*3*) storing the finished product in vacuum-sealed containers to prevent contamination by water and oxygen. Freeze-dried adult brine shrimp are available. Vacuum-freeze-dried, or simply *vacuum-dried* brine shrimp differ from the other freeze-dried product only in nuances of the manufacturing process (in vacuum-drying the freezing step is retained but the material is desiccated under lower vacuum).

Freeze-dried and vacuum-dried brine shrimp nauplii retain the same fatty acid composition and approximately the same total lipid concentration as freshly killed brine nauplii.[18] It has not been shown that freeze- or vacuum-dried nauplii or adults are a complete dietary substitute for live brine shrimp.

Moist Feeds

Dry feeds ordinarily contain <20% water, whereas the water content of moist feeds is 20 to 50%.[19] The manufacture of dry

TABLE 8-13 Essential amino acid composition in raw muscle tissue of representative commercial fishes and invertebrates. Units are g/100 g total protein; dashes indicate no data.

Common name	Scientific name	Arginine	Histidine	Threonine	Isoleucine	Leucine	Valine	Lysine	Methionine /cystine	Phenylalanine /tyrosine	Tryptophan
					Fishes						
Atlantic herring	*Clupea harengus harengus*	1.2	2.7	5.3	5.1	9.6	6.0	8.6	2.0/6.2	4.7/4.1	11.0
Pacific herring	*Clupea harengus pallasi*	5.5	2.2	4.4	4.8	7.4	5.2	8.4	2.7/1.1	3.9/—	0.9
Pacific anchovy	*Engraulis japonicus*	6.5	2.6	5.3	5.6	9.7	6.0	9.6	3.5/0.9	4.7/4.0	1.4
Atlantic cod	*Gadus morhua*	6.1	1.9	3.7	4.3	6.7	5.0	8.5	3.0/1.4	3.5/3.0	1.2
Haddock	*Melanogrammus aeglefinus*	6.4	2.1	4.2	5.1	7.7	5.3	9.4	3.1/1.0	3.8/3.0	1.2
Silver hake	*Merluccius bilinearis*	5.7	1.7	4.6	4.2	7.1	4.8	9.1	3.0/2.1	3.9/3.0	1.0
Red hake	*Urophycis chuss*	5.9	1.8	4.1	4.0	6.6	4.6	7.6	2.8/—	3.6/2.8	—
Pacific halibut	*Hippoglossus stenolepis*	5.8	2.5	4.3	4.3	7.7	5.0	8.8	3.0/1.5	3.6/3.4	—
Atlantic mackerel	*Scomber scombrus*	5.6	4.0	4.7	4.7	7.3	5.2	8.2	2.8/—	3.3/—	0.9
Chub mackerel	*Scomber japonicus*	6.0	3.2	5.0	6.8	7.7	7.1	9.2	3.0/1.1	4.4/3.9	1.2
Yellowfin tuna	*Thunnus albacares*	5.5	5.3	3.5	4.0	6.2	7.2	8.5	2.6/1.2	3.1/4.2	1.7
Blue runner	*Caranx crysos*	5.8	3.3	4.8	4.5	8.4	5.2	9.6	3.1/—	4.1/3.1	—
Striped mullet	*Mugil cephalus*	7.4	3.1	4.1	4.1	7.9	4.8	10.7	2.6/2.4	3.4/3.0	—
					Invertebrates						
Blue crab	*Callinectes sapidus*	8.6	1.8	3.7	4.1	7.0	4.3	7.3	2.4/1.5	3.5/3.3	1.3
Dungeness crab	*Cancer magister*	11.0	2.2	3.6	3.5	5.9	4.8	8.5	2.5/0.6	3.2/2.9	1.8
White shrimp	*Penaeus setiferus*	8.0	2.6	3.3	3.8	7.5	4.3	7.8	2.7/1.8	3.6/4.0	1.2
Brown shrimp	*Penaeus aztecus*	9.5	1.9	3.6	4.3	7.7	4.4	7.1	2.3/1.2	3.3/2.4	1.4
Quahog	*Mercenaria mercenaria*	5.8	1.4	4.1	3.5	6.2	3.6	5.2	1.9/—	2.4/2.9	1.4
Eastern oyster, whole	*Crassostrea virginica*	6.0	1.9	4.2	3.5	4.0	6.3	5.8	2.0/—	3.3/3.8	9.9
Pacific oyster, whole	*Crassostrea gigas*	6.2	2.0	3.8	4.9	6.7	4.3	6.0	2.2/1.4	3.5/2.8	0.8
Longfinned squid	*Loligo pealei*	5.7	1.5	3.5	3.7	6.9	3.0	7.2	2.3/—	2.7/1.8	10.7
Pacific squid	*Loligo opalescens*	6.3	2.5	3.7	3.7	6.9	3.3	7.5	2.2/—	2.7/1.8	—

Source: Sidwell (1981).

TABLE 8-14 Selected fatty acids in raw commercial fishes and invertebrates. Units are g/100 g total lipid; dashes indicate no data.

Common name	Scientific name	10:0	12:0	14:0	14:1	15:0	16:0	16:1	16:2	17:0	18:0	18:1	18:2	18:3	18:4	20:1	20:2	20:5	22:1	22:2	22:5	22:6
										Fishes												
Anchoveta[1]	*Engraulis ringens*	—	0.3	8.4	0.6	1.3	21.7	7.9	—	1.6	7.2	13.0	3.0	—	—	—	0.6	10.0	—	0.6	0.9	10.7
Rainbow smelt[2]	*Osmerus mordax*	—	—	3.0	0.2	1.4	17.8	10.2	0.5	0.8	2.6	21.7	0.8	0.3	0.9	1.3	0.2	13.3	0.0	—	0.6	18.1
Sprat[1]	*Sprattus sprattus*	—	0.1	7.6	0.1	0.7	20.8	5.7	0.3	0.3	2.0	17.9	1.4	1.0	2.1	8.6	0.3	5.2	13.7	—	0.7	8.1
Capelin[1]	*Mallotus villosus*	—	0.1	7.1	0.1	0.7	9.1	12.5	0.7	0.2	0.9	11.8	0.9	0.4	1.1	20.4	0.2	6.7	2.5	—	0.5	3.2
Hake[3]	Gadidae	—	—	2.8	—	0.5	34.6	4.9	—	—	11.4	23.7	4.0	0.5	—	—	—	—	2.5	—	1.4	9.6
Atlantic mackerel[3]	*Scomber scombrus*	—	0.1	5.5	0.0	0.5	17.3	5.6	—	0.3	3.3	14.2	1.6	0.9	1.6	8.8	0.4	6.5	12.8	—	1.7	12.9
Menhaden[1]	Clupeidae	—	—	6.6	0.0	0.3	13.0	11.2	0.0	1.6	3.6	21.8	3.2	3.0	2.9	3.2	0.2	13.7	—	—	2.1	10.6
Skipjack tuna[3]	*Euthynnus pelamis*	—	0.1	2.0	0.9	1.4	30.0	2.5	—	—	16.6	24.0	0.6	0.2	0.7	0.9	—	10.2	—	—	1.0	3.2
										Invertebrates												
Blue crab	*Callinectes sapidus*	—	1.7	1.2	0.6	1.1	13.2	5.1	0.8	1.5	14.6	3.0	0.7	—	—	1.3	—	9.8	—	—	—	—
Dungeness crab	*Cancer magister*	—	0.3	0.8	0.4	0.3	9.4	4.6	0.7	1.0	7.1	7.8	3.4	7.1	0.8	—	5.6	—	0.3	—	—	0.9
Brown shrimp	*Penaeus aztecus*	—	—	1.0	0.9	0.2	16.3	5.8	—	2.3	4.4	10.0	7.7	1.7	—	—	4.3	—	0.8	—	2.8	—

Source: Sidwell (1981).

TABLE 8-15 Mean concentrations of vitamins in raw muscle tissue of representative commercial fishes and invertebrates. Units are per 100 g; dashes indicate no data.

Common name	Scientific name	A, mg	Thiamin, μg	Riboflavin, μg	Niacin, mg	Ascorbic acid, mg	Folic acid, μg	Cyanocobalamin, μg
			Fishes					
Atlantic herring	*Clupea harengus harengus*	167.57	82.60	266.00	4.53	2.70	1.60	10.00
Pacific herring	*Clupea harengus pallasi*	100.00	64.33	195.67	2.20	—	—	1.72
Anchovy	*Engraulidae*	490.67	68.33	200.16	3.14	—	12.30	6.30
Atlantic cod	*Gadus morhua*	37.50	115.50	237.80	1.91	2.00	—	0.75
Pacific cod	*Gadus macrocephalus*	—	98.50	158.00	—	—	6.60	0.09
Haddock	*Melanogrammus aeglefinus*	36.50	64.02	145.27	3.02	—	0.81	1.21
Atlantic halibut	*Hippoglossus hippoglossus*	—	89.92	94.87	4.47	—	—	0.85
Atlantic mackerel	*Scomber scombrus*	131.67	84.60	372.86	7.68	4.00	1.30	5.25
Chub mackerel	*Scomber japonicus*	6.60	144.50	140.00	6.50	2.00	—	3.52
Yellowfin tuna	*Thunnus albacares*	30.00	211.33	70.80	12.17	1.00	1.92	0.52
Striped mullet	*Mugil cephalus*	150.00	85.50	82.00	5.16	0.60	8.50	0.22
			Invertebrates					
Blue crab	*Callinectes sapidus*	5.00	83.40	45.00	2.70	3.00	—	—
Dungeness crab	*Cancer magister*	—	176.00	20.00	—	—	—	—
Shrimp	Penaeidae	188.88	42.20	65.52	2.54	2.28	9.64	3.72
Eastern oyster	*Crassostrea virginica*	300.00	147.40	190.94	1.96	—	—	18.00
Pacific oyster	*Crassostrea gigas*	—	—	—	2.22	22.30	9.60	16.00
Squid	Unspecified	5.00	25.16	91.59	2.24	—	—	—

Source: Sidwell (1981).

TABLE 8-16 Mean concentrations of trace elements in raw muscle tissue of representative commercial fishes and invertebrates. Units are mg/kg; dashes indicate no data.

Common name	Scientific name	Fe	I	Se	Cu	Zn	Mn
		Fishes					
Atlantic herring	*Clupea harengus harengus*	10.00	—	0.421	0.918	6.42	0.279
Pacific herring	*Clupea harengus pallasi*	17.00	0.37	0.566	0.686	4.40	0.364
Northern anchovy	*Engraulis mordax*	—	—	0.531	1.066	23.15	4.872
Atlantic cod	*Gadus morhua*	17.50	0.41	0.395	0.247	3.82	0.144
Pacific cod	*Gadus macrocephalus*	—	—	0.566	0.235	3.83	0.138
Haddock	*Melanogrammus aeglefinus*	6.79	1.80	0.365	0.239	3.17	0.171
Silver hake	*Merluccius bilinearis*	—	—	0.449	0.280	4.49	0.149
Red hake	*Urophycis chuss*	—	—	0.375	0.401	2.75	0.162
Pacific halibut	*Hippoglossus stenolepis*	0.90	0.28	0.902	0.152	3.26	0.095
Atlantic Mackerel	*Scomber scombrus*	10.12	1.00	0.612	0.733	7.90	0.163
Chub mackerel	*Scomber japonicus*	4.20	—	0.612	0.658	8.79	0.143
Yellowfin tuna	*Thunnus albacares*	27.04	—	0.836	0.417	3.77	0.127
Blue runner	*Caranx crysos*	—	—	0.731	0.927	5.62	0.165
Striped mullet	*Mugil cephalus*	14.61	3.30	0.378	0.390	5.07	0.266
		Invertebrates					
Blue crab	*Callinectes sapidus*	—	—	0.943	4.521	22.74	0.300
Dungeness crab	*Cancer magister*	3.65	0.10	0.571	5.576	52.03	0.688
White shrimp	*Penaeus setiferus*	—	0.45	0.708	1.991	10.67	0.710
Brown shrimp	*Penaeus aztecus*	17.80	—	0.589	3.760	11.76	0.410
Quahog	*Mercenaria mercenaria*	30.00	0.16	0.451	5.168	27.41	17.111
Eastern oyster, whole	*Crassostrea virginica*	65.65	0.31	0.398	5.808	205.59	1.711
Pacific oyster, whole	*Crassostrea gigas*	62.25	—	0.798	18.559	119.71	10.150
Longfinned squid	*Loligo pealei*	—	—	0.593	3.962	12.40	0.256
Pacific squid	*Loligo opalescens*	—	—	0.407	3.078	10.87	0.333

Sources: Fe and I from Sidwell (1981); other elements from Hall et al. (1978).

TABLE 8-17 Carotenoid pigments in raw muscle tissue of representative commercial fishes and invertebrates.

Common name	Scientific name	β-carotene	Lutein	Cantha-xanthin	Asta-xanthin	Tuna-xanthin	Zea-xanthin
		Fishes					
Atlantic herring	*Clupea harengus harengus*		x	x	x		
Pacific herring	*Clupea harengus pallasi*		x			x	x
Anchovy	*Engraulis japonica*		x				x
Sardine	*Etrumeus micropus*		x			x	
Sardine	*Sardinops melanosticta*		x			x	x
Chub mackerel	*Scomber japonicus*		x			x	
Walleye pollock	*Theragra chalcogramma*		x			x	x
Yellowfin tuna	*Thunnus albacares*					x	

TABLE 8-17 (*Continued*)

Common name	Scientific name	β-carotene	Lutein	Cantha-xanthin	Asta-xanthin	Tuna-xanthin	Zea-xanthin
		Invertebrates					
Shrimp	*Penaeus japonicus*	x	x	x	x	x	x
White shrimp	*Penaeus setiferus*				x		
Short-necked clam	*Veneus japonica*	x					
Hard clam	*Meretrix lusoria*	x	x				x
Blue mussel	*Mytilus edulis*	x	x				x

Source: Simpson et al. (1981).

TABLE 8-18 Fishes and invertebrates known to be thiaminase-positive in the raw state.

Common name	Scientific name
Alewife	*Alosa pseudoharengus*
Common carp	*Cyprinus carpio*
Channel catfish	*Ictalurus punctatus*
Fathead minnow	*Pimephales promelas*
Goldfish	*Carassius auratus*
Sauger	*Stizostedion canadense*
Spottail shiner	*Notropis hudsonius*
Rainbow smelt	*Osmerus mordax*
White sucker	*Catostomus commersoni*
Lake whitefish	*Coregonus clupeaformis*
Atlantic herring	*Clupea harengus harengus*
Northern anchovy	*Engraulis mordax*
Chub mackerel	*Scomber japonicus*
Atlantic menhaden	*Brevoortia tyrannus*
Gulf menhaden	*Brevoortia patronus*
Butterfish	*Poronotus triacanthus*
Invertebrates	
American lobster	*Homarus americanus*
Scallop	*Placopecten grandis*
Blue mussel	*Mytilus edulis*
Clam	*Mya arenaria*
Ocean quahog	*Artica islandica*

Source: Stephen Spotte, compiled from references in Greig and Gnaedinger (1971).

feeds (pellets and flakes) and moist pellets requires special pelleting or extrusion equipment (Figs. 8-3 and 8-4), in addition to precise temperature and moisture control. Dry feeds are impractical to make in small quantities. Nonpelleted moist feeds, however, can be produced easily in limited amounts, and the procedures are much less stringent. Moist feeds have a texture closer to that of natural foods and sometimes are more readily accepted, particularly by unacclimated fishes. Factors to consider are (*1*) digestibility of the ingredients, (*2*) acceptability to fishes, (*3*) physical stability and nutrient retention in water, (*4*) nutrient balance, and (*5*) ease of mixing and storage. Cost is not significant if only small quantities of ingredients are required.

PROTEINS The purpose of adding proteins to feeds is to supply EAAs. In theory, these can be added either as protein (fresh or dried animal or plant tissue) or individually in purified form as free amino acids. In practice, the first option is more effective because (*1*) the EAA requirements have never been determined for any species of aquarium fish and surely are species dependent; (*2*) not all fishes can use free amino acids in feeds,[20] posing the question of whether most aquarium fishes can use them either; and (*3*) both dry and moist feeds often lose substantial

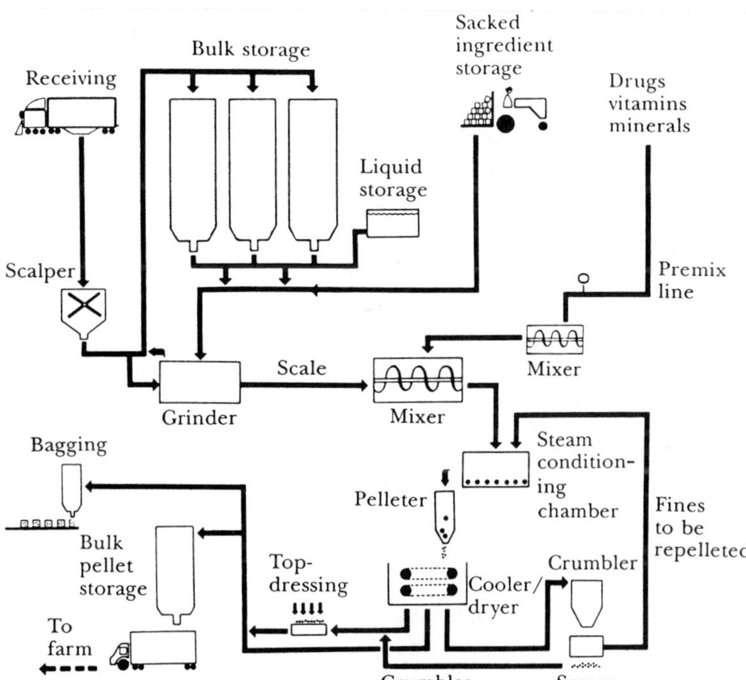

Figure 8-3 *Simplified flow diagram of compressed pellet manufacture.* Source: Hardy (1989).

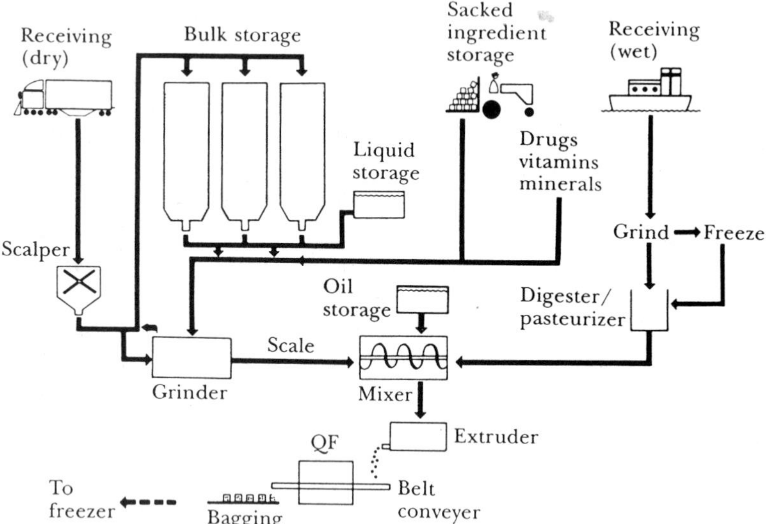

Figure 8-4 *Simplified flow diagram of moist pellet manufacture. QF = quick freezing.* Source: Hardy (1989).

amounts of EAAs when immersed in water (see the subsection below on leaching). Thus EAAs are preferably supplied as high-quality protein, often in the form of fish meal.

Protein quality is a measure of the relationship between the amino acid composition of food and the amino acid content of the animal to which it is fed. The highest-quality protein contains an amino acid composition that most closely matches that of the recipient. The proximate composition of whole fish is similar among species; moreover, all fish meals show comparable EAA patterns despite the origin of the fish used (freshwater or seawater) or the concentrations of lipids and other constituents (Tables 8-19 and 8-20). Fish meal provides the highest-quality protein available for fish feeds. Other protein sources in descending order of quality are meals prepared from crustaceans (crabs and shrimps), algae, terrestrial plants (e.g., soybeans, wheat, corn), and milk (whey). Some of these are listed in Table 8-21. It is sometimes stated that the chitin in crustacean meals provides an alternate source of nitrogen. However, the nitrogen in chitin is available only if the digestive tract of the fish contains *chitinases*, which are chitin-splitting enzymes; otherwise, the material is indigestible and passes unchanged in the feces. It can be reasoned that chitinases are present in many fishes that normally feed on crustaceans, but this has been demonstrated only in a few species. Until representative seawater aquarium fishes are tested it must be assumed that just the nonchitinous nitrogen fraction of total protein nitrogen in crustacean meals is available. Manufacturers who list

TABLE 8-19 Proximate composition and energy of desiccated fish meals. Units are g/100 g except energy, which is kcal/100 g.

Common name	Scientific name	Water	Protein	Lipid	Ash	Carbohydrate	Energy
Atlantic herring	*Clupea harengus harengus*	8.8	74.1	14.9	10.3	0.0	430
Herring	Clupidae	6.8	73.0	8.9	11.5	0.0	372
Anchovy	Engraulidae	6.8	64.7	7.8	17.1	3.6	343
European pilchard	*Clupea pilchardus*	2.2	65.2	26.9	5.5	0.2	504
Atlantic menhaden	*Brevoortia tyrannus*	6.0	63.5	12.5	17.4	0.6	369
Cisco	*Coregonus artedii*	9.8	68.3	7.8	12.8	1.3	349
Capelin	*Mallotus villosus*	13.6	68.4	8.8	8.3	0.8	353
Cod	Gadidae	6.3	72.7	2.8	19.4	0.0	394
Hake	Gadidae	5.9	80.4	2.1	16.8	0.0	340
Silver hake	*Merluccius bilinearis*	5.6	81.5	9.7	5.3	0.0	413
Haddock[1]	*Melanogrammus aeglefinus*	10.4	62.9	1.8	25.1	0.0	268
Walleye pollock	*Theragra chalogramma*	11.9	53.8	7.5	23.8	3.0	295
Flounder[1]	Bothidae/Pleuronectidae	6.3	59.9	10.2	23.2	0.4	330
Freshwater drum	*Aplodinotus grunniens*	8.9	62.4	8.4	20.5	0.0	325
Deepwater redfish	*Sebastes mentella*	6.0	73.0	5.7	18.5	0.0	343
Redfish (ocean perch)	*Sebastes marinus*	3.6	58.6	10.6	25.3	1.9	337
Albacore[1]	*Thunnus alalunga*	7.0	53.8	12.9	26.3	0.0	331
Tuna	Scombridae	6.1	60.9	9.7	21.0	2.3	340

Source: Sidwell (1981).

Note: Made from waste (offal).[1]

crab or shrimp meal as a protein source should, in my opinion, subtract chitinous nitrogen from total protein nitrogen to give an accurate assessment of digestible protein.[21]

The deposition of protein in fish tissues is independent of dietary concentration, and changes in the relative concentrations of protein in fish diets do not affect the amount deposited. Too much protein serves no useful purpose. The amount in excess of growth and tissue maintenance requirements is wasted. During digestion the carbon residues are burned as energy, which merely duplicates the function of dietary lipids. The excess nitrogen is excreted, increasing the potential concentration of ammonia in the water. Excessive dietary protein also affects food intake. In most food fishes tested, food intake declines when protein exceeds 45% (by dry mass) of the diet. If high-quality protein is used, a concentration of 35% is adequate.

As mentioned previously, proteins can serve as sources of metabolic energy, but ordinarily this occurs only if other energy sources (i.e., lipids and carbohydrates) are inadequate.[22] A basic understanding of how fishes use protein is an important prelude to formulating moist feeds. Aquarists have little hope of ever devising moist feeds that meet the needs of even a few

TABLE 8-20 Amino acid composition of desiccated fish meals. Units are g/100 g total protein; dashes indicate no data.

Common name	Scientific name	Arginine	Histidine	Threonine	Isoleucine	Leucine	Valine	Lysine	Methionine /cystine	Phenylalanine /tyrosine	Tryptophan
					Fishes						
Alewife	*Alosa pseudoharengus*	7.2	2.9	5.0	6.7	8.3	7.5	8.4	3.2/0.7	3.5/4.5	1.2
Anchovy	Engraulidae	4.4	2.3	3.5	4.0	6.6	4.5	6.5	2.5/0.9	3.6/2.9	0.7
Capelin	*Mallotus villosus*	5.8	2.2	4.4	4.2	8.4	4.8	7.6	3.0/1.2	3.8/3.5	1.2
Atlantic cod	*Gadus morhua*	7.1	2.1	3.8	3.8	6.4	4.6	6.9	3.0/0.8	3.7/2.8	—
Cod[1]	Gadidae	6.1	1.6	3.3	3.2	5.6	3.6	7.2	2.7/1.0	3.0/1.7	—
Flounder[1]	Bothidae/ Pleuronictidae	6.2	3.6	4.5	4.0	7.2	4.7	9.1	3.2/1.2	3.8/3.2	1.2
Haddock	*Melanogrammus aeglefinus*	5.7	1.9	6.0	6.0	8.2	6.0	10.6	4.4/2.0	4.2/—	1.0
Atlantic herring	*Clupea harengus harengus*	4.6	2.0	4.8	5.6	7.4	5.6	8.3	2.9/1.2	3.8/3.2	0.8
Herring	Clupidae	4.6	1.6	4.4	4.2	6.0	5.0	6.0	2.4/1.0	3.6/2.8	—
Atlantic menhaden	*Brevoortia tyrannus*	6.0	2.5	3.8	4.3	7.1	5.0	7.7	2.9/0.7	3.9/3.2	1.2
Pilchard	Clupeidae	5.2	2.5	4.4	4.8	7.8	6.0	8.1	3.0/2.4	4.0/3.4	1.0
Redfish (ocean perch)	*Sebastes marinus*	6.4	2.0	4.1	5.0	6.8	4.7	9.1	2.9/1.1	3.9/2.7	1.0
Tuna[1]	Scombridae	5.0	2.1	2.3	2.4	3.8	2.8	4.8	1.7/0.4	2.2/1.8	0.5
Whitefish	Salmonidae	6.6	2.0	4.1	4.2	6.8	4.7	7.0	2.6/1.2	3.4/3.0	1.0

Source: Sidwell (1981).

Note: Made from waste offal.

TABLE 8-21 Percentage of crude protein in dried meals and powders from sources other than fishes.

Yeasts (*Candida* spp.)[1]	58.2
Bacteria (*Pseudomonas* spp.)[1]	77.7
Algae (*Spirulina* spp.)[1]	49.8
Shrimps (dehydrated)[2]	37.3
Shrimps (sun dried)[2]	51.7
Crabs[3]	31.5
Whey[3]	12.2

Sources: Matty and Smith (1978),[1] Meyers et al. (1973),[2] Albritton (1954).[3]

species, much less the many that are kept routinely. Nonetheless, the exercise outlined here illustrates that protein use by fishes can, under some circumstances, be estimated.

The use of dietary protein by fishes is sometimes measured as *protein efficiency ratio*, PER, and *productive protein value*, PPV. These are expressed as

$$\text{PER} = \frac{\text{change in mass, g}}{\text{protein intake, g}} \tag{8.2}$$

$$\text{PPV (\%)} = \frac{\text{gain in nitrogen}}{\text{nitrogen intake}} \times 100 \tag{8.3}$$

The amount of protein eventually incorporated into the tissues relates strongly to how well dietary protein and lipid have been balanced; in other words, whether the dietary protein offered is ''spared'' after ingestion or deaminated and burned to meet energy needs. Depending on the species of fish maintained, its state of maturity, and relevant environmental factors (e.g., temperature), a diet containing 35% total protein by dry mass is often more effective than one of 55%, especially when steady growth rate, rather than maximum growth rate, is used as the indicator. Fishes typically use protein more efficiently at lower percentages because more of it is spared. Increasing the amount available reduces the PER value. This is partly attributable to increased energy demands for protein metabolism when dietary protein is high. After several days on a high-protein diet an upper threshold is reached. No further protein is required. The excess is then metabolized to supply energy or stored as fat in body tissues, suggesting that excess protein not only is wasted, but may ultimately be harmful.

The criterion of steady growth seems aptly suited to the long-term maintenance of fishes in public aquariums, although maximum growth rate is often more desirable in aquaculture. Most seawater aquarium fishes are late juveniles and adults. Sparse evidence gathered from studies of freshwater food and game fishes indicates that dietary protein requirements diminish with increasing age, but caloric needs do not. Nitrogen balances sustained by older fishes are determined by metabolic and tissue maintenance demands, rather than growth.[23]

LIPIDS As stated previously, a general tenet of nutrition science is that animals eat to satisfy energy requirements. High-energy diets are consumed in lesser amounts. Excess dietary energy subsequently prevents a fish from ingesting sufficient protein for growth. Unlike proteins, dietary lipids in excess of physiological requirements are deposited in the tissues, resulting in reduced activity and abnormal fatty acid ratios.[24] Fatty acids of the $\omega 3$ series are required by all fishes, and these are the real essential fatty acids. Fatty acids of the $\omega 6$ series evidently are not required by seawater fishes. Fish oils are high in PUFAs of the $\omega 3$ series, whereas vegetable oils are rich in the $\omega 6$ series. Some fishes can desaturate short-chain unsaturated fatty acids and lengthen them when the feed is deficient in EFAs,[6] but others (particularly the larger carnivores) are unable to do this even with moderately long-chain molecules such as $18{:}3\omega 3$. It is therefore not surprising that vegetable oils are used poorly by the seawater species tested so far, and none gives growth and survival rates comparable with fish oils. Clearly, direct addition of C_{20} and C_{22} $\omega 3$-PUFAs to feeds is the best procedure, and this is accomplished easily by using fish oil as the sole source of lipid. Lipids should make up 10 to 20% of the diet.

CARBOHYDRATES Seawater fishes apparently do not require carbohydrates. Their addition to feeds is probably unnecessary. The function of carbohydrates is to supply energy, but energy can be provided easily and more effectively in the form of lipids. Carbohydrates used as binders (see below) should make up $<2\%$ of feeds by dry mass.

VITAMINS Vitamins are added to moist feeds as *premixes*. A vitamin premix for fish feeds should contain the concentrations of essential vitamins shown in Table 8-22. The requirements of warm-water species other than the ones shown are less well understood.[25] Vitamin deficiencies are less likely if live foods are fed regularly as dietary supplements (see later sections).

CAROTENOIDS The normal skin coloration of some fishes can be intensified by adding carotenoids to feeds,[26] but whether

TABLE 8-22 Vitamin requirements for growth (mg/kg of dry feed except as indicated). R = required but concentration unknown. N = requirement not demonstrated. Dashes indicate no data.

Vitamin	Trout	Salmon	Carp	Channel catfish	Red(?) seabream
Thiamin	10–12	10–15	2–3	1–3	R
Riboflavin	20–30	20–25	7–10	9	R
Pyridoxine	10–15	15–20	5–10	3	5–6
Pantothenic acid	40–50	40–50	30–40	25–50	R
Niacin	120–150	150–200	30–50	14	R
Biotin	1–1.2	1–1.5	1–1.5	R	N
Folic acid	6–10	6–10	N	R	R
Cyanocobalamin	R	0.015–0.02	N	R	R
Ascorbic acid	100–150	100–150	30–50	60	R
*myo*inositol	200–300	300–400	200–300	R	300–900
Choline	R	600–800	1500–2000	R	R
Vitamin A[1]	2000–2500	2000–2500	1000–2000	1000–2000	1000–2000
Vitamin D[1]	2400	2400	N	500–1000	—
Vitamin E	30	30	80–100	30	—
Vitamin K	10	10	R	R	—

Source: Halver (1989).

Note: In IU.[1]

this is true for most species that deposit carotenoid pigments in the integument is unknown. Relatively few investigators have been concerned with the fading of captive fishes. Experimental work has emphasized improving market appearance (i.e., flesh coloration) of a few cultured species of commercial food value.[27] As dietary supplements, only canthaxanthin and astaxanthin appear capable of intensifying red skin coloration in fishes.[28] Several carotenoids, including these two, have been synthesized and are available as powders for addition to feeds.

BINDERS No feed is suitable if the ingredients do not hold together long enough to be ingested by a fish. In dry and moist feeds formulated for aquatic animals this function is performed by *binders*, which are proteins or carbohydrates derived from animal process wastes, seaweeds, and exudates of terrestrial plants. Typical binders are listed in Table 8-23.[29] The most useful of these are alginates[30] (specifically sodium alginate)[31] and gelatin. When sodium alginate is mixed with water it forms a liquid suspension called a *sol*.[32] If calcium ions are added, the suspension precipitates as a *gel*.[32] A *sequestrant* (e.g., sodium pyrophosphate) is added to prevent gelling before the ingredients are evenly distributed in the sol. Elimination of a sequestrant reduces the stability of the gel, and the final product destabilizes more quickly in water. All gels, regardless of how

TABLE 8-23 Common natural binding agents used in aquatic animal feeds.

Binding agent	Precursor
	Seaweed Derivatives
Agar	Red seaweed (*Gelidium* spp.)
Algin	Brown seaweed (*Macrocystis pyrifera*)
Carrageenin	Red seaweed (*Chondrus crispus, Gigartina stellata*)
Fucoidan	Brown seaweed (*Fucus* spp.)
Laminaran	Brown seaweed (*Laminaria* spp.)
	Plant Extracts and Exudates
Gum arabic	Thorn trees (*Acacia* spp.)
Locust bean	Carob tree (*Ceratonia siliqua*)
Pectin	Cell walls of all plants (commercial source is citrus processing wastes)
Starch	Cereal grains and tubers
	Animal Extracts
Chitin	Shells of arthropods, principally crustacean processing wastes
Gelatin	Collagen (skins, ligaments, and tendons of domestic animals)

Source: Stephen Spotte, compiled from various sources.

they are handled, are freely permeable to noncolloidal ions and molecules and allow nutrients to leach into the environment.

LEACHING *Leaching* is the diffusion of dissolved nutrients from foods and feeds into the water. Water-soluble vitamins and EAAs are the principal substances lost. The loss of EAAs is greater when these are added in the free form, rather than as protein. Contrary to popular belief, the degree of leaching does not necessarily depend on a feed's *stability* or resistance to physical deterioration after being immersed in water. Experiments have demonstrated that the stability of both dry and moist feeds bears no relationship to the concentrations of nutrients lost, or to the speed at which nutrient loss occurs.[33] Pellets and flakes often leach important dietary elements freely, but still remain firm for hours.

The problem of leaching has been largely overcome in aquaculture feeds by *encapsulation* (*microencapsulation* is a synonym if the feed particles are small). During encapsulation, feed particles are encased individually in digestible walls composed of synthetic polymers such as ethyl cellulose, polyvinyl alcohol or

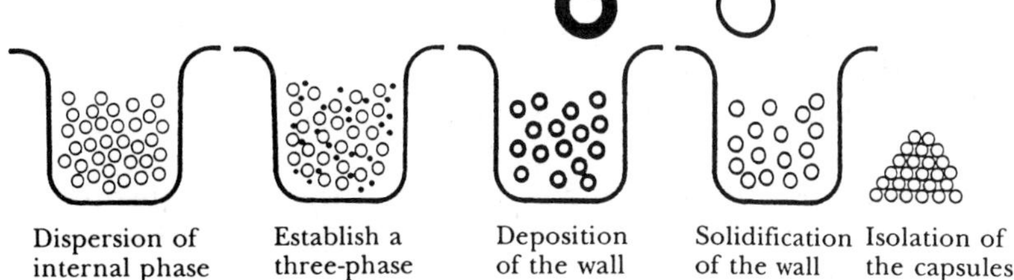

Figure 8-5 *Simplified flow diagram of the encapsulation process.* Source: Meyers et al. (1971).

polyethylene, or natural polymers (e.g., gelatin, gums, waxes). When manufactured correctly, the products retain nutrients exceptionally well in water and have a spongy texture that seems attractive to fishes. In one experiment it was shown that minimum leaching occurred even after 6 h when pelleted feeds were coated with ethyl cellulose.[34] Steps in the procedure are illustrated in Figure 8-5. The feed is first dispersed in a liquid medium. The liquid encapsulating material is added and forms deposits around the feed particles. The newly formed wall is solidified, and encapsulated feed grains are isolated for packaging.

STORAGE AND HANDLING Moist feeds should be cut into pieces of convenient size, sealed tightly in heavy plastic, and frozen. Dry feeds should be kept cool and dry. Oxidation and hydrolysis start immediately in tins of flakes left open at room temperature. The subsequent loss of nutrient value is substantial and almost instantaneous. Dry feeds left open to the atmosphere after refrigeration are particularly vulnerable to deterioration. Moisture from warm room air condenses on the cooler feed. After the temperature of the feed reaches equilibrium with the room air, increased dampness in the container stimulates rapid colonization by bacteria and fungi, resulting in microbial contamination. Touching feeds with wet hands should be avoided for the same reason. Flakes containing PUFAs should be packaged at the factory in airtight containers charged with dinitrogen to prevent *in vitro* oxidation and subsequent rancidity.

Live Foods—Brine Shrimp

Live foods seem superior to natural foods and feeds. Fishes fed live foods ordinarily grow faster and have higher survival rates than controls fed nonliving foods, and the disparity is most striking in young, growing animals.[35] Live foods retain active enzymes that make digestion more efficient.[36] These substances are sometimes destroyed when food organisms are killed during freezing or processing. If a central axiom can be stated for the nutrition of seawater aquarium fishes it is this: live foods are a basic requirement, fed either exclusively or as dietary supplements.

The most popular live food is the brine shrimp, and justifiably so. No other organism is so available, hardy, high in nutrient value, and easy to maintain. Dried, packaged *cysts*[37] can be obtained from distributors around the world.[38] The larvae or *nauplii* (the singular is *nauplius*) hatch in a few hours (Fig. 8-6) and can grow to ~1 cm in length within 2 weeks. Brine shrimp can be reared on either live or dead foods. If necessary, the same food can be used for both nauplii and adults, so long as the particle size is within the range of 6 to 15 μm. Brine shrimp are remarkably tolerant of adverse conditions. Cysts can survive desiccation for 15 years[39] and temperatures of −273 to 100°C.[40] Nauplii and adults can survive salinities ranging from 1‰ to nearly six times the strength of seawater (200‰).[41]

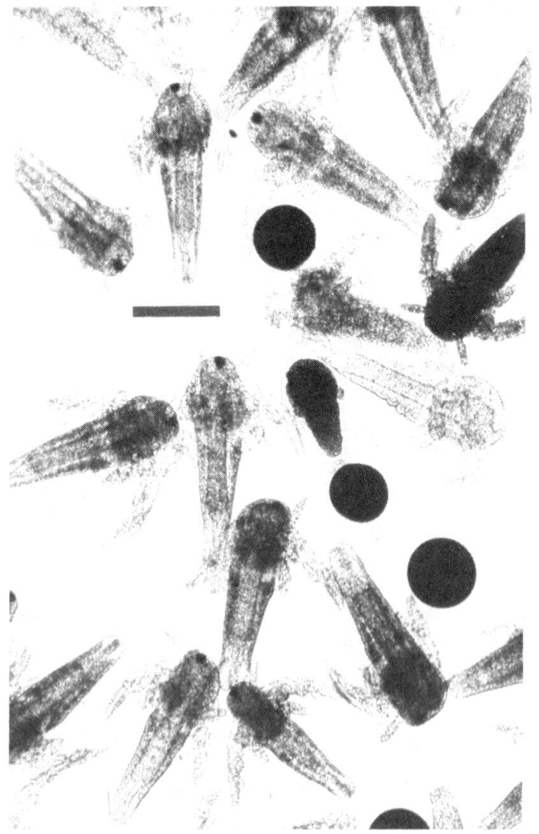

Figure 8-6 *Newly hatched brine shrimp nauplii* (Artemia franciscana). *Dark spheres are unhatched cysts. Scale bar = 0.25 mm.* Source: Spotte (1973) from New York Aquarium and Osborn Laboratories of Marine Sciences.

The brine shrimp is a primitive crustacean inhabiting salt pans and other high-salinity waters, but not the oceans. As of 1979, populations had been reported from 164 locations around the world.[40] It is thought that all brine shrimp belong to the genus *Artemia*, which includes at least five sibling species.[42] *Sibling species* do not interbreed because they are isolated geographically; however, they are similar (perhaps even identical) morphologically. The sibling species indigenous to the United States is *Artemia franciscana*.[42] In the United States, the two most convenient sources are San Francisco Bay and Great Salt Lake in Utah. Techniques for hatching dried cysts were developed at Steinhart Aquarium in San Francisco in the late 1920s.[43] Since then procedures for collecting, cleaning, drying, and packaging cysts have been refined considerably, and world consumption presently exceeds 100 metric tons annually.[44]

FOOD VALUE The food value of a brine shrimp depends on (*1*) its stage of development (see below), (*2*) the composition of the food it has been fed,[45] and (*3*) its geographic origin.[46] Operationally, only the first is important because the others cannot be controlled easily. A newly hatched brine shrimp emerges from the cyst as a stage 1 larva (Table 8-24). Within 24 h it molts and enters stage 2. Within the next 24 h it molts again, this time into stage 3. The interval between molts increases with each stage, ranging from 12 to 24 h in early molts to 24 to 30 h in later ones. Before development is finished at 8 to 14 d, a nauplius may complete 13 molts or more.[47] With each molt the shape and nutrient value of the animal change, and a brine

TABLE 8-24 Incremental growth (average length) of the San Francisco Bay brine shrimp (*Artemia franciscana*).

Stage	Length, mm
1	0.32
2	0.63
3	0.90
4	1.20
5	1.48
6	1.70
7	1.99
8	2.43
9	3.35
10	4.40
11	5.35
12	6.45

Source: Heath (1924).

TABLE 8-25 Lipid and caloric composition of San Francisco Bay brine shrimp (*Artemia franciscana*) nauplii.

Factor	Stage 1	Stages 2 and 3	Change, %
Dry mass, μg	1.85	1.48	−20
Ash, % dry mass(?)	6.03	11.28	+87
Energy per gram of ash-free dry mass, kcal(?)	5.557	5.503	−1
Individual energy value, kcal × 10^{-6}(?)	10.06	7.30	−27
Total lipid, % dry mass	19.3	13.7	−29
Fatty acids, % dry mass	14.7	10.9	−26

Source: Benijts et al. (1976).

shrimp nauplius is most nutritious at stage 1, newly hatched and rich with yolk from the cyst. The yolk provides a source of energy until the mouthparts develop, which happens by the end of stage 2. Table 8-25 shows that in the transition from stage 1 to stage 3 the energy content of a nauplius declines, and its food value subsequently diminishes.[48] It is therefore imperative that nauplii be used as soon as possible, and any remaining 24 h after hatching should be reared to maturity and fed to larger fishes, or discarded. The fatty acid composition of brine shrimp nauplii from different locations is summarized in Table 8-26. The amino acid composition of newly hatched nauplii (source unknown) is shown in Table 8-27. Brine shrimp nauplii may be deficient in threonine.[46]

As a brine shrimp approaches maturity it changes dramatically in length and mass, and its food value increases because of its larger size. An adult weighs 1 mg and is 8 mm long; a newly hatched nauplius is 0.002 mg and 0.4 mm.[49] Length and mass thus increase substantially.[49] The lipid concentration decreases from 23.2% of dry mass in a newly hatched nauplius to 7% shortly before sexual maturity at stage 12.[49] Protein increases from 43% (dry mass) in newly hatched nauplii to 63% in adults.[49]

FACTORS AFFECTING HATCH The number of nauplii obtained from a hatch is affected by several factors, mainly light, salinity, temperature, and the method of pre-treatment used on the cysts prior to packaging them. In low-salinity water (~5‰) pH becomes a limiting factor if the value falls below 8.0.[50] When all these factors are standardized, timing of the hatch, number of nauplii obtained, and survival rate of the nauplii are strain dependent.[51]

TABLE 8-26 Fatty acid composition of newly hatched brine shrimp from different locations. Units are g/100 g total lipid. Dashes indicate no detectable concentration.

Fatty acid[1]	Australia	Brazil	SF 313[2]	SF 321[2]	SP 1628[2]	Italy	Utah
14:0	1.34	1.57	0.99	1.57	0.43	1.53	0.93
14:1	2.23	0.81	1.27	0.74	2.26	3.30	1.45
15:0	0.34	0.67	0.16	0.58	0.25	0.11	0.11
15:1	0.15	0.24	0.20	0.13	0.46	0.54	0.37
16:0	13.45	15.42	10.33	12.13	7.79	15.23	11.78
16:1	9.97	10.79	13.27	19.52	5.24	10.38	5.64
16:2ω7	—	—	—	—	1.51	2.94	—
16:3ω4/ 17:1ω8	3.87	3.88	2.09	2.32	2.44	3.28	2.90
18:0	3.07	2.79	6.83	2.90	3.08	3.17	4.07
18:1ω9	28.23	35.86	26.97	31.20	29.15	29.05	28.58
18:2ω6	5.78	9.59	9.35	3.69	4.60	6.79	4.60
18:3ω3	14.77	4.87	17.33	5.16	33.59	6.35	31.46
18:4ω3	4.37	0.96	3.26	1.28	4.88	1.01	3.10
20:1ω9	0.37	0.52	0.41	0.35	0.35	0.42	0.37
20:2ω6/ ω9	0.12	0.06	0.06	—	0.24	0.20	0.09
20:3ω6	0.79	2.76	1.01	2.23	0.05	1.47	0.48
20:3ω3/ 20:4ω6	—	—	1.48	2.69	1.48	—	—
20:5ω3	10.50	8.98	4.06	12.44	1.68	13.63	3.55
22:6ω3	0.26	0.06	—	—	—	—	—

Source: Schauer et al. (1980); also see Webster and Lovell (1990).

Notes: Determined analytically as fatty acid methyl esters;[1] designations SF and SP stand for San Francisco and San Pablo Bays.[2]

TABLE 8-27 Comparative amino acid composition (EAAs for fishes) of rotifers and newly hatched brine shrimp nauplii. Units are g/100 g total protein.

Amino acid	Rotifers[1]	Brine shrimp nauplii[2]
Arginine	5.1	5.0
Histidine	1.7	1.3
Threonine	4.0	1.7
Isoleucine	4.0	2.6
Leucine	6.9	6.1
Valine	4.4	3.2
Lysine	6.6	6.1
Methionine/cystine	1.0/0.7	0.9/0.4
Phenylalanine/tyrosine	4.5/3.0	3.2/3.7
Tryptophan	1.1	1.0

Source: Watanabe et al. (1978a).

Notes: Brachionus plicatilis fed baker's yeast,[1] *Artemia* sp.[2]

Light somehow triggers hatching, but periods of light lasting several hours do not shorten hatching time or increase the number of nauplii obtained.[52] The highest percentage hatch is obtained when San Francisco Bay and Great Salt Lake cysts are illuminated with a minimum of 2000 lx after full wetting for 5 and 10 min, respectively.[52] *Wetting* occurs after the cysts have been placed in water and suspended in the hatch solution for several minutes. Afterward, the cysts can be kept in darkened containers or a darkened room until they hatch. Ordinary room light is sometimes inadequate to promote efficient hatching, and it is best to illuminate even transparent hatch vessels for several minutes after wetting. Once this is done it is unimportant whether the room lights are left on or off.

Cysts can be hatched either in brine (table salt dissolved in tap water), seawater, or artificial seawater. Total salt concentration is evidently more important than the species and concentrations of individual ions in solution, provided sodium and chloride dominate.[53] Seawater or artificial seawater is recommended, however.[54] Brine shrimp are found only in salt pans where the salinity periodically reaches 70 to 175‰,[41] but the cysts are unable to hatch until considerable dilution has occurred. In nature the fluctuation in salinity caused by alternate dilution and evaporation is generally seasonal. In the San Francisco Bay area, for example, cysts lie dormant in summer when inorganic ions in the pans are most concentrated and do not hatch until winter rains lower the salinity. Thus the hatch time is faster and the percentage hatch greater in low-salinity waters, and values as low as 5‰ give excellent results.[44] However, low-salinity seawater and artificial seawaters, and brine at any concentration, are poorly buffered, making it difficult to keep pH values between 8.0 and 9.0, the range within which cyst hatching enzymes function best.[50] Highly dilute brine, artificial seawaters, and seawater are not recommended hatch solutions.

The time required for brine shrimp cysts to hatch is temperature dependent, being shorter in warm water than in cold. The upper limit is 40°C, at which point embryonic development stops.[44] Optimal temperature is strain dependent, but 28 to 30°C is optimal for the two major U.S. strains.[52] At 30°C, hatching begins in 10 to 12 h.[55]

Cysts that have been pretreated with strong oxidants such as bleach (i.e., decapsulated; Method 8.3) to remove the outer shell, wetted and illuminated one or more times prior to final drying and packaging, or dried for 24 h before final packaging show different hatching characteristics from cysts that have simply been collected, dried, and packaged. It is known that repeated wetting and drying have a cumulative effect on embryonic development;[56] in other words, the cysts hatch in a shorter time when rewetted. For example, most strains start to hatch within ~13 h when conditions are favorable.[57] Wetting for 8 h followed by drying has a cumulative effect, and cysts hatch within 5 h of rewetting.[57] Similarly, pretreatment with light is cumulative and results in a high percentage hatch (often greater than 90%), even when the cysts are wetted in complete darkness.[57] Pretreatment by drying followed by storage for periods longer than 24 h lowers the number of nauplii obtained.[57] In my opinion, companies that package brine shrimp cysts should be encouraged to state on the container when the cysts were packaged. Other useful information would include the precise origin[58] and method of pretreatment.

Live Foods—Rotifers

The phylum Rotifera (or Rotatoria) includes ~1800 species of small (typically <3 mm), mostly free-living animals, the majority inhabiting freshwaters. The source of the name is the ciliated crown or *corona* (Fig. 8-7). When the cilia are beating the corona resembles a rotating wheel. Many rotifers are suspension feeders, and some are *raptors* (i.e., they capture prey). Captive planktivorous fishes can often be maintained on rotifers, which are smaller than brine shrimp but similar in amino acid composition (Table 8-27). In addition, rotifer cultures are less expensive to maintain.

REPRODUCTION I shall discuss rotifer reproduction briefly because certain features impinge directly on culture techniques. According to some authors, reproduction occurs both sexually and asexually, but this is incorrect. Reproduction in rotifers is entirely sexual (Fig. 8-8), although some species are *parthenogenetic,* and the eggs develop without fertilization. In most parthenogenetic rotifers, males appear in the population only at certain times. Members of one group, the bdelloids, exist entirely without males; at least males have never been observed, and only females hatch from the eggs. Other rotifers produce more than one type of egg. *Amictic eggs* have thin shells. They cannot be fertilized and develop parthenogenetically into amictic females. *Meiosis*—the series of special nuclear divisions that maintains constant chromosome numbers—does not occur, and amictic eggs are *diploid* (i.e., the chromosome number is not reduced). *Mictic eggs* are thin-shelled too, but *haploid,* and the chromosome number is reduced by half after meiosis. If fertilization does not take place, mictic eggs develop parthenogenetically into males. Fertilized mictic eggs secrete a thick shell

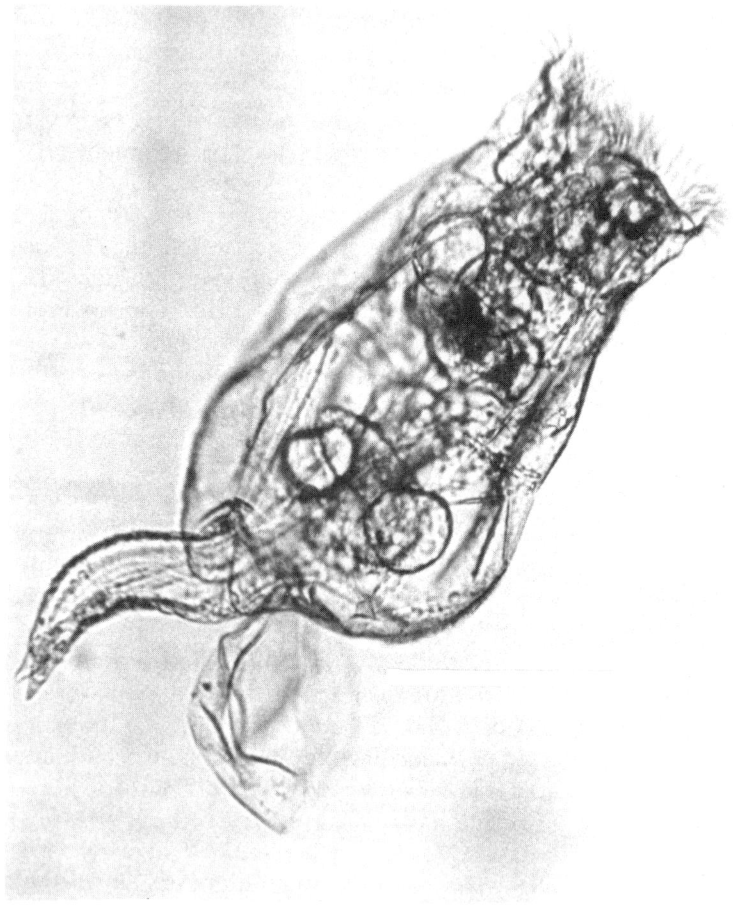

Figure 8-7 *Rotifer* (Brachionus plicatilis). *Note the corona at the top. Scale bar = 100 μm.* Source: Patricia M. Bubucis, Sea Research Foundation.

and become *dormant eggs*. Unfertilized amictic eggs hatch in a few days, but dormant eggs can survive desiccation, cold, and other adverse conditions for months. Dormant eggs always hatch into females. Production of dormant eggs apparently is an adaptation allowing populations to survive during unfavorable conditions. Dormant eggs are sold in rotifer ''starter kits.'' Cryopreservation has proved effective in preserving parthenogenetic eggs of *Brachionus plicatilis*.[59]

FACTORS AFFECTING SURVIVAL AND REPRODUCTION

The survival and reproduction of rotifers in culture are affected adversely by low dissolved oxygen[60] and high concentrations of ammonia.[61] Salinity influences the rate of reproduction,[62] and interactive effects of temperature and salinity affect body size.[63] Substantial deviation in water temperature from the optimal range (18 to 24°C) affects population growth adversely.[64]

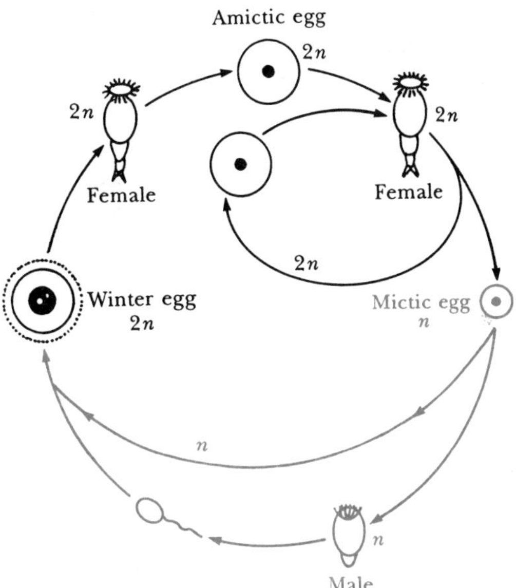

Figure 8-8 Rotifer life cycle. Amictic eggs produced in spring and summer develop parthenogenetically into new generations of females. Smaller mictic eggs produced in autumn develop parthenogenetically into males. If the males fertilize mictic eggs, dormant eggs result. In spring these hatch into females. The symbols n and 2n indicate one (haploid) and two (diploid) sets of chromosomes per cell. Source: Weisz and Keogh (1982).

Crowding has a negative effect on population growth.[65] However, environmental factors can be controlled with relative ease, and nutrition is perhaps the most important limitation in rotifer culture. Rotifers lose body mass and food value rapidly when starved.[66] Consequently, nutrient composition of the food is not always the principal consideration; particle size[67] and particle density[68] also exert a profound influence on population growth and reproduction. I found no general consensus in the literature about which foods are best for rotifers in culture, or even whether live foods are preferable.[69]

TECHNOLOGY

Method 8.1 Alginate- and Gelatin-Bound Moist Feeds[70]

Many fishes accept alginate- and gelatin-bound feeds in captivity (Table 8-28). Ingredients and concentrations of two recipes are listed in Table 8-29. Names and addresses of potential suppliers are provided in the footnotes. Table 8-30 lists concentrations of the vitamins. Dextrose has been eliminated because it represents an unwanted source of carbohydrate: the vitamin mix plus choline as routinely packaged and distributed by the listed manufacturer contains 84.7% dextrose (847.39 g/kg). Information on nutrient composition of the two feeds, derived from both moist (e.g., ready-to-feed) and desiccated samples, is provided in Tables 8-31 through 8-34.

TABLE 8-28 Captive fishes (by family) at Mystic Marinelife Aquarium that routinely eat alginate- and gelatin-bound moist feeds.

Acanthuridae	Mullidae
Atherinidae	Pleuronectidae
Balistidae	Poeciliidae
Bothidae	Pomacanthidae
Carangidae	Pomacentridae
Chaetodontidae	Pomatomidae
Clupeidae	Priacanthidae
Diodontidae	Salmonidae
Gadidae	Scaridae
Gobiidae	Scombridae
Grammidae	Scyliorhinidae
Haemulidae	Serranidae
Holocentridae	Sparidae
Labidae	Stromateidae
Lutjanidae	Tetraodontidae
Merluccidae	Zoarcidae
Monocanthidae	

Source: Spotte et al. (1985).

Stock solutions of vitamin mix and Roxanthin® Red 10 Beadlets (10% canthaxanthin, β-carotene-4,4′-dione) can be made to reduce preparation time. *Vitamin stock solution*: Add 0.0854 g of vitamin mix (Table 8-30) and 0.0825 g of choline (Table 8-29) per millilitre of distilled water, dH_2O. Use 2 mL/100 g of finished feed. *Canthaxanthin stock solution*: Dissolve 1.0 g of Roxanthin® Red 10 Beadlets in 60 mL dH_2O at 50°C and dilute to 100 mL for a final concentration of 10 mg/mL. This contains 1 mg/mL canthaxanthin. Use 6 mL/100 g of feed. Store the beadlets and both stock solutions at <8°C in a refrigerator.

How to Make Alginate-Bound Moist Feed

1 Refer to Table 8-29. Mix 1 kg of feed at a time.

2 Dissolve the sodium pyrophosphate in dH_2O after heating the water to ~60°C.

3 Place the solution in the bowl of a commercial mixer. Slowly add sodium alginate while mixing at high speed to form a suspension. Scrape the beater and sides of the bowl with a plastic food scraper, then mix at high speed for 1 min.

4 Stir in the canthaxanthin solution with the plastic food scraper.

TABLE 8-29 Ingredients in alginate- and gelatin-bound moist feeds for freshwater or seawater fishes. Units are g/100 grams of finished feed.

Ingredient	Alginate	Gelatin
Distilled water,[1] dH_2O	61.2	57.3
Sodium pyrophosphate,[2] $Na_4P_2O_7$	0.05	
Keltone®, sodium alginate[3]	2.0	
Animal gelatin[4]		7.0
Roxanthin® Red 10 Beadlets[5] (10% canthaxanthin), 10 mg/mL of primary stock solution	0.06 (6 mL)	0.06 (6 mL)
Vitamin mix (without choline),[6] Table 8-30	0.1708	0.1708
Choline,[7] Table 8-30	0.1650	0.1650
Calcium sulfate dihydrate,[8] $CaSO_4 \cdot 2H_2O$	1.0	
Sodium chloride,[9] NaCl	2.4	2.4
Fish meal[10]	25.0	25.0
Herring oil[11]	2.0	2.0

Source: Spotte et al. (1985).

Notes: Equivalent ingredients from other suppliers can be substituted:

[1]The following applies to gelatin-bound moist feeds only. For seawater fishes substitute 59.7 mL of full-strength seawater ($S = \sim 35‰$); the alternative is to use dH_2O and NaCl (footnote 9). For freshwater fishes substitute 59.7 mL of canned clam juice.

[2]P8010, Sigma Chemical Company, P.O. Box 14508, St. Louis MO 63178.

[3]Kelco, 75 Terminal Avenue, Clark NJ 07066.

[4]225 BL Edible PS Gelatin (Lot 49), Knox Gelatin Co., Inc., P.O. Box 725, Sioux City IA 51102.

[5]Roxanthin® Red 10 Beadlets, ABBA Products Corp., P.O. Box 122, Elizabeth NJ 07207. Canthaxanthin concentration is 10 mg/mL. Store refrigerated (<8°C).

[6]ICN Diet Fortification Mixture 904655 without dextrose. ICN Nutritional Biochemicals, 26201 Miles Road, Cleveland OH 44128. Store refrigerated (<8°C).

[7]Choline, ICN Nutritional Biochemicals (packaged separately as part of ICN Diet Fortification Mixture 904655 without dextrose). Store refrigerated (<8°C).

[8]C3771, Sigma Chemical Company.

[9]Sterling Evaporated Salt, TX-1 Granulated, International Salt Co., Inc., Clarks Summit PA 18411. Substitute 2.4 mL dH_2O for freshwater fishes (alginate), or omit if dH_2O and NaCl are replaced with seawater or clam juice (gelatin).

[10]Fish meal, The Lake Group, Gaultois, Newfoundland, Canada. Store refrigerated (<8°C).

[11]Herring oil, Seapro, Inc., Seapro Wharf, Rockland ME 04841. Store refrigerated (<8°C).

TABLE 8-30 Vitamin mix of Table 8-29. Choline is packaged separately, and dextrose has been omitted (see footnotes 6 and 7 of Table 8-29). Amounts shown are vitamin concentrations remaining after omission of 847.39 g dextrose. Store refrigerated (<8°C).

Ingredient	Mass as packaged, g/kg	g/100 g feed
Choline	75.0	1.65×10^{-1}
Ascorbic acid	45.0	9.90×10^{-2}
α-Tocopherol acetate, 250 IU/g	5.0	1.10×10^{-2}
Inositol	5.0	1.10×10^{-2}
p-Aminobenzoic acid (PABA)	5.0	1.10×10^{-2}
Vitamin A, 200,000 IU/g	4.5	9.90×10^{-3}
Niacin	4.5	9.90×10^{-3}
Calcium pantothenate	3.0	6.60×10^{-3}
Menadione	2.25	4.95×10^{-3}
Riboflavin	1.0	2.20×10^{-3}
Pyridoxine·HCl	1.0	2.20×10^{-3}
Thiamin·HCl	1.0	2.20×10^{-3}
Vitamin D_2, 400,000 IU/g	0.25	5.50×10^{-4}
Folic acid	0.090	1.98×10^{-4}
Biotin	0.020	4.40×10^{-5}
Cyanocobalamin	0.00135	2.97×10^{-6}

Source: Spotte et al. (1985).

TABLE 8-31 Proximate composition of alginate- and gelatin-bound feeds, either moist (as fed) or desiccated. Units are g/100 g (± the standard deviation), except as indicated.

		Alginate	Gelatin[1]	Gelatin[2]
Matter, %	Moist	33.56±0.28	37.50±0.81	37.21±0.38
	Dry	100	100	100
Crude protein, %	Moist	14.68±0.23	21.72±0.18	21.54±0.74
	Dry	43.74±0.69	57.92±0.48	57.89±1.99
Total lipid, %	Moist	9.90±0.25	9.32±0.13	9.29±0.03
	Dry	29.50±0.74	24.85±0.35	24.97±0.08
Ash, %	Moist	8.28±0.32	6.28±0.13	6.24±1.05
	Dry	24.67±0.95	16.75±0.35	16.77±2.82
Nitrogen-free	Moist	2.08±0.085	0.46±0.16	0.39±0.20
extract, %	Dry	6.20±0.25	1.23±0.43	1.05±0.54
Energy, kcal/g	Moist	1.594±0.012	1.855±0.014	1.844±0.024
	Dry	4.749±0.035	4.947±0.038	4.955±0.063
Protein/kcal ratio, mg/kcal (dry)				
Gross		92	117	117
Digestible[3]		108	137	137

Source: Spotte et al. (1985).

Notes: Formula for seawater fishes (NaCl dissolved in distilled water),[1] formula for freshwater fishes (clam juice),[2] estimated from Brett and Groves (1979).[3]

TABLE 8-32 **Essential amino acid (EAA) concentrations of alginate- and gelatin-bound feeds (moist as fed or dessicated) compared with the Maximum Composite Requirement (MCR) from literature values. Each MCR value is the highest requirement reported among chinook salmon, Japanese eel, and common carp.**

EAA	Requirement[1] MCR, g/100g of feed (dry)	Alginate,[2] % of MCR		Gelatin,[2] % of MCR	
		Moist	Dry	Moist	Dry
Arginine	2.4	36.7	109.4	60.4	161.7
Histidine	0.8	47.5	141.5	55.0	147.2
Isoleucine	1.5	52.0	154.9	56.8	152.0
Leucine	2.0	56.0	166.9	67.5	180.7
Lysine	2.2	55.4	165.1	68.6	183.6
Methionine[3]	1.9	33.7	100.4	37.9	101.4
Phenylalanine[4]	2.5	44.8	133.5	52.4	140.3
Threonine	1.5	41.3	123.1	50.0	133.8
Tryptophan	0.4	45.0	134.1	45.0	120.5
Valine	1.5	53.3	158.8	65.3	174.8

Sources: Cowey and Sargent (1979),[1] Spotte et al. (1985).[2]
Notes: Methionine + cystine,[3] phenylalanine + tyrosine.[4]

5 Let the suspension stand until all bubbles are gone (~2 h); if necessary, place in a refrigerator overnight to allow bubbles to dissipate.

6 Combine the vitamin mix, calcium sulfate dihydrate, sodium chloride, and fish meal in another bowl and mix thoroughly. If the food is to be fed only to freshwater animals omit sodium chloride and substitute 2.4 mL dH_2O.

7 Add herring oil to the dry ingredients (step 6) and mix thoroughly.

8 With the suspension containing sodium alginate bubble free and at room temperature or cooler, stir in the dry ingredients from step 7 and mix thoroughly and quickly by hand.

9 Pour the food into a mold or allow it to gel in the mixing container. Gelling occurs in a few minutes. Cut into suitable portions, wrap, and freeze.

How to Make Gelatin-Bound Moist Feed

1 Refer to Table 8-29. Any amount can be mixed.

2 Measure the total volume of solvent (dH_2O, seawater, clam juice) in a graduated cylinder and divide into two equal portions. Set one aside. Heat the second portion to ~100°C and dissolve the gelatin.

TABLE 8-33 Vitamin composition of alginate- and gelatin-bound (moist as fed or desiccated) feeds and general dietary requirements of fishes (per 100 g of feed).

	Alginate		Gelatin		Requirement
	Moist	Dry	Moist	Dry	(Moist)
Vitamin A, IU	1980	5900	1980	5300	45 to ≤1000[1-3]
Vitamin D, IU	220	656	220	589	≥100 to ≤400[4,5]
Vitamin E, IU	11	33	11	29	≤70[6-9]
Vitamin K, mg	5.0	14.9	5.0	13.4	0.05[10]
Thiamin, mg	2.2	6.6	2.2	5.9	0.06–0.26[11,12]
Riboflavin, mg	2.3	6.8	2.3	6.2	0.3–1.2[13-18]
Niacin, mg	11.3–12.1	34–36	11.3–12.1	30–32	1.4–2.8[19,20]
Pantothenic acid, mg	6.8–6.9	20	6.8	18.3	1.0–3.0[14,21]
Pyridoxine, mg	2.3	6.8	2.3	6.2	0.1–0.54[22-26]
Biotin, μg	44	131	44	118	100–600[27-29]
Folic acid, μg	205	611	205	550	?
Cyanocobalamin, ng	5.2–9.0	15–27	5.2–9.0	14–24	<180?[30]
Ascorbic acid, mg	99	295	113	302	4–70[31-34]
Choline, mg	220–265	656–790	220–265	589–709	50–100[36,37]
Inositol, mg	11	33	11	29	25–400[23,38,39]
p-Aminobenzoic acid, mg	11	33	11	29	None known

Source: Spotte et al. (1985).

Notes:

[1] Dupree (1966). Channel catfish (*Ictalurus punctatus*), 45 IU.
[2] Dupree (1970). Channel catfish, 100 IU.
[3] Poston et al. (1977). Rainbow trout (*Oncorhynchus mykiss*) and brook trout (*Salvelinus fontinalis*), 1000 IU.
[4] Barnett et al. (1979). Rainbow trout, 160–240 IU.
[5] Andrews et al. (1980). Channel catfish, ≥100 to ≤400 IU.
[6] Poston (1965). Brown trout (*Salmo trutta*), ≤50 IU.
[7] Murai and Andrews (1974). Channel catfish, 2.5–10 IU.
[8] Watanabe and Takashima (1977). Common carp (*Cyprinus carpio*), ≤70 IU.
[9] Poston et al. (1976). Atlantic salmon (*Salmo salar*), ≤50 IU.
[10] Poston (1976a). Lake trout (*Salvelinus namaycush*), 0.05 mg.
[11] Cowey et al. (1975). Turbot (*Scophthalmus maximus*), 0.06–0.26 mg.
[12] Murai and Andrews (1978a). Channel catfish, 0.1 mg.
[13] Aoe et al. (1967a). Common carp, 0.4 mg.
[14] Ogino (1967). Common carp, 1.0 mg B_2; 3.0 mg pantothenic acid.
[15] Hughes et al. (1981). Rainbow trout, 0.3 mg.
[16] Murai and Andrews (1978b). Channel catfish, 0.9 mg.
[17] Takeuchi et al. (1980). Rainbow trout, 0.4 mg; common carp, 0.5 mg.
[18] Woodward (1982). Rainbow trout, 1.2 mg.
[19] Aoe et al. (1967b). Common carp, 2.8 mg.
[20] Andrews and Murai (1978). Channel catfish, 1.4 mg.
[21] Murai and Andrews (1979). Channel catfish, 1.0 mg.
[22] Ogino (1965). Common carp, 0.54 mg.
[23] Yone (1975). Red seabream (*Chrysophrys major*), 0.20–0.50 B_6; 55–90 mg inositol.
[24] Adron et al. (1978). Turbot, 0.10–0.25 mg.
[25] Andrews and Murai (1979). Channel catfish, 0.30 mg.
[26] Kissil et al. (1981). Gilthead bream (*Sparus aurata*), 0.20 mg.
[27] Poston and McCartney (1974). Brook trout, 600 μg.
[28] Ogino et al. (1970b). Common carp, 100 μg.
[29] Poston (1976b). Lake trout, 100–500 μg.

TABLE 8-33 *(Continued)*

[30] Limsuwan and Lovell (1981). Channel catfish, ≤180 mg.
[31] Halver et al. (1969). Coho salmon (*Oncorhynchus kisutch*), 5 mg; rainbow trout, 10 mg.
[32] Andrews and Murai (1975). Channel catfish, 5 mg.
[33] Lim and Lovell (1978). Channel catfish, 6 mg.
[34] Hilton et al. (1978). Rainbow trout, 4 mg.
[35] Mahajan and Agrawal (1980). Indian major carp (*Cirrhina mrigala*), 70 mg.
[36] Ogino et al. (1970a). Common carp, 50 mg.
[37] Ketola (1976). Lake trout, ≤100 mg.
[38] Halver (1957). Chinook salmon (*Oncorhynchus tshawytscha*), 25–400 mg.
[39] Aoe and Masuda (1967). Common carp, 400 mg.

TABLE 8-34 Elemental composition of alginate- and gelatin-bound feeds (moist as fed or desiccated) and general dietary requirements of fishes. Units are mg/100 g of feed.

	Alginate		Gelatin		Requirement
Element	Moist	Dry	Moist	Dry	Dry
Ca	754–1548	2247–4613	498–1292	1333–3459	1500[1–4]
P	171–750	510–2235	159–738	426–1976	400–800[3–7]
Mg	35–68	104–203	35–68	94–192	40–70[8, 9]
Na	1243–1439	3704–4288	1037–1235	2776–3306	?
K	13–280	387–834	310–460	830–1231	?
Cl	1502–1740	4476–5185	1502–1740	4021–4658	?
S	205	611	—	—	?
Fe	2.0–10.9	6.0–32.5	2.4–11.3	6.4–30.2	15–20[10, 11]
Zn	2.5–3.8	7.4–11.3	2.5–3.8	6.7–10.2	1.5–4.1[12, 13]
Cu	0.11–0.28	0.33–0.83	0.11–0.28	0.29–0.75	0.07–0.30[14, 15]
Mn	0.05–0.9	0.15–2.7	0.5–0.9	0.13–2.4	1.2[14]
Se	?	?	?	?	0.25[16, 17]
I	?	?	?	?	11[18]

Source: Unpublished data, Stephen Spotte and Paul E. Stake (College of Agriculture and Natural Resources, The University of Connecticut); also see NAS/NRC (1981, pp. 17–19) and NAS/NRC (1983, pp. 23–29).

Notes:

[1] Andrews et al. (1973). Channel catfish (*Ictalurus punctatus*), 1500 mg.
[2] Sakamoto and Yone (1973). Red seabream (*Chrysophrys major*), 340 mg (Ca/P ratio).
[3] Ogino and Takeda (1976). Common carp (*Cyprinus carpio*), 30 mg Ca; 70 mg P.
[4] Ogino and Takeda (1978). Rainbow trout (*Oncorhynchus mykiss*), 340 mg Ca; 700–800 mg P.
[5] Ketola (1975). Atlantic salmon (*Salmo salar*), ≥600 mg.
[6] Lovell (1978). Channel catfish, 450 mg.
[7] Gatlin et al. (1982). Channel catfish, 400 mg.
[8] Ogino and Chiou (1976). Common carp, 40–50 mg.
[9] Ogino et al. (1978). Rainbow trout, 60–70 mg.
[10] Sakamoto and Yone (1978a). Red seabream, 15 mg.
[11] Sakamoto and Yone (1978b). Common carp, 20 mg.
[12] Ogino and Yang (1978). Rainbow trout, 1.5–3.0 mg.
[13] Ogino and Yang (1979). Common carp, 1.5–3.0 mg.
[14] Ogino and Yang (1980). Common carp, 0.30 mg Cu; rainbow trout, ≤0.07 mg Cu, ≤1.3 mg Mn.
[15] Murai et al. (1981). Channel catfish, ≤0.15 mg.
[16] Gatlin and Wilson (1984). Channel catfish, 0.025 mg.
[17] Bell et al. (1987). Atlantic salmon (*Salmo salar*), 0.094 mg with 4 mg α-tocopherol acetate.
[18] Woodall and LaRoche (1964). Chinook salmon (*Oncorhynchus tshawytscha*), 11 mg.

3 Stir the canthaxanthin solution into the heated solvent containing the gelatin and cool to ~26°C.
4 In another container combine the fish meal, sodium chloride (if dH_2O is the solvent instead of seawater), vitamin mix, and choline. Add the herring oil and mix thoroughly.
5 Add the first portion of the solvent (step 2) and allow to soak for at least 15 min.
6 Stir the solution of gelatin and canthaxanthin into the rest of the ingredients and mix by hand.
7 Pour into molds, refrigerate until fully gelled, then cut into suitable portions, wrap, and freeze.

Method 8.2 Hatch Procedure for Brine Shrimp Cysts

GENERAL PROCEDURES The procedure offered here can be adapted to any hatch vessel.

1 Dilute full-strength seawater or artificial seawater by about one-third with freshwater. If tap water is the diluent, aerate overnight or pass through activated carbon before use. This is the *hatch solution*.
2 Add a known volume of hatch solution to the hatch vessel (see below). If the temperature is <20°C insert a small immersion heater. Keep the temperature constant at 20 to 30°C.
3 Turn on the air and adjust the aeration rate to produce a slow stream of bubbles. Excessive aeration causes cysts to collect in "windrows" along the edges of the container. No aeration results in oxygen depletion of the water. The latter problem is partly offset by using low-salinity water as recommended here.[71]
4 Add the cysts to the hatch vessel (see subsections below).
5 After 10 min of wetting, illuminate with 2000 lx for 10 min. This can be accomplished by placing a 40-W, cool white fluorescent lamp with reflector 20 cm from the hatch vessel.[72] Do not illuminate without aeration because the density of the cysts will create a shading effect, shielding some cysts from the light.
6 After full hatch has occurred (ordinarily <35 h), shut off the air, allowing empty shells and unhatched cysts to stratify and separate from the nauplii. After 15 min draw the nauplii to a corner of the container using a flashlight or small spotlight. The nauplii are strongly *photopositive* (attracted to light). The time required to concentrate the nauplii with light depends on the distance they must swim to reach it, and this

depends in turn on the design of the hatch vessel. Usually 15 min is sufficient.

7 When the nauplii are concentrated, drain or siphon them into a net (~150 μm mesh size) and rinse well with seawater or artificial seawater.

HATCH VESSELS Cysts can be hatched easily in any container that holds water, including bottles of all shapes and sizes, unused aquariums, and plastic flats from gardening supply centers. But when it comes to concentrating the nauplii for separation from cyst debris and unhatched cysts, a well-designed hatch vessel is clearly superior to a simple container. Two basic designs are in general use. I shall call them *vertical* and *horizontal*. A vertical hatch vessel is deeper than it is wide, and often tapered near the bottom for easy concentration of nauplii and removal of debris. Conventional vertical hatch vessels can be adapted from plastic carboys or made from thin sheets of clear acrylic (Fig. 8-9). The model in Figure 8-10 shows two sizes of hatch vessels adapted from glass glucose bottles hung upside down from a wire bracket. The rest of the apparatus consists of a two-hole rubber laboratory stopper, some glass tubing, and a pinch clamp. Air is injected through one glass tube; the excess escapes into the atmosphere through the vent tube. Vertical hatch vessels of ~1 L are ideal for hatching and harvesting small numbers of nauplii. To use the apparatus follow the general hatch procedure given previously in conjunction with the one below.

How to Use a Vertical Glucose-Bottle Hatch Vessel

1 Remove the stopper and fill with 0.75 L of hatch solution.

2 Add the cysts. Do not exceed 1 g/L by mass or 0.25 tsp/L* by volume. In this example, do not exceed 0.75 g, or 0.20 tsp. Consider the cyst count to be 300,000/g.[73]

3 Replace the stopper, hang the bottle upside down, and adjust the air. Be sure the vent tube is well above the surface.

4 After 24 h shut off the air and shine a light at a right angle to the bottle as close to the stopper as possible.

5 After 15 min gently open the pinch clamp and drain the nauplii into a net (~150 μm mesh size). The shells and unhatched cysts, which are less dense than the nauplii, should remain in the hatch vessel.

6 Rinse the nauplii with seawater or artificial seawater.

*tsp = teaspoons.

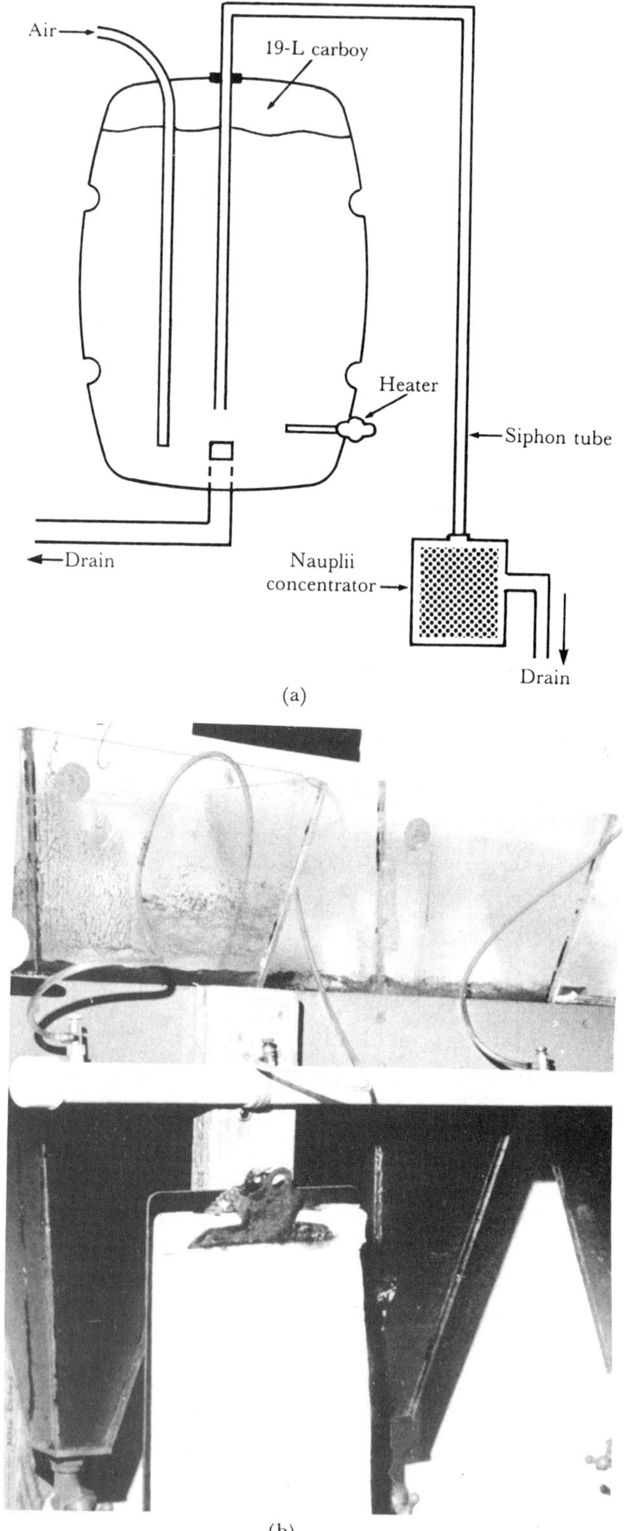

Figure 8-9 *Conventional vertical hatch vessels for brine shrimp cysts.* (a) *Carboy vessel.* (b) *Acrylic vessel.* Sources: (a) Kinne (1976); (b) Stephen Spotte.

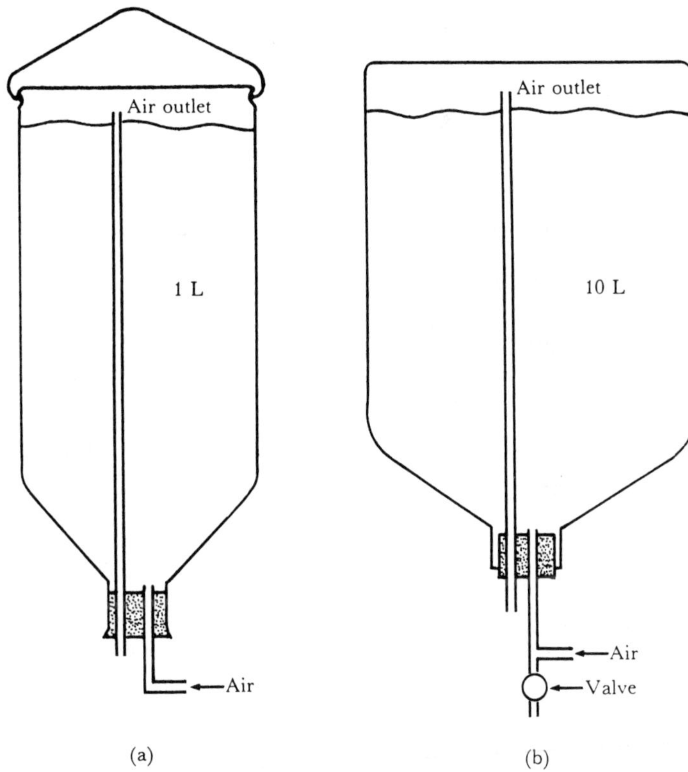

Figure 8-10 *Hatch vessels for brine shrimp cysts adapted from glucose bottles.* Source: Kinne (1976).

Horizontal hatch vessels are sometimes preferred when large numbers of nauplii are needed, despite their inferior design compared with vertical models.[74] Horizontal hatchers are wide and shallow. During hatching the increased surface area permits a greater number of cysts to accumulate in "windrows." Harvesting is less efficient than in vertical units because the reduced depth often does not permit adequate stratification and subsequent separation of nauplii from cyst debris. The horizontal hatch vessel pictured in Figure 8-11 consists of a tray with two compartments. The divider plate contains several holes drilled in a single plane approximately two-thirds the distance between the surface of the water and the bottom of the hatch vessel. A slide partition made of black acrylic keeps cysts placed in the incubator from drifting into the accumulator. Later, the slide partition serves as a light-proof lid over the incubator. Horizontal hatch vessels are usually made of acrylic, which can be cut with a hacksaw and sealed at the edges with acetone. Follow the general hatch procedure given previously, along with the instructions below.

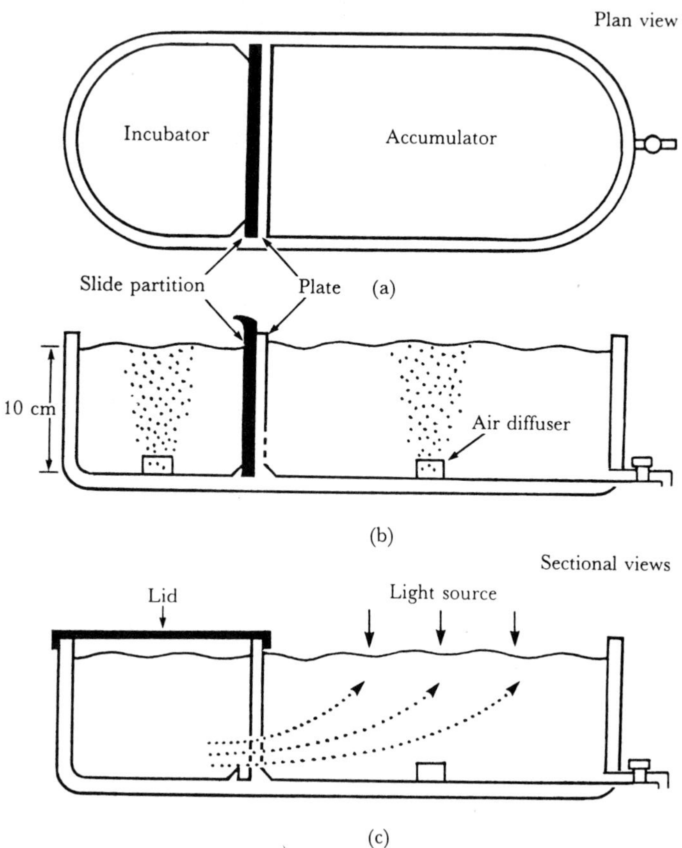

Figure 8-11 Horizontal hatch vessel for brine shrimp cysts. (a) Plan view illustrating the incubator (where cysts are placed to hatch) and accumulator (where nauplii are later concentrated and collected). (b) Cysts placed in the incubator are restrained by a slide partition made of black acrylic. (c) After the cysts hatch, the air diffusers are shut off; the slide partition becomes a light-proof lid with which to cover the incubator. Nauplii swim toward the illuminated accumulator through holes in the divider plate. Source: Kinne (1976).

How to Use a Horizontal Hatch Vessel

1. Insert the slide partition and add the hatch solution.
2. Add the cysts. Do not exceed 0.5 g/L by mass or 0.125 tsp/L by volume. Adjust the air in both compartments.
3. After 24 h shut off both air diffusers.
4. Cover the incubator with the slide partition to block all light.
5. Shine a light over the accumulator near the end, as far from the divider plate as possible. Aim the light straight down into the water.
6. Allow 2 h for nauplii to concentrate under the light, then replace the slide partition and drain the water from the accumulator into a net (~150 μm mesh size).
7. Rinse the nauplii with seawater or artificial seawater.

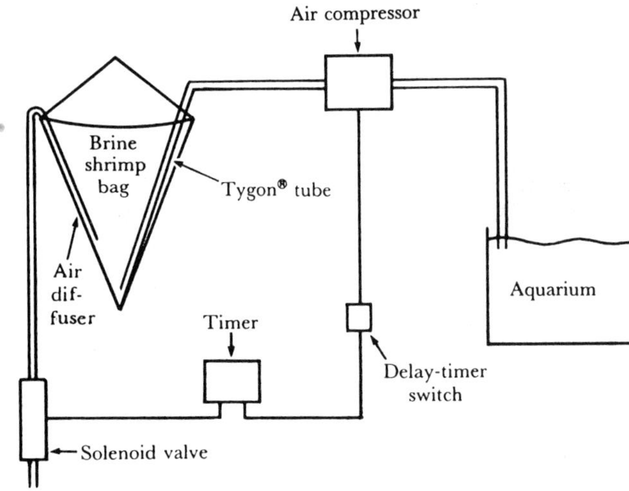

Figure 8-12 *Flow diagram for continuous feeding of brine shrimp nauplii to community aquarium exhibits containing planktivorous fishes.* Source: Kinne (1976).

Hatch vessels can be adapted for continuous addition of brine shrimp nauplii to large community exhibits containing planktivorous fishes (Fig. 8-12).

Method 8.3 Decapsulation of Brine Shrimp Cysts

The tough, dark-brown external layers of a brine shrimp cyst together constitute the *tertiary envelope*. This structure can be removed easily in strong hypochlorite solutions, leaving only the *cuticular membranes* surrounding the embryo. These make up the *embryonic cuticle*. The process is called *chemical decapsulation*, or simply *decapsulation* (Fig. 8-13). The embryonic cuticle, unlike the tertiary envelope, is resistant to hypochlorite oxidation.[75] Decapsulation is reported to offer five advantages: (*1*) more nauplii obtained from a hatch, (*2*) sterile cyst surfaces, (*3*) reduced cyst debris and easier isolation of nauplii in the hatch vessel, (*4*) a product that can serve as a safer (compared with undecapsulated cysts) and suitable food even before the nauplius emerges, and (*5*) nauplii of greater body mass.[76] The first is doubtful.[77] The second is based on some questionable assumptions (e.g., that commercial cysts are heavily contaminated, that many of the contaminant organisms present are dangerous pathogens, and that sterilizing the cysts prior to hatching them lowers the number of microorganisms in the hatch vessel).[78] The third reported advantage is a major consideration in aquaculture installations because of the large numbers of nauplii required; in public aquariums the problem of cyst debris and separation of nauplii is only a minor annoyance.

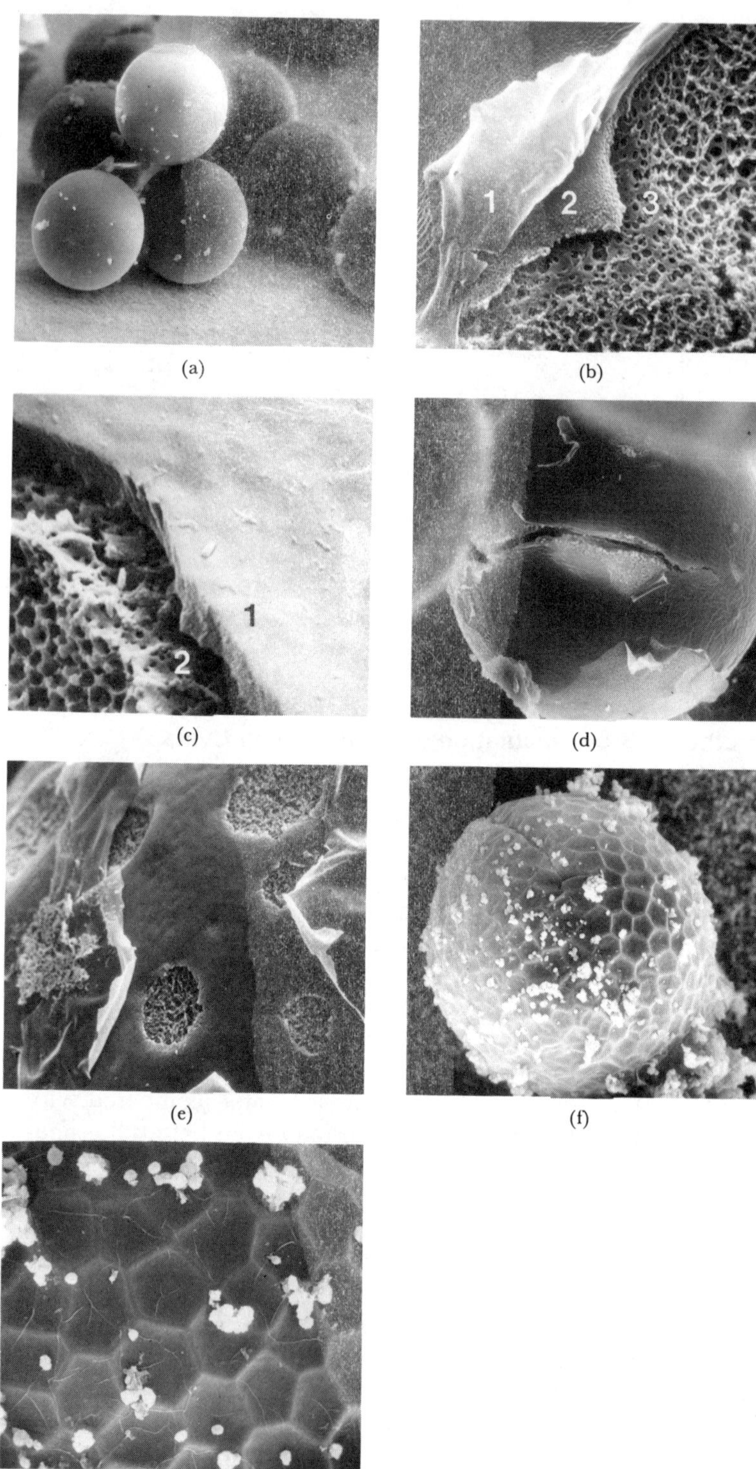

(a) (b) (c) (d) (e) (f) (g)

Figure 8-13 *Decapsulation sequence of desiccated* Artemia franciscana *cysts in equal parts Clorox® and seawater (~2.625% NaOCl by mass).* (a) *Untreated control cysts. 150x.* (b) *Tertiary envelope of a decapsulating cyst after 240 s: (1) outer membrane, (2) cortical layer, (3) alveolar layer. 5200x.* (c) *Fractured edge of an untreated cyst that was purposely squashed before being mounted: (1) cortical layer, (2) alveolar layer. 6400x.* (d) *Decapsulating cyst after 240 s showing the peeling edges of the outer membrane and underlying structures. The crack probably was not caused by decapsulation. 480x.* (e) *Decapsulating cyst at 240 s illustrating that the cortical layer is oxidized in a circular pattern. 1910x.* (f) *Decapsulated cyst at 840 s covered in debris of the oxidized tertiary envelope. The* polygonal septa *(underlying structures responsible for the hexagonal pattern) are clearly visible. 450x.* (g) *Closer view of the previous specimen (840 s). Wrinkles are visible in the outer cuticular membrane. This overlies the* fibrous layer, *which contains the polygonal septa. 1000x.* Source: Spotte and Anderson (1988).

The fourth appears to be valid, although the logic may be faulty.[79] The fifth reason to decapsulate cysts is based on limited evidence.[80] All these factors and the problems associated with them should be considered before implementing the decapsulation procedure outlined below.

How to Decapsulate Brine Shrimp Cysts[81]

1 Wet any amount of cysts up to 1 g in 100 mL of seawater or artificial seawater at room temperature.
2 After 1 h dilute the suspension with 100 mL of Clorox®, a commercial bleach. Clorox® contains 5.25% sodium hypochlorite, NaOCl, by mass; the final decapsulating solution will be ~2.625%. Simultaneously add 6 mL of a 1% sodium hydoxide, NaOH, solution (mass/vol). This is made by dissolving 1 g of NaOH pellets in a little seawater or artificial seawater and diluting to 100 mL with the same solvent. Both solutions should be cold (5 to 8°C) when used because the oxidation reaction generates heat. Clorox® should be stored in a refrigerator.
3 Decapsulate for 15 min. As the tertiary envelope is oxidized the cysts become white, then change to orange, the color of the embryo as seen through the thin cuticular membranes.[82]
4 If the cysts are to be hatched immediately, follow the general hatch procedure given previously.
5 If the cysts are to be stored, place them in saturated brine.[83] This is made by adding uniodized table salt to tap water, preferably between 20 and 30°C. Stir the water gently and continue adding salt until no more dissolves, as demonstrated by the appearance of salt crystals at the bottom of the container. Allow the solution to settle and decant the saturated brine. Store refrigerated.

Method 8.4 Rearing Brine Shrimp on Dead Foods and Feeds

Brine shrimp can be reared to maturity at a density of ~2 shrimp/mL. At a concentration of 0.75 g of cysts hatched in 0.75 L of hatch solution this results in 180,000 nauplii, assuming an average of 300,000 cysts/g and 80% hatch. For the first 3 d the nauplii can be fed dried rice bran; thereafter, use dried algae made either from phytoplankton or seaweeds.[84] Both the bran and the algae should be finely powdered to ensure particle sizes small enough to be ingested. A representative proximate analysis is presented in Table 8-35. Alternatively, use one of the encapsulated feeds devised for crustacean larvae and available

TABLE 8-35 Proximate analyses of a seaweed (*Enteromorpha* sp.), a species of phytoplankton (*Spirulina* sp.), and rice bran as percentage dry mass.

Food item	Protein	Lipid	Carbohydrate	Moisture	Ash
Enteromorpha sp.	31.1	2.2	49.2	10.4	7.1
Spirulina sp.	58.1	10.2	12.7	7.2	11.8
Rice bran	13.4	16.7	51.8	7.8	10.3

Source: Johnson (1980).

commercially. Feeding rate is an important factor; overfeeding retards growth even if the food particles are the proper size to be used efficiently. Rearing is most efficient in total darkness and at temperatures of 28 to 30°C.[85] In addition, brine shrimp grow faster if the salinity is higher than that of normal seawater. The nauplii can be transferred directly from a low-salinity hatch solution to a high-salinity rearing solution without stress. Addition of vitamins may enhance growth rate, but this is speculation. Vitamins known to be essential for growth are listed in Table 8-36. Appropriate amounts need to be determined experimentally.

How to Rear Brine Shrimp on Dead Foods and Feeds

1. Raise the temperature of the rearing solution (seawater or artificial seawater of normal salinity) to 30°C, then increase the specific gravity to ~1.085 with NaCl.
2. Estimate the number of nauplii to be reared based on 80% of 300,000 cysts/g added originally to the hatch vessel.
3. Fill the rearing container to give an estimated final density of ~2 brine shrimp/mL by count (Method 8.6).

TABLE 8-36 Vitamins essential for growth of brine shrimp.

Vitamin
Thiamin
Niacin
Pantothenate
Pyridoxamine
Riboflavin
Folic acid
Biotin[1]
Putrescine[1]
A, D, E[2]

Source: D'Agostino (1980).

Notes: "Extends longevity,"[1] thought to be essential.[2]

4 Adjust the water temperature to 30°C and provide very low aeration (no more than 0.5 L/min of air).

5 Transfer the nauplii directly to the rearing container after siphoning them into a net or sieve (~150 μm mesh size). Allow the excess hatch solution to drain off and rinse the nauplii with seawater or artificial seawater.

6 Feed powdered rice bran for the first 3 d at 0.1 mg/(d·mL) in two feedings. To make a stock suspension of rice bran powder:

Add 1 g to 250 mL of unused rearing solution, prepared according to step 1. This gives a concentration of 4 mg/mL.

Add 1 mL of stock suspension for each 40 mL in the rearing container.

Store in the refrigerator. Shake to resuspend immediately before use.

7 Feed algae powder in two feedings at 0.5 mg/(d·mL) from day 4 until harvest at 10 to 14 d. To make a stock suspension of algae powder:

Add 5 g to 250 mL of unused rearing solution, prepared according to step 1. This gives a concentration of ~20 mg/mL.

Add 1 mL of stock suspension for each 40 mL in the rearing container.

Store in the refrigerator. Shake to resuspend immediately before use.

Method 8.5 Rearing Brine Shrimp on Live Phytoplankton

Brine shrimp can be reared to adult size on live phytoplankton. This is sometimes more efficient and less expensive than Method 8.4. Light should be continuous and at intensities conducive to phytoplankton culture (Method 8.9).

How to Rear Brine Shrimp on Live Phytoplankton

1 Add newly hatched nauplii (~2/mL by count, Method 8.6) to a plastic carboy (18 to 20 L) containing phytoplankton in exponential growth (~5 d, Fig. 8-14). This growth phase is described in Method 8.13.

2 Aerate moderately with air diffusers.

3 Every 2 d siphon the growing brine shrimp into a net (~150 μ mesh size) and discard the old rearing solution.

4 Rinse debris from the brine shrimp with seawater or artificial seawater and transfer to another carboy of phytoplankton in

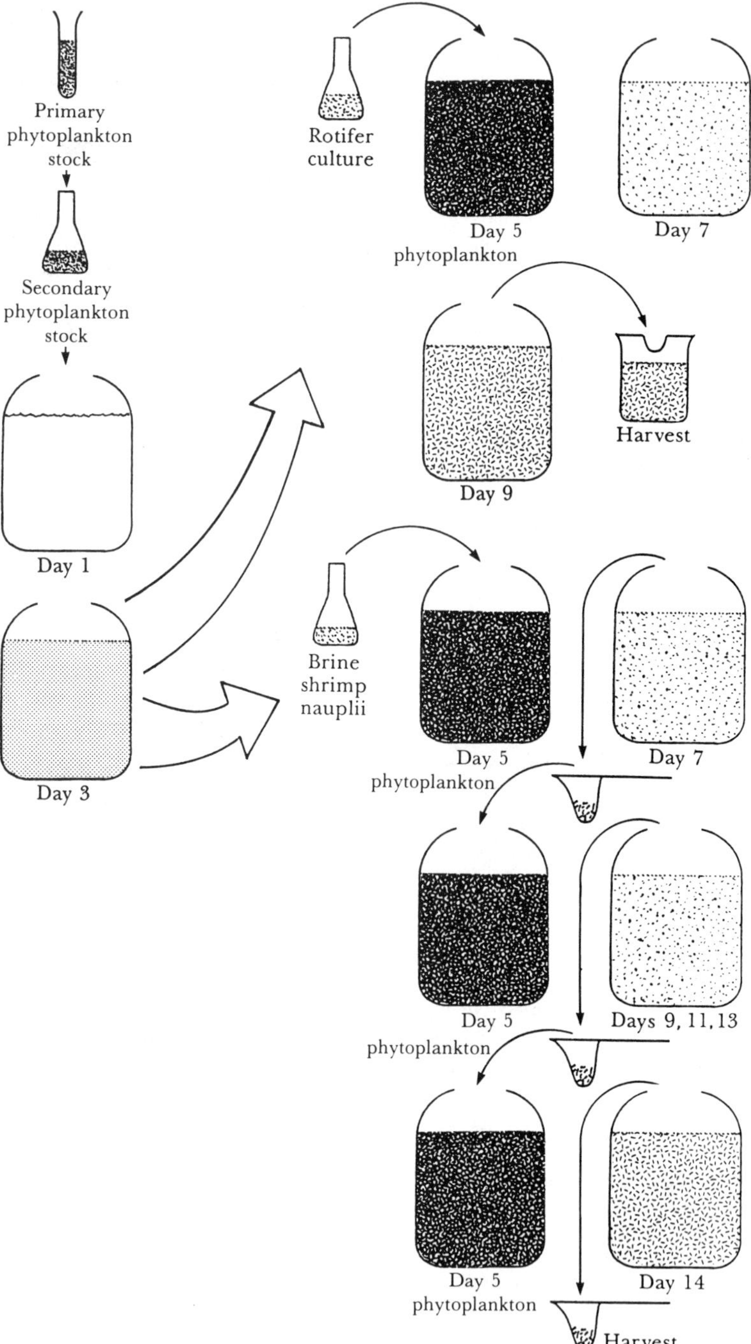

Figure 8-14 *Simplified flow diagram for culture of phytoplankton* (left), *rearing of rotifers* (top right), *and rearing of brine shrimp to adult size* (bottom right). *The right-hand portion of the graphic illustrates a common "green water" technique.* Source: Stephen Spotte and Patricia M. Bubucis, Sea Research Foundation.

exponential growth. The solutions turn clearer as the phytoplankton cells are consumed.

5 Adult size is attained within 2 weeks. Harvest by siphoning into a net and rinsing to remove debris.

This procedure requires some practice. ''Green-water'' inoculations may have to be made more frequently if either the growth or harvest is substandard. The amount of water replaced at each inoculation determines the density of phytoplankton cells.

Method 8.6 Breeding Brine Shrimp

When culture conditions are right brine shrimp breed readily, producing more than 100 offspring every 4 d, and the adults may live 6 months or longer. Brine shrimp ordinarily reproduce *ovoviviparously* (the eggs are retained internally and young are born as free-swimming nauplii), or *oviparously* (the eggs, which later become cysts, are shed into the water). The mode of reproduction can be controlled by manipulating environmental factors. Ovoviviparity is preferable because two steps are omitted (no cysts must be collected and hatched).[86] Factors affecting the mode of reproduction are poorly understood, but dissolved oxygen concentration appears to be important. At high oxygen concentrations ovoviviparity dominates.[87] Maintaining adequate dissolved oxygen concentrations can be difficult in warm, high-salinity water, and continuous aeration is required.

How to Breed Brine Shrimp

1 Determine the volume of a shallow tray and fill it with rearing solution (Method 8.4).

2 Adjust the temperature to 30°C.

3 Add two brine shrimp nauplii per 10 mL (see the counting procedure below).

4 Add several air diffusers spaced evenly apart; aerate moderately.

5 Feed algae powder at 0.5 mg/(d·mL) in two feedings. Use the stock suspension described in step 7 of Method 8.4.

6 Maintain the tray in continuous darkness.

7 Harvest adults periodically with a net (0.5 to 1.0 mm mesh size).

How to Count Brine Shrimp Nauplii

1. Distribute a 1.0-mL sample of hatch solution containing nauplii to a Boerner slide; add 0.1 mL to each of the 10 depressions.
2. If necessary, add a drop of formalin to each depression to fix the nauplii and stop their movements.
3. Count under low power (10x) using a dissecting microscope.
4. The number of nauplii per millilitre is the total count of the slide. If the nauplii are too numerous to count, dilute before counting and multiply the total count by the dilution factor to obtain original density.

Method 8.7 Rotifer Culture Procedures

Several species of rotifers have been cultured. The procedures I describe have been adapted from different sources and are meant for use in the culture of *Brachionus plicatilis*, an inhabitant of saline environments. Like the brine shrimp, *B. plicatilis* often appears in temporary ponds and is tolerant of extreme environmental conditions.[88] My use of the term ''rotifer'' refers to *B. plicatilis*, unless stated otherwise. The rotifer is cosmopolitan, and several strains have been described. Two are designated S and L, which I presume mean short and long. They differ slightly in morphology and noticeably in length. Lengths of 99 to 250 μm have been reported.[89]

Like brine shrimp, rotifers can be cultured either with live phytoplankton (''green water'' procedure) or nonliving particles (e.g., powdered yeasts and phytoplankton). ''Green water'' procedures are troublesome but ordinarily produce more rotifers. As in brine shrimp culture, either procedure is suitable if the apparatus is well designed and managed. Some authors recommend starting the culture with live phytoplankton and later switching to powdered food, which reduces the size of the phytoplankton culture that must be maintained. Several methods of rotifer culture have been published,[90] but I shall describe only two: *changing tanks* (Fig. 8-15) and *drain-down* (Figure 8-16).[91] A modified drain-down procedure is outlined in Fig. 8-14 (top right).

The changing tanks method requires several vessels of the same volume. All-glass aquariums or plastic carboys are adequate. Phytoplankton can be cultured directly in these vessels, and the addition of phytoplankton inoculants to each is staggered so that the stationary phase (Method 8.13) is reached sequentially. The actual time required depends on many factors (e.g., light intensity, temperature, nutrient composition of the culture solution, cell density of the inoculant, species).

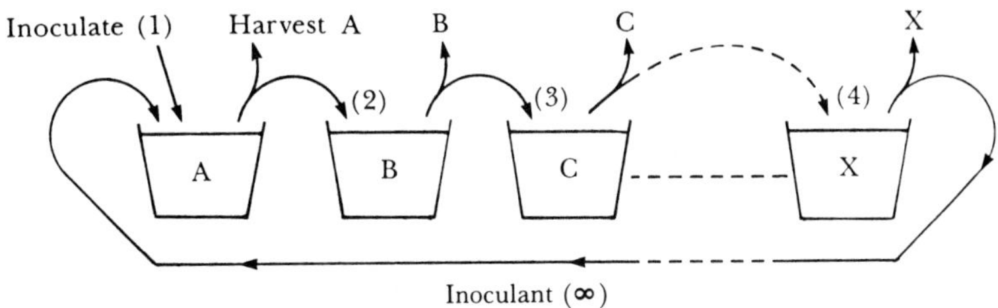

Figure 8-15 *The changing tanks method of rotifer culture.* Source: Hirata (1979).

Changing Tanks Procedure[92]

1 Fill a series of culture vessels (empty aquariums, plastic carboys) with equal volumes of phytoplankton culture solution (Method 8.8) and place an air diffuser in each.

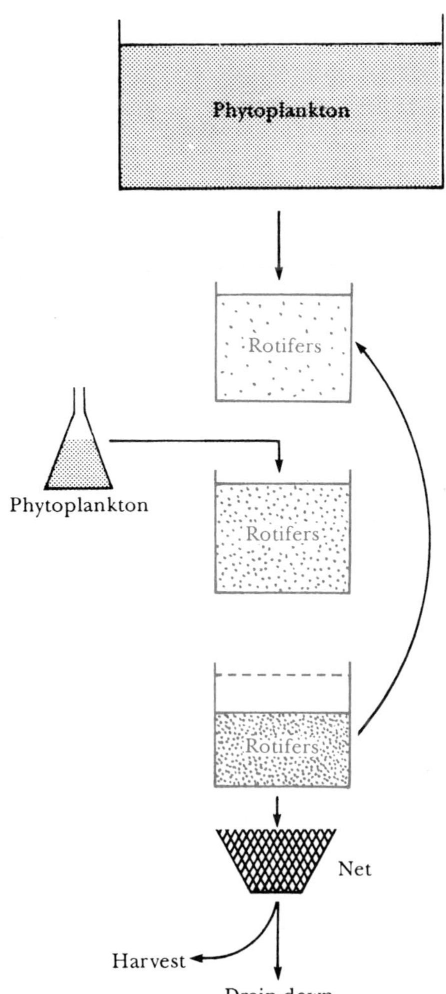

Figure 8-16 *The drain-down method of rotifer culture.* Source: Hirata (1979).

2 Inoculate the vessels with live phytoplankton and determine by periodic cell counts (Method 8.13) the time required to reach the stationary phase (maximum density). Repeat until the timing of this step is reproducible.
3 Inoculate vessels containing phytoplankton in the stationary phase with rotifers (10 to 50/mL). The phytoplankton have been consumed when the water turns clear. Note the time required. Repeat this step until the timing is reproducible.
4 Establish a series of culture vessels all subjected to the same conditions of light, temperature, and aeration rate as in the first three steps.
5 Inoculate the first vessel with phytoplankton.
6 When the stationary phase is reached (now determined by length of time, not cell counts), inoculate with rotifers (10 to 20/mL).
7 Inoculate the second and subsequent vessels with phytoplankton at appropriate intervals.
8 When phytoplankton in the first vessel have been consumed, siphon all the water through a plankton net (~69 μm mesh size). Determine the proper mesh size beforehand by measuring several rotifers under a microscope.
9 Transfer the rotifers to a second vessel with stationary phase phytoplankton.
10 Wash the first vessel and prepare it to receive a new inoculant of phytoplankton.
11 Repeat steps 8 and 9 until rotifer density is >200/mL, then harvest all but enough to inoculate another phytoplankton culture. Count rotifers at 20x using the procedure in Method 8.6 for brine shrimp nauplii.

Drain-Down Procedure[92]

1 Establish a large culture of phytoplankton and grow to the stationary phase.
2 Transfer the phytoplankton and phytoplankton culture solution (Method 8.8) to a suitable vessel and inoculate with rotifers (10 to 50/mL).
3 When the water becomes pale green, add a suspension of yeast or phytoplankton powder daily at a ratio of 1 g/10^6 rotifers.
4 When the rotifer density reaches >100/mL, remove part of the population by draining 25% of the water through a plankton net (~69 μm mesh size). Count rotifers at 20× using the procedure in Method 8.6.

5 Replace the harvested volume with culture solution.
6 Repeat daily until the culture water becomes fetid. The culture ordinarily can be maintained for 2 to 4 weeks.
7 Empty the vessel, clean it, and start again.

Method 8.8 Artificial Seawater—Culture Solutions

To be called a *culture solution* an artificial seawater must contain essential compounds necessary to complete the life cycle, excluding those supplied as dietary constituents when the organism being cultured is an animal. A culture solution differs in important respects from a maintenance solution, which is successful merely by keeping an organism in good condition at one stage of its life cycle (e.g., as an adult). The most completely defined culture solutions in marine biology have been devised for oceanic phytoplankton. All algae rely totally on the environment to supply essential growth factors. This method of obtaining nutrients distinguishes them from fishes, which probably can satisfy most of their needs through digestion of plant and animal tissues. A functional culture solution for phytoplankton contains every substance known to be essential, primarily major and minor ions (Table 8-37). In addition, many species are *auxotrophic* (require vitamins); most higher plants are not. The algae as a group need only three vitamins: thiamin, cyanocobalamin, and biotin. The first two are required alone or in combination by most auxotrophic species, and cyanocobalamin appears to be required more often than thiamin. Biotin is needed by only a few species. Of phytoplankton species studied to date approximately 70% require cyanocobalamin, 10% thiamin, and 2% biotin.[93]

TABLE 8-37 Elements essential to at least one species of algae. Those in the left column are essential to all algae.

Oxygen	Potassium
Hydrogen	Calcium
Carbon	Sulfur
Nitrogen	Sodium
Phosphorus	Cobalt
Magnesium	Vanadium
Iron	Silicon
Copper	Chlorine
Manganese	Boron
Zinc	Iodine
Molybdenum	

Source: O'Kelley (1974).

GP2 CULTURE SOLUTION Culture solutions can be complete or require enrichment additives. *Complete culture solutions* are chemically defined and contain major ions, minor ions, and vitamins.[94] "Chemically defined" is accompanied by the disclaimer that the composition of a complex solution cannot be known completely. *Enrichment additives* are minor ions and vitamins added to seawater or artificial seawater.[95] GP2 culture solution is a complete recipe. Others perhaps work as well, but I am most familiar with this one. Phytoplankton in general tolerate pH, alkalinity, salinity, and major ion ratios that deviate substantially from seawater values. Consequently, a number of formulas that support phytoplankton growth are unsuitable for fishes.

GP2 culture solution has salinity, pH, and alkalinity values comparable with offshore seawater. Most of the components reflect seawater concentrations (Table 8-38; compare with Table 1.1, molar scale). Solutions A through C (Table 8.39) can be autoclaved without precipitating;[96] solution D is sterilized by microfiltration. The major ions are identical in concentration to GP2 maintenance solution (Table 1-10), except that all components are reagent-grade to improve chemical definition. Minor ions and vitamins make up solutions C and D. Some of the

TABLE 8-38 Ionic species concentrations for GP2 culture solution.

Species	mol/L	μg/L of solution
Cl^-	5.45×10^{-1}	1.93×10^{7}
Na^+	4.68×10^{-1}	1.08×10^{7}
Mg^{2+}	5.32×10^{-2}	1.29×10^{6}
S	2.82×10^{-2}	9.04×10^{5}
Ca^{2+}	1.02×10^{-2}	4.09×10^{5}
K^+	1.02×10^{-2}	3.99×10^{5}
Br^-	8.40×10^{-4}	6.71×10^{4}
C[1]	3.21×10^{-3}	2.76×10^{4}
N[1]	1.53×10^{-3}	2.09×10^{4}
Sr^{2+}	9.10×10^{-5}	7.97×10^{3}
B	4.08×10^{-4}	4.41×10^{3}
P	9.31×10^{-5}	2.88×10^{3}
$Fe^{3+,2+}$[2]	3.50×10^{-6}	1.95×10^{2}
I^-	5.00×10^{-7}	6.34×10^{1}
Mo	1.00×10^{-7}	9.59×10^{0}
Zn^{2+}	7.60×10^{-8}	4.97×10^{0}
V	5.00×10^{-8}	2.55×10^{0}
Mn^{2+}	3.60×10^{-9}	1.98×10^{-1}

Source: Spotte et al. (1984a).

Notes: Concentrations in mol/L recalculated from original reference to include vitamin constituents,[1] concentrated 100 times seawater.[2]

TABLE 8-39 Component concentrations in GP2 culture solution. Calculated final salinity = 34.09‰.[1]

Solution	Salt	Formula	mol/L	g/L of solution
A	Sodium chloride	$NaCl$	4.09×10^{-1}	2.39×10^{1}
	Sodium sulfate	Na_2SO_4	2.82×10^{-2}	4.00×10^{0}
	Potassium chloride	KCl	9.36×10^{-3}	6.98×10^{-1}
	Sodium bicarbonate	$NaHCO_3$	2.30×10^{-3}	1.93×10^{-1}
	Potassium bromide	KBr	8.40×10^{-4}	1.00×10^{-1}
	Disodium borate	$Na_2B_4O_7 \cdot 10H_2O$	1.02×10^{-4}	3.90×10^{-2}
B	Magnesium chloride	$MgCl_2 \cdot 6H_2O$	5.32×10^{-2}	1.08×10^{1}
	Calcium chloride	$CaCl_2 \cdot 2H_2O$	1.02×10^{-2}	1.50×10^{0}
	Strontium chloride	$SrCl_2 \cdot 6H_2O$	9.10×10^{-5}	2.43×10^{-2}
C	Sodium dihydrogen phosphate[2]	$NaH_2PO_4 \cdot H_2O$	9.31×10^{-5}	1.28×10^{-2}
	Disodium EDTA[3]	$Na_2C_{10}H_{14}N_2O_8 \cdot 2H_2O$	7.16×10^{-6}	2.66×10^{-3}
	Ferric citrate	$Fe \cdot C_6H_5O_7 \cdot H_2O$	3.50×10^{-6}	9.20×10^{-4}
	Disodium molybdate	$Na_2MoO_4 \cdot 2H_2O$	1.00×10^{-7}	2.42×10^{-5}
	Potassium iodide	KI	5.00×10^{-7}	8.30×10^{-5}
	Zinc sulfate	$ZnSO_4 \cdot 7H_2O$	7.60×10^{-8}	2.18×10^{-5}
	Sodium vanadate	$NaVO_3$	5.00×10^{-8}	6.10×10^{-6}
	Manganese sulfate	$MnSO_4 \cdot H_2O$	3.60×10^{-9}	6.08×10^{-7}
D	Urea[2]	CH_4N_2O	7.45×10^{-4}	4.47×10^{-2}
	Thiamin hydrochloride	$C_{12}H_{18}Cl_2N_4OS$	5.79×10^{-6}	1.95×10^{-3}
	Biotin	$C_{10}H_{16}N_2O_3S$	4.09×10^{-9}	9.99×10^{-7}
	Cyanocobalamin	$C_{63}H_{88}CoN_{14}O_{14}P$	7.21×10^{-10}	9.77×10^{-7}

Source: Spotte et al. (1984a).

Notes: $S = (1.80655)(Cl)$ where Cl represents chlorinity, ‰ (Wilson 1975), which in this case (a chemically defined solution) is g Cl/kg of final solution at a measured final solution density (ρ) of 1.022857 g/cm^3 at 20°C;[1] N/P ratio = 16;[2] two molar equivalents added for iron, manganese, and zinc.[3]

minor ions are *complexed* (chemically bound to an organic substratum)[97] with EDTA;* the resultant compounds decompose little during autoclaving and are relatively resistant to bacterial oxidation in culture. The fact that EDTA *photodegrades* (is light labile) is advantageous because iron and perhaps other cations of low solubility are released for uptake and assimilation by phytoplankton.[98] Iron and manganese apparently are growth limiting at low concentrations, and levels of these constituents have been increased in excess of seawater values.[98] Moreover, complexed iron compounds are adsorbed strongly onto the walls of glass culture vessels, and much of the original concentration may be lost within a few hours.[99] Silicon has been omit-

*Ethylenediaminetetraacetate (EDTA) is one of the aminocarboxylates. Other examples are CDTA (cyclohexylenediaminetetraacetate), DTPA (diethylenetraminepentaacetate), and EDDHA or ethylenediamine di(o-hydroxyphenyl)acetate. Their relative strengths as complexing agents for metal cations in seawater increase in the order in which I have presented them.

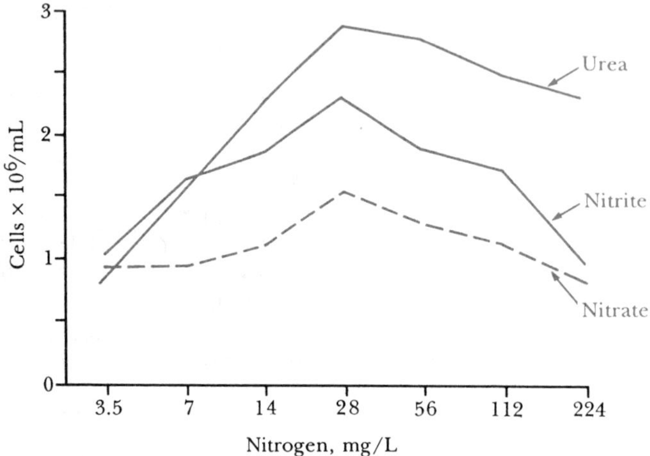

Figure 8-17 *Maximum cell density of* Dunaliella tertiolecta *in the s tionary growth phase at different sources and concentrations of nitrogen (data points omitted).* Source: Fabregas et al. (1989).

ted because it is required only by diatoms.[100] Copper has been excluded because of its toxicity to phytoplankton under certain conditions even at normal seawater concentrations.[101] Molybdenum and cobalt are important to seaweeds.[102] The greater concentrations of these elements in comparison with seawater values should enhance the performance of seaweed filters (Chapter 2). Urea was selected as the nitrogen source because ammonia is toxic at low concentrations to animals (Chapter 2) and many species of phytoplankton.[103] In addition, the uptake and assimilation of ammonia and nitrate by phytoplankton changes the alkalinity and pH of the culture solution.[104] One study has shown that growth of *Dunaliella tertiolecta* (Chlorophyceae) is superior in some respects when urea is the nitrogen source (Fig. 8-17). Addition of biotin is optional.[105]

MIXING GP2 CULTURE SOLUTION[106] To prevent precipitation, the original GP2 mixing procedure called for separate autoclaving of the major anhydrous (solution A) and hydrated (solution B) salts. After cooling, the two solutions are combined. In the revised procedure given here, solutions A and B are dissolved and autoclaved together, except for sodium bicarbonate, which is autoclaved separately either as a dry powder or stock solution and added later to the A + B solution. The major salts are still listed as groups A and B (Table 8-39) for those who prefer the original procedure. In either procedure the ingredients can be concentrated to five times tabular concentrations.

Solution C components are weighed to 1000 times the tabular values, combined in one flask with distilled-deionized water, and autoclaved. Solution D components also are concentrated to 1000 times. The ingredients decompose if autoclaved (unless acidified first), and sterilization is accomplished by microfiltration through a 0.22-μm cellulose acetate membrane filter. Urea is included with the vitamins because it is heat labile.

In the following procedures, distilled water can be substituted for distilled-deionized water if the objective is routine phytoplankton culture. This also holds true for the next subsection. Distilled-deionized water is recommended for experimental work. Throughout, I emphasize that additions are made volumetrically (i.e., in terms of the *final* volume of GP2 culture solution, *final* volume of stock solution, or *final* volumes of solutions C and D).

How to Mix Solutions A and B

The volume of solution A + B that can be mixed depends on the capacity of the autoclave and size of the culture vessels. A typical vessel holds 15 to 20 L. Polycarbonate water-cooler carboys, available through distributors of spring water, are less expensive than autoclavable, linear polyethylene units purchased from scientific equipment distributors. Fit each vessel with an aspirator spout, silicone tubing, and metal clamp; spigots and plastic clamps leak with repeated autoclaving. Plastic clamps can be used during culture and harvest of the phytoplankton. To prevent melting, autoclave the carboys at least two-thirds full, or sterilize them without heat (e.g., UV radiation, chlorine-based oxidants). Calibrate each carboy by marking the desired volume with indelible ink. If the autoclave is too small to receive upright carboys, concentrate solutions A + B to five times and autoclave in smaller vessels. Afterward, transfer to larger, sterile vessels and bring to volume and normal concentration.

1 Fill a carboy halfway with distilled-deionized water, ddH_2O, place on a magnetic stirrer, and add a large Teflon®-coated stir bar.

2 To calculate the amount of *final* GP culture solution, multiply the component concentrations (Table 8-39, g/L column) by the appropriate factor (e.g., multiply by 20 for 20 L of *final* GP2 culture solution) and weigh all A + B salts except sodium bicarbonate. In this procedure, the A + B salts are *not* concentrated. Add the salts to the carboy while stirring.

3 Autoclave appropriate portions of dry sodium bicarbonate (e.g., 3.68 g for 20-L volumes of *final* GP2 culture solution) in screw-capped test tubes at 120°C for 15 min at a pressure

of 103 kPa (15 lb/in^2). This step can be performed in advance. Cool to room temperature and dispense one portion to the carboy after the carboy has been autoclaved (step 8).

4 Alternatively, make a primary stock solution of sodium bicarbonate by adding 38.6 g of dry, sterile $NaHCO_3$ to a sterile 500-mL volumetric flask and diluting to volume with sterile ddH_2O. This step also can be performed in advance. Dispense at 2.5 mL/L of *final* GP2 culture solution (step 8).

5 When the salts have dissolved, remove the stir bar and dilute the carboy almost to volume with ddH_2O (i.e., almost to the predetermined volume level marked with indelible ink). Some water will be lost during autoclaving.

6 Plug the mouth of the carboy loosely with an autoclavable foam stopper or gauze-wrapped nonabsorbent cotton.

7 Autoclave at 120°C for 30 min at a pressure of 103 kPa. To prevent precipitation, open the autoclave to begin cooling immediately after the pressure has been released. The combined solution (A + B) is clear and colorless.

8 Cool to room temperature. Add sterile sodium bicarbonate. Also add solutions C and D (see below) at 1 mL each per litre of *final* GP2 culture solution.

9 Dilute to volume with sterile ddH_2O and seal the mouth with Parafilm® or a sterile screw cap.

How to Mix Stock Solution C Concentrated 1000 Times

1 Weigh 0.0608 g $MnSO_4 \cdot H_2O$. Transfer to a 100-mL volumetric flask and dilute to volume with ddH_2O to make a primary stock solution of 6.08×10^{-4} g/mL. The volume used (1 mL/L of *final* stock solution C) contains 1000 times the concentration of manganese sulfate shown in Table 8-39 (g/L column). The primary stock solution is clear and colorless.

2 Multiply the remaining constituents of solution C (Table 8-39, g/L column) by 1000 before weighing.

3 After each salt is weighed add it to a 1-L Erlenmeyer flask containing ~700 mL of hot ddH_2O and a Teflon®-coated stir bar. Also add 1.0 mL of primary manganese sulfate stock solution. Make salt additions while the flask is being heated and stirred on a magnetic stirrer at low speed.

4 When the salts have dissolved, cover the flask with Parafilm® and cool to room temperature.

5 Transfer to a 1-L volumetric flask. Rinse the Erlenmeyer flask (which still contains the stir bar) with a little ddH_2O and add the rinse water to the volumetric flask. Dilute to volume with

ddH_2O. Solution C stock concentrated 1000 times the values in Table 8-39 is clear and pale amber.

6 Transfer to the 1-L Erlenmeyer flask. Plug the flask with autoclavable foam or nonabsorbent cotton and autoclave at 120°C for 15 min at a pressure of 103 kPa.

7 Cool to room temperature. Transfer to a sterile 1-L volumetric flask and replace lost water by diluting to volume with sterile ddH_2O.

8 Dispense aseptically into sterile 100-mL flasks with sterile screw caps. Screw the caps on tightly and store in a darkened refrigerator at <8°C. Shelf life is at least 1 year. If a glass-fronted refrigerator is used, store in sterile amber glass bottles.

9 Use at a concentration of 1 mL/L of *final* GP2 culture solution.

How to Mix Stock Solution D Concentrated 1000 Times

1 Prepare a primary stock solution of biotin by weighing 0.0999 g biotin. Add to a 100-mL volumetric flask, dilute almost to volume with ddH_2O, heat, and mix to dissolve. Cool to room temperature and dilute to volume. Primary biotin stock solution is clear and colorless. The solution an be divided into smaller volumes and stored in sterile, tightly sealed containers in a freezer. Use 1.0 mL/L of *final* stock solution D.

2 Prepare a primary stock solution of cyanocobalamin by weighing 0.0977 g cyanocobalamin. Add to a 100-mL volumetric flask with ~60 mL ddH_2O, heat, and mix to dissolve. Cool to room temperature and dilute to volume with ddH_2O. Primary cyanocobalamin stock solution is dark red. The solution can be divided into smaller volumes and stored in sterile, tightly sealed containers in a freezer. Use 1.0 mL/L of *final* stock solution D.

3 For a stock solution of solution D that is concentrated 1000 times, add 900 mL ddH_2O to a 1-L volumetric flask.

4 Weigh 1000 times the component concentrations of urea and thiamin·HCl (Table 8-39, g/L column) and add them to the flask.

5 Add 1.0 mL each of the primary stock solutions of biotin and cyanocobalamin.

6 Dilute to volume with ddH_2O and mix well. Solution D stock concentrated 1000 times the values in Table 8-39 is pale pink.

7 Filter-sterilize by passing through a sterile, 0.22-μm membrane filter.

8 Distribute in suitable volumes and store frozen in tightly sealed containers, preferably glass or polyethylene bottles.

9 Use at a concentration of 1 mL/L of *final* GP2 culture solution.

Note In rare situations, urea causes toxic ammonia reactions in some phytoplankton, either directly or indirectly as a result of bacterial activity. If necessary, substitute sodium nitrate at the equivalent concentration of nitrogen in urea ($NaNO_3$, 0.127 g/L of *final* GP2 culture solution).

MIXING GP2 LOW-SALINITY CULTURE SOLUTION The GP2 formula has been modified[107] as shown in Tables 8-40 and 8-41 by (*1*) lowering the salinity to 30‰, (*2*) increasing the concentrations of nitrogen and phosphorus, (*3*) altering the relative proportions of nitrogen and phosphorus to yield an N/P ratio of 25, and (*4*) replacing urea with nitrate. The nitrogen concentration of the original formula (as urea-N) was included when calculating the NO_3-N concentration of the low-salinity version. Low-salinity solutions are less strongly buffered because the ionic species concentrations are proportional to the salinity.

TABLE 8-40 Ionic species concentrations for GP2 low-salinity culture solution.

Species	mol/L	μg/L of solution
Cl^-	4.80×10^{-1}	1.70×10^{7}
Na^+	4.12×10^{-1}	9.47×10^{6}
Mg^{2+}	4.67×10^{-2}	1.14×10^{6}
S	2.48×10^{-2}	7.95×10^{5}
Ca^{2+}	8.98×10^{-3}	3.60×10^{5}
K^+	8.92×10^{-3}	3.49×10^{5}
Br^-	7.39×10^{-4}	5.90×10^{4}
C	2.18×10^{-3}	2.62×10^{4}
N[1]	3.57×10^{-3}	5.00×10^{4}
Sr^{2+}	7.50×10^{-5}	6.57×10^{3}
B	3.56×10^{-4}	3.85×10^{3}
P[1]	1.43×10^{-4}	4.43×10^{3}
$Fe^{3+,2+}$	3.50×10^{-6}	1.95×10^{2}
I^-	5.00×10^{-7}	6.34×10^{1}
Mo	1.00×10^{-7}	9.59×10^{0}
Zn^{2+}	7.60×10^{-8}	4.97×10^{0}
V	5.00×10^{-8}	2.55×10^{0}
Mn^{2+}	3.60×10^{-9}	1.98×10^{-1}

Source: Steele and Thursby (1988).

Note: Nitrogen and phosphorus concentrations and N/P ratio of 25 based on Ukeles and Wikfors (1988).[1]

TABLE 8-41 Component concentrations in GP2 low-salinity culture solution. Calculated final salinity = 30.11‰.[1]

Solution	Salt	Formula	mol/L	g/L of solution
A	Sodium chloride	$NaCl$	3.60×10^{-1}	2.10×10^{1}
	Sodium sulfate	Na_2SO_4	2.48×10^{-2}	3.52×10^{0}
	Potassium chloride	KCl	8.18×10^{-3}	6.10×10^{-1}
	Sodium nitrate[2]	$NaNO_3$	3.53×10^{-3}	3.00×10^{-1}
	Sodium bicarbonate	$NaHCO_3$	2.02×10^{-3}	1.70×10^{-1}
	Potassium bromide	KBr	7.39×10^{-4}	8.80×10^{-2}
	Disodium borate	$Na_2B_4O_7 \cdot 10H_2O$	8.91×10^{-5}	3.40×10^{-2}
B	Magnesium chloride	$MgCl_2 \cdot 6H_2O$	4.67×10^{-2}	9.50×10^{0}
	Calcium chloride	$CaCl_2 \cdot 2H_2O$	8.98×10^{-3}	1.32×10^{0}
	Strontium chloride	$SrCl_2 \cdot 6H_2O$	7.50×10^{-5}	2.14×10^{-2}
C	Sodium dihydrogen phosphate[2]	$NaH_2PO_4 \cdot H_2O$	1.43×10^{-4}	1.97×10^{-2}
	Disodium EDTA[3]	$Na_2C_{10}H_{14}N_2O_8 \cdot 2H_2O$	7.16×10^{-6}	2.66×10^{-3}
	Ferric citrate	$Fe \cdot C_6H_5O_7 \cdot H_2O$	3.50×10^{-6}	9.20×10^{-4}
	Disodium molybdate	$Na_2MoO_4 \cdot 2H_2O$	1.00×10^{-7}	2.42×10^{-5}
	Potassium iodide	KI	5.00×10^{-7}	8.30×10^{-5}
	Zinc sulfate	$ZnSO_4 \cdot 7H_2O$	7.60×10^{-8}	2.18×10^{-5}
	Sodium vanadate	$NaVO_3$	5.00×10^{-8}	6.10×10^{-6}
	Manganese sulfate	$MnSO_4 \cdot H_2O$	3.60×10^{-9}	6.08×10^{-7}
D	Thiamin hydrochloride	$C_{12}H_{18}Cl_2N_4OS.$	5.79×10^{-6}	1.95×10^{-3}
	Biotin	$C_{10}H_{16}N_2O_3S$	4.09×10^{-9}	9.99×10^{-7}
	Cyanocobalamin	$C_{63}H_{88}CoN_{14}O_{14}P$	7.21×10^{-10}	9.77×10^{-7}

Source: Steele and Thursby (1988).

Notes: $S = (1.80655)(Cl)$ where *Cl* represents chlorinity, ‰ (Wilson 1975), which in this case (a chemically defined solution) is g Cl/kg of final solution at a measured final solution density (ρ) of 1.019857 g/cm^3 at 20°C;[1] nitrogen and phosphorus concentrations and N/P ratio of 25 based on Ukeles and Wikfors (1988);[2] two molar equivalents added for iron, manganese, and zinc.[3]

Dense phytoplankton cultures can alter the buffer properties when NO_3^- is substituted for urea, a neutral molecule, resulting in elevated alkalinity and pH.[104] This ordinarily does not affect production of the hardier phytoplankton species.

Follow mixing instructions in the previous subsection, but use concentrations displayed in Table 8-41 (g/L column). The primary stock solution of manganese sulfate and the amount of its addition to solution C is the same as given previously. Primary vitamin stock solutions and the amount of each added to solution D also are identical with the previous procedure: solutions C and D are added at 1 mL/L of *final* GP2 low-salinity culture solution. To prepare a primary stock solution of sodium bicarbonate, follow the previous procedure (step 4) but use 33.6 g of material. Use at a concentration of 2.5 mL/L of *final* GP2 low-salinity culture solution.

Method 8.9 Phytoplankton Culture—The Culture Room[108]

Phytoplankton is the food of choice for rearing brine shrimp and rotifers. Stock cultures can be obtained from commercial suppliers (Table 8-42). A list of equipment and glassware is provided in Table 8-43. It is important to identify the species being cultured before starting. Stock cultures must be kept free of contamination by bacteria, protozoans, and other algae. Phytoplankton should be cultured in an enclosed space where light intensity and air temperature can be controlled. A phytoplankton culture room is shown in Figure 8-18. Specific requirements are described below.

Space Stock cultures and small volumes of phytoplankton can be grown and maintained in water baths or commercial incubators. Large volumes require shelves large enough to accommodate carboys of up to 20 L.

Temperature Most of the phytoplankton species grown for zooplankton food reproduce well at 16 to 24°C. Some species (e.g., *Dunaliella* and *Pyramimonas*) grow best near

TABLE 8-42 Suppliers of phytoplankton cultures.

Culture Collection of Algae
Department of Botany
University of Texas at Austin
Austin TX 78712

Carolina Biological Supply Company
2700 York Road
Burlington NC 27215

Culture Collection of Algae
Institute of Applied Microbiology
University of Tokyo
Bunkyo-ku
Tokyo 113, Japan

Institute of Terrestrial Ecology
Culture Centre of Algae and Protozoa
36 Storey's Way
Cambridge CB3 0DT, England

Sammlung von Algenkulturen
Pflanzenphysiologisches Institute der Universität Göttingen
Nikolausberger Weg 18
D-3400 Göttingen, Federal Republic of Germany

Source: Stephen Spotte.

TABLE 8-43 Equipment and glassware required for the phytoplankton culture room and laboratory.

Culture Room

Air compressor
Air filter
Carboys (~20-L glass or polycarbonate with aspirator spout)
Flexible airline tubing
Lamps (cool white fluorescent, 40 W, 16.5 cm long)
Silicone tubing (each piece ~30 cm long)
Temperature control (air conditioning)
Timer and thermostat switch for lamps
Tubing clamps (metal and plastic)
Water trap

Laboratory

Autoclave
Bunsen burner
Compound microscope
Depression slides
Flasks (125-mL and 1-L Erlenmeyer)
Hand tally
Hemacytometer
Membrane filters (0.22-μm pore size)
Membrane filtration apparatus
Microscope slides and coverslips
Nichrome transfer loop
Pipette canisters
Pipette container for used pipettes
Pipettes (1.0, 5.0, 10.0 mL Pasteur)
Pipette washer
Stoppers (autoclavable foam or gauze-wrapped nonabsorbent cotton)
Test tube racks
Test tubes (screw-capped, 120 mm long, 20-mm diameter)

Source: Patricia M. Bubucis, Sea Research Foundation.

16°C. A room air conditioner is recommended for any phytoplankton culture room because the fluorescent lamps used to illuminate the cultures give off heat. Air conditioning is made more efficient if the room is insulated.

Aeration To avoid contamination, never aerate stock cultures. Flasks with cultures having a large surface/volume ratio (e.g., Fernbach flasks containing 1 L of solution or 1-L Erlenmeyer flasks with 300 mL) must be swirled or agitated by hand once daily. Carboys and larger flasks require aeration to keep the cells in suspension, provide carbon dioxide, and control pH. Air compressors give off

Figure 8-18 *Phytoplankton culture room at Mystic Marinelife Aquarium, Mystic, Connecticut. The room is 1.3 m wide × 2.3 m long × 2.6 m high.* Source: Stephen Spotte.

waste heat and should be located outside the culture room. Equip air lines in the room with valves to control the aeration rate in each culture vessel (Fig. 8-19).

Water traps Place traps at low points to catch water in the air lines. A water trap can be a thick-walled flask sealed securely with a silicone stopper. Drill two holes in the stopper, each fitted with rigid tubing. Air entering the trap passes through a piece of tubing extending nearly to the bottom of the flask and exits through a piece extending not far beyond the base of the stopper (Fig. 8-19).

Air filters Filter the incoming air to trap particles and other contaminants. The filter can be a simple cartridge or flask filled with clean glass wool or polyester fiber. Use flexible airline tubing between the airline valves and pipettes in the carboys. Disposable, plugged, sterile 1.0-mL pipettes are convenient and have self-contained filters.

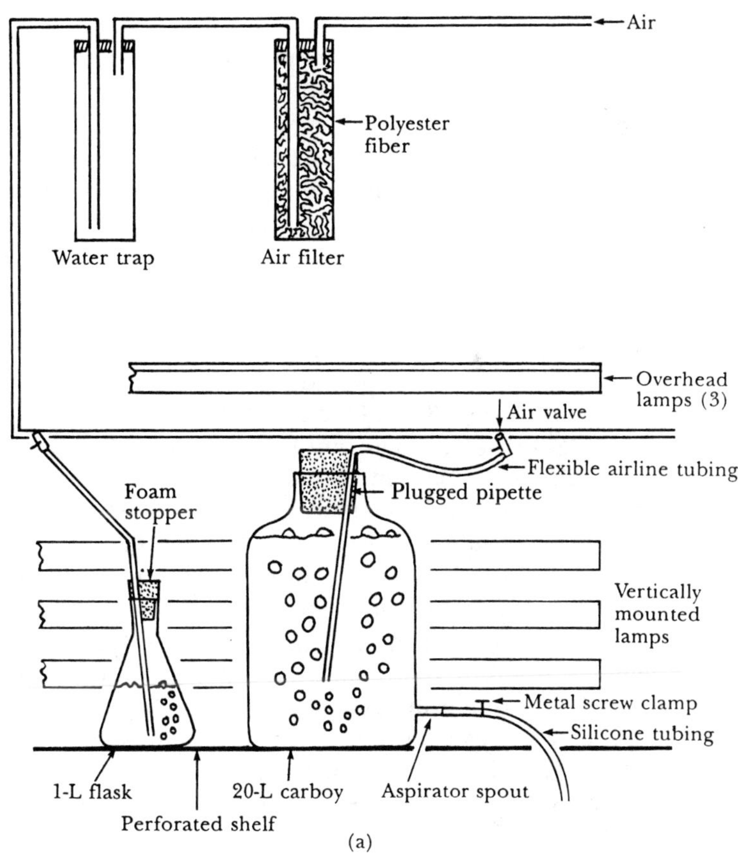

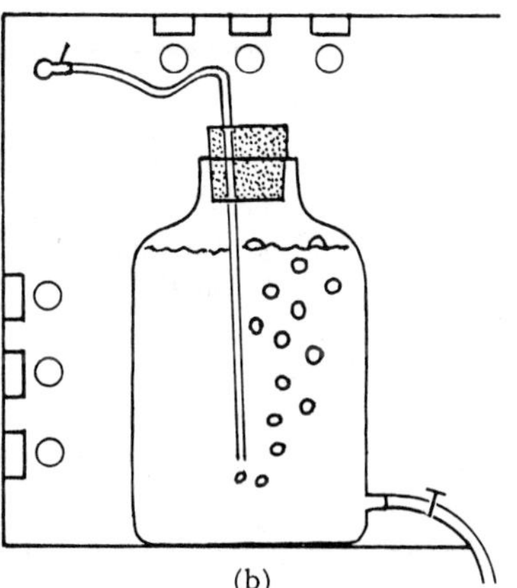

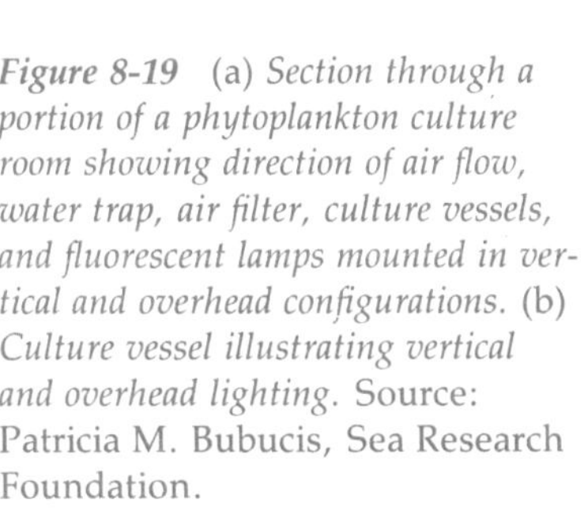

Figure 8-19 (a) *Section through a portion of a phytoplankton culture room showing direction of air flow, water trap, air filter, culture vessels, and fluorescent lamps mounted in vertical and overhead configurations.* (b) *Culture vessel illustrating vertical and overhead lighting.* Source: Patricia M. Bubucis, Sea Research Foundation.

Light intensity Measure light intensity at the midpoint of the culture vessels with a light meter capable of reading in lux. Intensities of 3000 to 4000 lx are suitable for routine culture; 10,000 lx is a safe maximum intensity. Long-term maintenance requires lower intensities of 500 to 1000 lx (Method 8.12).

Light sources Natural lighting is impractical in most situations, but a northern exposure that prevents entry of direct sunlight is sometimes acceptable. Consistent illumination is best provided by 40-W, cool white fluorescent lamps. The ballasts impart heat and should be mounted outside the culture room. Two lamps are adequate for stock cultures. Three or four lamps mounted both above and behind the carboys provide enough illumination for dense growth (Fig. 8-19). One set of lamps (either the upper or lower) is sufficient until growth becomes dense. Light efficiency can be increased with perforated shelves and by painting the room with high-gloss white paint.

Photoperiod The lighting circuit should have a timer to control hours of light and a thermostat switch that shuts off the lamps to prevent overheating of the room in case of air-conditioning failure. Ordinarily, little advantage is gained by lighting the room continuously. Some species of phytoplankton grow poorly under continuous light.[109] Light-dark cycles conserve energy and add a margin of safety if the air conditioning is shut off for any reason. Typical cycles are 14/10 (14 h of light, 10 h of darkness) and 16/8.

Method 8.10 Preparation of Glassware and GP2 Culture Solution[110]

The glassware and culture solution should be sterile. Method 8.8 gives procedures for preparing sterile GP2 culture solution. The salinity may need adjustment downward for some phytoplankton, but most species grown for food are tolerant within the range of 28 to 34‰.[111] Make all transfers using aseptic techniques. These require some dexterity (Method 8.11).

Carboys Modify commercial carboys by attaching a length of silicone tubing to the aspirator spout. Close the end of the tubing with a metal screw clamp. If there is no aspirator spout, make one by carefully drilling a hole near the base of a polycarbonate carboy and fitting it with a silicone stopper. Insert a piece of rigid plastic tubing through the stopper for connecting the silicone tubing. Inject the air through a pipette plugged with nonabsorbent cotton and inserted in the mouth of the carboy. Plug the mouth of the carboy with an autoclavable foam stopper or gauze-wrapped nonabsorbent cotton. Fill the carboys at least two-thirds full with liquid before autoclaving (Method 8.8). After autoclaving, add a plastic clamp to the silicone tubing for easier use.

Flasks and test tubes Plug empty flasks and test tubes with autoclavable foam stoppers or gauze-wrapped nonabsorbent cotton, or use screw caps. If screw caps are selected, wash and autoclave them several times beforehand to prevent toxicity. Screw the caps partly onto the flasks or tubes and tighten only after autoclaving and subsequent cooling.

Filtration and miscellaneous equipment Wrap equipment to be autoclaved in brown paper and make dust covers for plugged flasks and carboys by covering the tops and necks loosely with paper or heavy-duty aluminum foil

Pipettes Pipettes with nonabsorbent cotton should be baked (170°C for 4 h) or autoclaved for 15 min at 120°C and 103 kPa (15 lb/in) in a canister.[112] Pack the canisters loosely. Store used pipettes with tips down in a container of dilute liquid sterilizing agent (e.g., Clorox® or Wescodyne®) until enough have accumulated to wash. Unplug and wash the pipettes (tips up) with hot water in a pipette washer; rinse with distilled water, dH_2O. Dirty pipettes may require soaking in 10% HCl before being rinsed.

Sterile GP2 culture solution Prepare sterile GP2 culture solution (Method 8.8) for distribution in the following volumes: 10 mL (test tubes), 50 mL (125-mL Erlenmeyer flasks), 500 mL (1-L Erlenmeyer flasks), and 15 to 20 L (carboys). Do not tighten any screw caps until the containers have been autoclaved and cooled. Sterilize empty glassware and liquid volumes of <2 L in an autoclave for 15 min at 120°C and 103 kPa.[113] Carboys containing GP2 culture solution require 30 min.[114] Cool all vessels promptly after autoclaving. Small volumes are more easily prepared by filter-sterilizing the complete solution (solutions A through D) and distributing appropriate volumes aseptically to sterilized tubes or flasks over a flame.

Cleaning If glassware is cleaned with detergent, rinse thoroughly with tap water followed by at least three rinses with dH_2O. Alternatively, "acid strip" by rinsing with 10% (by volume) HCl for 10 min, then rinse three times with dH_2O.[114]

Method 8.11 Contamination Check[110]

Stock cultures are maintained in test tubes, and great care must be taken to avoid losses caused by contamination. Examine the original stock culture under the microscope for contamination and physical condition of the cells. Microscopic inspections should be made at several points in the culture procedure (Fig. 8-20). Check occasionally for bacterial contamination by transferring 0.5 mL of phytoplankton culture to tubes containing ~5 mL of sterile GP2 culture solution with 0.1% (mass/vol) of Bactopeptone.* Incubate at least 2 weeks in darkness at the same temperature used to culture the phytoplankton.[113] A cloudy culture indicates contamination. Clean contaminated stocks by

* Difco Laboratories, Detroit MI 48232.

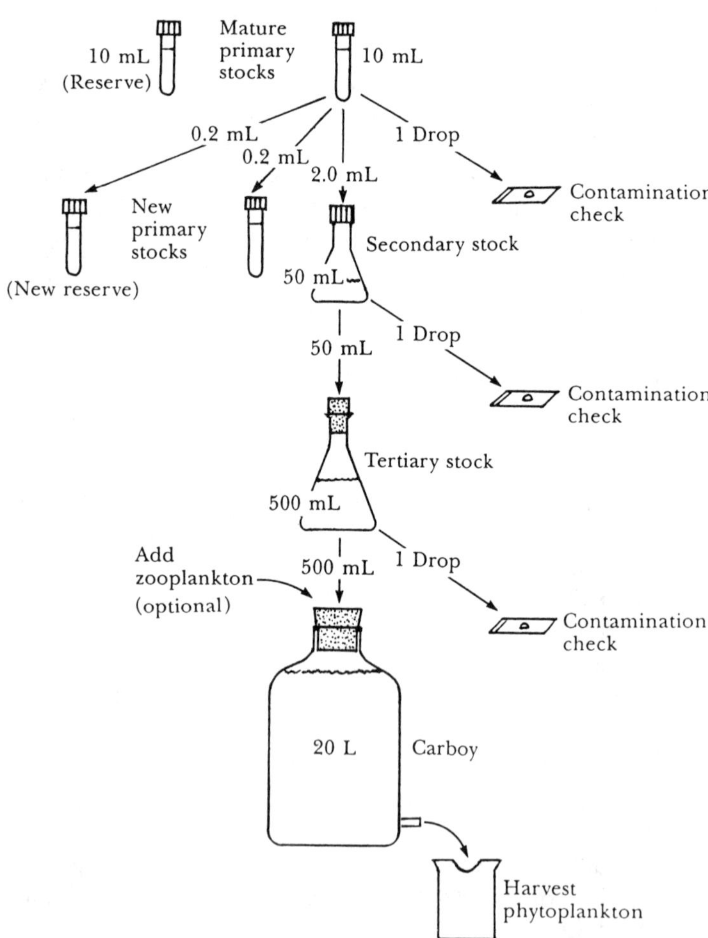

Figure 8-20 Flow diagram of a phytoplankton procedure. Source: Patricia M. Bubucis, Sea Research Foundation.

serial dilution or addition of antibiotics. Both procedures are described in subsections below.

How to Examine Cultures Microscopically for Contamination

1 Hold a test tube in your left hand and loosen the cap. With your right hand flame a nichrome transfer loop in a Bunsen burner until it turns red.
2 Remove the test tube cap with the heel and little finger of your right hand; pass the mouth of the tube over the flame while simultaneously inserting the loop.
3 Move the loop through the culture, remove it from the tube, and replace the cap, again using the heel and little finger of your right hand.
4 Set the tube in a rack.
5 Transfer the drop from the loop to a microscope slide, place a coverslip over it, and examine the contents at 200× and 400× with a light microscope.
6 Look for motility (in flagellated cells); also morphology and the presence of other algae, debris, bacteria, and protozoans. Motility may not be apparent if the cells have been compressed by the coverslip. If this is the case, use a sterile Pasteur pipette to transfer a drop or two of the culture to a depression slide, then cover with a coverslip and examine.

SERIAL DILUTION A series of transfers can be made into fresh GP2 culture solution until the contaminant has been removed by dilution. For example, transfer 1.0 mL of contaminated stock to 99.0 mL of sterile GP2 culture solution, mix well, transfer 1.0 mL to another 99.0 mL of sterile solution, and so forth (Fig. 8-21). Each step dilutes the stock by a hundredfold. Try a series of three or four dilutions, incubate them all, and check the cultures for contamination.

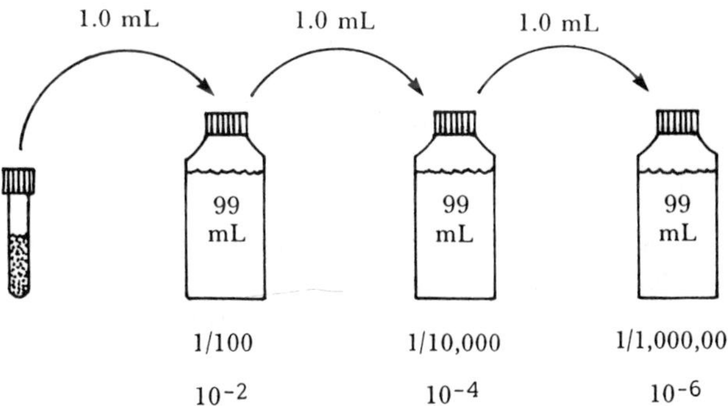

Figure 8-21 Serial dilution of a phytoplankton culture. Source: Patricia M. Bubucis, Sea Research Foundation.

ANTIBIOTIC TREATMENT[115] Contaminated cultures may require antibiotic treatment to rid them of bacteria.

How to Treat Contaminated Cultures with Antibiotics

1 Dissolve 100 mg penicillin G (potassium or sodium salt) and 50 mg streptomycin sulfate in 10 mL dH_2O.
2 Dissolve 1 mg chloramphenicol in 1.0 mL 95% ethanol (U.S.P. grade).
3 Combine the two solutions, mix well, and filter-sterilize by passing through a sterile 0.22-μm membrane filter.
4 Inoculate each of six 125-mL flasks containing 50 mL of sterile GP2 culture solution with 1.0 mL of the phytoplankton culture, then add these amounts of antibiotic solution: 3.0, 2.0, 1.0, 0.5, 0.25, and 0.125 mL.
5 Incubate the flasks at normal conditions for the phytoplankton species being cultured.
6 At 24 and 48 h, transfer 0.5 mL in triplicate from each flask to tubes of sterile GP2 culture solution.
7 Incubate the tubes for 2 to 3 weeks and check for bacterial contamination.

Method 8.12 Inoculation and Incubation of Stock Cultures[116]

Volumes of inoculant and incubation times are flexible and can be adjusted to suit personnel schedules. In general, heavy inoculation reduces incubation time. Incubation time is affected by many factors, including growth phase of the inoculant, composition of the culture solution, aeration rate, temperature, and light intensity. Stock cultures should be transferred at approximately one-half their expected life to allow time for use in case of equipment failures and accidents. Both situations occur more frequently than we like; for this reason, old and current stocks should not be kept in the same location. Stocks of typical laboratory ''weeds'' (e.g., *Dunaliella* and *Pyramimonas*) do well if transferred biweekly or monthly. Follow the procedures below.

PRIMARY STOCK CULTURES Mature stock cultures used to make new stocks can be sources of the inoculants for secondary cultures (Fig. 8-20). Keep unused stocks in dim light (500 to 1000 lx) as reserves. Do not use or discard them until the ''new'' stocks become ''old'' stocks.

How to Transfer Primary Stock Cultures

1. Start with 24 tubes of stock culture.
2. Store 12 tubes as reserves in a different location with low ambient light.
3. From the other 12 make two transfers of 0.5 mL from each tube into tubes with 10.0 mL of sterile GP2 culture solution.
4. Incubate these new stocks and check the mature stocks for contamination.

How to Inoculate Primary Stock Cultures

1. If an aseptic transfer hood is not available, make transfers in locations of low activity and no air currents.
2. Clean the surfaces in the work area by spraying or wiping with a disinfectant solution (e.g., dilute Clorox® or Wescodyne®) and wait 10 min.
3. Light a Bunsen burner and set up two test tube racks, one with mature stock cultures and the other with tubes of sterile GP2 culture solution (two for each mature stock).
4. Label the tubes (number, species, date) and arrange them in the racks in order of intended use. Also set up a row of labeled microscope slides.
5. Loosen the caps on all tubes. Pick up a canister of sterile, plugged 1.0-mL pipettes in your left hand. *Close the tube and canister before setting them down.*
6. With the heel and little finger of your right hand remove the lid of the canister and pass the pipette ends over the flame.
7. Gently shake the canister until one pipette can be removed with the right forefinger and thumb without touching the others. Pass the remaining pipette ends over the flame and replace the canister lid after passing it over the flame once again. *Do not set the pipette down until you are ready to discard it.*
8. Set down the canister, but now hold the pipette with the thumb and middle finger of your right hand. Pick up a stock culture with your left hand, agitate it gently, remove the cap with the heel and little finger of your right hand, pass the test tube mouth and pipette tip through the flame, and pipette 1.0 mL of stock culture.
9. Seal the pipette with your right forefinger and replace the cap on the stock culture tube after passing the mouth through the flame.

10 Place the stock culture tube in the rack and pick up the first labeled tube of sterile GP2 culture solution.

11 Remove the cap as described previously; after passing the test tube mouth and pipette tip through the flame, immerse the pipette tip in the tube and carefully release ~0.5 mL of stock culture. *Do not let the pipette touch the sides of the test tube.*

12 Pass the mouth of the test tube through the flame, replace the cap loosely, and return the tube to the rack.

13 Remove the second labeled tube of sterile GP2 culture solution. Follow step 11 and release the remaining ~0.5 mL of stock culture. *Do not blow out the pipette or let it touch the sides of the test tube.* Repeat step 12.

14 Blow out the remaining drop onto a labeled microscope slide, then discard the pipette.

15 Place a coverslip on the drops to be inspected for contamination. Repeat the above procedures until all transfers have been made.

How to Incubate Primary Stock Cultures

1 Incubate new stock cultures on a shelf directly in front of a double-lamp arrangement (Method 8.9). Keep the caps of the tubes loosened.

2 Occasionally tighten the caps, agitate the tubes, and loosen the caps again before replacing the tubes on the shelf.

3 When adequate growth has been attained, move the cultures farther from the light. Do not remove the caps from the tubes except to transfer to new stock cultures.

SECONDARY STOCK CULTURES If contamination is not detected in the mature cultures, transfer 2.0 mL to 125-mL Erlenmeyer flasks containing 50 mL of sterile GP2 culture solution (Fig. 8-19). As many as four flasks can be inoculated from one tube.

How to Inoculate Secondary Stock Cultures

1 Label the flasks (number, species, date).

2 Handle tubes and pipettes as in the procedures outlined for primary stock cultures.

3 Use a 10.0-mL pipette to remove 9.0 mL of inoculant from the tube.

4 Flame and close the tube and return it to the rack.

5 *Do not touch the mouth of the flask.* Hold the flask in your left hand, twist out the stopper (or remove the screw cap) with the heel and little finger of your right hand, then flame the mouth of the flask and the pipette tip.

6 Transfer 2.0 mL of stock culture to the flask, flame the mouth, and return the stopper by twisting it back in.

7 Set down the flask and pick up another. Continue until four flasks have been inoculated, then discard the pipette.

8 Swirl the flasks to suspend the cells evenly and incubate them in front of two fluorescent lamps. Swirl at least once daily.

TERTIARY STOCK CULTURES When growth in the secondary stocks is sufficient, each of the flasks can be used to inoculate a 1-L flask (Fig. 8-20). These flasks are the tertiary stock cultures. A 1-L flask containing 500 mL of culture can be used to inoculate a carboy when phytoplankton growth is in the exponential phase (Fig. 8-22). A growth curve must first be plotted to determine when the exponential phase occurs. At the same time, make notes of the cell density and color of the culture. Another technique is to take a series of color photographs and mount the prints in the culture area. Afterward, growth phases can be identified visually.

How to Inoculate Tertiary Cultures

1 Check cultures in the 125-mL flasks microscopically for contamination.

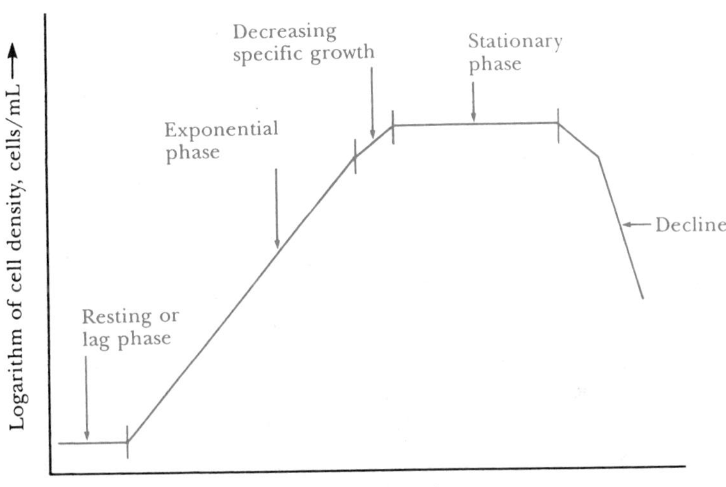

Figure 8-22 *Stylized growth curve of a phytoplankton culture.* Source: Patricia M. Bubucis, Sea Research Foundation; drawn from information in various sources.

2 If contamination is not detected, remove the stopper from a 1-L flask containing 500 mL of sterile GP2 culture solution. Remove the stopper with your right hand; do not set it down.
3 Pass the mouth of the flask through the flame and set the flask down.
4 With your left hand, remove and hold the stopper from a 125-mL flask containing stock culture.
5 Keep the small flask in your right hand, pick up the large one with your left hand, flame the mouths of both, and pour the culture into the large flask.
6 Set aside the small flask and its stopper, flame the mouth of the large flask, and return the stopper.
7 Remove a 1.0-mL disposable pipette aseptically by holding only the mouth end, remove the stopper from the 1-L flask, flame the mouth, drop in the pipette, and replace the stopper.
8 In the culture room, connect the flexible airline tubing to the pipette and adjust the air flow to keep cells in suspension without splashing the sides of the flask and wetting the stopper.
9 Incubate in front of three or four fluorescent lamps until growth is exponential (Method 8.13). Each flask can be used to inoculate a carboy.

CARBOY CULTURE Carboys of phytoplankton can be harvested when cells are at peak density; alternatively, carboys can be inoculated with zooplankton (brine shrimp, rotifers) when cells are in the exponential phase (Method 8.13).

How to Inoculate Carboys

1 To a carboy containing 15 to 20 L of sterile GP2 culture solution, add 500 mL of phytoplankton culture in the exponential phase.
2 Attach flexible airline tubing to the mouth of the pipette in a carboy. Keep the tubing outside the stopper.
3 Adjust the aeration rate high enough to mix the culture without wetting the stopper.
4 Incubate with three or four lamps until growth becomes dense, then double the illumination.
5 Harvest the phytoplankton by draining through the silicone tubing, or inoculate the carboy with zooplankton when phytoplankton growth is exponential (Method 8.13).

Method 8.13 Enumeration[117]

A plot on semilog paper of incubation time against cell density (this last variable on the log scale) should reveal a growth pattern similar to that illustrated in Figure 8-22. Enumeration involves daily collection and fixation of samples, followed by counting in a hemacytometer under the microscope. Electronic counters can be adapted for enumeration of phytoplankton cells.

SAMPLE COLLECTION AND FIXATION Sample collection is best performed at the same time every day. Record the time when samples are collected. Remove 5.0 mL with a 5.0-mL pipette. Use aseptic techniques. Transfer the sample to a clean (not necessarily sterile) test tube. Add 0.05 mL ($\sim$1 drop) of Lugol's iodine with a Pasteur pipette and mix gently. This fixes and immobilizes the cells, causing them to settle in the hemacytometer. Lugol's iodine is made by dissolving 2.0 g iodine crystals and 3.0 g potassium iodide, KI, in 300 mL dH_2O.

COUNTING The hemacytometer described here is an American Optical Bright-Line* hemacytometer counting chamber with Neubauer markings. The chamber is a glass slide with two counting platforms separated and surrounded by a "moat" (Fig. 8-23). Each platform contains an etched grid with a notched "loading port." On either side of the counting platforms is a raised ridge to support a coverslip exactly 0.1 mm above the grids. The coverslip is 0.4 mm thick and not disposable. The grid consists of nine large squares of 1.0 mm per side. The four remaining large squares are divided into 25 smaller squares. The central large square is subdivided even further by squares that are 0.05 mm per side. The volume of sample counted in one large square is 0.1 mm.

LOADING THE COUNTING CHAMBER Use and cleaning of the counting chambers and coverslips must be done carefully to avoid scratching or breaking. The components must be absolutely clean and dry before loading with a sample. Rinse with dH_2O followed by ethanol or acetone rinses; if necessary, dry both components carefully with lens tissue between uses.

How to Load the Counting Chamber

1 Place the coverslip on the coverslip supports.

2 Mix the fixed phytoplankton gently but thoroughly.

*American Optical, Buffalo NY 14215.

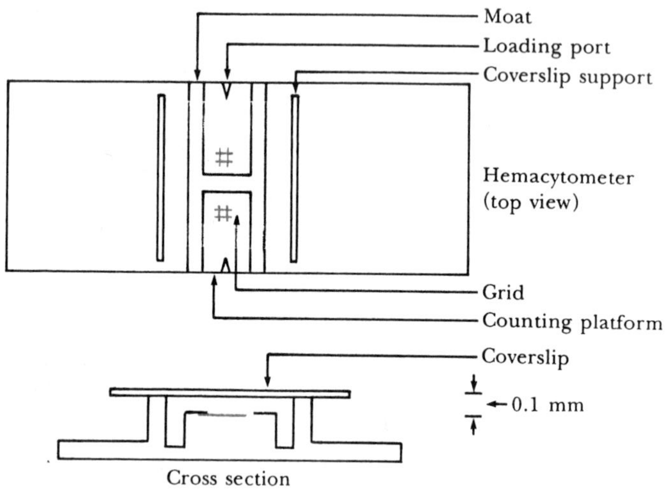

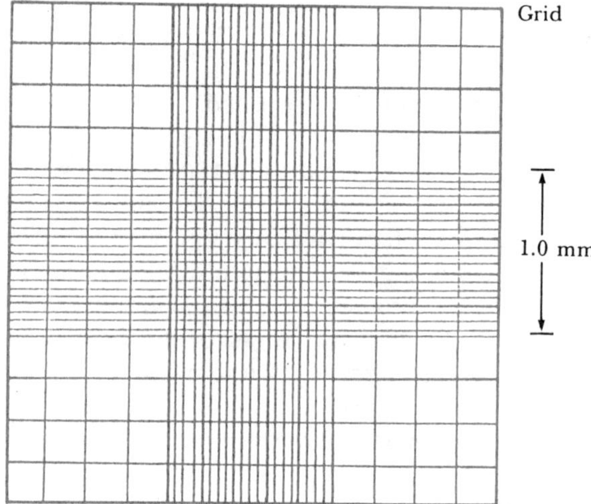

Figure 8-23 *Hemacytometer.* Source: Patricia M. Bubucis, Sea Research Foundation.

3 Collect a small subsample with a Pasteur pipette. Use separate subsamples to load the two platforms.

4 Touch a small drop to the notch and pull away the pipette. Capillary action should fill the chamber completely and evenly without overflowing or bulging into the moat. If the chambers do not fill properly, remove the coverslip by pressing down on one end. Clean and dry the coverslip and chambers and try again.

5 Allow the cells to settle for ~1 min before counting.

How to Count Phytoplankton Cells

1. Place the loaded hemacytometer on the stage of a compound microscope.
2. Focus on one of the grids with the lowest power objective, then change to the 10× objective.
3. Use a hand tally to count the cells in one to nine of the large (1 mm per side) squares for a total count no greater than ~400. The number and pattern of the squares counted should be the same for both platforms, with the number depending on the size and density of the cells.
4. Focus up and down within the chamber and count only cells more than halfway into the counting area.
5. To avoid recounting cells on lines, consistently count only cells positioned on the top and left lines, or on the bottom and right lines.
6. Record the cell counts and number of squares counted.
7. If counts of the two chambers are not within 20%, the cells were not distributed evenly. Reload the chambers and make another count.
8. Average the counts of the two platforms.
9. Each of the nine large squares contains 0.1 mm^3 of sample. Divide the count by the number of large squares counted and multiply by 10^4 to calculate the number of cells per millilitre (i.e., cm^3). Plot incubation time (hours or days) against the cell density (cells/mL) on semilog paper. Cell density should be on the logarithmic axis.
10. The steep upward slope indicates the time of exponential growth (Fig. 8-22).

C H A P T E R

9 Health

Books about aquarium fishes typically include one or more chapters on disease. I reject the notion that disease is a limiting factor in the successful operation of a public aquarium. Parasitic organisms exist as integral elements of the aquarium biota. These agents and the diseases they induce are components of life; they cannot be made to disappear simply by treating their effects. No disease, including those that afflict human beings, has ever been controlled effectively except by prevention. As such, diseases warrant less consideration than the factors that predispose fishes to contracting them. Aquarium fishes are often poorly nourished, exposed to seawater of inferior quality, and provided with physical settings that interrupt or impair normal behavior. In short, disease is often the result of stress and mismanagement. If the pertinent stress factors can be identified and controlled, diseases are less likely to flourish.

Emphasis throughout the chapter is on health, which connotes prevention. The Technology section contains advice on the treatment of individual diseases. One objective was to streamline the enormous body of information on remedies and regimens. Anecdotal material was ignored. The treatments offered have some empirical basis, however modest.

SCIENCE

Infection and Disease

A *parasite* lives on or in another organism called the *host* and is potentially damaging to it. The host-parasite relationship is dynamic because each organism modifies the activities and functions of the other. Whether the host or the parasite eventually gains dominance depends on the *virulence* of the parasite (its capacity to inflict damage) and the *resistance* or susceptibility of the host to the activities of the parasite. Neither the parasite's virulence nor the host's resistance is inflexible: each is influenced by external factors and by nuances of the host-parasite relationship itself.

Infectious diseases are caused by *microorganisms*: viruses, bacteria, protozoans, and yeasts (unicellular fungi).[1] All other diseases are *noninfectious*, including those produced by multicellular fungi, worms, and crustaceans. These organisms cause *infestations*.[1] It is important to realize that infection, infestation, and disease are not synonyms. To be *diseased* the host must be harmed extensively enough for its health to become impaired. Infections and infestations define conditions in which a parasite is established and growing, whether the host is harmed or not. Agents that cause infections and infestations are potentially *pathogenic* or disease producing. Viewed this way, the terms *parasite* and *pathogen* are interchangeable.[2]

Resistance to Disease

The capacity of the host to resist disease depends on (*1*) the maintenance of an intact physical barrier between the internal tissues and the environment; (2) the presence of natural resistance factors in the host's blood, tissues, and mucus; and (3) a facile immune response that can be mobilized quickly to attack specific invading organisms. In fishes, the principal physical barriers are the skin and mucus. When resistance is nonspecific—that is, directed against no particular pathogen—it is termed *natural resistance* or *nonspecific immunity*.[3] In contrast, *immunity* (by implication specific immunity) is the host's focused response to specific foreign particles, including pathogens.

PHYSICAL BARRIERS To induce disease a pathogen must gain access to its host's internal tissues. Only then can it multiply and have the potential to cause damage. The normal barrier against pathogens is a layer of tissue separating the animal from the environment. In fishes any *lesion* or breach in the gills, eyes, skin, or *intestinal mucosa* (lining of the intestine) provides pathogens with a site of entry to vulnerable tissues underneath. The outside layer of tissue is the *epidermis* (Fig. 9-1). Fish epidermis is similar to the lining of the human mouth, being composed of several layers of flattened epithelial cells.[4] Beneath the epidermis is the *dermis*, which contains blood vessels, nerves, sense organs, and other specialized tissues. The scales, for example, originate from specialized cells of the dermis (Fig. 9-1). The dermis also contains mucous cells that extend outward into the epidermis (Fig. 9-1). These secrete mucus, which forms a protective shield between the fish and the environment (Fig. 9-2). Mucous cells of the intestinal mucosa and gills provide

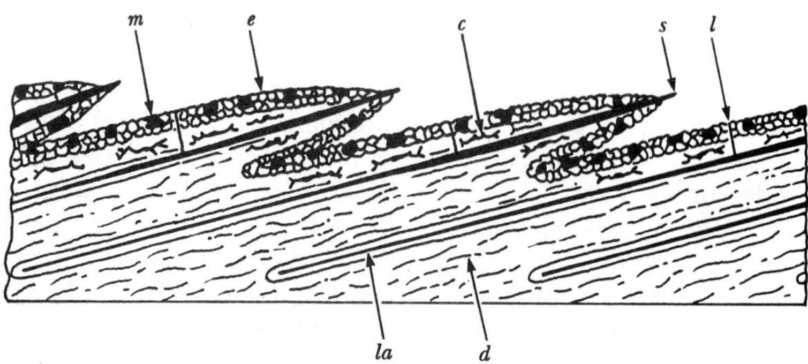

Figure 9-1 *Diagrammatic longitudinal section through the skin of a representative teleost, the common sole* (Solea solea)*: c = dermal chromatophore, d = dermis, e = epidermis, l = weak line where the skin fractures, la = bony lamina of the scale, m = epidermal mucous cell, s = spine.* Source: Kearn (1976).

similar defense against invading pathogens. The epidermis and dermis together comprise the *skin*. If the mucus and skin are breached, invading microorganisms can reproduce at the site of infection (*local infection*) or penetrate to tissue layers below, spreading to other organs and producing general or *systemic infections* (also called *septicemias*).

NATURAL RESISTANCE Natural resistance is an effective defense against bacteria and some viruses. Natural resistance factors can be present in the blood (serum and plasma), mucus,

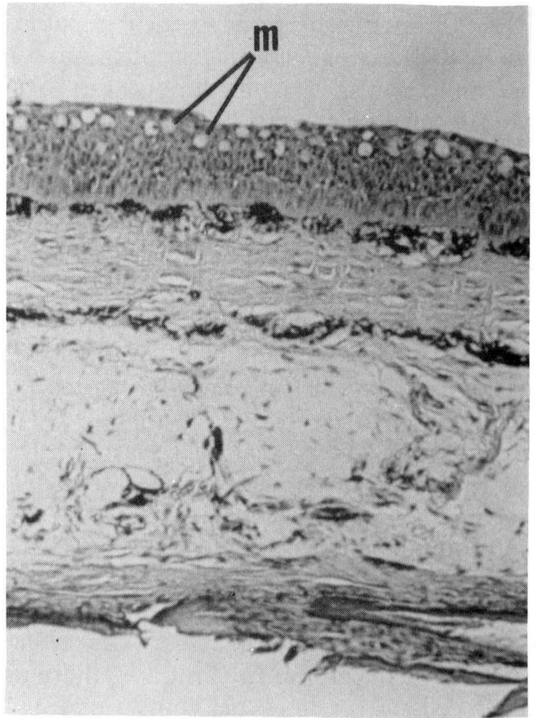

Figure 9-2 *Section through the normal epidermis of a striped bass* (Morone saxatilis)*: m = mucous cells. 100x.* Source: Richard E. Wolke, Marine Pathology Laboratory, University of Rhode Island.

TABLE 9-1 Representative natural resistance factors in fishes.

Factor group	Factor	Mechanistic group	Location	Function
Acute-phase proteins	C-reactive protein, CRP	Precipitin	Serum, mucus	Precipitates C-polysaccharides of certain bacteria in presence of Ca^{2+}
	Transferrin	Precipitin	Serum	Binds specifically and reversibly with two ferric ions and limits amount of iron available to pathogens
—	Lysozyme	Lysin	Serum, mucus	Dissolves mucopolysaccharide wall of some Gram-positive, nonpathogenic bacteria; bacteriolytic effect in Gram-negative bacteria with aid of complement; antiviral properties
—	Interferon	Virus-neutralizing	Serum	Interferes with viral replication
Natural lysins	Complement	Lysin	Serum, mucus	Causes lysis of cell membranes of Gram-negative bacteria, often in conjunction with CRP
	Properdin	Lysin	Serum	Initiates lysis of red blood cells and bacteria
Natural agglutinins	—	Agglutinins	Serum, mucus	Agglutinates red blood cells and bacteria

Source: Stephen Spotte, compiled from various sources.

and sometimes other specialized tissues (Table 9-1). Several have powerful, nonspecific defense functions.[5] *Lysozyme,* an enzyme in the mucus, blood, and certain types of *leukocytes* (white blood cells) of many fishes is believed to be important in defense against invading microorganisms by causing them to lyse or rupture.[6] *Interferon* is an antiviral agent produced mainly by macrophages (see below), although infected cells of all types can produce it. Interferon prevents viruses from replicating. *Complement* is a system of serum enzymes that lyses foreign cells to which specific antibodies are attached.

IMMUNITY Unlike natural resistance, *immunity* (also known as *humoral immunity*) is directed against specific diseases. It is a complex surveillance system dependent in part on *antibodies,* which neutralize foreign molecules called antigens (defined below). Antibodies, like natural resistance factors, are classed according to their mode of activity against antigens (e.g., precipitins, agglutinins, opsonins, antitoxins, lysins). Antibody-antigen reactions result in precipitation of soluble antigens and agglutination (i.e., clumping) of particulate forms. In addition, phagocytosis (defined below) of bacteria increases, toxins are neutralized, and susceptible cells (including those of bacteria) are lysed.

Five groups of antibodies are recognized, based on chemical structure and biological activity. The principal group is made up of IgG, IgM, and IgA; the minor group consists of IgD and IgE. Fishes are believed to possess only IgM.[7] All antibodies belong to a broader class of compounds, the *immunoglobulins,* which are glycoproteins.

An *antigen* is any foreign substance that initiates antibody formation. All complete proteins are antigens, as are many polysaccharides (including those derived from the cellular envelopes of bacteria), some nucleic acids, and a few lipids. Antigens enter animals in several ways (e.g., ingestion and skin contact), but most often by injection into the blood, skin, or other protected tissue through lesions. It is important to remember that all antigens are foreign; that is, the body does not recognize an antigen as being part of itself. An immune system that attempted to destroy its own molecules would be an obvious liability.

The response elicited by antigens (i.e., the mobilizing of antibodies) is the *immune response* (Fig. 9-3). This is a dual system poised to repel invading pathogens. The *cellular immune response* is especially effective against fungi, protozoans, and certain types of viruses. The *humoral immune response* defends mainly against other kinds of viruses and bacteria. The duality of the immune response is inherent in two types of white blood cells called *lymphocytes*. One type, the *T cells,* covers the cellular immune response by binding to the invader and lysing it. The

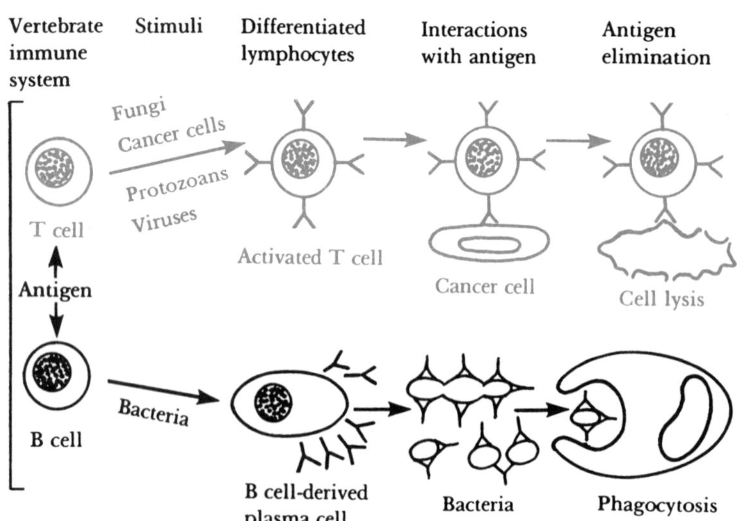

Figure 9-3 *Differentiation, interaction, and elimination events that may occur when T and B cells of the immune system are stimulated.* Source: Hood et al. (1978).

B cells are mobilized by the humoral immune response. They secrete antibodies that bind selectively to invading microorganisms, preparing them to be surrounded, engulfed, and digested by still other specialized lymphocytes, the *phagocytes*. Phagocytes include *polymorphonuclear leukocytes*, PMNs,. and *macrophages* (cells that wander about in the tissues engulfing antigens, Fig. 9-4). The process by which phagocytes remove infectious microorganisms is *phagocytosis*.

VIRULENCE If natural resistance and immunity are maintained effectively, an infection does not result in disease. Signs of disease are not evident, and the infection remains *subclinical*. *Latent infections* are subclinical infections in which the presence of the pathogen cannot be detected readily by available methods. However, if the immune response or natural resistance of the host is compromised (e.g., a sudden temperature change, injury, malnutrition), the subclinical or latent infection may flare up. Afterward, the infection is *clinical*, as demonstrated by evident signs of disease.

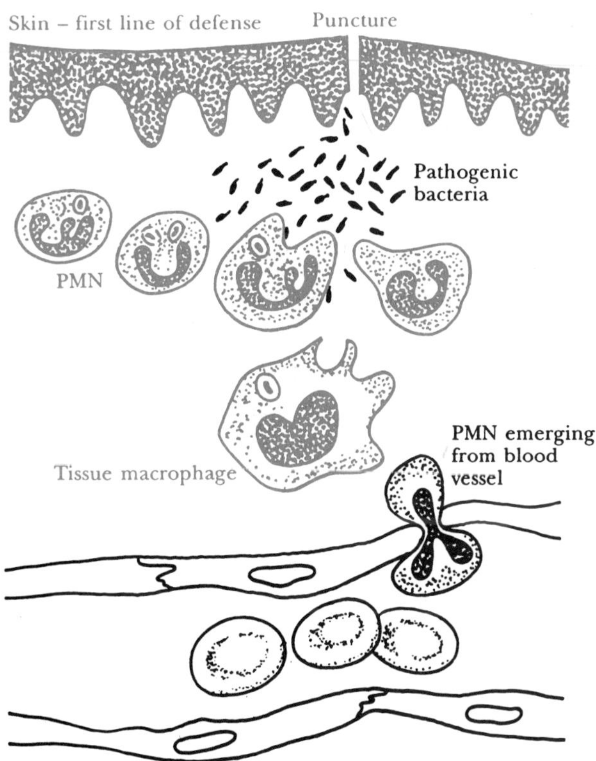

Figure 9-4 Diagrammatic representation of phagocytosis by polymorphonuclear leukocytes (PMNs) and tissue macrophages after penetration of the skin and introduction of pathogenic bacteria into the deeper tissues. The PMNs are more efficient at phagocytosis than the macrophages. Note that PMNs are mobilized into tissues from blood vessels during the inflammatory response. Source: Bellanti (1971).

Clinical Signs and Pathological Effects

Diseases are described in terms of clinical signs and pathological effects. *Clinical signs*[8] encompass all features used in diagnosis, excluding specific changes in cells and tissues, which comprise the pathological effects (see below). Clinical and pathological methods are both diagnostic, but in different ways. Ideally, they complement each other. As shown in Table 9-2, clinical signs in fishes can be behavioral, morphological, or physiological.

Pathological effects involve anatomical and functional changes in cells and tissues, and diagnosis by pathology must include categorizing disease-induced lesions. In fishes the three main categories of lesions are involved with (*1*) inflammation, (*2*) cellular degeneration, and (*3*) abnormal cell growth.

INFLAMMATION The most common and basic pathological reaction of injured cells is the *inflammatory response* or *inflammation,* which is the local reactive change in tissues after injury or irritation (Fig. 9-5). It accompanies or follows tissue repair and healing and represents efforts by the cells to contain the damage and protect tissues from further injury. Inflammation can be acute, subacute, or chronic. *Acute inflammation* develops swiftly, and the tissues affected appear to be ''inflamed'' (red and swollen). *Chronic inflammation* is prolonged. It can be a late stage of the acute process or chronic from the start. If the latter it typically is associated with pathogens of low virulence. *Subacute inflammation* is a transitional phase between the other stages. Factors that cause inflammation include chemical irritants in the water and injury, but the mobilization of phago-

TABLE 9-2 Some clinical signs often used to diagnose diseases in fishes.

Behavior	Appearance	Physiology
Anorexia	Loss of body sheen	Primary and secondary stress responses
Loss of equilibrium	Frayed fins	Change in normal blood constituents
Hyperventilation	Excessive mucus production	
	Opaque eyes	
	Skin ulcerations	
	Change in coloration	

Source: Stephen Spotte.

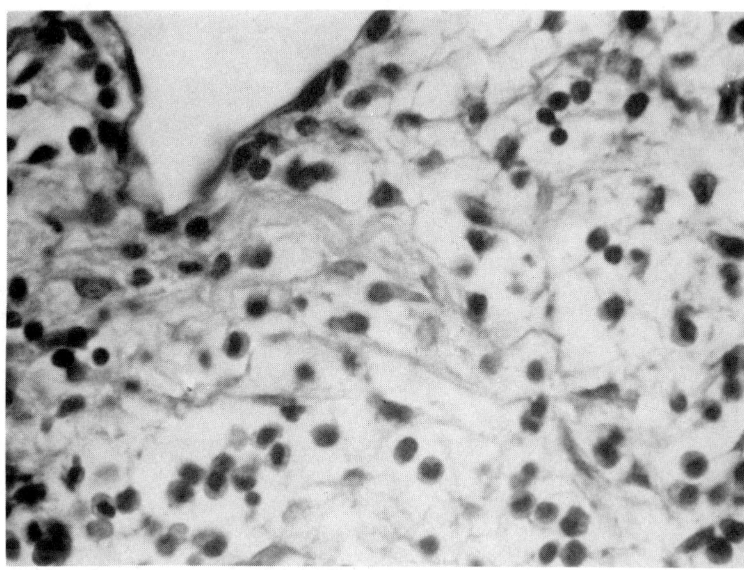

Figure 9-5 *Skin of a grouper* (Epinephelus *sp.*) *illustrating an inflammatory response. 400x.* Source: Richard E. Wolke, Marine Pathology Laboratory, University of Rhode Island.

cytes, which are associated with the inflammatory response, is initiated by the sudden entry of foreign particles (usually bacteria), and this requires a lesion. The phagocytes are all derived ultimately from the blood. They mass at the site of inflammation and surround and engulf invading organisms (Fig. 9-4), the elimination of which is a prerequisite to healing.

CELLULAR DEGENERATION Another fundamental pathological change in tissue resulting from injury is *necrosis* or cell death while the cells are still within the living organism (Fig. 9-6). Necrosis occurs when cells are exposed to noxious agents. These ordinarily are metabolic by-products of pathogenic microorganisms, but can include prolonged exposure to chemical irritants in the water. An *ulcer* combines elements of inflammation and necrosis and represents the loss of continuity from any surface (skin or mucous membrane), with inflammation of the adjacent tissue.

ABNORMAL CELL GROWTH *Hyperplasia* is an increase in the number of cells at a local site and therefore considered a disturbance of cell growth (Fig. 9-7). In fishes, gill hyperplasia is commonly associated with a chemical irritant in the water, but is also a reaction by the tissues to pathogens, especially protozoans. I shall not deal with *neoplasms* (i.e., tumors or new growth). Their appearance in exhibit aquariums is little more than a curiosity.[9]

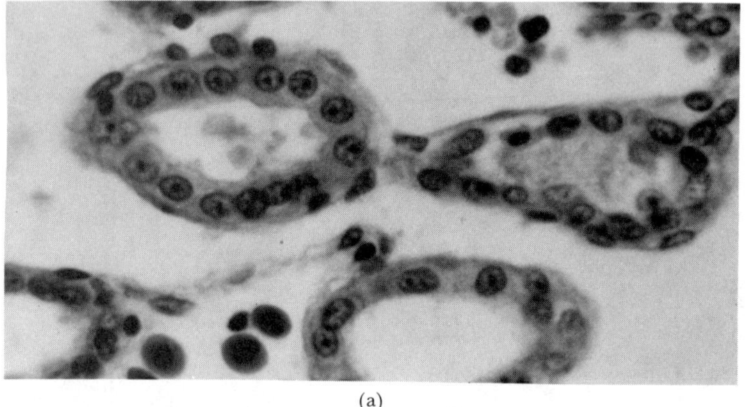

(a)

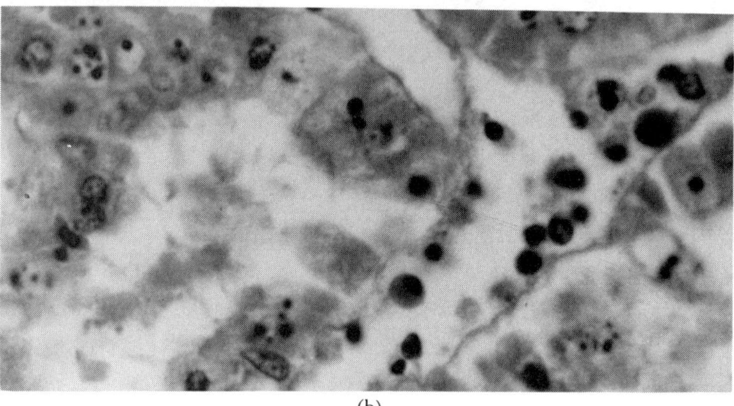

(b)

Figure 9-6 Kidney tissue of a teleost. 400x. (a) *Normal tissue.* (b) *Necrotic tissue.* Source: Richard E. Wolke, Marine Pathology Laboratory, University of Rhode Island.

Predisposition to Disease

Subclinical infections become clinical when aquarium fishes are exposed to situations that predispose them to disease. At such times natural resistance and immunity are impaired, and the delicate host-parasite relationship is tipped in favor of the parasite. Stress is the most important predisposing factor. From the standpoint of health, *stress* refers to physical injury or to any behavioral or environmental factor that suppresses the immune response. Typical stress factors are lesions, sudden fluctuations in temperature and salinity, exposure to chemical irritants such as copper and ammonia, harassment by other fishes, and handling. The physiology of the stress response is discussed in Chapter 4. The principal predisposing factors are described in the subsections that follow.

FASTING Well-nourished fishes resist disease-producing infections and infestations and recover from diseases faster than

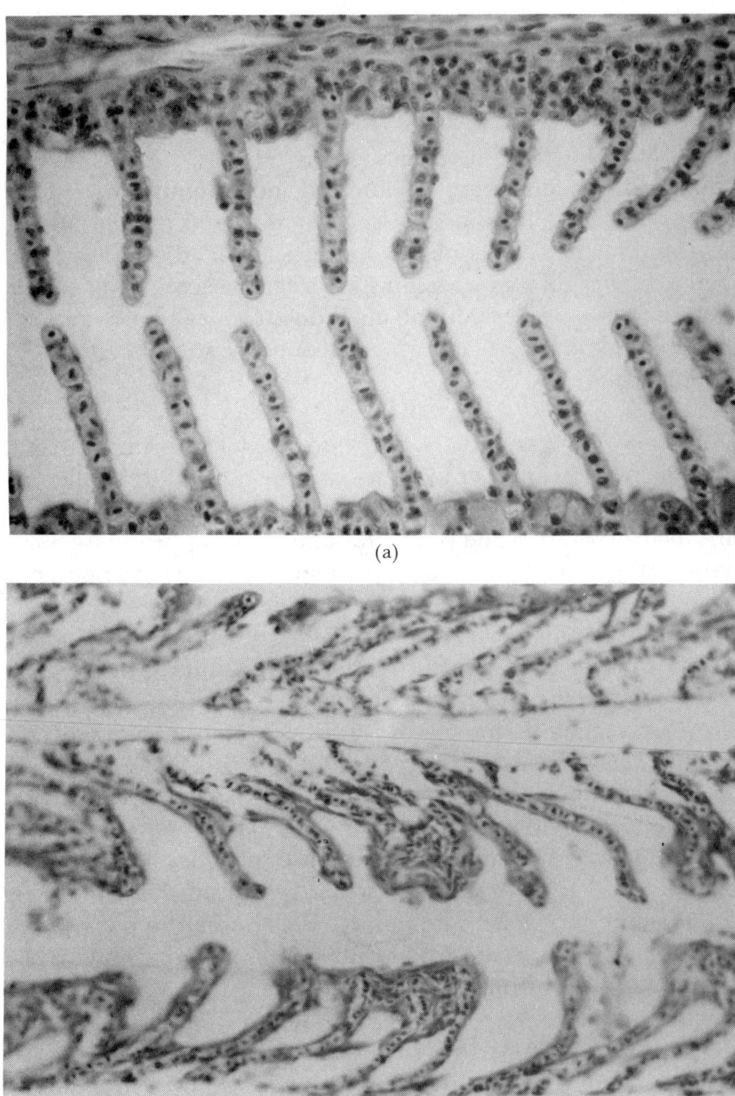

(a)

(b)

Figure 9-7 *Gills of a teleost.* (a) *Normal gill. 250x.* (b) *Hyperplastic gill. 160x.* Source: Richard E. Wolke, Marine Pathology Laboratory, University of Rhode Island.

fishes that are malnourished, in part because inadequate nutrition can induce immune suppression.[10] Fasted fishes often demonstrate higher blood corticosteroid levels when stressed, compared with fishes that are well fed.[11]

INJURY Lesions on the skin, eyes, gills, or intestinal mucosa are subject to invasion by *opportunistic pathogens*, normally bacteria. Pathogenic bacteria that invade wounds originally caused by other parasites produce *secondary infections*. Fishes with surface lesions caused by parasitic protozoans, worms, and crustaceans are prime candidates for secondary infections, as are specimens with scales missing from careless handling or with lesions on the eyes caused by capture with nets.

CROWDING Crowding facilitates the transfer of parasites by reducing the distance between infected and potential hosts. The aggressive nature of some fish species results in nipped fins if they are crowded. This has two effects. First, the lesions are open for invasion by opportunistic bacteria; second, the social stress imposed on less dominant individuals causes increases in hormone levels, leading to secondary stress responses (Chapter 4).

HANDLING[12] Handling, which involves capturing a fish, transferring it to another location, or transporting it, results in an immediate stress response. In some species several days must elapse before blood concentrations of the appropriate hormones return to normal. Forcing a fish to exercise strenuously by chasing it or letting it struggle in a net induces acidosis, a secondary stress effect. During respiratory acidosis the blood becomes more acidic, which interferes with uptake of oxygen by the hemoglobin. Another secondary effect of handling stress is hyperglycemia. Removing a fish from water even for a few seconds causes temporary hypoxia and a subsequent rise in blood glucose. The most severe form of handling stress is letting a fish struggle out of water in a net. Handling stress also may suppress the inflammatory response (phagocytosis and the migration of PMNs from the vascular system to the site of infection), interfering with immunity. This poses the possibility that the healing of lesions caused by handling may be delayed, resulting in death from bacterial infections.

ENVIRONMENTAL QUALITY[12] An increase in ammonia produces a rise in blood corticosteroid levels, as does treatment with copper. Corticosteroids rise during sudden and substantial increases in temperature or salinity, or as a result of physiological hypoxia induced by oxygen depletion of the water.

Transmission of Parasites

EPIZOOTIOLOGY The term *epizootiology* refers to the sum of all factors contributing to the presence of a disease; in other words, its natural history. The epizootiology of disease-producing infections and infestations depends on (*1*) the degree of adaptation of the parasite and host to each other, (*2*) the ability of the parasite to survive outside the host, and (*3*) the mode of transfer of the parasite to new hosts. Interruption of any of these processes reduces the overall incidence of infection or infestation and represents the first step in effective disease control. Parasites are troublesome only if their mode of development is direct (i.e., they are capable of replicating and inducing disease within the confines of the aquarium environment). Organisms that require one or more intermediate hosts before reaching the invasive or parasitic stage are seldom a problem. Suitable intermediate hosts typically are absent from aquarium exhibits, and the result is a natural break in the life cycle.

EPIZOOTIC AND ENZOOTIC DISEASES The discussion until now has centered on the intimate relationship between individual parasites and hosts. The concept of epizootiology involves the multiple interactions of parasite and host populations, with the environment as a third factor. Diseases spread quickly if the resistance of the host is low. In such instances the rate of infection or infestation and appearance of disease are rapid, resulting in an *epizootic*. This typically is the case when all fishes in an aquarium show signs of disease more or less simultaneously. If some individuals survive, the rate at which parasites are transmitted decreases, and the hosts may develop and retain some degree of immunity. The infection or infestation is then subclinical, and the situation becomes *enzootic* (i.e., one in which the parasite is present but the incidence of disease is low). Epizootics in nature often originate from interference with the ecological balance. If substantial numbers of host species are removed from a population, or the environment is disturbed, epizootics are one tangible result. In nature a given disease either is absent or enzootic, but only rarely epizootic.

MODES OF TRANSMISSION In aquariums, all parasites are transmitted through water, and the organisms must be able to survive for the necessary length of time away from the host. Pathogens in aquariums can be transmitted in several ways, including (*1*) infected or infested food, (*2*) infected or infested water, (*3*) direct contact with diseased aquarium-mates, (*4*) ingestion of tissues of dead aquarium-mates, and (*5*) direct inoculation through lesions.

Chemotherapy, Sterilization, Disinfection

Pathogens can exist on or inside the host, or in the water apart from the host. Pathogens associated directly with a fish already are potentially disease producing; the chance of those in the environment causing disease is more remote. The choice of a treatment regimen thus depends on whether the intent is to treat the animals or the water. Accordingly, there are three options: (*1*) chemotherapeutic agents, (*2*) sterilizing agents, and (*3*) disinfecting agents (or simply disinfectants). The last two probably never render fishes free of disease, and subclinical infections are likely to persist.

Chemotherapy, sterilization, and disinfection kill parasites or suppress their growth and reproduction. Lethal agents are "-cidal," with the prefix indicating the type of organism that is killed. A *bactericide* kills bacteria, an *algicide* destroys algae, and so forth. Agents that do not kill but only inhibit growth are "-static" (e.g., bacteriostatic, algistatic). Often agents that are "cidal" at high concentrations are "static" if the concentration is lowered. To be effective a "static" agent must be present at all times; if removed, growth resumes. Every antiparasitic compound has a *minimum inhibitory concentration*, MIC, if it is a "static" agent, or a *minimum lethal concentration*, MLC, if the primary activity is "cidal."

Chemotherapeutic Agents

Chemicals that attack parasites selectively causing little or no damage to the host's cells are *chemotherapeutic agents*. These are synthetic or natural chemicals. *Antibiotics* act selectively against many types of microorganisms, but the majority are formulated to combat diseases caused by bacteria. Antibiotics are chemotherapeutic agents of microbial origin. However, many other compounds with similar activity have been synthesized, and the term "antibiotic" is now too general to be useful. Chemotherapeutic agents are classified by the type of microorganism they are most selective against (e.g., *antibacterial, antifungal, antiprotozoal, anthelminthic*).

SELECTIVITY AND SENSITIVITY Only a *sensitivity test* can determine which antimicrobial compound and concentration are effective against a particular microorganism. Sensitivity testing is a standard medical procedure in which microorganisms cultured from an infected fish or some other animal (including humans) are subjected to different kinds and concentrations of antimicrobial compounds to determine which are most effective.

Sensitivity tests are necessary because an organism from one locality often is resistant to a course of treatment known to work effectively somewhere else. The indiscriminate dispensing of antimicrobial compounds (particularly those that are antibacterial) without first conducting sensitivity tests is one reason for the appearance worldwide of drug-resistant organisms. Their presence in the environment is of grave concern to medical scientists. There is a growing list of antibacterial compounds that once were effective in treating diseases of humans and domestic animals, but now are ineffective. Aquarists who use them at *subtherapeutic concentrations* (concentrations too low to be bactericidal or bacteriostatic), or as *chemoprophylactics* (antimicrobial compounds used to prevent future infection and disease), only contribute to this worsening situation.[13]

METHODS OF APPLICATION Chemotherapeutic agents can be applied in three ways: (*1*) orally (*per os* or by mouth), (*2*) by injection, or (*3*) by immersing the diseased fish in a solution of the agent for a measured period of time (*immersion treatment*).[14] Feeding a chemotherapeutic agent to a fish in a dry or moist feed is probably the most effective method of treatment, but this sometimes is impractical. Other problems of the *per os* method include (*1*) the occasional poor palatability of medicated feeds, which reduces the chances of their being eaten; (*2*) the fact that many fishes demonstrate *anorexia* (loss of appetite), often before clinical signs of disease appear; and (*3*) leaching of the agent from the feed. Antibacterial and antifungal agents sometimes are injected into fishes, but the practice is limited to large specimens. It also causes stress. Immersing a fish in a solution of the agent is often the only option available to aquarists, but the efficacy of this method also has limitations.

LIMITATIONS OF IMMERSION TREATMENTS It must be assumed that all bacterial and fungal infections are systemic and that application of a chemotherapeutic agent to surface lesions is ineffective. Infections caused by bacteria can be secondary, resulting in mortalities even if the primary infectious organism (e.g., fungus or protozoan) is controlled. Successful chemotherapy in the treatment of any infectious disease depends on two factors: (*1*) knowing the MIC or MLC of the agent against the pathogen and (*2*) being certain that *therapeutic concentrations* can be reached in the fish's blood and tissues.[15] In the treatment of primary diseases caused by bacteria, therapeutic concentrations are considered to be two to four times the MIC or MLC, but neither concentration can be ascertained without sensitivity testing. Failure to reach therapeutic concentrations is inevitable if the agent is assimilated poorly during immersion treatment, and no subsequent cure is achieved even if *in vitro* results show a high degree of sensitivity. Sensitivity tests of compounds not absorbed from solution serve no useful purpose. Immersion treatments devised from data obtained *in vitro* are meaningless if effective *in vivo* (in the living organism, in this case the host) concentrations are unattainable.

Relatively few studies have been performed on the efficacy of antibacterial and antifungal chemotherapeutic compounds in immersion treatment, and even fewer have been published in which seawater aquarium fishes were the test animals. The rate of assimilation and final blood and tissue concentrations of a chemotherapeutic agent are affected by environmental factors (e.g., temperature, salinity, pH) and species. Another determining factor is the surface/volume ratio of the fish to the treatment solution, because absorption occurs through the gills and skin and consequently is affected by how much of a fish's total surface is exposed to the water. Most chemotherapeutic agents are toxic when misused, and toxicity varies by species, size (surface area), duration of treatment, and condition of the fish (clinical stage of the disease). All this is complicated by the existence in the environment of microorganisms that are resistant to available compounds. This last factor has become so important that published dosage levels of specific compounds may not be valid if the data are more than a few years old.

Immersion treatments are effective only if the chemotherapeutic agent is absorbed by the fish to a concentration proportional to the treatment concentration. In other words, if the concentration of the agent in the treatment solution is doubled, the concentration of the chemotherapeutic agent in the blood and tissues should also double. Not all agents fit this description. Many are either untested or assimilated so poorly that therapeutic concentrations cannot be achieved at reasonable dosages.

No chemical compound used to treat diseased fishes should ever be added to the water of an established aquarium. Many antibacterial chemotherapeutic agents interrupt important bacteriological processes in the filter bed, resulting in increases in ammonia (Table 2-3). In addition, organic coatings on the surfaces of gravel grains and aquarium decorations absorb treatment compounds and make them unavailable to the fishes. Aquariums used for short immersion treatments should contain only a known volume of seawater. In aquariums used for long treatments, add a few plastic flower pots or short sections of PVC pipe to provide the fishes with hiding places. This reduces behavioral stress. The deterioration in water quality caused by no filtration is not an important consideration during short treatments. If treatment is prolonged, regular partial water changes must be made anyway to renew the concentration of the chemotherapeutic agent.

FORMULATED PRODUCTS Several companies formulate and market chemotherapeutic agents (including antibacterial compounds) for use in small aquariums. Research by Canadian scientists in the 1970s demonstrated that all antibacterial formulations tested *in vitro* were subtherapeutic and ineffective against bacteria present routinely in freshwater aquariums, even at dosages several times greater than the manufacturers' recommendations. Still higher concentrations would have been required to achieve positive results against organisms in surface lesions. In addition, some of the formulations were directly toxic to test fishes at dosages high enough to be bacteriostatic.[16] Perhaps the compounds now available have been improved.

Sterilizing Agents

Sterilizing agents by definition are ''cidal'' and nonselective, resulting in complete destruction of all life.[17] Sterilizing agents ordinarily are applied in a closed-loop arrangement. A side stream of contaminated water is recirculated continuously between the *bulk fluid* (i.e., the main portion of the water system where the exhibit fishes are confined) and the source of sterilization. The process is called *point contact sterilization* because most of the pathogens suspended in the water can be killed only if brought into direct contact with the sterilizing agent (Fig. 9-8). The two sterilizing agents used most often in point contact systems are ultraviolet (UV) radiation and ozone.

UV RADIATION The equipment used to produce UV radiation is a *UV sterilizer* (Fig. 9-9), and the process is *UV irradiation*. The radiation from ultraviolet light at ~254 nm produced inside

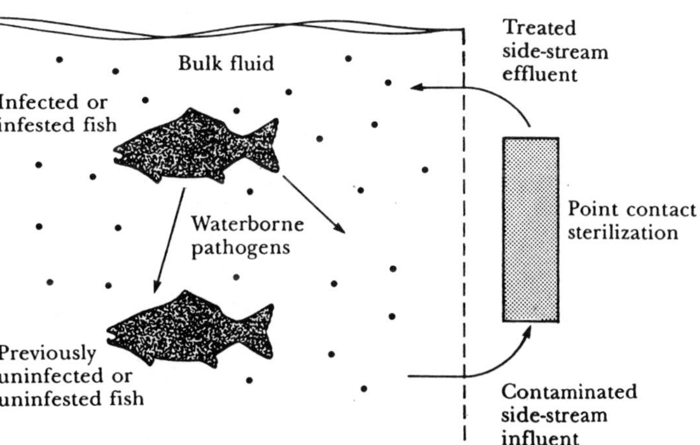

Figure 9-8 Point contact sterilization. Waterborne pathogens are killed primarily at the source of contact. The number of pathogens in the bulk fluid is not reduced substantially. Source: Stephen Spotte.

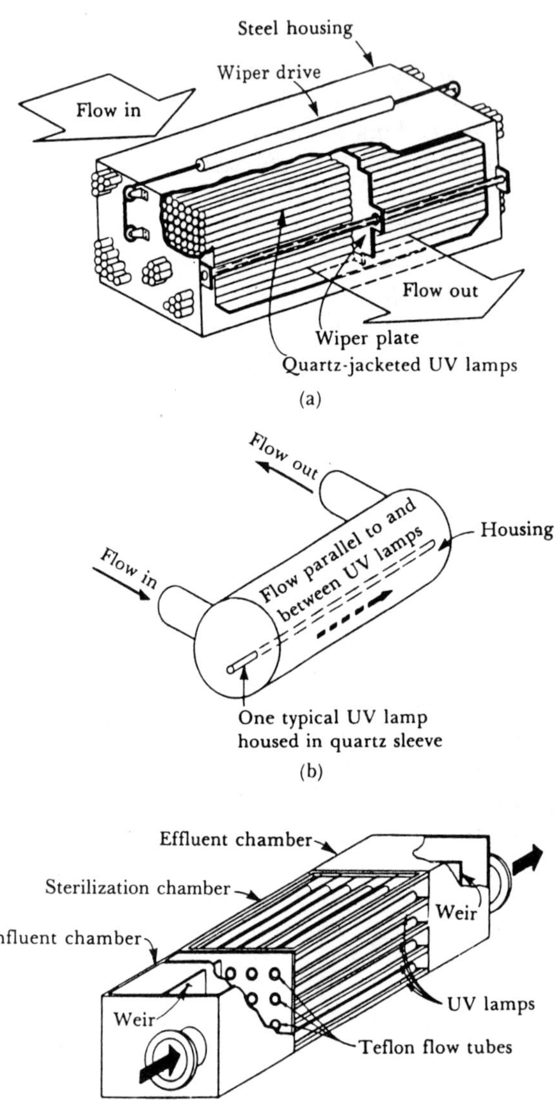

Figure 9-9 *Typical UV sterilization equipment configurations for large water systems. In all three designs a side stream of contaminated water is passed through batteries of tubes surrounded by lamps that emit UV radiation, and pathogens are killed by point contact. Quartz tubes are often used because UV rays cannot penetrate ordinary glass.* (a) *Perpendicular-to-lamp flow in a quartz unit.* (b) *Parallel-to-lamp flow in a quartz unit.* (c) *Teflon® tube unit.* Source: White et al. (1986).

the sterilizer by a UV lamp exerts a lethal effect on microorganisms (Fig. 9-10). Ultraviolet light alters genetic material within the cells, which interrupts respiration. This can occur without rupturing the cell wall or membrane of the organism. Microorganisms exposed to sublethal doses of UV radiation are able to repair the damage and survive.

UV irradiation does not lower clinical infections because the lethal elements are directed at the water and not at the fishes. Any benefit is derived from destroying organisms that are *po-*

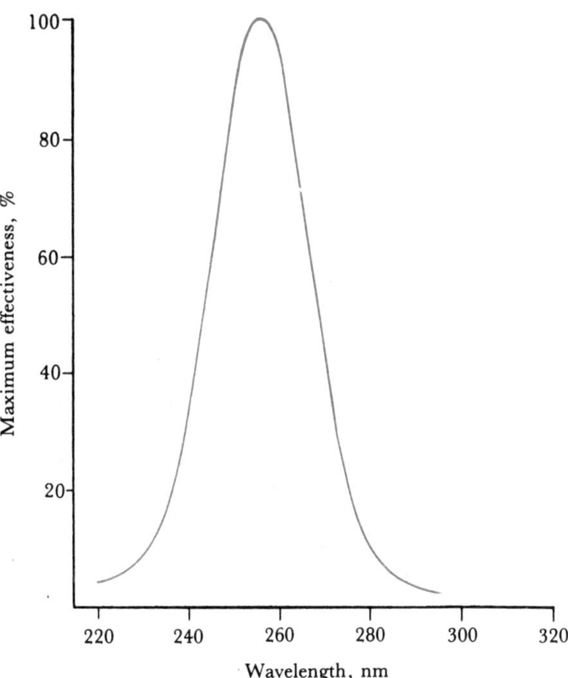

Figure 9-10 *Relative bactericidal effectiveness of ultraviolet light as a function of wavelength.* Source: Spotte (1979) after Wheaton (1977).

tentially infectious, rather than actually so, and the utility of such an approach is questionable. The aquarium literature attributes considerable importance to UV irradiation as a method of disease control, but not all the accolades are deserved. Experiments have demonstrated that in a properly operated UV sterilizer the kill rate of microorganisms inside the unit is nearly 100%, although the minimum lethal dosage of UV radiation depends on several factors, one being the size (i.e., surface area) of the pathogen. Small pathogens are killed more easily than large ones (Fig. 9-11). However, before the number of pathogens in the bulk fluid can be reduced, the kill rate must exceed the rate at which they are produced (Figs. 9-12 and 9-13). This occurs most effectively in *plug flow systems,* in which water from a contaminated aquarium is passed through a sterilizer and directed into a second aquarium. Plug flow and open systems are similar in the sense that the water is treated in a single pass instead of recirculated. Microorganisms multiply exponentially. During epizootics UV sterilizers cannot stop the spread of waterborne pathogens, and the process is of doubtful value in closed systems.[18] This should be clear from the example below.

The efficacy of a sterilizer depends on several factors: total volume of the system (V), volume flow rate through the sterilizer (F), fraction of the total number of microorganisms killed

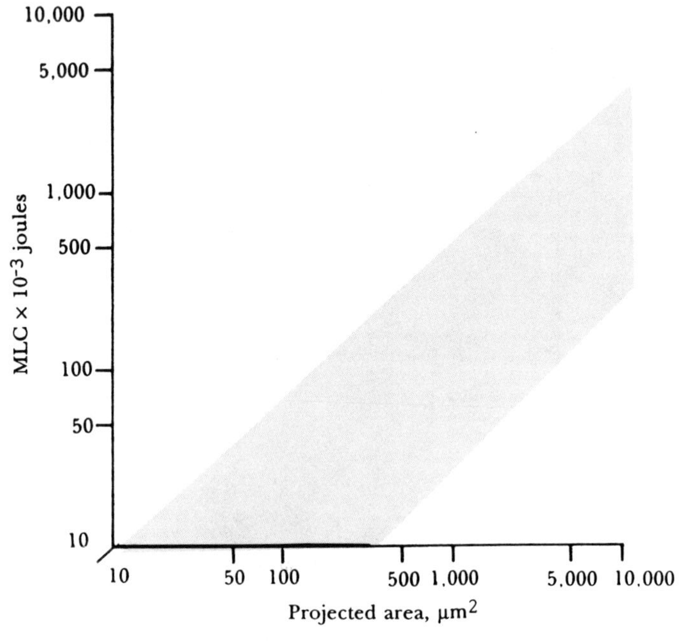

Figure 9-11 *Zone of effectiveness for the minimum lethal dosage of UV radiation at 254 nm versus projected area of the pathogen. Upper portion of the shaded area indicates UV-resistant organisms.* Source: Spotte (1979), drawn from data in Hoffman (1974).

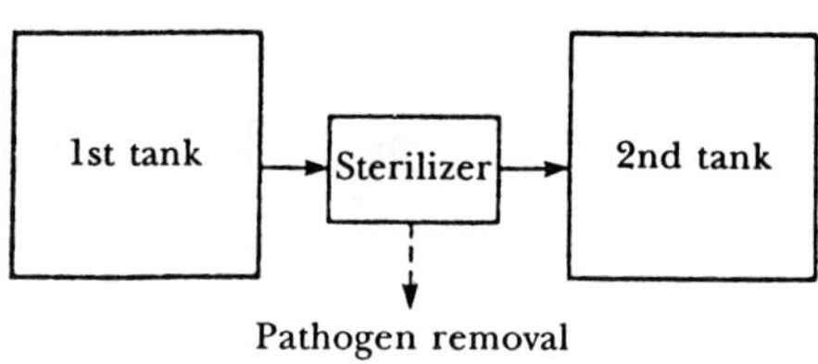

Plug flow

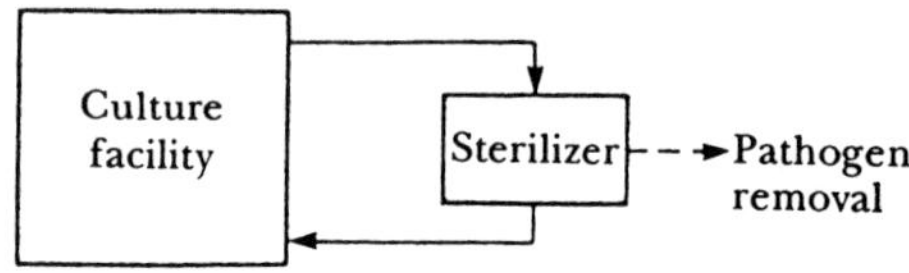

Idealized closed system

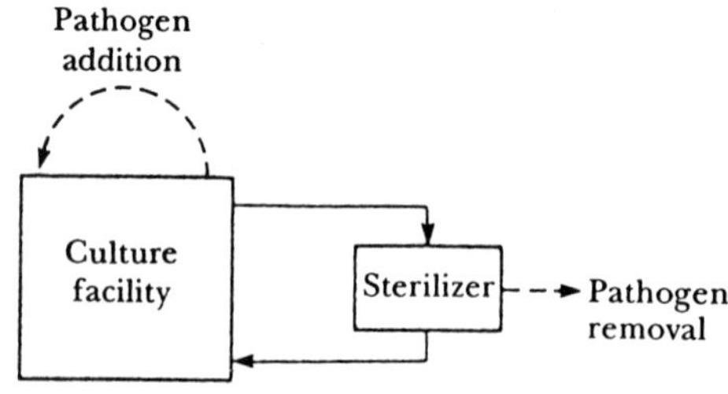

Conventional closed system

Figure 9-12 *In the plug flow scheme, water flows through the sterilizer in a single pass, and pathogens are removed at a constant rate. In the idealized closed system, all water is recycled, there is no new addition of pathogens, and pathogens are removed at a rate proportional to their concentration. In a conventional closed system all water is recycled; pathogens are added at a constant rate and removed at a rate proportional to their concentration.* Source: Spotte and Adams (1981).

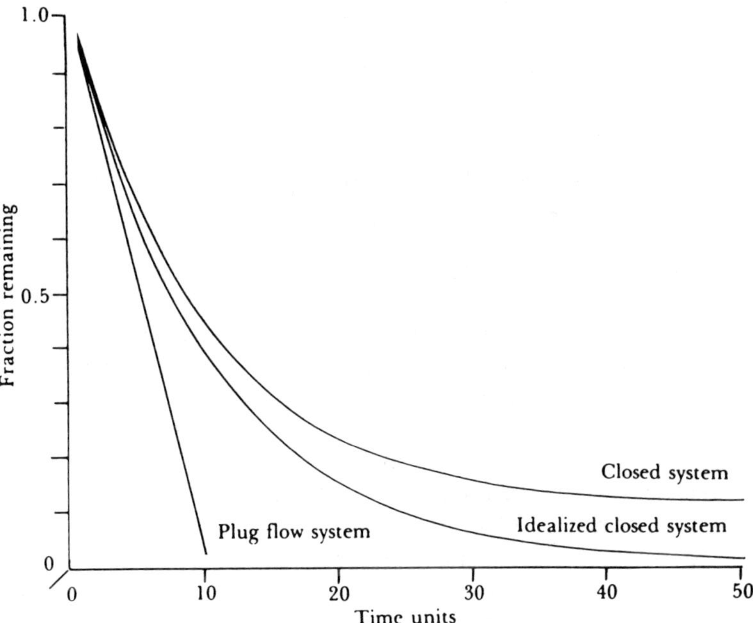

Figure 9-13 *Mass of pathogens remaining versus time after UV irradiation of the water in three types of flow schemes (Fig. 9-12). The rate of sterilization in all three schemes is assumed to be 100% (i.e., all organisms that pass through the sterilizer are killed). According to this model, complete sterilization of the bulk fluid in a conventional closed system is unattainable.* Source: Spotte and Adams (1981).

in a single pass through the sterilizer (E), and the rate at which microorganisms are added to the system (R). To construct a model of the system, two additional factors are required: t and c_0 as time and quantity of microorganisms present at time zero. The basic differential equation can be stated

$$dc = (-cEF/V + R)dt \qquad (9.1)$$

Integration yields

$$(-V/EF)\ \ln(-cEF/V + R) = t + k \qquad (9.2)$$

and substitution of the initial conditions produces

$$\ln[(-cEF/V + R)/(-c_0EF/V + R)] = -EFt/V \qquad (9.3)$$

Conversion to exponential form and rearranging gives

$$c = c_0\, e^{-EFt/V} + (1 - e^{-EFt/V})RV/EF \qquad (9.4)$$

For example, a 100,000-L aquarium in closed-system configuration has a UV sterilizer capable of removing 95% of the bacteria passing through it at a flow rate of 10,000 L/h. The aquarium initially contains 1.0×10^6 bacteria, and the captive fishes shed 2000 bacteria/h into the system. To calculate the number of bacteria remaining after 24 h,

$$c = 1.0 \times 10^6\, e^{-(0.95)(10,000)(24)/(100,000)} + (1 - e^{-(0.95)(10,000)(24)/(100,000)}) \cdot (2000)(100,000)/[(0.95)(10,000)]$$

$$c = 1 \times 10^6\, e^{-2.28} + (1 - e^{-2.28})(1.9 \times 10^4)$$

$$c = 1.19 \times 10^5 \text{ bacteria, only an 88\% reduction.}$$

OZONE Ozone, O_3, is another sterilizing agent used in seawater aquariums. The ozone molecule kills microorganisms by acting as a protoplasmic oxidant at the cell wall (bacteria) or membrane (protozoans). The use of ozone to treat fish diseases dates from at least October 1906, when freshwater fishes afflicted with a parasitic fungus were placed in ozonated water at Galatz, Germany.[19] Ozone is generated by an *ozonator*, and the process is *ozonation*. Ozone cannot be stored and must be produced continuously. Many of the smaller and older ozonators rely on UV lamps that generate UV radiation to produce O_3, but more modern and efficient models use the *silent discharge* method. Alternating voltage is applied across two electrodes separated by an insulator or *dielectric* (Fig. 9-14). The space between the electrodes is the *discharge gap*. Oxygen in the *feed gas* (gas entering the discharge gap) is converted into O_3. To apply ozone properly, contaminated water must be siphoned or pumped from the aquarium to a *contact chamber* (Figs. 9-15 and 9-16), where pathogens are placed in point contact with O_3 injected from the ozonator. Afterward, the treated effluent is returned to the bulk fluid. The arrangement is similar to the closed

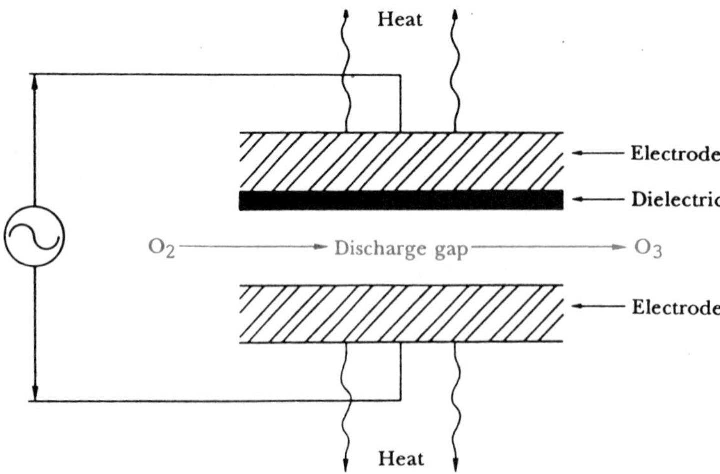

Figure 9-14 *Basic ozonator configuration.* Source: Spotte (1979) after Rosen (1973).

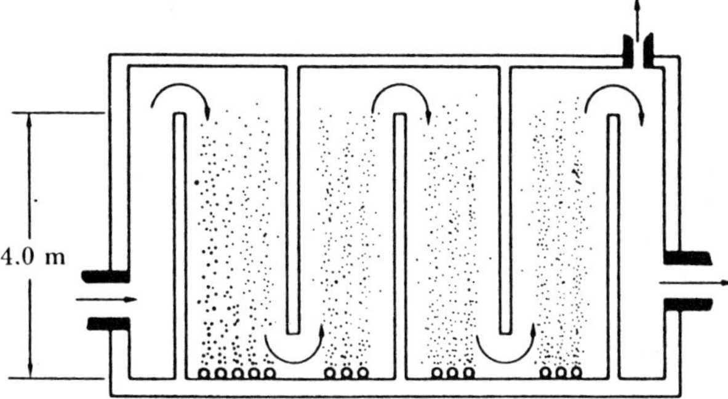

Figure 9-15 *Diffusion method of treating water with ozone.* Source: Spotte (1979) after Masschelein et al. (1975).

loop used to apply UV radiation. The effectiveness of ozonation is enhanced by extended contact time. This is achieved by contact chamber designs that prolong the time in which bubbles containing ozone remain in the treated water.

Disinfectants and Antiseptics

Disinfection is defined as the process of eliminating infection, a meaning quite different from sterilization, which is the elimination of all life.[17] *Antiseptics* disinfect without damaging the host's tissues. Disinfectants, unlike sterilizing agents, must be administered by methods that place them in contact with the surfaces of the fishes being treated. Antiseptics must be applied directly to the fish. Disinfectants are administered by immersion and can be ''cidal'' or ''static.'' Only chemotherapeutic

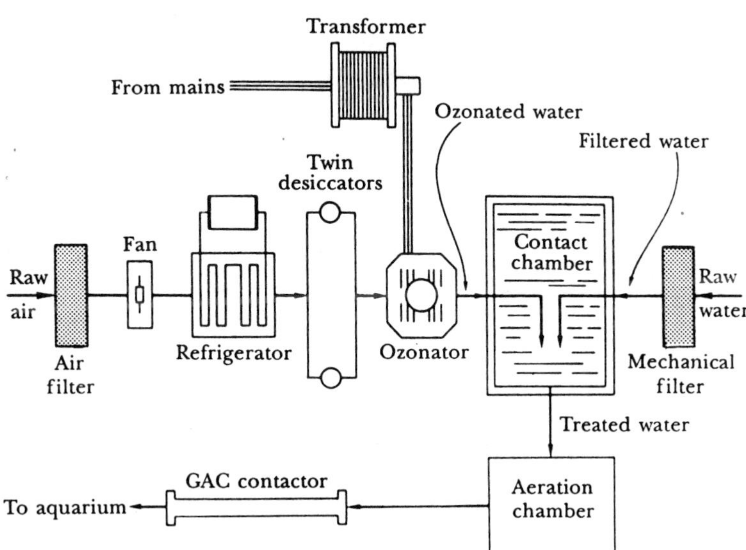

Figure 9-16 *Ozone treatment scheme for large water systems.* Source: Spotte (1979) after O'Donovan (1965).

agents are recommended for treating fish diseases, because of their selectivity. Disinfectants cause irritation or pathological changes in the host's tissues; antiseptics require handling the fish and must stay in place after the fish is returned to the water. Nothing further will be said about antiseptics.

The two most common disinfectants used to treat seawater aquarium fishes are ozone-produced oxidants and compounds of copper. These and some other common disinfectants are listed in Table 9-3. Many formulated products are available, but few have been tested against protozoan and fungal parasites of seawater fishes under proper experimental conditions. In one study, all products tested failed to lower the concentration of bacteria in freshwater aquariums significantly, and none was bacteriostatic *in vitro* at the manufacturer's recommended concentration.[20] If bacteria suspended in the water are not reduced, disinfection at the surface of a fish would be unlikely.

OZONE-PRODUCED OXIDANTS The ozone molecule is a sterilizing agent, but O_3 injected into seawater reacts with other constituents to form toxic residuals. These behave as persistent disinfectants. One study showed that the *half-life* of these substances in seawater (the time necessary for 50% to decompose) is at least 24 h. The situation in freshwater is different. In freshwater the instability of O_3 results in rapid decay of ozonated reaction products and little or no subsequent toxicity. Statements that O_3 in aquariums decomposes harmlessly are therefore truer of freshwater than of seawater.[21] The residuals formed

TABLE 9-3 Common disinfectants used to treat diseases of seawater aquarium fishes.

Acriflavin
Copper complexes
Chloramine-B
Dichlorophen
Formalin (dilute formaldehyde solution)
Halazone
Malachite green
Merbromin
Methylene blue
Ozone-produced oxidants
Silver oxide
Thimersal
2,4,5-Trichlorophenol
Zinc complexes

Source: Stephen Spotte; also see Meyer and Schnick (1989) and Schnick et al (1989).

in seawater are mainly brominated and chlorinated compounds, together called *ozone-produced oxidants*, OPOs. A more precise term is probably unnecessary because OPOs behave similarly to residual disinfectants formed by chlorination of seawater and called *chlorine-produced oxidants*, CPOs.[22] When added to seawater both chlorine gas, Cl_2, and O_3 react rapidly and preferentially with bromide, Br^-, and more slowly with Cl^- to form CPOs and OPOs.[23] Both groups of residuals are toxic at nearly identical concentrations, and their toxic effects appear to be the same.[24] The result of ozonating seawater containing bromide is therefore the same as chlorinating it.[25]

COPPER Copper at elevated concentrations in the marine environment is a pollutant, but spiking aquarium seawater with copper is thought by many to produce beneficial effects by killing parasites. This is a curious juxtaposition, considering that the chemical pathways of copper in the sea and in the aquarium are similar, and that its pathological effects in wild and captive fishes are identical. Copper should be eliminated from consideration in the treatment of aquarium fish diseases. I base this statement on several important facts, including a general failure to demonstrate the long-term effectiveness of copper experimentally. Added complications are the inability of all but the most sophisticated analytical techniques to distinguish the different chemical states of copper in either freshwaters or seawater,[26] an incomplete understanding of which chemical states are most toxic,[27] and the proved adverse effects of copper on fishes[28] (Table 9-4). Finally, the complicated and poorly known fate of copper compounds in seawater makes dosages impossible to predict.

The presumed efficacy of copper treatment is based to some extent on the assumption that free cupric ion, Cu(II), is available in substantial concentrations in solution. Copper is among the most extensively complexed of the trace metals. The different forms that exist at known conditions of temperature, pH, and ligand species and concentration can be projected using calculated values derived from assumptions of how copper reacts in different environments. These calculations constitute chemical models. A model for copper takes into consideration competition among the various cations such as Cu(II) for available complexation sites on ligands, and between inorganic and organic ligands for available cations.

Little of the total copper, TCu, in seawater exists as Cu(II), and the amount of soluble TCu becomes depleted in the presence of carbonate mineral filtrants. This suggests that it remains in copper-treated water systems indefinitely, desorbing during

TABLE 9-4 Adverse effects and functional impairments in fishes caused by environmental copper.

Enzyme activity

Impaired liver function and carbohydrate metabolism[13]
Lowered muscle and liver enzyme activity[3]
Inhibition of lactate oxidation by the gill[5]

Physiology

Reduced oxygen consumption[3, 11]
Increased mortality (salmon smolts) during freshwater-seawater transfer[7]
Tissue water imbalances[15]
Disruption of osmoregulation[9, 10] leading to potassium intoxication at acutely toxic concentrations[10]
Alteration of normal blood constituents[9, 21, 22]
Inhibition of chloride transport across the gill[12]
Disruption of normal sodium flux across the gill[19]

Growth

Anorexia[2, 20, 24]
Impairment of normal growth[4, 8, 11, 20, 24]

Health

Immune suppression[16, 23]
Decreased resistance to disease[2]

Behavior

Impaired locomotor activity, including hyper- and hypoactivity[25, 26]
Disorientation[11]
Abnormal schooling behavior suggestive of fright[17]

Pathology

Fatty liver degeneration[1]
Necrosis of kidney tissue[1, 14]
Destruction of hemopoietic tissue[1]
Pathological changes in the gill[1, 10]
Corneal lesions and visual impairment[6]
Possible accelerated senescence of neuronal cells[27]
Pathological changes to the lateral line[14, 18]
Degeneration of the olfactory sacs[14]
Brain hemorrhage[14, 29]
Dilation of blood vessels[14]
Permeation and destruction of the taste buds[28]

Sources: Baker (1969),[1] Baker et al. (1983),[2] Balavenkatasubbaiah et al. (1984),[3] Benoit (1975),[4] Bilinski and Jonas (1973),[5] Bodammer (1987),[6] Bouck and Johnson (1979),[7] Buckley et al. (1982),[8] Cardeilhac and Hall (1977),[9] Cardeilhac et al. (1979),[10] Collvin (1984),[11] Crespo and Karnaky (1983),[12] Dixon and Hilton (1981),[13] Gardner and LaRoche (1973),[14] Heath (1984),[15] Knittel (1981),[16] Koltes (1984),[17] LaRoche et al. (1973),[18] Laurén and McDonald (1986),[19] Lett et al. (1976),[20] Lewis and Lewis (1971),[21] McKim et al. (1970),[22] O'Neill (1981),[23] Ozaki et al. (1970),[24] Scarfe et al. (1982),[25] Steele (1983),[26] Totaro et al. (1985),[27] Vijayamadhavan and Iwai (1975),[28] Woodhead and Setlow (1982).[29]

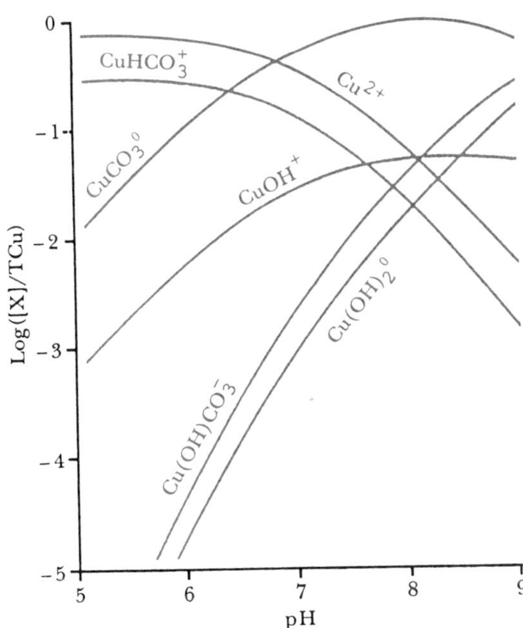

Figure 9-17 Distribution diagram of total copper, TCu, in a carbonate solution (total alkalinity = 2 mEq/kg) as a function of pH at the ionic strength of seawater (0.72 mol/kg). TCu = 1×10^{-10} mol/kg. Concentrations of individual species [X] were calculated from experimental data and plotted as the log of the fraction of TCu. Note that the model does not account for carbonate minerals, which also remove copper from solution (Figs. 9-18 and 9-19). Source: Symes and Kester (1985).

transient periods of localized acidity in the filter bed. Carbonato complexes in seawater (pH 8.2, total alkalinity 2.3 meq/kg, 25°C) account for 82% of the inorganic copper species (Fig. 9-17).[29] Only 2.9% exists as Cu(II). Hydrolysis products, $CuOH^+$ and $Cu(OH)_2^0$, account for 6.5%; $CuHCO_3^+$ and $Cu(OH)CO_3^-$ are 1.0 and 6.3% of the remainder.[29] Other models have yielded similar results.[30] The cuprous state—Cu^{1+} or Cu(I)—does not exist in aqueous solutions (Chapter 8, Note 101).

Copper is removed from solution rapidly in the presence of carbonate minerals. Its uptake in distilled water is directly proportional to the concentration in solution, and copper-based precipitates form on the surfaces of calcite (Fig. 9-18).[31] In seawater, the assimilation of copper onto calcite surfaces is also directly proportional to the concentration, but the affinity of copper for calcite is approximately an order of magnitude less than in distilled water[31] (Fig. 9-19). This is believed to be the result of several factors, including increased competition for adsorption sites by other ions.[31]

TECHNOLOGY

A few parasites cause most of the mortalities in captive seawater fishes. All others are comparatively unimportant. Literally hundreds of compounds have been proposed for the treat-

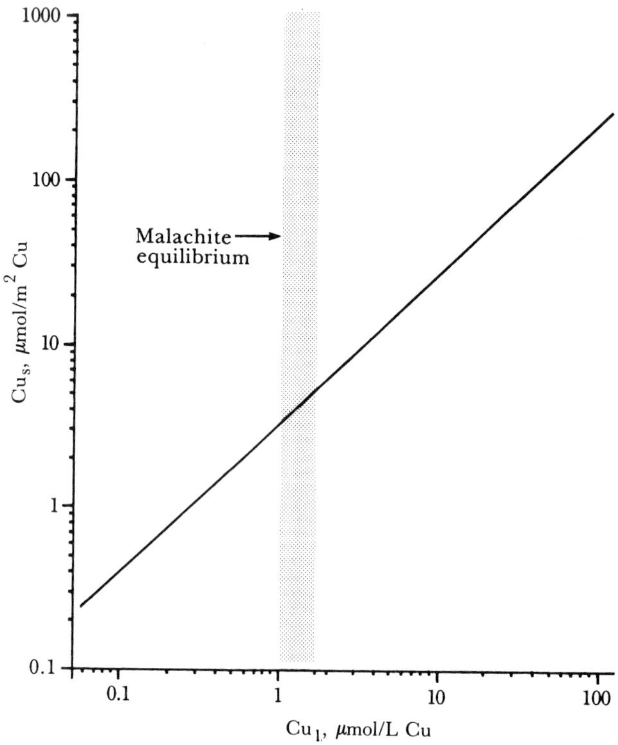

Figure 9-18 *Assimilation of copper by calcite in distilled water at a solid/solution ratio of 1 g/L (data points omitted). The shaded area represents the equilibrium copper concentration for the solubility of malachite, $Cu_2(OH)_2CO_{3(s)}$, over the pH range 7.5 to 8.4. The subscripts s and l represent solid and dissolved.* Source: Franklin and Morse (1982).

ment of fish diseases, but far fewer can be justified, having proved both efficacious and harmless to the host when used correctly. Sterilizing agents and disinfectants can be eliminated unilaterally until any beneficial properties are identified and measured. Sterilizing agents either fail to lower the number of suspended pathogens to levels adequate to prevent reinfection (UV radiation in recirculated water) or produce toxic residuals (ozone in seawater). In either case, when a sterilizing agent is applied to an aquarium the focus of activity is on the water, not on the infection. Disinfectants are placed in direct contact with the host and their toxicities are nonselective, damaging hosts and pathogens indiscriminately. Moreover, the reduction of unattached microorganisms and those on the surfaces of the host does not alleviate systemic infections. When used correctly, chemotherapeutic agents exert selective toxicities, causing little or no harm to the host's tissues. Chemotherapeutic agents are emphasized in the sections that follow. The rest of the chapter is devoted to descriptions of diseases and prophylactic techniques. As stated previously, not a single disease—fish or human—has ever been eradicated except by prevention. Vaccines offer the best hope. The subject of laboratory diag-

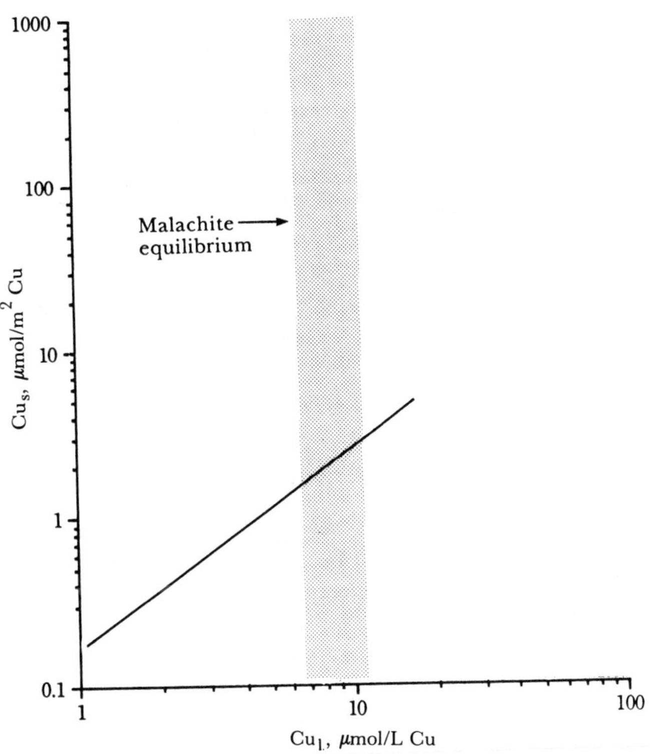

Figure 9-19 *Assimilation of copper by calcite in seawater at solid/solution ratios ranging from 1.0 to 10.0 g/L (data points omitted). The shaded area represents the equilibrium copper concentration for the solubility of malachite, $Cu_2(OH)_2CO_{3(s)}$, at pH 7.85 over a range of 0.006 to 0.010 in the total activity coefficient of copper. The subscripts s and l represent solid and dissolved.* Source: Franklin and Morse (1982).

nostics exceeds the scope of this text. A functional fish disease laboratory requires modern diagnostic equipment and personnel with specialized training.

Quarantine

Public aquariums receive fishes from many sources, including retailers and wholesalers, other institutions, hatcheries, and nature. All fishes—regardless of origin—should be kept in quarantine a minimum of 21 d before being placed in community exhibits. Consider these general guidelines when designing a quarantine area.

Disease organisms are easily transmitted to healthy fishes in contaminated water and food, aquarists' hands, and cleaning utensils. Establish the quarantine area in a remote place out of contact with the exhibits and fishes held in reserve. Encourage personnel to follow hygienic procedures. Use dedicated nets, hoses, and other equipment. After use, place equipment in a 2% Clorox® solution for a minimum of 45 min.

Newly acquired fishes are stressed and should be provided with ample hiding places. These can be short sections of discarded PVC pipe, plastic flowerpots, and other items with smooth, inert surfaces that can be disinfected easily.

An aquarium that has held diseased fishes should be sterilized before reuse. Start by stirring the gravel and siphoning out as much detritus as possible to reduce the oxidant demand of the water. Refill with tap water. Add sodium hypochlorite, NaOCl, to give a free available chlorine level of 3 to 5 mg/kg of water as determined crudely with a test kit. Let stand overnight. Dechlorinate with an appropriate reducing agent (e.g., sodium thiosulfate), drain, flush thoroughly with tap water, and refill with seawater or artificial seawater.

Lymphocystis Disease

SYNONYMS Cauliflower disease, lymphocystis.

ETIOLOGY Lymphocystis disease, which has a long and interesting history,[32] is caused by a virus classified tentatively as one of five genera (proposed name *Cystivirus*) in the iridovirus family.[33] It afflicts derived bony fishes[34] in both fresh and saline waters, warm and cold, in numerous regions of the world.[35] Through 1976 the disease had been reported from 83 species of teleosts representing 33 families and five orders.[36] The list has expanded since then.[37] Lymphocystis disease was first described in 1874,[38] but a virus was not isolated until 1966.[39] To date it is the only virus disease known with certainty from aquarium fishes, although many more undoubtedly await discovery.[40]

EPIZOOTIOLOGY Lymphocystis disease is benign, chronic, and nonlethal,[41] although infected fishes in nature may suffer increased mortality.[42] The incubation period is a few days[43] to several weeks.[44] Healthy fishes remain susceptible indefinitely in the presence of aquarium-mates with lesions.[44] Lymphocystis disease is transmitted easily among species, less easily among genera,[44] and perhaps never among families.[45] This suggests relatively high host specificity. The virus enters the water from epithelial cells shed by infected fishes, or from ruptured cells.[46] Healthy fishes have been infected experimentally by placing them in water containing emulsified lymphocystis-infected cells.[43] Modes of entry into new hosts are unknown, but suspected sites are surface lesions[47] and the gut wall after ingestion of the virus.[45] The rupture of infected cells is probably the principal route of transmission.[48] Epizootics in nature are thought to be seasonal, at least in temperate regions.[49]

CLINICAL SIGNS AND PATHOLOGICAL EFFECTS The name ''cauliflower disease'' is an apt description of the lesions, which are raised, whitish or opalescent, warty, and have a lumpy or ''raspberry'' texture[50] (Fig. 9-20). The lesions consist of hypertrophied connective tissue cells[37] (Fig. 9-21). Infected cells grow abnormally large, often increasing in volume by 100,000-fold.[44] Most range in diameter from 100 to 250 μm, occasionally reaching 2 mm in some species of flounders.[51] Lymphocystis is principally a disease of the body surfaces and fins,[44] although lesions sometimes occur on the internal organs,[52] in addition to the eyes and associated tissues.[53] Diseased fishes typically show few signs of distress and continue to feed and otherwise behave normally.

PROPHYLAXIS AND TREATMENT The most effective prophylaxis is avoidance.[40] No effective treatment is known. Infections often regress spontaneously as diseased tissue is sloughed, with recovery time ranging from 20 d to >4 months.[54] Degeneration of diseased cells may be caused by natural resistance and immune responses of the host;[55] the alternative possibility is that it represents a normal stage in the progression of the infection.[48] Fishes that recover are often not susceptible to recurrence of the disease.[56] According to one author, the lesions can be excised like human warts, although subsequent treatment with antibacterial agents is recommended to prevent secondary bacterial and fungal infections.[40]

Figure 9-20 Lymphocystis disease in an Atlantic croaker (Micropogonias undulatus). Source: Edward J. Noga, College of Veterinary Medicine, North Carolina State University.

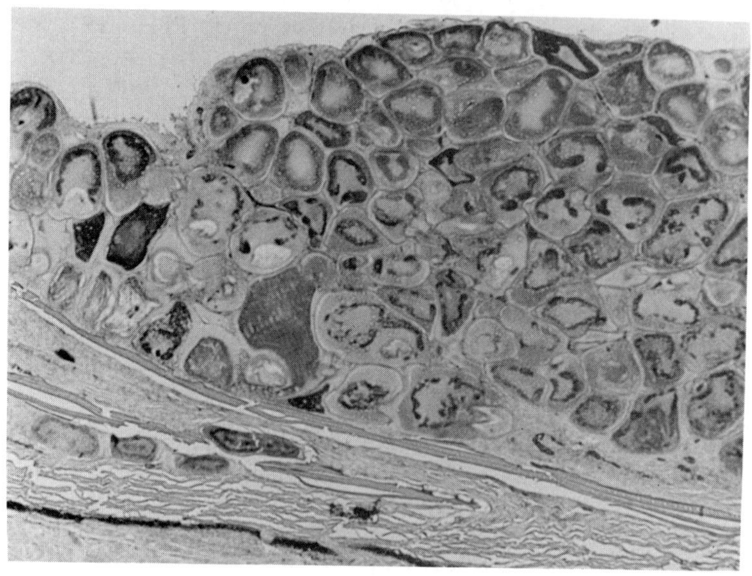

Figure 9-21 *Abnormally large epithelial cells of a teleost caused by lymphocystis virus. 400x.* Source: Richard E. Wolke, Marine Pathology Laboratory, University of Rhode Island.

Mycobacteriosis

SYNONYMS Fish tuberculosis,[57] wasting disease.

ETIOLOGY Mycobacteriosis is caused by rod-shaped,[58] Gram-positive,[59] acid-fast[60] bacteria of the genus *Mycobacterium*.[61] Mycobacteriosis was first described nearly 100 years ago from common carp (*Cyprinus carpio*) held in a pond in France.[62] The first publication describing the disease in seawater aquarium fishes appeared in 1926. The specimens were obtained from exhibits at the Fairmount Park Aquarium in Philadelphia.[63] Mycobacteriosis is widespread in hatcheries and public aquariums. One report listed the disease as having been reported in 151 species of freshwater and seawater fishes representing 40 families.[64]

EPIZOOTIOLOGY Mycobacteriosis-producing bacteria are transmitted orally through raw, infected fish flesh,[65] detritus,[66] and probably feces. Because the kidney is a primary site of infection (see the next subsection), it is thought that organisms are shed into the water along with urinary wastes and ingested directly.[67] Some researchers suspect that *Mycobacterium* can enter injured fishes as an opportunistic pathogen through lesions in the skin and gills.[68] Mycobacteriosis ordinarily is chronic.[69] Development to the clinical stage is slow, sometimes taking years,[70] which suggests low virulence. As a result, infections are more commonly enzootic than epizootic.[71] Once in the environment, bacteria remain viable at least 5 weeks at 4°C and for 18 d at 35°C.[72] The onset of clinical signs of the disease is probably mediated by predisposing factors, including crowding (which facilitates transmission),[73] capture and handling stress,[74] and temperature changes.[74] Fin-nipping that results in open lesions is still another predisposing factor.[75]

CLINICAL SIGNS AND PATHOLOGICAL EFFECTS External signs may be absent entirely.[76] A fish that seems outwardly healthy can be heavily infected internally, and the disease ordinarily is far advanced by the time skin lesions appear.[77] Infected fishes of some species often live a year or more before succumbing.[78] Young fishes may be stunted or fail to mature.[79] The coloration of salmonids becomes brighter than normal;[79] other species turn darker.[71] In the neon tetra (*Hyphessobrycon innesi*), a freshwater aquarium fish, the bright red lateral markings assume a yellowish discoloration.[77] In other species, skin lesions are gray, rounded, and slightly raised.[80] *Exophthalmia* ("popeye") is sometimes associated with the disease.[81] Other signs include *dyspnea* (labored breathing),[71] immobility or *ataxia* (incoordination of voluntary muscle action),[71] scale loss,[71] lifting of scales,[82] frayed fins,[82] depigmentation,[83] and *anorexia* (loss of appetite).[84] The most prevalent clinical sign is emaciation;[80] hence the term "wasting disease." On dissection numerous small, spherical lesions or *tubercles* are typically present (Fig. 9-22). These contain *Mycobacterium* (Fig. 9-23) and are diagnostic.[77] The tubercles can be found in the *mesenteries* (membranes

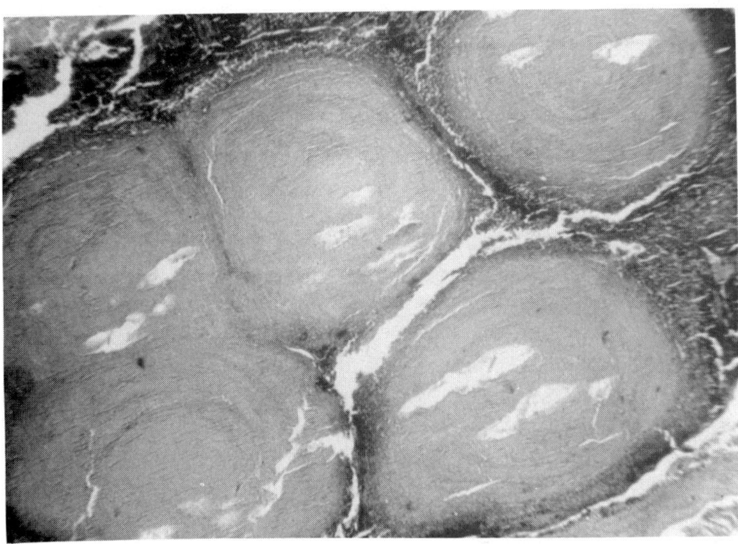

Figure 9-22 *Granulomatous lesions in the liver of a triggerfish* (Balistoides *sp.*) *caused by mycobacteriosis. 25x.* Source: George C. Blasiola.

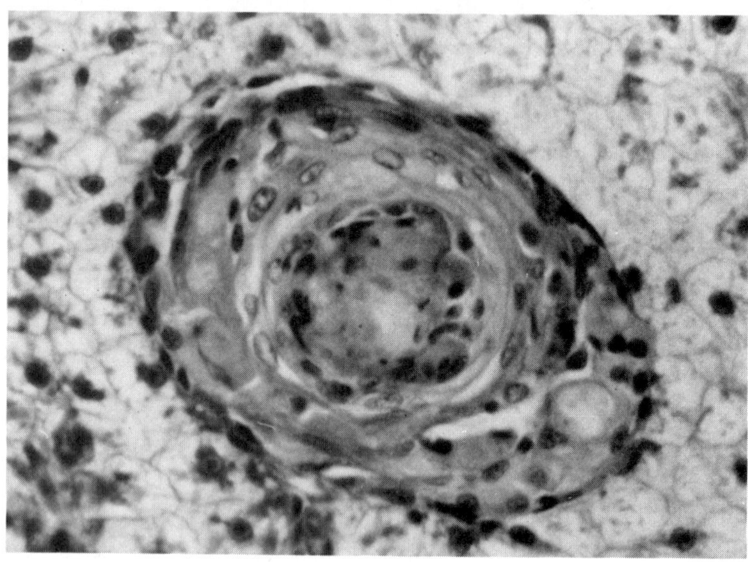

Figure 9-23 Mycobacterium *sp. in the tissues of a teleost. 400x.* Source: Richard E. Wolke, Marine Pathology Laboratory, University of Rhode Island.

that support the internal organs), muscles, skin, heart, eyes, gills, kidney, spleen, liver, pancreas, brain, and *gonads* (male and female sex organs, the *testes* and *ovaries*).[85] Curiously, tubercular lesions have not been found in the intestine, although ingestion appears to be the principal means of entry.[77]

PROPHYLAXIS AND TREATMENT The best prevention is to avoid feeding raw fish and shellfish. Destroy infected fishes. Discard the water and sterilize the aquarium and everything in it with a chlorine-based oxidant.[86] Remove uneaten food and dead specimens routinely. The threat of mycobacteriosis in public aquariums is serious because the organism cannot be eradicated from the liver and kidneys of infected fishes that do not show clinical signs of disease.[87] In addition, there is the possibility that *Mycobacterium* shed into the water can become disease producing when ingested.[67]

Recent data from *in vivo* treatment studies are lacking, although several compounds have shown high *in vitro* activity against *Mycobacterium*, notably erythromycin, rifampicin, and streptomycin (Table 9-5). These offer the hope of effective immersion treatment.

ZOONOSIS Aquarists can acquire granulomatous lesions, primarily on the hands and arms, caused by *M. marinum*.[88] Both freshwater and seawater aquariums can be sources of infection. Cuts and abrasions are the sites of entry[89] and can become infected during routine cleaning of aquariums.[90] The lesions ap-

TABLE 9-5 Efficacy of 10 antibacterial compounds against 20 strains of *Mycobacterium* sp. *in vitro*.

Compound	MIC, μg/mL	MLC, μg/mL
Ampicillin	1.56–3.13	1.56–3.13
Chloramphenicol	3.13–25	3.13–50
Erythromycin	0.025–0.78	0.025–0.78
Isoniazid	3.13–25	3.13–50
Josamycin	3.13–25	3.13–50
Lincomycin	3.13–25	3.13–50
Oxytetracycline	3.13–25	3.13–50
Rifampicin	0.025–0.78	0.025–0.78
Streptomycin	0.025–0.78	0.025–0.78
STM[1]	25–100	50–>100

Source: Stephen Spotte, compiled from data in Kawakami and Kusuda (1989).
Note: Identity omitted from English summary and legends.[1]

pear in 21 d,[91] enlarge,[91] and sometimes spread to the arms and legs.[92] Advanced lesions are large (0.5 to 5.0 cm in diameter),[93] bluish,[91] ulcerating nodules that drain serous fluid.[93] Infections often persist, sometimes requiring antibacterial treatment extending 2 years or longer.[94]

Vibriosis

SYNONYMS Saltwater furunculosis, boil disease, ulcer disease, vibrio disease, Hitra disease (also called cold-water vibriosis), red boil, red pest, red plague, red disease. The last four have been used to describe vibrosis in captive eels (*Anguilla* spp.).

ETIOLOGY Vibriosis is caused by motile, rod-shaped (straight or curved), Gram-negative bacteria of the genus *Vibrio*.[95] The organisms are 0.5 to 0.8 μm wide by 1.4 to 2.5 μm long.[95] *Vibrio* spp. inhabit mainly saline environments and are common constituents of the surface and intestinal flora of fishes and invertebrates (see below). Vibriosis is widespread,[96] and reports from western Europe of fishes afflicted with what probably was vibriosis date from the early eighteenth century.[97] Vibriosis occurs in brackish water and seawater environments and occasionally in freshwaters.[98] The fact that vibrios are often present as benign commensals indicates that epizootics are triggered and sustained by a complex array of factors. Host specificity is certainly one factor, and the virulence of the infectious agent is another. Host specificity is suggestive of a normal complement of vibrios that somehow becomes pathogenic, probably during times of stress.[99] Alternatively, epizootics develop with introduction of a new strain of *Vibrio* to which the host has limited immunity, or none at all.[99]

EPIZOOTIOLOGY Ten species of *Vibrio* are known or suspected fish pathogens:[100] *V. alginolyticus, V. anguillarum, V. carchariae, V. cholerae, V. damsela, V. furnissii, V. harveyi, V. ordalii, V. splendidus,* and *V. vulnificus*. Because vibrios are normal surface constituents of healthy fishes,[101] lesions are principal entry sites.[102] Waterborne transmission also occurs,[103] and clinical infections have been induced by oral transmission.[104] Changes in temperature have been implicated in natural epizootics of vibriosis.[105]

CLINICAL SIGNS AND PATHOLOGICAL EFFECTS Clinical signs, pathological effects, and predisposing factors in vibriosis are summarized in Table 9-6. Clinical signs vary with the species of *Vibrio* and species of host.[106] The terms ''chronic'' and ''acute'' are difficult to define,[107] and overlap in both clinical signs and pathological effects is inevitable. Chronic forms of the disease may result in *leukocytosis* (production of white blood cells), anemia, ulcers on the skin and lower jaw (hence the names ''ulcer disease'' and ''boil disease''), and sloughing of the gut epithelium.[108] In captive fishes, lesions often occur where the fish rubs against the walls of the aquarium.[109] Advanced stages are characterized by a hemorrhagic septicemia with concomitant anemia.[108] Other signs can include hemorrhaging of the gills, skin (Fig. 9-24), intestinal tract, and swimbladder;[110] pale gills;[110] *ecchymosis* (small hemorrhagic spots) and septicemia;[111] loose scales;[112] ocular opacity[113] (Fig. 9-25) or exophthalmia,[114] *erythema* (bloody patches) at the base of the fins and inside the mouth;[115] milky cloudiness of body surfaces;[113] *petechiae* (minute hemorrhagic spots) on the skin and base of the fins;[116] and ataxia.[109] The hemorrhages may be transformed into ulcers that deepen with time,[110] and ulcers later appear on the muscle tissue.[117] Diseased fishes sometimes become darker;[109] alternatively, dark patches appear on the body surfaces and spread rapidly.[110]

Acute vibriosis is accompanied by fewer clinical signs.[118] This suggests that toxemia is the cause of death,[119] which typically occurs within 4 d after exposure to the infectious agent,[120] often with darkened skin coloration as the only noticeable change.[110] In addition to darkened skin coloration,[121] clinical signs can include pale gills and copious amounts of peritoneal fluid,[110] ecchymosis,[122] massive bacteremia,[111] and *erythropenia* (depressed numbers of red blood cells)[113] and leukopenia,[111] indicating the

TABLE 9-6 Clinical signs, pathological effects, and predisposing factors in vibriosis. Every sign and effect is not always seen because each is dependent to some extent on the species of *Vibrio*.

Chronic vibriosis	Acute vibriosis
Anemia	Anemia
Ataxia	Massive bacteremia
Bacteremia	Darkened skin coloration
Darkened skin coloration or dark patches on body surfaces	Duration 2 to 4 days
Duration 2 to 6 weeks	Ecchymosis
Ecchymosis	Fin hemorrhaging
Erythema at base of fins and inside mouth	Inflamed digestive tract
Exophthalmia	Leukopenia
Hemorrhagic septicemia	Occurs all year
Hemorrhaging of the gills, skin, intestinal tract, swimbladder	Rectum distended
Lesions where the fish rubs against the aquarium walls	Ulcerative skin lesions
Leukocytosis	
Loose scales	
Milky cloudiness on body surfaces	
Occurs seasonally	
Ocular opacity	
Pale gills	
Petechiae on skin and base of fins	
Sloughing of gut epithelium	
Ulcers on skin and lower jaw; in muscle tissue as disease advances	
Predisposing Factors	
Careless use of sterilizing agents that damage gills and skin	
Copper treatment	
Crowding	
Handling and transport stress	
Osmotic stress	
Parasitism by potential vectors of vibrios	

Source: Stephen Spotte, compiled from various sources.

production of powerful erythrocytolytic and leukocytolytic factors by the bacteria.[123] Other reported signs are irregular breathing,[124] skin sloughing,[110] petechiae,[125] skin ulcers,[126] *vasculitis* (inflammation of a vessel),[127] and swelling and inflammation of the anal region.[125] Gray areas may appear around open wounds.[125] Fishes afflicted with either the chronic or acute form of the disease are anorexic, sluggish, and sometimes

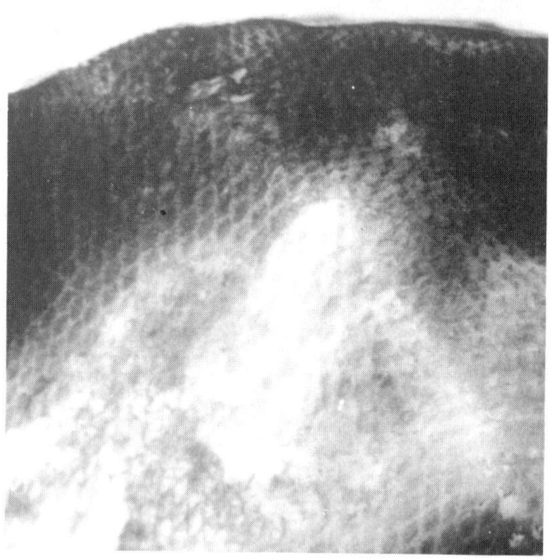

Figure 9-24 *Hemorrhagic skin of a batfish* (Platax pinnatus) *caused by vibriosis.* Source: George C. Blasiola.

ataxic.[128] Two additional illustrations of vibriosis are shown in Figures 9-26 and 9-27.

PROPHYLAXIS AND TREATMENT Handling stress is a major consideration in controlling vibriosis, and epizootics often occur following netting and transfer, presumably via lesions incurred.[129] At such times any vibrios present in the surface flora are located conveniently near the lesions. Crowding has also been implicated in epizootics.[130] Healthy lemon sharks (*Nega-*

Figure 9-25 *Milkfish* (Chanos chanos) *fingerlings: upper is a control fish; lower is a test fish with opaque corneas caused by an experimentally induced* Vibrio *sp. infection.* Source: Muroga et al. (1984b).

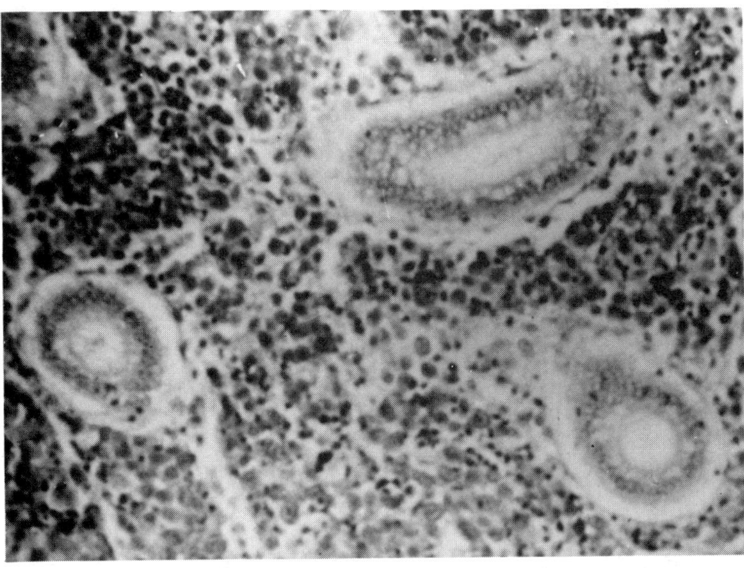

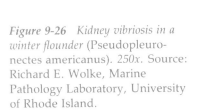

Figure 9-26 Kidney vibriosis in a winter flounder (Pseudopleuronectes americanus). *250x.* Source: Richard E. Wolke, Marine Pathology Laboratory, University of Rhode Island.

prion brevirostris) are commonly infected with *V. carchariae*, but clinical signs of disease are observed only after the host has been stressed.[131] In some teleosts osmotic stress is apparently a predisposing factor.[132] The careless use of sterilizing agents (e.g., chlorine-based oxidants) resulting in gill and skin damage has been known to initiate vibrio epizootics.[110] Exposing fishes to copper-treated water increases their susceptibility to vibriosis.[133]

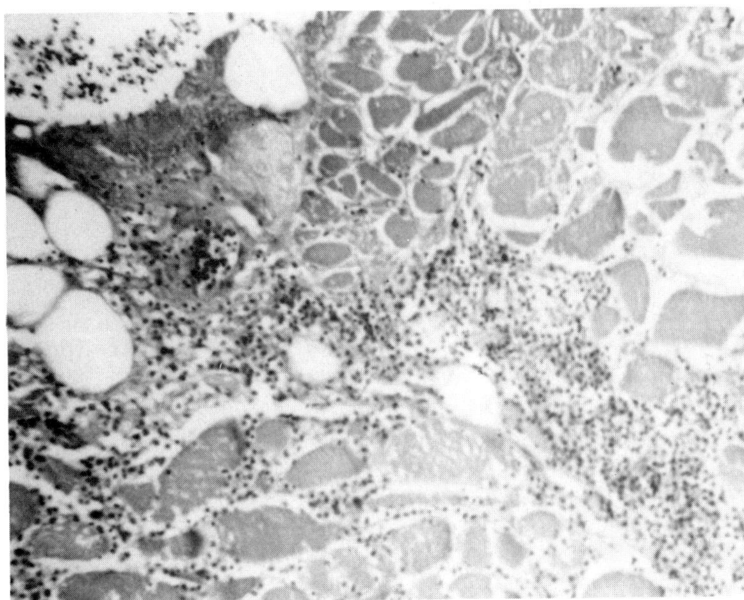

Figure 9-27 Skin vibriosis in an American eel (Anguilla rostrata). *100x.* Source: Richard E. Wolke, Marine Pathology Laboratory, University of Rhode Island.

If the vibrios are present as part of the normal bacterial flora of fishes (i.e., as commensals), stress is a primary consideration. However, introduction of other *Vibrio* species, or particularly virulent strains of species present already, warrants some thought. In addition, vibrios normally present in one species of host, and to which some degree of immunity has been acquired, can be pathogenic to newly introduced fishes lacking immunity.[98] Raw seafoods may harbor vibrios (Table 9-7), and their use is best avoided.[134]

Vaccines against *V. anguillarum* are available commercially, and vaccination of hatchery salmonids is common practice.[135] Intraperitoneal injection of vaccines appears to be the most effective method (Table 9-8), but it is labor intensive and stressful.[136] Vaccines have been used with seawater aquarium fishes on a limited basis[137] and with no demonstrable success. Their potential utility is untested. Public aquariums house hundreds of species of unknown susceptibility and tolerance to vibriosis. A general vaccine might immunize some specimens, but certainly not all.

Several treatments for vibriosis have been tried (Table 9-9 and Treatment Abstracts). Systemic vibriosis responds poorly to antibacterial compounds applied externally.[138]

ZOONOSIS *Vibrio cholerae* causes human cholera, but other vibrios can also be pathogenic in humans: *V. alginolyticus*, *V. fluvialis*, *V. metschnikovii*, *V. parahaemolyticus*, and *V. vulnificus*.[139] Among the etiologic paths suspected of leading to human vibriosis are consumption of raw seafoods[140] and exposure

TABLE 9-7 Invertebrates from which pathogenic vibrios have been isolated.

Common name	Scientific name
American lobster[6]	*Homarus americanus*
Blue crab[4]	*Callinectes sapidus*
Brown shrimp[1,2]	*Penaeus aztecus*
Eastern oyster[7,8]	*Crassostrea virginica*
European oyster[8]	*Ostrea edulis*
Kuruma prawn[3]	*Penaeus japonicus*
Quahog[8]	*Mercenaria mercenaria*
Rock crab[5]	*Cancer irroratus*
White shrimp[2]	*Penaeus setiferus*

Sources: Bowser et al. (1981),[1] Elston et al. (1982),[2] Elston et al. (1981),[3] Lewis (1973),[4] Lightner and Lewis (1975),[5] Newman and Feng (1982),[6] Sizemore (1985),[7] Takahashi et al. (1984).[8]

TABLE 9-8 Comparative success (as cumulative percentage mortality) of different methods of vaccination against *Vibrio anguillarum*. Controls received no treatment. All fishes were salmonids. Dashes indicate no data. Study numbers correspond with numerical superscripts in the list of sources.

Study	2	1	4	3
Controls	52	33.8	42	100
Oral	27	31.7	17.6	94
Immersion	4	2.1	12	53
Spray	1	—	—	—
Injection	0	1.4	2	7

Sources: Amend and Johnson (1981),[1] Baudin-Laurencin and Tangtrongpiros (1980),[2] Evelyn and Ketcheson (1980),[3] Horne et al. (1982).[4]

TABLE 9-9 Treatments for fish vibriosis caused by *V. alginolyticus*, *V. anguillarum*, and *V. ordalli*. Units are in concentration of the active ingredient: mg/L (immersion), mg/kg of fish (oral or *per os*). Dashes indicate no information. Chloramphenicol is effective but not included because its use should be restricted to human beings. Juvenile turbot (*Scophthalmus maximus*) immersed in halquinol for 10 min became ataxic, but recovered after transfer to untreated seawater (reference 3 of this table).

Compound	Dosage	Method	Duration
Halquinol[3]	10 mg/L	Immersion	15 min, repeat every other day for 8 d
	100 mg/kg	Oral	2x daily for 56 d
Halquinol[2]	25 mg/L	Immersion	15 min, 2x daily for 3 d
Nifurpirinol[6]	2 mg/L	Immersion	—
Nifurpirinol-oxytetracycline[7]	10 mg/L	Immersion	—
Trimethoprim[8]	30 mg/kg	Oral	3 d
UV radiation[10, 12]	19,400 J/cm^2	Immersion	Flow rate = 25 L/min
UV + ozone[10, 13]	19,400 J/cm^2	Immersion	Flow rate = 25 L/min

Sources: Austin and Austin (1987),[1] Austin et al. (1982),[2] Austin et al. (1981/1982),[3] Bullock (1987),[4] Colorni et al. (1981),[5] Egidius and Andersen (1979),[6] LeaMaster and Ostrowski (1988),[7] Sako and Kusuda (1978),[8] Sako et al. (1979),[9] Sako and Sorimachi (1985),[10] Tashiro et al. (1979).[11]

Notes: 3.4 × 10^5 cells (colony forming units/mL) of *V. anguillarum* reduced to 5,[12] 3.4 x 10^5 cells (colony forming units/mL) of *V. anguillarum* reduced to 10 or less.[13]

of open wounds to seawater and live seawater organisms.[140] Many of the clinical symptoms are similar to clinical signs in fishes, including septicemia, bacteremia, rapidly developing secondary cutaneous lesions (within 36 h of the onset of illness), erythematous or ecchymotic areas on the extremities, necrotic surface ulcers, vasculitis in the skin and muscles, and leukopenia or leukocytosis.[140] Depending on the species of *Vibrio*, other symptoms can include fever, chills, headache, abdominal cramps, nausea, vomiting, hypotension, ear infections, diarrhea, and gastroenteritis.[141] Vibriosis is more debilitating in patients with existing diseases, including cancers and hepatic disfunctions.[140] Public aquarium personnel who handle live animals are susceptible to zoonotic vibriosis, especially through superficial cuts and abrasions.[142]

Fin Rot

SYNONYMS Tail rot, fin erosion disease.

ETIOLOGY Most evidence implicates bacteria as the causative agents of fin rot, but cases are on record in which no infectious organisms could be isolated.[143] A definite bacterial etiology therefore has not been established.[144] It has been suggested that bacteria associated with fin rot are secondary invaders, with the primary etiologic agents being chemical irritants in the water.[145] Fin rot afflicts fishes in freshwater, brackish water, and seawater. Several different bacteria have been cultured from diseased fishes inhabiting each of these environments. However, the species and strains vary, and the infectivity of a particular organism may be limited by salinity.[146] The organisms most often associated with the disease in seawater fishes are opportunistic, Gram-negative bacteria of the genera *Aeromonas*, *Pseudomonas*, and *Vibrio*,[147] but *Achromobacter*, *Flavobacterium*, and *Flexibacter* have also been cultured from fin rot lesions.[148] Occasionally, *Aeromonas*, *Pseudomonas*, and *Vibrio* are present simultaneously.[149]

EPIZOOTIOLOGY The nonspecific nature of fin rot has led some researchers to class it as a *syndrome*, rather than as a specific disease.[150] Fin rot is one of the most prevalent diseases of captive seawater fishes.[151] The appearance of clinical signs probably results from captivity-imposed stresses. These can include (*1*) organic enrichment of the water,[152] (*2*) the presence of wounds and other surface lesions,[153] (*3*) crowding,[154] (*4*) exposure to chemical pollutants,[155] and (*5*) seasonal changes in water temperature (usually upward).[156] Infection occurs initially on the surface of the fish and probably is not acquired orally in food or water.[157] Experiments in which the flesh of diseased fish was fed to healthy specimens of the same species failed to produce signs of the disease.[157]

CLINICAL SIGNS AND PATHOLOGICAL EFFECTS On gross examination the most obvious feature of fin rot is necrosis of the fins, starting at the tips and advancing toward the body[158] (Fig. 9-28). As the disease progresses the edges of the fins become frayed and the fin rays separate. In extreme cases the entire fin is eroded away, leaving only a stump.[149] Areas of active necrosis appear mucoid, whitish, and opaque,[159] and most of the infected fin may be hemorrhagic.[160] In advanced stages the

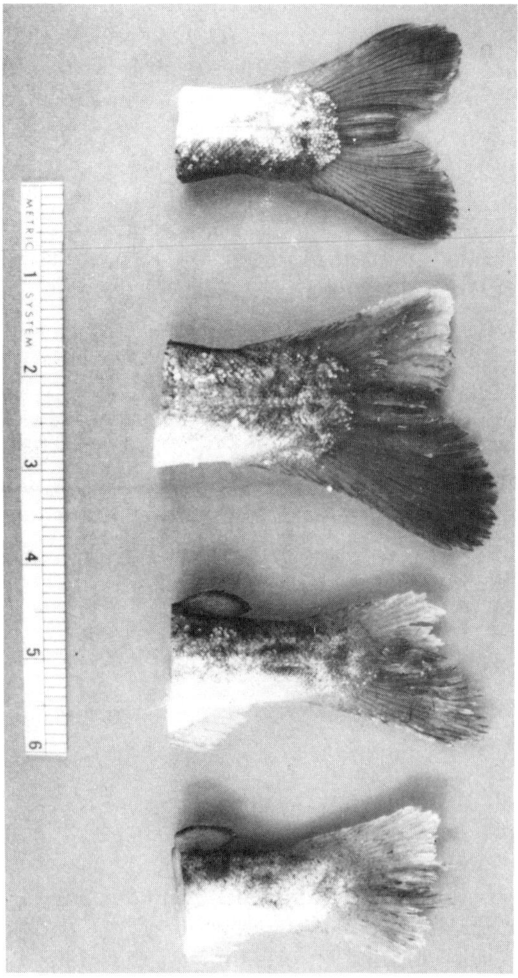

Figure 9-28 *Fin rot.* Source: Richard E. Wolke, Marine Pathology Laboratory, University of Rhode Island.

disease spreads to the skin, causing hemorrhaging and ulceration.[161] Further erosion results in muscle necrosis.[162] Other signs are alteration of normal blood constituents,[163] an increase in the number of mucous cells,[164] and corneal opacity and blindness.[157] Gill hyperplasia may be present[165] or absent.[162] Fin rot can be chronic[166] or acute.[167] It also can be local[165] or systemic.[157] In nonsystemic infections pathogenic bacteria and pathological changes are often absent from the internal organs.[162] During systemic infections yellow or bloody fluid may be present in the body cavity,[157] and the liver and kidney are sometimes hemorrhagic or necrotic.[168]

PROPHYLAXIS AND TREATMENT Fin rot epizootics are thought to reflect deteriorating water quality.[169] Observe correct husbandry practices, such as removing uneaten food and dead animals and plants, all of which are potential sources of excess dissolved organic carbon (DOC) and inorganic nitrogen and phosphorus. These substances contribute to eutrophic conditions by providing a nutrient ''broth'' for the growth of bacteria that are potential etiologic agents of fin rot.[157] Moreover, one form of inorganic nitrogen (ammonia) is a chemical irritant and a suspected agent of gill hyperplasia. The continuous use of granular activated carbon, as recommended in Chapter 2, is a demonstrated method of removing DOC from solution. Use plastic bags instead of nets to capture fishes and avoid other handling methods that cause injury. Lesions are potential sites of infection by bacteria associated with fin rot.[170] Crowding is a predisposing factor.[157] If two fishes are fighting, remove one of the combatants because nipped fins are potential sites of infection. Do not use disinfectants for treating other diseases. Copper in particular should be avoided, because fin rot epizootics in nature have been associated directly with increased copper concentrations in water and sediments.[171] See Treatment Abstracts (e.g., *Aeromonas, Vibrio*).

Amyloodinium Disease

SYNONYMS Oodinium disease, rust disease, velvet disease, oodiniasis.

ETIOLOGY Amyloodinium disease is caused by the dinoflagellate *Amyloodinium* (= *Oodinium*) *ocellatum*[172] and afflicts both brackish water and seawater fishes. The parasite's distribution in nature is uncertain. In North America it apparently is endemic to Sandy Hook Bay (New Jersey)[173] and Mississippi Sound.[174] Unconfirmed reports indicate that it may also be endemic to the Indo-West Pacific and Bermuda.[175]

EPIZOOTIOLOGY As of 1979 *A. ocellatum* had been reported from 111 species of North American fishes representing 46 families.[176] Some species appear to have partial or full immunity.[177] In adult fishes *A. ocellatum* is mainly a gill parasite,[178] although infections sometimes occur on the skin,[178] eyes,[179] fins,[179] esophagus,[179] membranes of the branchial cavity,[180] around the teeth,[179] and in the nasal passages.[179] In postlarvae and early juveniles the skin may be the most prevalent attachment site.[180] The organism also has been recovered from the intestinal tract, pharynx (submucosa, muscle, and connective tissue), kidney, and mesentery adjacent to the liver.[181]

The life cycle (Fig. 9-29) has three stages:[182] (*1*) the *trophont* or attached parasitic stage (Fig. 9-30); (2) the *tomont* or reproductive stage (Fig. 9-31); and (*3*) the *dinospore* or *tomite*, which is free swimming and infective.[183] The trophont is a single, pear-shaped cell that tends to become spherical as it matures,[184] measuring 12.4 × 9.9 to 103.7 × 80.5 μm with a mean of 61.1 × 50.1 μm.[185] Growth in length is linear, but volumetric growth is exponential.[186] The trophont is attached to the host by structures that emerge from its base (Fig. 9-29b). Descending

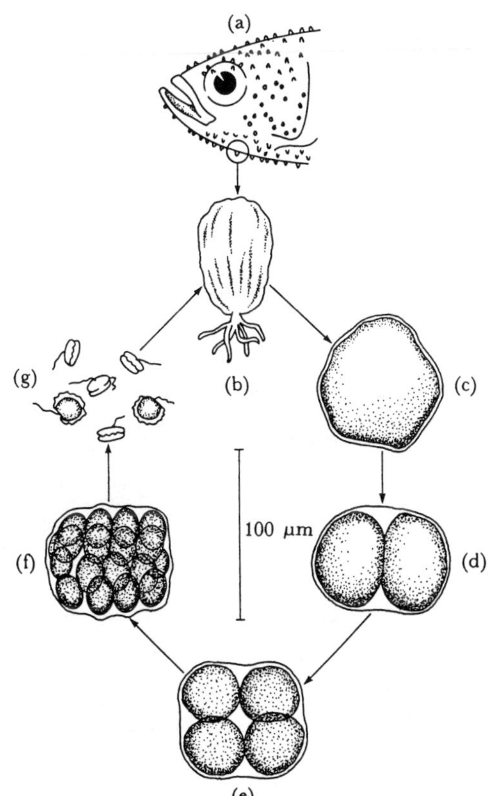

Figure 9-29 *Life cycle of* Amyloodinium ocellatum. (a) *Trophonts on an infected fish.* (b) *Enlarged view of a trophont.* (c-f) *Tomonts.* (g) *Dinospores.* Source: Bower et al. (1987).

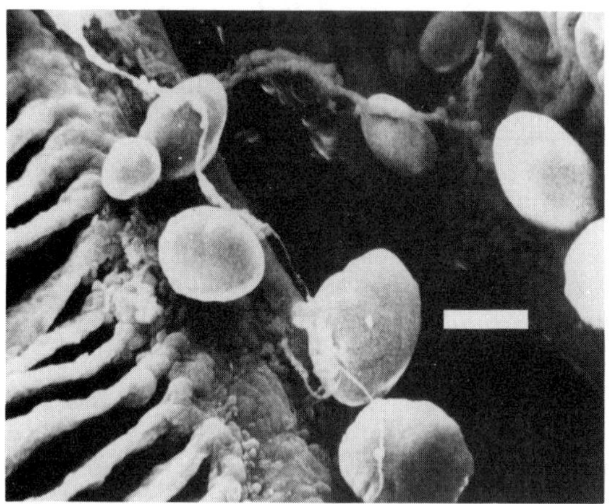

Figure 9-30 *Trophonts (Fig. 9-29a and b) of* A. ocellatum *attached to the surface of the gill filament of a yellow tang* (Zebrasoma flavescens). *Scale bar = 40 µm.* Source: Paul J. Cheung, New York Aquarium and Osborn Laboratories of Marine Sciences.

into the primary attachment structure or *attachment plate* is the *stomopode*. The edges of the attachment plate are evaginated into projections known as *rhizoids*, which are embedded in the epithelial cells of the host. The rhizoids resemble roots and anchor the trophont to epithelial tissues of its host. Early authors furthered the analogy by presuming the rhizoids also to absorb nutrients from the host, but this is unlikely.[187] The stomopode probably injects *lytic* (digestive) substances into the host, which break down its cells and allow the liquid to be assimilated by the trophont.[188] Larger cellular components probably are absorbed through a *temporary cytopharynx*, located in the *flagellar canal*.[188] The temporary cytopharynx is thought to ingest lumps of tissue too large to pass through the stomopode.

The trophont eventually detaches. It falls to the substratum,[189] becomes a tomont, and undergoes reproduction by cell division (i.e., *sporulation* or spore formation). The mechanisms

Figure 9-31 *Four-cell developmental stage of an* A. ocellatum *tomont (Fig. 9-29e). Scale bar = 10 µm.* Source: Paul J. Cheung, New York Aquarium and Osborn Laboratories of Marine Sciences.

controlling sporulation are unknown. The rate of cell division depends on several factors, including temperature and salinity. Development is arrested below 10°C, but completed in 3 to 5 d at 22 to 25°C[190] within the optimal salinity range of 16.7 to 28.5‰.[191] Ultimately, as many as 256 dinospores are released from a single tomont.[192] The dinospores measure 12 to 15 μm in length and are nearly as wide,[182] with some noticeable variation in size and shape.[193] They can survive at least 15 d without a host.[179] The dinospores are recognizable by a red *eyespot* and by the *flagellum* (the taillike locomotory organ characteristic of the flagellates).[194] One end of the flagellum is wrapped around the middle of the dinospore to form a *girdle*.[194]

CLINICAL SIGNS AND PATHOLOGICAL EFFECTS The trophont is large, compared with bacteria, and small fishes suffer more extensive damage and succumb more quickly than large ones. The skin of heavily infected fishes appears dull, patchy,[180] and velvetlike. The skin mucus occasionally appears pinkish.[192] The lighter patches signify damaged skin tissue;[180] white spots are often visible on sections of intact skin.[180] The behavior of the fishes often changes before clinical signs of disease appear, particularly if only the gills are infected. Behavior is variable, but can include anorexia,[179] gasping,[195] congregating near the surface,[196] scratching against objects or other animals,[180] sluggishness,[197] and ataxia.[179] In social species, diseased individuals often mill about in tightly knit groups, or close ranks when schooling. Heavily infected fishes harbor 200 to 500 trophonts on a single gill filament.[179] Epithelial cells where rhizoids attach become swollen, and the tissue undergoes extensive hyperplasia,[198] sometimes to the extent that the lamellae become fused, distorted, or even obliterated.[180] Congestion of blood vessels in the gill is common,[180] inducing physiological hypoxia as gas exchange becomes impaired.[192] The result is necrosis.[180] Death is probably caused by extensive destruction of the host's tissues, especially the epithelium.[199] Other factors perhaps enhance pathogenicity. When skin infections are heavy, the mass of the trophonts disrupts the normal streamlines of the fish, causing drag, turbulence, and stretching of the epithelial cells. Extensive gill damage interrupts ion exchange processes, perhaps leading to water and ion imbalances and interfering with the capacity to discharge ammonia, carbon dioxide, and other metabolic wastes. Mucous cell depletion compromises natural resistance. In combination with lesions caused by the trophonts, this leads to secondary infections by opportunistic bacteria.

PROPHYLAXIS AND TREATMENT No completely effective treatment is known, although several compounds either stop

TABLE 9-10 Compounds with some demonstrated effectiveness against *Amyloodinium ocellatum*: * = *in vitro*; † = *in vivo* (immersion). Dashes indicate no information.

Compound	Concentration, mg/L	Duration of exposure	Effect
*Acriflavin[3]	6	—	Interrupts tomont division
†Benzalkonium chloride[2]	1	24 h repeated after 2 d	Fishes free of trophonts
†Copper (TCu in cupric sulfate)[1]	0.5	10 d	Number of trophonts reduced: thought to be lethal to dinospores
†Cupric sulfate[2]	1	24 h	Number of trophonts reduced
*Cupric sulfate[3]	0.5, 1, 2, 4, 10	11 d	Lethal to dinospores
†Cutrine[2,4]	2, 6	24 h	Fishes free of trophonts
*Formalin[3]	25, 50, 100	11 d	Interrupts tomont division, lethal to dinospores
*Malachite green[3]	2	—	Interrupts tomont division
*Nifurpirinol[3]	5	4 d	Interrupts tomont division
*Nitrofurazone[3]	50	—	Interrupts tomont division

Sources: Dempster (1955),[1] Johnson (1984),[2] Paperna (1984a).[3]
Note: Not listed in the Merck Index (Budavari 1989).[4]

division of the trophonts or kill the dinospores (Table 9-10). Many more have been tried with little or no success.[200] Manipulation of environmental factors (e.g., temperature and salinity) stresses the host and fails to eradicate the parasite.[201] *Amyloodinium ocellatum* reproduces across temperature and salinity ranges that bracket the tolerance limits of most fishes. Disinfectants[202] and brief immersion in freshwater[203] sometimes dislodge trophonts from the host, but do not kill them. A few always remain to complete the life cycle and sustain the infection despite repeated treatments. Disinfectants probably fail because they cannot penetrate the cell membrane of the trophont, and trophonts attached to the gills are protected by the host's mucus. Their use is not justified. All are stressful, damage the host's tissues, and are only marginally effective. Formalin is also of doubtful efficacy.[204] Copper has been shown to control epizootics of *A. ocellatum* if used carefully,[205] but its detrimental effects on fishes are protean (Table 9-4).

Cryptocaryoniasis

SYNONYMS Cryptocaryon disease, white-spot disease, saltwater "ich." The last is sometimes used because the clinical signs and pathological effects are similar in appearance to "ich," a disease of freshwater fishes caused by a related parasite, *Ichthyophthirius multifiliis*.

ETIOLOGY Cryptocaryoniasis is caused by the ciliate protozoan *Cryptocaryon irritans*.[206] As is the case with amyloodinium disease, epizootics occur with distressing frequency in public aquariums,[207] home aquariums,[208] and warm seawater aquaculture installations.[209] Many species of teleosts are susceptible to infection, but elasmobranchs apparently are more resistant.[210] Little original research has been published on *C. irritans*, and its geographic origin is unknown.[211]

EPIZOOTIOLOGY The life cycle of *C. irritans* is depicted in Figure 9-32.[212] The parasitic *trophont* lives embedded in the skin, gills, and sometimes the eyes of the host fish. The *tomont* is the reproductive stage. The infective stage is represented by the *tomites*, which are free swimming when newly emerged (Fig. 9-33). The trophonts (Fig. 9-34) are large, ranging from 48×27 to 450×350 μm.[213] They move about in the skin and gills of the host ingesting blood, other fluids, and cellular debris through the *buccal apparatus*[212] (Fig. 9-35). Eventually, a tro-

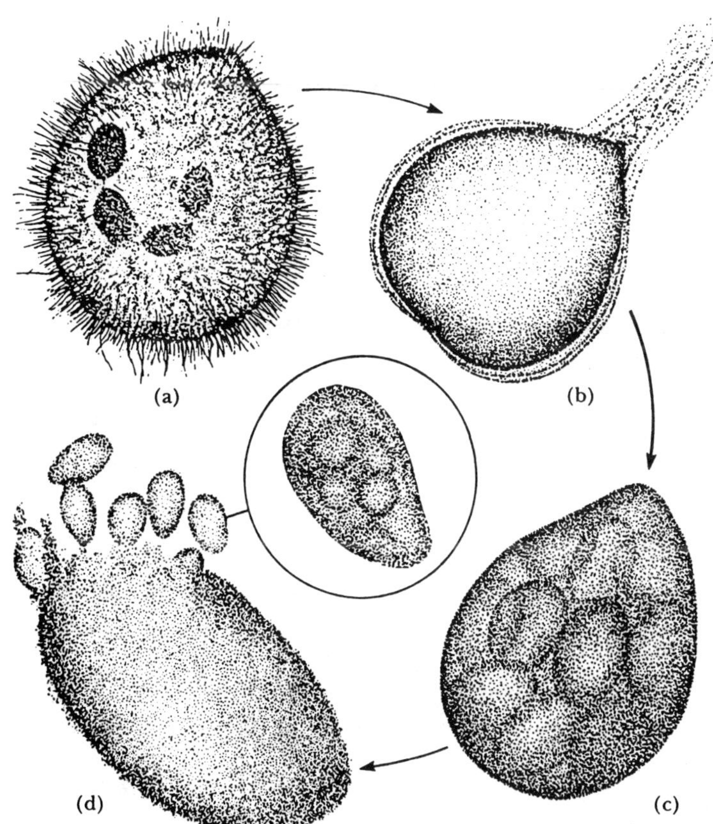

Figure 9-32 *Life-cycle of* Cryptocaryon irritans. (a) *Trophont or parasitic stage.* (b) *Tomont or reproductive stage (shape variable).* (c) *Tomont with developing tomites.* (d) *Free-swimming tomites (infective stage) from ruptured tomont.* Source: Spotte (1973) after Nigrelli and Ruggieri (1966).

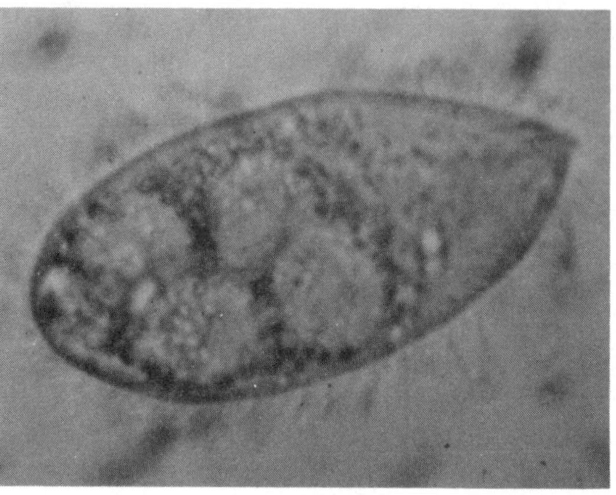

Figure 9-33 *Tomite of* C. irritans. *430x.* Source: Paul J. Cheung, New York Aquarium and Osborn Laboratories of Marine Sciences.

phont's activities slow, the *cilia* (hairlike projections that define the ciliates and which serve a locomotory function) are absorbed, and cyst membranes develop.[214] The resultant tomont drops off the host onto the substratum,[215] where it undergoes reproduction by cell division.[214] The mechanism triggering the onset of the tomont phase is obscure, but detachment occurs when the host dies.[216] Detachment is, however, unrelated to a sudden drop in temperature, which induces the process in *I. multifiliis*.[214]

The size of the tomont is variable, but large specimens can be 440 × 250 μm.[217] The new cells mature within the membranes of the tomont and become tomites. The time required to

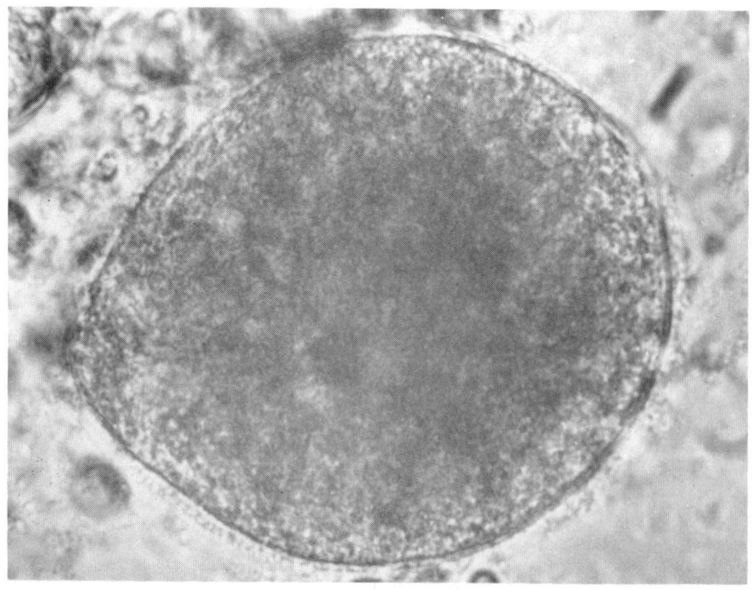

Figure 9-34 *Trophont of* C. irritans. *100x.* Source: George C. Blasiola.

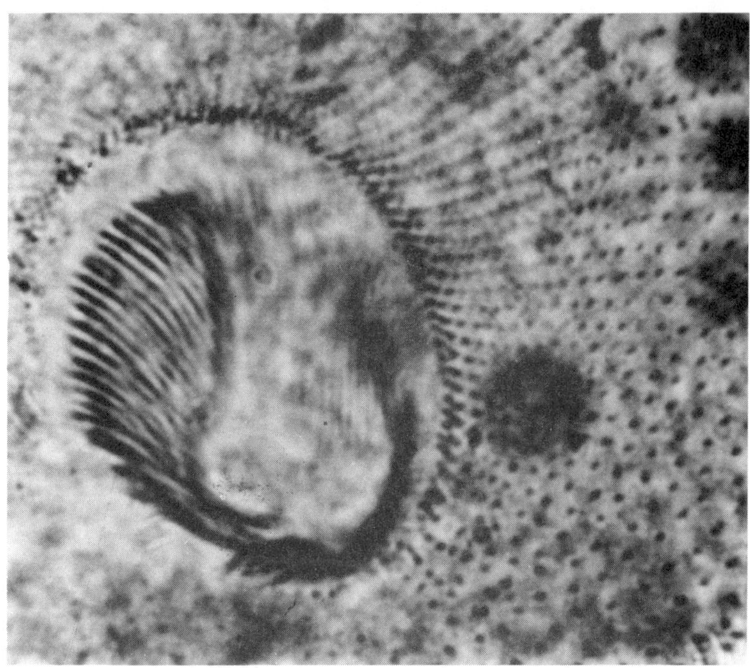

Figure 9-35 *Buccal apparatus of a* C. irritans *trophont. 1000x.* Source: Paul J. Cheung, New York Aquarium and Osborn Laboratories of Marine Sciences.

complete the life cycle varies, but can be summarized in general terms on the basis of two *in vitro* studies.[218] At temperatures of ~21 to 24°C, the trophont or parasitic stage lasts 3 to 7 d.[219] The trophont encysts and divides, sometimes within 20 h.[214] Tomites emerge 3 to 28 d later,[218] although most appear on day 8.[214] The optimal temperature for development is 30°C.[220] Tomonts begin to rupture at salinity values of 16‰ and lower[221] and become inactive or dead at salinities >55‰.[209] The effect of temperature and salinity is interactive: rupturing becomes even more prevalent at low salinity when the temperature falls outside the range of 25 to 30°C.[220]

As many as 200 tomites are produced from a large tomont.[218] The newly emerged tomites are 56.5 × 35 μm.[222] They swim toward a host, attach, develop the buccal apparatus, and burrow vigorously into the epidermis.[214] The tomites remain free swimming for <48 h and die if a host is not found.[219]

CLINICAL SIGNS AND PATHOLOGICAL EFFECTS Early signs of cryptocaryoniasis can include anorexia, corneal opacities, respiratory distress, excessive mucus production, and pale skin.[223] Diagnostic white papules appear on the skin, gills, and eyes, and death follows within a few days.[223] Some fishes are believed to acquire immunity.[224] The pathological effects have not been described in detail. Parasites attached to the gill lamellae cause marked erosion of the tissue;[214] blindness results when the eyes are invaded.[214]

PROPHYLAXIS AND TREATMENT *Cryptocaryon irritans* is principally a warm-water parasite that reproduces most effectively within the salinity range of seawater. These characteristics afford a greater measure of control than is the case with *Amyloodinium ocellatum*. Cryptocaryoniasis can be controlled to some extent by manipulating salinity and temperature. Success may depend ultimately on whether tolerance limits of the host fishes fall within or outside thresholds of these factors necessary to control the parasite. Fishes that can tolerate brackish water are easily treated by reducing the salinity to <16‰.[225] Infected seawater fishes pose a more difficult problem. *Cryptocaryon irritans* tolerates hypersaline environments;[209] many seawater fishes do not, especially if stressed by heavy parasite loads. Raising the salinity to 55‰ for 5 min kills or inactivates *C. irritans* trophonts, but can cause delayed mortality of the hosts.[209] Mortality may be greater if the treatment regimen is accompanied by handling, transfer, and other stressful procedures.[209] Lowering the temperature to <15°C halts reproduction of the parasite.[226] Copper at concentrations up to 0.4 mg/L has limited effectiveness against the trophont stage[227] and is perhaps lethal only to the tomites. The use of copper has yielded mixed results.[227]

Chemotherapeutic agents (e.g., antimalarial compounds) probably have limited effectiveness except when combined with salinity or temperature manipulation,[209] although treatment of infected fishes and water systems with quinine·HCl ($C_{20}H_{25}ClN_2O_2$, 40 to 60 mg/L) is reportedly effective against tomites.[228] A promising treatment consisted of the following regimen.[229] The salinity of the seawater was raised to 45 to 48‰ (presumably by addition of sodium chloride), and hypersaline conditions were maintained for 20 min. Afterward, the container was flushed with seawater (S = 36‰) until the salinity was normal. The flow was stopped, and two antimalarial compounds were added. The initial concentrations (quinine·HCl, 3.96 mg/L; chloroquine, $C_{18}H_{26}ClN_3$, 15.90 mg/L) were maintained for 2 d. Treated fish were not handled at anytime during the procedure. Reinfection was not seen after 120 d.

Uronema Disease[230]

SYNONYMS None.

ETIOLOGY Uronema disease is caused by the ciliate protozoan *Uronema marinum*. The origin of the parasite is unknown.

EPIZOOTIOLOGY Host specificity appears to be low. *Uronema marinum* infects captive fishes across a broad range of temperature and salinity values. At New York Aquarium, infected fishes were observed in aquariums ranging in temperature and salinity from 8 to 28°C and 20 to 31‰. The parasite is elongate with a rounded posterior; the anterior end is bluntly pointed (Figs. 9-36 and 9-37). Length and width of 20 specimens averaged 34.1 × 15.8 μm (range 38 to 32 and 20 to 13 μm).

CLINICAL SIGNS AND PATHOLOGICAL EFFECTS External ulceration is often associated with uronema disease, although some fishes (e.g., seahorses, Syngnathidae) may not display visible external lesions. Muscle and skin are hemorrhagic and necrotic, and the epidermis may slough extensively (Fig. 9-38a). Infected fishes are lethargic, but seldom anorexic and emaciated. Active ciliates are common in the skin, muscle, kidney, urinary bladder, neural canal, blood vessels, and gills of seahorses; in other species, the parasite occurs mainly in the musculature and on the skin. In seahorses, ciliates have been found around the vertebral column (Fig. 9-38b). Feeding parasites often contain blood cells (Fig. 9-38c). Penetration may

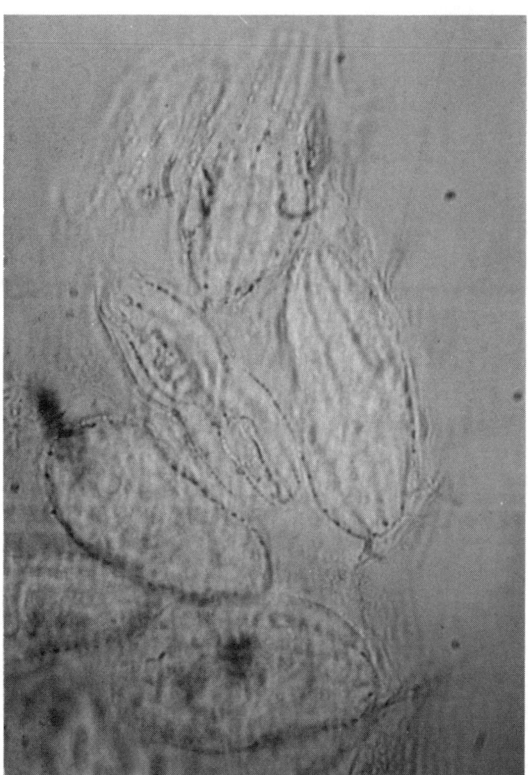

Figure 9-36 Uronema marinum. *1000x.* Source: Paul J. Cheung, New York Aquarium and Osborn Laboratories of Marine Sciences.

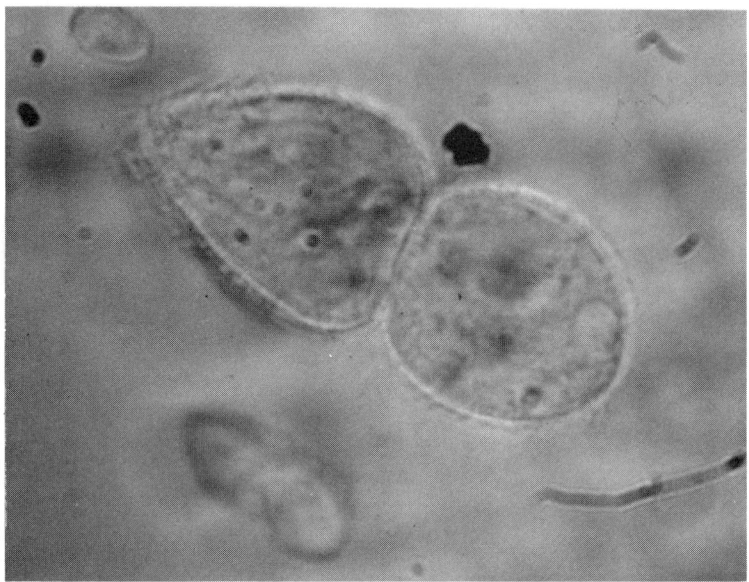

Figure 9-37 Uronema marinum *dividing. 450x.* Source: Paul J. Cheung, New York Aquarium and Osborn Laboratories of Marine Sciences.

cause muscle tissue to appear honeycombed. Ciliates can occur in the central cavity of the gill filament and in capillaries of the gill lamellae (Fig. 9-38d), causing restricted blood flow. *Aneurysms* (sacs formed by localized dilation of an artery or vein) and epithelial detachment of the gill lamellae are sometimes observed (Fig. 9-38e). Renal tubules and hematopoietic tissues of the kidney may become infected with little apparent damage (Fig. 9-38f).

Pathology is similar to that induced in freshwater fishes by *Tetrahymena corlissi*. No specific tissue reaction is apparent (an inflammatory response may not be evident), and damage appears to be mechanical, probably caused by penetration and subsequent movement of the parasites. Although the parasite feeds actively on blood cells and tissue debris, muscle may be the ''preferred'' tissue. Impaired circulation in the gills probably contributes to death of the host.

PROPHYLAXIS AND TREATMENT Not known.

Ichthyophonus Disease

SYNONYMS Staggers, whirling disease, Taumelkrankheit, and swinging disease refer to a characteristic form of ataxia. Sandpaper disease describes the roughened appearance of the skin in advanced cases. Ichthyosporidiosis should be considered obsolete (see below).

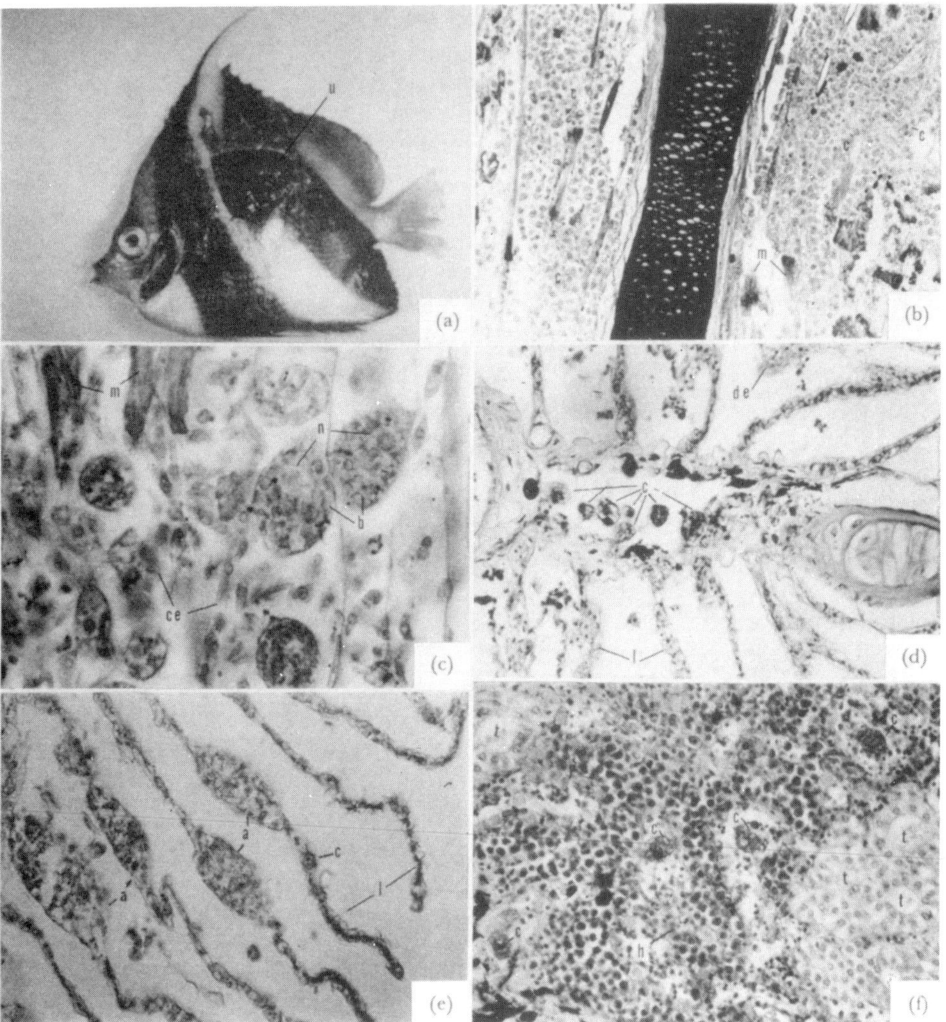

Figure 9-38 *Pathology of uronema disease.* (a) *Bannerfish or royal coachman* (Heniochus acuminatus) *infected with* Uronema marinum: u = *ulcer.* (b) *Ciliates on both sides of the vertebral column of a seahorse* (Hippocampus erectus): c = *ciliates,* m = *degenerated muscle tissue. 60x.* (c) *Actively feeding ciliates destroying the surrounding tissues of a bannerfish:* n = *macronucleus of ciliate,* b = *ingested blood cells,* ce = *cellular debris,* m = *degenerated muscle. 600x.* (d) *Numerous ciliates in the central cavity of the gill filament of a seahorse:* c = *ciliate,* de = *detached epithelial cells,* l = *lamellae. 250x.* (e) *Aneurysm and detachment of epithelial cells from the gill lamellae of an infected seahorse:* a = *aneurysm,* c = *ciliate,* l = *lamellae. 150x.* (f) *Ciliates in the hematopoietic tissues of the anterior head kidney of an infected seahorse:* c = *ciliates,* h = *hematopoietic tissue,* t = *renal tubule. 260x.* Source: Cheung et al. (1980).

ETIOLOGY Fungi are not uncommon in the oceans,[231] although only a few are confirmed parasites of seawater fishes.[232] Of these, none but *Ichthyophonus*, the agent of ichthyophonus disease, is known with certainty to be an obligate parasite.[233] These statements are presumptive, and I should qualify them before continuing. Attempts to classify *Ichthyophonus* have a long and cloudy history. In particular, confusion of *Ichthyophonus* with the protozoan genus *Ichthyosporidium* has continued for nearly 80 years.[234] The taxonomic affinity of the genus *Ichthyophonus* is still unresolved, although most consider the organism to be a fungus, probably of the Entomorphthorales group.[235] Whether one or more species exists, or a complex of species, is unknown.[235] *Ichthyophonus gasterophilum* and *I. hoferi* have gained acceptance by some mycologists.[233] Others are of the opinion that *I. hoferi* alone may be valid.[232] I shall refer to the parasite simply as *Ichthyophonus*.

Most records of ichthyophonus disease in wild fishes are from the North Atlantic, giving a false impression that only temperate seawater species are afflicted.[232] However, this may simply reflect sampling bias.[232] *Ichthyophonus* has worldwide distribution, and infestations have been observed in temperate and tropical fishes inhabiting both fresh and saline waters.[232] Authorities generally agree that *Ichthyophonus* is restricted to the oceans,[232] and it is doubtful whether ichthyophonus disease occurs naturally in wild freshwater fishes (see below).[236]

EPIZOOTIOLOGY The life cycle of *Ichthyophonus* is complex (Fig. 9-39) and incompletely understood.[237] Much of what is known has been muddied by the investigators themselves, who seem unable to agree on a common terminology. An attempt has been made to sort out these differences in the accompanying chapter notes. Reproduction is asexual.[238] The most frequent developmental stage observed in infested tissues is the thick-walled *resting spore*[232] (Fig. 9-40). The diameter increases with age and varies from 20 to 200 μm.[239] Older resting spores contain numerous nuclei.[239] At 20°C the resting spores germinate within 15 to 30 min of the host's death.[232] Germination begins when contents of the resting spore protrude through a rupture in the spore wall, leading within a few days to production of the vegetative branching stage or *hypha*.[240] The cellular contents of a spore are evacuated into growing hyphae and accumulate in the tips.[232] After 4 to 10 d these *hyphal bodies* become rounded and separate from the main hyphal mass[232] (Fig. 9-41). Often 20 or more are formed from an original resting spore, and they develop in the host's intestine.[232] Sometimes the hyphal bodies, which are large and multinucleate, form

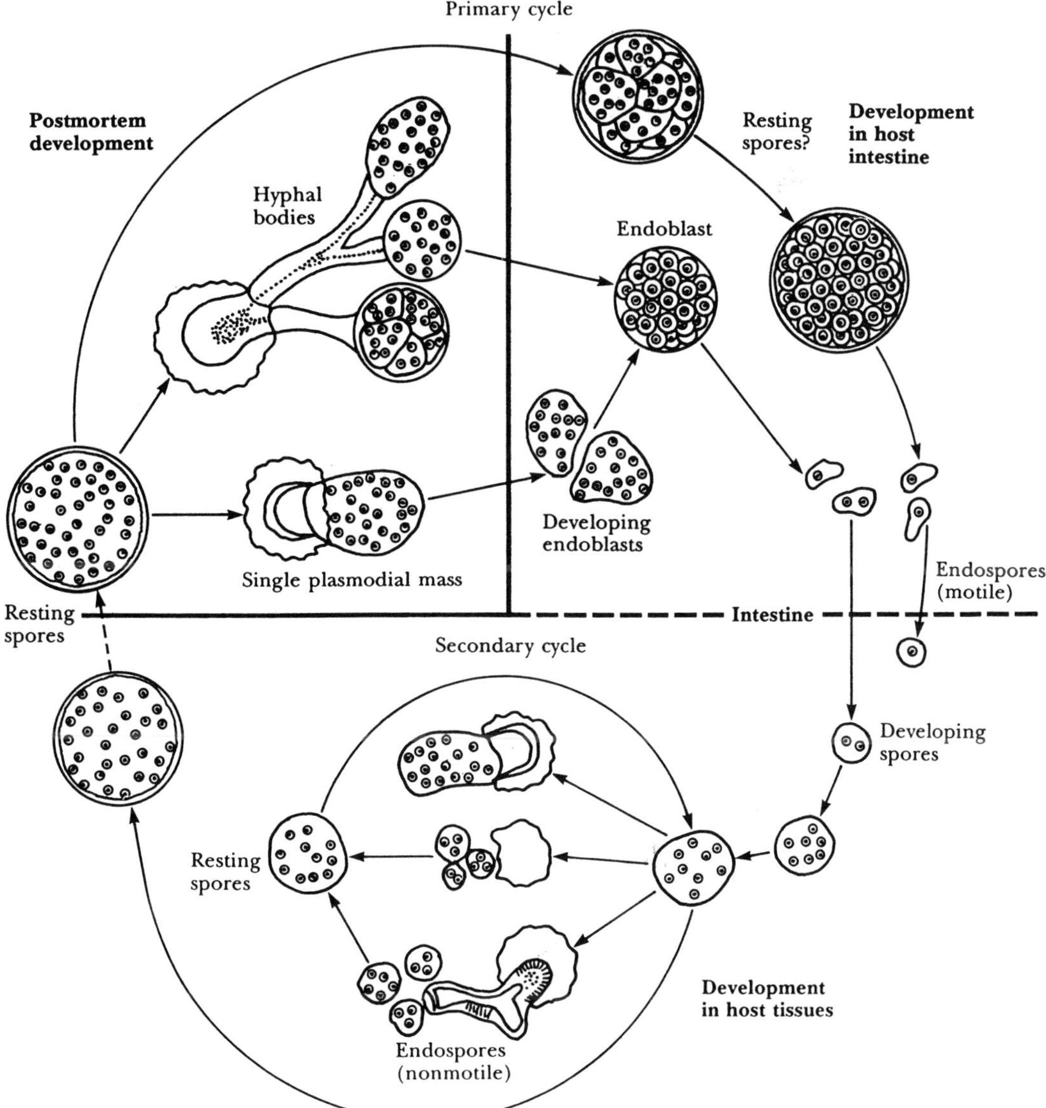

Figure 9-39 *Proposed life cycle of* Ichthyophonus. Source: Stephen Spotte after Lauckner (1984a).

thick walls and are indistinguishable from resting spores.[232] Alternatively, the cytoplasm divides, giving rise to hundreds of small (< 10 μm diameter) *endospores*. I shall call the stage giving rise to endospores the *endoblast*.[241] Endospores, which represent the infestive stage, can occur in both dead and living hosts and have been observed during secondary invasions by *Ichthyophonus* while the host is still alive.[232] The endospores penetrate

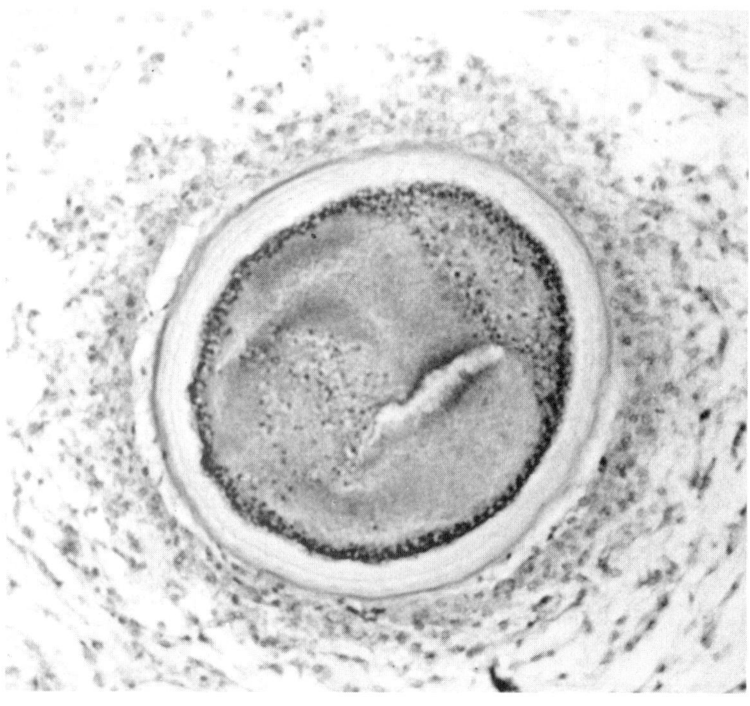

Figure 9-40 *Resting spore of* Ichthyophonus. *250x.* Source: Richard E. Wolke, Marine Pathology Laboratory, University of Rhode Island.

the intestine, are transported by the blood to organ and muscle tissues, and become transformed into uni- or binucleate, spherical *developing spores*.[242] The developing spores mature rapidly.[243] Some become resting spores[244] and perpetuate the principal loop of the life cycle (i.e., the *primary cycle*). Others form

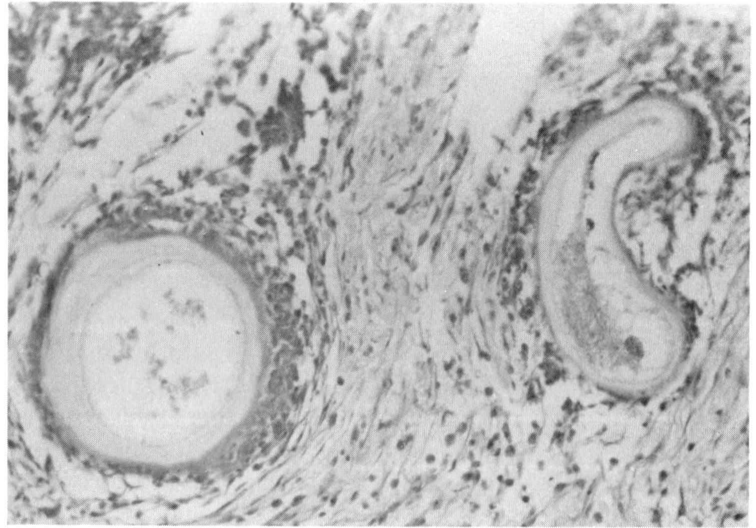

Figure 9-41 *Hyphal bodies of* Ichthyophonus. *160x.* Source: Richard E. Wolke, Marine Pathology Laboratory, University of Rhode Island.

nonmotile endospores, which are liberated by rupture of the spore wall or escape from the tips of irregular, nonseptate hyphae.[245] The production of nonmotile endospores initiates a *secondary cycle,* culminating in large numbers of new resting spores.[243] During decay of the host's tissues, resting spores germinate and form hyphae; alternatively, they develop into *single plasmodial masses,*[246] giving rise once again to endoblasts. New resting spores are formed within 20 d.[232] During virulent secondary infestations, endospores are sometimes produced within 8 d of the primary infestation, within either the original resting spore or diminished hyphae.[232] In such instances the parasite multiplies in the same organ, forming gross lesions (see below), or spreads by means of the circulatory system to other organs.[232]

In summary, reproduction in *Ichthyophonus* is asexual involving division of multinucleate resting spores into smaller endospores, with or without prior formation of hyphae and hyphal bodies. The motile or nonmotile endospores invade new hosts or tissues of the same host, forming new resting spores and perpetuating the life cycle.

Host specificity is low,[247] and ichthyophonus disease is transmitted easily among different families of fishes in waters of any salinity.[232] Transmission is thought to be mainly oral, because early stages of the disease are seen in the gut.[248] In coastal regions, free-floating endospores are a likely source of infestation in cage-cultured salmonids,[232] and waterborne transmission of ichthyophonus disease has been demonstrated under experimental conditions even in freshwater.[249] As stated previously, no evidence exists that *Ichthyophonus* is enzootic in wild freshwater fishes. All descriptions of ichthyophonus disease from freshwater environments apparently have involved captive fishes. *Ichthyophonus* infestations can be acquired in contaminated food, mainly raw fish products of seawater origin.[250] Captive brackish water and seawater fishes are also susceptible to infestations resulting from careless feeding practices.

CLINICAL SIGNS AND PATHOLOGICAL EFFECTS Ichthyophonus disease is systemic.[235] It also is chronic, and death may not occur until 2 months after the initial infestation.[251] Organ tissues with rich blood supplies (mainly the kidney, heart, spleen, and liver) are invaded preferentially and replaced by the fungus.[235] In heavy infestations the whole body can be invaded.[232]

Clinical signs can include emaciation,[232] spinal curvature,[232] impaired growth,[235] darkening[252] or paling[253] of the skin,

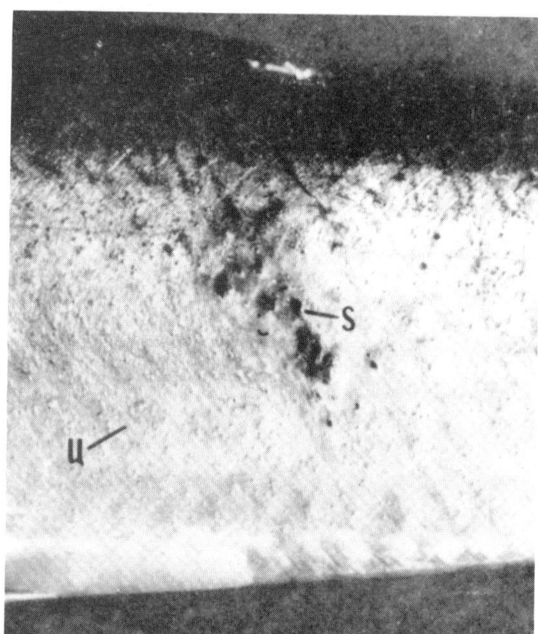

Figure 9-42 External signs of ichthyophonus disease in an Atlantic herring (Clupea harengus harengus). *Note the "sandpaper" effect* (s); *ulcers* (u) *in the center of the photograph indicate an advanced stage of infestation.* Source: Sindermann and Rosenfield (1954).

roughening of the skin (Fig. 9-42) caused by outward penetration through the epidermis,[252] fin erosion,[253] ataxia,[254] exophthalmia,[253] and skin ulcers[254] (Fig. 9-42). Female guppies (*Poecilia reticulatus*) with infested ovaries have been known to undergo sex reversal.[253] Some of these signs (e.g., fin erosion) are perhaps caused by associated bacterial infections, but this is my opinion. Roughened skin is evidence that most of the body has been invaded and the disease is far advanced. Survival at this stage is unlikely.

The most obvious pathological effect is the presence of nodular white lesions on the internal organs.[255] The lesions are necrotic.[256] Whether there is an inflammatory response is controversial.[257] If the gills are infested, both the filaments and lamellae may be deformed.[258]

PROPHYLAXIS AND TREATMENT The systemic nature of ichthyophonus disease makes treatment extremely difficult. No suitable therapeutic agent has been identified,[235] although some of the modern antifungal compounds (e.g., amphotericin B, ketoconazole, nystatin) warrant investigation. Prevention requires proper hygiene, in particular the prompt removal of infested fishes before uninfested aquarium-mates can ingest their tissues. Live specimens with suspected infestations should be removed and killed. The most effective practice is to avoid feeding raw seafood products, especially raw fish. Fish may be unsafe even if cooked. Some evidence suggests that *Ichthyophonus* spores remain viable even after having been heated to 60°C for 30 min.[235] It is doubtful whether any agent is effective unless adminstered orally, and then only during early stages of the disease.

Exophiala Disease

SYNONYMS None.

ETIOLOGY Exophiala disease is caused by fungi of the genus *Exophiala*. The species *E. pisciphilus* and *E. salmonis* are recognized fish pathogens.[259] Exophiala disease occurs in fresh and saline waters, both warm and cold. Reports are few. Curiously, *Exophiala* and *Exophiala*-like fungi have been described only in captive fishes from public aquariums, hatcheries, and floating pens.[260]

EPIZOOTIOLOGY Nothing is known about the epizootiology of exophiala disease. The disease is regarded as acute.[261]

CLINICAL SIGNS AND PATHOLOGICAL EFFECTS Clinical signs include ataxia and whirling movements followed by lethargy and death.[262] Exophthalmia sometimes accompanied by cephalic swelling often occurs shortly before death;[262] the swollen areas may be transformed into ulcers.[262] Others have reported the appearance of external dermal masses (Fig. 9-43); internally there may be round, yellowish areas on the liver, kidney, myocardium, swimbladder, and spleen that are raised as much as 5 mm.[261] The lesions are similar in gross appearance to those induced by mycobacteriosis.[261] A tissue section is shown in Figure 9-44.

PROPHYLAXIS AND TREATMENT Not known.[263]

Tang Turbellarian Disease

SYNONYMS None.

ETIOLOGY Turbellarians are flatworms (Class Platyhelminthes). Only a few are parasitic; most are free living. Genera that parasitize fishes include *Digenobothrium*, *Ichthyophaga*, *Mycropharynx*, *Paravortex*, and *Procerodes*.[264] Fishes infested with turbellarians have been reported from the eastern North Atlantic, Bering Sea, Mediterranean Sea, Sea of Japan, Indo-West Pacific, West Indies, and Australia.[265]

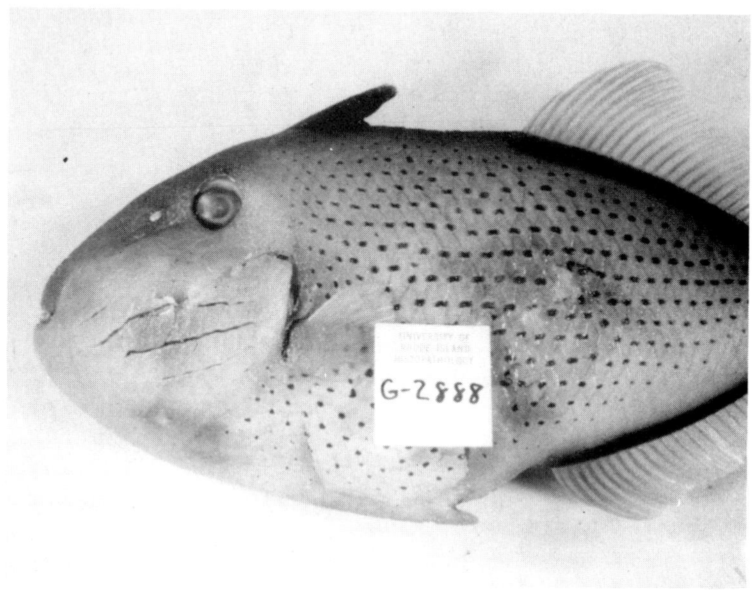

Figure 9-43 *Triggerfish* (Xanthichthys ringens) *with exophiala disease.* Source: Richard E. Wolke, Marine Pathology Laboratory, University of Rhode Island.

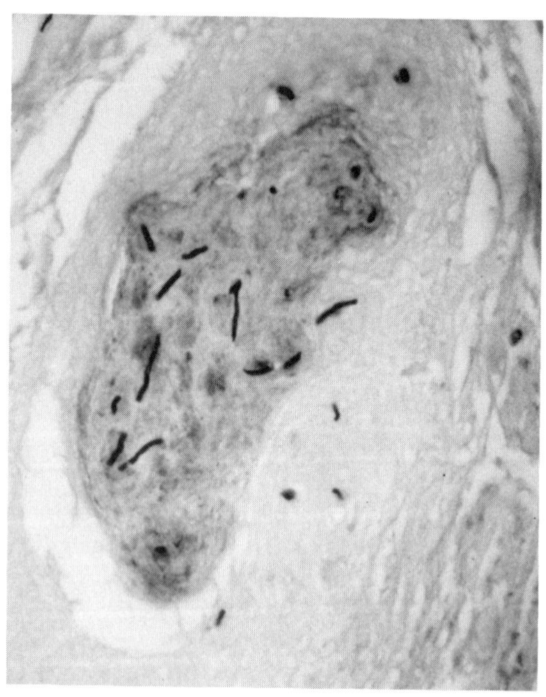

Figure 9-44 *Heart section from an Atlantic cod* (Gadus morhua) *infested with* Exophialia. *250x.* Source: Richard E. Wolke, Marine Pathology Laboratory, University of Rhode Island.

EPIZOOTIOLOGY Parasitic turbellarians are troublesome in seawater aquariums because they develop directly. The life cycle has the potential to proceed uninterrupted, resulting in increasingly heavier infestations with successive generations. Only worms placed provisionally in the genus *Paravortex*—in particular the "tang turbellarian" (*Paravortex* sp.)—have proved troublesome in closed-system seawater aquariums, although others perhaps await discovery.[266] The tang turbellarian is so-named because of its predeliction for parasitizing the yellow tang (*Zebrasoma flavescens*) of the Indo-West Pacific (Fig. 9-45). I shall focus on its life cycle in this subsection.[267]

Turbellarian reproduction is species dependent and can be asexual (i.e., by fission or fragmentation) or sexual.[268] Many species that reproduce sexually are simultaneous hermaphrodites, relying on internal fertilization.[268] Male organs have not been found in the tang turbellarian, and sexual reproduction may be parthenogenetic.[269] Despite its name, the tang turbellarian exhibits low host specificity. Other fishes are susceptible,[270] perhaps 25 species of 10 families.[269] The severity of infestation is cyclical. When the incidence is low, worms containing developing young can be found in the bottom detritus. Previously uninfested fishes become infested within 24 h and after 20 d can harbor as many as 4500 worms. Death can ensue in 10 to 23 d. Worms in the parasitic phase (i.e., on the host) range from 77 μm on day 1 to 440 μm on day 7 (Fig.

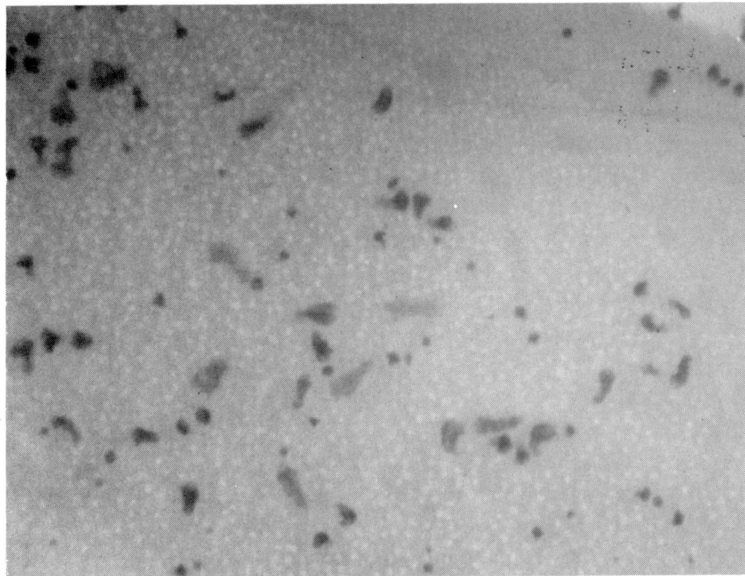

Figure 9-45 Yellow tang (Zebrasoma flavescens) *infested with tang turbellarians* (Paravortex *sp.*). Source: George C. Blasiola.

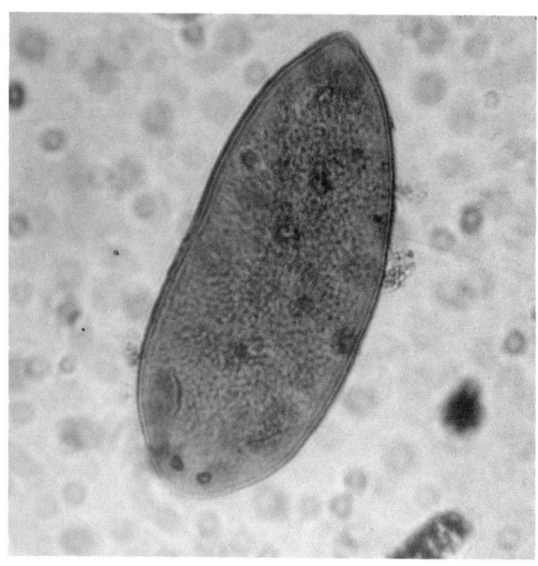

Figure 9-46 *Adult tang turbellarian* (Paravortex *sp.*); *note the eyespots. 25x.* Source: George C. Blasiola.

9-46). After 6 d the worms leave the host and increase in length to 737 μm by day 10. The young are brooded internally during this nonparasitic phase. Young worms develop eyespots after ~5 d. Unborn young are 70 to 90 μm long, and a single adult gives birth to as many as 160 juveniles. Whether the adult survives after giving birth is unknown. The young, which are free swimming, emerge through a rupture in the mid-lateral wall and actively seek a host. Alternatively, infestations spread when worms in the parasitic phase change hosts. The life cycle takes ~10 d at 24.5°C.

CLINICAL SIGNS AND PATHOLOGICAL EFFECTS Tang turbellarians in the parasitic phase appear as numerous dark spots distributed unevenly over the fins, gills, and body surface, but the parasites are difficult to see on dark-skinned fishes.[271] Clinical signs include anorexia, listlessness, opaqueness of the skin, inflamed lesions, scratching against objects in the aquarium, and paling of the skin.[271] Fishes near death are often emaciated.[269] Pathological effects include acute *focal dermatitis* (localized inflammation of the skin), congested capillaries, and *perivascular hemorrhages* (hemorrhages around blood vessels).[269] Secondary bacterial infections (e.g., *Vibrio* spp.) have been shown to occur.[269] Clinical signs and pathological effects caused by infestations of other turbellarian species are similar.[272]

PROPHYLAXIS AND TREATMENT Crowding facilitates infestation.[269] Several treatments have been proposed (Table

TABLE 9-11 Treatments for tang turbellarian disease caused by *Paravortex* sp. Praziquantel at the stated concentration and duration of treatment is not based on experimental evidence and should be considered provisional.

Compound	Dosage	Method	Duration
Formalin[1]	250 mg/L	Immersion	Three 50-min treatments administered evenly over 1 week
Praziquantel[3]	20 mg/L	Immersion	<3 h
Reduced salinity[2]	12–15‰	Immersion	3 d to 2 weeks
Trichlorfon[1]	0.80–1.0 mg/L	Immersion	3 d to 2 weeks

Sources: Blasiola (1976a),[1] G. Early (personal communication in Kent and Olson 1986),[2] Thoney (1989a).[3]

9-11), but their comparative effectiveness has not been determined. From the standpoint of the host, formalin is the most toxic of the substances listed. Many seawater fishes are unable to tolerate salinities in the low ranges recommended.

Monogenetic Trematode Infestations

SYNONYMS None

ETIOLOGY The *monogenetic trematodes* (or simply *monogeneans*) are arguably the most troublesome group of parasitic worms encountered by public aquarists. This is because they develop directly. Only one host—the fish—is involved, making infestations difficult to control by interrupting the life cycle. The *digenetic trematodes*, in contrast, require at least two and sometimes four intermediate hosts. The absence of just one is sufficient to stop the spread of infestation. Monogeneans are ectoparasites of the eyes and skin, or infest body cavities that open directly to the water (e.g., gills, mouth, urogenital openings). Digeneans are predominantly endoparasitic. Monogeneans gain entry to aquarium exhibits on the skin and gills of infested fishes, raw seafood products, and water infested with larvae. Many species have low host specificity. Their introduction into both ecosystems and public aquarium exhibits can cause extensive damage to hosts lacking resistance factors.[273]

EPIZOOTIOLOGY Monogenean eggs fall to the substratum, and free-swimming, ciliated larvae or *onchomiracidia* are the infestive stage of the life cycle. At hatching, an onchomiracidium seeks a host and upon finding one attaches by means of an attachment organ, the *opisthaptor*. The parasite matures, reproduces, and perpetuates the life cycle (Fig. 9-47). Relatively few monogeneans known to be fish parasites are troublesome in public aquariums. Not uncommonly, the worms are lost spontaneously through an unknown means of acquired toler-

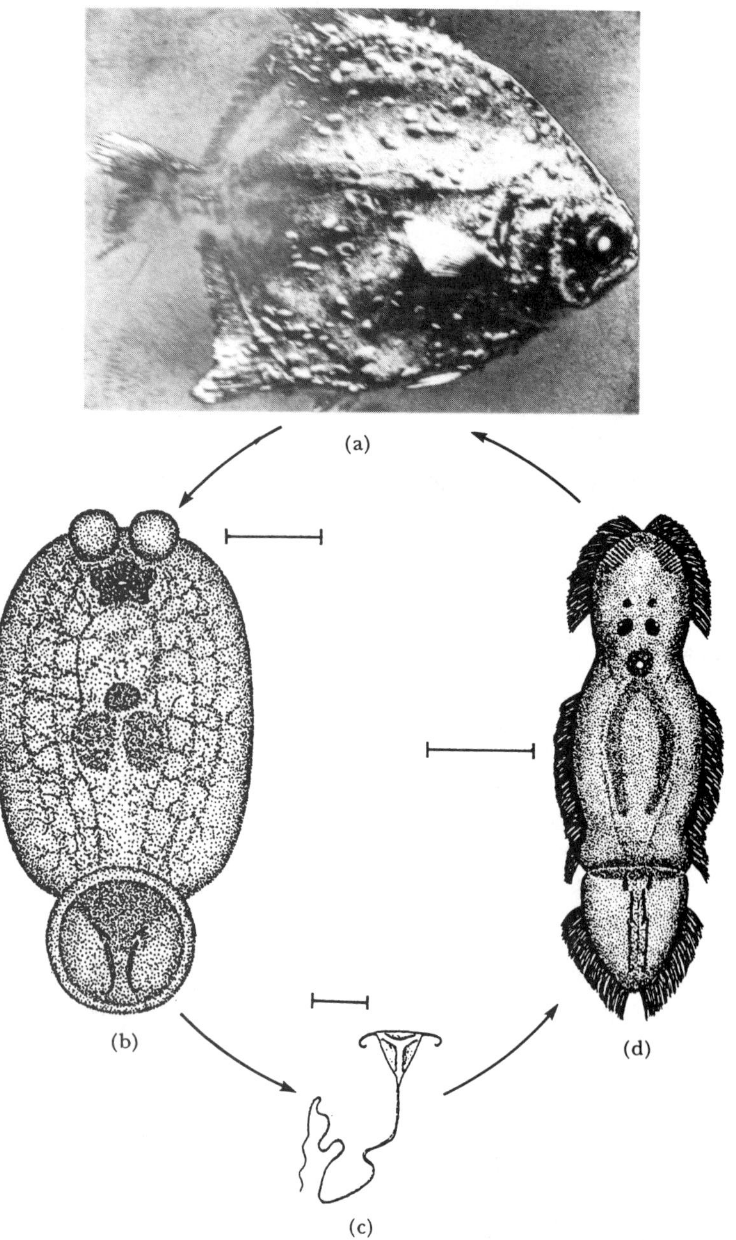

Figure 9-47 *Life cycle of* Benedenia (= Epibdella) melleni, *a monogenetic trematode parasitic on many species of seawater fishes.* (a) *Infested juvenile Florida pompano* (Trachinotus carolinus). (b) *Adult parasite. Scale bar = 1 mm.* (c) *Egg. Scale bar = 150 μm.* (d) *Onchomiricidium. Scale bar = 50 μm.* Sources: Stephen Spotte for the overall graphic; (a) Spotte (1973) from New York Aquarium and Osborn Laboratories of Marine Sciences, (b and d) Spotte (1973) after Jahn and Kuhn (1932), (c) Jahn and Kuhn (1932).

ance.[274] Mass mortalities in nature caused by monogeneans are rare, suggesting that infestation-related mortality in captive fishes is a result of crowding, malnutrition, and deteriorating environmental conditions.[275] In monogeneans that tolerate a range of temperatures, the trend is toward accelerated development with increasing temperature.[276] The life cycles of monogeneans are adapted exquisitely to the activity rhythms of their hosts. In nature, the severity of parasitic infestations is often seasonal.[275] Photoperiod is an important triggering event in the endogenous hatching cycles of monogenean eggs. The eggs often hatch when the host is most likely to be accessible (i.e., during the quiescent phase of its diel cycle).[277]

CLINICAL SIGNS AND PATHOLOGICAL EFFECTS Many species of monogeneans are small and difficult to observe without taking skin scrapings. Gill parasites are even more difficult to detect (Fig. 9-48). Infested fishes often damage themselves by rubbing against objects in the aquarium. The resulting lesions encourage secondary bacterial infections.[278]

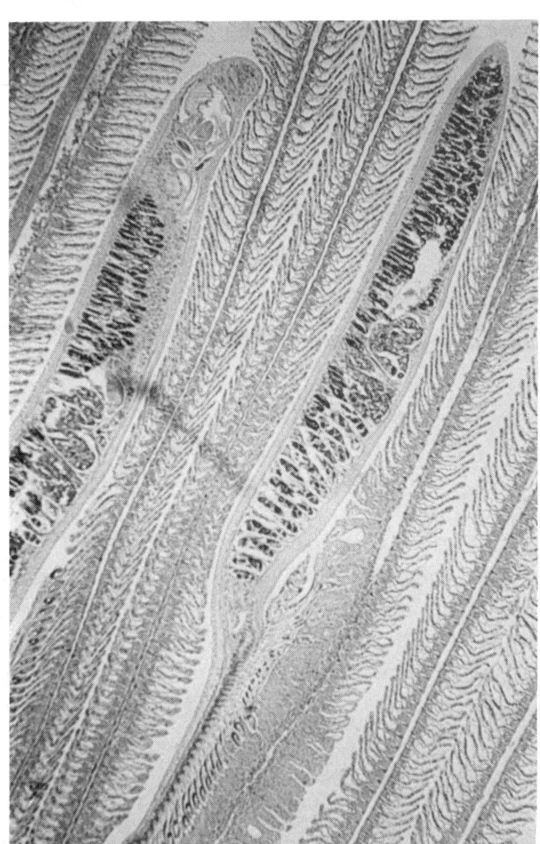

Figure 9-48 *Unidentified monogeneans embedded in the gills of a bluefish* (Pomatomus saltatrix). *25x.* Source: Richard E. Wolke, Marine Pathology Laboratory, University of Rhode Island.

PROPHYLAXIS AND TREATMENT Monogenean infestations are difficult to eradicate, and reports in the aquarium literature of how best to attack them often disagree. This is hardly surprising considering how little effort public aquarists have expended attempting to identify stages of life cycles most vulnerable to control. Increased emphasis on the biology of host-monogenean relationships might show that treatment regimens can be made more effective by manipulating photoperiod and other exogenous factors. Identification of any such developmental "windows" has obvious advantages. Suppose, for example, that free-swimming larvae of a specific monogenean are more susceptible than adults to known concentrations of an anthelminthic compound. Timing of the treatment to coincide with peak hatching would be more effective than waiting until infestations are heavy and many adult worms are present.

Anthelminthic compounds of demonstrated effectiveness against monogeneans include levamisole·HCl, mebendazole, niclosamide, praziquantel, and trichlorfon, all administered by immersion (see Treatment Abstracts). Praziquantel should be tried first at a concentration of no less than 10 mg/L for an exposure period of at least 3 h.[279] Praziquantel has been administered by intramuscular injection and *per os* by force feeding, but these methods sometimes fail to eradicate monogeneans.[280] Monogeneans belonging to the genus *Benedenia* can be controlled, but seldom eradicated, by immersing infested fishes in freshwater for 3 min.[278] Repeat after 2 weeks.[278] The eggs are likely to survive the procedure.[278]

Crustacean Infestations

SYNONYMS Copepod infestations, fish louse infestations.

ETIOLOGY Numerous species of crustaceans are fish parasites. Parasitic isopods are only of passing interest from the standpoint of aquarium keeping, although a few species are large enough to be visible from several metres (Fig. 9-49). Of the copepods, species comprising the orders Notodelphyoida, Monstrilloida, Caligoida, and Lernaeopodoida are exclusively parasitic. Members of the order Calanoida are free living. Two other orders (Cyclopoida and Harpacticoida) include some parasitic species. Branchiuran crustaceans of the family Argulidae (*Argulus* and related genera) are exclusively parasitic (Fig. 9-50).[281]

EPIZOOTIOLOGY The life cycles of crustacean fish parasites are varied, but most species develop directly and are able to

Figure 9-49 *Parasitic isopod (perhaps* Anilocra *sp.) on a foureye butterflyfish* (Chaetodon capistratus). *The isopod in view is a female; smaller males were probably present elsewhere on the fish. Note the eyespots. Pine Cay, Turks and Caicos Islands, 17 m.* Source: Stephen Spotte.

reinfest the same hosts, making severe infestations difficult to eradicate. Adult parasitic copepods mate on the surface of the host, and the female carries the eggs in *egg sacs*. The larvae are free living and typically hatch as nauplii before passing through several naupliar, instar, and copepodid stages. Contact with the

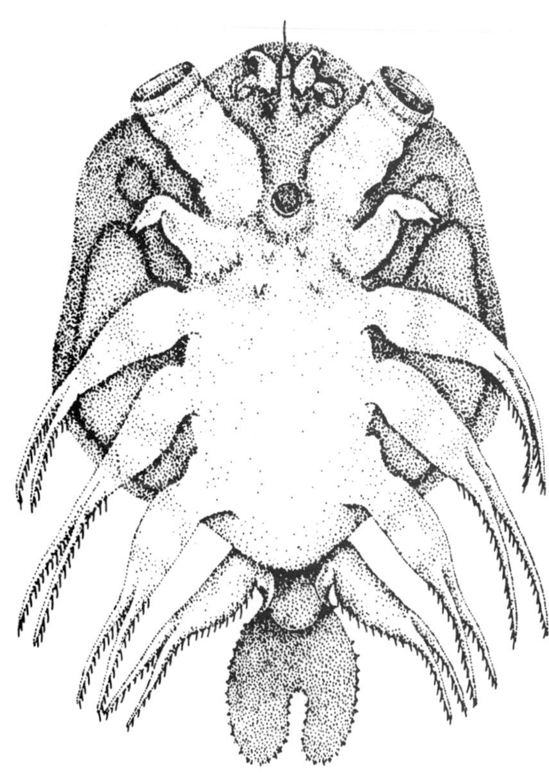

Figure 9-50 *Argulus* sp. Source: Spotte (1973).

host ordinarily occurs during one of the larval stages. Because adult copepods stay attached to their hosts, the principal sources of infestation are waterborne larvae.

Female argulids at maturity leave the host and deposit their egg masses on whatever hard surfaces are available.[282] The origin of argulid infestations can therefore be an infested host or water infested with either adults or larvae, but the aquarium glass, rocks, vegetation, and other surfaces are also potential sources.[283] The larvae (naupliar, metanaupliar, and in some species the copepodid stages) develop within the eggs.[284] At hatching they seek a host, but leave to molt and reproduce. Adults can survive in the free state for several days. A life cycle may require several weeks to complete, depending on the species. From 20 to 300 eggs are deposited in the egg mass. Hatching is stimulated by light and retarded by darkness. Hatching time is temperature dependent and variable, but in some freshwater species the process may take 2 months.

CLINICAL SIGNS AND PATHOLOGICAL EFFECTS Parasitic copepods are distinguished from argulids by their egg sacs. In addition, most copepods remain fixed in the same location; argulids are active and move freely over the surfaces of the host. Both copepods and argulids feed by piercing the host with the *preoral sting* or *stylet*.[285] In argulids, rapid thrusts of the stylet are accompanied by the release of toxic secretions that induce a severe hemorrhagic response.[286] The resulting mechanical and chemical damage to the tissues, coupled with the large size of many argulids (up to 22 mm in adults of some species),[287] can cause severe pathological effects. These often include rapid secondary stress responses (e.g., elevated blood glucose),[288] anemia,[289] and other changes in blood constituents.[288] Fishes with heavy infestations swim erratically, rub against objects, and jump.[287] Loss of equilibrium results if the lateral line has been damaged.[287] Bacteria often invade the lesions.[290]

PROPHYLAXIS AND TREATMENT In seawater aquariums, argulids ordinarily are more troublesome than copepods. However, remove fishes infested with either immediately. In the case of argulid infestations, also remove aquarium decorations and either dry them thoroughly to kill egg masses or immerse them in a 2% Clorox® solution for 2 h. Scrape the glass and walls of the aquarium to remove attached egg masses and let dry for several days. Treat infested fishes by immersion in the insecticides trichlorfon ($\sim$0.15 mg/L) or malathion ($\sim$0.20 mg/L).[291]

Gas-Bubble Trauma

SYNONYMS Gas-bubble disease, gas embolism, the "bends"

ETIOLOGY Gas-bubble trauma is seen when gases in seawater are present at supersaturated states (Chapter 3). Nitrogen appears to be the most important:[292] fatal *embolisms* (gas bubbles in the blood) consist of almost pure nitrogen.[293] Observations of afflicted fishes held in aquariums of the U.S. Fish Commission at Woods Hole, Massachusetts, about 1900 led to the first reports linking gas-bubble trauma directly with gas supersaturation.[294] The aquarium required restocking every few days, and sometimes more than 50% of the newly introduced fishes died within 48 h.[295] The mystery was solved when M. C. Marsh discovered that air drawn into the water system through leaks in the intake pipe was being forced into solution under pressure during pumping.[295] Leaks on the suction sides of seawater supply systems remain a problem today, nearly a century later (Chapter 3). Seawater supply systems require constant surveillance.

EPIZOOTIOLOGY Gas-bubble trauma is noninfectious. The malady has been reported in freshwaters and saline waters, but the effects may be magnified in seawater, probably because it supersaturates more easily.[296] Some species of fishes are more susceptible than others;[297] in addition, individuals near the surface succumb more quickly than those at depths of 3 m or more where the hydrostatic pressure is greater.[297]

CLINICAL SIGNS AND PATHOLOGICAL EFFECTS Bubbles collect on the surfaces of fishes within minutes if the water is highly supersaturated,[298] increasing in size within a few minutes more (Fig. 9-51) and ". . . enveloping the fish completely, body and fins, in a delicate, shimmering layer of silvery white."[298] Gross clinical signs are lesions of the oral cavity, skin, eyes, and fins.[299] These form after several hours as the result of intracellular gas bubbles.[298] Some individuals may be blinded completely.[300] More subtle signs include changes in blood chemistry,[301] sloughing of surface mucus,[302] and rarely exophthalmia.[303] Afflicted fishes become restless and excitable,[304] probably as small bubbles form in the bloodstream.[305] Other behavioral signs can include jumping,[306] erratic swimming,[307] loss of equilibrium,[308] darkened skin,[309] sensory deprivation caused by impaired lateral line function,[310] and anorexia.[311] Embolisms disrupt blood flow,[305] sometimes producing aneurysms in the gill lamellae[312] and distending the

Figure 9-51 *Chinook salmon* (Oncorhynchus tshawytscha) *fingerling with gas-bubble trauma.* Source: Western Fish Disease Laboratory.

heart.[298] The lamellae are often *edematous* (swollen) and contain lysed erythrocytes.[313] Embolisms may be produced in the gut,[314] pyloric ceca,[309] eye,[315] peritoneal cavity,[316] heart,[317] opercula,[309] mouth,[309] mesentery,[309] gill filaments,[318] and fin epithelium.[309] *Emphysemas* (gases formed in tissues) are sometimes apparent in the dermis,[317] between the dermis and epidermis,[319] in different connective tissues,[317] and in the fins,[320] opercula,[321] and oral cavity.[306] In larval fishes, supersaturated gases can increase the swimbladder volume at total gas pressures as low as 102.9%,[322] although swimbladder volume is affected in adult fishes too.[323] Death from gas-bubble trauma occurs when embolisms block the flow of blood,[321] resulting in cerebral anoxia and hemorrhage.[324]

PROPHYLAXIS AND TREATMENT Gas-bubble trauma is best controlled by prevention. Methods of removing supersaturated gases from seawater are described in Chapter 3.

Goiter Disease

SYNONYMS Goiter, thyroid hyperplasia.

ETIOLOGY Goiter disease of fishes is noninfectious, resulting from impaired thyroid function and the diminished production

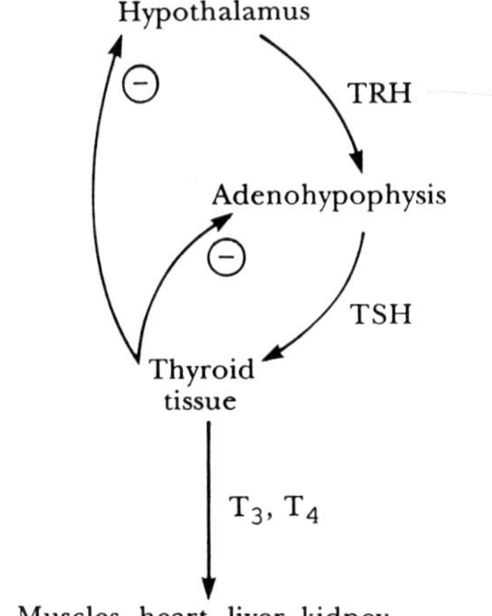

Figure 9-52 *Pathway for production of thyroid hormones. Minus signs indicate negative feedback.* Source: Stephen Spotte.

of thyroid hormones.[325] The disease is nonspecific, but some fishes are more susceptible than others.[326] With a few exceptions (e.g., elasmobranchs, lungfishes, parrotfishes), the thyroid is not a discrete gland but an unencapsulated agglomeration of follicles, mostly in the area of the subpharynx or pharynx between the first and second gill arches.[327]

The thyroid assimilates and concentrates iodide, I^-, derived from food and water. This is oxidized enzymatically to either iodine, I_2, or iodate, IO^-. A series of thyronines or *thyroid hormones* is formed during subsequent conversions: diiodothyronine, triiodothyronine (T_3), and tetraiodothyronine or thyroxine (T_4). The last two predominate, and T_4 is present in the greater concentration. *Thyroid stimulating hormone*, TSH, released from the adenohypophysis, regulates the thyroid gland and stimulates the release of thyroid hormones (Fig. 9-52). The release of TSH is controlled by *TSH releasing hormone*, TRH, from the hypothalamus. Thyroid hormones are distributed to the muscles, heart, liver, and kidney where they assist in regulating metabolic processes. The concentrations of thyroid hormones are controlled at the hypothalamus and adenohypophysis by *negative feedback* (i.e., elevated concentrations in the blood are detected by the hypothalamus and adenophypophysis, causing production to cease).[328] In fishes, thyroid hormones help control certain metabolic and developmental processes; in salmonids, these hormones are involved in adaptation to waters of different salinity during migration.

EPIZOOTIOLOGY Goiter disease is characterized by expansion of the thyroid tissue caused by hypertrophy and then hyperplasia of the epithelial cells.[329] Nothing is known about the epizootiology of goiter disease in captive seawater fishes. The most frequently cited causes are iodide depletion of the water, inadequate amounts of iodide in the food, and continuous exposure to environmental toxins or *goitrogens*. A less specific etiology triggered by the primary or neurohormonal stress response is seldom mentioned, although worthy of consideration. All are discussed below.

Seawater contains ~60 μg/L iodine, but far greater amounts are concentrated in organic surface sediments.[330] Recirculated seawater may lose iodine to the detritus[331] and perhaps to the atmosphere during aeration.[332] Only small amounts of iodide are required for normal functioning of the thyroid, but some assimilation from the environment may be necessary.[333] However, iodide deficiency is not necessarily the cause of goiter disease in fishes. It has been suggested that goitrogens are the causative agents.[334] Among the suspected compounds are ammonia[335] and urea,[335] although nitrate is another possibility. Nitrate often increases in closed-system seawater aquariums (Chapter 2), but any adverse effect it may have on the thyroid has not been confirmed. Concentrations of ~78 mg NO_3-N/L were demonstrated to inhibit iodide assimilation by the thyroid and other tissues (gill, muscle, liver, gonads) in several species of freshwater fishes, but thyroid function was unimpaired.[336] If fishes maintained in closed systems are indeed more likely to contract goiter disease, then depletion of compounds essential to sustain production of thyroid hormones (e.g., iodide) accounts for only some of the possibilities. Perhaps goitrogens that accumulate in the environment are more important.

The neurohormonal basis of the primary stress response of fishes was discussed in Chapter 4. Such stress factors as capture, handling, and transport cause an immediate increase in cortisol, one of the corticosteroids. Concomitantly, the levels of T_3 and T_4 in recently captured fishes often decline precipitously, sometimes not recovering for a month or more.[337]

CLINICAL SIGNS AND PATHOLOGICAL EFFECTS The opercula of fishes afflicted with goiter disease are flared permanently, and swollen thyroid tissue sometimes protrudes from the branchial cavity[327] (Fig. 9-53). Some specimens are emaciated, and breathing is often labored.[327] Pathological effects include enlargement of the thyroid, which may appear translucent,[338] flabby,[338] and occasionally hemorrhagic.[327] Areas near the edge may appear normal (i.e., follicles spherical in shape, bordered by low cuboidal epithelium and filled with eosinophilic colloid).[338] Follicles in the rest of the gland typically are distended with colloid and the diameters enlarged up to eight times, representing a volumetric increase of 80 times;[338] alternatively, there is very little colloid.[327] The follicular epithelium may be flattened and stretched; some follicles are hemorrhagic.[338] The follicular epithelium is hyperplastic with large papillae projected into the lumen.[338] In extreme cases, the gill lamellae are destroyed by proliferating thyroid tissue.[327]

PROPHYLAXIS AND TREATMENT Programs of prevention and treatment cannot be devised until the etiology of goiter disease has been identified. The problem seems to be more prevalent in closed systems, but this statement is speculative.[339] If goitrogens are the causative agents of goiter disease, addition of iodide to the food or water is of limited benefit. Fishes sometimes recover when transferred from closed to open seawater systems.[340] One report described the successful treatment of goiter in a goldfish (*Carassius auratus*).[341] The fish was admin-

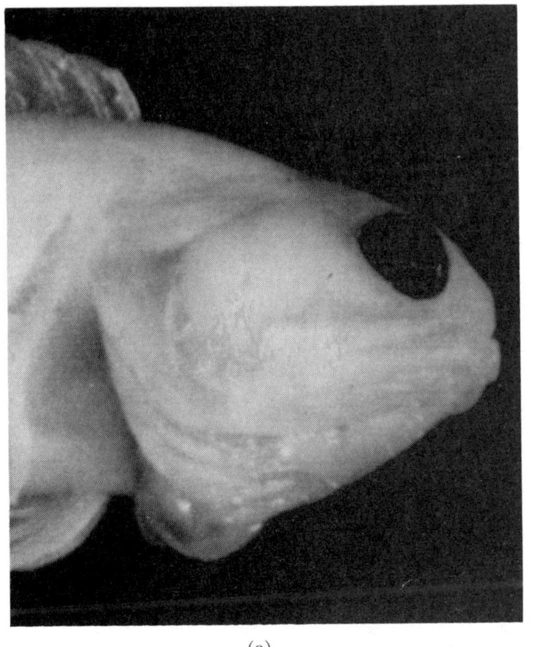

(a)

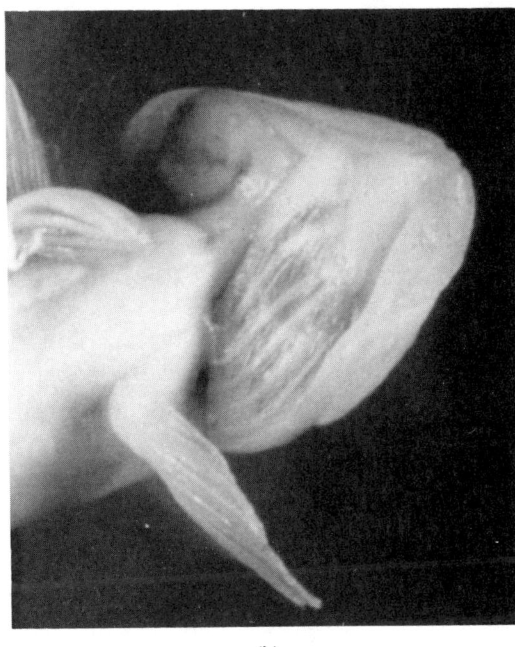

(b)

Figure 9-53 Goitrous yellowhead jawfish (Opistognathus aurifrons): *(a) lateral view.* (b) *ventral view.* Source: Richard E. Wolke, Marine Pathology Laboratory, University of Rhode Island.

istered an aqueous solution of "an organic iodine compound" (10 mg/L iodine) orally, followed by flushing of the buccal cavity with tap water. The treatment was repeated 2 d later. Another report stated that maintaining total iodine at 0.1 mg/L prevents goiter disease in elasmobranchs held in closed seawater systems.[342] No data were included. Preliminary results of studies at Mystic Marinelife Aquarium and National Aquarium in Baltimore indicate that injection of Synthroid®, a synthetic thyroid hormone, at dosage levels of 0.2 to 0.75 μg/kg sometimes initiates regression of thyroid lesions in sharks. Oral administration of Synthroid® at concentrations up to 400 μg/kg has also been tried. A firm treatment regimen for either injectable or oral administration of Synthroid® has not been devised.

Treatment Abstracts

The compounds and treatment regimens presented below are synopses of reports selected from the fish disease literature. They describe chemotherapeutic agents and methods of application demonstrated to be effective against specific pathogens, either a bacterium or monogenean. The literature contains hundreds of entries, but relatively few have been based on adequate research. Those offered here conform with certain criteria that, in my opinion, define research of good quality in terms of both scientific standards and practical application. The list is by no means complete; much excellent work was not included because of space limitations.

The problems of testing a chemotherapeutic agent are generally more complex when the pathogen is a bacterium. In my opinion, the results of research attempting to evaluate the efficacy of a compound against bacteria should include, at minimum, these eight features: (*1*) the origin, purity, and demonstrated strength of the chemotherapeutic agent; (*2*) pretests of factors that may influence the life and stability of the agent (e.g., temperature, light); (*3*) appropriate tests of efficacy *in vitro* against known organisms (e.g., minimum inhibitory concentration, MIC); (*4*) rate of assimilation by the test host, including blood and tissue assays; (*5*) residence time in blood and tissues at therapeutic concentrations; (*6*) toxicity to the host; (*7*) efficacy *in vivo* determined by challenging the host with known numbers of the test pathogen; and (*8*) evaluation of methods of administration (e.g., immersion, *per os*).

Experimental designs to test the effectiveness of chemotherapeutic agents and regimens against other groups of pathogens (e.g., protozoans, helminths) seldom include all eight features listed above. Except for bacteria, most pathogens of interest to aquarists are external or subepithelial. Residence time of the agent in blood and tissues may not be relevant, in which case assays are unnecessary. *In vitro* testing is seldom done when the parasite is a helminth or arthropod; instead, the test hosts are inspected visually for any parasites remaining after treatment. As mentioned, reports that provide the basis of the following synopses were selected from a large body of literature. Because they are presented without further evaluation, I have called them Treatment Abstracts. All stated concentrations are of the active ingredients unless otherwise indicated.

BACTERIA

Aeromonas spp.

Test compound: DS-677 K, Potassium-1-methyl-1,4-dihydro-7-[2-(5-nitro-2-furyl)-vinyl]-4-oxo-1,8-naphthyridine-3-carboxylate.[1]

Test hosts: Goldfish (*Carassius auratus*), freshwater-acclimated Japanese eels (*Anguilla japonica*).

MIC in vitro: 0.0125 to 0.05 μg/mL (*A. liquefaciens*), 0.0125 to 0.025 μg/mL (*A. salmonicida*) over 48 h at 30°C.

Toxicity: Depresses respiration rate of eels during immersion at 2.5 and 10 μg/mL for 245 min; not lethal to young eels during immersion at this regimen.

Assimilation: Absorbed rapidly. Concentrated sixfold in eel blood during immersion at 5 mg/L. Therapeutic concentrations are reached in the gill after 1 h, but not in the kidney, spleen, muscle, or liver.

Treatment regimen: Immersion in 10 mg/L for 30 min on three consecutive days; *per os* at 5 mg/kg (duration not stated).

Comments: Aqueous solutions of DS-677 K are unstable in light. Administer treatment in darkness; if aqueous solutions are saved, store in the dark.

Source: Oshima et al. (1970); not listed in The Merck Index (Budavari 1989).[1]

Pasteurella piscicida (pseudotuberculosis)

Test compound: Sodium nifurstyrenate (NFS·Na), sodium salt of 5-nitro-2-(*p*-carboxyl styryl)-furan.

Test host: Yellowtail (*Seriola quinqueradiata*).

MIC in vitro: 0.015 to 1.0 μg/mL (48 h at 25°C).

Toxicity: Not toxic at 1 g/kg for 96 h.

Assimilation: Absorbed quickly. Therapeutic levels are maintained in the blood, liver, kidney, and muscle for 36 h after one dose (74.6 and 100 mg/kg administered *per os*); residual is not detectable after 48 h.

Treatment regimen: 100 mg/kg administered *per os* daily for 5 d.

Comments: None.

Source: Sugimoto et al. (1976).

Streptococcus sp.

Test compound: Spiramycin embonate, SpE.

Test host: Yellowtail (*Seriola quinqueradiata*).

MIC in vitro: 0.78 to 3.12 μg/mL (duration and temperature not stated).

Toxicity: Not acutely toxic when administered at 200, 400, or 800 mg/kg *per os* in a single dose; not subacutely toxic at 40, 80, or 400 mg/(d·kg) for 10 d. In all cases, fish survived without clinical or pathological abnormalities.

Assimilation: Absorbed easily and distributed rapidly by the blood to major organs. Peak levels are reached in 24 h. Levels in the liver, spleen, kidney, and bile exceeded blood levels. Tissue levels were maintained at 11 mg/kg or less for 96 h in fish administered 40 mg/kg *per os* in a single dose.

Treatment regimen: 25 to 40 mg/(d·kg) *per os* for 10 d.

Comments: None.

Sources: Kubota et al. (1980), Kubota and Miyazaki (1980).

Vibrio anguillarum

Test compound: Piromidic acid, 8-ethyl-5,8-dihydro-5-oxo-2-(1 pyrrolidinyl)pyrido(2,3-*d*)pyrimidine-6-carboxylic acid.

Test hosts: Goldfish (*Carassius auratus*), freshwater-acclimated Japanese eels (*Anguilla japonica*).

MIC in vitro: 1 to 3 μg/mL (range for three strains of *V. anguillarum*); activity greater at pH 8.0 than at pH 6.0.

Toxicity: Goldfish receiving 750 mg/kg *per os* survived without clinical evidence of abnormality. Eels administered 2000 mg/kg *per os* also survived without clinical changes. Goldfish administered 125 mg/(d·kg) survived without clinical changes, as did eels receiving 1000 mg/(d·kg).

Assimilation: Absorbed rapidly. Goldfish administered 5 mg/kg *per os* had mean blood concentrations of 1 μg/mL after 1 to 3 h. Maximum concentration was 1.11 μg/mL after 2 h, followed by a gradual decline to one-half this level at 6 h and to levels below the detection limit of the assay (<0.25 μg/mL) at 24 h. In eels administered 5 mg/kg, plasma concentrations were 1.36 μg/mL (1 h), 2.32 μg/mL (2 h), 2 μg/mL (6 h), and below the detection limit at 48 h. Concentrations in the liver and kidney exceeded those in the blood for both fishes.

Treatment regimen: A treatment regimen was not offered, but the assimilation data suggest that 5 mg/kg is inadequate to sustain therapeutic concentrations in the blood if administered once daily. Toxicity is low, and a regimen of 50 mg/(d·kg) for 5 d might be a suitable starting point.

Comments: The effective dosage (i.e., defined here as the single dose at which growth is inhibited *in vivo* with no host mortalities) was 7.8 mg/kg.

Source: Katae et al. (1979).

Vibrio anguillarum

Test compound: Halquinol, 5,7-dichloro-8-hydroxyquinoline.

Test host: Juvenile turbot (*Scophthalmus maximus*).

MIC in vitro: At 100 mg/L, cultures of *V. anguillarum* were inactivated within 5 min; total inactivation was achieved within 1 h.

Toxicity: Bioassays were not performed. Treatment with halquinol causes mucus production.[2] Fish became ataxic within 5 min of immersion at 10 mg/L, but recovered completely within 30 min of transfer to untreated seawater. Fish that consumed feed containing 100 mg/kg survived well. Palatability apparently was excellent, and feed containing 5 g/kg was accepted, provided the disease had not advanced to the stage at which anorexia commenced.

Assimilation: No data.

Treatment regimen: Immerse infected fishes in a suspension of 10 mg/L halquinol in aerated seawater for 15 min, then transfer them immediately to untreated, aerated seawater.[1] Repeat every second day for 8 d. Alternatively, immerse in 25 mg/L for 15 min, then transfer to untreated, aerated seawater. Repeat twice daily ıor 3 d.[2] For *per os* treatment feed at 100 mg/(d·kg) for 10 d.[1]

Comments: Losses of test fish treated with halquinol either by immersion or *per os* was 10 to 15% after 21 d;[1] mortality of the control fish was 85 to 90%.[1] Most fishes with advanced vibriosis refuse to feed and must be treated by immersion.

Sources: Austin et al. (1981/1982,[1] 1982[2]).

Vibrio anguillarum

Test compound: Oxolinic acid, 1-ethyl-1,4-dihydro-6,7-methylenedixoy-4-oxo-3-quinolinecarboxylic acid.

Test host: Juvenile turbot (*Scophthalmus maximus*).

MIC in vitro: At 100 mg/L, cultures of *V. anguillarum* were inactivated within 5 min.

Toxicity: Bioassays were not performed. Treatment with oxolinic acid causes mucus production. Fish that consumed feed containing 75 mg/(d·kg) survived well. Palatability was acceptable.

Assimilation: No data.

Treatment regimen: Immerse infected fishes in a suspension of 25 mg/L oxolinic acid in aerated seawater for 15 min, then transfer them immediately to untreated, aerated seawater. Repeat twice daily for 3 d. Alternatively, feed twice daily for 10 d at 75 mg/(d·kg).

Comments: Losses of test fish treated either by immersion or *per os* was 25% after 42 d; mortality of the control fish was 85 to 90%. Most fishes with advanced vibriosis refuse to feed and must be treated by immersion.

Source: Austin et al. (1982).

MONOGENETIC TREMATODES

Bicotylophora trachinoti

Test compound: Trichlorfon (2,2,2-trichloro-1-hydroxyethyl)phosphonic acid dimethyl ester.

Test host: Florida pompano (*Trachinotus carolinus*).

Effectiveness in vitro: No data.

Treatment regimen: Immersion in 0.25 mg/L for 24 h (S = 30‰).

Toxicity: No mortalities observed in preliminary trials.

Assimilation: No data.

Comments: The treatment appeared to be completely effective (i.e., no attached worms were seen on fish examined).

Source: Williams (1974).

Pseudodactylogyrus anguillae and *P. bini*

Test compound: Mebendazole (10% active ingredient), 5-benzoyl-2-benzimidazolecarbamic acid methyl ester.

Test host: Freshwater-acclimated European eels (*Anguilla anguilla*) with simultaneous infestations of *P. anguillae* and *P. bini* (20 to 30 worms per eel).

Effectiveness in vitro: No data.

Toxicity: No data.

Assimilation: No data.

Treatment regimen: Eels in freshwater (see Comments) were administered a single immersion treatment of 10 mg/L (1 h) or 100 mg/L (10 or 20 min).

Comments: Effective doses (no mortalities, eels visibly free of worms when examined after treatment) in freshwater were 100 mg/L (10 min, 20 min), 10 mg/L and 40 mg/L (1 h), and 0.4 mg/L (24 h). Some worms did not die for as long as 6 d after treatment. Exposing eels to a 5% brine solution for 2 or 5 min prior to treatment for 20 min lowered the effective concentration by 90%. This should not be interpreted to mean that mebendazole is notably more effective in the treatment of seawater fishes. The eels were left in brine only long enough to disturb osmotic equilibrium. The increased assimilation rate across the integument is attributable to escalated water flux outward (and of mebendazole inward). Treatment with organophosphates, brine, and ammonia (concentrations and duration not given) were ineffective.

Source: Székely and Molnár (1987).

Benedeniella posterocolpa, Dermophthirioides pristidis, Dermophthirius nigrellii

Test compounds: Praziquantel (see next Treatment Abstract) trichlorfon, cupric sulfate; actual test concentrations not stated (i.e., dosages given in parts per million, ppm).

Test hosts: Juvenile cownose rays (*Rhinoptera bonasus*), two sawfish (*Pristis* sp.), and a lemon shark (*Negaprion brevirostris*).

Effectiveness in vitro: Adult *B. posterocolpa* removed from cownose rays and treated with praziquantel (20 ppm) were dead within 6 h. Newly hatched larvae of *B. posterocolpa* treated with praziquantel (20 ppm) and trichlorfon (0.7 ppm) did not survive past 12 h. Larvae treated with cupric sulfate (0.25 ppm) survived more than 36 h. Eggs of *B. posterocolpa* were affected most by trichlorfon and least by cupric sulfate (no data given).

Toxicity: Praziquantel appeared to be less stressful than trichlorfon to cownose rays.

Assimilation: No data.

Treatment regimen: Immersion. Ten cownose rays treated on one occasion for 90 min with praziquantel (20 ppm) were rendered parasite free. Cownose rays treated with trichlorfon (0.7 ppm) for 6 h and again 2 d later lost 81% of their worms (presumably the mean of 10 specimens). The sawfish and shark administered the same dosage were also rendered free of monogeneans after 90 min, although there were no controls and the number of worms present before and after treatment apparently was not monitored.

Comments: The test dosage of praziquantel apparently rids captive elasmobranchs of at least three species of monogeneans.

Source: Thoney (1989b).

Gyrodactylus aculeati

Test compound: Praziquantel, 2-(cyclohexylcarbonyl)-1,2,3, 6,7,1 1 *b*-hexahydro-4*H*-pyrazino(2,1-*a*)isoquinolin-4-one.

Test host: Threespine sticklebacks (*Gasterosteus aculeatus*) in freshwater.

Effectiveness in vitro: No data.

Toxicity: Behavior was normal except at 50 mg/L for 60 and 90 min and 20 mg/L for 120 min. At these regimens the fish swam upside down and respiration rate increased, although all recovered within 15 min after transfer to untreated water.

Assimilation: No data.

Treatment regimen: Immersion at concentrations of 0, 1, 5, 10, 20, or 50 mg/L for 15, 30, 60, 90, and 120 min and 4 and 16 h.

Comments: Praziquantel killed the worms by destroying the tegument. The recommended dosage was 10 mg/L for 3 h.

Source: Schmahl and Taraschewski (1987).

Gyrodactylus aculeati

Test compound: Niclosamide, 2′,5-dichloro-4′-nitrosalicylanilide.

Test host: Threespine sticklebacks (*Gasterosteus aculeatus*) in freshwater.

Effectiveness in vitro: No data.

Toxicity: No toxic effects observed.

Assimilation: No data.

Treatment regimen: Fish were treated by immersion at concentrations of 0.05, 0.075, or 0.1 mg/L for 30, 60, 90, and 120 min.

Comments: Niclosamide killed the worms by destroying the tegument. A recommended dosage was not offered; presumably, any of the above concentrations for 120 min would be acceptable.

Source: Schmahl and Taraschewski (1987).

Gyrodactylus aculeati

Test compound: Levamisole·HCl.

Test host: Threespine sticklebacks (*Gasterosteus aculeatus*) in freshwater.

Effectiveness in vitro: No data.

Toxicity: Levamisole·HCl was tolerated at regimens of 10 to 50 mg/L for 30 to 120 min, but adult sticklebacks ''did not tolerate the drug'' at 100 mg/L for 25 min (I presume this means they died). Juvenile sticklebacks survived if transferred to untreated water. No long-term effects were seen in fish that recovered.

Assimilation: No data.

Treatment regimen: Immersion at concentrations of 10, 20, 50, or 100 mg/L for 25, 30, 60, 90, and 120 min.

Comments: Levamisole·HCl killed the worms by destroying the tegument. A recommended dosage was not offered, although 50 mg/L for 120 min eliminated worms from the skin.

Source: Schmahl and Taraschewski (1987).

CHAPTER

10 Exhibition

It would be remiss in a book written mostly for public aquarists not to include a chapter on the exhibition of fishes. I saved this subject for last, in part because a fish exhibit is not defined easily. Seawater and fishes are integral components, of course, but not enough by themselves. Outstanding exhibits are provocative, unfinished statements containing an element of art, a sprinkling of magic, lingering images that taunt the imagination. To say simply that good exhibits are ''educational'' misses the mark. The mind functions best in a state of heightened awareness.

I was able to identify four additional features that require thought when designing exhibits: color, light, space, and decorations. The last can be missing, so long as the emptiness is filled by overflow from the rest. Color and light (including optics) are especially interesting, and sizable parts of the Science and Technology sections are devoted to them. Space is an abstraction, and I chose not to address it specifically. Space considerations are obviously important if everything else is to be manipulated successfully.

SCIENCE

Light

Waves are forms of energy that travel in an oscillatory motion. Ocean waves travel through water, and waves of a guitar string move along the string. Sound waves are vibrations in air or water. In all these examples the medium itself is moving back and forth as the wave passes (i.e., the waves cause atoms and molecules in their path to oscillate). Thus all require some form of matter through which to travel. *Electromagnetic waves* are different because they travel best in the absence of matter—in other words, in a vacuum. What vibrates is not matter but an electric field force. Many kinds of electromagnetic waves exist, including radio, radar, infrared, light, ultraviolet, and x-ray waves. These forms of *radiant energy* travel at the same speed (2.998 × 10^8 m/s); they differ only in frequency and wavelength. Both terms are defined below.

Every wave is characterized by its wavelength, period, and speed. On a plot of electric field strength (electromagnetic wave) or pressure (sound wave) against time, the *wavelength* is the distance between two points on the curve having the same phase. To state this differently, it is a measure of the distance over which the intensity of the wave is repeated. The time required for one wavelength to pass a given point in space is the *period*, and the reciprocal of the period is the *frequency* measured in hertz, Hz. The range of wavelengths within the electromagnetic spectrum is enormous (Fig. 10-1). The shortest gamma rays are only 5.7×10^{-4} nm; the longest radio waves extend for ~30 km (3×10^{13} nm). *Light* is the visible portion of the electromagnetic spectrum (i.e., the portion to which the human eye is sensitive), a narrow band of wavelengths restricted to ~360 to 780 nm. Thus light is radiant energy measured in terms of its capacity to produce visual sensations.

As light travels through air or water it is subjected to losses from absorption and scattering. *Absorption* is the conversion of light energy into heat, whereas *scattering* represents a change in the direction of light energy. Both are caused by the presence of matter. Scattering in the atmosphere is produced by gas molecules, raindrops, and dust and other particles; in the hydrosphere the primary factor is the presence of particulate organic carbon (POC) suspended in the water column. *Attenuation* is the sum of absorption and scattering and therefore the reduction in light intensity caused by these factors.

The change in density from the atmosphere to the hydrosphere causes some of the light that enters water to be reflected; the rest is refracted toward the vertical (broken line of Fig. 10-2). The law of refraction, or Snell's law, relates the angle of the

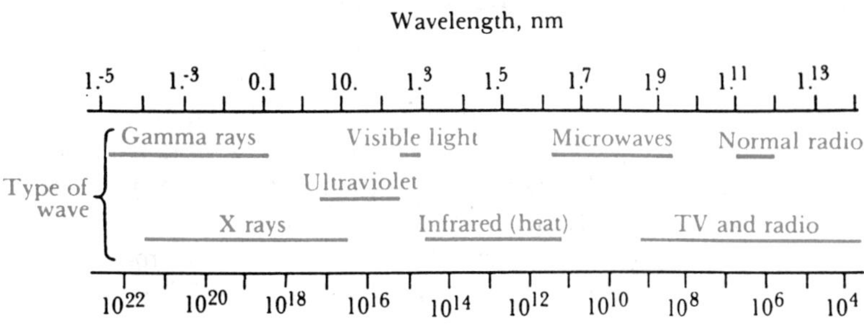

Figure 10-1 *Types of electromagnetic waves.* Source: Bueche (1985).

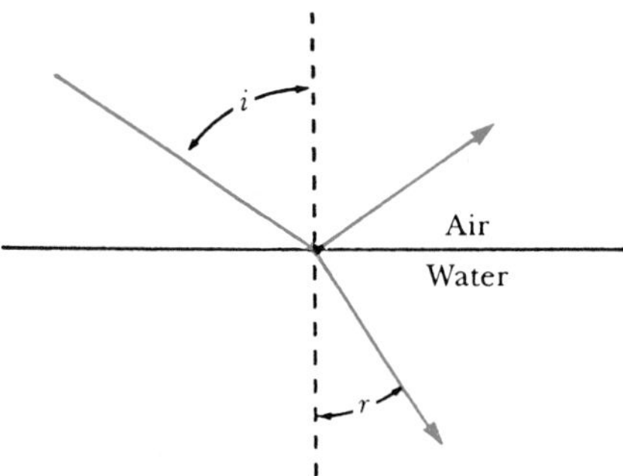

Figure 10-2 When light is directed at water a portion is reflected back into the atmosphere, and the remainder is refracted. The angle represented by r is the angle of refraction; i is the angle of incidence. The term refractive index denotes the phase speed of radiant energy in free space divided by the phase speed of the same energy in a specified medium such as seawater. It is equal to the ratio of the sine of the angle of incidence in a vacuum to the sine of the angle of refraction. If n stands for refractive index, n = sin i/sin r. Source: Stephen Spotte, drawn from various sources.

incoming incident light to that of the transmitted beam (i.e., bundle of light rays) by relative index of refraction.[1] This value is ~1.33 for pure water at 20°C and increases slightly with decreasing temperature and increasing salinity. Seawater has a refractive index of 1.34. Snell's law is expressed

$$n = \frac{\sin \theta_i}{\sin \theta_r} \tag{10.1}$$

where θ_i and θ_r represent the angle of incidence and refraction, and n is the relative index of refraction. The precise angle of refraction is variable if waves and ripples cause the surface to be unstable.

COLOR Different wavelengths of light correspond to different colors. Light containing wavelengths of 380 to 780 nm is *white light*, defined in practical terms as radiant energy with a wavelength distribution that evokes a neutral or "hueless" sensation (see below) in persons with normal color vision. White light passed through a prism is dispersed into a *color spectrum*, which is the range of visible wavelengths given off by a light source (Fig. 10-3, Table 10-1), with red and violet at the longer and shorter wavelengths, respectively. Persons with normal color vision can see blue at 480, green at 515, yellow at 575, and red at 650 nm.

Prisms allow all wavelengths of white light to pass through;

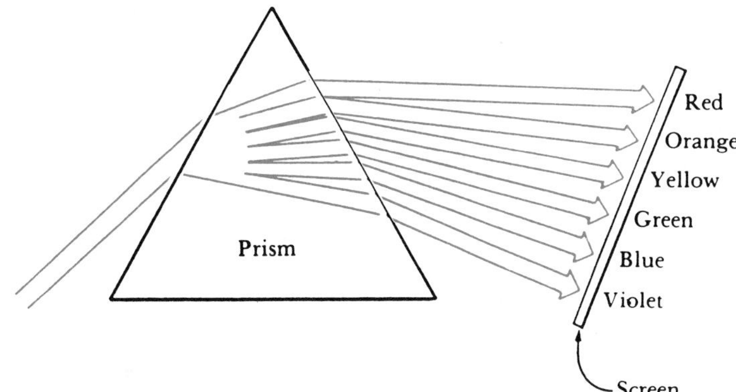

Figure 10-3 *White light passed through a prism is dispersed into a spectrum of colors.* Source: Feinberg (1983).

filters (including water) selectively remove them by absorption. Wavelengths that are not filtered (i.e., absorbed) are transmitted. Filtered light can be studied from the standpoint of the wavelengths removed (absorption) or remaining (transmittance). A white object appears white because all wavelengths of light are reflected. Black objects absorb all wavelengths and reflect none. Grays are intermediate.

The visual sensation resulting when light falls on the retina has three characteristics: hue, saturation, and brightness. Because color is a visual sensation, colors themselves can be said to possess these same attributes. *Hue* is what enables us to call a color red, green, or brown. The purity of a color defines its degree of *saturation*, or the extent to which it departs from a neutral gray and approaches a pure spectrum color. The attributes of hue and saturation in sum represent *chromaticity*. White, black, and gray are *achromatic* colors because they are without hue and saturation. (To be completely accurate it is preferable to say that the hue of gray is indeterminate.) Colors of the same hue or without hue can differ in *value* (also called *brightness* and *lightness*), defined as the equivalent visual sensation produced by one of a series of grays between black and

TABLE 10-1 Wavelengths of colors.

Color	Wavelength, nm
Violet	400–450
Blue	450–500
Green	500–570
Yellow	570–590
Orange	590–610
Red	610–700

Source: Stephen Spotte, compiled from various sources.

white. By definition all grays are unsaturated, provided they are completely neutral (i.e., contain no traces of chromatic colors). Snow (which is never pure white) and graphite are both neutral grays, but snow is brighter and has greater value. Similarly, light green is brighter than dark green, even if they have the same hue. Highly saturated colors have pronounced hues and greater chromaticity than colors of low saturation. They differ more from grays (achromatic standards) of equivalent value. Pink and other chromatic colors, which are of low hue but high value, are *tints*; a color of low hue and low value (e.g., brown) is a *shade*.

It is possible to see colors because sources of light emit energy. The objects on which light falls can absorb, transmit, or reflect light (sometimes all three). This capacity to selectively process the light received imparts *coloration*. Objects that reflect or transmit most of the light falling on them appear as white and transparent, respectively. Objects that absorb more light than they reflect or transmit appear black. As stated previously, white and black are achromatic (without color). An object that selectively absorbs more light at some wavelengths than at others ordinarily is chromatic and displays coloration.

LIGHT ABOVE THE OCEAN The appearance of the ocean depends on surface activity (calm or rough) and degree of cloudiness, in addition to the observer's distance and angle of view. If the surface is perfectly smooth the amount of radiant energy reflected is a function only of the sun's altitude. But if the ocean is disturbed its total surface area is increased, and the angles of incidence reflected from each wave and ripple (i.e., each distortion from a smooth state) fluctuate with time, resulting in *glitter* (Fig. 10-4). Because the configuration of the surface changes rapidly and continuously, periods of glitter from individual waves and ripples are short, even though the overall effect may last for hours. The ocean appears deep blue and dark if the sky is clear, the viewing angle steep, and the observer close (Fig. 10-5). From afar the surface can appear deep blue under a clear sky, or pale gray and light if cloud cover is reflected or the angle of view is shallow (Fig. 10-6). On clear days the blue color of the sky, which results from the scattering of sunlight by gas molecules, adds to blue light refracted and scattered off the water.

SUBMARINE LIGHT[2] Water is ~1000 times denser than air. Both air and clear water ordinarily are considered to be transparent and colorless, but light penetration through water is at least 2000 times less than in air. Absorption accounts for minor

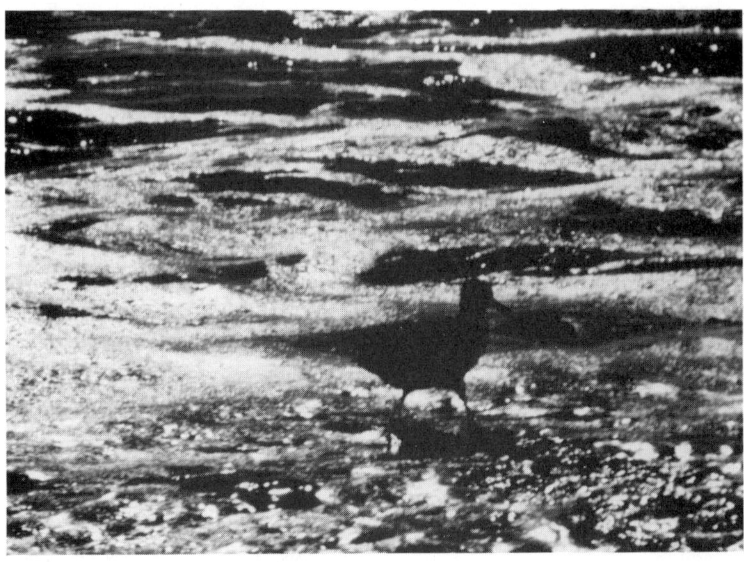

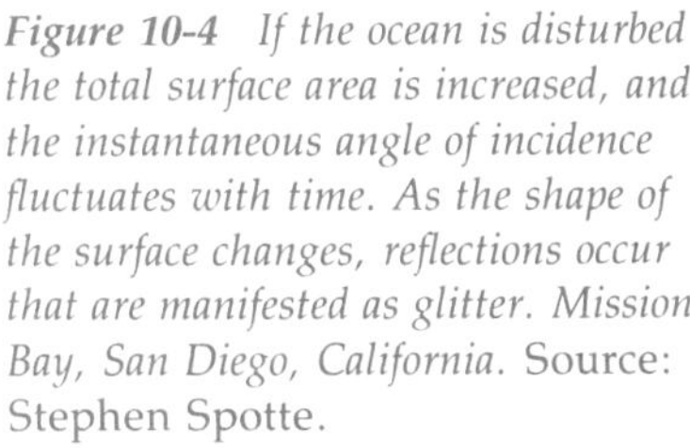

Figure 10-4 If the ocean is disturbed the total surface area is increased, and the instantaneous angle of incidence fluctuates with time. As the shape of the surface changes, reflections occur that are manifested as glitter. Mission Bay, San Diego, California. Source: Stephen Spotte.

losses of light energy in the atmosphere because gas molecules are widely dispersed, but in the hydrosphere the loss from attenuation (mainly absorption) is substantial (Fig. 10-7). Wavelengths are absorbed selectively with increasing depth (Fig. 10-8). As light penetrates deeper, the shorter and longer wavelengths are attenuated rapidly until substantial amounts of energy remain only in wavelengths near the middle of the visible spectrum. Thus water (both seawater and freshwater) is relatively opaque to ultraviolet and red light (particularly the lat-

Figure 10-5 The ocean photographed on a clear, sunny day from a steep angle appears deep blue and dark. Palos Verdes Peninsula, California. Source: Stephen Spotte.

Figure 10-6 The ocean photographed on an overcast day from a shallow angle appears pale gray and light. St. Paul Island, Pribilof Islands, Alaska. Source: Stephen Spotte.

ter), but comparatively transparent to blue and green wavelengths. Of all the wavelengths blue penetrates deepest, and the oceans become increasingly monochromatic with depth.[3] In addition, blue coloration is imparted through scattering by water molecules, just as the blue of the sky results from scat-

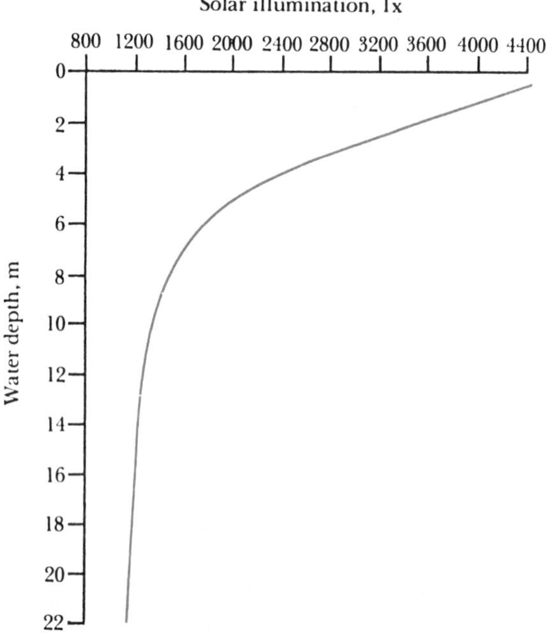

Figure 10-7 Attenuation of light at noon on 20 March 1985 in the Caribbean Sea off Bonaire, Netherlands Antilles (north latitude 12° 6′). The curve has been fitted by eye through 10 data points (omitted) plotted from a single series of measurements. The measurements were made with a photometer (Photo-Meter 1, Quantum Instruments Inc., Garden City NY 11530) housed in a watertight acrylic case. Source: Stephen Spotte, unpublished data.

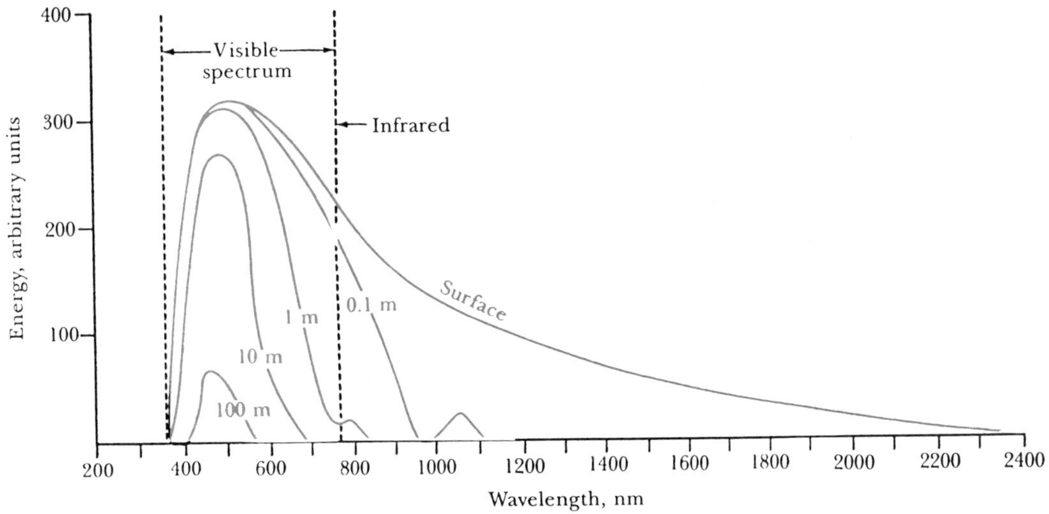

Figure 10-8 Schematic representation of the energy spectrum of radiation from the sun and sky penetrating the surface of the ocean, and of the energy spectrum in pure water at depths of 0.1, 1, 10, and 100 m. Source: Sverdrup et al. (1942).

tering of sunlight by molecules of gas.[4] Inorganic solutes have only a tiny effect on the optical properties of water,[5] and the attenuation of light in the cleanest seawater is almost identical with that of pure water.

Fine particles of POC increase scattering, with the effect being greatest at the ultraviolet and infrared wave ends of the spectrum.[6] Large particles of POC (e.g., plankton and detritus) scatter and absorb light. Scattering is independent of wavelength, but absorption is strongest in the blue range.[7] Coastal seawaters are productive and contain heavy concentrations of phytoplankton and humic compounds (pigmented yellow fractions of the dissolved organic carbon or DOC; Chapter 2). Humic compounds absorb blue light. Clear oceanic (i.e., offshore) seawaters and many tropical oceans are comparatively less productive and contain lower concentrations POC and pigmented DOC. The low light penetration in coastal seawaters is accompanied by a shift in the wavelength of maximum transmittance from blue at ~465 nm to yellow at ~575 nm (Fig. 10-9), and coastal and oceanic seawaters appear green and blue, respectively.

Submarine light just beneath the surface is characterized by an abrupt increase in the radiance of the sky in all directions. This is a purely geometric effect caused by the narrowing of a beam of refracted light (Fig. 10-10).[8] On a sunny day in shallow,

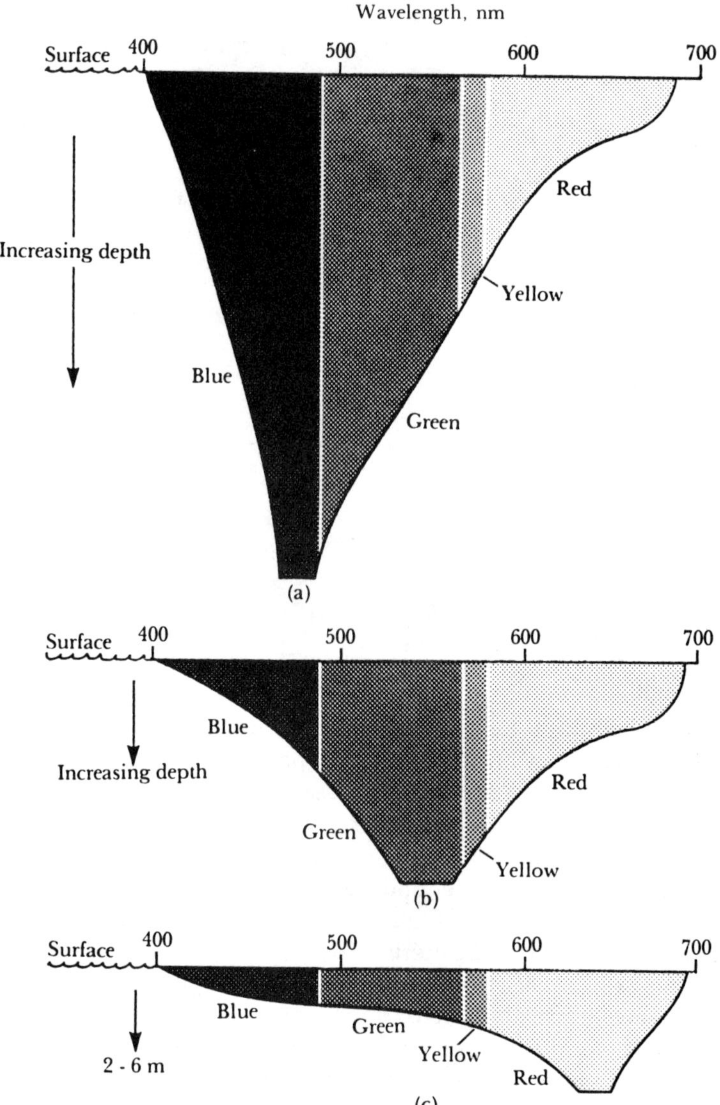

Figure 10-9 *Schematic representation of the energy spectrum of radiation from the sun and sky that penetrates the surface of the ocean.* (a) *Clear oceanic waters.* (b) *Coastal seawaters.* (c) *Estuarine waters.* Source: Levine (1980).

clear water a diver looking down sees a rippling mosaic of bright and dark areas on the bottom. This is produced by refracted rays of light converging and diverging at different points (Fig. 10-11).

Artificial Illumination

Most aquarium exhibits are constructed indoors, requiring the use of artificial light. This has advantages and disadvantages.

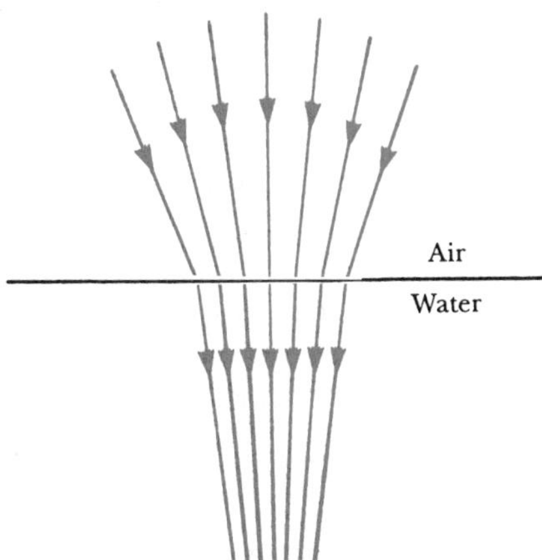

Figure 10-10 *Bundles of refracted light rays are narrowed as they enter water from the less dense air.* Source: Preisendorfer (1976).

No artificial light source is ever a completely suitable substitute for daylight, although exhibits placed beneath skylights or open to the sky cannot be viewed at night unless supplementary light is provided. In addition, viewing is diminished on overcast days and at times of the day or season of the year when daylight enters the surface of the water at long angles. Besides reducing the intensity of ambient light, such conditions limit the horizonal viewing depth by magnifying turbidity effects. The subsections that follow discuss how lamps can be used to simulate the intensity and spectrum of daylight beneath the oceans.

THE NATURE OF ARTIFICIAL ILLUMINATION Data for defining the color of a light source are given as a measure of the energy at each wavelength or group of wavelengths making up the light source. Different light sources emit energy in varying amounts and in different portions of the spectrum. Illuminated objects can reflect or transmit only those parts of the spectrum contained in the source. To see the true coloration of objects as they appear in shallow water—in other words, in daylight—it

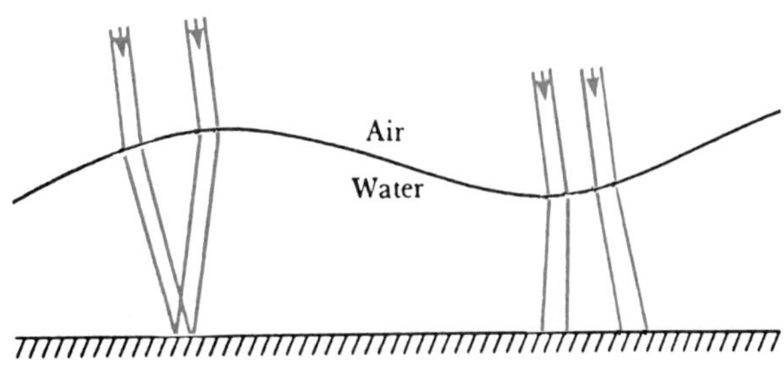

Figure 10-11 *Generation of light patterns on shallow ocean bottoms. When refracted light rays converge momentarily* (left) *the irradiance abruptly increases and is seen as a bright spot. If light rays are diverted* (right) *the spot is momentarily dark.* Source: Preisendorfer (1976).

is necessary that the source of illumination comprise all portions of the visible spectrum. The light source must contain energy for all visible wavelengths if the effect is to simulate daylight.

The range of colors of both daylight and artificial light vary widely. It is important to identify the composition of the "white" light used in the exhibition of fishes. The concept of color temperature is useful for this purpose. *Color temperature* is the absolute or Kelvin temperature, °K, of a perfect radiator (called a *blackbody*) that has a chromaticity (i.e., hue and saturation without regard to value) identical with the object being illuminated.

LAMPS The chromaticity of a lamp does not define how the coloration of an object will appear when illuminated. The light emitted by two different lamps can have the same chromaticity but render the coloration of the same object differently. For example, a warm white fluorescent lamp has approximately the same chromaticity as a high wattage incandescent lamp, but the former has much less deep red in its spectrum. Objects with red coloration therefore do not seem as bright. A problem arises in that lamps with color temperature ranges of 3000 to 6500°K are considered to represent the range of white light, with 5000°K accepted as typical (Table 10-2). Many lamps differ substantially from a blackbody spectral distribution. Consequently, the coloration of objects experience unnatural shifts (i.e., depart from normal coloration as observed in daylight) despite being illuminated under what would be considered "white light." It is possible for two lamps to match in color but differ in spectral distribution. This is because, as mentioned previously, objects reflect or transmit light at different portions of the spectrum only in the proportion in which these wavelengths are present in the light source. The spectral energy distribution of a light source and not simply its "white" color is the basis for its effect on the coloration of objects. Incandescent

TABLE 10-2 Color shift with changes in absolute temperature.

Color	Temperature, °K
Red	800–900
Yellow	3000
White (neutral)	5000
Pale blue	800–10,000
Brilliant blue	60,000–1,000,000

Source: Stephen Spotte, compiled from various sources.

and fluorescent lamps are the types used most commonly to illuminate aquarium exhibits.[9]

INCANDESCENT LAMPS Like the sun and other continuous-spectrum light sources, *incandescent lamps* emit all wavelengths of light, with the peak wavelength (i.e., the radiation emitted) varying with temperature. An incandescent lamp consists of a mounted filament made of wire that is enclosed in a glass bulb. The bulb contains either a gas (ordinarily a mixture of argon and dinitrogen) or a vacuum. The current produced when the lamp is plugged into an electrical circuit must overcome the resistance of the filament. The power consumed in the process heats the filament to incandescence, and it glows. The white-hot filament within the lamp emits a continuous spectrum, and the distribution of spectral energy follows a blackbody distribution closely. Incandescent lamps used in the home ordinarily are in the range 2800 to 3000°K. An incandescent lamp radiates only a small percentage of the total energy from the filament in the visible region. Most is in the infrared region with a comparatively small portion emitted as ultraviolet light (Fig. 10-12). As the figure shows, when the spectral distribution of energy is raised, the radiation in the visible spectrum increases more rapidly than in the infrared region.

FLUORESCENT LAMPS *Fluorescent* objects are self-luminous. They absorb energy at one wavelength and emit it at another that ordinarily is longer. *Fluorescent lamps* thus emit wave-

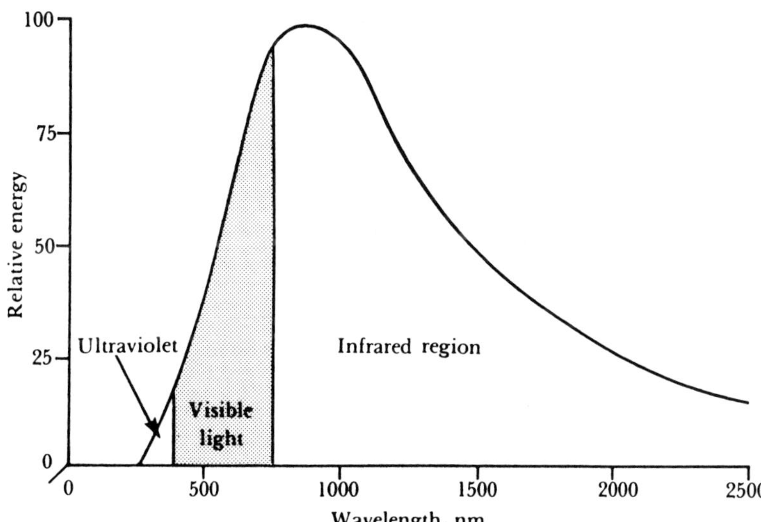

Figure 10-12 *Spectral energy distribution of an incandescent tungsten lamp with approximate color temperature of 3000°K.* Source: Anonymous (1974).

lengths selectively, rather than in a continuous spectrum (Fig. 10-13). A gas sealed inside ordinarily serves as the source of the spectrum, and phosphors used to coat the inside surfaces of the glass tube elicit fluorescent coloration. Radiation produced by the gases strikes the fluorescent phosphor, and the lamp glows and gives off light. The light can be made to appear nearly white if the mix of fluorescent materials is correct. Fluorescent lamps vary markedly in the distribution of spectral energy emitted. All fail to elicit the true coloration of objects they illuminate, partly because inexpensive, safe phosphors in the long wave-

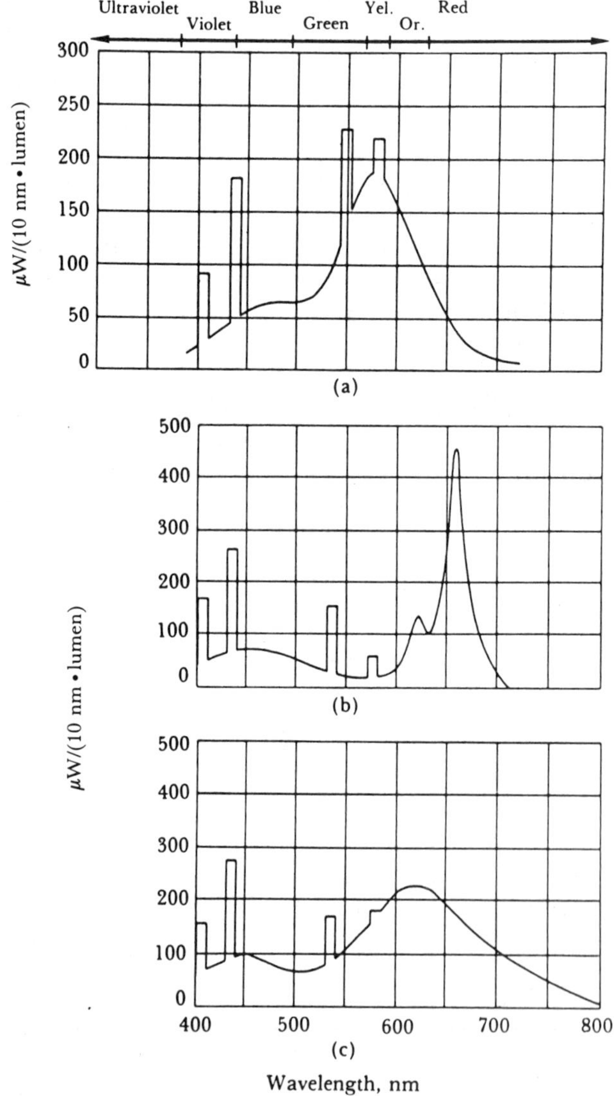

Figure 10-13 Actual spectral energy curves for three commercial 40-W fluorescent lamps. (a) *General Electric Cool White Panel Fluorescent.* (b) *Sylvania Standard Gro-Lux®.* (c) *Sylvania Wide Spectrum Gro-Lux®.* Sources: (a) General Electric Company, Nela Park, Cleveland OH 44112; (b and c) GTE Products Corporation, 630 Fifth Avenue, Suite 2670, New York NY 10111.

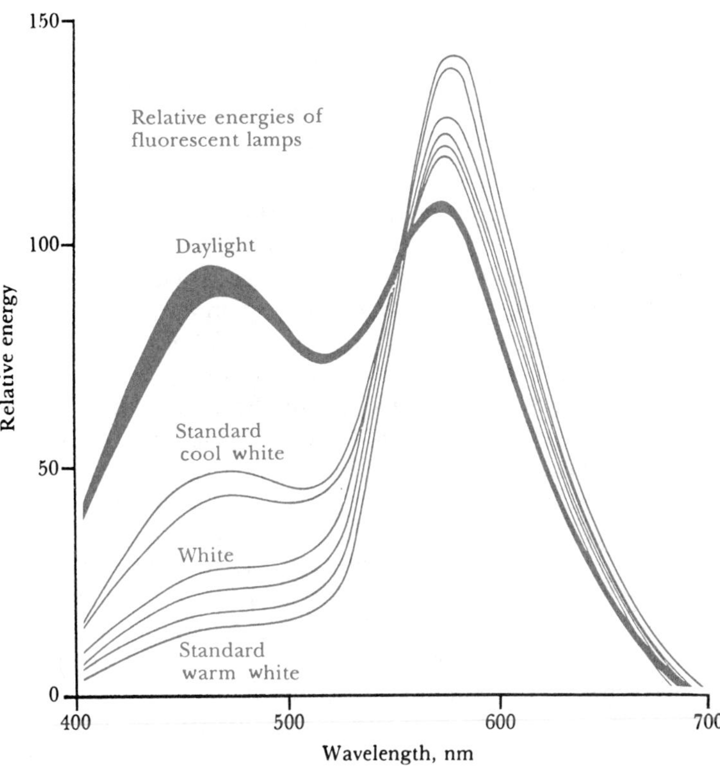

Figure 10-14 *Relative spectral energy curves of four white fluorescent lamps. Approximate corresponding color temperatures are warm white = 3000°K, white = 3500°K, cool white = 4200°K, and daylight = 6500°K.* Source: Nickerson (1983).

lengths (i.e., the reds) are not available. Fluorescent lamps that are able to compensate to some extent are manufactured with special phosphors. Fluorescent lamps are available in several "whites," commonly called warm white, white, cool white, and daylight (Fig. 10-14). Model choices are standard and deluxe. The latter emit more energy in the red wavelengths, and their relative energy distributions are more like those of incandescent lamps of corresponding color temperature.

Illumination and Background Coloration

Submarine illumination differs in important respects from that seen in a fish exhibit, and the aquarist must decide whether the purpose is to simulate nature or create a special effect. Each technique has a proper place in public aquarium exhibits.

NATURALISTIC ILLUMINATION Both the intensity of a light source and its spectrum of colors must be considered if the desired effect is to simulate submarine illumination. These factors are affected by (*1*) vertical depth of the exhibit, (2) coloration of the water (i.e., whether it contains a high concentration of humic compounds), (*3*) coloration of the background and objects in the display, and (*4*) the level of ambient light in front of the exhibit. I shall assume that the water is of maximum clarity and disregard the fact that most of the world ocean is characterized by poor visibility. Natural or not, turbid aquarium water is unpleasant to look at.

On a clear day a considerable amount of incident light is reflected from the surface of the ocean. Radiant energy generated by sources of artificial illumination is paltry in comparison (Table 10-3). The first problem of lighting an aquarium exhibit is to provide adequate illumination throughout the vertical depth of the exhibit; the second is to introduce the light at visible wavelengths simulating daylight. Solving both simultaneously can be accomplished only by using incandescent lamps of daylight color tempratures.

BACKGROUND COLORATION The walls of an exhibit aquarium should be considerably less bright than fishes and other objects of interest. To focus the visitor's concentration, the walls must be inconspicuous, giving only an unconscious illusion of horizontal depth. Hue, value, and color saturation of the paints require careful consideration. These factors must be viewed in terms of the spectrum and intensity of light emitted by the lamps, in addition to the selective light-absorbing properties of water. Incandescent lamps are weak in the blue wavelengths. In air, royal blue, navy blue, and black (listed in descending order of color saturation) are difficult to distinguish

TABLE 10-3 Illumination for normal human vision.

Object	Illumination, lx
Snow in sunlight[1]	97,000
White sand beach in noon sunlight[2]	44,000
Hospital operating table	27,000
Blue sky[1]	5,000
Drafting table	1,000
Office or classroom	400
150-W incandescent lamp in air (10 cm, 90°)	185
White book page in adequate reading light	50
Fish exhibit as seen from the publ:c viewing area at Mystic Marinelife Aquarium (10 cm, 90°)	22
Snow in full moonlight[1]	0.2
Full moonlight in an open pasture[1]	5.4×10^{-3}

Source: Stephen Spotte from measurements made with a photometer (Photo-Meter 1, Quantum Instruments Inc., Garden City NY 11530).

Notes: North latitude 41°19′,[1] north latitude 12°6′.[2]

under incandescent illumination. Underwater the effect is even more marked because of generally low levels of illumination. But any gain from the lamps is lost partly by the tendency of water to transmit blue and green wavelengths and accentuate these colors in paint.

Several systems of color standards are available, but the one described here has been developed jointly by the Inter-Society Color Council (ISCC) and National Bureau of Standards (NBS).[10] The ISCC-NBS system describes each color in terms of Munsell scales of hue, value, and saturation (Fig. 10-15). A given color is classified in three tiers. The first tier is hue (e.g., blue, green). The second indicates degree of saturation, frequently defined by an adjective with the suffix "-ish" (e.g., greenish, yellowish). The third indicates range of value or brightness. Finally, a color is assigned an ISCC-NBS number. There are 262 colors plus five degrees of gray (including white and black), making 267 centroids or "color-name blocks." Value ranges from very light to very dark. Deviations in saturation are described by such terms as grayish, strong, and vivid. A deviation in both value and saturation might be listed as light grayish, pale, blackish, brilliant, or deep. Color 163, for example, is "light bluish green," meaning that its hue is decidedly green but with a bluish cast, and its value is bright. The system is inexact and somewhat confusing, but with a little practice it allows color choices to be narrowed quickly. More important,

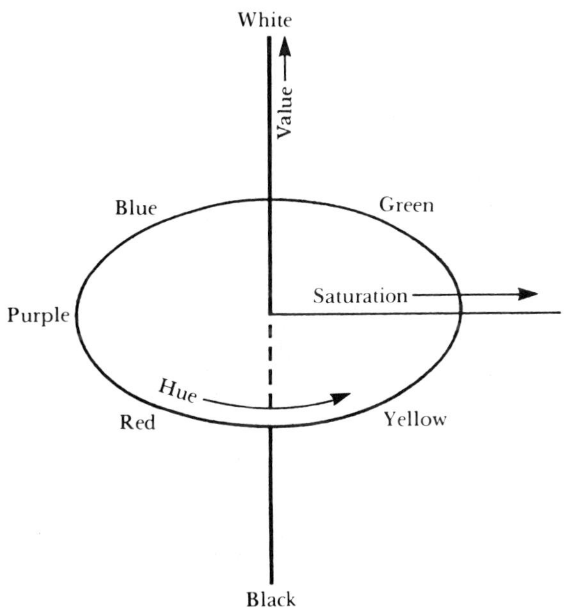

Figure 10-15 Diagrammatic illustration of the ISCC-NBS system of colors showing hue, value (i.e., brightness or lightness), and saturation. Visualize the illustration as a cylinder. The spectrum of hues ranges from violet to red. Degrees of value range from white at the top to black at the bottom with intermediate grays. Saturation increases with distance from the center. Colors nearest the center are least saturated because they contain gray. Colors in a vertical plane are of the same hue, those falling in one of the horizontal planes are of the same value, and ones that lie on concentric cylinders about the white-black axis are of the same saturation. Source: Kelly and Judd (1976a).

it provides a range of colors that are similar in hue and saturation but with varying degrees of value.

In Vitro Photography of Fishes

Photographs used to augment exhibits of living fishes serve either of two functions: (*1*) to identify the species displayed or (*2*) to illustrate some aspect of a fish's natural history that cannot be reproduced under conditions of captivity. Rarely can the same photograph accomplish both purposes. I shall refer to the first type as *species labels* and the second as *photographics* because they can be substituted for hand-drawn illustrations and other types of graphic art. A species label should illustrate just the fish. Bright background light and the presence of corals or other objects are distracting when the intention is to help viewers quickly identify the live specimens before them. A species label reveals nothing about the life of a fish—its courtship behavior, feeding habits, the plants and other animals with which it interacts, or the physical characteristics of its habitat. Photographics are useful to explain the natural history of fishes, and photographs taken in nature are best. Sometimes undersea photographs are unavailable, in which case exposures of live specimens can be made in the exhibit or a small aquarium set up just for photography. When staged and executed carefully, either type of photograph places fishes somewhat in natural context if appropriate background elements are included. I call techniques of this genre *in vitro* fish photography (i.e., photography of fishes through glass).

The subsections that follow deal sequentially with cameras, film, lamps, filters, equipment and procedures for producing species labels, procedures for *in vitro* fish photography, and equipment and techniques for undersea photography.

CAMERAS Any 35-mm SLR (single lens reflex) camera with a built-in light meter is suitable for both species label and *in vitro* fish photography. A "macro lens" is the only lens needed. It should have a focal length of ~55 mm and focus from 1/2 (i.e., the developed image is one-half life size) to infinity. Also required is a tripod. A cable release is useful in some situations because it allows the photographer to step back and avoid casting a shadow on the subject. The white letters and numbers around the lens should be painted out with flat black paint to prevent their reflections from appearing in the finished exposures.

FILTERS[11] For practical purposes (e.g., photography), white light can be considered a mixture of red, green, and blue light

Figure 10-16 *Glass photographic filter.* Source: Anonymous (1981).

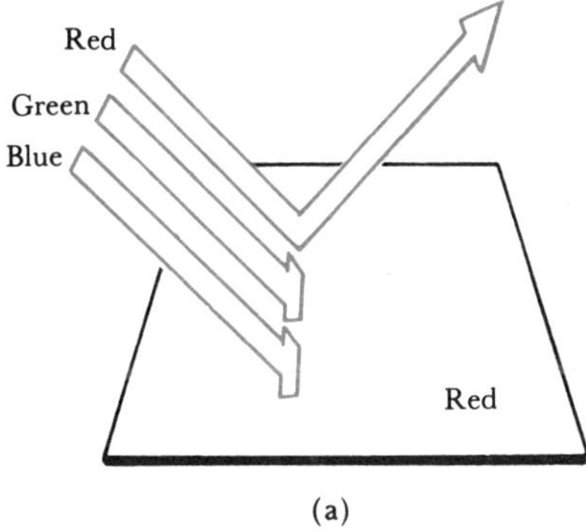

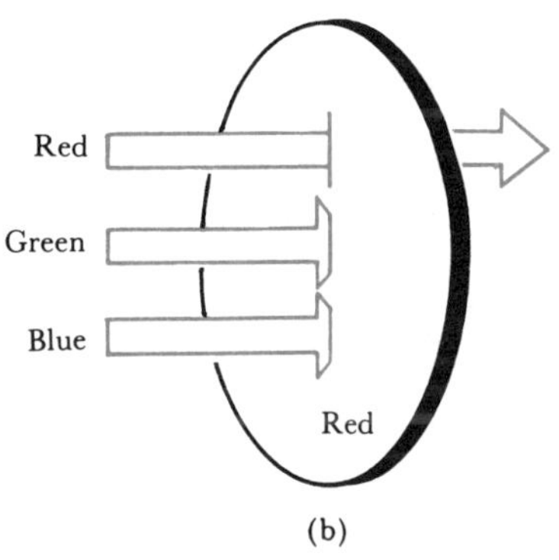

Figure 10-17 (a) *Reflection: an object that absorbs green and blue and reflects red appears red.* (b) *Transmission: a filter that absorbs green and blue and transmits red also appears red.* Source: Stephen Spotte, after Anonymous (1969).

in equal proportions. These are the *primary colors,*[12] which in different combinations comprise all other colors (i.e., every hue). This is possible because, although the number of primary colors is limited, the proportions in which they can be mixed is infinite. The three *secondary colors* are derived by eliminating one primary color and mixing the remaining two in equal proportions: yellow (red plus green), cyan (green plus blue), and magenta (red plus blue).

The most readily available photographic filters are made of optical glass and screw onto the front of the camera lens (Fig. 10-16). A photographic filter selectively absorbs certain wavelengths of light and transmits others. The color of a filter indicates the color of the light transmitted, but this is simply another way of describing which colors have been absorbed (Fig. 10-17). In other words, a red filter transmits red light because it absorbs green and blue light. The quantity of light absorbed depends on the *density* of the filter, or its degree of darkness. When color film is used, the filter imparts its own color to the exposure. Black and white film is achromatic, and objects are gray. They can only appear lighter or darker, and filters lighten objects of the same color.[13] The red markings of a fish photographed with black and white film and a red filter will appear light gray compared with adjacent colors.

Photographic filters have limited but critical application in the production of species labels and photographics. Their utility is confined mostly to situations involving photographs taken under artificial light with certain color films. Filters are not recommended for taking undersea photographs with either black and white or color films.

The most useful filter for species label photography is the *polarizing filter* because it reduces reflections from the surface of the fish. The effect is to remove highlights or ''hot spots'' and increase color saturation. Light rays oscillate in all directions along the path in which they travel (Fig. 10-18). When a light ray strikes a nonmetallic surface, the oscillation occurring in a single plane or direction is reflected completely. Oscillations in other planes are reduced or eliminated, depending on the angle from which the reflected light is viewed. Polarizing filters are manufactured in a double ring arrangement. The threaded ring screws onto the front of the camera lens. The outer ring can be rotated to control the amount of polarized light that is transmitted. Polarizing filters transmit light oscillating in a single plane. When the oscillation is that of polarized light, reflections are erased (Fig. 10-19). The maximum effect from a polarizing filter is achieved when the angle of view and the angle of light striking the object are the same.

Color conversion filters (Table 10-4) change the spectrum of a

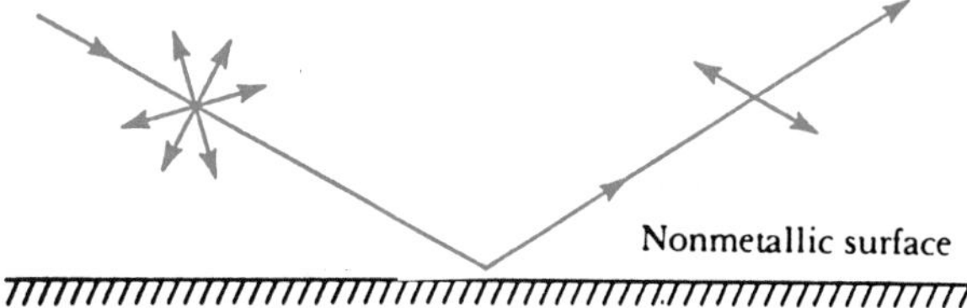

Figure 10-18 *When a light ray from the sun strikes a nonmetallic surface, only the vibrations in one plane are reflected completely. This reflected light, which travels at a right angle to the sun, is polarized light.* Source: Anonymous (1969).

light source to match the spectrum for which a color film is balanced. They are used exclusively with incandescent lamps (e.g., photo or tungsten) and only if the color temperatures of the film and the lamps are incompatible. Daylight films (i.e., films balanced for the color spectrum of daylight) exposed under photo or tungsten lamps have sepia overtones unless the appropriate filter is used. Conversely, tungsten and Type A films appear bluish green when exposed in unfiltered daylight. As the table demonstrates, daylight films exposed outdoors do not require color conversion filters. When used indoors the same film requires an 80B filter if exposed under photo lamps and an 85B filter if tungsten lamps are used.

Color compensating filters are necessary if fluorescent lamps are the sources of illumination. These differ from color conversion filters by adsorbing only red, blue, or green and allowing the remaining two wavelengths to be transmitted. Daylight films exposed under unfiltered fluorescent illumination appear greenish, whereas unfiltered exposures made with Type A and tungsten films have a bluish cast. Photographing fishes for any

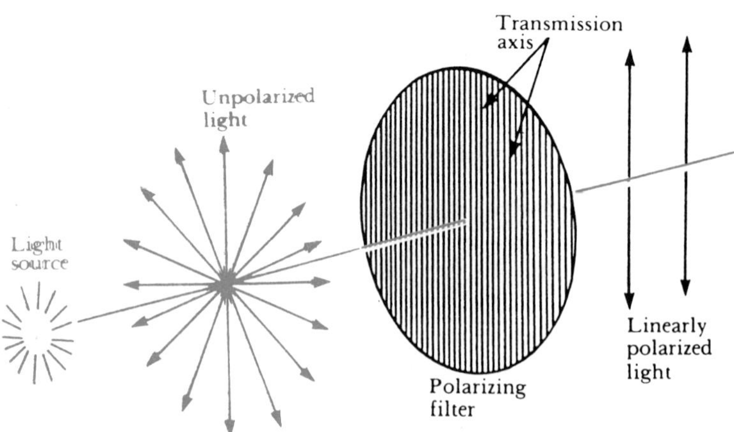

Figure 10-19 *A polarizing filter transforms nonpolarized light to polarized light by transmitting only light wave components having an electric field vector that is parallel to the axis of transmission. The light allowed to pass through the filter is polarized linearly.* Source: Feinberg (1983).

TABLE 10-4 Color conversion filters required for Kodak color films.

Film	Balanced for	Source of illumination: Daylight	Photo lamp (3400°K)	Tungsten (3200°K)
Kodachrome 25	Daylight, electronic strobe	None	80B	80A
Kodachrome 64	Daylight, electronic strobe	None	80B	80A
Kodachrome 25 Type A	Photo lamps	85	None	82A
Ektachrome 200	Daylight, electronic strobe	None	80B	80A
Ektachrome 400	Daylight, electronic strobe	None	80B	80A
Ektachrome (Tungsten)	Tungsten	85B	81A	None

Source: Stephen Spotte, compiled from various sources.

purpose under fluorescent illumination is not recommended because of the difficulty in achieving the correct color balance. If fluorescent lamps are the only light sources available use the filters listed in Table 10-5. Stick to one type of lamp. Mixing lamps only worsens the color balance problem. Color compensating filters are available in squares of gelatin, plastic, or glass and used with a special holder fastened to the front of the lens with an adapter ring.

TABLE 10-5 Kodak color compensating filters for exposures made under fluorescent lamps and the number of f stops that the exposure must be increased because of the subsequent loss of light.

Lamp type	Film type: Daylight	Tungsten	Type A
Daylight	40M + 30Y + 1 stop	85B + 30M + 10Y + 1 stop	85 + 30M + 10Y + 1 stop
White	20C + 30M + 1 stop	40M + 40Y + 1 stop	40M + 30Y + 1 stop
Warm white	40C + 40M + $1\frac{1}{3}$ stop	30M + 20Y + 1 stop	30M + 10Y + 1 stop
Warm white deluxe	60C + 30M + $1\frac{2}{3}$ stop	10Y + $\frac{1}{3}$ stop	No filter None
Cool white	30M + $\frac{2}{3}$ stop	50M + 60Y + $1\frac{1}{3}$ stop	50M + 50Y + $1\frac{1}{3}$ stop
Cool white deluxe	30C + 20M + 1 stop	10M + 30Y + $\frac{2}{3}$ stop	10M + 20Y + $\frac{2}{3}$ stop

Source: Anonymous (1969).

Undersea Photography of Fishes

CAMERAS The recent development of reliable equipment, principally the Nikonos camera (Fig. 10-20) and several models of watertight electronic strobes, has greatly simplified the technological aspects of undersea photography. The Nikonos is compact and does not require a watertight housing, but unfortunately it is a viewfinder camera and unsuitable for taking consistently acceptable photographs of fishes except in special situations. In *viewfinder cameras* a small optical viewfinder separate from the lens permits the photographer to see the image of the subject *approximately* as the lens sees it, but the boundaries of the two photographic fields are not identical because the angles are different. The lenses of viewfinder cameras are fixed and cannot be focused. The subject distance must be estimated and set manually. This is not troublesome with sessile subjects, but most fishes are active and seldom pose quietly while an adjustment is made. As a result, the chance that the subject will be out of focus is greatly increased. Viewfinder cameras also introduce problems of parallax or image displacement. *Parallax* is the difference in the position of the image from the vantage point of the viewfinder compared with that of the lens (Fig. 10-21a). The problem worsens as the camera-subject distance is decreased. In undersea photography few exposures are made at distances greater than ~1 m, and parallax is a major consideration. Contrary to advice offered by many of the experts, I recommend not using the Nikonos for fish photography except when wide-angle exposures are acceptable.

In my experience a single lens reflex or SLR camera encased in a watertight housing is preferable by far. The photographer must be able to frame swimming fishes quickly and bring them

Figure 10-20 *Nikonos V camera.* Source: Nikon Inc., 623 Stewart Avenue, Garden City NY 11530.

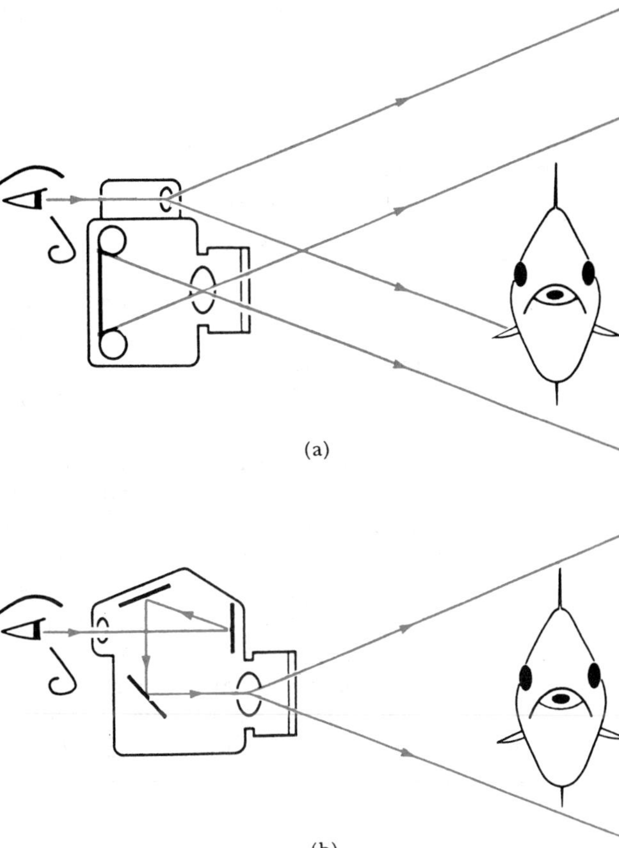

Figure 10-21 (a) *Parallax is troublesome when viewfinder cameras are used, because the angle of the object seen through the viewfinder is different from the angle seen by the lens.* (b) *With SLR cameras the eye and the lens see the object from the same angle.* Source: Stephen Spotte, drawn from various sources.

into focus with precision, a luxury not possible with viewfinder cameras. Single lens reflex cameras offer ''through-the-lens'' viewing; in other words, the photographer's eye and the lens see the image of the subject from the same angle (Fig. 10-21b). Parallax is not a factor. The manually operated light meters on older SLRs require the photographer to control the amount of light reaching the film by adjusting either the lens aperture or shutter speed (new models perform this step automatically). Typically, the electrical circuit linking the shutter speed and electronic strobe are synchronized (e.g., $\frac{1}{60}$ s), meaning that only the lens aperture could be varied. This seldom was a handicap because light meters are largely superfluous beneath the ocean. In most situations it is safe to assume that ambient light is nonexistent. The illumination required to expose film properly is supplied entirely by the electronic strobe. Any added effect from ambient light is apparent only in shallow, clear waters, or when the camera is aimed toward the surface from below. At depths of several metres photographs taken at midnight and at noon require essentially the same exposure. Modern SLRs have light metering systems capable of providing automatic exposure control, which in practical terms represents nothing more than the intensity of light reflected off the subject by the strobe. Either type of camera is suitable.

Any SLR used inside a watertight housing must have a ''sportfinder'' or comparable device to enlarge the field of vision (Fig. 10-22). This is necessary because the distance from the photographer's eye to the viewfinder is lengthened by the face mask and by the space between the viewfinder and viewing port of the housing. In older cameras the sportfinder replaced the light meter, and the latter device could not be used. As mentioned, this was seldom a problem.

The lens recommended previously for *in vitro* fish photography also is the one most suitable for photographing fishes in nature (a 55-mm lens that focuses from 1/2 to infinity). For panoramic photographs a 24-mm lens is suitable. These are the only lenses needed in most circumstances. Paint the front surfaces of the focusing gear rings and any white lettering around the lenses with flat black paint to prevent reflections in the finished exposure (Fig. 10-23). This is particularly important in the case of the 24-mm lens because panoramic exposures sometimes are framed by aiming the camera toward the surface, which allows ambient light to reflect off the lens and back onto the scene. The result is a faint image of the lens superimposed on the developed exposure.

ELECTRONIC STROBES[14] Undersea photographs can be illuminated with flash bulbs or electronic strobes. The flash bulb

Figure 10-22 *An SLR camera equipped with a ''sportfinder.'' The sportfinder is mandatory when an SLR camera is placed inside a watertight housing because the distance between the photographer's eye and the viewfinder is greater than in air. The added distance is a result of the presence of a face mask, the viewing port of the housing, and the space between the viewing port and the viewfinder.* Source: Stephen Spotte.

Figure 10-23 *An SLR camera mounted on the inside back plate of a watertight housing. The focusing gear ring and white lettering around the lens have been painted out with flat black paint.* Source: Stephen Spotte.

technique is rarely used today, and I shall not mention it again. A strobe (Fig. 10-24) consists of a high-voltage power supply (in more powerful models, dry cells or rechargeable nickel-cadmium power packs), one or more capacitors, a triggering circuit, and a flash tube. Firing the strobe converts the high-voltage direct current from the power supply into light. The capacitors are charged by the power supply, and energy is stored until released. The number of capacitors is determined by the range of light output adjustments. For example, if settings for 50, 100, and 150 J* of light output are provided, the

*J (joule) = 1 W-s (watt-second).

Figure 10-24 *Watertight electronic strobe.* Source: Ikelite Underwater Systems, P. O. Box 88100, Indianapolis IN 46208.

strobe typically will contain capacitors with these same quantities of energy.[15] The flash tube is a glass lamp filled with xenon gas. When the strobe is fired by triggering the shutter release of the camera, electrical energy stored in the capacitor is applied instantly between the electrodes at each end of the flash tube. Discharged voltage causes the xenon gas to glow brilliantly, producing a brief, intense light impulse or ''flash.''

A durable, coiled cord connects the strobe to the camera inside the watertight housing. The integrity of the electrical circuit is maintained with a coupling device. In one model the male or plug end is called an ''e. o. connector'' (Fig. 10-25) and is located at the end of the coiled cord. The female portion, often called a ''bulkhead connector,'' is bolted to the housing. When the coupling is joined, an electric current is conducted through contact points of beryllium copper. This design allows the device to be disconnected and rejoined underwater without short-circuiting the strobe.

The strobe is perhaps the most important piece of undersea photographic equipment. Its power and angle of coverage represent the margin between mediocre photographs and excellent ones. The energy storage rating of the capacitors should be at least 100 J, and 150 J is even better. Angle of coverage should be as great as possible. Weak strobes limit depth of field (i.e., exposures can be made only at large lens apertures), and narrow angles of coverage preclude the use of wide angle lenses.

WATERTIGHT HOUSINGS Modern watertight housings are often equipped with visual or audio leak detectors and internal lighting that enables the photographer to see the lens aperture, shutter speed, and exposure counter. Such amenities are convenient but not necessary. Any model is suitable, so long as it keeps out water. My own two housings have not been manu-

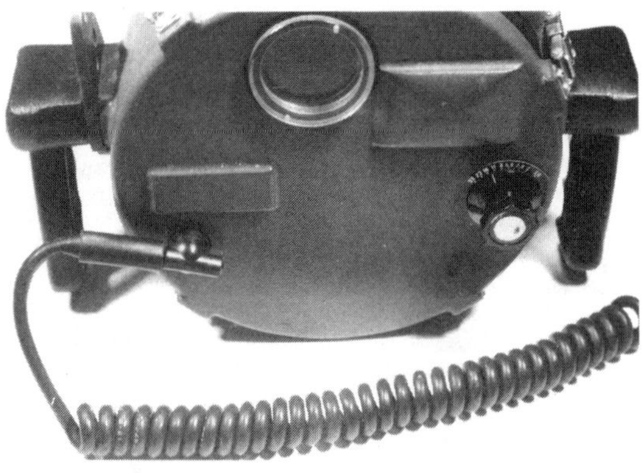

Figure 10-25 An e. o. connector attached to the bulkhead connector of a watertight SLR camera housing. Source: Stephen Spotte.

(a)

(b)

Figure 10-26 Watertight SLR camera housings made of cast aluminum. Sources: (a) Tussey Underwater Systems, 5724 Dolphin Place, La Jolla CA 92037. (b) Aqua Vision Systems Inc., Box 1097, Postal Station Point Claire, Quebec H9S 4H9, Canada.

factured for several years, but with good maintenance they have remained serviceable. The bodies of most housings are constructed of cast aluminum or aluminum alloys (Fig. 10-26), or of clear acrylic (Fig. 10-27). All camera controls are manipulated by stainless steel shafts attached to exterior control knobs made of hard plastic. The ends of the shafts that protrude into the housing are equipped with machined acrylic or aluminum devices shaped to the specific mechanisms on the camera they are intended to activate. The control knobs enable the photographer to trigger the shutter release and change shutter speeds and lens apertures. The interchangeable ''port'' or acrylic window in front of the lens can be convex (i.e., ''domed'') or flat. The same domed port is often suitable for lenses with focal lengths between 24 and 55 mm. Lenses longer than 55 mm ordinarily require flat ports.

Watertight seals throughout the housing are maintained with O-rings. The control knob shafts are inserted in ''packing glands'' in the body of the housing (Fig. 10-28). These are aluminum bolts with holes through the centers. A watertight seal is maintained around each bolt by an O-ring. Another O-ring set in a groove inside keeps water from leaking into the housing from around the shaft.

An O-ring serves its function so long as it remains round and intact. After several months under constant pressure an O-ring

Figure 10-27 Watertight SLR camera housing made of clear acrylic. Source: Ikelite Underwater Systems, P. O. Box 88100, Indianapolis IN 46208.

tends to flatten. Old O-rings crack. To prevent either possibility the housing should be stored in a cool location with the pressure on the O-rings released. The O-rings should be kept lightly moistened at all times with clear silicone grease. The kind used for laboratory glassware is suitable. Only a thin layer is neces-

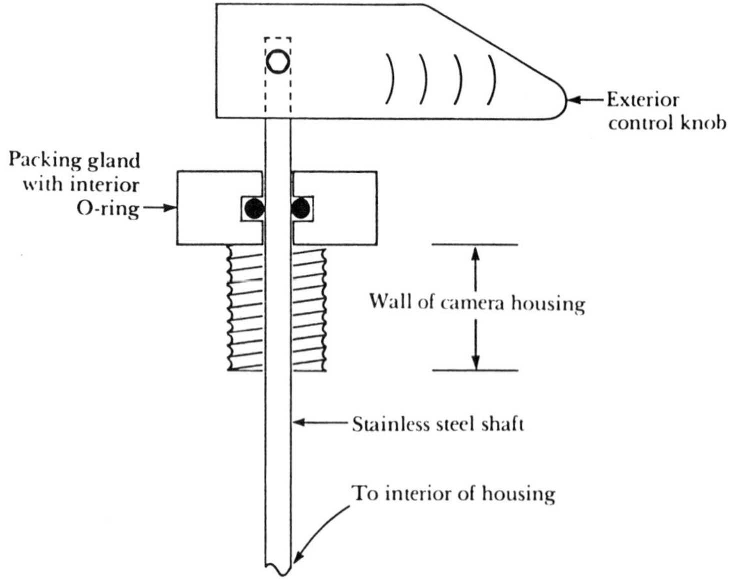

Figure 10-28 Packing gland used in watertight camera housings. Source: Stephen Spotte.

sary; too much grease serves no useful purpose. Control knob shafts should be greased each time the housing is used to prevent excess wear against the O-rings. If the housing has been stored for long periods, make a preliminary dive without the camera inside to check for leaks. The main O-ring (i.e., the one around the opening used to remove the camera or change film) should be taken out after each day of diving and wiped clean with tissue paper, then greased lightly and replaced. The groove should also be cleaned. A grain of sand pressing against the O-ring deforms the neoprene and is a site of potential leaks.

FILMS The flash tubes of electronic strobes have color temperatures that approximate daylight, and only daylight color films should be used. The color of the light emitted by strobes is slightly blue, and Ektachrome™ films or equivalent are not recommended, despite the ease of processing. In my opinion the best film for undersea fish photography is Kodachrome™ 64.

The Philosophy of Exhibiting a Fish[16]

Public aquarium visitors are sometimes disappointed when exhibits fail to coincide with imprinted images of the undersea world obtained at the movies. What a live exhibit gains over cinema in realism it necessarily loses in grandeur. Thus neither medium is completely successful simply because nature can never be copied. But if public aquariums have little in common with movies they have much in common with live stage plays, where adherence to realism has pragmatic limits that are understood and accepted by the audience. A drama skillfully produced gives an *illusion* of reality, provided the audience concentrates on the actors and not the stage settings. Once the curtain rises the *flats* (painted background panels) are never objects of attention, nor are the stage props. A chair is merely a chair, a place for an actor to sit. Light—its intensity and color—is a metaphor for emotion. In fact, only the actors matter—their actions and words.

The objective of a public aquarium exhibit is to place fishes in perspective, and the best approach is analogous to staging a play. Consider the walls and sides of the exhibit to represent flats. Simulated corals, rocks, and other inanimate objects become props, and mood is again focused by light. Directing attention to the fishes has everything to do with background, illumination, and the placement of objects. It has little to do with detail *per se,* just as paint peeling from the back of a chair used in a stage setting is of no importance. To replicate painstakingly the detail in every coral or rock serves no useful purpose if the focus of a fish exhibit is fishes, not rocks. The *illusion* of a coral

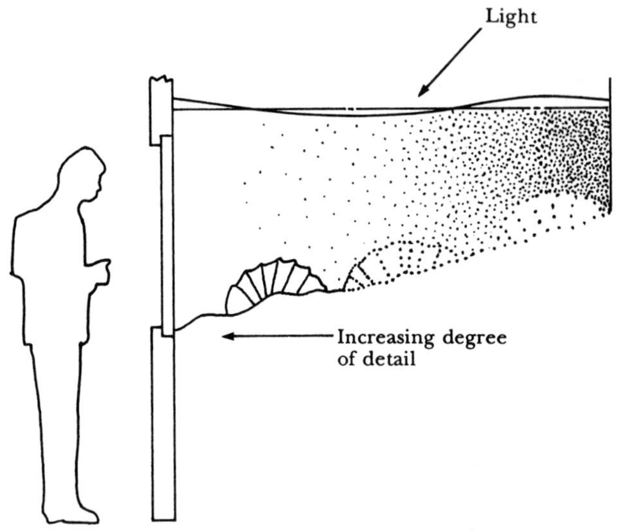

Figure 10-29 *Diagrammatic illustration of the relationship between light intensity and degree of detail required in an exhibit as a function of distance of the viewer's eye from the focal point.* Source: Stephen Spotte.

reef or tidal riverbed can be achieved by placing a few exquisitely detailed objects directly in front of the visitor. The illusion is sustained when objects of lesser detail are then placed in dimmer light farther from view (Fig. 10-29). A visual image of the closer objects is ''remembered'' when the eye shifts to others that are more distant but of the same general size, shape, and coloration.

Layout of Exhibits

Exhibit aquariums can be designed for specific functions or purely esthetic reasons. In the first instance form follows function; in the second only form matters, and the exhibits are transformed into *objets trouvés*. An arrangement of living exhibits (I much prefer this to ''fish tanks'') involves more than pleasant architectural symmetry. If visitors are to be informed, their attention must not be allowed to wander. The exhibit before them is the only one of importance, not those yet to be seen or seen already.

EXHIBIT AQUARIUM SHAPES The development of clear acrylics has made possible exhibit aquarium designs limited only by the imagination. Two popular shapes currently in use are the cylinder (Fig. 10-30) and half-cylinder (Fig. 10-31). Other shapes include hexagons, prisms, and even oversized cocktail glasses. None is more functional than a simple square or rectangle, and small convex viewing surfaces cause substantial dis-

Figure 10-30 *Free-standing cylindrical exhibit aquariums.* Source: Marine Science Museum, Tokai University, Tokai, Japan.

tortion, particularly at close range. All, however, are pleasing to look at, and therein lies their value.

LAYOUT AND VISITOR MOVEMENT No quantitative studies of what constitutes a superior layout of aquarium exhibits have been made. Perhaps a nearly perfect layout is impossible to achieve. Any treatment of the problem at this time is subjec-

Figure 10-31 *Half-cylinder exhibit aquariums placed against a wall.* Source: Sunshine International Aquarium, Tokyo, Japan.

tive. Logic and experience nonetheless indicate that some arrangements are better than others, provided certain assumptions are made. In the brief discussion that follows I shall assume that (*1*) visitors should be presented with one exhibit at a time and, (*2*) distractions such as reflected light and unnecessary physical barriers are esthetically unpleasing and detract from the learning experience. I emphasize again that this represents my own opinion.

The layout of aquarium exhibits has traditionally been patterned after art galleries and natural history museums: visitors are led first down one wall "gallery" and then back along another directly opposite (Fig. 10-32). Such an arrangement is unsatisfactory in all three types of exhibitions, but particularly so in the case of aquariums. This is because the public areas ordinarily are darker and contain more reflective glass surfaces. Exhibits should be placed strategically in the path of the visitor with perhaps just a hint of what lies beyond. The "art gallery" layout allows visitors to see exhibits other than the one directly before them (all of the exhibits in a nearly empty exhibition hall). This encourages aimless viewing. The absence of a traffic pattern obstructs the flow of people on crowded days and discourages any attempt to tell a story by incorporating separate elements into a sequence of individual exhibits. In addition, backlighting from the row of exhibits on the opposite wall casts a silhouette of the visitors' images on the windows of exhibits directly before them. These deficiencies can be remedied to some extent simply by construction of a dividing wall to serve as a light barrier.

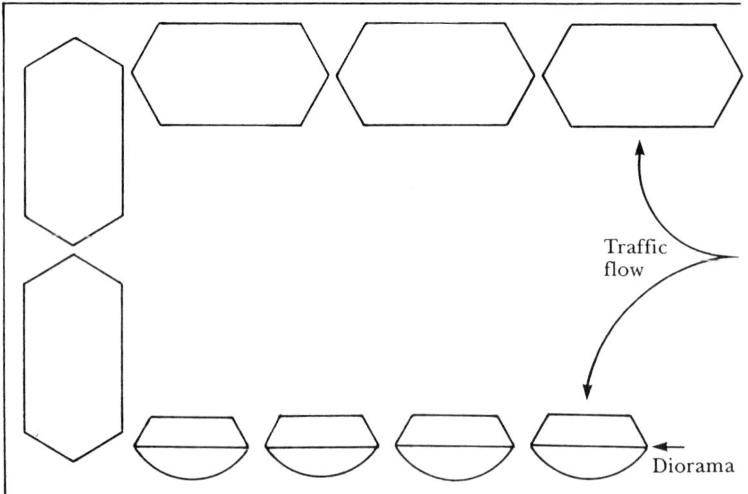

Figure 10-32 *Public aquarium exhibits in a "gallery" arrangement, a less desirable design than Figure 10-33.* Source: Stephen Spotte.

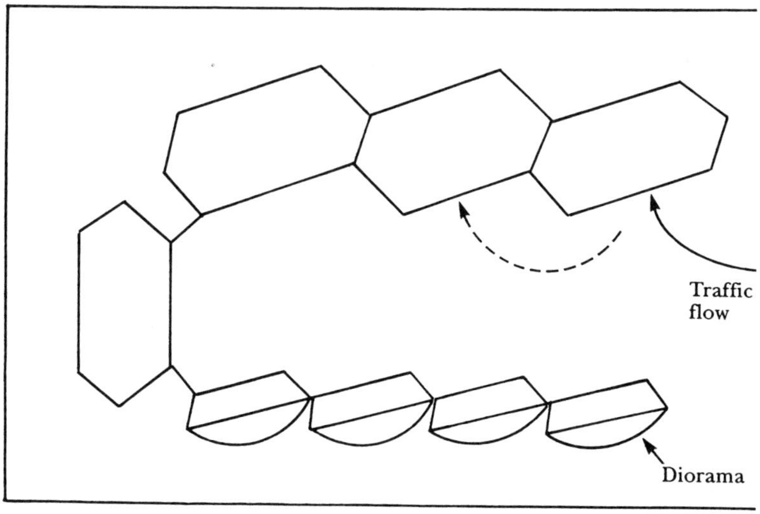

Traffic flow

Diorama

Figure 10-33 *Design in which the exhibits are angled. The visitor's interest is heightened because fewer exhibits are fully visible from any location.* Source: Kelley (1960b).

In a far more pleasing and functional layout, exhibits are oriented so that each is presented to the visitor without the distraction of adjacent or opposite exhibits (Fig. 10-33).

TECHNOLOGY

Method 10.1 Aquarium Optics

The viewing window of an aquarium exhibit can be flat (plane-surfaced) or curved. If curved, it can be concave or convex. The shape of a window and the visitor's distance from it affect the apparent location of fishes on display. Assume that a flat window of refractive index n_2 separates air and water having refractive indices of n_1 and n_3 (Fig. 10-34). Assume that n_1 and n_3

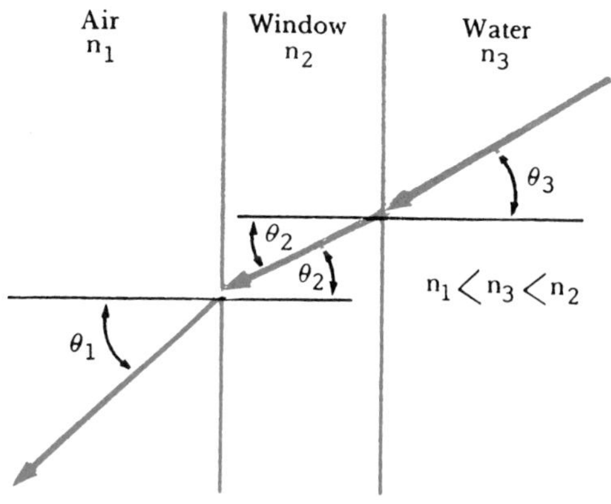

Figure 10-34 *Angles of a light beam traveling from water to air through glass. This situation is typical of an aquarium exhibit illuminated from above.* Source: Williams (1970).

are $<n_2$. Light from an underwater object is refracted first at the surface glass and again as it leaves the glass. By Snell's law

$$n_3 \sin \theta_3 = n_2 \sin \theta_2 \tag{10.2}$$

and

$$n_2 \sin \theta_2 = n_1 \sin \theta_1 \tag{10.3}$$

If the above equations are combined,

$$n_3 \sin \theta_3 = n_1 \sin \theta_1 \tag{10.4}$$

So long as the window has parallel faces, bending of the light rays passing from water to air (or vice versa) is independent of the refractive index of the glass. Thus a single interface can be used to calculate the angle of refraction without error, although thickness of the glass causes a lateral displacement of light rays.

How to Find the Maximum Angle of View Through a Flat Window

1 Look at Figure 10-35. Assume that the refractive index of water is 1.33 and that

$$\alpha = \arctan\left(\frac{h}{d}\right) \tag{10.5}$$

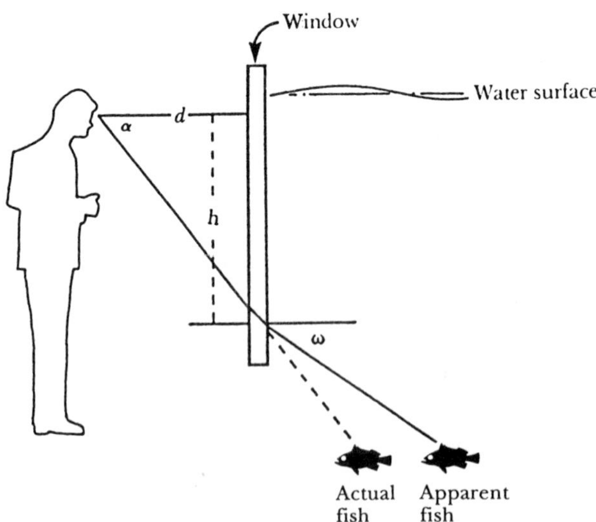

Figure 10-35 *Variation in apparent and actual positions of a fish in an aquarium exhibit caused by the angle of refraction.* Source: Gary Adams and Stephen Spotte, Sea Research Foundation.

where h = height (cm) and d = distance of the viewer from the window (cm). The maximum angle of view is represented by ω. To solve Snell's law for ω,

$$\omega = \arcsin\left(\frac{\sin \alpha}{1.33}\right) \tag{10.6}$$

or

$$\omega = \arcsin\left[\frac{\sin(\arctan [h/d])}{1.33}\right] \tag{10.7}$$

2 If d = 36 cm and h = 56 cm, find the maximum angle of view, ω. From equation 10.5,

$$\alpha = \arctan\left(\frac{56}{36}\right) = 52.7$$

From equation 10-6,

$$\omega = \arcsin(\sin 52.7/1.33) = \arcsin(0.841/1.33) = 39.2°$$

Therefore, any portion of the aquarium beyond the 39.2° line is invisible to the viewer.

How to Find the Maximum Angle of View Through a Convex Window

1 Look at Figure 10-36. Again assume that the refractive index of water is 1.33. According to Snell's law, $\sin \alpha / \sin \omega = 1.33$. However, $\alpha = 90°$ and $\sin 90° = 1$, so that $\omega = \arcsin(1/1.33) = 48.7°$.

2 Assume that the window is made of acrylic and has a refractive index of 1.54. The refractive angle in the window is

$$\omega - \arcsin\left(\frac{1}{1.54}\right) = 40.5°$$

The angle at the acrylic-water interface will be the same if the radius of the aquarium is large (inset of Fig. 10-36).

3 The angle in the water is described by

$$\frac{\sin 40.5°}{\sin \omega} = \frac{1.33}{1.54}$$

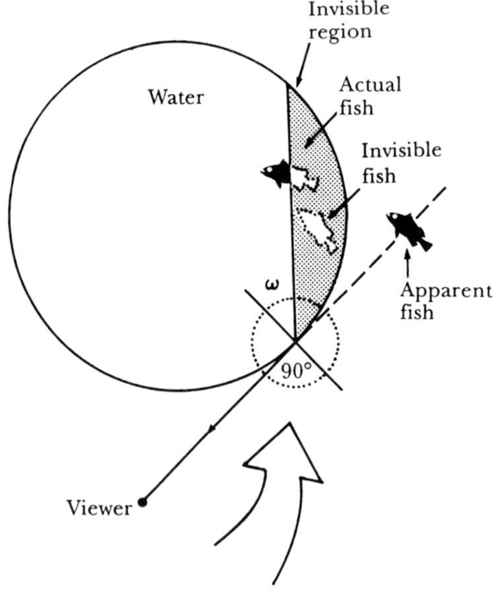

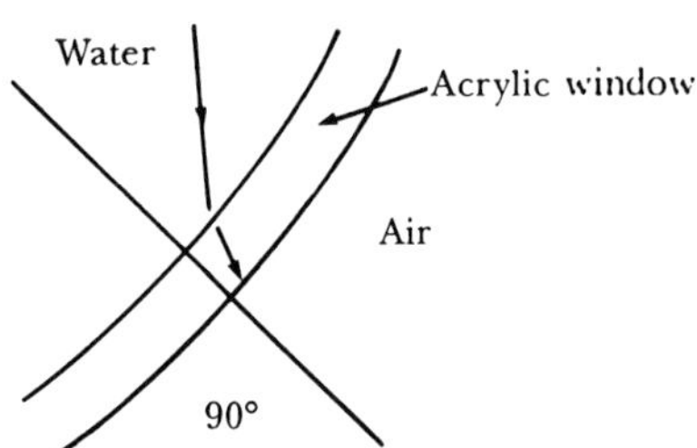

Figure 10-36 *Optics of a convex aquarium made of clear acrylic. A fish in the darkened area will be invisible from the viewer's position, even though the aquarium contains no structural mullions that would block the sightline.* Source: Gary Adams and Stephen Spotte, Sea Research Foundation.

or

$$\omega = \arcsin\left(\frac{1.5 \sin 40.5^\circ}{1.33}\right) = 48.8^\circ$$

Note that characteristics of the window have no important effect on the angle unless the thickness is large relative to the radius of the aquarium.

How to Calculate Angles of Disappearing Walls

The side walls of aquariums can be angled away to make them invisible to the viewer (Fig. 10-37). In this example, i (the angle of incidence) = arctan (L/d), r = the angle of refraction, L = length of the viewing window (cm), and d = distance of the viewer from the glass (cm). Assume the refractive index to be 1.34. By Snell's law

$$\frac{\sin i}{\sin r} = 1.34$$

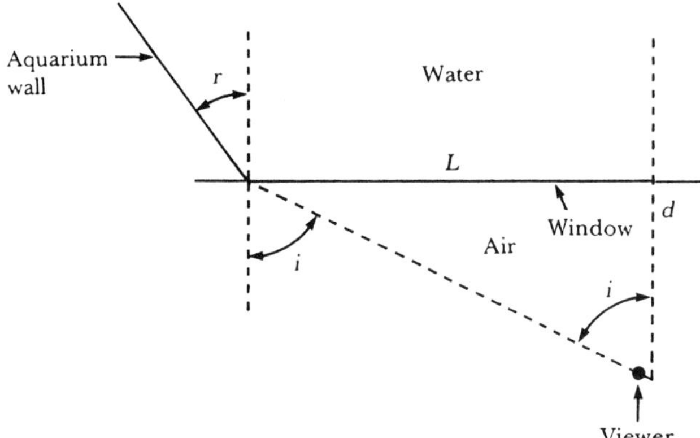

Figure 10-37 *Plan view of an aquarium with a disappearing wall. Calculations are provided in the text.* Source: Gary Adams and Stephen Spotte, Sea Research Foundation.

Therefore

$$r = \arcsin\left(\frac{\sin i}{1.34}\right) = \arcsin\left[\frac{\sin(\arctan[L/d])}{1.34}\right]$$

If $d = 30$ cm and $L = 50$ cm, then $r = 39.8°$. Similarly, if $L =$ 100, 200, and 300 cm, the value of r will be 45.6°, 47.6°, and 47.9°. These represent the angles that the side walls must be to disappear from view. The value of r is insensitive to large window lengths or decreases in viewing distance. The limiting value of r is $\sim$48.3°.

Method 10.2 Selection of Background Colors

In my opinion, backgrounds of aquarium exhibits should be painted several colors instead of just one. Single colors do not give an illusion of extended horizontal depth because contrast is missing. The colors selected are preferably of the same hue and saturation and differ only in value. All paints should be nonreflective (i.e., mat finish) blues and greens. Plates 15 and 16 are reproductions of a series of ISCC-NBS centroid colors. The layout of colored chips in each series follows the pattern illustrated diagrammatically in Fig. 10-15. The white-gray-black vertical axis (here called the gray axis) on the left is identical in every series of centroid colors, as is the degree of gray in the background. All colors depicted in a single figure are of the same hue. Colors in a vertical column contain the same degree of saturation. Saturation in each horizontal column increases with distance from the gray axis, or to the right. Value decreases from top to bottom in each vertical column. Colors of low saturation (i.e., those nearer the gray axis) are preferred.

Background coloration should match the coloration of seawater in the region of the world an exhibit is meant to depict. Seawater along the east coast of North America has a yellowish green appearance because it contains large amounts of humic compounds and POC. In other regions the coloration of the ocean may be green. An example is coastal southern California, represented here by the vertical bluish green series 162 to 166 (Plate 15). Clear, tropical seas are predominantly blue because concentrations of humic compounds and POC are low. The vertical series of centroid colors starting with 180 at the top and ending with 183 at the bottom (blue) would be a good choice (Plate 16). Any series of colors painted on a background will appear true only if the concentration of dissolved organic carbon, which includes humic compounds, is kept low (Chapter 2).

How to Apply Colors to Backgrounds

1 Select an appropriate vertical series of centroid colors from Plates 15 or 16, or from the original source publication.

2 Match each color with a paint available commercially. Unfortunately, paint manufacturers do not state whether their colors match ISCC-NBS centroid colors. This task is left to the aquarist. Use only one generic paint (e.g., epoxy).

3 Start at the bottom and work up. Apply the paint in horizontal streaks of increasing degrees of value from bottom to top (Fig. 10-38). For each color change, blend the top color into the one below. If light is then focused near the glass,

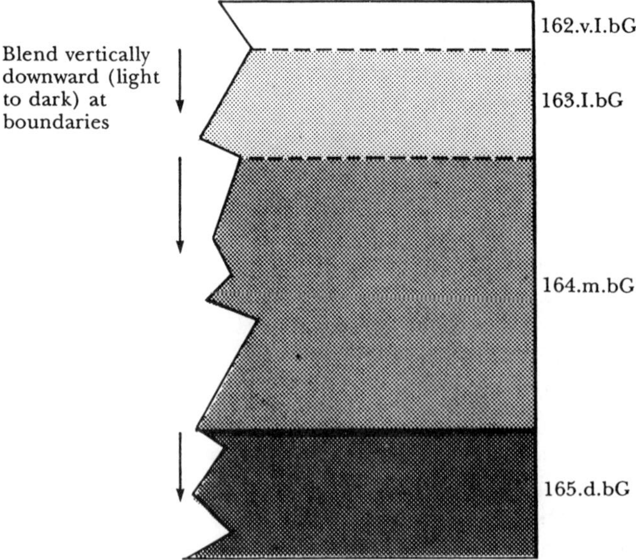

Figure 10-38 *Select several paints that match a series of ISCC-NBS centroid colors (in this case bluish green, Plate 15). Apply in horizontal streaks with the color of greatest value (i.e., brightness or lightness) at the top and the color of least value at the bottom. Where two colors meet, blend in the direction of the arrows.* Source: Stephen Spotte.

two effects are achieved. The first is an exaggerated impression of rapidly diminishing light in the vertical. The second is a softening of the walls.

Method 10.3 Demonstration of Light Reflection by Silvery Fishes

To illustrate how light is reflected from the sides of silvery fishes a light source must be placed inside the exhibit, and the area above must be kept in darkness (Fig. 10-39). The technique apparently was developed by Japanese public aquarists, but is now applied in the United States and Europe. Use a cool white fluorescent lamp sealed inside a length of clear acrylic pipe. To keep the lamp invisible, place it below the bottom of the viewing window but near the front of the exhibit. Stray light creates an undesirable effect by illuminating the space between the fishes and the window. This problem can be overcome by use of a reflector.

Method 10.4 Polarized Light Exhibits[17]

The semi-transparency of some fishes makes them excellent models for illustrating internal structures such as the swimbladder and spinal column. These features of fish anatomy can be revealed in a dark-field illuminator (Fig. 10-40). The illuminator consists of an incandescent lamp in a reflector, a diffusing screen, a sheet of polarizing plastic, an aquarium with fishes, and a second sheet of polarizing plastic. The polarizing screens are crossed to reduce the background brilliance (Fig. 10-19),

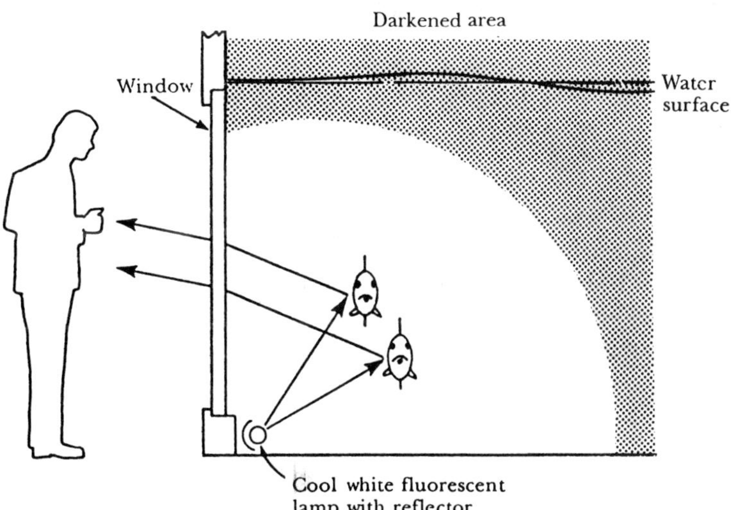

Figure 10-39 The reflective properties of silvery fishes can be demonstrated by illuminating them from the side. The illumination level must be greater than the level of illumination from above and behind. Source: Stephen Spotte.

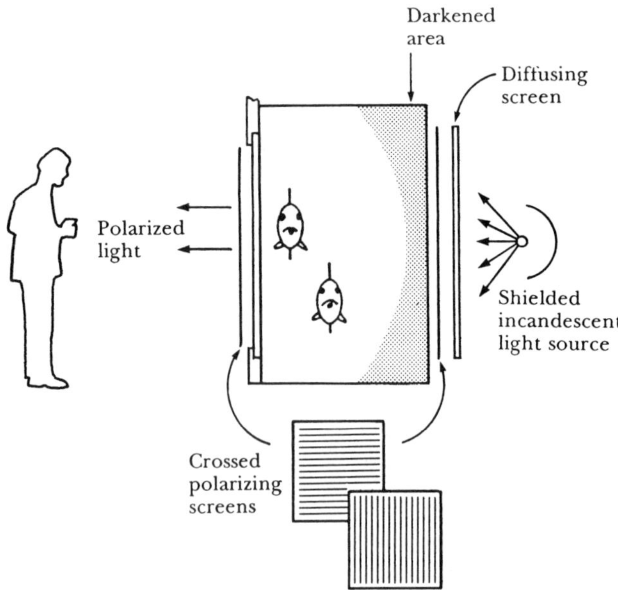

Figure 10-40 *Polarized light exhibit.* Source: Stephen Spotte after Kelley (1960a).

which extinguishes nearly all light. The fishes rotate the plane of polarization by diffusing the transmitted light, and by the *anisotropic* (doubly refractive) properties of their tissues. This causes their internal structures to glow brightly against the dark background.

Method 10.5 Species Label Photography

The best species labels are painted from live or freshly dead specimens. Paintings provide uniformity of size and coloration, features difficult to duplicate with a series of photographs. Photographs used as species labels frequently suffer from other inconsistencies, principally orientation of the specimens (they should all face in the same direction) and defects caused by careless technique. This last problem includes high-lights from surface reflections (which reduce color saturation), the use of damaged or decomposing specimens, and inclusion of backgrounds. Such flaws give the appearance of haphazard presentation. It bears mentioning again that the purpose of a species label is to enable visitors to identify the live fishes in the exhibit. Extraneous factors that distract from this purpose are undesirable.

How to Prepare the Specimen[18]

1 Fishes intended for species label photography must be sacrificed. Use only healthy, freshly dead specimens and store them on ice until just before use.

2 Standard taxonomic procedure calls for illustrating the left side of a fish (i.e., it should face left). Blot the right side dry with paper towels and use surgical scissors to remove any fins on the right side that may protrude into the photographic field. The pelvic fin ordinarily is the most troublesome. Lay the fish on its right side on a block of styrofoam covered with polyethylene. The polyethylene keeps the fins from sticking to the styrofoam.

3 Expand the fins by pulling them forward, then pin them in place. Do not puncture the membranes between the fin rays; instead, insert the pins behind the tips of the spines where they protrude beyond the membranes. Spread the pectoral fin and press it against the body. If the fin starts to collapse pin it to the flesh underneath. Pin the fins of thick specimens to small blocks of styrofoam to keep them in the same photographic plane as the rest of the fish (Fig. 10-41). It is important for the fins to be clearly visible. Fin ray characteristics are often important in distinguishing closely related species.

4 Move the fish to a location with good ventilation. Pin the mouth open and the operculum shut, then apply formaldehyde solution (37%, or 40 g of formaldehyde gas in 100 mL of solution) to the fins with a small paintbrush. Wait 5 min and apply a second coat. Fishes with thick, fleshy fins sometimes require a third application. Test a fin by removing the pins. If it starts to collapse reinsert the pins, apply still more formaldehyde solution, and wait 5 min. Remove all pins after the fins have been fixed.

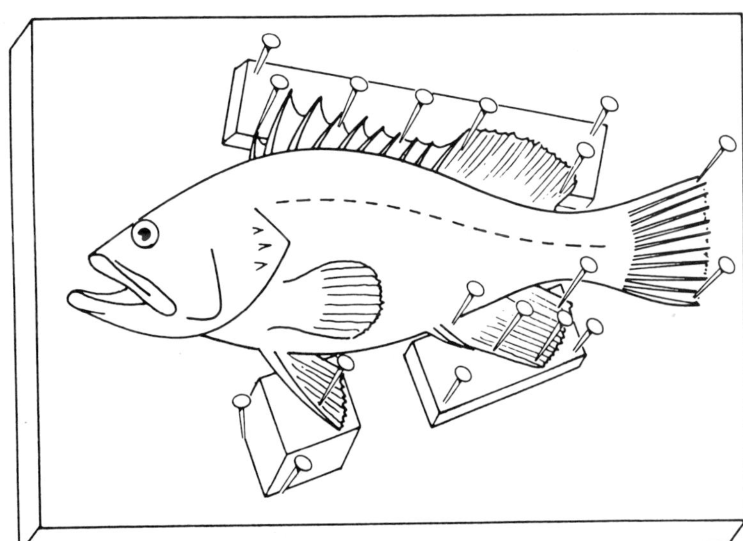

Figure 10-41 *To prepare a fish for photography, spread the fins and pin them. Use blocks of styrofoam to keep fins in the same horizontal plane.* Source: Flescher (1983).

5 Carefully blot the exposed surface of the fish dry with paper towels, but do not disturb the fins. Once fixed, the fins cannot be pinned again. Drying eliminates surface moisture that causes reflections.

How to Take the Photographs[19]

1 Place the fish on a glass surface with a colored surface directly below (Fig. 10-42). I recommend a gray mat finish. As an achromatic color gray imparts no wavelengths of light that might alter the surface coloration of the fish. Have backgrounds with several grays available, and always select one of lesser value (i.e., darker and less bright) than the specimen. Sheets of acrylic 0.6 cm thick that have been spray-painted work well.

2 Place the acrylic sheet with the fish on the table, preferably outdoors. A sunny day in late morning or early afternoon provides the most favorable light and permits surface reflections off the fish to be controlled with a polarizing filter. Position the camera with the sun behind so that sunlight falls directly on the subject. If photographing indoors always use two lamps (one lamp casts a shadow). Place them at either end of the fish (head and tail) and adjust the downward angle of the beams to ~45° (Fig. 10-43). The lamps must be of the same type (e.g., either photo or tungsten) and encased in studio reflectors made of brushed aluminum. If possible, match the film with the temperature of the lamps (Ta-

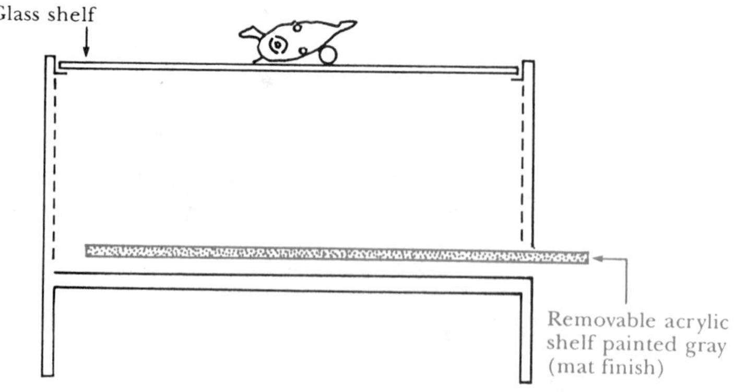

Figure 10-42 *Apparatus for photographing freshly dead fishes. The top shelf is glass; the bottom shelf is acrylic spray-painted the desired color. I recommend using only achromatic colors (i.e., grays) and mat finishes to prevent background reflections.* Source: Flescher (1983).

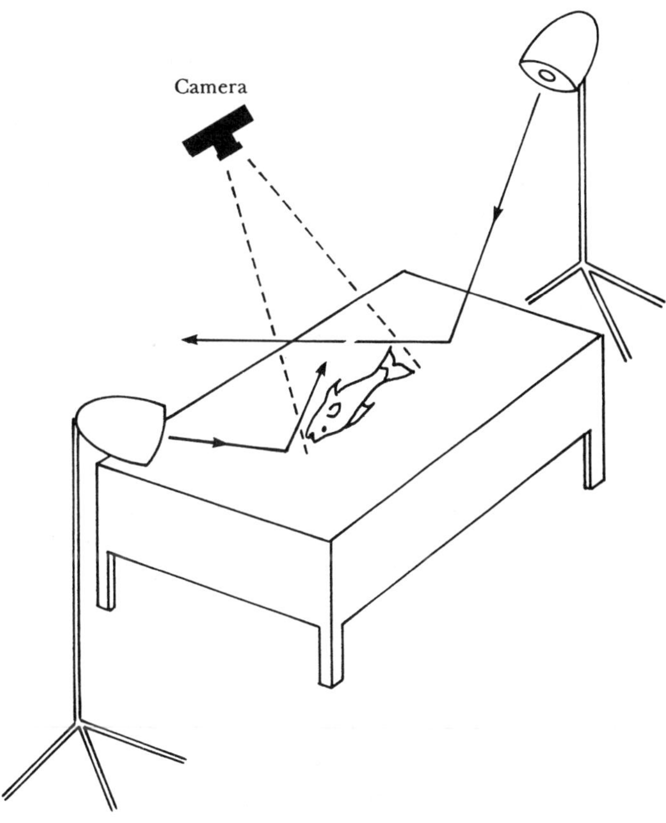

Figure 10-43 *Position the lamps in a way that prevents light from reflecting into the camera lens.* Source: Flescher (1983).

ble 10-2) so that a color conversion filter will not be required. Mounting a polarizing filter on top of a color conversion filter results in substantial light loss, which is particularly troublesome if the film speed is slow.

3 Prop the underneath dorsolateral part of the fish with styrofoam wedges so it tilts up (Fig. 10-42). This prevents reflections off the camera into the photographic field. To achieve maximum effect from the polarizing filter the angle of the camera lens should be the same as the angle of the light. The fish should also be tilted at this angle for all its features to be in the same photographic plane and therefore in focus.

4 The camera can be hand-held or mounted on a tripod. The tripod technique is preferable because it allows a cable release to be used; the absence of your shadow from the finished exposure is guaranteed. Adjust the distance so that the fish fills the frame almost completely (leave only a small margin all around). Maintaining a consistent margin for every specimen assures continuity of size in the finished species labels.

5 Screw the polarizing filter onto the front of the camera lens and rotate it until the surface reflections are erased. The automatic light meters of many cameras are relatively insensitive to polarized light. Polarizing filters have a ''filter factor'' of 2.5 (i.e., the exposure must be increased by $1\frac{1}{3}$ stops). Adjust the lens aperture as indicated by the light meter, then open it $1\frac{1}{3}$ stops. Add another $\frac{1}{2}$ stop if the fish is silvery or otherwise highly reflective. Alternatively, use the light meter to adjust the lens aperture without the filter, readjust it by the filter factor, and screw the filter in place. The filter factor applies regardless of how much the filter is rotated (i.e., whether all or none of the polarized light is transmitted).

6 Work quickly before the coloration of the fish starts to fade. ''Bracket'' the initial exposure by exposing a frame at lens apertures one stop larger and one stop smaller. For example, if the light meter indicates the correct exposure to be f5.6 at $\frac{1}{125}$ s, trip the shutter at this setting and again at f8 and f11.

Method 10.6 *In Vitro* Fish Photography

Photographs taken in aquariums ordinarily have limited educational value simply because the scenes depicted do not represent nature. However, such photographs can occasionally demonstrate aspects of natural history that are impossible to capture in the field, and for this reason the techniques are worth knowing. Fishes can be photographed in small ''photo aquariums'' or in large exhibits. Photographing fishes in large exhibits is preferable if the purpose is to achieve some semblance of nature (assuming the exhibit is decorated appropriately). In either case the principal consideration is light—its intensity and color. The source of illumination must be balanced with the correct film before the true coloration of a fish can be reproduced accurately.

How to Take *In Vitro* Fish Photographs[20]

1 Select an all-glass aquarium of the ''tall'' type. Aquariums with volumes of ~1.3 to 2.6 L (5 to 10 U.S. gal) are adequate unless the specimens to be photographed are large. The sides on the long axis must be free of scratches and distortions.

2 Cut a piece of plate glass 0.6 cm thick to appropriate size to serve as a divider when placed in the aquarium. The divider should be ~2 cm shorter than the length of the aquarium and extend ~2 cm above the top when placed at the angle illustrated in Figure 10-44. ''Seam'' the edges with emory cloth or a fine whetstone to avoid cutting yourself.

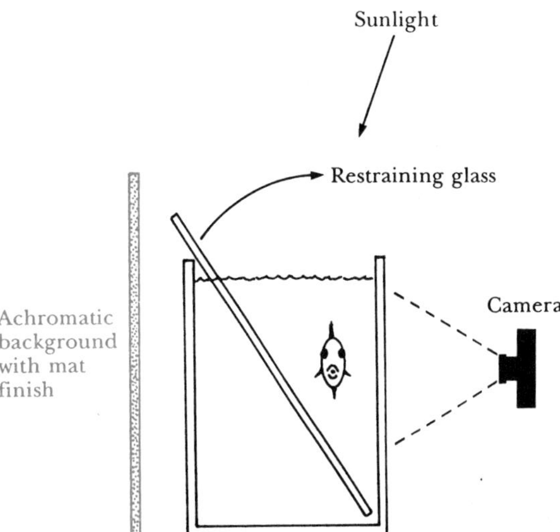

Figure 10-44 *A fish placed in front of a glass insert ordinarily stays in focus long enough to be photographed.* Source: Stephen Spotte.

3 Use an achromatic background of lesser value than the fish and place it ~2 cm behind the back glass of the aquarium.

4 Fill the aquarium with filtered seawater or artificial seawater and place the fish in front of the restraining glass. If water has dripped onto the front glass, wipe it off and clean the glass with commercial window cleaner. Seawater and artificial seawaters leave thin, opaque films on glass that impart a hazy appearance to the developed exposures.

5 Pull the restraining glass forward until the fish is sandwiched loosely against the front glass. Poke the fish into position with a thin glass rod, then clamp the divider in place with chunks of modeling clay at each corner where it meets the top of the aquarium.

6 If possible, set up the apparatus outdoors on a bright, sunny day. Late morning and early afternoon are the best times. Position the aquarium so the light is behind you. For indoor photography always use two lamps (a single lamp casts a shadow). Place one at each end of the aquarium and aim the light down on the fish at an angle of ~45° to avoid reflections and the subsequent color desaturation they cause in the developed exposures. Some photographers place a third lamp directly over the fish, aimed slightly toward the diorama (i.e., away from the camera). The lamps should be encased in studio reflectors made of brushed aluminum. Match the film with the temperature of the incandescent lamps or use the appropriate color conversion filter (Table 10-4). Use only lamps of the same type (e.g., either photo or tungsten).

7 Move the camera forward or backward until the fish fills the desired amount of space in the frame. Because the decor tends to look artificial, open the lens aperture so that the image of the fish is sharp but objects in the diorama appear slightly out of focus.

8 Use the automatic light meter reading on the camera for exposing the first frame, then ''bracket'' subsequent frames by exposing them at the next larger and next smaller lens aperture.

9 The developed exposure can be enlarged, cropped, and mounted near the exhibit as a color transparency or print.

Method 10.7 Undersea Photography of Fishes

The undersea photographer's objective is to take exposures of fishes that are properly framed in the photographic field, perfectly in focus, and evenly illuminated. For nonschooling species this is best accomplished by remaining in one place long enough for the subjects to overcome their initial discomfort that your presence causes. Few good exposures can be made by chasing a fish in the hope it will eventually become quiescent.

How to Take Undersea Photographs

1 Before putting film in the camera test the electrical circuit by coupling the connector, turning on the strobe, and triggering the shutter release.

2 Load the camera only if the strobe discharges properly. Use rolls of 36 exposures. Rolls of 20 require more frequent changes of film, which increase the risk of seawater dripping onto the camera, particularly when dives are being made from a boat.

3 Never jump from a boat or fall backward over the gunwales while holding camera equipment. The force of hitting the water can dislodge a seal, causing the strobe or housing to leak. Tie the equipment to a line fixed to the boat, or have someone on board hand it to you over the side. If a line is used, splice it with a doubled length of surgical tubing to dampen the vertical whipping action produced by swells.

4 Turn on the strobe before descending. The unit should be adjusted to the most powerful light output setting. Be sure the ''ready light'' is on. Cock the camera before entering the water.

5 A few minutes of observation will determine how close you can get to a fish before it moves out of camera range. Maximum effective range is <1.5 m. Focus on the subject once

or twice, then back away momentarily, leaving the lens focused at the selected setting. Estimate the range and adjust the lens aperture. The figures are merely guidelines; actual exposures can be determined only by experience.

6 Move toward the fish slowly until it comes into focus. The subject distance and lens aperture were established in step 5. All that remains is to frame the fish in the photographic field and position the strobe.

7 Most photographers use an adjustable strobe arm attached to the housing, but I find these devices cumbersome. Simply holding the strobe in your left hand is easier. The advantage of a strobe arm is to free the left hand to operate one of the camera controls, ordinarily the focusing knob, but this is unnecessary if the focus adjustment has been made beforehand. Moreover, each time the focus is changed the angle of the strobe arm must also be adjusted.

8 The angle of the strobe and its distance from the subject determine the quality of illumination (Fig. 10-45). In turbid waters it is important to illuminate the subject at an angle of ~45° to prevent backscatter of light from POC. Close sub-

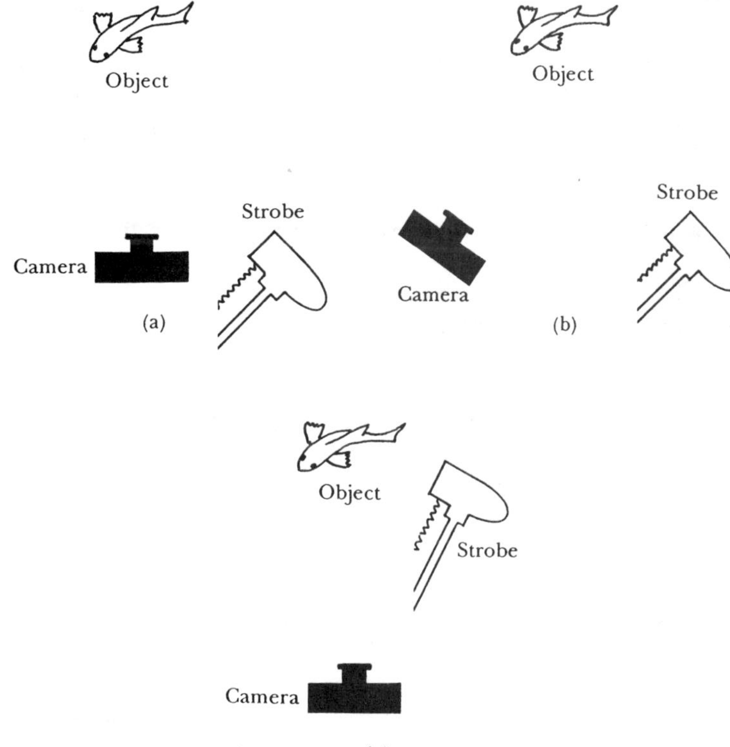

Figure 10-45 *Correct placement of the strobe is critical in undersea photography. Three typical positions are illustrated in increasing order of effectiveness. The position shown in* (c) *is best. Many potentially good photographs are ruined by the presence of suspended POC. The number of particles is reduced if the source of illumination is positioned close to the subject.* Source: Stephen Spotte.

jects can be illuminated from the front because at the shorter distance fewer suspended particles are present between the subject and lens.

Method 10.8 Fiberglass-Reinforced Plastic Decorations

Procedures for replicating natural objects in fiberglass-reinforced plastic evolved simultaneously at several public aquariums in the United States during the 1960s.[21] As techniques were perfected, the more progressive institutions largely abandoned the use of dead, bleached corals or piles of beach stones haphazardly placed. Exhibits decorated with such materials do not accurately represent the undersea world. The ability to "cast" natural objects using modern materials offers obvious advantages. First, aquarists can duplicate the true coloration of a coral head or some other object that once was alive. Second, the low masses of modern plastics reduce structural stresses on the walls and floors of exhibit aquariums. Third, the nature of the procedure permits a degree of visual continuity and realism not possible in the past. For example, large sections of a simulated coral reef can be cast and seamlessly pieced together, even in cantilevered configurations. Similarly, the steep slope of a gravelly beach can be replicated, making cobbles appear as if they had just been deposited by a falling tide. The capacity to represent nature more closely has added a new educational dimension to public aquarium exhibition. A list of materials and supplies needed to make fiberglass-reinforced plastic objects is given in Table 10-6.

How to Make Fiberglass-Reinforced Plastic Decorations[22]

1 Carefully examine the object to be reproduced. It must be clean, dry, and contain no tiny openings that might cause the latex mold to become stuck to any part of its surface (i.e., the finished mold must pull away cleanly). Brain and star corals, for example, should be sprayed with clear acrylic and allowed to dry before proceeding. The acrylic flows into deep recesses that were once inhabited by coral polyps without substantially altering the external appearance of the coral. Fill any large openings with modeling clay. Allow 24 h for the acrylic to harden.

2 The work area should be brightly illuminated (at least 400 lx), well ventilated, and relatively warm (>20°C). Spray the object thoroughly with silicone mold release to prevent the first layer of latex from sticking permanently (Fig. 10-46) and proceed immediately to the next step.

TABLE 10-6 Materials and supplies needed to make fiberglass-reinforced plastic aquarium decorations.

Liquid latex rubber
Polyester resin (USDA approved)
Acetone
Paintbrushes (artist's No. 8 and 1-inch)
Liquid polyester pigments (black, white, chocolate brown, yellow, dark green)
Plastic spoons
Mold release (silicone spray)
Clear acrylic spray
Resin thickener
Modeling clay
Catalyst (industrial methyl ethyl ketone, MEK)
Aluminum measuring spoons (1 set)
Safety goggles
Rubber or disposable plastic gloves
Disposable paint containers
Stirring sticks
Cheesecloth
Heavy scissors
Fiberglass (chopped fibers, mat, and woven cloth)

Source: Spotte (1973).

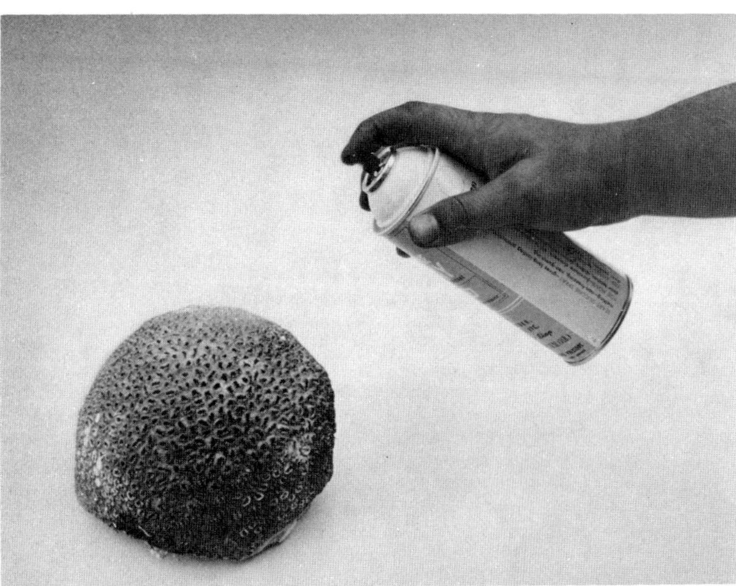

Figure 10-46 *Spray the object to be replicated with silicone to keep the latex rubber from sticking to it.* Source: Spotte (1973).

3 Latex molding rubber comes as a thick liquid and is applied at full strength. If necessary, thin the material by adding small amounts of an ammonia solution (8 mL of full-strength household ammonia in 500 mL of water; 2 tsp/pt).* Keep the container tightly sealed. The first coat of latex is the most important because it reproduces all surface characteristics of the object. Apply the latex with a paintbrush using an up-and-down dabbing motion to force the material into every depression. Allow 24 h to dry.

4 Apply two additional coats. These and subsequent coats ordinarily require less drying time (e.g., ~6 h each).

5 Thick molds are sturdier than thin ones and can be used to cast dozens of objects. To make a thick mold apply at least three more coats of latex with a layer of cheesecloth embedded in all but the last. Cut the cheesecloth to the correct size with scissors, drape it over the object, and paint it with latex.

6 When the last coat of latex has dried, peel off the mold by freeing it evenly around the edges and stripping it away (Fig. 10-47).

7 Pour a small amount of polyester resin into a disposable cardboard container. Wear goggles and disposable plastic gloves during steps 7 through 20. Use only polyester resins that have been approved by the U.S. Department of Agri-

*Teaspoons per pint.

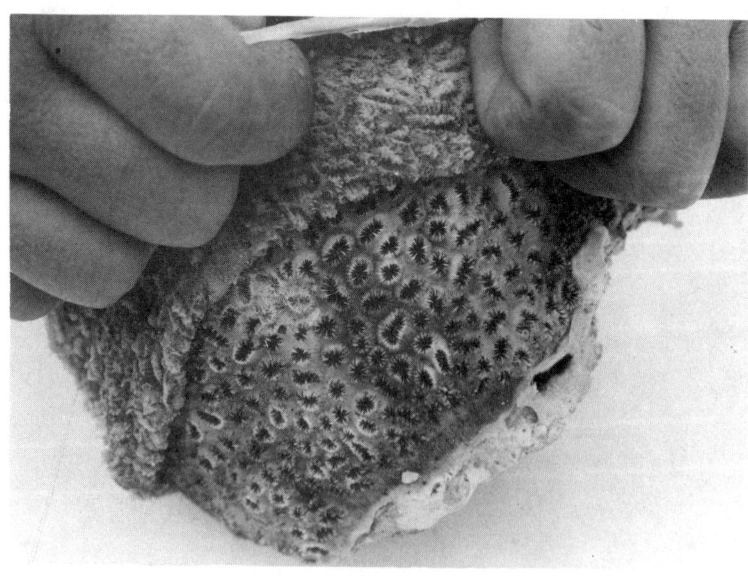

Figure 10-47 *Peel off the finished latex rubber mold by freeing the edges all around.* Source: Spotte (1973).

culture for meat lockers and similar food storage facilities. They have been bioassayed and are least likely to be toxic to fishes. The thicker, low-cobalt resins designed for coating and not casting are preferable. They are inexpensive and can assimilate up to 15% pigment by volume. The second factor is important because measuring pigments accurately in such messy circumstances is difficult, and the resin will not harden properly if excessive amounts of pigment are present. Polyester resins gradually harden if kept in warm locations (see step 11), and they should be stored at 10 to 15°C.

8 The coloration of fiberglass-reinforced plastic objects is blended into the resin; alternatively, coloration can be imparted to the unpigmented casts by application of acrylic paints. The steps that follow describe the use of pigments. Use only polyester resin pigments, which are sold as pastes and liquids; liquids are preferable. Drip pigments slowly into the resin from individual plastic spoons while stirring the contents of the container vigorously until the desired coloration is attained (Fig. 10-48). Use the minimum amount of pigments.

Figure 10-48 *Blend pigments into the resin by dripping small amounts into the mixing can with a plastic spoon while stirring. Alternatively, do not use pigments but color the finished casts with acrylic paints.* Source: Spotte (1973).

Figure 10-49 Add thickener until the resin is the correct consistency. Source: Spotte (1973).

9 When the correct coloration has been attained add thickener until the mixture assumes the consistency of molasses (Fig. 10-49). The thickener is made of fumed silica. It alters the consistency of the resin without changing its coloration or other properties, much as flour thickens gravy without affecting its flavor. Wear a disposable mask over your nose and mouth.

10 Turn the mold inside out and spray it lightly with mold release (Fig. 10-50).

11 Polyester resin hardener (also referred to as ''catalyst'') ordinarily is methyl ethyl ketone, $CH_3COCH_2CH_3$. Industrial grade stock is adequate. Approximately 8 mL/L of unpigmented resin (~2 tsp/qt)* are required, and curing time is 30 to 45 min at ~20°C. The presence of pigments prolongs curing by ~15 min. Polyester resins cure by heat. The hardener reacts with cobalt in the resin, which causes the temperature to rise. The reaction is noticeably exothermic, and the heat generated can be felt through the sides of the mixing container. Working in sunlight often accelerates curing time because the additional heat augments that initiated by catalytic action of the hardener. Add hardener to the container of resin from a measuring spoon and mix

*Teaspoons per quart.

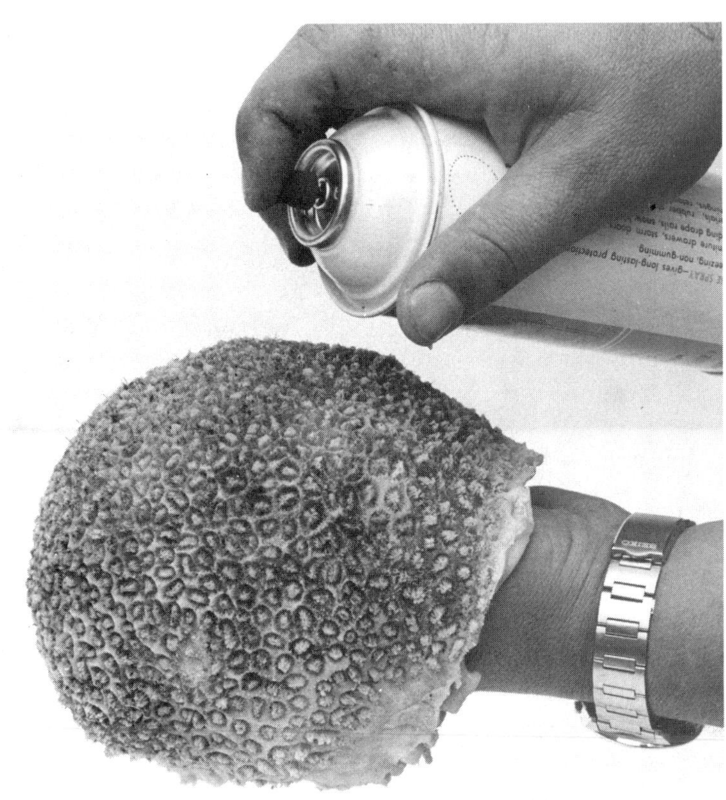

Figure 10-50 Turn the mold inside out and apply a light coat of silicone spray. Source: Spotte (1973).

thoroughly. This is the point of no return; proceed to the next step without delay.

12 With a small paintbrush (No. 8) apply resin to high points of the mold. If the resin runs it is too thin. Stop and stir in more thickener. Turn the mold right side out and set it aside so the resin will harden. The high points just painted represent crevices and areas of deep surface relief in the finished cast, and they should be darker than the second coat to provide contrast. At the end of this step and all the rest that require the use of resin, clean the brush in acetone immediately. Acetone is considered a carcinogen. Always wear disposable plastic gloves and avoid breathing the vapor.

13 The second color coat can be applied as soon as the first dries. Mix it the same way, only slightly thinner and lighter in color (i.e., similar in hue but lower in saturation and of greater value than the first coat).

14 Do not turn the mold inside out. With a 1-in. brush, paint the entire inside of the mold with the second color coat.

None of the latex nor any of the first color coat should be visible. Let the resin cure overnight.

16 The purpose of applying subsequent coats is to fill thin spots in the two color coats that may appear translucent in the finished cast, and to provide strength and durability. To block out potentially translucent places, the third coat (the next one after the second color coat) should be very dark, even black. It also should be thicker than the molasseslike consistency of the first color coat. If the third coat is too thin and the surface fractures after the cast has been placed in the exhibit, any embedded fiberglass (steps 17 through 20) will be visible.

17 Large casts should be reinforced with glass fibers (i.e., fiberglass). This material can be embedded in the cast in several forms, including short, chopped fibers purchased in bags, fiberglass ''mat,'' or thick, woven fiberglass cloth. The last two materials are available in rolls of different widths. Ordinarily, a roll of each (mat and cloth) is hung on a wall in the exhibit preparation area, and sections are cut to size with heavy scissors.

18 Use chopped fibers for strengthening small casts. They can be embedded in two ways. The first method involves painting a coat of resin containing only hardener (no pigment or thickener) over the third coat to form a sticky surface, then sprinkling on a handful of fibers and embedding them in place with a resin-soaked paintbrush. If a slightly thicker layer is required use the next technique, which is to add thickener, fibers, and hardener to the resin and apply the mixture to the inside of the mold with a paintbrush.

19 Fiberglass mat is embedded in casts in the same way that cheesecloth is embedded in latex molds (step 5). Sections are cut, placed inside the mold, and dabbed in place with a resin-soaked paintbrush. A cast is not strengthened properly unless sections of mat are cut small enough to fill parts of the mold that have deep surface relief. Hollow places between the mat and inside surface of the cast provide inadequate protection if the cast is bumped after being placed in the exhibit (Fig. 10-51).

20 Large casts (e.g., those larger than $\sim 1\ m^2$) should contain woven fiberglass cloth. This material is more difficult to embed than fiberglass mat because it is considerably less flexible. All deep surface relief inside the mold must be filled either with additional coats of thickened resin or with unthickened resin and several layers of mat.

21 Pigments formulated to color polyester resins frequently contain metal salts that are potentially toxic. Toxicity will

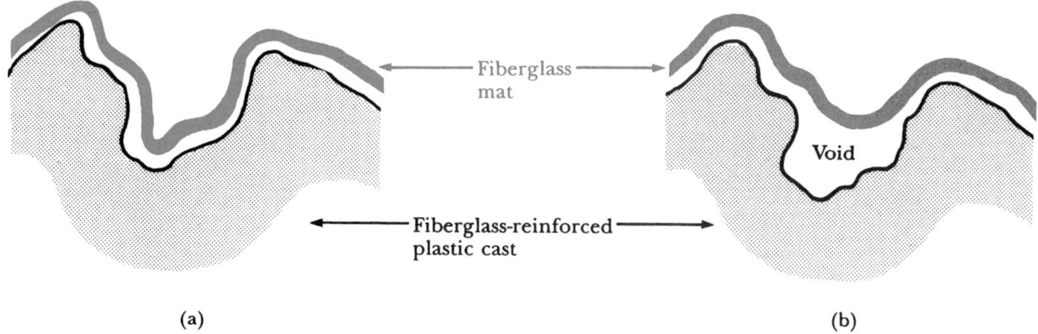

Figure 10-51 *Embed fiberglass mat into all low parts of the mold to prevent voids; otherwise, the finished cast may fracture.* (a) *Correct.* (b) *Incorrect.* Source: Stephen Spotte.

not be a problem if the cast has polymerized completely because the metallic elements will have formed chemical bonds and become integrated into the overall structure. To ensure complete polymerization the finished cast should be placed in a confined space and cured evenly at ~50°C for a minimum of 3 d. Afterward, the surface should feel dry. A sticky surface indicates that some pigments have not polymerized, probably because their total volume exceeded 15% of the combined volume of pigment and resin. Sticky casts should be discarded. The finished cast duplicates the shape and texture of the original object, but has natural coloration (Fig. 10-52).

Figure 10-52 *Finished cast of a head of star coral* (left) *in natural coloration, compared with the original bleached coral head* (right). Source: Spotte (1973).

Method 10.9 Moving Water Exhibits

Moving water exhibits duplicate the surge and wave motion of beaches and rocky intertidal areas.

SURGE ACTION[23] The apparatus in Figure 10-53 is the prototype of a surge action exhibit designed for Vancouver Public Aquarium. Overall dimensions are 75 cm (length) × 75 cm (width) × 35 cm (height). Water motion is generated by a paddle. The paddle mechanism protrudes an additional 30 cm above the back part of the aquarium. A divider separates the visible portion of the exhibit from the section containing the paddle. Corners are reinforced with gussets, which also make water flow more efficient. One rear gusset has been cut lower than the rest to serve as an overflow.

The total volume is ~160 L at a water depth of 30 cm. The paddle apparatus takes up ~70 L, the viewing area is ~30 L, and the rest is occupied by "surge channels" separating the viewing and paddle sections. The paddle is separated from the surge channels by screens consisting of fluorescent lamp diffuser grids. The paddle pivots on an aluminum shaft that penetrates holes drilled in the acrylic. The paddle gear drive is a small-gear motor used for store window displays with an output shaft speed of 5 rpm. The linkage between the motor and paddle includes a Scotch Yoke mechanism to provide two-speed

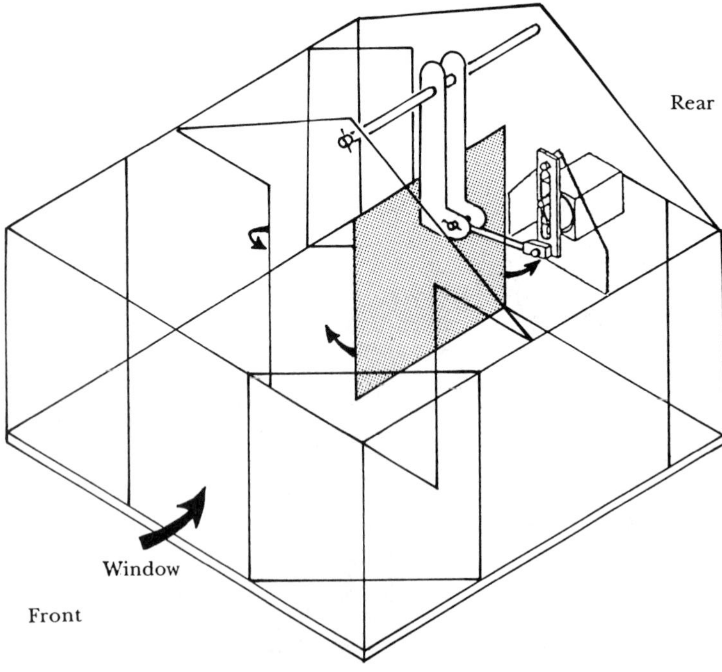

Figure 10-53 Prototype of a surge action exhibit. Source: Webb (1982).

action. The forward stroke requires 4 s, the return stroke 8 s. The volume displaced by a paddle stroke is similar to the volume of the viewing portion. The paddle is suspended with a clearance of 1 cm off the bottom of the aquarium at the midpoint of its stroke.

The actual exhibit has dimensions approximately twice those of the prototype (Fig. 10-54). The total volume is ~1500 L divided about equally between the viewing area and the paddle area plus surge channels. The paddle mechanism, which protrudes 15 cm above the top of the aquarium, was changed to a double-ended hydraulic cylinder powered by tap water. The paddle's movement is controlled by valves actuated electrically and fitted with limit switches. These are operated by a control arm mounted on the frame of the paddle. The paddle travels horizontally on plastic slider bearings in tracks of 316 stainless steel. All other stainless steel parts are also 316. The tracks are welded inside a frame of stainless steel and bolted to the edge of the aquarium. The same frame supports the divider separating the viewing and paddle areas. The ends of the hydraulic cylinder rods are attached to brackets on the frame. The viewing window is plate glass 1.27 cm thick installed in a frame of stainless steel. The paddle is supported on a stainless steel frame that carries the slider bearings on the upper four corners and is attached to the center of the hydraulic cylinder. In this design, the paddle area is not screened from the surge channels. For servicing, the paddle is "parked" at either end by activating a multiposition switch on the side of the aquarium.

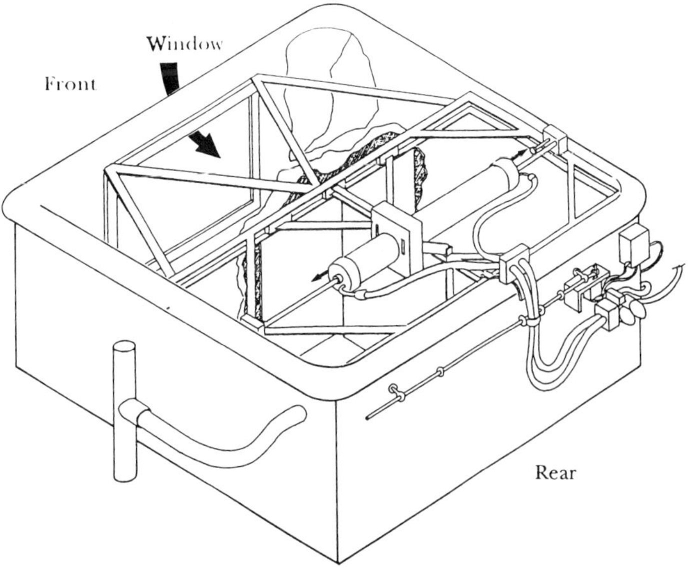

Figure 10-54 *Working exhibit based on the design in Figure 10-53.* Source: Webb (1982).

WAVE ACTION Wave action simulating rocky intertidal areas can be produced by either the "dump bucket" or continuous siphon method. The first operating models based on both methods were devised by David Powell in the 1960s. The "dump bucket" designs reproduced here were developed at New England Aquarium. Water from the exhibit is pumped continuously to an overhead pivoting chamber or "bucket" (Figs. 10-55 and 10-56). When filled to capacity the bucket tips, spilling the entire volume into the exhibit below, either near the

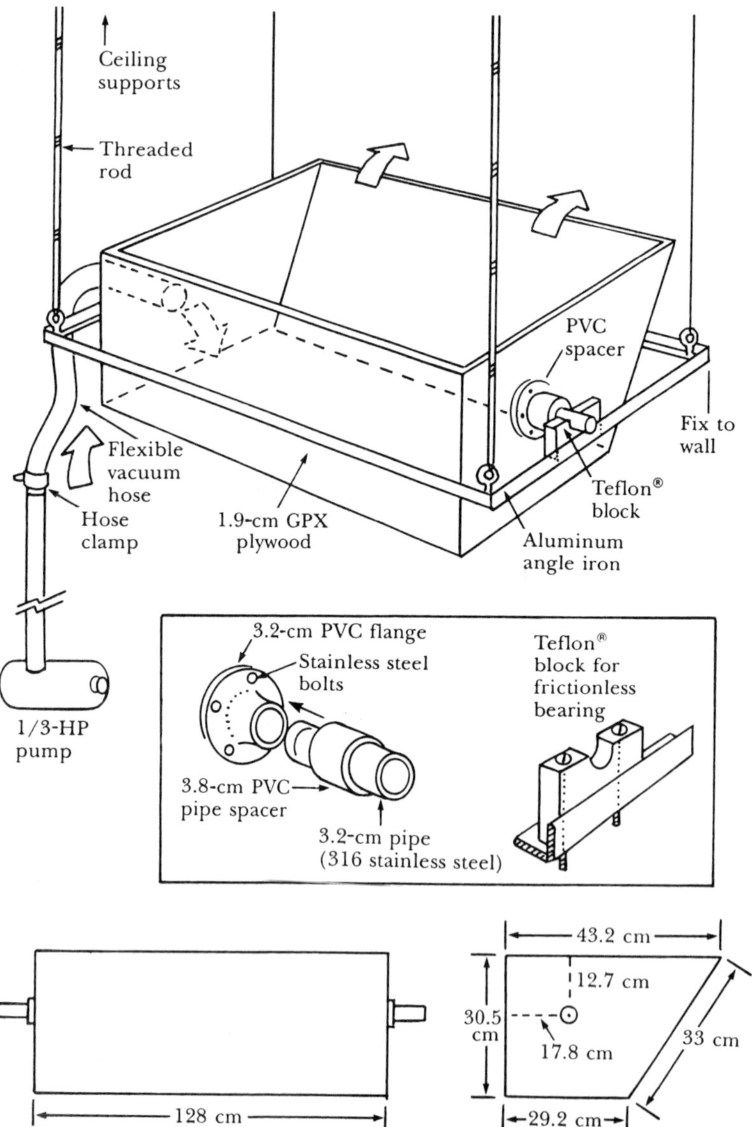

Figure 10-55 Wave action exhibit based on the "dump bucket" method. Source: Sieswerda (1979).

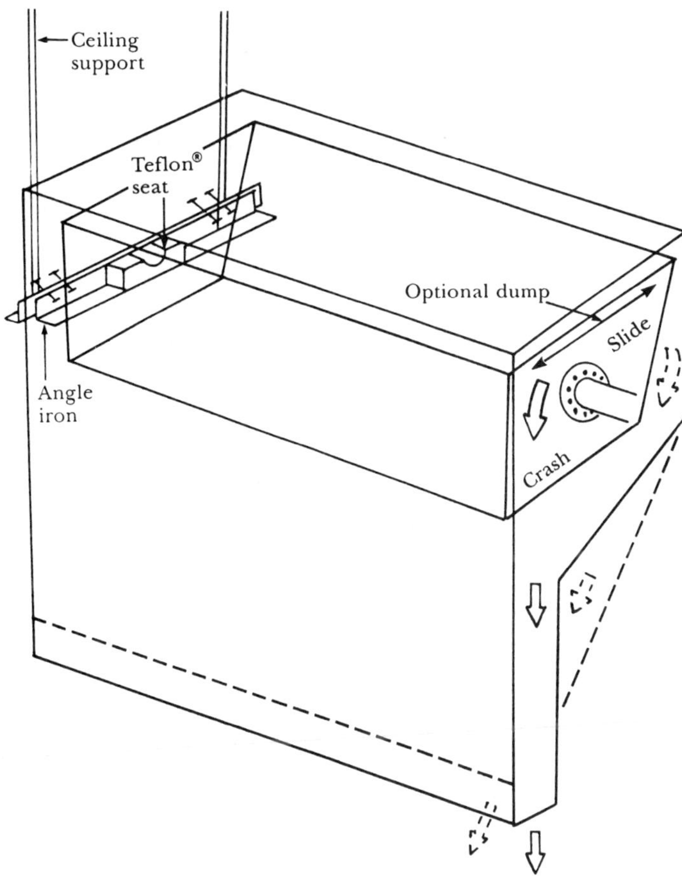

Figure 10-56 *Wave action exhibit based on the "dump bucket" method. This arrangement allows water to be emptied near the front or center of the exhibit down a long, narrow chute, or at the back down a sloping baffle.* Source: Sieswerda and Dayton (1982).

center or along the back walls (Fig. 10-56). The apparatus then rights itself in time for the refill part of the cycle. To retain the interest of viewers, the complete cycle should be <2 min. Because the bucket is emptied in a few seconds, the length of a cycle naturally depends on the refill rate. This is the quotient of the bucket volume divided by refill time. In other words, pumping rate is the limiting variable. The bucket should hold approximately two-thirds of the water contained in the exhibit. Cycles can be shortened and pumping costs reduced by keeping the volume of water as small as possible. This is achieved by displacing a sizable part of the exhibit volume with rocks and other decor. The substratum should be composed of heavy items (e.g., cobbles) to prevent it from shifting.

In the continuous siphon method (Fig. 10-57), water from the exhibit is pumped to an overhead reservoir that holds approximately two-thirds of the water in the exhibit. A PVC pipe of large diameter serves as the siphon. The curve of the pipe

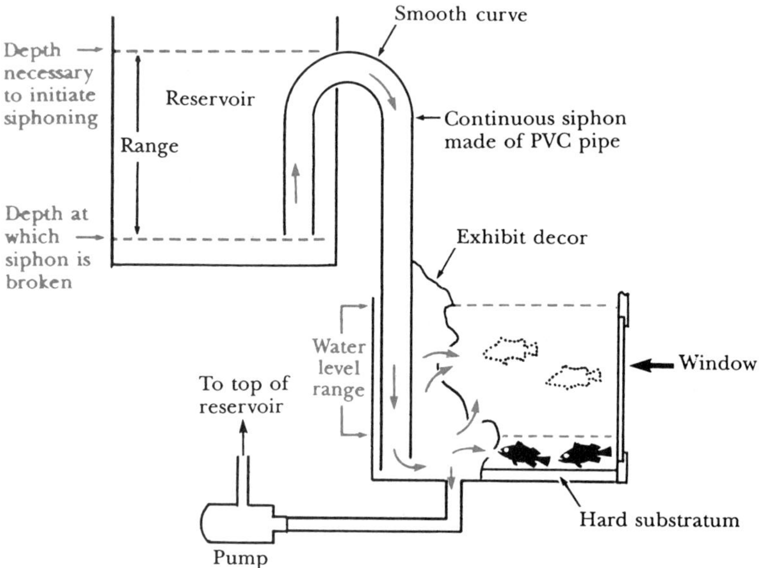

Figure 10-57 Wave action exhibit based on the continuous siphon method. Source: Stephen Spotte.

should be smooth. Siphoning is initiated when the water level reaches the highest point of the pipe, and the contents of the reservoir are emptied rapidly into the exhibit below. The pipe is hidden from view behind rocks and other heavy decor; water emerges from the spaces between them. The comments in the preceding paragraph on cycling time, pumping rate, water volume, and density of the substratum apply here as well.

Method 10.10 Angled Viewing Window Exhibits

Sometimes the best way to view fishes is by looking down at them. Submerged objects are difficult to see clearly in open water exhibits because of surface disturbance and reflected light. Many public aquariums have solved these problems by the use of angled viewing windows (Fig. 10-58). The exhibits mimic static museum cases. The angled window is flooded underneath to eliminate reflected light. Surface disturbance caused by aeration or the entrainment of influent water is confined to the highest part of the enclosure. Illumination provided by fluorescent lamps is soft and evenly distributed.

Method 10.11 Bioassay with Fertilized Sea Urchin Gametes[24]

Unlike standard bioassay tests in which the relative toxicity of substances used in exhibits is evaluated, the procedure below

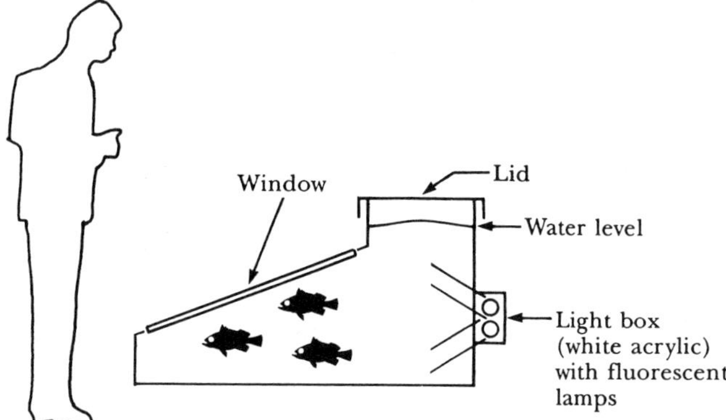

Figure 10-58 Angled viewing window exhibit. Source: Stephen Spotte.

gives a straightforward answer: proceed or do not proceed. It relies on one criterion: normal development of sea urchin gametes. If, under bioassay conditions the eggs cannot be fertilized *in vitro,* if fertilized eggs fail to develop or develop abnormally, or if subsequent embryonic stages show any morphological abnormalities, the test material (e.g., fiberglass-reinforced plastic casts) should be rejected. Most species of sea urchins are suitable, provided they are gravid. Developmental stages are easily recognized and similar in all species (Fig. 10-59).

How to Conduct the Bioassay Procedure

1 Seawater or artificial seawater can be used. Filter newly collected seawater through Whatman No. 1 filter paper (0.45 μm). Prepare artificial seawater by dissolving the components in distilled or deionized water (Chapter 8). Each test and control sample requires 1 L of solution.

2 Soak the material to be tested in 1 L of test solution for 24 h at 20°C.

3 After 24 h fill a 250-mL glass beaker with 200 mL of control solution at 20°C. Fill an identical beaker with 250 mL of test solution.

4 Hold a sea urchin upside down (oral side up). With a sterile syringe (24 to 26 gauge needle) inject 0.1 to 0.3 mL of 0.5 mol/L KCl into the body cavity through the soft peristomial membrane around the mouth. If performed correctly, the animal will survive and recover quickly.

5 Gametes will be expelled through the gonapores on the aboral (dorsal) side. Sperm is always white. Eggs vary in color by species, but ordinarily are yellow, brown, or reddish.

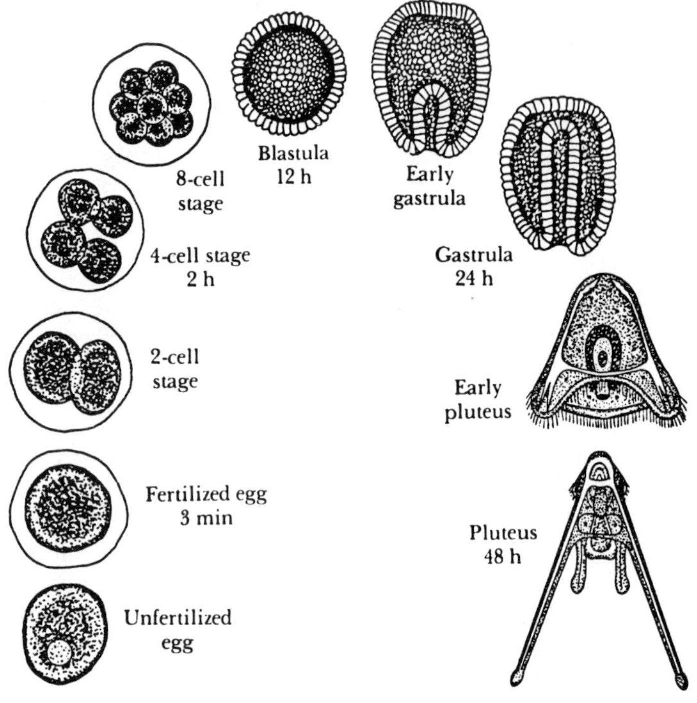

Figure 10-59 Early sea urchin development. Source: King and Spotte (1974); original source unknown.

6 Add 0.025 mL of sperm suspension to each beaker, swirl gently, and let stand for 5 min.

7 Add 0.15 mL of egg suspension to the beakers and swirl gently.

8 After 3 min check each beaker for fertilization. Check again at 2, 12, 24, and 48 h, or times correlating approximately with stages of development (Fig. 10-59).

Notes and References

CHAPTER 1

(1) A chemical equilibrium can be shown by the general reaction

$$A + B \underset{s_2}{\overset{s_1}{\leftrightharpoons}} C + D \tag{1.15}$$

where A, B, C, and D are individual reactants, and s_1 and s_2 represent the rates of the forward (right) and reverse (left) reactions. At equilibrium, $s_1 = s_2$. The *equilibrium constant, K*, is

$$K = \frac{[C]\,[D]}{[A]\,[B]} \tag{1.16}$$

where brackets stand for *molar concentration.** The numerical value of an equilibrium constant is essentially unchanged at a given temperature. Any change in the concentrations of the reactants by their addition or removal causes a shift in the equilibrium to keep K constant, provided the temperature does not change. In this example the addition of reactants C or D shifts

* A *mole* (the symbol is mol) is the quantity of a substance that has a mass in grams numerically equal to its molecular weight. The word is derived from the Latin ''moles,'' meaning heap or pile; thus a mole is the number of particles in a pile. The elements sodium and chlorine have atomic weights of 23 and 35.5, respectively. One molecule (literally, the diminutive of moles) has a *formula weight* (the sum of the elements it contains) of 58.5. One mole of NaCl therefore has a mass of 58.5 grams. The *molarity* of a solution is equal to the number of moles of the solute it holds, and a *molar concentration* is a solution containing one mole of solute per litre of solution (1 mol/L).

the equilibrium represented by reaction 1.15 in reverse; removal of *C* or *D* shifts it forward. The value of *K* does not change. When *K* has a large numerical value, *C* and *D* predominate; when *K* is small, *A* and *B* are present in greater amounts than *C* or *D*, and the sequence is reversed.

(2) The rate at which ions leave the solid depends only on the temperature and pressure of the solution; the rate at which they arrive back and precipitate is a function of temperature and their concentrations. The solution is saturated when the rates of dissolution and precipitation are equal at a given temperature and pressure and a particular solution concentration.

(3) This is a simplified definition. *Salinity* is traditionally defined as the total mass in grams of solutes dissolved in 1 kg of seawater after all bromide and iodide have been replaced by the equivalent mass of chloride and all bicarbonate and carbonate converted to *oxide* (compounds containing oxygen).

(4) In more than 97% of the world's seawater the salinity falls within the range 33 to 37‰ (Cox 1965).

(5) In 1819 Marcet wrote: "With the exception of the Dead Sea, and of the Lake Ourmia, which are mere salt ponds, perfectly unconnected with the ocean, all the specimens of seawater which I have examined, however different in their strength, contain the same ingredients all over the world, these bearing very nearly the same proportions to each other; so that they differ only as to the total amount of their saline contents."

(6) Forchhammer (1865) established the term "salinity." He stated: "The next question to be considered refers to the proportion between all the salts together and the water; or to express it in one word, I may allow myself to call it the salinity of sea-water. . . ."

(7) Today it is generally accepted that evaporation is carried out in an open container and distillation in one that is closed, but early chemists often used the terms interchangeably. Nonetheless, they were aware that attempting to separate the water from seawater resulted in false weights of the residues remaining. They also knew that the reason was because some of the solid components were lost in the process. Count Louis Ferdinand Marsilli reported in 1725 that distillates of seawater were consistently lighter in weight than they should have been. He also made artificial seawater, distilled it, and observed the same results (Wallace 1974, p. 36).

(8) If a solution of electrolytes (e.g., Na^+ and Cl^-) is placed in a beaker with two carbon electrodes connected to a voltage

source, an electric current is produced. One electrode is the *anode,* which has positive potential; the other, the *cathode,* has negative potential. The positive ions in the solution are attracted to the cathode and the negative ions to the anode. As a result of ion migration there is a transfer of positive and negative charges from the ions to the electrodes, which constitutes an electric current. The names ''cation'' and ''anion'' originate from the names of the electrodes to which ions migrate, not from the nature of their charges.

(9) No method exists for accurately measuring the density of seawater (Cox 1965, Wilson 1975), meaning that no *original* density determination of seawater has ever been made. However, the same is true of all liquids, simply because any measured value ultimately must be compared with the value of pure water at 4°C. In contrast, the density of a purified solid can be determined as an original measurement by weighing a known volume. Nonetheless, the density of seawater can be determined to six significant digits with a *pycnometer,* which is essentially a glass bottle of known volume. The pycnometer is calibrated by filling it with pure water at 4°C and weighing it. This gives

$$V = m/1.000 \tag{1.17}$$

where V and m represent volume and mass. Afterward, the pycnometer is filled with seawater of temperature T (°C), and the corrected volume, V_c, is determined by

$$V_c = V\,[1 + \beta(T - 4)] \tag{1.18}$$

where $\beta = 3\alpha$ and α is the linear expansion coefficient of glass. The value of $\beta(T - 4)$ is negligible for Pyrex®. Next the bottle is weighed and the density (represented by rho) of seawater is calculated from

$$\rho_{SW} = \frac{m}{V_c} \tag{1.19}$$

The inability to measure the density of seawater directly has resulted in historic misuse of the term. Many density determinations reported about 1900, when the subject was addressed by an international panel of oceanographers, are dimensionless ratios and actually represent specific gravity. Some of this information is still in use.

(10) Riley (1965) wrote: ''It is uncertain who invented the hydrometer, it may possibly have been Archimedes (287?–212

B.C.). The first clear description of the instrument is given in the fifteenth letter of Syrenius (A.D. 370–415) to his friend and mentor Hypatia (appointed Bishop of Ptolemāis, A.D. 410). 'I am so unfortunate as to need a Hydroscope. Have a bronze one constructed and assembled for me. It consists of a cylindrical tube the size and shape of a flute. On this tube in a vertical line are the notches by which you tell the weight of the waters we are testing. A cone fits over the tube so evenly that cone and tube have a common base. . . . Now whenever you place the tube in the water it will remain erect.' Robert Boyle (in 1675) designed a glass hydrometer very similar in design to the modern instrument.'' I surveyed Boyle's publications for 1675 and several years before and after, but found no description of a hydrometer.

(11) In mathematical terms the concept of p means to take the negative logarithm of the quantity that follows and multiply the result by minus one, in this case $pH = -\log[H^+]$. The ionization of pure water results in formation of equal portions of H^+ and OH^-. The *ion product*, IP, of pure water, K_w, is expressed by

$$K_w = [H^+]\,[OH^-] = (1 \times 10^{-7})(1 \times 10^{-7})$$
$$= 1 \times 10^{-14} \text{ at } 25°C \qquad (1.20)$$

where brackets represent molar concentration in water at neutrality (pH 7.0), H^+ is 10^{-7}, and pH is $-\log 10^{-7}$. If the water has a pH of less than 7 the concentration of H^+ is greater than 10^{-7}, and conditions are acidic. A pH of 3 indicates that the water contains 10^{-3} mol/L H^+. In this instance the concentration of OH^- is 10^{-11} because the product of the two concentrations ($10^{-3} \times 10^{-11}$) must always equal K_w, which is 10^{-14}. In other words, pH + pOH = 14, and the pH scale begins at 1 and ends at 14.

(12) Reactions 1.1 represent the essential steps in seawater carbonate equilibria if ion pairing is disregarded, mainly the pairing of HCO_3^- and CO_3^{2-} with Ca^{2+}, Mg^{2+}, and Na^+ (Skirrow 1975).

(13) The following discussion is based on Weyl (1970, p. 319). Seawater is a neutral mixture of ions in water (i.e., the sums of species with positive and negative charges are equal). The use of equivalents is one way of monitoring the total charge of all ion present. An *equivalent*, Eq, is the amount of an ion required to equal the charge of a mole of an ion with a single charge. For species such as Na^+ with only one charge, the number of equivalents is equal to the number of moles; for an ion with two

charges (e.g., CO_3^{2-}), one mole equals two equivalents. In a given amount of seawater the sum of the equivalents of positive and negative ions must be equal to maintain neutrality. Chemical oceanographers ordinarily use milliequivalents, mEq, when expressing alkalinity.

(14) Sillén (1961) first proposed that reactions between silicate minerals and seawater control the pH of the oceans over geologic time. Garrels (1965) and Pytkowicz (1968, 1973b) agreed. These authors and Sillén (1967) reasoned that all carbonates in the oceans are derived from atmospheric CO_2 and the weathering of igneous rocks. As time passed, sedimentary rocks were formed and the weathering of both carbonates and silicates began contributing to the alkalinity of the oceans. McDuff and Morel (1980) pointed out that the appropriate silicate phases in oceanic sediments have yet to be found in sufficient amounts to support quantitative aspects of this model.

It appears that ~88% of the alkalinity originates from weathering of $CaCO_3$ and the balance from weathering of aluminum silicates (Pytkowicz 1967). According to Pytkowicz (1967), pH fluctuations in the oceans that occur within nongeologic time scales of ~1000 years (the residence time of deep ocean waters) are controlled by the alkalinity, and the effect of silicates is negligible. Dissolution of the shells of calcareous organisms increases the alkalinity of ocean waters. Thus the pH at a given moment is determined by the amount of CO_2 and the alkalinity, both of which originate from photosynthesis, oxidation processes, and the formation and dissolution of the calcium carbonate shells of calcareous organisms. A more detailed explanation is presented in a later text subsection.

(15) Bissell and Chilingar (1967).

(16) As noted by Bissell and Chilingar (1967), some geologists prefer *dolostone* for the rock containing <50% dolomite. However, the term dolomite will probably continue to be used for both the mineral and the rock, despite possible confusion. Carozzi (1960, p. 264), for example, wrote: "Dolomites are carbonate rocks primarily composed of the mineral dolomite."

(17) Bathurst (1971).

(18) The composition of a "magnesian calcite" is arbitrary. Plummer and Mackenzie (1974) defined magnesian calcites as calcites in which $MgCO_3$ is >4 mol %* of the total composition.

*The *mole fraction* of a solute is the number of moles in the solution divided by the total moles of solutes present. *Mole percent* (mol %) is 100 times the mole fraction. The sum of all mole percents is 100; the sum of all mole fractions is 1.00.

To Berner (1966), low and high magnesian calcites contained <4 and >10 mol % $MgCO_3$, respectively. Morse et al. (1979) considered *biogenic* (biological in origin), low magnesian calcites to consist of <1 mol % $MgCO_3$.

(19) Wattenberg and Timmerman (1936) first showed that surface seawaters are supersaturated with respect to $CaCO_3$. Subsequent work has demonstrated that values between three and five times saturation are typical of the surface waters of temperate and tropical oceans (e.g., Li et al. 1969), although Möller and Parekh (1975) suggested that a more realistic estimation of carbonate saturation may be 1.0 to 2.2 times.

(20) The input of a given number of moles of CO_2 does not release twice as many moles of H^+ in reaction 1.3, but actually a much smaller quantity. In this manner the system is *buffered* (i.e., resists a change in H^+ concentration). Consequently, the pH of seawater seldom falls outside the range 7.8 to 8.3.

(21) When a slightly soluble solid is placed in water saturated with ions of the same composition, an equilibrium is established between the reactants already in solution (*liquid phase*) and the surface of the solid (*solid phase*). At saturation the concentration of the solid exceeds its solubility because no more can dissolve, and it exists as an *excess solid phase*. If calcium carbonate (which is only slightly soluble) in the excess solid phase is placed in contact with a saturated solution of calcium carbonate, the equilibrium is represented by

$$CaCO_{3(s)} \rightleftharpoons Ca^{2+} + CO_3^{2-} \qquad (1.21)$$

in which the subscript *s* represents the solid phase. This relationship can be further described by an equilibrium constant, K (see Note 1), and shown as

$$K = \frac{[Ca^{2+}][CO_3^{2-}]}{[CaCO_{3(s)}]} \qquad (1.22)$$

where brackets stand for molar concentration. Remember that two phases are involved, liquid and solid, and the equilibrium consequently is *heterogeneous*. The Ca^{2+} and CO_3^{2-} are dissociated and in the liquid phase, whereas $CaCO_{3(s)}$ is a solid. The solid phase, because it is undissociated and not dispersed in the solution has a constant concentration. As a result, $CaCO_{3(s)}$ can be incorporated into K as

$$[Ca^{2+}][CO_3^{2-}] = K[CaCO_{3(s)}] = K_{sp} \qquad (1.23)$$

The new constant formed, K_{sp}, is the *solubility product*, and the expression $[Ca^{2+}][CO_3^{2-}]$ is the ion product, *IP*. According to the last equation, *IP* must equal K_{sp} when the saturated solution is in equilibrium with an excess solid phase.

The value of K_{sp}, once determined experimentally, defines the limits of dissolution and precipitation. Because K_{sp} values are calculated from data derived from saturated or *supersaturated solutions* (i.e., solutions in excess of saturation), any ions in addition to those giving the proper K_{sp} will precipitate. The situation is thus reduced to a comparison of the magnitude of K_{sp} and *IP*. Three possibilities arise: (*1*) $IP > K_{sp}$, and precipitation occurs until $IP = K_{sp}$; (*2*) $IP = K_{sp}$, and there is no visible reaction because the solution is saturated; or (*3*) $IP < K_{sp}$, there is no precipitation, and the existing precipitate dissolves until $IP = K_{sp}$. The degree of saturation is represented by $\Omega = IP/K_{sp}$, and only when $\Omega = 1$ is the seawater saturated with $CaCO_3$.

The degree of saturation of a sample of seawater with respect to a carbonate mineral is sometimes determined in chemical oceanography with a *carbonate saturometer*, a modified pH meter devised by Weyl (1961). In principle, the dissolution or precipitation of $CaCO_3$ causes an increase and decrease in pH, respectively, by the reaction

$$CaCO_3 + H^+ \rightleftharpoons Ca^{2+} + HCO_3^- \tag{1.24}$$

The pH of the seawater sample inside the saturometer is measured, the carbonate mineral is added, and the pH is then measured continuously until water and mineral reach equilibrium (i.e., no further change in pH occurs). At this point the degree of saturation is determined by equilibrium calculations. See Plath et al. (1980) for a description of the instrument and advantages and disadvantages of its use.

(22) Simkiss (1964) compared the removal of $CaCO_3$ from seawater and artificial seawater supersaturated with calcite and placed in contact with powdered oyster shell, which is nearly pure calcite. The total degree of supersaturation was increased by addition of three times the normal concentration of sodium bicarbonate (0.6 compared with 0.2 g $NaHCO_3$/L) to a closed vessel containing 100 mg of oyster shell and 400 mL of artificial seawater from which free CO_2 had been removed. Afterward, 27.8 mg of $CaCO_3$ precipitated at pH 8.0 after 20 h. Addition of 0.6 g $NaHCO_3$/L to seawater and removal of CO_2 did not precipitate any $CaCO_3$ after 20 h. Addition of monobasic sodium phosphate, NaH_2PO_4, and three organic phosphorus compounds to the artificial seawater produced the same inhibitory effect observed in seawater.

(23) As Morse (1986) emphasized, interactions between dissolved organic carbon, DOC, and carbonate minerals are complex: ''The organic matter found associated with carbonates can be present as a true adsorbate, a precipitate or coprecipitate, occluded biogenic tissue, biogenic coatings or sheaths, bacterial 'slimes,' and even living organisms such as bacteria or boring algae.'' Chave and Suess (1970) demonstrated that the time required for $CaCO_3$ to precipitate from supersaturated surface and aquarium seawater increased with increasing concentrations of DOC. The time required in surface seawater of pH 8.09 was 22 min, as determined by a rapid pH decline at a DOC concentration of 1.1 mg/L. Aquarium seawater with a DOC concentration of 4.0 mg/L required >240 min. It was later shown that specific fractions of the DOC in seawater are adsorbed onto $CaCO_3$ in the solid phase. Specific compounds include lipids and fats (Meyers and Quinn 1971), stearic acid and albumin (Suess 1970), amino acids (Carter 1978, Carter and Mitterer 1978, Suess 1970), humic acids (Carter and Mitterer 1978), and fulvic acids (Carter 1978). Humic and fulvic acids are described in Chapter 2 and lipids in Chapter 8.

(24) Pytkowicz (1973a) studied the effect of magnesium ions on spontaneous precipitation of $CaCO_3$ from three artificial seawaters that varied in the concentration of magnesium. The formulas, designated ASW-1, ASW-2, and ASW-3 contained, respectively, no magnesium, magnesium at typical seawater concentrations (11.09 g/L $MgCl_2 \cdot 6H_2O$), and magnesium at twice the amount present in seawater (22.18 g/L $MgCl_2 \cdot 6H_2O$). The degree of saturation of each solution was changed by addition of known concentrations of sodium carbonate, Na_2CO_3. Under all experimental conditions the time required for precipitation of $CaCO_3$ decreased with increasing degree of saturation (i.e., with increasing concentrations of Na_2CO_3). Precipitation in ASW-1 occurred in minutes. In ASW-2 the time for precipitation varied from 700 to 800 h (0.70 mmol/L Na_2CO_3) to 13 to 20 h (9.10 mmol/L Na_2CO_3). In contrast, addition of 9.10 mmol/L Na_2CO_3 to ASW-3 resulted in precipitation being delayed for 22 to 29 h. Other researchers also have reported that magnesium ions in seawater delay precipitation of $CaCO_3$ (e.g., Berner 1974, Bischoff 1968, Bischoff and Fyfe 1968, de Groot and Duyvis 1966, Katz 1973, and Simkiss 1964).

(25) Pytkowicz (1973a).

(26) The ratio of magnesium to calcium in seawater is ~5 ($5.32 \cdot 10^{-2}$ versus $1.02 \cdot 10^{-2}$ mol/L). Magnesium is the most important of the ions and molecules thought to affect surface com-

position and thus the solubility of carbonate minerals. The surfaces of carbonate minerals placed in seawater or artificial seawater are enriched with magnesium, relative to their interiors, by the formation of magnesian calcite overgrowths (Berner 1966, Brätter et al. 1972, Morse et al. 1979, Weyl 1967). In addition, the composition attained ultimately by the overgrowth (i.e., the composition at equilibrium) is controlled mainly by the magnesium concentration in the liquid phase; the original composition of the mineral itself is less important (Brätter et al. 1972; Möller 1973, 1974; Möller and Parekh 1975; Morse et al. 1979; Weyl 1967).

Morse et al. (1979) reported that nearly pure calcite (Iceland spar) placed in supersaturated seawater acquired an overgrowth of $MgCO_3$ that averaged 4 mol % after 3 and 7 d. The overgrowth was 30% less soluble than calcite. They wrote: ''The fact that no major variation in the Mg content was found within the growth layer indicates that the composition of the solution is probably more important in determining the Mg content of the growth layer than the composition of the calcite on which the deposition is occurring.''

It is thought that an increase in the Mg^{2+}/Ca^{2+} ratio in the surrounding solution induces formation of magnesian calcites of lower stability (i.e., greater solubility) than pure calcite (Berner 1975; Möller and Parekh 1975; Plummer and Mackenzie 1974; Thorstenson and Plummer 1977, 1978; Wollast et al. 1980). Furthermore, the Mg^{2+}/Ca^{2+} ratio in the seawater or artificial seawater dictates the amounts of magnesium incorporated into magnesian calcite overgrowths that precipitate on calcite from supersaturated solutions (Mucci and Morse 1983). Brätter et al. (1972) wrote: ''Only the surface and any overgrowth, which are expected to differ in their chemical composition from that of the bulk [solution], form equilibria with the solution.'' Berner (1975) demonstrated that 7 to 10 mol % $MgCO_3$ precipitates as an overgrowth on nearly pure calcite crystals in artificial seawater of pH 8.40 (Fig. 1-14).

Magnesian calcite overgrowths, incidently, are not representative of a true ''solid phase'' (see Note 21). They actually are ''solid solutions.'' To quote Weyl (1967): ''In order that a solution be in thermodynamic equilibrium with a solid phase, the same phase must dissolve and precipitate from the solution. A solid phase is a solid whose composition and properties are uniform throughout. The solution contacts only the outer layer of the solid and is indifferent to its interior.'' Considering that the overgrowth is what dissolves and precipitates, it cannot represent a true solid phase because its composition is different. It therefore is a ''solid solution.'' Unless carbonate minerals are subjected to conditions of undersaturation, their interiors (i.e., the true solid phase) remain unchanged over geologic time, or millions of years (Brätter et al. 1972). This obviously is not the case with overgrowths.

(27) When placed in seawater all carbonate minerals incorporate magnesium into their surfaces, but the amount adsorbed depends on the original composition of the mineral. In the case of calcite, Mg^{2+}/Ca^{2+} ratios at the outer surface reach values of nearly 1 at Mg^{2+}/Ca^{2+} ratios between 2 and 10 in the surrounding solution (Möller and Parekh 1975). The exchange of Mg^{2+} and Ca^{2+} is unaffected by Na^+, Cl^-, and SO_4^{2-} up to concentrations of these ions in seawater (Möller and Parekh 1975). In the case of dolomite, the surface ion ratio approaches 1 when the Mg^{2+}/Ca^{2+} solution ratio is 5 (Brätter et al. 1972). It has been established that aragonite adsorbs less Mg^{2+} than calcite, although neither mineral contains Mg^{2+}. Both aragonite and calcite adsorb considerably less Mg^{2+} than dolomite and magnesite (de Groot and Duyvis 1966, Mucci and Morse 1985).

Mucci and Morse (1985) exposed polished surfaces of four carbonate minerals to seawater. The Mg^{2+}/Ca^{2+} ratios of the resulting surface layers were aragonite (0.63) < calcite (0.83) < dolomite (3.05) < magnesite (120). The numbers in parentheses represent surface ion composition at $\Omega = 1.2$ (saturation with respect to calcite). The magnesite contained 46.56% MgO and 0.84% CaO, compared with percentage compositions of 21.59% MgO and 30.46% CaO in the sample dolomite. The authors concluded that (*1*) Mg^{2+} is adsorbed much less than Ca^{2+} onto aragonite, (*2*) Ca^{2+} and Mg^{2+} are adsorbed about equally onto calcite, (*3*) Mg^{2+} is adsorbed almost exclusively onto magnesite, and (*4*) the ratio of adsorbed Mg^{2+}/Ca^{2+} onto dolomite is ~ 3. This suggests that minerals containing high concentrations of magnesium adsorb the greatest amounts of Mg^+ from the surrounding seawater.

(28) The decline in pH that occurs in closed-system seawater aquariums is well documented (e.g., Atkins 1922; Atz 1964a, 1964b; Bower et al. 1981; Breder and Howley 1931; Breder and Smith 1932; Brown 1929; Cooper 1932; Deguchi 1963, 1964; Hirayama 1970, 1974; Honig 1934; Kokubo 1933; Oliver 1957; Saeki 1958, 1962; Siddall 1974; Spotte 1979a, pp. 104–111 and 1979b, pp. 73–99; Stowell 1925; and Wilson and Griggs 1941).

(29) As Wollast et al. (1980) pointed out, if the precipitate did not recrystallize it would cease to grow when its Mg^{2+} content was so great that its "KCaCO$_2$" was equal that of the seawater. I interpret this to mean the point at which the K_{sp} of $CaCO_3$ equals that of the seawater (i.e., $IP = K_{sp}$; see Note 21).

(30) Möller and Sastri (1974) demonstrated that only cations in the outermost layers of the solid phase (i.e., solid solution) are gained and lost.

(31) The study of carbonate minerals involves nuances of solubility that pose some of the most difficult problems in chemical oceanography and geochemistry. Early research (e.g., Anderson 1889) was limited by insufficient knowledge of how carbonate minerals behave in the ocean environment. To appreciate the extent of the controversy, read the report of Thorstenson and Plummer (1977) and the comments that ensued (Garrels and Wollast 1978, Lafon 1978, Thorstenson and Plummer 1978). Briefly, Thorstenson and Plummer (1977) discovered that the Mg^{2+}/Ca^{2+} ratios of aqueous solutions in stable equilibrium with magnesian calcites are considerably greater than would be encountered in natural environments. Their conclusion was that reactions involving a carbonate mineral must always occur outside stable equilibrium, with the constraint being the constant composition of the minerals (see Note 21). This situation, which the authors called ''stoichiometric saturation,'' permitted them to examine states of equilibrium involving realistic aqueous Mg^{2+}/Ca^{2+} ratios. Lafon (1978) took issue with their approach, in effect disagreeing with the very nature of the theoretical framework. Lafon wrote: ''Nonetheless, it is very difficult to envisage natural mechanisms that could in fact precisely fix the composition of a solid-solution mineral in a reacting geochemical system.'' Lafon continued, ''Thus 'stoichiometric saturation' is an equilibrium model only in appearance, and its application to real situations presupposes a knowledge of the kinetics [reaction rates] of geochemical reactions which we do not yet have.'' Keep in mind that Thorstenson and Plummer tried merely to *describe* naturally occurring processes. Aquarists who use carbonate minerals as filtrants often do so with the mistaken intention of *controlling* these same processes.

(32) Magnesian calcite overgrowths are acquired soon after a carbonate mineral is placed in seawater. The average life of a calcite surface (i.e., the time required to dissolve or precipitate one monolayer) is ~1 d if the seawater and the mineral are in equilibrium (Berner and Morse 1974, Mucci and Morse 1985). Adams and Spotte (1985) demonstrated that crushed coral and crushed oyster shell with newly exposed surfaces cause a marked decline in alkalinity during the first few hours in both seawater and artificial seawater, whereas silica sand does not. The extent of the decline depends on the composition of the filtrant, but also on the solution/filtrant volume ratio. Silica sand (silica), coral (aragonite), and oyster shell (calcite) were ground

to similar particle sizes. Three volumes of each (1, 10, and 50 mL) were placed in 800 mL of aerated seawater and artificial seawater, and the pH was measured at times 0, 1, 2, 4, 8, and 24 h. Alkalinity measurements were made at 0 and 24 h. Changes in pH were negligible, but losses of alkalinity, particularly in the 50-mL samples, were substantial. All pH shifts were caused by changes in alkalinity. Alkalinity values of the silica samples remained essentially unchanged. Alkalinity of the seawater containing 50 mL of coral was 0.21 mEq/L (−12%) at 24 h; in the 50-mL oyster shell sample the decline amounted to 0.14 mEq/L (−7%) at 24 h. The effect was more pronounced in artificial seawater, even though the initial alkalinity exceeded that of the seawater. In the 50-mL coral sample, alkalinity dropped by 1.12 mEq/L (−46%); in the case of oyster shell the decline amounted to 0.71 mEq/L (−29%). In all instances alkalinity loss was attributed to precipitation of magnesium carbonate onto the surfaces of the minerals.

Siddall (1974) demonstrated that the tumbling of dolomite, which exposes new surfaces, temporarily increased its buffering activity 53%. According to Garrels et al. (1960), grinding or tumbling briefly increases the solubility of dolomite because the presence of two structurally nonequivalent cations (calcium and magnesium) makes the broken surfaces susceptible to *disordering effects* (i.e., the normal orderly arrangement of elements within the crystal is disrupted). The result is a reduction in stability at the surfaces of the mineral in contact with water. Stability of a solid is related to the rate of dissolution. Disordering effects are especially apparent in waters of low CO_2 (and therefore higher pH) because the overall solubility is less. Garrels and coauthors reported that exposing newly formed surfaces to distilled water saturated with CO_2 caused a rapid increase in pH (to an extrapolated equilibrium value of 6.2 after several hundred minutes), probably because dissolution is incongruent (uneven) under conditions of reduced stability: $MgCO_3$ is left behind. This effect, however, is short-lived. If the water is then decanted and replaced with new distilled water the solubility of the mineral returns to its original value, indicating that all exposed new material has been dissolved. Tests by Siddall (1974) with calcite revealed no substantial increase in pH above the equilibrium value. In my opinion, this happened in part because calcite contains a single cation (Ca^{2+}) and its dissolution is congruent.

(33) Bower et al. (1981).

(34) The quotation is from Weyl (1967).

(35) In chemical oceanography, *specific gravity* is traditionally defined as the ratio of the mass of a known volume of seawater at a specified temperature to that of an equal volume of pure water at 4°C (precisely 3.98°C). Operationally, the temperature of the standard solution can be any value, provided it matches that of the reference solution, or a correction is made to account for the difference when specific gravity is calculated.

(36) This method of correction is based on tables of Zerbe and Taylor (1953).

(37) At first glance Figure 1-23 appears to be wrong. Specific gravity values are known to increase with decreasing temperature because seawater becomes denser as the temperature is lowered. The opposite is depicted in the figure: the correction term is a positive value at high temperatures and negative at low ones. Thus a correction term applied to H (1.023 in the example in the text) at 23°C results in a larger number. This is because SG is corrected to 15.56°C, which in the example is lower than the sample temperature of 23°C. A specific gravity of 1.025 at 15.56°C, in other words, is the value that would have been obtained had the sample temperature been lowered to 15.56°C.

(38) Bidwell and Spotte (1985, p. 2) argued that "salinity" has meaning only in reference to seawater. The classic definition of salinity describes changes in the oxidation states of four minor constituents (carbonate, bromine, iodine, and chlorine; see Note 3). Consequently, salinity differs only slightly from the total mass of dissolved solids, with the two factors being within 0.5%. The exact seawater concentrations of the four constituents cannot be duplicated in artificial seawaters. Moreover, many artificial seawaters deviate from seawater in their concentrations and proportions of major ions. An artificial seawater can have a solute concentration comparable with seawater but differ in chemical composition. In other words, a reading of the total solute concentration of an artificial seawater obtained with a refractometer is not salinity. Bidwell and Spotte recommended the use of specific gravity at stated temperature when artificial seawaters are involved. The term "salinity" is deeply ingrained in our lexicon. I shall therefore use it when referring to either seawater or artificial seawater, but not without a certain queasiness.

(39) The equation was derived by Gary Adams of Sea Research Foundation.

(40) The following discussion is based on Spotte (1979b, pp. 321–322). A ''pH meter'' does not actually measure pH. Theoretically, the potential of a reversible electrochemical cell can be related directly to the *activity* (effective concentration) of the ions involved in the cell reaction, rather than actual concentration. Activity is a more useful concept because it considers the interionic forces involved. In a pH meter assembly, the cell consists in part of the two electrodes. The relationship

$$pH = -\log \{f'_{H^+}\} \tag{1.25}$$

where braces represent activity is valid if the buffers used to standardize and calibrate the electrode pair are similar in pH and ionic strength to seawater. Ordinarily, a dilute buffer solution of monobasic potassium phosphate, KH_2O_4P, is used. This buffer, specified by the National Bureau of Standards (NBS), has an ionic strength of 0.1 mol/kg, compared with 0.7 mol/kg for seawater at a salinity of 35‰. The differences in pH (7 compared with 8.2) are substantial. As a result, the theoretical definition of pH correlates only approximately with the measured value. As Hansson (1973) observed, when a cell is calibrated with a standard buffer solution of low ionic strength (e.g., NBS buffer standards), ''The pH-value of the sea water sample obtained by this procedure is not a measure of the concentration of H^+ or the activity of H^+. . . . It is just a value read on the pH-meter.'' Hansson (1973) developed a set of buffer standards close to the pH and ionic strength of seawater.

In aquarium management, consistency and convenience of data collection are what matter. The NBS buffer standards give highly reproducible results in seawater (Hawley and Pytkowicz 1973, Pytkowicz et al. 1975), and the fact that values obtained fall outside the framework of theoretical chemistry is of little consequence. In determining the acid-base status of aquarium seawater a value derived using a pH meter and dilute buffer standards is still ''pH'' from an operational standpoint. Further evidence that dilute buffer standards give excellent results can be found in Pytkowicz et al. (1966). They showed that pH measurements made with NBS standards are reproducible to ± 0.006 pH unit when the same reference electrode is used with different pH glass electrodes, and that reproducible values of ± 0.003 are possible with the same electrode pair.

Aquarists frequently monitor pH over a period of days or weeks, then average the values. However, there can be no such factor as mean pH. The notion of a series of pH values centered about the mean is inherently incorrect. Measuring the pH of a series of water samples and then dividing by the number of measurements yields a numerical value, but that value is not the mean. By definition, pH is the logarithm of the reciprocal of H^+ *normality*.* The p stands for *puissance* (power), and H is the symbol for hydrogen. As noted by Kinney (1973), summing a series of pH values multiplies the reciprocals of the normalities. Dividing by the number of samples gives the *n*th root of the product. The mean can only be determined by changing the original pH determinations to hydrogen normalities before dividing by the number of measurements. The logarithm of the reciprocal is then ''mean pH.'' An acceptable pH for aquarium seawater—and all other waters—should obviously be stated as a single value or a range of values.

(41) For a clear, concise description of how a pH assembly functions see Rothstein and Fisher (1985). My text discussion is based on theirs. As they explained, standardization and calibration rely on either of two basic design features of currently available pH meters. The first and more traditional method is used with analog and digital meters. It calls for adjustment of the input signal to the meter and involves addition or subtraction of DC voltage to correct for the offset voltage (standardization), in addition to adjustments in the gain of an amplifier to correct for non-Nernstian behavior of the glass membrane. The second method, which is relatively recent, uses microprocessors to handle standardization and interpret the electrode signal after it has been digitized.

The ideal behavior of inert membranes permeable only to H^+ is described by the Nernst equation:

$$E_s = -\frac{RT}{F}\ln\left(\frac{a_{H^+\text{ext}}}{a_{H^+\text{int}}}\right) \tag{1.26}$$

where E_s = the potential difference across the glass membrane (i.e., the difference in potential between the two phases separated by the membrane), R = the universal gas constant, T = temperature in °K, F = Faraday's constant, $a_{H^+\text{ext}}$ = H^+ activity outside the membrane, and $a_{H^+\text{int}}$ = H^+ activity internal to the membrane.

(42) Bates (1973) recommended that the two buffer standards bracket the anticipated pH of the sample solution. The anticipated pH of seawater is 8.2.

(43) The rules of calibration are from Rothstein and Fisher (1985).

*The *normality*, *N*, of a solution expresses the number of milliequivalents of dissolved solute contained in 1 mL of solution. Also see Note 13.

(44) The high precision method of alkalinity determination is from Almgren and Fonselius (1976). The original procedure is difficult to follow, and I have rewritten parts of it.

(45) The low precision method of alkalinity determination is from Spotte (1979a, pp. 134–135 and 1979b, pp. 319–320). Both references contain an error: the HCl concentration should be 0.01 *N* (or 0.01 mol/L), but is printed as 0.1 *N*.

(46) Adams and Spotte (1985) recommended this procedure.

(47) The procedure is from Spotte (1979b, pp. 98–99).

(48) Frakes et al. (1982) observed delayed metamorphosis in larval anemonefish (*Amphiprion ocellaris*) reared in artificial seawater deficient in iodine, I_2. Metamorphosis was delayed from 3 d to more than 8 d when iodine was absent, compared with time of metamorphosis in the same medium supplemented with iodine at the normal seawater concentration of 60 μg/L (the sum of iodate, IO_2^-, and iodide, I^-). Survival of larvae was independent of iodine, but delayed metamorphosis appeared to be detrimental to survival of postlarvae.

(49) See the survey of artificial seawater formulas by Bidwell and Spotte (1985). Hoffmann (1884) described the first artificial seawater formulated as a maintenance solution and used successfully in a public aquarium (Berlin). Kester et al. (1967) and Lyman and Fleming (1940) published nonspecific artificial seawater recipes for use in chemical oceanographic research. Segedi and Kelley (1964) produced a general formula for maintenance of marine animals. The Segedi-Kelley formula was later modified (Spotte 1979a, pp. 100–103 and 1979b, pp. 50–54); in another version it became Instant Ocean® Synthetic Sea Salts* (e.g., King and Spotte 1974).

(50) Called GP2 medium in previous publications (Bidwell and Spotte 1985, pp. 200–202; Spotte et al. 1984).

(51) Richard M. Segedi, formerly of Mystic Marinelife Aquarium, discovered that when technical-grade calcium chloride, $CaCl_2$, is dissolved in distilled water the pH value is often ~9, whereas the pH of a solution of reagent-grade material is ~7. The difference is sufficient to raise the pH of newly mixed artificial seawater above 8.2 when the technical-grade material is used. Segedi also observed that technical-grade $CaCl_2$ is frequently contaminated with ammonia, which is toxic to fishes (Chapter 2). Both high pH and ammonia contamination can be

* Aquarium Systems, 8141 Tyler Boulevard, Mentor OH 44060.

explained by the nature of the Solvay process, which is used to manufacture $CaCl_2$. According to Masterton and Slowinski (1969, pp. 474–477), raw materials used in the Solvay process are sodium chloride, water, and limestone (mainly calcium carbonate). Carbon dioxide, which is produced from the thermal decomposition of $CaCO_3$, is bubbled through a concentrated brine solution (NaCl dissolved in water) saturated with ammonia (NH_4^+ + NH_3) at ~0°C. Sodium bicarbonate precipitates. The ammonia is recovered by heating the remaining solution with slaked lime (calcium oxide, CaO). What remains is $CaCl_2$. The final pH of GP2 solution—or any other maintenance solution—cannot be predicted with greater accuracy than ±0.3 unit without mixing a batch. This is because the compositions of technical-grade salts and the chemistry of tap waters vary.

(52) This section is based on Spotte (1979a, pp. 97–102) and Spotte (1979b, pp. 43–47 and 51–54).

CHAPTER 2

(1) Spotte (1979b, pp. 23–24 and 100–164). Egotism was not the motive for relying heavily on my own work, nor was it my intention to induce narcolepsy among colleagues familiar with what I had written previously. Ordinarily, plagiarism is a form of flattery to the author whose work has been stolen. Someone who steals his own work merely draws attention to how little his writing skills have improved.

(2) Spotte (1979b, p. 117).

(3) This discussion is based on Spotte (1979b, pp. 106–111).

(4) Kester and Pytkowicz (1967).

(5) According to Owens and Esaias (1976), no evidence exists that algae can directly assimilate forms of phosphorus other than orthophosphate; however, DOP can be hydrolyzed at the the outer cell surfaces and used indirectly.

(6) Goldizen (1970) speculated that phosphorus precipitates as calcium salts; Saeki (1958, 1962) proposed that calcium and magnesium salts are formed in combination with phosphorus. However, Saeki's work was performed using water to which lime had been added to control alkalinity and pH. Logically, both magnesium and calcium would be involved in the precipitation of phosphorus compounds. Kester and Pytkowicz (1967) demonstrated that 96% of the PO_4^{3-} and 44% of the HPO_4^{2-} exist

in the sea as ion pairs, probably in association with calcium and magnesium. Siddall (1974), using X-ray diffraction, could not find evidence that phosphorus compounds coat old aquarium gravel, but this does not preclude surface adsorption as a possibility. As Stumm and Morgan (1981, p. 285) noted, X-ray diffraction not only has poor sensitivity, but is incapable of detecting impurities adsorbed onto the solid surfaces of minerals. Changes that result from occlusion can sometimes be detected. *Occlusion* is the process by which impurities become trapped in the solids. This is different from surface adsorption, in which impurities are adsorbed onto mineral surfaces under nonequilibrium conditions. The extent to which occlusion occurs depends on the rate of precipitation; in adsorption, the impurity is either adsorbed or reacts with the surface of the solid to form a surface complex. Occlusion alters the lattice dimension of the solid, and the changes are sometimes measurable by X-ray diffraction. However, surface adsorption causes no such changes, and the presence of impurities cannot be detected.

Malone and Towe (1970) showed that in cultures of aerated seawater, bacteria formed the mineral struvite, $NH_4MgPO_4 \cdot 6H_2O$, by a reaction between phosphorus and ammonium ions. The reaction occurred in the presence of magnesium and organic matter. The ammonia had been produced during the mineralization of DOC. Even if some of the orthophosphate is precipitated on gravel in the filter bed, it seems unlikely that much could be removed in this manner.

(7) Baylor et al. (1962).

(8) According to Sutcliffe et al. (1963), total phosphorus and orthophosphate are bound to these particles as they form in surface foam produced by aeration. This was demonstrated by the disappearance of both forms of phosphorus from an experimental aeration chamber. The suggestion put forth was that during particle formation orthophosphate is adsorbed onto insoluble organic particles and removed from solution.

(9) The distinction between DOC and POC is arbitrary. Ordinarily, the organic fraction that passes through a 0.45-μm filter is considered as DOC and the fraction retained as POC (Reuter and Perdue 1977). According to Parsons (1975), the lower size limit of POC is 0.5 to 1.0 μm. Johnson and Wangersky (1985) criticized the arbitrary selection of the 0.45-μm pore size and suggested that 2 μm might be more reasonable.

(10) Schnitzer and Khan (1972, p. 3) defined humic materials as ". . . amorphous, brown or black, hydrophilic, acidic, polydisperse substances of molecular weights ranging from several

hundreds to tens of thousands.'' Humus consists of two major fractions: (1) *humic acid*, which is soluble in dilute base and insoluble in alcohol and acid; and (2) *fulvic acid*, which is water-soluble and stays in solution after the humic acid has precipitated (Steelink 1977). Both definitions are strictly operational.

Harvey et al. (1983, 1984) reported that humic substances in seawater are water-soluble, aliphatic organic acids formed by the autoxidative cross-linking of two or more polyunsaturated fatty acids, a class of lipids (see Chapter 8 for a description of fatty acids). Humus allowed to form in the laboratory under controlled conditions was similar to humic substances that form naturally in seawater.

(11) Harvey et al. (1983).

(12) Hirayama et al. (1988).

(13) Soil humus is reported to vary in age from 50 to 3000 years, according to Gjessing (1976). The alkaline-extractable fraction (i.e., fulvic acid) is 50 to 250 years, whereas the portion resistant to extraction is considerably older (~2000 years). Bada and Lee (1977) concluded from radioactive carbon dating studies that ''. . . the dissolved organic material present in the sub-surface waters of the oceans has an apparent ^{14}C age of several thousand years. Since this age is greater than the mixing time of the oceans . . . this would imply that the bulk of the organic material in seawater has been recycled several times and has still not been degraded.'' Humification is immensely important. If all the carbon and nitrogen generated biologically were to be mineralized and recycled, none would accumulate in such refractory forms as coal and oil.

(14) The origin of aquatic humus is considered to be either *allochthonous* (leached or eroded from soil) or *autochthonous* (formed from the cellular constituents and exudates of aquatic organisms, primarily plants). The humus of freshwaters is mainly allochthonous (see the review of Reuter and Perdue 1977). The *pigmented fraction* of humus (the portion colored greenish-yellow) extracted from river and lake waters consists of mixtures of polyphenols and phenolic acids (Christman 1970), or essentially the same breakdown products derived from soil humus (Schnitzer and Khan 1972, pp. 137–201). Once transported to an aquatic environment humus is subject to alteration by chemical and microbial activities. Any resemblance of terrestrial to aquatic humus is therefore debatable (see Note 10). Accordingly, Liao et al. (1982) criticized earlier work claiming to have identified structural similarities. They wrote: ''Humic materials isolated from soils have been extensively studied

. . . but it is presumptive to conclude that aquatic humic materials are similar except for chemical complexity.'' Harvey et al. (1983) remarked that reports of humus formation and composition in freshwater and terrestrial environments are ''irrelevant to seawater humus.'' Kalle (1966) and Williams and Gordon (1970) considered allochthonous pathways to be unlikely sources of organic matter in the oceans, and recent writers have generally agreed (Bada and Lee 1977; Harvey et al. 1983, 1984; Jackson 1975). Much of the organic matter transported by rivers and streams precipitates on contact with seawater (Sholkovitz 1976). In addition, the allochthonous component diminishes markedly in concentration with increasing distance from land (Breger and Brown 1962, Kalle 1966, Nissenbaum and Kaplan 1972, Sieburth and Jensen 1968). Present evidence supports a mainly autochthonous origin of oceanic humus, derived from phytoplankton in offshore waters (Kalle 1966, Prieur and Sathyendranath 1981) and seaweeds in coastal regions (Craigie and McLachlan 1964; Sieburth and Jensen 1968, 1969, 1970).

(15) Many of the brown seaweeds are intertidal and able to withstand desiccation at low tide. During reimmersion, phenols are released into the water as normal exudates (Zavodnik 1981). Sieburth and Jensen (1969, 1970) reported that phenolic substances in fresh exudates of the seaweeds *Ascophyllum nodosum* were nontoxic to plaice (*Pleuronectes platessa*) larvae. Under the alkaline conditions of seawater the polyphenols were converted to free polyphenols, which had an LC_{50} (lethal concentration at which 50% of the test animals die) of 0.32 mg/L. Free polyphenol rapidly ''tanned'' proteinaceous and carbohydrate materials to form humus, after which it again was nontoxic to plaice larvae.

So few studies have been done on the toxicity of humus that no general conclusions can be made. The work cited above suggests that some portions of the DOC may be more toxic during humification than afterward, when they become biologically and chemically stable and inert. If so, it is important to remove these transitional compounds as they form. The degree of pigmentation of the water is probably not a relative indication of toxicity. The initial polyphenolic compounds described by Sieburth and Jensen (1969, 1970) are colorless. However, during reaction with other organics (i.e., during humification) they are highly toxic. The strongly pigmented fraction of aquarium seawater, if truly inert, is perhaps less toxic than its paler precursor. During humification, polyphenols may precipitate carbohydrate and proteinaceous materials in the tissues of living animals. The toxic effect is manifested at that instant, but not afterward when a visible yellow pigment has appeared.

(16) Schnitzer and Khan (1972, pp. 5–6).

(17) This discussion is based on Spotte (1979b, pp. 118–121).

(18) The toxicity of ammonia to aquatic animals was reviewed by API (1981) and Spotte (1979b, pp. 276–289). In fishes the effects include (*1*) extensive damage to tissues, especially the gills and kidney (Burkhalter and Kaya 1977; Burrows 1964; Flis 1968a, 1968b; Larmoyeux and Piper 1973; Redner and Stickney 1979; Reichenbach-Klinke 1967; Schreckenbach et al. 1975; Sigel et al. 1972; Smart 1976; Smith and Piper 1975; Thurston et al. 1978, Yang and Chun 1986); (*2*) physiological imbalances (Lloyd and Orr 1969, Shaffi 1980, Smart 1978, Sousa and Meade 1977, Swift 1981, Tomasso et al. 1981); (*3*) impaired growth (Alderson 1979, Brockway 1950, Burkhalter and Kaya 1977, Burrows 1964, Colt and Tchobanoglous 1978, Kawamoto 1961, Larmoyeux and Piper 1973, Robinette 1976, Sadler 1981/1982); (*4*) diminished resistance to disease (Burkhalter and Kaya 1977, Burrows 1964, Smart 1976, Wolf 1957); and (*5*) alteration of normal predator–prey interactions (Woltering et al. 1978).

(19) Lewis and Morris (1986) reviewed the toxicity of nitrite to fishes, although my comments are not based on their assessment. Nitrite toxicity studies have focused either on strictly freshwater species such as the channel catfish (*Ictalurus punctatus*), or salmonids and other species capable of acclimating to either freshwater or saline environments. The results of experiments attempting to identify which ions exert protective effects when the two fish types are compared often differ markedly, suggesting different protective mechanisms. Chloride ion, Cl^-, produces a clearly protective effect in both types (Bowser et al. 1983, 1989; Eddy et al. 1983; Huey et al. 1982; Iwai et al. 1974; Perrone and Meade 1977; Russo et al. 1981; Schwedler and Tucker 1983; Tomasso et al. 1980b; Wedemeyer and Yasutake 1978). Calcium, Ca^{2+}, does not reduce the incidence of toxicity or magnitude of the toxic response (i.e., methemoglobin formation) in salmonids acclimated to seawater, but raises the threshold of nitrite toxicity substantially (Crawford and Allen 1977). However, calcium exerts no such protective effect in channel catfish (Tomasso et al. 1980b). Preliminary work has shown that sodium bicarbonate, $NaHCO_3$, protects channel catfish against nitrite toxicity, but sodium sulfate, Na_2SO_4, does not. This suggests that in this species monovalent cations such as sodium, Na^+, perhaps lower toxicity, whereas multivalent anions (e.g., SO_4^{2-}) may not (Tomasso et al. 1979).

In salmonids acclimated to seawater, Cl^- is thought to compete with NO_2^- for adsorption sites on the gill surface (Perrone and Meade 1977, Tomasso et al. 1979). The concentration of Cl^-

in full-strength seawater is ~19 g/L. The addition of chloride as a sodium or calcium salt dramatically lowers nitrite toxicity in salmonids acclimated to freshwater. Wedemeyer and Yasutake (1978), for example, showed that addition of 200 mg NaCl/L reduced nitrite toxicity in steelhead trout (*Oncorhynchus mykiss*) by threefold. Addition of 200 mg/L calcium chloride, $CaCl_2$, lowered the toxic threshold by a factor of fifty. Almendras (1987) found nitrite to be fifty-five times more toxic to juvenile milkfish (*Chanos chanos*) in freshwater than in brackish water ($S = 16‰$). The 48-h median LC_{50} values were, respectively, 12 and 675 mg NO_2-N/L.

Seawater fishes are notably resistant to nitrite toxicity. Postlarval red drums (*Sciaenops ocellatus*) tolerate 100 mg NO_2-N/L with no decrease in growth rate (Holt and Arnold 1983). Wise and Tomasso (1989), however, reported increased toxicity of nitrite to red drum fingerlings in dilute seawater (1.4‰). Saroglia et al. (1981) reported that in the seabass (*Dicentrarchus labrax*) the 96-h LC_{50} at 23°C was 220 mg NO_2-N/L; in European eel (*Anguilla anguilla*) elvers the LC_{50} at 96 h ($S = 30‰$) was 503 mg NO_2-N/L. Concentrations >3 mg NO_2-N/L are unusual in seawater aquarium exhibits.

Nitrate appears to be less toxic than nitrite. Frakes and Hoff (1982) reported that survival of juvenile anemonefish (*Amphiprion ocellaris*) was 100% at 100 mg NO_3-N/L, but growth was impaired. Otte and Rosenthal (1978) maintained tilapia (*Oreochromis mossambica, O. nilotica, O. zilli*) and European eels without adverse effects in a closed system containing brackish water. Concentrations of NO_3-N typically ranged from 200 to 400 mg/L with occasional peaks of 1100 mg/L. In my opinion, concentrations <50 mg NO_3-N/L are safe for adult fishes in seawater aquarium exhibits.

(20) See Hellebust (1974). Of the macroscopic forms, brown algae of the genera *Ascophyllum, Ectocarpus, Fucus,* and *Laminaria* are known to liberate complex proteinaceous materials (Fogg and Boalch 1958, Sieburth 1969). Similar substances are present in the extracellular products of the unicellular red alga *Porphyridium* and the red seaweeds *Chondrus* and *Polysiphonia* (Jones 1962, Sieburth 1969).

(21) Painter (1970).

(22) Johnson and Sieburth (1976) claimed that heterotrophic bacteria in aquarium water compete with nitrifiers for inorganic nitrogen. Culter and Crump (1933) reported that at least 104 species of soil heterotrophs could oxidize ammonia to nitrite. Tate (1977) found that cultures of the soil heterotroph *Anthrobacter* could oxidize ammonia directly to both nitrite and nitrate.

In other instances, heterotrophic bacteria have been known to convert nitrogenous organic compounds directly to nitrite and nitrate without first forming ammonia (Doxtader and Alexander 1966, Jensen and Gundersen 1955, Quastel et al. 1950).

The traditional role of oceanic heterotrophs has been that of net mineralizers. However, recent research has shown that heterotrophic bacteria consume substantial quantities of ammonia and nitrate in direct competition with phytoplankton. In this capacity they strongly influence oceanic nitrogen budgets, and therefore nitrogen cycling (Laws et al. 1985). Natural assemblages of oceanic heterotrophs in culture reproduced threefold when supplemented with inorganic nitrogen (Horrigan et al. 1988).

Tupas and Koike (1990) showed that the contribution of NH_4^+ to total microbial nitrogen demand in natural assemblages of seawater bacteria in culture ranged from 50 to 88%, even when large amounts of dissolved organic nitrogen were also taken up. In addition, 80% of the dissolved organic nitrogen assimilated was converted intracellularly to NH_4^+, refuting the idea that NH_4^+ assimilation is restricted to times and locations where organic nitrogen is limiting.

(23) This discussion is based on Spotte (1979b, pp. 112–116 and 121–123).

(24) Nitrification was reviewed by Sharma and Ahlert (1977).

(25) Watson et al. (1981) reviewed the taxonomy of nitrifying bacteria.

(26) Oceanic nitrifiers may be obligate chemoautotrophs (Glover 1983, Watson and Waterbury 1971).

(27) Wallace et al. (1970) demonstrated that cultures of *Nitrosomonas europaea* and *Nitrobacter winogradsky* (= *N. agilis*, see Note 25) assimilate organic compounds in both the presence and absence of their respective inorganic energy sources. Clark and Schmidt (1967b) showed that *N. europaea* could assimilate several amino acids, but the rate of uptake was enhanced in the presence of ammonia (see Note 22). Smith and Hoare (1968) found that cell suspensions of *N. winogradsky* took up acetate in the presence of nitrite, although more slowly than when nitrite was absent.

(28) See Smith and Hoare (1968). Delwiche and Finstein (1965) determined that labeled isotopes of acetate and glycine contributed substantially to cellular carbon. In the case of acetate, 42.2% of the amount supplied exogenously was incorporated into cellular carbon by resting suspensions of *Nitrobacter wino-*

gradsky. When glycine was used, 22.8% of the glycine-*1*-^{14}C and 20% of the glycine-2-^{14}C were incorporated into cellular carbon. Smith and Hoare (1968) found that *N. winogradsky* could grow under heterotrophic conditions in the absence of nitrite. The organism assimilated acetate-*1*-^{14}C; acetate-2-^{14}C and acetate carbon accounted for 33 to 39% of the newly synthesized cellular carbon. Moreover, carbon from the acetate was used in the synthesis of all cellular materials, including most of the amino acids and cell proteins. Steinmüller and Bock (1977) reported that *N. winogradsky* could be grown autotrophically on nitrite, mixotrophically on nitrite together with either acetate or pyruvate, and heterotrophically on acetate and casamino acids, pyruvate and casamino acids, and pyruvate and nitrate.

Clark and Schmidt (1967a) reported that cultures of *Nitrosomonas europaea* incorporated ^{14}C isotopes of several amino acids. Both protein synthesis and formation of nitrite were increased in the presence of L-glutamic acid, L-aspartic acid, L-serine, and L-glutamine. Other amino acids tested either were toxic or had no effect. However, all were taken up and metabolized by growing cells when present at low concentrations, regardless of whether their effects at higher levels were stimulatory, inhibitory, or inconsequential. Further evidence that low concentrations of ^{14}C-amino acids (1 μg/mL or less) added to the environment were taken up by *N. europaea* was presented in another work (Clark and Schmidt 1967b). Wallace et al. (1970) incubated cell suspensions of *N. europaea* and *N. winogradsky* with ^{14}C isotopes of CO_2, acetate, pyruvate, α-ketoglutarate, succinate, glutamate, and aspartate. After incubation periods of up to 1 h, these tracer substances were found in proteins, soluble amino and organic acids, and neutral cell fractions.

(29) This discussion is based on Spotte (1979b, pp. 123–139).

(30) Audic et al. (1984) demonstrated that the rate of oxidation of nitrite by a pure strain of *Nitrobacter winogradsky* was 130% greater in colonies attached to glass beads than in free cells. Saeki (1958) attributed 25% of the nitrifying capacity of the filter bed of an experimental aquarium to accumulated detritus, which provided additional surface area.

(31) Khailov and Finenko (1970) concluded that DOC in the sea must be adsorbed onto solid substrates before it can be used by microorganisms. They saw the process as consisting of two steps: (*1*) physical (adsorption onto a substratum) and (*2*) biochemical (conversion of the DOC once it has been adsorbed). The important feature of this concept is the role assigned to detritus in the conversion of organic carbon to inorganic substances. Khailov and Finenko did not believe that heterotrophs

assimilate DOC directly; rather, the high surface activity demonstrated by many of these compounds suggests a mechanism by which they are adsorbed onto particulate material populated by bacteria. The authors went on to say, ''The data give the impression that the traditional question: 'do micro-organisms populating detritus decompose organic matter dissolved in the surrounding water or organic matter of detritus itself?' was posed inexactly. Apparently the answer is that micro-organisms populating detrital particules decompose dissolved surfactants of sea water, but only after their adsorption on to the detritus surface.''

(32) Lees and Quastel (1946a, 1946b) thought that nitrification rates were increased in the presence of soil particles, supposedly because the nutrient ions available for use by nitrifiers are fixed at particle surfaces. According to this hypothesis, ammonium ions, NH_4^+, are held in base exchange combinations, and nutrient uptake occurs by ion exchange. Later work by Allison et al. (1951, 1953a, 1953b, 1953c) produced different results: as more NH_4^+ was adsorbed onto soil particles, less became available for nitrification. Kholdebarin and Oertli (1977) studied the effects of suspended solids from a freshwater river on nitrification in culture. They concluded that nitrification rates are indeed enhanced in the presence of particles, but not because of any chemical affinity of the organisms to their attachment sites. Instead, the particles seem to provide places for physical attachment and nothing more. The greater the number of particles in suspension, the greater the surface area available for potential colonization.

(33) Johnson and Sieburth (1976) measured films that varied from 1 to 5 mm thick on the surfaces of membrane filters submerged for 20 to 40 d in a freshwater salmon culture facility. In comparison, little slime was evident in the filtrant of a sparsely populated seawater aquarium. Heavy films have been reported from the surfaces of gravel grains in trickling filters (Hoehn and Ray 1973), in which wastewater is sprayed over a gravel bed exposed to the air. Nutrients are oxidized by aerobic bacteria as the wastewater ''trickles'' through the gravel. Thick films are possible partly because wastewater contains high nutrient levels. In addition, exposure to the atmosphere allows a cross section of the film to remain aerobic to a greater depth because of the larger concentration of oxygen in air compared with water. Biological films rely on the diffusion of oxygen from the environment to sustain aerobic bacteria. In submerged filters, where dissolved oxygen concentrations are much lower than in the atmosphere, thick films often become oxygen limited near the base.

Film formation is a common process in nature. Bacteriologists in the 1930s first discovered that solid surfaces submerged in freshwater or seawater promote microbial activity. Clean glass slides suspended beneath the surface in lakes (Henrici and Johnson 1935, Smith and ZoBell 1937) or in the sea (ZoBell and Anderson 1936) are soon covered with an assortment of bacteria, in addition to other microorganisms and particulate matter. To explain this phenomenon, Stark et al. (1938) and Heukelekian and Heller (1940) proposed that solid surfaces enhance the concentration of nutrients, promoting microbial activity indirectly.

Microorganisms that attach to solid surfaces are called *periphytes* (ZoBell 1970). Heterotrophic and autotrophic bacteria attached to the walls or gravel grains in the filter beds of seawater aquariums are therefore periphytic. Once attached, periphytic bacteria form microcolonies. The microcolonies, in turn, produce a biological film composed of their own products (Corpe 1970). Many periphytic microorganisms that live in biological films are stalked, budding, or filamentous and therefore truly sessile (Corpe 1974). Others presumably move about within the matrix.

(34) Williamson and McCarty (1976).

(35) Hoehn and Ray (1973).

(36) Heukelekian and Crosby (1956a, 1956b) estimated that most wastewater films break apart regularly about every 14 d. Corpe (1974) found that microcolonies, consisting of pseudomonads that became attached to a glass slide suspended in seawater, turned over every 3 to 4 d.

(37) Lees (1952).

(38) As Lees (1952) noted, care must be taken when interpreting data on the effects of inhibiting substances, especially when the experimental work was extended for days or weeks. Many compounds inhibit cell growth in culture, but may not affect the capacity of the remaining cells to oxidize the energy source. During prolonged experiments, the distinction becomes more nebulous if neither factor has been controlled. For instance, by limiting the duration of the experiments to a few hours, cell proliferation as a variable can be eliminated. If, for example, the suspected inhibitor X is added to an experimental culture but not to the control, and if the nitrite or nitrate formed in the culture containing X is less than in the control, there still is no indication of how X behaved. If X inhibited oxidation directly, less ammonia or nitrite would be formed in its presence. But if X actually had no effect on oxidation but inhibited cell growth,

the accumulation of ammonia-oxidizing enzymes would naturally be less than in the controls, and a smaller amount of nitrite or nitrate would appear in the experimental culture than in the controls. The quantity of substance formed in each experimental culture might be the same, but the mechanisms of formation would be different. To say that compound *X* inhibits the oxidation of ammonia is not necessarily synonymous with the statement that *X* inhibits the growth of ammonia-oxidizing bacteria.

(39) Meiklejohn (1954) wrote: ''The electrolytes to which the nitrifiers are sensitive include their own substrates, and in each case, the substrate of the other species was found to be much more toxic than the organisms' own substrate. Nitrite depressed both respiration and growth of *Nitrosomonas*. . . . *Nitrobacter* was sensitive to the ammonium ion, but even more so to free ammonia. . . . Nitrate . . . was only slightly toxic to both species.''

(40) Anthonisen et al. (1976).

(41) Srna and Baggaley (1975) reported that sulfide ion at concentrations of 0.03 mg/L severely inhibited the oxidation of ammonia in aquarium seawater at 20 to 24°C. Inhibition continued until the sulfide ion concentration was reduced to 0.015 mg/L. Conversion of nitrite to nitrate was 14% slower when sulfide was present at 0.1 mg/L. Yoshida (1967) found that nitrite formation in nearly pure cultures of seawater oxidizers was not inhibited by addition of Na_2S until the concentration reached 3 mg/L; all activity stopped at 30 mg/L.

(42) Gundersen (1955) reported that five amino acids—L-tryptophan, L-glutamic acid, L-histidine, L-tyrosine, and L-phenylalanine—inhibited the growth of *Nitrosomonas europaea* in culture when present at 100 mg/L. Clark and Schmidt (1967a), however, found that in the case of the first three compounds, only L-histidine inhibited the growth of *N. europaea* at lower concentrations (4 mg/L).

(43) The results of toxicity studies must be interpreted cautiously because the experimental method can affect the results. The findings of Collins et al. (1975, 1976) are not directly comparable with those of Levine and Meade (1976) because the experiments involved different protocols. Collins and coauthors measured the effects of the compounds they tested by taking water samples directly from aquariums containing fish and functional filter beds. Levine and Meade used inoculates of mixed bacteria, and their measurements were performed in culture. Levine and Meade acknowledged that their assays were

possibly more sensitive than might have been the case under actual operating conditions. They showed, for example, that formalin, malachite green, and nifurpirinol (Furanace®) were mildly toxic to nitrifying bacteria, whereas Collins and coauthors had determined the same compounds to be harmless. Levine and Meade attributed the sensitivity of their cultures to the greater percentage of autotrophs in the original inoculants and suggested that low inhibition thresholds for these substances might not exist in the presence of greater numbers of heterotrophs and higher concentrations of organic matter.

(44) The concentration of dissolved oxygen required for maximum growth and activity of nitrifying bacteria varies widely. Part of the reason has been the failure of investigators to control certain experimental variables (Stenstrom and Poduska 1980). Another reason is the adaptability of nitrifying bacteria, and future experimental work should note the partial pressure of O_2 to which the organisms had been acclimated previously. The general statement can be made that nitrifying bacteria adapted to seawater are aerobic, although their oxygen requirements are lower than those of many other aerobic species.

Carlucci and McNally (1969) showed that nitrifying bacteria isolated from the open sea oxidized low concentrations of substrate in a liquid medium containing <0.14 mg O_2/L and in a solid medium when the concentration was <0.002 atm O_2.* More carbon was assimilated per unit of substratum oxidized in low than in high oxygen concentrations. This confirmed the earlier work of Gundersen (1966), who reported that nitrification occurred under conditions of low oxygen. *Nitrosococcus* (= *Nitrosocystis*) *oceanus* grew more efficiently when the oxygen concentration was <0.05 atm than in air (0.2 atm O_2); that is, more carbon was assimilated per unit of nitrogen oxidized. In a liquid medium, the lowest oxygen concentration at which nitrification still occurred was ~ 0.05 mg/L.

Kimata et al. (1961) demonstrated how aeration can harm cultures of nitrifying bacteria isolated from seawater, and Kawai et al. (1965) wrote that high aeration rates actually lowered the activities of nitrifiers in seawater, although the effects were shown to be the opposite in freshwater. Kawai and coauthors noted that nitrifying activity was greatest at higher oxygen concentrations, but some activity continued under near anaerobic conditions. Forster (1974) found that ammonia oxidation in aquarium seawater was inhibited at dissolved oxygen concentrations below 0.6 to 0.7 mg O_2/L. Sugiyama and Kawai (1978) determined the turnover rate of ammonia in aerated aquariums

*The abbreviation atm stands for atmosphere.

with mud on the bottoms and no filtration to be 4.5%/h, compared with 0.6%/h in aquariums without aeration.

(45) Watson (1965) found that pure cultures of *Nitrosococcus* (= *Nitrosocystis*) *oceanus* grew best at 30°C. Carlucci and Strickland (1968), working with the same species, determined an optimal temperature of 28°C, with 20°C the next best temperature for activity (oxidation of ammonia). A second (unknown) ammonia oxidizer performed most efficiently at 37°C, as did an undetermined species of nitrite oxidizer.

Kawai et al. (1965) reported that nitrifying bacteria in seawater aquarium filter beds demonstrated greatest activity at 30 to 35°C; activity diminished when the temperature was raised or lowered. The optimal temperature for freshwater nitrifiers was ~30°C. Below 20°C the differences in activity between seawater and freshwater nitrifiers become more conspicuous. Yoshida (1967) noted an optimal temperature of 27 to 28°C for growth of seawater nitrifiers. His organisms, however, had been isolated in culture at 25°C, and an optimal growth rate near the acclimation temperature is not surprising. The greatest level of activity for ammonia oxidizers occurred at 30 to 35°C. In another study (Yoshida et al. 1967), the optimal temperature of a seawater ammonia oxidizer was 50 to 55°C.

Srna and Baggaley (1975) studied the kinetics of nitrification in seawater aquariums. An increase in water temperature of 4°C in conditioned aquariums increased ammonia and nitrite conversion rates by 50 and 12%, respectively, compared with calculated values. Lowering the temperature 1°C slowed down the oxidation rate of ammonia by 30%, and a 1.5°C decrease dropped the rate of nitrite conversion by 8%, compared with calculated values.

Nitrification evidently is more efficient in warm water. As to ideal temperatures >30°C, Carlucci and Strickland (1968) pointed out that it is not uncommon for seawater bacteria in culture to demonstrate optimal temperatures much higher than the temperature of the natural environment. None of the cultures tested by Carlucci and Strickland (1968) was able to carry out nitrification at 5°C, even after 4 months of incubation. However, Collos et al. (1988) measured efficient nitrification in the water column of a shallow coastal pond at subzero temperatures.

Carlucci and Strickland (1968) determined the rate constant, *k*, for several ammonia and nitrite oxidizers growing in a range of substrate concentrations. At concentrations typical of seawater, *k* was ~0.05/d at 25°C, indicating slow oxidation. Buswell et al. (1954) found that *k* values in pure cultures of *Nitrosomonas europaea* increased from 0.5/d at 15°C to 2/d at 32°C.

The calculated increase from these data is 8.2%/°C (Knowles et al. 1965). As shown by Knowles and coauthors, the *k* values of nitrifying bacteria vary widely.

(46) Reports of the ideal pH ranges for efficient nitrification are variable. Srna and Baggaley (1975) analyzed data from several sources; all but one dealt with freshwater. They suggested that the numbers did not agree because of the varied conditions under which the test organisms had been maintained. Evidently, nitrifying bacteria can be conditioned to function through a wide pH range, provided they are given time to adjust to new conditions. Kawai et al. (1965) determined the optimal pH for seawater nitrifiers to be 9.0. Saeki (1958) had earlier reported optimal pH values of 7.8 and 7.1 for ammonia and nitrite oxidation, respectively, in seawater aquariums. Srna and Baggaley (1975) found that the seawater nitrifiers used in their study functioned best at pH 7.45, with an effective range of 7.0 to 8.2. Yoshida (1967) reported optimal values for four strains of unidentified seawater ammonia oxidizers that varied from 7.0 to 9.0, and Yoshida et al. (1967) found the optimal pH range for a seawater ammonia oxidizer to be 8.5 to 8.7. Forster (1974) lowered the pH slowly in an experimental seawater aquarium; nitrification stopped at pH 5.5.

(47) Kawai et al. (1965) reported this observation. In addition, no activity was observed when the seawater was replaced with freshwater, but some remained even when the salinity of the full-strength seawater was doubled. As might be expected, the nitrifying activity of the freshwater filter sand was greatest before addition of any seawater. Activity stopped when the salinity reached the value of full-strength seawater. Kawai and coauthors found that nitrifying activities in a warm seawater aquarium were greatest at the salinity to which the filter bed bacteria had been acclimated, in this case full-strength seawater. Nitrifying activity diminished as the water was made more dilute or concentrated, although some activity remained even after the salinity was doubled. Srna and Baggaley (1975) demonstrated that a decrease in salinity of 8‰ and an increase of 5‰ did not affect the rate of nitrification in aquarium seawater.

The unknown seawater ammonia oxidizers cultured by Yoshida (1967) grew best in 50 to 60% seawater. Growth rates declined gradually as the solution was either concentrated or diluted. Four strains of these organisms demonstrated greatest activity in seawater concentrations of 40 to 100%.

(48) This discussion is based on Spotte (1979b, pp. 139–144).

(49) Jeris and Owens (1975).

(50) Many species of heterotrophic and autotrophic bacteria are capable of dissimilation, but heterotrophs are more important. Painter (1970) listed these genera: *Achromobacter, Micrococcus, Pseudomonas, Denitrobacillus, Spirillum,* and *Bacillus*. Davies and Toerien (1971) isolated members of the first three genera from domestic sewage, in addition to *Alcaligenes, Aerobacter, Brevibacterium, Paracolobactrum, Enterobacter, Proteus, Serratia, Anthrobacter, Leptotricha,* and *Lactobacillus*. Ozretich (1977) reported on nitrate reduction by four species of bacteria isolated from seawater. Three belonged to the genus *Pseudomonas,* and the fourth was *Vibrio anguillarum*.

(51) The definition of denitrification is from Knowles (1982), but also see Delwiche and Bryan (1976), Goering (1972), Painter (1970), Payne (1981), and Stewart (1988).

(52) Knowles (1982).

(53) Davies and Toerien (1971) monitored the rise and fall of denitrifying bacteria in a mixed-species population cultured from domestic sewage. When the carbon source was changed from glucose to malate some species disappeared, and the numbers of the others declined. New forms better able to use malate became dominant. There was a time lag while species better suited to the new carbon source proliferated and the activity and numbers of the rest gradually diminished.

(54) Dodd and Bone (1975) described denitrification systems for treating wastewaters.

(55) St. Amant and McCarty (1969).

(56) Meade (1974).

(57) Dawson and Murphy (1972).

(58) Dodd and Bone (1975).

(59) Davies and Toerien (1971).

(60) See references in Note 51.

(61) Bishop et al. (1976).

(62) Kawai et al. (1964) noticed that nitrate decreased after 3 months in seawater aquariums kept at 22°C, and they attributed this to dissimilation by filter bed bacteria. Aerobic bacteria in the filter sand numbered 10^7/g after 3 months, and 10% of these organisms could reduce NO_3^-. Aerobes outnumbered anaerobes by tenfold, but 50% of the anaerobic forms could reduce NO_3^-. Kawai and coauthors concluded that portions of the filter bed must have been anaerobic, despite continuous aer-

ation and circulation of the water. This is a logical but seldom-considered characteristic of aquariums, especially those with deep filter beds. Most of the oxygen is consumed in the first few centimetres of filtrant, and the remaining layers may become oxygen deficient. Mulbarger (1971), working with cultures of mixed bacteria from activated sludge, found that even when relatively high levels of oxygen were present (1 mg O_2/L), denitrification was possible. This was attributed to local oxygen depletion, meaning that denitrification occurred during anaerobic conditions. Perhaps the situation in aquarium filter beds is similar. High concentrations of dissolved oxygen in the water column do not preclude local anoxia deep within the filtrant.

(63) St. Amant and McCarty (1969) reported that denitrification was efficient in a pilot plant wastewater treatment column down to 12°C; below that, efficiency tapered off rapidly. In working with activated sludge, Dawson and Murphy (1972) noted that the denitrification rate declined 80% when the temperature was lowered from 20 to 5°C. However, after the bacteria had acclimated to the lower temperature, denitrification once again became efficient. The authors concluded that denitrification is practical in water treatment at temperatures of 5 to 27°C.

(64) The optimal pH value for denitrifiers depends on the concentration of NO_3^-, age of the culture, and species of organism (Delwiche 1956). *Pseudomonas aeruginosa* was most active between pH 7 and 8.2, although denitrification occurred within a much wider range (5.8 to 9.2). Delwiche also noted that pH affects both the rate of denitrification and composition of the end products. Above pH 7.3, N_2 was the principal end product; below this value the percentage of N_2O was greater. Wuhrmann and Mechsner (1965), working with denitrifying isolates from activated sludge, found that at pH values of 7 and higher the inhibitory effects of oxygen increased. This suggests the possibility of synergism between oxygen and pH in alkaline solutions such as seawater.

(65) This discussion is based on Spotte (1979b, pp. 144–147).

(66) *Uptake* refers to transport across the outer membranes (the *plasmalemma*); *assimilation* is the sequence of reactions involving the incorporation of inorganic ions into organic cellular components (Lobban et al. 1985, p. 87).

(67) Hanisak (1983) reviewed the uptake and assimilation of nitrogen by seaweeds. Most can remove both NH_4^+ and NO_3^-. Prince (1974) reported that the rockweed *Fucus vesiculosus*, a brown alga, grew equally well on ammonia and nitrate. When

the biomass of plants in culture was high, 65 to 92% of the ammonia was removed. Ammonia concentrations varied from 1.75 to 2.8 g total NH_4-N/L; phosphorus was 450 mg PO_4-P/L. Topinka and Robbins (1976) found that greatest growth in *Fucus spiralis* occurred when ammonia and nitrate levels were raised from 23.8 mg NH_4-N/L and 16.8 mg NO_3-N/L to concentrations of 490 mg/L for both nutrients. Waite and Mitchell (1972) measured increased photosynthetic activity in sea lettuce (*Ulva lactuca*), a green seaweed, when ammonia was added to the culture water. Greatest stimulation took place when the level of total NH_4-N was raised to ~602 mg/L.

Some seaweeds can take up urea from the environment. Mohsen et al. (1974) tested the efficiency of amino acid synthesis in sea lettuce (*Ulva fasciata*) using three concentrations each of urea and nitrate supplied as KNO_3. The best growth was obtained with urea. The optimal concentration in the water for maximum amino acid synthesis was 0.5 g/L; a concentration of 0.125 g/L resulted in substantially less amino acid synthesis. When KNO_3 was present, 0.8 g NO_3-N/L yielded maximum amino acid synthesis, followed by a concentration of 0.4 g/L. The third concentration tested (1.6 g/L) inhibited amino acid synthesis.

(68) In an earlier publication (Spotte 1979b, p. 144) I wrote, ''Overall, living plants probably improve the quality of aquarium water.'' The qualifier ''probably'' was necessary then and still is. Far more research is needed before it can be known whether seaweed filters are distinctly advantageous in the routine maintenance of aquarium seawater. The decision to supplement bacteriological filtration with seaweed filters should be considered carefully, simply because there is no evidence that algae actually do improve captive seawater environments.

Seaweed filters have been used by aquarists for a number of years, but literature on the subject is sparse. Yang et al. (1989) evaluated closed aquarium systems for squid culture. In systems with seaweeds (*Enteromorpha* spp. and *Gracilaria tikvahiae*), neither positive nor negative effects could be seen. Gerhardt (1981) reported that a filter containing *Chaetomorpha* sp. and *Rhizoclonium* sp. prevented increases in ammonia and nitrate, but were ineffective in controlling the concentration of nitrite. Adey (1983) described an ''algal turf scrubber'' contiguous with a 6800-L seawater system at the National Museum of Natural History. The algae were cultured under intense light on plastic screen (2-mm mesh size). Influent water flowing over the screen in a thin sheet carried nutrients from the aquarium. The screens were scraped of excess algae every 10 to 14 d. Oxygen ranged from 5.5 to 8.3 mg/L, comparable with values on a coral reef at

St. Croix (U.S. Virgin Islands) having moderate wave action; the pH of the system was 8.2 to 8.3. Ammonia, nitrite, nitrate, and orthophosphate were maintained near the upper limit of the ranges recorded at St. Croix (ammonia data from St. Croix were not available). Nitrate fluctuated diurnally in accordance with primary production.

The principal function of seaweed filters appears to be nitrate removal, but whether this is beneficial when balanced against possible negative factors has yet to be demonstrated. Seaweeds produce natural exudates in micromolar concentrations, and the potential adverse effects of these substances should not be discounted completely. Several are toxic, and the few compounds isolated to date may represent only a fraction of the number that actually exist. According to Paul (1984), tropical green seaweeds, including species often kept in aquarium exhibits, routinely produce toxic compounds that prevent herbivory by grazing fishes and benthic invertebrates. Some are biologically active terpenoid metabolites with known cellular toxicity, antimicrobial effects, and direct toxicity to fishes and various larvae. Norris and Fenical (1982) studied toxins produced by seaweeds on the barrier reef off Belize, Central America. Of six species of *Caulerpa* tested (*C. cupressoides, C. mexicana, C. racemosa, C. serrulata, C. sertularoides,* and *C. verticillata*), all but *C. mexicana* contained the toxic compound caulerpin. Species of *Caulerpa, Halimeda, Penicillus, Rhipocephalus,* and *Udotea* also were found to produce complex terpenoids. Two other compounds isolated from *Rhipocephalus phoenix* proved toxic to a damselfish (the beaugregory, *Stegastes leucostictus*) at 2 and 10 μg/mL. An isolate of a tropical brown alga (*Stypopodium zonale*) was toxic to *S. leucostictus* at ~3 μg/mL. A compound from the tropical red alga *Laurencia caraibica* was toxic to fertilized eggs of the temperate sea urchin *Strongylocentrotus purpuratus*. Also see Note 15.

(69) Schramm et al. (1984), Brylinski (1977), Fankboner and DeBurgh (1977), Guterstam et al. (1978).

(70) Sieburth (1969) is the source of this statement. As Schramm et al. (1984) pointed out, Sieburth's experimental protocol may have caused extensive tissue damage, perhaps accounting for the unusually high concentration of organic exudates.

(71) This discussion is based on Spotte (1979b, pp. 147–151).

(72) Kawai et al. (1964) considered a filter bed to be conditioned when it had acquired sufficient nitrifying capability, which takes ~2 months under warm conditions. His definition, although useful on a practical basis, is incomplete because nitrification is

only one mechanism by which nutrients in solution are used by bacteria. Mineralization, for example, precedes nitrification under real aquarium conditions. Conditioning is not complete until *all* bacteria have acclimated to the aquarium environment (Spotte 1979b, p. 147).

(73) Most of the following discussion is from Spotte (1979b, p. 148). Kimata et al. (1961) reported a time lag of 30 to 60 d before activity could be detected in cultures of marine nitrifiers maintained at 25°C. In an earlier study by Carey (1938), 90 d at room temperature were required before nitrification was evident. Yoshida (1967) mentioned 60 to 90 d of incubation at 25°C as having elapsed before nitrification could be detected with almost pure cultures of seawater nitrifiers. Two months is more than twice the time required to enumerate soil nitrifiers (Matulewich et al. 1975). Similar lag phases are evident in filter beds of new seawater aquariums. Kawai et al. (1964) showed that the population of nitrifiers in a filter bed stabilized at ~60 d, and Srna and Baggaley (1975) found that 40 d were required to generate a large population of nitrifiers in a new filter bed. Based on tests conducted at 26°C, Forster (1974) suggested that a 30-d period is necessary for a new filter bed to reach full nitrifying potential, but his study included only ammonia conversion; the rest of the nitrification sequence was not monitored.

(74) Kawai et al. (1964) discovered that in a warm seawater aquarium, the numbers of bacteria increased tenfold within 2 weeks after addition of animals. Most of the organisms were heterotrophs. The level reached nearly 10^8/g of filter sand. Afterward, the total population was not much different at 134 d than at 90 d, indicating that populations of the different groups had become stable.

(75) Kawai et al. (1964) determined that the numbers of both ammonia and nitrite oxidizers seemed to stabilize after reaching maximum density. Populations were, respectively, 10^5 and 10^6 cells/g of filter sand. However, ammonia oxidizers yielded higher cell counts after the first 2 weeks, which was apparent from the increased concentration of nitrite compared with nitrate. Kimata et al. (1961) found that the concentration of ammonia oxidizers and nitrite oxidizers in the filter beds of conditioned seawater aquariums averaged, respectively, 10^4 and 10^5 cells/g of filter sand. The numbers in the water were less, only 10^2 and 10^3 cells/mL. Kimata and coauthors reported that values in surface seawater were much lower: ammonia and nitrite oxidizers together averaged 0.3 cells/mL. Yoshida and Kimata (1967) found nitrifiers in surface seawater to be 10^0 to 10^2 cells/mL. Yoshida (1967) observed seawater nitrifiers at concentra-

tions of 10^1 to 10^3 cells/mL in the water and 10^4 to 10^6/g of filter sand at two public aquariums in Japan (Misaki Aquarium and Sakai Aquarium). The concentrations of nitrifying bacteria in a fish culture pond were found by Sugahara and Hayashi (1974) to be 1 to 10^5/g of filter sand and 10 to 10^5 per 100 mL of water.

(76) Hirayama (1974) noted that in a newly established seawater aquarium at 20 to 21°C, ammonia accumulated rapidly until day 10. Subsequently, nitrite accumulated before peaking at day 35; by day 50 most of it had disappeared. Kawai et al. (1964) reported nitrite values peaking on day 30 at 22°C. Yoshida (1967), working with an experimental aquarium at 22°C, stated that nitrite peaked after 20 to 30 d.

(77) In a 4000-L conditioned exhibit at Mystic Marinelife Aquarium, the warm-water animals were removed, the temperature lowered abruptly from 20 to 12°C, and cold-water animals were added. Ammonia and nitrite did not peak until 29 and 62 d, respectively, even though the filter bed had been conditioned fully at the higher temperature (unpublished in Spotte 1979b, p. 151).

(78) This discussion is based on Spotte (1979b, pp. 151–152).

(79) Srna and Baggaley (1975) reported that when water in an experimental aquarium was spiked with ammonium chloride, NH_4Cl, equal to twice the ammonia concentration to which the filter bed had been conditioned, the conversion rate was similar, suggesting no net increase in the population density of ammonia oxidizers.

(80) Bower and Turner (1981) compared conditioning times using different ''seeding'' techniques. The experimental aquariums were small (38 L) and contained artificial seawater. Methods tested were: (*1*) 10% wet filtrant from a conditioned filter, (*2*) 5% wet filtrant, (*3*) 20% artificial seawater from an aquarium with a conditioned filter, (*4*) 10% air-dried filtrant from a conditioned filter, (*5*) 10% wet filtrant from a conditioned freshwater aquarium, and (*6*) three commercial additives purported to contain liquid or freeze-dried cultures of nitrifying bacteria. The authors did not culture and enumerate nitrifying bacteria, but relied on laboratory analyses of total NH_4-N and NO_2-N as indicators of nitrifying activity. None of the commercial additives accelerated conditioning time, and one product appeared to inhibit nitrite oxidation. ''Seeding'' with air-dried filtrant decreased the time required for complete oxidation of ammonia by 48%, compared with controls, but the time necessary for nitrite oxidation was reduced only 25%. ''Seeding'' with water from an aquarium with a conditioned filter resulted in acceler-

ated conversions of 19 and 29% for ammonia and nitrite, respectively. When 5% wet filtrant was used, ammonia and nitrite oxidation were accelerated 74 and 81%, respectively, and the use of 10% wet filtrant reduced conditioning time even further (81% for ammonia and 89% for nitrite). Addition of 10% filtrant from the conditioned freshwater aquarium did not improve conditioning time noticeably.

These results are consistent with two established facts: (*1*) nitrification is limited at first by an insufficient number of organisms, and (*2*) nitrifiers are sensitive to important changes in the environment (e.g., desiccation, an abrupt change from freshwater to saline water). Commercially prepared cultures cannot be expected to reduce conditioning time substantially unless the bacteria were grown under the same conditions of temperature, pH, salinity, and dissolved oxygen as the new aquarium (Spotte 1979b, pp. 123–132). Moreover, it is doubtful whether even a large commercial culture can supply enough bacteria to have an immediate impact on ammonia and nitrite oxidation, particularly in large water systems. The use of commercial preparations appears not only to be a questionable technique but a needlessly expensive one. It is well known that in aquatic environments bacteria are concentrated on solid surfaces, and comparatively few are suspended in the water. It therefore is not surprising that addition of water from an aquarium with a conditioned filter bed reduces conditioning time less effectively than adding a portion of the filter itself. Nor is it surprising to think that the period of conditioning is reduced in increments of time corresponding with the proportion of the filtrant that is already conditioned.

(81) Saeki (1962) demonstrated that nitrification in new filter beds took 60 d to become established at 19°C. The time could be reduced to 2 weeks when new filter sand was placed in an old (uncleaned) aquarium containing old seawater. Saeki attributed the shortened time to nitrifying bacteria in the water and attached to the walls of the aquarium.

(82) This discussion is based on Spotte (1979b, pp. 152–153).

(83) Meade (1974).

(84) Hirayama (1966b, 1974).

(85) This discussion is based on Spotte (1979b, pp. 153–158).

(86) Gary Adams of Sea Research Foundation and I devised the half-depth model in an attempt to overcome deficiencies in Hirayama's method of estimating carrying capacity. Whether the effort is an improvement remains to be seen. Our inspira-

tion and the slope of the void-fractions graph (Fig. 2-19) came from Hess (1981). A temperature correction is needed because nitrification proceeds faster in warm water than in cold (see Note 45).

(87) This discussion is based on Spotte (1979b, pp. 158–162).

(88) Kawai et al. (1965) determined that heterotrophic bacteria were most numerous at the surfaces of filter beds (10^8/g of filter sand) and decreased 90% at a depth of 10 cm. The same trend held true for autotrophic bacteria. The surface sand populations of ammonia and nitrite oxidizers, which were 10^5 and 10^6/g of filter sand, respectively, fell 90% at a depth of only 5 cm. Based on these findings, Kawai and coauthors recommended that filter beds be designed with large surface areas and shallow depths. Yoshida (1967) reported that maximum nitrifying activity occurred in the upper layer of filtrant. Activity diminished rapidly with increasing depth. Such changes are not so marked when larger-grained filtrants are used, although the filter bed must be deeper.

Hirayama (1966a) demonstrated that the effect of filter bed depth on nutrient conversion in aquarium water is indirect when OCF is used as an index. Conversely, the time taken for the water to pass through the filter bed could be correlated directly with OCF. Hirayama's data showed that the apparent depth effects were misleading, because flow rate and filter bed depth are proportional. Hirayama designed an experiment in which aquarium water was passed through four filter columns that differed only in depth. The time necessary for water to move through each column was kept constant by adjusting the flow rate. It was shown that OCF values were the same.

(89) This discussion is based on Spotte (1979b, pp. 161–162).

(90) Kawai et al. (1965) found that gently washing the filter sand of a seawater aquarium reduced nitrifying activity 40%; still more activity was lost with subsequent washings. When the sand was washed vigorously, activity diminished by approximately two-thirds, and another 20% was lost with a second vigorous washing.

Bower and Turner (1983) assessed the effects of washing filtrants in small aquariums and obtained different results. The fish were removed from aquariums with conditioned filter beds. Afterward, the filtrant was transferred to buckets containing new artificial seawater and washed by hand stirring. The wash water and suspended detritus were discarded. The washed filtrant, fish, and original artificial seawater were reinstated. A second procedure was identical to the first, except that tap water was used for washing. The controls were treated by removing the fish and filtrant, but the filtrant was not washed. Concentrations of total NH_4-N and NO_2-N were monitored at 24-h intervals for 3 d. The removal of detritus did not affect nitrite oxidation, but large, transient increases in ammonia were observed. Nonetheless, the levels remained substantially lower than those seen in unconditioned aquariums. The authors proposed that, although the numbers of nitrifiers were reduced, compensation was achieved by organisms attached to the filtrant grains and aquarium walls, and suspended in the water. Gentle washing with either freshwater or saline water was not considered detrimental to nitrification.

(91) Balderston and Sieburth (1976) stated correctly that a source of exogenous carbon is necessary to achieve complete nitrate reduction in denitrification columns because the endogenous carbon is too low to support sustained removal.

(92) Hooper and Terry (1973).

(93) Balderston and Sieburth (1976) established experimental denitrification columns using freshwater from a high density salmon hatchery. Columns filled with unconditioned 11-mm crushed limestone could remove 95 to 100% of the influent nitrate after a conditioning period of 20 to 22 d at the C/N ratio of 1. The time required to reach this capacity depended partly on the carbon concentration (methanol in this case). At C/N ratios >1, 100% nitrate removal could be achieved 6 d sooner. I emphasize that 100% removal is *not* the same as 100% reduction. It is possible to remove all the nitrate by reducing it to nitrite and ammonia. According to Balderston and Sieburth, ". . . 95 to 100% nitrate removal does not necessarily mean that the column effluent is of a high quality (i.e., quality sufficient for the culture of fish); nitrite was produced in the developing columns and is correlated with C/N ratios of <1 as well as time from the start of carbon supplementation." In addition, the concentration of DOC in the treated effluent fluctuated widely during the startup period.

(94) Balderston and Sieburth (1976).

(95) Balderston and Sieburth (1976) concluded that in conditioned columns a C/N ratio of 1 is adequate, although exogenous DOC was never removed completely from their treated effluent. The ratio of 1 allowed 100% nitrate removal and produced an effluent low in carbon and nitrite. Ratios greater and less than 1 were inadequate: even the increase in columnar biomass that occurred after conditioning did not result in complete denitrification, and some nitrite persisted.

(96) Jaubert (1989), on whose report my discussion is based, called this a "living sand" system. The only data compared concentrations of ammonia, nitrite, nitrate, and pH in the "living sand" aquarium with these factors in a conventional aquarium equipped with a subgravel filter. Ten sets of values representing 10 months were recorded. Whether they represent single measurements or the means of several is unknown. A rationale for the plenum containing stagnant water was not offered. Nitrogen in various stages of reduction could diffuse into the stagnant water or upward, as it must to enter the atmosphere. In diffusing upward, incompletely reduced forms would be subject to reoxidation in the aerobic layers of sediment. Jaubert failed to describe these and other processes. The statement about DOC removal in the "living sand" aquarium was unsupported. That pH values >8 could be sustained in the aquarium with the subgravel filter is surprising. The report did not describe the extent of oxygen depletion along the sediment gradient. A chemical description of the stagnant layer was a crucial omission. The mechanisms of transformation and transport of nitrogen leading to its eventual loss require a mass-balance analysis. Jaubert's report offers a tantalizing glimpse of what might be an improved method of aquarium keeping, one certainly worth investigation.

(97) This discussion is based on Spotte (1979b, pp. 23–24 and 163–164).

(98) Spotte (1979b, p. 163).

(99) Kain (1966).

(100) Chapman (1973).

(101) Shelbourne (1964).

(102) Ozone generally is incapable of oxidizing most organic matter in water completely to CO_2. Adams and Spotte (1980) exposed saline water from a whale and dolphin pool to ozone. Initial TOC concentrations of 13.66 and 12.85 mg/L were unchanged by sequential contact periods of 25, 30, and 30 min (first trial) and 30, 30, and 30 min (second trial) at dosage levels of 4.13, 4.03, and 4.52 mg O_3/L. The results are consistent with similar experiments described in the wastewater treatment literature. Nebel et al. (1973) showed that low TOC concentrations (~10 mg/L) were not reduced further by oxidation with 15 mg O_3/L. Elia et al. (1978) found that even higher dosage levels of ozone (31 mg/min) did not remove appreciable amounts of TOC from wastewater. Farooq et al. (1977) suggested that ozone oxidizes a portion of the TOC in wastewater

to intermediate organic species. The same evidently is true of other types of waters and explains why TOC values are seldom altered very much by contact with ozone. Gjessing (1976), for example, showed that increasing the dosage level of O_3 has little effect on DOC in natural freshwaters. A rise in O_3 of 12 to 100 mg/L lowered the amount of carbon by <10 %.

(103) The micropores are formed by burning away individual complete layers of fused carbon rings (Snoeyink and Weber 1967). The structure of activated carbon is disorganized compared with graphite because the oxidation of these layers is random. The ultimate molecular structure of a brand or type of activated carbon depends on carbonization and activation temperatures (Cookson 1978).

(104) The distinction between PAC and GAC is arbitrary. Tchobanoglous (1972, p. 350) considered GAC to have a grain size >0.1 mm. According to U.S. EPA (1973), the smallest GACs start at Tyler sieve size 50, which is ~ 0.295 mm (Table 3-9).

(105) The pore surface area of activated carbon is measurable as iodine, methylene blue, and molasses numbers. Each substance is a distinct chemical compound; consequently, each has a distinctly different molecular diameter. The extent to which one of these can be adsorbed depends on how many pores of that particular size are available. Iodine, being the smallest, is used to estimate the total pore surface area of a batch or brand of activated carbon. It provides a measure of all pores with diameters >1 nm. The methylene blue and molasses numbers account for all pores with diameters >1.5 and 2.8 nm, respectively. Total surface area also is measured by adsorption of dinitrogen gas (called the Brunauer-Emmett-Teller, or BET method). The distribution of pores of different diameters is determined by the amount of nitrogen desorbed (i.e., released from the pores) at intermediate pressures.

(106) Hutchins (1981).

(107) In wastewater, the rate of adsorption increases with decreasing pH, probably because nonpolar molecules are adsorbed more readily than charged particles (Hutchins 1981). Logically, the adsorption rate should decrease with increasing water temperature, but the reverse ordinarily is true. This is because decreasing viscosity and increasing molecular activity at high temperatures may allow organic compounds to penetrate the pores more easily (Hutchins 1981). Viscosity is defined and discussed in Chapter 8, Note 32.

(108) Li and DiGiano (1983), Lowery and Burkhead (1980), Maqsood and Benedek (1977), Ying and Weber (1979).

(109) AWWA (1981).

(110) Bancroft et al. (1983) reported on the removal of TOC from wastewater by microorganisms attached to solid surfaces. They found no significant difference between removal on GAC versus sand. Sand is nonporous and has a much smaller surface area. Peel and Benedek (1983) demonstrated that the presence of microorganisms in GAC beds did not affect TOC reduction in simulated wastewater and suggested that biological enhancement is restricted to situations in which the compounds removed are biodegradable and ample oxygen is available. Peel and Benedek used scanning electron microscopy to illustrate that the surfaces of GAC grains were populated only sparsely with microorganisms, and that the internal pores were devoid of cells.

Servais et al. (1991) compared changes in the concentrations of refractory and nonrefractory DOC components of wastewater entering and leaving an exhausted GAC bed. Degradable or nonrefractory fractions in the influent water varied from 0.4 to 0.9 mg DOC/L, representing 21 to 49% of the total DOC (i.e., including the refractory component). Of the total DOC, an average of 40% of the nonrefractory component was removed in a single pass, compared with 8% of the refractory component. The authors wrote: "This strongly suggests that biological activity, instead of adsorption processes, is responsible for most of the reduction of DOC during GAC filtration [in exhausted GAC contactors]. . . ." It would seem that exhausted GAC is no better than nonporous filtrants for promoting bacteriological mineralization.

(111) The study of Spotte and Adams (1984), in which artificial seawater in an operating aquarium was used, produced results similar to those described in Note 110. The authors speculated that vigorous activity in the biological filter perhaps reduced the concentration of biodegradable organic carbon before the influent water reached the experimental flasks containing GAC.

(112) Diffusion is slow, and long contact times are desirable. Schuliger (1978) cited several studies showing that in purification of industrial wastewater the percentage removal of adsorbates increases when flow rate through an activated carbon contactor is increased but contact time is kept constant.

(113) Reactivation has been studied extensively. Several inorganic and organic compounds have proved effective, resulting in recovery rates approaching 100%. However, most of these substances pose physical dangers to human beings during the reactivation process, or leave toxic residues that may be harm-

ful to aquatic animals and plants. Interested readers should consult Cairo et al. (1982), Cooney et al. (1983), Dreusch (1978, 1981), Koffskey and Lykins (1990), Martin and Ng (1984), and McGinnis (1981).

The most common method of reactivation is a three-step process that involves drying, *pyrolysis* (oxygen-free burning), and gasification (Cairo et al. 1982). A multiple-hearth furnace or rotary kiln is required, and the process takes ~30 min. The wet, exhausted material is dried at 94°C. The temperature is then raised to 400 to 540°C in an oxygen-free environment. Volatile organics are driven off, and adsorbates are pyrolyzed to ash, which is retained in the pores. During gasification the temperature is raised again, this time to 934 to 990°C, and steam is introduced at 1 kg/kg GAC (Lyman 1978). The remaining residues are oxidized with little damage to the pore structures.

Koffskey and Lykins (1990) described GAC reactivation in an infrared furnace. The drying (dewatering) zone of the furnace was maintained at 130 to 156°C with heat from the pyrolysis zone (364°C). The reactivation zone was kept at 442°C. The GAC was baked for 25 min, quenched with water, then reactivated with flue gas from the furnace in combination with steam. Adsorptive capacity after three cycles of use and reactivation was comparable with that of unused GAC.

(114) The method for determining orthophosphate is from Spotte (1979b, pp. 310–312) and has been adapted from APHA et al. (1985, pp. 448–450), Martin (1968, pp. 113–120), and Murphy and Riley (1962). It works well in waters of all salinities. Goulden and Brooksbank (1975) described a procedure for determining total phosphorus in natural waters. Ridal and Moore (1990) reviewed methods for determining dissolved organic phosphorus in seawater, and Broberg and Pettersson (1988) discussed analytical methods for orthophosphate in water.

(115) Koroleff (1976a, p. 117).

(116) Spotte (1979b, p. 310).

(117) Murphy and Riley (1962) reported that samples could be preserved by addition of chloroform (1 mL/150 mL). Morse et al. (1982) found all conventional methods of storage and preservation inadequate and recommended analyzing samples as soon as possible after collection. Samples can be stored in polyethylene containers if they are quick-frozen. Hassenteufel et al. (1963) and Heron (1962) observed loss of orthophosphate from polyethylene containers at room temperature.

(118) The pipetting of reagents does not have to be done as carefully if the final volume is measured accurately. Volumetric

flasks are therefore preferable to Erlenmeyer flasks, and the same is true for the other spectrophotometric methods given in this chapter.

(119) The method for determining total NH_4-N is modified from Liddicoat et al. (1975); the standard additions portion is from Spotte (1979a, pp. 129–133 and 1979b, pp. 313–314). Liddicoat et al. (1975) reported high and erratic blank values in initial trials with Solórzano's method (Solórzano 1969), which they attributed partly to the instability of commercial hypochlorite solutions. They suggested using sodium dichloroisocyanurate instead. However, Bower and Holm-Hansen (1980a) observed no change in absorbance during a 4-month period in which the same bottle of Clorox® was used.

The practice of stating ammonia as nitrogen should, in my opinion, be reserved for expressions of concentration. It is the molecule (NH_3) or ion (NH_4^+) that exerts a toxic effect and not the nitrogen component alone. For example, it would be correct to say that free ammonia is toxic at a concentration of 0.5 mg NH_3-N/L.

(120) Several methods of ammonia determination have been published, most of them modifications of previous methods. These include fluorescence (Aoki et al. 1983); enzymatic assay (Knight and Toom 1981, Verdouw 1973); indophenol blue (Boyd 1978, Brzezinski 1987, Catalano 1987, González 1984, Grasshoff and Johannsen 1974, Hampson 1977b, Harwood and Kühn 1970, Helder and de Vries 1979, Liddicoat et al. 1975, Manabe 1969, Newell 1967, Newell and dal Pont 1964, Nimura 1973, Riley and Mix 1981, Solórzano 1969, Zadorojny et al. 1973); salicylate (Benesch and Mangelsdorf 1972, Bower and Holm-Hansen 1980a, Skjemstad and Reeve 1978); gas-sensing or specific ion electrode (Barica 1973, 1975; Beckett and Wilson 1974; Cuenco and Stickney 1980; Evans and Patridge 1974; Gilbert and Clay 1973; Maugle and Meade 1980; Meyerhoff 1980; Shibata 1976; Siegal 1980; Simeonov et al. 1979; Srna et al. 1973; Thomas and Booth 1973; Willason and Johnson 1986); gas-sensing electrode with immobilized nitrifying bacteria (Hikuma et al. 1980, O'Kelley and Nason 1970); hydrazine reduction fluorometry (Danielson and Conroy 1982); chemical oxidation and measurement as nitrite (Shinagawa and Tsunogai 1978); centrifugal analysis (McCurdy et al. 1989); and infrared spectrometry (Ataman and Mark 1977). Procedures that use nesslerization do not work in saline waters without modification (Manabe 1969).

(121) This discussion is based on Koroleff (1976b, p. 128).

(122) According to Hampson (1977b), nitrite interference is minimal so long as NO_2-N $<$ total NH_4-N. The percentage of

total NH_4-N underestimated by Solórzano's indophenol blue method (Solórzano 1969) increases rapidly when this relationship is reversed. Helder and de Vries (1979) also showed that nitrite in saline waters causes underestimation of ammonia by the indophenol blue method. However, this does not appear to be a problem in aquarium seawater, except perhaps when new filters are being conditioned. At such times nitrite can reach high concentrations. The concentrations depicted in Figure 2-41 considerably exceed those typical of aquariums. In my experience, concentrations during conditioning of new biological filters in large water systems range from ~0.1 to ~3 mg NO_2-N/L, equivalent to 0.007 to 0.2 mmol/L. As shown by Figure 2-41, a concentration of 0.007 mg NO_2-N/L would cause no underestimation of ammonia, whereas 3 mg/L would result in an underestimation of ~40%.

(123) Storage of seawater alters the original concentrations of nutrient ions. The two factors mainly responsible are adsorption onto walls of the storage container and bacteriological degradation (mineralization) of POC, which releases nutrients and causes falsely high readings. Samples destined for storage traditionally are treated to eliminate or minimize the effects of microbial activity. Common techniques include (*1*) quick freezing in a dry ice-alcohol or dry ice-acetone bath followed by storage at ~ −15°C; (*2*) slow freezing to ~ −15°C and subsequent storage at that temperature; (*3*) microfiltration through a cellulose acetate, glass fiber, or polycarbonate filter (ordinarily with a pore size of 0.45 μm) to eliminate as much POC as possible; and (*4*) addition of a toxicant such as mercuric chloride ($HgCl_2$), chloroform ($CHCl_3$), or phenol (C_6H_6O) to minimize microbial activity. Even the compositions of different storage containers have been compared (Teflon®, glass, polyethylene) to evaluate their nutrient adsorption characteristics. Most of these efforts appear to be ineffective. Morse et al. (1982) performed an exhaustive evaluation of preservation and storage methods for samples of offshore seawater. They wrote: "One interesting finding was that the degree of preservation was not substantially improved by going to complex techniques involving freezing and chemical additives." Their recommendations for collection and storage of seawater samples are what I have given in the text.

If the sample is filtered, the composition of both a filter and the frit used to hold it affect the nutrient composition of seawater samples, but to a lesser extent than freshwater ones. Cellulose acetate filters release compounds containing phosphorus during filtration of freshwater (Jenkins 1968). Riemann and Schierup (1978) reported that adsorption of ammonia from freshwater passed through polycarbonate filters is negligible, but that up to 30% of the ammonia in the first 50 mL is retained by cellulose acetate filters. Eaton and Grant (1979) observed that glass support frits used to hold filters rapidly adsorb ammonia from freshwater and brackish water ($S < 5‰$). Distilled-deionized water was not an effective cleaning agent for either the frits or cellulose acetate filters they used. However, the adsorbed ammonia could be released readily by flushing with water of greater salinity. Polypropylene frits did not retain ammonia, nor did glass frits soaked in a 5% solution of trimethylchlorosilane in dichloromethane and dried at 100°C. This last technique adds another step to the procedure and is unnecessary if the proper filters and frits are used.

(124) The specific ion electrode method is based on Srna et al. (1973), who explained how an ''ammonia probe'' works. A hydrophobic membrane separates the sample solution from the solution inside the electrode. The membrane allows small quantities of NH_3 and some amines to pass into the cell until the partial pressure of NH_3 is the same on both sides of the membrane. The ammonia reacts with the internal solution to produce hydroxyl ions, OH^-. The change in OH^- concentration is detected by the internal reference, which develops a potential in accordance with the Nernst equation (Chapter 1, Note 41).

Garside et al. (1978) described the use of ''ammonia probes'' in seawater. Gilbert and Clay (1973) and Srna et al. (1973) evaluated these instruments for aquarium seawater analysis specifically. The last publication is especially useful.

(125) The method of analysis can be by standard additions or by preparation of standard curves. Srna et al. (1973) recommended standard additions because it is faster and reduces problems associated with loss of free ammonia to the atmosphere. Klein and Hach (1977) pointed out that the standard additions technique gives more realistic values than calibration curves because the sample and standard are measured under the same conditions. Dean (1974, pp. 379–381) and Klein and Hach (1977) described the theory of standard addition. Tables are available from Orion Research Incorporated (a manufacturer of ''ammonia probes'') that simplify standard additions calculations and allow rapid computation of concentrations in a sample solution.

(126) This discussion is based on Srna et al. (1973).

(127) Estimation of the allowable upper limit of total NH_4-N is based on Spotte and Adams (1983).

(128) The dissociation of aqueous ammonia has been studied by Bates and Pinching (1949), Johansson and Wedborg (1980), Khoo et al. (1977), and Whitfield (1974, 1978). Useful tables for predicting the dissociation of NH_4^+ at known values of pH and temperature in freshwater were published by Emerson et al. (1975), Messer et al. (1984), Rogers and Klemetson (1985), and Trussell (1972). Bower and Bidwell (1978) published a table for saline waters of known pH, temperature, and salinity; Hampson (1977a) and Rogers and Klemetson (1985) provided comparable computer programs for seawater and freshwater, respectively.

(129) The empirical argument favoring the greater toxicity of NH_3 has not been confirmed, despite the belief by most that it has. Early investigators demonstrated that the toxicity of total NH_4-N increases with increasing pH (e.g., Downing and Merkens 1955, Wuhrmann and Woker 1948). Because the ratio of NH_4^+/NH_3 diminishes as the pH rises, these and subsequent observations have been interpreted to mean that NH_3 is the toxic species, despite its small relative concentration. Most investigators have attributed any increase in toxicity to the greater concentration of NH_3 available at higher pH, while ignoring possible additive or synergistic effects of pH and ammonia. In other words, the increased concentration of NH_3 is only one factor and offers no insight as to how higher pH values might influence toxicity. The dissociation of NH_4^+ is not simply pH dependent, but greatly so. As Erickson (1985) noted, any toxic effects of NH_3 and pH may be inseparable.

Investigators usually have shown the toxicity to be pH dependent (e.g., Broderious et al. 1977, Lloyd and Herbert 1960, Tabata 1962, Thurston et al. 1981), although the study of Tomasso et al. (1980a) is an exception. All these studies were conducted in freshwaters. Data on ammonia toxicity in animals living in brackish waters and seawater are limited (Miller et al. 1990, Spotte and Anderson 1989). As Miller et al. (1990) pointed out, evidence gathered to date suggests that because of salinity effects the pH-toxicity relationship with respect to NH_3 in these environments may be less predictable than in freshwaters. None of this is evidence that the toxicity of NH_3 is substantially greater, but indicates only that the toxicity of total NH_4-N—not necessarily one of its calculated components—correlates positively with increasing pH. Similarly, the concentration of NH_3 correlates positively with increasing pH. Correlation and cause, however, are not synonyms.

Early work reported an apparent increase in ammonia toxicity with increasing temperature when total NH_4-N was the effect variable, but the pH was not measured (e.g., Powers

1920). Wuhrmann and Woker (1953) demonstrated that toxicity increases with increasing temperature when ammonia is expressed as NH_3, although pH effects were again disregarded. According to more recent information, the toxicity of NH_3 declines markedly with rising temperature (Colt and Tchobanoglous 1976, Hazel et al. 1971, Thurston and Russo 1983, Thurston et al. 1983) because an increase in lethal concentration represents a decrease in toxicity. This effect is consistent even though the concentration of NH_3 doubles with each incremental rise of 10°C. However, the metabolic rates of cold-blooded animals rise with temperature, and it is impossible to know whether the toxic response has been altered by accelerated metabolism (Erickson 1985).

It is probable that both NH_3 and NH_4^+ are toxic, as first suggested by Tabata (1962). If so, the dozens of publications that have expressed toxicity values in terms of NH_3-N are subject to serious criticism, especially if pH, temperature, and salinity were not stated. Thurston et al. (1981) pointed out that if NH_3 alone is toxic then the same concentration of total NH_4-N should be 10 times more toxic when the pH is raised one unit, because the concentration of NH_3 increases logarithmically. In other words, the toxicity of NH_3 over a range of pH values is nonlinear, although why it should not be is unclear to me. Thurston et al. (1981) conducted an experiment using freshwater-acclimated rainbow trout and fathead minnows (*Pimephales promelas*) to observe the relationship between NH_3 toxicity and pH. They found that the LC_{50} was signficantly less at lower pH values. A lower LC_{50} indicates greater toxicity, because the lower the lethal concentration of a compound, the more toxic it is. The authors offered two possible explanations: (*1*) an increase in H^+ brought about by lowering the pH in some way increases the toxicity of NH_3, or (2) NH_4^+ is also toxic. They favored the second possibility. In an experiment with larvae of a brackish water prawn (*Macrobrachium rosenbergii*), Armstrong et al. (1978) noticed growth reduction when the concentration of NH_3-N was 90 μg/L (26.2 mg total NH_4-N/L) at pH 6.8. However, growth was not affected when the NH_3-N concentration was 805 μg/L and the pH and concentration of NH_4^+-N were, respectively, 8.34 and 7.4 mg/L. The difference in toxicity was attributed to the action of NH_4^+.

(130) Bower and Bidwell (1978).

(131) This concentration is well below limits known to be lethal to fishes, as determined by bioassay. Values of 0.2 to 0.4 mg NH_3-N/L are typically stated (Burkhalter and Kaya 1977). Bioassays measure effects of relatively high concentrations of a tox-

icant for short periods, and the data are not always useful to aquarists. When fishes are maintained for extended periods, as in aquarium keeping, concentrations far below lethal limits are sometimes harmful. The effects may be subtle and difficult to quantify (e.g., reduced growth rates, diminished capacity to resist infectious diseases). Colt and Armstrong (1981) wrote: ". . . a 'no-effects' level of ammonia does not exist; that is, any level of ammonia will have an effect on growth." Even from this rather extreme viewpoint an arbitrary limit of 0.01 mg NH_3-N/L does not seem unreasonable.

(132) Figure 2-42 and Tables 2-17 through 2-20 were calculated by Spotte and Adams (1983) from p*K* data of Khoo et al. (1977). The ionization of NH_4^+ in seawater can be expressed by

$$pK = 0.09018 + \frac{2729.92}{T + 273.1} + (0.1552 - 0.000314T)I \qquad (2.25)$$

where T represents temperature (°C). Ionic (molal) strength, I, is shown by

$$I = 19.973 \frac{S}{1000 - 1.2005109S} \qquad (2.26)$$

where S represents salinity. However, the paper of Spotte and Adams contained a typographical error, and the second term of the first equation was written $2727.92/(T + 273.1)$. The figure and tables are correct as published, but calculation of intermediate values using the equation will be incorrect unless the error is taken into account.

(133) The method for determining NO_2-N has been modified from Spotte (1979b, pp. 317–318), who adapted it from Strickland and Parsons (1972, pp. 77–80). Zafiriou and True (1977) discussed problems of standardization.

(134) APHA et al. (1985, pp. 404–405).

(135) The low-concentration NO_3-N test has been adapted primarily from APHA et al. (1985, pp. 394–396), but also see Grasshoff (1976, pp. 137–145) and Strickland and Parsons (1972, pp. 71–76). Grasshoff's description contains several errors.

(136) According to Mullin and Riley (1955), the relationship between optical density and nitrate concentration is linear up to 50 μg NO_3-N/L. Above this value the optical density increment per microgram of NO_3-N decreases slightly. At concentrations

>250 μg NO_3-N/L, Beer's law is again obeyed. The relationship, in other words, is linear at low and high concentrations only. The concentration of NO_3-N in aquarium seawater occasionally exceeds 250 $\mu g/L$; if the estimated concentration is less, dilutions can be made prior to analysis. The alternative is to plot a calibration curve.

(137) This method was adapted from Strickland and Parsons (1965) and Mullin and Riley (1955) and reprinted with revisions from Spotte (1979b, pp. 318–319). Another hydrazine reduction method was published by Bower and Holm-Hansen (1980b). A brucine method for use in saline waters was given by Kahn and Brezenski (1967).

CHAPTER 3

(1) Public aquarium waters can become turbid for several reasons, including excessive growth of bacteria and phytoplankton (Lackey 1956) and the entrainment of POC with influent seawater supplies (see text). Because ''turbidity'' is a term used frequently (if loosely), it deserves more than a passing remark. Much of the following discussion is based on Austin (1974), Gibbs (1974), and Jerlov (1968). Also see APHA et al. (1985, pp. 133–140).

The first attempts to define and measure turbidity began about the turn of the century and arose from a need to monitor the amount of silt in municipal water supplies. Someone (presumably D. D. Jackson) devised a simple *extinction photometer* now called the Jackson candle turbidimeter. In its most basic form the instrument consists of a graduated cylinder with a glass bottom supported on a stand above a standard candle (originally specified to be made of spermaceti). Sample water is poured into the graduated cylinder until the image of the candle flame disappears (i.e., is extinguished) in the glow field caused by the forward-scattered light. The distance at which this occurs is used as a measure of the turbidity. However, any attempt to relate extinction distance to concentration of POC presents an insurmountable problem, simply because of the variability among waters. Light transmission is affected by more than just the number of particles present (Chapter 10). Also of significance are the size distribution of the particles and their refractive indices, shapes, and colors. Dissolved organic molecules, which are DOC and not POC, interfere with transmitted light by absorbing some of it. Humic substances, for example, absorb blue light more strongly than other wavelengths and in doing so cause water to appear yellow.

The problem today is still how to devise a standard suspension that is valid for all waters. The first standard consisted of a known concentration of diatomaceous earth in distilled water. A calibration curve was plotted using depth of the suspension (actually length of the light path) against ''parts per million silica'' (i.e., ''turbidity units''), and this became the *Jackson turbidity unit*, JTU.

What happens when a different diatomaceous earth is used to make the standard solution? As Austin (1974) noted, in such instances ''. . . the JTU reading indicates only that the suspension being measured has the same turbidity, opacity, obscuration or, more precisely, *contrast transmittance* as the suspension used by Jackson having a concentration in PPM [parts per million] equal to the JTU reading. The reading does *not* tell us the concentration for other materials nor is it necessarily simply related to it. The calibration, therefore, becomes quite arbitrary. . . .''

The difficulty experienced by Jackson led to a new standard developed in the 1920s. This consisted of a suspension of formazin. Formazin is still used to calibrate extinction photometers, and the modern trend is to refer to the unit as the *formazin turbidity unit*, FTU. However, the basic standard is still a table of turbidity units versus length of the light path and not the concentration of formazin. Consequently, the FTU is no more a viable unit of measure than the JTU.

Most modern wastewater treatment plants rely on nephelometric measurement of turbidity. *Nephelometry* is based on the scattering of light through a water sample, measured at a single angle or a small range of angles. Unfortunately, nephelometers are commonly calibrated using a suspension of formazin, which is then expressed in FTUs or NTUs (*nephelometric turbidity units*). Extinction photometers account for effects of both scattering (particularly forward scattering) and absorption; nephelometers ignore absorption and simply make a ''turbidity'' determination that is proportional to the volume scattering function at some known angle from the light source. When calibrated with formazin the results have little physical significance and can be correlated only with measurements made using instruments of identical design, or instruments that have been calibrated using the same standard suspension.

Transmissometers measure the intensity of image-forming light remaining at some distance from the light source. This ordinarily is recorded as the percentage of transmitted light relative to transmission in perfectly clear water. The percentage transmission value is then converted to the volume attenuation coefficient, α, by the equation

$$\alpha = \frac{L}{(\ln)(X)} \tag{3.13}$$

where L is beam length (m), ln represents the natural logarithm of X, and X = percentage transmission (Drake et al. 1974, Jerlov et al. 1972). Oceanographers prefer transmissometers to turbidimeters because the measurements obtained are based on actual optical properties of seawater. Nonetheless, transmissometers cannot resolve changes in POC of <1 mg/L because of the variable characteristics of suspended particulate matter and the presence of DOC. Without a reproducible means of measuring the optical properties of seawater there can be no reliable rules for sizing filtration systems. Often an existing analytical method suffices until a suitable substitute is developed, but this is not the case with turbidity. As observed by Austin et al. (1974), the term ''. . . is qualitative and relative . . . to the same manner as warmth. One does not measure warmth; one measures temperature.''

(2) This discussion is based mainly on Herzig et al. (1970). Also see Adin et al. (1971), Amirtharajah (1988), Boyd and Ghosh (1974), Craft (1966), O'Melia and Stumm (1967), Selmeczi (1971), Tchobanoglous (1970), Tchobanoglous and Eliassen (1970), Tobiason and O'Melia (1988), and Yao et al. (1971).

(3) Experts disagree about which capture mechanisms are most important. Filtration theory has historically been explained by mathematical models, an approach subject to obvious pitfalls (i.e., models are quantitatively incorrect by definition). Perhaps most important, analyses of capture mechanisms can seldom be applied to filter design and operation (Selmeczi 1971). Kawamura (1975a), whose pragmatic design data are excellent, shunned the theoretical approach ''. . . because many published theories and formulas have a tendency to be too complicated or time-consuming to apply.'' The opinion of O'Melia and Stumm (1967) is largely valid today: ''It does not appear unfair to state that current physical theories of filtration are either too simple to be flexible enough to apply in practice, or too complex (i.e., require an excessive amount of experimentation) to be useful. In either case, they disagree to such an extent that their general applicability may be questioned.''

(4) I am unaware of any bioassay studies detailing the toxicity of polyelectrolytes to fishes. Olson et al. (1973) described the treatment of influent water to a trout hatchery with several

polyelectrolytes. A cationic product at a concentration of 0.5 mg/L worked best. The gills of trout (species unstated) were normal after a year in treated water. The authors reported that cationic polyelectrolytes are harmful to fishes in the absence of POC, but gave no data. McDonald and Thomas (1970) described treatment of a freshwater pond with polyelectrolytes but did not conduct toxicity studies.

(5) The void fraction of a clean filter is the ratio of total filtrant volume to the total volume without the filtrant. Filtrant volume is computed from the mass and specific gravity of the material.

(6) It is sometimes stated in the water filtration literature that abrasion of filtrant grains during backwash is an important cleaning mechanism, but the extensive research of Cleasby and Baumann (1977) demonstrated otherwise.

(7) Caolo and Spotte (1990).

(8) This discussion is based on Colt (1986).

(9) Colt (1984).

(10) Colt and Westers (1982), Cornacchia and Colt (1984).

(11) Kils (1976/1977).

(12) Kanwisher (1963).

(13) The following discussion is from Spotte (1979b, p. 58). In several studies of air-water gas exchange an empirical factor called the exit coefficient, f, has been used. Ordinarily, f is treated as a measure of gas exchange through a stagnant laminar layer. However, Higbie (1935) used it to account for the uptake of gas by water in which new surfaces are created too rapidly for steady state (stagnant diffusion) to be established. The rate of gas exchange depends on the amount of oxygen that can diffuse into newly formed surfaces during the split seconds they are exposed to the air. Subsequently, the exit coefficient can be expressed by

$$f = 2\sqrt{\frac{D}{\pi\theta}} \tag{3.14}$$

where θ = time of exposure to the surface and D = the diffusion coefficient of oxygen in water. If the surfaces are renewed randomly,

$$f = \sqrt{DS} \tag{3.15}$$

where S = average rate of renewal. The uptake of oxygen becomes highly temperature dependent once the surface of the water is agitated. Downing and Truesdale (1955) found the exit coefficient of oxygen (the rate at which O_2 dissolved in water) to increase linearly with increasing temperature, doubling between 5 and 25°C.

(14) The following discussion is from Spotte (1979b, pp. 58–59). Kanwisher (1963) reported that small bubbles (0.05 cm in diameter) are rapid gas exchangers. Bubbles of this size with laminar layers 0.0010 to 0.0015 cm thick were ~90% equilibrated with CO_2 after rising through only 5 cm of water in 2.5 s. Kanwisher noted that the relative amounts of the different gases moved by a bubble are directly proportional to their differences in partial pressure in air versus water. If it is assumed that a fish consumes 1 mL O_2/L and produces 1 mL CO_2/L, the partial pressure of CO_2 in water will be ~0.04% of an atmosphere, compared with 0.03% in an air bubble injected beneath the surface. Air is ~21% O_2, whereas the partial pressure of oxygen in seawater will be ~17% (5 to 6 mL O_2/L). Thus an air bubble can move ~4% of its volume of O_2 and only ~0.01% of its volume of CO_2. In other words, oxygen and nitrogen (see below) in air bubbles proceed toward steady state with seawater at several hundred times the rate of carbon dioxide.

Differences in equilibration rates of gases decrease if the laminar layer around a bubble is made thinner. Consequently, forces that erode away the laminar layer are important in establishing rates of gas exchange. Liebermann (1957) found that freely ascending air bubbles showed a "diffusion coefficient" twice that of stationary bubbles. The turbulence surrounding a rising bubble probably exerts a shearing effect, causing the laminar layer to become thinner in places and increasing the rate of gas loss to the surrounding water.

Wyman et al. (1952) determined that air bubbles rising in seawater become depleted of oxygen and richer in nitrogen. This can also be explained in terms of solubility differences and hydrostatic pressure. If the pressure in an aquarium is considered to be 1 atm, and if the gases in an air bubble at the surface are also at 1 atm, there can be no diffusion because a diffusion gradient does not exist. The system is at steady state. But if the hydrostatic pressure is increased by releasing a bubble near the bottom of the aquarium, a concentration gradient is immediately established because the partial pressures of gases in the bubble have been increased. Oxygen is approximately twice as soluble as nitrogen, and it moves quickly across the laminar layer and into solution. Differences in solubility and the fact that the diffusion constants for oxygen and nitrogen are nearly the same cause the percentage loss of oxygen from the air bubbles to exceed the percentage of nitrogen lost, and nitrogen is left behind to enrich the interior of the bubble.

(15) This discussion is based mainly on Rooney and Huibregtse (1980).

(16) According to Rooney and Huibregtse (1980), ''Any flow striking a vertical wall produces a downward flow at reduced velocity. Since losses at the bend are proportional to the velocity squared, the greater the distance to the wall or the lower the velocity approaching the wall, the lower the reduction.''

(17) Castro et al. (1975) reported that the airlift pump principle was discovered in 1797 by Carl Loescher, a German mining engineer, but did not cite their source. Murray et al. (1981) also gave a brief history of the airlift but cited no references.

(18) The discussion on airlift design considerations in the remainder of the subsection is based on Reinemann and Timmons (1989). Also see Bronikowski and McCormick (1983), Castro and Zielinski (1980), Parker and Suttle (1987), Rousseau and Bu'Lock (1980), Spotte (1979a, pp. 75–82 and 1979b, pp. 61–70), and Stewart and Lidkea (1976). Castro et al. (1975) reported on the performance of airlift pumps of short length and small diameter. Német (1961) developed a correlation based on a large number of airlifts of different lengths, diameters, and submergence ratios.

(19) This discussion is based mainly on Spotte (1979a, pp. 46–48 and 1979b, pp. 209–213).

(20) Ng and Mueller (1975).

(21) See Peltzer and Griffin (1987/1988) for an analysis of foam stability in seawater.

(22) Wallace and Wilson (1969).

(23) Sebba (1962, pp. 62–64)

(24) This discussion is based on Spotte (1979b, pp. 1–9).

(25) This discussion is based on Spotte (1979b, pp. 185–186).

(26) This discussion is based on Spotte (1979b, pp. 186–187).

(27) This discussion is based on Spotte (1979b, pp. 187–190).

(28) The choice of multimedia over dual media is hard to justify. Culp (1977), Culp and Culp (1974), and Culp et al. (1978) touted multimedia as superior in terms of effluent clarity and headloss characteristics, but comparative testing was not done.

Experimental evidence shows that from a practical standpoint effluent clarities are indistinguishable (Tate et al. 1977). Moreover, headloss actually is greater in multimedia filters (Cleasby and Baumann 1977, Qureshi 1981) because garnet or ilmenite has a smaller grain size than the sand above it. Headloss ultimately is a function of reduced void fraction, and at any interface of two filtrants the one with the smaller grain size controls this factor (Cleasby and Baumann 1977).

(29) This discussion is based on Spotte (1979b, pp. 172–178).

(30) This discussion is based on Spotte (1979b, p. 173). One problem in filter design is the error inherent in effective size. Camp (1964) warned that because the hydraulic gradient is a function of the square of the filtrant grain diameter, d^2, effective size is critical. He noted that a manufacturer's rating of the size of a sieve opening may be 10 to 15% less than random samples actually counted and weighed. If the manufacturer's rating is then used, the resultant error in d^2 is 21 to 32%.

(31) This discussion is based on Spotte (1979b, pp. 180–183).

(32) Culp and Culp (1974) and Culp et al. (1978) recommended placing two 3.8-cm layers of high density gravel (garnet or ilmenite) on top of the support media to form an interface with the lowest layer of filtrant (garnet or ilmenite in multimedia filters, sand in dual media units). This prevents disruption of the support media during backwash and keeps the smallest filtrants from migrating downward into the support media. They suggested that the top 3.8 cm have a d_e of 0.85 mm and that the bottom 3.8 cm be 1 mm. The authors offered an option, which I have incorporated into Table 3-10. Simply add another 7.6 cm of the top level of support medium. In Leopold and pipe lateral underdrain systems this material is 3.2 × 6.4 cm silica gravel. Wheeler filter bottoms require an additional 7.6 cm of 4.8 × 9.5 cm silica gravel.

(33) This discussion is based on Cleasby and Baumann (1977) and Spotte (1979b, pp. 176–177).

(34) This discussion is based on Bouck et al. (1984). Also see Colt and Bouck (1984), Marking (1987), Marking et al. (1983), and Penrose and Squires (1976). Lasker and Vlymen (1969) described a splash tower design.

(35) Bouck et al. (1984) found the change in ΔP with movement through the column to be a log function described by

$$\ln \Delta P_h = a + bh \tag{3.16}$$

where the starting hyperbaric gas pressure (ΔP) = 210 mm Hg (>125% saturation), $\Delta P_h = \Delta P$ at height h (cm), $a = 5.2494$ (intercept of the regression), $b = -0.0626$ (slope of the regression), and $r^2 = 0.9728$ (coefficient of determination). The value of ΔP was reduced to <25 mm Hg. Packing consisted of 2.54-cm rings. For additional design criteria see Colt and Bouck (1984).

(36) This discussion is based on Caolo and Spotte (1990).

(37) This discussion is based on Spotte (1979a, pp. 79–80 and 1979b, pp. 64–68).

(38) Német (1961).

(39) Castro et al. (1976) obtained approximately 140 sets of data over a range of s, L, and D values appropriate for aquarium or aquaculture airlift design. Lee C. Eagleton (personal communication 1978; see Note 42) fitted most applicable sets of data to an equation of the form developed by Német (1961). The flow rate dependence on diameter shown by the Castro data were fit more reliably by a 2.2 power on the diameter than 2.5, as suggested by Német (1961). Equation 3.11, which resulted from the linear regression, fits the Castro data well enough for design purposes, although a better equation could perhaps be developed.

(40) Castro et al. (1975), Castro et al. (1976).

(41) Spotte (1979a, p. 76 and 1979b, p. 65) suggested that the minimum acceptable submergence ratio is 0.8. The experiments of Reinemann and Timmons (1989) demonstrated that greatest efficiency is attained at submergence ratios >0.85.

(42) Lee C. Eagleton, Department of Chemical Engineering, Pennsylvania State University, cited in Spotte (1979a, p. 79 and 1979b, p. 66).

(43) Castro et al. (1975).

(44) This discussion is based on Spotte (1979a, pp. 48–50 and 1979b, pp. 213–217).

(45) Lemlich (1972).

(46) These ideal factors were determined by Wace and Banfield (1966). Wallace and Wilson (1969) studied the removal of surfactants from seawater and artificial seawaters. They used bubble sizes varying from 0.1 to 2 mm and a gas flow rate of 0.46 $cm/(s \cdot cm^2)$ of contact column cross sectional area. The extreme differences between these results and those of Wace and Banfield are attributable partly to variations in surface activity of

the surfactants studied. Wallace and Wilson used highly proteinaceous substances such as bovine serum albumin, which were removed readily by foam fractionation. Consequently, the design criteria of Wace and Banfield are recommended.

(47) Wallace and Wilson (1969) found that joints in their column promoted turbulence and resulted in reduced recovery rates of surfactants.

(48) Sebba (1962, pp. 65–67).

(49) Nebel et al. (1973) noted that draining of the foam depended on the distance between the lip of the collection chamber and the effluent water level (the point at which the residue is returned). They recommended that the distance not exceed 0.63 cm.

(50) Sebba (1962, p. 64).

CHAPTER 4

(1) Hughes (1980), Hughes and Morgan (1973), Hughes and Shelton (1962), and Randall (1982) gave detailed descriptions of the morphology of fish gills.

(2) In most fishes the gill rakers are simply knobs on each side of the gill arch. In plankton feeders such as the Atlantic herring (*Clupea harengus harengus*) they have evolved into finely divided, netlike structures and strain out particulate matter.

(3) Gosline (1971, p. 51) described the movement of water this way: "The oral cavity may be viewed as a sort of intake pipe with a filtering device on the outflow sides. . . . Each filtering device is usually double; an inner (or medial) series of gill rakers . . . screens out the larger material (i.e., food), and the remaining water then passes through a finer (peripheral) screen made up of gill filaments. . . ." Also see Saunders (1961).

(4) Epithelial cells of the secondary lamellae ordinarily vary in thickness from 1 to 10 μm, depending on the species of fish. According to Hughes and Morgan (1973), those of the spiny dogfish, *Squalus acanthias*, and skipjack, *Euthynnus* (= *Katsuwanus*) *pelamis*, are 10 and 0.6 μm, respectively.

(5) This discussion is based on Spotte (1979, pp. 27–31). More detailed treatments were published by Hoar (1975, pp. 363–396), Prosser (1973), and Schmidt-Nielsen (1975, pp. 371–396).

(6) *Osmolality* is the term used to describe concentrations of biological solutions (e.g., blood and urine) in terms of particles

that affect osmotic pressure. An *osmole* is the amount of solute that when dissolved in 1000 g of water exerts the same osmotic pressure as a mole of an ideal nonelectrolyte. For solutes an osmole equals the number of ions *plus* undissociated molecules that give the same osmotic pressure as a mole of ideal nonelectrolyte. Biological fluids ordinarily are dilute, and the *milliosmole*, mOm, is the preferred unit of expression.

(7) Isosmotic is not the same as isotonic. According to Prosser (1973) an *isotonic solution* is one in which a cell or whole organism does not change volume. An isosmotic solution of a substance to which a cell is permeable but initially is absent from the cell is not isotonic. As an example Prosser cited red blood cells, which demonstrate no change in volume in 0.3 mol/L sucrose because they are impermeable to sucrose. When placed in an isosmotic solution of urea the cells swell because urea enters and water follows. Hoar (1975, p. 368) explained the difference this way: ''Solutions which produce no osmotic stress are isotonic; those which are theoretically of the same osmotic pressure are isosmotic.'' The term isosmotic is preferable when referring to equal osmotic concentrations.

(8) It sometimes is stated that freshwater fishes drink no water at all, but this is incorrect (e.g., Evans 1979, 1980b).

(9) Fredericq (1901) discovered that the ionic concentration of the body fluids of teleosts is relatively constant and similar to that of higher vertebrates (i.e., about one-third that of seawater). This rule holds whether a fish is freshwater, seawater, or transitional (brackish water or *euryhaline*). The only isosmotic vertebrates in which blood osmolality is attributable almost entirely to inorganic ions are the primitive hagfishes, which have internal concentrations of Na^+ and Cl^- that are similar to seawater. In this respect they resemble seawater invertebrates.

(10) The elasmobranchs are predominantly marine. Stingrays of the family Potamotrygonidae are the only elasmobranchs known to reside permanently in freshwater.

(11) Payan and Maetz (1973) termed these compounds ''osmotic fillers'' in describing their use by elasmobranchs.

(12) Data on all aspects of ionic and osmotic regulation in elasmobranchs are limited. Payan and Maetz (1971) reported that the smaller spotted dogfish (*Scyliorhinus canicula*) ingests only ~0.01% of its body mass per hour, or 1 to 10% of the drinking rate typical of seawater teleosts. Nonetheless, elasmobranchs carry on a high rate of water exchange with the environment.

Payan and Maetz measured water exchange with the external environment in three elasmobranchs: the smaller spotted dogfish, a skate (*Raja montagu*), and a ray (*Torpedo marmorata*). The rate was very high, amounting to, respectively, 157, 167, and 97%/h. The gills were the major sites of water exchange. In all cases, water turnover rates of elasmobranchs exceed those of freshwater teleosts, which are faced with continuous osmotic loading (Pang et al. 1977). Payan and Maetz compared their findings with data from a number of aquatic vertebrates and invertebrates. They concluded that isosmotic animals are more water-permeable than animals that are hyposmotic or hyperosmotic.

(13) Excellent reviews on branchial ion flux in freshwater teleosts were published by Cameron and Heisler (1985), Evans (1979, 1980b, 1982), Evans and Cameron (1986), Kirschner (1970, 1973), Maetz (1971, 1974), and Maetz et al. (1976). Krogh (1937, 1939) first proposed that environmental Na^+ and Cl^- are taken up by freshwater teleosts in exchange for blood NH_4^+ and HCO_3^-, respectively. Supporting evidence was later provided by Maetz and García Romeu (1964) using radioactive isotopes. They showed that adding NH_4^+ to the water as ammonium chloride, NH_4Cl, depresses uptake of Na^+ by goldfish (*Carassius auratus*); injecting goldfish with NH_4Cl stimulates uptake of Na^+. The work of de Vooys (1968) demonstrated that common carp (*Cyprinus carpio*) kept in deionized water, which contains no Na^+, still excrete NH_4^+, indicating an alternate mechanism to Na^+/NH_4^+ exchange. Kerstetter et al. (1970) reported similar results with rainbow trout. They found that when the rate of Na^+ uptake is stimulated by raising the concentration of Na^+ in the water, the excretion rate of H^+ also increases, but the rate at which NH_4^+ is excreted remains unchanged. In other words, an elevated influx of Na^+ could also indicate stimulated Na^+/H^+ exchange (Heisler 1989). Kirschner (1970) had proposed that in certain situations H^+ serves as a counterion for Na^+ instead of NH_4^+. Cameron and Heisler (1983) obtained results in apparent agreement with this hypothesis. Cameron (1986) found that when the normal concentration of ammonia is reversed (i.e., the amount in the water is greater than in the blood), channel catfish (*Ictalurus punctatus*) appear to exchange NH_4^+ only for H^+. This process has been termed the *Na^+-free effect*, because Na^+, even when present in sufficient quantities, does not affect NH_4^+ conductance (Evans and Cameron 1986). Goldfish were also discovered to make use of H^+ as a counterion for NH_4^+, and in this species Na^+ uptake appeared at first to correlate best with the sum of NH_4^+ and H^+ efflux (Maetz 1973). Cameron and Heisler (1983), however, repeated the ex-

periments of Maetz and García-Romeu (1964) and demonstrated that the results could be explained in terms of Na^+ influx by Na^+/H^+ exchange (Evans and Cameron 1986). Maetz's 1973 results are therefore inconclusive (Evans and Cameron 1986).

Krogh (1939) also was the first to suggest that blood HCO_3^- is exchanged for environmental Cl^-. This was confirmed experimentally by Maetz and García Romeu (1964): when HCO_3^- was injected into goldfish the uptake of Cl^- from the water was stimulated. Additional evidence of Cl^-/HCO_3^- exchange was provided by Dejours (1969), who reported that excretion of CO_2 by goldfish depends on the concentration of Cl^- in the environment.

(14) The form in which ammonia is transported by the blood to the branchial epithelium of teleosts and seawater elasmobranchs and later extruded into the environment is an important problem in comparative physiology (Claiborne and Evans 1988; Claiborne et al. 1982; Evans 1980b; Goldstein 1982; Goldstein et al. 1982; Maetz 1972; Randall and Wright 1987; Spotte 1979, pp. 275–281), but its solution has proved elusive. Krogh (1939) proposed that in freshwater teleosts the Na^+/NH_4^+ exchange maintains a nearly neutral electrochemical gradient across the gills. Maetz and García Romeu (1964) suggested that Na^+/NH_4^+ is apical and that blood NH_3 enters the serosal surface of the gill cell, joins with H^+ produced by the hydration of CO_2 (and subsequent dissociation of carbonic acid, H_2CO_3), and enters the environment across the apical surface in exchange for Na^+. Kerstetter et al. (1970) suggested a different mechanism: Na^+/H^+ and not Na^+/NH_4^+ occurs at the apical surface. Payan (1978) confirmed the findings of Maetz and García Romeu (1964). Kerstetter and Keeler (1976) conducted experiments indicating that Na^+/NH_4^+ is a serosal exchange process. Payan's work demonstrated that Na^+ influx across the apical surface is linked with ammonia (NH_4^+ plus NH_3) efflux. However, his data suggested that not all ammonia released depends on external Na^+. In fact, the efflux of ammonia in his Na^+-free solutions was 75% of that in normal (1 mmol/L Na^+) freshwater. The studies of de Vooys (1968), Kerstetter et al. (1970), and Maetz (1973) also suggested that any link in the Na^+/NH_4^+ exchange processes in freshwater teleosts is loose. Were this not so then manipulation of the environmental Na^+ concentration would affect NH_4^+ excretion more strongly than the data showed. Moreover, the net movement of Na^+ across the gills of seawater teleosts is outward, but the magnitude of NH_4^+ excretion is as great as in freshwater species (Maetz 1972). More recently, McDonald and Prior (1988) demonstrated that over 20 min the

exchange of blood NH_4^+ for environmental Na^+ in rainbow trout maintained in low-NaCl freshwater (0.05 mEq/L Na^+) is nearly 1.0. After 40 h the Na^+/NH_4^+ ratio was ~0.33. In these experiments Na^+/NH_4^+ appeared to be ". . . the sole mechanism for movement of ammonia across the gill."

Evidence for Na^+/NH_4^+ exchange in seawater teleosts is substantial. Evans (1973, 1975a) found that increasing the concentration of external NH_4^+ inhibited assimilation of Na^+ in the euryhaline sailfin molly (*Poecilia latipinna*) acclimated to seawater. Similar data derived from pinfish (*Lagodon rhomboides*) were published by Carrier and Evans (1976) and by Evans (1977) for the lined seahorse (*Hippocampus erectus*), lined sole (*Archirus lineatus*), striped burrfish (*Chilomycterus schoepfi*), and gulf toadfish (*Opsanus beta*). Injection of gulf toadfish with NH_4^+ stimulates both Na^+ assimilation and excretion of NH_4^+, the latter process being dependent on the external concentration of Na^+. Evans (1977) observed that in this species a sizable increase in the concentration of external NH_4^+ (200 mmol/L NH_4^+ added as NH_4Cl) actually reverses the ion exchange process, and Na^+ excretion (measured with radioactive isotopes) increases.

But if Na^+/NH_4^+ exchange accounts for only part of the ammonia excreted, how is the remainder released? Logic favors passive outward movement of NH_3. Historically, the assumption has been that NH_3 crosses living membranes readily but that NH_4^+ does not (Milne et al. 1958, Warren and Schenker 1962). The difference was attributed to greater solubility of NH_3 in lipids and the fact that free ammonia carries no electrical charge to entrap it before the membrane is traversed. Such reasoning is attractive, and it encouraged belief in the exclusive movement of NH_3 across cell membranes, including fish gill epithelia. Goldstein (1982) wrote: ". . . the hypothesis that ammonia moves across branchial membranes as free ammonia has not been tested. In fact the assumption that free ammonia is sufficiently soluble in lipids to allow it to move across the branchial membranes has not been examined." Evans and Cameron (1986) pointed out that NH_3 is barely soluble in lipids. They reasoned that if other ions could traverse epithelial membranes, so could NH_4^+. This was confirmed by Kikeri et al. (1989) in work demonstrating that the apical membrane of the human renal tubule cell is nearly impermeable to NH_3 but highly permeable to NH_4^+.

Freshwater-acclimated rainbow trout perfused with ammonium sulfate, $(NH_4)_2SO_4$, become acidotic (McDonald and Prior 1988). Acid excretion was believed to occur mainly as NH_4^+ because of the favorable gradient and large loss of blood ammonia. After perfusion there was only slight inward movement of

Na^+, suggesting that most of the NH_4^+ loss was paracellular. Following NH_4Cl infusion (5 mmol/kg), longhorn sculpins (*Myoxocephalus octodecemspinosus*) experience a rapid decrease in blood pH of 0.36 unit (Claiborne and Evans 1988). Ammonia is lost as NH_3 and NH_4^+ in equal proportions after an outwardly direct NH_3 diffusion gradient has been established. Longhorn sculpins placed in seawater to which NH_4Cl had been added ($\sim$1 mmol/L total NH_4-N) assimilate NH_4^+ initially, but after 4 h ammonia efflux resumes despite the negligible NH_3 diffusion gradient. Excretion of NH_4^+ is therefore likely.

Goldstein et al. (1982) designed experiments to test the possibility of the outward movement of NH_3. If NH_3 is the form excreted, and the gill is assumed to be relatively impermeable to NH_4^+, then the rate of NH_3 excretion is determined by the concentration on either side of the apical membrane (i.e., by the diffusion gradient). If NH_3 in the water is negligible the excretion rate is a function only of the concentration of NH_3 in the blood. Isolated heads of longhorn sculpins were used. The gills were perfused with artificial seawater containing ammonium chloride (1 mmol/L NH_4Cl). The concentration of NH_3 was varied by adjusting the pH of the perfusate to 7.8 or 6.9. The concentration of NH_3 is greater at the higher pH (Chapter 2). At pH values of 7.8 and 6.9 the concentrations of NH_3 were 0.04 and 0.005 mmol/L. By calculation, the rate of ammonia excretion would be directly related to the blood NH_3 concentration, or approximately eight times faster at the higher pH, assuming that NH_3 is the form excreted. However, the excretion rate was only slightly greater than at the lower pH. The concentration of NH_3 in the blood could not have been the determining factor, and NH_4^+ appears to have been exchanged actively with Na^+; the remainder diffused into the environment. Diffusion of NH_3 evidently did not occur.

Ion exchange also appears to function in elasmobranchs (see the brief discussion of Evans 1980b). Payan and Maetz (1973) injected ammonium sulfate, ammonium acetate ($NH_4C_2H_3O_2$), and ammonium bicarbonate (NH_4HCO_3) into smaller spotted dogfish and found that Na^+ influx was enhanced. Injection of acetazolamide (which inhibits production of H^+ and of NH_4^+ to a lesser extent) diminished Na^+ influx. Evans et al. (1979) reported that efflux of acid in the little skate (*Raja erinacea*) is stopped when the animal is placed in artificial seawater devoid of Na^+ and K^+, but that ammonia excretion is unaffected. Whether Na^+ or H^+ is exchanged for NH_4^+ may be species dependent in elasmobranchs.

The evidence favors excretion of both NH_3 and NH_4^+, but not necessarily under the same conditions. Evidently, NH_4^+ is the principal form excreted by fishes in seawater. Under other conditions NH_3 may predominate. Heisler (1980) speculated that low-pH freshwaters are promising environments for such a mechanism to occur. In freshwaters of pH 7.4, ~1% of the ammonia exists as NH_3 (Emerson et al. 1975), whereas at a pH of 5.1 ". . . the relative concentration is already so low that the environment can be considered as [an] infinite sink for NH_3. This makes it likely that most of the ammonia produced is eliminated by non-ionic diffusion. . . ." Other authors (Maetz 1971, 1972, 1973; Maetz and García Romeu 1964; Payan 1978; Payan and Maetz 1973) postulated that NH_4^+ is the main form of ammonia excreted by the gills, with NH_3 excretion occurring when the pH of the water is low or environmental Na^+ is absent.

Channel catfish used in experiments by Cameron and Kormanik (1982) appeared to excrete ammonia as NH_3. The fish were fitted with catheters surgically implanted in the dorsal aorta, which permitted acids or bases to be infused directly into the arterial blood. Each fish was then placed in a small chamber containing a volume of freshwater three to five times the volume of the fish. One compound infused into the dorsal aorta was NH_4Cl. If ammonia as NH_3 were transferred to the external environment a proton, H^+, would be left behind in the blood, making the blood more acidic. Conversely, loss of ammonia as NH_4^+ would entail loss of the proton as well. Cameron and Kormanik (1982) reasoned that an "H^+ load" in the blood ". . . is only generated by an excess of NH_3 excretion over net H^+ excretion." Moreover, ". . . if NH_3 is excreted, it will subsequently combine with a proton in the external water, and with our methods we will measure zero net H^+ excretion. In that case the ammonia excretion all contributes to the expressed H^+ load. If NH_4^+ is excreted, or NH_3 and a proton simultaneously, we would measure net H^+ excretion equal to the ammonia excretion, and in this case no contribution to the expressed H^+ load." During the first 6 h after injection, 0.65 mmol/kg of acid in excess of that produced by the control fish (which received no injections) was excreted, or 32.5% of the infused acid load. The authors concluded: "The effective acid load is produced, of course, by diffusive loss of NH_3, and not by direct excretion of NH_4^+. . . . With our methods, excretion of NH_4^+ would appear as net H^+ excretion, whereas NH_3 excretion would not. During the first hour after infusion, ammonia excretion exceeded net H^+ excretion by nearly 4.5 to 1, confirming diffusive loss of NH_3. . . ."

Hillaby and Randall (1979) used a similar experimental procedure to study ammonia extrusion in freshwater-acclimated rainbow trout. Compounds infused into the arterial blood were NH_4Cl and NH_4HCO_3. These authors also concluded that ammonia is lost to the external environment as NH_3. Blood pH increased after infusion of NH_4HCO_3, resulting in a greater proportion of blood ammonia as NH_3, whereas infusion of NH_4Cl caused a decrease in blood pH and the concomitant shift in ammonia toward NH_4^+. The data indicated that ammonia was excreted more rapidly following infusion of NH_4HCO_3, favoring rapid diffusion of NH_3 outward into the surrounding water. The work of Avella and Bornancin (1989) also supported the outward diffusion of NH_3 in freshwaters. In experiments involving isolated, perfused heads of rainbow trout in low-Na^+ water (200 μmol/L), no significant change in Na^+ uptake was seen when the internal concentration of ammonia was raised from 0 to 1 mmol/L at constant pH. However, ammonia excretion increased with the internal ammonia concentration, demonstrating ". . . complete uncoupling between sodium and ammonia transport." When 20 mmol/L ammonia were added to the water for 20 min and then removed, Na^+ uptake was reduced 40%. The pH changes in arterial effluents gave evidence that NH_3 diffuses into the branchial epithelium (either by transcellular or paracellular means) and ". . . could argue for an intracellular alkalinization responsible for sodium influx inhibition." In other words, addition of ammonia to the external solution results in rapid inward diffusion of NH_3, subsequent binding of intracellular H^+, and alkalinization (Boron and de Weer 1976).

Cameron and Heisler (1985) speculated that an operational mechanism for Na^+/NH_4^+ exchange is not required because most natural waters contain low concentrations of ammonia. Therefore, ". . . NH_4^+ may only incidently substitute for H^+ . . . ." In unpolluted waters the normal gradients for NH_4^+ and NH_3 are outward and steep, and at least 60 to 90% of the total ammonia is excreted as NH_3. As such, plasma ammonia becomes elevated only if the external ammonia increases to levels that interfere with the outward diffusion of NH_3 (Heisler 1989). Cameron and Heisler (1985) emphasized that, until recently, few investigations of ammonia uptake and excretion have included a simultaneous measure of the acid-base status of the test animals. Changes in plasma pH affect not only the form of ammonia transported, but also the mechanisms involved. Experiments in which the external ammonia concentration was low have failed to rule out Na^+/H^+ exchange. Conversely, an Na^+/NH_4^+ exchange mechanism is likely if the test fishes have been exposed to high concentrations of ammonia for prolonged periods, or if the blood ammonia is elevated suddenly (Claiborne and Evans 1988, McDonald and Prior 1988). In this instance, NH_4^+ is exchanged for Na^+ or possibly H^+ and also excreted paracellularly.

(15) McDonald and Prior (1988), McDonald et al. (1989).

(16) The following discussion is based on Evans (1979, 1980a, 1980b, 1982). Also see Maetz (1971, 1974, 1976). Seawater teleosts have body fluids of lower ionic concentration than the environment (see Note 9). However, ion distribution on either side of any semipermeable membrane must account for electrochemical gradients, in addition to chemical concentrations. Potts et al. (1973) noted that a hyposmotic animal conserves energy if it can sustain differential permeability so that an electrical potential gradient of a given ion develops between the blood and the outside environment. The gradient potential then favors diffusion outward, which reduces the need for active excretion. No net influx occurs if the gradient is steep enough. The steepness of the gradient (i.e., the electrical or equilibrium potential) necessary to maintain passive ionic equilibrium is defined for monovalent ions by the Nernst equation:

$$\mathrm{V} = \frac{RT}{F} \ln \frac{[c_\mathrm{m}]}{[c_\mathrm{b}]} \tag{4.2}$$

in which V = the electrical potential across the epithelial tissue in volts (*transepithelial potential*, TEP), R = the universal gas constant, T = temperature in °K, F = Faraday's constant, c_m and c_b are the concentrations of a monovalent ion in the external solution and blood (actually, the activities), and RT/F reduces to 26 mV at 23°C. As the TEP approaches the Nernst potential necessary for an ionic species to become regulated, the energy required for its active excretion approaches zero. However, the electrochemical gradient against which the ion of opposite charge must be excreted increases; consequently, the energy needed for excretion also increases. Overall, the process still results in an energy savings (Potts et al. 1973), and some seawater teleosts appear to use it.

Both Na^+ and Cl^- are maintained at <200 mmol/L in the plasma, compared with individual values of ~ 500 mmol/L in seawater. Based on these concentrations the Nernst potential is $\sim +26$ mV for Na^+ and ~ -30 mV for Cl^-. (The sign of the TEP represents blood relative to external solution.) In all seawater teleosts studied so far the equilibrium potential of Cl^- is substantially different from the measured TEP, and it therefore can be assumed that Cl^- must be excreted actively before blood

Cl^- can be maintained below the electrochemical equilibrium. The case for Na^+ is less clear.

In species evaluated to date the TEPs are near the Na^+ equilibrium potential or lower, suggesting the possibility of either active or passive excretion (Evans 1982). The considerable data in print can thus be evaluated in two ways. The first interpretation is that Na^+ is actively exchanged with K^+ in the environment. Transfer of a seawater teleost to K^+-free artificial seawater results in a decline in the amount of Na^+ it excretes, as measured with radioactive isotopes (Evans et al. 1973, Maetz 1969, Motais and Isaia 1972), and an increase in blood Na^+ concentration (Maetz 1969). Addition of ouabain to seawater, which inhibits an enzyme in the gills that mediates or controls the rate of the exchange process (sodium-potassium-activated adenosine triphosphatase or Na^+-K^+-activated ATPase), halts both Na^+ excretion and ion exchange (Evans et al. 1973, Motais and Isaia 1972). This also is followed by an increase in blood Na^+ concentration (Motais and Isaia 1972).

The second interpretation is that an active excretion mechanism is unnecessary because Na^+ is at, or very close to, electrochemical equilibrium (i.e., any movement would be passive). Several lines of reasoning support this position, not all of them discussed here. Potts and Fleming (1971) removed K^+ from artificial seawater and saw no effect on excretion of Na^+ by the plains killifish, *Fundulus zebrinus* (= *F. kansae*). Similar results were reported by Motais and Isaia (1972) for European eels (*Anguilla anguilla*), Kirschner et al. (1974) for rainbow trout, and Sanders and Kirschner (1983a, 1983b) for Pacific staghorn sculpins (*Leptocottus armatus*) and seawater-acclimated rainbow trout. Motais and Isaia (1972) proposed that in European eels Na^+/K^+ exchange is transformed to a process involving Na^+/Na^+. In such circumstances any Na^+ efflux would be masked.

Confirmation of a passive excretion mechanism for Na^+ is clouded by the uncertain role of K^+ as a driving force. Evans (1979) suggested that removal of K^+ from the environment may affect the TEP enough to cause major changes in the passive efflux of Na^+. In other words, the effects on Na^+ efflux caused by K^+ described in the preceding paragraph may actually originate from alterations in electrochemical potential and not from shifts in the Na^+/K^+ exchange rate. Removal of K^+ perhaps lowers the TEP, which in turn reduces Na^+ efflux by passive transfer. In such cases the effect would be potential mediated. But this evidently is not a viable mechanism in some species. Evans et al. (1974) reported that removal of K^+ from artificial seawater reduced Na^+ efflux in the fat sleeper (*Dormitator maculatus*) without affecting the TEP. Evans (1979) summarized data for other species in which the K^+-stimulated efflux of Na^+ is also greater than can be explained by changes in TEP.

(17) Silva et al. (1977a) showed that ouabain injected into European eels inhibits both Na^+ and Cl^- efflux. The location of Na^+–K^+-activated ATPase (see Note 16) is on the serosal surface. These authors proposed the existence of a membrane carrier linking the movements of Na^+ and Cl^- tightly together. Thus Cl^- is transported actively into cells of the gill epithelium. The necessary energy would be derived from passive movement of Na^+ along its electrochemical gradient. At this point Cl^- diffuses down its concentration gradient, across the apical membrane, and into the environment. Part of the Na^+ is recycled into the blood in active exchange with K^+; the rest moves passively by paracellular means and enters the seawater. As noted by Evans et al. (1982), the model does not account for Na^+ excretion by fishes known to maintain Na^+ in electrochemical disequilibrium.

(18) Silva et al. (1977b) conducted the first study that elucidated essential mechanisms of ion exchange by this organ. They used a perfused rectal gland preparation from spiny dogfish. The authors suggested that the rectal gland functions in the same manner as their model of the teleost branchial epithelium (Silva et al. 1977a). Both models resemble Figure 4-8.

(19) The contents of the rectal gland epithelial cell are negative with respect to the *lumen* (internal cavity), which accounts for the active transport of Cl^-. Loosely speaking, the lumen and external environmental are equivalent because they are in contact. Presumably, Na^+ is concentrated in the lumen, which maintains a TEP that is negative to the blood (Evans 1980b, Silva et al. 1977b). An important finding of Silva et al. (1977b) is the dependence of Cl^- movement on Na^+ concentration (i.e., transport of the two ions is linked), which was confirmed in experiments of Epstein et al. (1983) and Kinne et al. (1982). In the words of Epstein and coauthors, "Secretion of chloride from blood to lumen is accomplished in the rectal gland of elasmobranchs by a process of secondary active transport involving the co-transport of Cl^- with Na^+ across the basolateral [serosal] membranes of rectal gland cells. Energy is provided by ATP *via* membrane Na-K-ATPase, which establishes an electrochemical gradient favouring Na^+ influx into the cell." As noted by Kinne and coauthors, such mechanisms exclude the possibility of Na^+ and Cl^- transport by exchange with protons and hydroxide ions. Thus the exchanges $Na^+/(H^+ + NH_4^+)$ and Cl^-/OH^- do not appear to occur in the elasmobranch rectal gland.

(20) Evans (1980b) briefly reviewed excretion of Na^+ and Cl^- across the branchial epithelium of elasmobranchs. Evidence for such a process is strong but indirect. Published studies indicate that the sum of Na^+ and Cl^- loss at extrabranchial sites (e.g., rectal gland, urine) accounts for <50% of total concentration excreted.

(21) This provocative idea was proposed by Evans (1975b). He wrote: ''Excretion of HCO_3^- provides for the net loss of respiratory CO_2, excretion of H^+ provides for the net loss of both acid and nitrogenous waste. . . . It appears therefore that the fish gill has . . . provided for four metabolic needs via the acquisition of two ionic exchange systems. These metabolic needs are divided between the kidney and lung in terrestrial vertebrates.'' Evans' reasoning assumes that some of these processes are more important than others. The uptake of Na^+ and Cl^- is ''necessary'' only to freshwater fishes, which face a net loss of ions to the environment. However, the net losses of acids (represented by H^+) and nitrogenous wastes (represented by NH_4^+) are mandatory in all waters. He concluded that because seawater fishes appear to exchange Na^+ for either H^+ or NH_4^+ while simultaneously coping with a ''salt load'' (i.e., net influx of ions), ''. . . one can only conclude that the physiological necessity for excretion of H^+ and NH_4^+ outweighs the problems of adding to the Na^+ imbalance.'' In Evans' view, the ''reason'' for the uptake of Na^+ and Cl^- in seawater is not ionic regulation *per se,* but to provide ions for exchange with other (unwanted) species. As the author observed, this hypothesis has yet to be subjected to rigorous testing.

(22) To convert mg O_2/L to partial pressure expressed in mm Hg, multiply by the constant 0.00195; multiply the product obtained by (T + 273) where T = temperature in degrees Celsius (°C) and 273 = absolute temperature in degrees Kelvin (°K). Two examples follow:

Example 1 Convert 8 mg O_2/L at 15°C to mm Hg:

$$8(0.00195)(288) = 4.5 \text{ mm Hg}$$

Example 2 Convert 6.0 mm Hg at 21°C to mg O_2/L:

$$\frac{6.0}{(0.00195)(294)} = 10.5 \text{ mg } O_2/L$$

(23) This discussion is based on Randall (1982) and Randall et. al. (1982).

(24) In my opinion, "relative alkalinity" should be abandoned because it is misleading. The term was proposed by Rahn (1966, 1967) and perpetuated in subsequent publications by Rahn and others of his working group (e.g., Howell 1970; Howell et al. 1970; Rahn 1967, 1974a, 1974b; Rahn and Baumgardner 1972; Reeves 1969, 1977). The concept of the blood being maintained on the basic side of neutral is perfectly valid, but the term itself bears no relationship to the definition of alkalinity, and it is here that misinterpretations arise. Alkalinity, which is the net negative charge of all ions that interact with H^+, has obvious relevance to studies of acid-base regulation in fishes because pH*a* is controlled by $[HCO_3^-]a$. Rahn and his colleagues worked mainly with amphibians and reptiles. In these animals "relative alkalinity" is controlled by changes in $PaCO_2$, whereas $[HCO_3^-]a$ remains essentially constant (Heisler 1980). Any mechanism linked with HCO_3^- would naturally affect alkalinity (chemical definition), but CO_2 does not because it contains no electrical charge (Fig. 1-8). According to Howell et al. (1970), ". . . pH, per se, is not being maintained but rather a constant relationship between hydroxyl and hydrogen ions [constant OH^-/H^+ ratio] even though their absolute concentrations will vary greatly." This suggests that *relative pH* is a more appropriate term.

The concept of "relative alkalinity" is based mainly on the work of Rahn (1966) and Robin (1962). Rahn (1966) demonstrated that the degree to which the blood of cold-blooded, air-breathing vertebrates remains on the basic side of neutral (i.e., the degree to which it is alkaline) is an inverse linear function of temperature. The values of K_w (concentration ion product of pure water; Chapter 1, Note 11) at neutrality vary with temperature. The pH at which water is neutral increases by 0.6 pH unit when the temperature drops from 37 to 3°C.

(25) Heisler (1980, 1989).

(26) Rahn and Baumgardner (1972) plotted pH*a* values from 11 species of fishes against the respective environmental temperature of each and showed that all maintain normal blood pH within 0.25 unit of constant relative pH (see Note 24). This work also confirmed that a decrease in pH*a* with a rise in temperature is valid for fishes as well as amphibians and reptiles. However, the authors went further by proposing that fishes, like these other animals, maintain their blood at constant relative pH, which was later demonstrated not to be true. The validity of such a concept had been questioned earlier. Houston (1971) reviewed acid-base regulation in fishes and stated that ". . . the data are not generally compatible with the hypothesis that the

teleosts, like amphibians and reptiles, direct their regulation of acid-base balance towards a stabilization of the OH^-/H^+ ratio when challenged by variations in environmental temperature.'' Data supporting Houston's conclusions subsequently were published by Cameron (1978) for sand seatrout (*Cynoscion arenarius*), Heisler (unpublished, cited in Heisler 1980) for larger spotted dogfish, and Randall and Cameron (1973) for rainbow trout. A South American swamp-eel (*Synbranchus marmoratus*) is the only fish known to maintain constant relative blood pH with changes in temperature (unpublished, cited in Heisler 1980). In this respect it behaves like an amphibian or reptile.

(27) This discussion is based on Heisler (1978, 1980, 1989) and McDonald and Prior (1988).

(28) Two of the more controversial species involved in ion exchange processes are H^+ and OH^-. Whether H^+ and NH_4^+ are both exchanged for Na^+ has not been resolved to everyone's satisfaction, nor is it clear that Cl^- is exchanged for HCO_3^-, OH^-, or both. However, Cameron (1978) pointed out that from the standpoint of acid-base balance it makes no difference because the effects are the same. Cameron (1979) later wrote: ''It is the *difference* in rates of H^+ and HCO_3^- excretion . . . that acts to change pH[*a*], and so even if *all* CO_2 produced by the animal is excreted as bicarbonate, there is no pH[*a*] effect so long as an equivalent amount of H^+ (or NH_4^+) is also excreted.'' Also see Heisler (1982).

(29) This discussion is based on Heisler (1978, 1980).

(30) As noted by Heisler (1980), the mechanisms used by fishes to assimilate HCO_3^- from the water during environmental hypercapnia are unclear. Cameron (1976) subjected Arctic graylings (*Thymallus arcticus*) to hypercapnic conditions. A reduction in branchial Cl^- assimilation was accompanied by increased influx of Na^+, suggesting Cl^-/HCO_3^- and $Na^+/(H^+ + NH_4^+)$ exchange. These would be appropriate responses to an increase in $[HCO_3^-]w$.

(31) Compensation times for the larger spotted dogfish and rainbow trout are from Heisler et al. (1976) and Janssen and Randall (1975), respectively. Heisler (1980) pointed out that the considerable difference may be a function of the larger $[HCO_3^-]$ gradients between the blood and the environment in the freshwater-acclimated rainbow trout, compared with the seawater shark. He further noted that the rate at which $[HCO_3^-]w$ is assimilated by larger spotted dogfish during hypercapnia depends on the pH gradient between the blood and the seawater (Fig. 4-15). In this species the blood/seawater gradient (pH*a*/

p*Hw*) is >0.6 unit (Heisler and Neumann 1977). At identical values of $PaCO_2$ and $PwCO_2$ the rate of assimilation depends on the $[HCO_3^-]a/[HCO_3^-]w$ gradient. Perry (1982) observed a similar disparity in the recovery rate from hypercapnia between freshwater-acclimated rainbow trout and seawater-acclimated coho salmon (*Oncorhynchus kisutch*). The salmon accumulated HCO_3^- from the water more rapidly and recovered much faster. Perry attributed this to the greater buffer capability (in this situation, greater $[HCO_3^-]w$) of the seawater.

Cross et al. (1969) showed that shifts in $[HCO_3^-]a$ in the spiny dogfish cannot be attributed exclusively to active uptake of HCO_3^- from the surrounding seawater. Cross and coauthors and Randall et al. (1976), who worked with larger spotted dogfish, suggested that intracellular transfer could support $[HCO_3^-]a$ at least transiently during environmental hypercapnia. Intracellular transfer of HCO_3^- during environmental hypercapnia in the larger spotted dogfish was confirmed and quantified by Heisler et al. (1976). Initially, HCO_3^- is transferred from intracellular sites to the blood. A portion is then transferred to the seawater, increasing the $[HCO_3^-]w$. This loss from the $[HCO_3^-]a$ pool indicates that the gill epithelium has not yet adjusted to hypercapnic conditions, and the transfer represents an ''overflow'' resulting from increased $[HCO_3^-]a$. Assimilation of HCO_3^- from seawater begins ~15 min after the onset of hypercapnia and is accompanied by the simultaneous influx of HCO_3^- back into intracellular compartments. The next phase of the process involves a net uptake of HCO_3^- from the seawater. This is followed by return to the intracellular compartments of the amount transferred initially, at which point both p*Ha* and the pH of the intracellular compartments are compensated by active uptake of HCO_3^- from the seawater. Heisler et al. (1976) concluded: ''Even though bicarbonate exchange with the seawater is the more important means by which extracellular pH[*a*] is restored in the longer term, the action of the intracellular space appears to be valuable in order to maintain extracellular pH[*a*]. It diminishes the maximal pH variations at a time where no other mechanisms for compensation of serious $P[a]CO_2$ changes are available and it may help to extend the range of tolerance to such external disturbances in these animals.''

(32) Stephen Spotte, Gary Adams, Patricia M. Bubucis, and John D. Buck (1989, unpublished data).

(33) This discussion is based mainly on findings of Truchot et al. (1980) in which smaller spotted dogfish were the experimental animals. The pattern is typical of other elasmobranchs and derived teleosts subjected to the same conditions, as shown by

Dejours (1973, 1979) for common carp, Dejours (1975) for the brown trout (*Salmo trutta* = *S. fario*), and Dejours et al. (1977) for the smaller spotted dogfish, larger spotted dogfish, and five species of seawater teleosts (a wrasse, *Labrus bergylta*; a temperate bass, *Morone labrax*; a mullet, *Mugil labrosus*; a gurnard, *Trigla lyra*; and the pollock, *Pollachius virens*). In the study of Truchot et al. (1980), pH*i* and $PiCO_2$ averaged 8.15 and 0.32 torr,* respectively, during conditions of normcapnia. During environmental hypercapnia these factors averaged 7.70 and 1.025 torr. Pairs of values (pH*i* and $PiCO_2$) matched for normcapnia (NoNc, HoNc); similarly, pairs matched for hypercapnia (HoHc, NoHc). Under both sets of circumstances $PeCO_2$ was substantially higher (and the pH of expired water, pH*e*, correspondingly lower) as a result of the ventilatory depression induced by hyperoxia. At the same time, $PaCO_2$ was higher (and pH*a* correspondingly lower) in hyperoxic than in normoxic water. It did not matter whether $PiCO_2$ was low (HoNc, NoNc) or high (HoHc, NoHc). The authors concluded that in the smaller spotted dogfish ventilatory depression during hyperoxic conditions is always accompanied by arterial hypercapnia. This also appears to be true of other fishes.

(34) This ratio, termed the oxygen extraction coefficient, E_w, is shown by

$$E_w = \frac{PiO_2 - PeO_2}{PiO_2} \tag{4.3}$$

and the oxygen concentration difference is defined by

$$CiO_2 - CeO_2 = \alpha O_2 w(PiO_2 - PeO_2) \tag{4.4}$$

where $\alpha O_2 w$ is the solubility coefficient of oxygen in seawater at stated temperature and salinity; in other words, at 18°C and 35‰ the value is 1.53 μmol/(L·mm Hg). The reciprocal of the oxygen concentration difference is the ventilatory convection requirement (also called specific ventilation), $Vw/\dot{M}O_2$, where Vw = the flow rate of water and $\dot{M}O_2$ = oxygen consumption (i.e., the volume of water that must pass over the gills for one unit of O_2 to be extracted). See Dejours (1975, pp. 22–26 and 113–119), Dejours et al. (1970, 1977), and Truchot et al. (1980).

(35) Dejours (1979).

(36) Dejours (1973, 1975), Glass et al. (1990), Holeton (1980), Randall (1970, 1982).

*1 torr = 1 mm Hg at 0°C.

(37) Dejours (1979) did not state the species of fishes and crustaceans. He noted only that ". . . for normoxic water . . . [the values] correspond [to] ventilatory requirements of some fishes (carp, trout, mullet, bass, dogfish) and two crustaceans (crayfish and crab). . . ." The caption of the figure referred to data in Dejours (1975) and Dejours et al. (1970). Both works are reviews that make extensive use of primary literature sources. They list animals by common name only, and the mullet is not mentioned.

(38) Randall (1982).

(39) The shift from perfusion to diffusion limitation was demonstrated in the rainbow trout by Daxboeck et al. (1982). It had been thought previously that fish gills are mainly—perhaps exclusively—diffusion limited because differences in PO_2 between blood and gill water are often large, suggesting that the two solutions are not in equilibrium (Hughes 1980, Jones and Randall 1978, Randall 1970).

(40) This was demonstrated in the tench (*Tinca tinca*) by Eddy (1974); rainbow trout by Holeton and Randall (1967), Nikinmaa and Soivio (1982), and Soivio et al. (1980); winter flounder (*Pseudopleuronectes americanus*) by Cech et al. (1977); and European eel by Wood and Johansen (1973a).

(41) This was demonstrated in the plaice (*Pleuronectes platessa*) by Wood et al. (1975), mummichog (*Fundulus heteroclitus*) by Greaney and Powers (1978), rainbow trout by Soivio et al. (1980), and European eel by Wood and Johansen (1973b). Riggs (1979) discussed specific biochemical pathways.

(42) Other factors, notably temperature and the combined effect of CO_2 and pH, also influence the binding of oxygen. A rise in temperature weakens the bond between oxygen and hemoglobin, causing the hemoglobin-oxyhemoglobin reaction to shift in reverse and the oxygen dissociation curve to shift forward. An increase in $PaCO_2$ lowers pH*a*, which also weakens the oxygen-hemoglobin bond, a phenomenon known as the *Bohr effect*. In some fishes the Bohr effect is even more pronounced, and the blood cannot be saturated at any PaO_2. This is the *Root effect* (Dafré and Wilhelm F° 1989, Pelster and Weber 1990, Brittain 1987). In elasmobranchs, both effects typically are weak or absent (e.g., Dafré and Wilhelm F° 1989, Wells and Davie 1985).

(43) The quotation is from Pickering (1981). Also see Schreck (1981) and Stebbing (1981). Selye (1950, 1973) was among the first to consider stress in terms of the nonspecific response, (i.e.,

any number of stress factors can elicit the same physiological stress response), but see Moberg (1987) for a dissenting opinion. According to Hattingh (1988), ''stress'' refers to the response.

(44) Adedire and Oduleye (1984), Haux and Sjöbeck (1985), Houston et al. (1971b), Maetz (1974), Pic et al. (1974), Stevens (1972), Woodward and Strange (1987).

(45) Wedemeyer (1969).

(46) Wells and Davie (1985).

(47) Cliff and Thurman (1984), Holeton and Heisler (1983), Jensen (1987), Soivio and Oikari (1976), Wells et al. (1984).

(48) Bilinsky (1974), White and Fletcher (1989).

(49) Bourne (1986), Casillas and Smith (1977), Chavin and Young (1970), Cliff and Thurman (1984), Haux and Sjöbeck (1985), Ishioka (1984a, 1984b), Kirk (1974), Martem'yanov (1986), Soivio and Oikari (1976), Spieler and Nickerson (1976), Yamamoto et al. (1980).

(50) Bagarinao and Kungvankij (1986), Ellsaesser and Clem (1987), Mazeaud et al. (1977), Pickford et al. (1971b, 1971c), Simpson (1975/1976), Tripp et al. (1987), Wedemeyer (1976), Woo et al. (1987).

(51) Leach and Taylor (1980), Leloup-Hatey (1985), Mazeaud (1964), Robertson et al. (1987), Sumpter et al. (1986).

(52) Barton and Peter (1982), Black and Connor (1964), Bourne (1984), Chavin and Young (1970), Davis et al. (1982), Ferreira et al. (1981), Houston et al. (1971a), Limsuwan et al. (1983), Nishimura et al. (1976), Soivio et al. (1977), Spieler and Nickerson (1976), Strange and Schreck (1978), Wedemeyer (1970).

(53) Ainsworth et al. (1985), Peters (1982), Schreck (1981).

(54) Barton et al. (1980), Carmichael et al. (1984), Davis and Parker (1983), Davis et al. (1979), Leach and Taylor (1980), Mazeaud et al. (1977), Pickering et al. (1987), Strange (1980), Strange et al. (1978), Sumpter et al. (1986), Wedemeyer (1976), White and Fletcher (1986), Woodward and Strange (1987).

(55) Leach and Taylor (1980), Wahlqvist and Nilsson (1980).

(56) Rasquin and Rosenbloom (1954).

(57) Butler et al. (1978), Chavin and Young (1970), Leach and Taylor (1980), Kirk (1974), Mazeaud et al. (1977), Pettersson and Johansen (1982), White and Fletcher (1986, 1989).

(58) Barton and Peter (1982), Mazeaud et al. (1977), Pickford et al. (1971a), Stanley and Colby (1971), Strange et al. (1977).

(59) Leloup-Hatey (1985), Singley and Chavin (1971).

(60) Barton and Peter (1982), Barton and Schreck (1987), Barton et al. (1980, 1987, 1988), Bouck and Ball (1966), Bouck et al. (1978), Carmichael et al. (1983, 1984), Chavin and Young (1970), Cliff and Thurman (1984), Fletcher (1975), Fuller et al. (1974), Hattingh (1976), Hattingh and van Pletzen (1974), Houston et al. (1971a), Martem'yanov (1986), Mazeaud et al. (1977), Pickering et al. (1982), Redgate (1974), Robertson et al. (1987), Soivio and Oikari (1976), Specker and Schreck (1980), Strange et al. (1977), Sumpter et al. (1985, 1986), Umminger and Gist (1973), Wedemeyer (1972), Wells and Davie (1985), White and Fletcher (1986), Wydoski et al. (1976), Yamamoto et al. (1980).

(61) Dejours (undated).

(62) Barton et al. (1988), Giesy (1988), Martini (1978), Soivio and Oikari (1976), Storer (1967).

(63) Toxicants include ammonia (Spotte and Anderson 1989, Tomasso et al. 1981b), copper (Donaldson and Dye 1975, Schreck and Lorz 1978), and formalin (Wedemeyer 1971).

(64) To my knowledge, Chavin (1973) and Mazeaud et al. (1977) were the first investigators to employ the concept of primary, secondary, and tertiary stress responses to fishes.

(65) Donaldson (1981) reviewed the biochemistry of the stress response.

(66) The following discussion is based mainly on Bern and Nandi (1964). The location and distribution of interrenal and chromaffin tissues vary greatly among aquatic vertebrates. In elasmobranchs the interrenal is a well defined gland located on the posterior surface of the kidney. The chromaffin bodies are small and paired; they extend along the anterior part of the kidney but are distinctly separate from the interrenal tissue. In teleosts the interrenal tissue is located inside or just forward of the head kidney or pronephros and associated with the postcardinal veins or their branches. Chromaffin cells are scattered in the walls of these veins, but do not necessarily intermingle with cells of the interrenal tissue. The chromaffin tissues, incidently, are named for a characteristic staining reaction.

(67) Axelrod and Reisine (1984), Donaldson (1981).

(68) As used here the term ''strenuous exercise'' is applicable only to forced movement caused by a disturbance. In undis-

turbed fishes the normal level of activity is species dependent and thus a product of evolutionary factors. Forced movement that causes exercise stress in a sedentary fish might not be stressful to a species that typically is more active. Piiper et al. (1977) reported that larger spotted dogfish become oxygen-depleted even during moderate (and apparently normal) swimming. The tissues recover during intermittent periods in which the animals rest on the bottom.

(69) Wood et al. (1983) fitted rainbow trout with dorsal aortic catheters, then chased them vigorously with a prod for 6 min. Delayed post-exercise mortality was 40% with most deaths occurring 4 to 8 h later. Blood samples were withdrawn before exercise (experimental controls) and at 0, 0.5, 1, 2, 4, 8, and 12 h after application of the stress. Respiratory acidosis was manifested by a tripling of $PaCO_2$ to ~9 torr from prestress (control) values. Subsequent changes in $PaCO_2$ were the same in trout that survived as in those that died, returning to prestress values within 1 h. After 0.5 h the remaining acidosis was almost entirely metabolic.

Wood et al. (1977) studied secondary stress effects after severe exercise in starry flounders (*Platichthys stellatus*). Catheters were implanted in the caudal artery of each experimental fish. After recovery the flounders were chased for 10 min, at which point they failed to respond to further stimulation and were unable to right themselves. Venous blood samples were withdrawn at 0 (immediately after application of the stress) and 20 min and at 1, 2, 4, 6, and 24 h. The initial (prestress) lactate concentration was 0.28 mmol/L. The concentration had risen only to 1.8 mmol/L at 0 min, but continued to rise to six and then seven times the prestress value at 2 and 4 h. Initial values were reestablished by 24 h. The authors wrongly assumed that lactate and H^+ ions are produced and removed in equivalent quantities (see Note 71), ". . . so the amount of . . . lactic acid added can be considered equal to that of the measured L-lactate ion."

The pH values of the same venous blood samples indicated a very different pattern. The pH fell markedly from an average prestress value of 7.900 to 7.516 at 9 min, then increased slowly despite the subsequent increase in lactate concentration. The pH was still depressed at 6 h but had returned to normal by 24 h. The initial partial pressure of CO_2 in the venous blood ($PvCO_2$) was ~2.0 mm Hg based on calculations (as opposed to direct analytical determination). At 0 min $PvCO_2$ rose to 6.5 mm Hg, then declined gradually to prestress values by 24 h. The time course varied inversely with changes in pH but not lactate. In interpreting their results the authors observed that at 9 min the acidosis was caused almost entirely by the increase in $PvCO_2$; by 2 h the contribution of this factor was ~50%. However, by 4 h, when the respiratory acidosis was diminishing, the contribution of lactate had become important (51%). Mean lactate contribution to the total pH change increased from 2.3 to 48.3% at 6 h, but the magnitude of the total change in pH had decreased substantially by this time. Thus the overall influence of lactate on blood pH was considered minor.

(70) Wood et al. (1983).

(71) Increased lactic acid levels have long been suspected of being a primary cause of delayed post-exercise mortality in fishes (see Bennett 1978 for supporting arguments). Wood et al. (1983) were skeptical. They pointed out that in no study implicating lactic acid as a direct cause of death had the blood lactic acid concentration actually been measured; instead, the concentration of lactate anion alone had been the factor determined. In mammals that have just exercised, lactate is fully dissociated at normal physiological pH values, and H^+ and lactate are formed in equivalent amounts (i.e., the concentration of lactate anion accurately represents the concentration of "lactic acid"). However the same is not always true of cold-blooded vertebrates, and discrepancies between blood lactate and metabolic proton levels often are evident (e.g., Piiper et al. 1972).

(72) Holeton and Heisler (1983) fitted larger spotted dogfish with dorsal aortic catheters. The animals were then stimulated to exhaustion by the administration of mild electric shocks. Blood samples were withdrawn at intervals starting at 9 min (end of the stress period). Values for pH*a* and $[HCO_3^-]a$ fell sharply at 0 min, and $PaCO_2$ increased. Lactate rose slowly and attained peak values 4 to 6 h after removal of the stress. In one group, respiratory acidosis was characterized by a drop in pH*a* from 7.8 to 7.2 and a decline in $[HCO_3^-]a$ from ~7 to ~3 mmol/L within 30 min. After 2 h $[HCO_3^-]a$ began to rise, and prestress concentrations were regained by 10 h. Normal pH*a* values were not achieved for several more hours. Blood lactate increased to ~20 mmol/L after 8 h before starting to decline, and prestress concentrations still had not been attained by 24 h.

Jensen et al. (1983) fitted the dorsal aortas of tench with catheters and forced them to exercise vigorously by continuous prodding for periods of 5 min. Blood for analysis was withdrawn at intervals. A characteristic finding was a drastic decline in arterial blood pH, with the lowest values occurring immediately after exercise. During recovery, pH*a* moved slowly toward resting (i.e., prestress) values. Arterial lactate approximately doubled immediately after exercise from resting concentrations of <5 mmol/L, and $PaCO_2$ rose steeply and remained elevated for as long as 3 h; PaO_2 values demonstrated a similar pattern.

(73) Yamamoto et al. (1980) placed catheters in the dorsal aortas of yellowtails (*Seriola quinqueradiata*) and chased them continuously for 5 min. Hematocrit concentrations increased 41% (mean prestress value of 26.1 to 36.9%) in blood withdrawn immediately after the stress ended, then rapidly decreased to the prestress values after 1 h. Hemoglobin increased 44% (7.69 to 11.04 g/dL)* immediately after the stress and also decreased to prestress concentration after 1 h. The mean spleen mass in exercised yellowtails decreased 71%; prestress values were gradually recovered 5 h after exercise. Spleen hemoglobin concentrations decreased 45% from a mean prestress concentration of 22.73 to 12.53 g per 100 g of spleen. Gross changes in spleens of exercised fish were apparent: ''The spleen of resting fish was large, soft and of fresh blood color, and the organ of exercised fish was small, hard and dark red.''

(74) Wedemeyer (1972) wrote: ''There are . . . many instances in which the physiological consequences of handling are not . . . immediately obvious. There may be few behavioral changes after handling, and thus little visible evidence that stress has even occurred. Accordingly, in the absence of actual death as an indicator, the severity of handling stress and the length of time a fish needs for recovery are frequently unclear.''

(75) Tomasso et al. (1980) confined freshwater-acclimated striped bass × white bass hybrids (male *Morone saxatilis* × female *M. chrysops*) for 10 min in a net, which resulted in significantly elevated corticosteroid levels (242 ng/mL compared with control values of 8 ng/mL).** Leach and Taylor (1980) confined mummichogs in shallow water for 24 h and monitored changes in serum cortisol levels. Values peaked at 400 ng/mL compared with base-line levels of 10 to 50 ng/mL, then fell and became constant at 8 h. Restricting movement of the fish had a similar effect, although return to nearly normal values was delayed an additional 4 h.

The primary stress response varies widely even among closely related fishes. Davis and Parker (1983) confined rainbow trout, Atlantic salmon (*Salmo salar*), and lake trout (*Salvelinus namaycush*) in a net just beneath the surface in freshwater. Fishes were sacrificed at 2-min intervals for 40 min and at 5-min

*1 dL (decalitre) = 10^{-1} L.
**1 ng (nanogram) = 10^{-9} g.

intervals for 20 min, and blood corticosteroid concentrations were measured. Base-line values in all three species were <40 ng/mL. Corticosteroid secretion was prolonged in rainbow trout in comparison with the other two species, and concentrations were markedly higher at 1 h (six times the base-line value compared with three and two times for lake trout and Atlantic salmon, respectively).

Strange et al. (1977) confined juvenile chinook salmon (*Oncorhynchus tshawytscha*) in a small cage suspended in the container to which they had been acclimated (whether the environment was freshwater or seawater was not stated). Experimental fish from the cage and control specimens from the container below were removed and sacrificed at intervals of 0, 1, 6, 12, 18, 24, and 48 h. The concentrations of cortisol (termed ''corticoids'') in blood of the control fish remained consistently below 10 ng/mL during the entire period. Values in confined fish rose steadily from similar values at 0 h to ~500 ng/mL in the first 24 h, then declined by ~50% at 24 h. In another experiment the same authors dip-netted 50 juvenile chinook salmon (12 to 14 cm in length) into a 10-L bucket of aerated water. Thirty serial samples were collected at intervals of 90 s. Cortisol concentrations increased linearly from <10 to almost 100 ng/mL in <20 min, or at a rate of 5 ng/(min·mL). The rate of increase slowed substantially after a rapid initial rise, and no fish died.

Barton et al. (1980) measured the primary stress response of fingerling rainbow trout (mean length 127 mm) to handling and confinement using blood cortisol as an indicator. Approximately 100 fingerlings were acclimated to an aquarium at 0.4 fish/L. The fish were captured with a net and transferred to a 25-L tub at 5 fish/L. After 90 s the fish were again captured and returned to the original aquarium. Before starting the experiment specimens had been removed from the aquarium and sampled at intervals of 0, 5, 15, and 30 min. After return to the aquarium, fish were removed and sampled at intervals of 1, 2, and 4 h. A control group was sampled as above but handling and transfer were omitted from the protocol. Blood cortisol concentrations in the experimental fish rose rapidly to a peak (~44 ng/mL) within 12 min of exposure to handling and confinement, then returned to base-line levels (~5 ng/mL) by 2 h. These results are similar to those reported by Strange and Schreck (1978) for juvenile chinook salmon.

In a second experiment ~350 fish were acclimated to an aquarium at 0.4 fish/L, then exposed to continuous ''mild agitation'' (quotation marks added; the nature of the agitation was not described) and repeated capture and release back into the aquarium for 1 h. Specimens were removed at intervals of 0, 5,

15, 30, and 60 min for blood cortisol determination. Concentrations rose steadily starting at 15 min (~7 ng/mL) to ~35 ng/mL at 30 min and ~68 ng/mL at 60 min. The authors remarked that these findings did not agree qualitatively with values published for other salmonids and the goldfish and suggested that ". . . for a particular species, the timing and magnitude of the corticoid response are dependent upon both the severity and duration of the specific stressor."

Effects of continuous, intense handling and severe confinement were tested in a third experiment. A group of fish acclimated to an aquarium at 0.4 fish/L was transferred to a small cage with a dip net. The cage, suspended in the same aquarium, was confining enough that the fish were constantly touching. The fish also were stirred with a hand net every 10 to 20 min. Specimens were removed for blood cortisol analysis at intervals of 0, 0.5, 1, 2, 3, and 4 h and then at 2- or 3-h intervals until 50% of those remaining were dead. The cage was raised slightly as fish were removed so that a constant 15 or 16 fish/L was maintained. Cortisol concentrations rose rapidly: ~90 ng/mL at 0.5 h, ~143 ng/mL at 3 h, and ~210 ng/mL at 16.5 h. Some fish were moribund at 2 h, and the first mortalities were recorded at 3.5 h. The rate of mortality increased progressively, reaching 56% at 16.5 h.

In a final experiment, effects of capture and transport were evaluated. Two rearing ponds containing ~3700 fish at 0.4 fish/L (mean length 137 mm) were drained. The fish were captured with dip nets, loaded onto a hatchery truck at 2.0 fish/L, transported to another site, and "planted by hand" (presumably removed from the truck with dip nets) in a lake (second site). At the second site groups of fish were placed in live cages anchored off the bottom. Fish for analysis were removed from each rearing pond prior to the disturbance, and also 35 and 55 min after the capture process commenced. Additional sample fish were taken at 80 min when all had been loaded onto the truck, after 2.5 h in transit, and at 6.1 h (arrival at the second site). Fish from the live cages were removed for analysis at 1, 2, 4, 8, 11, and 14 d. Blood cortisol concentrations peaked at ~50 ng/mL after capture in the rearing ponds, declined to ~22 ng/mL while the truck was in transit, rose again to ~42 ng/mL when stocking of the lake commenced, and fell to nearly normal levels 8 d later.

Mazeaud et al. (1977) measured the primary stress response in sexually mature coho salmon using both corticosteroids and catecholamines as indicators. Unstressed (control) fish were netted and stunned by a blow to the head, and blood was withdrawn within 2 min of capture. Experimental fish were either captured and anesthetized with 2-phenoxyethanol (concentration unstated) or forced to struggle out of water in a net for 5 min. Blood samples were collected 5 to 20 min after capture in the two experimental groups and after anesthetization in those administered 2-phenoxyethanol. Fish that struggled in a net had substantially higher corticosteroid levels than controls and anesthetized specimens, but because of sexual and individual variations no clear pattern emerged.

Nakano and Tomlinson (1967) monitored the effects of repeated disturbance on rainbow trout by measuring changes in blood catecholamine concentrations. Fish acclimated to aquarium conditions were disturbed by repeatedly being grabbed by the tail, which forced them to swim vigorously. Afterward, the fish were allowed to recover. Periods of disturbance varied between 2 and 120 min and recovery periods between 1 and 48 h. Adrenaline in disturbed fish (values for all disturbance periods pooled) averaged 132 ng/mL, compared with a mean concentration of 5 ng/mL in undisturbed fish. Blood noradrenaline concentrations averaged 25 ng/mL (data from all disturbance periods again pooled); those of undisturbed fish averaged 3 ng/mL. Values for both catecholamines returned to normal in fish disturbed for 10 min and allowed 24 h to recover.

(76) Soivio and Oikari (1976) studied the effect of handling stress on blood glucose concentrations in northern pike (*Esox lucius*) captured from different bodies of water, one fresh and the other brackish ($S = 6.2‰$). The two groups were acclimated in water similar to their natural habitats prior to start of the experiments. Each fish was fitted with a catheter implanted in the dorsal aorta. Stress was induced by capturing a fish with a net and transferring it to a small container of water, then lifting it out of the water for 20 s and returning it to the water for 10 s. The last part of the cycle was repeated three times in succession. Blood samples were withdrawn at 0, 5, 20, and 60 min and at 4, 12, 24, and 48 h after application of the stress. The average blood glucose concentration in the freshwater group tripled at 60 min from a prestress value of 530 μg/mL and did not return to normal until the last sampling time (48 h). In the brackish water group blood glucose concentrations rose from an average prestress value of 228 μg/mL to >300 μg/mL at 20 min, then fell to below normal values at 12 h and did not approach prestress levels until 48 h later.

Scott (1921) reported that blood glucose concentrations of smooth dogfish (*Mustelis canis*) rose from 700 to 1700 μg/mL in 2.5 min when the animals were held out of the water for 80 s. Chavin and Young (1970) discovered that simply netting goldfish and transferring them rapidly to another aquarium nearby caused hyperglycemia that persisted for 2 d. Maximum values occurred 1 d after the transfer (mean glucose concentration 536 μg/mL compared with a mean prestress value of 285 μg/mL). Hyperglycemia was apparent 15 min after aquarium transfer (422 μg/mL) and increased to a mean value of 1030 μg/mL at 59 to 61 min.

Hattingh (1976) described the effect of capture and transport on blood glucose in the mudfish (*Labeo capensis*), a freshwater teleost. The fish were seined from a lake and transported for 4 h in large, aerated tanks. Glucose increased from a mean concentration of 196 μg/mL (normal prestress value for this species) to 518 μg/mL. The hyperglycemia then abated, and blood glucose concentrations returned to normal within 24 h.

(77) Soivio and Oikari (1976).

(78) Isaia et al. (1978) pointed out that to cross the gill epithelium water molecules must traverse two barriers—the apical and serosal membranes. Between them lies a pool of intracellular water, which is the water that is exchanged. Either or both membranes can limit diffusion, and the volume of intracellular water available to participate in diffusional exchanges is small. Isaia and colleagues performed experiments using perfused, isolated heads of rainbow trout from freshwater. When trout heads were prefused without adrenaline the permeability of the apical membrane to water exceeded that of the serosal membrane by approximately eightfold. Thus it is the serosal membrane that limits water diffusion. Perfusion of trout heads with a solution containing 10^{-5} mol/L adrenaline produced two effects: (*1*) a comparable increase in the permeability of both apical and serosal membranes and (2) a quadrupling of the water transport pool. Also see McDonald and Rogano (1986) and Pic et al. (1974).

(79) Stevens (1972) showed that stresses resulting from handling or exercise affect the body mass of tilapia (*Oreochromis mossambica*), a species that acclimates easily to freshwater or seawater. Fish were handled by being quickly netted from an aquarium, blotted once on a paper towel, weighed, and transferred to another aquarium. After 4 min the procedure was repeated. Fish subjected to exercise stress were treated the same except they were forced to swim vigorously for 4 min after being placed in the second aquarium. Both procedures caused a slight but measureable increase in the body masses of freshwater-acclimated fish. Conversely, both stresses resulted in body mass losses of similar magnitude in seawater-acclimated specimens. The author did not measure blood catecholamine concentra-

tions but performed other experiments indicating that catecholamines were involved.

Hemodilution after handling stress was demonstrated in the mudfish by Hattingh and van Pletzen (1974). Yamamoto et al. (1980) showed that the opposite occurred in a seawater teleost: blood water content of yellowtails declined 5.5% (from 83.63 to 79.04%) after the fish were chased continuously for 5 min and returned to prestress values 1 h later.

(80) Pic et al. (1974) studied effects of epinephrine, a catecholamine, on water transport by gills of seawater-adapted mullet (*Mugil capito*). Outward movements of water, Na^+, and Cl^- were measured simultaneously with radioactive isotopes. The drinking rate of fish injected with epinephrine declined sharply to 337 μL/h per 100 g of body mass, compared with 1533 μL/h per 100 g in control fish. Loss of body mass was just as dramatic (2500 mg per 100 g compared with 200 mg per 100 g in control fish).

(81) Strange et al. (1977) studied the primary stress response of cutthroat trout (*Salmo clarki*) exposed to sudden and substantial changes in temperature. The temperature of the water to which the fish were acclimated (13°C) was raised to 26°C in 20 min. The higher temperature was maintained for the duration of the experiment (210 min). Blood "corticoid" concentrations increased from ~20 to ~70 ng/mL in 25 min and remained nearly constant. The last sampling point (210 min) represented approximately one-half the median survival time of 6 h.

Fryer (1975) determined the effect of thermal stress on blood corticosteroid concentrations in goldfish by placing fish acclimated to 20°C directly into water of 35°C. In the first experiment blood samples were taken after 15 min at the higher temperature. In the second, groups of fish were returned to water of 20°C after spending 10 min at 35°C before blood was sampled. The first group had blood corticosteroid concentrations similar to the control group (41 ng/mL). However, fish from the group sampled 15 min after return to 20°C had concentrations substantially greater than the controls (137 ng/mL compared with 19 ng/mL), indicating that in this species the primary effects are delayed slightly after exposure to thermal stress.

(82) Redgate (1974) reported that "inadequate oxygenation" of the water in which common carp were held resulted in elevated blood cortisol concentrations, but gave no data. Tomasso et al. (1981a) observed that corticosteroid concentrations of yearling channel catfish rose in response to environmental hypoxia. The environment was made hypoxic by stopping the flow of aerated water into the container, and soon the fish were gasping at the

surface. Blood corticosteroids increased from base-line levels of 10 ng/mL during normoxia (4.3 mg O_2/L) to 59 ng/mL under conditions of environmental hypoxia (0.1 mg O_2/L).

Hattingh (1976) exposed mudfish to O_2 concentrations of 90, 75, 53, 20, and 9% O_2 saturation. Mean normal blood glucose concentrations ($\sim$190 μg/mL) were sustained until 20% O_2 saturation, then rose to 250 μg/mL, although behavioral evidence of physiological hypoxia (gasping at the surface) was apparent when O_2 levels fell below 40% saturation.

(83) It is known from perfusion experiments with isolated fish heads that deoxygenating the perfusion medium causes vascular constriction in the gills (Ristori and Laurent 1977). Vascular resistance that suggests constriction increases in live rainbow trout exposed to hypoxic water (Holeton and Randall 1967). Constriction of the gill blood vessels would appear superficially to be a maladaptive response to increased O_2 demand unless, as pointed out by Pettersson and Johansen (1982), blood is diverted to sites of improved gas exchange or the blood-water diffusion barrier is somehow enhanced. Pettersson and Johansen (1982) used perfused, isolated heads of Atlantic cod (*Gadus morhua*) to study effects of adrenaline on the gas exchange efficiency of fish gills. The exterior surfaces of the gills were irrigated with seawater; the perfusion medium was a saline solution. The design of the experimental apparatus permitted either the seawater or the perfusion medium to be made hypoxic. It was found that the vascular constriction response could be elicited by rendering either fluid hypoxic (i.e., ''external'' seawater or ''internal'' perfusion medium). Adding 10^{-6} mol/L adrenaline to the perfusion medium caused the flow of blood in the dorsal aorta to increase and the perfusion pressure to decrease. In an experiment in which the PO_2 gradient was $\sim$135 mm Hg (seawater to perfusion medium) the presence of adrenaline resulted in substantial increases in blood flow through the dorsal aorta and in PaO_2. The results demonstrated that adrenaline increases systemic blood flow and enhances O_2 transfer. This is indirect evidence of lamellar recruitment from vascular constriction of blood vessels in the gills.

(84) Most reports of ammonia toxicity in fishes have relied on LC_{50} determinations. Comparatively few studies have documented the physiological changes (e.g., primary and secondary responses) in living fishes exposed to ammonia. Ammonia toxicity varies widely among species, suggesting that the magnitude of the physiological response is variable too.

Tomasso et al. (1981b) exposed channel catfish to total ammonia nitrogen (total NH_4-N) concentrations of 0, 50, 100, 150, and 200 mg/L for 24 h in water of neutral pH. In fish exposed to 200 mg/L the mean blood corticosteroid concentration rose from a prestress value of 13 ng/mL to ~112 ng/mL at 8 h, then fell to ~45 ng/mL at 24 h. The decline indicates that channel catfish can adapt to high concentrations of ammonia in the environment.

Hattingh (1976) found that elevated ammonia in the water of freshwater aquariums caused hyperglycemia in mudfish. The fish had normal blood glucose concentrations (184 μg/mL) at an ammonia concentration of 800 μg/L (presumably total NH_4-N but stated as ''ammonium''); the mean concentration rose to 224 μg/mL when ammonia was increased to 4.6 mg/L.

The length of time that a fish is exposed to ammonia may be less critical than the concentration. Spotte and Anderson (1989) exposed seawater-adapted mummichogs to total NH_4-N concentrations of 1, 2, 5, 10, 25, 50, 100, 150, and 200 mg/L for periods of 2, 4, 8, 12, 18, 24, 36, and 48 h. Duration of exposure and the ammonia concentration accounted for, respectively, <4% and ~35% of the blood cortisol response. The effective concentration (in this series of experiments, the concentration of total NH_4-N inducing a mean cortisol response equivalent to two standard deviations above the mean of the controls) was 47.14 mg total NH_4-N/L, corresponding with a mean blood cortisol of 134.4 ng/mL. Mummichogs sampled in the field had mean cortisol concentrations comparable with values published previously in the literature and did not differ significantly from the mean of untreated fish acclimated to aquarium conditions. This suggests that captivity *per se* had not induced a primary stress response.

CHAPTER 5

(1) This discussion is based mainly on Levine (1980).

(2) Density alone has no effect on visual acuity. The text statement means simply that optical elements in the eyes of terrestrial animals function differently from comparable elements in the eyes of aquatic animals. I am grateful to Joseph S. Levine for emphasizing this point in a personal communication.

(3) This is the concept used by Munz and McFarland (1977) to define color vision.

(4) According to Levine (1980), the ''reason'' (in an evolutionary sense) for these enlarged cone cells is as follows. The number of photons (i.e., photon flux density) striking a cone dimin-

ishes as light intensity falls. A specific number of regular photon absorptions must occur in a cone before a neural signal is induced. It is thought that the chances of a cone capturing enough photons at low flux density—meaning in dim light—are improved if the cell size is increased.

(5) This discussion is based mainly on Levine (1980), Loew and Lythgoe (1978), and Lythgoe (1966). Also see McFarland and Munz (1975a, 1975b) and Munz and McFarland (1975, 1977).

(6) The following discussion is based on Levine and MacNichol (1982). The molecules of a visual pigment undergo structural changes when struck by photons. Absorption of photons initiates electrochemical responses in the visual cells containing pigment. How each rod and cone responds is determined partly by the number of photons absorbed by its pigment, but not by the wavelengths of the photons. The wavelength of an absorbed photon does not affect the output of the visual cell. Consequently, ''The only means the visual system has of extracting information about the color of incident light is to take into account the statistical probability that one of its pigments will absorb a photon with a given wavelength.''

(7) Levine (1980) used an interesting analogy to explain this point. Imagine yourself wearing sunglasses and sitting in a theater. The light is dim, and the color of your sunglasses represents the spectral sensitivity of your only visual pigment. If the stage lighting is blue, you could see reasonably well provided the sunglasses also are blue, because the sensitivity of your visual pigment would match the spectrum of the light. Green or rose-colored glasses would markedly diminish visual sensitivity, thus darkening the scene. A comparable situation can be imagined if the visual pigments of deepwater fishes were to become mismatched. But visual pigments in the rods cluster tightly around the absorption maximum of the color of the seawater in which the fish is typically found.

(8) Attenuation narrows the width of the visible spectrum as light passes vertically from air into water, and the same effect naturally is true for light traveling through water horizontally. In both instances the light becomes increasingly *monochromatic* (tending toward a single wavelength), a situation that critically impairs contrast perception. Thus the spectral distribution of light reflected from a submerged object depends on its distance beneath the surface and the distance between the object and the eye. Light reflected from a nearby object will have traveled a shorter distance than the light in the background. The spectral distribution of reflected light will therefore be broader than the spectrum of the background spacelight.

The importance of contrast perception cannot be underestimated. McFarland and Munz (1975a) wrote: ''It is the background spacelight which is visually relevant, for against it a fish must detect targets, be they predator, prey or mate.'' Walls (1963) even suggested that color vision (see Note 10) evolved specifically as a mechanism of enhancing contrast between objects and the background.

(9) Offset visual pigments can be contained in either the rod or the cone cells. The rod visual pigments of shallow-water fishes are almost always offset. For example, inshore fishes indigenous to the North Atlantic have rod pigments most sensitive to wavelengths between 500 and 510 nm, although the dominant wavelength of the background spacelight is 525 to 550 nm (Levine and MacNichol 1982). Perhaps not surprisingly, Sager et al. (1985) found that juvenile Atlantic menhaden (*Brevoortia tyrannus*) are attracted most strongly to light of wavelengths between 460 and 500 nm.

(10) Animals that possess only single pigments are color blind. The majority of shallow-water, diurnal fishes possess at least two visual pigments and appear to meet the basic requirement for color vision, as do most epipelagic species. Deepwater, crepuscular, and nocturnal species typically do not. Color blindness in their case does not limit visual acuity because the photic environment is either monochromatic or devoid of light. Even if the appropriate visual pigments were present, color vision would be impossible.

Color vision is mediated by cone cells, which occupy the retina as both paired and single units. Single cone cells contain single pigments, but paired cones can have either one or two pigments. Many fishes have two or more classes of paired cone cells, each containing a different visual pigment. The retinas of diurnal, shallow-water fishes ordinarily are of two types, distinguished by the nature of the paired cones. In some species each member of the pair contains a different pigment, and the cells are called ''doubles.'' In others the cones are referred to as ''twins'' because they contain the same visual pigment.

The terminology used to classify cone cells is arbitrary. Levine and MacNichol (1979) gave a concise, historical review of paired cone cell nomenclature. They restricted use of the terms ''double'' and ''twin'' to descriptions of pigments, effectively sidestepping any mention of paired cone cell morphology. In the estimation of these authors, morphological distinctions are too poorly understood at present to be useful in nomenclature.

(11) The use of λ_{max} to describe the wavelength absorbed most strongly is potentially confusing. When comparing the optical properties of different waters the same symbol defines the wavelength transmitted most strongly. Lythgoe (1966) avoided the problem by letting λ_{max} represent optical density and using λ_{min} to indicate the wavelength of maximum transmission (i.e., minimum attenuation) in water. *Optical density* is the degree of opacity of a translucent medium expressed by log I_0/I where I_0 = the intensity of the incident ray and I = the intensity of the transmitted ray (Chapter 10).

(12) The following discussion is based on Munz and McFarland (1977), who conducted their work in the blue waters of the tropical Pacific Ocean. The matching and offset pigments they found are not necessarily representative of fishes generally. Also keep this in mind when reading Note 13. Offset visual pigments in all fishes tested so far are limited to the green region of the spectrum. In tropical seawater fishes the λ_{max} values lie between 518 and 541 nm. This raises an interesting question: what factors account for the presence of green-sensitive visual pigments instead of pigments that are yellow- or red-sensitive? Munz and McFarland suggested three. First, light reflected from the sides of a silvery fish is white light and contains a broad spectrum of wavelengths (see the text section on coloration). However, the reflected light is rapidly attenuated toward blue with increasing distance. For contrast perception to be enhanced at long distances, an offset visual pigment must not be positioned too far toward the longer wavelengths (i.e., toward the red end of the spectrum). Photosensitivity at long distances perhaps limits the degree to which a pigment is offset. Second, if predators are to find prey both near the surface and in deeper water, an offset visual pigment must be positioned within a range of wavelengths available at the maximum depth. In this situation the "blue shift" (i.e., shift toward shorter wavelengths) would limit the degree of offset. Third, objects in the epipelagic zones typically are countershaded or transparent (see the text section on coloration). Because blue is the most prevalent color (in combination with silver) in countershaded pelagic fishes, the color range of targets is limited. Possession of a yellow-sensitive pigment would not be very useful, considering that few pelagic species are yellow. Incidently, Shlaifer (1942) found that captive chub mackerels (*Scomber japonicus* = *S. colias*) could detect wavelengths of ~650 to 700 nm.

(13) The following discussion is based on Loew and Lythgoe (1978) and McFarland and Munz (1975b). The offset pigment hypothesis was established by Lythgoe (1966), who considered

that visual pigments offset from each other enhance contrast perception against the background spacelight. However, his argument encompassed only scotopic vision. Munz and McFarland (1975) and McFarland and Munz (1975b) agreed with the essential features of Lythgoe's concept, but considered it more appropriate for photopic vision. Their conclusions were based on data from retinal extracts of 179 tropical Pacific species (Munz and McFarland 1973). Of these, 113 had two pigments, and two species possessed three. In their summary paper, McFarland and Munz (1975b) pointed out that Lythgoe (1966) had properly applied his argument to scotopic visual function, considering that the data he obtained were from rod pigments. Lack of a spectral match between a visual pigment and the available light indicated that ". . . evolutionary forces molding scotopic vision had selected for enhanced contrast rather than for maximum photosensitivity." At the time of Lythgoe's work, however, it was thought that the twilight spectrum near the surface in clear seas was similar to that of daylight, but with a slight "red shift" (i.e., a shift toward longer wavelengths). Munz and McFarland (1973) had demonstrated that the submarine spectrum undergoes a blue shift at twilight (see Note 12), and that the absorbance properties of the scotopic pigments in their extensive sample of coral reef fishes matched the bluish twilight spectrum. The conclusion reached by McFarland and Munz (1975b) was that offsetting of visual pigments in the rods does not occur. Instead, evolutionary forces ". . . have operated to maximize photosensitivity rather than contrast, as suggested by Lythgoe." Thus the visual problem of deepwater, crepuscular, and nocturnal fishes appears to be one of light gathering, or photosensitivity, not contrast. Contrast perception is of greater importance to diurnal species. Offset visual pigments in these fishes enhance contrast perception against the background spacelight. The detection of objects in different directions is best achieved when at least two cone pigments are present, one matched to the wavelength of the background spacelight and the other offset from that wavelength. McFarland and Munz (1975b) considered the possession of two visual pigments an essential prelude to the evolution of color vision.

(14) The following discussion is based on McFarland and Munz (1975b). Background spacelight framing either a bright (reflective) or dark (nonreflective) object in tropical seas is very blue. To match it a fish requires a photopic visual pigment of ~470 nm. The object can appear bright only if reflected light within the absorption spectrum of the matched visual pigment is more

intense than the background spacelight. Yellow and red wavelengths cannot be detected even at a depth of 1 m, although they would be reflected horizontally for several metres. But a dark object stands out readily from the brighter background spacelight because it has no stimulating affect on the cone cells. Thus an eye with a matched visual pigment detects an object literally by not ''seeing'' it, because both contrast and photosensitivity are at maximum for dark objects.

Consider next what happens if the spectral photosensitivity of a visual pigment differs from that of a matched pigment. To simplify the prose let C_m represent conditions described in the above paragraph, in which C represents a cone cell and m is a visual pigment matched spectrally to the background spacelight (λ_{max} = 460 nm), and assume that C_o stands for an offset visual pigment (λ_{max} = 520 nm). The contrast of a bright object seen in a horizontal plane is greater with C_m because of its enhanced sensitivity to background spacelight. A dark object produces less contrast for C_o than C_m for the same reason. As Lythgoe (1966) observed, offset visual pigments reduce photosensitivity to available light but enhance contrast to reflective objects. Detection of nonreflective objects is more facile through use of a matched visual pigment. Clearly, maximum visibility of both bright and dark objects requires more than one visual pigment. McFarland and Munz (1975b) wrote: ''The evolution of high visual acuity with maximum contrast under varied photic conditions would favor the selection and maintenance of separate visual pathways for these different cones. In other words, we have described the elements necessary for color vision.''

Finally, consider whether a multiple visual pigment system functions as well at greater depths (25 m versus 1 m). The λ_{max} of the visual pigment must be ~460 nm to match wavelengths available at 25 m. Few long wavelengths penetrate to this depth, and consequently both the background spacelight and the reflected light from objects are blue. A C_o of λ_{max} near 520 nm is a poorer contrast enhancer at 25 m than at 1 m. For dark objects at either depth C_o is less photosensitive to background spacelight than C_m. As the available light becomes increasingly monochromatic C_o visual pigments become progressively less effective at enhancing contrast. It therefore is not surprising that single, matched photopic visual pigments are typical of fishes that dwell in deeper waters; multiple pigments (both matched and offset) are characteristic of shallow-water species.

(15) Munz and McFarland (1973, 1977) discussed briefly the transition in fish populations at twilight. Others described this

behavior in fishes indigenous to the Hawaiian Islands (Hobson 1972), Great Barrier Reef (Domm and Domm 1973), and West Indies (Collette and Talbot 1972, Smith and Tyler 1972).

(16) Hobson (1972).

(17) See Collette and Talbot (1972) and Hobson (1972). Hobson (1968) found that twilight also is a critical time of predator-prey interaction in the Gulf of California in areas consisting of sand and rock.

(18) This discussion is based on Munz and McFarland (1973, 1977).

(19) Munz and McFarland (1973) raised the question of why the predator has a visual advantage at twilight. They observed that predators are subjected to the same adjustments as diurnal and nocturnal fishes. Moreover, the scotopic visual pigments of crepuscular predators are not unique compared with these other fishes. Munz and McFarland concluded, ". . . as in diurnal and nocturnal fishes, their rhodopsins have been selected to provide a relatively close spectral match to the light available near the surface during twilight. Thus, they should be maximally sensitive to downwelling light." *Rhodopsin* or *visual purple* is the deep red pigment contained in the rods.

(20) Hobson (1973).

(21) To quote Munz and McFarland (1973): "Significantly, the wrasses (labrids), which may even seek cover before sunset and are the last diurnal reef fishes to emerge at dawn, possess a variety of visual pigments with no apparent relationship to either twilight or moonlight. . . . They go to bed too early and rise too late to be involved. High visual sensitivity, therefore, has little to do with their survival."

(22) This discussion is based mainly on Fujii and Oshima (1986). Morphology of the chromatophore was described by Hawkes (1974). Fujii and Oshima (1986) and Obika (1986) reviewed mechanisms of pigment transport within chromatophores. See Pickford and Atz (1957, pp. 39–59) for a review of early literature.

(23) The hormone that stimulates transport of melanin has traditionally been called *melanophore* (or *melanocyte*) *stimulating hormone*, MSH; its historical antithesis has been known as *melanophore* (or *melanocyte*) *release inhibiting hormone*, MRH. Fujii and Oshima (1986) advocated replacing these terms with *melanin dispersing hormone*, MDH, and *melanin aggregating hormone*, MAH. This struck me as logical, and after assessing their ar-

guments I thought of two additional reasons why the new terminology should be accepted. First, the terms ''releasing'' and ''release-inhibiting,'' although accurate reflections of the hormonal mechanisms involved, fail in a descriptive sense. Functionally, the pigments are dispersed and aggregated. Second, melanin is the substance in flux. As the stationary target tissues, melanophores (or melanocytes) can be neither released nor release-inhibited.

(24) This discussion is based on Denton (1970, 1971) and Fujii and Oshima (1986).

(25) The problem of how ''hearing'' and ''sound'' ought to be defined has not passed unnoticed. In his review of the evolution of vertebrate hearing, van Bergeijk (1967) wrote: ''The most formidable obstacle to be overcome in the proper interpretation of 'hearing' is the formation of a precise concept of what the stimulus is, i.e., what we shall call 'sound.' ''

(26) This discussion is based on Lindsay (1982), Morse (1981), and Tavolga (1971).

(27) The following discussion is based on Morse (1981). Sounds differ considerably in intensity, which is best measured logarithmically. The decibel scale is a relative measure because it relies on a ratio of two intensities, one being the standard. The intensity in decibels is defined by

$$\mathrm{dB} = 10 \log \left(\frac{I}{I_0}\right) \tag{5.4}$$

where I = intensity (W/m^2) and I_0 = some standard intensity, ordinarily 1×10^{-2} W/m^2. On such a scale a sound 20 dB higher than another is 100 times greater in intensity, whereas one 30 dB higher has an intensity that is 1000 times greater.

(28) Pressure waves ordinarily are measured with a hydrophone, and their intensity diminishes as the *square* of the distance from the source. Displacements can be detected only at distances very close to the sound source because their intensity diminishes as the *cube* of the distance.

(29) The 1960s model was explained by van Bergeijk (1964, 1967). The text discussion of the two models of underwater sound propagation borrows heavily from pertinent sections of both reports. Tavolga (1967) treated the subject briefly, and Harris (1964) described the same concepts mathematically.

(30) Accurate acoustic measurements are extremely difficult to make in shallow waters and impossible in aquariums (e.g., Chapman 1973; Hawkins 1981; Parvulescu 1964, 1967; Popper and Fay 1973; Sand and Enger 1973; Tavolga 1967). In both situations the relationship between displacement and pressure approaches conditions that exist in air. The theoretical *acoustic impedance* (i.e., the resistance to the passage of acoustic waves) of water is ~150,000 acoustic ohms compared with ~42 acoustic ohms in air. In volumes of water restricted by boundaries the entire system vibrates in complex fashion, and impedances in the two media tend toward a common value. Under such conditions, according to Tavolga (1967), "The terms near-field and far-field cease to have any real meaning, and, thus far, no mathematical treatment of the situation is available. The only available approach is an empirical one, i.e., to measure directly the pressure and displacement at various points in the [aquarium] tank."

(31) As van Bergeijk (1964) emphasized, two facts are apparent. First, the magnitude of both terms (radial and displacement)—and thus the magnitude of their sum—is inversely proportional to the cube of the distance. Second, along the axis of motion the angular component vector is zero because sin 0° = 0. In addition, the radial component in a plane perpendicular to the direction of vibration is zero because cos 90° = 0. Along the axis, only radial displacement occurs. Angular displacement in the perpendicular plane is evident in the opposite direction to the motion of the sphere. Movements in these locations therefore occur in opposite directions. Everywhere in the near-field the direction of d is determined by the angle θ from a line drawn between the point of observation and the sphere's center, and the axis of motion.

(32) Lekander (1949) discussed the embryology and structure of the lateral line and included an extensive bibliography.

(33) The idea that the lateral line might be a tactile receptor, a sound receptor, or both, is old. Knox (1825) concluded that what today we call the ordinary lateral line organs occupy ". . . an intermediate place between touch and hearing, but approaching nearest to the latter." According to Parker (1904), the situation at the turn of the century was as follows: ". . . the majority of investigators disagree, some maintaining that the [ordinary] lateral line organs are simply organs of touch . . . others that they are organs belonging to an independent class, probably intermediate between touch and hearing . . . and, lastly, those that believe them to be accessory auditory

organs. . . .'' There the matter rested until Dijkgraaf's experiments starting in the 1930s.

Dijkgraaf (1934) popularized the notion that both the ordinary and specialized lateral line organs (see the text subsection on electroreception) are tactile receptors and was an early proponent of Ferntastsinn to describe their mode of action. The argument was expanded in a later review (Dijkgraaf 1963). That article is probably the most widely cited and influential ever written about the lateral line, but its central thesis—what I refer to in the text as Dijkgraaf's tactile modality model—is flawed. Dijkgraaf (1963) made his position clear: ''Physiologically, the lateral-line sensory cell with its delicate hair is to be regarded as a specialized organ of touch; analogous structures are the tactile hairs of mammals and particularly the vibrissae. . . .'' In the same article Dijkgraaf distinguished between what he called ''damming phenomena,'' which the lateral line could detect, and pressure waves, which it could not detect. Only pressure waves were considered to represent sound. Dijkgraaf characterized ''damming phenomena'' as ''. . . a local rise of pressure . . . as well as a local displacement of water. . . .'' Because ''damming phenomena'' did not constitute sound, and only ''damming phenomena'' could be detected, the ordinary lateral line was considered not to be a sound receptor.

Dijkgraaf's tactile modality model was refuted by van Bergeijk (1964, 1967). As he correctly observed (van Bergeijk 1964), Dijkgraaf erred in thinking that a sound is necessarily periodic; many natural sounds are not. For example, when a fish glides (i.e., as opposed to undulates) past a displacement detector, what is perceived is a pulse of near-field acoustic energy (Fig. 5-28). The frequency of the pulse is a function of the *velocity* of the fish. Harris (1964) and Harris and van Bergeijk (1962) pointed out that the near-field amplitude is independent of frequency (i.e., the velocity of the fish) and related only to the fish's volume and distance from the detector.

Harris and van Bergeijk (1962) showed unequivocally that the ordinary lateral line organs respond to near-field displacements of sound sources. As van Bergeijk (1967) later wrote, ''. . . the question seemed to be solved: the 'local water motions' [Dijkgraaf's alternate term for ''damming effects''] and 'sound' are identical phenomena, and the controversy appeared to have been a matter of semantics.'' But van Bergeijk subsequently admitted, ''This evidence, however, does not decide the other question: should the lateral line be considered a 'near-field hearing organ' or a 'distant-touch organ'? The mere fact that the adequate stimulus *can* be described as an acoustic phenomenon does not make the organ an acoustic receptor any more than the electrical excitability of the skin makes it an electricity detector. Clearly, some independent definitions of 'hearing' and 'touch' are needed before the issue can be decided.'' He then quoted Pumphrey (1950): ''The primitive function of touch is the location of moving objects in contact with the animal. The primitive function of hearing is the location of moving objects not in contact with the animal. So we can define hearing as follows: an animal *hears* when it *behaves as if* it has located a moving object (a sound source) not in contact with it. And *sound* can be defined as any mechanical disturbance whatever which is potentially referable to an external and localized source.''

In my opinion, Pumphrey's description fails in some respects. I would substitute ''sensed'' for ''located.'' An animal can be capable of hearing but still not be able to locate the direction of the sound. Moreover, whether the object is moving or stationary is irrelevant in this instance. Finally, a qualifying phrase is needed to exclude other sensory modes (e.g., vision). With my modifications, Pumphrey's definition of hearing now reads: an animal *hears* when it behaves as if it has sensed an object (a sound source) not in contact with it *through the motion of the surrounding medium*. The qualifying phrase is in italics.

Dijkgraaf (1963) emphasized correctly that the ability of aquatic vertebrates to detect distant, moving objects is not in doubt. However, ''touch'' is local and perceived by an animal at its surface. As van Bergeijk (1967) noted, it does not take place ''. . . 'out there' in the environment. . . . The notion that the lateral line is 'touched' by the stimulus via the medium is a bit of semantic legerdemain that, applied consistently, leads inevitably to the conclusion that hearing in the conventional sense (i.e., sensitivity to pressure waves) is really a form of touch also, since the same medium and the same form of energy (viz., acoustical energy) are involved.'' The point is that the distinction between touch and hearing is not predicated on definition of the stimulus, the nature of the medium, or peripheral reception. Rather, it is the *perceptual* difference that can be estimated from an animal's behavior. When the lateral line is impinged upon, ''. . . the animal behaves as if it *heard* something, not as if it were touched.''

The acoustic modality model of van Bergeijk does not reject all of Dijkgraaf's contentions, and van Bergeijk (1967) acknowledged that Dijkgraaf was correct in considering single, ordinary lateral line organs to be receptors of water motion, particularly in the near-field. He emphasized, however, that a single, ordinary lateral line organ does not allow a fish to locate the source of motion. Only a *system* of such organs permits localization: ''Through the lateral line *system* the animal *perceives* an external sound source, and thus, by Pumphrey's definition, *hears*; this interpretation disagrees with Dijkgraaf's.''

Which model is truer? In my opinion, van Bergeijk's. Dijkgraaf's ''damming phenomena'' were simply near-field effects. Both near- and far-field effects are acoustic phenomena, and there can be no doubt that the ordinary lateral line organs respond to near-field displacements of sound sources, as demonstrated convincingly by Harris and van Bergeijk (1962).

(34) This discussion is based mainly on Moyle and Cech (1982, pp. 137–141) and van Bergeijk (1967), and to a lesser extent on information presented by Lagler et al. (1977, pp. 100–102), Lowenstein (1971), Platt and Popper (1981), and Tavolga (1971).

(35) As van Bergeijk (1967) observed, the response of the swimbladder to sound pressures varies with stimulus frequency. It therefore has a resonance (defined below). Harris (1964) calculated that most fishes probably have swimbladder resonances between 100 and 1000 Hz, depending on the species. It should not be assumed that all fishes with swimbladders are sensitive to far-field effects. Macula of the proper sensitivity also are required (van Bergeijk 1967). A physical system exhibits *resonance* if capable of existing in a well defined state longer than the period for internal motion in that state. Audible or acoustic resonances of musical instruments have been known since antiquity.

(36) Early experiments indicated that in sharks the most sensitive sound detection apparently occurs in the labyrinths, not the ordinary lateral line organs. Parker (1909) first suggested the importance of sound detection by the labyrinths in the smooth dogfish (*Mustelus canis*). After extirpating appropriate cranial nerves and noting responses to a pendulum striking the wall of a wood aquarium, Parker showed the labyrinths to be more sensitive than the ordinary lateral line organs. Similar results were obtained by Dijkgraaf (unpublished information in Dijkgraaf 1963) for the smaller spotted dogfish (*Scyliorhinus canicula*). According to Corwin (1979, 1981b), the most sensitive sound detection in the lemon shark (*Negaprion brevirostris*) is mediated by the labyrinths. Both the lemon shark and horn shark (*Heterodontus francisci*) appear to be strictly displacement sensitive (Banner 1967, Kelly and Nelson 1975). Banner (1967) emphasized that regardless of which organ system functions in sound detection, displacement energy and not pressure energy is the stimulus involved. Popper and Fay (1977) gave an overview of hearing in elasmobranchs.

(37) This discussion is based on Schneider (1967) and Tavolga (1971). Also see the articles assembled by Tavolga (1977).

(38) Myrberg (1978, Table 1) listed 19 species of sharks of five families that have been tested and shown to react positively to synthesized sounds. As reviewed briefly by Klimley and Myrberg (1979), synthesized sounds that attract sharks in nature are characterized by low frequency (Myrberg et al. 1969, 1972; Nelson and Gruber 1963), broad *bandwidth* or wide frequency range (Myrberg et al. 1969), and amplitude modulation (Myrberg et al. 1972, Nelson and Gruber 1963). The intensity of the behavioral response is enhanced by decreasing the frequency and increasing the pulse rate (Myberg et al. 1972). In addition, irregularly pulsed sounds attract sharks more readily than those that are regularly pulsed (Nelson and Johnson 1972, Myberg et al. 1972).

(39) As Myrberg (1978) pointed out, field experiments require that enough sharks be attracted to constitute an adequate sample. To achieve this, researchers typically have used unrealistically high intensity levels to project synthesized sounds over a broad area. The resulting far-field could extend hundreds of metres before attenuating to background intensities. Few biological sounds have comparable intensity levels. Myrberg concluded that ". . . most biological sounds of interest to sharks probably are detected only at distances much less than 100 m from the source."

(40) The characteristics of sounds that repel sharks have been of interest to the military, but the findings have no obvious application in aquarium technology. The reports of Myrberg (1978), Myrberg et al. (1978), and Klimley and Myrberg (1979) contain interesting data and brief literature reviews.

(41) Richard (1968) reported that in the West Indies, predatory teleosts could be attracted predictably (although from unknown distances) with irregularly pulsed frequencies of 25 to 50 Hz. Included were grunts, snappers (Lutjanidae), and groupers (Serranidae). Olsen (1976) conditioned a large group of free-ranging pollocks (*Pollachius virens*) to locate and swim toward sounds generated at distances up to 80 m. No response was observed at 1000 Hz, but the fish could locate a regularly pulsed signal of 150 Hz.

(42) Richard (1968) found that synthesized sounds used to attract predators on a coral reef evoked no response from herbivorous fishes. Olsen (1976) observed the responses of Atlantic herrings (*Clupea harengus harengus*) to synthesized sound of regularly pulsed frequencies. The fish were confined inside a large

net enclosure in a fjord. All responses were negative and directional (i.e., the fish were repelled and moved away from the direction of the source). Directional responses could be elicited with frequencies ranging from 30 to 5000 Hz, but not at signals >5000 Hz, and no responses were detected at 10,000 Hz. Directional responses were stronger at lower (<500 Hz) than higher frequencies. Increasing the distance of the sound source from 6 to 20 m did not visibly alter directional responses.

(43) This discussion is based mainly on Myrberg (1978) and Popper et al. (1973). Reports of van Bergeijk (1964, 1967) perpetuated the idea that aquatic animals could orient only to sounds produced in the near-field, and that subsequent responses were mediated solely through the ordinary lateral line organs (i.e., the labyrinths did not participate). The argument of van Bergeijk stated that location of a sound source by pressure alone would be impossible because pressure is nonvectorial. Teleosts have one swimbladder, not two. A fish could thus locate sounds only in the near-field, where vectorial energy is available to stimulate the ordinary lateral line organs. Directional information in the far-field was considered unavailable because the velocity of the sound would be too weak to be detected.

Evidence for van Bergeijk's hypothesis had been obtained under laboratory conditions. Confined spaces inevitably present difficult acoustic problems (see Note 30). The responses of teleosts tested soon after van Bergeijk's publications seemed to confirm his hypothesis, but sharks proved an exception. However, most experimental work with sharks had been performed at sea, not in laboratories. More recent field and laboratory experiments (e.g., Olsen 1976, Myrberg et al. 1972, Richard 1968, van den Berg and Schuijf 1983) indicate that some elasmobranchs and teleosts demonstrate directional responses to far-field sounds. Orientation in certain cases is mediated through the labyrinths, but the matter has not been settled, (e.g., Popper et al. 1973). Schuijf (1976, 1981) produced models of directional hearing.

(44) Moulton and Dixon (1967), Popper and Fay (1977).

(45) In the study of van den Berg and Schuijf (1983) it was demonstrated that *Chiloscyllium griseum* responds to a frequency of 84 Hz in both the near-field and far-field, despite not having a swimbladder with which to transform pressure energy to displacement energy. The authors proposed that two mechanisms are used in locating a sound source: sound pressure in the far-field, and displacement energy reflected back from the surface of the ocean.

(46) The opening portion of this subsection is based on Alexander (1974, pp. 133–136), Bennett (1971), and Kalmijn (1974).

(47) Kalmijn (1974).

(48) Kalmijn (1966, 1971, 1972) measured bioelectric potentials in the water ~1 mm from the body surfaces of 120 specimens of seawater invertebrates and vertebrates. The animals represented 60 species of nine phyla. Results were summarized by Kalmijn (1974).

(49) As pointed out by Bennett (1971) and Kalmijn (1974), the distinction between active and passive modes is arbitrary. Electroreceptors in active sensory systems can sometimes operate passively. For example, the skates (Rajidae) are weakly electric elasmobranchs, but their electric organs discharge infrequently and appear to function passively most of the time.

(50) This designation includes the few rays that are weakly electric. Despite their possession of electric organs, none is phasic (Bennett 1971).

(51) Dijkgraaf (1963), Murray (1974), and Waltman (1966) gave detailed descriptions of the morphology and physiology of the ampullae of Lorenzini. When reading Dijkgraaf's summary keep in mind that he classified all electroreceptor organs as "ampullary." In writing this subsection I followed terminology proposed by Bennett (1971) and Szabo (1974). Their convention is reflected graphically in Figure 5-35. Szabo suggested replacing Dijkgraaf's generic use of "ampullary" with "strict" (i.e., specific) usage. This makes sense to me. Both Bennett and Szabo classified electroreceptors as ampullary (tonic) and tuberous (phasic). As described in the text, ampullary and tuberous are morphological (i.e., structural) classifications; tonic and phasic pertain to physiological or functional attributes.

(52) The listing by family (Fig. 5-35) gives a false impression that more species are known to possess electroreceptors than actually is the case. Comparatively few species have been examined, and some families to which they belong are small. Gymnarchidae contains only *Gymnarchus niloticus*. The Siluridae (catfishes) is a large family of teleosts, and several genera possess electroreceptors. The only seawater teleost known to have electroreceptors is *Plotosus anguillaris*, a silurid. Polyodontidae contains two species. The one examined (the paddlefish, *Polyodon spathula*) has electroreceptors. The single member of the Polypteridae (bichirs) with demonstrated electroreceptors is *Calamoichthys calabricus*. Lepidosirenidae is represented by a lungfish (*Protopterus dolloi*), Gymnotidae by the electric eel

(*Electrophorus electricus*), and Mormyridae by several species of elephantfishes. For discussions of the morphology and physiology of electroreception in freshwater teleosts see Bennett (1971), Kalmijn (1974), and Szabo (1974).

(53) Kalmijn (1966).

(54) Blonder and Alevizon (1988) found the Atlantic stingray (*Dasyastis sabina*) incapable of distinguishing between apparent nonprey (a tunicate, *Molgula* sp.) and prey (a shrimp, *Penaeus* sp.) using only electroreception.

CHAPTER 6

(1) The quotation is from Woolf (1967).

(2) One discordant voice was that of Williams (1964). He wrote: ". . . there has been a notable lack of success in relating schooling to general biological principles, and there are no really convincing ethological, ecological, or evolutionary explanations. I believe that this deficiency can be ascribed to the absence of any immediately apparent 'purpose' for schooling. There is no vital function to which it seems to make an efficient contribution, and it can not be immediately assigned to reproductive, defensive, or any other category of adaptive behavior."

Radakov (1973, p. 6), writing in a more encouraging voice, indicated how difficult it has been to demonstrate any fundamental value for schooling behavior. As he pointed out, the subject has been studied from two perspectives, one mechanistic and the other ecological. The first attempts to explain "how" schools are maintained (e.g., modes of sensory input, hydrodynamic aspects); the second tries to demonstrate some adaptive advantage within a broader context. Unfortunately, isolated information derived from either viewpoint is applicable to the other only by inference. In my opinion, the answers have eluded everyone, and the data as we know them have mostly descriptive value.

(3) Several authors have tried to reconcile the terms intended to define group behaviors of fishes, notably Breder (1967), Partridge (1982), Pitcher (1983), Radakov (1973, pp. 1–43), and Shaw (1970). Pitcher's terminology is among the most recent, but elements of it left me dissatisfied. A term is still needed that describes a generic gathering of fishes, orientation or "purpose" aside. I prefer "assemblage" to "shoal," the term suggested by Pitcher to serve this function. "Shoal" has not yet

shed its heritage as a synonym of "school," especially in the European literature. Confusion arises if "school" is then considered a subgroup of "shoal," as Pitcher proposed. Some might argue that "shoal" makes a suitable generic term if orientation is not implied, but I disagree. A term should not be both specific and general unless no other choice is available. If a school is always a shoal, and some shoals occasionally are schools, misuse is inevitable. An "assemblage" is simply a gathering of fishes. A "shoal" is an assemblage of fishes in which the individuals do not demonstrate uniform orientation. This distinguishes a shoal from both a school and a mill. Pitcher did not mention "mill," which has long been in disfavor, although I consider it useful and timely (see Note 5).

Disagreements over terminology perhaps begin with failure to acknowledge that all these configurations are temporary. For example, it is irrelevant to argue that a rigid definition of schooling is unacceptable because fishes cannot feed or reproduce while in a schooling mode (see Note 4). Feeding and reproduction obviously occur when individuals are *not* schooling. Consequently, a "school" can still be defined as collective swimming behavior in which the individuals demonstrate uniform orientation, swimming speed, and spacing.

Knowing whether fishes have gathered for a social "purpose" presents problems of a different kind. I maintain that the answer is seldom known or knowable. "Aggregation," a term used in older publications in reference to nonschooling assemblages of fishes, presupposes purpose, or the lack of it. Atz (1955), Breder and Halpern (1946), and Keenleyside (1955) basically agreed that fishes assemble for social interactions (i.e., mutual attraction), not because of a common and incidental affinity for a particular location. Breder and Nigrelli (1935), Morrow (1948), Parr (1927), and Williams (1964) disagreed. In their opinion, site attraction alone adequately explains why fishes gather in nonschooling assemblages. Morrow (1948) wrote: "Under such an interpretation, the apparent expression of social behavior represented by the school can be considered . . . merely as an incidental result of the mechanically integrated reactions of individuals." One curious attempt to fuse the two hypotheses must be mentioned. According to Shaw (1970), behaviorists at the 11th International Ethological Congress held in Rennes, France, agreed that the term aggregation ". . . should not be used when referring to fish that are socially attracted to each other. It could still be employed to indicate that fish come together as a direct response to extrinsic conditions or when there is reasonable doubt as to whether or not fish are socially attracted to each other." Shaw's brief discussion offered no definition of ''social.'' In other words, social behavior (whatever that may be) cannot contribute to the formation of aggregations, or else it can, depending on whether the observer interprets what he sees as representing social behavior.

In my opinion, assemblages—or generic gatherings by any such definition—are inherently social, which makes any discussion of ''purpose'' irrelevant if the objective is to identify behavior in a purely descriptive context. Some might argue that human beings on a crowded street (i.e., an assemblage of people) are not interacting directly and not part of a social situation, but this would be at least partly incorrect. When among strangers, many people are keenly—if not always consciously—aware of their own behavior and that of others. In this sense, individuals in an assemblage of fishes also are aware, after their fashion, of the fishes around them. To say this another way, the fact that fishes in an assemblage remain together by responding to each other's movements is sufficient evidence of mutual ''awareness.''

(4) As Radakov (1973, p. 21) wrote, ''In fact, if fish in schools . . . were permanently oriented the same way, were moving in one direction, and were at equal distances from each other, they could not exist for any length of time, since it would be difficult or even impossible to carry out the functions of feeding, reproduction, and other vital necessities.''

(5) To my knowledge, Parr (1927) first used ''mill'' when he described the behavior of captive chub mackerels, *Scomber japonicus* (= *S. colias*), at New York Aquarium. Parr defined milling as ''. . . a ceaseless swimming in circles on part of the single individuals, while the school as a whole remains stationary and apparently retains its normal density.'' Keenleyside (1955) described similar behavior in rudds (*Scardinius erythrophthalmus*) kept in an outdoor pond, although the term ''mill'' was not mentioned. He wrote: ''After swimming a certain distance, perhaps determined by the dimensions of the pond, the school stopped, became briefly disorganized, as each fish turned around through 180°, and then returned to approximately its former position.'' Breder (1951) described milling in *Jenkinsia* sp. (probably the dwarf herring, *J. lamprotaenia*) kept in a round pool. Recent critiques of terminology used to describe social behavior in fishes (e.g., Partridge 1982, Pitcher 1983) have omitted ''mill'' from consideration, although a few authors (e.g., Koltes 1984) have used it in an experimental context. In my opinion, the term adequately describes behavior—particularly in captivity—for which shoal is too indefinite and school too restrictive.

(6) Response times in fish schools are literally less than a second. Those measured by Hunter (1968) in captive jack mackerels (*Trachurus symmetricus*) took 0.15 to 0.25 s.

(7) It was believed at one time that positions occupied by individuals of a school could be described either by sphere-packing schemes or in the same context as crystal lattice structures. Several authors developed models that described individual distance in terms of regular geometric patterns. Those of Cullen et al. (1965) and Pitcher (1973) depicted a school as a three-dimensional arrangement of tightly packed spheres. Breder (1976) argued for the lattice structure model. Still others (e.g., Healey and Prieston 1973, van Olst and Hunter 1970) showed that the space around each individual tends to be elliptical: the distance between an individual and its neighbor directly in front or behind is less than the distance from neighbors positioned laterally.

(8) Individual distance is variable. Major (1977) watched as captive silversides (*Pranesus insularum*) increased individual distances by five to ten body lengths or more in the absence of predators. In the presence of a predator their ranks closed to less than one or two body lengths. Major (1978) noted that schools of Hawaiian anchovies (*Stolephorus purpureus*) feeding leisurely on plankton had individual distances of 0.3 m. When under attack by jacks (*Caranx ignobilis*) all feeding activity stopped, a tight school quickly formed, and individual distances shrank to 1 to 5 cm. Separate, captive groups of threespine sticklebacks (*Gasterosteus aculeatus*) and mummichogs (*Fundulus heteroclitus*) demonstrate uniform individual distances when the closest fish is less than a fish length away (Symons 1971). At greater distances the space between individuals becomes irregular. Zuyev and Belyayev (1970) reported individual distances in captive horse mackerels from the Black Sea (*Trachurus mediterraneous ponticus*?) as 0.5 to 1 times body thickness.

(9) Parr (1927) first concluded that schools are maintained by vision after watching schooling fishes of several species both in captivity and at sea. Historically, the case for vision has been based on three general observations: (*1*) nocturnal disintegration of schools in diurnal species, (*2*) mutual attraction of conspecifics in aquariums divided by transparent barriers but not opaque ones, and (*3*) failure of blinded fishes to school. The last is not universally true (see Note 10).

Nocturnal disintegration of shoals and schools has been reported in several species: by Bowen (1931) for black bullheads,

Ictalurus (= *Ameiurus*) *melas*, Breder (1929) for shortband herrings (*Jenkinsia stolifera*), Breder and Nigrelli (1935) for redbreast sunfish (*Lepomis auritus*), Newman (1876) for Atlantic herrings (*Clupea harengus harengus*), and Shlaifer (1942) for chub mackerels, *Scomber japonicus* (= *Pneumatophorus grex*?). Breder (1951) reviewed the earlier literature. Shlaifer remarked that chub mackerels in aquariums are able to school at very low light intensities, but illumination levels were not measured. This ". . . leaves unsolved the condition of mackerel schools in nature where dim light may obtain [*sic*] at night." Other authors later reported a substantial range of visual thresholds for schooling: 1.08 to 4 lx for Mexican cavefish, *Astyanax mexicanus* (John 1964) and 5.4 lx for silversides, *Menidia* sp. (Shaw 1961). Shaw also summarized published values obtained for other species prior to her work.

John (1964) suggested that the disparate findings may reflect arbitrary definitions of schooling and photometry errors. Shaw (1961) pointed out a more obvious flaw: "The problem appears not to be one of whether or not fish form schools at night, but rather, one of what is meant by night—in terms of the amount of light available to the fish and whether or not this amount is sufficient for schooling orientation to be present." Night vision in fishes is discussed in Chapter 5.

Spooner (1931) noted that a single fish isolated from three conspecifics attempted to join the others across a transparent barrier, but this behavior was not seen if the barrier was visually opaque. Single fish were also attracted to their own images in a mirror. Keenleyside (1955) confined five threespine sticklebacks in a glass jar submerged in an aquarium. A single individual was then released. This fish spent most of its time attempting to school with those inside the jar. In another experiment, six rudds were placed in the jar and a single rudd temporarily blinded with eye covers was placed in the aquarium. The blinded fish was unable to follow movements of its confined conspecifics, often bumping into the jar or the sides of the aquarium. When the eye covers were removed the rudd swam directly to the jar and followed the movements of the other fish closely. Six blinded rudds placed in an aquarium showed no synchrony of movement. When three blinded rudds were placed in an aquarium with three normal conspecifics, the fish with normal sight schooled; the blind ones did not.

Shaw (1969) studied crevalle jacks (*Caranx hippos*) in a large container that was either undivided or divided by transparent acrylic or a gray screen. The screen partially obscured vision, although water could pass through freely. The transparent acrylic offered optimal vision but prevented any mixing of water. Schooling was interrupted the least when the container was undivided. However, the fish were able to school (i.e., maintain a quantifiable semblance of individual distance and polarization) with conspecifics on the other side of either barrier, suggesting that a clear visual image is perhaps not a requisite for schooling, and that olfaction or other means of sensory contact might also be important. Olla and Samet (1974) placed juvenile striped mullets (*Mugil cephalus*), bluefish (*Pomatomus saltatrix*), and Atlantic mackerels (*Scomber scombrus*) in adjacent aquariums where only visual contact was possible. Response of the striped mullets to conspecifics and the other species was tested. Isolated striped mullets were attracted strongly to conspecifics in an adjacent aquarium, as indicated by vigorous attempts to join them. The attraction was successively less to bluefish and Atlantic mackerels. The results indicated that striped mullets can recognize conspecifics visually.

Breder and Halpern (1946) discovered that blinded goldfish (*Carassius auratus*) do not shoal, and Breder (1951) reported that schooling does not occur in darkness. Shlaifer (1942) found that chub mackerels blinded in one eye school readily with conspecifics, but a fish blinded in both eyes makes no attempts to school. Conversely, a single chub mackerel with normal vision does not school with a totally blind conspecific. Shlaifer attributed this to the abnormal swimming behavior of the blinded individual. He concluded that in the chub mackerel both vision and normal swimming movements appear to be requisites for schooling.

(10) Behaviorists generally agree that vision alone does not adequately explain some aspects of schooling, including maintenance of individual distance and degree of polarization. It is difficult to believe that visual acuity is not diminished when a school closes ranks. Breder (1929) suggested that the uniform spacing seen in fish schools is determined by the distance at which clear visual images are possible. The idea has merit, although to my knowledge no one has tested it. Springer (1957) described just how closely spaced the individuals of a school can be. He captured a dense school of dwarf herrings at night in a lift net after the fish had been attracted to a lamp. The entire school was captured. Springer estimated its volume at ~ 1 ft^3 (~ 0.028 m^3). The school weighed 25 lb (~ 11 kg), contained an estimated 7500 individuals, and was so dense that at first glance it appeared to be a single organism. Springer discounted the importance of vision under such conditions (the school was captured at night and appeared under the light already formed). He considered that the level of illumination at night was too low for visual contact and suggested that the fish ". . . main-

tained their positions by the sense of touch.'' Keenleyside (1955) noticed that rudds kept in a completely darkened aquarium swam slowly about and stayed together. This suggested to him that senses other than vision must be operational, otherwise the fish would have been scattered farther apart. Experiments using combinations of rudds that were blinded or with their olfactory sense destroyed suggested that olfaction might be important in mutual attraction among conspecifics, but the results were inconclusive.

A lateral line function seems the most promising alternative sensory system, but supporting evidence is mostly circumstantial. Laboratory experiments have included two basic protocols. In the first, the behavior of fish in full sensory contact is compared with their behavior when separated from conspecifics by a transparent barrier. The barrier allows visual contact but eliminates any perception of near-field effects (Chapter 5). The second method involves blinding fish or cutting their lateral lines and observing the subsequent effect on schooling with conspecifics. In research by Cahn (1972) and Shaw (1969), fish separated by transparent barriers approached each other more closely than when the barriers were absent. This suggested to Shaw (1970) that image size might not be critical in the maintenance of individual distance. She wrote: ''It appears that the visual system functions in the approach mechanism but that other systems may function in a withdrawal mechanism, keeping fish spacing within maximum and minimum limits.''

Cahn (1972) used captive specimens of kawakawa (*Euthynnus affinis*) in her study. The kawakawa is a species of small tuna. Fish were observed in groups of two, three, four, and six in channels with and without transparent acrylic barriers. Spacing between fish and angles of orientation were more variable when the barrier was present. Cahn suggested that vision alone is inadequate for maintenance of polarization associated with schooling in this species. In her opinion, group polarization in the kawakawa depends to an unknown extent on detection of water turbulence generated by individuals in the school.

Pitcher et al. (1976) demonstrated that pollocks (*Pollachius virens*) blinded with opaque eye covers are able to school with conspecifics, a finding contrary to previous reports (see Note 9). Blinded fish with their lateral lines cut could not. The authors wrote: ''Although it is unlikely that blind saithe [pollocks] could school in the wild, the constraints of the apparatus permitted a demonstration of a role of the lateral line organ in schooling.'' The constraints referred to were spatial. Pitcher (1979) remarked that the blinded pollocks were able to school because their normal conspecifics swam past them repeatedly.

Pitcher (1979) claimed that both vision and perception of hydrodynamic pressure waves (presumed to be received by the lateral line) are used simultaneously by breams (*Abramis brama*) for maintaining individual distance. Rendering the lateral line nonfunctional by placing fish in adjacent channels divided by transparent acrylic barriers increased the proportion of time spent in synchronous swimming. Fish in full sensory contact (i.e., those placed in a channel together) made periodic forays away from each other. This suggested that the fish were ''anxious'' and less inclined to leave the others when only visual contact was possible. In another series of experiments, breams attempted to approach their mirror images when a mirror was placed some distance away and separated from the fish by an empty channel with transparent acrylic dividers. The fish learned to avoid mirror images approachable directly because ''. . . unlike a real fish behind a transparent barrier [the mirror image] did not turn away at the 'individual distance'.'' Pitcher concluded that vision, the lateral line, and olfaction are all used by breams, but olfaction probably is unimportant in the maintenance of schools.

Shaw (1970) predicted that future research would show the dependence of fish assemblages on multisensory reception. Her idea seemed logical then and still does, but confirming evidence remains elusive. A primary obstacle has been the design of experiments in which potential mediating factors can be isolated and measured. Visual tests are comparatively simple: fishes can be separated by transparent dividers in a single aquarium or placed in adjacent aquariums. Interference from near-field effects and olfaction is manageable. These last-named factors, however, are more difficult to study in isolation.

(11) Fishes that are predisposed to school ordinarily do so when threatened by a predator. This is easily observed while scuba diving: diurnal shoals move out of a diver's way by forming temporary schools and increasing swimming speed. Seghers (1974) described how guppies (*Poecilia reticulata*) form schools in the presence of a predator. Hobson (1973) observed that planktivorous fishes in feeding ''aggregations'' tend to ''. . . draw themselves close together when threatened; if the danger intensifies they may then dive to the sheltering rocks below.''

(12) Schooling behavior of some fishes—particularly temperate species—is affected strongly by changing seasons, which control migration. Unlike diel rhythms, these have little or nothing to do with feeding. Seasonal rhythms seldom are apparent in aquariums unless temperate fishes are kept in open water systems without temperature controls. Captive Atlantic silversides (*Menidia menidia*) school actively in spring and fall (Koltes 1984).

The fish were maintained in an aquarium with an open water system, and the temperature matched that of the natural environment. Milling behavior replaced schooling in summer and winter, and the fish moved to the bottom of the aquarium and became quiescent. Spring and fall are times when Atlantic silversides migrate.

(13) Hobson (1972, 1973).

(14) The categories of diel rhythms and much of my subsequent description of them are based on Hobson (1973).

(15) Fishes that feed on zooplankton are true carnivores. My distinction of ''planktivores'' from ''carnivores'' is simply for convenience.

(16) Hobson (1965, 1968).

(17) The text description is based on the behavior of *Pempheris oualensis* by Fishelson et al. (1971).

(18) Descriptions of the behavior of *Pranesus pinquis* are based on Hobson and Chess (1973). Diel rhythms of diurnal planktivorous fishes sometimes mirror those of nocturnal species. The behavior of *P. pinquis*, for example, is similar in some respects to that of the inland silverside (*Menidia beryllina*), an introduced species in Clear Lake, California. According to Wurtsbaugh and Li (1985), inland silversides form inactive shoals along the shore at night. At dawn they migrate offshore to feed and return to the shoaling site 3 to 4 h later by a route parallel with the shore. The numbers of returning fish increase until about noon. Shoals remain quiescent throughout the day and do not feed, but a second offshore movement occurs in the evening.

(19) Starck and Davis (1966).

(20) Descriptions of the behavior of French and white grunts are based on Ogden and Ehrlich (1977).

(21) My dictionary defines *teleology* as the use of design or purpose to explain natural phenomena. No trap likely to be encountered by a scientist is more cleverly camouflaged. Behaviorists, who should be most wary of all, are regularly captured in the greatest numbers. Teleology is rife in the fish schooling literature, particularly those aspects that are believed to have survival value, and I approached the subject reluctantly. Readers will have to look elsewhere for explanations of ''why'' fishes school. The comments in this subsection should be read with active skepticism, whether they are mine or someone else's.

Wright (1985) provided an everyday explanation of teleology: ''Thinkers of a teleological bent have what in science is considered a peculiar habit. When they hear the word 'why,' they think of the future. For example: Why does dropped toast seem always to land jelly-side-down? Most of us, and certainly the scientists among us, would seek the answer in the stretch of time preceding the toast's landing: perhaps the laws of aerodynamics dictated that the toast stabilize in mid-descent with the heavier side down. But someone teleologically inclined would answer the question by reference to the stretch of time after the landing: the toast ends up jelly-side-down so that your day will get off to a terrible start.''

(22) The quotation is from Klopfer (1973, p. 4).

(23) Figure 6-4 is, of course, blatantly teleological. I have no confidence in having linked the presumed effects with the correct causes, nor in whether the presumed causes are real.

(24) Fishes that school typically are open-water species. They inhabit an environment devoid of shelter (e.g., Brock and Riffenburgh 1960, Williams 1964). Hamilton (1971), Koltes (1984), Vine (1971, 1973), and Williams (1964) proposed that schooling evolved as a cover-seeking mechanism in which a threatened individual becomes less conspicuous by positioning itself among others. Williams called this behavior ''defensive hiding;'' Hamilton (1971) gave it a theoretical framework that he termed ''geometry of the selfish herd.''

(25) Milinski (1977a) cultured water fleas (*Daphnia magna*) under conditions that either stimulated or inhibited production of hemoglobin. The high-hemoglobin group was more conspicuous to threespine sticklebacks. Water fleas from both groups (pale and cryptic, dark and conspicuous) were then presented to threespine sticklebacks both as a dense swarm and a sparse swarm consisting of a few individuals. If both swarms were pale (i.e., relatively inconspicuous), individuals of the sparse group were chosen significantly less often than when both groups were more conspicuous. Milinski concluded, ''From this it follows that the risk from becoming separated from the group is much higher for a conspicuous prey species than for a cryptic one.''

Fish in a homotypic school are often the same size. Their striking uniformity is thought to submerge individuality. According to Major (1978), ''This apparently serves to mask the individuals, making it impossible for predators to align themselves with individual prey for a successful strike.''

In a study of predation by hawks, Mueller (1971) purported to demonstrate that oddity is more important than conspicuousness in prey selection. Captive American kestrels (*Falco sparverius*) and broad-winged hawks (*Buteo platypterus*) were offered live white laboratory mice, some dyed gray with food coloring. Individual birds were offered nine mice of one color and one of the other color. A single odd mouse—either white or gray—was presented in each trial. The 10 mice were placed on a substratum painted gray or white. A trial ended when a mouse had been captured. All hawks showed a significant preference for odd mice, but only of one color. Mueller wrote: "Thus mice of a particular color were preferred, but only when they were odd, and the conspicuousness of the mouse [as dictated by the color of the substratum] had relatively little influence on the results."

The results of this experiment seem inconclusive to me. They reveal nothing of "color preference" because gray and white (which is also gray) are achromatic; in other words, preference from the standpoint of chromaticity or degree of color saturation. What actually was shown is that hawks can distinguish their preferred prey against backgrounds having different degrees of brightness (i.e., value). The terms achromatic, chromaticity, saturation, and value are defined and discussed in Chapter 10.

(26) Hobson (1973) speculated that the survival value of schooling may be partly attributable to a reduction in variable behavior, ". . . especially when precise timing or a particular type of response is required in a given stimulus situation." Hobson framed this statement not with predation in mind, but within the context of navigation and the general ability of fishes that forage away from the reef to find their home resting locations. He added the qualifier that variable behavior by an individual in a school makes it conspicuous and no longer anonymous.

(27) It has long been believed that schooling has survival value through safety in numbers. Parr (1927) correlated schooling with the ". . . general defenselessness of the forms in which it is found." He wrote: "If for instance the individuals of a much sought species like the sprat [*Sprattus sprattus*] or herring [*Clupea harengus*] would travel around separately, scarcely a single one of them would escape the enemies sufficiently long to be able to propagate, while the occurrence of a great number of specimens united in schools among scattered enemies may give a certain percentage a chance to survive and continue the existence of the species." This ignores schooling predatory fishes such as mackerels, tunas, bluefish, and many others.

Neill and Cullen (1974) observed that captive prey fishes (several species of teleosts) survive longer in schools than as isolated individuals. Capture attempts lasted longer when 20 or more schooling prey were present than when single prey or schools of six were used. The longer the "hunt" the lower the capture rate. The effect was most noticeable in the case of the two predatory cephalopods, a squid (*Loligo vulgaris*) and a cuttlefish (*Sepia officinalis*). It was insignificant in the case of perches (*Perca fluviatilis*) and barely significant when northern pikes (*Esox lucius*) were the predators. The conclusions: (*1*) longer hunts are more likely when schools of prey are large, and (*2*) longer hunts result in a lower rate of success. Major (1978) reported that isolated Hawaiian anchovies were nearly three times more vulnerable to predation by jacks (*Caranx ignobilis*) than were anchovies in schools.

According to Milinski (1977a, 1977b), threespine sticklebacks presented with a "swarm" of water fleas preferentially attack the stragglers. Milinski (1977b) concluded (somewhat cryptically), "As stragglers were more often attacked than any portion of a swarm itself, natural selection favours all individual swarm members, although differentially."

Major (1978) studied predator-prey interactions in two schooling fishes, a jack (*Caranx ignobilis*) and the Hawaiian anchovy. In all combinations tested, which involved varying the numbers of predators and prey, Hawaiian anchovies in schools suffered the lowest rate of predation.

Foster and Treherne (1981) reviewed several of these reports and noted that any dilution effect is likely to be masked by other advantages of group living ". . . such as improved efficiency of feeding and reproduction or, more importantly, improved detection and confusion of the predator." As they pointed out, in most published studies the prey has been visible to predators, and ". . . it is unclear to what extent the benefits of increased group size are the result of a dilution effect or of some other effects, such as improved avoidance behaviour." Foster and Treherne conducted field studies on predator-prey interactions between Pacific sardines (*Sardinops sagax*) and a surface-dwelling marine insect, the ocean skater (*Halobates robustus*), that often congregates in groups. The ocean skaters could not see the fish beneath them and presumably were unable to detect their presence. Observations of attacks on individual versus grouped ocean skaters closely followed a statistical pattern predictable on the basis of a dilution effect.

Brock and Riffenburgh (1960) proposed that if schooling protects the prey (by a dilution effect), two seemingly incompatible devices are at work. They reasoned that if a single fish is regarded as a group of unit size, schooling has two consequences. First, it reduces the number of groups and thus lowers the frequency of encounters with predators. Second, it increases the sizes of the groups, thereby increasing the probability of their detection. The authors offered a second possible advantage: the inability of the predator to consume all individuals in the school. Their model showed frequency of detection to correlate negatively with the number of grouped individuals. The number of individuals that a predator can consume in a single encounter is limited, presumably by satiation. Once the size of the school exceeds this number, further increases in size reduce the frequency of individual predator-prey encounters without necessarily altering the number of prey consumed at each encounter. This in turn may reduce the rate of prey consumption. Moreover, the number of prey consumed is considerable if (*1*) the sighting distance of predator to prey exceeds individual distances within the prey school, and (*2*) the total number of prey is high. In other words, any survival advantage of schooling is quickly eliminated after predators move into short range.

Olson (1964) reached similar conclusions using equations for predicting the probability of attack on unescorted surface ships by enemy submarines. The Koopman theory of search, published after World War II, included equations that describe the comparative safety of ships alone and in groups (e.g., Koopman 1956). Olson applied Koopman's equations to fishes with these results. First, the probability of predation on a lone fish is substantially greater than on an individual in a school. Second, a school is more likely than a single fish to be detected by a predator. Koopman's model for naval warfare thus confers a distinct advantage on schooling, although the comparative advantage is less than when the probability of detection is high. My opinion is that James Thurber's dictum is worth remembering: there is no safety in numbers, or in anything else.

(28) Several authors have suggested that schooling of prey fishes may have survival value by ''confusing'' predators (e.g., Allen 1920; Eibl-Eibesfeldt 1962; Foster and Treherne 1981; Hobson 1965, 1968; Neill and Cullen 1974; Starck and Davis 1966). It is important to recognize, however, that ''confusion'' has limited descriptive value without reproducible methods of measurement. These are currently lacking.

I offer no new evidence to confirm or deny the ''confusion'' hypothesis. What follows is my opinion of what happens after having witnessed numerous attacks on schooling fishes by both solitary and grouped predators. These observations, made while scuba diving, are unquantified and subjective, but any ''confusion'' on the part of the predator seems to occur at the end of an attack sequence, not at the start of one. An attack sequence appears to begin confidently as predators dash into a school of prey fish. If an attack fails, a predator—particularly a solitary one—may simply stop, giving the appearance of being confused.

Most agree that vision is used extensively by predators attacking schooling prey. By implication, any confusion would be visually mediated. Fishes tend toward hyperopia (Chapter 5), a factor that perhaps influences the outcome of the attack sequence. Initiation of the sequence can be visually mediated in either of two ways: (*1*) the predator selects an individual from a school of prey fish and pursues it to the exclusion of the others; or (*2*) the predator rushes into the school, scatters it, and then selects an individual to pursue. In the first situation a prey fish selected for attack may be an individual positioned at what I shall call the *optimal visual distance* (i.e., the distance that provides the clearest visual image). Stragglers and individuals on the periphery of a school would offer the clearest images against the background spacelight (Chapter 5). After selecting its prey the predator must close the intervening gap to make a capture. In the process optimal visual distance is sacrificed, and the visual image of the prey becomes increasingly less distinct as predator and prey draw together. In other words, the prey fish is in sharp focus only at the beginning of an attack sequence, and success depends on split-second timing. In effect, the predator must "remember" the prey's location as the attack sequence proceeds. The prey fish can escape by moving perpendicular to the direction of the attack for a distance that exceeds the spatial boundaries of the predator's visual "memory." This is quite different from stating that the prey has only to move away from the predator's field of vision to avoid capture. Clear visual contact was lost earlier in the attack sequence at the predator's initiation (i.e., as it moved toward the prey).

Now consider the second situation. If a predator rushes into a school of prey without first focusing on a particular fish, the school scatters, momentarily isolating some individuals. In such cases it appears that the beginning of the attack sequence is intended only to penetrate the school (see Note 29). An isolated fish is more visible against the background spacelight than individuals in the school itself. The sequential elements of the attack then occur in the same order as in the first situation. As before, the predator's success depends largely on evasive action of the prey.

(29) This observation was made by Major (1978) in his study of predator-prey interactions between jacks (*Caranx ignobilis*) and Hawaiian anchovies. The predators' "intent" was evident in this case because they dashed into the anchovies without striking (by Major's definition, without opening their mouths and

attempting to make a capture). The strike portion of the attack sequence occurred afterward and was directed at individual prey fish, ordinarily those that had not immediately rejoined the school. This suggested to Major that ". . . predators may not be confused by tightly grouped or schooled prey, but lack the time necessary to align themselves with an individual prey for a successful strike." They could also have lost clear visual contact (see Note 28).

(30) Milinski (1977a, 1977b) showed that prey (water fleas in this case) on the periphery or a group of "swarm" are more vulnerable to attack than those in the center.

(31) The report of Healey and Prieston (1973) is the most quantified. These authors sought answers to two questions. First, is a particular fish found in all possible positions within the school with equal probability? Second, do fish tend to associate specifically with others in the school? The school studied consisted of 12 sockeye salmon (*Oncorhynchus nerka*) fingerlings that had been hatched and reared in captivity. Each fish was marked with a distinctive tattoo. The school was photographed as it passed through the center of the experimental aquarium. Each photograph recorded the side and top view of the school, and coordinates of the position of the individual fish were recorded. The data provided a three-dimensional observation of every fish in context with its conspecifics and indicated how positions within the school changed with time. To answer the first question, "There seems little doubt . . . that the fish are not moving at random but are occupying a restricted space within the school." Some fish swam at the edges of the school significantly more often than others. These were neither the largest nor the smallest individuals. Moreover, they did not prefer any particular location and appeared at the sides, front, and rear of the school with similar frequency. Healey and Prieston speculated on what they had seen: "One possible cause of the pattern observed is that individual fish prefer to stay a specific distance from all other fish. Fish which prefer to stay relatively far from other fish can only achieve this by staying at the edge of the school while those which prefer short distances can best achieve this near the center of the school." As to the second question, there was no obvious tendency for a fish to swim beside particular conspecifics. The authors cautioned against application of their findings to large schools.

(32) Planktivorous fishes are predators if they feed on zooplankton, but the limited information available suggests that schooling may have an adverse effect on prey consumption because of competition among individuals. This supposedly is a

result of overlapping visual fields. In such situations the prey is seen and subsequently attacked by more than one fish in the school, resulting in decreased consumption compared with single fish. Eggers (1976) published a model purporting to show how schooling fishes capture fewer plankton than isolated individuals, presumably because the visual field of each fish overlaps partially with the visual fields of its nearest companions. No experimental data were included. Seghers (1981) reached a similar conclusion (also without supporting data) after studying spottail shiners (*Notropis hudsonius*) in the field.

Earlier writers believed that schooling confers an advantage on planktivorous fishes. After observing Atlantic mackerels in an outdoor pool, Sette (1950) proposed that schooling makes prey capture more efficient. The school disintegrated when large food particles were present, and each fish fed on its own. When feeding on plankton the fish schooled as a compact unit. They ". . . opened their mouths to the fullest extent and extended their operculums widely. . . . In this condition the school formed a group of miniature tow-nets spaced hardly more than their own diameter apart." Sette suggested that if copepods anticipate the presence of predators and try to escape by darting 1 cm or more, the "tow-net" would greatly reduce their chances: "This theory supposes that the copepods and other planktonic food organisms are capable of detecting a mackerel at a small distance, and it needs support from critical experiments or observations indicating the sensory ability of a copepod in such a situation. If they do not possess this faculty the individual mackerel would be at no disadvantage as compared with a school in catching copepods." Sette believed that the large number of schooling planktivorous species offered "strong indication" of evidence for his hypothesis. He considered the situation of schooling piscivorous predators feeding on schooling prey to be similar.

(33) Major (1978) compared the success rate of single and grouped jacks (*Caranx ignobilis*) in capturing isolated and schooling Hawaiian anchovies. Single jacks were more successful at capturing isolated prey than schooling prey, and less successful than groups of jacks at capturing schooling anchovies. Partridge et al. (1983) analyzed the structure of bluefin tuna (*Thunnus thynnus*) schools from aerial photographs and proposed that this species uses schooling formations to hunt cooperatively.

Hiatt and Brock (1948) observed three black skipjacks, *Euthynnus lineatus* (= *E. yaito*), herding a dense school of several hundred scads (*Decapterus sanctaebelenae*?). They wrote: "The three tuna usually followed the school of scads rather closely, with one tuna at each rear flank of the school and the third lagging behind them. Now and then the scads would turn off to one side, at which time the tuna on that side would move forward swiftly and herd them back into line. It became obvious that the school of scads was prevented from leaving the area . . . being herded back whenever it moved over deep water. On one occasion a laggard scad was swiftly picked off by the rear-most black skipjack; however, except for this incident the tuna made no attempt to prey upon the scads during our period of observation.''

Schmitt and Strand (1982) observed what in their opinion was cooperative hunting by yellowtails (*Seriola lalandei*) on jack mackerels and Cortez grunts (*Lythrulon flaviguttatum*; Fig. 6-9). The authors distinguished cooperative foraging from less complex hunting behaviors by two criteria: (*1*) individuals adopt different but complementary roles, and (2) individuals exercise ''temporary restraint,'' not attacking until the prey has been rendered more vulnerable.

(34) The study of Major (1978, see Note 33) showed that relatively few prey are captured by jacks from schools of Hawaiian anchovies during an attack, but individual anchovies are inevitably isolated. These are attacked before they can locate the original school or form a new one. Experiments were conducted in large net enclosures in a Hawaiian lagoon. The degree of predation depended on the numbers of both prey and predator. Jacks released into an enclosure containing anchovies were less successful as single predators than in groups. The mean number of anchovies captured increased as the numbers of predators and prey increased. However, the percentage of anchovies captured decreased as their numbers rose. Major acknowledged that satiation of the jacks may have influenced this last observation. Isolated anchovies were more vulnerable to predation than those in schools. Single jacks were more successful in capturing isolated prey than were groups of jacks, but less successful at capturing schooling prey. All capture attempts (single or grouped jacks) were less successful with schooling, as opposed to isolated, anchovies. When a school of anchovies was attacked, several individuals became momentarily isolated before the school could reform, and these were preyed on most heavily. If an anchovy left the school to feed, failed to synchronize movements with the school, or fell behind, the chances of its survival decreased. The author wrote: ''The major value of school or group formation in predators in the experiments appeared to be related to their increased ability

to break up schools of prey, and to create increased confusion, such that more individual prey became isolated. As had been shown, isolated prey were easier to catch. . . .''

(35) As pointed out by Belyayev and Zuyev (1969), any importance derived from studies that attempt to measure the hydrodynamics of group motion in fishes depends on demonstrable advantages, compared with the hydrodynamics of individual fishes. Thus although models may show the way (e.g., Belyayev and Zuyev 1969; Breder 1965, 1976; Childress 1981, pp. 98–115; Inagaki et al. 1976; Weihs 1973, 1975), only experimental results really matter. These have failed to uphold the hypothesis that schooling confers a hydrodynamic advantage (Partridge 1981).

(36) According to my dictionary, agonist and antagonist are synonyms. The adjective agonistic means striving to overcome in argument; competitive or combative. This seems simple enough. However, to animal behaviorists the agonist can be either the aggressor or the recipient of aggression. According to Miller (1978), agonistic behavior encompasses attacking, threat, submissive, and fleeing behaviors. Inclusion of so many disparate activities in a single definition is confusing. If the dictionary definition is inadequate to explain some aspect of science, then a new, more specific and descriptive term should be proposed. Miller (1978) also discussed the difficulties of animal behaviorists in defining aggression, although as I shall use the term it means simply hostile action or behavior, which is straight from the dictionary. Aggression and agonistic behavior will therefore be used interchangeably.

(37) Kaufmann (1983) argued that from an evolutionary standpoint it is irrelevant whether dominance is interpreted as *conferring* priority of access to a resource or is simply defined as priority of access. Natural selection is affected only when increased fitness results, ordinarily by access to limited resources.

(38) The idea of territorial dominance (''territoriality'' is a horrible word) is subjective and burdened with multiple interpretations. A good analysis is that of Kaufmann (1983). The thoughts expressed here are derived mainly from his review. Everyone apparently accepts the idea that maintenance of territories is a type of dominance, but the agreement ends there. The general dictionary definition of territory is the land and waters under jurisdiction of a state, nation, or sovereign. Kaufmann noted this and offered the following advice: ''To avoid the proliferation of useless jargon, it would be sensible for the more specialized biological definition to depart as little as pos-

sible from the general definition. There is no excuse for using the word territory unless it refers to a specific geographical location—an identifiable volume of land, air and water. Control, dominion and jurisdiction are expressions of dominance, not of exclusive occupation.'' This makes sense, because the mere occupation of a space and the social implications associated with that occupation should properly be separated. Historically, biological definitions have included elements of three concepts. A territory has been considered (*1*) a defended area, (*2*) an exclusive area, and (*3*) an area of dominance. These will be discussed briefly.

Territorial dominance was first described in birds, and the earliest definition, formulated in 1868, regarded a territory as the space defended aggressively by a male bird against conspecific males. Noble (1939) reduced the definition to ''any defended area'' and included animals other than birds. Wilson (1975, p. 257) considered that a territory ''. . . need not be a fixed piece of geography. It can be 'floating' or *spatiotemporal* in nature, meaning that the animal defends only the area it happens to be in at the moment, or during a certain time of day or season, or both.'' Wilson insisted that aggression be included in any definition of territory. He wrote (p. 261), ''. . . defense must be the diagnostic feature of territoriality. More precisely, territory should be defined as an area occupied more or less exclusively by animals or groups of animals by means of repulsion through overt aggression or advertisement.''

The idea of exclusive use was first proposed by Pitelka (1959). He offered an ecological—as opposed to a strictly behavioral—definition. Pitelka defined territory simply as an area used exclusively by an animal. The means by which the space came to be identified with the owner had little or no relevance, although some form of social interaction was implied. Thus defense and dominance (see below) were not necessarily unimportant.

According to Kaufmann (1983), Emlen (1957) was the first to propose social dominance as a necessary component of territorial behavior. Emlen defined territory as ''. . . an area of space in which a particular bird is aggressive and largely if not supremely dominant with regard to certain categories of intruder.'' Emlen purposely ignored defense and exclusion. He considered the first to imply a state of motivation that could not be confirmed by observation and the second to be irrelevant. Marler and Hamilton (1966, p. 171) wrote, ''When the external reference for dominance is more or less fixed in space it is commonly spoken of as a 'territory.' '' These authors considered dominance to be ''territorial'' or ''individual,'' a convention I agree with and adopted because it reinforces the fact that territorial behavior is a form of dominance. Marler and Hamilton (1966, p. 171) pointed out that in the context proposed by Pitelka (1959), ''Active defense is not a necessary condition for the maintenance of some degree of exclusive occupation of an area—the most important ecological consequence of territoriality. . . .'' A combination of *site attachment* (attachment to a particular place) and mutual avoidance by individuals also can result in exclusive use. Willis (1967) considered submission to be as important as aggression. Dominance could include either submissive or escape behavior by the subordinate animal.

Willis (1967) also considered dominance reversal to be important. Operationally, trespassers are tolerated under certain conditions. According to Wolf (1970), trespassers may sometimes be tolerated if they do not try to use the defended resources. In still other cases, trespassers are tolerated so long as they remain subordinate (Owen-Smith 1977). In all these situations space-related dominance reversal is the determining factor in territorial behavior, rather than exclusive use of space. Trespassers are tolerated unless the owner's priority of access to resources is threatened. Consequently, Kaufmann redefined territorial dominance as ''space-related dominance.'' He emphasized that his definition is valid only if the meaning of dominance is extended to include mutual assessment and avoidance without ''overt defence'' (presumably Wilson's phrase). The brief summary given here has been synthesized from reports that have mostly described territorial behavior of birds and mammals. Whether the same principles pertain unilaterally to fishes is uncertain.

(39) The definition of territory is from Kaufmann (1983).

(40) This definition has long applied to home ranges of mammals (e.g., Burt 1943, Jewell 1966). I have applied it to fishes as well.

(41) These are the designations listed by Sale (1978). Much of the information in this subsection is from his report.

(42) Descriptions of lekking—including principles used to define it—originated primarily from studies of birds. As pointed out by Loiselle and Barlow (1978), lekking patterns of fishes differ in important respects, and use of a common terminology may be inappropriate.

(43) Kaufmann (1983).

(44) This discussion is based on Robertson and Lassig (1980).

(45) Curiously, this possibility has been overlooked, at least in the reports I read. It seems logical that if a species is planktiv-

orous and obtains its food from the water column, maintenance of a benthic territory may serve some function other than protection of the food supply. Planktivorous damselfishes typically are territorial only during the breeding season.

(46) Bakus (1966, 1967, 1969, 1972), Borowitzka (1981), Brock (1979), Earle (1972), Hay (1984), Littler and Doty (1975), Miller (1982), Montgomery et al. (1980), Randall (1961), Vine (1974), Wanders (1977).

(47) The cultivation of algal lawns has been reported in damselfishes from the Indo-West Pacific, eastern North Pacific, and West Indies. Species include *Stegastes apicalis* (Kamura and Choonhabandit 1986), *S. fasciolatus* (Hixon and Brostoff 1983), and *S. planifrons* (Brawley and Adey 1977, Hinds and Ballantine 1987); *Hypsypops rubicundus* (Clarke 1970, Foster 1972); *Microspathodon dorsalis* (Montgomery 1980); *Dischistodus perspicillatus* (Potts 1977); and *Pomacentrus lividus* (Vine 1974).

According to some authors, tertiary algal lawns are composed of species preferred as food. To suggest that preferences exist in the case of herbivorous damselfishes implies a motivational state that has not been demonstrated. There appear to be two clear mechanisms by which algal lawns are established and subsequently maintained, and they are species dependent. I shall classify them simply as "weeding" and "grazing." The garibaldi (*Hypsypops rubicundus*) is a "weeder." As a carnivore it eats none of the algae growing inside its territory. Algal lawns are used exclusively as nest sites. Clarke (1970) and Foster (1972) observed territorial males removing unwanted species of algae, debris, and even sessile and slow-moving invertebrates from nest sites during the breeding season. At other times these items were allowed to remain, and the nests had an unkempt appearance. The giant blue damselfish (*Microspathadon dorsalis*) is a nonselective herbivore (Montgomery 1980). Algal lawns are established and maintained by heavy grazing, to be dominated ultimately by *Polysiphonia*, a red alga (Rhodophyceae). Continuous cropping keeps the plants in a phase of early, rapid growth, and slower growing forms are precluded.

(48) Clarke (1970) and also the last paragraph of Note 49.

(49) Myrberg and Thresher (1974) showed that threespot damselfish (*Stegastes planifrons*) exhibit agonistic behavior of variable intensity toward intruders. Other herbivores are attacked vigorously, but carnivores are often ignored. Conspecifics are attacked at the greatest distance from the center of a territory, *congenerics* (members of the same genus) at the next greatest distance (with one exception), and then other species. Bicolor

damselfish (*S. partitus*) were often allowed closer to the center of the territory than noncongeners. However, *S. partitus* is a planktivore and does not compete with *S. planifrons* for food resources. In this study, relative size of the intruder did not affect the maximum distance of attack. The authors suggested that threespot damselfish recognize food competitors. Thresher (1976) obtained similar results in a study of *S. planifrons* and reported that fishes of 22 species were repelled. Most agonistic responses were elicited by surgeonfishes, parrotfishes, and grunts. The latter are nocturnal carnivores and not food competitors. Only 5% of the chases involved conspecifics. Intervals between chases averaged 6 min.

The beaugregory (*S. leucostictus*), another West Indies damselfish, also repels food competitors selectively (Ebersole 1977). Conspecifics do not always elicit the most intense agonistic responses. Ebersole concluded that ". . . if interspecific territorialty is a nonadaptive behavior . . . conspecifics should be the most vigorously attacked intruders." Protection of food resources apparently is the most important functional aspect in this species, followed by defense of the nest from egg predators.

Clarke (1970) reported that the garibaldi defends its territory selectively against other teleost species. Most "bottom-grazing" fishes are repelled vigorously by adult garibaldis, but "carnivores" ordinarily are tolerated inside territorial boundaries. As an adult, the garibaldi's principal foods are benthic invertebrates. In this instance, "bottom-grazers" referred to teleosts of other species that feed on different sessile invertebrates and are not food competitors. According to Clarke's usage, "carnivores" evidently meant piscivores. Other large fishes and invertebrates share space within the territories of adult garibaldis on a permanent basis. Clarke concluded that territorial defense is not predicated on interspecific competition for either food or space.

(50) Sammarco and Williams (1982), Williams (1978).

(51) Kaufman (1977), Risk and Sammarco (1982).

(52) Myrberg and Thresher (1974) measured intensity of the agonistic response in male threespot damselfish as the maximum distance of attack. Attacks occurred farthest from the center of the territory during the breeding season and declined noticeably at other times. Clarke (1970) reported similar behavior in the garibaldi when males were guarding nests, but did not quantify it.

(53) Most of this discussion is based on Norman and Jones (1984).

(54) This was the conclusion of Norman and Jones (1984). They wrote: ''We contend that in reality no . . . optimal territory size exists. That is, spatial and temporal variability in the costs and benefits of defence are so large that there is no clear relationships [*sic*] between these variables and territory size.'' Others have disagreed. Ebersole (1980), for example, stated that ''. . . there must be an optimal territory size if there is to be territoriality at all.''

(55) Schoener (1971) introduced the concepts of ''energy maximization'' and ''time minimization'' to relate potential fitness to the time and energy invested in foraging. Hixon (1980) produced a model showing identical responses when food abundance is increased, and Hixon (1982) suggested that the relative proportion of available time spent foraging is perhaps the only distinction. Thus ''. . . any animal during any given time period becomes strictly one or the other type of forager.'' If true, he continued, perhaps these foragers should be renamed ''feeding-time minimizers'' and ''feeding-time maximizers.'' This terminology was retained in a later review (Hixon 1987). However, Hixon (1982) concluded that to accurately place animals in either category probably is impossible under most circumstances.

At least one experiment offered partial confirmation of Schoener's predictions, although the experimental protocol—and consequently the results—were criticized by Norman and Jones (1984). Ebersole (1980) tested the hypothesis with beaugregories. Females were predicted to be feeding-time maximizers and males feeding-time minimizers. When algal abundance was increased experimentally inside territories of both sexes, females and males expanded and decreased their occupied space, respectively.

(56) For examples of this viewpoint see Simon (1975) and Stimson (1973).

(57) Franzblau and Collins (1980); Myers et al. (1979, 1981).

(58) Mares et al. (1982), Simon (1975), Stimson (1973), Taitt (1981), Taitt and Krebs (1981).

(59) This conclusion is based mainly on the work of Norman and Jones (1984), Nursall (1977), and Sale (1975). Ebersole (1980) and Hixon (1981) showed that food abundance influenced the amount of space occupied by territorial fishes they studied. However, Norman and Jones (1984) pointed out that in most cases the territories were not contiguous and suggested that the results may not be applicable in a broad sense.

(60) My discussion of sex reversal is based almost entirely on Warner (1984). Terminology follows Warner and Robertson (1978).

(61) The following information is from the brief summary of Warner (1984). See his report for references, in particular Policansky (1982). At least 14 families of teleosts have representative species that are protogynous as a normal part of their life histories. Of these, 10 commonly inhabit coral reefs. In the wrasses (Labridae), parrotfishes, and larger groupers (Serranidae), protogyny is evident in the majority of species for which observations have been made. Other families in which female-to-male sex reversal occurs in some species are the Gobiidae (gobies), Grammistidae (soapfishes), Lethrinidae (emperors), Pomacanthidae (angelfishes), Pomacentridae (damselfishes), Pseudochromidae (dottybacks), and Sparidae (porgies). Protandry evidently is less common and known in eight teleost families. Three of these are found on coral reefs: damselfishes, porgies, and morays (Muraenidae).

(62) According to Warner and Robertson (1978), parrotfishes are different in this respect, and further distinctions are necessary. Some hermaphroditic males are functional females before changing sex (*post-maturational secondary males*), but others experience sex reversal before maturing as females (*pre-maturational secondary males*).

(63) The size advantage hypothesis was developed by Ghiselin (1969).

(64) Robertson (1972).

(65) Social control of sex reversal in anemonefishes (*Amphiprion* spp.) was described by Fricke and Fricke (1977) and Moyer and Nakazono (1978). Fricke (1974) claimed that in colonies of *A. bicinctus,* growth and development of juveniles are repressed by the presence of the adult pair.

(66) Allen (1972, pp. 40–45) recognized *Premnas* and *Amphiprion* as subgenera of *Amphiprion*.

(67) The largest sea anemone yet measured may have been a specimen of *Stichodactyla* (= *Stoichactis*) *giganteum* at Pipidon Island off Phuket, western Thailand. It was 3 ft 11 in. (~ 1.24 m) in diameter (Mariscal 1970b). Fishes do not appear to be primary dietary items of any sea anemone, although some species are capable of killing small fishes with their stinging structures and feeding on them opportunistically. *Cnidocytes* are located in the epidermis of cnidarians and are especially numerous in the

tentacles. The everting organelles are *cnidae*; some cnidae have stinging structures called *nematocysts*.

(68) Richard N. Mariscal studied symbiotic associations between damselfishes and sea anemones at several locations and published the results in a series of papers in the 1960s and 1970s. Several were summaries in which descriptions and data were repeated. He considered all species of *Amphiprion*, including species of *Premnas* (see Note 66), to be obligate anemone dwellers as juveniles and adults (e.g., Mariscal 1970b, 1970c, 1972). In the 1970b publication he wrote, ''Although there are occasional reports that *Amphiprion* may be found without anemones in the field, it is doubtful that this is actually the case.'' In nature, *Dascyllus albisella* and *D. trimaculatus* were seen to associate with anemones only as juveniles (e.g., Mariscal 1972). Captive adult *D. trimaculatus* commonly nestle among the tentacles of sea anemones.

(69) Eibl-Eibesfeldt (1960), Mariscal (1970c).

(70) Mariscal (1970b, 1970c) conducted microscopic examinations of gut contents of anemonefishes collected in the wild and found cnidae and other anemone tissues. The subject of anemonefishes eating food captured by their hosts was reported without comment by Mariscal (1970c).

(71) When placed in aquariums, some species of anemonefishes take objects (including food) to their hosts and either deposit the material among the tentacles or push it into the oral cavity (e.g., Allen 1980; Fishelson 1965; Gohar 1934, 1948; Mariscal 1970b; Verwey 1930). Researchers with extensive field experience consider this an artifact of captivity and dismiss any notion of its ecological importance. Mariscal (1970b) saw anemonefishes take food to sea anemones ''several hundred times,'' always in aquarium settings. Allen (1980) wrote: ''During my own extensive underwater observations and those of Fricke (1974), this behaviour was noted on only three occasions. . . .''

That anemonefishes take objects to their hosts is not in doubt. The problem lies with the interpretation. In my opinion, any reference to anemones being ''fed'' connotes mutualism and should be avoided. I therefore use ''taking objects to the anemone'' throughout this note. Mariscal (1970b) used the phrase, ''returned food to the anemone,'' but this implies a circular pattern of behaviors that begins and ends with the anemone, rather than a linear sequence starting with the fish and ending with the anemone. I shall begin by describing the behavior as others have reported it.

Fishelson (1965) discussed a series of simple laboratory experiments with *Amphiprion bicinctus* and anemones of the genus *Stichodactyla* (= *Stoichactis*). Fish were seen pushing food into the oral cavities of their hosts. Alternatively, a fish would accept food from the observer, then ". . . dive between the tentacles and agitate them with its head until the meat sticks." In reporting one incident Fishelson wrote, ". . . the *Amphiprion* ate the first three small pieces of fish that were dropped in the aquarium. However, when a large piece was introduced, one of the fish seized it and immediately swam across the aquarium to the anemone. The food was released about 1 to 2 cm away from the anemone's tentacles but it did not contact them and started to drop to the bottom. As the fish turned away and had nearly reversed course, it observed that the piece of food had missed the anemone's tentacles. The fish then abruptly turned and dove down to seize the food again. This time the fish swam directly to the tentacles where the food was rather forcefully pushed among them. It then held the food there until firmly grasped by the tentacles before swimming away. The tentacles contracted towards the mouth and the food was ingested by the anemone."

Fishelson (1965) and Gohar (1934, 1948) intepreted such behavior as "feeding" of the anemones by their symbionts, and Gohar claimed that anemonefishes assist the anemones in prey capture, although neither author's experimental work justified his conclusions. Fishelson (1965) wrote, "Observations both in nature and in captivity, have shown that *A. bicinctus* serves its anemone-host by supplying food." However, observations "in nature" were abetted by Fishelson feeding the fish. Factors necessary to elicit the "feeding" sequence in the oceans—if indeed it is that—are now thought to be rare or absent. The arbitrary introduction and subsequent manipulation of factors presumed to be natural without experimental controls is not a test of the hypothesis.

Gohar (1934, 1948) and Mariscal (1970b) observed captive anemonefishes taking live fishes to their anemones. Gohar stated, "The fish—it is true—would swallow pieces of food that are not too big, pushing to the anemone those that they cannot swallow. This is simply natural, as fish—like all animals—have to feed themselves first, but when they help the anemone to capture its own food, they clearly seem to do so as a help to their host rather than as a vain attempt to devour the food themselves. This is shown beyond doubt when they drag to the anemone living fish almost their own size." Gohar's statement implies that an anemonefish somehow distinguishes two kinds of food items: its own and the anemone's. But if the fish recognizes an object as food, and food is taken to the anemone for whatever "purpose," its condition (alive or dead) is irrelevant. It is doubtful whether anemonefishes even recognize "anemone foods" as such. Mariscal (1970b) noted that a captive *A. clarkii* (= *A. xanthurus*) took *all* objects offered—including inedible pieces of paper—to its anemone. Allen (1980) reported three occasions in which anemonefishes in the wild took objects to their hosts. One was a piece of fish feces and the other a string of algae. In his opinion, both were of doubtful nutritional value.

Factors other than an innate drive on the part of the fish to "feed" the anemone should be considered. Possibilities are (*1*) a proclivity for taking food or other objects inside the territory, which includes the anemone; (*2*) size of the food; and (*3*) the extent to which the fish is satiated. All have been mentioned, but none adequately tested. Allen (1980) favored the territory hypothesis: "All damselfishes are territorial [*sic*] and in the case of *Amphiprion* and *Premnas* the anemone is the focal point of the territory; in other damselfishes a hole or crevice in the reef serves this same function. Therefore, rather than deliberately attempting to feed the anemone, the fishes are bringing the food items back to their protective shelter. . . ." Fishelson (1965) described behavior that could be interpreted similarly. He placed an anemonefish (*A. bicinctus*) in an aquarium that did not contain anemones. "When fed, the fish swallowed a few morsels of meat [cut fish or shrimp], then carried another into a corner of the aquarium and there spit it out. It continued to transport food until it had assembled quite a store in the corner. After the feeding, the fish went to its store and gambolled [*sic*] about in the exact way that is typical of *A. bicinctus* when playing [*sic*] between the tentacles of a host anemone. The fish spent the whole night hovering over its store. This entire pattern of behaviour was repreated on twelve consecutive days . . . while spoiled pieces of meat were being removed every morning." Mariscal (1970b) dropped food into an aquarium some distance away from an anemonefish (species unstated) and its host anemone. As the fish swam to the food, the anemone was removed. The fish returned and, not finding the anemome, swam to the nearest corner and deposited the food. The corner was one that the fish had occupied prior to introduction of the anemone. When the anemone was returned to its original place, the fish left the corner and took the food to the anemone. Afterward, it remained with the anemone.

Fishelson (1965) conducted four aquarium experiments with *A. bicinctus* and anemones of the genus *Stichodactyla* (= *Stoichactis*): (*1*) hungry fish and small pieces of food, (*2*) hungry fish and large pieces, (3) satiated fish and small pieces, and (4) satiated fish and large pieces. Fishelson's experiments were completely descriptive. Interpretation of the results can only be inferred. In the first experiment all food was eaten and none taken to the anemone. To me, this infers normal behavior in a planktivorous fish. Similar behavior was described by Mariscal (1970b). In the second experiment the fish took food to the anemone, deposited it among the tentacles, tore off pieces and ate them, and pushed the remainder into the oral cavity of the anemone. By inference, this might represent taking food inside the territory. All food in the third experiment was taken to the anemone, but the pieces were spit into the tentacles from some distance away. Results of the fourth experiment were similar to the third, except that the fish deposited the food directly among the tentacles. I attribute no importance to where or how on the anemone the food was deposited. The results again infer taking food to the territory, although perhaps with a different twist. Plankton drifts across coral reefs more or less continuously, and diurnal planktivores feed throughout the day. Satiation in wild planktivorous fishes may be atypical. Researchers and aquarists tend to feed captive fishes intermittently, as Fishelson did. Satiation may have been the relevant factor, rather than size of the food.

The tendency of anemonefishes to take objects to sea anemones is stronger in some species than others. Evidently, *A. ocellaris* never does this, *A. ephippium* and *A.* (= *Premnas*) *biaculeatus* do on occasion, and *A. bicinctus*, *A. nigripes*, and *A. clarkii* (= *A. polymnus* of Verwey 1930) do so frequently (Fishelson 1965; Gohar 1948; Mariscal 1970b, 1970c, 1972; Verwey 1930). A specimen of *A. nigripes* was seen depositing food in a sea anemone occupied and defended by other anemonefishes after its own anemone had been removed. According to Mariscal (1970b), ". . . an *A. nigripes* deprived of its anemone persisted in taking food to an *R. ritteri* anemone inhabited by two *A. percula*, deposit its food and then turn to flee from the anemone before being attacked. On one occasion, however, the *A. nigripes* required 11 minutes of getting past the vigorous territorial defense of the resident *A. percula* to deposit its food."

(72) Mariscal (1970b).

(73) Mariscal (1972).

(74) Eibl-Eibesfeldt (1960), Mariscal (1970b).

(75) Davenport and Norris (1958) reported that newly introduced *Amphiprion percula* began the acclimation process by swimming cautiously above and below the anemone. "Even-

tually, on one of these trips over the [oral] disk, the fish would touch a tentacle or two, usually with the ventral edge of its anal fin or the lower margin of its caudal fin. Commonly this resulted in a moderate adherence of the tentacles to the fin and contraction of the tentacle. The fish then jerked itself free with a violent flexure of its body and usually raced off the disk.'' The time from introduction to first contact ranged from <1 to 65 min. Afterward, the fish approached the tentacles more closely and touched them with increasing regularity. ''The reaction to the clinging of tentacles became less and less violent. . . . Mouthing or nipping of tentacles was often observed in this and later stages. . . . The clinging and contraction of tentacles upon contact with the fish gradually became less until it ceased altogether. At the same time the fish began to swim deeper among the tentacles, using the same slow undulating movements as when it had cruised above the disk.'' The fish increased its activity until it appeared to be ''bathing'' itself among the tentacles. Fish at this stage were considered to be fully acclimated. The entire process required ~1 min to ~3 h with a mean time of 1 h. Descriptions of the acclimation process also were published by Mariscal (1970a, 1972).

(76) Mariscal (1970a, 1970b).

(77) An interesting experimental problem has been to determine the identity and origin of the protective mechanism. The situation can be summarized in two questions. First, does protection originate with the fish or the anemone? Second, is a specific biochemical compound responsible or simply a physical barrier? Researchers agree almost unanimously that protection is acquired during acclimation, and most have considered it to originate with the fish. However, D. Schlichter has steadfastly favored the anemone (Schlichter 1967, 1968a, 1968b, 1970, 1972, 1975, 1976).

Early proponents of the fish-origin hypothesis (e.g., Blösch 1961, Gohar 1948, Graefe 1963) suggested that discharge of the anemone's cnidae is inhibited or altered by a behavioral, physical, or chemical feedback mechanism from the fish. Others saw a strictly passive role for the anemone, with the fish gaining protection through alteration of its mucous coating (e.g., Brooks and Mariscal 1984; Davenport and Norris 1958; Eibl-Eibesfeldt 1960; Fukui 1973; Lubbock 1980; Mariscal 1965, 1970a). Davenport and Norris, for example, concluded that ''. . . an active principle is present in the mucus [of the fish] secreted on the outer surface of the integument . . . which raises the threshold of mechanically-induced discharge of the host's nematocysts.'' They demonstrated that exterior surfaces of acclimated *Amphi-*

prion percula devoid of mucus elicited cnidal discharges from *Stichodactyla* (= *Stoichactis*). Mariscal (1965, 1970a) reported similar findings using *A. clarkii* (= *A. xanthurus*) and the eastern North Pacific anemone *Anthropleura xanthogrammica*. He wrote that ". . . if the surface of an acclimated fish is carefully wiped off with soft absorbent tissue, the previously acclimated fish becomes 'unacclimated' and is stung by both acclimated and unacclimated [to the fish] anemones."

Schlichter's hypothesis that the fish gains protection by coating itself with the anemone's mucus was widely accepted until recently. Schlichter used radioactive isotopes and other techniques to show that mucus is transferred from the anemone to the fish during acclimation. In theory, the anemone recognizes only itself (i.e., the fish's presence is masked), and cnidal discharge is not elicited. Lubbock (1980) agreed that anemonefishes acquire mucus from their hosts, perhaps with limited beneficial effects, but doubted whether the anemone's mucus afforded the fish substantial protection. According to Lubbock's conclusions, no inhibitory mechanism is involved; instead, protection is achieved by a mucous layer up to four times thicker than typically found in fishes. Activity of the mucous layer is neutral and serves as a physical barrier. Chemical masking is apparently not involved.

(78) Hanlon et al. (1983), Hanlon and Kaufman (1976).

(79) Information for the subsection on refuge associations came mostly from three sources: Tyler and Böhlke (1972) described West Indies fish-sponge associations, and Lassig (1977a, 1977b) reported on fish-shrimp and fish-crab relationships on the Great Barrier Reef.

(80) The definition of cleaning behavior is from Gorlick et al. (1978). Gorlick and coauthors actually said, "Cleaning behavior involves feeding by cleaner organisms on ectoparasites, scales, mucus, and other materials from the body surfaces and oral and gill cavies of 'cooperating' host fishes." I narrowed the definition to cleaning fishes, although other animals—in particular, shrimps—also clean fishes (e.g., Johnson and Ruben 1988, Limbaugh et al. 1961, Sargent and Wagenbach 1975, Spotte et al. 1991).

(81) Losey (1971).

(82) Limbaugh (1961) discussed the results of cursory experiments in the West Indies. After all cleaning organisms had been removed from a section of reef he observed fewer fishes, a noticeable increase in parasitism, and what appeared to be infectious diseases in those that remained. Limbaugh was critical of

his own work (e.g., lack of experimental controls) and considered the findings preliminary, but as Losey (1971) pointed out, Limbaugh's paper has been cited uncritically ever since. Youngbluth (1968) conducted tests similar to Limbaugh's in Hawaii and saw no subsequent changes in the host fish population.

(83) In most of the reports I consulted, evidence of cleaning was indirect, based on the authors having witnessed activities considered by them to represent ''cleaning behavior'' (e.g., Johnson and Ruben 1988). Direct evidence can be obtained only by observing such behavior, then capturing the cleaner fish and examining its gut contents for ectoparasites, scales, and mucus (e.g., Losey 1974). Gorlick (1984) studied the behavior of captive cleaner wrasses (*Labroides phthirophagus*). Periods of cleaning were longer and more frequent with parasitized hosts, compared with hosts that had been treated to remove their external parasites.

(84) Losey (1972) suggested that cleaning symbiosis may be mutualistic on coral reefs when infections or infestations are high, but perhaps represents commensalism or even parasitism at other times. See Chapter 9 for definitions of infection and infestation.

(85) Brockmann and Hailman (1976), Hobson (1969).

(86) Youngbluth (1968) found that juveniles of the cleaner wrasse *Labroides phthirophagus* can be maintained on unnatural diets in the laboratory, but adults cannot. Adults were considered obligate cleaners.

(87) Eibl-Eibesfeldt (1955) published an early description of this behavior in the trumpetfish. Having witnessed it, Collette and Talbot (1972) called it ''riding'' and suggested a camouflage function: ''[In the U.S. Virgin Islands] we observed trumpetfish 'riding' half over the back of a larger fish, such as a grouper, which was swimming over the reef. When suitable prey was below the pair of fish, the trumpetfish would suddenly shoot down past the fish behind which it had been camouflaged. Normally colored (brown or reddish brown) trumpetfish were observed 'riding' graysbys, *Epinephelus cruentatus*. Yellow phase trumpetfish were seen 'riding' over red and yellow Spanish hogfish, *Bodianus rufus*. This type of camouflage behavior, but with herbivorous parrotfishes instead of carnivorous groupers was photographed and discussed by Eibl-Eibesfeldt (1955: 216–217) at Bonaire.'' The trumpetfish I have observed ''riding'' Spanish hogfish at Bonaire were usually yellow, but some were brown.

(88) Parr (1927) claimed that milling behavior was unaffected by the size of the aquarium because ''. . . the length of the latter . . . was about ten times the diameter of the mill, which . . . was never found in the center of the tank but always close to the walls.'' Parr's observation actually shows the opposite: milling behavior in the chub mackerels he watched was a direct result of restricted space. Mackerels of all species tend to school, not mill. By selecting the outer perimeter of the aquarium in preference to the center, the fish used the greatest amount of linear space. In other words, they could swim forward in a school for the longest possible distance before being forced to turn.

(89) Levin et al. (1989) proposed that the orientation of fishes in a circular channel is affected by two mechanisms: (*1*) maintenance of a constant angle with the source of light and (*2*) an inertial guidance system that in nature ''. . . allows for straight course navigation by equating the amount of turns to the right and to the left.'' Levin and coauthors noted that an inertial guidance system would be zeroed with reference to the sun. After having been placed in a circular space, ''. . . the zero of the inertial mechanism would be adjusted to the curvature of the channel. Hence, fish would fix a random initial direction, and become unable to respond to a light change which demands a discrete double fold adjustment. Therefore, swimming would anchor in the original direction.'' Once the unique direction has been established, there is no response to changes in the angle of light.

(90) Levin et al. (1989) compared swimming orientation in two groups of a schooling characinid (*Cheirodon pulcher*). One group was placed in a circular channel and the other in a channel shaped like a figure eight. Fish in the circular channel swam in the same direction regardless of the angle of light (see Note 89). In contrast, fish in the figure-eight channel responded to light shifts, indicating that the angle of light took precedence over shape of the channel.

(91) Clarke et al. (1977).

(92) Casimir and Fricke (1971).

(93) Colin (1971, 1973) and Leong (1967) described burrows of the yellowhead jawfish. Colin's 1973 report is the most detailed. Elements of the text discussion came from all three sources, plus personal observation.

(94) Mounds of the sand tilefish were described briefly by Colin (1973) and in more detail by Clarke et al. (1977) and Clifton and Hunter (1972).

CHAPTER 7

(1) Cohen (1970) estimated that ~8000 species representing 40% of all known extant fishes inhabit warm, coastal regions. Most are found in association with coral reefs.

(2) Smith and Tyler (1972) treated a Virgin Islands patch reef that was 3 m in diameter with rotenone and recorded 75 species. Clarke (1977) obtained 53 to 55 species (two juveniles were identified only to genus) from a patch reef of 120 m^3 near Bimini, Bahamas, after treating it with rotenone. Detonation of a single explosive charge on a section of east African reef covered with a dense stand of hard corals (*Acropora* spp.) yielded 240 specimens of 66 species (Talbot 1965).

(3) This is the definition proposed by Smith and Tyler (1973b).

(4) For detailed treatment of the terms niche, habitat, biotope, and ecotope see Kulesza (1975), Udvardy (1959), and Whittaker et al. (1973, 1975). Whittaker et al. (1973) emphasized that niche does not connote a sense of place. In other words, niche is not a subdivision of habitat when the definition of habitat includes location. The concept of niche ". . . is a construct, one of a class of concepts not subject to direct observation but postulated to explain a range of observations. A niche is as much an attribute of a species as a personality (as expressed in interaction with others) is of a person. . . ."

(5) Proponents of at least some aspects of the resource specialist hypothesis include Abrams (1984), Anderson et al. (1981), Brock et al. (1979), Clarke (1977), Galzin and Legendre (1987), Gladfelter et al. (1980), Macpherson (1981), Ogden and Ebersole (1981), Robertson and Lassig (1980), Smith (1978), Smith and Tyler (1972, 1973a, 1973b, 1975), Smith (1979), and Thresher (1983).

(6) That species is *Acanthochromis polyacanthus*, a damselfish indigenous to the Indo-West Pacific. As reported by Robertson (1973), *A. polyacanthus* broods its larvae for perhaps 2 months. Afterward, the young disperse over the reef with no intermediate pelagic phase. Some damselfish species protect nests with eggs, but in all cases the newly hatched larvae rise immediately into the plankton.

(7) Proponents of at least some aspect of the resource generalist hypothesis include Ayal and Safriel (1982), Doherty (1982, 1983), Robertson et al. (1981), Sale (1974, 1975, 1977, 1978a, 1978b), Sale and Douglas (1984), Sale and Dybdahl (1975, 1978), Sale and Williams (1982), and Talbot et al. (1978). Sale (1978a, 1978b) referred to it as a "lottery" for living space because more

than one species can compete. Marliave (1985) pointed out that neither the resource specialist nor the resource generalist hypothesis questions the veracity of the central assumption that a great diversity of species actually exists on coral reefs. As Marliave suggested, perhaps there are fewer species than we think. If the central assumption of great species diversity is false, so are the postulates derived from it. Marliave noted that captive-reared offspring from a single pair of anemonefish (in this case *Amphiprion frenatus*) display different color polymorphs, a fact observed previously by others (see Marliave's report for references). The numerous species of anemonefishes that have been identified can perhaps be reduced to very few. Marliave reasoned that the same may be true of a substantial number of other "species." If so, he asked, "Is the reef-fish lottery rigged?"

(8) The guild concept was formulated by Root (1967).

(9) Critics have claimed that both hypotheses are valid in certain situations, or that neither is. The end of this note is a synopsis of a series of experiments in which neither hypothesis could be falsified. Greenfield and Greenfield (1982) observed habitat partitioning on a very fine scale by two West Indies clinids of the genus *Acanthemblemaria*. On the basis of their own study and the work of others the authors concluded that the resource generalist hypothesis may apply only to larger species. Kaufman and Ebersole (1984) claimed that coral reef fish communities are influenced by both deterministic and stochastic factors. In their opinion, strict adherence to either hypothesis results in a limited perspective. Instead, the focus should be ". . . on the morphological and behavioral features of fish species in relation to the microtopographic features of their environment." Shulman et al. (1983) observed elements of both hypotheses in a study of juvenile recruitment on artificial reefs in the U.S. Virgin Islands. Recruitment of three species of settling juveniles decreased significantly when adult territorial damselfish (beaugregories, *Stegastes leucostictus*) were in residence, and prior settlement of a juvenile predator (either mahogany or blackfin snappers (*Lutjanus mahogoni* and *L. buccanella*) lowered the rate of successful recruitment of two juvenile prey species. Shulman and coauthors wrote: "The first effect increases determinism in the structure of coral reef fish assemblages, while the second decreases their predictability." The conclusion: ". . . in unoccupied habitat (created by storms, mortality, changes in reef structure), the order of settlement, particularly of predators and prey, will partially determine composition of the initial assemblage; in occupied areas, resi-

dents are likely to determine which species can possibly invade, but within this group of 'permissible' invaders, order of settlement may determine which will successfully recruit into the habitat.''

Talbot et al. (1978) followed the recruitment of 64 species onto artificial reefs in the lagoon of One Tree Island, Great Barrier Reef, and concluded that ''. . . for most species, interspecific actions between adults and newly settling juveniles are unimportant. . . .'' Jones (1984) decided that neither hypothesis applied consistently to *Pseudolabrus celidotus*, a New Zealand temperate wrasse, in all habitats in which it is found. Brock et al. (1979) suggested that chance factors may explain colonization on a small scale but that entire coral reef ecotopes are regulated by deterministic factors. Bohnsack (1979) studied fish communities on Florida Keys patch reefs and predicted species turnover rates on the basis of island biogeographic theory (see MacArthur and Wilson 1967). Reefs examined after long intervals gave an impression of stability because most departures and arrivals were not detected. When examined after short intervals, the high turnover rates observed suggested instability.

Victor (1983) studied recruitment patterns of the bluehead wrasse (*Thalassoma bifasciatum*) onto a patch reef in the San Blas Islands, Panama. Bluehead wrasses spawn every day. Recruitment patterns bore no correlation with patterns of mortality on the reef, and the composition of the adult population was a direct reflection of juvenile recruitment from the previous year. Victor concluded that population fluxes are probably determined by the supply of recruits and not the amount of space or some other resource. In his opinion, rates of recruitment and reproduction are affected severely and unpredictably by factors in pelagic environments that influence survival of planktonic larvae.

Robertson and Lassig (1980) studied the distribution of six species of damselfishes that coexist on the Great Barrier Reef. The space occupied by one species consistently overlapped with the spaces of two others, and these three species formed guilds. Five species demonstrated varying degrees of space partitioning. The authors concluded that (*1*) in many habitats competition occurs regularly, (*2*) among competing species those that are dominant have priority to space, and (*3*) subordinate species persist because dominant ones do not saturate the habitat. The findings thus supported both deterministic and stochastic elements.

A popular experimental protocol involves removing or transplanting a known number of resident individuals from or to one or more small reefs or artificial reefs, then monitoring the subsequent recruitment rate of newly metamorphosed larvae. If space is a limiting factor, the recruitment rate offers a measure of which hypothesis—resource specialist or resource generalist—is the driving force. Representative of this genre are the experiments of Doherty (1982), Ogden and Ebersole (1981), Victor (1983), and Williams (1980). To give an idea of how the data are gathered and interpreted, a synopsis of one experiment is given below. Sale (1980) reviewed methods used for estimating species abundance in the field, and Ross (1986) summarized field methods for assessing space (habitat) partitioning.

In an experimental study, Williams (1980) monitored the recruitment dynamics in seven species of damselfishes (Pomacentridae) on 12 small adjacent patch reefs along the Great Barrier Reef. All adult damselfishes were removed from three of the reefs, all juveniles from three more, both juveniles and adults from three others, and the remaining three were left undisturbed to serve as controls. Recruitment was subsequently determined by counting newly metamorphosed larval damselfishes (which I shall refer to as juveniles) that appeared on each reef. In a parallel observational study, natural changes in damselfish populations were monitored on 66 undisturbed patch reefs and rubble patches in the same vicinity. The total observation period for both studies was 2.5 years.

Williams noted that because each reef in the experimental study differed in both indigenous species and the number of each, and different protocols were applied, the number of individuals removed initially was variable. If the settlement of juveniles were limited in some way by resident fishes, a correlation might exist between the number of fishes removed from a reef and later recruitment. In other words, recruitment should be lowest on the control reefs and greatest on reefs from which the most fishes had been removed. The data, however, showed no such correlation. The presence or absence of resident adult or juvenile damselfishes did not affect the recruitment rate. Some reefs had greater recruitment rates than nearby reefs that on superficial examination appeared similar. Thus the number of juveniles settling on one of these reefs in the first year should correlate positively with the number settling there the next year. The data did demonstrate a positive correlation, indicating the number of recruits to be nonrandom, but for reasons other than the densities of the resident populations. Moreover, a correlation between the size of a reef and its number of resident fishes was not seen. Finally, the numbers of juveniles recruited were low relative to the numbers of resident adults or juveniles removed.

Recruitment patterns were considered further in the observational study. The patch reefs and rubble patches were populated primarily by two species. For both, the number of juveniles recruited at a particular site showed good correlation from one year to the next. This suggested that if recruitment patterns were similar a positive correlation should be evident between recruitment of the two species in the same year, but this was not the case. Some sites had consistently high recruitment of both species, whereas in others the recruitment was consistently low. Still other sites showed differential rates of recruitment.

Williams' results are more complex than my brief summary indicates, but enough has been said to discuss some of the conclusions. Williams suggested that space limitations imposed on the damselfishes he observed might be manifested in two ways. Recruitment is inhibited by resident fishes, in which case recruitment rate would depend on space becoming available through death or departure of one or more resident fishes. Alternatively, percentage survival of new recruits may depend on the density of other fishes in the area. Nothing specific was said about the second possibility, but I presume Williams meant that these "other fishes" might represent competition for the same resources. Williams' data did not support either possibility. If a population of fishes on a reef is resource limited—regardless of the mechanism—the number of individuals should remain relatively constant, yet Williams found considerable temporal variation in the observational study. Moreover, stable population size alone is inadequate evidence of space limitation. Williams proposed instead that stable populations reflected in the low recruitment rates seen were barely sufficient to replace resident fishes and that this occurred independently of interactions with other damselfish species. Thus the recruitment rate was considered inadequate for damselfish populations to become resource limited. Such a scenario could account for the "relatively precarious balance" that was apparent in the observational study.

The resource specialist hypothesis is based on competitive exclusion. Because space is a limited resource, the use of space must be different for all species before they can coexist. The resource generalist hypothesis argues that although space limits the number of species, the composition of the community is regulated by chance recruitment. This depends on chance mortality or departure of at least some of the resident fishes. As a result, coexistence is possible even when resource use overlaps, as it does in guilds. Williams found no clear support for either hypothesis. Space apparently was of little importance in determining the number of individuals, and recruitment did not depend on interactions with resident fishes.

(10) The resource specialist and resource generalist hypotheses resemble models that have long served as cornerstones of terrestrial vertebrate ecology (for a synopsis of how terrestrial vertebrate communities are organized see Pianka 1978, pp. 271–304). The similarity has been largely ignored by researchers who have reported on coral reef fish communities. By not integrating their findings with mainstream ecology, they have allowed a subset of principles to evolve instead of a badly needed synthesis. Anderson et al. (1981) recognized the problem. They argued that communities of coral reef fishes differ little from communities of terrestrial vertebrates: "We do not imply that community theory has been well established in terrestrial vertebrate communities. What we do assert is that community theory is not automatically destined to be less successful with reef fish than with terrestrial vertebrate communities simply because reef fish and their larvae are under water."

The concept of resource specialization parallels models used to define competition among terrestrial vertebrates. Similarly, resource generalization could easily be mistaken for what terrestrial ecologists call rarefaction (defined below). Vertebrate populations of tropical rainforests are considered to be near maximum size as a result of keen intra- and interspecific competition. Selection for competitive ability (i.e., *k selection*; see MacArthur and Wilson 1967, pp. 68–69 and 149) is strong. Successful organisms exist within zones of competition in which they demonstrate superiority over competitors. Successful species specialize in some aspect of resource use to gain a competitive advantage. The overall effects are small niche size and great species diversity. For example, rainforest bird communities are more diverse than bird communities of temperate regions. This is attributed to four factors: (*1*) extreme variation in habitat structure, (*2*) the presence of numerous guilds, (*3*) larger guild niches buoyed by a broader spectrum of resources, and (*4*) tighter packing of species (Terborgh 1985). The same features describe coral reefs and their resident fish communities.

Rarefaction is the continuous, density-independent removal of organisms from a community. The competition and rarefaction hypotheses essentially are mutually exclusive in the same way that resource specialization and resource generalization appear incompatible. Rarefaction considers a community to be below saturation. Competition is reduced, and coexistence is possible without competitive exclusion of species. Accordingly, communities can exceed saturation in numbers of species because more can coexist than if the system were permitted to become saturated. Rarefaction occurs through environmental disturbances, predation, and other factors proposed by the resource generalist hypothesis.

(11) Milliman (1973).

(12) This discussion is based mainly on Ladd (1977). The origin of fringing reefs, barrier reefs, and atolls was discussed by Steers and Stoddart (1977).

(13) Hopley (1982, pp. 384–386).

(14) Reef structure and the diversity of hermatypic corals are affected strongly by water movement and other factors listed in the text. Stoddart (1973) emphasized that the reef structure itself affects water movement, rendering causal relationships difficult to discern. Inevitably, descriptive accounts of coral reefs vary greatly, and a ''typical'' coral reef—not to mention a ''typical'' vertical zone—does not exist. The chapters edited by Jones and Endean (1973) attest to the immense variability of coral reefs. The problem of adequate description is worsened by casual use of the few generic terms available. To avoid muddying the situation more than necessary, I largely adopted the simplified terminology proposed by Tracy et al. (1955). For examples of more diversified terminology see Bouchon et al. (1981), Burke (1982), Dustan (1985), Goreau (1959), Hopley (1982, pp. 247–397), Lang (1974), Pichon (1981), and Stearn et al. (1977).

(15) Shinn (1963), Shinn et al. (1981).

(16) Glynn (1973) discovered well developed algal ridges on reefs of eastern Panama, disproving the earlier view that they are absent in the West Indies. Also see Hopley (1982, pp. 395–396).

(17) The discussion of patch reef formation in the Florida Keys is based on Jones (1977). Maxwell and Swinchatt (1970) speculated on the origin of patch reefs in the Great Barrier Reef system.

(18) Alcyonarians grow profusely in the West Indies, but are less abundant in the Indo-West Pacific (Hopley 1982, p. 395).

(19) The discussion of dome patch reef formation is based on Smith and Tyler (1975).

(20) To my knowledge, this point has been mentioned only by Edwards and Rosewell (1981).

(21) See Gladfelter et al. (1980), but before accepting their conclusions read Shulman's criticisms of the statistical methods used (Shulman 1983).

(22) These are the designations listed by Luckhurst and Luckhurst (1978b), except for open areas of the reef near particular landmarks, which is my addition. Grunts (Haemulidae) and snappers (Lutjanidae) in the West Indies are nocturnal feeders and often found in the same locations during the day. These are commonly open sites, rather than caves, crevices, or ledges.

(23) Randall (1963) was among the first to relate structural and surface features of coral reefs with the diversity and abundance of fish species. Others have since confirmed it (e.g., Alevizon and Brooks 1975; Gladfelter and Gladfelter 1978; Gladfelter et al. 1980; Goldman and Talbot 1976; Gosline 1965; Grovhoug and Henderson 1978; Jones and Chase 1975; Luckhurst and Luckhurst 1978a, 1978c; Risk 1972; Talbot 1965; Talbot and Goldman 1972).

(24) Gladfelter et al. (1980) showed that species diversity in patch-reef fish communities at Enewetak Atoll and St. Croix, U.S. Virgin Islands, correlates positively with certain morphological features of the reef. Species richness (number of species) at St. Croix correlates well with reef surface area, reef surface complexity, and reef height in that order. At Enewetak Atoll good correlation was seen only with surface complexity. Molles (1978) investigated patch reefs in the Gulf of California. Substratum complexity did not correlate positively with either species diversity or abundance. In most cases reef height showed positive correlation with both factors. Alevizon and Brooks (1975) compared the fish populations at Key Largo, Florida, and Islas las Aves, Venezuela. Key Largo reefs had more species and larger populations. This was attributed partly to the more substantial coral development at the Key Largo sites. Bell and Galzin (1984) found a strong positive correlation between live coral cover and both species richness and species abundance (numbers of individuals) on a reef in French Polynesia. Changes in live coral cover of <2% produced significant increases in both parameters; changes of 2% to <5% increased species richness significantly.

Risk (1972) collected data from a patch reef in the U.S. Virgin Islands. He wrote: ''It is interesting that there is no significant correlation between fish species diversity [richness] and the biological nature of the substrate; the choice [by fishes] . . . would seem to be controlled by predation pressure, rather than feeding preferences. There is also no significant positive correlation between total numbers of fishes and either substrate topographic complexity or substrate biological diversity; the relationship does not appear to be a simple one of 'more holes, more fish.' '' Sale and Douglas (1984) studied several structural characteristics of lagoon patch reefs at One Tree Island, Great Barrier Reef: (*1*) surface area, (*2*) volume, (*3*) maximum height, (*4*) mean reef diameter, (*5*) substratum diversity, (*6*) topographic complexity, and (*7*) percentage of cover. The last factor was measured in terms of branched hard corals, massive hard corals, sponges, and bare or algae covered rock surfaces. Gross surface area could be used most consistently to predict fish density. This factor, plus the percentage of cover provided by bare or algae covered rock surfaces, most closely predicted the number of species. The conclusion: ". . . topographic complexity is not a useful predictor of the species richness of reef fish assemblages on patch reefs at One Tree Reef. Substratum diversity appears a similarly weak predictor. Percent bare or algae-covered rock, however, does significantly assist in predicting total species richness."

Luckhurst and Luckhurst (1978a) investigated the fish community of a fringing reef at Curacao, Netherlands Antilles, and found poor correlation between species richness and abundance and the percentage of substratum covered by corals, although good correlation was obtained when substratum complexity was used as the reef structural parameter. They concluded that ". . . substrate complexity . . . provides a greater diversity of shelter sites, thus enhancing [fish] species richness. . . . This relationship may not be valid for a single-species coral stand because of the limited diversity of shelter sites. . . ."

When artificial reefs have been assembled in tropical waters, no relationship has been discerned between structure (e.g., sizes of holes) and species composition of the fishes that are subsequently attracted (Molles 1978, Ogden and Ebersole 1981, Randall 1963, Talbot et al. 1978), although the same generality does not always hold true for artificial reefs in temperate waters (Gascon and Miller 1982). It has been presumed that temperate fish populations exist well below steady state levels, or at densities too low for competitive interactions to be important (Gascon and Miller 1982).

(25) Goldman and Talbot (1976).

(26) Several authors (e.g., Luckhurst and Luckhurst 1978b) have employed the terms "partitioning" and "sharing" interchangeably, but I believe a distinction is warranted. Partitioning to me implies exclusion; sharing suggests species overlap and dual- or multiple-species use of the same space.

(27) Luckhurst and Luckhurst (1978c) reported seeing the same creole wrasses (*Clepticus parrai*), which they suggested were the same individuals, sheltering consistently in a reef crevice in

Curacao, Netherlands Antilles, over a period of 5 months. Collette and Talbot (1972) found C. *parrai* sheltering at night several times over a period of 2 weeks in the U.S. Virgin Islands. Bluehead wrasses have been reported returning to the same sponge at night (Luckhurst and Luckhurst 1978c, Smith and Tyler 1972, Tyler and Böhlke 1972).

CHAPTER 8

(1) According to Spotte et al. (1985), all seawater fishes that can be maintained in captivity—without exception—accept animal matter. Weatherley and Gill (1987, p. 25) wrote: "The natural diet of carnivorous and herbivorous fish is quite different but in culture situations both types of fish can utilize similar ingredients in formulated diets and grow well."

(2) Because nitrogen is the key element in proteins, the most common way of determining the protein content of a food is by measuring total nitrogen, ordinarily by the Kjeldahl method. It is usually assumed that the nitrogen content of proteins is 16%, but this varies within wide limits (15 to 19%). Total protein is obtained by multiplying the nitrogen value determined in the laboratory by the standard factor 6.25 (i.e., 100/16).

(3) This statement is based on Wilson (1985); for earlier summaries see Cowey and Sargent (1979) and Ketola (1982).

(4) Cowey and Sargent (1977) suggested that most lipids probably can be assimilated by fishes, with the nutrient value being limited by factors other than digestibility (i.e., ease of dissolution of the food). For reviews of fatty acid metabolism and dietary requirements in fishes see Castell (1979), Cowey and Sargent (1977, 1979), Henderson and Sargent (1985), Kanazawa (1985), Leger (1985), Sargent et al. (1989), and Watanabe (1982).

(5) Cowey and Sargent (1979) pointed out that most foods of freshwater fishes originate from terrestrial sources. In their opinion this may account for the differences in PUFA composition between freshwater and seawater fishes. Linoleic acid ($18{:}2\omega6$) and arachidonic acid ($20{:}4\omega6$) are the main PUFAs of terrestrial animals. In contrast, most fatty acids of seawater animals and plants are of the $\omega3$ type (Ackman 1964, Lovern 1964, Sargent et al. 1989, Sidwell 1981). The information available indicates that seawater fishes require long-chain PUFAs, whereas some freshwater teleosts need both short- and long-chain PUFAs (Watanabe 1982). A large body of knowledge is accu-

mulating on the EFA requirements of a few fishes of commercial value, and evidence suggests critical differences among species, even those that are closely related (e.g., the salmonids). Whether any of the data are applicable to even a single, noncommercial species of the hundreds kept routinely in public aquarium exhibits is not known.

(6) The capacity to chain-elongate PUFAs is found in teleosts of both freshwater and seawater origin (Castell 1979; Cowey and Sargent 1977, 1979; Watanabe 1982). According to preliminary evidence (Fujii et al. 1976), seawater fishes may be less adept at such conversions than freshwater species. In the common carp, rainbow trout, Japanese eel, and ayu (*Plecoglossus altivelis*) the concentration of $20{:}5\omega3$ increases when $18{:}3\omega3$ is the dietary lipid, which is interpreted as evidence of chain elongation. However, the conversion does not occur under the same circumstances in plaice (*Pleuronectes platessa*), as demonstrated by Owen et al. (1972), or in the red seabream (Fujii et al. 1976) and turbot (Cowey et al. 1976, Owen et al. 1975).

(7) Sinclair (1964) argued that the word ''glucose,'' introduced about 1840, should have been ''glycose'' because the Greek upsilon becomes ''y'' in English. He stated: ''It is time that an international conference of senile professors pronounce authoritatively that glucose should be called glycose; much more radical and less intelligent changes in anatomical nomenclature are made every few years.''

(8) Furuichi and Yone (1980) showed that the yellowtail (*Seriola quinqueradiata*), an obligate carnivore, uses 10% of total carbohydrate supplied in the diet as complex sugars (olio- and polysaccharides). The seabass (*Dicentrarchus labrax*) demonstrates some protein sparing action (defined in the text) when carbohydrate is added to the diet, but high concentrations result in poor growth and elevated liver glycogen (Alliot et al. 1979).

(9) Common carp, rainbow trout (*Oncorhynchus mykiss*), and channel catfish tolerate 25 to 40% of the total dietary energy as carbohydrate (Brett and Groves 1979, Page and Andrews 1973). Red seabream (*Chrysophyrys major*) use glucose, dextrin AH, and dextrin E efficiently during growth, but dextrin H and α-potato starch are used less efficiently (Furuichi and Yone 1971). When common carp are starved, tissue stores of lipid are used in preference to carbohydrate (Nagai and Ikeda 1971a).

The capacity of herbivorous and omnivorous species to use dietary carbohydrate may depend on whether sufficient protein is also available. If protein is insufficient, EFA depletion may result. Csengeri et al. (1979) reported that common carp fed protein and vegetable oil (30 and 13.5%, respectively) grew normally and deposited linolenic acid in the liver. Those fed diets low in protein (7.7 to 13.7%) and lipids (3.4 to 3.7%), but high in carbohydrate (81 to 87%), had increased levels of oleic acid and intensive desaturation of linoleic acid to arachidonic acid (20:4ω6) and decosapentenoic acid (22:5ω6). (In my opinion, desaturation seems inconsistent with chain-elongation.) The authors concluded that diets rich in carbohydrate and poor in linolenic acid increased the rate of oleic acid synthesis, resulting in low PUFA content of the liver. Common carp on a low linolenic acid diet accumulated a high proportion of eicosatrienoic acid in their tissue lipids and were probably in early stages of EFA deficiency.

Nagai and Ikeda (1971a, 1971b) established that common carp do not require carbohydrate as a primary energy source. Common carp were maintained on diets containing different proportions of protein and glucose. When the diet contained >50% protein, glucose oxidation decreased markedly. A subsequent study (Nagai and Ikeda 1971c) revealed that amino acids are used in preference to glucose as sources of energy.

(10) Lipids are metabolized preferentially to carbohydrates when both are included in the diet (Brett and Groves 1979, Cowey and Sargent 1979).

(11) Simpson et al. (1981).

(12) This is a strictly practical definition and admittedly incomplete. Pigmentation is not always visible. In some crustaceans, for example, the red coloration is masked and the living animal appears green, brown, or blue. This is because the carotenoids are bound chemically with proteins. When the animal is dropped into boiling water the protein complex is destroyed, and the shell becomes red. The carotenoids can be extracted by placing a piece of the shell in alcohol or some other lipid solvent.

(13) Liaaen-Jensen (1978), Tanaka (1978).

(14) Katsuyama et al. (1987), Matsuno et al. (1985), Tanaka (1978).

(15) Liaaen-Jensen (1978).

(16) Katayama et al. (1973) made this statement; also see Meyers and Chen (1982), Simpson (1982), and Simpson and Kamata (1979). In their Figure 1, Meyers and Chen (1982) showed canthaxanthin as being deposited directly in both Class 1 and Class

2 fishes. In his discussion of the subject, Simpson (1982) omitted any mention of canthaxanthin.

(17) Rey (1975).

(18) Liou and Simpson (1989).

(19) Sloberg (1979).

(20) Young common carp and channel catfish reportedly are unable to assimilate FAAs when the diet is devoid of crude protein, amino acid deficient, or unbalanced (Andrews and Page 1974, Andrews et al. 1977, Aoe et al. 1970, Dupree and Halver 1970, Nose et al. 1974).

(21) This is accomplished by measuring chitinous nitrogen, subtracting the value from total nitrogen, and multiplying by the standard factor 6.25 to obtain corrected crude protein. Often the difference is substantial. In the two shrimp meal samples given in Table 8-21, corrected crude protein values were 28.5 (dehydrated) and 47.8 (sun-dried), as shown by Meyers et al. (1973).

(22) For a concise description of how proteins can be a source of calories see Weatherley and Gill (1987, pp. 32–36).

(23) Gerking (1971), Weatherley and Gill (1987, p. 34).

(24) Schauer and Simpson (1979) reported that deposition of tissue lipid in captive Atlantic silversides (*Menidia menidia*) increased drastically when tissue concentrations of the essential fatty acid 22:6ω3 declined to 1.95% of the total fatty acid concentration. They suggested that lipid storage is related to a minimum level of 22:6ω3, and that ". . . a mechanism may exist which enhances the absorption and deposition of lipids to ensure minimal 22:6ω3 tissue levels." Thus excessive fat deposition in captive seawater fishes cannot be considered entirely in terms of too much dietary lipid; the type of lipid fed (i.e., the amount of EFAs) appears to affect fat deposition substantially.

(25) NAS/NRC (1983).

(26) Katayama et al. (1965) observed that red seabreams reared in captivity were nearly devoid of the red coloration characteristic of wild fish. Loss of coloration was attributable to the small concentration of astaxanthin. Enhancement of normal coloration has been reported in several species fed carotenoids from different sources. Examples include the pearl gourami (*Trichogaster leeri*) fed dry flake feeds containing canthaxanthin (Fey and Meyers 1980) and astaxanthin (Meyers and Thibodeaux 1983), brook trout (*Salvelinus fontinalis*) fed shrimp and crab

wastes (Saito and Regier 1971) and crawfish wastes (Peterson et al. 1966), red seabream fed frozen krill and mysids (Ibrahim et al. 1984) and astaxanthin diester purified from krill oil (Fujita et al. 1983), and "fancy carp" fed astaxanthin (Iwahashi and Wakui 1976).

(27) Salmonids with pink flesh are more marketable than those with pale flesh. Recent work by food scientists involved in aquaculture has dealt with ways to enhance flesh coloration of salmonids by addition of carotenoids to feeds (Bauernfeind 1976; Choubert and Storebakken 1989; Ellis 1979; Foss et al. 1984, 1987; Harris 1984; Inoue et al. 1988; Kuo et al. 1976; Mori et al. 1989; Peterson et al. 1966; Schmidt and Baker 1969; Simpson 1973; Simpson and Chichester 1981; Simpson and Kamata 1979; Storebakken et al. 1986, 1987; Torrissen 1985; Torrissen and Braekkan 1979; Torrissen et al. 1981/1982). Much of the information, however, applies only to salmonids. Few other fishes deposit carotenoids so extensively in the muscle tissue.

(28) Meyers and Chen (1982).

(29) Some authors include all items listed in Table 8-23 with the *natural gums*, which is incorrect. Chitin is a nitrogenous carbohydrate in the shells of arthropods. Gelatin is a derivative of collagen, the most abundant protein in the animal kingdom. *Collagen* constitutes most of the white fiber in connective tissues of animals and is obtained industrially by hydrolyzing and boiling the skins, muscles, and tendons of domestic animals. Natural gums are carbohydrates exclusively and occur as exudates of various trees and shrubs, or as complex colloidal compounds in algae. Thus animal products are not properly called gums (Hawley 1977).

(30) The terms alginic acid, algin, and alginate are used loosely and interchangeably by many authors. I prefer the distinctions drawn by Hoppe and Schmid (1969). To them *alginic acid* is the raw substance obtained from kelp. *Alginates* are salts of alginic acid and therefore derivatives. *Algin* is a name applied collectively to alginic acid and alginates.

(31) Alginic acid can be processed into a number of salts (e.g., calcium, sodium, potassium). Sodium and potassium alginates are the most soluble; of these, sodium alginate is the more available.

(32) The term *sol* is synonymous with *colloidal suspension*. A *gel* is a slightly rigid colloid system. To precipitate a sol and form a gel all that is required is addition of an electrolyte (salt, acid, or base). The process is reversible, and most precipitated gels

can be resuspended by placing them in water and extracting the adsorbed electrolytes by dialysis (West et al. 1966).

A *suspension* is a two-phase (heterogeneous) system consisting of a solid dispersed in another solid or fluid. In coarse suspensions the particles of solid are visible, although a microscope may be required. If undisturbed they eventually settle to the bottom of the vessel. If the particles are subdivided to the molecular or elemental level they become invisible and do not settle. The result is a single-phase (homogeneous) system or *solution*. Between coarse suspensions and true solutions is a transitional phase from heterogeneity to homogeneity. In this region the particles are too small to be seen but not small enough to form a solution. This is the *colloidal state,* and sols and gels are *colloids*. When gelatin or sodium alginate is dispersed in water the result is properly called a suspension, not a solution, because the material is not actually dissolved.

Viscosity is the resistance experienced by one layer of a liquid in moving over another layer. Liquids such as ether and gasoline have little (i.e., low) viscosity and are very mobile; the viscosities of honey and tar are high. When alginates and similar substances are suspended in water they are sols and still fluid, and their viscosities are relatively low. Once they ''harden'' and turn into gels their viscosities become so high that they can be made to flow only under pressure. Reference to viscosities of different binders in the fish nutrition literature has limited importance because binders are fed as gels, not sols, and the gelling properties of a binder are what matter.

(33) Goldblatt et al. (1979) emphasized that stability of a feed is not a measure of its capacity to retain nutrients. A feed can remain firm after immersion in water, but leak important nutrients freely. Goldblatt and coauthors reported that substantial amounts of amino acids added as FAAs were lost rapidly from test feeds submerged for 2 h. Leaching of FAAs is apparently more serious when these are added to moist feeds in the free form rather than in the form of crude protein. This is seldom troublesome because aquarists expect feeds to be consumed within minutes of being immersed, not hours.

The amount of ascorbic acid lost from experimental feeds (presumably dry) depends on time of immersion, storage temperature, exposure to light during storage, and the chemical form of the vitamin (Soliman et al. 1987). Percentage retention can be increased by raising the concentration of ascorbic acid in the feed, storage of feed at temperatures below freezing, and packaging feeds in light-proof containers. Soliman and coauthors found ascorbic acid 2-sulfate (AA2S) and glyceride-coated ascorbic acid (GCAA) to be more stable than ascorbic acid and its sodium salt. Ascorbic acid as GCAA proved to be the most stable chemical form.

(34) Goldblatt et al. (1980) demonstrated that losses of riboflavin and choline could be reduced by encapsulating dry feeds with ethyl cellulose. Substantial losses of ascorbic acid still occurred, although the loss was less than in unencapsulated control feeds.

(35) The survival of individual fishes fed only natural and prepared foods is not evidence of nutritional parity with live foods, and the subject is not controversial among fish culturists. To quote Beck (1979a): "It appears there are no published studies of marine fishes where growth or survival of fish was superior or equal on artificial or non-living diets to those reared on live natural foods." Also see Adron et al. (1973), Beck (1979b), Beck and Bengston (1979), Beck and Simpson (1979), Bengston et al. (1978), Colesante (1989), Ehrlich et al. (1989), Flüchter (1980), Kirk (1972), Marliave (1989), Schauer and Simpson (1979), and Seidel et al. (1980b).

(36) Several authors have reported inferior growth and survival of larval fishes on diets of frozen and freeze-dried zooplankton, including brine shrimp. Two factors apparently are responsible: (*1*) adverse changes during freezing and freeze-drying that reduce available nutrients and (*2*) additional loss of nutrients or nutrient conversion activity when the foods are immersed in water. The second factor is especially interesting. K. L. Simpson (in Beck and Simpson 1979) postulated that the ". . . live food is being digested within itself as well as on the surface by enzymes in the live food." Flüchter (1980) observed that slowly frozen brine shrimp are poor food, whereas those that have been quick-frozen retain nutrient elements essential to larval whitefish (*Coregonus* spp.) These *proteolytic enzymes* or *proteases* catalyze the cleavage of peptide bonds in other proteins (Neurath 1984). They serve many physiological functions in addition to generalized protein digestion (also see Dabrowski and Glogowski 1977). When frozen or freeze-dried zooplankton are immersed in water, proteolytic enzyme activity is lost rapidly (Grabner et al. 1981/1982).

(37) Use of the term "egg" is incorrect. The structure is a dormant *blastula* or *gastrula* (arrested stages of early embryonic development) and properly called a *cyst* or *resting egg* (Bagshaw 1979, Nash 1973).

(38) Sorgeloos (1979) published a list of harvesters and distributors of brine shrimp cysts worldwide.

(39) Bowen (1962).

(40) Simpson (1979).

(41) Croghan (1958b).

(42) Barigozzi (1980) stated that the binomial *Artemia salina* no longer has taxonomic validity, except in reference to brine shrimp collected from salt ponds in Lymington, England, in the eighteenth century. These were the type specimens to which the name was given. The Lymington salt ponds have since disappeared, and no brine shrimp occur in England. The type species (*A. salina*) is extinct. Bowen et al. (1980), however, recognized the name *Artemia salina* and considered its use with extant brine shrimps permissible as a general designation when further subdivision is unnecessary or unimportant. In their view, *Artemia salina* is not one species but a complex of sibling species. At least five sibling species were recognized in a later paper (Bowen et al. 1985): *Artemia franciscana* (native to North and Central America), *A. persimilia* (Argentina), *A. tunisiana* (Mediterranean salterns), *A. urmiana* (Iran), and *A. parthenogenetica* (Europe, Asia, and Australia).

(43) Dempster (1953), Jenné (1960), Seale (1933).

(44) Sorgeloos (1980).

(45) The degree to which the nutrient composition of brine shrimp is affected by diet is unclear. Most studies have compared fatty acid patterns of nauplii with those of their different food sources. Claus et al. (1979) reported the relationship to be direct (i.e., nauplii used in their experiments assumed a fatty acid pattern similar to that of the food source). Fujita et al. (1980) and Watanabe et al. (1978b) stated that nauplii deficient in a fatty acid known to be essential to seawater fishes could be "enriched" by feeding them marine algae (*Chlorella*) or baker's yeast (*Saccharomyces cerevisiae*) mixed with squid liver oil. Hinchcliffe and Riley (1972), however, observed little resemblance in fatty acid pattern between nauplii and their food sources. These authors found *Artemia* to be flexible in its ability to modify dietary fatty acids and incorporate altered forms into the tissues. They wrote: "It is suggested that the metabolic requirements of the [brine] shrimps is of at least equal importance to the composition of their food in determining the component fatty-acid distribution of their lipids." These disparate findings reinforce how difficult it would be to consistently modify the nutrient composition of brine shrimp by manipulating dietary components. Claus et al. (1977), for example, showed that the fatty acid pattern of nauplii even depends on the environmental and nutritional conditions under which the cysts were produced.

Gozalbo and Amat (1988) reported on the compositions of five *Artemia* strains. They found no relationship between composition and mode of sexual reproduction (e.g., ovoviviparous), geographical origin, or ploidy (e.g., parthogenetic diploid) and concluded that environmental conditions affect nutrient composition the most. Food was not mentioned specifically.

(46) Some brine shrimp appear superior to others in terms of nutrient concentration, but again most assessments have been based mainly on fatty acid patterns. Schauer et al. (1980) determined the fatty acid composition of newly hatched nauplii of different origin. The cysts were obtained from Australia, Brazil, San Francisco Bay (batch numbers 313 and 321), San Pablo Bay (batch number 1628), Great Salt Lake, and Italy. Only the Australian and Brazilian nauplii contained detectable concentrations of 22:6ω3, but all had adequate amounts of 20:5ω3. Both fatty acids are essential to seawater fishes. Deficiencies in EFAs probably are unimportant when brine shrimp nauplii are used as a supplementary food for aquarium fishes. In aquaculture they can be critical because nauplii are often the only source of food. Fujita et al. (1980), for example, fed EFA-deficient nauplii to larval red seabream and observed heavy mortalities. Based on this experience they concluded: ". . . the nutritional value of *Artemia* should be determined in terms of EFA content." More recently, Léger et al. (1987) altered the fatty-acid profiles of brine shrimp nauplii by feeding them foods enriched with oils (e.g., rice bran coated with cod liver oil). Similar products are now available commercially. Léger et al. (1986) reviewed nutrient enhancement of brine shrimp nauplii.

Seidel et al. (1980a) analyzed amino acids of newly hatched nauplii from five regions of the world: Australia, Brazil, San Pablo Bay (California), Great Salt Lake (Utah), and Italy. In the estimation of the authors, no amino acid was so low as to be limiting in the diets of cultured fishes or invertebrates. In contrast, Watanabe et al. (1978a) discovered a batch of newly hatched nauplii low in threonine.

(47) The number of molts depends on salinity. Heath (1924) reported 13 molts in brine shrimp collected from the wild (San Francisco Bay), each representing a different stage of development. Water temperature at the collection site was not stated, but the "specific gravity" was 1.086. Weisz (1946) studied the effect of a range of specific gravities (1.022, 1.033, 1.047, 1.066, and 1.085) on number of molts in brine shrimp cultured from commercially available cysts (source unstated). He observed a range of 12 to 16 molts between hatching and maturity at a specific gravity of 1.085 in water of 21 to 22°C, which agrees with

the findings of Heath (1924). However, brine shrimp reared in water of 1.022 at the same temperature underwent 25 to 29 molts. Molting frequency decreased gradually with increasing specific gravity. Weisz (1946) noted that 13 molts, each representing a developmental stage, is valid only at a specific gravity near 1.085.

(48) After each molt a nauplius acquires additional chitin and increases in length; if it is starved, the result is an increase in the ratio of inert material (chitin) to organic (nutrient) matter and a concomitant decrease in food value. This has been confirmed in nutrient analyses performed by Benijts et al. (1976) on dried San Francisco Bay nauplii before and after the first molt. Dry body mass decreased 20% (caused by less organic matter), and ash mass (inorganic matter) increased 87% (Table 8-25). In other words, a fish fed stage 2 larvae would have to ingest 20% more by dry mass than another fish fed only stage 1 nauplii to obtain the equivalent nutrient value. The caloric value of the organic portion decreased 4% after the first molt. Total lipid concentration (the major source of calories) decreased 29% and total fatty acids dropped 26%. In individual nauplii the decrease in lipids alone represents 60% of the total decrease in energy value after the first molt. Claus et al. (1979) reported that the ash content of San Francisco Bay nauplii starved for the first 48 h doubled (8.17 to 19.97% of dry body mass). The ash content of Great Salt Lake nauplii increased 40% (9.52 to 13.29% of dry body mass). Carbohydrates and lipids decreased in both strains. In larvae that were fed, the organic content exceeded the increase in organic matter, and the percentage of ash was lower. Obviously, brine shrimp not meant to be reared to maturity should be used soon, preferably within the first 24 h of hatching.

(49) References in Sorgeloos and Persoone (1975).

(50) Sato (1967).

(51) Survival of San Francisco Bay nauplii exceeds 90% through a wide range of temperatures and salinities. Survival is primarily temperature dependent (e.g., at 30°C survival rate is constant between salinity values of 20 and 60‰). Conditions for holding or rearing Great Salt Lake nauplii are different: there is, for example, a negative effect of increasing temperature on survival, but this is offset by increasing salinity. The Great Salt Lake strain, in other words, prefers higher salinities than the strain from San Francisco Bay (Sorgeloos et al. 1976).

(52) Information in the text is from Sorgeloos and Persoone (1975). Also see Sorgeloos (1973) and van der Linden et al. (1985, 1988).

(53) Croghan (1958a).

(54) Sodium chloride is essential, but calcium chloride, $CaCl_2$, and sodium bicarbonate, $NaHCO_3$, promote hatching. Calcium chloride promotes hatching effectively only in combination with $NaHCO_3$, but the reverse is not true (Sato 1967). There can be little doubt that the presence of other ions makes seawater a better hatch solution than brine.

(55) Boone and Bass-Becking (1931).

(56) Morris (1971).

(57) Sorgeloos et al. (1976).

(58) As an example, in the past some cysts marketed as originating from San Francisco Bay actually came from San Pablo Bay, and hatching characteristics of the two strains differ (Sorgeloos 1980).

(59) Okamoto et al. (1987).

(60) Yamasaki et al. (1987).

(61) Schlüter and Groeneweg (1985) reported that free ammonia nitrogen (NH_3-N) concentrations of 3 to 5 mg/L caused a decline in the reproductive rate of *Brachionus rubens*. Raising the concentration to >5 mg NH_3-N/L for 2 d killed the cultures. According to Lincoln et al. (1983), rotifer infestations can be eliminated from ponds by temporarily raising the concentration of NH_3-N (added as ammonium hydroxide, NH_4OH) to 20 mg/L. Snell et al. (1987) developed a test for the effect of environmental stress factors based on the degree of swimming activity of rotifers across a grid. The effective concentration, EC_{50} (the concentration that reduced swimming activity to 50% of the untreated controls) was 2.3 mg NH_3-N/L. After exposure to 10 mg NH_3-N/L for 10 min, swimming activity was reduced 16%. The 24-h LC_{50} value (the concentration at which 50% of the test animals died) was 20.4 mg NH_3-N/L.

(62) Lubzens et al. (1985) and Minkoff et al. (1984/1985) described effects of salinity on the reproductive rate of *Brachionus plicatilis*; Hino and Hirano (1988) reported a *chlorinity* (total chlorine per kilogram of seawater) effect. Gatesoupe and Luquet (1981) did not see any detrimental effect of seawater on reproduction in *B. plicatilis*.

(63) Serra and Miracle (1987).

(64) Hirayama and Kusano (1972) reported this effect. Optimal temperature range for the culture of *Brachionus plicatilis* is 20 to 24°C (Hirata 1974, Schlosser and Anger 1982), but suitable re-

sults can be obtained between 18 and 23°C (Anderson and Smith 1983).

(65) Hirata (1974) reported a negative relationship between food uptake and rotifer density. Schlosser and Anger (1982) saw no negative effects at rotifer densities up to 1000/mL.

(66) Scott and Baynes (1978).

(67) Hino and Hirano (1984).

(68) Hirayama et al. (1973).

(69) Discriminatory feeding by *Brachionus plicatilis* is based on particle size (Hino and Hirano 1984) and type and condition of the food (Chotiyaputta and Hirayama 1978, Lubzens and Minkoff 1988). These and numerous other factors, some mentioned in the preceding notes, affect the rates of filtration and ingestion (Hirayama and Ogawa 1972) and ultimately the growth and nutrient composition of adult rotifers. Not surprisingly, experiments designed to demonstrate optimal foods and food densities have yielded disparate results. Scott and Baynes (1978) fed rotifers with four species of live phytoplankton. Differences in the test factors (growth rate, body mass, and levels of total protein, carbohydrate, and lipid) attributable to the species of algae used were minor. Hirayama and Nakamura (1976) found that a live seawater clone of *Chlorella* (Chlorophyceae) produced better growth than dried *Chlorella* powder, and that both were superior to living caked yeast (*Rhodotorula* sp.). Hirayama and Watanabe (1973) reported similar results. Segner et al. (1984) published an indirect comparison of the nutrient value of rotifers cultured with three species of phytoplankton. Milkfish (*Chanos chanos*) fry fed with the rotifers were later sacrificed, and liver hepatocytes were used as an index of nutritional status. Best results were obtained with *Isochrysis galbana* (Prymnesiophyceae), followed by *Platymonas* sp. (= *Tetraselmis* sp., Chlorophyceae). *Chlorella* of marine origin yielded the poorest results. Gatesoupe and Luquet (1981) substituted a combined diet of prepared food and freeze-dried phytoplankton for live phytoplankton and observed good population growth.

(70) Procedures in this section are from Spotte et al. (1985). Moist feeds were described several times in the edited volumes of Halver and Tiews (1979a, 1979b). Also see Fowler and Burrows (1971), Kellems and Sinnhuber (1982), Peterson et al. (1967), Quick (1982), and Roa et al. (1982). Spotte et al. (1985) recommended against using moist feed formulas designed for aquatic invertebrates, because many contain high carbohydrate concentrations. The compound *p*-aminobenzoic acid (often ab-

breviated as PABA) is a constituent of pantothenic acid. It is not known to be required by any species of fish (Halver 1985, 1989).

(71) Sorgeloos and Persoone (1975) noted that brine shrimp nauplii are sensitive to vigorous aeration (many are injured) and stated that a rate of 1 L/min of air is sufficient. No data to substantiate this claim were provided.

(72) The method is from Sorgeloos et al. (1983). Light stimulates embryonic development of *Artemia* resting cysts (Sorgeloos 1973). After wetting and subsequent exposure to light, the time of hatch varies by geographic origin (Vanhaecke et al. 1981) and also depends on the wavelength and intensity of the light source (van der Linden et al. 1985). The last authors reported that wavelengths between 400 and 600 nm (characteristic of fluorescent lamps; Fig. 10-13) are the most effective. San Pablo Bay (California) cysts hatch best after exposure to light intensities of 100 to 500 lx (Vanhaecke et al. 1981).

(73) Nash (1973) estimated the number of San Francisco Bay cysts at 300,000/g and reported that cysts from other regions (sources unstated) were ~275,000/g. Spotte et al. (1984b) weighed 30 replicates of San Francisco Bay cysts from a single lot to 0.01 mg. The mean mass of a single cyst was 2.597 μg ($\pm$ 0.040 μg, 95% confidence interval).

(74) Sorgeloos and Persoone (1975) reviewed some of the problems of using horizontal hatchers and remarked that because of their poorer performance maximum cyst densities are generally less than in vertical types, ranging from 0.3 to 1 g/L.

(75) Decapsulation oxidizes only the tertiary envelope because it is composed of lipoprotein complexes (Brown 1950). The embryonic cuticle beneath is chitinous and resistant to hypochlorite (Linder 1960). Spotte and Anderson (1988, 1989) reviewed decapsulation of anostracan cysts. Also see Campton and Busack (1989).

Bogatova and Erofeyeva (1985) claimed that ''preliminary activation'' of brine shrimp cysts with hydrogen peroxide, H_2O_2, increased the number of nauplii obtained by 3 to 5%, or to ~80% of cysts in the hatch vessel. The results were attributed to the increase in dissolved oxygen, although slight modifications in the tertiary envelope of the wetted cysts might also have occurred. The authors recommended adding 1.1 to 0.3 mL/L of a 33% H_2O_2 solution directly to the hatch vessel.

(76) Bruggeman et al. (1979, 1980), Liao et al. (1983), Sorgeloos (1980), Sorgeloos et al. (1977, 1978, 1983).

(77) Vanhaecke and Sorgeloos (1983) reported that decapsulation increased the number of nauplii obtained from *Artemia franciscana* cysts by 15%. However, Spotte and Anderson (1989) found the reverse to be true: in most cases, decapsulation of *A. franciscana* cysts lowered the number of nauplii obtained significantly.

(78) Decapsulation probably sterilizes *Artemia* cysts, although I found no evidence of it in the literature. Nonetheless, *Artemia* used in aquaculture installations or public aquariums are not hatched and reared *axenically* (i.e., in an environment that is sterile except for the organism being cultured), and sterilizing the cysts does not eliminate subsequent contamination from the air, the water supply, and handling. The unspoken assumption that these sources of contamination are somehow less important (e.g., Sumitra-Vijayarghavan et al. 1988) is unfounded. Austin and Allen (1981/1982) cultured aerobic, heterotrophic bacteria associated with cysts and nauplii. Bacterial counts from desiccated cysts were relatively lower than counts obtained during hatch, suggesting increased contamination with time. Of the five genera of bacteria recovered from desiccated cysts, only one (*Vibrio*) is a known pathogen of aquatic animals. Vibrios are common in coastal waters (Barbay et al. 1984, Buck and Spotte 1986, Buck et al. 1984, Colwell et al. 1984, Seidler and Evans 1984), and their introduction is likely to occur anyway. Austin and Allen also showed that bacteria associated with nauplii can be removed easily by rinsing. Rinse procedures are faster, simpler, and cheaper than decapsulation. Gilmour et al. (1975) cultured commercially packaged brine shrimp cysts straight from the container and reported, ". . . it would seem that there is little danger of introducing pathogenic bacteria to fish tanks by feeding brine shrimps, hatched from canned brine shrimp eggs. . . ." Finally, Bruggeman et al. (1979) suggested that decapsulated cysts may be contaminated with chlorinated hydrocarbons.

(79) The same group of authors (Sorgeloos et al. 1977, 1983) has stated more than once that ingestion of undecapsulated cysts by larval fishes and crustaceans causes "gut blockages," but the evidence cited is anecdotal. Whether this actually happens remains to be demonstrated. On the other hand, decapsulated cysts evidently are suitable food for at least some species of larval fishes and crustaceans (Santos et al. 1980, Yan et al. 1982).

(80) Bruggeman et al. (1980) claimed that nauplii of greater body mass are obtained from decapsulated *Artemia* cysts, although Vanhaecke and Sorgeloos (1983) determined later that this was true for only a few strains.

(81) The decapsulation procedure is from Spotte and Anderson (1989). I see problems with decapsulation in general. Sorgeloos et al. (1977) stated that either freshwater or seawater could be used in the first step of decapsulation, but in a later publication (Bruggeman et al. 1979) it was claimed that embryonic viability is greater in seawater solutions. No explanation was provided, although the paper of Bruggeman and coauthors contains a stylized curve depicting the effect of pH on the dissociation of hydrated chlorine. The curve is misleading because it describes only the hydrolysis of chlorine species in freshwater. Full-strength seawater contains ~65 mg/L of bromide (Table 1-1), and brominated oxidants form preferentially to chlorinated species when seawater is chlorinated (Chapter 9, Note 23). The presence of ammonia is a further complication. According to Inman and Johnson (1978), reaction rates associated with the formation of HOBr (hypobromous acid) and NH_2Cl (monochloramine) are first order and depend on the concentration of HOCl (hypochlorous acid). Small volumes of water containing heavy concentrations of brine shrimp cysts are ammonia- and organic-rich, high chlorine demand solutions. Until *breakpoint* is exceeded (i.e., all ammonia and oxidizable organic carbon are consumed in the oxidation process) the formation of HOBr and NH_2Cl is independent of the initial chlorine dosage. Breakpoint is unlikely to be reached during decapsulation, as implied by Sorgeloos et al. (1977) and Bruggeman et al. (1979), who cautioned against leaving the cysts in the oxidant solutions for too long. Their comments suggest that perhaps the concentrations are too strong, and that the different reaction products formed during chlorination of freshwater versus seawater are what prompt the need to use separate oxidant strengths for the two solutions. In addition, neither paper quantified the ratio of cysts to oxidant solution. Sorgeloos et al. (1977) merely stated that it should not exceed 1 g/15 mL. The chemical reaction, however, involves the surfaces of the cysts, and decapsulation is a surface phenomenon (Spotte and Anderson 1988). I suspect that the surface area/volume ratio at a given concentration of oxidant is important.

(82) The change in color of *Artemia* cysts was described by Sorgeloos et al. (1977, 1983) and Spotte and Anderson (1988, 1989).

(83) Decapsulated cysts apparently can be stored for several months at room temperature in saturated brine. After 6 months, however, the percentage of nauplii obtained drops below 60% (Bruggeman et al. 1979). Lowering the brine temperature below −4°C results in greater retention of viability.

(84) Johnson (1980) found that early nauplii have higher carbohydrate requirements than later stages. He recommended using rice bran powder to feed nauplii for the first 3 d and switching to algae powder starting on day 4.

(85) Sorgeloos and Persoone (1975).

(86) Some brine shrimp reproduce parthenogenetically, but North American strains are not among them (Bowen 1962).

(87) Lavens and Sorgeloos (1984).

(88) Howell (1973).

(89) Ito (1960) reported lengths of 99 to 198 μm for *B. plicatilis*, whereas the organism used by Howell (1973) "fell into the range" 180 to 250 μm (no data were given). Fukusho and Okauchi (1982) listed the lengths of *B. plicatilis* from six countries in southeast Asia as ranging from 169.1 (Philippines) to 221.4 μm (Indonesia).

(90) Solangi and Ogle (1977) published a partial bibliography on mass culture of rotifers with emphasis on *Brachionus plicatilis*. Many descriptions in the literature refer to culture in test tubes, flasks, and other small vessels, and the techniques are not directly applicable to mass culture. Other descriptions are incomplete, especially when the culture method is incidental to the subject of the report. Reports emphasizing the mass culture of *B. plicatilis* and some other species include Anderson and Smith (1983), Fontaine and Revera (1980), Giliberto and Mazzola (1981), Hirata (1979), Liao et al. (1983), Stemberger (1981), and Theilacker and McMaster (1971). Stemberger's work dealt with freshwater rotifers.

(91) Hirata (1979) referred to these methods as "daily tank-transfer" and "drain-down;" to Liao et al. (1983) they were the "changing tank" and "partial harvest" methods.

(92) Essential features of the changing tanks and drain down procedures are from Hirata (1979).

(93) Provasoli and Carlucci (1974).

(94) Culture solutions for growing algae were reviewed by Bidwell and Spotte (1985) and McLachlan (1973).

(95) Droop (1961), McLachlan (1973), and Provasoli et al. (1957) reviewed enrichment formulas. These are still referred to on occasion as "enriched media," which is incorrect. Additives alone do not constitute a culture medium; instead, the additives and base solution (seawater or artificial seawater) together

do. The earliest enrichment additives were soil extracts and thus chemically undefined. When these are mixed with seawater the resultant media are called *Erdschreiber*. Gross (1937) described one procedure: ''The soil extract is made up by boiling for one hour 1 kg. of good garden or potting soil with 1 litre glass distilled water in an autoclave. (More recently I have been using tap water with equal success.) After 2–3 days the resulting brown and rather dirty fluid is decanted into a flask and sterilized by heating up to the boiling point. After standing for 3–4 weeks the rougher particles settle to the bottom and the fluid becomes transparent, brown or red in colour and ready for use.'' Published enrichment formulas include versions of Erdschreiber (Gross 1937, Schreiber 1927); Grund (von Stosch 1969); ES (Provasoli 1968, West in McLachlan 1973); f (Guillard 1963, Guillard and Ryther 1962); f/2, the f formula at half strength (Guillard in McLachlan 1973, Guillard 1975); SWM-3 Medium (Chen et al. 1969); SWM-1 Medium (McLachlan 1964) and several subsequent versions (McLachlan 1973); and ESAW (Harrison et al. 1980). Also see Bidwell and Spotte (1985).

(96) Precipitates form when seawater is autoclaved. This also occurs when artificial seawaters are autoclaved, unless certain precautions are taken. Provasoli et al. (1957) considered precipitation to be a major obstacle in making effective artificial seawaters for axenic culture of phytoplankton, an opinion still generally accepted. The reasoning is that precipitation removes essential constituents from solution, rendering them unavailable to cells. This may be true in certain cases, although McLachlan (1959) demonstrated that removal of a precipitate inhibited growth of *Dunaliella tertiolecta* (= *D. euchlora*), indicating ''. . . that there is a rapid resolution of salts from the initially formed precipitate, or at least enough so that the rate of growth is not affected.'' Nonetheless, the formation of precipitates often causes erratic growth (McLachlan 1964, Provasoli et al. 1957), which is sufficient reason to consider cloudy solutions undesirable.

Jones (1967) analyzed precipitates formed during autoclaving of seawater and artificial seawater. Major fractions of aluminum, tin, chromium, copper, silver, selenium, and lead were precipitated. In terms of total mass of precipitate, magnesium was 4%, silicon 4%, calcium variable but averaged 2%, and aluminum 0.5%. The other elements accounted for another 1 to 2% of the total precipitated mass. Calcium carbonate, $CaCO_3$, was the most consistent precipitate identified by X-ray diffraction, and it was thought to coprecipitate with other elements.

Harrison et al. (1980) listed six ways in which precipitation during autoclaving has historically been reduced: (*1*) adding complexing agents to reduce loss of metal ions; (*2*) adding organic buffers such as tris (2-amino-2-hydroxymethyl-1,3-propanediol)* and glycylglycine; (*3*) reducing the salinity, which lowers the concentrations of major ions available for precipitation; (*4*) partially replacing calcium and magnesium with more soluble cations (i.e., those with single positive charges); (*5*) replacing inorganic phosphorus with an organic form (e.g., sodium glycerophosphate) to minimize precipitation; and (*6*) introducing weak solubilizers, which are acids (e.g., citric acid) that form soluble salts with calcium.

Kester et al. (1967) separated hydated major salts (magnesium, calcium, and strontium chlorides) from anhydrous major species to keep carbonate and sulfate salts of calcium and strontium from precipitating. The same approach was used by Spotte et al. (1984a) in formulating GP2 maintenance and culture solutions. In their procedure for mixing GP2 low-salinity culture solution Steele and Thursby (1988) dissolve the major salts as a common solution, which is then autoclaved; the only omission is sodium bicarbonate. Preweighed, dry sodium bicarbonate is dissolved in a little water and autoclaved separately. The two solutions are cooled, mixed, and diluted to volume with deionized water. The alternative procedure suggested by Steele and Thursby is to autoclave dry sodium bicarbonate in a Teflon® squeeze bottle, dissolve it in sterile deionized water, and add it directly to the culture vessel.

(97) Numerous natural *ligands* or chemical bonding sites exist in seawater. Some are inorganic, whereas others contain carbon. All are anionic, having negative electrical charges. The strength of a ligand, or its ability to *complex* or join with a free cation, is variable, depending on such factors as temperature, pH, and competition from other ligands of different composition. Ligands can be *labile* (easily dissociated or broken apart) or *refractory* (i.e., nonlabile). Minor cations containing more than one electrical charge traditionally are complexed with an organic ligand before being added to culture solutions. The process ordinarily is called *chelation*. However, not every organic compound can properly be called a chelate after being complexed with a cation. Acetate-based compounds are examples (Stumm and Brauner 1975). I shall therefore refer to all cation-ligand compounds simply as complexes.

(98) Iron in seawater exists in the inorganic state mainly as $Fe(OH)_2$ (ferrous hydroxide) and $Fe(OH)_2$ (ferric hydroxide). The latter is dominant. Hydroxides are almost insoluble in

*Trizma®, Sigma Chemical Company, P. O. Box 14508, St. Louis MO 63178.

aqueous solutions, and iron is one of the least soluble minor cations in seawater. It also is among the most important growth factors for phytoplankton. Iron's low solubility led earlier marine biologists to speculate that phytoplankton somehow could assimilate it as a precipitate (Harvey 1937), but precipitated iron in culture was generally considered undesirable. Circumstantial evidence suggested that iron in usable forms could be sustained in culture solutions by complexing it with organic ligands. The assumed effect was to maintain iron in a ''soluble'' (i.e., unprecipitated and more biologically useful) chemical state. However, Goldberg (1952) showed that iron complexed to an organic ligand such as citrate or EDTA is unavailable to the marine diatom *Asterionella japonica*. Nonetheless, adding complexed iron to culture solutions increased the number of phytoplankton species cultured successfully (Droop 1961), although how this happened remained obscure.

Anderson and Morel (1982) conducted extensive experiments designed to detect and quantify iron uptake mechanisms by the coastal diatom *Thalassiosira weissflogii*. The organism was cultured in AQUIL, an artificial seawater formulated for physiological studies of phytoplankton (Morel et al. 1979). The results can be applied directly only to *T. weissflogii*, but the provocative insights of these investigators furthered understanding of how complexing agents can be used in the culture of all phytoplankton species. I shall therefore discuss some of their findings.

The uptake of iron in the dark by *T. weissflogii* in the presence of a strong complexing agent showed that the rate is controlled by the concentration of ferric ion, Fe(III)*—in other words, by iron in the free or uncomplexed state. Many complexing agents including the aminocarboxylates photodegrade in light. When culture solutions are illuminated the complexing agent degrades, releasing ferrous ion, Fe(II). This is a form of iron taken up by algae (Anderson and Morel 1980). Anderson and Morel (1982) discovered that Fe(II) released during photodegradation serves as an important nutrient source. Cells evidently can compete with some of the aminocarboxylates (at least EDTA and CDTA) for Fe(II); however, they cannot compete with DTPA. Uptake of released Fe(II) was verified by adding ascorbic acid, $C_6H_8O_6$, a chemical reductant known to promote Fe(II) formation in the presence of Fe(III)-aminocarboxylate complexes (Kahn and Martell 1967a, 1967b). Addition of 10^{-3} mol/L ascorbic acid to cultures maintained in darkness gave the same relative enhanced uptake of iron as those kept in light. Addi-

* Ferric ion can be expressed as Fe^{3+} and ferrous ion as Fe(II) and Fe^{2+}.

tion of a very strong complexing agent (EDDHA) resulted in lack of any detectable uptake of iron either in light or darkness. Thus highly stable Fe(III) complexes are not photodegraded appreciably, nor are they reduced by ascorbic acid addition. This confirms earlier work by Johnston (1964), who reported poor growth of phytoplankton in the presence of excess EDDHA. Anderson and Morel (1982) also found that iron was assimilated from the culture solution when no complexing agents were present, but uptake in precipitated form was considered unlikely. Uptake followed a saturation curve with increasing iron concentration. When ascorbic acid was added to uncomplexed AQUIL the uptake of iron was inhibited by ~50%. Inhibition by a reductant suggests that oxidation of Fe(II) and subsequent transport of Fe(III) to the cell surface is probable, considering that ascorbate does not interfere with the growth of phytoplankton cells (at least not *T. weissflogii*), nor does it complex Fe(II) appreciably.

At present, no general model of iron assimilation by phytoplankton is available, rendering an evaluation of which chemical form to use in culture solutions obscure. Available evidence suggests that complexing agents of moderate strength such as EDTA are suitable. Goldberg (1952) demonstrated that after 6 d in light at pH 8.25, 85% of the iron complexed with EDTA in seawater had hydrolyzed. He considered this to reflect negatively on EDTA, although recent evidence favors the opposite opinion: EDTA provides a chemical time release mechanism for Fe(III) and Fe(II), triggered by light.

(99) Goldberg (1952) studied the effects of complexation on uptake of radioactive iron by marine diatoms. He observed that 80 to 90% of iron added to cultures as a ferric citrate complex was adsorbed onto the walls of the culture flasks within 24 h.

(100) Guillard (1975) and McLachlan (1973) wrote that silicon can be omitted from culture solutions except when diatoms are cultured. McLachlan (1973) recommended adding silicon as sodium metasilicate, Na_2SiO_3, from prepared stock solutions. The salt dissolves easily in warm water. The solution is strongly alkaline and precipitates or polymerizes when added to seawater or artificial seawater. The same problem occurs during autoclaving. McLachlan suggested that stock solutions be stabilized by acidification to pH 2 with concentrated hydrochloric acid, HCl. Haines and Guillard (in Guillard 1975) reported that f/2-enriched seawater with silicon omitted dissolves as much as 290 μmol/L silicon from 125-mL borosilicate glass flasks during autoclaving. Lesser concentrations were recovered from larger vessels. The amount removed from the sides of 125-mL flasks

was adequate to supply the needs of diatoms. Jones (1967) observed the formation of long, fine, highly refractive crystals during autoclaving of seawater and artificial seawater. The crystals contained 12 to 16% silicon thought to have originated from the sides of the flasks.

(101) Copper is an essential micronutrient to algae (Manahan and Smith 1973), but can be toxic at very low concentrations. In my opinion, adding it to culture solutions is risky and unnecessary. Enough probably exists as a contaminant in other salts to satisfy the physiological requirements of most phytoplankton species. Toxicity and the chemical state of copper in solution are directly related. Under oxidizing conditions (aerated seawater), uncomplexed copper is present in the cupric form, expressed Cu^{2+} or Cu(II). The cuprous state, Cu^{1+} or Cu(I), cannot exist in aqueous solution because it oxidizes and reduces itself by the reaction

$$2Cu^{+} \rightleftharpoons Cu^{2+} + Cu(s) \tag{8.4}$$

The complexing of cupric ions by organic ligands reduces toxicity markedly (Barber 1973, Davey et al. 1973, Jackson and Morgan 1978, Petersen 1982, Sunda and Guillard 1976, Sunda and Lewis 1978), even at low initial concentrations. Nielsen and Wium-Andersen (1970) first proposed that cupric ions at naturally occurring seawater concentrations can be toxic to phytoplankton under certain conditions. They suggested that the capacity of organic ligands to increase growth rates of phytoplankton, as observed by Johnston (1964), was caused by reduced concentrations of Cu(II) in the presence of complexing agents. In culture solutions at least 99.5% of all dissolved copper at normal seawater concentrations is complexed by EDTA at equilibrium (Jackson and Morgan 1978), and any observed toxicity results from release of Cu(II) during photodegradation of the complexing agent.

According to Jackson and Morgan (1978), phytoplankton respond to abnormally high levels of copper in two ways. One way is by a decrease in growth rate that changes little with time. The second, seen in at least one green alga (*Chlorella pyrenoidosa*), is by a *lag phase* (temporary interruption in growth) that is extended with increasing concentrations of copper. The lag phase is followed by exponential growth at a rate independent of the initial copper concentration. If algae respond to high levels of copper by excreting organic matter, the time necessary to change the concentration of Cu(II) will vary with the amount initially present and the concentration of organic ligands that must be excreted.

(102) O'Kelley (1974).

(103) Ammonia is toxic to some phytoplankton, and many species are unable to tolerate even 0.1 μmol/L, presumably as total NH_4-N (Guillard 1963). Guillard (1975) found that adding 0.5 to 1.0 mmol/L ammonium chloride, NH_4Cl, to seawater autoclaved in 50-mL batches resulted in a 25 to 30% loss of ammonia. This is not surprising, considering that the pH of autoclaved seawater increases as CO_2 is driven into the atmosphere. The result is a shift from ammonium ion, NH_4^+, to free ammonia, NH_3, a gas.

(104) Phytoplankton can be cultured on any of four nitrogen sources: nitrate (NO_3^-), nitrite (NO_2^-), ammonia (mainly ammonium ion, NH_4^+, at the normal pH of seawater), and urea (Goldman and Peavey 1979). Brewer and Goldman (1976) and Goldman and Brewer (1980) showed that changes in alkalinity occurring in culture solutions during assimilation of nitrogen are consistent with a simple model in which production of hydroxyl ions, OH^-, is balanced by the uptake of NO_3^- or NO_2^-; production of H^+ is balanced by the uptake of NH_4^+. Alkalinity and pH increase when the nitrogen source is either nitrate or nitrite and decline when ammonia is used (Goldman et al. 1982; also see Table 1-3). No change in alkalinity or pH occurs when urea is the nitrogen source because it contains no electrical charge. The authors recommended using urea exclusively in phytoplankton culture. Price and Harrison (1988) found that *in situ* assimilation of urea by phytoplankton in the Sargasso Sea occurs near the maximum rate, indicating a high affinity for urea.

(105) Guillard (1975) wrote: "By no means [do] all useful species of algae need vitamins, though some without a requirement are stimulated by them. Vitamin B_{12} [cyanocobalamin] is one most often needed, with thiamine following and biotin a poor third (only a few flagellates need it). However, it is just as well to supply all three vitamins if any are required at all, because the cost is slight, while the trouble of making an auxiliary solution if needed later is considerable."

(106) The procedure is modified from Spotte et al. (1984a), except that Solutions A and B are autoclaved together and sodium bicarbonate is autocalved separately as recommended by Steele and Thursby (1988; see Note 96, last paragraph).

(107) Steele and Thursby (1988) modified GP2 culture solution to culture seaweed gametophytes. They lowered the salinity to 30‰, increased the concentrations of nitrogen and phosphorus, and replaced urea with nitrate. The specific concentrations of

nitrogen and phosphorus and the N/P ratio of 25 stated in the text subsection were based on ENV, a seawater enrichment solution devised by Ukeles and Wikfors (1988) for phytoplankton culture.

(108) Patricia M. Bubucis of Sea Research Foundation compiled the information in this section. Literature sources were Guillard (1973, 1975), Starr (1973), Steele and Thursby (1988), and Ukeles (1976). Also see Belcher and Swale (1982).

(109) Brand and Guillard (1981).

(110) Patricia M. Bubucis of Sea Research Foundation compiled the information in this section.

(111) Guillard (1975), Ukeles (1976).

(112) APHA et al. (1985, p. 853).

(113) Guillard (1975).

(114) Steele and Thursby (1988).

(115) The procedure for antibiotic treatment is from Hoshaw and Rosowski (1973).

(116) Patricia M. Bubucis of Sea Research Foundation compiled the information in this section. Information on inoculants and culture solution volumes are from Fox (1983) and Guillard (1975). Also see Belcher and Swale (1982).

(117) Patricia M. Bubucis of Sea Research Foundation compiled the information in this section. See Elnabarawy and Welter (1984) and Parsons (1973).

CHAPTER 9

(1) Overstreet (1978, p. 138) defined infection and infestation differently than I have. In his view, an infection ". . . is the invasion or state resulting from an invasion of a parasite or pathogen into a host. An infestation is an external rather than internal invasion. If both internal and external organisms occur on one host, all the associations are collectively referred to as infections. Some biologists, however, restrict the term 'infestation' to either internal or external associations with metazoans." In this chapter I use the term "infection" to mean simply the *presence* of an infectious organism without regard to its location. "Infestation" is used in reference to metazoans. Not even this distinction is straightforward, however.

(2) Mahmoud (1989) wrote: ''Parasitism involves a specialized and dependent mode of life; as such, all infectious organisms are parasites.'' Mahmoud's use of ''infectious organisms'' included both microbial and metazoan parasites.

(3) A synonym of natural resistance is *natural immunity*, a term that connotes specific activity. As such, I prefer to avoid it. In a similar context, Ingram (1980) wrote: ''It is difficult to assign an appropriate definition to the term 'natural antibody.' '' To lessen the confusion, Ingram defined natural antibody ''. . . in the broad sense, in contrast to 'antigen-induced antibody' or immunoglobulin.'' Fauve (1976) considered immunity to be nonspecific (i.e., natural) ''. . . when it develops in the absence of prior contact with the antigen(s) specific for the pathogenic agent.'' For reviews of fish immunology, both natural and specific, see Avtalion (1981), Corbel (1975), Cushing (1970), Ellis (1978, 1982), Ingram (1980), Manning et al. (1982), and Manning and Tatner (1985). For a survey of early work on natural resistance and immunity of seawater fishes, see Lewis et al. (1970, pp. 63–75).

(4) Kearn (1976) described the structure of fish skin.

(5) Ingram (1980).

(6) The presence of lysozyme varies by species (Fletcher and White 1973).

(7) Ellis (1978) and Ingram (1980) stated that only IgM has been found in fishes. In reviewing the literature, Ingram (1980) pointed out that in some fishes, notably the sharks, IgM activity is broad. This is unusual, considering that immunoglobulins ordinarily demonstrate antigen-specific activity. Consequently, some authors have concluded that fish IgM functions as a ''naturally occurring immunoglobulin'' (i.e., IgM may actually be a natural resistance factor).

(8) The term *symptom* ordinarily is used only in reference to human beings. Overstreet (1978, p. 139) made this distinction: ''A sign is any objective evidence of a disease or disorder, as opposed to a symptom, which is the subjective complaint of a patient.''

(9) For reviews of neoplasms in fishes see Mawdesley-Thomas (1972), Mix (1986), and Nigrelli (1954).

(10) Blazer et al. (1989), Blazer and Wolke (1984a, 1984b), Durve and Lovell (1982), Li and Lovell (1985), Segner and Möller (1984).

(11) Barton et al. (1988), Giesy (1988).

(12) See the section on stress in Chapter 4.

(13) Bacteria are able to transfer genetic material by cell-to-cell contact (see Kelch and Lee 1978 and the reviews by Koch 1981, Lyon and Skurray 1987, Richmond 1972, and Watanabe 1963). The process is called *conjugation* and the genetic package is a *plasmid*. Under certain conditions the recipient cell becomes a *donor*, capable of transferring plasmids to other recipients. Conjugative plasmids then spread rapidly through a population of bacteria (even to organisms of different species) in the manner of an infection. When conditions are optimal a few plasmid-positive cells can rapidly convert an entire population of recipients. Among the known plasmids are the resistance transfer factors, or *R factors*, which confer resistance to antibacterial compounds and other growth inhibitors. Bacteria have been found that are resistant to more than one antibacterial compound, a condition called *multiple drug resistance*.

The appearance of microorganisms with *R* factors in natural waters and sewage is a worsening problem. Indiscriminate use of antibacterial compounds in aquaculture and the ornamental fish trade, particularly at subtherapeutic concentrations, has contributed to widespread resistance in many strains of important pathogenic bacteria (Aoki 1974; Aoki and Egusa 1971; Aoki et al. 1981; Hilton and Wilson 1980; Shotts et al. 1976a, 1976b; Toranzo et al. 1983; Trust and Whitby 1976). These organisms pose an immediate health hazard to humans and domestic animals (Brown 1989, Richmond 1972, Shotts et al. 1976b, Trust and Whitby 1976). Already there are reports of aquarium-borne mycobacterioses that are resistant to chemotherapy (Janssen 1970). More frightening is the specter of antibiotic therapy becoming less effective and attempting to project the impact it will have on human and veterinary medicine. According to Hammond and Lambert (1978), ''It would not be alarmist to say that we are only a half-step ahead of the ability of many bacteria to overcome modern chemotherapy, with the possibility of a return to the dark days of the preantibiotic era.'' It has been suggested that antibacterial compounds be developed exclusively for the treatment of fish diseases (Trust and Whitby 1976), and that products used to treat humans and domestic animals be banned from use in fish culture (Trust and Chipman 1974, Trust and Whitby 1976).

(14) The immersion method can be accomplished by *bath* or *dip*. These supposedly differ in duration of treatment and concentration of the chemical, but I consider such distinctions arbitrary. According to Herman (1970, 1972), dips last for 1 min or less and contain high concentrations because of the short ex-

posure. A bath treatment can extend from slightly more than a minute to several weeks. Because of the longer treatment period the concentration of the agent is lower. No chemotherapeutic agent is applied in dips, because none can be assimilated from solution that rapidly. Dips are therefore reserved for treatment with disinfectants. I have avoided both terms and used immersion instead. Duration of treatment is stated if provided in the primary literature source.

(15) In my opinion, the term *therapeutic concentration* should always refer to the amount of a chemotherapeutic agent present in the blood and tissues of the animals being treated, not to the immersion concentration. Successful treatment of systemic infections depends on how well the agent is assimilated. This may be unrelated to the solution concentration, because many chemotherapeutic agents are assimilated poorly or not at all by fishes.

(16) Trust and Chipman (1974) tested eight solid products (capsules and tablets), including neomycin sulfate, tetracycline hydrochloride, streptomycin sulfate, merbromin, sodium sulfathiozole, acriflavin, sodium sulfamerazine, erythromycin, nifurpirinol, and potassium penicillin. All are chemotherapeutic agents with selective toxicity to bacteria, except acriflavin and merbromin, which are disinfectants. The products were tested *in vitro* against 16 different bacteria, some known fish pathogens. None inhibited the growth of all test bacteria at dosages recommended by the manufacturers. Minimum inhibitory concentrations ranged from 8 to 83 times the manufacturers' recommendations. It appears doubtful whether any of these products could have been bactericidal at reasonable concentrations.

(17) Sykes (1965, p. 6).

(18) Under typical operating conditions, UV sterilization does not reduce the number of pathogens in closed systems and therefore does not alter the incidence of infection and disease, as demonstrated experimentally by Gratzek et al. (1983), Herald et al. (1970), Ross (1977), Spanier (1978), and Spotte and Buck (1981). The effectiveness of UV irradiation in single-pass applications (e.g., wastewater and drinking water treatment) has encouraged fish culturists to transfer the same technology to closed systems, where it probably is misapplied. The example in the mathematical model of Spotte and Adams (1981) demonstrates that in closed systems in which the influx of pathogens is continuous, only a 90% reduction can be achieved even after infinite time. The authors concluded: "If the water is re-

cycled . . . any apparent efficacy of a UV sterilizer, based on kill rate, is an artifact, because the mass of pathogens in the immediate vicinity of the cultured animals is always greater than the mass in the sterilizer effluent. Equilibrium is never attained, and the entire system cannot be rendered disease-free, even when the sterilization process is 100% effective.'' In other words a sterilizer may indeed kill 100% of the organisms passing through it, but because of the closed-loop arrangement the volume of water inside the unit is only a fraction of the total volume. It is unlikely that the kill rate at this single point contact site can equal or exceed the rate at which pathogens are introduced to the main part of the water system, particularly during epizootics. UV irradiation is therefore ineffective if the objective is to lower the incidence of infection by reducing the concentration of potential (unattached) pathogens. Equations 9.1 to 9.4 in the text are based on the original equations (Spotte and Adams 1981) and are the work of Gary Adams.

(19) Zirzow (1910).

(20) Trust (1972) tested 14 liquid products manufactured for hobbyists and reputed to be disinfectants when added to small freshwater aquariums. The active ingredients were disinfectants (e.g., formalin, malachite green, methylene blue, potassium permanganate, silver oxide). An organic compound with a quaternary ammonium base formulated for disinfecting empty aquariums also was tested. All products failed to inhibit the growth of test bacteria (i.e., were not bacteriostatic) at the manufacturers' recommended dosages, and none significantly reduced the concentration of bacteria in aquarium water when fishes were present.

(21) The use of ozonation in closed-system seawater aquariums is a misapplication of the technology, for two reasons. First, ozone reacts so differently in freshwater than in seawater that data derived experimentally in one medium are irrelevant to the other. Second, sterilization at a single point contact site may not lower the concentration of suspended microorganisms significantly if the input is continuous (see Note 17). The equations of Spotte and Adams (1981) can be used to demonstrate that if only the O_3 molecule and its immediate hydrated radicals are considered, sterilization is potentially ineffective even if the kill of microorganisms at the contact site is 100%.

(22) In using the terms OPO and CPO I am following current protocol. Both refer to the total residual oxidant concentration, measured amperometrically as ''total residual chlorine.'' In other words, ozonated and chlorinated compounds in seawater

are difficult to distinguish by conventional analytical methods, mainly because they consist of identical chemical species (see Note 23).

Ozone in water can be determined spectrophotometrically at 600 nm by decolorization of indigo trisulfonate after acidification of the sample to pH <4. The procedure, developed by Bader and Hoigné (1981), is stoichiometric, rapid, and uses stable reagents. Precision is at the 2% level (3 μg O_3/L). Oxidation products (at least in the inorganic state) do not interfere. The direct measurement of O_3, however, is of doubtful value in the daily management of saline water systems. Of greater concern are the longer-lived oxidation products.

(23) The ozonation and chlorination of seawater cause brominated sterilizing agents to form, including bromite, OBr^-, hypobromous acid, HOBr, and bromate, BrO_3^-, as shown by Blogoslawski et al. (1975), Crecelius (1979), Haag (1981), Midgley (1980), Williams et al. (1978), and Wong and Davidson (1977). Ozonation of seawater also results in formation of chlorinated reaction products. Blogoslawski et al. (1975), Kosak-Channing and Helz (1979), and Yeatts and Taube (1949) suggested that ozone reacts with Cl^- to form residual oxidants. Williams et al. (1978) gave equivocal evidence that Cl^- and OCl^- (hypochlorite) are produced during ozonation of seawater and proposed that other chlorinated reaction products, including chlorate, ClO_3^-, are possible thermodynamically. According to Haag (1981), bromate and chlorate are the two main reaction products produced during chlorination of seawater. Haas (1981) showed that sodium hypochlorite, NaOCl, forms as a result of ion pairing when waters of high ionic strength are chlorinated. Assuming that ozonation produces OCl^-, it is possible that NaOCl forms as a later reaction product. Sodium hypochlorite is the sterilizing agent commonly added to swimming pools.

(24) In estuarine waters (which in some respects are low-salinity seawaters), equal concentrations of OPOs and CPOs result in similar delays in the percentage hatch of fish eggs (Hall et al. 1981) and percentage mortalities of larvae and juveniles of fishes and invertebrates (Hall et al. 1981, Richardson and Burton 1981). This is not surprising, considering that similar reaction products form during chlorination and ozonation of estuarine waters and seawater.

(25) Aquarists have been slow to realize that ozonating seawater achieves the same effect as chlorinating it, particularly in the presence of bromide. However, the large water processing industries understand and accept this as fact, and many are abandoning the use of ozone in seawater applications because

it costs more than chlorine and is no safer to marine organisms. For example, in a discussion of methods used to sterilize power plant cooling water, Garey (1980) wrote: ". . . in seawater ozone reacts in a manner similar to chlorine, oxidizing bromide to bromine. Therefore, none of the advantages seen in freshwater are realized. . . . [and] ozone is not considered an alternative [to chlorine] for seawater applications."

(26) Few analytical methods are able to distinguish the different forms of copper in seawater (see Hasle and Abdullah 1981, Lazar et al. 1981, Mills and Quinn 1981, Zirino and Seligman 1981, and the reviews by Hart 1979 and Schmidt 1978). Only total copper, TCu, can be determined by conventional laboratory testing.

(27) Because copper is a disinfectant and not a chemotherapeutic agent, a proper dosage level would be one that is lethal to the parasite but sublethal to the host. In my opinion, the distinction between these terms when referring to disinfectants is too nebulous to be meaningful. Any assessment of the effectiveness of copper should include a measure of delayed mortality because toxicity is relative and not always demonstrable from conventional bioassays. The harmful effects of copper on fishes are well documented, and it seems reasonable that concentrations below the acute toxicity level could still produce pathological changes that are irreversible and ultimately fatal. Second, what constitutes a lethal concentration depends a great deal on chemical and physical factors (e.g., temperature, pH, mass/volume ratios, the nature and concentrations of ionic species in solution). These are impossible to replicate precisely in bioassays. Biological differences in the test animals also are important, and such factors as age, size, previous exposure history, and general health can affect bioassay results significantly.

(28) In phytoplankton probably only the free ion or Cu(II) exerts a toxic effect at the boundary between water and the external surfaces. The concentration of total copper is not a factor (Allen et al. 1980). Toxicity in phytoplankton is reduced substantially when Cu(II) is complexed with inorganic and organic substances in solution and becomes unavailable for uptake by the cell walls (Nielsen and Wium-Andersen 1970, Sunda and Guillard 1976). The same may be true of the cell membranes of protozoan parasites.

In invertebrates capable of assimilating organic molecules through their external membranes, organic complexes of copper definitely are toxic. Certain marine *polychaetes* (segmented worms) assimilate organically complexed copper at the same rate regardless of what form the metal is in (Milanovich et al.

1976). In still other polychaetes death is caused not by the total amount of copper accumulated in the tissues, but by the rate of uptake (McLusky and Phillips 1975, Milanovich et al. 1976).

The toxicity of Cu(II) to fishes may be limited to pathological changes in the gills, lateral line, taste buds, and other tissues exposed to the water; otherwise, the rapid complexation of Cu(II) with living tissue probably restricts toxicity to the amount of TCu ingested or digested, as is the case with some invertebrates (Sutherland and Major 1981). The fact that fishes exposed to increased concentrations of copper deposit the metal in tissues of the eyes, vertebrae, muscles, ovaries, kidneys, and liver (Brungs et al. 1973, LaRoche et al. 1973, Shackley et al. 1981, Solbé and Cooper 1976) is clear evidence that external toxicity is only one consideration. Calamari et al. (1980), in fact, considered it meaningless to view the toxicity of any metal in terms of speciation and effects on gill tissue and suggested that all inorganic and organic states contribute to the toxicity.

The relative toxicities of the different chemical states of copper in seawater are extremely difficult to identify and measure. Results from freshwater experiments are instructive, even if the data cannot be extrapolated directly to describe seawater environments. The trend in freshwater bioassays is clearly toward increased copper toxicity to fishes in waters of low alkalinity and pH, conditions favoring Cu(II) formation (Howarth and Sprague 1978, Pagenkopf et al. 1974, Shaw and Brown 1974, Waiwood and Beamish 1978). The ''acute toxicity'' of copper (i.e., availability of the free ion) therefore correlates negatively with the ligand concentration. If substantial amounts of ligands are present, as in seawater, it is doubtful whether free copper ions exist at all except in transitional states.

After ingestion, copper becomes toxic in different ways. One mechanism is to cause the redistribution of other ions. Copper assimilated by the blue mussel (*Mytilus edulis*) is concentrated in all organs and causes immediate redistribution of other elements in the tissues (Sheppard 1977, Sutherland and Major 1981). One species displaced is zinc, which is released from the kidney in such huge quantities that its level in the gill rises 300% (Sutherland and Major 1981). Any apparent ''copper poisoning'' may actually be caused by the reapportionment of zinc, even when zinc in the surrounding seawater is at normal concentrations.

(29) Symes and Kester (1985).

(30) Models that preceded those of Franklin and Morse (1982) and Symes and Kester (1985) indicated that in seawater containing no organic matter, borate, $B(OH)_4^-$, may be the principal

ligand that complexes copper (Sposito 1981). In the absence of both organic ligands and borate, hydroxyl, OH^-, and carbonate, CO_3^{2-}, become the most important ligands (Stumm and Brauner 1975, Stumm and Morgan 1981, Zirino and Yamamoto 1972). When they react with cations, the anions $B(OH)_4^-$, OH^-, and CO_3^{2-} form borato, hydroxo, and carbonato complexes. Other anions (e.g., chloride, sulfate) are insignificant where complexation of copper is concerned (Stumm and Brauner 1975, Stumm and Morgan 1981, Zirino and Yamamoto 1972).

As indicated previously, the assumption that free copper ions can exist in solution probably is correct for waters of low pH and alkalinity, but not for seawater. In the absence of organic compounds, borato complexes form preferentially (Sposito 1981). When organics are present, approximately 73% of the TCu is complexed with organic substances; the remaining 27% consists of borato complexes (Sposito 1981). Seawaters containing no borate (e.g., many artificial seawaters) would complex copper as hydroxo and carbonato compounds, as described in earlier seawater models that did not consider borate as a complexing agent of the minor trace metals (Zirino and Yamamoto 1972). If borato complexes are eliminated from consideration, the concentration of Cu(II) is ~30% of the TCu in organic-free seawater acidified to pH 7.0, but accounts for only 1% at pH 8.1, and for <0.1% at pH 8.6 (Zirino and Yamamoto 1972). Consequently, there is no reason to think that any appreciable concentration of Cu(II) can exist in seawater within the normal pH range (8.1 to 8.3), even in the complete absence of borate and organic matter. In such situations most of the complexed copper species are hydroxides, which are insoluble or nearly so. In other words, they are nonlabile and release Cu(II) to the water either slowly or not at all.

Aquarium seawater ordinarily contains organic ligands, in addition to the inorganic species $B(OH)_4^-$, OH^-, and CO_3^{2-}. The most important organic ligands are humic acids, composed of large molecules with weak negative electrical charges. Humic acids originate from several sources, including the cellular constituents of bacteria and algae, and give old aquarium water its characteristic yellow color (Chapter 2). Seawater also contains calcium and magnesium, commonly referred to as the *hardness metals*. The far greater concentrations of calcium and magnesium compared with copper suggests that they might compete with copper for complexation sites on ligands, freeing Cu(II). But this is not what happens.

Immediately on dissociation the Cu(II) in copper salts forms very strong and complete nonlabile complexes with humic acids. The hardness metals are not involved, being unable to compete with copper for complexation sites. This is because the hardness metals are generally more weakly complexed than the minor metals (Stumm and Morgan 1981). Carbonate and hydroxyl ions are not involved either, because they cannot compete as ligands with borate and humic acids, even if the latter are present only in trace amounts. When humic acids are available, nonlabile copper complexes form preferentially to labile ones, but as more Cu(II) is added the excess shifts to form labile complexes. The extent of nonlabile complexation is pH-dependent and increases with increasing pH. In other words, as the pH rises the concentrations of OH^- and CO_3^{2-} increase, effectively increasing the fraction of copper that they complex. Calcium and magnesium produce no noticeable effect on nonlabile interactions at pH values greater than 8.0 and probably are unable to release Cu(II) from nonlabile ligands by ion exchange (O'Shea and Mancy 1978).

The controversy over whether copper precipitates in aquarium seawater is of no consequence. If precipitates are considered to be one class of nonlabile complexes, it makes little difference whether Cu(II) is chemically unavailable as an insoluble borato, hydroxo, or carbonato complex, or complexed with a nonlabile organic ligand. The chances of Cu(II) being available by ion exchange from formulated copper compounds are remote, considering how weakly the hardness metals are complexed. Any Cu(II) released is quickly and preferentially complexed by trace organic compounds in solution. The resulting substances are nonlabile at the normal pH range of seawater.

(31) Franklin and Morse (1982).

(32) Wolf (1988, pp. 268–271).

(33) See references in Darai (1986).

(34) According to Pilcher and Fryer (1980), lymphocystis disease has been reported only from ''certain higher orders'' of fishes and presumably does not occur in elasmobranchs and ancestral teleosts.

(35) For example, lymphocystis disease has been reported in fishes from freshwaters of North America (Clifford and Applegate 1970, Margenau et al. 1988, Nigrelli and Ruggieri 1965, Walker and Weissenberg 1965, Weissenberg 1954), coastal waters of northern Europe (Hussein and Mills 1982, Wolthaus 1984), western North Atlantic (Murchelano and Bridges 1976), eastern North Pacific (McCosker 1969, McCosker and Nigrelli 1971), Bering Sea (Alpers et al. 1977), Gulf of Mexico (Cook 1972, Dukes and Lawler 1975, Johnson 1978), Caribbean

(Urdaneta 1982, Williams et al. 1984), and Red Sea (Paperna et al. 1982). Also see the summary of Wolf (1988, pp. 271 and 284).

(36) McCosker et al. (1976).

(37) Anderson et al. (1988), Pilcher and Fryer (1980).

(38) Lowe (1874).

(39) Wolf et al. (1966).

(40) Wolf (1980).

(41) Nigrelli and Ruggieri (1965), Pilcher and Fryer (1980), Wolf (1968).

(42) Margenau et al. (1988).

(43) Weissenberg (1965).

(44) Wolf (1968).

(45) Hetrick (1984).

(46) Hetrick (1984), Nigrelli and Ruggieri (1965).

(47) Hetrick (1984) mentioned this possibility. Clifford and Applegate (1970) reported a greater incidence of lymphocystis in tagged walleyes (*Stizostedion vitreum*) than in untagged fish. Lesions were common near the tags.

(48) Paperna et al. (1987).

(49) Epizootics occur in both summer and winter, but centrarchids are more susceptible in winter (Weissenberg 1954). Nigrelli (1954) observed a greater incidence of disease among North American freshwater fishes in summer. Lymphocystis disease in dabs (*Limanda limanda*) is most prevalent in winter and spring (Wolthaus 1984).

(50) Pilcher and Fryer (1980), Wolf (1968).

(51) McAllister (1981).

(52) Nigrelli and Ruggieri (1965) reported that enlarged cells are sometimes recovered from the gills, pharynx, ovary, spleen, heart walls, and gastrointestinal tract. They provided an annotated bibliography.

(53) Dukes and Lawler (1975).

(54) Cook (1972), Paperna et al. (1982, 1987), Weissenberg (1954).

(55) Russell (1974).

(56) Paperna et al. (1982), Weissenberg (1954).

(57) Parisot and Wood (1959, 1960) proposed the term ''mycobacteriosis'' based on the absence of typical inflammatory responses to infections in salmonids. Nigrelli and Vogel (1963) disagreed with their assessment: ''However, since this [inflammatory response] is not true for fishes generally and since typical tubercles and other classical tissues [*sic*] reactions are present, tuberculosis is a valid term for the disease in fish as well as in other cold-blooded animals.'' Both terms seem acceptable.

(58) The shape of a bacterium as seen under a microscope is a useful diagnostic tool. Those shaped like cylinders are known as *rods*.

(59) Bacteria are often identified by staining. Dyes increase the visibility of bacterial cells under magnification. Each dye has an affinity for specific cellular material. Many are positively charged (cationic) and combine with negatively charged (anionic) constituents of cells (e.g., nucleic acids). One such dye is methylene blue. Others are anionic (e.g., Congo red, eosin) and combine with cationic cellular constituents such as proteins. Among the important dyes used in bacteriology is *Gram's stain*, named after Christian Gram, a Dane, who devised the procedure in 1884 (Lautrop 1981). Gram's stain is *differential* because it permits the differentiation of bacteria that are morphologically indistinguishable, but of different species. Based on how bacterial cells react to the procedure (application of a crystal violet solution followed by an iodine solution), they can be classified as *Gram-positive* or *Gram-negative*. The portion of the organism that accepts stain is the *cell wall*, which separates the intracellular constituents from the external environment. The cell walls of Gram-negative bacteria are complex and comprised of several layers; the walls of Gram-positive organisms generally consist of a single, thicker layer. If, after staining, the cells are washed with alcohol, those that are Gram-positive retain the stain and appear blue under a microscope. Gram-negative cells relinquish the stain and must be *counterstained* with another material (e.g., safranin) to be visible.

(60) *Acid-fast* cells are those that when stained with dyes such as basic fuchsin resist decolorization with dilute acid. Bacteria that are not acid-fast are decolorized readily. Acid-fastness, which is limited to *Mycobacterium* and a few species of *Nocardia*, is caused by the presence of large amounts of waxy substances on the cell surfaces that bind the dye molecules tightly.

(61) Several species and subspecies of *Mycobacterium* are associated with mycobacteriosis in fishes: *M. chelonae, M. chelonae abscessus, M. chelonae chelonae, M. chelonae piscarius, M. fortui-*

tum, *M. marinum*, and *M. salmoniphilum*. *Mycobacterium chelonae* was formerly *M. chelonei* (von Graevenitz and Berger 1980). Wayne and Kubica (1986) did not list (and apparently did not recognize) *M. chelonae piscarius* (see Arakawa and Fryer 1984) and *M. salmoniphilum* (see Ross 1960).

(62) Bataillon et al. (1897).

(63) Aronson (1926), Winsor (1946).

(64) The list was published by Nigrelli and Vogel (1963). Giavenni et al. (1980) described an epizootic involving 97 captive coral reef fishes of 17 species.

(65) The inclusion of raw carcasses and viscera of adult salmon in unpasteurized feeds used to rear juveniles was a primary source of infection in salmonid hatcheries in the 1950s (Ross 1963, 1970; Snieszko 1978). The incidence of mycobacteriosis diminished markedly when pasteurized salmonid by-products were substituted (Fryer and Sanders 1981, Snieszko 1978). Nigrelli (1963) reported that aquarium fishes can become infected by eating the carcasses of infected aquarium-mates.

(66) Dulin (1979).

(67) This possibility was suggested by Parisot and Wood (1959). Later, Clark and Shepard (1963) demonstrated that tadpoles can become infected by waterborne *Mycobacterium marinum*, and that infected fishes were the sources.

(68) Nigrelli and Vogel (1963), Snieszko (1978).

(69) Arakawa and Fryer (1984).

(70) Snieszko (1978).

(71) Giavenni et al. (1980).

(72) Daoust et al. (1989).

(73) Conroy (1970), Snieszko (1978).

(74) Daoust et al. (1989) reported that 8% of the yellow perch (*Perca flavescens*) sampled from a freshwater Canadian lake were infected with *Mycobacterium chelonae*. No signs of disease were evident initially, but some fish died after several weeks in captivity. The authors suggested that immune suppression at low temperature could be a predisposing factor. They noted that warm temperatures strengthen immunity in fishes, but also favor bacterial growth. Conroy (1970) mentioned the possibility that sudden temperature changes induce clinical mycobacteriosis in captive fishes.

(75) Winsor (1946).

(76) External signs do not appear in young salmonids (Parisot and Wood 1959).

(77) Nigrelli and Vogel (1963).

(78) Nigrelli (1963).

(79) Parisot and Wood (1959).

(80) Conroy (1970).

(81) Giavenni et al. (1980), Nigrelli and Vogel (1963).

(82) Gratzek (1981).

(83) Majeed et al. (1981).

(84) Dulin (1979).

(85) Daoust et al. (1989), Nigrelli and Vogel (1963), Sakanari et al. (1983).

(86) Snieszko (1978) stated that *Mycobacterium* is notably resistant to disinfectants, but provided no literature citations.

(87) Reichenbach-Klinke (1972).

(88) Faoagali et al. (1977).

(89) Adams et al. (1970), Faoagali et al. (1977).

(90) Adams et al. (1970), Faoagali et al. (1977), Swift and Cohen (1962), van Dyke and Lake (1975).

(91) Adams et al. (1970).

(92) Adams et al. (1970), van Dyke and Lake (1975).

(93) Adams et al. (1970), Swift and Cohen (1962).

(94) van Dyke and Lake (1975).

(95) Baumann et al. (1984).

(96) Anderson and Conroy (1970) listed 63 species of fishes from which vibriosis has been described. Austin and Austin (1987, p. 266) wrote: ''An authoritative publication [no citation] reported that vibriosis occurs in more than 14 countries, where it has ravaged approximately 48 species of marine fish.''

(97) See Anderson and Conroy (1970) for a brief history of vibriosis.

(98) For summaries see Austin and Austin (1987, pp. 263–296), Bullock (1987), and Colwell and Grimes (1984). Larsen (1983) and Larsen and Mellergaard (1984) published comprehensive surveys of *V. anguillarum* strains known to be fish pathogens.

(99) Horne (1982) removed samples of *V. anguillarum* from the posterior gut of young Atlantic salmon (*Salmo salar*), cultured the organism, and injected it intramuscularly into the same fish. Vibriosis did not develop. However, *V. anguillarum* isolated from the lymphoid organs of moribund Atlantic salmon during an epizootic induced disease in healthy fish when injected intramuscularly. The situation is more complex when different hosts are involved. Egidius and Andersen (1978) found that *V. anguillarum* isolated from rainbow trout (*Oncorhynchus mykiss*) induce vibriosis in salmonids, but the incidence of disease was low when the same organism was injected into healthy pollocks (*Pollachius virens*). *Vibrio anguillarum* isolated from diseased pollocks were pathogenic when injected into healthy pollocks, but without apparent effect when administered to rainbow trout. Horne (1982, p. 175) concluded that each species of fish probably has a range of tolerance to a particular vibrio. Host specificity ". . . may act as a barrier to infection which lowers the likelihood of cultured stocks being infected from wild populations; on the other [hand], the [harmless] commensals of one fish species may be the pathogens of another." Horne (1982, p. 176) continued, "Despite the ambiguity and scarcity of the evidence it is still widely held that the commensal strains of *Vibrio* sp. found in healthy fish are a common origin of disease outbreaks either in their own host or another species."

Differences in host specificity are not the only consideration. As Horne (1982) noted, vibrios can also be viewed simply as pathogenic bacteria. In this context, pathogenic vibrios are genetic variants of the larger, commensal population, and their mere introduction from extraneous sources is sufficient to increase the risk of epizootics. A virulence mechanism, typically present only in highly virulent strains of *Vibrio*, has been identified (Austin and Austin 1987, p. 273).

(100) Bullock (1987) stated that seven species of *Vibrio* had been identified as fish pathogens, but did not list them. Austin and Austin (1987, p. 263) listed seven species, including *V. cholerae*, but considered infectivity of *V. cholerae* and *V. parahaemolyticus* in fishes to be tentative (Austin and Austin 1987, pp. 263 and 280). Colwell and Grimes (1984) also discussed *V. parahaemolyticus* as a tentative fish pathogen, but felt certain that *V. cholerae* (the organism that causes cholera in humans) is a legitimate fish pathogen. I have included *V. cholerae* in my list (see the text) and added three others: Grimes et al. (1985a) cultured *V. furnissii* and *V. harveyi* from sharks in Bahamian waters; Kraxberger-Beatty et al. (1990) recovered *V. harveyi* and *V. splendidus* from ocular lesions of captive snook (*Centropomus undecimalis*) and also from the aquarium water. None of these species was mentioned by Austin and Austin (1987).

On the basis of Koch's postulates, only a few vibrios qualify as confirmed fish pathogens; the rest must be listed as suspected pathogens. Koch's postulates state that before a microorganism can be said to induce a specific disease it must (1) always be found in the diseased animal but never in healthy ones, (2) be isolated from diseased animals and grown in pure culture, (3) initiate and reproduce the disease when reinoculated into susceptible hosts, and (4) be reisolated from animals infected experimentally.

At one time *V. anguillarum* was believed to exist as two biochemical isolates, labeled biotypes 1 and 2. Biotype 2 is now *V. ordalii* (see Schiewe 1981, 1983; Schiewe et al. 1981). The range of *V. ordalii* is limited at present to the Pacific Northwest and Japan; that of *V. salmonicida* to Norway and Scotland (Bullock 1987). The last-named species was described by Egidius et al. (1986).

(101) Grimes et al. (1985a) examined the bacterial flora of 28 sharks of five species in the Bahamas and isolated *V. alginolyticus, V. carchariae, V. damsela, V. furnissii, V. harveyi,* and *Vibrio* spp. Buck et al. (1984) cultured *V. alginolyticus, V. fluvialis,* and *V. parahaemolyticus* from the teeth of an adult white shark (*Carcharodon carcharias*) harpooned by fishermen in the western North Atlantic. Love et al. (1981) reported finding *V. damsela* on marine algae.

(102) Grimes et al. (1985b) suggested that a monogenetic trematode (*Dermophthirius nigrellii*) parasitic on lemon sharks is a vector for *V. carchariae*. Roberts et al. (1973) showed that *V. anguillarum* is a secondary invader in Atlantic salmon through dermal lesions caused by tagging. Colorni et al. (1981) observed extensive mortality of cultured gilthead breams (*Sparus aurata*) after handling. The deaths were associated with *V. alginolyticus*, although clinical infections could not be induced experimentally. Moring (1982) reported epizootics of vibriosis in pen-raised chinook salmon (*Oncorhynchus tshawytscha*) after routine handling and transfer.

(103) Haastein and Holt (1972) added *V. anguillarum* to water containing Atlantic salmon; death occurred within 10 to 27 d at 10°C. Hjeltnes et al. (1987) monitored the waterborne transmission of a species of *Vibrio* implicated in Hitra disease. Atlantic salmon exposed to inoculated water for 1 h died a week later. Some of the fish had been wounded by the removal of scales, but death ensued almost as quickly in unwounded fish. Similar findings with *V. damsela* were reported by Love et al. (1981). Scales were removed from blacksmiths (*Chromis punctipinnis*), after which the skin was scarified and inoculated. Ulcers formed within 3 d, and all fish died within 4 d. Cultures of *V. damsela*

swabbed onto 10 healthy blacksmiths with scales intact produced ulcers in five of the fish, all of which died within 4 d.

In the experiment of Hjeltnes et al. (1987), other Atlantic salmon were anesthetized, and dense suspensions of bacteria were placed on the gills. The fish started to die after 2 weeks, indicating that the gill may be a primary site of waterborne infections. In still another aspect of the study it was shown that fish-fish infections took place: some of the fish kept in UV-sterilized influent water died after infected fish were transferred to the same water system (see Note 17). The authors speculated that although the gills are a primary site of initial infection, induction of disease is enhanced in the presence of open wounds. In a study that produced different results, Chart and Munn (1980) were unable to induce vibriosis in wounded European eels (*Anguilla anguilla*) maintained in freshwater contaminated with a virulent strain of *V. anguillarum*. Lewis (1985) could not find *V. anguillarum* in cultures of aquarium water inhabited by uninfected channel catfish (*Ictalurus punctatus*). However, concentrations of $\sim 10^4$ cells/mL were recovered 48 h after the fish were inoculated with *V. anguillarum*. Waterborne transmission is the principal means by which healthy fishes become diseased (Kanno et al. 1989).

(104) Chart and Munn (1980) failed to induce clinical signs of vibriosis in European eels fed inocula of *V. anguillarum* for 3 weeks. Haastein and Holt (1972), however, reported that when Atlantic salmon were fed *V. anguillarum* in water of 15°C, death occurred within 24 h.

(105) *Vibrio anguillarum* in culture ordinarily has an optimal growth temperature near 25°C (Larsen 1984), but epizootics in salmonid hatcheries and other cold-water environments occur at much lower temperatures. Epizootics in temperate seawater fishes are reportedly more prevalent in summer and early autumn when the water is warmest (Bolinches and Egidius 1987, Haastein and Holt 1972, Love et al. 1981). Muroga et al. (1984a) stated that juvenile ayu (*Plecoglossus altivelis*) captured during warm months had a higher incidence of vibriosis than winter juveniles.

Epizootics occur at other times of the year if the temperature suddenly rises several degrees above ambient (Haastein and Holt 1972), conditions that presumably promote bacterial growth. However, the reverse situation is not uncommon, perhaps because the immune response of temperate fishes may be lower in winter (Corbel 1975). Watkins et al. (1981) found that juvenile winter flounders (*Pseudopleuronectes americanus*) collected in winter were more susceptible to vibriosis than specimens obtained in summer and suggested that suppression of the immune response at low temperature is a predisposing factor. Olafsen et al. (1981) observed the same phenomenon in several species of cold-water fishes from coastal Norway. Optimal growth temperature for the four strains of *V. anguillarum* described was 15 to 18°C. These authors also associated epizootics with immune suppression of the host fishes at low temperatures.

(106) Austin and Austin (1987, pp. 263–286).

(107) I have used these terms previously without defining them. In general, *chronic* diseases progress more slowly and often are enzootic, resulting ultimately in remission or death. *Acute* forms of the same disease develop rapidly with severe clinical signs and ordinarily result in death. Both chronic and acute diseases can develop into epizootics. Epizootics of acute vibriosis may be less sensitive to seasonal changes (Watkins et al. 1981). Watkins et al. (1981) provided a clear distinction between chronic and acute vibriosis in juvenile winter flounders (see their Table 4, p. 1049).

(108) Bullock (1987) gave a general overview.

(109) LeaMaster and Ostrowski (1988).

(110) Richards (1980).

(111) Watkins et al. (1981).

(112) Colorni et al. (1981), LeaMaster and Ostrowski (1988).

(113) May et al. (1982).

(114) Haastein and Holt (1972).

(115) Bullock (1987), May et al. (1982).

(116) Bullock (1987), Fryer et al. (1972), Haastein and Holt (1972), Hjeltnes et al. (1987), Sako and Hara (1984).

(117) Anderson and Conroy (1970), Haastein and Holt (1972).

(118) Hjeltnes et al. (1987), Hodgins et al. (1977), Richards (1980).

(119) *Vibrio anguillarum* produces an exotoxin that kills host fishes (Inamura et al. 1984). The anemia that accompanies vibriosis is believed to be caused by a potent *hemolytic toxin* (a substance of metabolic origin that destroys red blood cells) produced by the infectious agent. This possibility was proposed by Wolke (1975), and tentative confirmation was obtained by Munn (1980). However, Watkins et al. (1981) were unable to induce lesions or death in captive winter flounders by injecting them with cell supernatants, killed cell suspensions, cell extracts, and

cell debris of *V. anguillarum*. More recently, Sakata et al. (1989) showed that *V. damsela* has demonstrable hemolytic activity to fish erythrocytes.

Vibrio carchariae and *V. damsela* also produce virulent cytotoxins (Sakata et al. 1989) in cells other than erythrocytes. These compounds are potentially fatal within hours. Grimes et al. (1984b) isolated *V. carchariae* and *V. damsela* from a sandbar shark (*Carcharhinus plumbeus*) that died at National Aquarium in Baltimore during an epizootic of vibriosis. Cultures of the organisms were administered separately to spiny dogfish (*Squalus acanthias*, one shark for each species of *Vibrio*) by intraperitoneal injection (Grimes et al. 1984a, 1984b). Both sharks died <18 h later. *Vibrio damsela* was recovered from the kidney and peritoneal cavity, but not from spleen, liver, or skin tissues; kidney, liver, peritoneum, and skin tissues of the shark were positive for *V. carchariae*. Healthy lemon sharks administered the same isolates by intraperitoneal injection were resistant to *V. damsela* (Grimes et al. 1984a, 1984b). After 46 h, *V. damsela* could not be recovered from the tissues. The shark injected with *V. carchariae* survived the 46-h period, but abnormalities were observed in kidney, liver, and spleen tissues. In other lemon sharks, *V. damsela* was isolated from the stomach of a healthy specimen, *V. carchariae* from a whitish skin lesion, and *V. carchariae* from trematodes (*Dermophthirius nigrellii*) infesting the skin of still another individual.

Vibrio carchariae and *V. damsela* were shown to hydrolyze urea, an uncommon trait in vibrios. In the case of *V. carchariae*, urea is the only source of metabolic nitrogen and carbon; *V. damsela* can use urea as a carbon and nitrogen source, but only in the presence of yeast extract. In elasmobranchs, the high concentration of urea in the blood and tissues serves an osmoregulatory function (Chapter 4). For additional information see Grimes et al. (1989) and Knight et al. (1988).

(120) Fryer et al. (1972), Love et al. (1981), Watkins et al. (1981).

(121) Hjeltnes et al. (1987), Richards (1980).

(122) Lewis (1985), Watkins et al. (1981).

(123) Schiewe (1983) suggested that *V. ordalli* produces a leukocytolytic factor.

(124) Lewis (1985).

(125) Hjeltnes et al. (1987).

(126) Love et al. (1981).

(127) Grimes et al. (1985b) reported that *V. carchariae* causes vasculitis in lemon sharks.

(128) Anderson and Conroy (1970), Hjeltnes et al. (1987), Richards (1980).

(129) LeaMaster and Ostrowski (1988) described vibriosis in captive dolphins (*Coryphaena hippurus*) that they associated with handling. Richards (1980), noting that epizootics often occur after netting of wild flatfishes and transfer to holding facilities, recommended minimum handling as a standard husbandry practice.

(130) Anderson and Conroy (1970), Ross (1970).

(131) Grimes et al. (1985b).

(132) Itami and Kusuda (1984) reported that in ayu, the stress of transfer from freshwater to saline water can induce vibriosis. Virulence of the infectious agent (*V. anguillarum*) was enhanced in water of greater ionic strength. Richards (1980) suggested that osmotic imbalances resulting from open ulcers and subsequent loss of skin surface contribute to mortality during advanced stages of vibriosis.

(133) Baker et al. (1983), Rødsaether et al. (1977).

(134) Vibrios introduced into salmonid hatcheries in seafood products (e.g., herring) have been a source of vibriosis (Anderson and Conroy 1970).

(135) Colwell and Grimes (1984) reviewed the literature on vaccination of fishes against vibriosis. Vaccines found to be effective against *V. anguillarum* in salmonids were described by Austin and Austin (1987, pp. 275–278), Baudin-Laurencin and Tangtrongpiros (1980), Baum et al. (1982), Evelyn and Ketcheson (1980), Gould et al. (1979), Håstein et al. (1980), Holm and Jørgensen (1987), Johnson et al. (1982a, 1982b), and Lillehaug (1990). Baudin-Laurencin and Batellier (1986) reported that a *V. anguillarum* vaccine for turbot (*Scophthalmus maximus*) is marketed in France.

(136) Bullock (1987).

(137) Prescott (1977) claimed partial success in immunizing three species of tropical damselfishes (Pomacentridae) and one species of snapper (Lutjanidae) against *V. anguillarum* with an oral vaccine. However, the data sets were too small for proper statistical analysis, and the method was incompletely described.

(138) Fryer et al. (1972).

(139) Blake (1980), Love et al. (1981).

(140) Blake et al. (1979).

(141) Blake (1980), Blake et al. (1979).

(142) Buck and Spotte (1986a, 1986b).

(143) Mearns and Sherwood (1974), Murchelano (1975), Wellings et al. (1976).

(144) Sindermann (1979).

(145) Mearns and Sherwood (1974) and Murchelano (1975) failed to isolate bacteria from fin rot lesions of wild-caught fishes. They suggested that the principal etiologic agent is a chemical irritant. This possibility was given credence by Mearns and Sherwood (1974), who observed slight gill hyperplasia in some specimens, a condition not ordinarily associated with fin rot but a typical effect of chemical irritants in the environment.

(146) Mahoney et al. (1973) isolated 60 cultures of *Aeromonas, Pseudomonas,* and *Vibrio* from fin rot lesions of fishes collected in New York Bight. They stated: ''Almost all of the 60 cultures belonging to the three genera did not grow well or at all in the absence of salt, therefore, presumably all were 'marine' types.''

(147) Khan et al. (1981), Levin et al. (1972), Mahoney et al. (1973), Oppenheimer (1958).

(148) Murchelano (1975), Murchelano and Ziskowski (1979), Wakabayashi et al. (1984).

(149) Khan et al. (1981), Mahoney et al. (1973).

(150) Mahoney et al. (1973), Mearns and Sherwood (1974).

(151) Sindermann (1977).

(152) Mahoney et al. (1973), Murchelano and Ziskowski (1976).

(153) Bullock (1968), Khan et al. (1981), Mahoney et al. (1973).

(154) Mahoney et al. (1973), Schneider and Nicholson (1980).

(155) Mahoney et al. (1973), Mearns and Sherwood (1974), Pippy and Hare (1969).

(156) Temporal effects in temperate seawater and brackish water fishes are not well defined and may be species dependent to an extent. Khan et al. (1981) found that Atlantic cod (*Gadus morhua*) captured in winter and kept in laboratory aquariums at winter temperatures had higher incidences of fin rot than specimens caught in summer. They speculated that the immune response in Atlantic cod is suppressed or absent at low temperatures (0 to 3°C in their studies). Wellings et al. (1976) wrote that incidences of fin rot in wild-caught starry flounders (*Platichythys stellatus*) are highest in March and lowest in July. Ma-

honey et al. (1973) noted that the observations of fin rot in wild-caught silver hake (*Merluccius tenuis*) and red hake (*Urophycis chuss*) increases in late autumn, but in 20 other species the incidence of disease tends to parallel increases in water temperature, being highest in summer and early autumn. Mahoney et al. (1973) and Murchelano and Ziskowski (1977) suggested that elevated bacterial counts in warm water are responsible for the greater prevalence of fin rot in summer, compared with winter. Schneider and Nicholson (1980) observed that Atlantic salmon in a freshwater hatchery had a higher incidence of active fin rot lesions as the water temperature decreased. The rise in spring temperatures could be correlated with an abatement of active lesions and healing. Wakabayashi et al. (1984) isolated an unknown species of *Flexibacter* from fin rot lesions of pen-reared red seabreams (*Chrysophrys major*) and black seabreams (*Acanthopagrus schlageli*). The organism grew *in vitro* at temperatures ranging from 15 to 34°C; optimal temperature for growth was 30°C.

(157) Mahoney et al. (1973).

(158) Khan et al. (1981), Mahoney et al. (1973), Murchelano (1975), Murchelano and Ziskowski (1977), Wellings et al. (1976).

(159) Schnieder and Nicholson (1980), Wakabayashi et al. (1984).

(160) Mahoney et al. (1973), Murchelano (1975), Murchelano and Ziskowski (1977).

(161) Khan et al. (1981), Mahoney et al. (1973), Wakabayashi et al. (1984), Wellings et al. (1976).

(162) Khan et al. (1981), Murchelano and Ziskowski (1977).

(163) Khan et al. (1981).

(164) Murchelano (1975).

(165) Mearns and Sherwood (1974).

(166) Murchelano (1975), Schneider and Nicholson (1980).

(167) Khan et al. (1981), Murchelano (1975), Murchelano and Ziskowski (1977).

(168) Mahoney et al. (1973), Wellings et al. (1976).

(169) Murchelano and Ziskowski (1979) referred to fin rot as ". . . a sentinel of environmental quality."

(170) Mahoney et al. (1973) conducted an experiment in which two isolates each of *Aeromonas*, *Pseudomonas*, and *Vibrio* were

rubbed onto the lightly abraded caudal fins of mummichogs (*Fundulus heteroclitus*) kept in laboratory aquariums. Fin rot resulted in every case.

(171) Pippy and Hare (1969).

(172) The genera *Amyloodinium* and *Oodinium* are both retained in the literature with the specific name *ocellatum*. In her original description, Brown (1931) named the parasite *Oodinium ocellatum*, but Brown and Hovasse (1946) transferred it to the genus *Amyloodinium*. By their analysis, members of genus *Oodinium* contain no starch and attach to the host by an adhesive disk instead of rootlike rhizoids (see the text description). *Amyloodinium*, in contrast, was believed to possess both starch and rhizoids. Perhaps these distinctions are no longer valid. In describing a new parasitic dinoflagellate, Lawler (1967) noted that it had both starch and rhizoids, but named the organism *Oodinium cyprinodontum*. Brown and Hovasse (1946) were cited by Lawler, but in a different context. *Amyloodinium* seems to be favored in current usage, although some authors prefer *Oodinium* (e.g., Cheung et al. 1979a, 1981a, 1981b). Lawler (1980) briefly reviewed the literature on *Amyloodinium ocellatum* and related species.

(173) Nigrelli (1936) listed 16 species of teleosts from Sandy Hook Bay found to harbor *A. ocellatum*. Some were late-summer transients in the Gulf Stream from southern waters.

(174) Lawler (1972) reported finding *A. ocellatum* attached to 13 species indigenous to Mississippi Sound, and Lawler (1980) examined 99 fishes of 43 species from 20 families; 16 species of 13 families carried natural infections of *A. ocellatum*. These fishes had low-level (enzootic?) infections (~100 organisms), a number ". . . far short of the several thousand necessary to kill the host."

(175) This was discussed briefly by Brown (1934), Lawler (1980), and Nigrelli (1936). *Amyloodinium ocellatum* has been introduced into aquaculture installations on the Red Sea (Paperna 1980).

(176) The number of North American fishes known to be susceptible to amyloodinium disease is from Lawler (1979). Brown (1934) listed 28 infected species at the Aquarium of the Zoological Society of London.

(177) The fishes placed in this category by Lawler (1977, 1980) are species he studied. All are brackish water and indigenous to the southern United States: sheepshead minnow (*Cyprinodon variegatus*), gulf killifish (*Fundulus grandis*), American eel (*Anguilla rostrata*), gulf toadfish (*Opsanus beta*), sailfin molly (*Poecilia

latipinna), fat sleeper (*Dormitator maculatus*), and inland silverside (*Menidia beryllina*). Brown (1934) noted that fishes in residence at the Aquarium of the Zoological Society of London were less likely to die of amyloodinium disease than newly acquired specimens and stated that some species seemed more susceptible than others. This suggests the possibility of immunity, although stress would appear to be a mediating factor. Paperna (1980) reported that survivors of amyloodinium epizootics in an Israeli hatchery survived subsequent exposure to the disease. The species were the gilthead bream, seabass (*Dicentrarchus labrax*), and rabbitfish (*Siganus rivulatus*).

(178) Brown (1934), Paperna (1980).

(179) Lawler (1980).

(180) Paperna (1980).

(181) Brown (1934) found unattached tomonts in the stomach of an infected fish, as did Lawler (1980), who suggested that they might have been ingested after detachment. Cheung et al. (1981a) reported *A. ocellatum* from the pharynx, head kidney, and mesentery adjacent to the liver of infected porkfish (*Anisotremus virginicus*).

(182) Brown (1934), Nigrelli (1936).

(183) Brown and Hovasse (1946) stated that only two stages exist, the trophont and tomont, but included the tomite separately in a later section of their paper.

(184) Brown (1934) described the trophonts as ". . . colourless, opaque, rounded cysts, easily distinguished from other parasites of similar form occurring on fish gills by a pearly lustre which is very striking."

(185) Dimensions of the trophonts given in the text are from Nigrelli (1936), who isolated the organism from fishes at New York Aquarium. Trophonts studied by Paperna (1984b) in Israel measured 50 to 90 μm in length. Lawler (1980) reported that trophonts of *A. ocellatum* recovered from Mississippi Sound fishes occasionally attained lengths of 350 μm, but most were < 150 μm. These differences are considerable, and perhaps more than one species exists.

(186) Paperna (1984b).

(187) Lom and Lawler (1973) discounted any presumed function of the rhizoids in nutrient assimilation.

(188) Lom and Lawler (1973) provided an extensive description of the ultrastructure of *Amyloodinium* sp. and discussed how the

different components might function in nutrient uptake. My text description, which is based largely on their discussion, may not be completely valid for *A. ocellatum*. However, no specific description of the feeding mechanisms of *A. ocellatum* is possible at this time, because the two existing papers on the subject (Brown 1934, Nigrelli 1936) are dated and may be incorrect.

(189) Brown (1934) stated that in severe infections the trophonts detach ". . . from the gill filaments . . . and fall into the water in clouds, like fine powder."

(190) *Amyloodinium ocellatum* is primarily a warm-water parasite. Bower and Turner (1988) claimed that tomonts survive storage in seawater at 10°C for 9 weeks and at 15°C for at least 12 weeks. No data were provided. According to Brown (1934), development is halted below 10°C. Sporulation occurs slowly between 10 and 20°C, quickens at 20 to 25°C, and reaches peak rate (in ~3 d) at 25°C. Paperna (1984b) observed delayed detachment of trophonts at 16°C, although full growth (>100 μm) was still attained by days 6 or 7, compared with days 3 to 5 at 19 to 24°C. Delayed division and sporulation were seen at 15°C; at 8 and 35°C there was total interruption of division followed by mortality. The optimal temperature range for reproduction was 18 to 30°C, although minimum division time took place between 23 and 27°C. Nigrelli (1936) studied the rate of development at constant salinity (37.6‰) and different temperatures. Sporulation was slow at 12.5°C, with only a few nonmotile dinospores seen after 7 d. Most dinospores did not become free swimming until after 10 d. At 25°C a few nonmotile dinospores were formed as soon as day 3, and motile cells were observed after 5 d. At 35°C development accelerated, and the rates were similar to those observed at 22°C and S = 20.6‰. The work of Nigrelli (1936) and Paperna (1984b) suggests that the effects of temperature and salinity are interactive.

(191) Bower and Turner (1988) stated that tomonts in their cultures reproduced after having been stored in freshwater for 6 weeks, but provided no data. The percentage survival was greater in tap water than either distilled water or distilled water to which calcium or sodium salts had been added. Nigrelli (1936) reported that tomont development was arrested at the four-cell stage in freshwater, with only 18% reaching the eight-cell stage. Similar results were obtained with water of S = 1.5‰. At 22°C development proceeded over a wide range of salinities (20.6 to 43‰), with the optimal range being 16.7 to 28.5‰. According to Paperna (1984b), salinity tolerance depends on the ambient temperature, and he observed the greatest tolerance range at

24 to 25°C. Division occurred between 1 and 78‰, but normal reproductive processes were observed between 10 and 60‰. Brown (1934) wrote that the development of tomonts in freshwater continued, although slowly, and not all cells divided. Fifty percent of a culture kept in freshwater for 3 d divided normally after transfer to seawater, and the author was of the opinion that tomonts could survive immersion in freshwater for even longer periods.

(192) Nigrelli (1936).

(193) Lawler (1980), Nigrelli (1936).

(194) Brown (1934), Lawler (1980), Nigrelli (1936).

(195) Dempster (1955), Lauckner (1984b), Lawler (1980).

(196) Dempster (1955).

(197) Lawler (1980), Paperna (1980).

(198) Lom and Lawler (1973), Paperna (1980).

(199) Lom and Lawler (1973) wrote: "The extensive damage done by a single trophont to many epithelial cells in which its rhizoids are embedded, as well as avid feeding on large lumps of host cell cytoplasm, explains the high pathogenicity of dinoflagellates for fish."

(200) Numerous compounds have been tried with varying success in attempts to control amyloodinium disease. The published reports often provide tantilizing hope but too often are devoid of experimental details. Bower and Turner (1988) listed a number of compounds that either kill dinospores or interrupt tomont division, but offered no information on concentration and exposure time. According to these authors, dinospores *in vitro* were killed within 48 h by acriflavin neutral, amphotericin B, benzalkonium chloride, chiniofon, chloramphenicol, chloroquine, dehydroemetine, emetine, formalin, hydrogen peroxide, Lugol's iodine, malachite green, methylene blue, nifurpirinol, primaquine, and quinacrine. Dinospores were unaffected by cupric sulfate, cupric sulfate complexed with citric acid or EDTA, chlortetracycline, difluoromethylornithine, furazolidone, ipronidazole, ivermectin, metronidazole, nitrofurazone, pentamidine, sulfamethazine, sulfathiazole, and suramin. Cupric sulfate alone and complexed with citric acid or EDTA inhibited tomont division or sporulation over 5 d of continuous treatment *in vitro*, but only chiniofon, formalin, ipronidazole, malachite green, and pentamidine impaired reproduction completely.

According to Lawler (1977), several compounds yielded poor

results during continuous immersion of infected fishes, but no data were provided. The compounds evaluated: aureomycin, Clorox®, chlortetracycline, formalin, glacial acetic acid, malachite green, malachite green plus formalin, Microcide®, potassium permanganate, tetracycline, and Wardley's Aqua Tonic. The concentrations and dosages were unclear.

(201) Højgaard (1960) claimed that coral reef fishes could be "cured" of amyloodinium disease by lowering the salinity to 10‰. However, no data were presented, and the statement is doubtful.

(202) Brown (1934) wrote: "I am informed that chlorine was used unsuccessfully [at the aquarium] in Amsterdam . . ."

(203) According to Lawler (1977), immersion of infected fishes in freshwater for 2 to 5 min dislodges the trophonts, but some are retained in the mucus.

(204) The effectiveness of formalin treatment depends on several factors, notably the concentration and exposure time. Trophonts respond to formalin (25, 50, and 100 mL/L prepared with formaldehyde solution) by retracting the rhizoids and metamorphosing into tomonts in 1 to 3 h (Paperna 1984a). In Paperna's experiments, the tomonts were actually harmed only at the highest formalin concentration, and the detrimental effect was enhanced by increasing the concentration and time of exposure. Reproductive success—measured as the number of tomonts observed to divide and undergo sporulation, and the number of motile dinospores—declined with increased formalin concentration and exposure time. Division appeared to be inhibited after exposure to 200 mL/L formalin for 24 h, although a few motile dinospores developed even after 12 h. Division was delayed 24 h in tomonts exposed to 100 mL/L formalin and 9 d after exposure to 100 mL/L for 12 h.

(205) According to Bower and Turner (1988), cupric citrate, cupric sulfate, and cupric sulfate complexed with EDTA failed to kill dinospores of *A. ocellatum* when tested *in vitro*. These same compounds, however, prevented or inhibited tomont division or sporulation during 5 d of treatment. Test concentrations were not stated. Paperna (1984a) obtained opposite results from *in vitro* studies carried out at 20°C for 11 d (S = 40‰): concentrations of 0.5, 1.0, 2.0, 4.0, and 10.0 mg/L $CuSO_4 \cdot 5H_2O$ had no effect on tomont division, although all concentrations inhibited sporulation and were lethal to developing dinospores. Paperna (1984a) emphasized that if copper treatment is interrupted before sporulation and then resumed, normal dinospores develop. Højgaard (1960) warned that copper treatments could

never rid afflicted fishes completely of *A. ocellatum*, because some organisms in the gut would survive. No confirming evidence was offered.

(206) The organism was named *Ichthyophthirius marinus* by Sikama (1961), who was unaware that Brown (1951) had previously assigned the name *Cryptocaryon irritans*. Nigrelli and Ruggieri (1966) reviewed the history of *C. irritans* prior to publication of their paper. Also see Wilkie and Gordin (1969).

(207) Araga (1962), Cheung et al. (1979b, 1982), Hirayama and Shiomi (1962), Nigrelli and Ruggieri (1966), Wilkie and Gordin (1969).

(208) Blasiola (1976b).

(209) Huff and Burns (1981).

(210) Nigrelli and Ruggieri (1966), Sikama (1964), and Wilkie and Gordin (1969) published lists of fish species that in captivity are susceptible to *C. irritans* infections. Wilkie and Gordin reported that elasmobranchs, gobies of the genus *Lythrypnus*, moray eels (Muraenidae), and flounders (Pleuronectidae) are resistant.

(211) Public aquariums receive exhibit fishes from numerous sources, making the origin of any pathogen difficult to trace. Nigrelli and Ruggieri (1966) gave a brief history of the disease through the mid-1960s, with emphasis on epizootics at New York Aquarium (also see Cheung et al. 1979b, 1982). Epizootics involving captive fishes have been reported from Japan (Hirayama and Shiomi 1962; Sikama 1938, 1960, 1961, 1964), England (Brown 1951), Holland (de Graaf 1960), possibly Singapore (M. Laird 1965, personal communication in Nigrelli and Ruggieri 1966), and California (Wilkie and Gordin 1969). The parasite has become a widespread pest of seawater aquarium fishes throughout the United States.

(212) Brown (1963), Nigrelli and Ruggieri (1966), and Sikama (1961) described the life cycle of *C. irritans*. My description follows Nigrelli and Ruggieri (1966).

(213) Trophont dimensions in the text are from Nigrelli and Ruggieri (1966); Sikama (1961) reported ranges of 452×360 and 66×34 μm.

(214) Nigrelli and Ruggieri (1966).

(215) The life cycle of *C. irritans* depicted by Brown (1963, p. 285) is generally accurate, but her text description is not. She evidently believed that the trophonts are contained inside a

cyst, are motile in the water, and reproduce to become what she called ''blisters'' (i.e., the visible white spots on infected fishes). The white spots are actually large individual trophonts; the developmental stage is the tomont, and it produces tomites. According to Brown (1963, p. 284), these ''blisters'' swell and eventually burst. The released trophonts then ''. . . swim to the bottom, encyst, divide within the cyst and liberate tomites, which are the infective bodies and attack new hosts.'' Sikama (1938, 1960, 1961, 1964) also described the life cycle.

(216) Encystment and detachment with death of the host was reported by Colorni (1985), Nigrelli and Ruggieri (1966), and Sikama (1961).

(217) Tomont dimensions in the text are from Nigrelli and Ruggieri (1966). Tomonts measured by Sikama (1961) averaged 200 to 300 μm in diameter (range 90 to 400 μm); those described by Colorni (1985) ranged from 370 $\times$ 310 to 60 $\times$ 60 μm.

(218) Colorni (1985), Nigrelli and Ruggieri (1966).

(219) Colorni (1985).

(220) Cheung et al. (1979b) reported that at 30°C, 70% of a group of trophonts observed *in vitro* had encysted within 16 h. The percentages at 37 and 7°C were, respectively, 44 and 10. Optimal temperature for *excystment* (leaving the tomont) was 30°C: 50% had excysted within 5 d and 100% within 7 d. Excystment was slower at higher and lower temperatures and did not occur at the two extremes tested (37 and 7°C).

(221) Cheung et al. (1979b) found that 35% of the tomonts maintained *in vitro* at 37, 20, and 7°C ruptured (S = 16‰); at 30 and 25°C only 30% ruptured (S = 8‰). None of the tomonts developed normally at either dilution.

Colorni (1985) tested the salinity tolerance of *C. irritans* at 0 to 60‰ in increments of 5‰. Dilutions were made with dechlorinated tap water; salinities >40 ‰ were attained by evaporation. *In vitro* evaluation involved three factors: time to encystment of trophonts, survival time of tomites, and time to excystment of tomonts. Tomonts were maintained at 27°C for 3, 6, 12, and 48 h before the test solutions were replaced with seawater (40‰). The test fish was the gilthead bream, a species that tolerates a wide range of salinities. For the *in vivo* evaluation infected fish were acclimated to different salinities, then examined for trophonts. Trophonts were able to encyst at all salinities between 15 and 60‰, but tomites excysted only from tomonts maintained between 25 and 50‰. Time to excystment varied widely. Under identical conditions of temperature and salinity, maximum time to excystment was 17 d (40‰), 13 d (30 and 35‰), and 25 d (25‰). At 25‰ some did not emerge for 28 d. Tomonts could tolerate 70‰ for 1 week and 20‰ for 48 h without loss of viability when the test solutions were replaced with seawater. Some excystment occurred in tomonts kept at 15‰ for 24 h. Between 0 and 10‰ the tomonts often ruptured, and all were killed within this salinity range if exposed for 3 h. Trophonts in the *in vivo* experiments survived even freshwater emersion for 18 h. If the host was then transferred to seawater the trophonts encysted, developed, and produced tomites.

(222) Tomite dimensions in the text are from Nigrelli and Ruggieri (1966). Sikama (1961) gave the size range of tomites as 40×30 μm; those measured by Colorni (1985) were 50×20 and 70×30 μm.

(223) Wilkie and Gordin (1969).

(224) Nigrelli and Ruggieri (1966) made this statement, but provided no evidence. Some species apparently are more susceptible to *C. irritans* infections than others. Colorni (1985, p. 21) wrote that after repeated exposure these hardier species ". . . survived several waves of tomite attacks after which they apparently acquired immunity, sustaining little or no infection for several months."

(225) Cheung et al. (1979b) experimentally infected mummichogs, which are estuarine killifishes. Serial dilutions of seawater (31‰) with distilled water at ratios of 1, 0.5, and 0.33 all resulted in cures within 6 d (i.e., no signs of disease reappeared within 25 d). Embedded trophonts and tomonts were both eradicated. Colorni (1985) found during *in vitro* experiments that if the salinity was reduced to 10‰ for 3 h four times in succession at 3-d intervals, some tomonts were destroyed each time. Fish subjected to this treatment were rendered free of infection in 5 to 8 d. Elimination of *C. irritans* could be achieved within 10 d by transferring the fish to other aquariums, then drying and cleaning the infected aquariums. Four transfers at 3-d intervals were required.

(226) According to Nigrelli and Ruggieri (1966), cryptocaryoniasis is an important disease ". . . at temperatures ranging from 20 to 26°C." Wilkie and Gordin (1969) stated that cryptocaryoniasis did not appear on fishes maintained at <15°C. They noted that fishes kept at 20 and 26°C required regular treatment to control infections.

(227) Cheung et al. (1979b) stated that treatment with cupric sulfate failed to kill trophonts, but details of the regimen (e.g., concentration, duration of exposure) were not provided. Wilkie and Gordin (1969) were able to control cryptocaryoniasis *in vivo*

at 19.4°C by continuous copper treatment (cupric sulfate complexed with citrate and maintained at 0.15 mg/L total copper). Cures could be achieved with concentrations of 0.1 to 0.4 mg TCu/L, provided treatment began in the early infectious stages. Trophonts were unaffected and remained active and abundant in skin smears of fishes treated with 0.4 mg TCu/L for 24 h.

Wilkie and Gordin (1969) also used a ''shock treatment'' with some success, although the procedure was stressful even to hardy species such as scorpionfishes and seabasses. Dilution is necessary at the end of the treatment period, and the procedure is impractical except in open systems. Infected fishes are immersed for 30 min in seawater containing formalin (formaldehyde solution, 0.4 mL/L). Afterward, the calculated concentration of TCu (as cupric sulfate complexed with citrate) is brought abruptly to 2.0 mg/L. The seawater supply is turned on and adjusted to a rate that reduces the TCu concentration to 0.4 mg/L over 2 h, with simultaneous dilution of the formalin. Dilution is maintained until the water is free of copper and formalin. No analytical method for determining formalin in seawater was given.

(228) Hirayama and Shiomi (1962) used quinine·HCl against *C. irritans* at Suma Aquarium (Japan). The authors made two assumptions: (*1*) reproductive division is most prevalent in the dark, and (*2*) tomites are the stage in the life cycle most vulnerable to quinine treatment. Quinine·HCl was applied each night at 40 to 60 mg/L after the influent seawater had been shut off. Normal flow was resumed the next morning. Experiments were not performed, but a table was provided showing that diligent application of this regimen over 3 years all but eliminated the parasite from the water systems.

(229) The treatment regimen described is from Huff and Burns (1981). Unfortunately, important details were omitted from their report, which makes replication of the experiment impossible. For example, the authors did not state how the saline water was prepared; in my text description I assumed that NaCl was used. The flow rate of influent seawater after the 20-min hypersaline treatment also was not stated, leaving the reader to wonder how long the fish remained at salinities <45‰ but >36‰. Parasite counts were not made, nor was there an untreated group of control fish. Because quinine·HCl and chloroquine were used in combination, it is unclear whether just one of the compounds might have been effective, or if the positive results observed were caused by additive or synergistic effects.

(230) Cheung et al. (1980).

(231) Kohlmeyer (1984).

(232) McVicar (1982).

(233) Alderman (1982).

(234) Alderman (1982), Reichenbach-Klinke and Elkan (1965), and Wolke (1975) reviewed the history of the generic name *Ichthyophonus*, which is no less intricate than the parasite's life cycle. According to Alderman, one problem has been ". . . a tendency to use the genus as a convenient 'waste basket' for partially observed organisms, often with only superficial resemblances to each. . . ." Ichthyophonus disease was first observed by von Hofer (1893) to cause Taumelkrankheit or "staggers" in rainbow trout. Robertson (1909) described what is generally agreed to have been *Ichthyophonus* in several species of seawater fishes, including sea-run brown trout (*Salmo trutta*). The genus *Ichthyophonus* had not yet been established when Robertson published her paper. The problems started when Caullery and Mesnil (1905) assigned two previously undescribed organisms to a new genus, *Ichthyosporidium*. These were *I. gastrophilum* and *I. phymogenes*. Robertson believed that the parasite she had observed was *I. gastrophilum*. Subsequent to this other work, Plehn and Mulsow (1911) described *Ichthyophonus hoferi* as a parasitic fungus of rainbow trout. Pettit (1913), in an effort to allay the mounting confusion, transferred *Ichthyophonus hoferi* to *Ichthyosporidium* and assigned the name *Ichthyosporidium hoferi*. Alderman (1982) wrote, "Over the years various authors have accepted, rejected, misunderstood or ignored this transfer." Sprague (1965), following accepted rules of nomenclature, resolved the dilemma in the following way. Because *Ichthyosporidium* is actually a protozoan, it is unrelated to the type species of the original genus, *Ichthyophonus*, which is based on a description of a fungus. The name *Ichthyophonus* has priority, and *Ichthyophonus hoferi* is the type species.

(235) McVicar (1986).

(236) Alderman (1982), McVicar (1982).

(237) The best account I found was that of McVicar (1982). Unfortunately, the life cycle was not illustrated. Also see Chien et al. (1979), Lauckner (1984a), and Miyazaki and Kubota (1977c).

(238) McVicar (1982), Reichenbach-Klinke and Elkan (1965, p. 130).

(239) McVicar (1982), Miyazaki and Kubota (1977a).

(240) Chien et al. (1979), McVicar (1982).

(241) The nature of this developmental stage is controversial (McVicar 1982). Some may disagree with my designation

''endoblast,'' but the logic seems sound. Lauckner (1984a, p. 93) referred to it as an ''amoeboblast,'' stating that it gives rise to ''plasmodia'' or ''amoeboid forms'' capable of motility. In using these terms he distinguished plasmodia from endospores. McVicar (1982) considered amoeboid forms to be motile endospores, a convention I have adopted for simplicity, although they may indeed be a different stage; in other words, ''endospore-like,'' according to McVicar (1982). As McVicar (1982) noted, ''Further studies on the motile bodies could be rewarding, particularly with respect to the taxonomic position of *Ichthyophonus*.'' According to McVicar, the reported disparities in size and even structure of hyphal bodies (resting spores and endospores) may be artifacts of environmental conditions (e.g., nutrient availability).

(242) Lauckner (1984a, p. 93) used the term ''cyst.'' McVicar (1982) did not give a term. I substituted ''developing spore'' for cyst to avoid introducing another term. Whatever the nature of this stage, it gives rise (i.e., develops) into either resting spores or endospores.

(243) Lauckner (1984a).

(244) Lauckner (1984a) also used the term resting spore for this stage of the life-cycle.

(245) Lauckner (1984a, p. 93) called these ''endospores.'' A synonym based on this terminology might be nonmotile plasmodia, unless the combination of terms is contradictory.

(246) Lauckner (1984a, p. 93) used the term ''plasmodial bodies.''

(247) McVicar (1982, 1986).

(248) Reichenbach-Klinke and Elkan (1965, p. 132).

(249) Gustafson and Rucker (1956).

(250) Epizootics of ichthyophonus disease in freshwater fish hatcheries in Europe, North America, Australia, and Japan have been traced to feeding practices that include the use of raw fish products of seawater origin (McVicar 1982, 1986). McVicar (1986) cited an example. A rainbow trout farm in Scotland experienced heavy mortalities from *Ichthyophonus*. On investigation it was discovered that smoking facilities were used to cure seawater fishes and, on a single occasion, the trout were fed raw haddock (*Melanogrammus aeglefinus*) viscera.

(251) The period of 2 months cited in the text has been confirmed in experimentally infested plaice (*Pleuronectes platessa*) described by McVicar (1982). As noted by McVicar (1986), the

response varies by species. Rainbow trout demonstrate variable susceptibility, and mortality may be low (McVicar 1986, Miyazaki and Kubota 1977b) or high (Miyazaki and Kubota 1977a, Okamoto et al. 1987).

(252) McVicar (1982), Okamoto et al. (1987).

(253) Reichenbach-Klinke and Elkan (1965, p. 133).

(254) McVicar (1982), Reichenbach-Klinke and Elkan (1965, p. 133).

(255) Okamoto et al. (1987), Ruggieri et al. (1970).

(256) Ruggieri et al. (1970).

(257) Ruggieri et al. (1970) stated that there is no inflammatory response; Miyazaki and Kubota (1977a) described what they considered to be inflammation.

(258) Paperna (1986).

(259) Alderman (1982), McGinnis and Ajello (1974).

(260) Blazer and Wolke (1979), in the most extensive work to date, described exophiala disease from several temperate and tropical seawater fishes at Mystic Marinelife Aquarium. Lieberman and Early (1979) reported an exophiala-like fungus from an alewife (*Alosa pseudoharengus*) at New England Aquarium. Carmichael (1966) observed a series of epizootics at a freshwater salmonid hatchery in Alberta, Canada. The species involved were cutthroat trout (*Oncorhynchus clarkii*) and lake trout (*Salvelinus namaycush*). Richards et al. (1978) described the disease in pen-reared Atlantic salmon in Scotland.

(261) Blazer and Wolke (1979).

(262) Carmichael (1966).

(263) Carmichael (1966) stated that sulfamerazine, salt, and formalin treatments did not arrest the course of the disease. No further details were provided.

(264) Cannon and Lester (1988).

(265) See Cannon and Lester (1988) for references. In particular, refer to their Table 1 (p. 21) for a summary of turbellarians known to be symbiotic with vertebrates.

(266) Blasiola (1976a) first drew attention to the tang turbellarian as a parasite of tropical seawater aquarium fishes. At the time of his report the organism's taxonomic status was unknown. Kent and Olson (1986) placed it provisionally in the genus *Paravortex*.

(267) My text description of the life cycle of the tang turbellarian is based on Kent and Olson (1986).

(268) Barnes (1980, pp. 223–228).

(269) Kent and Olson (1986).

(270) Blasiola (1976a), Condé (1976).

(271) Blasiola (1976a).

(272) Cannon and Lester (1988), Condé (1976), Menitskii (1963).

(273) Bauer and Hoffman (1976), Jahn and Kuhn (1932), Nigrelli and Breder (1934).

(274) Jahn and Kuhn (1932), Nigrelli and Breder (1934), Paperna et al. (1984).

(275) Paperna et al. (1984).

(276) Hoshina (1968), Imada and Muroga (1978).

(277) Eggs of the monogenean skin parasite *Entobdella soleae* hatch in bottom sediment soon after dawn (Kearn 1973). The host, which is the common sole (*Solea solea*), is active at night but buries itself in the sediment at dawn. During its inactive period the common sole is susceptible to infestation by slow-swimming larvae of *E. solea* (Kearn 1973). A "hatching factor" in skin mucus of the common sole stimulates hatching of *E. soleae* (Kearn 1974b). The endogenous hatching rhythm of a related parasite, *Entobdella hippoglossi*, is out of phase with *E. solea* by ~12 h, suggesting that its host, the Atlantic halibut (*Hippoglossus hippoglossus*), is active in daylight and quiescent at night (Kearn 1974a).

(278) Hoshina (1968).

(279) Schmahl and Taraschewski (1987) reported that 10 mg/L praziquantel administered for 3 h was lethal to adult *Gyrodactylus aculeati* from freshwater fishes. Earlier, Schmahl and Melhorn (1985) had shown that praziquantel was effective against two other freshwater monogeans (*Dactylogyrus extensus* and *D. vastator*), also at 10 mg/L for 3 h. Neither study assessed the effectiveness of praziquantel in quantitative terms, leaving unanswered the question of whether all parasites had been killed. The results are therefore provisional.

(280) Moser et al. (1986) found praziquantel to be ineffective against the gill fluke *Amphibdelloides* sp. when administered once to Pacific electric rays (*Torpedo californica*) either by injection with 0.3 mL of a commercial compound (56.8 mg/mL active ingredient) or *per os* by force feeding in tablet form (17 mg active

ingredient). Praziquantel administered *per os* is not always effective against other trematodes. Foreyt and Gorham (1988) reported that a dosage of 100 mg/kg did not eradicate metacercariae of the trematode *Nanophyetus salmincola* from kidney tissues of chinook salmon (*Oncorhynchus tshawytscha*).

(281) Paperna and Overstreet (1981) noted that argulids are sometimes included with the copepods, which is incorrect. I found several incidences of this in the older literature (e.g., Bere 1936, Wilson 1902).

(282) My general description of an argulid life cycle is from Hoffman (1977), who restricted his discussion to freshwater species. The life cycles of seawater argulids are similar.

(283) Wilson (1902).

(284) Shimura (1981) described the developmental stages of *Argulus coregoni*, a freshwater species. See his report for references on other species.

(285) See van Niekerk and Kok (1989), Shimura (1983), and Sutherland and Wittrock (1986) for scanning electron photomicrographs illustrating the mouthparts of branchiurans.

(286) Shimura and Inoue (1984).

(287) Hoffman (1977).

(288) Shimura et al. (1983).

(289) Shimura and Inoue (1984), Shimura et al. (1983).

(290) Kubota and Takakuwa (1963).

(291) Paperna and Overstreet (1981).

(292) See Marking (1987), Marsh and Gorham (1905), and Rucker (1972). Samuelsen (1989) cited O_2 at up to 100% saturation as a cause of death from gas-bubble trauma in exhibits at Bergen Aquarium (Norway), but presented no data.

(293) Marking (1987); no references cited.

(294) Experiments by Marsh (1903) led to the discovery that exophthalmia could be induced by lowering the atmospheric pressure over a vessel of seawater containing live fish. Marsh (1903) and Marsh and Gorham (1905) were therefore among the first to correctly identify supersaturated gases as the cause of gas-bubble trauma. According to Marking (1987), ". . . the term 'supersaturation' was used as early as 1866 to describe an excess of any gas in solution."

(295) Marsh (1903), Marsh and Gorham (1905).

(296) Bouck and King (1983).

(297) Heggberget (1984).

(298) Marsh and Gorham (1905)

(299) Krise and Herman (1989), Krise et al. (1990), Marsh and Gorham (1905), McLeod (1978).

(300) Westgard (1964).

(301) Newcomb (1974).

(302) Clay et al. (1976), McLeod (1978).

(303) According to Bouck (1980), exophthalmia is a relatively rare occurrence in gas-bubble trauma except in salmonids. However, Marcello and Fairbanks (1976) reported exophthalmia in Atlantic menhaden (*Brevoortia tyrannus*), and Marsh and Gorham (1905) described it in a number of seawater teleosts kept in the aquariums at Woods Hole. According to the last authors, ''Though not necessarily always occurring in all cases of supersaturated water, this affection [exophthalmia] is so prominent among symptoms of gas disease as to deserve special consideration.''

(304) Bouck (1980), McLeod (1978).

(305) Bouck (1980).

(306) Marcello and Fairbanks (1976).

(307) Bouck (1980), Clay et al. (1976), McLeod (1978).

(308) Jones and Lewis (1976), Marcello and Fairbanks (1976), Marsh and Gorham (1905).

(309) McLeod (1978).

(310) Schiewe and Weber (1976).

(311) Bentley et al. (1976).

(312) Bouck et al. (1976).

(313) Pauley and Nakatani (1967).

(314) Cornacchia and Colt (1984), Krise and Herman (1989), McLeod (1978).

(315) Bouck et al. (1976), Krise et al. (1990), McLeod (1978).

(316) Jones and Lewis (1976).

(317) Smith (1988).

(318) McLeod (1978), Smith (1988).

(319) Marcello and Fairbanks (1976), Smith (1988).

(320) Marcello and Fairbanks (1976), Stroud and Nebeker (1976).

(321) Marsh (1903), Marsh and Gorham (1905), Stroud and Nebeker (1976).

(322) Cornacchia and Colt (1984).

(323) Shrimpton et al. (1990a, 1990b).

(324) R. E. Wolke (1973, unpublished) cited in Marcello and Fairbanks (1976).

(325) Guternatsch (1911) and Mawdesley-Thomas (1972) described the structure of the teleostean thyroid; Novales et al. (1973) discussed thyroid function in the vertebrates.

(326) Nigrelli (1952) listed fishes from New York Aquarium in which goiter disease and other thyroid abnormalities had been observed.

(327) Nigrelli and Ruggieri (1974).

(328) Negative feedback is similar to the workings of a room thermostat. When the temperature falls below the setpoint an electronic sensor signals for heat, and the furnace turns on. When the setpoint temperature has been reached, signals again relayed to the furnace shut it off. The shutoff part of the cycle is negative feedback (i.e., the required ''concentration'' of heat has been attained). By analogy, heat represents the thyroid hormones; the furnace compares favorably with the hypothalamus and adenohypophysis, and the electronic sensors represent glandular receptor or target cells.

(329) The following discussion of how hypertrophy and hyperplasia arise is based on Leatherland and Sonstegard (1984). Hypertrophy results from excessive TSH production in the absence of negative feedback. Goiter in humans arises from iodine deficiency, and the condition can be controlled by including ''iodized'' salt in the diet. The origin of goiter disease in fishes is less clear, although iodide is required for normal functioning of the thyroid. If available iodide is inadequate, the amount of T_4 that can be produced by the thyroid is lowered, resulting in reduced blood T_4 concentrations. Secretion of TSH, which is controlled by negative feedback, depends on the concentration of T_4. A reduction in the amount of circulating T_4 causes increased secretion of TSH and a concomitant rise in blood TSH. The TSH stimulates iodide assimilation, which is followed by the synthesis and subsequent release of thyroid

hormones. If insufficient iodide is available to address these demands, secretion of TSH escalates, and the concentration of blood TSH rises. High levels of circulating TSH deplete the reserves of thyroid hormones in the thyroid tissue, causing hypertrophy and hyperplasia.

(330) Malcolm and Price (1984) measured 208 to 721 mg/L iodine in the estuarine surface sediments of Loch Etive, Scotland.

(331) Frakes et al. (1983).

(332) The loss of iodine from aquarium seawater to the atmosphere is possible, but unproved. Moyers and Duce (1972) showed that gaseous and particulate iodine are expelled into the atmosphere over the surfaces of the oceans. They suggested as possible mechanisms the release of gaseous iodine during decomposition of iodine-rich particulate organic carbon and expulsion on sea-salt particles.

(333) Iodide balance in seawater fishes is not well understood; most of the available information has been obtained from fishes living in freshwaters, mainly salmonids. Hunt and Eales (1979) maintained rainbow trout in freshwater with 1.85 $\mu g\ I^-/L$. The fish were fed food containing 0.48 $\mu g\ I^-/g$. Iodide flux into the plasma was 148 ng/h per 100 g (wet fish mass), of which <1% was contributed by deiodination of thyroid hormones. As much as 16% originated from the diet and perhaps 84% from the water. Of the total iodide assimilated, <5% was necessary to sustain normal thyroid functions.

(334) Leatherland and Sonstegard (1984) reviewed research on goiter disease in coho (*Oncorhynchus kisutch*) and chinook salmon introduced into the Great Lakes from the Pacific Northwest during the 1950s and 1960s. Within 10 years thyroid hyperplasia was being reported. The data do not exclude iodide deficiency as a causative agent, but suggest that it is not a critical factor. The authors reasoned that if iodide deficiency is the principal etiologic agent, concentrations in the water or in the tissues, or both, should correlate with the degree of thyroid hyperplasia. No such correlation has been found, and tissue iodide levels in salmon from Lake Ontario are comparable with those of conspecifics migrating from the Pacific Ocean. The authors further reasoned that because salmon are near the top of Great Lakes food chains, sufficient iodide can be accumulated from prey, even if environmental levels are inadequate.

(335) Nigrelli and Ruggieri (1974) suggested the possibility that goitrogens accumulate in closed systems and mentioned ammonia and urea, but not nitrate, as possible causative agents.

They suggested that lack of a protective capsule increases the vulnerability of thyroid follicles to environmental toxins, but this contradicts a previous observation. The authors remarked on p. 285 that yellowhead jawfish (*Opistognathus aurifrons*) are especially susceptible to goiter disease, and that the gland is ". . . surrounded by a thin capsule, reminiscent of the gland of higher vertebrates."

(336) Lahti et al. (1985).

(337) Simpson (1975/1976) reported that T_3 and T_4 blood levels of rainbow trout transported ~100 km declined to <25% of resting values and did not recover during the next 30 d. Intravenous injection of TSH on day 34 caused a rapid rise in blood T_4, indicating a hypothalamus deficit and not thyroid impairment. When a second group of trout was captured and immediately returned to the original enclosure, blood T_4 concentrations after 5 d were still <40% of resting values. These fish, like the first group, also responded quickly to injection of TSH. In Simpson's opinion, the results indicated reduced hormone production by the thyroid, perhaps resulting from inactivation of the hypothalamus.

(338) Woodhead and Woodhead (1980).

(339) According to results of an informal survey of Japanese public aquariums (Uchida and Abe 1987), incidences of goiter disease in captive sharks have been observed in 24 or 38 facilities with closed seawater systems.

(340) Blum and Luer (1985) monitored serum TSH and T_3 in two nurse sharks (*Ginglymostoma cirratum*) after transfer from artificial seawater to seawater and reported associated changes in the sizes of hyperplastic lesions. It was unclear whether just one shark was transferred, or both. Visible swelling of the thyroid of at least one shark was apparent after 10 weeks in artificial seawater. Blood T_3 fell from 460 to 60 ng/mL between weeks 8 and 12, and TSH increased from 2.2 to 3.0 μIU/mL* between weeks 12 and 20. Placing a shark in seawater resulted in gradual reduction of the swollen area, although complete regression of the goiter was not achieved. Blood T_3 rose from 80 to 190 ng/mL during the first 4 weeks in seawater; TSH fell from 3.6 to 2.7 μIU/mL and decreased over the next 20 weeks to 1.9 μIU/mL.

(341) Conroy and Santacana (1979).

(342) Uchida and Abe (1987).

*IU = International units.

CHAPTER 10

(1) The ratio represented by n is called the relative index of refraction because the speed of light in air, water, or any other medium is less than its speed in a vacuum. A vacuum represents the ideal reference point for defining *absolute* indices of refraction. The refractive index in a vacuum equals 1 by definition; consequently, all other media must have absolute refractive indices >1.

(2) This discussion is based mainly on Dring (1982, pp. 13–19).

(3) In the 1930s William Beebe and Otis Barton made the first mid-ocean descents in the New York Zoological Society's *Bathysphere*, a steel sphere 145 cm in diameter equipped with three small viewing ports of fused quartz. Physicists by that time had predicted that submarine light becomes a definite color (i.e., is increasingly monochromatic) with depth, but Beebe and Barton were the first to witness the effect, and it left them profoundly impressed. Their deep descents were made off Bermuda, and the first took place on 6 June 1930. At ~213 m (700 ft) Beebe (1934, p. 109) recorded these observations: "We were the first living men to look out at the strange illumination: And it was stranger than any imagination could have conceived. It was of an indefinable translucent blue quite unlike anything I have ever seen in the upper world, and it excited our optic nerves in a most confusing manner. We kept thinking and calling it brilliant, and again and again I picked up a book to read the type, only to find that I could not tell the difference between a blank page and a colored plate. I brought all my logic to bear, I put out of mind the excitement of our position in watery space and tried to think sanely of comparative color, and I failed utterly. I flashed on the searchlight, which seemed the yellowest thing I have ever seen, and let it soak into my eyes, yet the moment it was switched off, it was like the long vanished sunlight—it was as though it never had been—and the blueness of the blue, both outside and inside our sphere, seemed to pass materially through the eye into our very beings."

Even after subsequent descents Beebe could not forget the sensation and mentioned it repeatedly. On p. 119 he wrote: "On this and other dives I carefully studied the changing colors, both by direct observation and by means of the spectroscope. Just beneath the surface the red diminished to one-half its normal width. At 20 feet there was only a thread of red and at 50 the orange was dominant. This in turn vanished at 150 feet. 300 feet found the whole spectrum dimmed, the yellow almost gone and the blue appreciably narrowed. At 350 I should give as a rough summary of the spectrum fifty per cent blue violet, twenty-five percent green, and an equal amount of colorless pale light. At 450 feet no blue remained, only violet, and green too faint for naming. At 800 feet there was nothing visible but a narrow line of pale grayish-white in the green-blue area, due of course to the small amount of light reaching my eye. Yet when I looked outside I saw only the deepest, blackest-blue imaginable. On every dive this unearthly color brought excitement to our eyes and minds.'' After another descent (p. 129) he recorded that between 1250 and 1300 ft (~ 380 and ~ 396 m) ''. . . was 50 feet of terrible emptiness, with the blue mostly of some wholly new color term—a term quite absent from any human language. It was probably sheer imagination but the characteristic most vivid was its transparency. As I looked out I never thought of feet or yards of visibility, but of the hundreds of miles of this color stretching over so much of the world.''

(4) Technically, the means by which light is scattered in air and water are different. Scattering in the pure atmosphere is caused by molecules of gas, but scattering in pure water is not caused by diffraction of light from water molecules. It results instead from irregular Brownian motion of water molecules, which induces slight density fluctuations that cause optical distortions. The distortions lead to irregular variations of light refraction characterized as scattering (Neumann and Pierson 1966, p. 63).

(5) Jerlov (1968, p. 53).

(6) This is because scattering is inversely proportional to wavelength to the fourth power.

(7) According to Neumann and Pierson (1966, p. 63), attenuation of light in the long wavelengths results almost entirely from absorption. Only between ~380 and 500 nm is scattering equal to absorption. The maximum effect from scattering is apparent at ~460 nm.

(8) According to Preisendorfer (1976), this phenomenon is not detectable to the unaided eye because the apparent radiance associated with a beam of light depends only on the indices of refraction at the beginning and end of the light beam's path. Because the beam begins in air and ends on the retina *inside* the eye, water situated in the middle has no apparent effect.

(9) The workings of incandescent and fluorescent lamps rely on different principles of physics. The following discussion is based on Feinberg (1983). The process of light emission depends on the transition of an atomic system from a higher to a lower level

of energy. During this process a *photon* (a quantity of electromagnetic energy devoid of mass) is emitted. The energy of the photon represents the difference in the energy between the two levels of the atom (high and low) and the energy corresponding to light of a definite frequency. For a substantial amount of light to be emitted a large number of atoms must undergo transitions from higher energy levels to lower ones. This can occur in several ways. Thermal light sources, in which a solid body is heated, are representative of one such method. Solid objects that are hot enough to give off light are incandescent sources such as the sun and incandescent lamps. In both examples the light given off by each atom is influenced (through collisions) by other atoms, resulting in frequencies different from those that would be radiated by isolated atoms. The radiation emitted at room temperature by even the best incandescent lamps is nearly all infrared (i.e., invisible), but at ~500°C enough light is produced in the visible range to permit the lamp to be seen by its own light (it appears red). Progressively more colors appear as the temperature is increased.

In fluorescent lamps the radiation of the atoms is mostly independent, and the spectrum contains wavelengths characteristic of the atoms involved. Fluorescent lamps use gas discharge with a substantial ultraviolet component. The ultraviolet light excites electrons in fluorescent centers on the walls of the tube, causing an immediate drop in the energy state and the simultaneous emission of visible light. Thus the atoms are not excited by high temperature but as a result of being struck by electrons in the electric current passed through the tube.

(10) The ISCC-NBS system of color designation was described in detail by Kelly and Judd (1976b). They listed the other systems and provided a method of integrating them with the ISCC-NBS system.

(11) Most of the information in this section is derived from Anonymous (1969) and Anonymous (1981).

(12) The following discussion is based mainly on Sears (1956, pp. 365–367). The mixing of light differs from the mixing of inks and other pigments. When lights are mixed the colors are additive. In the mixing of inks they are subtractive (Anonymous 1981, p. 10, footnote), and control is obtained by altering the concentration of each color. The particular portion of the spectrum that each color controls is the portion in which it absorbs. Light absorption increases with increasing concentration. The widest range of colors can be obtained in a three-color subtractive process if the same ones are *controlled* that give the widest

range in an additive process (i.e., red, green, and blue). In a subtractive process these are ''minus-red,'' ''minus-green,'' and ''minus-blue.'' When applied to a white surface and seen in white light, ''minus-red'' appears blue, ''minus-green'' magenta, and ''minus-blue'' yellow. ''Minus-green'' is ordinarily (and incorrectly) called ''red.''

Many people mistakenly believe that the primary colors are red, yellow, and blue. This is partly the result of wrongly describing magenta as ''red'' and also from failure to understand the subtractive process (i.e., that each color controls the specific region of the spectrum in which it absorbs). The three colors *controlled* are the same as those giving the widest range of colors in an additive process: red, green, and blue. Blue (''minus-red'') controls red, magenta (''minus-green'') controls green, and yellow (''minus-blue'') controls blue.

(13) The following discussion is based on Anonymous (1981, p. 11). In an unfiltered exposure the reds, greens, and blues appear in their correct color combinations to render a proper exposure. If the object is then photographed with a red filter, green and blue light are absorbed (i.e., they never reach the film). The loss of these colors is compensated by red light at an increased exposure, and the film is exposed almost entirely by red light. The added red that is allowed to reach the film makes red objects in the photographic field appear lighter (i.e., they are selectively over exposed).

(14) This discussion is based on Strykowski (1974, pp. 119–122).

(15) As noted by Strykowski (1974, p. 120), the ''watt-second'' is actually a measure of electrical energy that can be stored in the capacitor of the strobe. A true measure of light output must account for the light field of the flash reflector, light disbursement and efficiency of the reflector, and the efficiency of electrical energy actually discharged into the flash tube. The last factor represents the energy left after the portion converted into heat and dissipated has been subtracted. The light output of electronic strobes traditionally is measured in beam candle power seconds, BCPS. Unfortunately, some manufacturers fail to provide this information.

(16) I am indebted to Jerry M. Johnson for teaching me this concept.

(17) This discussion is based on Kelley (1960a).

(18) The procedure given in the text follows that of Flescher (1983), which in turn is based on a technique described originally by Randall (1961).

(19) Basic elements of this procedure are from Flescher (1983), although I have made extensive modifications.

(20) Also see Baugh (1982), Emery and Winterbottom (1980), Goodbred and Occhiogrosso (1979), Hodge (1977), Holm (1989), Page and Cummings (1984), Pletcher (1966), Reighard (1910), and Rinne and Jakle (1981).

(21) This discussion is based on Spotte (1973), although I did not devise the techniques described. Credit belongs to Charles Beck, who was my colleague at Aquarium of Niagara Falls in the 1960s. That facility, which opened 12 June 1965, was the first public aquarium to feature exhibit decorations made of fiberglass-reinforced plastic. The techniques have since become widespread in the profession, but little has been written about them. A general description was published by Brady (1984).

(22) This procedure is based on Spotte (1973, pp. 143–158).

(23) The designs of the moving water exhibits are from Webb (1982). See the original publication for maintenance problems.

(24) This procedure is based on King and Spotte (1974), with modifications.

Appendix I

Appendix I outlines what coral reef fishes eat in nature. Table I-A is a breakdown of foods by item or phylogenetic category and serves as a key to Tables I-B and I-C. Table I-B lists foods of Hawaiian teleosts (Hawaii) as percentage by volume in increasing order. Table I-C offers the same information for teleosts of the West Indies. Table 8-1 is a summary of information contained in Appendix I.

TABLE I-A Key to Tables I-B and I-C.

Cyanobacteria (''blue-green algae'') [A_1]
Diatoms [A_2]
Boring algae [A_3]
Benthic seaweeds [A_4]
Detached and floating seaweeds [A_5]
Algae and detritus [A_6]
Algal fragments [A_7]
Algal fragments and diatoms [A_8]

Attached or detached and floating seagrasses [B_1]
Spermatophytes including seagrasses [B_2]

Unqualified plant material [B_3] including [A_2], [A_4], and [B_1]

Phylum Protozoa [C]
    Class Rhizopoda
        Order Foraminifera—foraminiferans [C]

Phylum Porifera [D]—sponges

Phylum Cnidaria (= Coelenterata) [E]
    Class Hydrozoa—hydroids [E_1]
        Order Siphonophora—siphonophores [E_2]
    Class Scyphozoa—sea jellies [E_3]
    Class Anthozoa
      Subclass Octocorallia (= Alcyonaria)
        Order Gorgonacea—soft corals [E_4]
      Subclass Zoantharia
        Order Zoanthiniaria—zoanthids [E_5]
        Order Actinaria—sea anemones [E_6]
        Order Scleractinia—hard corals [E_7], coral mucus [E_8], coral polyps [E_9]
        Order Corallimorpharia—corallimorpharians [E_{10}]

Phylum Ctenophora [F]—comb jellies

Phylum Bryozoa [G]—moss animals

Phylum Nemertinea [H]—nemerteans

Phylum Mollusca [I]—mollusks [I_1], mollusk eggs [I_2]
    Class Polyplacophora—chitons [I_3]
    Class Gastropoda—snails, slugs—gastropods [I_4], gastropod larvae [I_5], gastropod egg masses [I_6]
      Subclass Prosobranchia—limpets, top shells, whelks, cone shells—prosobranchs [I_7], prosobranch larvae [I_8]
      Subclass Opisthobranchia—opisthobranchs [I_9]
        Order Thecosomata—planktonic pteropods [I_{10}]
        Order Gymnosomata—fast-swimming planktonic pteropods [I_{10}]
        Order Nudibranchia—nudibranchs [I_{11}]
    Class Scaphopoda—tusk shells [I_{12}]
    Class Bivalvia—scallops, mussels, oysters, clams—pelecypods [I_{13}], pelecypod larvae [I_{14}]
    Class Cephalopoda—cephalopods [I_{15}], cephalopod larvae [I_{16}]
      Subclass Coleoida
        Order Octopoda—octopuses [I_{17}], octopus larvae [I_{18}]
        Order Teuthidida—squids [I_{19}]
    veligers [I_{20}]

Phylum Sipuncula [J]—peanut worms

Phylum Annelida [K]—segmented worms
    Class Polychaeta—polychaetes [K_1]; polychaete larvae [K_2]; tentacular crowns of sabellid, serpulid, and terebellid polychaetes [K_3]; polychaete fragments [K_4]

TABLE I-A *(Continued)*

Phylum Arthropoda [L]—joint-footed invertebrates
- Subphylum Chelicerata
  - Class Pycnogonida—sea spiders [L_1]
- Subphylum Mandibulata
  - Class Crustacea—crustacean fragments [L_2]
    - Subclass Ostracoda—ostracods [L_3]
    - Subclass Copepoda—copepods [L_4]
    - Subclass Cirripedia—barnacles—barnacle appendages [L_5], barnacle larvae [L_6], barnacle appendages and larvae [L_7]
    - Subclass Malacostraca—lobsters, crabs, shrimps
      - Superorder Syncarida
        - Order Mysidacea—mysids [L_8]
        - Order Tanaidacea—tanaids [L_9]
        - Order Isopoda—isopods [L_{10}]
        - Order Amphipoda—amphipods [L_{11}]
      - Superorder Hoplocarida
        - Order Stomatopoda—mantis shrimps—stomatopods [L_{12}], stomatopod larvae [L_{13}]
      - Superorder Eucarida—true shrimps
        - Order Decapoda
          - Suborder Natantia—shrimps [L_{14}], shrimp larvae [L_{15}], shrimps and shrimp larvae [L_{16}]
          - Suborder Reptantia—crabs [L_{17}], crab larvae [L_{18}], crabs and crab larvae [L_{19}], spiny lobsters [L_{20}], scyllarid (slipper) lobsters [L_{21}], scyllarid lobster larvae [L_{22}]

Phylum Chaetognatha [M]—arrowworms

Phylum Echinodermata [N]—spiny-skinned invertebrates
- Class Holothuroidea—sea cucumbers [N_1]
- Class Echinoidea—sea urchins, sand dollars—echinoids [N_2], echinoid tube feet [N_3], echinoid pedicellariae [N_4]
  - Subclass Regularia—sea urchins [N_5]
  - Subclass Irregularia—sand dollars [N_6]
- Class Asteroidea—sea stars [N_7]
- Class Ophiuroidea—serpent stars, brittle stars [N_8]

Phylum Hemichordata [O]—acorn worms

Phylum Protochordata [P]
- Subphylum Urochordata
  - Class Ascidiacea—tunicates [P_1], tunicate larvae (appendicularians) [P_2]
  - Class Thaliacea—salps [P_3]
  - Class Larvacea—larvaceans [P_4]

Phylum Chordata [Q]—vertebrates,
- Class Teleostei—bony fishes [Q_1], fish larvae [Q_2], fish eggs [Q_3], planktonic fish eggs [Q_4], demersal fish eggs [Q_5], fish scales [Q_6]

Unidentified eggs [R]
Unidentified worms [S]
Unidentified animal matter [T]
Sea turtles [U]
Vertebrate muscle tissue [V]
Insects [W]
Detritus [X]
Fish ectoparasites (isopods) [Y]
Invertebrates [Z]

Source: Stephen Spotte.

TABLE I-B Foods of Hawaiian teleosts (see Table I-A for key). Items are listed as percentage by volume in increasing order. Families and species are listed alphabetically. ***Note:*** **Columns read across.**

ACANTHURIDAE—SURGEONFISHES

Acanthurus thompsoni:

L_{14}	0.3	L_{11}	0.7	K_1	0.9
Q_4	1.3	A_1	1.6	R	1.7
P_4	7.4	L_4	8.7	E_2	10.0
T	11.7	P_3	18.6	M	37.1

Naso hexacanthus:

I_{20}	0.3	L_{11}	0.8	K_1	1.3
E_2	2.0	L_4	2.3	L_{14}	2.3
T	10.0	P_4	16.3	A_5	18.4
M	21.3	Q_4	25.0		

A. menesemus:

L_4	0.1	I_5	0.1	L_{10}	0.2
L_{11}	0.8	Q_1	2.0	L_8	2.9
L_{17}	6.9	T	13.7	L_{14}	15.7
L_{18}	17.6	L_2	40.0		

A. snyderi:

J	0.2	T	0.6	L_{11}	1.3
L_4	1.3	L_8	2.1	K_1	2.9
Q_1	5.6	L_{18}	7.5	L_{17}	18.8
L_2	25.4	L_{14}	34.3		

APOGONIDAE—CARDINALFISHES

Apogon erythrinus:

L_{11}	20.0	L_2	30.0	L_{17}	50.0

ATHERINIDAE—SILVERSIDES

Pranesus insularum:

L_1	0.4	L_{18}	1.7	P_4	2.1
L_4	4.2	C	6.3	L_{15}	6.7
L_8	14.2	T	23.6	L_2	40.8

TABLE I-B (*Continued*)

AULOSTOMIDAE—TRUMPETFISHES

Aulostomus chinensis:
L_{14} 37.0; Q_1 63.0

BALISTIDAE—LEATHERJACKETS

Cantherines dumerili:
I_{13} 0.1; N_2 7.4; G 12.5
E_7 80.0

C. sandwichiensis:
N_8 0.1; L_9 0.1; I_7 0.3
I_6 0.3; E_1 0.4; I_{13} 0.6
sand 0.7; G 1.0; A_2 1.1
K_1 1.4; D 2.2; L_{11} 4.6
E_7 5.0; P_1 6.1; T 8.3
A_4 67.8

Melichthys niger:
I_{20} 0.1; L_{11} 0.1; I_4 0.1
L_3 0.1; Q_4 0.1; I_7 0.3
C 0.3; W 0.4; L_{18} 0.4
L_{14} 1.1; E_7 2.1; sand 2.9
L_4 3.9; T 17.1; A_4 18.7
A_5 52.3

Pervagor spilosoma:
L_4 0.2; sand 0.2; L_{18} 0.2
I_9 0.2; N_8 0.2; L_3 0.2
E_1 0.3; A_2 0.3; Q_3 0.5
L_9 0.5; L_{11} 0.7; N_2 0.8
K_1 1.5; D 3.3; A_4 27.0
T 28.1; E_7 35.8

Rhinecanthus rectangulus:
L_{18} 0.2; I_{13} 0.3; G 0.7
I_7 2.4; L_{10} 2.6; L_9 2.9
N_2 2.9; L_{14} 4.2; L_2 6.2
K_1 6.3; L_{17} 6.7; P_1 8.6
A_4 10.4; L_{11} 20.0; T 25.6

Sufflamen bursa (original dietary data total 99.2%):
L_5 0.1; G 0.1; J 0.1
L_{18} 0.3; C 0.4; L_3 0.4
L_{14} 0.8; I_{13} 1.0; L_4 1.3
A_7 1.2; L_{10} 1.3; I_9 2.3
D 2.6; L_9 2.8; L_2 3.8
I_7 3.8; K_1 4.6; L_{17} 4.8
L_{11} 8.3; N_2 9.1; T 50.8

Xanthichthys ringens:
I_7 0.3; L_{11} 0.4; L_3 0.6
I_{20} 0.8; E_2 1.2; I_{10} 1.2
M 1.3; Q_4 1.4; L_2 4.6
T 43.5; L_4 44.7

BLENNIDAE—COMBTOOTH BLENNIES

Cirripectus variolosus:
E_7 3.0; A_6 40.0; X 57.0

Exallias brevis:
A_8 5.0; E_7 95.0

Plagiotremus goslinei:
Q_8 100.0

BOTHIDAE—LEFTEYE FLOUNDERS

Bothus mancus:
Q_1 100.0

BROTULIDAE—CUSK-EELS

Brotula multibarbata:
L_{18} 0.3; L_8 5.0; L_{14} 6.3
T 9.6; Q_1 16.3; L_{17} 25.0
L_2 37.5

CARANGIDAE—JACKS

Caranx melampygus:
T 10.0; L_8 20.0; Q_1, Q_2 70.0

CHAETODONTIDAE—BUTTERFLYFISHES

Chaetodon auriga:
K_4 0.2; E_1 0.2; L_{11} 0.4
J 0.4; L_{14} 1.4; A_7 1.8
N_3 2.0; D 3.1; E_6 4.0
K_4 5.4; I_6 8.8; K_3 20.6
T 20.7; E_4 31.0

C. corallicola:
A_1 <0.1; E_1 0.1; L_{15} 0.2
P_3 0.2; L_8 0.3; L_{22} 0.5
L_{11} 0.5; L_3 0.5; Q_4 1.3
P_4 5.5; T 26.0; L_4 64.7

C. fremblii:
L_{14} 0.1; I_4 0.1; I_9 1.4
L_{10} 1.6; O 2.3; E_1 2.9
K_4 3.1; I_6 3.6; A_7 11.2
L_{11} 12.4; J 15.0; T 21.3
K_3 25.0

C. lunula:
E_1 0.1; E_6 0.1; L_9 0.1
L_4 0.1; L_{17} 0.1; P_1 0.1
K_3 0.2; N_3 0.2; E_4 0.3
L_{14} 0.3; L_2 0.4; L_{11} 0.4
A_7 0.5; I_7 0.7; Q_3 1.1
N_1 1.3; J 1.7; K_4 2.2
K_3 10.6; I_9 29.2; T 50.3

TABLE I-B (*Continued*)

CHAETODONTIDAE—BUTTERFLYFISHES (*Continued*)

C. miliaris:

L_8	0.1	L_3	0.1	R	0.4
Q_4	0.4	L_{11}	0.4	P_4	0.9
P_3	3.0	T	23.2	L_4	71.5

C. multicinctus:

L_4	0.1	E_1	0.2	K_4	0.4
A_8	1.2	J	1.3	L_{11}	1.8
T	3.4	E_4	91.6		

C. ornatissimus:

A_8	0.2	E_8	99.8

C. quadrimaculatus:

L_4	0.1	L_{11}	0.6	I_9	1.3
E_1	1.6	J	1.9	A_8	2.1
T	4.5	K_4	6.2	E_4	81.4

C. unimaculatus:

L_4	0.3	L_{11}	1.3	J	1.6
I_{13}	3.2	A_8	6.8	D	12.4
T	29.1	E_7	45.3		

Forcipiger flavissimus:

Q_5	0.1	L_{18}	0.1	L_{10}	0.1
A_7	0.2	I_6	0.5	J	0.6
L_2	0.9	E_1	1.0	L_{14}	1.3
L_{11}	2.8	K_3	3.6	L_4	4.1
N_4	7.0	H	11.9	K_3	15.4
T	50.4				

F. longirostris:

Q_1	0.5	L_{17}	1.9	L_2	9.2
L_{14}	88.4				

Hemitaurichthys thompsoni:

P_4	0.2	R	0.2	L_8	0.2
I_4	0.3	L_{11}	0.3	Q_4	1.0
A_1	3.5	T	8.2	L_4	86.1

H. zoster:

I_{14}	0.1	I_5	0.1	L_{14}	0.2
I_5	0.3	P_4	1.0	A_1	1.3
E_1	1.9	Q_4	1.9	L_2	3.2
T	9.9	E_4	18.2	L_4	61.7

CIRRHITIDAE—HAWKFISHES

Cirrhitops fasciatus:

L_{11}	0.6	T	5.0	L_{18}	7.8
I_{17}	6.3	N_8	6.3	L_{14}	20.9
L_2	22.2	L_{17}	30.9		

Cirrhitus pinnulatus:

L_{14}	2.9	N_2	3.2	I_{17}	7.1
N_8	7.1	L_2	11.1	L_{17}	68.6

Paracirrhites arcatus:

L_{11}	0.5	T	1.3	L_{18}	1.8
L_4	4.3	N_8	5.0	Q_1	10.5
L_2	13.5	L_{14}	15.5	L_{17}	47.6

P. forsteri:

L_{17}	4.8	L_2	12.4	L_{14}	16.2
Q_1	66.6				

CONGRIDAE—CONGER EELS

Conger marginatus:

Z	50.0	Q_1	50.0

DIODONTIDAE—PORCUPINEFISHES

Diodon holocanthus:

N_8	3.9	N_2	18.0	L_{17}	24.0
I_7	54.1				

D. hystrix:

I_{13}	0.8	T	4.2	L_{17}	12.9
I_7	27.1	N_2	55.0		

FISTULARIIDAE—CORNETFISHES

Fistularia petimba:

Q_1	100.0

HOLOCENTRIDAE—SQUIRRELFISHES

Holocentrus diadema:

I_9	0.2	N_2	0.2	I_{13}	0.4
L_9	0.4	L_4	0.5	N_1	0.6
L_8	0.8	L_{10}	1.4	I_3	1.7
L_{11}	1.7	T	3.9	K_1	6.1
I_7	6.3	L_2	11.3	N_8	12.0
L_{14}	12.0	L_{18}	12.4	L_{17}	27.9

H. lima:

L_{11}	0.5	L_{18}	7.0	Q_1	3.5
L_2	24.5	L_{14}	31.5	L_{17}	33.0

H. sammara:

Q_1	7.8	L_2	13.8	L_{14}	18.1
L_{17}	60.3				

H. tiere:

J	0.1	K_1	0.2	Q_1	1.8
L_{18}	4.8	L_{14}	24.7	L_2	29.7
L_{17}	38.7				

H. xantherythrus:

L_{10}	0.1	L_8	0.1	L_9	0.2
I_{13}	0.6	J	0.8	I_9	0.9
L_{12}	1.9	I_7	2.3	L_{18}	14.8
L_{14}	15.4	L_2	20.3	L_{17}	42.6

TABLE I-B *(Continued)*

Myripristis amaenus:

L_{12} .... 0.1 L_4 .... 0.1 L_{10} 0.1
L_{11} .... 0.2 L_8 .... 0.3 K_1 .... 0.4
I_7 .... 0.4 I_{15} .... 1.4 Q_1 .... 2.9
L_{14} .... 9.3 L_2 .... 9.7 L_{18} 75.1

M. kuntee:

L_3 .... 0.1 L_9 .... 0.1 R 0.1
L_{11} .... 0.9 L_{10} .... 1.8 T 2.7
L_{12} .... 2.8 Q_1 .... 4.6 K_1 .... 4.8
L_4 .... 8.0 L_8 .... 9.3 L_{14} 11.8
L_{18} .... 25.2 L_2 .... 27.8

M. murdjan:

L_4 .... 0.1 L_3 .... 0.1 I_7 .... 0.3
L_{11} .... 0.5 L_{12} .... 0.9 I_{15} 1.2
K_1 .... 1.5 Q_1 .... 2.0 L_8 .... 6.5
L_{14} .... 9.3 T .... 9.6 L_2 .... 14.5
L_{18} 53.5

Sargocentron lacteoguttatum:

N_8 .... 0.1 N_2 .... 0.18 L_4 .... 1.1
I_7 .... 1.2 J .... 1.8 L_{14} 1.9
L_9 .... 3.7 K_1 .... 4.9 L_{11} 5.1
T .... 6.7 L_{18} .... 8.0 L_2 .... 28.1
L_{17} 36.6

S. spiniferum:

L_{21} .... 11.0 L_2 .... 24.0 L_{17} 31.0
L_{14} 34.0

KUHLIIDAE—AHOLEHOLES

Kuhlia sandvicensis:

L_1 .... 100.0

KYPHOSIDAE—SEA CHUBS

Kyphosus cinerascens:

A_4 .... 100.0

LABRIDAE—WRASSES

Anampses cuvier:

L_{10} .... 0.3 L_9 .... 0.3 P_1 .... 0.3
L_{17} .... 1.8 A_7 .... 1.9 N_2 .... 1.9
C+sand ... 4.3 K_1 .... 4.3 Q_5 .... 5.0
L_2 .... 14.1 I_1 .... 18.1 T 18.8
L_{11} 28.9

Bodianus bilunatus:

I_1 .... 100.0

Chilinus rhodochrous:

L_{17} .... 8.0 T .... 10.0 L_2 .... 12.0
L_{14} .... 30.0 Q_1 .... 40.0

Coris gaimard:

L_{11} .... 0.2 P_1 .... 0.6 L_{17} 2.2
N_2 .... 9.8 L_2 .... 15.0 I_1 .... 72.2

Gomphosus varius:

I_4 .... 2.1 I_{13} .... 4.2 L_{14} 6.7
T .... 23.3 L_2 .... 25.8 L_{17} 37.9

Halichoeres ornatissimus:

L_3 .... 0.1 N_2 .... 0.4 L_{10} 0.5
R .... 0.8 J .... 1.2 A_7 .... 1.2
K_1 .... 1.5 L_9 .... 1.5 L_4 .... 2.5
N_8 .... 3.1 C+sand ... 4.5 A_2 .... 6.9
L_{11} .... 7.7 P_1 .... 8.8 L_2 .... 10.8
I_1 .... 13.5 T 35.0

Labroides phthirophagus:

L_{10} 100.0

Macropharyngodon geoffroy:

L_{11} .... 0.1 L_4 .... 0.4 L_2 .... 0.6
A_6 .... 8.4 T .... 17.4 C 35.3
I_7 .... 37.8

Pseudocheilinus octotaenia:

L_4 .... 0.1 Q_5 .... 1.0 N_2 .... 5.0
L_{17} .... 22.0 L_2 .... 71.9

Stethojulis balteata:

L_4 .... 0.4 J .... 0.6 N_2 .... 1.0
L_{10} .... 2.4 C .... 2.4 K_1 .... 4.0
L_9 .... 5.0 L_{11} .... 8.6 X+sand ... 10.2
L_2 .... 15.0 T .... 15.4 I_7 .... 15.6
L_4 .... 19.4

Thalassoma duperrey:

Q_1 .... 0.2 C .... 0.2 J 0.2
Q_3 .... 0.6 L_{10} .... 0.9 L_9 .... 1.3
N_8 .... 1.5 P_1 .... 1.5 L_{11} 1.9
K_1 .... 2.1 E_7 .... 2.5 I_{13} 5.0
L_{17} .... 6.5 I_4 .... 7.5 L_4 .... 7.7
N_2 .... 7.9 L_2 .... 9.4 A_7 .... 11.5
T 31.5

T. fuscum:

L_{10} .... 0.1 L_{11} .... 0.7 J 1.4
K_1 .... 1.8 L_4 .... 2.0 Q_1 .... 2.5
L_{18} .... 2.8 L_2 .... 3.7 N_8 .... 5.0
I_{17} .... 7.1 I_1 .... 17.2 T 20.2
L_{17} 35.5

LUTJANIDAE—SNAPPERS

Aphareus furcatus:

L_{18} .... 25.0 L_{11} .... 25.0 Q_1 .... 50.0

TABLE I-B (*Continued*)

MULLIDAE—GOATFISHES

Mulloidichthys auriflamma:

L_{14}	0.5	I_{13}	0.5	J	0.5
L_3	0.6	A_7	1.0	L_{10}	1.1
L_{11}	1.3	N_2	4.7	I_7	4.7
L_{17}	7.2	L_2	8.5	L_{18}	11.5
K_1	11.7	T	12.0	N_8	14.5
C+sand	19.7				

M. samoensis:

L_{14}	0.2	N_2	0.8	L_{17}	1.2
L_{10}	2.8	I_7	3.1	L_{18}	3.1
J	5.4	L_{11}	6.7	L_2	7.1
I_{13}	10.0	K_1	11.2	T	11.6
C+sand	36.8				

Parupeneus bifaciatus:

L_{11}	0.3	K_1	0.4	I_7	0.6
I_{17}	3.9	X	4.2	L_{14}	8.0
L_2	15.5	Q_1	17.0	L_{18}	19.4
L_{17}	30.7				

P. chryserydros:

L_{14}	1.3	T	7.3	L_{17}	8.3
Q_1	83.1				

P. multifasciatus:

L_3	0.1	L_{11}	0.4	L_9	0.6
T	0.8	I_7	1.8	L_{18}	8.6
X	11.7	L_{14}	16.0	L_2	29.4
L_{17}	30.6				

P. porphyreus:

L_{11}	0.2	I_3	0.2	I_7	0.2
X	1.0	L_{14}	2.0	L_2	21.2
L_{17}	75.2				

MURAENIDAE—MORAYS

Echidna zebra:

L_{11}	100.0

Gymnothorax eurostus:

L_{14}	50.0	L_{17}	50.0

G. flavimarginatus:

Q_1	100.0

G. meleagris:

L_{17}	50.0	Q_1	50.0

G. petelli:

L_{17}	50.0	Q_1	50.0

OSTRACIIDAE—BOXFISHES

Ostracion meleagris:

L_4	0.4	I_{13}	1.0	I_7	1.0
D	2.0	X	6.0	A_4	7.4
K_1	13.0	T	26.4	P_1	42.8

POMACANTHIDAE—ANGELFISHES

Centropyge potteri (original dietary data total 89.9%):

L_4	0.3	D	2.3	A_2	3.3
A_4	41.7	X+C+sand	42.3		

Holacanthus arcuatus:

A_7	0.7	D	98.3

POMACENTRIDAE—DAMSELFISHES

Abudefduf abdominalis:

I_5	0.1	I_{14}	0.2	L_{15}	0.3
A_1	1.3	L_{14}	1.7	K_1	1.9
Q_4	2.0	A_7	2.6	P_4	4.0
T	24.6	L_4	61.3		

A. imparipennis:

D	0.3	L_{10}	0.4	A_2	0.5
I_6	0.8	A_7	0.8	I_9	1.7
R	1.8	J	1.9	Q_5	3.1
L_4	7.1	L_{11}	12.6	K_1	17.6
T	50.9				

A. sindonis:

J	0.2	W	0.2	L_4	1.0
E_1	1.0	L_{11}	2.2	K_1	2.2
L_{14}	7.0	A_8	39.4	X	46.8

A. sordidus:

G	0.4	L_1	0.4	K_1	0.4
W	0.4	E_1	0.4	L_9	0.6
I_6	1.2	L_{11}	4.4	I_7	9.2
D	12.2	T	15.4	L_{17}	20.0
A_8	35.0				

Chromis leucurus:

A_7	2.0	Q_4	2.8	A_1	3.6
P_4	22.0	L_4	23.4	T	46.2

C. ovalis:

L_8	2.5	L_{14}	2.5	P_4	7.5
T	37.0	L_4	50.5		

C. vanderbilti (original dietary data total 99.5%):

L_{11}	0.1	L_3	0.5	A_1	0.5
Q_4	0.9	K_1	0.9	E_2	1.7
L_{14}	1.7	P_4	21.7	T	31.1
L_4	40.4				

C. verater:

K_1	0.2	L_8	0.4	M	0.4
E_2	0.8	Q_4	2.4	L_{14}	7.0
T	20.8	L_4	32.0	P_4	36.0

Dascyllus albisella:

L_{11}	0.2	E_1	0.2	I_{14}	0.2
Q_4	1.1	A_7	1.5	L_{15}	2.2
A_1	7.2	L_4	20.6	T	23.7
P_4	43.1				

TABLE I-B (*Continued*)

Plectroglyphidodon johnstonianus:

J ... 0.2 | A_7 ... 2.0 | T ... 3.5
E_4, E_8 ... 94.3

Pomacentrus jenkinsi:

L_5 ... 0.1 | I_{13} ... 0.1 | L_{11} ... 0.2
Q_5 ... 1.0 | sand ... 1.7 | K_1 ... 2.0
L_4 ... 5.0 | D ... 5.7 | A_8 ... 24.1
X ... 60.1

PRIACANTHIDAE—BIGEYES

Priacanthus cruentatus:

L_{12} ... 0.1 | L_8 ... 0.4 | L_{14} ... 3.6
L_{17} ... 7.6 | T ... 11.0 | Q_1 ... 11.2
L_2 ... 13.4 | I_{15} ... 20.4 | L_{18} ... 32.3

SCARIDAE—PARROTFISHES

Scarus rubroviolaceus:

A_6+sand ... 100.0

S. sordidus:

A_6+sand ... 100.0

S. taeniurus:

A_6+sand ... 100.0

SCORPAENIDAE—SCORPIONFISHES

Pterois sphex (original dietary data total 100.1%):

L_{17} ... 14.4 | L_2 ... 29.4 | L_{14} ... 56.3

Scorpaena coniorta:

Q_1 ... 6.7 | L_2 ... 26.0 | L_{14} ... 28.3
L_{17} ... 39.0

Scorpaenopsis cacopsis:

I_{17} ... 35.0 | Q_1 ... 65.0

SERRANIDAE—SEA BASSES

Epinephelus argus:

Q_1 ... 100.0

SPARIDAE—PORGIES

Monotaxis grandoculis:

N_1 ... 0.8 | A_7 ... 1.3 | R ... 1.3
L_2 ... 2.5 | P_1 ... 2.5 | K_1 ... 3.8
L_{17} ... 6.3 | I_9 ... 11.8 | N_2 ... 21.3
I_7 ... 21.3 | N_8 ... 27.1

SYNODONTIDAE—LIZARDFISHES

Saurida garcilis:

Q_1 ... 100.0

Synodus variegatus:

Q_1 ... 100.0

TETRAODONTIDAE—PUFFERS

Arothron hispidus:

I_7 ... 0.1 | A_4 ... 0.3 | D ... 2.9
E_1 ... 2.9 | T ... 3.8 | L_{17} ... 6.5
N_7 ... 8.3 | N_8 ... 13.4 | N_2 ... 28.1
P_1 ... 33.7

A. meleagris:

I_{13} ... 0.6 | T ... 11.9 | E_7 ... 43.1
P_1 ... 44.4

Canthigaster amboinensis:

K_1 ... 0.2 | C ... 0.2 | L_{11} ... 0.2
P_1 ... 0.3 | J ... 0.3 | G ... 0.6
I_7 ... 0.6 | D ... 1.3 | N_2 ... 2.4
N_8 ... 4.9 | L_{17} ... 7.3 | E_7 ... 7.7
L_{13} ... 7.8 | T ... 14.3 | A_4 ... 51.9

C. jactator:

L_{14} ... 0.2 | L_{10} ... 0.2 | L_3 ... 0.2
L_{11} ... 0.2 | N_8 ... 0.3 | C ... 0.3
A_2 ... 0.7 | L_{17} ... 1.3 | G ... 1.3
sand ... 1.5 | J ... 4.3 | L_2 ... 5.0
N_2 ... 5.5 | P_1 ... 6.0 | D ... 6.8
E_7 ... 10.0 | I_7 ... 11.2 | A_4 ... 19.4
T ... 25.6

ZANCLIDAE—MOORISH IDOL

Zanclus cornutus:

L_9 ... 0.1 | L_{14} ... 0.1 | L_5 ... 0.2
P_1 ... 0.2 | E_1 ... 0.2 | C ... 0.3
L_{11} ... 0.5 | K_1 ... 0.6 | I_{13} ... 0.9
G ... 1.1 | A_4 ... 11.3 | D ... 84.5

Source: Stephen Spotte and Patricia M. Bubucis, Sea Research Foundation; calculated from data in Hobson (1974); names have been changed where appropriate to reflect current usage.

TABLE I-C Foods of West Indies teleosts (see Table I-A for key). Items are listed as percentage by volume in increasing order. Families and species are listed alphabetically. ***Note:*** **Columns read across.**

ACANTHURIDAE—SURGEONFISHES

Acanthurus bahianus:

B_2	8.2	A_3, A_6	91.8

A. chirurgus:

I_4	0.1	I_9	0.1	K	0.2
B_1	5.7	A_3, A_6	93.9		

A. coeruleus:

E_4	0.1	L_2	0.3	B_2	6.8
A_3, A_6	92.8				

ANTENNARIIDAE—FROGFISHES

Antennarius multiocellatus:

L_{17}	12.5	L_{12}	12.5	Q_1	75.0

A. scaber:

Q_1	100.0

APOGONIDAE—CARDINALFISHES

Apogon maculatus:

L_{11}	0.7	L_{10}	1.1	K_1	3.7
L_4	9.1	L_2	12.7	L_{17}	23.7
L_{16}	49.0				

Phaeoptyx conklini:

Q_2	1.8	L_9	2.7	L_{10}	5.3
L_4	5.9	K_1	5.9	P_2	7.3
L_{18}	10.0	L_2	18.2	L_{11}	18.8
L_{15}	24.1				

ATHERINIDAE—SILVERSIDES

Atherinomorus stipes:

C	2.2	Q_3	2.2	L_7	10.0
Q_6	20.0	L_4	30.0	L_{15}	35.6

Hypoatherina harringtonensis:

K_2	2.7	Q_2	8.1	L_4	89.2

AULOSTOMIDAE—TRUMPETFISHES

Aulostomus maculatus:

L_{14}	26.5	Q_1	73.5

BALISTIDAE—LEATHERJACKETS

Aluterus schoepfi:

L_{17}	0.6	I_4	0.6	A_4	31.8
B_1	67.0				

A. scriptus:

L_{14}	0.3	D	0.4	I_4	0.6
P_1	1.1	E_5	2.4	B_1	9.0
E_4	12.6	A_4	34.2	E_1	39.4

Balistes vetula:

E_5+E_6	0.02	L_{11}	0.03	L_{12}	0.05
L_{21}	0.10	I_3	0.10	Q_1	0.20
E_7	0.20	L_2	0.20	P_1	0.60
L_{14}	0.80	J	0.90	A_4	1.20
N_7	1.40	I_4	1.60	K_1	2.10
T	2.50	N_8	3.30	I_{13}	4.60
L_{17}	7.30	N_2	72.80		

Cantherines macrocerus:

N_1	0.8	A_4	2.9	E_4	4.8
E_1	5.0	D	86.5		

C. pullus:

N_2	0.1	L_{14}	0.1	I_6	0.1
L_{11}	0.1	I_{13}	0.2	E_7	0.7
L_2	0.8	E_5	1.7	E_4	1.7
N_8	1.9	G	2.3	T	2.9
E_1	3.1	B_2	4.6	P_1	6.0
D	30.9	A_6	42.8		

C. sufflamen:

L_{15}	1.2	L_6	1.2	L_{10}	2.5
A_4	2.5	L_{18}	3.7	L_{11}	6.0
E_2	8.5	I_5	13.2	T	15.0
I_{10}	21.2	N_2	25.0		

Melichthys niger:

I_{13}	0.1	C	0.1	L_6	0.2
L_4	0.2	L_{16}	0.6	E_7	0.6
L_{17}	1.2	I_5	1.3	P_1+P_3	1.8
E_2	2.3	L_2	2.9	Q_1	3.1
B_1	4.4	L_{19}	4.9	I_{10}	5.5
A_4+A_5	70.8				

Monacanthus ciliatus:

I_1	0.3	I_4	1.5	T	1.9
I_{13}	2.3	L_{10}	3.1	L_{12}	3.9
K_1	4.2	L_9	4.6	L_{11}	5.4
L_2	8.5	L_{16}	13.1	L_4	14.6
B_1	15.4	A_6	21.2		

M. tuckeri:

L_{11}	3.0	L_{10}	3.3	L_9	4.0
I_5	6.7	L_2	6.7	L_4	35.0
T	41.3				

BELONIDAE—NEEDLEFISHES

Platybelone argalus:

W	3.0	Q_1	97.0

Strongylura timucu:

L_{14}	4.0	Q_1	96.0

Tylosurus acus:

L_{13}	0.9	L_{18}	1.4	W	1.4
Q_1	96.3				

TABLE I-C (*Continued*)

T. crocodilus:
L_{14} .... 9.1 Q_1 .... 90.9

BLENNIIDAE—COMBTOOTH BLENNIES

Entomacrodus nigricans:
K_1 .... 3.6 A_6 .... 96.4

Ophioblennius atlanticus:
Q_3 .... 0.5 A_6 .... 99.5

Parablennius marmoreus:
E_1 .... 2.4 N_8 .... 9.2 K_1 .... 9.2
A_6 .... 79.2

Scartella cristata:
I_4 .... 0.8 A_6 .... 99.2

BOTHIDAE—LEFTEYE FLOUNDERS

Bothus lunatus:
I_{17} .... 2.9 L_{12} .... 11.4 Q_1 .... 85.7

B. ocellatus:
L_{12} .... 2.8 L_2 .... 11.1 L_{11} 15.0
L_{14} .... 17.8 L_{17} .... 25.0 Q_1 .... 28.3

CARANGIDAE—JACKS

Caranx bartholomaei:
Q_1 ....100.0

C. crysos:
L_4 .... 0.6 E_2 .... 0.7 T 1.1
I_{10} .... 1.2 L_{12} .... 3.5 L_{17} 5.9
Q_1 .... 87.0

C. latus:
L_{10} .... 0.7 L_{14} .... 3.8 I_{10} 8.4
Q_1 .... 87.1

C. lugubris:
Q_1 ....100.0

C. ruber:
L_2 .... 0.1 L_{17} .... 0.4 I_4 .... 0.4
L_{12} .... 0.6 I_{19} .... 1.4 L_8 .... 2.2
L_{14} .... 3.4 Q_1 .... 91.5

Decapterus macarellus:
L_8 .... 0.5 L_{18} .... 0.5 L_{15} 0.5
L_2 .... 0.8 L_4 .... 1.2 I_{10} 96.5

D. punctatus:
L_{15} .... 1.0 T .... 6.0 I_{10} 6.0
L_3 .... 8.5 I_5 .... 18.5 L_4 .... 60.0

Oligoplites saurus:
L_{15} .... 1.3 Q_1 .... 98.7

Selar crumenophthalmus:
I_5 .... 0.8 L_4 .... 2.1 Q_1+Q_2 ..... 9.6
L_{18} .... 12.5 L_{15} .... 25.0 Q_6 .... 50.0

Seriola dumerili:
Q_1 ....100.0

Trachinotus falcatus:
L_{17} .... 10.0 I_{13} .... 17.2 N_2 .... 25.0
I_4 .... 47.8

T. goodei:
L_{17} .... 0.9 L_{10} .... 1.7 I_{13} 3.9
I_4 .... 8.3 Q_1 .... 85.2

CHAETODONTIDAE—BUTTERFLYFISHES

Chaetodon (= Prognathodes) aculeatus:
L_9 .... 1.0 L_8 .... 4.7 L_4 .... 4.9
L_2 .... 5.7 L_{14} .... 7.2 N_2+N_3 ..... 11.4
T .... 26.6 K_1 .... 38.5

Chaetodon capistratus:
P_1 .... 2.1 E_4 .... 4.7 R 6.4
T .... 16.8 K_1 .... 31.4 E_5 .... 38.6

C. sedentarius:
E_1 .... 11.7 L_{11} .... 13.3 L_{14} 15.0
K_1 .... 16.7 T 43.3

C. striatus:
I_2 .... 2.5 L_2 .... 6.3 E_4 .... 32.5
K_1 .... 58.7

CIRRHITIDAE—HAWKFISHES

Amblycirrhitus pinos:
T .... 0.8 L_9 .... 1.4 L_{11} 2.1
L_{10} .... 2.5 K_1 .... 12.1 L_{19} 14.2
L_{16} .... 21.1 L_4 .... 45.8

CLINIDAE—CLINIDS

Labrisomus guppyi:
L_{10} .... 2.5 I_4 .... 5.0 I_3 .... 20.0
L_{17} 72.5

L. kalisherae:
N_8 ....100.0

L. nuchipinnis:
L_{11} .... 5.3 L_{14} .... 7.7 K_1 .... 10.0
N_2 .... 10.5 Q_1 .... 10.5 N_8 .... 12.3
I_4 .... 16.5 L_{17} 27.2

CLUPEIDAE—HERRINGS

Harengula clupeola:
Q_3 .... 2.0 I_{10} .... 5.0 K_1 .... 5.0
L_{15} .... 8.0 L_{18} .... 25.0 L_4 .... 55.0

TABLE I-C (*Continued*)

CLUPEIDAE—HERRINGS (*Continued*)

H. humeralis:

L_{18} .... 1.0 T .... 2.0 B_1 .... 2.5
L_{15} .... 5.0 K_1 .... 29.0 Q_1 .... 60.5

Jenkinsia lamprotaenia:

Q_3 .... 1.1 L_{11} .... 1.7 L_{18} 3.8
L_2 .... 3.8 T .... 4.2 L_{15} 11.4
L_4 .... 74.0

Opisthonema oglinum:

I_{10} .... 0.3 Q_3 .... 0.5 L_3 .... 0.5
I_{14} .... 0.6 E_2 .... 0.7 I_5 .... 1.6
L_{13} .... 2.5 R .... 2.5 P_2 .... 3.0
L_8 .... 5.5 L_{18} .... 6.4 Q_1 .... 9.8
L_{16} .... 17.1 K_1 .... 22.4 L_4 .... 26.6

CONGRIDAE—CONGER EELS

Nystachtichthys halis:

I_5 .... 1.9 R .... 2.4 L_{15} 2.5
L_3 .... 3.8 I_{10} .... 4.5 P_1 .... 18.6
L_4 .... 66.3

DACTYLOPTERIDAE—FLYING GURNARDS

Dactylopterus volitans:

L_{11} .... 1.4 Q_1 .... 5.0 L_{14} 5.4
I_{13} .... 7.2 L_{12} .... 19.3 L_{17} 61.7

DIODONTIDAE—PORCUPINEFISHES

Chilomycterus antennatus:

L_{14} .... 0.4 L_{10} .... 20.6 L_{17} 22.4
I_4 .... 56.6

Diodon holocanthus:

L_{17} .... 7.9 N_2 .... 11.6 I_{13} 12.8
I_4 .... 67.7

D. hystrix:

T .... 0.3 I_{13} .... 13.0 L_{17} 20.8
I_4 .... 31.3 N_2 .... 34.6

ECHENEIDAE—REMORAS

Echeneis naucrates:

L_2 .... 5.0 L_{10} .... 20.0 T 35.0
Q_1 .... 40.0

Remora remora:

L_{11} .... 8.0 L_{18} .... 10.0 Q_1 .... 10.0
L_2 .... 10.0 L_{10} .... 20.0 Q_8 .... 20.0
L_4 .... 22.0

ELOPIDAE—TARPONS

Megalops atlantica:

Q_1 ....100.0

EPHIPPIDAE—SPADEFISHES

Chaetodipterus faber:

L_{11} .... 0.1 L_{15} .... 0.1 L_{18} 0.2
L_{20} .... 0.2 I_7 .... 0.5 B_1 .... 2.3
N_1 .... 2.3 E_7 .... 2.3 I_6 .... 3.2
A_4 .... 5.0 E_4 .... 6.3 P_1 .... 12.6
K_1 .... 13.7 E_5+E_6 ...... 18.5 D 32.7

EXOCOETIDAE—FLYINGFISHES

Hemiramphus balao:

L_4 .... 1.2 L_{15} .... 2.9 L_{18} 4.7
K_1 .... 8.9 T .... 11.8 I_{10} 31.4
Q_1 .... 39.1

H. brasiliensis:

Q_1 .... 19.0 B_1 .... 81.0

FISTULARIIDAE—CORNETFISHES

Fistularia tabacaria:

Q_1 ....100.0

GERREIDAE—MOJARRAS

Eucinostomus argenteus:

I_4 .... 1.6 L_4 .... 2.0 T 2.1
J .... 2.6 L_2 .... 2.6 I_{13} 3.4
L_9 .... 5.9 L_{14} .... 7.6 L_{17} 10.9
K_1 .... 19.5 L_{11} 41.8

Gerres cinereus:

L_{11} .... 0.4 T .... 1.1 N_8 .... 1.9
O .... 1.9 L_{12} .... 2.8 L_{14} 4.3
L_2 .... 4.4 J .... 6.0 K_1 .... 12.7
I_4 .... 14.5 I_{13} .... 23.0 L_{17} 27.0

GOBIDEA—GOBIES

Coryphopterus glaucofraenum:

L_4 .... 8.0 R .... 10.0 I_{13} 10.0
N_8 .... 10.0 L_3 .... 12.0 A_6 .... 50.0

Gnatholepis thompsoni:

L_3 .... 2.0 L_2 .... 2.0 L_{11} 4.0
L_4 .... 18.0 A_6 .... 74.0

Gobiosoma genie:

L_{11} 100.0

GRAMMISTIDAE—SOAPFISHES

Rypticus saponaceous:

L_{12} .... 8.3 L_{17} .... 9.6 L_{14} 34.2
Q_1 .... 47.9

TABLE I-C (*Continued*)

HAEMULIDAE—GRUNTS

Anisotremus surinamensis:

L_{10}	0.05	D	0.08	T	0.12
L_3	0.25	K_1	0.40	L_{21}	0.50
E_4	0.75	L_2	1.10	I_{13}	1.30
Q_1	1.50	N_7	1.75	L_{12}	2.30
L_{14}	2.30	N_8	5.30	L_{17}	12.80
I_4	16.00	N_2	53.50		

A. virginicus:

I_{12}	0.2	J	0.4	C	0.5
I_3	0.8	L_3	0.9	L_9	1.1
P_1	1.5	L_4	1.8	L_{11}	3.0
I_4	3.8	L_{12}	4.7	I_{13}	5.5
L_2	5.6	L_{10}	8.2	K_1	14.0
L_{14}	14.7	N_8	16.5	L_{17}	16.8

H. album:

G	0.1	D	0.1	I_{12}	0.2
L_{11}	0.5	I_3	0.8	S_2	0.8
S_1	1.0	L_{12}	1.4	T	1.9
Q_1	2.0	I_4	2.7	L_2	3.3
O	3.5	L_{14}	3.9	N_8	5.2
I_{13}	5.4	L_{17}	8.1	K_1	14.0
N_2	19.9	J	25.2		

H. aurolineatum:

L_{10}	0.2	I_{12}	0.4	L_9	0.9
L_6	1.2	I_{13}	1.6	I_4	2.1
L_4	2.5	L_{11}	3.4	R	6.2
L_{19}	8.1	L_2	8.8	K_1	31.0
L_{16}	33.6				

H. carbonarium:

L_3	0.05	L_{11}	0.20	Q_1	0.70
L_5	1.90	L_{14}	4.10	J	4.85
N_8	6.00	K_1	8.00	I_3	9.80
N_2	10.90	I_4	15.20	L_{17}	38.30

H. chrysargyreum:

I_{15}	0.2	Q_1	0.4	J	1.2
I_4	1.8	L_{17}	1.8	R	3.5
L_{10}	4.7	L_{11}	5.7	L_2	5.7
L_{12}	5.9	I_{13}	14.7	L_{16}	15.9
K_1	19.1	L_{19}	19.4		

H. flavolineatum:

T	0.2	I_4	0.5	L_{11}	0.6
L_{12}	0.7	I_{12}	0.8	N_2	1.5
L_2	2.2	N_8	3.1	I_{13}	3.2
I_{17}	3.3	L_{14}	3.3	L_{10}	3.8
N_1	5.0	I_3	5.7	J	10.2
L_{17}	16.3	K_1	39.6		

H. macrostomum:

T	5.3	L_{17}	7.9	N_2	86.8

H. parrai:

I_{12}	0.2	L_{10}	0.5	L_{12}	0.5
L_2	0.9	N_8	2.4	I_{13}	2.8
K_1	2.9	N_1	3.3	E_6	3.4
I_4	5.1	L_{11}	7.1	L_{17}	33.3
L_{14}	37.6				

H. plumieri:

L_9	0.3	L_{11}	0.5	I_3	0.7
I_{13}	1.3	N_1	2.7	T	3.0
O	3.3	Q_1	3.3	L_2	5.3
N_8	5.7	L_{14}	5.8	I_4	6.9
J	8.3	N_2	12.4	K_1	14.5
L_{17}	26.0				

H. sciurus:

L_9	0.07	I_{12}	0.20	G	0.30
L_3	0.60	P_1	1.00	L_{10}	1.40
I_{17}	1.50	L_2	1.80	L_{11}	1.90
Q_1	2.90	J	3.00	L_{12}	4.40
I_4	4.50	K_1	5.00	T	5.20
N_8	5.60	N_2	8.70	L_{14}	10.00
I_{13}	15.00	L_{17}	26.93		

HOLOCENTRIDAE—SQUIRRELFISHES

Flammeo marianus:

L_4	1.1	L_{13}	3.3	L_2	13.3
L_{17}	30.6	L_{14}	51.7		

Holocentrus ascensionis:

L_{10}	0.6	I_4	1.0	K_1	3.9
L_{14}	10.6	L_2	10.6	L_{17}	73.3

H. rufus:

L_{12}	0.4	I_3	0.6	Q_1	1.2
L_3	1.2	L_8	1.4	L_{10}	1.5
L_2	2.4	K_1	4.5	N_8	7.1
I_4	7.8	L_{14}	15.0	L_{17}	56.9

Myripristis jacobus:

T	0.1	L_3	0.3	L_{18}	0.9
L_{22}	0.9	I_{16}	1.5	L_{10}	1.8
L_4	2.4	L_2	2.7	L_{11}	3.2
Q_2	5.4	K_1	7.0	L_8	11.2
L_{19}	14.9	L_{13}	17.4	L_{16}	30.3

Plectrypops retrospinis:

K_1	50.0	L_{17}	50.0

Sargocentron coruscum:

L_2	2.7	L_{17}	27.3	L_{14}	70.0

S. vexillarium:

L_4	0.4	L_2	1.6	K_1	4.0
Q_1+Q_2	5.2	L_{10}	5.7	I_3	10.3
L_{16}	20.8	I_4	25.1	L_{19}	26.9

TABLE I-C (*Continued*)

INERMIIDAE—BONNETMOUTHS

Inermia vittata:

K_1 .... 1.3 L_{18} .... 2.0 Q_6 .... 3.3
E_2 .... 16.7 L_4 .... 76.7

KYPHOSIDAE—SEA CHUBS

Kyphosus incisor:

A_4 .... 100.0

K. sectatrix:

B_1 .... 0.5 A_4 .... 99.5

LABRIDAE—WRASSES

Bodianus rufus:

K_1 .... 0.2   T .... 0.6 L_{10} 0.7
I_3 .... 0.7 L_{12} .... 1.2 L_2 .... 2.2
L_{14} .... 6.0 I_{13} .... 8.0 I_4 .... 10.4
N_2 .... 14.4 N_8 .... 19.5 L_{17} 36.1

Clepticus parrai:

L_{13} .... 0.3   T .... 0.3 I_5 .... 1.4
L_3 .... 1.5   R .... 1.7 L_{18} 2.3
P_1+P_3 ...... 4.7 L_{15} .... 5.0 I_{10} 19.2
E_2 .... 20.0 L_4 .... 43.6

Halichoeres bivittatus:

C .... 0.1 L_2 .... 1.0 L_{12} 3.0
Q_1 .... 3.2 I_3 .... 3.3 L_{14} 3.5
I_{13} .... 3.7   T .... 4.0 N_8 .... 7.3
I_4 .... 12.4 K_1 .... 17.4 N_2 .... 17.9
L_{17} 23.2

H. garnoti:

J .... 0.5 I_3 .... 2.0 Q_1 .... 3.0
N_2 .... 3.0 L_{14} .... 5.0 K_1 .... 5.5
I_{13} .... 7.0   T .... 7.5 I_4 .... 13.5
L_2 .... 14.0 N_8 .... 15.5 L_{17} 23.5

H. maculipinna:

I_{12} .... 0.2   T .... 0.8   J 0.9
I_3 .... 1.5 L_9 .... 1.5   R 1.6
L_{10} .... 1.7 L_2 .... 1.9 I_{13} 2.4
L_{17} .... 3.1 I_{17} .... 4.3 L_{11} 5.1
I_4 .... 5.3 L_3 .... 5.9 L_{14} 6.5
L_4 .... 10.2 K_1 .... 47.1

H. poeyi:

L_{12} .... 0.2 L_{10} .... 0.3 N_1 .... 1.6
K_1 .... 1.9 I_{13} .... 2.2   T 3.9
I_3 .... 4.4 Q_1 .... 5.0 L_{17} 5.1
J .... 5.2 N_2 .... 6.8 L_2 .... 7.4
N_8 .... 10.2 I_4 .... 21.3 L_{14} 24.5

H. radiatus:

I_3 .... 0.2 L_{12} .... 0.9 L_2 .... 1.1
K_1 .... 1.4 N_8 .... 6.8 N_2 .... 19.9
I_4 .... 21.3 L_{17} .... 23.3 I_{13} 25.1

Hemipteronotus novacula:

L_{11} .... 0.6 L_{10} .... 3.1 L_2 .... 4.2
I_{12} .... 5.6 L_{14} .... 6.3   T 6.3
K_1 .... 7.5 I_{13} .... 27.9 I_4 .... 38.5

H. splendens:

L_{10} .... 0.8 Q_3 .... 1.4   T 1.7
I_{13} .... 3.3 L_2 .... 3.3 I_4 .... 5.0
L_{14} .... 11.2 L_{11} .... 12.5 L_4 .... 60.8

Lachnolaimus maximus:

L_5 .... 0.5 I_{12} .... 0.6 L_{11} 1.0
N_2 .... 4.6 L_{17} .... 11.0 I_4 .... 39.7
I_{13} 42.6

Thalassoma bifasciatum:

L_{12} .... 0.8 I_2 .... 1.3 N_2 .... 1.5
L_1 .... 1.9 L_9 .... 1.9 K_1 .... 5.1
L_{10} .... 6.0 L_{16} .... 6.5 N_8 .... 7.5
T .... 7.7 L_2 .... 7.9 Q_1 .... 8.7
I_4+I_5 .... 11.4 L_{19} .... 13.0 L_4 .... 18.8

LUTJANIDAE—SNAPPERS

Lutjanus analis:

L_{12} .... 0.8 L_{20} .... 1.9   T 1.9
L_{14} .... 2.3 I_{17} .... 3.1 I_4 .... 13.0
Q_1 .... 29.8 L_{17} 47.2

L. apodus:

I_4 .... 0.50 L_{14} .... 3.45 I_{17} 3.45
L_{12} .... 3.70 L_2 .... 6.00 L_{17} 22.20
Q_1 .... 60.70

L. cyanopterus:

Q_1 .... 100.0

L. griseus:

L_{21} .... 0.9 I_4 .... 6.8 L_{14} 13.2
Q_1 .... 39.1 L_{17} 40.0

L. jocu:

L_2 .... 0.9 Q_3 .... 1.8 L_{21} 1.8
I_{19} .... 2.2 I_4 .... 3.6 L_{20} 6.6
I_{17} .... 7.0 L_{17} .... 15.4 Q_1 .... 60.7

L. mahogoni:

L_{17} .... 3.1 I_{17} .... 9.4 L_{14} 12.5
Q_1 .... 75.0

L. synagris:

L_{12} .... 50.0 L_{17} 50.0

TABLE I-C (*Continued*)

Ocyurus chrysurus:

L_{11}	0.5	W	0.5	I_5	0.7
L_{14}	0.8	Q_3	0.9	I_{13}	1.2
L_{22}	1.9	L_{12}	2.4	I_4	2.4
T	2.5	P_2+P_3	2.7	F	2.7
L_8	2.9	$I_{15}+I_{16}$	3.8	L_4	5.1
E_2	7.1	I_{10}	7.3	Q_1+Q_2	15.1
L_{16}	16.2	L_{19}	23.3		

MALACANTHIDAE—TILEFISHES

Malacanthus plumieri:

L_{14}	1.4	L_{11}	1.6	N_2	2.7
I_3	5.7	S	6.4	J	7.2
K_1	7.2	Q_1	12.4	L_{12}	15.0
L_{17}	18.5	N_8	21.9		

MUGILIDAE—MULLETS

Mugil curema:

B_3	100.0

MULLIDAE—GOATFISHES

Mulloidichthys martinicus:

L_2	0.3	L_4	0.3	N_2	0.4
I_{12}	0.4	I_4	0.7	L_{12}	0.8
L_8	0.9	T	1.5	L_3	1.6
L_{11}	4.3	L_{10}	5.7	J	6.8
I_3	7.9	N_8	8.9	L_{16}	11.9
I_{13}	13.1	L_{19}	15.9	K_1	18.6

Pseudopeneus maculatus:

R	0.2	L_9	0.2	L_3	0.4
N_8	0.8	I_4	0.8	L_{11}	1.8
L_{10}	1.9	T	2.7	L_{12}	3.2
Q_1	4.3	J	4.4	I_{13}	6.7
L_2	7.3	K_1	13.3	L_{14}	21.8
L_{17}	30.2				

MURAENIDAE—MORAYS

Echidna catenata:

L_{14}	3.7	L_{17}	96.3

Gymnothorax funebris:

Q_1	50.0	L_{17}	50.0

G. moringa:

Q_1	100.0

G. vicinus:

I_{17}	12.5	L_{17}	25.0	Q_1	62.5

OGCOCEPHALIDAE—BATFISHES

Ogcocephalus nasutus:

L_5	0.6	I_{13}	1.7	K_1	4.4
Q_1	8.8	A_4	11.1	I_4	25.9
L_{17}	47.5				

OPHICHTHIDAE—SNAKE EELS

Myrichthys acuminatus:

L_{12}	7.0	N_2	7.0	L_{17}	86.0

M. oculatus:

K_1	1.2	Q_1	3.2	L_{14}	3.2
L_{12}	12.5	L_2	18.7	L_{17}	61.2

Ophichthys ophis:

Q_1	50.0	I_{17}	50.0

OPISTOGNATHIDAE—JAWFISHES

Opisthognathus aurifrons:

K_1	0.3	L_6	0.6	E_2	1.3
Q_3	1.5	T	1.9	L_{15}	9.4
L_4	85.0				

O. macrognathus:

L_{14}	100.0

O. maxillosus:

L_4	0.4	L_8	5.4	K_1	14.3
Q_1	22.7	L_{10}	28.6	L_{14}	28.6

O. whitehursti:

L_{17}	5.0	N_8	8.0	L_{10}	11.0
Q_1	22.0	L_{14}	54.0		

OSTRACIIDAE—BOXFISHES

Lactophrys bicaudalis:

I_4	1.0	L_{17}	4.0	K_1	6.0
N_7	6.0	A_4	7.0	T	7.0
B_1	8.0	N_2	10.0	N_8	12.5
N_1	19.0	P_1	19.5		

L. polygonia:

I_4	1.7	L_{14}	10.0	D	11.7
E_4	23.3	T	25.0	P_1	28.3

L. quadricornis:

L_{11}	0.3	I_{13}	0.3	L_{14}	0.3
R	0.8	K_1	1.8	E_3	2.5
B_1	3.0	E_4	4.2	A_1	7.2
L_{17}	8.3	E_5	10.8	T	11.5
P_1	18.3	D	30.7		

TABLE I-C (*Continued*)

OSTRACIIDAE—BOXFISHES (*Continued*)

L. trigonus:

L_{14}	0.3	I_3	0.8	R	1.0
S	1.0	N_8	1.6	L_{11}	1.8
I_4	2.1	N_7	2.4	N_1	2.6
T	2.9	B_1	3.0	P_1	4.5
A_4	4.9	N_2	7.1	K_1	8.6
I_{13}	10.1	L_{17}	45.3		

L. triqueter:

L_3	0.2	R	0.3	I_3	0.7
A_4	0.9	S	1.0	B_2	1.2
L_{11}	1.3	I_{13}	1.7	N_2	2.3
I_4	2.9	O	3.3	D	6.0
P_1	6.7	L_{14}	7.1	T	8.2
L_{17}	11.3	J	15.7	K_1	29.2

PEMPHERIDAE—SWEEPERS

Pempheris schomburgki:

L_{11}	1.1	L_2	2.8	I_{18}	3.3
L_{13}	16.7	L_{15}	18.9	K_1	27.3
L_{18}	29.9				

POMACANTHIDAE—ANGELFISHES

Centropyge argi:

A_6	100.0

Holacanthus ciliaris:

G	0.4	E_1	0.5	P_1	0.9
A_4	1.4	D	96.8		

H. tricolor:

A_4	0.8	E_5	2.1	D	97.1

Pomacanthus arcuatus:

G	0.1	B_1	0.1	E_1	0.4
R	1.5	E_4	1.6	T	3.3
E_5	4.4	A_4	8.3	P_1	10.1
D	70.2				

P. paru:

B_2	0.1	R	0.1	G	0.2
E_1	0.3	E_4	1.4	P_1	4.8
E_5	4.9	A_4	13.4	D	74.8

POMACENTRIDAE—DAMSELFISHES

Abudefduf saxatilis:

E_2	0.8	K_1	0.9	W	1.2
L_5	3.0	L_{15}	3.2	T	3.7
Q_1	4.5	Q_3	4.7	I_9	5.3
P_1	7.1	A_4	8.8	L_4	13.6
E_4	43.2				

A. taurus:

I_3	0.1	E_1	0.1	I_4	0.2
L_{17}	0.3	E_4	5.3	A_4	94.0

Chromis cyanea:

L_3	0.3	Q_3	2.1	E_2	2.9
L_{15}	8.4	P_1	33.9	L_4	52.4

C. multilineatus:

L_3	0.2	L_{18}	0.8	T	1.2
L_2	1.3	I_{10}	1.6	E_2	1.8
L_{15}	2.1	P_1	3.2	L_4	87.8

Microspathodon chrysurus:

Q_6	0.1	L_{11}	0.1	I_4	0.1
D	0.2	L_3	0.2	N_8	1.0
L_{14}	1.2	L_2	1.8	E_7	2.2
T	3.8	A_6	89.3		

Stegastes fuscus:

P_1	0.2	E_1	0.2	I_{13}	0.5
L_{14}	0.9	L_2	0.9	E_3	1.1
L_8	1.1	R	1.2	L_{11}	1.2
L_{10}	1.6	B_1	1.9	L_{17}	2.4
E_4	3.0	I_4	3.3	Q_1	4.9
L_4	5.2	K_1	5.6	T	8.6
A_6	56.2				

S. leucostictus:

I_4	0.3	L_4	0.5	L_{14}	1.0
C	1.5	E_7	1.5	L_{11}	1.6
P_1	2.9	L_{17}	3.9	E_9	5.1
Q_1	7.1	K_1	12.6	T	18.2
I_2+Q_3	21.2	A_6	22.6		

S. planifrons:

E_7	0.6	P_1	0.6	R	2.4
L_4	2.8	N	3.3	B_1	3.9
K_1	5.6	L_2	11.1	E_4	19.4
A_6	24.4	T	25.9		

S. variabilis:

I_{13}	0.6	L_9	0.6	L_{11}	0.7
N_8	0.85	L_{14}	0.85	I_4	1.1
E_7	1.7	D	1.7	L_2	2.6
E_1	2.8	T	9.3	L_{10}	10.0
K_1	15.7	A_6	51.5		

PRIACANTHIDAE—BIGEYES

Priacanthus arenatus:

L_{22}	1.4	L_{10}	1.6	L_{13}	1.7
I_{15}	2.2	L_{19}	9.8	K_1	11.1
L_{14}	34.7	Q_1+Q_2	37.5		

P. cruentatus:

L_{11}	0.7	I_4	1.2	T	1.2
L_{10}	4.9	L_{13}	5.4	L_8	7.8

TABLE I-C (*Continued*)

$I_{15}+I_{16}$ ...... 8.9 L_{16} .... 10.0 L_{19} 14.4
K_1 .... 16.8 Q_1 .... 28.7

RACHYCENTRIDAE—COBIAS

Rachycentron canadum:
Q_1 ....100.0

SCARIDAE—PARROTFISHES

Scarus coelestinus:
D .... 0.1 N_2 .... 0.1 A_7 .... 0.2
C .... 0.2 I_1 .... 0.4 L_2 .... 0.4
B_1 .... 1.3 A_3+A_4 ..... 97.3

S. guacamaia:
B_1 .... 8.0 A_3+A_4 ..... 92.0

S. iserti:
A_3+A_4 .....100.0

S. taeniopterus:
D .... 1.5 B_1 .... 17.3 A_3+A_4 ..... 81.2

S. vetula:
D .... 1.0 E_4 .... 1.8 B_1 .... 3.2
A_3+A_4 ..... 94.0

Sparisoma aurofrenatum:
E_7 .... 0.2 E_4 .... 0.7 B_1 .... 1.3
A_3+A_4 ..... 97.8

S. chrysopterum:
B_1 .... 16.8 A_3+A_4 ..... 83.2

S. radians:
A_3+A_4 ..... 12.0 B_1 .... 88.0

S. rubripinne:
D .... 0.4 B_1 .... 7.0 A_3+A_4 ..... 92.6

S. viride:
E_4 .... 0.1   D .... 0.1 B_1 .... 2.5
A_3+A_4 ..... 97.3

SCIAENIDAE—DRUMS

Equetus acuminatus:
L_{11} .... 0.3 L_4 .... 1.6 L_{13} 2.3
L_{10} .... 3.1 Q_1+Q_2 ..... 3.7 L_{17} 5.3
L_2 .... 10.5 L_{16} 73.2

E. lanceolatus:
L_{17} .... 6.2 K_1 .... 31.3 L_{14} 62.5

E. punctatus:
L_{12} .... 0.3 L_3 .... 0.3 Q_1 .... 0.4
I_{10} .... 0.6 L_{10} .... 1.0 I_4 .... 3.2
K_1 .... 5.4 L_{16} .... 20.6 L_2 .... 22.5
L_{17} 45.7

Odontoscion dentex:
L_{13} .... 1.2 L_{17} .... 5.2 L_{10} 17.8
Q_1+Q_2 ..... 37.8 L_{16} 38.0

SCOMBRIDAE—MACKERELS

Euthynnus alletteratus:
K_1 .... 6.7 I_{19} .... 36.6 Q_1 .... 56.7

Scomberomorus cavalla:
I_{19} .... 7.7 Q_1 .... 92.3

S. regalis:
L_{14} .... 0.4 L_2 .... 1.2 I_{19} 2.3
Q_1 .... 96.1

SCORPAENIDAE—SCORPIONFISHES

Scorpaena brasiliensis:
L_{17} .... 7.1 Q_1 .... 14.3 L_{12} 14.3
L_2 .... 28.6 L_{14} 35.7

S. grandicornis:
L_2 .... 12.5 Q_1 .... 12.5 L_{14} 75.0

S. inermis:
Q_1 .... 0.3 L_{17} .... 0.6   T 6.3
L_{12} .... 7.5 L_{14} 85.3

S. plumieri:
I_{17} .... 6.2 L_{14} .... 18.7 L_{17} 32.9
Q_1 .... 42.2

Scorpaenodes carribaeus:
Q_1 .... 7.7 L_2 .... 9.1 L_{17} 17.3
L_{14} 65.9

SERRANIDAE—SEA BASSES

Epinephelus adscensionis:
I_3 .... 1.6 I_4 .... 3.2 L_2 .... 4.0
L_{14} .... 4.4 Q_1 .... 20.1 L_{17} 66.7

E. afer:
I_{17} .... 2.5 L_2 .... 6.7 L_{14} 6.8
Q_1 .... 7.0 L_{17} 77.0

E. cruentatum:
I_4 .... 3.8 L_{17} .... 3.8 L_{12} 8.9
L_{14} .... 17.3 Q_1 .... 66.2

E. fulvus:
L_2 .... 3.7 L_{12} .... 12.4 L_1 .... 17.2
L_{14} .... 20.7 Q_1 .... 46.0

E. guttatus:
S_1 .... 2.0 L_2 .... 3.3 I_{17} 7.0
L_{14} .... 10.5 L_{12} .... 16.6 Q_1 .... 21.1
L_{17} 39.5

TABLE I-C *(Continued)*

PRIACANTHIDAE—BIGEYES *(Continued)*

E. itajara:

Q_7 5.6 | L_{17} 12.2 | Q_1 13.3
L_{21} 23.3 | L_{20} 45.6

E. morio:

Q_1 16.7 | L_{17} 33.3 | L_2 50.0

E. striatus:

L_{10} 0.2 | L_2 0.6 | I_{13} 0.7
I_4 1.6 | L_{20} 3.5 | L_{14} 5.0
I_{15} 5.2 | L_{12} 5.5 | L_{17} 23.7
Q_1 54.0

Hypoplectrus unicolor:

L_2 6.7 | L_{17} 17.1 | Q_1 25.0
L_{14} 51.2

Mycteroperca bonaci:

Q_1 100.0

M. interstitialis:

Q_1 100.0

M. tigris:

Q_1 100.0

M. venenosa:

L_{14} 0.8 | I_{19} 3.9 | Q_1 95.3

Paranthias furcifer:

R 0.1 | L_2 0.2 | I_5 0.2
Q_2 0.6 | L_8 2.3 | L_{11} 3.1
T 7.7 | L_{16} 11.9 | P_1 12.2
L_4 61.7

Serranus tabacarius:

Q_1 100.0

S. tigrinus:

L_2 1.7 | L_{17} 7.8 | L_{12} 8.9
Q_1 9.7 | L_{14} 71.9

S. tortugarum:

Q_3 8.0 | L_4 92.0

SPARIDAE—PORGIES

Archosargus rhomboidalis:

L_{11} 0.2 | K_1 0.4 | I_{13} 3.4
R 3.5 | I_4 4.3 | L_{17} 4.8
A_4 38.8 | B_1 44.6

Calamus bajonado:

T 0.3 | K_1 6.7 | I_4 11.1
I_{13} 13.4 | L_{17} 23.3 | N_2 45.2

C. calamus:

J 0.6 | T 0.9 | I_3 1.8
L_2 3.6 | I_4 8.3 | N_2 8.9
I_{13} 15.0 | N_8 15.5 | K_1 19.2
L_{17} 26.2

C. penna:

L_{17} 50.0 | I_4 50.0

C. pennatula:

L_{12} 3.0 | N_2 4.0 | N_1 4.0
J 5.0 | L_{14} 5.8 | I_4 8.2
I_{13} 12.3 | K_1 14.0 | N_8 14.2
L_{17} 29.5

Diplodus caudimaculata:

I_3 2.0 | L_{17} 2.0 | I_4 16.0
A_4 80.0

SPHYRAENIDAE—BARRACUDAS

Sphyraena barracuda:

L_{22} 1.9 | I_{17} 2.6 | Q_1 95.5

S. picudilla:

I_{19} 17.9 | Q_1 82.1

SYNODONTIDAE—LIZARDFISHES

Synodus foetens:

Q_1 100.0

S. intermedius:

L_{14} 0.5 | I_{19} 5.0 | Q_1 94.5

S. synodus:

Q_1 100.0

TETRAODONTIDAE—PUFFERS

Canthigaster rostrata:

P_1 0.6 | L_4 1.2 | L_1 1.2
A_6 2.2 | L_2 2.3 | E_1 2.7
L_{14} 2.9 | L_{11} 3.1 | N_7 3.8
N_2 3.8 | S 4.6 | I_{13} 5.2
K_1 7.2 | I_4 7.8 | T 8.2
L_{17} 12.1 | D 15.0 | B_2 16.1

Sphaeroides spengleri:

Q_1 0.7 | L_4 0.9 | P_1 0.9
L_{10} 1.1 | I_3 1.4 | T 2.1
R 2.1 | O 3.4 | A_6 3.5
B_2 5.3 | L_{14} 5.5 | L_{11} 5.7
N_8 6.0 | N_2 6.9 | K_1 7.6
I_4 9.6 | I_{13} 16.0 | L_{17} 21.3

Source: Stephen Spotte and Patricia M. Bubucis, Sea Research Foundation; calculated from data in Randall (1967); names have been changed where appropriate to reflect current usage.

Literature Cited

Chapter 1

Adams, G. and S. Spotte. 1985. Carbonate mineral filtrants with new surfaces remove alkalinity from seawater and artifical seawater. Aquacult. Eng'g. 4: 305–311.

Almgren, T. and S. H. Fonselius. 1976. Determination of alkalinity and total carbonate. *In* Methods of seawater analysis, K. Grasshoff (ed.). Verlag Chemie, Weinheim, pp. 97–115.

Anderson, W. S. 1889. The solubility of carbonate of lime in fresh and sea water. Proc. R. Soc. Edinburgh 16: 319–324.

Anikouchine, W. A. and R. W. Sternberg. 1981. The world ocean: an introduction to oceanography, 2nd ed. Prentice-Hall, Englewood Cliffs, 513 pp.

Anonymous. 1982. The Beckman handbook of applied electrochemistry, 2nd ed. Bull. 7707-A, Beckman Instruments, Inc., Irvine, 128 pp.

Atkins, W. R. G. 1922. Hydrogen ion concentration of sea water in its biological relations. J. Mar. Biol. Assoc. U.K. 12: 717–771.

Atz, J. W. 1964a. Some principles and practices of water management for marine aquariums. *In* Seawater systems for experimental aquariums: a collection of papers, J. R. Clark and R. L. Clark (eds.). Res. Rpt. 63, U.S. Fish and Wildlife Service, Washington, pp. 3–16.

Atz, J. W. 1964b. Principles and practices of water management for marine aquaria. Int. Zoo Ybk. 5: 173–181.

Bates, R. G. 1973. Determination of pH: theory and practice, 2nd ed. Wiley, New York, 479 pp.

Bathurst, R. G. C. 1971. Carbonate sediments and their diagenesis. Elsevier, Amsterdam, 620 pp.

Berner, R. A. 1966. Diagenesis of carbonate sediments: interaction of magnesium in sea water with mineral grains. Science 153: 188–191.

Berner, R. A. 1974. Physical chemistry of carbonates in the oceans. *In* Studies in paleo-oceanography, W. W. Hay (ed.). Spec. Pub. No. 20, Society of Economic Paleontologists and Mineralogists, Tulsa, pp. 37–43.

Berner, R. A. 1975. The role of magnesium in the crystal growth of calcite and aragonite from sea water. Geochim. Cosmochim. Acta 39: 489–504.

Berner, R. A. and J. W. Morse. 1974. Dissolution kinetics of calcium carbonate in seawater. IV. Theory of calcite dissolution. Am. J. Sci. 274: 108–135.

Bidwell, J. P. and S. Spotte. 1985. Artificial seawaters: formulas and methods. Jones and Bartlett, Boston, 349 pp.

Bischoff, J. L. 1968. Kinetics of calcite nucleation: magnesium ion inhibition and ionic strength catalysis. J. Geophys. Res. 73: 3315–3322.

Bischoff, J. L. and W. S. Fyfe. 1968. Catalysis, inhibition, and the calcite-aragonite problem. I. The aragonite-calcite transformation. Am. J. Sci. 266: 65–79.

Bissell, H. J. and G. V. Chilingar. 1967. Classification of sedimentary carbonate rocks. *In* Carbonate rocks: origin, occurrence and classification, G. V. Chilingar (ed.). Elsevier, Amsterdam, pp. 87–168.

Bower, C. E., D. T. Turner, and S. Spotte. 1981. pH maintenance in closed seawater culture systems: limitations of calcareous filtrants. Aquaculture 23: 211–217.

Boyd, C. E. 1979. Water quality in warmwater fish ponds. Agricultural Experiment Station, Auburn University, Auburn, 359 pp.

Brätter, P., P. Möller, and U. Rösick. 1972. On the equilibrium of coexisting sedimentary carbonates. Earth Planet. Sci. Lett. 14: 50–54.

Breder, C. M. Jr. and T. H. Howley. 1931. The chemical control of closed circulating systems of sea water in aquaria for tropical marine fishes. Zoologica (N.Y.) 9: 403–442.

Breder, C. M. Jr. and H. W. Smith. 1932. On the use of sodium bicarbonate and calcium in the rectification of sea-water in aquaria. J. Mar. Biol. Assoc. U.K. 18: 199–200.

Brewer, P. G. 1975. Minor elements in sea water. *In* Chemical oceanography, 2nd ed., Vol. 1, J. P. Riley and G. Skirrow (eds.). Academic Press, London, pp. 415–496.

Brown, E. M. 1929. Notes on the hydrogen ion concentration, excess base, and carbon-dioxide pressure of marine aquarium waters. Proc. Zool. Soc. London 44: 601–613.

Carozzi, A. V. 1960. Microscopic sedimentary petrography. Wiley, New York, 485 pp.

Carter, P. W. 1978. Adsorption of amino acid-containing organic matter by calcite and quartz. Geochim. Cosmochim. Acta 42: 1239–1242.

Carter, P. W. and R. M. Mitterer. 1978. Amino acid composition of organic matter associated with carbonate and non-carbonate sediments. Geochim. Cosmochim. Acta 42: 1231–1238.

Chave, K. E. and E. Suess. 1970. Calcium carbonate saturation in seawater: effects of dissolved organic matter. Limnol. Oceanogr. 15: 633–637.

Cooper, L. H. N. 1932. On the effect of long continued additions of lime to aquarium sea-water. J. Mar. Biol. Assoc. U.K. 18: 201–202.

Cox, R. A. 1965. The physical properties of sea water. *In* Chemical oceanography, Vol. 1, J. P. Riley and G. Skirrow (eds.). Academic Press, London, pp. 73–120.

Deguchi, Y. 1963. Contribution to the study of aquarium conditions—IV. Titration curve of circulating aquarium. Bull. Coll. Agricult. Vet. Med., Nihon Univ. (17): 33–37.

Deguchi, Y. 1964. Some studies on the quality of water fish rearing aquarium. III. Titration curve and carbon dioxide system. Kaiyō Kagaku (6): 95–116.

Fofonoff, N. P. 1985. Physical properties of seawater: a new salinity scale and equation of state for seawater. J. Geophys. Res. 90: 3332–3342.

Forchhammer, G. 1865. On the composition of seawater in the different parts of the ocean. Phil. Trans. R. Soc. London 155: 203–262.

Frakes, T. A., F. H. Hoff Jr., and W. G. Hoff. 1982. Delayed metamorphosis of larval anemonefish (*Amphiprion ocellaris*) due to iodine deficiency. *In* Proceedings of the warmwater fish culture workshop, R. R. Stickney and S. P. Meyers (eds.). Spec. Pub. No. 3, World Mariculture Society, Baton Rouge, pp. 117–123.

Garrels, R. M. 1965. Silica: role in the buffering of natural waters. Science 148: 69.

Garrels, R. M., M. E. Thompson, and R. Siever. 1960. Stability of some carbonates at 25°C and one atmosphere total pressure. Am. J. Sci. 258: 402–418.

Garrels, R. and R. Wollast. 1978. Discussion. Am. J. Sci. 278: 1469–1474.

Goldberg, E. D. 1980. Composition of sea water. *In* Encyclopedia of ocean and atmospheric sciences, S. P. Parker (ed.). McGraw-Hill, New York, pp. 415–417.

Groot, K. de and E. M. Duyvis. 1966. Crystal form of precipitated calcium carbonate as influenced by adsorbed magnesium ions. Nature 212: 183–184.

Hansson, I. 1973. A new set of pH-scales and standard buffers for sea water. Deep-sea Res. 20: 479–491.

Hawley, J. E. and R. M. Pytkowicz. 1973. Interpretation of pH measurements in concentrated electrolyte solutions. Mar. Chem. 1: 245–259.

Hirayama, K. 1970. Studies of water control by filtration through sand bed in a marine aquarium with closed circulating system.—VI. Acidification of aquarium water. Bull. Jap. Soc. Sci. Fish. 36: 26–34.

Hirayama, K. 1974. Water control by filtration in closed culture systems. Aquaculture 4: 369-385.

Hoffmann, R. E. 1884. Artificial sea water for aquaria. Bull. U.S. Fish Comm. 4: 465-467.

Honig, C. 1934. Nitrates in aquarium water. J. Mar. Biol. Assoc. U.K. 19: 723-725.

International Salt Company. 1972. The Sterling® brine handbook. International Salt Company, Clarks Summit, 32 pp.

Katz, A. 1973. The interaction of magnesium with calcite during crystal growth at 25-90°C and one atmosphere. Geochim. Cosmochim. Acta 37: 1563-1586.

Kester, D. R., I. W. Duedall, D. N. Connors, and R. M. Pytkowicz. 1967. Preparation of artificial seawater. Limnol. Oceanogr. 12: 176-179.

King, J. M. and S. Spotte. 1974. Marine aquariums in the research laboratory. Aquarium Systems, Inc., Eastlake, 38 pp.

Kinney, E. C. 1973. Average or mean pH. Prog. Fish-cult. 35: 93.

Kokubo, S. 1933. A study of the respiratory conditions in sea water aquarium. Sci. Rpt. Tôhoku Imp. Univ. 8(Ser. 4): 111-125.

Lafon, G. M. 1978. Discussion. Am. J. Sci. 278: 1455-1468.

Li, Y. H., T. Takahashi, and W. S. Broecker. 1969. Degree of saturation of $CaCO_3$ in the oceans. J. Geophys. Res. 74: 5507-5525.

Lyman, J. and R. H. Fleming. 1940. The composition of sea water. J. Mar. Res. 3: 134-146.

MacIntyre, F. 1976. Concentration scales: a plea for physico-chemical data. Mar. Chem. 4: 205-224.

Marcet, A. 1819. On the specific gravity, and temperature, in different parts of the ocean, and in particular seas; with some account of their saline contents. Phil. Trans. R. Soc. London 109: 161-208.

Masterton, W. L. and E. J. Slowinski. 1969. Chemical principles, 2nd ed. Saunders, Philadelphia, pp. 474-477.

McDuff, R. E. and F. M. M. Morel. 1980. The geochemical control of seawater (Sillen revisited). Environ. Sci. Technol. 14: 1182-1186.

Meyers, P. A. and J. G. Quinn. 1971. Interaction between fatty acids and calcite in seawater. Limnol. Oceanogr. 16: 992-997.

Millero, F. J. and A. Poisson. 1981. International one-atmosphere equation of state of seawater. Deep-sea Res. 28A: 625-629.

Möller, P. 1973. Determination of the composition of surface layers of calcite in solutions containing Mg^{2+}. J. Inorgan. Nucl. Chem. 35: 395-401.

Möller, P. 1974. Bestimmung der Oberflächenzusammensetzung von Calcit in Mg^{2+}-haltigen Ca-45-markierten Lösungen. Z. Anal. Chem. 268: 28-30. [English summary]

Möller, P. and P. P. Parekh. 1975. Influence of magnesium on the ion-activity product of calcium and carbonate dissolved in seawater: a new approach. Mar. Chem. 3: 63-77.

Möller, P. and C. S. Sastri. 1974. Estimation of the number of surface layers of calcite involved in *Ca*-^{45}*Ca* isotopic exchange with solution. Z. Phys. Chem. (N.F.) 89: 80-87.

Morse, J. W. 1986. The surface chemistry of calcium carbonate minerals in natural waters: an overview. Mar. Chem. 20: 91-120.

Morse, J. W., A. Mucci, L. M. Walter, and M. S. Kaminsky. 1979. Magnesium interaction with the surface of calcite in seawater. Science 205: 904-905.

Mucci, A. and J. W. Morse. 1983. The incorporation of Mg^{2+} and Sr^{2+} into calcite overgrowths: influences of growth rate and solution composition. Geochim. Cosmochim. Acta 47: 217-233.

Mucci, A. and J. W. Morse. 1985. Auger spectroscopy determination of the surface-most adsorbed layer composition on aragonite, calcite, dolomite, and magnesite in synthetic seawater. Am. J. Sci. 285: 306-317.

Oliver, J. H. 1957. The chemical composition of sea water in the aquarium. Proc. Zool. Soc. London 129: 137-145.

Peffer, E. L. and M. G. Blair. 1949. Testing of hydrometers. Nat. Bur. Stand. Circ. 477, U.S. Department of Commerce, Washington, 9 pp.

Plath, D. C., K. S. Johnson, and R. M. Pytkowicz. 1980. The solubility of calcite—probably containing magnesium—in seawater. Mar. Chem. 10: 9-29.

Plummer, L. N. and F. T. Mackenzie. 1974. Predicting mineral solubility from rate data: application to the dissolution of magnesian calcites. Am. J. Sci. 274: 61-83.

Pytkowicz, R. M. 1967. Carbonate cycle and the buffer mechanism of recent oceans. Geochim. Cosmochim. Acta 31: 63–73.

Pytkowicz, R. M. 1968. The carbon dioxide-carbonate system at high pressures in the oceans. Oceanogr. Mar. Biol. Ann. Rev. 6: 83–135.

Pytkowicz, R. M. 1973a. Calcium carbonate retention in supersaturated seawater. Am. J. Sci. 273: 515–522.

Pytkowicz, R. M. 1973b. The carbon dioxide system in the oceans. Schweizer. Z. Hydrol. 35: 8–28.

Pytkowicz, R. M., E. Atlas, and C. H. Culberson. 1975. Chemical equilibrium in seawater. *In* Marine chemistry in the coastal environment, T. M. Church (ed.). American Chemical Society, Washington, pp. 1–24.

Pytkowicz, R. M., D. R. Kester, and R. C. Burgener. 1966. Reproducibility of pH measurements in seawater. Limnol. Oceanogr. 11: 417–419.

Riley, J. P. 1965. Historical introduction. *In* Chemical oceanography, Vol. 1, J. P. Riley and G. Skirrow (eds.). Academic Press, London, pp. 1–41.

Rothstein, F. and J. E. Fisher. 1985. pH measurement: the meter. Am. Lab. 17(9): 124–133.

Saeki, A. 1958. Studies on fish culture in the aquarium of closed-circulating system: its fundamental theory and standard plan. Bull. Jap. Soc. Sci. Fish. 23: 684–695. [Japanese with English summary and legends]

Saeki, A. 1962. The composition and some chemical control of the sea water of the closed circulating aquarium. Bull. Mar. Biol. Sta. Asamushi, Tôhoku Univ. 11: 99–104.

Segedi, R. and W. E. Kelley. 1964. A new formula for artificial sea water. *In* Sea-water systems for experimental aquariums: a collection of papers, J. R. Clark and R. L. Clark (eds.). Res. Rpt. 63, U.S. Fish and Wildlife Service, Washington, pp. 17–19.

Siddall, S. E. 1974. Studies of closed marine culture systems. Prog. Fish-cult. 36: 8–15.

Sillén, L. G. 1961. The physical chemistry of seawater. *In* Oceanography, M. Sears (ed.). American Association for the Advancement of Science, Washington, pp. 549–581.

Sillén, L. G. 1967. The ocean as a chemical system. Science 156: 1189–1197.

Simkiss, K. 1964. The inhibitory effects of some metabolites on the precipitation of calcium carbonate from artificial and natural sea water. J. Conseil Int. Explor. Mer 29: 6–18.

Skirrow, G. 1975. The dissolved gases—carbon dioxide. *In* Chemical oceanography, 2nd ed., Vol. 2, J. P. Riley and G. Skirrow (eds.). Academic Press, London, pp. 1–192.

Spotte, S. 1979a. Fish and invertebrate culture: water management in closed systems, 2nd ed. Wiley, New York, 179 pp.

Spotte, S. 1979b. Seawater aquariums: the captive environment. Wiley, New York, 413 pp.

Spotte, S., G. Adams, and P. M. Bubucis. 1984. GP2 medium is an artificial seawater for culture or maintenance of marine oganisms. Zoo. Biol. 3: 229–240.

Stowell, F. P. 1925. Physical and chemical conditions in the sea-water of the Zoological Society's aquarium—a comparison with the water of the open sea. Proc. Zool. Soc. London 82: 1241–1258.

Stumm, W. and J. J. Morgan. 1981. Aquatic chemistry: an introduction emphasizing chemical equilibria in natural waters, 2nd ed. Wiley, New York, 780 pp.

Suess, E. 1970. Interaction of organic compounds with calcium carbonate—I. Association phenomena and geochemical implications. Geochim. Cosmochim. Acta 34: 157–168.

Thorstenson, D. C. and L. N. Plummer. 1977. Equilibrium criteria for two-component solids reaction with fixed composition in an aqueous phase—example: the magnesian calcites. Am. J. Sci. 277: 1203–1223.

Thorstenson, D. C. and L. N. Plummer. 1978. Reply. Am. J. Sci. 278: 1478–1488.

Wallace, W. J. 1974. The development of the chlorinity/salinity concept in oceanography. Elsevier, Amsterdam, 227 pp.

Wattenberg, H. and E. Timmerman. 1936. Über die Sattigung des Seewassers an $CaCO_3$ und die anorganogene Bildung von Kalksedimenten. An. Hydrogr. Mar. Met. 24: 23–31.

Wescott, C. C. 1978. pH measurements. Academic Press, New York, 172 pp.

Weyl, P. K. 1961. The carbonate saturometer. J. Geol. 69: 32–44.

Weyl, P. K. 1967. The solution behavior of carbonate materials in sea water. Stud. Trop. Oceanogr. 5: 178–228.

Weyl, P. K. 1970. Oceanography: an introduction to the marine environment. Wiley, New York, 535 pp.

Wilson, J. P. and M. A. Griggs. 1941. Analysis of sea water in a closed aquarium. Trans. N.Y. Acad. Sci. 3(Ser. 2): 218–221.

Wilson, T. R. S. 1975. Salinity and the major elements of sea water. *In* Chemical oceanography, Vol. 1, 2nd ed., J. P. Riley and G. Skirrow (eds.). Academic Press, London, pp. 365–413.

Wollast, R., R. M. Garrels, and F. T. Mackenzie. 1980. Calcite-seawater reactions in ocean surface waters. Am. J. Sci. 280: 831–848.

Zerbe, W. B. and C. B. Taylor. 1953. Sea water temperature and density reduction tables. Spec. Pub. 198, U.S. Coast and Geodetic Survey, Washington, 21 pp.

Chapter 2

Adams, G. and S. Spotte. 1980. Effects of tertiary methods on total organic carbon removal in saline, closed-system marine mammal pools. Am. J. Vet. Res. 41: 1470–1474.

Adey, W. H. 1983. The microcosm: a new tool for reef research. Coral Reefs 1: 193–201.

Alderson, R. 1979. The effect of ammonia on the growth of juvenile sole, *Solea solea* (L) and turbot, *Scophthalmus maximus* (L). Aquaculture 17: 291–309.

Allison, F. E., J. H. Doetsch, and E. M. Roller. 1951. Ammonium fixation and availability in Harpster clay loam. Soil. Sci. 72: 187–200.

Allison, F. E., E. M. Roller, and J. H. Doetsch. 1953a. Ammonium fixation and availability in vermiculite. Soil Sci. 75: 173–180.

Allison, F. E., J. H. Doetsch, and E. M. Roller. 1953b. Availability of fixed ammonium in soils containing different clay minerals. Soil Sci. 75: 373–381.

Allison, F. E., M. Kefauver, and E. M. Roller. 1953c. Ammonium fixation in soils. Soil Sci. Soc. Am. Proc. 17: 107–110.

Almendras, J. M. E. 1987. Acute nitrite toxicity and methemoglobinemia in juvenile milkfish (*Chanos chanos* Forsskal). Aquaculture 61: 33–40.

Anonymous. 1971. Starting with sea water. II. Aeration and filtration. Petfish Mon. 6: 21–22.

Anthonisen, A. C., R. C. Loehr, T. B. S. Prakasam, and E. G. Srinath. 1976. Inhibition of nitrification by ammonia and nitrous acid. J. Water Pollut. Contr. Fed. 48: 835–852.

Aoki, T., S. Uemura, and M. Munemori. 1983. Continuous flow fluorometric determination of ammonia in water. Anal. Chem. 55: 1620–1622.

API (American Petroleum Institute). 1981. The sources, chemistry, fate, and effects of ammonia in aquatic environments. American Petroleum Institute, Washington, 145 pp.

APHA et al. (American Public Health Association, American Water Works Association, and Water Pollution Control Federation). 1985. Standard methods for the examination of water and wastewater, 16th ed. American Public Health Association, Washington, 1268 pp.

Armstrong, D. A., D. Chippendale, A. W. Knight, and J. E. Colt. 1978. Interaction of ionized and unionized ammonia on short-term survival and growth of prawn larvae, *Macrobrachium rosenbergii*. Biol. Bull. 154: 15–31.

Ataman, O. Y. and H. B. Mark Jr. 1977. Determination of ammonia in aqueous solutions by infrared spectrometry following preconcentration on zeolite. Anal. Chem. 49: 1331–1335.

Audic, J. M., G. M. Faup, and J. M. Navarro. 1984. Specific activity of *Nitrobacter* through attachment on granular media. Water Res. 18: 745–750.

AWWA (American Water Works Association). 1981. An assessment of microbial activity on GAC. J. Am. Water Works Assoc. 73: 447–454.

Bada, J. L. and C. Lee. 1977. Decomposition and alteration of organic compounds dissolved in seawater. Mar. Chem. 5: 523–534.

Balderston, W. L. and J. McN. Sieburth. 1976. Nitrate removal in closed-system aquaculture by columnar denitrification. Appl. Environ. Microbiol. 32: 808–818.

Bancroft, K., S. W. Maloney, J. McElhaney, I. H. Suffet, and W. O. Pipes. 1983. Assessment of bacterial growth and total organic carbon removal on granular activated carbon contactors. Appl. Environ. Microbiol. 46: 683–687.

Barica, J. 1973. Reliability of an ammonia probe for electrometric determination of total ammonia nitrogen in fish tanks. J. Fish. Res. Board Can. 30: 1389–1392.

Barica, J. 1975. Electrochemical detection of NH_4^+-NH_3 systems in water. *In* Water quality parameters, ASTM (ed.). American Society for Testing and Materials, Philadelphia, pp. 20–24.

Bates, R. G. and G. D. Pinching. 1949. Acidic dissociation constant of ammonium ion at 0° to 50° C, and the base strength of ammonia. J. Res. Natl. Bureau Stand. 42: 419–430.

Baylor, E. R., W. H. Sutcliffe, and D. S. Hirschfield. 1962. Adsorption of phosphate onto bubbles. Deep-sea Res. 2: 120–124.

Beckett, M. J. and A. L. Wilson. 1974. The manual determination of ammonia in fresh waters using an ammonia-sensitive membrane-electrode. Water Res. 8: 333–340.

Benesch, R. and P. Mangelsdorf. 1972. Eine Methode zur colorimetrischen Bestimmung von Ammoniak in Meerwasser. Helgoländer Meeresunters. 23: 365–375. [English summary]

Bishop, D. F., J. A. Heidman, and J. B. Stamberg. 1976. Single-stage nitrification-denitrification. J. Water Pollut. Contr. Fed. 48: 520–532.

Bower, C. E. and J. P. Bidwell. 1978. Ionization of ammonia in seawater: effects of temperature, pH, and salinity. J. Fish. Res. Board Can. 35: 1012–1016.

Bower, C. E. and T. Holm-Hansen. 1980a. A salicylate-hypochlorite method for determining ammonia in seawater. Can. J. Fish. Aquat. Sci. 37: 794–798.

Bower, C. E. and T. Holm-Hansen. 1980b. A simplified hydrazine-reduction method for determining high concentrations of nitrate in recirculated seawater. Aquaculture 21: 281–286.

Bower, C. E. and D. T. Turner. 1981. Accelerated nitrification in new seawater culture systems: effectiveness of commercial additives and seed media from established systems. Aquaculture 24: 1–6.

Bower, C. E. and D. T. Turner. 1982. Effects of seven chemotherapeutic agents on nitrification in closed seawater culture systems. Aquaculture 29: 331–345.

Bower, C. E. and D. T. Turner. 1983. Nitrification in closed seawater culture systems after washing of filter beds. Prog. Fish-cult. 45: 198–200.

Bowser, P. R., G. A. Wooster, and A. L. Aluisio. 1989. Plasma chemistries of nitrite stressed Atlantic salmon *Salmo salar*. J. World Aquacult. Soc. 20: 173–180.

Bowser, P. R., W. W. Falls, J. VanZandt, N. Collier, and J. D. Phillips. 1983. Methemoglobinemia in channel catfish: methods of prevention. Prog. Fish-cult. 45: 154–158.

Boyd, C. E. 1978. Determination of total ammonia nitrogen and chemical oxygen demand in fish culture systems. Trans. Am. Fish. Soc. 108: 314–319.

Breger, I. A. and A. Brown. 1962. Kerogen in the Chattanooga Shale. Science 137: 221–224.

Broberg, O. and K. Pettersson. 1988. Analytical determination of orthophosphate in water. Hydrobiologia 170: 45–59.

Brock, T. D. 1966. Principles of microbial ecology. Prentice-Hall, Englewood Cliffs, 306 pp.

Brock, T. D. 1970. Biology of microorganisms. Prentice-Hall, Englewood Cliffs, 737 pp.

Brockway, D. R. 1950. Metabolic products and their effects. Prog. Fish-cult. 12: 127–129.

Broderius, S. J., L. L. Smith Jr., and D. T. Lond. 1977. Relative toxicity of free cyanide and dissolved sulfide forms to the fathead minnow (*Pimephales promelas*). J. Fish. Res. Board Can. 34: 2323–2332.

Brylinski, M. 1977. Release of dissolved matter by some marine macrophytes. Mar. Biol. 39: 213–220.

Brzezinski, M. A. 1987. Colorimetric determination of nanomolar concentrations of ammonium in seawater using solvent extraction. Mar. Chem. 20: 277–288.

Burkhalter, D. E. and C. M. Kaya. 1977. Effects of prolonged exposure to ammonia on fertilized eggs and sac fry of rainbow trout (*Salmo gairdneri*). Trans. Am. Fish. Soc. 106: 470–475.

Burrows, R. E. 1964. Effects of accumulated excretory products on hatchery-reared salmonids. Res. Rpt. 66, U.S. Fish and Wildlife Service, Washington, 12 pp.

Buswell, A. M., T. Shiota, N. Lawrence, and V. van Meter. 1954. Laboratory studies on the kinetics of the growth of *Nitrosomonas* with relation to the nitrification phase of the B.O.D. test. Appl. Microbiol. 2: 21–25.

Cairo, P. R., J. T. Coyle, J. J. Davis, H. M. Neukrug, I. H. Suffet, and A. Wicklund. 1982. Evaluating regenerated activated carbon through laboratory and pilot-column studies. J. Am. Water Works Assoc. 74: 84–102.

Carey, C. 1938. The occurrence of nitrifying bacteria in the sea. J. Mar. Res. 1: 291–304.

Carlucci, A. F. and P. M. McNally. 1969. Nitrification by marine bacteria in low concentrations of substrate and oxygen. Limnol. Oceanogr. 14: 736–739.

Carlucci, A. F. and J. D. H. Strickland. 1968. The isolation, purification and some kinetic studies of marine nitrifying bacteria. J. Exp. Mar. Biol. Ecol. 2: 156–166.

Catalano, G. 1987. An improved method for the determination of ammonia in seawater. Mar. Chem. 20: 289–295.

Chao-yuan, W., Z. Yan-xia, L. Ren-zhi, P. Zuosheng, Z. Ying-fang, L. Qing-chen, Z. Jing-pu, and F. Xiao. 1984. Utilization of ammonium-nitrogen by *Porphyra yezoensis* and *Gracilaria verrucosa*. *In* Proceedings of the eleventh international seaweed symposium, C. J. Bird and M. A. Ragan (eds.). Dr W. Junk, Dordrecht, pp. 475–477.

Chapman, A. R. C. 1973. Methods for macroscopic algae. *In* Handbook of phycological methods: culture methods and growth measurements, J. R. Stein (ed.). Cambridge University Press, Cambridge, pp. 87–104.

Christman, R. F. 1970. Chemical structures of color producing organic substances in water. *In* Symposium on organic matter in natural waters, D. W. Hood (ed.). Occas. Pub. No. 1, Institute of Marine Science, University of Alaska, College, pp. 181–198.

Clark, C. and E. L. Schmidt. 1967a. Growth response of *Nitrosomonas europaea* to amino acids. J. Bacteriol. 93: 1302–1308.

Clark, C. and E. L. Schmidt. 1967b. Uptake and utilization of amino acids by resting cells of *Nitrosomonas europea*. J. Bacteriol. 93: 1309–1315.

Colinvaux, L. H., K. M. Wilbur, and N. Watabe. 1965. Tropical marine algae: growth in laboratory culture. J. Phycol. 1: 69–78.

Collins, M. T., J. B. Gratzek, D. L. Dawe, and T. G. Nemetz. 1975. Effects of parasiticides on nitrification. J. Fish. Res. Board Can. 32: 2033–2037.

Collins, M. T., J. B. Gratzek, D. L. Dawe, and T. G. Nemetz. 1976. Effects of antibacterial agents on nitrification in an aquatic recirculating system. J. Fish. Res. Board Can. 33: 215–218.

Collos, Y., E. A. S. Linley, M. G. Frikha, and B. Ravail. 1988. Phytoplankton death and nitrification at low temperatures. Estuar. Coast. Shelf Sci. 27: 341–347.

Colt, J. E. and D. A. Armstrong. 1981. Nitrogen toxicity to crustaceans, fish, and molluscs. *In* Bio-engineering symposium for fish culture, L. J. Allen and E. C. Kinney (eds.). FCS Pub. 1, American Fisheries Society, Bethesda, pp. 34–47.

Colt, J. and G. Tchobanoglous. 1976. Evaluation of the short-term toxicity of nitrogenous compounds to channel catfish, *Ictalurus punctatus*. Aquaculture 8: 209–224.

Colt, J. and G. Tchobanoglous. 1978. Chronic exposure of channel catfish, *Ictalurus punctatus*, to ammonia: effects on growth and survival. Aquaculture 15: 353–372.

Cookson, J. T. Jr. 1978. Adsorption mechanisms: the chemistry of organic adsorption on activated carbon. *In* Carbon adsorption handbook, P. N. Cheremisinoff and F. Ellerbusch (eds.). Ann Arbor Science, Ann Arbor, pp. 241–279.

Cooney, D. O., A. Nagerl, and A. L. Hines. 1983. Solvent regeneration of activated carbon. Water Res. 17: 403–410.

Corpe, W. A. 1970. An acid polysaccharide produced by a primary film forming marine bacterium. Develop. Indus. Microbiol. 11: 402–412.

Corpe, W. A. 1974. Periphytic marine bacteria and the formation of microbial films on solid surfaces. *In* Effect of the ocean environment on microbial activities, R. R. Colwell and R. Y. Morita (eds.). University Park Press, Baltimore, pp. 397–417.

Craigie, J. S. and J. McLachlan. 1964. Excretion of colored ultraviolet-absorbing substances by marine algae. Can. J. Bot. 42: 23–33.

Crawford, R. E. and G. H. Allen. 1977. Seawater inhibition of nitrite toxicity to chinook salmon. Trans. Am. Fish. Soc. 106: 105–109.

Cuenco, M. L. and R. R. Stickney. 1980. Reliability of an electrode and a water analysis kit for determination of ammonia in aquaculture systems. Trans. Am. Fish. Soc. 109: 571–576.

Culter, D. W. and L. M. Crump. 1933. Some aspects of the physiology of certain nitrite-forming bacteria. Ann. Appl. Biol. 20: 291–296.

Danielson, N. D. and C. M. Conroy. 1982. Fluorometric determination of hydrazine and ammonia separately or in mixtures. Talanta 29: 401–404.

Davies, T. R. and D. F. Toerien. 1971. Population description of a denitrifying microbial system. Water Res. 5: 553–564.

Dawson, R. N. and K. L. Murphy. 1972. The temperature dependency of biological denitrification. Water Res. 6: 71–83.

Dean, W. M. 1974. Instrumental methods of analysis, 5th ed. D. van Nostrand, New York, 860 pp.

Delwiche, C. C. 1956. Denitrification. *In* Symposium on inorganic nitrogen metabolism, W. D. McElroy and B. Glass (eds.). Johns Hopkins Press, Baltimore, pp. 233–256.

Delwiche, C. C. and B. A. Bryan. 1976. Denitrification. Ann. Rev. Microbiol. 30: 241–262.

Delwiche, C. C. and M. S. Finstein. 1965. Carbon and energy sources for the nitrifying autotroph *Nitrobacter*. J. Bacteriol. 90: 102–107.

Dodd, D. J. R. and D. H. Bone. 1975. Nitrate reduction by denitrifying bacteria in single and two stage continuous flow reactors. Water Res. 9: 323–328.

Downing, K. M. and J. C. Merkens. 1955. The influence of dissolved-oxygen concentration on the toxicity of un-ionized ammonia to rainbow trout (*Salmo gairdneri* Richardson). Ann. Appl. Biol. 43: 243–246.

Doxtader, K. G. and M. Alexander. 1966. Nitrification by heterotrophic soil microorganisms. Soil Sci. Soc. Am. Proc. 30: 351–355.

Dreusch, C. von Jr. 1978. Process aspects of regeneration in a multiple-hearth furnace. *In* Carbon adsorption handbook, P. N. Cheremisinoff and F. Ellerbusch (eds.). Ann Arbor Science, Ann Arbor, pp. 923–953.

Dreusch, C. von. 1981. Regeneration systems. *In* Activated carbon adsorption for wastewater treatment, J. R. Perrich (ed.). CRC Press, Boca Raton, pp. 137–153.

Eaton, A. D. and V. Grant. 1979. Sorption of ammonium by glass frits and filters: implications for analyses of brackish and freshwater. Limnol. Oceanogr. 24: 397–399.

Eddy, F. B., P. A. Kunzlik, and R. N. Bath. 1983. Uptake and loss of nitrite from the blood of rainbow trout, *Salmo gairdneri* Richardson, and Atlantic salmon, *Salmo salar* L. in fresh water and in dilute sea water. J. Fish Biol. 23: 105–116.

Elia, V. J., C. S. Clark, K. T. McGinnis, T. E. Cody, and R. N. Kinman. 1978. Ozonation in a wastewater reuse system: examination of products formed. J. Water Pollut. Contr. Fed. 50: 1727–1732.

Emerson, K., R. C. Russo, R. E. Lund, and R. V. Thurston. 1975. Aqueous ammonia equilibrium calculations: effect of pH and temperature. J. Fish. Res. Board Can. 32: 2379–2383.

Erickson, R. J. 1985. An evaluation of mathematical models for the effects of pH and temperature on ammonia toxicity to aquatic organisms. Water Res. 19: 1047–1058.

Evans, W. H. and B. F. Partridge. 1974. Determination of ammonia levels in water and wastewater with an ammonia probe. Analyst 99: 367–375.

Fankboner, P. U. and M. E. DeBurgh. 1977. Diurnal exudation of ^{14}C-labelled compounds by the large kelp *Macrocystis integrifolia* Bory. J. Exp. Mar. Biol. Ecol. 28: 151–162.

Farooq, S., E. S. K. Chian, and R. S. Engelbrecht. 1977. Basic concepts in disinfection with ozone. J. Water Pollut. Contr. Fed. 49: 1818–1831.

Flis, J. 1968a. Anatomicohistopathological changes induced in carp (*Cyprinus carpio* L.) by ammonia water. Part I. Effects of toxic concentrations. Acta Hydrobiol. 10: 205–224.

Flis, J. 1968b. Anatomicohistopathological changes induced in carp (*Cyprinus carpio* L.) by ammonia water. Part II. Effects of subtoxic concentrations. Acta Hydrobiol. 10: 225–238.

Fogg, G. E. and G. T. Boalch. 1958. Extracellular products in pure cultures of a brown alga. Nature 181: 789–790.

Forster, J. R. M. 1974. Studies on nitrification in marine biological filters. Aquaculture 4: 387–397.

Frakes, T. and F. H. Hoff Jr. 1982. Effect of high nitrate-N on the growth and survival of juvenile and larval anemonefish, *Amphiprion ocellaris*. Aquaculture 29: 155–158.

Garside, C., G. Hull, and S. Murray. 1978. Determination of submicromolar concentrations of ammonia in natural waters by a standard addition method using a gas-sensing electrode. Limnol. Oceanogr. 23: 1073–1076.

Gerhardt, H. V. 1981. The effect of algal and bacterial filters on sea water quality during closed system culture. S. Afr. J. Zool. 16: 127–131.

Gilbert, T. R. and A. M. Clay. 1973. Determination of ammonia in aquaria and in sea water using the ammonia electrode. Anal. Chem. 45: 1758–1759.

Gjessing, E. T. 1976. Physical and chemical characteristics of aquatic humus. Ann Arbor Science, Ann Arbor, 120 pp.

Glover, H. E. 1983. Measurement of chemoautotrophic CO_2 assimilation in marine nitrifying bacteria: an enzymatic approach. Mar. Biol. 74: 295–300.

Goering, J. J. 1972. The role of nitrogen in eutrophic processes. *In* Water pollution microbiology, R. Mitchell (ed.). Wiley, New York, pp. 43–68.

Goldizen, V. C. 1970. Laboratory culture of marine organisms. *In* Food-drugs from the sea. Proceedings of the Marine Technological Society 1969, H. W. Youngken Jr. (ed.). Marine Technological Society, Washington, pp. 113–117.

González, J. F. 1984. On the ammonia-nitrogen determination in fisheries wastewaters by means of the indophenol method. Environ. Technol. Lett. 5: 345–348.

Goulden, P. D. and P. Brooksbank. 1975. The determination of total phosphate in natural waters. Anal. Chim. Acta 80: 183–187.

Grasshoff, K. 1976. Determination of nitrate. *In* Methods of seawater analysis, K. Grasshoff (ed.). Verlag Chemie, Weinheim, pp. 137–145.

Grasshoff, K. and H. Johannsen. 1974. A critical review of the method by Benesch and Mangelsdorf for the colorimetric determination of ammonia in sea water. J. Conseil Int. Explor. Mer 36: 90–92.

Grosjean, D., P. M. Whitmore, and G. R. Cass. 1988. Ozone fading of natural organic colorants: mechanisms and products of the reaction of ozone with indigos. Environ. Sci. Technol. 22: 292–298.

Gundersen, K. 1955. Effects of B-vitamins and amino-acids on nitrification. Physiol. Plant. 8: 136–141.

Gundersen, K. 1966. The growth and respiration of *Nitrosocystis oceanus* at different partial pressures of oxygen. J. Gen. Microbiol. 42: 387–396.

Guterstam, B., I. Wallentinus, and R. Iturriaga. 1978. In situ primary production of *Fucus vesiculosus* and *Cladophora glomerata*. Kieler Meeresforsch. (4): 257–266.

Hampson, B. L. 1977a. Relationship between total ammonia and free ammonia in terrestrial and ocean waters. J. Conseil Int. Explor. Mer 37: 117–122.

Hampson, B. L. 1977b. The analysis of ammonia in polluted sea water. Water Res. 11: 305–308.

Hanisak, M. D. 1983. The nitrogen relationships of marine macroalgae. *In* Nitrogen in the marine environment, E. J. Carpenter and D. G. Capone (eds.). Academic Press, New York, pp. 699–730.

Harlin, M. M., B. Thorne-Miller, and G. B. Thursby. 1978. Ammonium uptake by *Gracilaria* sp. (Florideophyceae) and *Ulva lactuca* (Chlorophyceae) in closed system fish culture. *In* Proceedings of the ninth international seaweed symposium, A. Jensen and J. R. Stein (eds.). Science Press, Princeton, pp. 285–292.

Harvey, G. R., D. A. Boran, L. A. Chesal, and J. M. Tokar. 1983. The structure of marine fulvic and humic acids. Mar. Chem. 12: 119–132.

Harvey, G. R., D. A. Boran, S. R. Piotrowicz, and C. P. Weisel. 1984. Synthesis of marine humic substances from unsaturated lipids. Nature 309: 244–246.

Harwood, J. E. and A. L. Kühn. 1970. A colorimetric method for ammonia in natural waters. Water Res. 4: 805–811.

Hassenteufel, W., R. Jagitsch, and F. F. Koczy. 1963. Impregnation of glass surface against sorption of phosphate traces. Limnol. Oceanogr. 8: 152–156.

Haug, R. T. and P. L. McCarty. 1972. Nitrification with submerged filters. J. Water Pollut. Contr. Fed. 44: 2086–2102.

Hazel, C. R., W. Thomsen, and S. J. Meith. 1971. Sensitivity of striped bass and stickleback to ammonia in relation to temperature and salinity. Calif. Fish and Game 57: 138–153.

Helder, W. and R. T. P. de Vries. 1979. An automatic phenol-hypochlorite method for the determination of ammonia in sea- and brackish waters. Nethl. J. Sea Res. 13: 154–160.

Hellebust, J. A. 1974. Extracellular products. *In* Algal physiology and biochemistry, W. D. P. Stewart (ed.). University of California Press, Berkeley and Los Angeles, pp. 838–863.

Henrici, A. T. and D. E. Johnson. 1935. Studies on fresh-water bacteria. II. Stalked bacteria, a new order of Schizomycetes. J. Bacteriol. 30: 61–93.

Heron, J. 1962. Determination of phosphate in water after storage in polyethylene. Limnol. Oceanogr. 7: 316–321.

Hess, H. J. 1981. Performance ratings for submerged nitrification biofilters development of a design calculation procedure [*sic*]. *In* Proceedings of the bioengineering symposium for fish culture, L. J. Allen and E. C. Kinney (eds.). FCS Pub. 1, American Fisheries Society, Bethesda, pp. 63–70.

Heukelekian, H. and E. S. Crosby. 1956a. Slime formation in polluted waters. Sew. Indus. Wastes 28: 78–92.

Heukelekian, H. and E. S. Crosby. 1956b. Slime formation in sewage. Sew. Indus. Wastes 28: 206–210.

Heukelekian, H. and A. Heller. 1940. Relation between food concentration and surface for bacterial growth. J. Bacteriol. 40: 547–558.

Hikuma, M., T. Kubo, T. Yasuda, I. Karube, and S. Suzuki. 1980. Ammonia electrode with immobilized nitrifying bacteria. Anal. Chem. 52: 1020–1024.

Hirayama, K. 1966a. Studies on water control by filtration through sand bed in a marine aquarium with closed circulating system—III. Relation of grain size of filter sand to purification of breeding water. Bull. Jap. Soc. Sci. Fish. 32: 11–19. [Japanese with English summary and legends]

Hirayama, K. 1966b. Studies on water control by filtration through sand bed in a marine aquarium with closed circulating system—IV. Rate of pollution by fish, and the possible number and weight of fish kept in an aquarium. Bull. Jap. Soc. Sci. Fish. 32: 20–27. [Japanese with English summary and legends]

Hirayama, K. 1974. Water control by filtration in closed systems. Aquaculture 4: 369–385.

Hirayama, K., H. Mizuma, and Y. Mizue. 1988. The accumulation of dissolved organic substances in closed recirculation culture systems. Aquacult. Eng'g. 7: 73–87.

Hoehn, R. C. and A. D. Ray. 1973. Effects of thickness on bacterial film. J. Water Pollut. Contr. Fed. 45: 2302–2320.

Holt, G. J. and C. R. Arnold. 1983. Effects of ammonia and nitrite on growth and survival of red drum eggs and larvae. Trans. Am. Fish. Soc. 112: 314–318.

Hooper, A. B. and K. R. Terry. 1973. Specific inhibitors of ammonia oxidation in *Nitrosomonas*. J. Bacteriol. 115: 480–485.

Horrigan, S. G., Å. Hagström, I. Koike, and F. Azam. 1988. Inorganic nitrogen utilization by assemblages of marine bacteria in seawater culture. Mar. Ecol. Prog. Ser. 50: 147–150.

Huey, D. W., M. C. Wooten, L. A. Freeman, and T. L. Beitinger. 1982. Effect of pH and chloride on nitrite-induced lethality in bluegill (*Lepomis macrochirus*). Bull. Environ. Contam. Toxicol. 28: 3–6.

Hutchins, R. A. 1981. Activated carbon. *In* Activated carbon adsorption for wastewater treatment, J. R. Perrich (ed.). CRC Press, Boca Raton, pp. 29–40.

Iwai, T., T. Ito, and K. Tamura. 1974. The toxicity of nitrite on ayu-fry, *Plecoglossus altivelis*, and the chlorinity in the culturing water. Bull. Fac. Fish., Mie Univ. 1: 43–51. [Japanese with English summary and legends]

Jackson, T. A. 1975. Humic matter in natural waters and sediments. Soil Sci. 119: 56–64.

Jaubert, J. 1989. An integrated nitrifying-denitrifying biological system capable of purifying sea water in a closed circuit aquarium. Bull. Inst. Océanogr., Monaco, Num. spéc. 5: 101–106.

Jenkins, D. 1968. The differentiation, analysis, and preservation of nitrogen and phosphorus forms in natural waters. *In* Trace inorganics in water, R. G. Gould (ed.). American Chemical Society, Washington, pp. 265–280.

Jensen, H. L. and K. Gundersen. 1955. Biological decomposition of nitro-compounds. Nature 175: 341.

Jeris, J. S. and R. W. Owens. 1975. Pilot-scale, high-rate biological denitrification. J. Water Pollut. Contr. Fed. 47: 2043–2057.

Johansson, O. and M. Wedborg. 1980. The ammonia-ammonium equilibrium in seawater at temperatures between 5 and 25°C. J. Soln. Chem. 9: 37–44.

Johnson, B. D. and P. J. Wangersky. 1985. Seawater filtration: particle flow and impaction considerations. Limnol. Oceanogr. 30: 966–971.

Johnson, P. W. and J. McN. Sieburth. 1976. *In situ* morphology of nitrifying-like bacteria in aquaculture systems. Appl. Environ. Microbiol. 31: 423–432.

Jones, R. F. 1962. Extracellular mucilage of the red alga *Porphyridium cruentum*. J. Cell. Comp. Physiol. 60: 61–64.

Kabasawa, H. and M. Yamada. 1971. The effect of copper sulfate ($CuSO_4 \cdot 5H_2O$) and Neguvon on the function of filtering bacteria in a closed circulating sea water system. Sci. Rpt. Keikyu Aburatsubo Mar. Park Aquar. (4): 18–22. [Japanese with English summary and legends]

Kahn, L. and F. T. Brezenski. 1967. Determination of nitrate in estuarine waters: comparison of a hydrazine reduction and a brucine procedure. Environ. Sci. Technol. 1: 488–491.

Kain, J. M. 1966. The role of light in the ecology of *Laminaria hyperborea*. *In* Light as an ecological factor, R. Bainbridge, C. G. Evans, and O. Rackman (eds.). Oxford University Press, Oxford, pp. 109–130.

Kalle, K. 1966. The problem of the Gelbstoff in the sea. Oceanogr. Mar. Biol. Ann. Rev. 4: 91–104.

Kawai, A., M. Sugiyama, R. Shiozaki, and I. Sugahara. 1971. Microbiological studies on the nitrogen cycle in aquatic environments. I. Effects of oxygen tension on the microflora and the balance of nitrogenous compounds in the experimental aquarium. Mem. Res. Inst. Food Sci., Kyoto Univ. (32): 7–15.

Kawai, A., Y. Yoshida, and M. Kimata. 1964. Biochemical studies on the bacteria in aquarium with circulating system—I. Changes of the qualities of breeding water and bacterial population of the aquarium during fish cultivation. Bull. Jap. Soc. Sci. Fish. 30: 55–62. [Japanese with English summary and legends]

Kawai, A., Y. Yoshida, and M. Kimata. 1965. Biochemical studies on the bacteria in the aquarium with circulating system— II. Nitrifying activity of the filter-sand. Bull. Jap. Soc. Sci. Fish. 31: 65–71. [Japanese with English summary and legends]

Kawamoto, N. Y. 1961. The influence of excretory substances of fishes on their own growth. Prog. Fish-cult. 23: 70–75.

Kester, D. R. and R. M. Pytkowicz. 1967. Determination of the apparent dissociation constants of phosphoric acid in seawater. Limnol. Oceanogr. 12: 243–252.

Khailov, K. M. and Z. P. Burkalova. 1969. Release of dissolved organic matter by marine seaweeds and distribution of their total organic products to inshore communities. Limnol. Oceanogr. 14: 521–527.

Khailov, K. M. and Z. Z. Finenko. 1970. Organic macromolecular compounds dissolved in sea-water and their inclusion into food chains. *In* Marine food chains, J. H. Steele (ed.). Oliver and Boyd, Edinburgh, pp. 6–18.

Kholdebarin, B. and J. J. Oertli. 1977. Effect of suspended particles and their sizes on nitrification in surface water. J. Water Pollut. Contr. Fed. 49: 1693–1697.

Khoo, K. H., C. H. Culberson, and R. G. Bates. 1977. Thermodynamics of the dissociation of ammonium ion in seawater from 5 to 40°C. J. Soln. Chem. 6: 281–290.

Kimata, M., A. Kawai, and Y. Yoshida. 1961. Studies on marine nitrifying bacteria (nitrite formers and nitrate formers)—I. On the method of cultivation and on the distribution (preliminary report). Bull. Jap. Soc. Sci. Fish. 27: 593–597. [Japanese with English summary and legends]

Klein, R. Jr. and C. Hach. 1977. Standard additions: uses and limitations in spectrophotometric analysis. Am. Lab. 9(7): 21–27.

Knight, C. B. and P. M. Toom. 1981. An enzymatic assay for the measurement of ammonia in seafood products. Mississippi-Alabama Sea Grant Consortium, NTIS PB81-23139 1, National Technical Information Service, Springfield, 14 pp.

Knowles, G., A. L. Downing, and M. J. Barrett. 1965. Determination of kinetic constants for nitrifying bacteria in mixed culture, with the aid of an electronic computer. J. Gen. Microbiol. 38: 263–278.

Knowles, R. 1982. Denitrification. Microbiol. Rev. 46: 42–70.

Koffskey, W. E. and B. W. Lykins Jr. 1990. GAC adsorption and infrared reactivation: a case study. J. Am. Water Works Assoc. 82: 48–56.

Koroleff, F. 1976a. Determination of phosphorus. *In* Methods of seawater analysis, K. Grasshoff (ed.). Verlag Chemie, Weinheim, pp. 117–126.

Koroleff, F. 1976b. Determination of ammonia. *In* Methods of seawater analysis, K. Grasshoff (ed.). Verlag Chemie, Weinheim, pp. 126–133.

Larmoyeux, J. D. and R. G. Piper. 1973. Effects of water reuse on rainbow trout in hatcheries. Prog. Fish-cult. 35: 2–8.

Laws, E. A., W. G. Harrison, and G. R. DiTullio. 1985. A comparison of nitrogen assimilation rates based on ^{15}N uptake and autotrophic protein synthesis. Deep-sea Res. 32: 85–95.

Lees, H. 1952. The biochemistry of the nitrifying organisms. 1. The ammonia-oxidizing systems of *Nitrosomonas*. Biochem. J. 52: 134–139.

Lees, H. and J. H. Quastel. 1946a. Biochemistry of nitrification in soil. 2. The site of soil nitrification. Biochem. J. 40: 815–823.

Lees, H. and J. H. Quastel. 1946b. Biochemistry of nitrification in soil. 3. Nitrification of various organic nitrogen compounds. Biochem. J. 40: 824–828.

Levine, G. and T. L. Meade. 1976. The effects of disease treatment on nitrification in closed system aquaculture. Proceedings of the 7th annual meeting, World Mariculture Society, J. W. Avault Jr. (ed.). Louisiana State University, Baton Rouge, pp. 483–490.

Lewis, W. M. Jr. and D. P. Morris. 1986. Toxicity of nitrite to fish: a review. Trans. Am. Fish. Soc. 115: 183–195.

Li, A. Y. L. and A. DiGiano. 1983. Availability of sorbed substrate for microbial degradation on granular activated carbon. J. Water Pollut. Contr. Fed. 55: 392–399.

Liao, W., R. F. Christman, J. D. Johnson, D. S. Millington, and J. R. Hass. 1982. Structural characterization of aquatic humic material. Environ. Sci. Technol. 16: 403–410.

Liddicoat, M. I., S. Tibbitts, and E. I. Butler. 1975. The determination of ammonia in seawater. Limnol. Oceanogr. 20: 131–132.

Lloyd, R. and D. W. M. Herbert. 1960. The influence of carbon dioxide on the toxicity of un-ionized ammonia to rainbow trout (*Salmo gairdneri*). Ann. Appl. Biol. 48: 399–404.

Lloyd, R. and L. D. Orr. 1969. The diuretic response by rainbow trout to sub-lethal concentrations of ammonia. Water Res. 3: 335–344.

Lobban, C. S., P. J. Harrison, and M. J. Duncan. 1985. The physiological ecology of seaweeds. Cambridge University Press, Cambridge, 242 pp.

Lowery, J. D. and C. E. Burkhead. 1980. The role of adsorption in biologically extended activated carbon columns. J. Water Pollut. Contr. Fed. 52: 389–398.

Lyman, W. J. 1978. Applicability of carbon adsorption to the treatment of hazardous industrial wastes. *In* Carbon adsorption handbook, P. N. Cheremisinoff and F. Ellerbusch (eds.). Ann Arbor Science, Ann Arbor, pp. 131–165.

Malone, P. G. and K. M. Towe. 1970. Microbial carbonate and phosphate precipitates from sea water cultures. Mar. Geol. 9: 301–309.

Manabe, T. 1969. New modification of Lubrochinsky's indophenol method for direct microanalysis of ammonia-N in sea water. Bull. Jap. Soc. Sci. Fish. 35: 897–906. [Japanese with English summary and legends]

Maqsood, R. and A. Benedek. 1977. Low-temperature organic removal and denitrification in activated carbon columns. J. Water Pollut. Contr. Fed. 49: 2107–2117.

Martin, D. F. 1968. Marine chemistry, Vol. 1. Marcel Dekker, New York, 280 pp.

Martin, R. J. and W. J. Ng. 1984. Chemical regeneration of exhausted activated carbon—I. Water Res. 18: 59–73.

Mathieson, A. C. and C. J. Dawes. 1986. Photosynthetic responses of Florida seaweeds to light and temperature: a physiological survey. Bull. Mar. Sci. 38: 512–524.

Matulewich, V. A., P. F. Strom, and M. S. Finstein. 1975. Length of incubation for enumerating nitrifying bacteria present in various environments. Appl. Microbiol. 29: 265–268.

Maugle, P. D. and T. L. Meade. 1980. Use of specific-ion electrode for the determination of un-ionized ammonia in fish blood. Prog. Fish-cult. 42: 224–228.

McCurdy, R. F., R. Boss, and J. Dale. 1989. Determination of ammonia in water by centrifugal analysis. Water Res. 23: 779–784.

McGinnis, F. K. 1981. Infrared furnaces for reactivation. *In* Activated carbon adsorption for wastewater treatment, J. R. Perrich (ed.). CRC Press, Boca Raton, pp. 155–176.

McGuire, M. J. and I. H. Suffet. 1978. Adsorption of organics from domestic water supplies. J. Am. Water Works Assoc. 70: 621–636.

Meade, T. L. 1974. The technology of closed system culture of salmonids. Tech. Rpt. 30, Animal Sci./NOAA Sea Grant, University of Rhode Island, Kingston, 30 pp.

Meiklejohn, J. 1954. Some aspects of the physiology of the nitrifying bacteria. *In* Symposium on autotrophic microorganisms, B. A. Fry and J. L. Peel (eds.). Cambridge University Press, Cambridge, pp. 68–83.

Messer, J. J., J. Ho, and W. J. Grenney. 1984. Ionic strength correction for extent of ammonia ionization in freshwater. Can. J. Fish. Aquat. Sci. 41: 811–815.

Meyerhoff, M. E. 1980. Polymer membrane electrode based potentiometric ammonia gas sensor. Anal. Chem. 52: 1532–1534.

Miller, D. C., S. Poucher, J. A. Cardin, and D. Hansen. 1990. The acute and chronic toxicity of ammonia to marine fish and a mysid. Arch. Environ. Contam. Toxicol. 19: 40–48.

Mohsen, A. F., A. F. Khaleata, M. A. Hashem, and A. Metwalli. 1974. Effect of different nitrogen sources on growth, reproduction, amino acid, fat and sugar contents in *Ulva fasciata* Delile. Bot. Mar. 17: 218–222.

Morse, J. W., M. Hunt, H. Zullig, A. Mucci, and T. Mendez. 1982. A comparison of techniques for preserving dissolved nutrients in open ocean seawater samples. Ocean Sci. Eng'g. 7: 75–106.

Mulbarger, M. C. 1971. Nitrification and denitrification in activated sludge systems. J. Water Pollut. Contr. Fed. 43: 2059–2070.

Mullin, J. D. and J. P. Riley. 1955. The spectrophotometric determination of nitrate in natural waters, with particular reference to sea-water. Anal. Chim. Acta 12: 464–480.

Murphy, J. and J. P. Riley. 1962. A modified single solution method for the determination of phosphate in natural waters. Anal. Chim. Acta 27: 31–36.

Nebel, C., R. D. Gottschling, R. L. Hutchinson, T. J. McBride, D. M. Taylor, J. L. Pavoni, M. E. Tittlebaum, H. E. Spencer, and M. Fleischman. 1973. Ozone disinfection of industrial-municipal secondary effluents. J. Water Pollut. Contr. Fed. 45: 2493–2507.

Newell, B. S. 1967. The determination of ammonia in sea water. J. Mar. Biol. Assoc. U.K. 47: 271–280.

Newell, B. and G. Dal Pont. 1964. Ammonia in sea water. Nature 201: 36–37.

Nimura, Y. 1973. A direct estimation of microgram amounts of ammonia in water without salt-error. Bull. Jap. Soc. Sci. Fish. 39: 1315–1324.

Nissenbaum, A. and I. R. Kaplan. 1972. Chemical and isotopic evidence for the *in situ* origin of marine humic substances. Limnol. Oceanogr. 17: 570–582.

Norris, J. N. and W. Fenical. 1982. Chemical defense in tropical marine algae. *In* The Atlantic barrier reef ecosystem at Carrie Bow Cay, Belize, I Structure and communities, K. Rützler and I. G. Macintyre (eds.). Smithsonian Institution Press, Washington, pp. 417–431.

O'Kelley, J. C. and A. Nason. 1970. Use of the nitrifying chemoautotroph *Nitrosomonas* for assay of ammonia. Anal. Biochem. 33: 454–459.

Otte, G. and H. Rosenthal. 1978. Water quality during a one year operation of a closed intensive fish culture system. Int. Council Explor. Sea, C.N. 1978/F:7, 1–18. [Manuscript report]

Owens, O. v. H. and W. E. Esaias. 1976. Physiological responses of phytoplankton to major environmental factors. Ann. Rev. Plant Physiol. 27: 461–483.

Ozretich, R. J. 1977. An investigation of the transition from aerobic to nitrate respiration in marine bacteria in continuous culture. Diss. Abst. Int. 38: 1002-B.

Painter, H. A. 1970. A review of literature on inorganic nitrogen metabolism in microorganisms. Water Res. 4: 343–450.

Parsons, T. R. 1975. Particulate organic carbon in the sea. *In* Chemical oceanography, Vol. 2, 2nd ed., J. P. Riley and G. Skirrow (eds.). Academic Press, London, pp. 365–383.

Paul, V. J. 1984. Chemical defense in tropical green algae of the order Caulerpales. Am. Zool. 24: 24A. [Abstract]

Payne, W. J. 1981. Denitrification. Wiley, New York, 214 pp.

Peel, R. G. and A. Benedek. 1983. Biodegradation and adsorption within activated carbon adsorbers. J. Water Pollut. Contr. Fed. 55: 1168–1173.

Perrone, S. J. and T. L. Meade. 1977. Protective effect of chloride on nitrite toxicity in coho salmon (*Oncorhynchus kisutch*). J. Fish. Res. Board Can. 34: 386–492.

Powers, E. B. 1920. Influence of temperature and concentration on the toxicity of salts to fishes. Ecology 1: 95–112.

Prieur, L. and S. Sathyendranath. 1981. An optical classification of coastal and oceanic waters based on the specific spectral absorption curves of phytoplankton pigments, dissolved organic matter, and other particulate materials. Limnol. Oceanogr. 26: 671–689.

Prince, J. S. 1974. Nutrient assimilation and growth of some seaweeds in mixtures of sea water and secondary sewage effluents. Aquaculture 4: 69–79.

Quastel, J. H., P. G. Scholefield, and J. W. Stevenson. 1950. Oxidation of pyruvic-oxime by soil organisms. Nature 166: 940–942.

Quinlan, A. V. 1984. Prediction of the optimum pH for ammonia-N oxidation by *Nitrosomonas europaea* in well-aerated natural and domestic-waste waters. Water Res. 18: 561–566.

Redner, B. D. and R. R. Stickney. 1979. Acclimation to ammonia by *Tilapia aurea*. Trans. Am. Fish. Soc. 108: 383–388.

Reichenbach-Klinke, von H-H. 1967. Untersuchungen über die Einwirkung des Ammoniakgehalts auf den Fischorganismus. Arch. Fischereiwiss. 17: 122–132. [English summary]

Reuter, J. H. and E. M. Perdue. 1977. Importance of heavy metal-organic matter interactions in natural waters. Geochim. Cosmochim. Acta. 41: 325–334.

Ridal, J. J. and R. M. Moore. 1990. A re-examination of the measurement of dissolved organic phosphorus in seawater. Mar. Chem. 29: 19–31.

Riemann, B. and H-H. Schierup. 1978. Effects of storage and conservation on the determination of ammonia in water samples from four lake types and a sewage plant. Water Res. 12: 849–853.

Riley, R. T. and M. C. Mix. 1981. An ion-exchange technique for concentrating ammonia from small volumes of seawater. Mar. Chem. 10: 159–164.

Robinette, H. R. 1976. Effect of selected sublethal levels of ammonia on the growth of channel catfish (*Ictalurus punctatus*). Prog. Fish-cult. 38: 26–29.

Rogers, G. L. and S. L. Klemetson. 1985. Calculation of un-ionized ammonia concentrations. J. Aquaricult. Aquat. Sci. 4: 61–65.

Russo, R. C., R. V. Thurston, and K. Emerson. 1981. Acute toxicity of nitrite to rainbow trout (*Salmo gairdneri*): effects of pH, nitrite species, and anion species. Can. J. Fish. Aquat. Sci. 38: 387–393.

Ryther, J. H. 1976. Marine polyculture based upon natural food chains and recycled wastes, July, 1975–June, 1976. Woods Hole Oceanographic Institution, Woods Hole, 20 pp. [Manuscript report]

Sadler, K. 1981/1982. The toxicity of ammonia to the European eel (*Anguilla anguilla* L.). Aquaculture 26: 173–181.

Saeki, A. 1958. Studies on fish culture in filtered closed-circulation aquaria. I. Fundamental theory and system design standards. Bull. Jap. Soc. Sci. Fish. 23: 684–695. [Japanese with English summary and legends]

Saeki, A. 1962. The composition and some chemical control of the sea water of the closed circulating aquarium. Bull. Mar. Biol. Sta. Asamushi, Tôhoku Univ. 11: 99–104.

Saroglia, M. G., G. Scarano, and E. Tibaldi. 1981. Acute toxicity of nitrite to sea bass (*Dicentrarchus labrax*) and European eel (*Anguilla anguilla*). J. World Maricult. Soc. 12: 122–126.

Schnitzer, M. and S. U. Khan. 1972. Humic substances in the environment. Marcel Dekker, New York, 327 pp.

Schramm, W., E. Gualberto, and C. Orosco. 1984. Release of dissolved organic matter from marine tropical reef plants: temperature and desiccation effects. Bot. Mar. 27: 71–77.

Schreckenbach, K. von, R. Spangenberg, and S. Krug. 1975. Die Ursache der Kiemennekrose. Z. Binnenfisch. DDR 22: 257–288.

Schuliger, W. G. 1978. Purification of industrial liquids with granular activated carbon: techniques for obtaining and interpreting data and selecting the type of commercial system. *In* Carbon adsorption handbook, P. N. Cheremisinoff and F. Ellerbusch (eds.). Ann Arbor Science, Ann Arbor, pp. 55–83.

Schwedler, T. E. and C. S. Tucker. 1983. Empirical relationship between percent methemoglobin in channel catfish and dissolved nitrite and chloride in ponds. Trans. Am. Fish. Soc. 112: 117–119.

Servais, P., G. Billen, C. Ventresque, and G. P. Bablon. 1991. Microbial activity in GAC filters at the Choisy-le-Roi treatment plant. J. Am. Water Works Assoc. 83: 62–68.

Shaffi, S. A. 1980. Ammonia toxicity: metabolic disorder in nine freshwater teleosts. Toxicol. Lett. 6: 349–356.

Sharma, B. and R. C. Ahlert. 1977. Nitrification and nitrogen removal. Water Res. 11: 897–925.

Shelbourne, J. E. 1964. Sea-water systems for rearing fish larvae. *In* Sea-water systems for experimental aquariums: a collection of papers, J. R. Clark and R. L. Clark (eds.). Res. Rpt. 63, U.S. Fish and Wildlife Service, Washington, pp. 81–93.

Shibata, N. 1976. Improvements in the determination of trace levels of ammonia with an ammonia electrode. Anal. Chim. Acta 83: 371–373.

Shinagawa, T. and S. Tsunogai. 1978. Determination of small amounts of ammonia in natural water and air. Bull. Fac. Fish., Hokkaido Univ. 29: 173–181. [Japanese with English summary and legends]

Sholkovitz, E. R. 1976. Flocculation of dissolved organic and inorganic matter during the mixing of river water and sea water. Geochim. Cosmochim. Acta 40: 831–845.

Siddall, S. E. 1974. Studies of closed marine culture systems. Prog. Fish-cult. 36: 8–15.

Sieburth, J. McN. 1969. Studies on algal substances in the sea. III. The production of extracellular organic matter by littoral algae. J. Exp. Mar. Biol. Ecol. 3: 290–309.

Sieburth, J. McN. and A. Jensen. 1968. Studies on algal substances in the sea. I. Gelbstoff (humic material) in terrestrial and marine waters. J. Exp. Mar. Biol. Ecol. 2: 174–189.

Sieburth, J. McN. and A. Jensen. 1969. Studies on algal substances in the sea. II. The formation of Gelbstoff (humic material) by exudates of Phaeophyta. J. Exp. Mar. Biol. Ecol. 3: 275–289.

Sieburth, J. McN. and A. Jensen. 1970. Production and transformation of extracellular organic matter from littoral marine algae: a résumé. *In* Symposium on organic matter in natural waters, D. W. Hood (ed.). Occas. Pub. No. 1, Institute of Marine Science, University of Alaska, College, pp. 203–223.

Siegal, R. S. 1980. Determination of nitrate and exchangeable ammonium in soil extracts by an ammonia electrode. Soil Sci. Soc. Am. J. 44: 943–947.

Sigel, M. M., G. Ortiz-Muniz, and R. B. Shouger. 1972. Toxic effect of ammonia dissolved in seawater. Comp. Biochem. Physiol. 42A: 261–262.

Simeonov, V. D., G. A. Andreyev, and A. S. Stoyanov. 1979. Successive determination of pH and ammonia nitrogen in seawater. C. R. Acad. Bulgare Sci. 32: 329–332.

Skjemstad, J. O. and R. Reeve. 1978. The automatic determination of ppb levels of ammonia, nitrate plus nitrite, and phosphate in water in the presence of added mercury(II) chloride. J. Environ. Qual. 7: 137–141.

Smart, G. 1976. The effect of ammonia exposure on gill structure of the rainbow trout (*Salmo gairdneri*). J. Fish Biol. 8: 471–475.

Smart, G. R. 1978. Investigations of the toxic mechanisms of ammonia to fish-gas exchange in rainbow trout (*Salmo gairdneri*) exposed to acutely lethal concentrations. J. Fish Biol. 12: 93–104.

Smith, A. J. and D. S. Hoare. 1968. Acetate assimilation by *Nitrobacter agilis* in relation to its obligate autotrophy. J. Bacteriol. 95: 844–855.

Smith, C. E. and R. G. Piper. 1975. Lesions associated with chronic exposure to ammonia. *In* The pathology of fishes, E. W. Ribelin and G. Migaki (eds.). University of Wisconsin Press, Madison, pp. 497–514.

Smith, W. W. and C. E. ZoBell. 1937. Direct microscopic evidence of an autochthonous bacterial flora in Great Salt Lake. Ecology 18: 453–458.

Snoeyink, V. L. and W. J. Weber Jr. 1967. The surface chemistry of active carbon. A discussion of structure and surface functional groups. Environ. Sci. Technol. 1: 228–234.

Solórzano, L. 1969. Determination of ammonia in natural waters by the phenolhypochlorite method. Limnol. Oceanogr. 14: 799–801.

Sousa, R. J. and T. L. Meade. 1977. The influence of ammonia on the oxygen delivery system of coho salmon hemoglobin. Comp. Biochem. Physiol. 58A: 23–28.

Spotte, S. 1979a. Fish and invertebrate culture: water management in closed systems, 2nd ed. Wiley, New York, 179 pp.

Spotte, S. 1979b. Seawater aquariums: the captive environment. Wiley, New York, 413 pp.

Spotte, S. and G. Adams. 1983. Estimation of the allowable upper limit of ammonia in saline waters. Mar. Ecol. Prog. Ser. 10: 207–210.

Spotte, S. and G. Adams. 1984. The type of activated carbon determines how much dissolved organic carbon is removed from artificial seawater. Aquacult. Eng'g. 3: 207–220.

Spotte, S. and G. Anderson. 1989. Plasma cortisol changes in seawater-adapted mummichogs (*Fundulus heteroclitus*) exposed to ammonia. Can. J. Fish. Aquat. Sci. 46: 2065–2069.

Srna, R. F. and A. Baggaley. 1975. Kinetic response and perturbed marine nitrification systems. J. Water Pollut. Contr. Fed. 47: 472–486.

Srna, R. F., C. Epifanio, M. Hartman, G. Pruder, and A. Stubbs. 1973. The use of ion specific electrodes for chemical monitoring of marine systems. I. The ammonia electrode as a sensitive water quality indicator probe for recirculating mariculture systems. DEL-SG-73, College of Marine Studies, University of Delaware, Newark, 20 pp.

St. Amant, P. P. and P. L. McCarty. 1969. Treatment of high nitrate waters. J. Am. Water Works Assoc. 61: 659–662.

Stark, W. H., J. Stadler, and E. McCoy. 1938. Some factors affecting the bacterial population of fresh water lakes. J. Bacteriol. 36: 653–654.

Steelink, C. 1977. Humates and other organic substances in the aquatic environment. J. Chem. Educ. 54: 599–603.

Steinmüller, W. and B. Bock. 1977. Enzymatic studies on autotrophically, mixotrophically and heterotrophically grown *Nitrobacter agilis* with special reference to nitrite oxidase. Arch. Microbiol. 115: 51–54.

Stenstrom, M. K. and R. A. Poduska. 1980. The effect of dissolved oxygen concentration on nitrification. Water Res. 14: 643–649.

Stewart, V. 1988. Nitrate respiration in relation to facultative metabolism in Enterobacteria. Microbiol. Rev. 52: 190–232.

Strickland, J. D. H. and T. R. Parsons. 1965. A manual of sea water analysis, 2nd ed. Bull. 125, Fisheries Research Board of Canada, Ottawa, 203 pp.

Strickland, J. D. H. and T. R. Parsons. 1972. A practical handbook of seawater analysis, 2nd ed. Bull. 167, Fisheries Research Board of Canada, Ottawa, 310 pp.

Stumm, W. and J. J. Morgan. 1981. Aquatic chemistry: an introduction emphasizing chemical equilibria in natural waters, 2nd ed. Wiley, New York, 780 pp.

Sugahara, I. and K. Hayashi. 1974. Microbiological studies on the artificial seedling production of ayu fish, *Plecoglossus altivelis* (Temminck et Schlegel)—I Distribution and activity of nitrogen-cycle bacteria in fishponds. Bull. Fac. Fish., Mie Univ. 1: 11–23.

Sugiyama, M. and A. Kawai. 1978. Microbiological studies on the nitrogen cycle in aquatic environments—IV Metabolic rate of ammonium nitrogen in freshwater regions. Bull. Jap. Soc. Sci. Fish. 44: 351–355.

Sutcliffe, W. H., E. R. Baylor, and D. W. Menzel. 1963. Sea surface chemistry and Langmuir circulation. Deep-sea Res. 10: 233–243.

Swift, D. J. 1981. Changes in selected blood component concentrations of rainbow trout, *Salmo gairdneri* Richardson, exposed to hypoxia or sublethal concentrations of phenol or ammonia. J. Fish Biol. 19: 45–61.

Tabata, K. 1962. [Toxicity of ammonia to aquatic animals with reference to the effect of pH and carbon dioxide.] Bull. Tokai Reg. Fish. Res. Lab. (34): 67–74. [Japanese with English summary]

Tate, R. L. 1977. Nitrification in histosols: a potential role for the heterotrophic nitrifier. Appl. Environ. Microbiol. 33: 911–914.

Tchobanoglous, G. (ed.). 1972. Wastewater engineering: collection, treatment, disposal. McGraw-Hill, New York, 782 pp.

Thomas, R. F. and R. L. Booth. 1973. Selective electrode measurements of ammonia in water and wastes. Environ. Sci. Technol. 7: 523–526.

Thurston, R. V. and R. C. Russo. 1983. Acute toxicity of ammonia to rainbow trout. Trans. Am. Fish. Soc. 112: 696–704.

Thurston, R. V., R. C. Russo, and G. R. Phillips. 1983. Acute toxicity of ammonia to fathead minnows. Trans. Am. Fish. Soc. 112: 705–711.

Thurston, R. V., R. C. Russo, and C. E. Smith. 1978. Acute toxicity of ammonia and nitrite to cutthroat trout fry. Trans. Am. Fish. Soc. 107: 361–368.

Thurston, R. V., R. C. Russo, and G. A. Vinogradov. 1981. Ammonia toxicity to fishes. Effect of pH on the toxicity of the un-ionized ammonia species. Environ. Sci. Technol. 15: 837–840.

Tomasso, J. R., B. A. Simco, and K. B. Davis. 1979. Chloride inhibition of nitrite-induced methemoglobinemia in channel catfish (*Ictalurus punctatus*). J. Fish. Res. Board Can. 36: 1141–1144.

Tomasso, J. R., C. A. Goudie, B. A. Simco, and K. B. Davis. 1980a. Effects of environmental pH and calcium on ammonia toxicity in channel catfish. Trans. Am. Fish. Soc. 109: 229–234.

Tomasso, J. R., M. I. Wright, B. A. Simco, and K. B. Davis. 1980b. Inhibition of nitrite-induced toxicity in channel catfish by calcium chloride and sodium chloride. Prog. Fish-cult. 42: 144–146.

Tomasso, J. R., K. B. Davis, and B. A. Simco. 1981. Plasma corticosteroid dynamics in channel catfish

(*Ictalurus punctatus*) exposed to ammonia and nitrite. Can. J. Fish. Aquat. Sci. 38: 1106–1112.

Topinka, J. A. and J. V. Robbins. 1976. Effects of nitrate and ammonium enrichment on growth and nitrogen physiology in *Fucus spiralis*. Limnol. Oceanogr. 21: 659–664.

Trussell, R. P. 1972. The percent un-ionized ammonia in aqueous ammonia solutions at different pH levels and temperatures. J. Fish. Res. Board Can. 1505–1507.

Tupas, L. and I. Koike. 1990. Amino acid and ammonium utilization by heterotrophic marine bacteria grown in enriched seawater. Limnol. Oceanogr. 35: 1145–1155.

U.S. EPA (U. S. Environmental Protection Agency). 1973. Process design manual for carbon adsorption. NTIS PB-227 157, National Technical Information Service, Springfield, 195 pp.

Verdouw, H. 1973. Enzymatic NH_3-N determination: a specific method for the determination of ammonia in water and sediments. Water Res. 7: 1129–1136.

Waite, T. and R. Mitchell. 1972. The effect of nutrient fertilization on the benthic alga *Ulva lactuca*. Bot. Mar. 15: 151–156.

Walker, P. L. Jr. 1962. Carbon—an old but new material. Am. Sci. 50: 259–293.

Wallace, W., S. E. Knowles, and D. J. D. Nicholas. 1970. Intermediary metabolism of carbon compounds by nitrifying bacteria. Arch. Mikrobiol. 70: 26–42.

Watson, S. W. 1965. Characteristics of a marine nitrifying bacterium, *Nitrosocystis oceanus* sp. n. Limnol. Oceanogr. 10(Suppl.): R274-R289.

Watson, S. W. and J. B. Waterbury. 1971. Characteristics of two marine nitrite oxidizing bacteria, *Nitrospina gracilis* nov. gen. nov. sp. and *Nitrococcus mobilis* nov. gen. nov. sp. Arch. Mikrobiol. 77: 203–230.

Watson, S. W., F. W. Valois, and J. B. Waterbury. 1981. The Family Nitrobacteraceae. *In* The prokaryotes: a handbook on habitats, isolation, and identification of bacteria, Vol. 1, M. P. Starr, H. Stolp, H. G. Trüper, A. Balows, and H. G. Schlegel (eds.). Springer-Verlag, Berlin, pp. 1005–1022.

Wedemeyer, G. A. and W. T. Yasutake. 1978. Prevention and treatment of nitrite toxicity in juvenile steelhead trout (*Salmo gairdneri*). J. Fish. Res. Board Can. 35: 822–827.

Whitfield, M. 1974. The hydrolysis of ammonium ions in sea water—a theoretical study. J. Mar. Biol. Assoc. U.K. 54: 565–580.

Whitfield, M. 1978. The hydrolysis of ammonium ions in sea water—experimental confirmation of predicted constants at one atmosphere pressure. J. Mar. Biol. Assoc. U.K. 58: 781–787.

Willason, S. W. and K. S. Johnson. 1986. A rapid, highly sensitive technique for the determination of ammonia in seawater. Mar. Biol. 91: 285–290.

Williams, P. M. and L. I. Gordon. 1970. Carbon-13:carbon-12 ratios in dissolved and particulate organic matter in the sea. Deep-sea Res. 17: 19–27.

Williamson, K. and P. L. McCarty. 1976. A model of substrate utilization by bacterial films. J. Water Pollut. Contr. Fed. 48: 9–24.

Wise, D. J. and J. R. Tomasso. 1989. Acute toxicity of nitrite to red drum *Sciaenops ocellatus*: effect of salinity. J. World Aquacult. Soc. 20: 193–198.

Wolf, K. 1957. Blue-sac disease investigations: microbiology and laboratory induction. Prog. Fish-cult. 19: 14–18.

Woltering, D. M., J. L. Hedtke, and L. J. Weber. 1978. Predator-prey interactions of fishes under the influence of ammonia. Trans. Am. Fish. Soc. 107: 500–504.

Wuhrmann, K. and K. Mechsner. 1965. Über den influss von Sauerstoffspannung und Wasserstoffionen Konzentration des Mileus auf die mikrobielle Denitrification. Pathol. Microbiol. 28: 199–206.

Wuhrmann, K. and H. Woker. 1948. Bieträge zur Toxikologie der Fische. II. Experiementelle Untersuchungen über die Ammoniak- und Blausäurevergiftung. Schweiz. Z. Hydrol. 11: 210–244. [English summary]

Wuhrmann, K. and H. Woker. 1953. Beiträge zur Toxikologie der Fische. VIII. Über die Giftwirkungen von Ammoniak- und Zyanidlösungen mit verschiedener Sauerstoffspannung und Temperatur auf Fische. Schweiz. Z. Hydrol. 15: 235–260.

Yang, H. C. and S. K. Chun. 1986. Histopathological study of acute toxicity of ammonia on common carp, *Cyprinus carpio*. Bull. Korean Fish. Soc. 19: 249–256 [Korean with English summary and legends]

Yang, W. T., R. T. Hanlon, P. G. Lee, and P. E. Turk. 1989. Design and function of closed seawater systems for culturing squids. Aquacult. Eng'g. 8: 47–65.

Ying, W-C. and W. J. Weber Jr. 1979. Bio-physiochemical adsorption model systems for wastewater treatment. J. Water Pollut. Contr. Fed. 51: 2661–2667.

Yoshida, Y. 1967. Studies on the marine nitrifying bacteria, with special reference to characteristics and nitrite formation of marine nitrite formers. Bull. Misaki Mar. Biol. Inst., Kyoto Univ. (11): 1–58.

Yoshida, Y., A. Kawai, and M. Kimata. 1967. Studies on marine nitrifying bacteria (nitrite formers and nitrate formers)—V. Effects of environmental factors on the nitrite formation of cell free extracts of a marine nitrifying bacterium. Bull. Jap. Soc. Sci. Fish. 33: 421–425. [Japanese with English summary and legends]

Yoshida, Y. and M. Kimata. 1967. Studies on marine nitrifying bacteria (nitrite formers and nitrate formers)—VII. Distribution of marine nitrifying bacteria and the role played by them in the offshore region. Bull. Jap. Soc. Sci. Fish. 33: 578–585. [Japanese with English summary and legends]

Zadorojny, C., S. Saxton, and R. Finger. 1973. Spectrophotometric determination of ammonia. J. Water Pollut. Contr. Fed. 45: 905–912.

Zafiriou, O. C. and M. B. True. 1977. The determination of nitrite in sea waters—a revision concerning standardization. Anal. Chim. Acta 92: 223–225.

Zavodnik, N. 1981. Studies on phenolic content of some brown algae from Adriatic Sea. *In* Proceedings of the Xth international seaweed symposium, T. Levring (ed.). Walter de Gruyter, Berlin, pp. 543–548.

ZoBell, C. E. 1970. Substratum as an environmental factor for aquatic bacteria, fungi and blue-green algae. *In* Marine ecology: a comprehensive treatise on life in oceans and coastal waters, Vol. 1, Part 3, O. Kinne (ed.). Wiley, London, pp. 1251–1270.

ZoBell, C. E. and D. Q. Anderson. 1936. Observations on the multiplication of bacteria in different volumes of stored seawater. Biol. Bull. 71: 324–342.

Chapter 3

Adin, A., E. R. Baumann, and J. L. Cleasby. 1971. The application of filtration theory to pilot-plant design. J. Am. Water Works Assoc. 71: 17–27.

APHA et al. (American Public Health Association, American Water Works Association, and Water Pollution Control Federation). 1985. Standard methods for the examination of water and wastewater, 16th ed. American Public Health Association, Washington, 1268 pp.

Amirtharajah, A. 1988. Some theoretical and conceptual views of filtration. J. Am. Water Works Assoc. 80: 36–46.

Austin, R. W. 1974. Instrumentation used in turbidity measurement. *In* Proceedings NOIC turbidity workshop, R. Austin, J. A. Llewellyn, R. van Haagan, J. Shannon, and B. Pijanowski (eds.). National Oceanographic Instrumentation Center, Washington, pp. 45–74.

Austin, R., J. A. Llewellyn, R. van Haagan, J. Shannon, and B. Pijanowski. 1974. Workshop conclusions and recommendations. *In* Proceedings NOIC turbidity workshop, R. Austin, J. A. Llewellyn, R. van Haagan, J. Shannon, and B. Pijanowski (eds.). National Oceanographic Instrumentation Center, Washington, pp. 3–5.

Benson, B. B. and D. Krause. 1984. The concentration and isotopic fractionation of oxygen dissolved in freshwater and seawater in equilibrium with the atmosphere. Limnol. Oceanogr. 29: 620–632.

Bouck, G. R., R. E. King, and G. Bouck-Schmidt. 1984. Comparative removal of gas supersaturation by plunges, screens and packed columns. Aquacult. Eng'g. 3: 159–176.

Boyd, R. H. and M. M. Ghosh. 1974. An investigation of the influences of some physicochemical variables on porous-media filtration. J. Am. Water Works Assoc. 66: 94–98.

Bronikowski, E. J. Jr. and D. J. McCormick. 1983. The airlift pump as an energy conservation tool. *In* AAZPA 1983 annual conference proceedings. American Association of Zoological Parks and Aquariums, Wheeling, pp. 250–264.

Camp, T. R. 1964. Theory of water filtration. Am. Soc. Civil Engr. J.—Sanit. Eng'g. Div. 90: 1–30.

Caolo, A. C. and S. Spotte. 1990. Design of a rapid-flow seawater supply system for the University of

Connecticut's marine laboratory at Noank. Ocean Eng'g. 17: 171–178.

Castro, W. E. and P. B. Zielinski. 1980. Pumping characteristics of small airlift pumps. Proc. World Maricult. Soc. 11: 163–174.

Castro, W. E., P. B. Zielinski, and P. A. Sandifer. 1975. Performance characteristics of air lift pumps of short length and small diameter. Proceedings of the 6th annual meeting, World Mariculture Society, J. W. Avault Jr. and R. Miller (eds.). World Mariculture Society, Baton Rouge, pp. 451-461.

Castro, W. E., P. B. Zielinski, and P. A. Sandifer. 1976. Performance characteristics of air lift pumps of short length and small diameter. Manuscript report, 24 pp.

Cleasby, J. L. and E. R. Baumann. 1977. Backwash of granular filters used in wastewater filtration. Rpt. No. EPA-600/2-77-016, U.S. Environmental Protection Agency, Cincinnati, 356 pp.

Colt, J. undated. Dissolved oxygen. Department of Civil Engineering, University of California, Davis, 4 pp.

Colt, J. 1984. Computation of dissolved gas concentrations as functions of temperature, salinity, and pressure. Spec. Pub. No. 14, American Fisheries Society, Bethesda, 154 pp.

Colt, J. 1986. Gas supersaturation—impact on the design and operation of aquatic systems. Aquacult. Eng'g. 5: 49–85.

Colt, J. and G. Bouck. 1984. Design of packed columns for degassing. Aquacult. Eng'g. 3: 251–273.

Colt, J. and H. Westers. 1982. Production of gas supersaturation by aeration. Trans. Am. Fish. Soc. 111: 342–360.

Cornacchia, J. W. and J. E. Colt. 1984. The effects of dissolved gas supersaturation on larval striped bass, *Morone saxatilis* (Walbaum). J. Fish Dis. 7: 15–27.

Craft, T. F. 1966. Review of rapid sand filtration theory. J. Am. Water Works Assoc. 58: 428–439.

Culp, G. L. and R. L. Culp. 1974. New concepts in water purification. Van Nostrand Reinhold, New York, 305 pp.

Culp, R. L. 1977. Direct filtration. J. Am. Water Works Assoc. 69: 375–378.

Culp, R. L., G. M. Wesner, and G. L. Culp. 1978. Handbook of advanced wastewater treatment, 2nd ed. Van Nostrand Reinhold, New York, 632 pp.

Downing, A. L. and G. A. Truesdale. 1955. Some factors affecting the rate of solution of O_2 in water. J. Appl. Chem. 5: 570–581.

Drake, D. E., D. A. Segar, R. L. Charnell, and G. A. Maul. 1974. Comparison of optical measurements and suspended solids concentrations in the ocean. *In* Proceedings NOIC turbidity workshop, R. Austin, J. A. Llewellyn, R. van Haagan, J. Shannon, and B. Pijanowski (eds.). National Oceanographic Instrumentation Center, Washington, pp. 123–142.

Fair, G. M., J. C. Geyer, and D. A. Okun. 1971. Elements of water supply and wastewater disposal, 2nd ed. Wiley, New York, 752 pp.

Fuss, J. T. 1983. Effective flow-through vacuum degasser for fish hatcheries. Aquacult. Eng'g. 2: 301–307.

Gibbs, R. J. 1974. Fundamentals of turbidity measurements in nature. *In* Proceedings NOIC turbidity workshop, R. Austin, J. A. Llewellyn, R. van Haagan, J. Shannon, and B. Pijanowski (eds.). National Oceanographic Instrumentation Center, Washington, pp. 17–22.

Herzig, J. P., D. M. Leclerc, and P. Le Goff. 1970. Flow of suspensions through porous media—application to deep filtration. Indus. Eng'g. Chem. 62(5): 8–35.

Hettler, W. 1971. Open seawater system with controlled temperature and salinity. Prog. Fish-cult. 33: 3–11.

Higbie, R. 1935. The rate of absorption of a pure gas into a still liquid during short periods of exposure. Trans. Am. Inst. Chem. Engr. 31: 365–389.

Jerlov, N. G. 1968. Optical oceanography. Elsevier, Amsterdam, 194 pp.

Jerlov, N. G., H. Postma, and B. Zeitschel. 1972. Suspended solids and turbidity. *In* A guide to marine pollution, E. D. Goldberg (ed.). Gordon and Breach, New York, pp. 111–127.

Kanwisher, J. 1963. On the exchange of gases between the atmosphere and the sea. Deep-sea Res. 10: 195–207.

Kawamura, S. 1975a. Design and operation of high-rate filters—Part 1. J. Am. Water Works Assoc. 67: 535–544.

Kawamura, S. 1975b. Design and operation of high-rate filters—Part 2. J. Am. Water Works Assoc. 67: 653–662.

Kester, D. R. 1975. Dissolved gases other than CO_2. *In* Chemical oceanogrphy, Vol. 1, 2nd ed., J. P. Riley and G. Skirrow (eds.). Academic Press, London, pp. 497–556.

Kils, U. 1976/1977. The salinity effect on aeration in mariculture. Meeresforschung 25: 210–216.

Lackey, E. W. 1956. Some visibility problems in large aquaria, II. A bacteriological study of the sea water used in Marineland. Quart. J. Fla. Acad. Sci. 19: 266–273.

Lasker, R. and L. L. Vlymen. 1969. Experimental sea-water aquarium. Circ. 334, U.S. Fish and Wildlife Service, Washington, 14 pp.

Lemlich, R. 1972. Adsubble processes: foam fractionation and bubble fractionation. J. Geophys. Res. 77: 5204–5210.

Liebermann, L. 1957. Air bubbles in water. J. Appl. Phys. 28: 205–211.

Marking, L. L. 1987. Gas supersaturation in fisheries: causes, concerns, and cures. Fish Wildl. Leaf. 9, U.S. Fish and Wildlife Service, Washington, 10 pp.

Marking, L. L., V. K. Dawson, and J. R. Crowther. 1983. Comparison of column aerators and a vacuum degasser for treating supersaturated culture water. Prog. Fish-cult. 45: 81–83.

McDonald, R. and R. Thomas. 1970. A preliminary evaluation of polyelectrolytes as possible water clarification aids for treatment of turbid fish ponds. Prog. Fish-cult. 32: 174–177.

Murray, K. R., M. G. Poxton, B. T. Linfoot, and D. W. Watret. 1981. The design and performance of low pressure air lift pumps in a closed marine recirculation system. *In* Aquaculture in heated effluents, Vol. 1, K. Tiews (ed.). Satz und Druck: H. Heenemann GmbH, Berlin, pp. 413–428.

Nebel, C., R. D. Gottschling, R. L. Hutchinson, T. J. McBride, D. M. Taylor, J. L. Pavoni, M. E. Tittlebaum, H. E. Spencer, and M. Fleischman. 1973. Ozone disinfection of industrial-municipal secondary effluents. J. Water Pollut. Contr. Fed. 45: 2493–2507.

Ng, K. S. and J. C. Mueller. 1975. Foam separation—a technique for water pollution abatement. Water Sew. Works 122(6): 48–55.

Német, A. G. 1961. Flow of gas-liquid mixtures in vertical tubes. Indus. Eng'g. Chem. 53(2): 151–154.

Olson, W. H., D. L. Chase, and J. N. Hanson. 1973. Preliminary studies using synthetic polymers to reduce turbidity in a hatchery water supply. Prog. Fish-cult. 35: 66–73.

O'Melia, C. R. and W. Stumm. 1967. Theory of water filtration. J. Am. Water Works Assoc. 59: 1393–1412.

Parker, N. C. and M. A. Suttle. 1987. Design of airlift pumps for water circulation and aeration in aquaculture. Aquacult. Eng'g. 6: 97–110.

Peltzer, R. D. and O. M. Griffin. 1987/1988. The stability and decay of foam in sea water. Ocean Phys. Eng'g. 12: 101–126.

Penrose, W. R. and W. R. Squires. 1976. Two devices for removing supersaturating gases in aquarium systems. Trans. Am. Fish. Soc. 105: 116–118.

Qureshi, N. 1981. Comparative performance of dual- and mixed-media filters. J. Am. Water Works Assoc. 73: 490–496.

Reinemann, D. J. and M. B. Timmons. 1989. Prediction of oxygen transfer and total dissolved gas pressure in airlift pumping. Aquacult. Eng'g. 8: 29–46.

Rich, L. G. 1973. Environmental systems engineering. McGraw-Hill, New York, 448 pp.

Rooney, T. C. and G. L. Huibregtse. 1980. Increased oxygen transfer efficiency with coarse bubble diffusers. J. Water Pollut. Contr. Fed. 52: 2315–2326.

Rousseau, I. and J. D. Bu'Lock. 1980. Mixing characteristics of a simple air-lift. Biotechnol. Lett. 2: 475–480.

Sander, E. 1967. Skimmers in the marine aquarium. Petfish Mon. 2: 49–51.

Scholes, P. 1980. The sea-water well system at the fisheries laboratory, Lowestoft and the methods in use for keeping marine fish. J. Mar. Biol. Assoc. U.K. 60: 215–225.

Sebba, F. 1962. Ion flotation. Elsevier, Amsterdam, 154 pp.

Selmeczi, J. G. 1971. Capture mechanisms in deep-bed filtration. Indus. Water Eng'g. 8(6): 25–28.

Spotte, S. 1973. Marine aquarium keeping: the science, animals, and art. Wiley, New York, 171 pp.

Spotte. S. 1979a. Fish and invertebrate culture: water management in closed systems, 2nd. ed. Wiley, New York, 179 pp.

Spotte, S. 1979b. Seawater aquariums: the captive environment. Wiley, New York, 413 pp.

Stewart, M. J. and T. R. Lidkea. 1976. Vertical static tube aerators: evaluating their performance. Water Sew. Works (Ref. No.): R80–R84.

Tate, C. H., J. S. Lang, and H. L. Hutchinson. 1977. Pilot plant tests of direct filtration. J. Am. Water Works Assoc. 69: 379–384.

Tchobanoglous, G. 1970. Filtration techniques in tertiary treatment. J. Water Pollut. Contr. Fed. 42: 604–623.

Tchobanoglous, G. and E. D. Schroeder. 1985. Water quality: characteristics, modeling, modification. Addison-Wesley, Reading, 768 pp.

Tchobanoglous, G. and R. Eliassen. 1970. Filtration of treated sewage effluent. Am. Soc. Civil Engr. Proc.—Sanit. Eng'g. Div. 96: 243–265.

Tobiason, J. E. and C. R. O'Melia. 1988. Physicochemical aspects of particle removal in depth filtration. J. Am. Water Works Assoc. 80: 54–64.

Uhlig, H. H. 1971. Corrosion and corrosion control, 2nd ed. Wiley, New York, 419 pp.

Wace, P. F. and D. L. Banfield. 1966. Foam separation. Rpt. AERE-R5189, United Kingdom Atomic Energy Research Establishment, Harwell, Berkshire, 24 pp.

Wallace, G. T. Jr. and D. F. Wilson. 1969. Foam separation as a tool in chemical oceanography. Rpt. 6958, U.S. Naval Research Laboratory, Washington, 17 pp.

Weiss, R. F. 1970. The solubility of nitrogen, oxygen and argon in water and seawater. Deep-sea Res. 17: 721–735.

Wyman, J. Jr., P. F. Scholander, G. A. Edwards, and L. Irving. 1952. On the stability of gas bubbles in seawater. J. Mar. Res. 11: 47–62.

Yao, K. M., M. T. Habibian, and C. R. O'Melia. 1971. Water and waste water filtration: concepts and applications. Environ. Sci. Technol. 5: 1105–1112.

Chapter 4

Adedire, C. O. and S. O. Oduleye. 1984. Stress-induced water permeability changes in the tropical cichlid, *Oreochromis niloticus* (Trewavas). J. Fish Biol. 25: 463–471.

Ainsworth, A. J., P. R. Bowser, and M. H. Beleau. 1985. Serum cortisol levels in channel catfish, from production ponds. Prog. Fish-cult. 47: 176–181.

Avella, M. and M. Bornancin. 1989. A new analysis of ammonia and sodium transport through the gills of the freshwater rainbow trout (*Salmo gairdneri*). J. Exp. Biol. 142: 155–175.

Axelrod, J. and T. D. Reisine. 1984. Stress hormones: their interaction and regulation. Science 224: 452–459.

Bagarinao, T. and P. Kungvankij. 1986. An incidence of swimbladder stress syndrome in hatchery-reared sea bass (*Lates calcarifer*) larvae. Aquaculture 51: 181–188.

Barton, B. A. and R. E. Peter. 1982. Plasma cortisol stress response in fingerling rainbow trout, *Salmo gairdneri* Richardson, to various transport conditions, anaesthesia, and cold shock. J. Fish Biol. 20: 39–51.

Barton, B. A. and C. B. Schreck. 1987. Metabolic cost of acute physical stress in juvenile steelhead. Trans. Am. Fish. Soc. 116: 257–263.

Barton, B. A., C. B. Schreck, and L. D. Barton. 1987. Effects of chronic cortisol administration and daily acute stress on growth, physiological conditions, and stress responses in juvenile rainbow trout. Dis. Aquat. Organ. 2: 173–185.

Barton, B. A., C. B. Schreck, and L. G. Fowler. 1988. Fasting and diet content affect stress-induced changes in plasma glucose and cortisol in juvenile chinook salmon. Prog. Fish-cult. 50: 16–22.

Barton, B. A., R. E. Peter, and C. R. Paulencu. 1980. Plasma cortisol levels of fingerling rainbow trout (*Salmo gairdneri*) at rest, and subjected to handling, confinement, transport, and stocking. Can. J. Fish. Aquat. Sci. 37: 805–811.

Bennett, A. F. 1978. Activity metabolism of the lower vertebrates. Ann. Rev. Physiol. 40: 447–469.

Bern, H. A. and J. Nandi. 1964. Endocrinology of poikilothermic vertebrates. *In* The hormones: physiology, chemistry, and applications, Vol. 4, G. Pincus, K. V. Thimann, and E. B. Astwood (eds.). Academic Press, New York, pp. 199–298.

Bilinsky, E. 1974. Biochemical aspects of fish swimming. *In* Biochemical and biophysical perspectives in marine biology, Vol. 1, D. C. Malins and

J. R. Sargent (eds.). Academic Press, London, pp. 239–288.

Black, E. C. and A. R. Connor. 1964. Effects of MS 222 on glycogen and lactate levels in rainbow trout (*Salmo gairdneri*). J. Fish. Res. Board Can. 21: 1539–1542.

Boron, W. F. and P. de Weer. 1976. Intracellular pH transient in squid giant axons caused by CO_2, NH_3 and metabolic inhibitors. J. Gen. Physiol. 67: 91–112.

Bouck, G. R. and R. C. Ball. 1966. Influence of capture methods and blood characteristics on mortality in the rainbow trout (*Salmo gairdneri*). Trans. Am. Fish. Soc. 95: 170–176.

Bouck, G. R., M. A. Cairns, and A. R. Christian. 1978. Effect of capture stress on plasma enzyme activities in rainbow trout (*Salmo gairdneri*). J. Fish. Res. Board Can. 35: 1485–1488.

Bourne, P. K. 1984. The use of MS 222 (tricaine methanesulphonate) as an anaesthetic for routine blood sampling in three species of marine teleosts. Aquaculture 36: 313–321.

Bourne, P. K. 1986. Changes in haematological parameters associated with capture and captivity of the marine teleost, *Pleuronectes platessa*. L. Comp. Biochem. Physiol. 85A: 435–443.

Brock, T. D. 1970. Biology of microorganisms. Prentice-Hall, Englewood Cliffs, 737 pp.

Brittain, T. 1987. The root effect. Comp. Biochem. Physiol. 86B: 473–481.

Butler, P. J., E. W. Taylor, M. F. Capra, and W. Davison. 1978. The effect of hypoxia on the levels of circulating catecholamines in the dogfish *Scyliorhinus canicula*. J. Comp. Physiol. 127: 325–330.

Cameron, N. N. 1976. Branchial ion uptake in arctic grayling: resting values and effects of acid-base disturbance. J. Exp. Biol. 64: 711–725.

Cameron, J. N. 1978. Regulation of blood pH in teleost fish. Respir. Physiol. 33: 129–144.

Cameron, J. N. 1979. Excretion of CO_2 in water-breathing animals—a short review. Mar. Biol. Lett. 1: 2–13.

Cameron, J. N. 1986. Responses to reversed NH_3 and NH_4^+ gradients in a teleost (*Ictalurus punctatus*), an elasmobranch (*Raja erinacea*), and a crustacean (*Callinectes sapidus*): evidence for NH_4^+/H^+ exchange in the teleost and the elasmobranch. J. Exp. Zool. 239: 183–195.

Cameron, J. N. and N. Heisler. 1983. Studies of ammonia in the rainbow trout: physico-chemical parameters, acid-base behaviour and respiratory clearance. J. Exp. Biol. 105: 107–125.

Cameron, J. N. and N. Heisler. 1985. Ammonia transfer across fish gills: a review. *In* Circulation, respiration, and metabolism, R. Gilles (ed.). Springer-Verlag, Berlin, pp. 91–100.

Cameron, J. N. and G. A. Kormanik. 1982. The acid-base responses of gills and kidneys to infused acid and base loads in the channel catfish, *Ictalurus punctatus*. J. Exp. Biol. 99: 143–160.

Carmichael, G. J., J. R. Tomasso, B. A. Simco, and K. B. Davis. 1984. Confinement and water quality-induced stress in largemouth bass. Trans. Am. Fish. Soc. 113: 767–777.

Carmichael, G. J., G. A. Wedemeyer, J. P. McCraren, and J. L. Millard. 1983. Physiological effects of handling and hauling stress on smallmouth bass. Prog. Fish-cult. 45: 110–113.

Carrier, J. C. and D. H. Evans. 1976. The role of environmental calcium in freshwater survival of the marine teleost, *Lagodon rhomboides*. J. Exp. Biol. 65: 529–538.

Casillas, E. and L. S. Smith. 1977. Effect of stress on blood coagulation and haematology in rainbow trout (*Salmo gairdneri*). J. Fish Biol. 10: 481–491.

Cech, J. J. Jr., D. M. Rowell, and J. S. Glasgow. 1977. Cardiovascular responses of the winter flounder *Pseudopleuronectes americanus* to hypoxia. Comp. Biochem. Physiol. 57A: 123–125.

Chavin, W. 1973. Teleostean endocrine and para-endocrine alterations of utility in environmental studies. *In* Responses of fish to environmental changes, W. Chavin (ed.). Thomas, Springfield, pp. 199–239.

Chavin, W. and J. E. Young. 1970. Factors in the determination of normal serum glucose levels of goldfish, *Carassius auratus* L. Comp. Biochem. Physiol. 33: 629–653.

Claiborne, J. B. and D. H. Evans. 1988. Ammonia and acid-base balance during high ammonia exposure in a marine teleost (*Myoxocephalus octodecimspinosus*) [*sic*]. J. Exp. Biol. 140: 89–105.

Claiborne, J. B., D. H. Evans, and L. Goldstein. 1982. Fish branchial Na^+/NH_4^+ exchange is via basolateral Na^+-K^+-activated ATPase. J. Exp. Biol. 96: 431–434.

Cliff, G. and G. D. Thurman. 1984. Pathological effects of stress during capture and transport in the juvenile dusky shark, *Carcharhinus obscurus*. Comp. Biochem. Physiol. 78A: 167–173.

Cockrum, E. L. and W. J. McCauley. 1965. Zoology. Saunders, Philadelphia, 705 pp.

Cross, C. E., B. S. Packer, J. M. Linta, H. V. Murdaugh Jr., and E. D. Robin. 1969. H^+ buffering and excretion in response to acute hypercapnia in the dogfish *Squalus acanthias*. Am. J. Physiol. 216: 440–452.

Dafré, A. L. and D. Wilhelm F°. 1989. Root effect hemoglobins in marine fish. Comp. Biochem. Physiol. 92A: 467–471.

Davis, K. B. and N. C. Parker. 1983. Plasma corticosteroid and chloride dynamics in rainbow trout, Atlantic salmon, and lake trout during and after stress. Aquaculture 32: 189–194.

Davis, K. B., N. C. Parker, and M. A. Suttle. 1979. Plasma corticosteroid concentrations and secretion rates in channel catfish (*Ictalurus punctatus*): effect of temperature, time of day and fish density. Am. Zool. 19: 900. [Abstract]

Davis, K. B., N. C. Parker, and M. A. Suttle. 1982. Plasma corticosteroids and chlorides in striped bass exposed to tricaine methanesulfonate, quinaldine, etomidate, and salt. Prog. Fish-cult. 44: 205–207.

Daxboeck, C. P., S. Davie, S. F. Perry, and D. J. Randall. 1982. Oxygen uptake in a spontaneously ventilating, blood-perfused trout preparation. J. Exp. Biol. 101: 35–45.

Dejours, P. 1969. Variation of CO_2 output of a freshwater teleost upon change of the ionic composition of the water. J. Physiol. 202: 113P–114P.

Dejours, P. 1973. Problems of control of breathing in fishes. *In* Comparative physiology, L. Bolis, K. Schmidt-Nielsen, and S. H. P. Maddrell (eds.). North-Holland, Amsterdam, pp. 117–133.

Dejours, P. 1975. Principles of comparative respiratory physiology. North-Holland, Amsterdam, 253 pp.

Dejours, P. 1979. Respiratory controls: oxygenation, CO_2 clearance, or acid-base equilibrium? *In* Claude Bernard and the internal environment, E. D. Robin (ed.). Marcel Dekker, New York, pp. 161–177.

Dejours, P. undated. Problems of O_2 delivery and CO_2 clearance in metazoa. *In* Oxygen and physiological function, F. F. Jobsis (ed.). Professional Information Library, Dallas, pp. 1–13.

Dejours, P., W. F. Garey, and H. Rahn. 1970. Comparison of ventilatory and circulatory flow rates between animals in various physiological conditions. Respir. Physiol. 9: 108–117.

Dejours, P., A. Toulmond, and J. P. Truchot. 1977. The effect of hyperoxia on the breathing of marine fishes. Comp. Biochem. Physiol. 58A: 409–411.

Donaldson, E. M. 1981. The pituitary-interrenal axis as an indicator of stress in fish. *In* Stress and fish, A. D. Pickering (ed.). Academic Press, London, pp. 11–47.

Donaldson, E. M. and H. M. Dye. 1975. Corticosteroid concentrations in sockeye salmon (*Oncorhynchus nerka*) exposed to low concentrations of copper. J. Fish. Res. Board Can. 32: 533–539.

Eddy, F. B. 1974. Blood gases of the tench (*Tinca tinca*) in well aerated and oxygen-deficient waters. J. Exp. Biol. 60: 71–83.

Ellsaesser, C. F. and L. W. Clem. 1987. Cortisol-induced hematologic and immunologic changes in channel catfish (*Ictalurus punctatus*). Comp. Biochem. Physiol. 87A: 405–408.

Emerson, K., R. C. Russo, R. E. Lund, and R. V. Thurston. 1975. Aqueous ammonia equilibrium calculations: effect of pH and temperature. J. Fish. Res. Board Can. 32: 2379–2383.

Epstein, F. H., J. S. Stoff, and P. Silva. 1983. Mechanisms and control of hyperosmotic NaCl-rich secretion by the rectal gland of *Squalus acanthias*. J. Exp. Biol. 106: 24–41.

Evans, D. H. 1973. Sodium uptake by the sailfin molly, *Poecilia latipinna*: kinetic analysis of a carrier system present in both fresh-water-acclimated and sea-water-acclimated individuals. Comp. Biochem. Physiol. 45A: 843–850.

Evans, D. H. 1975a. The effects of various external cations and sodium transport inhibitors on sodium uptake by the sailfin molly, *Poecilia latipinna*, acclimated to seawater. J. Comp. Physiol. 96: 111–115.

Evans, D. H. 1975b. Ionic exchange mechanisms in fish gills. Comp. Biochem. Physiol. 51A: 491–495.

Evans, D. H. 1977. Further evidence for Na/NH_4 exchange in marine teleost fish. J. Exp. Biol. 70: 213–220.

Evans, D. H. 1979. Fish. *In* Osmotic and ionic regulation in animals, Vol. 1, G. M. O. Maloiy (ed.). Academic Press, London, pp. 305–390.

Evans, D. H. 1980a. Kinetic studies of ion transport by fish gill epithelium. Am. J. Physiol. 238: R224-R230.

Evans, D. H. 1980b. Osmotic and ionic regulation by freshwater and marine fishes. *In* Environmental physiology of fishes, M. A. Ali (ed.). Plenum, New York, pp. 93–122.

Evans, D. H. 1982. Salt and water exchange across vertebrate gills. *In* Gills, D. F. Houlihan, J. C. Rankin, and T. J. Shuttleworth (eds.). Cambridge University Press, New York, pp. 149–171.

Evans, D. H. and J. N. Cameron. 1986. Gill ammonia transport. J. Exp. Zool. 239: 17–23.

Evans, D. H., J. C. Carrier, and M. B. Bogan. 1974. The effect of external potassium ions on the electrical potential measured across the gills of the teleost, *Dormitator maculatus*. J. Exp. Biol. 61: 277–283.

Evans, D. H., J. B. Clairborne, L. Farmer, C. Mallery, and E. J. Krasny Jr. 1982. Fish gill ionic transport: methods and models. Biol. Bull. 163: 108–130.

Evans, D. H., G. A. Kormanik, and E. J. Krasny Jr. 1979. Mechanisms of ammonia and acid extrusion by the little skate, *Raja erinacea*. J. Exp. Zool. 208: 431–437.

Evans, D. H., C. H. Mallery, and L. Kravitz. 1973. Sodium extrusion by a fish acclimated to sea water: physiological and biochemical description of a Na-for-K exchange system. J. Exp. Biol. 58: 627–636.

Ferreira, J. T., G. L. Smit, and H. J. Schoonbee. 1981. Haematological evaluation of the anaesthetic benzocaine hydrochloride in the freshwater fish *Cyprinus carpio* L. J. Fish Biol. 18: 291–297.

Fletcher, G. L. 1975. The effects of capture, ''stress,'' and storage of whole blood on the red blood cells, plasma proteins, glucose, and electrolytes of the winter flounder (*Pseudopleuronectes americanus*). Can. J. Zool. 53: 197–206.

Fredericq, L. 1901. Sur la concentration moléculaire du sang et 'des tissus chez les animaux aquatiques. Bull. Acad. R. Belg. Cl. Sci. 38: 428–454.

Fryer, J. N. 1975. Stress and adrenocorticosteroid dynamics in the goldfish, *Carassius auratus*. Can. J. Zool. 53: 1012–1020.

Fuller, J. D., D. B. C. Scott, and R. Fraser. 1974. Effects of catching techniques, captivity and reproductive cycle on plasma cortisol concentration in the powan (*Coregonus lavaretus*), a freshwater teleost from Loch Lomond. J. Endocrinol. 63: 24*P*. [Abstract]

Giesy, J. P. 1988. Phosphoadenylate concentrations and adenylate energy charge of largemouth bass (*Micropterus salmoides*): relationship with condition factor and blood cortisol. Comp. Biochem. Physiol. 90A: 367–377.

Glass, M. L., N. A. Andersen, M. Kruhøffer, E. M. Williams, and N. Heisler. 1990. Combined effects of environmental P_{O_2} and temperature on ventilation and blood gases in the carp *Cyprinus carpio* L. J. Exp. Biol. 148: 1–17.

Goldstein, L. 1982. Gill nitrogen excretion. *In* Gills, D. F. Houlihan, J. C. Rankin, and T. J. Shuttleworth (eds.). Cambridge University Press, New York, pp. 193–206.

Goldstein, J., J. B. Clairborne, and D. H. Evans. 1982. Ammonia excretion by the gills of two marine teleost fish: the importance of NH_4^+ permeance. J. Exp. Zool. 219: 395–397.

Gosline, W. A. 1971. Functional morphology and classification of teleostean fishes. University Press of Hawaii, Honolulu, 208 pp.

Greaney, G. S. and D. A. Powers. 1978. Allosteric modifiers of fish hemoglobins: in vitro and in vivo studies of the effect of ambient oxygen and pH on erythrocyte ATP concentrations. J. Exp. Zool. 203: 339–350.

Hall, F. G. and F. H. McCutcheon. 1938. The affinity of hemoglobin for oxygen in marine fishes. J. Cell. Comp. Physiol. 11: 205–212.

Hattingh, J. 1976. Blood sugar as an indicator of stress in the freshwater fish *Labeo capensis* (Smith). J. Fish Biol. 10: 191–195.

Hattingh, J. 1988. The semantics of ''animal stress.'' S. Afr. J. Sci. 84: 731–732.

Hattingh, J. and A. J. J. van Pletzen. 1974. The influence of capture and transportation on some blood parameters of fresh water fish. Comp. Biochem. Physiol. 49A: 607–609.

Haux, C. and M-L. Sjöbeck. 1985. Physiological stress responses in a wild fish population of perch (*Perca fluviatilis*) after capture and during subsequent recovery. Mar. Environ. Res. 15: 77–95.

Heisler, N. 1978. Bicarbonate exchange between body compartments after changes in temperature in the larger spotted dogfish (*Scyliorhinus stellaris*). Respir. Physiol. 33: 145–160.

Heisler, N. 1980. Regulation of the acid-base status in fishes. *In* Environmental physiology of fishes, M. A. Ali (ed.). Plenum, New York, pp. 123–162.

Heisler, N. 1982. Transepithelial ion transfer processes for fish acid-base regulation in hypercapnia and lactacidosis. Can. J. Zool. 60: 1108–1122.

Heisler, N. 1989. Interactions between gas exchange, metabolism, and ion transport in animals: an overview. Can. J. Zool. 67: 2923–2935.

Heisler, N. and P. Neumann. 1977. Influence of seawater pH upon bicarbonate uptake induced by hypercapnia in an elasmobranch fish (*Scyliorhinus stellaris*). Pflüger Arch. 368(Suppl. R): 19. [Abstract]

Heisler, N., H. Weitz, and A. M. Weitz. 1976. Hypercapnia and resultant bicarbonate transfer processes in an elasmobranch fish (*Scyliorhinus stellaris*). Bull. Europ. Physiopathol. Respir. 12: 77–86.

Hillaby, B. A. and D. J. Randall. 1979. Acute ammonia toxicity and ammonia excretion in rainbow trout (*Salmo gairdneri*). J. Fish. Res. Board Can. 36: 621–629.

Hoar, W. S. 1975. General and comparative physiology, 2nd ed. Prentice-Hall, Englewood Cliffs, 848 pp.

Holeton, G. F. 1980. Oxygen as an environmental factor of fishes. *In* Environmental physiology of fishes, M. I. Ali (ed.). Plenum, New York, pp. 7–32.

Holeton, G. F. and M. Heisler. 1983. Contribution of net ion transfer mechanisms to acid-base regulation after exhausting activity in the larger spotted dogfish (*Scyliorhinus stellaris*). J. Exp. Biol. 103: 31–46.

Holeton, G. and D. J. Randall. 1967. Changes in blood pressure in the rainbow trout during hypoxia. J. Exp. Biol. 46: 297–305.

Houston, A. H. 1971. Some comments upon acid-base balance in teleost fishes and its relationship to environmental temperature. Comp. Biochem. Physiol. 40A: 535–542.

Houston, A. H., J. A. Madden, R. J. Woods, and H. M. Miles. 1971a. Some physiological effects of handling and tricaine methanesulphonate anesthetization upon the brook trout, *Salvelinus fontinalis*. J. Fish. Res. Board Can. 28: 625–633.

Houston, A. H., J. A. Madden, R. J. Woods, and H. M. Miles. 1971b. Variations in the blood and tissue chemistry of brook trout, *Salvelinus fontinalis*, subsequent to handling, anaesthesia, and surgery. J. Fish. Res. Board Can. 28: 635–642.

Howell, B. J. 1970. Acid-base balance in transition from water breathing to air breathing. Fed. Proc. 29: 1130–1134.

Howell, B. J., F. W. Baumgardner, K. Bondi, and H. Rahn. 1970. Acid-base balance in poikilotherms as a function of body temperature. Am. J. Physiol. 218: 600–606.

Hughes, G. M. 1961. How a fish extracts oxygen from water. New Sci. 11: 346–348.

Hughes, G. M. 1980. Functional morphology of fish gills. *In* Epithelial transport in the lower vertebrates, B. Lahlou (ed.). Cambridge University Press, Cambridge, pp. 15–36.

Hughes, G. M. and M. Morgan. 1973. The structure of fish gills in relation to their respiratory function. Biol. Rev. 48: 419–475.

Hughes, G. M. and G. Shelton. 1962. Respiratory mechanisms and their nervous control in fish. Adv. Comp. Physiol. Biochem. 1: 275–364.

Isaia, J., J. P. Girard, and P. Payan. 1978. Kinetic study of gill epithelial permeability to water diffusion in fresh water trout, *Salmo gairdneri*: effect of adrenaline. J. Membrane Biol. 41: 337–347.

Ishioka, H. 1984a. Stress responses to transportation in the red sea bream, *Pagrus major* (Temminck *et* Schlegel). Bull. Nansei Reg. Fish. Res. Lab. (16): 63–71. [Japanese with English summary and legends]

Ishioka, H. 1984b. Physiological and biochemical studies on the stress responses of the red sea bream, *Pagrus major* (Temminck et Schlegel). Bull. Nansei Reg. Fish. Res. Lab. (17): 1–133. [Japanese with English summary and legends]

Janssen, R. G. and D. J. Randall. 1975. The effects of changes in pH and P_{CO_2} in blood and water on breathing in rainbow trout, *Salmo gairdneri*. Respir. Physiol. 25: 235–245.

Jensen, F. B. 1987. Influences of exercise-stress and adrenaline upon intra- and extracellular acid-base status, electrolyte composition and respiratory properties of blood in tench (*Tinca tinca*) at different seasons. J. Comp. Physiol. 157B: 51–60.

Jensen, F. B., M. Nikinmaa, and R. E. Weber. 1983. Effects of exercise stress on acid-base balance and respiratory function in blood of the teleost *Tinca tinca*. Respir. Physiol. 51: 291–301.

Jones, D. R. and D. J. Randall. 1978. The respiratory and circulatory systems during exercise. *In* Fish physiology, 2nd ed., Vol. 7, W. S. Hoar and D. J. Randall (eds.). Academic Press, New York, pp. 425–501.

Kerstetter, T. H. and M. Keeler. 1976. On the interaction of NH_4^+ and Na^+ fluxes in the isolated trout gill. J. Exp. Biol. 64: 517–527.

Kerstetter, T. H., L. B. Kirschner, and D. D. Rafuse. 1970. On the mechanisms of sodium ion transport by the irrigated gills of rainbow trout (*Salmo gairdneri*). J. Gen. Physiol. 56: 342–359.

Kikeri, D., A. Sun, M. L. Seidel, and S. C. Hebert. 1989. Cell membranes impermeable to NH_3. Nature 339: 478–480.

Kinne, R., D. Friedman, J. Hannafin, and E. Kinne-Saffran. 1982. Further evidence for the presence of a sodium-chloride cotransport system in the rectal gland of *Squalus acanthias*. Bull. Mt. Desert Island Biol. Lab. 22: 67–69.

Kirk, W. L. 1974. The effects of hypoxia on certain blood and tissue electrolytes of channel catfish, *Ictalurus punctatus* (Rafinesque). Trans. Am. Fish. Soc. 103: 593–600.

Kirschner, L. B. 1970. The study of NaCl transport in aquatic animals. Am. Zool. 10: 365–376.

Kirschner, L. B. 1973. Electrolyte transport across the body surface of fresh water fish and Amphibia. *In* Transport mechanisms in epithelia, H. H. Ussing and N. A. Thorne (eds.). Munksgaard, Copenhagen, pp. 447–463.

Kirschner, L. B., L. Greenwald, and M. Sanders. 1974. On the mechanism of sodium extrusion across the irrigated gill of sea water-adapted rainbow trout (*Salmo gairdneri*). J. Gen. Physiol. 64: 148–165.

Krogh, A. 1937. Osmotic regulation in fresh water fishes by active absorption of chloride ions. Z. Vergl. Physiol. 24: 656–666.

Krogh, A. 1939. Osmotic regulation in aquatic animals. Cambridge University Press, Cambridge, 242 pp. [Dover reprint, 1965]

Leach, G. J. and M. H. Taylor. 1980. The role of stress-induced metabolic changes in *Fundulus heteroclitus*. Gen. Comp. Endocrinol. 42: 219–227.

Leloup-Hatey, J. 1985. Environmental effects on the fish interrenal gland. *In* The endocrine system and the environment, B. K. Follett, S. Ishii, and A. Chandola (eds.). Japan Scientific Society Press, Tokyo, pp. 13–21.

Limsuwan, C., T. Limsuwan, J. M. Grizzle, and J. A. Plumb. 1983. Stress response and blood characteristics of channel catfish (*Ictalurus punctatus*) after anesthesia with etomidate. Can. J. Fish. Aquat. Sci. 40: 2105–2112.

Maetz, J. 1969. Sea water teleosts: evidence for a sodium-potassium exchange in the branchial sodium-excreting pump. Science 166: 613–615.

Maetz, J. 1971. Fish gills: mechanisms of salt transfer in fresh water and sea water. Phil. Trans. R. Soc. London 262B: 209–249.

Maetz, J. 1972. Interaction of salt and ammonia transport in aquatic organisms. *In* Nitrogen metabolism and the environment, J. W. Campbell and L. Goldstein (eds.). Academic Press, New York, pp. 105–154.

Maetz, J. 1973. Na^+/NH_4^+ exchanges and NH_3 movement across the gills of *Carassius auratus*. J. Exp. Biol. 58: 255–275.

Maetz, J. 1974. Aspects of adaptation to hypo-osmotic environments. *In* Biochemical and biophysical perspectives in marine biology, Vol. 1, D. C. Malins and J. R. Sargent (eds.). Academic Press, London, pp. 1–166.

Maetz, J. 1976. Transport of ions and water across the epithelium of fish gills. *In* Lung liquids, P. Porter and M. O'Connor (eds.). Elsevier, Amsterdam, pp. 133–159.

Maetz, J. and F. García Romeu. 1964. The mechanism of sodium and chloride uptake by the gills of a fresh-water fish, *Carassius auratus*. II. Evidence of NH_4^+/Na^+ and HCO_3^-/Cl^- exchanges. J. Gen. Physiol. 47: 1209–1227.

Maetz, J., P. Payan, and G. de Renzis. 1976. Controversial aspects of ionic uptake in freshwater animals. *In* Perspectives in experimental biology, Vol. 1, P. S. Davies (ed.). Pergamon, Oxford, pp. 77–92.

Martem'yanov, V. I. 1986. Sensitivity of fish to natural and laboratory conditions. J. [Prob.] Ichthyol. 26: 162–164.

Martini, F. H. 1978. The effects of fasting confinement on *Squalus acanthias*. *In* Sensory biology of sharks, skates and rays, E. S. Hodgson and R. F. Mathewson (eds.). Office of Naval Research, Arlington, pp. 609–646.

Mazeaud, M. 1964. Influence de divers facteurs sur l'adrénalinémie et de la noradrénalinémie de la carpe. C. R. Séanc. Soc. Biol. 158: 2018–2021.

Mazeaud, M. M., F. Mazeaud, and E. M. Donaldson. 1977. Primary and secondary effects of stress in fish: some new data with a general review. Trans. Am. Fish. Soc. 106: 201–212.

McCauley, W. J. 1971. Vertebrate physiology. Saunders, Philadelphia, 422 pp.

McDonald, D. G. and E. T. Prior. 1988. Branchial mechanisms of ion and acid-base regulation in the freshwater rainbow trout, *Salmo gairdneri*. Can. J. Zool. 66: 2699–2708.

McDonald, D. G. and M. S. Rogano. 1986. Ion regulation by the rainbow trout, *Salmo gairdneri*, in ion-poor water. Physiol. Zool. 59: 318–331.

McDonald, D. G., Y. Tang, and R. G. Boutilier. 1989. Acid and ion transfer across the gills of fish: mechanisms and regulation. Can. J. Zool. 67: 3046–3054.

Milne, M. D., B. H. Schribner, and M. A. Crawford. 1958. Non-ionic diffusion and excretion of weak acids and bases. Am. J. Med. 24: 709–729.

Moberg, G. P. 1987. Problems in defining stress and distress in animals. J. Am. Vet. Med. Assoc. 191: 1207–1211.

Motais, R. and J. Isaia. 1972. Evidence for an effect of ouabain on the branchial sodium-excreting pump of marine teleosts: interaction between the inhibitor and external Na and K. J. Exp. Biol. 57: 367–373.

Nakano, T. and N. Tomlinson. 1967. Catecholamine and carbohydrate concentrations in rainbow trout (*Salmo gairdneri*) in relation to physical disturbance. J. Fish. Res. Board Can. 24: 1701–1715.

Nikinmaa, M. and A. Soivio. 1982. Blood oxygen transport of hypoxic *Salmo gairdneri*. J. Exp. Zool. 219: 173–178.

Nishimura, H., W. H. Sawyer, and R. F. Nigrelli. 1976. Renin, cortisol and plasma volume in marine teleost fishes adapted to dilute media. J. Endocrinol. 70: 47–59.

Pang, P. K. T., R. W. Griffith, and J. W. Atz. 1977. Osmoregulation in elasmobranchs. Am. Zool. 17: 365–377.

Payan, P. 1978. A study of the Na^+/NH_4^+ exchange across the gill of the perfused head of the trout (*Salmo gairdneri*). J. Comp. Physiol. 124: 181–188.

Payan, P. and J. Maetz. 1971. Balance hydrique chez les Elasmobranches: Arguments en faveur d'un contrôle endocrinien. Gen. Comp. Endocrinol. 16: 535–554. [English summary]

Payan, P. and J. Maetz. 1973. Branchial sodium transport mechanisms in *Scyliorhinus canicula*: evidence for Na^+/NH_4^+ and Na^+H^+ [*sic*] exchanges and for a role of carbonic anhydrase. J. Exp. Biol. 58: 487–502.

Pelster, B. and R. E. Weber. 1990. Influence of organic phosphates on the Root effect of multiple fish haemoglobins. J. Exp. Biol. 149: 425–437.

Perry, S. F. 1982. The regulation of hypercapnic acidosis in two salmonids, the freshwater trout (*Salmo gairdneri*) and the seawater salmon (*Onchorynchus kisutch*). Mar. Behav. Physiol. 9: 73–79.

Peters, G. 1982. The effect of stress on the stomach of the European eel, *Anguilla anguilla* L. J. Fish Biol. 21: 497–512.

Pettersson, K. and K. Johansen. 1982. Hypoxic vasoconstriction and the effects of adrenaline on gas exchange efficiency in fish gills. J. Exp. Biol. 97: 263–272.

Pic, P., N. Mayer-Gostan, and J. Maetz. 1974. Branchial effects of epinephrine in the seawater-adapted mullet. I. Water permeability. Am. J. Physiol. 226: 698–702.

Pickering, A. D. 1981. Introduction: the concept of biological stress. *In* Stress and fish, A. D. Pickering (ed.). Academic Press, London, pp. 1–9.

Pickering, A. D., T. G. Pottinger, J. Carragher, and J. P. Sumpter. 1987. The effects of acute and chronic stress on the levels of reproductive hormones in the plasma of mature male brown trout, *Salmo trutta* L. Gen. Comp. Endocrinol. 68: 249–259.

Pickering, A. D., T. G. Pottinger, and P. Christie. 1982. Recovery of brown trout, *Salmo trutta* L., from acute handling stress: a time-course study. J. Fish Biol. 20: 229–244.

Pickford, G. E., A. K. Srivastava, A. M. Slicher, and P. K. T. Pang. 1971a. The stress response in the abundance of circulating leucocytes in the killifish, *Fundulus heteroclitus*. I. The cold-shock sequence and the effects of hypophysectomy. J. Exp. Zool. 177: 89–96.

Pickford, G. E., A. K. Srivastava, A. M. Slicher. and P. K. T. Pang. 1971b. The stress response in the abundance of circulating leucocytes in the killifish, *Fundulus heteroclitus*. II. The role of catecholamines. J. Exp. Zool. 177: 97–108.

Pickford, G. E., A. K. Srivastava, A. M. Slicher, and P. K. T. Pang. 1971c. The stress response in the abundance of circulating leucocytes in the killifish, *Fundulus heteroclitus*. III. The role of adrenal cortex and a concluding discussion of the leucocyte-stress syndrome. J. Exp. Zool. 177: 109–118.

Piiper, J., M. Meyer, and F. Drees. 1972. Hydrogen ion balance in the elasmobranch *Scyliorhinus stellaris* after exhausting activity. Respir. Physiol. 16: 290–303.

Piiper, J., M. Meyer, H. Worth, and H. Willmer. 1977. Respiration and circulation during swimming activity in the dogfish *Scyliorhinus stellaris*. Respir. Physiol. 30: 221–239.

Potts, W. T. W. and W. R. Fleming. 1971. The effect of environmental calcium and ovine prolactin on sodium balance in *Fundulus kansae*. J. Exp. Biol. 54: 63–75.

Potts, W. T. W., C. R. Fletcher, and B. Eddy. 1973. An analysis of the sodium and chloride fluxes in the flounder *Platichtys flesus*. J. Comp. Physiol. 82: 21–28.

Prosser, C. L. 1973. Water: osmotic balance; hormonal regulation. *In* Comparative animal physiology, 3rd ed., C. L. Prosser (ed.). Saunders, Philadelphia, pp. 1–78.

Rahn, H. 1966. Evolution of the gas transport system in vertebrates. Proc. R. Soc. Med. 59: 493–494.

Rahn, H. 1967. Gas transport from the external environment to the cell. *In* Development of the lung, A. V. S. DeReuck and R. Porter (eds.). Little, Brown, Boston, pp. 3–29.

Rahn, H. 1974a. Body temperature and acid-base regulation. Pneumonologie 151: 87–94.

Rahn, H. 1974b. PCO_2, pH, and body temperature. *In* Carbon dioxide and metabolic regulation, G. Nahas and K. E. Schaefer (eds.). Springer-Verlag, New York, pp. 152–162.

Rahn, H. and F. W. Baumgardner. 1972. Temperature and acid-base regulation in fish. Respir. Physiol. 14: 171–182.

Randall, D. 1982. The control of respiration and circulation in fish during exercise and hypoxia. J. Exp. Biol. 100: 275–288.

Randall, D. J. 1970. Gas exchange in fish. *In* Fish physiology, Vol. 4, 2nd ed., W. S. Hoar and D. J. Randall (eds.). Academic Press, New York, pp. 253–292.

Randall, D. J. and J. N. Cameron. 1973. Respiratory control of arterial pH as temperature changes in rainbow trout *Salmo gairdneri*. Am. J. Physiol. 225: 997–1002.

Randall, D. J., N. Heisler, and F. Drees. 1976. Ventilatory response to hypercapnia in the larger spotted dogfish *Scyliorhinus stellaris*. Am. J. Physiol. 230: 590–594.

Randall, D. J., S. F. Perry, and T. A. Heming. 1982. Gas transfer and acid/base regulation in salmonids. Comp. Biochem. Physiol. 73B: 93–103.

Randall, D. J. and P. A. Wright. 1987. Ammonia distribution and excretion in fish. Fish Physiol. Biochem. 3(3): 107–120.

Rasquin, P. and L. Rosenbloom. 1954. Endocrine imbalance and tissue hyperplasia in teleosts maintained in total darkness. Bull. Am. Mus. Nat. Hist. 104: 359–426 + 26 plates.

Redgate, E. S. 1974. Neural control of pituitary-adrenal activity in *Cyprinus carpio*. Gen. Comp. Endocrinol. 22: 35–41.

Reeves, R. B. 1969. Role of body temperature in determining the acid-base state in vertebrates. Fed. Proc. 28: 1204–1208.

Reeves, R. B. 1977. The interaction of body temperature and acid-base balance in ectothermic vertebrates. Ann. Rev. Physiol. 39: 559–586.

Riggs, A. 1979. Studies of the hemoglobins of Amazonian fishes: an overview. Comp. Biochem. Physiol. 62A: 257–271.

Ristori, M. T. and P. Laurent. 1977. Action de l'hypoxie sur le système vasculaire branchial de la tête perfusée de truite. C. R. Séanc. Soc. Biol. 171: 809–813.

Robertson, L., P. Thomas, C. R. Arnold, and J. M. Trant. 1987. Plasma cortisol and secondary stress responses of red drum to handling, transport, rearing density, and a disease outbreak. Prog. Fish-cult. 49: 1–12.

Robin, E. D. 1962. Relationship between temperature and pH and carbon dioxide tension in the turtle. Nature 195: 249–251.

Sanders, M. J. and L. B. Kirschner. 1983a. Potassium metabolism in seawater teleosts. I. The use of ^{86}Rb as a tracer for potassium. J. Exp. Biol. 104: 15–28.

Sanders, M. J. and L. B. Kirschner. 1983b. Potassium metabolism in seawater teleosts. II. Evidence for active potassium extrusion across the gill. J. Exp. Biol. 104: 29–40.

Saunders, R. L. 1961. The irrigation of the gills in fishes. I. Studies on the mechanism of branchial irrigation. Can. J. Zool. 39: 637–653.

Schmidt-Nielsen, K. 1975. Animal physiology: adaptation and environment. Cambridge University Press, New York, 699 pp.

Schreck, C. B. 1981. Stress and compensation in teleostean fishes: response to social and physical factors. *In* Stress and fish, A. D. Pickering (ed.). Academic Press, London, pp. 295–321.

Schreck, C. B. and H. W. Lorz. 1978. Stress response of coho salmon (*Oncorhynchus kisutch*) elicited by cadmium and copper and potential use of cortisol as an indictor of stress. J. Fish. Res. Board Can. 35: 1124–1129.

Scott, E. L. 1921. Sugar in the blood of the dog-fish and the sand shark. Am. J. Physiol. 55: 349–354.

Selye, H. 1950. Stress and the general adaptation syndrome. Br. Med. J. 1: 1383–1392.

Selye, H. 1973. The evolution of the stress concept. Am. Sci. 61: 692–699.

Silva, P., R. Solomon, K. Spokes, and F. H. Epstein. 1977a. Ouabain inhibition of gill Na^+-K^+-ATPase: relationship to active chloride transport. J. Exp. Zool. 199: 419–426.

Silva, P., J. Stoff, M. Field, L. Fine, J. N. Forrest, and F. H. Epstein. 1977b. Mechanism of active chloride secretion by shark rectal gland: role of Na-K-ATPase in chloride transport. Am. J. Physiol. 233: F298-F306.

Simpson, T. H. 1975/1976. Endocrine aspects of salmonid culture. Proc. R. Soc. Edinburgh 75B: 241–252.

Singley, J. A. and W. Chavin. 1971. Cortisol levels of normal goldfish, *Carassius auratus* L., and response to osmotic change. Am. Zool. 11: 653. [Abstract]

Soivio, A., M. Nikinmaa, and K. Westman. 1980. The blood oxygen binding properties of hypoxic *Salmo gairdneri*. J. Comp. Physiol. 136: 83–87.

Soivio, A., K. Nyholm, and M. Huhti. 1977. Effects of anaesthesia with MS 222, neutralized MS 222 and benzocaine on the blood constituents of rainbow trout, *Salmo gairdneri*. J. Fish Biol. 10: 91–101.

Soivio, A. and A. Oikari. 1976. Haematological effects of stress on a teleost, *Esox lucius* L. J. Fish Biol. 8: 397–411.

Specker, J. L. and C. B. Schreck. 1980. Stress responses to transportation and fitness for marine survival in coho salmon (*Oncorhynchus kisutch*) smolts. Can. J. Fish. Aquat. Sci. 37: 765–769.

Spieler, R. E. and M. A. Nickerson. 1976. Effect of handling and methypentynol anaesthesia on serum glucose levels in goldfish, *Carassius auratus* Linnaeus. Trans. Wisc. Acad. Sci. Arts Lett. 64: 234–239.

Spotte, S. 1979. Seawater aquariums: the captive environment. Wiley, New York, 413 pp.

Spotte, S. and G. Anderson. 1989. Plasma cortisol changes in seawater-adapted mummichogs (*Fundulus heteroclitus*) exposed to ammonia. Can. J. Fish. Aquat. Sci. 46: 2065–2069.

Stanley, J. C. and P. J. Colby. 1971. Effects of temperature on electrolyte balance and osmoregulation in the alewife (*Alosa pseudoharengus*) in fresh and sea water. Trans. Am. Fish. Soc. 100: 624–638.

Stebbing, A. R. D. 1981. Stress, health and homeostasis. Mar. Pollut. Bull. 12: 326–329.

Stevens, E. D. 1972. Change in body weight caused by handling and exercise in fish. J. Fish. Res. Board Can. 29: 202–203.

Storer, J. H. 1967. Starvation and the effects of cortisol in the goldfish (*Carassius auratus* L.). Comp. Biochem. Physiol. 20: 939–948.

Storer, T. I. and R. L. Usinger. 1957. General zoology, 3rd ed. McGraw-Hill, New York, 664 pp.

Strange, R. J. 1980. Acclimation temperature influences cortisol and glucose concentrations in stressed channel catfish. Trans. Am. Fish. Soc. 109: 298–302.

Strange, R. J. and C. B. Schreck. 1978. Anesthetic and handling stress on survival and cortisol concentration in yearling chinook salmon (*Oncorhynchus tshawytscha*). J. Fish. Res. Board Can. 35: 345–349.

Strange, R. J., C. B. Schreck, and R. D. Ewing. 1978. Cortisol concentrations in confined juvenile chinook salmon (*Oncorhynchus tshawytscha*). Trans. Am. Fish. Soc. 107: 812–819.

Strange, R. J., C. B. Schreck, and J. T. Golden. 1977. Corticoid stress responses to handling and temperature in salmonids. Trans. Am. Fish. Soc. 106: 213–218.

Sumpter, J. P., H. M. Dye, and T. J. Benfey. 1986. The effects of stress on plasma ACTH, α-MSH, and cortisol levels in salmonid fishes. Gen. Comp. Endocrinol. 62: 377–385.

Sumpter, J. P., A. D. Pickering, and T. G. Pottinger. 1985. Stress-induced elevation of plasma α-MSH and endorphin in brown trout, *Salmo trutta* L. Gen. Comp. Endocrinol. 59: 257–265.

Tomasso, J. R., K. B. Davis, and N. C. Parker. 1980. Plasma corticosteroid and electrolyte dynamics of hybrid striped bass (white bass × striped bass) during netting and hauling. Proc. World Maricult. Soc. 11: 303–310.

Tomasso, J. R., K. B. Davis, and N. C. Parker. 1981a. Plasma corticosteroid dynamics in channel catfish, *Ictalurus punctatus* (Rafinesque), during and after oxygen depletion. J. Fish Biol. 18: 519–526.

Tomasso, J. R., K. B. Davis, and B. A. Simco. 1981b. Plasma corticosteriod dynamics in channel catfish (*Ictalurus punctatus*) exposed to ammonia and nitrite. Can. J. Fish. Aquat. Sci. 38: 1106–1112.

Tripp, R. A., A. G. Maule, C. B. Schreck, and S. L. Kaattari. 1987. Cortisol mediates suppression of salmonid lymphocyte responses *in vitro*. Dev. Comp. Immunol. 11: 565–576.

Truchot, J-P., A. Toulmond, and P. Dejours. 1980. Blood acid-base balance as a function of water oxygenation: a study at two different ambient CO_2 levels in the dogfish, *Scyliorhinus canicula*. Respir. Physiol. 41: 13–28.

Umminger, B. L. and D. H. Gist. 1973. Effects of thermal acclimation on physiological responses to handling stress, cortisol and aldosterone injections in the goldfish, *Carassius auratus*. Comp. Biochem. Physiol. 44A: 967–977.

Vooys, C. G. N. de. 1968. Formation and excretion of ammonia in Teleostei. I. Excretion of ammonia through the gills. Arch. Int. Physiol. Biochim. 76: 268–272.

Wahlqvist, I. and S. Nilsson. 1980. Adrenergic control of the cardiovascular system of the Atlantic cod, *Gadus morhua*, during "stress." J. Comp. Physiol. 137: 145–150.

Warren, K. W. and S. Schenker. 1962. Differential effect of fixed acid and carbon dioxide on ammonia toxicity. Am. J. Physiol. 203: 903–906.

Wedemeyer, G. 1969. Stress-induced ascorbic acid depletion and cortisol production in two salmonid fishes. Comp. Biochem. Physiol. 29: 1247–1251.

Wedemeyer, G. 1970. Stress of anesthesia with M.S. 222 and benzocaine in rainbow trout (*Salmo gairdneri*). J. Fish. Res. Board Can. 27: 909–914.

Wedemeyer, G. A. 1971. The stress of formalin treatments in rainbow trout (*Salmo gairdneri*) and coho salmon (*Oncorhynchus kisutch*). J. Fish. Res. Board Can. 28: 1899–1904.

Wedemeyer, G. 1972. Some physiological consequences of handling stress in the juvenile coho salmon (*Oncorhynchus kisutch*) and steelhead trout (*Salmo gairdneri*). J. Fish. Res. Board Can. 29: 1780–1783.

Wedemeyer, G. A. 1976. Physiological response of juvenile coho salmon (*Oncorhynchus kisutch*) and rainbow trout (*Salmo gairdneri*) to handling and crowding stress in intensive fish culture. J. Fish. Res. Board Can. 33: 2699–2702.

Wells, R. M. G. and P. S. Davie. 1985. Oxygen binding by the blood and hematological effects of capture stress in two big gamefish: mako shark and striped marlin. Comp. Biochem. Physiol. 81A: 643–646.

Wells, R. M. G., V. Tetons, and A. L. DeVries. 1984. Recovery from stress following capture and anaesthesia of antarctic fish: haematology and blood chemistry. J. Fish Biol. 25: 567–576.

White A. and T. C. Fletcher. 1986. Serum cortisol, glucose and lipids in plaice (*Pleuronectes platessa* L.) exposed to starvation and aquarium stress. Comp. Biochem. Physiol. 85A: 649–653.

White, A. and T. C. Fletcher. 1989. The effect of physical disturbance, hypoxia and stress hormones on serum components of the plaice, *Pleuronectes platessa* L. Comp. Biochem. Physiol. 93A: 455–461.

Woo, P. T. K., J. F. Leatherland, and M. S. Lee. 1987. *Cryptobia salmositica*: cortisol increases the susceptibility of *Salmo gairdneri* Richardson to experimental cryptobiosis. J. Fish Dis. 10: 75–83.

Wood, C. M., B. R. McMahon, and D. G. McDonald. 1977. An analysis of changes in blood pH following exhausting activity in the starry flounder, *Platichthys stellatus*. J. Exp. Biol. 69: 173–185.

Wood, C. M., J. D. Turner, and M. S. Graham. 1983. Why do fish die after severe exercise? J. Fish Biol. 22: 189–201.

Wood, S. C., K. Johansen, and R. E. Weber. 1975. Effects of ambient P_{O_2} on hemoglobin-oxygen affinity and red cell ATP concentrations in a benthic fish, *Pleuronectes platessa*. Respir. Physiol. 25: 259–267.

Wood, S. C. and K. Johansen. 1973a. Blood oxygen transport and acid-base balance in eels during hypoxia. Am. J. Physiol. 225: 849–851.

Wood, S. C. and K. Johansen. 1973b. Organic phosphate metabolism in nucleated red cells: influence of hypoxia on eel HbO_2 affinity. Nethl. J. Sea Res. 7: 328–338.

Woodward, C. C. and R. J. Strange. 1987. Physiological stress responses in wild and hatchery-reared rainbow trout. Trans. Am. Fish. Soc. 116: 574–579.

Wydoski, R. S., G. A. Wedemeyer, and N. C. Nelson. 1976. Physiological response to hooking stress in hatchery and wild rainbow trout (*Salmo gairdneri*). Trans. Am. Fish. Soc. 105: 601–606.

Yamamoto, K-I., Y. Itazawa, and H. Kobayashi. 1980. Supply of erythrocytes into the circulating blood from the spleen of exercised fish. Comp. Biochem. Physiol. 65A: 5–11.

Chapter 5

Alexander, R. McN. 1974. Functional design in fishes, 3rd ed. Hutchinson, London, 160 pp.

Banner, A. 1967. Evidence of sensitivity to acoustic displacements in the lemon shark, *Negaprion brevirostris* (Poey). *In* Lateral line detectors, P. H. Cahn (ed.). Indiana University Press, Bloomington, pp. 265–273.

Bennett, M. V. L. 1971. Electroreception. *In* Fish physiology, Vol. 5, 2nd ed., W. S. Hoar and D. J. Randall (eds.). Academic Press, New York, pp. 493–574.

Berg, A. V. van den and A. Schuijf. 1983. Discrimination of sounds based on the phase difference between particle motion and acoustic pressure in the shark *Chiloscyllium griseum*. Proc. R. Soc. London 218B: 127–134.

Bergeijk, W. A. van. 1964. Directional and nondirectional hearing in fish. *In* Marine bio-acoustics, W. N. Tavolga (ed.). Pergamon, Oxford, pp. 281–299.

Bergeijk, W. A. van. 1967. The evolution of vertebrate hearing. *In* Contributions to sensory physiology, Vol. 2, W. D. Neff (ed.). Academic Press, New York, pp. 1–49.

Blonder, B. I. and W. S. Alevizon. 1988. Prey discrimination and electroreception in the stingray *Dasyatis sabina*. Copeia 1988: 33–36.

Chapman, C. J. 1973. Field studies of hearing in teleost fish. Helogänder Meeresunters. 24: 371–390.

Collette, B. B. and F. W. Talbot. 1972. Activity patterns of coral reef fishes with emphasis on nocturnal-diurnal changeover. Nat. Hist. Mus. Los Angeles County Sci. Bull. 14: 98–124.

Collins, B. A. and E. F. MacNichol Jr. 1984. Morphological observations and microspectrophometric data from photoreceptors in the retina of the sea raven, *Hemitripterus americanus*. Biol. Bull. 167: 437–444.

Corwin, J. T. 1979. Parallel channels for sound detection in the fish ear. Soc. Neurosci. Abstr. 5: 18.

Corwin, J. T. 1981a. Audition in elasmobranchs. *In* Hearing and sound communication in fishes, W. N. Tavolga, A. N. Popper, and R. R. Fay (eds.). Springer-Verlag, New York, pp. 81–102.

Corwin, J. T. 1981b. Peripheral auditory physiology in the lemon shark: evidence of parallel otolithic and non-otolithic sound detection. J. Comp. Physiol. 142A: 379–390.

Denton, E. 1970. On the organization of reflecting surfaces in some marine animals. Phil. Trans. R. Soc. London 258: 285–313.

Denton, E. 1971. Reflectors in fishes. Sci. Am. 224(2): 65–72.

Dijkgraaf [Dykgraaf], S. 1934. Untersuchungen über die Funktion der Seitenorgane an Fischen. Z. Vergl. Physiol. 20: 162–214.

Dijkgraaf, S. 1952. Bau und Funktionen der Seitenorgane und des Ohrlabyrinths bei Fischen. Experientia 8: 205–216. [English summary]

Dijkgraaf, S. 1963. The functioning and significance of the lateral-line organs. Biol. Rev. 38: 51–105.

Dijkgraaf, S. and A. J. Kalmijn. 1963. Untersuchengen über die Funktion der Lorenzinischen Ampullen an Haifischen. Z. Vergl. Physiol. 47: 438–456. [English summary]

Domm, S. B. and A. J. Domm. 1973. The sequence of appearance at dawn and disappearance at dusk of some coral reef fishes. Pac. Sci. 27: 128–135.

Ebert, J. D., A. G. Loewy, R. S. Miller, and H. A. Schneiderman. 1973. Biology. Holt Rinehart and Winston, New York, 798 pp.

Frisch, K. von. 1938. Über die Bedeutung des Sacculus und der Lagena für den Gehörsinn der Fische. Z. Vergl. Physiol. 25: 703–747.

Fujii, R. and N. Oshima. 1986. Control of chromatophore movements in teleost fishes. Zool. Sci. 3: 13–47.

Harris, G. G. 1964. Considerations on the physics of sound production by fishes. *In* Marine bio-acoustics, W. N. Tavolga (ed.). Pergamon, Oxford, pp. 233–247.

Harris, G. G. and W. A. van Bergeijk. 1962. Evidence that the lateral-line organ responds to near-field displacements of sound sources in water. J. Acoust. Soc. Am. 34: 1831–1841.

Hawkes, J. W. 1974. The structure of fish skin. II. The chromatophore unit. Cell Tiss. Res. 149: 159–172.

Hawkins, A. D. 1981. The hearing abilities of fish. *In* Hearing and sound communication in fishes, W. N. Tavolga, A. N. Popper, and R. R. Fay (eds.). Springer-Verlag, New York, pp. 109–133.

Hobson, E. S. 1968. Predatory behavior of some shore fishes in the Gulf of California. Res. Rpt. 73, U.S. Fish and Wildlife Service, Washington, 92 pp.

Hobson, E. S. 1972. Activity of Hawaiian reef fishes during the evening and morning transitions between daylight and darkness. Fish. Bull. (NOAA) 70: 715–740.

Hobson, E. S. 1973. Diel feeding migrations in tropical reef fishes. Helgoländer Meeresunters. 24: 361–370.

Kalmijn, A. J. 1966. Electro-perception in sharks and rays. Nature 212: 1232–1233.

Kalmijn, A. J. 1971. The electric sense of sharks and rays. J. Exp. Biol. 55: 371–383.

Kalmijn, A. J. 1972. Bioelectric fields in sea water and the function of the ampullae of Lorenzini in elasmobranch fishes. SIO Ref. 72-83, Scripps Institution of Oceanography, La Jolla, 21 pp.

Kalmijn, A. J. 1974. The detection of electric fields from inanimate and animate sources other than electric organs. *In* Handbook of sensory physiology, Vol. III/3, A. Fessard (ed.). Springer-Verlag, Berlin, pp. 147–200.

Kelly, J. C. and D. R. Nelson. 1975. Hearing thresholds of the horn shark, *Heterodontus francisci*. J. Acoust. Soc. Am. 58: 905–909.

Klimley, A. P. and A. A. Myrberg Jr. 1979. Acoustic stimuli underlying withdrawal from a sound source by adult lemon sharks, *Negaprion brevirostris* (Poey). Bull. Mar. Sci. 29: 447–458.

Knox, R. 1825. On the theory of the existence of a sixth sense in fishes; supposed to reside in certain peculiar tubular organs, found immediately under the integuments of the head in sharks and rays. Edinburgh J. Sci. 2: 12–16.

Lagler, K. F., J. E. Bardach, R. R. Miller, and D. R. M. Passino. 1977. Ichthyology, 2nd ed. Wiley, New York, 506 pp.

Lekander, B. 1949. The sensory line system and the canal bones in the head of some Ostariophysi. Acta Zool. 30: 1–131.

Levine, J. S. 1980. Vision underwater. Oceanus 23(3): 19–26.

Levine, J. S. and E. F. MacNichol Jr. 1979. Visual pigments in teleost fishes: effects of habitat, microhabitat, and behavior on visual system evolution. Sensory Process. 3: 95–131.

Levine, J. S. and E. F. MacNichol Jr. 1982. Color vision in fishes. Sci. Am. 246(2): 140–149.

Lindsay, R. B. 1982. Sound. *In* Encylopedia of science and technology, Vol. 12, 5th ed. McGraw-Hill, New York, pp. 656–667.

Loew, E. R. and J. N. Lythgoe. 1978. The ecology of cone pigments in teleost fishes. Vision Res. 18: 715–722.

Lowenstein, O. 1971. The labyrinth. *In* Fish physiology, Vol. 5, 2nd ed., W. S. Hoar and D. J. Randall (eds.). Academic Press, New York, pp. 207–240.

Lythgoe, J. N. 1966. Visual pigments and underwater vision. *In* Light as an ecological factor, R. Bainbridge, G. C. Evans, and O. Rackham (eds.). Blackwell, Oxford, pp. 375–391.

McFarland, W. N. and F. W. Munz. 1975a. Part II: The photic environment of clear tropical seas during the day. Vision Res. 15: 1063–1070.

McFarland, W. N. and F. W. Munz. 1975b. Part III: The evolution of photopic visual pigments in fishes. Vision Res. 15: 1071–1080.

Morse, R. W. 1981. Sound and acoustics. *In* Collier's encyclopedia, Vol. 21. Collier, New York, pp. 221–244.

Moulton, J. M. and R. H. Dixon. 1967. Directional hearing in fishes. *In* Marine bio-acoustics, Vol. 2, W. N. Tavolga (ed.). Pergamon, Oxford, pp. 187–232.

Moyle, P. B. and J. J. Cech Jr. 1982. Fishes: an introduction to ichthyology. Prentice-Hall, Englewood Cliffs, 593 pp.

Munz, F. W. and W. N. McFarland. 1973. The significance of spectral position in the rhodopsins of tropical marine fishes. Vision Res. 13: 1829–1874.

Munz, F. W. and W. N. McFarland. 1975. Part I: Presumptive cone pigments extracted from tropical marine fishes. Vision Res. 15: 1045–1062.

Munz, F. W. and W. N. McFarland. 1977. Evolutionary adaptations of fishes to the photic environment. *In* Handbook of sensory physiology, Vol. VII/5, F. Crescitelli (ed.). Springer-Verlag, Berlin, pp. 193–274.

Murray, R. W. 1974. The ampullae of Lorenzini. *In* Handbook of sensory physiology, Vol. III/3, A. Fessard (ed.). Springer-Verlag, Berlin, pp. 125–146.

Myrberg, A. A. Jr. 1978. Underwater sound—its effect on the behavior of sharks. *In* Sensory biology of sharks, skates, and rays, E. S. Hodgson and R. F. Mathewson (eds.). Office of Naval Research, Arlington, pp. 391–417.

Myrberg, A. A. Jr., A. Banner, and J. D. Richard. 1969. Shark attraction using a video-acoustic system. Mar. Biol. 2: 264–276.

Myrberg, A. A. Jr., C. R. Gordon, and A. P. Klimley. 1978. Rapid withdrawal from a sound source by open-ocean sharks. J. Acoust. Soc. Am. 64: 1289–1297.

Myrberg, A. A. Jr., S. J. Ha, S. Walewski, and J. C. Banbury. 1972. Effectiveness of acoustic signals in attracting epipelagic sharks to an underwater sound source. Bull. Mar. Sci. 22: 926–949.

Nelson, D. R. and S. H. Gruber. 1963. Sharks: attraction by low-frequency sounds. Science 142: 975–977.

Nelson, D. R. and R. H. Johnson. 1972. Acoustic attraction of Pacific reef sharks: effect of pulse intermittency and variability. Comp. Biochem. Physiol. 42A: 85–95.

Obika, M. 1986. Intracellular transport of pigment granules in fish chromatophores. Zool. Sci. 3: 1–11.

Olsen, K. 1976. Evidence for localization of sound by fish schools. *In* Sound reception in fish, A. Schuijf and A. D. Hawkins (eds.). Elsevier, Amsterdam, pp. 257–270.

Parker, G. H. 1904. The function of the lateral-line organs in fishes. Bull. U.S. Bur. Fish. 24: 185–207.

Parker, G. H. 1909. The sense of hearing in the dogfish. Science 29: 428.

Parvulescu, A. 1964. Problems of propagation and processing. *In* Marine bio-acoustics, W. N. Tavolga (ed.). Pergamon, Oxford, pp. 87–100.

Parvulescu, A. 1967. The acoustics of small tanks. *In* Marine bio-acoustics, Vol. 2, W. N. Tavolga (ed.). Pergamon, Oxford, pp. 7–13.

Pickford, G. E. and J. W. Atz. 1957. The physiology of the pituitary gland of fishes. New York Zoological Society, New York, 613 pp.

Platt, C. and A. N. Popper. 1981. Fine structure and function of the ear. *In* Hearing and sound communication in fishes, W. N. Tavolga, A. N. Popper, and R. R. Fay (eds.). Springer-Verlag, New York, pp. 3–38.

Popper, A. N. and R. R. Fay. 1973. Sound detection and processing by teleost fishes: a critical review. J. Acoust. Soc. Am. 53: 1515–1529.

Popper, A. N. and R. R. Fay. 1977. Structure and function of the elasmobranch auditory system. Am. Zool. 17: 443–452.

Popper, A. N., M. Salmon, and A. Parvulescu. 1973. Sound localization by the Hawaiian squirrelfishes, *Myripristis berndti* and *M. argyromus*. Anim. Behav. 21: 86–97.

Pumphrey, R. J. 1950. Hearing. Symp. Soc. Exp. Biol. 4: 1–18.

Richard, J. D. 1968. Fish attraction with pulsed low-frequency sound. J. Fish. Res. Board Can. 25: 1441–1452.

Sager, D. R., C. H. Hocutt, and J. R. Stauffer Jr. 1985. Preferred wavelengths of visible light for juvenile Atlantic menhaden. N. Am. J. Fish. Mgt. 5: 72–77.

Sand, O. and P. S. Enger. 1973. Function of the swimbladder in fish hearing. *In* Basic mechanisms of hearing, A. R. Møller (ed.). Academic Press, New York, pp. 893–910.

Shlaifer, A. 1942. The schooling behavior of mackerel: a preliminary experimental analysis. Zoologica (N.Y.) 27: 75–80 + 1 plate.

Schneider, H. 1967. Morphology and physiology of sound-producing mechanisms in teleost fishes. *In* Marine bio-acoustics, Vol. 2, W. N. Tavolga (ed.). Pergamon, Oxford, pp. 135–158.

Schuijf, A. 1976. The phase model of directional hearing in fish. *In* Sound reception in fish, A. Schuijf and A. D. Hawkins (eds.). Elsevier, Amsterdam, pp. 63–86.

Schuijf, A. 1981. Models of acoustic localization. *In* Hearing and sound communication in fishes, W. N. Tavolga, A. N. Popper, and R. R. Fay (eds.). Springer-Verlag, New York, pp. 267–327.

Smith, C. L. and J. C. Tyler. 1972. Space resource sharing in a coral reef community. Nat. Hist. Mus. Los Angeles County Sci. Bull. 14: 125–170.

Szabo, T. 1974. Anatomy of the specialized lateral line organs of electroreception. *In* Handbook of sensory physiology, Vol. III/3, A. Fessard (ed.). Springer-Verlag, Berlin, pp. 13–58.

Tavolga, W. N. 1967. Underwater sound in marine biology. *In* Underwater acoustics, Vol. 2, V. M. Albers (ed.). Plenum, New York, pp. 35–41.

Tavolga, W. N. 1971. Sound production and detection. *In* Fish physiology, 2nd ed., Vol. 5, W. S. Hoar and D. J. Randall (eds.). Academic Press, New York, pp. 135–205.

Tavolga, W. N. (ed.). 1977. Sound production in fishes. Dowden, Hutchinson and Ross, Stroudsburg, 363 pp.

Walls, G. L. 1963. The vertebrate eye and its adaptive radiation. Hafner, New York, 785 pp.

Waltman, B. 1966. Electrical properties and fine structure of the ampullary canals of Lorenzini. Acta Physiol. Scand. 66(Suppl. 264): 1–60.

Wilson, E. O., T. Eisner, W. R. Briggs, R. E. Dickerson, R. L. Metzenberg, R. D. O'Brien, M. Susman, and W. E. Boggs. 1978. Life on earth, 2nd ed. Sinauer, Sunderland, 846 pp.

Chapter 6

Abel, E. F. 1961. Freiwasserstudien über das Fortpflanzungverhalten des Mönchfisches *Chromis chromis* Linné, einem Vertreter der Pomacentriden im Mittelmeer. Z. Tierpsychol. 18: 441–449. [English summary]

Allen, G. R. 1972. The anemonefishes: their classification and biology. T.F.H. Publications, Neptune City, 288 pp.

Allen, G. R. 1980. The symbiotic relationship. *In* The anemonefishes of the world: species, care, and breeding, rev. ed., G. R. Allen (ed.). Aquarium Systems, Mentor, pp. 16–18.

Allen, W. E. 1920. Behavior of loon and sardines. Ecology 1: 309–310.

Atz, J. W. 1955. Orientation in schooling fishes. *In* Proceedings of a conference on orientation in animals. Office of Naval Research, Washington, pp. 103–130.

Bakus, G. J. 1966. Some relationships of fishes to benthic organisms on coral reefs. Nature 210: 280–284.

Bakus, G. J. 1967. The feeding habits of fishes and primary production at Eniwetok, Marshall Islands. Micronesica 3: 135–149.

Bakus, G. J. 1969. Energetics and feeding in shallow marine waters. Int. Rev. Gen. Exp. Zool. 4: 275–369.

Bakus, G. J. 1972. Effects of feeding habits of coral reef fishes on the benthic biota. *In* Proceedings of the symposium on corals and coral reefs, C. Mukundan and C. S. G. Pillai (eds.). Marine Biological Association of India, Cochin, pp. 445–448.

Bartels, P. J. 1984. Extra-territorial movements of a perennially territorial damselfish, *Eupomacentrus dorsopunicans* Poey. Behaviour 91: 312–322.

Belyayev, V. V. and G. V. Zuyev. 1969. Hydrodynamic hypothesis of school formation in fishes. J. [Prob.] Ichthyol. 9: 578–584.

Blösch, M. 1961. Was ist die Grundlage der Korallenfischsymbiose: Schutzstoff oder Schutzverhalten? Naturwissenshaften 48: 387.

Borowitzka, M. A. 1981. Algae and grazing in coral reef ecosystems. Endeavour (N.S.) 5: 99–106.

Bowen, E. S. 1931. The role of the sense organs in aggregations of *Ameiurus melas*. Ecol. Monogr. 1: 3–35.

Brawley, S. H. and W. H. Adey. 1977. Territorial behavior of threespot damselfish (*Eupomacentrus planifrons*) increases reef algal biomass and productivity. Environ. Biol. Fish. 2: 45–51.

Breder, C. M. Jr. 1929. Certain effects in the habits of schooling fishes, as based on the observation of *Jenkinsia*. Am. Mus. Nov. (382): 1–5.

Breder, C. M. Jr. 1951. Studies on the structure of the fish school. Bull. Am. Mus. Nat. Hist. 98: 1–27.

Breder, C. M. Jr. 1965. Vortices and fish schools. Zoologica (N.Y.) 50: 97–114.

Breder, C. M. Jr. 1967. On the survival value of fish schools. Zoologica (N.Y.) 52: 25–40.

Breder, C. M. Jr. 1976. Fish schools as operational structures. Fish. Bull. (NOAA) 74: 471–502.

Breder, C. M. Jr. and F. Halpern. 1946. Innate and acquired behavior affecting the aggregation of fishes. Physiol. Zool. 19: 154–190.

Breder, C. M. Jr. and R. F. Nigrelli. 1935. The influence of temperature and other factors on the winter aggregations of the sunfish, *Lepomis auritus*, with critical remarks on the social behavior of fishes. Ecology 16: 33–47.

Brock, R. E. 1979. An experimental study on the effects of grazing by parrotfishes and the role of refuges in benthic community structure. Mar. Biol. 51: 381–388.

Brock, V. E. and R. H. Riffenburgh. 1960. Fish schooling: a possible factor in reducing predation. J. Conseil Int. Explor. Mer 25: 307–317.

Brockmann, H. J. and J. P. Hailman. 1976. Fish cleaning symbiosis: notes on juvenile angelfishes (*Pomacanthus*, Chaetodontidae) and comparisons with other species. Z. Tierpsychol. 42: 129–138.

Brooks, W. R. and R. N. Mariscal. 1984. The acclimation of anemone fishes to sea anemones: protection by changes in the fish's mucous coat. J. Exp. Mar. Biol. Ecol. 81: 277–285.

Burt, W. H. 1943. Territoriality and home range concepts as applied to mammals. J. Mamm. 24: 346–352.

Cahn, P. H. 1972. Sensory factors in the side to side spacing and positional orientation of the tuna, *Euthynnus affinis*, during schooling. Fish. Bull. (NOAA) 70: 197–204.

Casimir, M. J. and H. W. Fricke. 1971. Zur Funktion, Morphologie und Histochemie der Schwanzdrüse bei Röhrenaalen (Pisces, Apodes, Heterocongridae). Mar. Biol. 9: 339–346. [English summary]

Childress, S. 1981. Mechanics of swimming and flying. Cambridge University Press, Cambridge, 155 pp.

Clarke, D. G., G. F. Crozier, and W. W. Schroeder. 1977. Observations on the ecology and behavior of the sand tilefish, *Malacanthus plumieri*. *In* Proceedings of the third international coral reef symposium, Vol. 1. Rosenstiel School of Marine and Atmospheric Science, University of Miami, pp. 579–583.

Clarke, T. A. 1970. Territorial behavior and population dynamics of a pomacentrid fish, the garibaldi, *Hypsypops rubicunda*. Ecol. Monogr. 40: 189–212.

Clifton, H. E. and R. E. Hunter. 1972. The sand tilefish, *Malacanthus plumieri*, and the distribution of coarse debris near West Indian coral reefs. Nat. Hist. Mus. Los Angeles County Sci. Bull. 14: 87–92.

Colin, P. L. 1971. Interspecific relationships of the yellowhead jawfish, *Opistognathus aurifrons* (Pisces, Opistognathidae). Copeia 1971: 469–473.

Colin, P. L. 1973. Burrowing behavior of the yellowhead jawfish, *Opistognathus aurifrons*. Copeia 1973: 84–90.

Collette, B. B. and F. H. Talbot. 1972. Activity patterns of coral reef fishes with emphasis on nocturnal-diurnal changeover. Nat. Hist. Mus. Los Angeles County Sci. Bull. 14: 98–124.

Cullen, J. M., E. Shaw, and H. A. Baldwin. 1965. Methods for measuring the three-dimensional structure of fish schools. Anim. Behav. 13: 534–543.

Davenport, D. and K. S. Norris. 1958. Observations on the symbiosis of the sea anemone *Stoichactis* and the pomacentrid fish, *Amphiprion percula*. Biol. Bull. 115: 397–410.

Dunn, D. F. 1981. The clownfish sea anemones: Stichodactylidae (Coelenterata: Actinaria) and other sea anemones symbiotic with pomacentrid fishes. Trans. Am. Philos. Soc. 71 (Part 1): 1–115.

Earle, S. A. 1972. The influence of herbivores on the marine plants of Great Lameshur Bay, with an annotated list of plants. Nat. Hist. Mus. Los Angeles County Sci. Bull. 14: 17–44.

Ebersole, J. P. 1977. The adaptive significance of interspecific territoriality in the reef fish *Eupomacentrus leucostictus*. Ecology 58: 914–920.

Ebersole, J. P. 1980. Food density and territory size: an alternative model and a test on the reef fish (*Eupomacentrus leucostictus*). Am. Nat. 115: 492–509.

Eggers, D. M. 1976. Theoretical effect of schooling by planktivorous fish predators on rate of prey consumption. J. Fish. Res. Board Can. 33: 1964–1971.

Eibl-Eibesfeldt, I. 1955. Über Symbiosen, Parasitismus und andere besondere zwischenartliche Beziehungen tropischer Meeresfische. Z. Tierpsychol. 12: 203–219.

Eibl-Eibesfeldt, I. 1960. Beobachtungen und Versuche an Anemonenfischen (*Amphiprion*) der Malediven und der Nicobaren. Z. Tierpsychol. 17: 1–10. [English summary]

Eibl-Eibesfeldt, I. 1962. Freiwasserbeobachtungen zur Deutung des Schwarmverhaltens verschiedener Fische. Z. Tierpsychol. 19: 165–182. [English summary]

Emlen, J. T. Jr. 1957. Defended area?—a critique of the territory concept and of conventional thinking. Ibis 99: 352.

Fischer, E. A. 1981. Sexual allocation in a simultaneously hermaphroditic coral reef fish. Am. Nat. 117: 64–82.

Fishelson, L. 1965. Observations and experiments on the Red Sea anemones and their symbiotic fish *Amphiprion bicinctus*. Bull. Sea Fish. Res. Sta., Haifa (39): 1–14.

Fishelson, L., D. Popper, and N. Gunderman. 1971. Diurnal cyclic behavior of *Pempheris oualensis* Cuv. & Val. (Pempheridae: Teleostei). J. Nat. Hist. 5: 503–506.

Foster, M. S. 1972. The algal turf community in the nest of the ocean goldfish, *Hypsypops rubicunda*. *In* Proceedings of the seventh international seaweed symposium, K. Nisizawa (ed.). University of Tokyo Press, Tokyo, pp. 55–60.

Foster, W. A. and J. E. Treherne. 1981. Evidence for the dilution effect in the selfish herd from fish predation on a marine insect. Nature 293: 466–467.

Franzblau, M. A. and J. P. Collins. 1980. Test of a hypothesis of territory regulation in an insectivorous bird by experimentally increasing prey abundance. Oecologia 46: 164–170.

Fricke, H. W. 1974. Öko-Ethologie des monogamen Anemonenfisches *Amphiprion bicinctus* (Freiwasseruntersuchung aus dem Roten Meer). Z. Tierpsychol. 36: 429–512. [English summary]

Fricke, H. and S. Fricke. 1977. Monogamy and sex change by aggressive dominance in coral reef fish. Nature 266: 830–832.

Fukui, Y. 1973. Some experiments on the symbiotic association between sea anemone and *Amphiprion*. Pub. Seto Mar. Biol. Lab. 20: 419–430.

Ghiselin, M. T. 1969. The evolution of hermaphroditism among animals. Quart. Rev. Biol. 44: 189–208.

Gohar, H. A. F. 1934. Partnership between fish and anemone. Nature 134: 291.

Gohar, H. A. F. 1948. Commensalism between fish and anemone (with a description of the eggs of *Amphiprion bicinctus* Rüppell). Pub. Mar. Biol. Sta., Ghardaqa (6): 35–44.

Gorlick, D. L. 1984. Preference for ectoparasite-infected host fishes by the Hawaiian cleaning wrasse, *Labroides phthirophagus* (Labridae). Copeia 1984: 758–762.

Gorlick, D. L., P. D. Atkins, and G. S. Losey Jr. 1978. Cleaning stations as water holes, garbage dumps, and sites for the evolution of reciprocal altruism? Am. Nat. 112: 341–353.

Graefe, G. 1963. Die Anemonen-Fisch-Symbiose und ihre Grundlage—nach Freilanduntersuchungen bei Eilat/Rotes Meer. Naturwissenshaften 50: 410.

Hamilton, W. D. 1971. Geometry of the selfish herd. J. Theor. Biol. 31: 295–311.

Hanlon, R. T., R. F. Hixon, and D. G. Smith. 1983. Behavioral associations of seven West Indian reef fishes with sea anemones at Bonaire, Netherlands Antilles. Bull. Mar. Sci. 33: 928–934.

Hanlon, R. T. and L. Kaufman. 1976. Association of seven West Indian reef fishes with sea anemones. Bull. Mar. Sci. 26: 225–232.

Hay, M. E. 1984. Patterns of fish and urchin grazing on Caribbean coral reefs: are previous results typical? Ecology 65: 446–454.

Healey, M. C. and R. Prieston. 1973. The interrelationships among individuals in a fish school. Tech. Rpt. No. 389, Fisheries Research Board of Canada, Winnipeg, 15 pp.

Hiatt, R. W. and V. E. Brock. 1948. On the herding of prey and the schooling of the black skipjack *Euthynnus yaito* Kishinouye. Pac. Sci. 2: 297–298.

Hinds, P. A. and D. L. Ballantine. 1987. Effects of the Caribbean threespot damselfish, *Stegastes planifrons* (Cuvier), on algal lawn composition. Aquat. Bot. 27: 299–308.

Hixon, M. A. 1980. Food production and competitor density as the determinants of feeding territory size. Am. Nat. 115: 510–530.

Hixon, M. A. 1981. An experimental analysis of territorialty in the California reef fish *Embiotoca jacksoni* (Embiotocidae). Copeia 1981: 663–665.

Hixon, M. A. 1982. Energy maximizers and time minimizers: theory and reality. Am. Nat. 119: 596–599.

Hixon, M. A. 1987. Territory area as a determinant of mating systems. Am. Zool. 27: 229–247.

Hixon, M. A. and W. N. Brostoff. 1983. Damselfish as keystone species in reverse: intermediate disturbance and diversity of reef algae. Science 220: 511–513.

Hobson, E. S. 1965. Diurnal-nocturnal activity of some inshore fishes in the Gulf of California. Copeia 1965: 291–302.

Hobson, E. S. 1968. Predatory behavior of some shore fishes in the Gulf of California. Res. Rpt. 73, U.S. Fish and Wildlife Service, Washington, 92 pp.

Hobson, E. S. 1969. Comments on certain recent generalizations regarding cleaning symbiosis in fishes. Pac. Sci. 23: 35–39.

Hobson, E. S. 1972. Activity of Hawaiian reef fishes during the evening and morning transitions between daylight and darkness. Fish. Bull. (NOAA) 70: 715–740.

Hobson, E. S. 1973. Diel feeding migrations in tropical reef fishes. Helgoländer Meeresunters. 24: 361–370.

Hobson, E. S. and J. R. Chess. 1973. Feeding oriented movements of the atherinid fish *Pranseus pinguis* at Majuro Atoll, Marshall Islands. Fish. Bull. (NOAA) 71: 777–786.

Hunter, J. R. 1968. Effects of light on schooling and feeding of jack mackerel, *Trachurus symmetricus*. J. Fish. Res. Board Can. 25: 393–407.

Inagaki, T., W. Sakamoto, and T. Kuroki. 1976. Studies on the schooling behavior of fish—II Mathematical modeling of schooling form depending on the intensity of mutual force between individuals. Bull. Jap. Soc. Sci. Fish. 42: 265–270.

Jewell, P. A. 1966. The concept ot home range in mammals. Symp. Zool. Soc. London 18: 85–109.

John, K. R. 1964. Illumination, vision, and schooling of *Astyanax mexicanus* (Fillipi). J. Fish Res. Board Canada 21: 1453–1473.

Johnson, W. S. and P. Ruben. 1988. Cleaning behavior of *Bodianus rufus*, *Thalsassoma bifasciatum*, *Gobiosoma evelynae*, and *Periclimenes pedersoni* along a depth gradient at Salt River Submarine Canyon, St. Croix. Environ. Biol. Fish. 23: 225–232.

Kamura, S. and S. Choonhabandit. 1986. Algal communities within territories of the damselfish *Stegastes apicalis* and the effects of grazing by the sea urchin *Diademo* spp. in the Gulf of Thailand. Galaxea 5: 175–193.

Kaufman, L. 1977. The three spot damselfish: effects on benthic biota of Caribbean coral reefs. *In* Proceedings of the third international coral reef symposium, Vol. 1. Rosenstiel School of Marine and Atmospheric Science, University of Miami, pp. 560–564.

Kaufmann, J. H. 1983. On the definitions and functions of dominance and territoriality. Biol. Rev. 58: 1–20.

Keenleyside, M. H. A. 1955. Some aspects of the schooling behaviour of fish. Behaviour 8: 183–248.

Keenleyside, M. H. A. 1972. The behaviour of *Abudefduf zonatus* (Pisces, Pomacentridae) at Heron Island, Great Barrier Reef. Anim. Behav. 20: 763–774.

Klopfer, P. H. 1973. Behavioral aspects of ecology, 2nd ed. Prentice-Hall, Englewood Cliffs, 200 pp.

Koltes, K. H. 1984. Temporal patterns in three-dimensional structure and activity of schools of the Atlantic silverside *Menidia menidia*. Mar. Biol. 78: 113–122.

Koopman, B. O. 1956. The theory of search. II. Target detection. Oper. Res. 4: 503–531.

Lassig, B. R. 1977a. Socioecological strategies adapted by obligate coral-dwelling fishes. *In* Proceedings of the third international coral reef symposium, Vol. 1. Rosenstiel School of Marine and Atmospheric Science, University of Miami, pp. 565–570.

Lassig, B. R. 1977b. Communication and coexistence in a coral community. Mar. Biol. 42: 85–92.

Leong, D. 1967. Breeding and territorial behavior in *Opistognathus aurifrons* (Opistognathidae). Naturwissenshaften 54: 97.

Levin, L. E., R. Salazar, P. Belmonte, and A. Romero. 1989. Light-oriented swimming of schooling fish in continuous channels. Environ. Biol. Fish. 24: 145–150.

Limbaugh, C. 1961. Cleaning symbiosis. Sci. Am. 205(2): 42–49.

Limbaugh, C., H. Pederson, and F. A. Chase Jr. 1961. Shrimps that clean fishes. Bull. Mar. Sci. Gulf Carib. 11: 237–257.

Littler, M. M. and M. S. Doty. 1975. Ecological components structuring the seaward edges of tropical Pacific reefs: the distribution, communities and productivity of *Porolithon*. J. Ecol. 63: 117–129.

Loiselle, P. V. and G. W. Barlow. 1978. Do fishes lek like birds? *In* Contrasts in behavior: adaptations in the aquatic and terrestrial environments, E. S. Reese and F. J. Lighter (eds.). Wiley, New York, pp. 31–75.

Losey, G. S. Jr. 1971. Communication between fishes in cleaning symbiosis. *In* Aspects of the biology of symbiosis, T. C. Cheng (ed.). University Park Press, Baltimore, pp. 45–76.

Losey, G. S. Jr. 1972. The ecological importance of cleaning symbiosis. Copeia 1972: 820–833.

Losey, G. S. Jr. 1974. Cleaning symbiosis in Puerto Rico with comparison to the tropical Pacific. Copeia 1974: 960–970.

Losey, G. S. Jr. 1982. Ecological cues and experience modify interspecific aggression by the damselfish, *Stegastes fasciolatus*. Behaviour 81: 14–37.

Low, R. M. 1971. Interspecific territoriality in a pomacentrid reef fish, *Pomacentrus flavicauda* Whitley. Ecology 52: 648–654.

Lubbock, R. 1980. Why are clownfishes not stung by sea anemones? Proc. R. Soc. London 207B: 35–61.

Major, P. F. 1977. Predator-prey interactions in schooling fishes during periods of twilight: a study of the silverside *Pranesus insulatum* in Hawaii. Fish. Bull. (NOAA) 75: 415–426.

Major, P. F. 1978. Predator-prey interactions of two schooling fishes, *Caranx ignobilis* and *Stolephorus purpureus*. Anim. Behav. 26: 760–777.

Mares, M. A., T. E. Lacher Jr., M. R. Willig, N. A. Bitar, R. Adams, A. Klinger, and D. Tazik. 1982. An experimental analysis of social spacing in *Tamias striatus*. Ecology 63: 267–273.

Mariscal, R. N. 1965. Observations on acclimation behavior in the symbiosis of anemone fish and sea anemones. Am. Zool. 5: 694. [Abstract]

Mariscal, R. N. 1970a. An experimental analysis of the protection of *Amphiprion xanthurus* Cuvier & Valenciennes and some other anemone fishes from sea anemones. J. Exp. Mar. Biol. Ecol. 4: 134–149.

Mariscal, R. N. 1970b. A field and laboratory study of the symbiotic behavior of fishes and sea anemones from the tropical Indo-Pacific. Univ. Calif. Pub. Zool. 91: 1–43.

Mariscal, R. N. 1970c. The nature of the symbiosis between Indo-Pacific anemone fishes and sea anemones. Mar. Biol. 6: 58–65.

Mariscal, R. N. 1972. Behavior of symbiotic fishes and sea anemones. *In* Behavior of marine animals: current perspectives in research, Vol. 2, H. E. Winn and B. L. Olla (eds.). Plenum, New York, pp. 327–360.

Marler, P. and W. J. Hamilton III. 1966. Mechanisms of animal behavior. Wiley, New York, 771 pp.

Milinski, M. 1977a. Experiments on the selection by predators against spatial oddity of their prey. Z. Tierpsychol. 43: 311–325.

Milinski, M. 1977b. Do all members of a swarm suffer the same predation? Z. Tierpsychol. 45: 373–388.

Miller, A. C. 1982. Effects of differential fish grazing on the community structure of an intertidal reef flat at Enewetak [*sic*] Atoll, Marshall Islands. Pac. Sci. 36: 467–482.

Miller, R. J. 1978. Agonistic behavior in fishes and terrestrial vertebrates. *In* Contrasts in behavior: adaptations in the aquatic and terrestrial environments, E. S. Reese and F. J. Lighter (eds.). Wiley, New York, pp. 281–311.

Montgomery, W. L. 1980. The impact of non-selective grazing by the giant blue damselfish, *Microspathodon dorsalis*, on algal communities in the Gulf of California, Mexico. Bull. Mar. Sci. 30: 290–303.

Montgomery, W. L., T. Gerrodette, and L. D. Marshall. 1980. Effects of grazing by the yellowtail surgeonfish, *Prionurus punctatus*, on algal communities in the Gulf of California, Mexico. Bull. Mar. Sci. 30: 901–908.

Morrow, J. E. Jr. 1948. Schooling behavior in fishes. Quart. Rev. Biol. 23: 27–38.

Moyer, J. T. and A. Nakazono. 1978. Protandrous hermaphroditism in six species of the anemonefish genus *Amphiprion* in Japan. Jap. J. Ichthyol. 25: 101–106.

Mueller, H. C. 1971. Oddity and specific searching image more important than conspicuousness in prey selection. Nature 233: 345–346.

Myers, J. P., P. G. Connors, and F. A. Pitelka. 1979. Territory size in wintering sanderlings: the effects of prey abundance and intruder density. Auk 96: 551–561.

Myers, J. P., P. G. Conners, and F. A. Pitelka. 1981. Optimal territory size and the sanderling: compromises in a variable environment. *In* Foraging behavior: ecological, ethological and psychological approaches, A. C. Kamil and T. D. Sargent (eds.). Garland STPM Press, New York, pp. 135–158.

Myrberg, A. A., B. D. Brahy, and A. R. Emery. 1967. Field observations on reproduction of the damselfish, *Chromis multilineata* (Pomacentridae), with additional notes on general behavior. Copeia 1967: 819–827.

Myrberg, A. A. Jr. and R. E. Thresher. 1974. Interspecific aggression and its relevance to the concept of territoriality in reef fishes. Am. Zool. 14: 81–96.

Neill, J. St. S. R. and J. M. Cullen. 1974. Experiments on whether schooling by their prey affects the hunting behaviour of cephalopods and fish predators. J. Zool. (London) 172: 349–369.

Newman, E. 1876. Mr. Saville Kent's lecture, at the Society of Arts, on 'The aquarium: construction and management.' Zoologist 11(2nd Ser.): 4853–4858.

Noble, G. K. 1939. The role of dominance in the social life of birds. Auk 56: 263–273.

Norman, M. D. and G. P. Jones. 1984. Determinants of territory size in the pomacentrid reef fish, *Parma victoriae*. Oecologia 61: 60–69.

Nursall, J. R. 1974. Character displacement and fish behavior, especially in coral reef communities. Am. Zool. 14: 1099–1118.

Nursall, J. R. 1977. Territoriality in redlip blennies (*Ophioblennius atlanticus*—Pisces: Blenniidae). J. Zool. (London) 182: 205–223.

Ogden, J. C. and P. R. Ehrlich. 1977. The behavior of heterotypic resting schools of juvenile grunts (Pomadasyidae). Mar. Biol. 42: 273–280.

Olla, B. L. and C. Samet. 1974. Fish-to-fish attraction and the facilitation of feeding behavior as mediated by visual stimuli in striped mullet, *Mugil cephalus*. J. Fish. Res. Board Can. 31: 1621–1630.

Olson, F. C. W. 1964. The survival value of fish schooling. J. Conseil Int. Explor. Mer 29: 115–116.

Olst, J. C. van and J. R. Hunter. 1970. Some aspects of the organization of fish schools. J. Fish. Res. Board Can. 27: 1225–1238.

Owen-Smith, N. 1977. On territoriality in ungulates and an evolutionary model. Quart. Rev. Biol. 52: 1–38.

Parr, A. E. 1927. A contribution to the theoretical analysis of the schooling behavior of fishes. Occas. Pap. Bingham Oceanogr. Collect. (1): 1–32.

Partridge, B. L. 1981. Lateral line function and the internal dynamics of fish schools. *In* Hearing and sound communication in fishes, W. N. Tavolga, A. N. Popper, and R. R. Fay (eds.). Springer-Verlag, New York, pp. 515–522.

Partridge, B. L. 1982. Rigid definitions of schooling behaviour are inadequate. Anim. Behav. 30: 298–299.

Partridge, B. L., J. Johansson, and J. Kalish. 1983. The structure of schools of giant bluefin tuna in Cape Cod Bay. Environ. Biol. Fish. 9: 253–262.

Pitcher, T. J. 1973. The three-dimensional structure of schools in the minnow *Phoxinus phoxinus* (L.). Anim. Behav. 21: 673–686.

Pitcher, T. 1979. Sensory information and the organization of behaviour in a shoaling cyprinid fish. Anim. Behav. 27: 126–149.

Pitcher, T. J. 1983. Heuristic definitions of fish schooling behaviour. Anim. Behav. 31: 611–613.

Pitcher, T. J., B. L. Partridge, and C. S. Wardle. 1976. A blind fish can school. Science 194: 963–965.

Pitelka, F. A. 1959. Numbers, breeding schedule, and territoriality in pectoral sandpipers of northern Alaska. Condor 61: 233–264.

Policansky, D. 1982. Sex change in plants and animals. Ann. Rev. Ecol. Syst. 13: 471–495.

Potts, D. C. 1977. Suppression of coral populations by filamentous algae within damselfish territories. J. Exp. Mar. Biol. Ecol. 28: 207–216.

Potts, G. W. 1970. The schooling ethology of *Lutianus monostigma* (Pisces) in the shallow reef environment of Aldabra. J. Zool. (London) 161: 223–235.

Radakov, D. V. 1973. Schooling in the ecology of fish. Wiley, New York, 173 pp.

Randall, J. E. 1961. Overgrazing of algae by herbivorous marine fishes. Ecology 42: 812.

Risk, M. J. and P. W. Sammarco. 1982. Bioerosion of corals and the influence of damselfish territoriality: a preliminary study. Oecologia 52: 376–380.

Robertson, D. R. 1972. Social control of sex reversal in a coral reef fish. Science 197: 1007–1009.

Robertson, D. R. 1973. Field observations on the reproductive behaviour of a pomacentrid fish, *Acanthochromis polyacanthus*. Z. Tierpsychol. 32: 319–324.

Robertson, D. R. and B. Lassig. 1980. Spatial distribution patterns and coexistence of a group of territorial damselfishes from the Great Barrier Reef. Bull. Mar. Sci. 30: 187–203.

Robertson, D. R. and R. R. Warner. 1978. Sexual patterns in the labroid fishes of the western Caribbean, II: The parrotfishes (Scaridae). Smithsonian Contrib. Zool. (255): 1–26.

Sadovy, Y. 1985. Field analysis of the dominance hierarchy of the bicolor damselfish *Stegastes partitus* (Poey) (Pisces: Pomacentridae). *In* The ecology of coral reefs, Vol. 3, No. 1, M. L. Reaka (ed.). Symposia Series for Undersea Research, NOAA's Undersea Research Program, U.S. Department of Commerce, Washington, pp. 129–137.

Sale, P. F. 1971. Extremely limited home range in a coral reef fish, *Dascyllus aruanus* (Pisces; Pomacentridae). Copeia 1971: 324–327.

Sale, P. F. 1975. Patterns of use of space in a guild of territorial reef fishes. Mar. Biol. 29: 89–97.

Sale, P. F. 1978. Reef fishes and other vertebrates: a comparison of social structures. *In* Contrasts in behavior: adaptations in the aquatic and terrestrial environments, E. S. Reese and F. J. Lighter (eds.). Wiley, New York, pp. 313–346.

Sammarco, P. W. and A. H. Williams. 1982. Damselfish territoriality: influence on *Diadema* distribution and implications for coral community structure. Mar. Ecol. Prog. Ser. 8: 53–59.

Sargent, R. C. and G. E. Wagenbach. 1975. Cleaning behavior of the shrimp, *Periclimenes anthophilus* Holthuis and Eibl-Eibesfeldt (Crustacea: Decapoda: Natantia). Bull. Mar. Sci. 25: 466–472.

Schlichter, D. 1967. Zur Klärung der "Anemonen-Fisch-Symbiose." Naturwissenshaften 54: 569.

Schlichter, D. 1968a. Das Zusammenleben von Riffanemonen und Anemonenfischen. Z. Tierpsychol. 25: 933–954. [English summary]

Schlichter, D. 1968b. Der Nesselschutz der Anemonenfische. Vehr. Dt. Zool. Ges. 32: 327–333.

Schlichter, D. 1970. Chemischer Nachweis der Übernahme anemoneneigener Schutzstoffe durch Anemonenfische. Naturwissenschaften 57: 312–313.

Schlichter, D. 1972. Chemische Tarnung. Die stoffliche Grundlage der Anpassung von Anemonenfischen an Riffanemonen. Mar. Biol. 12: 137–150. [English summary]

Schlichter, D. 1975. Produktion oder Übernahme von Schutzstoffen als Ursache des Nesselschutzes von Anemonenfischen? J. Exp. Mar. Biol. Ecol. 20: 49–61. [English summary]

Schlichter, D. 1976. Macromolecular mimicry: substances released by sea anemones and their role in the protection of anemone fishes. *In* Coelenterate ecology and behavior, G. O. Mackie (ed.). Plenum, New York, pp. 433–441.

Schmitt, R. J. and S. W. Strand. 1982. Cooperative foraging by yellowtail, *Seriola lalandei* (Carangidae) on two species of fish prey. Copeia 1982: 714–717.

Schoener, T. W. 1971. Theory of feeding strategies. Ann. Rev. Ecol. Syst. 2: 369–404.

Seghers, B. H. 1974. Schooling behavior in the guppy (*Poecilia reticulata*): an evolutionary response to predation. Evolution 28: 486–489.

Seghers, B. H. 1981. Facultative schooling behavior in the spottail shiner (*Notropis hudsonius*): possible costs and benefits. Environ. Biol. Fish. 6: 21–24.

Sette, O. E. 1950. Biology of the Atlantic mackerel (*Scomber scombrus*) of North America. Part II: Migration and habits. Fish. Bull. (U.S. FWS) 51: 251–358.

Shaw, E. 1961. Minimal light intensity and the dispersal of schooling fish. Bull. Inst. Océanogr., Monaco (1213): 1–8.

Shaw, E. 1969. The duration of schooling among fish separated and those not separated by barriers. Am. Mus. Nov. (2373): 1–13.

Shaw, E. 1970. Schooling in fishes: critique and review. *In* The Development and evolution of behavior: essays in memory of T. C. Schneirla; L. R. Aronson, E. Tobach, D. S. Lehrmann, and J. S. Rosenblatt (eds.). Freeman, San Francisco, pp. 452–480.

Shlaifer, A. 1942. The schooling behavior of mackerel: a preliminary experimental analysis. Zoologica (N.Y.) 27: 75–80 + 1 plate.

Simon, C. A. 1975. The influence of food abundance on territory size in the iguanid lizard *Sceloporus jarrovi*. Ecology 56: 993–998.

Spooner, G. M. 1931. Some observations on schooling in fish. J. Mar. Biol. Assoc. U.K. 17: 421–448.

Spotte, S., R. W. Heard, P. M. Bubucis, R. R. Manstan, and J. A. McLelland. 1991. Pattern and coloration of *Periclimenes rathbunae* from the Turks and Caicos Islands, with comments on host associations in other anemone shrimps of the West Indies and Bermuda. Gulf Res. Rpt. 8: 301–311.

Springer, S. 1957. Some observations on the behavior of schools of fishes in the Gulf of Mexico and adjacent waters. Ecology 38: 166–171.

Starck, W. A. II and W. P. Davis. 1966. Night habits of fishes of Alligator Reef, Florida. Ichthyologica 38: 313–356.

Stevenson, R. A. 1963. Behavior of the pomacentrid reef fish *Dascyllus albisella* Gill in relation to the anemone *Marcanthia cookei*. Copeia 1963: 612–614.

Stimson, J. 1973. The role of the territory in the ecology of the intertidal limpet *Lottia gigantea* (Gray). Ecology 54: 1020–1030.

Symons, P. E. K. 1971. Spacing and density in schooling threespine stickleback (*Gasterosteus aculeatus*) and mummichog (*Fundulus heteroclitus*). J. Fish. Res. Board Can. 28: 999–1004.

Taitt, M. J. 1981. The effect of extra food on small rodent populations: I. Deermice (*Peromyscus maniculatus*). J. Anim. Ecol. 50: 111–124

Taitt, M. J. and C. J. Krebs. 1981. The effect of extra food on small rodent populations: II. Voles (*Microtus townsendii*). J. Anim. Ecol. 50: 125–137.

Thresher, R. E. 1976. Field analysis of the territorialty of the threespot damselfish, *Eupomacentrus planifrons* (Pomacentridae). Copeia 1976: 266–276.

Turner, C. H. and E. E. Ebert. 1962. The nesting of *Chromis punctipinnis* (Cooper) and a description of their eggs and larvae. Calif. Fish and Game 48: 243–248.

Tyler, J. C. and J. E. Böhlke. 1972. Records of sponge-dwelling fishes, primarily of the Caribbean. Bull. Mar. Sci. 22: 601–642.

Verwey, J. 1930. Coral reef studies. I. The symbiosis between damselfishes and sea anemones in Batavia Bay. Treubia 12: 305–366 + 2 figs.

Vine, I. 1971. Risk of visual detection and pursuit by a predator and the selective advantage of flocking behaviour. J. Theor. Biol. 30: 405–422.

Vine, I. 1973. Detection of prey flocks by predators. J. Theor. Biol. 40: 207–210.

Vine, P. J. 1974. Effects of algal grazing and aggressive behaviour of the fishes *Pomacentrus lividus* and *Acanthurus sohal* on coral-reef ecology. Mar. Biol. 24: 131–136.

Wanders, J. B. W. 1977. The role of benthic algae in the shallow reef of Curacao (Netherlands Antilles) III: The significance of grazing. Aquat. Bot. 3: 357–390.

Warner, R. R. 1975. The adaptive significance of sequential hermaphroditism in animals. Am. Nat. 109: 61–82.

Warner, R. R. 1984. Mating behavior and hermaphroditism in coral reef fishes. Am. Sci. 72: 128–136.

Warner, R. R. and D. R. Robertson. 1978. Sexual patterns in the labroid fishes of the western Caribbean, I: The wrasses (Labridae). Smithsonian Contrib. Zool. (254): 1–27.

Weihs, D. 1973. Hydromechanics of fish schooling. Nature 241: 290–291.

Weihs, D. 1975. Some hydrodynamical aspects of fish schooling. *In* Swimming and flying in nature, Vol 2, Y-T. Wu, C. J. Brokaw, and C. Brennan (eds.). Plenum, New York, pp. 703–718.

Williams, A. H. 1978. Ecology of threespot damselfish: social organization, age structure, and population stability. J. Exp. Mar. Biol. Ecol. 34: 197–213.

Williams, G. C. 1964. Measurement of consociation among fishes and comments on the evolution of schooling. Mich. State Univ. Pub. Mus. 2: 349–383.

Willis, E. O. 1967. The behavior of bicolored antbirds. Univ. Calif. Pub. Zool. 79: 1–132.

Wilson, E. O. 1975. Sociobiology: the new synthesis. Belknap/Harvard University Press, Cambridge, 697 pp.

Wolf, L. L. 1970. The impact of seasonal flowering on the biology of some tropical hummingbirds. Condor 72: 1–14.

Woolf, V. 1967. The sun and the fish. *In* Collected essays, Vol. 4. Harcourt Brace and World, New York, pp. 178–183.

Wright, R. 1985. Destination: point omega. The Sciences 25(3): 7–9.

Wurtsbaugh, W. and H. Li. 1985. Diel migrations of a zooplanktivorous fish (*Menidia beryllina*) in relation to the distribution of its prey in a large eutrophic lake. Limnol. Oceanogr. 30: 565–576.

Youngbluth, M. J. 1968. Aspects of the ecology and ethology of the cleaning fish, *Labroides phthirophagus* Randall. Z. Tierpsychol. 25: 915–932.

Zuyev, G. V. and V. V. Belyayev. 1970. An experimental study of the swimming of fish in groups as exemplified by the horse mackerel *Trachurus mediterraneus ponticus* Aleev. J. [Prob.] Ichthyol. 10: 545–549.

Chapter 7

Abrams, P. A. 1984. Recruitment, lotteries, and coexistence in coral reef fish. Am. Nat. 123: 44–55.

Alevizon, W. S. and M. G. Brooks. 1975. The comparative structure of two western Atlantic reef-fish assemblages. Bull. Mar. Sci. 25: 482–490.

Anderson, G. V. R., A. H. Ehrlich, P. R. Ehrlich, J. D. Roughgarden, B. C. Russell, and F. H. Talbot. 1981. The community structure of coral reef fishes. Am. Nat. 117: 476–495.

Ayal, Y. and U. N. Safriel. 1982. Species diversity of the coral reef—a note on the role of predation and of adjacent habitats. Bull. Mar. Sci. 32: 787–790.

Bagnis, R., R. Galzin, and J. Bennett. 1979. Poissons de Takapoto. J. Soc. Océan. 35: 69–74. [English summary]

Bardach, J. E. 1959. The summer standing crop of fish on a shallow Bermuda reef. Limnol. Oceanogr. 4: 77–85.

Bell, J. D. and R. Galzin. 1984. Influence of live coral cover on coral-reef fish communities. Mar. Ecol. Prog. Ser. 15: 265–274.

Bohnsack, J. A. 1979. The ecology of reef fishes on isolated coral heads: an experimental approach with emphasis on island biogeographic theory. Dissertation, University of Miami, 296 pp.

Bouchon, C., J. Jaubert, L Montaggioni, and M. Pichon. 1981. Morphology and evolution of the coral reefs of the Jordanian coast of the Gulf of Aqaba (Red Sea). *In* Proceedings of the fourth international coral reef symposium, Vol. 1, E. D. Gomez, C. E. Birkeland, R. W. Buddemeier, R. E. Johannes, J. A. Marsh Jr., and R. T. Tsuda (eds.). Marine Sciences Center, University of the Philippines, Quezon City, pp. 559–565.

Bouchon-Navaro, Y. and M. L. Harmelin-Vivien. 1981. Quantitative distribution of herbivorous reef fishes in the Gulf of Aqaba (Red Sea). Mar. Biol. 63: 79–86.

Bradbury, R. H. and G. B. Goeden. 1974. The partitioning of the reef slope environment by resident fishes. Proceedings of the second international coral reef symposium, Vol. 1. Great Barrier Reef Committee, Brisbane, pp. 167–178.

Brock, R. E., C. Lewis, and R. C. Wass. 1979. Stability and structure of a fish community on a coral patch reef in Hawaii. Mar. Biol. 54: 281–292.

Burke, R. B. 1982. Reconnaissance study of the geomorphology and benthic communities of the outer barrier reef platform, Belize. Smithsonian Contrib. Mar. Sci. (12): 509–526.

Chave, E. H. and D. B. Eckert. 1974. Ecological aspects of the distributions of fishes at Fanning Island. Pac. Sci. 28: 297–317.

Clarke, R. D. 1977. Habitat distribution and species diversity of chaetodontid and pomacentrid fishes near Bimini, Bahamas. Mar. Biol. 40: 277–289.

Clarke, T. A., A. O. Flechsig, and R. W. Grigg. 1967. Ecological studies during Project Sealab II. Science 157: 1381–1389.

Cohen, D. M. 1970. How many recent fishes are there? Proc. Calif. Acad. Sci. 38: 341–345.

Colin, P. L. 1974. Observation and collection of deep-reef fishes off the coasts of Jamaica and British Honduras (Belize). Mar. Biol. 24: 29–38.

Collette, B. B. and F. H. Talbot. 1972. Activity patterns of coral reef fishes with emphasis on nocturnal-diurnal changeover. Nat. Hist. Mus. Los Angeles County Sci. Bull. 14: 98–124.

Colton, D. E. and W. S. Alevizon. 1981. Diurnal variability in a fish assemblage of a Bahamian coral reef. Environ. Biol. Fish. 6: 341–345.

Doherty, P. J. 1982. Some effects of density on the juveniles of two species of tropical, territorial damselfish. J. Exp. Mar. Biol. Ecol. 65: 249–261.

Doherty, P. J. 1983. Tropical territorial damselfishes: density limitation limited by aggression or recruitment? Ecology 64: 176–190.

Dustan, P. 1985. Community structure of reef-building corals in the Florida Keys: Carysfort Reef, Key Largo and Long Key Reef, Dry Tortugas. Atoll Res. Bull. (288): 1–17 + 16 figs.

Edwards, A. and J. Rosewell. 1981. Vertical zonation of coral reef fishes in the Sudanese Red Sea. Hydrobiologia 79: 21–31.

Fourmanoir, P. 1963. Distribution ecologique des poissons de recifs coralliens et d'herbiers de la cote quest de Madagascar. Terre Vie 110: 81–100.

Galzin, R. 1987. Structure of fish communities of French Polynesian coral reefs. I. Spatial scales. Mar. Ecol. Prog. Ser. 41: 129–136.

Galzin, R. and P. Legendre. 1987. The fish communities of a coral reef transect. Pac. Sci. 41: 158–165.

Gascon, D. and R. A. Miller. 1982. Space utilization in a community of temperate reef fishes inhabiting small experimental artificial reefs. Can. J. Zool. 60: 798–806.

Gilbert, C. R. 1973. Characteristics of the western Atlantic reef-fish fauna. Quart. J. Fla. Acad. Sci. 35: 130–144.

Gladfelter, W. B. and E. H. Gladfelter. 1978. Fish community structure as a function of habitat structure on West Indian patch reefs. Revista Biol. Trop. 26(Suppl. 1): 65–84.

Gladfelter, W. B., J. C. Ogden, and E. H. Gladfelter. 1980. Similarity and diversity among coral reef fish communities: a comparison between tropical western Atlantic (Virgin Islands) and tropical central Pacific (Marshall Islands) patch reefs. Ecology 61: 1156–1168.

Glynn, P. W. 1973. Aspects of the ecology of coral reefs in the western Atlantic region. *In* Biology and geology of coral reefs, Vol. II: Biology 1, O. A. Jones and R. Endean (eds.). Academic Press, New York, pp. 271–324.

Goldman, B. and F. H. Talbot. 1976. Aspects of the ecology of coral reef fishes. *In* Biology and geology of coral reefs, Vol. III: Biology 2, O. A. Jones and R. Endean (eds.). Academic Press, New York, pp. 125–154.

Goreau, T. F. 1959. The ecology of Jamaican coral reefs. I. Species composition and zonation. Ecology 40: 67–90.

Gosline, W. A. 1965. Vertical zonation of inshore fishes in the upper water layers of the Hawaiian Islands. Ecology 46: 823–831.

Greenfield, D. W. and T. A. Greenfield. 1982. Habitat and resource partitioning between two species of *Acanthemblemaria* (Pisces: Chaenopsidae), with comments on the chaos hypothesis. Smithsonian Contrib. Mar. Sci. (12): 499–507.

Grovhoug, J. G. and R. S. Henderson. 1978. Distribution of inshore fishes at Canton Atoll. Atoll Res. Bull. (221): 99–157.

Gundermann, N. and D. Popper. 1975. Some aspects of recolonization of coral rocks in Eilat (Gulf of Aqaba) by fish populations after poisoning. Mar. Biol. 33: 109–117.

Gushima, K. and Y. Murakami. 1976. The reef fish fauna of Kuchierabu, offshore island of southern Japan. J. Fac. Fish. Anim. Husb., Hiroshima Univ. 15: 47–56.

Gushima, K. and Y. Murakami. 1979. Mixed-species groupings in reef fishes of Kuchierabu Island. J. Fac. Appl. Biol. Sci., Hiroshima Univ. 18: 103–121. [Japanese with English summary and legends]

Hiatt, R. W. and D. W. Strasburg. 1960. Ecological relationships of the fish fauna on coral reefs of the Marshall Islands. Ecol. Monogr. 30: 65–127.

Hobson, E. S. 1965. Diurnal-nocturnal activity of some inshore fishes in the Gulf of California. Copeia 1965: 291–302.

Hobson, E. S. 1968. Predatory behavior of some shore fishes in the Gulf of California. Res. Rpt. 73, U.S. Fish and Wildlife Service, Washington, 92 pp.

Hobson, E. S. 1972. Activity of Hawaiian reef fishes during the evening and morning transitions between daylight and darkness. Fish. Bull. (NOAA) 70: 715–740.

Hobson, E. S. 1974. Feeding relationships of teleostean fishes on coral reefs in Kona, Hawaii. Fish. Bull. (NOAA) 72: 915–1031.

Hobson, E. S. 1984. The structure of reef fish communities in the Hawaiian archipelago. *In* Proceedings of the second symposium on resource investigations in the northwestern Hawaiian Islands, Vol. 1, R. C. Grigg and K. Y. Tanoue (eds.). UNIHI-Seagrant-MR-84-01, University of Hawaii, Honolulu, pp. 101–122.

Hopley, D. 1982. The geomorphology of the Great Barrier Reef: quaternary development of coral reefs. Wiley, New York, 449 pp.

Jones, G. P. 1984. Population ecology of the temperate reef fish *Pseudolabrus celidotus* Bloch & Schneider (Pisces: Labridae). II. Factors influencing adult density. J. Exp. Mar. Biol. Ecol. 75: 277-303.

Jones. J. A. 1977. Morphology and development of southeastern Florida patch reefs. *In* Proceedings of the third international coral reef symposium, Vol. 2. Rosentiel School of Marine and Atmospheric Science, University of Miami, pp. 231-235.

Jones, O. A. and R. Endean (eds.). 1973. Biology and geology of coral reefs, Vol. I: Geology 1. Academic Press, New York, 410 pp. + map.

Jones, R. S. and J. A. Chase. 1975. Community structure and distribution of fishes in an enclosed high island lagoon in Guam. Micronesica 11: 127–148.

Jones, R. S. and M. J. Thompson. 1978. Comparison of Florida reef fish assemblages using a rapid visual technique. Bull. Mar. Sci. 28: 159–172.

Kaufman, L. S. and J. P. Ebersole. 1984. Microtopography and the organization of two assemblages of coral reef fishes in the West Indies. J. Exp. Mar. Biol. Ecol. 78: 253–268.

Kinsey, D. W. 1981. The Pacific/Atlantic reef growth controversy. *In* Proceedings of the fourth international coral reef symposium, Vol. 1, E. D. Gomez, C. E. Birkeland, R. W. Buddemeier, R. E. Johannes, J. A. Marsh Jr., and R. T. Tsuda (eds.). Marine Sciences Center, University of the Philippines, Quezon City, pp. 493–498.

Kulesza, G. 1975. Comment on "niche, habitat, and ecotope." Am. Nat. 109: 476–479.

Ladd, H. S. 1977. Types of coral reefs and their distribution. *In* Biology and geology of coral reefs, Vol. IV: Geology 2, O. A. Jones and R. Endean (eds.). Academic Press, New York, pp. 1–19.

Lang, J. C. 1974. Biological zonation at the base of a reef. Am. Sci. 62: 272–281.

Luckhurst, B. E. and K. Luckhurst. 1978a. Analysis of the influence of substrate variables on coral reef fish communities. Mar. Biol. 49: 317–323.

Luckhurst, B. E. and K. Luckhurst. 1978b. Diurnal space utilization in coral reef fish communities. Mar. Biol. 49: 325–332.

Luckhurst, B. E. and K. Luckhurst. 1978c. Nocturnal observations of coral reef fishes along depth gradients. Can. J. Zool. 56: 155–158.

MacArthur, R. H. and E. O. Wilson. 1967. The theory of island biogeography. Princeton University Press, Princeton, 203 pp.

Macpherson, E. 1981. Resource partitioning in a Mediterranean demersal fish community. Mar. Ecol. Prog. Ser 4: 183–193.

Marliave, J. B. 1985. Color polymorphism in sibling *Amphiprion*: is the reef-fish lottery rigged? Environ. Biol. Fish. 12: 63–68.

Maxwell, W. G. H. and J. P. Swinchatt. 1970. Great Barrier Reef: regional variation in a terrigenous-carbonate province. Geol. Soc. Am. Bull. 81: 691–724.

Miller, G. C. and W. J. Richards. 1980. Reef fish habitat, faunal assemblages, and factors determining distributions in the South Atlantic Bight. Proc. Gulf Carib. Fish. Inst. 1979: 114–130.

Milliman, J. D. 1973. Caribbean coral reefs. *In* Biology and geology of coral reefs, Vol. I: Geology 1, O. A. Jones and R. Endean (eds.). Academic Press, New York, pp. 1–50.

Mochek, A. D. and A. Silva. 1975. The group behavior of fishes of the genus *Haemulon*. J. [Prob.] Ichthyol. 15: 790–793.

Mochek, A. D. and E. Valdes-Munoz. 1984/1985. Behavior of fishes in a coastal tropical community. J. [Prob.] Ichthyol. 24: 147–155.

Molles, M. C. Jr. 1978. Fish species diversity on model and natural reef patches: experimental insular biogeography. Ecol. Monogr. 48: 289–305.

Newell, N. D. 1971. An outline history of tropical organic reefs. Am. Mus. Nov. (2465): 1–37.

Odum, H. T. and E. P. Odum. 1955. Trophic structure and productivity of a windward coral reef community on Eniwetok Atoll. Ecol. Monogr. 25: 291–320.

Ogden, J. C. and J. P. Ebersole. 1981. Scale and community structure of coral reef fishes: a long-term study of a large artificial reef. Mar. Ecol. Prog. Ser. 4: 97–103.

Pianka, E. R. 1978. Evolutionary ecology, 2nd ed. Harper and Row, New York, 397 pp.

Pichon, M. 1981. Dynamic aspects of coral reef benthic structures and zonation. *In* Proceedings of the fourth international coral reef symposium, Vol. 1, E. D. Gomez, C. E. Birkeland, R. W. Buddemeier, R. E. Johannes, J. A. Marsh Jr., and R. T. Tsuda (eds.). Marine Sciences Center, University of the Philippines, Quezon City, pp. 581–594.

Potts, G. W. 1980. The littoral fishes of Little Cayman (West Indies). Atoll Res. Bull. (241): 43–52.

Randall, J. E. 1963. An analysis of the fish populations of artificial and natural reefs in the Virgin Islands. Carib. J. Sci. 3: 31–47.

Risk, M. J. 1972. Fish diversity on a coral reef in the Virgin Islands. Atoll Res. Bull. (153): 1–4 + 2 pp.

Robertson, D. R. 1973. Field observations on the reproductive behavior of a pomacentrid fish, *Acanthochromis polyacanthus*. Z. Tierpsychol. 32: 319–324.

Robertson, D. R., S. G. Hoffman, and J. M. Sheldon. 1981. Availability of space for the territorial Caribbean damselfish *Eupomacentrus planifrons*. Ecology 62: 1162–1169.

Robertson, D. R. and B. Lassig. 1980. Spatial distribution patterns and coexistence of a group of territorial damselfishes from the Great Barrier Reef. Bull. Mar. Sci. 30: 187–203.

Robins, C. R. 1971. Distributional patterns of fishes from coastal and shelf waters of the tropical western Atlantic. *In* Symposium to investigate resources of the Caribbean and adjacent regions. Fish. Rpt. 71.2, Food and Agriculture Organization of the United Nations, Rome, pp. 249–255.

Root, R. B. 1967. The niche-exploitation pattern of the blue-grey gnatcatcher. Ecol. Monogr. 37: 317–350.

Ross, S. T. 1986. Resource partitioning in fish assemblages: a review of field studies. Copeia 1986: 352–388.

Roughgarden, J. 1974. Species packing and the competition function with illustrations from coral reef fish. Theor. Pop. Biol. 5: 163–186.

Russ, G. R. 1989. Distribution and abundance of coral reef fishes in the Sumilon Island Reserve, central Philippines, after nine years of protection from fishing. Asian Mar. Biol. 6: 59–71.

Sale, P. F. 1974. Mechanisms of coexistence in a guild of territorial fishes at Heron Island. *In* Proceedings of the second international coral reef symposium, Vol. 1. Great Barrier Reef Committee, Brisbane, pp. 193–206.

Sale, P. F. 1975. Patterns of use of space in a guild of territorial reef fishes. Mar. Biol. 29: 89–97.

Sale, P. F. 1977. Maintenance of high diversity in coral reef fish communities. Am. Nat. 111: 337–359.

Sale, P. F. 1978a. Coexistence of coral reef fishes—a lottery for living space. Environ. Biol. Fish. 3: 85–102.

Sale, P. F. 1978b. Chance patterns of demographic change in populations of territorial fish in coral rubble patches at Heron Reef. J. Exp. Mar. Biol. Ecol. 34: 233–243.

Sale, P. F. 1980. The ecology of fishes on coral reefs. Oceanogr. Mar. Biol. Ann. Rev. 18: 367–421.

Sale, P. F. and W. A. Douglas. 1984. Temporal variability in the community structure of fish on coral patch reefs and the relation of community structure to reef structure. Ecology 65: 409–422.

Sale, P. F. and R. Dybdahl. 1975. Determinants of community structure for coral reef fishes in an experimental habitat. Ecology 56: 1343–1355.

Sale, P. F. and R. Dybdahl. 1978. Determinants of community structure for coral reef fishes in isolated coral heads at lagoonal and reef slope sites. Oecologia 34: 57–74.

Sale, P. F. and D. McB. Williams. 1982. Community structure of coral reef fishes: are the patterns more than those expected by change? Am. Nat. 120: 121–127.

Shinn, E. 1963. Spur and groove formation on the Florida Reef Tract. J. Sed. Petrol. 33: 291–303.

Shinn, E. A., J. H. Hudson, D. M. Robbin, and B. Lidz. 1981. Spurs and grooves revisited: construction versus erosion Looe Key Reef, Florida. *In* Proceedings of the fourth international coral reef symposium, Vol. 1, E. D. Gomez, C. E. Birkeland, R. W. Buddemeier, R. E. Johannes, J. A. Marsh Jr., and R. T. Tsuda (eds.). Marine Sciences Center, University of the Philippines, Quezon City, pp. 475–483.

Shulman, M. J. 1983. Species richness and community predictability in coral reef fish faunas. Ecology 64: 1308–1311.

Shulman, M. J., J. C. Ogden, J. P. Ebersole, W. N. McFarland, S. L. Miller, and N. G. Wolf. 1983. Priority effects in the recruitment of juvenile coral reef fishes. Ecology 64: 1508–1513.

Smith, C. L. 1978. Coral reef fish communities: a compromise view. Environ. Biol. Fish. 3: 109–128.

Smith, C. L. and J. C. Tyler. 1972. Space resource sharing in a coral reef community. Nat. Hist. Mus. Los Angeles County Sci. Bull. 14: 125–170.

Smith, C. L. and J. C. Tyler. 1973a. Direct observations of resource sharing in coral reef fish. Helgoländer Meeresunters. 24: 264–275.

Smith, C. L. and J. C. Tyler. 1973b. Population ecology of a Bahamian suprabenthic shore fish assemblage. Am. Mus. Nov. (2528): 1–38.

Smith, C. L. and J. C. Tyler. 1975. Succession and stability in fish communities of dome-shaped patch reefs in the West Indies. Am. Mus. Nov. (2572): 1–18.

Smith, G. B. 1979. Relationship of eastern Gulf of Mexico reef-fish communities to the species equilibrium theory of insular biogeography. J. Biogeogr. 6: 49–61.

Smith, S. V., K. E. Chave, and D. T. O. Kam (eds.). 1973. Atlas of Kaneohe Bay: a reef ecosystem under stress. UNIHI-Seagrant-TR-72-01, University of Hawaii, Honolulu, 128 pp.

Starck, W. A. II. 1968. A list of fishes of Alligator Reef, Florida with comments on the nature of the Florida reef fish fauna. Undersea Biol. 1: 4–40.

Starck, W. A. II and W. P. Davis. 1966. Night habits of fishes of Alligator Reef, Florida. Ichthyologica 38: 313–356.

Stearn, C. W., T. P. Scoffin, and W. Martindale. 1977. Calcium carbonate budget of a fringing reef on the west coast of Barbados. Part I—zonation and productivity. Bull. Mar. Sci. 27: 479–510.

Steers, J. A. and D. R. Stoddart. 1977. The origin of fringing reefs, barrier reefs, and atolls. *In* Biology and geology of coral reefs, Vol. IV: Geology 2, O. A. Jones and R. Endean (eds.). Academic Press, New York, pp. 21–57.

Stephens, J. S. Jr., R. K. Johnson, G. S. Key, and J. E. McCosker. 1970. The comparative ecology of three sympatric species of California blennies of the genus *Hypsoblennius* Gill (Teleostomi, Blenniidae). Ecol. Monogr. 40: 213–233.

Stoddart, D. R. 1973. Coral reefs of the Indian Ocean. *In* Biology and geology of coral reefs, Vol. I: Geology 1, O. A. Jones and R. Endean (eds.). Academic Press, New York, pp. 51–92.

Talbot, F. H. 1965. A description of the coral structure of Tutia Reef (Tanganyika Territory, East Africa) and its fish fauna. Proc. Zool. Soc. London 145: 431–470.

Talbot, F. H. and B. Goldman. 1972. A preliminary report on the diversity and feeding relationships of the reef fishes of One Tree Island, Great Barrier Reef system. *In* Proceedings of the symposium on corals and coral reefs, C. Mukundan and C. S. G. Pillai (eds.). Marine Biological Association of India, Cochin, pp. 425–443.

Talbot, F. H., B. C. Russell, and G. R. V. Anderson. 1978. Coral reef fish communities: unstable, high-diversity systems? Ecol. Monogr. 48: 425–440.

Terborgh, J. 1985. Habitat selection in Amazonian birds. *In* Habitat selection in birds, M. L. Cody (ed.). Academic Press, Orlando, pp. 311–338.

Thomson, D. A. and C. E. Lehner. 1976. Resilience of a rocky intertidal fish community in a physically unstable environment. J. Exp. Mar. Biol. Ecol. 22: 1–29.

Thresher, R. E. 1983. Habitat effects on reproductive success in the coral reef fish, *Acanthochromis polyacanthus* (Pomacentridae). Ecology 64: 1184–1199.

Tracey, J. I. Jr., P. E. Cloud Jr., and K. O. Emery. 1955. Conspicuous features of organic reefs. Atoll Res. Bull. (146): 1–3 + 2 figs.

Tyler, J. C. 1971. Habitat preferences of the fishes that dwell in shrub corals on the Great Barrier Reef. Proc. Acad. Nat. Sci. Philadelphia 123: 1–26.

Tyler, J. C. and J. E. Böhlke. 1972. Records of sponge-dwelling fishes, primarily of the Caribbean. Bull. Mar. Sci. 22: 601–642.

Udvardy, M. F. D. 1959. Notes on the ecological concepts of habitat, biotope and niche. Ecology 40: 725–728.

Victor, B. C. 1983. Recruitment and population dynamics of a coral reef fish. Science 219: 419–420.

Vivien, M. 1973. Ecology of the fishes of the inner coral reef flat in Tulear (Madagascar). J. Mar. Biol. Assoc. India 15: 20–45.

Whittaker, R. H., S. A. Levin, and R. B. Root. 1973. Niche, habitat, and ecotope. Am. Nat. 107: 321–338.

Whittaker, R. H., S. A. Levin, and R. B. Root. 1975. On the reasons for distinguishing "niche, habitat, and ecotope." Am. Nat. 109: 479–482.

Williams, D. McB. 1980. Dynamics of the pomacentrid community on small patch reefs in One Tree Lagoon (Great Barrier Reef). Bull. Mar. Sci. 30: 159–170.

Williams, D. McB. 1982. Patterns in the distribution of fish communities across the central Great Barrier Reef. Coral Reefs 1: 35–43.

Chapter 8

Ackman, R. G. 1964. Structural homogeneity in unsaturated fatty acids of marine lipids. A review. J. Fish. Res. Board Can. 21: 247–264.

Adron, J. W., A. Blair, and C. B. Cowey. 1973. Rearing of plaice (*Pleuronectes platessa*) larvae to metamorphosis using an aritifical diet. Fish. Bull. (NOAA) 73: 353–357.

Adron, J. W., D. Knox, C. B. Cowey, and G. T. Ball. 1978. Studies on the nutrition of marine flatfish. The pyridoxine requirement of turbot (*Scophthalmus maximus*). Br. J. Nutr. 40: 261–268.

Albritton, E. C. (ed.). 1954. Standard values in nutrition and metabolism. Saunders, Philadelphia, 380 pp.

Alliot, E., A. Pastoureaud, and J. Nedelec. 1979. Etude de l'apport calorique et du rapport calorico-azote dans l'alimentation du bar, *Dicentrarchus labrax*. Influence sur la croissance et la composition corporelle. *In* Finfish nutrition and fishfeed technology, Vol. 1, J. E. Halver and K. Tiews (eds.). Satz und Druck: H. Heenemann GmbH, Berlin, pp. 241–251. [English summary]

Anderson, D. W. and N. Smith. 1983. The culture of larval foods at the Oceanic Institute, Waimanalo, Hawaii. *In* Handbook of mariculture, Vol. 1, J. P. McVey (ed.). CRC Press, Boca Raton, pp. 97–101.

Anderson, M. A. and F. M. Morel. 1980. Uptake of Fe(II) by a diatom in oxic culture medium. Mar. Biol. Lett. 1: 263–268.

Anderson, M. A. and F. M. M. Morel. 1982. The influence of aqueous iron chemistry on the uptake of iron by the coastal diatom *Thalassiosira weissflogii*. Limnol. Oceanogr. 27: 789–813.

Andrews, J. W. and T. Murai. 1975. Studies on the vitamin C requirements of channel catfish (*Ictalurus punctatus*). J. Nutr. 105: 557–561.

Andrews, J. W. and T. Murai. 1978. Dietary niacin requirements of channel catfish. J. Nutr. 108: 1508–1511.

Andrews, J. W. and T. Murai. 1979. Pyridoxine requirements of channel catfish. J. Nutr. 109: 533–537.

Andrews, J. W., T. Murai, and C. Campbell. 1973. Effects of dietary calcium and phosphorus on growth, food conversion, bone ash and hematocrit levels of catfish. J. Nutr. 103: 766–771.

Andrews, J. W., T. Murai, and J. W. Page. 1980. Effects of dietary cholecalciferol and ergocalciferol on catfish. Aquaculture 19: 49–54.

Andrews, J. W. and J. W. Page. 1974. Growth factors in the fishmeal component of catfish diets. J. Nutr. 104: 1091–1096.

Andrews, J. W., J. W. Page, and M. W. Murray. 1977. Supplementation of a semipurified casein diet for catfish with free amino acids and gelatin. J. Nutr. 107: 1153–1156.

Aoe, H., I. Masuda, I. Abe, T. Saito, T. Toyoda, and S. Kitamura. 1970. Nutrition of protein in young carp. I. Nutritive value of free amino acids. Bull. Jap. Soc. Sci. Fish. 36: 407–413.

Aoe, H. and I. Masuda. 1967. Water-soluble vitamin requirements of carp—II. Requirements for *p*-aminobenzoic acid and inositol. Bull. Jap. Soc. Sci. Fish. 33: 674–680.

Aoe, H., I. Masuda, T. Saito, and A. Komo. 1967a. Water-soluble vitamin requirements of carp—I. Requirement for vitamin B_2. Bull. Jap. Soc. Sci. Fish. 33: 355–360.

Aoe, H., I. Masuda, and T. Takada. 1967b. Water-soluble vitamin requirements of carp—III. Requirement for niacin. Bull. Jap. Soc. Sci. Fish. 33: 681–685.

APHA et al. (American Public Health Association, American Water Works Association, and Water Pollution Control Federation). 1985. Standard methods for the examination of water and wastewater, 16th ed. American Public Health Association, Washington, 1268 pp.

Austin, B. and D. A. Allen. 1981/1982. Microbiology of laboratory-hatched brine shrimp (*Artemia*). Aquaculture 26: 369–383.

Bagshaw, J. C. 1979. Molecular biology of *Artemia* development: progress and prospects. *In* Biochemistry of *Artemia* development, J. C. Bagshaw and A. H. Warner (eds.). Department of Biochemistry, Wayne State University School of Medicine, Detroit, pp. 1–4.

Barbay, J. R., H. B. Bradford Jr., and N. C. Roberts. 1984. The occurrence of halophilic vibrios in Louisiana coastal waters. *In* Vibrios in the environment, R. R. Colwell (ed.). Wiley, New York, pp. 511–520.

Barber, R. T. 1973. Organic ligands and phytoplankton growth in nutrient-rich seawater. *In* Trace metals and metal-organic interactions in natural waters, P. Singer (ed.). Ann Arbor Science, Ann Arbor, pp. 321–338.

Barigozzi, C. 1980. Genus *Artemia*: problems of systematics. *In* The brine shrimp *Artemia*, Vol. 1, G. Persoone, P. Sorgeloos, O. Roels, and E. Jaspers (eds.). Universa Press, Wetteren, pp. 147–153.

Barnett, B. J., C. Y. Cho, and S. J. Slinger. 1979. The requirement for vitamin D_3 and relative biopotency of dietary vitamin D_2 and D_3 in rainbow trout. J. Nutr. 109: xxiii. [Abstract]

Bauernfeind, J. C. 1976. Canthaxanthin: a pigmenter for salmonids. Prog. Fish-cult. 38: 180–183.

Beck, A. D. 1979a. Recommended procedures for comparative evaluation experiments of artificial and live diets for marine finfish. *In* Finfish nutrition and fishfeed technology, Vol. 2, J. E. Halver and K. Tiews (eds.). Satz und Druck: H. Heenemann GmbH, Berlin, pp. 555–559.

Beck, A. D. 1979b. Laboratory culture and feeding of the Atlantic silverside, *Menidia menidia*. *In* Cultivation of fish fry and its live food, E. Styczynska-Jurewicz, T. Backiel, E. Jaspers, and G. Persoone (eds.). Spec. Pub. No. 4, European Mariculture Society, Bredene, pp. 63–85.

Beck, A. D. and D. A. Bengston. 1979. Evaluating effects of live and artificial diets on survival and growth of the marine atherinid fish Atlantic silverside, *Menidia menidia*. *In* Finfish nutrition and fishfeed technology, Vol. 1, J. E. Halver and K. Tiews (eds.). Satz und Druck: H. Heenemann GmbH, Berlin, pp. 479–489.

Beck, A. and K. L. Simpson. 1979. Panel discussion: live food versus artificial feed in fish fry. *In* Cultivation of fish fry and its live food, E. Styczynska-Jurewicz, T. Backiel, E. Jaspers, and G. Persoone (eds.). Spec. Pub. No. 4, European Mariculture Society, Bredene, pp. 517–527.

Belcher, H. and E. Swale. 1982. Culturing algae: a guide for schools and colleges. Institute of Terrestrial Ecology, Cambridge (U.K.), 25 pp.

Bell, J. G., C. B. Cowey, J. W. Adron, and B. J. S. Pirie. 1987. Some effects of selenium deficiency on enzyme activities and indices of tissue peroxidation in Atlantic salmon parr (*Salmo salar*). Aquaculture 65: 43–54.

Bengston, D. A., A. D. Beck, and H. A. Poston. 1978. Comparative effects of live and artificial diets on growth and survival of juvenile Atlantic silverside, *Menidia menidia*. Proc. World Maricult. Soc. 9: 159–173.

Benijts, F., E. van Voorden, and P. Sorgeloos. 1976. Changes in the biochemical composition of the early larval stages of the brine shrimp, *Artemia salina* L. *In* 10th European symposium on marine biology, Vol. 1, G. Persoone and E. Jaspers (eds.). Universa Press, Wetteren, pp. 1–9.

Bidwell, J. P. and S. Spotte. 1985. Artificial seawaters: formulas and methods. Jones and Bartlett, Boston, 349 pp.

Bogatova, I. B. and Z. I. Erofeyeva. 1985. Incubation of dormant *Artemia salina* eggs without preliminary stimulation of hatching. Hydrobiol. J. 21: 65–68.

Boone, E. and L. G. M. Baas-Becking. 1931. Salt effects on eggs and nauplii of *Artemia salina* L. J. Gen. Physiol. 14: 753–763.

Bowen, S. T. 1962. The genetics of *Artemia salina*. I. The reproductive cycle. Biol. Bull. 122: 25–32.

Bowen, S. T., M. L. Davis, S. R. Fenster, and G. A. Lindwall. 1980. Sibling species of *Artemia*. *In* The brine shrimp *Artemia*, Vol. 1, G. Persoone, P. Sorgeloos, O. Roels, and E. Jaspers (eds.). Universa Press, Wetteren, pp. 155–167.

Bowen, S. T., E. A. Fogarino, K. N. Hitchner, G. L. Dana, V. H. S. Chow, M. R. Buoncristiani, and J. R. Carl. 1985. Ecological isolation in *Artemia*: population differences in tolerance of anion concentrations. J. Crust. Biol. 5: 106–129.

Brand, L. E. and R. R. L. Guillard. 1981. The effects of continuous light and light intensity on the reproduction rates of twenty-two species of marine phytoplankton. J. Exp. Mar. Biol. Ecol. 50: 119–132.

Brett, J. R. and T. D. D. Groves. 1979. Physiological energetics. *In* Fish physiology, 2nd ed., Vol. 8, W. S. Hoar, D. J. Randall, and J. R. Brett (eds.). Academic Press, New York, pp. 279–352.

Brewer, P. G. and J. C. Goldman. 1976. Alkalinity changes generated by phytoplankton growth. Limnol. Oceanogr. 21: 108–117.

Brown, C. H. 1950. A review of the methods available for the determination of the types of forces stabilizing structural proteins in animals. J. Microscop. Sci. 91: 331–339.

Bruggeman, E., M. Baeza-Mesa, E. Bossuyt, and P. Sorgeloos. 1979. Improvements in the decapsulation of *Artemia* cysts. *In* Cultivation of fish fry and its live food, E. Styczynska-Jurewicz, T. Backiel, E. Jaspers, and G. Persoone (eds.). Spec. Pub. No. 4, European Mariculture Society, Bredene, pp. 309–315.

Bruggeman, E., P. Sorgeloos, and P. Vanhaecke. 1980. Improvements in the decapsulation technique of *Artemia* cysts. *In* The brine shrimp *Artemia*, Vol. 3, G. Persoone, P. Sorgeloos, O. Roels, and E. Jaspers (eds.). Universa Press, Wettern, pp. 261–269.

Buck, J. D. and S. Spotte. 1986. The occurrence of potentially pathogenic vibrios in marine mammals. Mar. Mam. Sci. 2: 319–324.

Buck. J. D., S. Spotte, and J. J. Gadbaw Jr. 1984. Bacteriology of the teeth from a great white shark: potential medical implications for shark bite victims. J. Clin. Microbiol. 20: 849–851.

Campton, D. E. and C. A. Busack. 1989. Simple procedure for decapsulating and hatching cysts of brine shrimp (*Artemia* spp.). Prog. Fish-cult. 51: 176–179.

Castell, J. D. 1979. Review of lipid requirements of finfish. *In* Finfish nutrition and fishfeed technology, Vol. 1, J. E. Halver and K. Tiews (eds.). Satz und Druck: H. Heenemann GmbH, Berlin, pp. 59–84.

Chen, L. C-M., T. Edelstein, and J. McLachlan. 1969. *Bonnemaisonia hamifera* Hariot in nature and in culture. J. Phycol. 5: 211–220.

Chotiyaputta, C. and K. Hirayama. 1978. Food selectivity of the rotifer *Brachionus plicatilis* feeding on phytoplankton. Mar. Biol. 45: 105–111.

Choubert, G. and T. Storebakken. 1989. Dose response to astaxanthin and canthaxanthin pigmentation of rainbow trout fed various dietary carotenoid concentrations. Aquaculture 81: 69–77.

Claus, C., F. Benijts, and P. Soregloos, 1977. Comparative study of different geographical strains of the brine shrimp, *Artemia salina*. *In* Fundamental and applied research on the brine shrimp *Artemia salina* (L.), E. Jaspers (ed.). Spec. Pub. No. 2, European Mariculture Society, Bredene, pp. 95–105.

Claus, C., F. Benijts, and G. Vandeputte. 1979. The biochemical composition of the larvae of two strains of *Artemia salina* (L.) reared on two different algal foods. J. Exp. Mar. Biol. Ecol. 36: 171–183.

Colesante, R. T. 1989. Improved survival of walleye fry during the first 30 days of intensive rearing on brine shrimp and zooplankton. Prog. Fish-cult. 51: 109–111.

Colwell, R. R., P. A. West, D. Maneval, E. F. Remmers, E. L. Elliot, and N. E. Carlson. 1984. Ecology of pathogenic vibrios in Chesapeake Bay. *In* Vibrios in the environment, R. R. Colwell (ed.). Wiley, New York, pp. 367–387.

Cowey, C. B., J. W. Adron, D. Knox, and G. T. Ball. 1975. Studies on the nutrition of marine flatfish. The thiamin requirement of turbot (*Scophthalmus maximus*). Br. J. Nutr. 34: 383–390.

Cowey, C. B., J. W. Adron, J. M. Owen, and R. J. Roberts. 1976. The effect of different dietary oils on tissue fatty acids and tissue pathology in turbot *Scophthalmus maximus*. Comp. Biochem. Physiol. 53B: 399–403.

Cowey, C. B. and J. R. Sargent. 1977. Lipid nutrition in fish. Comp. Biochem. Physiol. 57B: 269–273.

Cowey, C. B. and J. R. Sargent. 1979. Nutrition. *In* Fish physiology, 2nd ed., Vol. 8, W. S. Hoar, D. J. Randall, and J. R. Brett (eds.). Academic Press, New York, pp. 1–69.

Croghan, P. C. 1958a. The survival of *Artemia salina* (L.) in various media. J. Exp. Biol. 35: 213–218.

Croghan, P. C. 1958b. The osmotic and ionic regulation of *Artemia salina* (L.). J. Exp. Biol. 35: 219–233.

Csengeri, I., F. Majoros, J. Oláh, and T. Farkas. 1979. Investigations on the essential fatty acid requirement of carp (*Cyprinus carpio*). *In* Finfish nutrition and fishfeed technology, Vol. 1, J. E. Halver and K. Tiews (eds.). Satz und Druck: H. Heenemann GmbH, Berlin, pp. 157–172.

Dabrowski, K. and J. Glogowski. 1977. Studies on the role of exogenous proteolytic enzymes in digestion processes in fish. Hydrobiologia 54: 129–134.

D'Agostino, A. 1980. The vital requirements of *Artemia*: physiology and nutrition. *In* The brine shrimp *Artemia*, Vol. 2, G. Persoone, P. Sorgeloos, O. Roels, and E. Jaspers (eds.). Universa Press, Wetteren, pp. 55–82.

Davey, E. W., M. J. Morgan, and S. J. Erickson. 1973. A biological measurement of the copper complexation capacity of seawater. Limnol. Oceanogr. 18: 993–997.

Dempster, R. P. 1953. The use of larval and adult brine shrimp in aquarium fish culture. Calif. Fish and Game 39: 355–364.

Droop, M. R. 1961. Some chemical considerations in the design of synthetic culture media for marine algae. Bot. Mar. 2: 231–246.

Dupree, H. K. 1966. Vitamins essential for growth of channel catfish (*Ictalurus punctatus*). Tech. Pap. 7, U.S. Fish and Wildlife Service, Washington, 12 pp.

Dupree, H. K. 1970. Dietary requirements of vitamin A acetate and beta-carotene. Resource Pub. 88, U.S. Fish and Wildlife Service, Washington, pp. 148–150.

Dupree, H. K. and J. E. Halver. 1970. Amino acids essential for the growth of channel catfish, *Ictalurus punctatus*. Trans. Am. Fish. Soc. 99: 90–92.

Ellis, J. N. 1979. The use of natural and synthetic carotenoids in the diet to color the flesh of salmonids. *In* Finfish nutrition and fishfeed technology, Vol. 2, J. E. Halver and K. Tiews (eds.). Satz und Druck: H. Heenemann GmbH, Berlin, pp. 353–364.

Elnabarawy, M. T. and A. N. Welter. 1984. A technique for the enumeration of unicellular algae. Bull. Environ. Contam. Toxicol. 32: 333–338.

Ehrlich, K. F., M-C. Cantin, and M. B. Rust. 1989. Growth and survival of larval and postlarval smallmouth bass fed a commercially prepared dry feed and/or *Artemia* nauplii. J. World Aquacult. Soc. 20: 1–6.

Fabregas, J., J. Abalde, B. Cabezas, and C. Herrero. 1989. Changes in protein, carbohydrates and gross energy in the marine microalga *Dunaliella tertiolecta* (Butcher) by nitrogen concentrations as nitrate, nitrite and urea. Aquacult. Eng'g. 8: 223–239.

Fey, M. and S. P. Meyers. 1980. Evaluation of carotenoid-fortified flake diets with the pearl gourami *Trichogaster leeri*. J. Aquaricult. 1: 15–19.

Flüchter, J. 1980. Review of the present knowledge of rearing whitefish (Coregonidae) larvae. Aquaculture 19: 191–208.

Fontaine, C. T. and D. B. Revera. 1980. The mass culture of the rotifer, *Brachionus plicatilis*, for use as foodstuff in aquaculture. Proc. World Maricult. Soc. 11: 211–218.

Foss, P., T. Storebakken, E. Austreng, and S. Liaaen-Jensen. 1987. Carotenoids in diets for salmonids. V. Pigmentation of rainbow trout and sea trout with astaxanthin and astaxanthin dipalmitate in comparison with canthaxanthin. Aquaculture 65: 293–305.

Foss, P., T. Storebakken, K. Schiedt, S. Liaaen-Jensen, E. Austreng, and K. Streiff. 1984. Carotenoids in diets for salmonids. I. Pigmentation of rainbow trout with the individual optical isomers of astaxanthin in comparison with canthaxanthin. Aquaculture 41: 213–226.

Fowler, L. G. and R. E. Burrows. 1971. The Abnernathy salmon diet. Prog. Fish-cult. 33: 67–75.

Fox, J. M. 1983. Intensive algal culture techniques. *In* Handbook of mariculture, Vol. 1, J. P. McVey (ed.). CRC Press, Boca Raton, pp. 15–41.

Fujii, M., H. Nakayama, and Y. Yone. 1976. Effect of ω3 fatty acids on growth, feed efficiency and fatty acid composition of red sea bream (*Chrysophrys major*). Rpt. Fish. Res. Lab., Kyushu Univ. (3): 65–86.

Fujita, S., T. Watanabe, and C. Kitajima. 1980. Nutritional quality of *Artemia* from different localities as a living feed for marine fish from the viewpoint of essential fatty acids. *In* The brine shrimp *Artemia*, Vol. 3, G. Persoone, P. Sorgeloos, O. Roels, and E. Jaspers (eds.). Universa Press, Wetteren, pp. 277–290.

Fujita, T., M. Satake, T. Watanabe, C. Kitajima, W. Miki, K. Yamaguchi, and S. Konosu. 1983. Pigmentation of cultured red sea bream with astaxanthin diester purified from krill oil. Bull. Jap. Soc. Sci. Fish. 49: 1855–1861.

Fukusho, K. and M. Okauchi. 1982. Strain and size of the rotifer, *Brachionus plicatilis*, being cultured in southeast Asian countries. Bull. Natl. Inst. Aquacult. 3: 107–109.

Furuichi, M. and Y. Yone. 1971. Studies on nutrition of red sea bream—IV Nutritive value of dietary carbohydrate. Rpt. Fish. Res. Lab., Kyushu Univ. (1): 75–81. [Japanese with English summary and legends]

Furuichi, M. and Y. Yone. 1980. Effect of dietary dextrin levels on the growth and feed efficiency, and chemical composition of liver and dorsal muscle, and the absorption of dietary protein and dextrin in fishes. Bull. Jap. Soc. Sci. Fish. 46: 225–229.

Gatesoupe, F-J. and P. Luquet. 1981. Practical diet for mass culture of the rotifer *Brachionus plicatilis*: application to larval rearing of sea bass, *Dicentrarchus labrax*. Aquaculture 22: 149–163.

Gatlin, D. M., E. H. Robinson, W. E. Poe, and R. P. Wilson. 1982. Phosphorus requirement of channel catfish. Fed. Proc. 41: 787. [Abstract]

Gatlin, D. M. and R. P. Wilson. 1984. Dietary selenium requirement of fingerling catfish. J. Nutr. 114: 627–633.

Gerking, S. D. 1971. Influence of rate of feeding and body weight on protein metabolism of bluegill sunfish. Physiol. Zool. 44: 9–19.

Giliberto, S. and A. Mazzola. 1981. Mass culture of *Brachionus plicatilis* with an integrated system of *Tetraselmis suecica* and *Saccharomyces cerevisiae*. J. World Maricult. Soc. 12: 61–62.

Gilmour, A., M. F. McCallum, and M. C. Allan. 1975. Antibiotic sensitivity of bacteria isolated from the canned eggs of the Californian brine shrimp (*Artemia salina*). Aquaculture 6: 221–231.

Goldberg, E. D. 1952. Iron assimilation by marine diatoms. Biol. Bull. 102: 243–248.

Goldblatt, M. J., D. E. Conklin, and W. D. Brown. 1979. Nutrient leaching from pelleted rations. *In* Finfish nutrition and fishfeed technology, Vol. 1, J. E. Halver and K. Tiews (eds.). Satz und Druck: H. Heenemann GmbH, Berlin, pp. 117–129.

Goldblatt, M. J., D. E. Conklin, and W. D. Brown. 1980. Nutrient leaching from coated crustacean rations. Aquaculture 19: 383–388.

Goldman, J. C. and P. G. Brewer. 1980. Effect of nitrogen source and growth rate on phytoplankton-mediated changes in alkalinity. Limnol. Oceanogr. 25: 352–357.

Goldman, J. C. and D. G. Peavey. 1979. Steady-state growth and chemical composition of the marine chlorophyte *Dunaliella tertiolecta* in nitrogen-limited continuous cultures. Appl. Environ. Microbiol. 38: 894–901.

Goldman, J. C., Y. Azov, C. B. Riley, and M. R. Dennett. 1982. The effect of pH in intensive microalgal cultures. I. Biomass regulation. J. Exp. Mar. Biol. Ecol. 57: 1–13.

Gozalbo, A. and F. Amat. 1988. Composición bioquímica de biomasas silvestres de *Artemia* (Crustacea, Branchiopoda, Anostraca). Inv. Pesq. 52: 375–385.

Grabner, M., W. Wieser, and R. Lackner. 1981/1982. The suitability of frozen and freeze-dried zooplankton as food for fish larvae: a biochemical test program. Aquaculture 26: 85–91.

Greig, R. A. and R. H. Gnaedinger. 1971. Occurrence of thiaminase in some common aquatic animals of the United States and Canada. Spec. Sci. Rpt.—Fish. No. 631, U.S. National Marine Fisheries Service, Seattle, 7 pp.

Gross, F. 1937. Notes on the culture of some marine plankton organisms. J. Mar. Biol. Assoc. U.K. (N.S). 21: 753–768.

Guillard, R. R. L. 1963. Organic sources of nitrogen for marine centric diatoms. *In*: Symposium on marine microbiology, C. H. Oppenheimer (ed.). Thomas, Springfield, pp. 93–104.

Guillard, R. R. L. 1973. Methods for microflagellates and nannoplankton. *In* Handbook of phycological methods: culture methods and growth measurements, J. R. Stein (ed.). Cambridge University Press, Cambridge, pp. 69–85.

Guillard, R. R. L. 1975. Culture of phytoplankton for feeding marine invertebrates. *In* Culture of marine invertebrate animals, W. L. Smith and M. H. Chanley (eds.). Plenum, New York, pp. 29–60.

Guillard, R. R. L. and J. H. Ryther. 1962. Studies of marine planktonic diatoms. I. *Cyclotella nana* Hustedt, and *Detonula confervacea* (Cleve) Gran. Can. J. Microbiol. 8: 229–239.

Hall, R. A., E. G. Zook, and G. M. Meaburn. 1978. National Marine Fisheries Service survey of trace elements in the fishery resource. NOAA Tech. Rpt. NMFS SSRF-721, U.S. National Marine Fisheries Service, Washington, 313 pp.

Halver, J. E. 1957. Nutrition of salmonoid fishes. III. Water soluble vitamin requirements of chinook salmon. J. Nutr. 62: 225–243.

Halver, J. E. 1985. Recent advances in vitamin nutrition and metabolism in fish. *In* Nutrition and feeding in fish, C. B. Cowey, A. M. Mackie, and J. G. Bell (eds.) Academic Press, London, pp. 415–429.

Halver, J. E. 1989. The vitamins. *In* Fish nutrition, 2nd ed., J. E. Halver (ed.). Academic Press, San Diego, pp. 32–109.

Halver, J. E., L. M. Ashley, and R. R. Smith. 1969. Ascorbic acid requirement of coho salmon and rainbow trout. Trans. Am. Fish. Soc. 98: 762–771.

Halver, J. E. and K. Tiews (eds.). 1979a. Finfish nutrition and fishfeed technology, Vol. 1. Satz und Druck: H. Heenemann GmbH, Berlin, 593 pp.

Halver, J. E. and K. Tiews (eds.). 1979b. Finfish nutrition and fishfeed technology, Vol. 2. Satz und Druck: H. Heenemann GmbH, Berlin, 622 pp.

Hardy, R. W. 1989. Diet preparation. *In* Fish nutrition, 2nd ed., J. E. Halver (ed.). Academic Press, San Diego, pp. 475–548.

Harris, L. E. 1984. Effects of a broodfish diet fortified with canthaxanthin on female fecundity and egg color. Aquaculture 43: 179–183.

Harrison, P. J., R. E. Waters, and F. J. R. Taylor. 1980. A broad spectrum artificial seawater medium for coastal and open ocean phytoplankton. J. Phycol. 16: 28–35.

Harvey, H. W. 1937. The supply of iron to diatoms. J. Mar. Biol. Assoc. U.K. 22: 205–219.

Hawley, G. G. 1977. The condensed chemical dictionary, 9th ed. Van Nostrand Reinhold, New York, 957 pp.

Heath, H. 1924. The external development of certain phyllopods. J. Morphol. 38: 453–483.

Henderson, R. J. and J. R. Sargent. 1985. Fatty acid metabolism in fish. *In* Nutrition and feeding in fish, C. B. Cowey, A. M. Mackie, and J. G. Bell (eds.). Academic Press, London, pp. 349–364.

Hiatt, R. W. and W. Strasburg. 1960. Ecological relationships of the fish fauna on coral reefs of the Marshall Islands. Ecol. Monogr. 30: 65–127.

Hilton, J. W., C-Y. Cho, and S. J. Slinger. 1978. Effect of graded levels of supplemental ascorbic acid in practical diets fed to rainbow trout (*Salmo gairdneri*). J. Fish. Res. Board Can. 35: 431–436.

Hinchcliffe, P. R. and J. P. Riley. 1972. The effect of diet on the component fatty-acid composition of *Artemia salina*. J. Mar. Biol. Assoc. U.K. 52: 203–211.

Hino, A. and R. Hirano. 1984. Relationship between body size of the rotifer *Brachionus plicatilis* and the minimum size of particles ingested. Bull. Jap. Soc. Sci. Fish. 50: 1139–1144.

Hino, A. and R. Hirano. 1988. Relationship between water chlorinity and bisexual reproduction rate in the rotifer *Brachionus plicatilis*. Nippon Suisan Gakkaishi 54: 1329–1332.

Hirata, H. 1974. An attempt to apply an experimental microcosm for the mass culture of marine rotifer, *Brachionus plicatilis* Müller. Mem. Fac. Fish., Kagoshima Univ. 23: 163–172.

Hirata, H. 1979. Rotifer culture in Japan. *In* Cultivation of fish fry and its live food, E. Styczynska-Jurewicz, T. Backiel, E. Jaspers, and G. Persoone (eds.). Spec. Pub. No. 4, European Mariculture Society, Bredene, pp. 361–375.

Hirayama, K. and T. Kusano. 1972. Fundamental studies on physiology of rotifer for its mass culture—II. Influence of water temperature on population growth of rotifer. Bull. Jap. Soc. Sci. Fish. 38: 1357–1363.

Hirayama, K. and K. Nakamura. 1976. Fundamental studies on the physiology of rotifers in mass culture—V. Dry *Chlorella* powder as a food for rotifers. Aquaculture 8: 301–307.

Hirayama, K. and S. Ogawa. 1972. Fundamental studies on physiology of rotifer for its mass culture—I. Filter feeding of rotifer. Bull. Jap. Soc. Sci. Fish. 38: 1207–1214.

Hirayama, K. and K. Watanabe. 1973. Fundamental studies on physiology of rotifer for its mass culture—IV. Nutritional effect of yeast on population growth of rotifer. Bull. Jap. Soc. Sci. Fish. 39: 1129–1133.

Hirayama, K., K. Watanabe, and T. Kusano. 1973. Fundamental studies on physiology of rotifer for its mass culture—III. Influence of phytoplankton density on population growth. Bull. Jap. Soc. Sci. Fish. 39: 1123–1127.

Hobson, E. S. 1974. Feeding relationships of teleostean fishes on coral reefs in Kona, Hawaii. Fish. Bull. (NOAA) 72: 915–1031.

Hoppe, H. A. and O. J. Schmid. 1969. Commercial products. *In* Marine algae: a survey of research and utilization, T. Levring, H. A. Hoppe, and O. J. Schmid (eds.). Cram, de Gruyter, Hamburg, pp. 288–368.

Hoshaw, R. W. and J. R. Rosowski. 1973. Methods for microscopic algae. *In* Handbook of phycological methods: culture methods and growth measurements, J. R. Stein (ed.). Cambridge University Press, Cambridge, pp. 53–68.

Howell, B. R. 1973. Marine fish culture in Britain VIII. A marine rotifer, *Brachionus plicatilis* Muller, and the larvae of the mussel, *Mytilus edulis* L., as foods for larval flatfish. J. Conseil Int. Explor. Mer 35: 1–6.

Hughes, S. G., G. L. Rumsey, and J. G. Nickum. 1981. Riboflavin requirement of fingerling rainbow trout. Prog. Fish-cult. 43: 167–172.

Ibrahim, A., C. Shimizu, and M. Kono. 1984. Pigmentation of cultured red sea bream *Chrysophrys major*, using astaxanthin from antarctic krill, *Euphausia superba*, and a mysid, *Neomysis* sp. Aquaculture 38: 45–57.

Inman, G. W. Jr. and J. D. Johnson. 1978. The effect of ammonia concentration on the chemistry of chlorinated sea water. *In* Water chlorination: environmental impact and health effects, Vol. 2, R. L. Jolley, H. Gorchev, and D. H. Hamilton Jr. (eds.). Ann Arbor Science, Ann Arbor, pp. 235–252.

Inoue, T., K. L. Simpson, Y. Tanaka, and M. Sameshima. 1988. Condensed astaxanthin of pigmented oil from crayfish carapace and its feeding experiment. Nippon Suisan Gakkaishi 54: 103–106.

Ito, T. 1960. On the culture of mixohaline rotifer *Brachionus plicatilis* O. F. Müller in the sea water. Rpt. Fac. Fish., Pref. Univ. Mie 3: 708–740.

Iwahashi, M. and H. Wakui. 1976. Intensification of color of fancy carp with diet. Bull. Jap. Soc. Sci. Fish. 42: 1339–1344. [Japanese with English summary and legends]

Jackson, G. A. and J. J. Morgan. 1978. Trace metal-chelator interactions and phytoplankton growth in seawater media: theoretical analysis and comparison with reported observations. Limnol. Oceanogr. 23: 268–284.

Jenné, F. 1960. Story of the brine shrimp. Aquar. J. 31: 331–335.

Johnson, D. A. 1980. Evaluation of various diets for optimal growth and survival of selected life stages of *Artemia*. *In* The brine shrimp *Artemia*, Vol. 3, G. Persoone, P. Sorgeloos, O. Roels, and E. Jaspers (eds.). Universa Press, Wetteren, pp. 185–192.

Johnston, R. 1964. Sea water, the natural medium of phytoplankton. II. Trace metals and chelation, and general discussion. J. Mar. Biol. Assoc. U.K. 44: 87–109.

Jones, G. E. 1967. Precipitates from autoclaved seawater. Limnol. Oceanogr. 12: 165–167.

Kahn, M. M. T. and A. E. Martell. 1967a. Metal ion and metal chelate catalyzed oxidation of ascorbic acid by molecular oxygen. I. Cupric and ferric ion catalyzed oxidation. J. Am. Chem. Soc. 89: 4176–4185.

Kahn, M. M. T. and A. E. Martell. 1967b. Metal ion and metal chelate catalyzed oxidation of ascorbic acid by molecular oxygen. II. Cupric and ferric chelate catalyzed oxidation. J. Am. Chem. Soc. 89: 7104–7111.

Kanazawa, A. 1985. Essential fatty acid and lipid requirement of fish. *In* Nutrition and feeding in fish, C. B. Cowey, A. M. Mackie, and J. G. Bell (eds.). Academic Press, London, pp. 281–298.

Katayama, T., N. Ikeda, and K. Harada. 1965. Carotenoids in seabream, *Chrysophrys major* Temminch and Schlegel—I. Bull. Jap. Soc. Sci. Fish. 31: 947–952. [Japanese with English summary and legends]

Katayama, T., Y. Kunisaki, M. Shimaya, K. L. Simpson, and C. O. Chichester. 1973. The biosynthesis of astaxanthin—XIV. The conversion of labelled β-carotene-15,15′-$^3H_2$ into astaxanthin in the crab, *Portunus trituberculatus*. Comp. Biochem. Physiol. 46B: 269–272.

Katsuyama, M., T. Komori, and T. Matsuno. 1987. Metabolism of three stereoisomers of astaxanthin in the fish, rainbow trout and tilapia. Comp. Biochem. Physiol. 86B: 1–5.

Kellems, R. O. and R. O Sinnhuber. 1982. Performance of rainbow trout fed gelatin-bound diets of fish protein concentrate of casein containing 25 to 45 percent herring oil. Prog. Fish-cult. 44: 131–134.

Kester, D. R., I. W. Duedall, D. N. Connors, and R. M. Pytkowicz. 1967. Preparation of artificial seawater. Limnol. Oceanogr. 12: 176–179.

Ketola, H. G. 1975. Requirement of Atlantic salmon for dietary phosphorus. Trans. Am. Fish. Soc. 104: 548–551.

Ketola, H. G. 1976. Choline metabolism and nutritional requirements of lake trout (*Salvelinus namaycush*). J. Anim. Sci. 43: 474–477.

Ketola, H. G. 1982. Amino acid nutrition of fishes: requirements and supplementation of diets. Comp. Biochem. Physiol. 73B: 17–24.

Kinne, O. 1976. Cultivation of animals: research cultivation. *In*: Marine ecology: a comprehensive, integrated treatise on life in oceans and coastal waters, Vol. 3, Part 2, O. Kinne (ed). Wiley, Chichester, pp. 579–1293. [Brine shrimp are discussed on pp. 743–761]

Kirk, R. G. 1972. Anomalous growth of young plaice (*Pleuronectes platessa* L.) on diets of live, frozen and freeze-dried *Lumbricillus rivalis* Levensen. Aquaculture 1: 35–37.

Kissil, G. W., C. B. Cowey, J. W. Adron, and R. H. Richards. 1981. Pyridoxine requirements of the gilthead bream, *Sparus aurata*. Aquaculture 23: 243–255.

Kuo, H. C., T. C. Lee, T. Kamata, and K. L. Simpson. 1976. Red crab processing waste as a carotenoid source for rainbow trout. Mar. Reprint No. 61, Food and Resource Chemistry, NOAA/Sea Grant, University of Rhode Island, Narragansett, 6 pp.

Lavens, P. and P. Sorgeloos. 1984. Controlled production of *Artemia* cysts under standard conditions in a recirculating culture system. Aquacult. Eng'g. 3: 221–235.

Leger, C. 1985. Digestion, absorption and transport of lipids. *In* Nutrition and feeding in fish, C. B. Cowey, A. M. Mackie, and J. G. Bell (eds.). Academic Press, London, pp. 299–331.

Léger, P., D. A. Bengston, K. L. Simpson, and P. Sorgeloos. 1986. The use and nutritional value of *Artemia* as a food source. Oceanogr. Mar. Biol. Ann. Rev. 24: 521–623.

Léger, P., E. Naessens-Foucquaert, and P. Sorgeloos. 1987. International study on *Artemia* XXXV. Techniques to manipulate the fatty acid profile in *Artemia* nauplii, and the effect on its nutritional effectiveness for the marine crustacean *Mysidopsis bahia* (M.). *In Artemia* research and its applications, Vol. 3, P. Sorgeloos, D. A. Bengston, W. Decleir, and E. Jaspers (eds.). Universa Press, Wetteren, pp. 411–424.

Liaaen-Jensen, S. 1978. Marine carotenoids. *In* Marine natural products: chemical and biological perspectives, Vol. 2, P. J. Scheuer (ed.). Academic Press, New York, pp. 1–73.

Liao, I-C., H-M. Su, and J-H. Lin. 1983. Larval foods for penaeid prawns. *In* Handbook of mariculture, Vol. 1, J. P. McVey (ed.). CRC Press, Boca Raton, pp. 43–69.

Lim, C. and R. D. Lovell. 1978. Pathology of the vitamin C deficiency syndrome in channel catfish (*Ictalurus punctatus*). J. Nutr. 108: 1137–1146.

Limsuwan, T. and R. T. Lovell. 1981. Intestinal synthesis and absorption of vitamin B-12 in channel catfish. J. Nutr. 111: 2125–2132.

Lincoln, E. P., T. W. Hall, and B. Koopman. 1983. Zooplankton control in mass algal cultures. Aquaculture 32: 331–337.

Linden, A. van der, R. Blust, and W. Decleir. 1985. The influence of light on the hatching of *Artemia* cysts (Anostraca: Branchiopoda: Crustacea). J. Exp. Mar. Biol. Ecol. 92: 207–214.

Linden, A. van der, R. Blust, A. J. van Laere, and W. Decleir. 1988. Light-induced release of *Artemia* dried embryos from diapause: analysis of metabolic status. J. Exp. Zool. 247: 131–138.

Linder, H. J. 1960. Studies on the fresh water fairy shrimp *Chirocephalopsis bundyi* (Forbes). II. Histochemistry of egg-shell formation. J. Morphol. 107: 259–284.

Liou, S-R. and K. L. Simpson. 1989. Lipid stability in the drying of *Artemia* by several methods. Aquacult. Eng'g. 8: 293–305.

Lovell, R. T. 1978. Dietary phosphorus requirement of channel catfish. Trans. Am. Fish. Soc. 107: 617–621.

Lovern, J. A. 1964. The lipids of marine organisms. Oceanogr. Mar. Biol. Ann. Rev. 2: 169–191.

Lubzens, E. and G. Minkoff. 1988. Influence of the age of algae fed to rotifers (*Brachionus plicatilis* O. F. Müller) on the expression of mixis in their progenies. Oecologia 75: 430–435.

Lubzens, E., G. Minkoff, and S. Marom. 1985. Salinity dependence of sexual and asexual reproduction in the rotifer *Brachionus plicatilis*. Mar. Biol. 85: 123–126.

Mahajan, C. L. and N. K. Agrawal. 1980. Nutritional requirement of ascorbic acid by Indian major carp, *Cirrhina mrigala*. Aquaculture 19: 37–48.

Manahan, S. E. and M. J. Smith. 1973. Copper micronutrient requirement for algae. Environ. Sci. Technol. 7: 829–833.

Marliave, J. B. 1989. Live first-food and the health of cultured chum salmon fry (*Oncorhynchus keta*). Bull. Inst. Océanogr., Monaco, Num. spéc. 5: 247–254.

Matsuno, T., M. Katsuyama, T. Maoka, T. Hirono, and T. Komori. 1985. Reductive metabolic pathways of carotenoids in fish (3S,3S′)-astaxanthin to tunaxanthin A, B and C. Comp. Biochem. Physiol. 80B: 779–789.

Matty, A. J. and P. Smith. 1978. Evaluation of a yeast, a bacterium and an alga as a protein source for rainbow trout. I. Effect of protein level on growth, gross conversion efficiency and protein conversion efficiency. Aquaculture 14: 235–246.

McLachlan, J. 1959. The growth of unicellular algae in artificial and enriched seawater media. Can. J. Microbiol. 5: 9–15.

McLachlan, J. 1964. Some considerations of the growth of marine algae in artificial media. Can. J. Microbiol. 10: 769–782.

McLachlan, J. 1973. Growth media—marine. *In* Handbook of phycological methods: culture methods and growth measurements, J. R. Stein (ed.). Cambridge University Press, Cambridge, pp. 25–51.

Meyers, S. P., D. P. Butler, and G. F. Sirine. 1971. Encapsulation: a new approach to larval feeding. Am. Fish Farm. 2(8): 15–20.

Meyers, S. P. and H-M. Chen. 1982. Astaxanthin and its role in fish culture. *In* Proceedings of the warmwater fish culture workshop, R. R. Stickney and S. P. Meyers (eds.). Spec. Pub. No. 3, World Mariculture Society, Baton Rouge, pp. 153–165.

Meyers, S. P., J. E. Rutledge, and S. C. Sonu. 1973. Variability in proximate analysis of different processed shrimp meals. Feedstuffs 45(47): 34.

Meyers, S. P. and P. Thibodeaux. 1983. Crawfish wastes and extracted astaxanthin as pigmentation sources in aquatic diets. J. Aquaricult. Aquat. Sci. 3: 64–70.

Minkoff, G., E. Lubzens, and E. Meragelman. 1984/1985. Improving asexual reproduction rates in a rotifer (*Brachionus plicatilis*) by salinity manipulations. Israel J. Zool. 33: 195–203.

Morel, F. M. M., J. G. Reuter, D. M. Anderson, and R. R. L. Guillard. 1979. Aquil: a chemically defined phytoplankton culture medium for trace metal studies. J. Phycol. 15: 135–141.

Mori, T., K. Makabe, K. Yamaguchi, S. Konosu, and S. Arai. 1989. Comparison between krill astaxanthin diester and synthesized free astaxanthin supplemented to diets in their absorption and deposition by juvenile coho salmon (*Oncorhynchus kisutch*). Comp. Biochem. Physiol. 93B: 255–258.

Morris, J. E. 1971. Hydration, its reversibility, and the beginning of development in the brine shrimp *Artemia salina*. Comp. Biochem. Physiol. 39A: 843–857.

Murai, T. and J. W. Andrews. 1974. Interactions of dietary α-tocopherol, oxidized menhaden oil and ethoxyquin on channel catfish (*Ictalurus punctatus*). J. Nutr. 104: 1416–1431.

Murai, T. and J. W. Andrews. 1978a. Thiamin requirement of channel catfish fingerlings. J. Nutr. 108: 176–180.

Murai, T. and J. W. Andrews. 1978b. Riboflavin requirement of channel catfish fingerlings. J. Nutr. 108: 1512–1517.

Murai, T. and J. W. Andrews. 1979. Pantothenic acid requirements of channel catfish fingerlings. J. Nutr. 109: 1140–1142.

Murai, T., J. W. Andrews, and R. G. Smith Jr. 1981. Effects of dietary copper on channel catfish. Aquaculture 22: 353–357.

Nagai, M. and S. Ikeda. 1971a. Carbohydrate metabolism in fish—I. Effects of starvation and dietary composition on the blood glucose level and the hepatopancreative glycogen and lipid contents in carp. Bull. Jap. Soc. Sci. Fish. 37: 404–409.

Nagai, M. and S. Ikeda. 1971b. Carbohydrate metabolism in fish—II. Effect of dietary composition on metabolism of glucose-6-^{14}C in carp. Bull. Jap. Soc. Sci. Fish. 37: 410–414.

Nagai, M. and S. Ikeda. 1971c. Carbohydrate metabolism in fish—III. Effect of dietary composition on metabolism of glucose-U-^{14}C and glutamate-U-^{14}C in carp. Bull. Jap. Soc. Sci. Fish. 38: 137–143.

Nash, C. E. 1973. Automated mass-production of *Artemia salina* nauplii for hatcheries. Aquaculture 2: 289–298.

NAS/NRC (National Academy of Sciences/National Research Council). 1981. Nutrient requirements of coldwater fishes. National Academy Press, Washington, 63 pp.

NAS/NRC (National Academy of Sciences/National Research Council). 1983. Nutrient requirements of warmwater fishes and shellfish. National Academy Press, Washington, 102 pp.

Neurath, H. 1984. Evolution of proteolytic enzymes. Science 224: 350–357.

Nielsen, E. S. and S. Wium-Andersen. 1970. Copper ions as poison in the sea and in freshwater. Mar. Biol. 6: 93–97.

Nose, T., S. Arai, D-L. Lee, and Y. Hashimoto. 1974. A note on amino acids essential for growth of young carp. Bull. Jap. Soc. Sci. Fish. 40: 903–908.

Ogino, C. 1965. B vitamins requirements [*sic*] of carp, *Cyprinus carpio*—I. Deficiency symptoms and requirement of vitamin B_6. Bull. Jap. Soc. Sci. Fish. 31: 546–551. [Japanese with English summary and legends]

Ogino, C. 1967. B vitamins requirements [*sic*] of carp—II. Requirements for riboflavin and pantothenic acid. Bull. Jap. Soc. Sci. Fish. 33: 351–354. [Japanese with English summary and legends]

Ogino, C. and J. Y. Chiou. 1976. Mineral requirements in fish. II Magnesium requirements of carp. Bull. Jap. Soc. Sci. Fish. 42: 71–75.

Ogino, C. and H. Takeda. 1976. Mineral requirements in fish—III Calcium and phosphorus requirements in carp. Bull. Jap. Soc. Sci. Fish. 42: 793–799.

Ogino, C. and H. Takeda. 1978. Requirements of rainbow trout for dietary calcium and phosphorus. Bull. Jap. Soc. Sci. Fish. 44: 1019–1022. [Japanese with English summary and legends]

Ogino, C., F. Takeshima, and J. Y. Chiou. 1978. Requirement of rainbow trout for dietary magnesium. Bull. Jap. Soc. Sci. Fish. 44: 1105–1108. [Japanese with English summary and legends]

Ogino, C., N. Uki, T. Watanabe, Z. Iida, and K. Ando. 1970a. B vitamin requirements of carp—IV. Requirement for choline. Bull. Jap. Soc. Sci. Fish. 36: 1140–1146.

Ogino, C., T. Watanabe, J. Kakino, N. Iwanaga, and M. Mizuno. 1970b. B vitamin requirements of carp—III. Requirement for biotin. Bull. Jap. Soc. Sci. Fish. 36: 734–740.

Ogino, C. and G-Y. Yang. 1978. Requirement of rainbow trout for dietary zinc. Bull. Jap. Soc. Sci. Fish. 44: 1015–1018.

Ogino, C. and G-Y. Yang. 1979. Requirement of carp for dietary zinc. Bull. Jap. Soc. Sci. Fish. 45: 967–969. [Japanese with English summary and legends]

Ogino, C. and G-Y. Yang. 1980. Requirements of carp and rainbow trout for dietary manganese and copper. Bull. Jap. Soc. Sci. Fish. 46: 455–458. [Japanese with English summary and legends]

Okamoto, S., M. Tanaka, H. Kurokura, and S. Kasahara. 1987. Cryopreservation of parthenogenetic eggs of the rotifer *Brachionus plicatilis*. Nippon Suisan Gakkaishi 53: 2093.

O'Kelley, J. C. 1974. Inorganic nutrients. *In* Algal physiology and biochemistry, W. D. P. Stewart (ed.). University of California Press, Berkeley and Los Angeles, pp. 610–635.

Owen, J. M., J. W. Adron, C. Middleton, and C. B. Cowey. 1975. Elongation and desaturation of dietary fatty acids in turbot *Scophthalmus maximus* L., and rainbow trout, *Salmo gairdneri*. Lipids 10: 528–531.

Owen, J. M., J. W. Adron, J. R. Sargent, and C. B. Cowey. 1972. Studies on the nutrition of marine flatfish. The effect of dietary fatty acids on the tissue fatty-acids of the plaice *Pleuronectes platessa*. Mar. Biol. 13: 160–166.

Page, J. W. and J. W. Andrews. 1973. Interactions of dietary levels of protein and energy on channel catfish (*Ictalurus punctatus*). J. Nutr. 103: 1339–1346.

Parsons, T. R. 1973. Coulter counter for phytoplankton. *In* Handbook of phycological methods: culture methods and growth measurements, J. R. Stein (ed.). Cambridge University Press, Cambridge, pp. 345–358.

Peterson, D. H., H. K. Jäger, and G. M. Savage. 1966. Natural coloration of trout using xanthophylls. Trans. Am. Fish. Soc. 95: 408–415.

Peterson, E. J., R. C. Robinson, and H. Willoughby. 1967. A Meal-gelatin diet for aquarium fishes. Prog. Fish-cult. 29: 170–171.

Petersen, R. 1982. Influence of copper and zinc on the growth of a freshwater alga, *Scenedesmus quadricauda*: the significance of chemical speciation. Environ. Sci. Technol. 16: 443–447.

Poston, H. A. 1965. Effect of dietary vitamin E on microhematocrit, mortality and growth of immature brown trout. Fish. Res. Bull. (N.Y. State) 28: 6–9.

Poston, H. A. 1976a. Relative effect of two dietary water-soluble analogues of menaquinone on coagulation and packed cell volume of blood of lake trout (*Salvelinus namaycush*). J. Fish. Res. Board Can. 33: 1791–1793.

Poston, H. A. 1976b. Optimum level of dietary biotin for growth, feed utilization, and swimming stamina of fingerling lake trout (*Salvelinus namaycush*). J. Fish. Res. Board Can. 33: 1803–1806.

Poston, H. A., G. F. Combs Jr., and L. Leibowitz. 1976. Vitamin E and selenium interrelations in the diet of Atlantic salmon (*Salmo salar*): gross, histological and biochemical deficiency signs. J. Nutr. 106: 892–904.

Poston, H. and T. H. McCartney. 1974. Effect of dietary biotin and lipid on growth, stamina, lipid metabolism and biotin-containing enzymes in brook trout (*Salvelinus fontinalis*). J. Nutr. 104: 315–322.

Poston, H. A., R. C. Riis, G. L. Rumsey, and H. G. Ketola. 1977. Effect of supplemental dietary amino acids, minerals and vitamins on salmonids fed cataractogenic diets. Cornell Vet. 67: 472–509.

Price, N. M. and P. J. Harrison. 1988. Urea uptake by Sargasso Sea phytoplankton: saturated and *in situ* uptake rates. Deep-sea Res. 35: 1579–1593.

Provasoli, L. 1968. Media and prospects for the cultivation of marine algae. *In* Cultures and collections of algae, H. Watanabe and A. Hattori (eds.). Japanese Society of Plant Physiologists, Hakone, pp. 63–75.

Provasoli, L. and A. F. Carlucci. 1974. Vitamins and growth regulators. *In* Algal physiology and biochemistry, W. D. P. Stewart (ed.). University of California Press, Berkeley and Los Angeles, pp. 741–787.

Provasoli, L., J. A. McLaughlin, and M. R. Droop. 1957. The development of artificial media for marine algae. Arch. Mikrobiol. 25: 392–428.

Quick, A. J. Jr. 1982. Preparation and administration of a defined laboratory diet for culture and maintenance of aquatic toxicity testing fishes. SOP Ref. No. ESR-ES-23, Dow Chemical U.S.A., Midland, 12 pp. [Manuscript report]

Randall, J. E. 1967. Food habits of reef fishes of the West Indies. Stud. Trop. Oceanogr. 5: 665–847.

Rey, L. 1975. Freezing and freeze-drying. Proc. R. Soc. London 191B: 9–19.

Roa, M. C., C. Huelvan, Y. Le Borgne, and R. Métailler. 1982. Use of rehydratable extruded pellets and attractive substances for the weaning of sole (*Solea vulgaris*). J. World Maricult. Soc. 13: 246–253.

Saito, A. and L. W. Regier. 1971. Pigmentation of brook trout (*Salvelinus fontinalis*) by feeding dried crustacean wastes. J. Fish. Res. Board Can. 28: 509–512.

Sakamoto, S. and Y. Yone. 1973. Effect of dietary calcium/phosphorus ratio upon growth, feed efficiency and blood serum Ca and P Level in red sea bream. Bull. Jap. Soc. Sci. Fish. 39: 343–348.

Sakamoto, S. and Y. Yone. 1978a. Requirement of red sea bream for dietary iron—II Bull. Jap. Soc. Sci. Fish. 44: 223–225.

Sakamoto, S. and Y. Yone. 1978b. Iron deficiency symptoms of carp. Bull. Jap. Soc. Sci. Fish. 44: 1157–1160.

Santos, C. de los Jr., P. Sorgeloos, E. Laviña, and A. Bernardino. 1980. Successful inoculation of *Artemia* and production of cysts in man-made salterns in the Philippines. *In* The brine shrimp *Artemia,* Vol., 3, G. Persoone, P. Sorgeloos, O. Roels, and E. Jaspers (eds.). Universa Press, Wettern, pp. 159–163.

Sargent, J., R. J. Henderson, and D. R. Tocher. 1989. The lipids. *In* Fish nutrition, 2nd ed., J. E. Halver (ed.). Academic Press, San Diego, pp. 153–218.

Sato, N. L. 1967. Enzymatic contribution to the excystment of *Artemia salina.* Sci. Rpt. Tôhoku Univ. 33(Ser. 4): 319–327.

Schauer, P. S., D. M. Johns, C. E. Olney, and K. L. Simpson. 1980. International study on *Artemia.* IX. Lipid level, energy content and fatty acid composition of the cysts and newly hatched nauplii from five geographical strains of *Artemia. In* The brine shrimp *Artemia,* Vol. 3, G. Persoone, P. Sorgeloos, O. Roels, and E. Jaspers (eds.). Universa Press, Wetteren, pp. 365-371.

Schauer, P. S. and K. L. Simpson. 1979. Fatty acids as biochemical indicators of dietary assimilation in the marine fish Atlantic silverside: a review of comparisons between cultured and wild fish. *In* Finfish nutrition and fishfeed technology, Vol. 2, J. E. Halver and K. Tiews (eds.). Satz und Druck: H. Heenemann GmbH, Berlin, pp. 565–590.

Schlosser, H. J. and K. Anger. 1982. The significance of some methodological effects on filtration and ingestion rates of the rotifer *Brachionus plicatilis.* Helgoländer Meeresunters. 35: 215–225.

Schlüter, M. and J. Groeneweg. 1985. The inhibition by ammonia of population growth of the rotifer, *Brachionus rubens,* in continuous culture. Aquaculture 46: 215–220.

Schmidt, P. J. and E. G. Baker. 1969. Indirect pigmentation of salmon and trout flesh with canthaxanthin. J. Fish. Res. Board Can. 26: 357–360.

Schreiber, E. 1927. Die Reinkulture von marienem Phytoplankton und deren Bedeutung für die Erforschung der Produktionsfähig keit des Meerwassers. Wiss. Meeresuntersuch. (N.F.) 16: 1–34.

Scott, A. P. and S. M. Baynes. 1978. Effect of algal diet and temperature on the biochemical composition of the rotifer, *Brachionus plicatilis.* Aquaculture 14: 247–260.

Seale, A. 1933. The brine shrimp (*Artemia*) as a satisfactory live food for fishes. Trans. Am. Fish. Soc. 63: 129–130.

Segner, H., B. Orejana-Acosta, and J. V. Juario. 1984. The effect of *Brachionus plicatilis* grown on three different species of phytoplankton on the ultrastructure of the hepatocytes of *Chanos chanos* (Forskål) fry. Aquaculture 42: 109–115.

Seidel, C. R., J. Kryznowek, and K. L. Simpson. 1980a. International study on *Artemia.* XI. Amino acid composition on electrophoretic protein patterns of *Artemia* from five geographical locations. *In* The brine shrimp *Artemia,* Vol. 3, G. Persoone, P. Sorgeloos, O. Roels, and E. Jaspers (eds.). Universa Press, Wetteren, pp. 375–382.

Seidel, C. R., P. S. Schauer, T. Katayama, and K. L. Simpson. 1980b. Culture of Atlantic silversides fed artificial diets and brine shrimp nauplii. Bull. Jap. Soc. Sci. Fish. 46: 237–245.

Seidler, R. J. and T. M. Evans. 1984. Computer-assisted analysis of *Vibrio* field data: four coastal areas. *In* Vibrios in the environment, R. R. Colwell (ed.). Wiley, New York, pp. 411–425.

Serra, M. and M. R. Miracle. 1987. Biometric variation in three strains of *Brachionus plicatilis* as a direct response to abiotic variables. Hydrobiologia 147: 83–89.

Sidwell, V. D. 1981. Chemical and nutritional composition of finfishes, whales, crustaceans, mollusks, and their products. NOAA Tech. Memo. NMFS F/SEC-11, U.S. Department of Commerce, Washington, 432 pp.

Simpson, K. L. 1973. Why salmon are pink and goldfish gold. Maritimes 17(1): 4–5.

Simpson, K. L. 1979. Focusing on the modest and minute brine shrimp. Maritimes 23(4): 9–11.

Simpson, K. L. 1982. Carotenoid pigments in seafood. *In* Chemistry and biochemistry of marine food products, R. E. Martin, G. J. Flick, C. E. Hebard, and D. R. Ward (eds.). Avi, Westport, pp. 115–136.

Simpson, K. L. and C. O. Chichester. 1981. Metabolism and nutritional significance of carotenoids. Ann. Rev. Nutr. 1: 351–374.

Simpson, K. L. and T. Kamata. 1979. Use of carotenoids in fish feeds. *In* Finfish nutrition and fishfeed technology, Vol. 2, J. E. Halver and K. Tiews (eds.). Satz und Druck: H. Heenemann GmbH, Berlin, pp. 415–424.

Simpson, K. L., T. Katayama, and C. O. Chichester. 1981. Carotenoids in fish feeds. *In* Carotenoids as colorants and vitamin A precursors: technological and nutritional applications, J. C. Bauernfeind (ed.). Academic Press, New York, pp. 463–538.

Sinclair, H. M. 1964. Carbohydrates and fats. *In* Nutrition: a comprehensive treatise, Vol. 1, G. H. Beaton and E. W. McHenry (eds.). Academic Press, New York, pp. 41–114.

Sloberg, S. O. 1979. Formulation and technology of moist feed— moist pellets. *In* Finfish nutrition and fishfeed technology, Vol. 2, J. E. Halver and K. Tiews (eds.). Satz und Druck: H. Heenemann GmbH, Berlin, pp. 41–45.

Snell, T. W., M. J. Childress, and E. M. Boyer. 1987. Assessing the status of rotifer mass cultures. J. World Aquacult. Soc. 18: 270–277.

Solangi, M. A. and J. T. Ogle. 1977. A selected bibliography on the mass propagation of rotifers with emphasis on the biology and culture of *Brachionus plicatilis*. Gulf Res. Rpt. 6: 59–68.

Soliman, A. K., K. Jauncey, and R. J. Roberts. 1987. Stability of L-ascorbic acid (vitamin C) and its forms in fish feeds during processing, storage and leaching. Aquaculture 60: 73–83.

Sorgeloos, P. 1973. First report of the triggering effect of light on the hatching mechanism of *Artemia salina* dry cysts. Mar. Biol. 22: 75–76.

Sorgeloos, P. 1979. List of commercial harvesters-distributors of *Artemia* cysts of different geographical origin. Aquaculture 16: 87–88.

Sorgeloos, P. 1980. The use of the brine shrimp *Artemia* in aquaculture. *In* The brine shrimp *Artemia*, Vol. 3, G. Persoone, P. Sorgeloos, O. Roels, and E. Jaspers (eds.). Universa Press, Wetteren, pp. 25–46.

Sorgeloos, P., M. Baeza-Mesa, F. Benijts, and G. Persoone. 1976. Research on the culturing of the brine shrimp *Artemia salina* L. at the State University of Ghent (Belgium). *In* 10th European symposium on marine biology, Vol. 1, G. Persoone and E. Jaspers (eds.). Universa Press, Wetteren, pp. 473–495.

Sorgeloos, P., E. Bossuyt, P. Lavens, P. Léger, P. Vanhaecke, and D. Versichele. 1983. The use of brine shrimp *Artemia* in crustacean hatcheries and nurseries. *In* Handbook of mariculture, Vol. 1, J. P. McVey (ed.). CRC Press, Boca Raton, pp. 71–96.

Sorgeloos, P., E. Bossuyt, E. Laviña, M. Baeza-Mesa, and G. Persoone. 1977. Decapsulation of *Artemia* cysts: a simple technique for the improvement of the use of brine shrimp in aquaculture. Aquaculture 12: 311–315.

Sorgeloos, P. and G. Persoone. 1975. Technological improvements for the cultivation of invertebrates as food for fishes and crustaceans. II. Hatching and culturing of the brine shrimp, *Artemia salina* L. Aquaculture 6: 303–317.

Sorgeloos, P., G. Persoone, M. Baeza-Mesa, E. Bossuyt, and E. Bruggeman. 1978. The use of *Artemia* cysts in aquaculture: the concept of ''hatching efficiency'' and description of a new method for cyst processing. Proceedings of the 9th annual meeting, World Mariculture Society, J. W. Avault Jr. (ed.). Louisiana State University, Baton Rouge, pp. 715–721.

Spotte, S. 1973. Marine aquarium keeping: the science, animals, and art. Wiley, New York, 171 pp.

Spotte, S., G. Adams, and P. M. Bubucis. 1984a. GP2 medium is an artificial seawater for culture or maintenance of marine organisms. Zoo Biol. 3: 229–240.

Spotte, S., G. Adams, and P. E. Stake. 1984b. PROBIT analysis predicts hatching rates of brine shrimp (*Artemia sp.*) cysts. Aquacult. Eng'g. 2: 305–317.

Spotte, S. and G. Anderson. 1988. Chemical decapsulation of resting cysts of the anostracans *Artemia franciscana* and *Streptocephalus seali* as revealed by scanning electron microscopy. J. Crust. Biol. 8: 221–231.

Spotte, S. and G. Anderson. 1989. Chemical decapsulation of *Artemia franciscana* resting cysts does not necessarily produce more nauplii. J. World Aquacult. Soc. 20: 127–133.

Spotte, S., P. E. Stake, P. M. Bubucis, and J. D. Buck. 1985. Alginate- and gelatin-bound foods for exhibit fishes. Zoo Biol. 4: 33–48.

Starr, R. C. 1973. Apparatus and maintenance. *In* Handbook of phycological methods: culture methods and growth measurements, J. R. Stein (ed.). Cambridge University Press, Cambridge, pp. 171–179 + 2 pp.

Steele, R. L. and G. B. Thursby. 1988. Laboratory culture of gametophytic stages of the marine macroalgae *Champia parvula* (Rhodophyta) and *Lam-*

inaria saccharina (Phaeophyta). Environ. Toxicol. Chem. 7: 997–1002.

Stemberger, R. S. 1981. A general approach to the culture of planktonic rotifers. Can. J. Fish. Aquat. Sci. 38: 721–724.

Storebakken, T., P. Foss, I. Huse, A. Wandsvik, and T. B. Lea. 1986. Carotenoids in diets for salmonids. II. Utilization of canthaxanthin from dry and wet diets by Atlantic salmon, rainbow trout and sea trout. Aquaculture 51: 245–255.

Storebakken, T., P. Foss, K. Schiedt, E. Austreng, S. Liaaen-Jensen, and U. Manz. 1987. Carotenoids in diets for salmonids. IV. Pigmentation of Atlantic salmon with astaxanthin, astaxanthin dipalmitate and canthaxanthin. Aquaculture 65: 279–292.

Stosch, H. A. von. 1969. Observations on *Corallina, Jania* and other red algae in culture. *In* Proceedings of the sixth international seaweed symposium, R. Margalef (ed.). Dirección General de Pesca Maritima, Madrid, pp. 389–399.

Stumm, W. and P. A. Brauner. 1975. Chemical speciation. *In* Chemical oceanography, Vol. 1, 2nd ed., J. P. Riley and G. Skirrow (eds.). Academic Press, London, pp. 173–239.

Sumitra-Vijayaraghavan, N. Ramaiah, and D. Chandramohan. 1988. Effect of indophor treatment on the hatching of *Artemia* cysts. Curr. Sci. 57(5): 278–280.

Sunda, W. G. and R. R. Guillard. 1976. Relationship between cupric ion activity and the toxicity of copper to phytoplankton. J. Mar. Res. 34: 511–529.

Sunda, W. G. and J. A. M. Lewis. 1978. Effect of complexation by natural organic ligands on toxicity of copper to a unicellular alga, *Monochrysis lutheri*. Limnol. Oceanogr. 23: 870–876.

Takeuchi, L., T. Takeuchi, and C. Ogino. 1980. Riboflavin requirements in carp and rainbow trout. Bull. Jap. Soc. Sci. Fish. 46: 733–737. [Japanese with English summary and legends]

Tanaka, Y. 1978. Comparative biochemical studies on carotenoids in aquatic animals. Mem. Fac. Fish., Kagoshima Univ. 27: 355–422.

Theilacker, G. H. and M. F. McMaster. 1971. Mass culture of the rotifer *Brachionus plicatilis* and its evaluation as a food for larval anchovies. Mar. Biol. 10: 183–188.

Torrissen, O. J. 1985. Pigmentation of salmonids: factors affecting carotenoid deposition in rainbow trout (*Salmo gairdneri*). Aquaculture 46: 133–142.

Torrissen, O. and O. R. Braekkan. 1979. The utilization of astaxanthin-forms by rainbow trout (*Salmo gairdneri*). *In* Finfish nutrition and fishfeed technology, Vol. 2, J. E. Halver and K. Tiews (eds.). Satz und Druck: H. Heenemann GmbH, Berlin, pp. 377–382.

Torrissen, O., E. Tidemann, F. Hansen, and J. Raa. 1981/1982. Ensiling in acid—a method to stabilize astaxanthin in shrimp processing by-products and improve uptake of this pigment by rainbow trout (*Salmo gairdneri*). Aquaculture 26: 77–83.

Ukeles, R. 1976. Cultivation of plants. Unicellular plants. *In* Marine ecology: a comprehensive, integrated treatise on life in oceans and coastal waters, Vol. 3, Part 1, O. Kinne (ed.). Wiley, London, pp. 367–466.

Ukeles, R. and G. H. Wikfors. 1988. Nutritional value of microalgae cultured in the absence of vitamins for growth of juvenile oysters, *Crassostrea virginica*. J. Shellfish Res. 7: 381–387.

Vanhaecke, P., A. Cooreman, and P. Sorgeloos. 1981. International study on *Artemia*. XV. Effect of light intensity on hatching rate of *Artemia* cysts from different geographical origin. Mar. Ecol. Prog. Ser. 5: 111–114.

Vanhaecke, P. and P. Sorgeloos. 1983. International study on *Artemia* XIX. Hatching data for ten commercial sources of brine shrimp cysts and re-evaluation of the "hatching efficiency" concept. Aquaculture 30: 43–52.

Watanabe, T. 1982. Lipid nutrition in fish. Comp. Biochem. Physiol. 73B: 3–15.

Watanabe, T., T. Arakawa, C. Kitajima, and S. Fujita. 1978a. Nutritional evaluation of proteins of living feeds used in seed production of fish. Bull. Jap. Soc. Sci. Fish. 44: 985–988. [Japanese with English summary and legends]

Watanabe, T., F. Oowa, C. Kitajima, and S. Fujita. 1978b. Nutritional quality of brine shrimp, *Artemia salina*, as a living feed from the viewpoint of essential fatty acids for fish. Bull. Jap. Soc. Sci. Fish. 44: 1115–1121. [Japanese with English summary and legends]

Watanabe, T. and F. Takashima. 1977. Effect of α-tocopherol deficiency on carp—VI Deficiency symptoms and changes of fatty acid and triglyceride distributions in adult carp. Bull. Jap. Soc. Sci. Fish. 43: 819–830.

Weatherley, A. H. and H. S. Gill. 1987. The biology of fish growth. Academic Press, London, 443 pp.

Webster, C. D. and R. T. Lovell. 1990. Quality evaluation of four sources of brine shrimp *Artemia* spp. J. World Aquacult. Soc. 21: 180–185.

Weisz, P. B. 1946. The space-time pattern of segment formation in *Artemia salina*. Biol. Bull. 91: 119–140.

Weisz, P. B. and R. N. Keogh. 1982. The science of biology, 5th ed. McGraw-Hill, New York, 1009 pp.

West, E. S., W. R. Todd, H. S. Mason, and J. T. Van Bruggen. 1966. Textbook of biochemistry. Macmillan, New York, 1595 pp.

Wilson, R. P. 1985. Amino acid and protein requirements of fish. *In* Nutrition and feeding in fish, C. B. Cowey, A. M. Mackie, and J. G. Bell (eds.). Academic Press, London, pp. 1–16.

Wilson, T. R. S. 1975. Salinity and the major elements of sea water. *In* Chemical oceanography, 2nd ed., Vol. 1, J. P. Riley and G. Skirrow (eds.). Academic Press, London, pp. 365–413.

Woodall, A. N. and G. LaRoche. 1964. Nutrition of salmonoid fishes. XI. Iodide requirements of chinook salmon. J. Nutr. 82: 475–482.

Woodward, P. 1982. Riboflavin supplementation of diets for rainbow trout. J. Nutr. 112: 908–913.

Yamasaki, S., D. H. Secor, and H. Hirata. 1987. Population growth of two types of rotifer (L and S) *Brachionus plicatilis* at different dissolved oxygen levels. Nippon Suisan Gakkaishi 53: 1303.

Yan, Z., L. Maotang, and T. Fengqin. 1982. The effects of the decapsulated *Artemia* cysts as food for mysid (*Neomysis awatschensis*). Chin. J. Mar. Sci. 4: 39–43. [Chinese with English summary]

Yone, Y. 1975. Nutritional studies of red sea bream. *In* Proceedings of the first international conference on aquaculture nutrition, K. S. Price Jr., W. N. Shaw, and K. S. Danberg (eds.). College of Marine Studies, University of Delaware, Newark, pp. 39–64.

Chapter 9

Adams, R. M., J. S. Remington, J. Steinberg, and J. S. Seibert. 1970. Tropical fish aquariums: a source of *Mycobacterium marinum* infections resembling sporotrichosis. J. Am. Med. Assoc. 211: 457–461.

Alderman, D. J. 1982. Fungal disease of aquatic animals. *In* Microbial diseases of fish, R. J. Roberts (ed.). Academic Press, London, pp. 189–242.

Allen, H. E., R. H. Hall, and T. D. Brisbin. 1980. Metal speciation. Effects on aquatic toxicity. Environ. Sci. Technol. 14: 441–443.

Alpers, C. E., B. B. McCain, M. S. Meyers, and S. R. Wellings. 1977. Lymphocystis disease in yellowfin sole (*Limanda aspera*) in the Bering Sea. J. Fish. Res. Board Can. 34: 611–616.

Amend, D. F. and K. A. Johnson. 1981. Current status and future needs of *Vibrio anguillarum* bacterins. Dev. Biol. Stand. 49: 403–417.

Anderson, B. E., J. A. Brock, T. Hayashi, S. Teruya, and L. K. Nakagawa. 1988. The occurrence of lymphocystis in a new host species, *Sargocentron punctatissimum* Cuvier and Valenciennes, collected and maintained in Hawaii. Pac. Sci. 42: 214–216.

Anderson, J. I. W. and D. A. Conroy. 1970. Vibrio disease in marine fishes. *In* A symposium on diseases of fishes and shellfishes, S. F. Snieszko (ed.). Spec. Pub. No. 5, American Fisheries Society, Washington, pp. 266–272.

Aoki, T. 1974. Studies of drug-resistant bacteria isolated from water of carp ponds and intestinal tracts of carp. Bull. Jap. Soc. Sci. Fish. 40: 247–254. [Japanese with English summary and legends]

Aoki, T. and S. Egusa. 1971. Drug sensitivity of *Aeromonas liquefaciens* isolated from freshwater fishes. Bull. Jap. Soc. Sci. Fish. 37: 176–185.

Aoki, T., T. Kitao, and K. Kawano. 1981. Changes in drug resistance of *Vibrio anguillarum* in cultured ayu, *Plecoglossus altivelis* Temminck and Schlegel, in Japan. J. Fish Dis. 4: 223–230.

Araga, C. 1962. On fish rearing in the "oceanarium." Bull. Mar. Biol. Sta. Asamushi, Tôhoku Univ. 11: 105–112.

Arakawa, C. K. and J. L. Fryer. 1984. Isolation and characterization of a new subspecies of *Mycobacterium chelonei* infectious for salmonid fish. Helgoländer Meeresunters. 37: 329–342.

Aronson, J. D. 1926. Spontaneous tuberculosis in salt water fish. J. Infect. Dis. 39: 315–320.

Austin, B. and D. A. Austin. 1987. Bacterial fish pathogens: disease in farmed and wild fish. Ellis Horwood, Chichester, 364 pp.

Austin, B., C. Johnson, and D. J. Alderman. 1982. Evaluation of substituted quinolines for the control of vibriosis in turbot (*Scophthalmus maximus*). Aquaculture 29: 227–239.

Austin, B., D. A. Morgan, and D. J. Alderman. 1981/1982. Comparison of antimicrobial agents for control of vibriosis in marine fish. Aquaculture 26: 1–12.

Avtalion, R. R. 1981. Environmental control of the immune response in fish. CRC Crit. Rev. Environ. Contr. 11: 163–188.

Bader, H. and J. Hoigné. 1981. Determination of ozone in water by the indigo method. Water Res. 15: 449–456.

Baker, J. T. P. 1969. Histological and electron microscopical observations on copper poisoning in the winter flounder (*Pseudopleuronectes americanus*). J. Fish. Res. Board Can. 26: 2785–2793.

Baker, R. J., M. D. Knittel, and J. L. Fryer. 1983. Susceptibility of chinook salmon, *Oncorhynchus tshawytscha* (Walbaum), and rainbow trout, *Salmo gairdneri* Richardson, to infection with *Vibrio anguillarum* following sublethal copper exposure. J. Fish Dis. 6: 267–275.

Balavenkatasubbaiah, M., A. U. Rani, K. Geethanjali, K. R. Purushotham, and R. Ramamurthi. 1984. Effect of cupric chloride on oxidative metabolism in the freshwater teleost, *Tilapia mossambica*. Ecotoxicol. Environ. Safety 8: 289–293.

Barnes, R. D. 1980. Invertebrate zoology, 4th ed. Saunders College/Holt, Rinehart and Winston, Philadelphia, 1089 pp.

Barton, B. A., C. B. Schreck, and L. G. Fowler. 1988. Fasting and diet content affect stress-induced changes in plasma glucose and cortisol in juvenile chinook salmon. Prog. Fish-cult. 50: 16–22.

Bataillon, Dubard, and Terre. 1897. Un nouveau type de Tuberculose. C. R. Séanc. Soc. Biol. 4: 446–449.

Baudin-Laurencin, F. and F. Y. Batellier. 1986. Protection immunitaire du turbot (*Scophthalmus maximus*) contre la vibriose. *In* Pathology in marine aquaculture, C. P. Vivarès, J-R. Bonami, and E. Jaspers (eds.). Spec. Pub. No. 9, European Aquaculture Society, Breden, pp. 391–403. [English summary]

Baudin-Laurencin, F. and J. Tangtrongpiros. 1980. Some results of vaccination against vibriosis in Brittany. *In* Fish diseases: third COPRAQ-session, W. Ahne (ed.). Springer-Verlag, Berlin, pp. 60–68.

Bauer, O. N. and G. L. Hoffman. 1976. Helminth range extension by translocation of fish. *In* Wildlife diseases, L. A. Page (ed.). Plenum, New York, pp. 163–172.

Baum, E. T., E. S. Sawyer, and R. G. Strout. 1982. Survival of hatchery-reared Atlantic salmon smolts vaccinated with a *Vibrio anguillarum* bacterin. N. Am. J. Fish. Mgt. 4: 409–411.

Baumann, P., A. L. Furniss, and J. V. Lee. 1984. Genus I. *Vibrio* Pacini 1854. *In* Bergey's manual of systematic bacteriology, Vol. 1, N. R. Krieg (ed.). Williams and Wilkins, Baltimore, pp. 518–538. [References at end of volume]

Bellanti, J. A. 1971. Protective mechanisms involved in the immune response to infectious agents. *In* Immunity II, J. A. Bellanti (ed.). Saunders, Philadelphia, pp. 355–384.

Benoit, D. A. 1975. Chronic effects of copper on survival, growth, and reproduction of the bluegill (*Lepomis macrochirus*). Trans. Am. Fish. Soc. 104: 353–358.

Bentley, W. W., E. M. Dawley, and T. W. Newcomb. 1976. Some effects of excess dissolved gas on squawfish, *Ptychocheilus oregonensis* (Richardson). *In* Gas bubble disease, D. H. Fickeisen and M. J. Schneider (eds.). Energy Research and Development Administration, Oak Ridge, pp. 41–46.

Bere, R. 1936. Parasitic copepods from Gulf of Mexico fish. Am. Midl. Nat. 17: 577–625.

Bilinski, E. and R. E. E. Jonas. 1973. Effects of cadmium and copper on the oxidation of lactate by rainbow trout (*Salmo gairdneri*) gills. J. Fish. Res. Board Can. 30: 1553–1558.

Blake, P. A. 1980. Diseases of humans (other than cholera) caused by vibrios. Ann. Rev. Microbiol. 34: 341–367.

Blake, P. A., M. H. Merson, R. E. Weaver, D. G. Hollis, and P. G. Heublein. 1979. Disease caused by a marine vibrio. New Eng. J. Med. 300: 1–5.

Blasiola, G. C. 1976a. Ectoparasitic Turbellaria. Mar. Aquarist 7(2): 53–58.

Blasiola, G. C. 1976b. A review of "white spot," *Cryptocaryon irritans*. Mar. Aquarist 7(4): 5–14.

Blazer, V. S., G. T. Ankley, and D. Finco-Kent. 1989. Dietary influences on disease resistance factors in channel catfish. Develop. Comp. Immunol. 13: 43–48.

Blazer, V. S. and R. E. Wolke. 1979. An *Exophiala*-like fungus as the cause of a systemic mycosis of marine fish. J. Fish Dis. 2: 145–152.

Blazer, V. S. and R. E. Wolke. 1984a. The effects of α-tocopherol on the immune response and non-specific resistance factors of rainbow trout (*Salmo gairdneri* Richardson). Aquaculture 37: 1–9.

Blazer, V. S. and R. E. Wolke. 1984b. Effect of diet on the immune response of rainbow trout (*Salmo gairdneri*). Can. J. Fish. Aquat. Sci. 41: 1244–1247.

Blogoslawski, W., L. Farrell, R. Garceau, and P. Derrig. 1975. Production of oxidants in ozonized seawater. *In* Aquatic applications of ozone, R. G. Rice, P. Pichet, and M-A. Vincent (eds.). Ozone Press International, Jamesville, pp. 671–681.

Blum, P. and C. A. Luer. 1985. Observations on the occurrence of thyroid hyperplasia in captive sharks. Fla. Sci. 48(Suppl. 1): 32.

Bodammer, J. E. 1987. A preliminary study on the corneas of American sand lance larvae exposed to copper. *In* Pollution physiology of estuarine organisms, W. B. Vernberg, A. Calabrese, F. P. Thurberg, and F. J. Vernberg (eds.). University of South Carolina Press, Columbia, pp. 439–448.

Bolinches, J. and E. Egidius. 1987. Heterotrophic bacterial communities associated with the rearing of halibut *Hippoglossus hippoglossus* with special reference to *Vibrio* spp. J. Appl. Ichthyol. 3: 165–173.

Bouck, G. R. 1980. Etiology of gas bubble disease. Trans. Am. Fish. Soc. 109: 703–707.

Bouck, G. R., G. A. Chapman, P. W. Schneider Jr., and D. G. Stevens. 1976. Observations on gas bubble disease among wild adult Columbia River fishes. Trans. Am. Fish. Soc. 105: 114–115.

Bouck, G. R. and D. A. Johnson. 1979. Medication inhibits tolerance to seawater in coho salmon smolts. Trans. Am. Fish. Soc. 108: 63–66.

Bouck, G. R. and R. E. King. 1983. Tolerance to gas supersaturation in fresh water and sea water by steelhead trout, *Salmo gairdneri* Richardson. J. Fish Biol. 23: 293–300.

Bower, C. E. and D. T. Turner. 1988. Drug and chemical effects on the behavior and survival in vitro of the dinoflagellate fish parasite *Amyloodinium ocellatum*. Proc. Int. Assoc. Aquat. Anim. Med. 19: 24. [Abstract]

Bower, C. E., D. T. Turner, and R. C. Biever. 1987. A standardized method of propagating the marine fish parasite, *Amyloodinium ocellatum*. J. Parasitol. 73: 85–88.

Bowser, P. R., R. Rosemark, and C. R. Reiner. 1981. A preliminary report of vibriosis in cultured American lobsters, *Homarus americanus*. J. Invert. Pathol. 37: 80–85.

Brown, E. M. 1931. Note on a new species of dinoflagellate from the gills and epidermis of marine fishes. Proc. Zool. Soc. London 1931 (Part 1): 345–346.

Brown, E. M. 1934. On *Oodinium ocellatum* Brown, a parasitic dinoflagellate causing epidemic disease in marine fish. Proc. Zool. Soc. London 1934: 583–607.

Brown, E. M. 1951. Agenda and abstracts of the scientific meetings of the Zoological Society of London. *Cryptocaryon irritans* gen. et sp. n. Proc. Zool. Soc. London 1950(11): 1–2.

Brown, E. M. 1963. Studies on *Cryptocaryon irritans* Brown. *In* Progress in protozoology. Czechoslovak Academy of Sciences, Prague, pp. 284–287.

Brown, E. M. and R. Hovasse. 1946. *Amyloodinium ocellatum* (Brown), a peridinian parasitic on marine fishes. A complementary study. Proc. Zool. Soc. London 116: 33–46.

Brown, J. H. 1989. Antibiotics: their use and abuse in aquaculture. World Aquacult. 29(2): 34–35, 38–39, and 42–43.

Brungs, W. A., E. N. Leonard, and J. M. McKim. 1973. Acute and long-term accumulation of copper by the brown bullhead, *Ictalurus nebulosus*. J. Fish. Res. Board Can. 30: 583–586.

Buck, J. D. and S. Spotte. 1986a. Microbiology of captive white-beaked dolphins (*Lagenorhynchus albirostris*) with comments on epizootics. Zoo Biol. 5: 321-329.

Buck, J. D. and S. Spotte. 1986b. The occurrence of potentially pathogenic vibrios in marine mammals. Mar. Mamm. Sci. 2: 319–324.

Buck, J. D., S. Spotte, and J. J. Gadbaw Jr. 1984. Bacteriology of the teeth from a great white shark: potential medical implications for shark bite victims. J. Clin. Microbiol. 20: 849–851.

Buckley, J. T., M. Roch, J. A. McCarter, C. A. Rendell, and A. T. Matheson. 1982. Chronic exposure of coho salmon to sublethal concentrations of copper—I. Effect on growth, on accumulation and distribution of copper, and on copper tolerance. Comp. Biochem. Physiol. 72C: 15–19.

Budavari, S. (ed.). 1989. The Merck index, 11th ed. Merck and Co., Rahway, 1606 pp. + tables, appendices, and indices.

Bullock, G. L. 1987. Vibriosis in fish. Fish Dis. Leaf. 77, U.S. Fish and Wildlife Service, Washington, 11 pp.

Bullock, G. L. 1968. The bacteriology of brook trout with tail rot. Prog. Fish-cult. 30: 19–22.

Calamari, D., R. Marchetti, and G. Vailati. 1980. Influence of water hardness on cadmium toxicity to *Salmo gairdneri* Rich. Water Res. 14: 1421–1426.

Cannon, L. R. G. and R. J. G. Lester. 1988. Two turbellarians parasitic in fish. Dis. Aquat. Organ. 5: 15–22.

Cardeilhac, P. T. and E. R. Hall. 1977. Acute copper poisoning of cultured marine teleosts. Am. J. Vet. Res. 38: 525–527.

Cardeilhac, P. T., C. F. Simpson, R. L. Lovelock, S. F. Yosha, H. W. Calderwood, and J. C. Gudat. 1979. Failure of osmoregulation with apparent potassium intoxication in marine teleosts: a primary effect of copper. Aquaculture 17: 231–239.

Carmichael, J. W. 1966. Cerebral mycetoma of trout due to a *Phialophora*-like fungus. Sabouraudia 5: 120–123.

Caullery, M. and F. Mesnil. 1905. Sur des haplosporides parasites de poissons marins. C. R. Séanc. Soc. Biol. 58: 640–643.

Chart, H. and C. B. Munn. 1980. Experimental vibriosis in the eel (*Anguilla anguilla*). *In* Fish diseases: third COPRAQ-session, W. Ahne (ed.). Springer-Verlag, Berlin, pp. 30–44.

Cheung, P. J., R. F. Nigrelli, and G. D. Ruggieri. 1979a. Scanning electron microscopic observation on the various stages of the life cycle of *Oodinium ocellatum* Brown. Trans. Am. Microscop. Soc. 98: 157. [Abstract]

Cheung, P. J., R. F. Nigrelli, and G. D. Ruggieri. 1979b. Studies on cryptocaryoniasis in marine fish: effect of temperature and salinity on the reproductive cycle of *Cryptocaryon irritans*, Brown 1951. J. Fish Dis. 2: 93–97.

Cheung, P. J., R. F. Nigrelli, and G. D. Ruggieri. 1980. Studies on the morphology of *Uronema marinum* Dujardin (Ciliatea: Uronematidae) with a description of the histopathology of the infection in marine fishes. J. Fish Dis. 3: 295–303.

Cheung, P. J., R. F. Nigrelli, and G. D. Ruggieri. 1981a. *Oodinium ocellatum* (Brown, 1931) (Dinoflagellata) in the kidney and other internal tissues of pork fish, *Anisotremus virginicus* (L.) J. Fish Dis. 4: 523–525.

Cheung, P. J., R. F. Nigrelli, and G. D. Ruggieri. 1981b. Development of *Oodinium ocellatum* (dinoflagellida): a scanning electron microscopic study. Trans. Am. Microscop. Soc. 100: 415–420.

Cheung, P. J., R. F. Nigrelli, and G. D. Ruggieri. 1982. Scanning electron microscopy on *Cryptocaryon irritans* Brown 1951, a parasitic ciliate in marine fishes. J. Aquaricult. 2: 70–72.

Chien, C-H., T. Miyazaki, and S. S. Kubota. 1979. Studies on ichthyophonus disease of fish—VII Morphology and life cycle. Bull. Fac. Fish., Mie Univ. 6: 161–172.

Clark, H. F. and C. C. Shepard. 1963. Effect of environmental temperatures on infection with *Mycobacterium marinum* (Balnei) of mice and a number of poikilothermic species. J. Bacteriol. 86: 1057–1069.

Clay, A., A. Barker, S. Testaverde, R. Marcello, and G. C. McLeod. 1976. Observations on the effects of gas embolism in captured adult menhaden. *In* Gas bubble disease, D. H. Fickeisen and M. J. Schneider (eds.). Energy Research and Development Administration, Oak Ridge, pp. 81–84.

Clifford, J. T. and R. L. Applegate. 1970. Lymphocystis disease of tagged and untagged walleyes in a South Dakota lake. Prog. Fish-cult. 41: 177.

Collvin, L. 1984. The effects of copper on maximum respiration rate and growth rate of perch, *Perca fluviatilis* L. Water Res. 18: 139–144.

Colorni, A. 1985. Aspects of the biology of *Cryptocaryon irritans*, and hyposalinity as a control measure in cultured gilt-head sea bream *Sparus auratus*. Dis. Aquat. Organ. 1: 19–22.

Colorni, A., I. Paperna, and H. Gordin. 1981. Bacterial infections in gilt-head sea bream *Sparus aurata* cultured at Elat. Aquaculture 23: 257–267.

Colwell, R. R. and D. J. Grimes. 1984. *Vibrio* diseases of marine fish populations. Helgoländer Meeresunters. 37: 265–287.

Condé, B. 1976. Parasitism de Labridés de la région Caraibes par une Planaire. Rev. Fr. Aquariol. Herpetol. 3(1): 23–24.

Conroy, D. A. 1970. Piscine tuberculosis in the sea water environment. *In* A symposium on diseases of fishes and shellfishes, S. F. Snieszko (ed.). Spec. Pub. No. 5, American Fisheries Society, Washington, pp. 273–278.

Conroy, D. A. and J. A. Santacana. 1979. A case of goitre and its treatment in a goldfish *Carassius auratus* (L.). J. Fish Dis. 2: 555–556.

Cook, D. W. 1972. Experimental infection studies with lymphocystis virus from Atlantic croaker. Proc. World Maricult. Soc. 3: 329–335.

Corbel, M. J. 1975. The immune response in fish: a review. J. Fish Biol. 7: 539–563.

Cornacchia, J. W. and J. E. Colt. 1984. The effects of dissolved gas supersaturation on larval striped bass, *Morone saxatilis* (Walbaum). J. Fish Dis. 7: 15–27.

Crecelius, E. A. 1979. Measurements of oxidants in ozonized seawater and some biological reactions. J. Fish. Res. Board Can. 36: 1006–1008.

Crespo, S. and K. J. Karnaky Jr. 1983. Copper and zinc inhibit chloride transport across the opercular epithelium of seawater-adapted killifish *Fundulus heteroclitus*. J. Exp. Biol. 102: 337–341.

Cushing, J. E. 1970. Immunology of fish. *In* Fish physiology, 2nd ed., Vol. 4, W. S. Hoar and D. J. Randall (eds.). Academic Press, New York, pp. 465–500.

Daoust, P-Y., B. E. Larson, and G. R. Johnson. 1989. Mycobacteriosis in yellow perch (*Perca flavescens*) from two lakes in Alberta. J. Wildl. Dis. 25: 31–37.

Darai, G. 1986. Molecular biology of fish lymphocystis disease virus. *In* Pathology in marine aquaculture, C. P. Vivarès, J-R. Bonami, and E. Jaspers (eds.). Spec. Pub. No. 9, European Aquaculture Society, Breden, pp. 261–280.

Dempster, R. P. 1955. The use of copper sulfate as a cure for fish diseases caused by parasitic dinoflagellates of the genus *Oodinium*. Zoologica (N.Y.) 40: 133–138.

Dixon, D. G. and J. W. Hilton. 1981. Influence of available dietary carbohydrate content on tolerance of waterborne copper by rainbow trout, *Salmo gairdneri* Richardson. J. Fish Biol. 19: 509–517.

Dukes, T. W. and A. R. Lawler. 1975. The ocular lesions of naturally occurring lymphocystis in fish. Can. J. Comp. Med. 39: 406–410.

Dulin, M. P. 1979. A review of tuberculosis (mycobacteriosis) in fish. Vet. Med. Small Anim. Clin. 74: 731–735.

Durve, V. S. and R. T. Lovell. 1982. Vitamin C and disease resistance in channel catfish (*Ictalurus punctatus*). Can. J. Fish. Aquat. Sci. 38: 948–951.

Dyke, J. J. van and K. B. Lake. 1975. Chemotherapy for aquarium granuloma. J. Am. Med. Assoc. 233: 1380–1381.

Egidius, E. and K. Andersen. 1978. Host-specific pathogenicity of strains of *Vibrio anguillarum* isolated from rainbow trout (*Salmo gairdneri*) and saithe (*Pollachius virens*). J. Fish Dis. 1: 45–50.

Egidius, E. and K. Andersen. 1979. The use of Furanace against vibriosis in rainbow trout *Salmo gairdneri* Richardson in salt water. J. Fish Dis. 2: 79–80.

Egidius, R., R. Wiik, K. Andersen, K. A. Hoff, and B. Hjeltnes. 1986. *Vibrio salmonicida* sp. nov., a new fish pathogen. Int. J. Syst. Bacteriol. 36: 518–520.

Ellis, A. E. 1978. The immunology of teleosts. *In* Fish pathology, R. J. Roberts (ed.). Baillière Tindall, London, pp. 92–104.

Ellis, A. E. 1982. Differences between the immune mechanisms of fish and higher vertebrates. *In* Microbial diseases of fish, R. J. Roberts (ed.). Academic Press, London, pp. 1–29.

Elston, R., E. L. Elliot, and R. R. Colwell. 1982. Conchiolin infection and surface coating *Vibrio*: shell fragility, growth depression and mortalities in cultured oysters and clams, *Crassostrea virginica*, *Ostrea edulis* and *Mercenaria mercenaria*. J. Fish Dis. 5: 265–284.

Elston, R., L. Leibovitz, D. Relyea, and J. Zatila. 1981. Diagnosis of vibriosis in a commercial oyster hatchery epizootic: diagnostic tools and management features. Aquaculture 24: 53–62.

Evelyn, T. P. T. and J. E. Ketcheson. 1980. Laboratory and field observations on antivibriosis vaccines. *In* Fish diseases: third COPRAQ-session, W. Ahne (ed.). Springer-Verlag, Berlin, pp. 45–52.

Faoagali, J. L., A. D. Muir, P. J. Sears, and G. P. Paltridge. 1977. Tropical fish granuloma. New Zealand Med. J. 85: 332–335.

Fauve, R. M. 1976. Nonspecific immunity. *In* Immunology, J-F. Bach (ed.). Wiley, New York, pp. 395–444.

Fletcher, T. C. and A. White. 1973. Lysozyme activity in the plaice (*Pleuronectes platessa* L.). Experientia 29: 1283–1285.

Foreyt, W. J. and J. R. Gorham. 1988. Preliminary evaluation of praziquantel against metacercariae of *Nanophyetus salmincola* in chinook salmon (*Oncorhynchus tshawytscha*). J. Wildl. Dis. 24: 551–554.

Frakes, T. A., F. H. Hoff Jr., and W. Hoff. 1983. Delayed metamorphosis of larval anemonefish (*Amphiprion ocellaris*) due to iodine deficiency. *In* Proceedings of the warmwater fish culture workshop, R. R. Stickney and S. P. Meyers (eds.). Spec. Pub. No. 3, World Mariculture Society, Baton Rouge, pp. 117–123.

Franklin, M. L. and J. W. Morse. 1982. The interaction of copper with the surface of calcite. Ocean Sci. Eng'g. 7: 147–174.

Fryer, J. L., J. S. Nelson, and R. L. Garrison. 1972. Vibriosis in fish. *In* Progress in fish food science, R. W. Moore (ed.). College of Fisheries, University of Washington, Seattle, pp. 129–133.

Fryer, J. L. and J. E. Sanders. 1981. Bacterial kidney disease of salmonid fish. Ann. Rev. Microbiol. 35: 273–298.

Gardner, G. R. and G. LaRoche. 1973. Copper induced lesions in estuarine teleosts. J. Fish. Res. Board Can. 30: 363–368.

Garey, J. F. 1980. A review and update of possible alternatives to chlorination for controlling biofouling in cooling water systems of steam electric generating stations. *In* Water chlorination: environmental impact and health effects, Vol. 3, R. L. Jolley, W. A. Brungs, and R. B. Cumming (eds.). Ann Arbor Science, Ann Arbor, pp. 453–467.

Giavenni, R., M. Finazzi, G. Poli, and E. Grimaldi. 1980. Tuberculosis in marine tropical fishes in an aquarium. J. Wildl. Dis. 16: 161–168.

Giesy, J. P. 1988. Phosphoadenylate concentrations and adenylate energy charge of largemouth bass (*Micropterus salmoides*): relationship with condition factor and blood cortisol. Comp. Biochem. Physiol. 90A: 367–377.

Gould, R. W., R. Antipa, and D. F. Amend. 1979. Immersion vaccination of sockeye salmon (*Oncorhynchus nerka*) with two pathogenic strains of *Vibrio anguillarum*. J. Fish. Res. Board Can. 36: 222–225.

Graaf, F. de. 1960. A new parasite causing epidemic infection in captive coralfishes. Bull. Inst. Océanogr., Monaco, Num. spéc. IA: 93–96.

Graevenitz, A. von and U. Berger. 1980. A plea for linguistic accuracy. Int. J. Syst. Bacteriol. 30: 520.

Gratzek, J. B. 1981. An overview of ornamental fish diseases and therapy. *In* Waltham Symposium No. 3: The diseases of ornamental fishes, D. M. Ford (ed.). J. Small Anim. Prac. 22: 345–366.

Gratzek, J. B., J. P. Gilbert, A. L. Lohr, E. B. Shotts Jr., and J. Brown. 1983. Ultraviolet light control of *Ichthyophthirius multifiliis* Fouquet in a closed fish culture recirculation system. J. Fish. Dis. 6: 145–153.

Grimes, D. J., R. R. Colwell, J. Stemmler, H. Hada, D. Maneval, F. M. Hetrick, E. B. May, R. T. Jones, and M. Stoskopf. 1984a. *Vibrio* species as agents of elasmobranch disease. Helogoländer Meeresunters. 37: 309–315.

Grimes, D. J., J. Stemmler, H. Hada, E. B. May, D. Maneval, F. M. Hetrick, R. T. Jones, M. Stoskopf, and R. R. Colwell. 1984b. *Vibrio* species associated with mortality of sharks held in captivity. Microb. Ecol. 10: 271–282.

Grimes, D. J., P. Brayton, R. R. Colwell, and S. H. Gruber. 1985a. Vibrios as autochthonous flora of neritic sharks. System. Appl. Microbiol. 6: 221–226.

Grimes, D. J., S. H. Gruber, and E. B. May. 1985b. Experimental infection of lemon sharks, *Negaprion brevirostris* (Poey), with *Vibrio* species. J. Fish Dis. 8: 173–180.

Grimes, D. J., J. Burgess, J. A. Crunkleton Jr., P. R. Brayton, and R. R. Colwell. 1989. Potential invasive factors associated with *Vibrio carchariae*, an opportunistic pathogen for sharks. J. Fish Dis. 12: 69–72.

Gustafson, P. V. and R. R. Rucker. 1956. Studies on an *Ichthyosporidium* infection in fish: transmission and host specificity. Spec. Sci. Rpt.—Fish. No. 166, U.S. Fish and Wildlife Service, Washington, 8 pp.

Guternatsch, J. F. 1911. The thyroid gland of teleosts. J. Morphol. 21: 709–782.

Haag, W. R. 1981. On the disappearance of chlorine in sea-water. Water Res. 15: 937–940.

Haas, C. N. 1981. Sodium alteration of chlorine equilibria. Quantitative description. Environ. Sci. Technol. 15: 1243–1244.

Håstein, [Haastein], T., F. Hallingstad, T. Refsti, and S. O. Roald. 1980. Recent experience of field vaccination trials against vibriosis in rainbow trout (*Salmo gairdneri*). *In* Fish diseases: third COPRAQ-session, W. Ahne (ed.). Springer-Verlag, Berlin, pp. 53–59.

Haastein, T. and G. Holt. 1972. The occurrence of vibrio disease in wild Norwegian fish. J. Fish Biol. 4: 33–37.

Hall, L. W. Jr., D. T. Burton, and L. B. Richardson. 1981. Comparison of ozone and chlorine toxicity to the developmental stages of striped bass, *Morone saxtilis*. Can. J. Fish. Aquat. Sci. 38: 752–757.

Hammond, S. M. and P. A. Lambert. 1978. Antibiotics and antimicrobial action. Edward Arnold, London, 63 pp.

Hart, B. T. 1979. Trace metal complexing capacity of natural waters: a review. Environ. Technol. Lett. 2: 95–110.

Hasle, J. R. and M. I. Abdullah. 1981. Analytical fractionation of dissolved copper, lead and cadmium in coastal seawater. Mar. Chem. 10: 487–503.

Heath, A. G. 1984. Changes in tissue adenylates and water content of bluegill, *Lepomis macrochirus*, exposed to copper. J. Fish Biol. 24: 299–309.

Heggberget, T. G. 1984. Effect of supersaturated water on fish in the River Nidelva, southern Norway. J. Fish Biol. 24: 65–74.

Herald, E. S., R. P. Dempster, and M. Hunt. 1970. Ultraviolet sterilization of aquarium water. Spec. ed., Drum and Croaker, W. Hagen (ed.). U.S. Department of the Interior, Washington, pp. 57–71.

Herman, R. L. 1970. Chemotherapy of fish diseases: a review. J. Wildl. Dis. 6: 31–34.

Herman, R. L. 1972. The principles of therapy in fish diseases. Symp. Zool. Soc. London 30: 141–151.

Hetrick, F. M. 1984. DNA viruses associated with diseases of marine and anadromous fish. Helogoländer Meeresunters. 37: 289–307.

Hilton, L. R. and J. L. Wilson. 1980. Terramycin-resistant *Edwardsiella tarda* in channel catfish. Prog. Fish-cult. 42: 159.

Hirayama, K. and M. Shiomi. 1962. On the countermeasure against disease in marine fishes at the Suma Aquarium of Kobe City. Bull. Mar. Biol. Sta. Asamushi, Tôhoku Univ. 11: 91–98.

Hjeltnes, B., K. Andersen, H-M. Ellinsen, and E. Egidius. 1987. Experimental studies on the pathogenicity of a *Vibrio* sp. isolated from Atlantic salmon, *Salmo salar* L., suffering from Hitra disease. J. Fish Dis. 10: 21–27.

Hodgins, H. O., M. H. Schiewe, A. J. Novotny, and L. W. Harrell. 1977. Vibriosis of salmon. *In* Disease diagnosis and control in North American marine aquaculture, C. J. Sindermann (ed.). Elsevier, Amsterdam, pp. 231–236.

Hofer, B. von. 1893. Eine Salmonidenerkrankung. Allg. Fisch. (N.F.) 8: 168–171.

Hoffman, G. L. 1974. Disinfection of contaminated water by ultraviolet irradiation, with emphasis on whirling disease (*Myxosoma cerebralis*) and its effect on fish. Trans. Am. Fish. Soc. 103: 541–550.

Hoffman, G. L. 1977. *Argulus*, a branchiuran parasite of freshwater fishes. Fish Dis. Leaf. 49, U.S. Fish and Wildlife Service, Washington, 9 pp.

Højgaard, M. 1960. Experiences made in Danmarks Akvarium concerning the treatment of *Oodinium ocellatum*. Bull. Inst. Océanogr., Monaco, Num. spéc. IA: 77–79.

Holm, K. O. and T. Jørgensen. 1987. A successful vaccination of Atlantic salmon, *Salmo salar* L., against "Hitra disease" or coldwater vibriosis. J. Fish Dis. 10: 85–90.

Hood, L. E., I. L. Weissman, and W. B. Wood. 1978. Immunology. Benjamin/Cummings, Menlo Park, 467 pp.

Horne, M. T. 1982. The pathogenicity of *Vibrio anguillarum* (Bergman). *In* Microbial diseases of fish, R. J. Roberts (ed.). Academic Press, London, pp. 171–187.

Horne, M. T., M. F. Tatner, S. McDerment, and C. Agius. 1982. Vaccination of rainbow trout, *Salmo gairdneri* Richardson, at low temperatures and the long-term persistence of protection. J. Fish Dis. 5: 343–345.

Hoshina, T. 1968. On the monogenetic trematode, *Benedenia seriolae*, parasitic on yellow-tail, *Seriola quinqueradiata*. Bull. Off. Int. Epizootiol. 69: 1179–1191.

Howarth, R. S. and J. B. Sprague. 1978. Copper lethality to rainbow trout in waters of various hardness and pH. Water Res. 12: 455–462.

Huff, J. A. and C. D. Burns. 1981. Hypersaline and chemical control of *Cryptocaryon irritans* in red snapper, *Lutjanus campechanus*, monoculture. Aquaculture 22: 181–184.

Hunt, D. W. C. and J. G. Eales. 1979. Iodine balance in rainbow trout (*Salmo gairdneri*) and effects of testosterone propionate. J. Fish. Res. Board Can. 36: 282–285.

Hussein, S. A. and D. H. Mills. 1982. The prevalence of "cauliflower disease" of the eel, *Anguilla anguilla* L., in tributaries of the River Tweed, Scotland. J. Fish Dis. 5: 161–165.

Imada, R. and K. Muroga. 1978. *Pseudodactylogyrus microrchis* (Monogenea) on the gills of cultured eels—II Oviposition, hatching and development on the host. Bull. Jap. Soc. Sci. Fish. 44: 571–576. [Japanese with English summary and legends]

Inamura, H., K. Muroga, and T. Nakai. 1984. Toxicity of extracellular products of *Vibrio anguillarum*. Fish Pathol. 19: 89–96.

Ingram, G. A. 1980. Substances involved in the natural resistance of fish to infection—a review. J. Fish Biol. 16: 23–60.

Itami, T. and R. Kusuda. 1984. Viability and pathogenicity of *Vibrio anguillarum*, in NaCl solutions of various concentrations, isolated from ayu cultured in freshwater. J. Shimonoseki Univ. Fish. 32: 33–39. [Japanese with English summary and legends]

Jahn, T. L. and L. R. Kuhn. 1932. The life history of *Epibdella melleni* McCallum 1927, a monogenetic trematode parasitic on marine fishes. Biol. Bull. 62: 89–111.

Janssen, W. A. 1970. Fish as potential vectors of human bacterial diseases. *In* A symposium on diseases of fishes and shellfishes, S. F. Snieszko (ed.). Spec. Pub. No. 5, American Fisheries Society, Washington, pp. 284–290.

Johnson, K. A., J. K. Flynn, and D. F. Amend. 1982a. Onset of immunity in salmonid fry vaccinated by direct immersion in *Vibrio anguillarum* and *Yersinia ruckeri* bacterins. J. Fish Dis. 5: 197–205.

Johnson, K. A., J. K. Flynn, and D. F. Amend. 1982b. Duration of immunity in salmonids vaccinated by direct immersion with *Yersinia ruckeri* and *Vibrio anguillarum* bacterins. J. Fish Dis. 5: 207–213.

Johnson, K. S. 1978. Lymphocystis disease of Texas coastal fishes. FDDL-M2, Fish Disease Diagnostic Laboratory, Texas A & M University, College Station, 3 pp.

Johnson, S. K. 1984. Evaluation of several chemicals for control of *Amyloodinium ocellatum*, a parasite of marine fishes. FDDL-M5, Fish Disease Diagnostic Laboratory, Texas A & M University, College Station, 4 pp.

Jones, D. and D. H. Lewis. 1976. Gas bubble disease in fry of channel catfish (*Ictalurus punctatus*). Prog. Fish-cult. 38: 41.

Kanno, T., T. Nakai, and K. Muroga. 1989. Mode of transmission among ayu *Plecoglossus altivelis*. J. Aquat. Anim. Health 1: 2–6.

Katae, H., K. Kouno, Y. Takase, H. Miyazaki, M. Hashimoto, and M. Shimizu. 1979. The evaluation of piromidic acid as an antibiotic in fish: an *in vitro* and *in vivo* study. J. Fish Dis. 2: 321–335.

Kawakami, K. and R. Kusuda. 1989. *In vitro* effect of some chemotherapeutics on the causative mycobacterium infection in yellowtail. Nippon Suisan Gakkaishi 55: 2111–2114. [Japanese with English summary and legends]

Kearn, G. C. 1973. An endogenous circadian hatching rhythm in the monogenean skin parasite *Entobdella soleae* and its relationship to the activity rhythm of the host (*Solea solea*). Parasitology 66: 101–122.

Kearn, G. C. 1974a. Nocturnal hatching in the monogenean skin parasite *Entobdella hippoglossi* from the halibut, *Hippoglossus hippoglossus*. Parasitology 68: 161–172.

Kearn, G. C. 1974b. The effects of fish skin mucus on hatching in the monogenean parasite *Entobdella soleae* from the skin of the common sole, *Solea solea*. Parasitology 68: 173–188.

Kearn, G. C. 1976. Body surface of fishes. *In* Ecological aspects of parasitology, C. R. Kennedy (ed.). North-Holland, Amsterdam, pp. 185–208.

Kelch, W. J. and J. S. Lee. 1978. Antibiotic resistance patterns of Gram-negative bacteria isolated from environmental sources. Appl. Environ. Microbiol. 36: 450–456.

Kent, M. L. and A. C. Olson Jr. 1986. Interrelationships of a parasitic turbellarian, (*Paravortex* sp.) (Graffillidae, Rhabdocoela) and its marine fish hosts. Fish Pathol. 21: 65–72.

Khan, R. A., J. Campbell, and H. Lear. 1981. Mortality in captive Atlantic cod, *Gadus morhua*. J. Wildl. Dis. 17: 521–527.

Knight, I. T., D. J. Grimes, and R. R. Colwell. 1988. Bacterial hydrolysis of urea in the tissues of carcharinid sharks. Can. J. Fish. Aquat. Sci. 45: 357–360.

Knittel, M. D. 1981. Susceptibility of steelhead trout *Salmo gairdneri* Richardson to redmouth infection *Yersinia ruckeri* following exposure to copper. J. Fish Biol. 4: 33–40.

Koch, A. L. 1981. Evolution of antibiotic resistance gene function. Microbiol. Rev. 45: 355–378.

Kohlmeyer, J. 1984. Tropical marine fungi. Mar. Ecol. (Napoli) 5: 329–378.

Koltes, K. H. 1984. Temporal patterns and environmental responses in the three-dimensional structure and activity of the Atlantic silverside, *Menidia menidia*. Diss. Abst. Int. 44B: 2041.

Kosak-Channing, L. and G. R. Helz. 1979. Ozone reactivity with seawater components. Ozone Sci. Eng'g. 1: 39–46.

Kraxberger-Beatty, T., D. J. McGarey, H. J. Grier, and D. V. Lim. 1990. *Vibrio harveyi*, an opportunistic pathogen of common snook, *Centropomus undecimalis* (Bloch), held in captivity. J. Fish Dis. 13: 557–560.

Krise, W. F. and R. L. Herman. 1989. Tolerance of lake trout, *Salvelinus namaycush* (Walbaum), sac fry to dissolved gas supersaturation. J. Fish Dis. 12: 269–273.

Krise, W. F., J. W. Meade, and R. A. Smith. 1990. Effect of feeding rate and gas supersaturation on survival and growth of lake trout. Prog. Fish-cult. 52: 45–50.

Kubota, S. S., T. Miyazaki, N. Funahashi, T. Ochiai, and Y. Suga. 1980. Studies on therapy of fish diseases with spiramycin—I Absorption, distribution, excretion and toxicity in cultured yellowtail (*Seriola quinqueradiata*). Bull. Fac. Fish., Mie Univ. 7: 151–166. [Japanese with English summary and legends]

Kubota, S. S. and T. Miyazaki. 1980. Studies on therapy of fish diseases with spiramycin—II Its clinical studies against *Streptococcus* sp. infection in cultured yellowtail (*Seriola quinqueradiata*). Bull. Fac. Fish., Mie Univ. 7: 167–172. [Japanese with English summary and legends]

Kubota, S. S. and M. Takakuwa. 1963. Studies on the diseases of marine-culture fishes. I General description and preliminary discussion of fish diseases in Mie Prefecture. J. Fac. Fish., Pref. Univ. Mie 6: 107–124. [Japanese with English summary and legends]

Lahti, E., M. Harri, and O. V. Lindquist. 1985. Uptake and distribution of radioiodine and the effect of ambient nitrate, in some fish species. Comp. Biochem. Physiol. 80A: 337–342.

LaRoche, G., G. R. Gardner, R. Eisler, E. H. Jackim, P. P. Yevish, and G. E. Zaroogian. 1973. Analysis of toxic responses in marine poikilotherms. *In* Bioassay techniques and environmental chemistry, G. E. Glass (ed.). Ann Arbor Science, Ann Arbor, pp. 199–216.

Larsen, J. L. 1983. *Vibrio anguillarum*: a comparative study of fish pathogenic, environmental, and reference strains. Acta Vet. Scand. 24: 456–476.

Larsen, J. L. 1984. *Vibrio anguillarum*: Influence of temperature, pH, NaCl concentration and incubation on growth. J. Appl. Bacteriol. 57: 237–246.

Larsen, J. L. and S. Mellergaard. 1984. Agglutination typing of *Vibrio anguillarum* isolates from diseased fish and from the environment. Appl. Environ. Microbiol. 47: 1261–1265.

Lauckner, G. 1984a. Agents: fungi. *In* Diseases of marine animals, O. Kinne (ed.). Biologische Anstalt Helgoland, Hamburg, pp. 89–113.

Lauckner, G. 1984b. Diseases caused by protophytans (algae). *In* Diseases of marine animals, O. Kinne (ed.). Biologische Anstalt Helgoland, Hamburg, pp. 169–179.

Laurén, D. J. and D. G. McDonald. 1986. Influence of water hardness, pH, and alkalinity on the mechanisms of copper toxicity in juvenile rainbow trout, *Salmo gairdneri*. Can. J. Fish. Aquat. Sci. 43: 1488–1496.

Lautrop, H. 1981. Christian Gram on the Gram stain in letters to Carl Julius Salomonsen, 1883–1884. ASM News 47(2): 44–49.

Lawler, A. R. 1967. *Oodinium cyprinodontum* n. sp., a parasitic dinoflagellate on gills of Cyprinodontidae of Virginia. Ches. Sci. 8: 67–68.

Lawler, A. R. 1972. Preliminary studies on *Amyloodinium ocellatum* (Brown, 1931) in the Gulf of Mexico: natural hosts, experimental hosts, and control. NMFS Compl. Rpt. 2-85-R, Gulf Coast Research Laboratory, Ocean Springs, 41 pp.

Lawler, A. R. 1977. The parasitic dinoflagellate *Amyloodinium ocellatum* in marine aquaria. Drum and Croaker 77(2): 17–20.

Lawler, A. R. 1979. North American fishes reported as hosts of *Amyloodinium ocellatum* (Brown, 1931). Drum and Croaker 19(1): 8–14.

Lawler, A. R. 1980. Studies on *Amyloodinium ocellatum* (Dinoflagellata) in Mississippi Sound: natural and experimental hosts. Gulf Res. Rpt. 6: 403–413.

Lazar, B., A. Katz, and S. Ben-Yaakov. 1981. Cooper complexing capacity of seawater: a critical appraisal of the direct ASV method. Mar. Chem. 10: 221–231.

LeaMaster, B. R. and A. C. Ostrowski. 1988. Vibriosis in captive dolphins. Prog. Fish-cult. 50: 251–254.

Leatherland, J. F. and R. A. Sonstegard. 1984. Pathobiological responses of feral teleosts to environmental stressors: interlake studies of the physiology of Great Lakes salmon. *In* Contaminant effects on fisheries, V. W. Cairns, P. V. Hodson, and J. O. Nriagu (eds.). Wiley, New York, pp. 115–149.

Lett, P. F., G. J. Farmer, and F. W. H. Beamish. 1976. Effect of copper on some aspects of bioenergetics of rainbow trout (*Salmo gairdneri*). J. Fish. Res. Board Can. 33: 1335–1342.

Levin, M. A., R. E. Wolke, and V. J. Cabelli. 1972. *Vibrio anguillarum* as a cause of disease in winter flounder (*Pseudopleuronectes americanus*). Can. J. Microbiol. 18: 1585–1592.

Lewis, D. H. 1973. Response of brown shrimp to infection with *Vibrio* sp. Proc. World Maricult. Soc. 4: 333–338.

Lewis, D. H. 1985. Vibriosis in channel catfish, *Ictalurus punctatus* (Rafinesque). J. Fish Dis. 8: 539–545.

Lewis, D. H., G. W. Klontz, S. McConnell, and L. C. Grumbles. 1970. Infectious diseases and host response of marine fish: a partially annotated bibliography. Sea Grant Pub. No. TAMU-SG-71-401, Texas A & M University, College Station, 104 pp.

Lewis, S. D. and W. M. Lewis. 1971. The effect of zinc and copper on the osmolality of blood serum of the channel catfish, *Ictalurus punctatus* Rafinesque, and the golden shiner, *Notemigonus crysoleucas* Mitchill. Trans. Am. Fish. Soc. 100: 639–643.

Li, Y. and R. T. Lovell. 1985. Elevated levels of dietary ascorbic acid increase immune responses in channel catfish. J. Nutr. 115: 123–131.

Lieberman, D. and G. Early. 1979. Exophiala-like fungus in an alewife *Alosa pseudoharengus*. Drum and Croaker 19(2): 37–39.

Lightner, D. V. and D. H. Lewis. 1975. A septicemic bacterial disease syndrome of penaeid shrimp. Mar. Fish. Rev. 37(5/6): 25–28.

Lillehaug, A. 1990. A field trial of vaccination against cold-water vibriosis in Atlantic salmon (*Salmo salar* L.). Aquaculture 84: 1–12.

Lom, J. and A. R. Lawler. 1973. An ultrastructural study on the mode of attachment in dinoflagellates invading gills of Cyprinodontidae. Protistologica 9: 293–309.

Love, M., D. Teebken-Fisher, J. E. Hose, J. J. Farmer III, and G. R. Fanning. 1981. *Vibrio damsela*, a marine bacterium, causes skin ulcers on the damselfish *Chromis punctipinnis*. Science 214: 1139–1140.

Lowe, J. 1874. Fauna and flora of Norfolk. Part IV. Trans. Norfolk Norwich Nat. Soc. Fish., pp. 21–56.

Lyon, B. R. and R. Skurray. 1987. Antimicrobial resistance of *Staphylococcus aureus*: genetic basis. Microbiol. Rev. 51: 88–134.

Mahmoud, A. A. F. 1989. Parasitic Protozoa and helminths: biological and immunological challenges. Science 246: 1015–1022.

Mahoney, J. B., F. H. Midlige, and D. G. Deuel. 1973. A fin rot disease of marine and euryhaline fishes in the New York Bight. Trans. Am. Fish. Soc. 102: 596–605.

Majeed, S. K., C. Gopinath, and D. W. Jolly. 1981. Pathology of spontaneous tuberculosis and pseudotuberculosis in fish. J. Fish Dis. 4: 507–512.

Malcolm, S. J. and N. B. Price. 1984. The behaviour of iodine and bromine in estuarine surface sediments. Mar. Chem. 15: 263–271.

Manning, M. J., M. F. Grace, and C. J. Secombes. 1982. Developmental aspects of immunity and tolerance in fish. *In* Microbial diseases of fish, R. J. Roberts (ed.). Academic Press, London, pp. 31–46.

Manning, M. J. and M. F. Tatner (eds.). 1985. Fish immunology. Academic Press, London, 374 pp.

Marcello, R. A. Jr. and R. B. Fairbanks. 1976. Gas bubble disease mortality of Atlantic menhaden, *Brevoortia tyrannus*, at a coastal nuclear power plant. *In* Gas bubble disease, D. H. Fickeisen and

M. J. Schneider (eds.). Energy Research and Development Administration, Oak Ridge, pp. 75–80.

Margenau, T. L., S. T. Schram, and W. H. Blust. 1988. Lymphocystis in a walleye population. Trans. Am. Fish. Soc. 117: 308–310.

Marking, L. L. 1987. Gas supersaturation in fisheries: causes, concerns, and cures. Fish Wildl. Leaf. 9, U.S. Fish and Wildlife Service, Washington, 10 pp.

Marsh, M. C. 1903. A fatality among fishes in water containing an excess of dissolved air. Trans. Am. Fish. Soc. 32: 192–199.

Marsh, M. C. and F. P. Gorham. 1905. The gas disease in fishes. *In* Report of the U.S. Bureau of Fisheries 1904, pp. 343–376 + 3 plates.

Masschelein, W., G. Fransolet, and J. Genot. 1975. Techniques for dispersing and dissolving ozone in water. Part 1. Water Sew. Works 122(12): 57–60.

Mawdesley-Thomas, L. E. 1972. Some tumours of fish. Symp. Zool. Soc. London 30: 191–283.

May, E. G., G. L. Bullock, W. D. Sheffield, M. W. Stoskopf, and A. G. Smith. 1982. Vibriosis in a marine aquarium involving *Vibrio alginolyticus* and *Vibrio anguillarium* [*sic*]: a review of gross and histopathological lesions, and bacteriological results. *In* International Association for Aquatic Animal Medicine: 13th annual conference and workshop and 7th eastern fish health workshop, Baltimore, p. 15. [Abstract]

McAllister, P. E. 1981. Viral diseases of freshwater fish—a review of agents affecting cold-water species. *In* Proceedings of Republic of China-United States cooperative science seminar on fish diseases, G-H. Kou, J. L. Fryer, and M. L. Landolt (eds.). NSC Symp. Ser. No. 3, National Science Council, Taipei, pp. 47–57.

McCosker, J. E. 1969. A behavioral correlate for the passage of lymphocystis disease in three blennioid fishes. Copeia 1969: 636–637.

McCosker, J. E., M. D. Lagios, and T. Tucker. 1976. Ultrastructure of lymphocystis virus in the quillback rockfish, *Sebastes maliger*, with records of infection in other aquarium-held fishes. Trans. Am. Fish. Soc. 105: 333–337.

McCosker, J. E. and R. F. Nigrelli. 1971. New records of lymphocystis disease in four eastern Pacific fish species. J. Fish. Res. Board Can. 28: 1809–1810.

McGinnis, M. R. and L. Ajello. 1974. A new species of *Exophiala* isolated from channel catfish. Mycologia 66: 518–520.

McKim, J. M., G. M. Christensen, and E. P. Hunt. 1970. Changes in the blood of brook trout (*Salvelinus fontinalis*) after short-term and long-term exposure to copper. J. Fish. Res. Board Can. 27: 1883–1889.

McLeod, G. C. 1978. The gas bubble disease of fish. *In* The behavior of fish and other aquatic animals, D. I. Mostofsky (ed.). Academic Press, New York, pp. 319–339.

McLusky, D. S. and C. N. K. Phillips. 1975. Some effects of copper on the polychaete *Phyllodoce maculata*. Estuar. Coast. Mar. Sci. 3: 103–108.

McVicar, A. H. 1982. *Ichthyophonus* infections of fish. *In* Microbial diseases of fish, R. J. Roberts (ed.). Academic Press, London, pp. 243–269.

McVicar, A. H. 1986. Fungal infection in marine fish and its importance in mariculture. *In* Pathology in marine aquaculture, C-P. Vivarès, J-R. Bonami, and E. Jaspers (eds.). Spec. Pub. No. 9, European Aquaculture Society, Bredene, pp. 189–196.

Mearns, A. J. and M. Sherwood. 1974. Environmental aspects of fin erosion and tumors in southern California Dover sole. Trans. Am. Fish. Soc. 103: 799–810.

Menitskii, Yu. L. 1963. [Structure and systematic position of the turbellarian *Ichthyophaga subcutanea* Syromjatnikova 1949, parasitizing fish.] Parazitol. Sbornik 21: 245–258. [English translation from Russian by Al Ahram Center for Scientific Translations, Cairo, 19 manuscript pages, 1979]

Meyer, F. P. and R. A. Schnick. 1989. A review of chemicals used for the control of fish diseases. Rev. Aquat. Sci. 1: 693–710.

Midgley, D. 1980. Chlorine disappearance in sea water. Water Res. 14: 1559–1560.

Milanovich, F. P., R. Spies, M. S. Guram, and E. E. Sykes. 1976. Uptake of copper by the polychaete *Cirriformia spirabrancha* in the presence of dissolved yellow organic matter of natural origin. Estuar. Coast. Mar. Sci. 4: 585–588.

Mills, G. L. and J. G. Quinn. 1981. Isolation of dissolved organic matter and copper-organic complexes from estuarine waters using reverse-phase liquid chromatography. Mar. Chem. 10: 93–102.

Mix, M. C. 1986. Cancerous diseases in aquatic animals and their association with environmental pollutants: a critical literature review. Mar. Environ. Res. 20: 1–141.

Miyazaki, T. and S. S. Kubota. 1977a. Studies on ichthyophonus disease of fishes—I Rainbow trout fry. Bull. Fac. Fish., Mie Univ. 4: 45–56. [Japanese with English summary and legends]

Miyazaki, T. and S. S. Kubota. 1977b. Studies on ichthyophonus disease of fishes—II Yearling rainbow trout—clonic [*sic*] infection. Bull. Fac. Fish., Mie Univ. 4: 57–65. [Japanese with English summary and legends]

Miyazaki, T. and S. S. Kubota. 1977c. Studies on ichthyophonus disease of fishes—III Life cycle of *Ichthyophonus* affected rainbow trout. Bull. Fac. Fish., Mie Univ. 4: 67–80. [Japanese with English summary and legends]

Moring, J. R. 1982. Fin erosion and culture-related injuries of chinook salmon raised in floating net pens. Prog. Fish-cult. 44: 189–191.

Moser, M., J. Sakanari, and R. Heckmann. 1986. The effects of praziquantel on various larval and adult parasites from freshwater and marine snails and fish. J. Parasitol. 72: 175–176.

Moyers, J. L. and R. A. Duce. 1972. Gaseous and particulate iodine in the marine atmosphere. J. Geophys. Res. 77: 5229–5238.

Munn, C. B. 1980. Production and properties of a haemolytic toxin by *Vibrio anguillarum*. *In* Fish diseases: third COPRAQ-session, W. Ahne (ed.). Springer-Verlag, Berlin, pp. 69–74.

Murchelano, R. A. 1975. The histopathology of fin rot disease in winter flounder from the New York Bight. J. Wildl. Dis. 11: 263–268.

Murcheleno, R. A. and D. W. Bridges. 1976. Lymphocystis disease in the winter flounder, *Pseudopleuronectes americanus*. J. Wildl. Dis. 12: 101–103.

Murchelano, R. A. and J. Ziskowski. 1976. Fin rot disease studies in the New York Bight. *In* Proceedings of a symposium on the middle Atlantic continental shelf and the New York Bight, M. G. Gross (ed.). Spec. Symp. 2, American Society of Limnology and Oceanography, Seattle, pp. 329–336.

Murchelano, R. A. and J. Ziskowski. 1977. Histopathology of an acute fin lesion in the summer flounder, *Paralichthys dentatus*, and some speculations on the etiology of fin rot disease in the New York Bight. J. Wildl. Dis. 13: 103–106.

Murchelano, R. A. and J. Ziskowski. 1979. Fin rot disease—a sentinel of environmental stress? C.M. 1979/E:25, Mar. Environ. Committee, Int. Council Explor. Sea, 5 pp. + 2 plates. [Manuscript report]

Muroga, K., H. Yamanoi, Y. Hironaka, S. Yamamoto, M. Tatani, Y. Jo, S. Takahashi, and H. Hanada. 1984a. Detection of *Vibrio anguillarum* from wild fingerlings of ayu *Plecoglossus altivelis*. Bull. Jap. Soc. Sci. Fish. 50: 591–596.

Muroga, K., G. Lio-po, C. Pitogo, and R. Imada. 1984b. *Vibrio* sp. isolated from milkfish (*Chanos chanos*) with opaque eyes. Fish Pathol. 19: 81–87.

Newcomb, T. W. 1974. Changes in blood chemistry of juvenile steelhead trout, *Salmo gairdneri*, following sublethal exposure to nitrogen supersaturation. J. Fish. Res. Board Can. 31: 1953–1957.

Newman, M. C. and S. Y. Feng. 1982. Susceptibility and resistance of the rock crab, *Cancer irroratus*, to natural and experimental bacterial infection. J. Invert. Pathol. 40: 75–88.

Niekerk, J. P. van and D. K. Kok. 1989. *Chonopeltis australis* (Branchiura): structural, developmental and functional aspects of the trophic appendages. Crustaceana 57: 51–56.

Nielsen, E. S. and S. Wium-Andersen. 1970. Copper ions as poison in the sea and in freshwater. Mar. Biol. 6: 93–97.

Nigrelli, R. F. 1936. The morphology, cytology and life-history of *Oodinium ocellatum* Brown, a dinoflagellate parasite on marine fishes. Zoologica (N.Y.) 21: 129–164 + 9 plates.

Nigrelli, R. F. 1952. Spontaneous neoplasms in fishes. VI. Thyroid tumors in marine fishes. Zoologica (N.Y.) 37: 185–189 + 9 plates.

Nigrelli, R. F. 1954. Tumors and other atypical cell growths in temperate freshwater fishes of North America. Trans. Am. Fish. Soc. 83: 262–296.

Nigrelli, R. F. 1963. Two diseases of the neon tetra *Hyphessobrycon innesi*. Aquar. J. 24: 203–208.

Nigrelli, R. F. and C. M. Breder Jr. 1934. The susceptibility and immunity of certain marine fishes to *Epibdella melleni*, a monogenetic trematode. J. Parasitol. 20: 259–269.

Nigrelli, R. F. and G. D. Ruggieri. 1965. Studies on virus diseases of fishes. Spontaneous and experimentally induced cellular hypertrophy (lymphocystis disease) in fishes of the New York Aquarium, with a report of new cases and an annotated bibliography (1874–1965). Zoologica (N.Y.) 50: 83–96 + 10 plates.

Nigrelli, R. F. and G. D. Ruggieri. 1966. Enzootics in the New York Aquarium caused by *Cryptocaryon irritans* Brown, 1951 (=*Ichthyophthirius marinus* Sikama, 1961), a histophagous ciliate in the skin, eyes and gills of marine fishes. Zoologica (N.Y.) 51: 97–102 + 7 plates.

Nigrelli, R. F. and G. D. Ruggieri. 1974. Hyperplasia and neoplasia of the thyroid in marine fishes. Mt. Sinai J. Med. 41: 283–293.

Nigrelli, R. F. and H. Vogel. 1963. Spontaneous tuberculosis in fishes and in other cold-blooded vertebrates with special reference to *Mycobacterium fortuitum* Cruz from fish and human lesions. Zoologica (N.Y.) 48: 131–144 + 6 plates.

Novales, R. R., L. I. Gilbert, and F. A. Brown Jr. 1973. Endocrine mechanisms. *In* Comparative animal physiology, 3rd ed., C. L. Prosser (ed.). Saunders, Philadelphia, pp. 857–908.

O'Donovan, D. C. 1965. Treatment with ozone. J. Am. Water Works Assoc. 57: 1157–1194.

Okamoto, N., H. Suzuki, K. Nakase, and T. Sano. 1987. Experimental oral infection of rainbow trout with spherical bodies of *Ichthyophonus hoferi* cultivated. Nippon Suisan Gakkaishi 53: 407–409. [Japanese with English summary and legends]

Olafsen, J. A., M. Christie, and J. Raa. 1981. Biochemical ecology of psychrotrophic strains of *Vibrio anguillarum* isolated from outbreaks of vibriosis at low temperature. Zbl. Bakt. Hyg. 2 (I. Abt. Orig. C): 339–348.

O'Neill, J. G. 1981. The humoral immune response of *Salmo trutta* L. and *Cyprinus carpio* L. exposed to heavy metals. J. Fish Biol. 19: 297–306.

Oppenheimer, C. 1958. A bacterium causing tail rot in the Norwegian codfish. Pub. No. 5, Institute of Marine Science, University of Texas, pp. 160–164.

O'Shea, T. A. and K. H. Mancy. 1978. The effect of pH and hardness metal ions on the competitive interaction between trace metal ions and inorganic and organic complexing agents found in natural waters. Water Res. 12: 703–711.

Oshima, Y., Y. Osada, M. Akagawa, and N. Nakazawa. 1970. Potassium-1-methyl-1,4-dihydro-7-[2-(5-nitro-2-furyl)-vinyl]-4-oxo-1,8-naphthyridine-3-carboxylic acid (DS-677 K). Bull. Jap. Soc. Sci. Fish. 36: 1186–1199. [Japanese with English summary and legends]

Overstreet, R. M. 1978. Marine maladies? Worms, germs, and other symbionts from the northern Gulf of Mexico. MASGP-78-021, Mississippi-Alabama Sea Grant Consortium, Ocean Springs, 140 pp.

Ozaki, H., K. Uematsu, and K. Tanaka. 1970. Survival and growth of goldfish and carp in dilute solutions of copper sulphate. Jap. J. Ichthyol. 17: 166–172. [Japanese with English summary and legends]

Pagenkopf, G. K., R. C. Russo, and R. V. Thurston. 1974. Effect of complexation on toxicity of copper to fishes. J. Fish. Res. Board Can. 31: 462–465.

Paperna, I. 1980. *Amyloodinium ocellatum* (Brown, 1931) (Dinoflagellida) infestations in cultured marine fish at Eilat, Red Sea: epizootiology and pathology. J. Fish Dis. 3: 363–372.

Paperna, I. 1984a. Chemical control of *Amyloodinium ocellatum* (Brown 1931) (Dinoflagellida) infections: in vitro tests and treatment trials with infected fishes. Aquaculture 38: 1–18.

Paperna, I. 1984b. Reproduction cycle and tolerance to temperature and salinity of *Amyloodinium ocellatum* (Brown, 1931) (Dinoflagellida). Ann. Parasitol. Hum. Comp. 59: 7–30.

Paperna, I. 1986. *Icythyophonus* infection in grey mullets from southern Africa: histopathological and ultrastructural study. Dis. Aquat. Organ. 1: 89–97.

Paperna, I., A. Diamant, and R. M. Overstreet. 1984. Monogenean infestations and mortality in wild and cultured Red Sea fishes. Helgoländer Meeresunters. 37: 445–462.

Paperna, I. and R. M. Overstreet. 1981. Parasites and diseases of mullets (Mugilidae). *In* Aquaculture of grey mullets, O. H. Oren (ed.). Cambridge University Press, Cambridge, pp. 411–493.

Paperna, I., I. Sabnai, and A. Colorni. 1982. An outbreak of lymphocystis in *Sparus aurata* L. in the Gulf of Aqaba, Red Sea. J. Fish Dis. 5: 433–437.

Paperna, I., T. M. Ventura, and A. P. de Matos. 1987. Lymphocystis infection in snakeskin gourami, *Trichogaster pectoralis* (Regan), (Anabantidae). J. Fish Dis. 10: 11–19.

Parisot, T. J. and J. W. Wood. 1959. Fish mycobacteriosis (tuberculosis). Fish. Leaf. 494, U.S. Fish and Wildlife Service, Washington, 3 pp.

Parisot, T. J. and E. M. Wood. 1960. A comparative study of the causative agent of a mycobacterial disease of salmonid fishes. 2. A description of the histopathology of the disease in chinook salmon (*Oncorhynchus tshawytscha*) and a comparison of the staining characteristics of the fish disease with leprosy and human tuberculosis. Am. Rev. Respir. Dis. 82: 212–222.

Pauley, G. B. and R. E. Nakatani. 1967. Histopathology of "gas-bubble" disease in salmon fingerlings. J. Fish. Res. Board Can. 24: 867–871.

Pettit, A. 1913. Observations sur l'*Ichthyosporidium* et sur la maladie qui'il provoque chez la truite. Ann. Inst. Pasteur 27: 986–1008.

Pilcher, K. S. and J. L. Fryer. 1980. The viral diseases of fish: a review through 1978. Part 1: Diseases of proven viral etiology. CRC Crit. Rev. Microbiol. 7: 287–363.

Pippy, J. H. C. and G. M. Hare. 1969. Relationship of river pollution to bacterial infection in salmon (*Salmo salar*) and suckers (*Catostomus commersoni*). Trans. Am. Fish. Soc. 98: 685–690.

Plehn, M. and K. Mulsow. 1911. Der Erreger der "Taumelkrankheit" der Salmoniden. Centr. Bakt. Parasit. Infekt. 59(Abt. I): 63–68 + 1 plate.

Prescott, S. R. 1977. A technical report on oral immunization of marine tropical fish against *Vibrio anguillarum*. Aquaculture 11: 281–283.

Reichenbach-Klinke, H-H. 1972. Some aspects of mycobacterial infections in fish. Symp. Zool. Soc. London 30: 17–24.

Reichenbach-Klinke, H. and E. Elkan. 1965. The principal diseases of lower vertebrates. Academic Press, London, 600 pp.

Richards, R. H. 1980. Observations on vibriosis in cultured flatfish. *In* Fish diseases: third COPRAQ-session, W. Ahne (ed.). Springer-Verlag, Berlin, pp. 75–81.

Richards, R. H., A. Holliman, and S. Helgason. 1978. *Exophiala salmonis* infection in Atlantic salmon *Salmo salar*. L. J. Fish Dis. 1: 357–368.

Richardson, L. B. and D. T. Burton. 1981. Toxicity of ozonated estuarine water to juvenile blue crabs (*Callinectes sapidus*) and juvenile Atlantic menhaden (*Brevoortia tyrannus*). Bull. Environ. Contam. Toxicol. 26: 171–178.

Richmond, M. H. 1972. Some environmental consequences of the use of antibiotics: or "what goes up must come down." J. Appl. Bacteriol. 35: 155–176.

Roberts, R. J., A. McQueen, W. M. Shearer, and H. Young. 1973. The histopathology of salmon tagging. III. Secondary infections associated with tagging. J. Fish Biol. 5: 621–623.

Robertson, M. 1909. Notes on an ichthyosporidian causing a fatal disease in sea-trout. Proc. Zool. Soc. London 1909: 399–402.

Rødsaether, M. C., J. Olafsen, J. Raa, K. Myhre, and J. B. Steen. 1977. Copper as an initiating factor of vibriosis (*Vibrio anguillarum*) in eel (*Anguilla anguilla*). J. Fish Biol. 10: 17–21.

Rosen, H. M. 1973. Use of ozone and oxygen in advanced wastewater treatment. J. Water Pollut. Contr. Fed. 45: 2521–2536.

Ross, A. J. 1960. *Mycobacterium salmoniphilum* sp. nov. from salmonid fishes. Am. Rev. Respir. Dis. 81: 241–250.

Ross, A. J. 1963. Mycobacteria in adult salmonid fishes returning to national fish hatcheries in Washington, Oregon, and California in 1958–59. Spec. Sci. Rpt.—Fish. No. 462, U.S. Fish and Wildlife Service, Washington, 5 pp.

Ross, A. J. 1970. Mycobacteriosis among Pacific salmonid fishes. *In* A symposium on diseases of fishes and shellfishes, S. F. Snieszko (ed.). Spec. Pub. No. 5, American Fisheries Society, Washington, pp. 279–283.

Ross, M. 1977. Factors affecting the survival and growth of striped bass, *Morone saxatilis* (Walbaum), fry in recirculating systems. Diss. Abst. Int. 38: 1969B–1970B.

Rucker, R. R. 1972. Gas-bubble disease of salmonids: a critical review. Tech. Pap. 58, U.S. Fish and Wildlife Service, Washington, 11 pp.

Ruggieri, G. D., R. F. Nigrelli, P. M. Powles, and D. G. Garnett. 1970. Epizootics in yellowtail flounder, *Limanda ferruginea* Storer, in the western North Atlantic caused by *Ichthyophonus*, an ubiquitous parasitic fungus. Zoologica (N.Y.) 55: 57–62 + 10 plates.

Russell, P. H. 1974. Lymphocystis in wild plaice *Pleuronectes platessa* (L.), and flounder, *Platichthys flesus* (L.), in British coastal waters: a histopathological and serological study. J. Fish Biol. 6: 771–778.

Sakanari, J. A., C. A. Reilly, and M. Moser. 1983. Tubercular lesions in Pacific coast populations of striped bass. Trans. Am. Fish. Soc. 112: 565–566.

Sakata, T., M. Matsuura, and Y. Shimokawa. 1989. Characteristics of *Vibrio damsela* isolated from diseased yellowtail *Seriola quinqueradiata*. Nippon Suisan Gakkaishi 55: 135–141.

Sako, H. and T. Hara. 1984. Pathogenicity of vibrio isolated from anadromous amago salmon. Bull. Natl. Res. Inst. Aquacult. (5): 71–76. [Japanese with English summary and legends]

Sako, H. and R. Kusuda. 1978. Chemotherapeutical studies on trimethoprim against vibriosis of pond-cultured ayu—I. Microbiological evaluation of trimethoprim and sulfonamides on the causative agent *Vibrio anguillarum*. Fish Pathol. 13: 91–96.

Sako, H., R. Kusuda, and T. Tabata. 1979. Chemotherapeutical studies on trimethoprim against vibriosis of pond cultured ayu—II. Tissue levels after administration of trimethoprim-sulfadoxine mixture. Fish Pathol. 14: 65–70.

Sako, H. and M. Sorimachi. 1985. Susceptibility of fish pathogenic viruses, bacteria and fungus to ultraviolet irradiation and the disinfectant effect of U.V.-ozone water sterilizer on the pathogens in water. Bull. Natl. Res. Inst. Aquacult. (8): 51–58. [Japanese with English summary and legends]

Samuelsen, T. J. 1989. The water system at the Bergen Aquarium—long term experience. Bull. Inst. Océanogr., Monaco, Num. spéc. 5: 93–99.

Scarfe, A. D., K. A. Jones, C. W. Steele, H. Kleerekoper, and M. Corbett. 1982. Locomotor behavior of four marine teleosts in response to sublethel copper exposure. Aquat. Toxicol. 2: 335–353.

Schiewe, M. H. 1981. Taxonomic status of marine vibrios pathogenic for salmonid fish. Develop. Biol. Stand. 49: 149–158.

Schiewe, M. H. 1983. *Vibrio ordalii* as a cause of vibriosis in salmonid fish. *In* Bacterial and viral diseases of fish: molecular studies, J. H. Crosa (ed.). Washington Sea Grant Program, University of Washington, Seattle, pp. 31–40.

Schiewe, M. H., T. J. Trust, and J. H. Crosa. 1981. *Vibrio ordalii* sp. nov.: a causative agent of vibriosis in fish. Curr. Microbiol. 6: 343–348.

Schiewe, M. H. and D. D. Weber. 1976. Effect of gas bubble disease on lateral line function in juvenile steelhead trout. *In* Gas bubble disease, D. H. Fickeisen and M. J. Schneider (eds.). Energy Research and Development Administration, Oak Ridge, pp. 89–92.

Schmahl, G. and H. Mehlhorn. 1985. Treatment of fish parasites. 1. Praziquantel effective against Monogenea (*Dactylogyrus vastator, Dactylogyrus extensus, Diplozoon paradoxum*). Z. Parasitenkunde 71: 727–737.

Schmahl, G. and H. Taraschewski. 1987. Treatment of fish parasites. 2. Effects of praziquantel, niclosamide, levamisol-HCl, and metrifonate on Monogenea (*Gyrodactylus aculeati, Diplozoon paradoxum*). Parasitol. Res. 73: 341–351.

Schmidt, R. L. 1978. Copper in the marine environment—Part I. CRC Crit. Rev. Environ. Contr. 8: 101–152.

Schneider, R. and B. L. Nicholson. 1980. Bacteria associated with fin rot disease in hatchery-reared Atlantic salmon (*Salmo salar*). Can. J. Fish. Aquat. Sci. 37: 1505–1513.

Schnick, R. A., F. P. Meyer, and D. L. Gray. 1989. A guide to approved chemicals in fish production and fishery resource management. MP241-5M-3-89RV, University of Arkansas Cooperative Extension Service and U.S. Fish and Wildlife Service, Little Rock and La Crosse, 27 pp.

Segner, H. and H. Möller. 1984. Electron microscopical investigations on starvation-induced liver pathology in flounders *Platichthys flesus*. Mar. Ecol. Prog. Ser. 19: 193–196.

Shackley, S. E., P. E. King, and S. M. Gordon. 1981. Vitellogenesis and trace metals in a marine teleost. J. Fish Biol. 18: 349–352.

Shaw, T. L. and V. M. Brown. 1974. The toxicity of some forms of copper to rainbow trout. Water Res. 8: 377–392.

Sheppard, C. R. C. 1977. Relationships between heavy metals and major cations along pollution gradients. Mar. Pollut. Bull. 8: 163–164.

Shimura, S. 1981. The larval development of *Argulus coregoni* (Crustacea: Branchiura). J. Nat. Hist. 15: 331–348.

Shimura, S. 1983. SEM observation on the mouth tube and preoral sting of *Argulus coregoni* Thorell and *Argulus japonicus* Thiele (Crustacea: Branchiura). Fish Pathol. 18: 151–156.

Shimura, S. and K. Inoue. 1984. Toxic effects of extract from the mouth-parts of *Argulus coregoni* THORELL (Crustacea: Branchiura). Bull. Jap. Soc. Sci. Fish. 50: 729.

Shimura, S., K. Inoue, K. Kasai, and M. Saito. 1983. Hematological changes of *Oncorhynchus masou* (Salmonidae) caused by the infection of *Argulus coregoni* (Crustacea: Branchiura). Fish Pathol. 18: 157–162. [Japanese with English summary and legends]

Shotts, E. B. Jr., V. L. Vanderwork, and L. M. Campbell. 1976a. Occurrence of R factors associated with *Aeromonas hydrophila* isolates from aquarium fish and waters. J. Fish. Res. Board Can. 33: 736–740.

Shotts, E. B., V. L. Vanderwork, and W. J. Long. 1976b. Incidence of R factors associated with *Aeromonas hydrophila* complex isolated from aquarium fish. *In* Wildlife diseases, L. A. Page (ed.). Plenum, New York, pp. 493–501.

Shrimpton, J. M., D. J. Randall, and L. E. Fidler. 1990a. Factors affecting swim bladder volume in rainbow trout (*Oncorhynchus mykiss*) held in gas supersaturated water. Can. J. Zool. 68: 962–968.

Shrimpton, J. M., D. J. Randall, and L. E. Fidler. 1990b. Assessing the effects of positive buoyancy on rainbow trout (*Oncorhynchus mykiss*) held in gas supersaturated water. Can. J. Zool. 68: 969–973.

Sikama, Y. 1938. Über die Weisspünktchenkrankheit bei Seefischen. J. Shanghai Sci. Inst. 4(Sect. III): 113–128.

Sikama, Y. 1960. [White spot disease in marine fish and some similar diseases.] Sogo-Kaiyokagaku 2: 189–200. [Japanese]

Sikama, Y. 1961. On a new species of *Ichthyophthirius* found in marine fishes. Sci. Rpt. Yokosuka City Mus. (6): 66–70.

Sikama, Y. 1964. [Study on the white spot disease in marine fish.] Aquiculture 19(2?): 29–90 + 97 figs. [Japanese]

Simpson, T. H. 1975/1976. Endocrine aspects of salmonid culture. Proc. R. Soc. Edinburgh 75B: 241–252.

Sindermann, C. J. 1977. Fin rot disease of striped bass. *In* Disease diagnosis and control in North American marine aquaculture, C. J. Sindermann (ed.). Elsevier, Amsterdam, pp. 276–277.

Sindermann, C. J. 1979. Pollution-associated diseases and abnormalities of fish and shellfish: a review. Fish. Bull. (NOAA) 76: 717–749.

Sindermann, C. and A. Rosenfield. 1954. Diseases of fishes of the western North Atlantic. I. Diseases of the sea herring (*Clupea harengus*). Res. Bull. No. 18, Department of Sea and Shore Fisheries, Augusta (Maine), 23 pp.

Sizemore, R. K. 1985. Involvement of *Vibrio* spp. in soft crab mortality. *In* Proceedings of a national symposium on the soft-shelled blue crab fishery, H. M. Perry and R. F. Malone (eds.). Gulf Coast Research Laboratory, Biloxi, pp. 21–22.

Smith, C. E. 1988. Histopathology of gas bubble disease in juvenile rainbow trout. Prog. Fish-cult. 50: 98–103.

Snieszko, S. F. 1978. Mycobacteriosis (tuberculosis) of fishes. Fish Dis. Leaf. 55, U.S. Fish and Wildlife Service, Washington, 9 pp.

Solbé, J. F. de L. G. and V. A. Cooper. 1976. Studies on the toxicity of copper sulphate to stone loach *Noemacheilus barbatulus* (L.) in hard water. Water Res. 10: 523–527.

Spanier, E. 1978. Preliminary trials with an ultraviolet liquid sterilizer. Aquaculture 14: 75–84.

Sposito, G. 1981. Trace metals in contaminated waters. Environ. Sci. Technol. 15: 396–403.

Spotte, S. 1973. Marine aquarium keeping: the science, animals, and art. Wiley, New York, 171 pp.

Spotte, S. 1979. Seawater aquariums: the captive environment. Wiley, New York, 413 pp.

Spotte, S. and G. Adams. 1981. Pathogen reduction in closed aquaculture systems by UV radiation: fact or artifact? Mar. Ecol. Prog. Ser. 6: 295–298.

Spotte, S. and J. D. Buck. 1981. The efficacy of UV irradiation in the microbial disinfection of marine mammal water. J. Wildl. Dis. 17: 11–16.

Sprague, V. 1965. *Ichthyosporidium* Caullery and Mesnil, 1905, the name of a genus of fungi or a genus of sporozoans? Syst. Zool. 14: 110–114.

Steele, C. W. 1983. Effects of exposure to sublethal copper on the locomotor behavior of the sea catfish, *Arius felis*. Aquat. Toxicol. 4: 83–93.

Stroud, R. K. and A. V. Nebeker. 1976. A study of the pathogenesis of gas bubble disease in steelhead trout (*Salmo gairdneri*). *In* Gas bubble disease, D. H. Fickeisen and M. J. Schneider (eds.).

Energy Research and Development Administration, Oak Ridge, pp. 66–71.

Stumm, W. and P. A. Brauner. 1975. Chemical speciation. *In* Chemical oceanography, Vol. 1, 2nd ed., J. P. Riley and G. Skirrow (eds.). Academic Press, London, pp. 173–239.

Stumm, W. and J. J. Morgan. 1981. Aquatic chemistry, 2nd ed. Wiley, New York, 780 pp.

Sugimoto, N., S. Ishibashi, and Y. Yone. 1976. On the effectiveness and safety of sodium nifurstyrenate as a chemotherapeutic agent for pseudotuberculosis of yellowtail. Rpt. Fish. Res. Lab., Kyushu Univ. (3): 33–43. [Japanese with English summary and legends]

Sunda, W. and R. R. L. Guillard. 1976. The relationship between cupric ion activity and the toxicity of copper to phytoplankton. J. Mar. Res. 24: 511–529.

Sutherland, D. R. and D. D. Wittrock. 1986. Surface topography of the branchiuran *Argulus appendiculosus* Wilson, 1907 as revealed by scanning electron microscopy. Z. Parasitenkunde 72: 405–415.

Sutherland, J. and C. W. Major. 1981. Internal heavy metal changes as a consequence of exposure of *Mytilus edulis*, the blue mussel, to elevated external copper(II) levels. Comp. Biochem. Physiol. 68C: 63–67.

Swift, S. and H. Cohen. 1962. Granulomas of the skin due to *Mycobacterium balnei* after abrasions from a fish tank. New Eng. J. Med. 267: 1244–1246.

Sykes, M. 1965. Disinfection and sterilization: theory and practice, 2nd ed. Spon, London, 486 pp.

Symes, J. L. and D. R. Kester. 1985. Copper(II) interaction with carbonate species based on malachite solubility in perchlorate medium at the ionic strength of seawater. Mar. Chem. 16: 189–211.

Székely, C. and K. Molnár. 1987. Mebendazole is an efficacious drug against pseudodactylogyrosis in the European eel *Anguilla anguilla*. J. Appl. Ichthyol. 3: 183–186.

Takahashi, Y., H. Nagoya, and K. Momoyama. 1984. Pathogenicity and characteristics of *Vibrio* sp. isolated from diseased postlarvae of Kuruma prawn, *Penaeus japonicus* Bate. J. Shimonoseki Univ. Fish. 32: 23–31.

Tashiro, F., S. Morikawa, A. Motonishi, I. Sanjo, N. Kimura, K. Inoue, T. Nomura, M. Ushiyama, Y. Jo, F. Hayashi, and I. Kunimine. 1979. Studies on chemotherapy of fish diseases with piromidic acid—II. Its clinical studies against bacterial infections in cultured salmonids and eels. Fish Pathol. 14: 93–101.

Thoney, D. A. 1989a. Praziquantel update. Seascope (Aquarium Systems) 6(Fall issue): 3.

Thoney, D. A. 1989b. The effects of various chemicals on monogeneans parasitizing the skin of elasmobranchs. *In* AAZPA 1989 annual conference proceedings. American Association of Zoological Parks and Aquariums, Wheeling, pp. 217–222.

Toranzo, A. E., J. L. Barja, R. R. Colwell, and F. M. Hetrick. 1983. Characterization of plasmids in bacterial fish pathogens. Infect. Immun. 39: 184–192.

Totaro, E. A., F. A. Pisanti, and P. Glees. 1985. A rôle of copper level in the formation of neuronal lipofuscin in the spinal ganglia of *Torpedo m.* Mar. Environ. Res. 15: 153–163.

Trust, T. J. 1972. Inadequacy of aquarium antibacterial formulations for the inhibition of potential pathogens of freshwater fish. J. Fish. Res. Board Can. 29: 1425–1430.

Trust, T. J. and D. C. Chipman. 1974. Evaluation of aquarium antibiotic formulations. Antimicrob. Agents Chemother. 6: 379–386.

Trust, T. J. and J. L. Whitby. 1976. Antibiotic resistance of bacteria in water containing ornamental fishes. Antimicrob. Agents Chemother. 10: 598–603.

Uchida, H. and Y. Abe. 1987. The prevention of goitre in captive sharks. Int. Zoo Ybk. 26: 59–61.

Urdaneta, H. E. 1982. Lymphocystis in róbalo, *Centropomus undecimalis* (Bloch), in Lake Maracaibo, Venezuela. J. Fish Dis. 5: 347–348.

Velji, M. I., L. J. Albright, and T. P. T. Evelyn. 1990. Protective immunity in juvenile coho salmon *Oncorhynchus kisutch* following immunization with *Vibrio ordalii* lipopolysaccharide or from exposure to live *V. ordalii* cells. Dis. Aquat. Organ. 9: 25–29.

Vijayamadhavan, K. T. and T. Iwai. 1975. Histochemical observations on the permeation of heavy metals into taste buds of goldfish. Bull. Jap. Soc. Sci. Fish. 41: 631–639.

Waiwood, K. G. and F. W. H. Beamish. 1978. Effects of copper, pH and hardness on the critical swimming performance of rainbow trout (*Salmo gairdneri* Richardson). Water Res. 12: 611–619.

Wakabayashi, H., M. Hikida, and K. Masumura. 1984. *Flexibacter* infection in cultured marine fish in Japan. Helgoländer Meeresunters. 37: 587–593.

Walker, R. and R. Weissenberg. 1965. Conformity of light and electron microscopic studies on virus particle distribution in lymphocystis tumor cells of fish. Ann. N.Y. Acad. Sci. 126: 375–385.

Watanabe, T. 1963. Infective heredity of multiple drug resistance in bacteria. Bacteriol. Rev. 27: 87–115.

Watkins, W. D., R. E. Wolke, and V. J. Cabelli. 1981. Pathogenicity of *Vibrio anguillarum* for juvenile winter flounder, *Pseudopleuronectes americanus*. Can. J. Fish. Aquat. Sci. 38: 1045–1051.

Wayne, L. G. and G. P. Kubica. 1986. Family Mycobacteriaceae Chester 1897. *In* Bergey's manual of systematic bacteriology, Vol. 2, P. H. A. Sneath, N. S. Mair, and M. E. Sharpe (eds.). Williams and Wilkins, Baltimore, pp. 1436–1457. [References at end of volume]

Weissenberg, R. 1954. Studies on virus diseases of fish. IV. Lymphocystis disease in Centrarchidae. Zoologica (N.Y.) 30: 169–176.

Weissenberg, R. 1965. Fifty years of research on the lymphocystis virus disease of fish (1914–1964). Ann. N.Y. Acad. Sci. 126: 362–374.

Wellings, S. R., C. E. Alpers, B. B. McCain, and B. S. Miller. 1976. Fin erosion disease of starry flounder (*Platichthys stellatus*) and English sole (*Parophrys vetulus*) in the estuary of the Duwamish River, Seattle, Washington. J. Fish. Res. Board Can. 33: 2577–2586.

Westgard, R. L. 1964. Physical and biological aspects of gas-bubble disease in impounded adult chinook salmon at NcNary spawning channel. Trans. Am. Fish. Soc. 93: 306–309.

Wheaton, F. W. 1977. Aquacultural engineering. Wiley, New York, 708 pp.

White, S. C., E. B. Jernigan, and A. D. Venosa. 1986. A study of operational ultraviolet disinfection equipment at secondary treatment plants. J. Water Pollut. Contr. Fed. 58: 181–192.

Wilkie, D. W. and H. Gordin. 1969. Outbreak of cryptocaryoniasis in marine aquaria at Scripps Institution of Oceanography. Calif. Fish and Game 55: 227–236.

Williams, E. H. Jr. 1974. Treatments employed for control of parasites of selected fishes stocked in mariculture experiments (1969–1972). Proc. World Maricult. Soc. 5: 291–295.

Williams, E. H., L. B. Williams, and J. M. Grizzle. 1984. Lymphocystis from West Indian marine fishes. J. Wildl. Dis. 20: 51–52.

Williams, P. M., R. J. Baldwin, and K. J. Robertson. 1978. Ozonation of seawater: preliminary observations on the oxidation of bromide, chloride and organic carbon. Water Res. 12: 385–388.

Wilson, C. B. 1902. North American parasitic copepods of the family Argulidae, with a bibliography of the group and a systematic review of all known species. Proc. U.S. Nat. Mus. 25: 635–742 + Plates 8–28.

Winsor, H. 1946. Cold-blooded tuberculosis from the Fairmount Park Aquarium, Philadelphia. Penn. Acad. Sci. 20: 43–46.

Wolf, K. 1968. Lymphocystis disease of fish. Fish Dis. Leaf. 13, U.S. Fish and Wildlife Service, Washington, 4 pp.

Wolf, K. 1980. Virology of aquarium fishes, a review. J. Aquaricult. 3: 58–62.

Wolf, K. 1988. Fish viruses and viral diseases. Comstock/Cornell University Press, Ithaca, 476 pp.

Wolf, K., M. Gravell, and R. G. Malsberger. 1966. Lymphocystis virus: isolation and propagation in centrarchid fish cell lines. Science 151: 1004–1005.

Wolke, R. E. 1975. Pathology of bacterial and fungal diseases affecting fish. *In* The pathology of fishes, W. E. Ribelin and G. Migaki (eds.). University of Wisconsin Press, Madison, pp. 33–116.

Wolthaus, B-G. 1984. Seasonal changes in frequency of diseases in dab, *Limanda limanda*, from the southern North Sea. Helgoländer Meeresunters. 37: 375–387.

Wong, G. T. F. and J. A. Davidson. 1977. The fate of chlorine in sea-water. Water Res. 11: 971–978.

Woodhead, A. D. and R. B. Setlow. 1982. Toxicity of copper to the Amazon molly, *Poecilia formosa*. Drum and Croaker 29(1): 10–13.

Woodhead, A. D. and P. M. J. Woodhead. 1980. A thyroid neoplasm in the spiny dogfish, *Squalus acanthias*. Bull. Mt. Desert Island Biol. Lab. 19: 19–21.

Yeatts, LeR. B. Jr. and H. Taube. 1949. The kinetics of the reaction of ozone and chloride ion in acid aqueous solution. J. Am. Chem. Soc. 71: 4100–4105.

Zirino, A. and P. F. Seligman. 1981. A note on the polarographic behavior of the Cu(II) ion selective electrode in seawater. Mar. Chem. 10: 249–255.

Zirino, A. and S. Yamamoto. 1972. A pH-dependent model for the chemical speciation of copper, zinc, cadmium, and lead in seawater. Limnol. Oceanogr. 17: 661–671.

Zirzow, P. 1910. A new method of combating fungus on fishes in captivity. Bull. Bur. Fish. 28(1908): 939–940.

Chapter 10

Anonymous. 1969. Filters for black-and-white and color pictures. Kodak Pub. AE-90, Eastman Kodak, Rochester, 44 pp.

Anonymous. 1974. Incandescent lamps. Eng'g. Bull. 0-324, GTE Sylvania, Danvers, 17 pp.

Anonymous. 1981. Using filters. Kodak Pub. KW-13, Eastman Kodak, Rochester, 96 pp.

Baugh, T. M. 1982. Technique for photographing small fish. Prog. Fish-cult. 44: 99–101.

Beebe, W. 1934. Half mile down. Harcourt, Brace, New York, 344 pp.

Brady, P. 1984. Coral reef magic: a new exhibit in the giant ocean tank. Aquasphere 18(1): 2–9.

Bueche, F. 1985. Technical physics, 3rd ed. Harper and Row, New York, 758 pp.

Dring, M. J. 1982. The biology of marine plants. Edward Arnold, London, 199 pp.

Emery, A. R. and R. Winterbottom. 1980. A technique for fish specimen photography in the field. Can. J. Zool. 58: 2158–2162.

Feinberg, G. 1983. Light. 1. Behavior of light. *In* Encyclopedia Americana, Int. ed., Vol. 17. Grolier, Danbury, pp. 438–455.

Flescher, D. D. 1983. Fish photography. Fisheries 8(4): 2–6.

Goodbred, S. and T. Occhiogrosso. 1979. Method for photographing small fish. Prog. Fish-cult. 41: 76–77.

Hodge, R. P. 1977. A photographic tank for aquatic organisms. Drum and Croaker 77(2): 14–16.

Holm, E. 1989. Improved technique for fish specimen photography in the field. Can. J. Zool. 67: 2329–2332.

Jerlov, N. G. 1968. Optical oceanography. Elsevier, Amsterdam, 194 pp.

Kelley, W. E. 1960a. An aquarium exhibit with polarized light. Bull. Inst. Océanogr., Monaco, Num. spéc. IB: 83–84.

Kelley, W. E. 1960b. Some optical properties of aquaria and their application to lighting and design. Bull. Inst. Océanogr., Monaco, Num. spéc. IC: 93–97.

Kelly, K. L. and D. B. Judd. 1976a. The ISCC-NBS method of designating colors and a dictionary of color names. *In* Color: universal language and dictionary of names, K. L. Kelly and D. B. Judd (eds.), 7th printing. NBS Spec. Pub. 440, National Bureau of Standards, Washington, pp. 1–14.

Kelly, K. L. and D. B. Judd (eds.). 1976b. Color: universal language and dictionary of names, 7th printing. NBS Spec. Pub. 440, National Bureau of Standards, Washington, 184 pp. [ISCC-NBS Color-Name Charts Illustrated with Centroid Colors is the first supplement]

King, J. M. and S. Spotte. 1974. Marine aquariums in the research laboratory. Aquarium Systems, Eastlake, 38 pp.

Levine, J. S. 1980. Vision underwater. Oceanus 23(3): 19–26.

Neumann, G. and W. J. Pierson Jr. 1966. Principles of physical oceanography. Prentice-Hall, Englewood Cliffs, 545 pp.

Nickerson, D. 1983. Color. *In* The encyclopedia Americana, Int. ed., Vol. 7. Grolier, Danbury, pp. 305–315.

Page, L. M. and K. S. Cummings. 1984. A portable camera box for photographing small fishes. Environ. Biol. Fish. 11: 160.

Pletcher, T. F. 1966. A portable aquarium for use at sea to photograph fish and aquatic life. J. Fish. Res. Board Can. 23: 1271–1275.

Preisendorfer, R. W. 1976. Hydrologic optics, Vol. 1. NOAA Environmental Research Laboratories, Honolulu, 218 pp.

Randall, J. E. 1961. The Randall technique. Copeia 1961: 241–242.

Reighard, J. 1910. Methods of studying the habits of fishes, with an account of the breeding habits of the horned dace. Bull. Bur. Fish. 1910(1908): 1111–1136 + 7 plates.

Rinne, J. N. and M. D. Jakle. 1981. The photarium: a device for taking photographs of live fish. Prog. Fish-cult. 43: 201–204.

Sears, F. W. 1956. Optics, 3rd ed. Addison-Wesley, Cambridge, 386 pp.

Sieswerda [Seiswerda], P. L. 1979. Wave tank—splash tank— dump bucket (call it what you will) here's one that works. Drum and Croaker 19(2): 9–10.

Sieswerda, P. and J. Dayton. 1982. Son of dump bucket. Drum and Croaker 20(2): 18–19.

Spotte, S. 1973. Marine aquarium keeping: the science, animals, and art. Wiley, New York, 171 pp.

Strykowski, J. 1974. Divers and cameras. Dacor, Northfield, 212 pp.

Sverdrup, H. U., M. W. Johnson, and R. H. Fleming. 1942. The oceans: their physics, chemistry, and general biology. Prentice-Hall, New York, 1087 pp.

Webb, G. 1982. Moving water display tanks: design and construction of a prototype and a public viewing tank. Drum and Croaker 20(1): 34–37.

Williams, J. 1970. Optical properties of the sea. U.S. Naval Institute, Annapolis, 123 pp.

Index

Abramis brama (see Bream)
Abscissa, 25
Acanthemblemaria spp.
habitat partitioning, 722
Acanthochromis polyacanthus
brooding of larvae, 721
occupation of pair territories, 289
Acanthopagrus schlageli (see Black seabream)
Acanthuridae (see Surgeonfishes)
Acanthurus coeruleus (see Blue tang)
Acetate
use by nitrifying bacteria, 611, 612
use in denitrification, 75
Acetazolamide, 651
Acetic acid
in activated carbon manufacture, 101
Achromobacter spp.
dissimilation by, 619
fin rot, 486
Acid–base balance
ammonia excretion and, 653
aquarium seawater, 602
control by ion exchange, 659
importance, 201
effect of environmental hypercapnia, 217, 218, 230, 659, 660
effect of environmental hypoxia, 218–221
effect of exercise stress, 227
effect of lactate ions, 665, 666
effect of lactic acid, 665, 666
effect of oxygen, 660, 661
effect of temperature, 658, 659
maintenance, 213, 214
regulation, 214–216
Acidity
as a stress factor, 229
Acids, 9, 19, 734, 747
Acoustic gradient hypothesis, 269
Acoustic impedance, 682
Acoustic pressure (see Excess pressure)
Acousticolateralis system (also see Labyrinth, Lateral line, Ordinary lateral line organs), 261
Acoustic organs (see Labyrinth, Lateral line)
Acoustics, 257
Acriflavin
as a formulated disinfectant, 755
Acriflavin neutral, 777
Acropora spp., 721
Acrylic
pipe, 565
refractive index, 561
spray, 574
use in brine shrimp hatch vessels, 407, 409
use in fish behavior studies, 693, 695, 696
use in species label photography, 568
watertight camera housings, 553
Acrylic paints (also see Epoxy paints, Paints), 577
ACTH, 227
Activated carbon (also see Granular, Powdered activated carbon)
determination of pore surface area, 629
factors affecting adsorption efficiency, 102–104, 330, 629
manufacture, 101, 102, 629
tap water treatment, 406
wastewater treatment, 629, 630
Activated carbon contactors, 53, 630
Activating agents, 102
Active denitrification method (see Columnar denitrification)
Active metabolism, 372
Active transport
definition, 205
of ions, 208, 209
in acid-base balance, 217
solution concentration during, 205
transepithelial potentials and, 655
Adenohypophysis
negative feedback and, 789
secretion of melanin dispersing hormone, 247
secretion of thyroid stimulating hormone, 517
Adrenaline (also see Catecholamines)
effect of handling stress, 670
effect of hypoxia, 230
effect on gill blood flow, 673
effect on lamellar recruitment, 230
effect on water permeability, 671
primary stress response and, 225
Adsorbate, 100, 102, 104
Adsorbent, 100, 103, 104
Adsorption
capacity, 103, 104, 107, 629
definition, 100
efficiency, 102–104
rate, 102, 104, 106, 107, 629
Aeration
aquariums, 45
artificial seawaters, 48, 153
breeding brine shrimp and, 417
brine shrimp cysts, 406
by airlift pumps, 157
definition, 153
dinitrogen solubility and, 151
effect on brine shrimp nauplii, 742
effect on nitrification, 616, 617

Aeration *(Continued)*
effect on phytoplankton growth, 438
energy, 157
gas transfer and, 154–157
introduction, 136
iodine loss by, 517
patterns, 156, 157
phosphorus precipitation, 57, 58, 606
phytoplankton cultures, 442
phytoplankton-rotifer cultures, 420
rearing brine shrimp nauplii, 415
requirements for phyto-plankton culture, 431, 432
seawater, 153
tap water, 406
Aeration tanks
depth, 156
mixing patterns, 156, 157
preparation for painting, 170
Aerators, 155, 156
Aerobacter spp., 619
Aerobic bacteria
denitrification, 75, 77
dissimilation, 77, 619
in biological films, 69, 613
Aerobic conditions
biological films, 68
dissimilation and, 71, 619
filter beds, 72
for nitrification, 75
Aerobic respiration, 55
Aeromonas spp.
DS-677 K treatment, 520, 521
fin rot, 486, 488, 772, 773
Agaricia agaricites (see Lettuce coral)
Agglutination
in antibody-antigen reactions, 449
Agglutinins, 449
Aggregations (of fishes), 690, 691, 696
Aggression
as a synonym for agonistic behavior, 706
in defining territory, 706
in dominance hierarchies, 287, 288
in territorial dominance, 707
Agonistic behavior
as a synonym for aggres-sion, 706
breeding and, 295
by captive anemonefishes, 304
by crabs, 309
definition, 286, 287, 706
in community exhibits, 287
inter- and intraspecific, 290
territorial boundary and, 293, 709, 710
Air
as an elastic medium, 256
compressibility, 257, 258
density compared with water, 532
sound velocity in, 257
Airborne contaminants, 106
Air bubbles
adsorption of dissolved organic carbon, 163
as model sound sources, 258–260
as transducers, 265
brine shrimp cysts and, 406
compressibility, 265
containing ozone, 467
effect of drag and friction, 193
effect on foam stability, 166
factors affecting size, 167
formation, 151, 153
gas supersaturation and, 151
gas transfer from, 154, 642, 643
in airlift pumps, 159
in foam fractionators, 164, 166, 192–195
in moist feeds, 403
interference in refractom-eters, 33
laminar layer, 153, 642
nitrogen release from, 64
orthophosphate adsorption on, 57, 58
oxygen transfer from, 155
partial pressure in, 642
rate of ascent, 156
shapes, 154, 167
surface area, 167
surface energy, 167, 168
surface tension, 167
swimbladders as, 265
Air compressors, 431, 432
Air diffusers
fish gills and, 201
in airlift pumps, 159
in brine shrimp breeding vessels, 417
in brine shrimp hatch vessels, 410
in brine shrimp rearing vessels, 415
in foam fractionators, 194
in phytoplankton culture vessels, 419
in vacuum degassers, 187
placement, 156
pore size, 167, 194
pressure drop across, 167
Air filter, 432
Air flow rate
in airlift pumps, 188–192
in foam fractionators, 192, 195
Airlift pumps
air bubbles in, 56
bubble flow patterns, 159–163
circulation by, 64
circulation of artificial seawaters, 49
designs, 157–159, 188–191
flow rate, 136
flow rate calculations, 191, 192
history, 643
hydrostatic pressure, 159
performance, 162, 163
principles, 156, 159–163
use with foam fractionators, 192, 193
pumping rate, 159
working parts, 159
Airlifts (see Airlift pumps)
Airline tubing, 49
Air scour, 146, 148
Airstripping (see Foam fractionation)
Alarm response, 267
Albumin, 596
Alcaligenes spp., 619
Alcyonarians (see Corals, soft)
Alewife
exophiala disease, 785
Algae (also see Phytoplankton, Seaweeds)
as contaminants in phytoplankton stock cultures, 430, 437
as sources of meal, 384
as sources of natural gums, 734
carotenoid synthesis and, 370
coralline, 292, 328, 330
culture solutions and, 421, 745
copper requirements, 750
copper toxicity, 750
enrichment of brine shrimp nauplii, 737
digestibility, 371
exudates, 99, 608, 610, 750
formation of humic acids, 760
in humification, 59
in seawater yellowing, 61, 760
nitrogen assimilation, 55
nitrogen excretion, 64, 67
on coral reefs, 323
phosphorus assimilation, 57, 605
phosphorus release, 57
photosynthesis, 17
powdered as foods, 413, 415, 417, 741, 745
predation by blue tangs, 250
predation by fishes, 325
"turf," 291
Vibrio damsela on, 767
vitamin requirements, 421, 751
Algal lawns, 292, 293, 709
Algicides, 458
Algin, 734
Alginate-bound moist feeds
nutrient composition, 399
procedure, 399, 400, 403
Alginates (also see Sodium alginate)
as feed encapsulating agents, 389
definition, 734
Alginic acid, 734
Alkalinity
bicarbonate ion and, 10–12
borate ion and, 10
carbonate ion and, 10–12, 44
carbonate minerals and, 9
control in aquariums, 44, 45
control in the oceans, 593
definition, 10, 658
effect of ammonia uptake and assimilation, 424, 751
effect of ammonium ions, 12, 13
effect of calcium carbonate dissolution, 13
effect of denitrification, 13
effect of filtrants, 599, 600
effect of hydrochloric acid, 12
effect of lime, 605
effect of nitrate uptake and assimilation, 12, 424, 429, 751
effect of nitrite uptake and assimilation, 751
effect of nitrification, 13
effect of inorganic nitrogen, 423, 429, 751
effect of sodium hydroxide, 12
effect of sulfate reduction, 13
effect of sulfide oxidation, 13
effect on copper chemistry, 759, 760

effect on copper toxicity, 759
expression, 41–44, 593
high precision determination, 41–43, 604
inorganic carbon and, 58
introduction, 1, 9
loss in artificial seawater, 44
loss in closed systems, 44
loss in seawater, 44, 45
low precision determination, 43, 44, 604
magnesian calcite overgrowths and, 23
of aquarium water, 45
of artificial seawaters, 23
of seawater, 10, 23, 45
pH and, 9
pH buffer standards, 38
pH control and, 11
phytoplankton tolerance of, 442
total CO_2 and, 11, 12

Alosa pseudoharengus (see Alewife)

α-potato starch, 731

Alpheus lottini, 308

Alum (see Hydrated aluminum sulfate)

American eel
immunity to *Amyloodinium ocellatum*, 774

American kestrel, 698, 699

Amictic eggs, 397, 398

Amines
decarboxylation and, 62

Amino acids (also see Essential amino acids, Free amino acids, Nonessential amino acids)
adsorption onto calcium carbonate, 596
assimilation by nitrifying bacteria, 612
brine shrimp, 394
brine shrimp nauplii, 738
from proteins, 371
inhibition of nitrification, 615
in proteins, 360
metabolism by animals, 66
mineralization, 62
of rotifers, 397
preferential use, 732
release by seaweeds, 66, 78
requirements for, 361
synthesis by nitrifying bacteria, 612
synthesis by seaweeds, 621
use by nitrifying bacteria, 612

Aminocarboxylates
as iron complexing agents, 423, 747, 748
photodegradation, 748–750

Ammonia (also see Ammonium ions, Free ammonia)
adsorption by microfiltration apparatus, 634
as a contaminant in calcium chloride, 604, 605
as a goitrogen, 517, 790
as a nitrogen source for phytoplankton, 751
as an irritant in fin rot, 488
as a stress factor, 454, 456, 664, 673
as energy, 373
breakthrough, 83
control by nitrification, 78
control by seaweed filters, 621, 622
determination, 110–117, 632
effect of amyloodinium disease on excretion, 491
effect of autoclaving seawater, 751
effect on acid-base balance, 214
effect of uptake and assimilation on alkalinity and pH, 424, 751
effect on blood pH, 651, 653
effect on chemotherapeutic agents, 460
effect of corticosteroids, 456, 674
effect on rotifers, 398
excretion by animals, 67, 82, 83, 210, 214
excretion by fishes, 206–210, 214, 230, 231, 649–654
expression, 110, 632
from dissimilation, 67, 74, 95
from excess dietary protein, 385
from mineralization, 67, 606
from nitrogen metabolism, 62, 67
in aquarium seawater, 90
latex rubber diluent, 576
loss from autoclaved seawater, 751
nitrite interference in determination, 111, 632, 633
organic precursors, 62
oxidation, 64, 67, 70–72, 74, 80, 82, 83, 95, 610, 611
"peaking" in unconditioned bacteriological filters, 80
percentage of protein nitrogen, 83
precursors in seawater, 62, 63
reaction with chlorine-based oxidants, 744
reduction by denitrification, 75
toxicity, 54, 62, 230, 635–637
toxicity to fishes, 604, 609, 673, 674
toxicity to nitrifying bacteria, 71
toxicity to phytoplankton, 423, 428, 751
uptake and assimilation by seaweeds, 78, 620, 621

Ammonia oxidizers (see Nitrifying bacteria)

"Ammonia probes," 115, 634

Ammonium ions
adsorption onto soil particles, 613
assimilation by plants, 12
calculation of p*K*, 637
dissociation in water, 117, 635
effect of autoclaving seawater, 751
effect of uptake and assimilation on alkalinity, 12
in acid-base balance, 214
in the environment, 230
physiological regulation, 206–209, 214, 230, 231, 648–654, 656, 657, 659
reaction with phosphorus, 606
toxicity, 117, 635, 636
toxicity to fishes, 117–122
toxicity to nitrifying bacteria, 71, 615
uptake and assimilation by seaweeds, 620, 621
use by heterotrophic bacteria, 611

Amphibdelloides sp.
praziquantel treatment, 786

Amphibians,
blood pH, 213
effect of temperature on blood pH, 658, 659
maintenance of constant blood pH, 658
mycobacteriosis, 764

Amphiprion (= *Premnas*) *biaculeatus*, 716

Amphiprion bicinctus
"feeding" of sea anemones, 714–716
protandry, 303
social repression of growth, 712

Amphiprion clarkii
acclimation to sea anemones, 718
"feeding" of sea anemones, 715, 716
protandry, 303

Amphiprion ephippium, 716

Amphiprion frenatus
color polymorphs, 722

Amphiprion nigripes, 716

Amphiprion ocellaris
effect of iodine on metamorphosis, 604
"feeding" of sea anemones, 716
nitrate toxicity, 610

Amphiprion percula
acclimation to sea anemones, 716–718

Amphiprion spp. (see Anemonefishes)

Amphotericin B
treatment of amyloodinium disease, 777
treatment of ichthyophonus disease, 504

Amplitude, 211

Ampullae of Lorenzini, 270, 688

Ampullary electroreceptors, 270, 688

Amyloodinium disease (also see *Amyloodinium ocellatum*)
clinical signs and pathological effects, 491, 777
epizootiology, 489–491, 775–777
etiology, 488, 493, 774
immunity to, 489, 775
prophylaxis and treatment, 491, 492, 777–779
synonyms, 488

Amyloodinium ocellatum (also see Amyloodinium disease)
dinospores (tomites), 775–778
distribution, 488, 774, 775
effect of temperature on development, 776
feeding mechanism, 775, 776
life cycle, 489–491, 496
optimal salinity range *in vitro*, 776
optimal temperature *in vitro*, 776
rhizoids, 774, 775, 777, 778
sporulation, 490, 491, 776–778
survival and development in freshwaters, 776, 777

Amyloodinium ocellatum (Continued)
taxonomic history, 774
tomonts, 775–778
trophonts, 775–778
Amyloodinium sp., 775
Anaerobic bacteria
dissimilation, 77, 619
in biological films, 69
respiration, 74
Anaerobic conditions
dissimilation and, 72, 74, 75, 77, 619
effect on nitrification, 616
in biological films, 68
in deep filter beds, 620
in filter beds, 71, 72
Anaerobic respiration, 55
Anemia
argulid infestations, 514
vibriosis, 480, 769
Anemonefishes
acclimation to sea anemones, 306, 716–718
agonistic behavior, 304
as obligate sea anemone symbionts, 713
association with sea anemones, 304
feeding in nature, 713
"feeding" of sea anemones, 304, 713–716
host specificity, 306
occupation of pair territories, 289
protandry and, 302, 303, 712
sound production, 267
speciation, 722
taxonomy, 712
territorial dominance, 304
Anesthesia
as a stress factor, 227
Aneurysms
gas-bubble trauma, 515
uronema disease, 498
Angelfishes
protogyny, 712
Anguilla anguilla (see European eel)
Anguilla japonica (see Japanese eel)
Anguilla rostrata (see American eel)
Anguilla spp. (see Eels)
Angled viewing window exhibits, 586
Animals
amino acid requirements, 361
ammonia excretion, 67, 82, 83, 210, 214
assimilation of oxygen, 210
bioelectric fields, 269
biological films and, 68
carbohydrates in, 365
carbon in, 58
carotenoids and, 370
cellulose digestion, 365
cold-blooded, 213, 214, 373, 636, 658, 666, 763
density of, 94
digestibility of, 358, 371
effect on nitrification, 623
energy requirements, 371, 373, 374
energy storage, 372
fatty acids, 730
hyposmotic, 654
in biotopes, 334
in defining culture solutions, 421
isosmotic, 648
lipid soluble vitamins and, 366
metabolism, 53, 66, 372
nutrient sources for, 358
nitrogen excretion, 66, 84
perfect protein for, 360
phosphorus excretion, 57
physiological hypercapnia, 217
protein quality and, 384
proteins in, 383
shelter on patch reefs, 332
sound detection, 258, 684, 687
sound localization by, 268
symbiosis and, 303
terrestrial, 256, 364, 730, 674, 726
toxicity of reactivated activated carbon, 631
vitamin synthesis, 366
warm-blooded, 213
Anions
alkalinity and, 10
as ligands, 747
definition, 1, 591
dyes as, 763
from dissolution of overgrowths, 23
in pH control, 19
in table salt, 2
Anisotremus virginicus (see Porkfish)
Anisotropic tissues, 566
Anode, 591
Anonymity
expressions, 283
in schools, 283, 285
Anorexia
amyloodinium disease, 491
cryptocaryoniasis, 495
definition, 459, 477
gas-bubble trauma, 515
mycobacteriosis, 477
tang turbellarian disease, 508
uronema disease, 497
vibriosis, 481
Anoxic sediment denitrification, 94–96, 628
Antagonistic behavior (also see Agonistic behavior), 706
Anthelminthic agents
monogenean life cycles and, 512
treatment of monogenean infestations, 512
Anthopleura xanthogrammica, 718
Anthracite
dual media filters, 140
granular media filters, 137
multimedia filters, 140
intermixing with sand, 181
relative grain size, 175
60% size, 177, 183
specific gravity, 175
transport to surface, 183
uniformity coefficients, 175, 177
*Anthrobacte*r spp., 610, 619
Antibacterial agents
effect on filter bed bacteria, 460
effect on nitrifying bacteria, 71
efficacy of formulated products, 461, 755
human *Mycobacterium* infections, 479
lymphocystis disease and, 475
production by freeze-drying, 377
sensitivity testing, 458, 459
systemic vibriosis, 484
use at subtherapeutic concentrations, 754
Antibiotics, 458
Antibodies
complement and, 449
definition, 449
groupings, 450
in defining antigen, 450
secretion by B cells, 451
Antigens
definition, 449, 450
effect of macrophages, 451
entry into hosts, 450
specificity, 753
Antifungal agents
treatment of ichthyophonus disease, 504
Antimalarial compounds
treatment of cryptocaryoniasis, 496
Antimicrobial compounds, 458, 459
Antiseptics, 467, 468
Antitoxins, 449
Anus
bioelectric fields, 269
inflammation from vibriosis, 481
Apogon maculatus (see Flamefish)
Aquarium of Niagara Falls, 796
Aquarium of the Zoological Society of London, 774, 775
Aqueous humor, 233
Arachidonic acid, 730, 732
Aragonite
as a polymorph of calcium carbonate, 14
crushed coral, 9, 599, 600
definition, 13
magnesium adsorption, 598
Archirus lineatus (see Lined sole)
Arctic grayling, 659
Arena behavior (see Lekking)
Argenteum, 250
Argon, 151, 539
Argulids (also see Crustacean infestations, Copepods)
as fish parasites, 512
life cycles, 514, 787
taxonomic distinction from copepods, 787
Argulus spp., 512
Arius spp. (see Sea catfishes)
Artemia franciscana (also see Brine shrimp), 393, 737, 743
Artemia spp. (see Brine shrimp)
Artificial reefs
competition and, 729
recruitment onto, 722, 723
species diversity and abundance, 729
Artificial seawaters (also see Culture solutions, GP2 culture solution, Maintenance solutions)
aeration, 153
alkalinity loss in, 23, 44
AQUIL, 748, 749
as base for enrichment additives, 745
as brine shrimp nauplii rearing solutions, 414
as hatch solutions for brine shrimp cysts, 396, 406, 413
as maintenance solutions,

46-48
bioassay in, 587
brine additions to, 51, 52
calcium carbonate saturation, 595
calcium carbonate precipitation, 595, 596
carbonate mineral solubility, 597
chemical definition, 46
complexing of copper, 760
definition of "salinity" and, 601
effect of autoclaving, 48, 746, 747, 750, 751
effect of distillation, 590
effect of filtrants on alkalinity, 599, 600
effect of filtrants on pH, 600
formulas, 604
gas saturation, 136
goiter disease, 791
GP2 maintenance solution, 46–49, 442, 747
in defining culture solutions, 421
in vitro fish photography, 571
ionic strength, 46
magnesian calcite overgrowths, 18, 597
maintenance of adult fishes, 46
maintenance of animals and plants, 48
major ions, 46, 601
mixing containers for, 48, 49
mixing, 1
pH reduction, 23, 44
precipitation from autoclaving, 746, 750
precipitation of calcium carbonate, 595
quarantine procedures and, 474
salts, 48
similarity to seawater, 46
sodium bicarbonate, 45
sterilization, 48
storage vats, 48, 49
tap water for mixing, 48, 49
trace ions, 46
unconditioned bacteriological filters and, 81

Ascophyllum nodosum, 608
Ascophyllum spp., 610
Ascorbic acid
as an iron complexing agent, 748, 749
depletion in plasma from stress, 226
glycerine-coated, 735, 736
leaching from feeds, 735
stability in feeds, 735, 736
2-sulfate, 735

Ash
determination in foods, 374
in activated carbon manufacture, 100
in brine shrimp, 739
in leafy green vegetables, 375

Assemblages (of fishes), 275, 689–691, 722
Assimilation
definition, 620
introduction, 54
of nitrate, 74
nitrogen removal, 54, 55

Astaxanthin
addition to dry feeds, 733
carotenoid metabolism and, 370
crustaceans and, 371
effect on skin coloration, 370, 371, 389, 733, 734
occurrence in fishes, 370, 371

Asterionella japonica
iron availability, 748

Astyanax mexicanus (see Mexican cavefish)
Ataxia
amyloodinium disease, 491
definition, 477
exophiala disease, 505
ichthyophonus disease, 598
halquinol treatment, 523
mycobacteriosis, 477
vibriosis, 480, 482

Atherinidae (see Silversides)
Atlantic cod
effect of adrenaline on branchial gas exchange, 673
fin rot, 772
quarantine procedures and, 474

Atlantic halibut
monogenean infestations, 786

Atlantic herring
gill rakers, 646
nocturnal disintegration of schools, 693
safety in numbers, 699
sound localization, 686, 687

Atlantic mackerel
feeding efficiency, 704
hemoglobin, 223
vision in schooling, 694

Atlantic menhaden
gas-bubble trauma, 788
wavelength attraction, 676

Atlantic salmon
effect of confinement stress, 667, 668
exophiala disease, 785
fin rot, 773
vibriosis, 766–768

Atlantic silverside
effect of season on schooling and milling, 696, 697
lipid deposition, 733

Atlantic stingray
electroreception, 689

Atmosphere
carbon dioxide release to, 58, 100
dinitrogen loss to, 67
effect on light, 529
gases in, 210
iodine loss to, 517
light energy, 533
light scattering, 532, 534, 535, 793
nitrogen gain from, 64, 66
nitrogen loss to, 55, 96
phosphorus loss to, 58

Atolls
description, 326, 328, 331, 332, 727

Atoms
carbon, 358, 362, 363, 365
definition, 1
hydrogen, 362
light emission and, 794
iron, 222
waves and, 528

ATP, 222
Attachment plate, 490
Attack sequence, 283, 701–703
Aulostomus maculatus (see Trumpetfish)
Aureomycin, 778
Autoclaving
carboys, 425, 426, 435
effect on seawater ammonia, 751
GP2 culture solutions A to C, 422, 424, 425, 435, 751
GP2 low-salinity culture solution, 747
methods of preventing precipitation, 746, 747
seawater and artificial seawaters, 48, 746, 747, 750, 751
sodium bicarbonate, 424, 747, 751

Autolysis, 56
Autotrophic bacteria
as periphytes, 614
definition, 55
effect of filter bed depth, 626
in biological films, 68
inorganic nitrogen conversion, 64
nitrification, 80–82
obligate, 64

Auxotrophic, 421
Axenic culture, 743, 746
Axial (aeration) pattern, 156
Ayu
chain elongation of fatty acids, 731
vibriosis, 768, 771

Bacillus spp., 619
Background spacelight
camouflage and, 249, 250
contrast perception and, 675–679
definition, 236
in underwater vision, 237–239, 241, 243
photosensitivity and, 679
predation and, 702

Backwash
as a limiting factor, 174, 175
design factors, 179, 180–184
effect of filtrant characteristics, 176
effect of support media, 644
effluent disposal, 182, 183
filtrant intermixing, 176
filtrant loss, 176
intervals, 140
of coarse sand filters, 148
with tap water, 184

Backwash holding tanks, 182, 183
Backwash mode variables, 144–147
Backwash rate
bulk density and, 181
design criteria, 179
filtrant intermixing and, 181
fluidization and, 145, 181
for seawater supplies, 182
in wastewater treatment, 181, 182
of high rate filters, 181
optimal, 183, 184
removal of particulate organic carbon, 145
void fraction and, 145

Backwash water, 144–146
Bacteria
acid-fast, 476, 763
as causes of secondary infections, 455, 456, 508, 511, 514
as microorganisms, 447
as opportunistic pathogens, 455, 476, 486, 491
as secondary infectious

Bacteria *(Continued)*
agents, 455, 456, 459, 475, 486
attached to detritus, 67
attached to filtrants, 44, 56
autotrophic, 55, 64, 68, 80–82, 614, 626
biological film formation, 68
cell wall, 763
chemoautotrophic, 64
chemotherapeutic agents and, 520
conjugation, 754
contaminants in phytoplankton stock cultures, 430, 436–438
disinfection and, 468
effect of antibiotics, 458
effect of ozone, 466
effect of temperature on growth, 764, 773
effect of the humoral immune response, 450
effect of UV radiation, 462, 465, 466
effect on turbidity, 638
efficacy of formulated antibacterial agents, 461, 755
efficacy of formulated disinfectants, 468, 756
feed contamination by, 391
fin rot lesions, 772
formation of humic acids, 760
Gram-positive, 476, 763
Gram-negative, 479, 763
ichthyophonus disease and, 504
identification by staining, 763
in conditioned bacteriological filters, 79
in fin rot, 486, 488
lysis, 57, 61, 449
metabolism, 53, 82, 99
mineralization, 55, 62
natural resistance and, 448
nitrogen conversion, 54, 67
oxidation of culture solution components, 423
phagocytosis, 449, 453
phosphorus input, 57
photoautotrophic, 64
plasmids, 754
polysaccharides in, 450
resistance transfer factors, 754
respiration, 62, 64
rods, 476, 479, 763
seaweed filters and, 78
size compared with *Amyloodinium ocellatum*, 491
struvite formation, 606
systemic infections and, 459
vitamin synthesis, 366
Bactericides, 458
Bacteriological filtration
definition, 54, 56
efficiency, 67–74
mineralization, 64
nitrification, 64
supplemental seaweed filtration, 621
Bacteriological filters (also see Filter beds)
acceleration of conditioning, 79, 81–83, 624, 625
carrying capacity, 79
conditioning, 79–83
conditioning defined, 79, 622, 623
filter plates, 91
location, 99
maintenance, 94, 626
nitrogen fixation, 66
preconditioning, 83, 624, 625
seaweed filters and, 78
time lags, 79, 80
Bactopeptone, 436
Bagre spp. (see Sea catfishes)
Baker's yeast, 737
Balistidae (see Leatherjackets)
Balistes vetula (see Queen triggerfish)
Bandwidth, 686
Barnacles, 147
Barometric pressure, 150, 151, 257
Barrier reefs, 326, 328, 331, 332, 727
Basal lamellae, 212
Bases, 9, 734
Basic fuchsin, 763
Basolateral cell surface (see Epithelium, serosal cell surface)
Bathysphere, 792
β-carotene, 370, 371
Bdelloids, 397
Beaugregory
effect on recruitment, 722
optimal territory size, 711
territorial defense, 710
toxicity of seaweed compounds, 622
Beef tallow, 364
Beer's law, 638
"Bends" (see Gas-bubble trauma)
Benedenia spp.
freshwater treatment, 512
Benedeniella posterocolpa
praziquantel treatment, 525
Benzalkonium chloride, 777
Bergen Aquarium, 787
Bicarbonate ions
carbonate equilibrium and, 17
control of blood pH, 658–660, 666
effect on alkalinity, 10–12
effect on pH, 17
formation, 10
function in acid-base balance, 214–218, 221, 230
in defining salinity, 590
ionization of ammonia and, 214
ion pairing and, 592
physiological regulation, 207–209, 648, 649, 657, 659
Bichirs, 688
Bicolor damselfish
dominance hierarchies, 288
territorial dominance, 288
threespot damselfish and, 709, 710
Bicotylophora trachinoti
trichlorfon treatment, 524
Binders, 389
Bioelectric potentials, 688
Bioassay
copper toxicity and, 758, 759
free ammonia toxicity in, 636
polyelectrolyte toxicity and, 640
procedure using fertilized sea urchin gametes, 586–588
Biofouling, 147
Biogenesis, 15
Biological films
composition, 68
cycling, 68, 69
definition, 68
effective depth, 68
factors affecting, 68
formation in nature, 614
in aquaculture installations, 68
in aquarium filter beds, 69
in public aquariums, 68
in wastewater treatment, 68, 69
metabolism, 68
on granular activated carbon, 104, 630
removal, 94
thickness, 68, 613
Biological filtration
definition, 54, 55
disruption, 182
introduction, 53
mineralization, 64
nitrification, 64
Biological oxygen demand, 84
Biotin
optional addition to culture solutions, 424
primary stock solution, 427
requirements of algae, 751
requirements of phytoplankton, 421
Biotope
communities and, 321, 334, 335, 341
coral reefs as, 323
definition, 319, 721
habitats and, 343
standing crop density and, 349
zonation and, 334, 335
Blackbody, 538, 539
Black bullhead
nocturnal disintegration of schools, 692, 693
Black seabream
fin rot, 773
Black skipjack
cooperative hunting, 704, 705
Blackfin snapper
effect on recruitment, 722
Blacksmith
vibriosis, 767, 768
Blastula, 736
Blindness
cryptocaryoniasis, 496
effect on schooling, 693–695
fin rot, 488
gas-bubble trauma, 515
Blood (also see Plasma)
acidosis, 456
ammonia, 206, 208, 649–653
antigen entry and, 450
assay for chemotherapeutic agents, 520
assimilation of chemotherapeutic agents, 460
buffers, 214, 217
chemotherapeutic agents, 755
chloride concentration, 654
effect of blood pressure, 212
electrochemical gradients, 654–656
flow through gills, 212, 213, 222
gas-bubble trauma and, 515
gas exchange, 202, 203, 212, 213

hemoglobin transfer to, 228, 662
ichthyophonus disease and, 502
ion exchange, 205–210
lysosome in, 449
natural resistance factors, 447, 448
osmolality, 647
oxygen, 662
partial pressure of carbon dioxide, 214, 216, 217, 220, 221, 227
partial pressure of oxygen, 222, 223
pH, 213–217, 221
phagocytes and, 453
pumping of, 221
release of hormones into, 225
restricted flow from uronema disease, 498
sodium concentration, 654
therapeutic concentrations in, 459
thyroid hormones and, 517

Blood glucose (also see Hyperglycemia)
effect of ammonia, 674
effect of argulid parasites, 514
effect of capture stress, 670, 671
effect of handling stress, 670
effect of physiological hypoxia, 456, 670, 671
effect of transport stress, 671

Blood pH
control by ion exchange, 659, 660
effect of ammonia perfusion, 651, 653
effect of bicarbonate ions, 658
effect of environmental stress factors, 230
effect of exercise stress, 665, 666
effect of hypercapnia, 217
effect of hyperoxia, 221
effect of temperature, 213–217, 658, 659
effect on hemoglobin oxygen affinity, 662
range in cold-blooded animals, 213

Blood pressure
effect of adrenaline, 673
effect of brachycardia, 221
effect of stroke volume, 221
effect on blood, 212
effect on lamellar recruitment, 221
effect on secondary lamellae, 212

Blood vessels
congestion from amyloodinium disease, 491
gas exchange and, 203
in dermis, 447
hemorrhaging from tang turbellarian disease, 508
Uronema marinum in, 497

Bluefin tuna
cooperative hunting, 704

Bluefish
as a schooling predator, 699
vision in schooling, 694

Bluehead wrasse
as a facultative sea anemone symbiont, 306
recruitment, 723
site attachment, 730

Blue mussel, 759
Blue shift, 677, 678
Blue tang,
coloration, 250, 251
Bodianus rufus (see Spanish hogfish)
Boerner slide, 418
Bohr effect, 662
Boil disease (see Vibriosis)
Bondex®, 170
Bones
sound production by, 267
Borate ions
alkalinity and, 10
as copper complexing agents, 759–761
Brachionus plicatilis (see Rotifer)
Brachionus rubens, 740
Brachycardia, 221
Brackish waters
ammonia toxicity, 635
amyloodinium disease, 488, 774
control of cryptocaryoniasis, 496
effect of ozonation and chlorination, 757
fin rot, 486
ichthyophonus disease, 503
nitrifying bacteria, 64
nitrate and nitrite toxicity, 610
vibriosis, 479
Brain
Mycobacterium tubercles, 478
Brain corals
fiberglass-reinforced plastic, 574
growth on patch reefs, 332
Branchial cavity
amyloodinium disease, 489
goiter disease, 518
Branchial epithelium (see Epithelium)
Breakpoint, 744
Bream
functional factors in schooling, 696
Breathing
effect of goiter disease, 518
effect of vibriosis, 481
Brevibacterium spp., 619
Brevoortia tyrannus (see Atlantic menhaden)
Brightness (also see Value), 531
Brine
as a hatch solution for brine shrimp cysts, 396, 740
in artificial seawaters, 49–52
insoluble impurities, 52
pumping, 52
saturation, 52
specific gravity, 52
storage of decapsulated brine shrimp cysts, 413, 744
Brine shrimp
amino acid composition, 394
as live foods, 358
breeding procedure, 417
development, 393, 394
effect of diet on nutrient composition, 737, 738
effect of freezing on food value, 736
energy content, 394
fatty acid composition, 377, 394
food size requirements, 392
food value, 394
freeze-dried, 358, 374, 377
growth, 392, 394
inoculation of phytoplankton cultures, 442
lipid concentration, 394
nutrient value, 392–394
protein concentration, 394
reproduction, 417, 738, 745
taxonomy, 393, 737
tolerance, 392
vacuum-dried, 377
Brine shrimp cysts
addition of hydrogen peroxide to hatch solutions, 742
associated bacteria, 743
availability, 392, 736
concentration for hatch, 407, 410, 413, 414
contamination, 743
cuticular membranes, 411, 413
cyst debris, 407, 411
decapsulation, 396, 411, 742–744
decapsulation procedure, 413
effect of light on development, 742
embryonic cuticle, 407, 411
embryonic development, 396, 397
factors affecting hatch, 394, 396, 397
fatty acid patterns of nauplii and, 737
hatch procedures, 406, 407, 409–411
hatch solutions, 396, 406, 407, 413–415, 740
hatch time, 397
hatch vessels, 406, 407, 409–411, 742
individual mass, 742
illumination, 406
sterility of surfaces, 411
storage of decapsulated cysts, 413, 743, 744
terminology, 736
tertiary envelope, 411, 413
wetting, 396, 397, 406, 413, 742
world consumption, 393
Brine shrimp nauplii
amino acid patterns, 738
associated bacteria, 743
carbohydrate requirements, 745
chitin increase, 739
counting procedure, 418
effect of aeration, 742
effect of growth on nutrient value, 739
effect of salinity on growth, 414
enhancement of nutrient value, 737, 738
fatty acid patterns, 737, 738
freeze- and vacuum-dried, 377
hatch time, 392
inoculation density for rearing, 414, 415, 417
molts, 393, 738, 739
number obtained from a hatch, 394, 396, 397
nutrient value, 393, 394
rearing on dead foods and feeds, 413–415
rearing on live phytoplankton, 415, 417, 430

Brine shrimp nauplii *(Continued)*
 rearing procedures, 414, 415, 417
 rearing solutions, 414, 415, 417
 rinsing, 407, 410, 415, 743
 threonine deficient, 394, 738
 vitamins and, 414
 separation procedure, 406, 407, 409–411
 survival, 394, 739
Broad-winged hawk, 699
Bromide ions
 formation in ozonated seawater, 757
 in defining salinity, 590, 601
 reactions with chlorine-based oxidants and ozone, 469, 744
Bromite ions
 formation in ozonated seawater, 757, 758
Brook trout
 effect of carotenoids, 733
Brown seaweeds
 in humification, 59
 phenols in, 59, 97
 proteinaceous exudates, 610
 toxic exudates, 608
 uptake and assimilation of inorganic nitrogen, 620, 621
Brown trout
 effect of oxygen on acid base balance, 661
 ichthyophonus disease, 783
Brunauer-Emmett-Teller (BET) method, 629
Bubble columns (see Airlift pumps)
Bubble flow pattern, 159, 161–163
Bubbly slug flow pattern, 161–163
Buccal apparatus
 Cryptocaryon irritans trophonts, 493, 495
Buccal cavity (see Oral cavity)
Buffer adjustment (see Standardization)
Buffering, 594
Bulk density, 181
Bulk fluid
 definition, 461
 ozonation and, 466
 UV irradiation and, 463
Bulk minerals, 23
Bunsen's coefficient, 150
Buteo platypterus (see Broad-winged hawk)
Butterflyfishes
 territorial dominance, 289

Cadmium columns
 in nitrate nitrogen determination, 130–132
Calamoichthys calabricus, 688
Calanoida, 512
Calcareous organisms, 15, 593
Calcites
 as filtrants, 20, 21
 as polymorph of calcium carbonate, 14
 copper precipitation onto, 471
 definition, 13
 magnesium in, 20, 593, 594
 magnesium adsorption, 597, 598
 oyster shell, 9, 595, 599, 600
 pure, 14
 solubility, 597, 599, 600
Calcium carbonate
 algal sand, 316
 biogenic removal, 18
 dissolution, 17, 594, 595
 effect on alkalinity, 13
 in artificial seawaters, 595–600
 in dolomite, 14
 ion product, 595
 loss from carbonate minerals, 17, 44
 magnesian calcite overgrowths, 596–599
 precipitation, 17, 20, 593, 595, 596
 precipitation from autoclaved seawater, 746, 747
 saturation, 22
 solubility in deep oceans, 16
 solubility product, 594, 595, 598
 supersaturation, 16, 17, 20, 21, 594–597
Calcium chloride
 effect on nitrite toxicity, 610
 in artificial seawaters, 48
 in the Solvay process, 605
 requirement for brine shrimp cysts, 740
 use in artificial seawater, 604, 605
Calcium ions
 congruent dissolution, 600
 coprecipitation with magnesium, 20, 605
 coprecipitation with phosphorus, 605
 effect on copper complexing, 760, 761
 effect on gel precipitation, 389
 excretion in urine, 205
 in saturated solutions, 594
 in seawater, 21
 ion pairing, 6, 592, 606
 loss from carbonate minerals, 17
 magnesium ion ratio in seawater, 596, 597
 nitrite toxicity and, 609
 precipitation from autoclaved seawater, 746
Calcium sulfate dihydrate
 in alginate-bound moist feeds, 403
Calibration
 definition in pH determination, 38
 hydrometers, 26, 30
 pH meters, 36–41, 43, 603
 refractometers, 31
 thermometers, 24–26
Caligoida, 512
calorie, 372, 373
Camera lenses
 in vitro fish photography, 572
 in watertight housings, 553
 "macro" lens, 544, 550
 photographic filters and, 545, 547
 single lens reflex cameras and, 549
 viewfinder cameras and, 548
 wide angle, 550, 552
Cameras
 light meters, 544, 549, 550, 568, 570, 572
 Nikonos, 548
 parallax, 548
 35-mm single lens reflex, 544, 548–550
 viewfinder, 548, 549
Camouflage, 249, 250
Canthaxanthin
 addition to dry feeds, 733
 addition to moist feeds, 400, 406
 carotenoid metabolism and, 370
 direct deposition, 732, 733
 effect on skin coloration, 370, 371, 389, 733
 occurrence in fishes, 370, 371
Capture stress, 224, 227
Carangidae (see Jacks)
Caranx hippos (see Crevelle jack)
Caranx ignobilis
 as a schooling predator, 700, 702, 704
 individual distance, 692
 isolation of prey, 705
Carbohydrates
 as binders, 389
 as energy *vs.* proteins, 385
 as nutrients, 366
 chitin as, 734
 description, 365, 366
 determination, 374
 effect on growth, 731
 in moist feeds, 399
 in brine shrimp, 739
 in fish and invertebrate flesh, 375
 in humification, 59
 in leafy green vegetables, 375
 in protoplasm, 359
 lipids and, 365, 366
 natural gums as, 734
 physiological fuel value, 372
 protein sparing, 731
 reduction to simple sugars, 371
 requirements for, 365, 366, 388, 732
 requirements for brine shrimp nauplii, 745
 tolerance, 365, 366, 731, 732
Carboline Carbomastic®, 172
Carbon
 amorphous and crystalline, 101
 as a polymorph of calcium carbonate, 14
 cellular, 58
 cycling in aquariums, 58
 in carbohydrates, 365
 in eutrophication, 53
 in fatty acids, 362, 363
 in organic compounds, 100
 in proteins, 385
 in protoplasm, 358
 in seawater, 6
 limits for denitrification, 95
 primary, 100, 101
Carbonate ions
 as copper complexing agents, 760, 761
 bicarbonate equilibrium and, 17
 effect on alkalinity, 10–12, 44
 effect on pH, 17, 44
 equivalents in seawater, 593
 in defining salinity, 590, 601
 in saturated solutions, 594
 in seawater, 21
 ion pairing, 592
Carbonate minerals
 alkalinity and, 9
 as filtrants, 9, 44, 45, 599

at interface with seawater, 17–19
behavior in the oceans, 14, 15, 599
definition, 13
dissolution, 16, 19, 22
dissolved organic carbon and, 596
effect of magnesium on solubility, 597
effect of undersaturation on solubility, 597, 598
effect on copper chemistry, 469, 471
effect on seawater pH, 595
in aquariums, 19–24
in carbonate rocks, 13
in sediments, 58
magnesian calcite overgrowths, 597–599
pH and, 9
pH control, 19, 24
precipitation, 16, 18, 19, 22
preparation, 44, 45
solubilities, 16–18, 23, 24
surface occlusion, 606
Carbonate rocks, 9, 13, 14
Carbonate saturometer, 595
Carbon dioxide
as an activating agent, 102
atmospheric, 10, 16, 17, 45, 593
biogenic production, 16, 17
concentration in seawater, 221
concentration in water, 210
decarboxylation and, 62
dissolution, 10, 17, 45
effect of amyloodinium disease on excretion, 491
effect of salinity, 210
effect of temperature, 210
effect on acid-base balance, 659–661, 665–667
effect on alkalinity, 10–12, 658
effect on calcium carbonate saturation, 595
effect on calcium carbonate solubility, 16, 17
effect on carbonate mineral solubility, 600
effect on hemoglobin oxygen affinity, 662
equilibrium in rising air bubbles, 642
excretion, 657
fixing, 64
formation from metabolism, 210
free (gaseous), 10, 11, 17
in Solvay process, 605
from metabolism, 17, 66
from mineralization, 58
from respiration, 58
hydration, 10, 16, 17
in activated carbon manufacture, 101
in ammonia metabolism, 649
in atmosphere, 210
influx, 16
in freshwaters, 210
in hypercapnia, 217, 218
in phytoplankton culture, 431
in the oceans, 210
in seawater buffering, 594
loss to atmosphere, 58, 100
loss from autoclaved seawater, 751
partial pressure, 151, 154
partial pressure in blood, 214–217, 220, 221, 227, 230
partial pressure in water, 210, 217, 218, 221
physiological formation, 208
production by ozonation, 628
production during exercise stress, 227
release by erythrocytes, 213
release by gills, 220
removal by photosynthesis, 17
solubility, 154
total CO_2, 11
Carbon monoxide, 101
Carbonic acid
dissociation, 17
effect on alkalinity, 10–12
formation, 10, 17
in ammonia metabolism, 649
Carbonic anhydrase, 208
Carbonization, 100, 101
Carboys (also see Phytoplankton culture)
aeration, 431
autoclaving, 425, 426, 435
phytoplankton culture, 430, 431, 434, 435, 442
plastic, 415, 418, 419
polycarbonate, 425, 434
polyethylene, 425
Carcharhinus plumbeus (see Sandbar shark)
Carcharodon carcharias (see White shark)
Cardinalfishes
association with sponges, 308
Care-giving behavior, 319
Carotenoid pigmentation
definition, 370, 732
mechanisms of deposition, 370, 371
of crustaceans, 732
Carotenoids
addition to feeds, 388
binding with proteins, 732
definition, 368
deposition, 370
effect of dietary addition, 389, 733, 734
forms, 370
synthesis, 370
Carrying capacity
calculation, 83–90, 97
definition, 79, 83
factors affecting, 84
fish standing crop density and, 355
half-depth method, 86–90, 625
Hirayama's method, 84, 85, 625
nitrogen cycling and, 84
Cartilage, 202
Catecholamines (also see Adrenaline, Noradrenaline)
definition, 225
effect of exercise stress, 671, 672
effect of handling stress, 228, 670–672
effect on water permeability, 228
primary stress response and, 225
secretion, 227
Cathode, 591
Cathodic protection, 171–173
Cations
assimilation by phytoplankton, 423
definition, 1, 591
disordering effects and, 600
dyes as, 763
formation of complexes, 747
in magnesian calcite overgrowths, 599
in magnesite, 14
in table salt, 2
ion pairing, 6
loss, 44
Caulerpa spp. (listed), 622
Caulerpin, 622
Cauliflower disease (see Lymphocystis disease)
CDTA (also see Aminocarboxylates, Complexing agents)
as an iron complexing agent, 423, 748
Cells
active transport, 205
passive transport, 208, 209
Cellular immune response, 450
Celluloses, 365
Centropomus undecimalis (see Snook)
Cephalic swelling
exophiala disease, 505
Cerebral anoxia
gas-bubble trauma, 516
Chaetodon baronessa, 289
Chaetodontidae (see Butterflyfishes)
Chaetomorpha sp.
in seaweed filters, 621
Chain pipefish, 267
Changeover, 242, 351
Channel catfish
ammonia excretion, 648, 652
assimilation of free amino acids, 733
carbohydrate tolerance, 731
effect of ammonia, 673, 674
effect of environmental hypoxia, 672
essential amino acid requirements, 361
nitrite toxicity, 609
vibriosis, 768
Chanos chanos (see Milkfish)
Characinids, 266, 720
Cheirodon pulcher, 720
Chelation, 747
Chemoautotrophic, 64
Chemotherapeutic agents
application, 459–461, 519, 755
assimilation, 755
classification, 458
cryptocaryoniasis, 496
definition, 458
effect of light and temperature, 520
efficacy of formulated products, 461, 755
factors affecting absorption, 460
leaching from feeds, 459
selectivity, 467, 468, 472, 519
testing, 520
therapeutic concentrations, 755
toxicity, 460, 461, 472, 520
treatment regimens, 458
Chilomycterus schoepfi (see Striped burrfish)
Chiloscyllium griseum
response to near- and far-field effects, 269, 687
Chiniofon, 777

Chinook salmon
effect of confinement stress, 668
essential amino acid requirements, 361
goiter disease, 790
monogenean infestations, 787
vibriosis, 767
Chitin
acquisition by growing brine shrimp, 739
as a nitrogen source, 384, 385
composition, 734
in brine shrimp cysts, 742
Chitinases, 384
Chloramphenicol
toxicity to nitrifying bacteria, 72
treatment of amyloodinium disease, 777
treatment of contaminated phytoplankton stock cultures, 438
Chlorate ions
formation in ozonated seawater, 757
Chlorella pyrenoidosa
response to copper toxicity, 750
Chlorella spp.
as rotifer foods, 741
enrichment of brine shrimp nauplii, 737
Chlorinated hydrocarbons, 743
Chloride ions
as electrolytes, 509
concentration in blood, 654
effect at carbonate mineral surfaces, 598
effect on nitrite toxicity, 609, 610
in defining salinity, 590, 601
in table salt, 2
physiological regulation, 205–209, 648, 649, 654–659
reactions with ozone- and chlorine-produced oxidants, 469, 757
requirements for brine shrimp, 396
seawater concentration, 610
Chlorine
activated carbon and, 104
free available, 474
reactions in seawater, 469, 757, 758
treatment of amyloodinium disease, 778
Chlorine-based oxidants
predisposing factor in vibriosis, 483
sterilization of aquariums, 478
sterilization of plastic carboys, 425
Chlorine-produced oxidants, CPOs
as disinfectants, 469
determination, 756, 757
formation in seawater, 469, 757, 758
toxicity, 469, 757
Chlorinity, 740
Chloroform
preservation of seawater samples, 631, 633
Chlorophytes
red light absorption, 98
Chloroquine
treatment of amyloodinium disease, 777
treatment of cryptocaryoniasis, 496
Chlorotetracycline
toxicity to nitrifying bacteria, 72
treatment of amyloodinium disease, 777, 778
Choline
addition to moist feeds, 399, 400
leaching from feeds, 736
Chondrus spp.
proteinaceous exudates, 610
Chromaffin tissues, 664
Chromaticity
definition, 531
in predation, 699
lamps, 538
saturated colors and, 532
Chromatophores, 246, 247, 680
Chromis punctipinnis (see Blacksmith)
Chrysophrys major (see Red seabream)
Chub mackerel
milling, 691, 720
nocturnal disintegration of schools, 693
vision in schooling, 694
wavelength detection, 677
Cigarette smoke, 106
Cilia, 494
Ciliates, 494, 497, 498
Citrate
as a copper complexing agent, 778, 782
as an iron complexing agent, 748, 749
use in denitrification, 75
Citric acid
addition to culture solutions, 747
as a copper complexing agent, 777
Clam juice
addition to moist feeds, 403
Cleaning behavior
cryptic coloration and, 256
definition, 309, 718
ecological importance, 309, 718, 719
evidence for, 719
specific behaviors, 309, 310
symbiotic category, 310, 719
Cleaning stations, 256, 309
Clepticus parrae (see Creole wrasse)
Clinical infections
definition, 451
effect of UV radiation, 462
predisposition to disease and, 454
vibriosis by oral transmission, 480
Clinical signs, 452, 753
Clinids, 306, 722
Clorox® (also see Sodium hypochlorite)
decapsulation of brine shrimp cysts, 413
eradication of parasitic crustaceans, 514
in total ammonia nitrogen determination, 632
quarantine procedures and, 473
sterilization of pipettes, 435
sterilization of work surfaces, 439
treatment of amyloodinium disease, 778
Closed systems
alkalinity loss, 44
carbonate minerals, 22
definition, 21
goiter disease and, 518, 519, 791
nitrate accumulation, 518
ozonation, 756
pH reduction, 44, 598
UV irradiation and, 463, 465, 466, 755, 756
water changes, 94
Clupea harengus harengus (see Atlantic herring)
Clupidae (see Herrings)
Cnidae, 713, 717, 718
Cnidocytes, 712
Coal tar epoxy, 172, 173
Coarse sand filters
air scour, 148
backwash, 148
definition, 140
sand size, 148
seawater supplies and, 147, 148
subfluidization and, 146
support media, 145, 146
underdrains for, 146
Cobalt
in polyester resins, 577, 578
requirements for seaweeds, 423
Cobbles
as support media, 173
fiberglass-reinforced plastic as, 574
in seaweed filters, 99
in wave action exhibits, 585
Coho salmon
effect of environmental hypercapnia, 660
effect of physiological hypoxia, 669, 670
goiter disease, 790
Cold-water vibriosis (see Vibriosis)
Colloids
definition, 735
enlarged thyroids and, 518
Coloration
crustaceans, 732
definition, 532
effect of carotenoids, 368, 370, 388, 389, 733, 734
effect of gas-bubble trauma, 515
effect of ichthyophonus disease, 503
effect of vibriosis, 480
exhibit backgrounds and artifacts, 542
fiberglass-reinforced plastic decorations, 574, 577, 578, 581
in exhibits, 537, 538
in fish skin, 366
in fishes, 246–256
lamps, 538, 540
sexual chromatism and, 299, 300
sexual dimorphism and, 298
species labels, 566, 570
water, 541
Colors
achromatic, 531, 532, 545, 568, 571, 699
chromatic, 531, 532
effect of mixing light, 794
effect of mixing pigments, 794, 795

effect of photographic filters, 545
effect of temperature, 794
energy, 537
hue, 530–532, 538, 542–545, 563, 579
in exhibit design, 528
of light in stage plays, 555
primary, 544, 795
saturation, 531, 532, 538, 542–544, 563, 566, 579, 699
secondary, 545
shades and tints, 532
value, 531, 532, 538, 542–544, 563, 568, 571, 579, 699
wavelength and, 530

Color saturation
chromaticity and, 532, 538
definition, 531
effect of polarizing filters, 545
fiberglass-reinforced plastic decorations, 579
paints, 542–544
paint selection and, 563
species label photography and, 566

Color spectrum (also see Visible spectrum)
definition, 530
effect of color conversion filters, 545, 546
in exhibits, 541
mixing of paints and, 794, 795
paint selection and, 542

Color vision
color blindness and, 676
cone visual pigments and, 239
contrast perception and, 676
definition, 235, 674
evolution, 678
monochromatic light and, 240
perception of white light, 530
visual acuity and, 679

Columnar denitrification, 94, 95, 627

Combination electrodes, 35, 36

Commensalism
anemonefishes and sea anemones, 304
cleaning behavior as, 719
definition, 304
feeding associations, 312

Common carp
ammonia excretion, 648
assimilation of free amino acids, 733
carbohydrate tolerance, 731, 732
chain elongation of fatty acids, 731
effect of environmental hypoxia, 672
effect of oxygen on acid-base balance, 660
essential amino acid requirements, 361
first description of mycobacteriosis, 476

Common sole
monogenean infestations, 780

Community
biotopes and, 321, 335, 341
definition, 319
fish standing crop density, 349, 351
influencing factors, 722, 726

Complement, 449

Complex (also see Aminocarboxylates, Complexing agents), 747

Complexing agents (also see Aminocarboxylates)
effect on copper toxicity, 750
inorganic, 471, 759–761
photodegradation, 748–750

Complex sugars (see Polysaccharides)

Compressibility, 257, 258, 265

Concrete
backwash holding tanks, 182
effect of seawater, 170
filter tank design and, 169, 170
in steel pressure filters, 173
preparation for painting, 170, 171

Conditioned bacteriological filters
acceleration of conditioning, 79, 81–83, 624, 625
carrying capacity, 79
definition, 79, 622, 623
time lags, 79, 80

Conductivity meters, 6, 31

Condylactis gigantea, 306

Cones
color vision and, 676
definition, 235
density, 243
diurnal fishes, 235
effect of photons, 675
enlarged, 674
nocturnal fishes, 236
offset visual pigments, 676, 678
photosensitivity and, 679
visual pigments in, 237, 243

Confinement stress, 227

Confusion
definition in predation, 283
in cooperative hunting, 284, 285

Congeneric, 709

Congo red, 763

Congridae (see Garden eels)

Constant relative alkalinity, 213, 658

Contact time
airlift pumps, 159
denitrification columns, 95
effect on adsorption efficiency, 104
effect on ozonation, 467
foam fractionators, 167, 192, 193
granular activated carbon contactors, 104
packed column degassers, 185

Contrast perception
color vision and, 676
enhancement, 677–679
functioning, 237–239
importance, 676
light attenuation and, 675
photopic and scotopic vision and, 678

Copepodid stage, 513, 514

Copepods (also see Argulids, Crustacean infestations)
as prey, 704
parasitic, 512, 514
taxonomic distinction from argulids, 512, 787

Copper
as a disinfectant, 468, 758
as a stress factor, 454, 456, 664
beryllium, 552
chemistry in freshwaters, 759
chemistry in seawater, 469, 471, 759, 760
complexing, 758–761, 777, 782
deposition in fish tissues, 759
determination in seawater, 758
effect on *Amyloodinium ocellatum* development, 777, 778
effect on corticosteroids, 456
factors affecting toxicity, 758, 759
fate in seawater aquariums, 761
immersion treatment, 496, 525, 778, 779, 781, 782
in freshwaters, 469
in sediments, 488
parasites and, 469
pathological effects, 469
precipitation from autoclaved seawater, 746
predisposing factor in fin rot, 488
predisposing factor in vibriosis, 483
toxicity, 469
toxicity to fishes, 469, 492, 758, 759
toxicity from evaporator coils, 195
toxicity to phytoplankton, 423, 750, 758
toxic mechanisms, 759
treatment of amyloodinium disease, 492, 778
treatment of cryptocaryoniasis, 496, 781, 782

Coral reef exhibits
carbonate mineral filtrants, 45
ecology and, 274

Coral reefs
as ecotopes, 321
as symbiotic associations, 303
breeding on, 295
classification, 326, 727
competition for resources on, 321, 322
distribution, 323–326
factors shaping, 323
fish abundance, 349, 351, 728, 729
fish behavior on, 274
fish diversity, 319, 349, 721, 722, 728, 729
fish standing crop density, 351, 355
illusion of, in exhibits, 555, 556
simulated in fiberglass-reinforced plastic, 574
zonation, 326, 328–331, 727

Corals
artificial, 355
associations, 326
bioerosion, 293, 332
destruction by damselfishes, 293
effect on fish diversity and abundance, 334, 341, 349, 351, 721, 728, 729
factors affecting growth and diversity, 323, 727

Corals *(Continued)*
glomerate, 349
growth, 326, 328–330
hard, 325, 326, 328, 332, 333, 721, 729
hermatypic, 323, 325, 326, 727
morphology, 325
on fringing reefs, 326
on patch reefs, 332, 333
ramose, 349
rubble, 317
shelter spaces in, 349
soft, 332, 347, 727
Coregonus spp., 736
Corn, 384
Cornea, 233, 234
Corneal opacity
cryptocaryoniasis, 495
fin rot, 488
Corona, 397
Correction term
for specific gravity determinations, 30, 31, 33
Cortez grunt
as schooling prey, 705
Corticosteroids (also see Cortisol, Cortisone)
definition, 225, 226
effect of ammonia, 456, 674
effect of capture stress, 670
effect of confinement stress, 667–669
effect of copper, 456
effect of environmental hypoxia, 672, 673
effect of fasting, 454
effect of handling stress, 228
effect of thermal stress, 672
primary stress response and, 225, 226
secretion, 227
Cortisol (also see Corticosteroids)
effect of ammonia, 674
effect of capture stress, 669
effect of confinement stress, 669
effect of environmental hypoxia, 672
effect of handling stress, 669
effect of stress factors, 518
effect of transport stress, 669
primary stress response and, 225
Cortisone (also see Corticosteroids)
primary stress response and, 225
Coryphaena hippurus (see Dolphin)
Counterions, 207, 648
Countershading, 677
Courtship
territorial defense and, 267
Cownose ray
treatment for monogeneans, 525
Crabs
agonistic behavior, 309
as sources of meal, 384, 385
sheltering with fishes, 308, 309
wastes as carotenoid sources, 733, 734
Crawfish wastes
as carotenoid sources, 734
Creole-fish
nocturnal coloration, 251
Creole wrasse
mating system, 295
site attachment, 729, 730
Crepuscular
definition, 234
predators, 242, 243, 246
Crevelle jack
vision in schooling, 693, 694
Cross (aeration) pattern, 156, 157
Crowding
as a stress factor, 227
effect on predisposition to disease, 456
effect on rotifers, 398, 399, 741
predisposing factor in fin rot, 486, 488
predisposing factor in monogenean infestations, 511
predisposing factor in mycobacteriosis, 477
predisposing factor in tang turbellarian disease, 508
predisposing factor in vibriosis, 482
Crustacean infestations (also see Argulids, Copepods)
clinical signs and pathological effects, 514
epizootiology, 512–514, 787
etiology, 512
prophylaxis and treatment, 514
synonyms, 512
Crustaceans
as sources of meal, 384
carotenoid conversion, 371
carotenoid pigmentation, 732
decapsulated brine shrimp cysts as food, 743
diseases and, 447
feeds for larvae, 413
lesions caused by, 455, 456
sheltering with fishes, 308
Cryptocaryon disease (see Cryptocaryoniasis)
Cryptocaryoniasis (also see *Cryptocaryon irritans*)
clinical signs and pathological effects, 495, 496, 780, 781
epizootiology, 493–495, 779–781
etiology, 493, 779
immunity to, 495, 781
prophylaxis and treatment, 496, 781, 782
synonyms, 492
Cryptocaryon irritans (also see Cryptocaryoniasis)
distribution, 493, 779
effect of freshwater on development, 781
effect of salinity on development, 496, 780, 781
effect of temperature on development, 495, 780
immunity to, 495, 781
life cycle, 493–495, 779, 780
optimal *in vitro* temperature for excystment, 780
taxonomic history, 779
tomites, 780–782
tomonts, 780, 781
trophonts, 779–782
Cryptic coloration, 253–256
Culture solutions (also see Artificial seawaters, GP2 culture solution)
autoclaving, 422, 424
complete, 422, 745
definition, 421
enrichment additives, 422, 745, 746, 749, 752
precipitation, 422, 746, 747
AQUIL, 748, 749
silicon addition for diatoms, 749
Cutthroat trout
effect of thermal stress, 672
exophiala disease, 785
Cyanocobalamin
primary stock solution, 427
requirement for algae, 751
requirement for phytoplankton, 421
Cyclopoida, 512
Cynoscion arenarius (see Sand seatrout)
Cyprinids
hearing, 266
Cyprinodon variegatus (see Sheepshead minnow)
Cyprinus carpio (see Common carp)
Cystivirus (also see Lymphocystis disease), 474
Cytoplasm
ingestion by *Amyloodinium ocellatum*, 777
in *Ichthyophonus* life cycle, 501
refractive index, 248, 249

Dab
lymphocystis disease, 762
Dactylogyrus spp.
praziquantel treatment, 786
"Damming phenomena," 683, 685
Damselfishes
agonistic behavior, 295
algal lawns, 291–293
as sea anemone symbionts, 304, 306, 713
as territory holders, 293, 295
brooding of larvae, 721
competition and size, 291
defense of food supplies, 293, 709, 710
destruction of corals, 293
dominance hierarchies, 288
group territories, 290
guilds, 723
home ranges, 287
lekking, 290
nest guarding, 319
predation on, 272
recruitment, 723–726
sex reversal, 712
space partitioning, 723
territorial dominance, 288, 289
territories, 287, 709, 710
Daphnia magna (see Water flea)
Dark-field illuminator, 565
Dascyllus albisella
as a facultative sea anemone symbiont, 713
Dascyllus aruanus, 290
Dascyllus trimaculatus
as a facultative sea anemone symbiont, 713
Dascyllus spp.
association with sea anemones, 304
Dasyastis sabina (see Atlantic stingray)
Daylight
color films, 546, 555
electronic strobes and, 555

  fishes active in, 235
  in exhibits, 537, 538
  light spectrum, 238, 240–242, 678
  predation in, 245
  simulation in exhibits, 542
Deaeration (see Packed column degassers)
Deamination, 62, 387
Decapterus sanctaebelenae (see Scad)
Decarboxylation, 62
Decosapentenoic acid, 732
Dehydroemetine, 777
Dehydrogenation, 62
Delayed post-exercise mortality
  definition, 227
  effect of exercise stress, 666
  effect of lactic acid, 228
Denitrification
  carbon/nitrogen ratio, 94, 95, 627
  complete, 95, 627
  definition, 75, 619
  effect of carbon source, 619
  effect on alkalinity, 13
  enzymes for, 77
  in seawater, 620
  pH requirements, 78, 620
  stimulation by carbon, 75, 77
  temperature requirements, 78, 620
Denitrification columns, 95, 627
Denitrification systems, 94–96, 627, 628
Denitrifying bacteria, 75
Denitrobacillus spp., 619
Density
  coarse sand, 146
  cones, 243
  confusion with specific gravity, 591
  definition, 7
  determination of seawater, 591
  effect of temperature, 7
  effect on refractive index, 233
  expression, 7, 30, 33
  in defining sound, 256, 257
  introduction, 1
  particulate organic carbon, 141, 142
  photographic filters, 545
  pure water, 26, 27, 591
  salinity and, 7
  seawater, 7, 141, 142, 167, 601
  specific gravity and, 7–9, 33
  water, 232–234, 674
Denticles, 267
Depigmentation
  mycobacteriosis, 477
Dermis
  definition, 447, 448
  gas-bubble trauma, 516
Dermophthirius nigrellii
  as a vector in vibriosis, 767, 770
  praziquantel treatment, 525
Dermophthirioides pristidis
  praziquantel treatment, 525
Desorption, 100
Detritus
  as particulate organic carbon, 535
  digestibility, 371
  effect on ammonia oxidation, 627
  effect on mineralization, 613
  effect on nitrification, 612
  iodine loss to, 517
  mineralization, 57
  mycobacteriosis transmission in, 476
  nutrient adsorption, 67
  organic phosphorus and, 56
  phosphorus adsorption, 57
  removal, 94
  surface area, 67, 94
  tang turbellarian disease and, 507
Developing spores, 502
Dextrin (AH, E, H), 731
Dextrose
  addition to moist feeds, 399
Diadema antillarum (see Longspine sea urchin)
Diagenesis, 15
Diandric fishes, 300
Diatomaceous earth, 639
Diatoms
  iron requirements, 748
  silicon requirements, 423, 749, 750
Dicentrarchus labrax (sea basses)
  carbohydrate tolerance, 731
  immunity to amyloodinium disease, 775
  nitrite toxicity, 610
  protein sparing, 731
Dichocoenia stokesii, 332
Dielectrics, 466
Diel rhythms
  categories, 280–282
  effect on schooling, 278
  effect on shoaling, 278, 280
  monogeneans, 511
Diets
  carotenoids, 371, 389
  definition, 357, 358
  digestibility, 371
  effect on growth, 47
  effect on iodide balance, 790
  effect on metamorphosis, 47
  effect on skin coloration, 366
  energy, 371, 372
  lipid composition, 388
  live food supplements, 393
  of carnivores, 366
  polyunsaturated fatty acids, 365
  protein composition, 387
  vitamins and, 388
Differential hyperbaric gas pressure, 151, 185, 644, 645
Diffusion, 203, 204, 212
Diffusivity, 154, 641, 642
Difluoromethylornithine, 777
Digeneans, 508
Digenetic trematodes (see Digeneans)
Digenobothrium spp., 505
Digestible energy, 373
Digestibility, 370, 371
Digestion rate, 371
Diiodothyronine, 517
Dijkgraaf's tactile modality model, 263, 683, 684
Dinitrogen
  diffusion into aquariums, 64, 66
  from denitrification, 75, 620
  from dissimilation, 75
  in incandescent lamps, 539
  in packaging of dry feeds, 391
  loss to atmosphere, 67
  partial pressure, 66
  solubility, 151
Dinospores (also see Tomites)
  Amyloodinium ocellatum, 489, 491, 492
Diploid, 397
Diploria spp. (see Brain corals)
Dipoles, 2, 6
Disaccharides, 365
Discharge gap, 466
Dischistodus perspicillatus
  cultivation of algal lawns, 709
Diseases
  acute defined, 769
  as a limiting factor, 446
  as stress factors, 227
  chronic defined, 769
  definition, 447
  diagnosis, 472, 473
  immunity and, 449
  infectious and, 447, 451
  infestations and, 447
  Koch's postulates and, 767
  noninfectious, 447
  physiology and, 201
  predisposition to, 226, 454–456
  resource partitioning and, 322
  sensitivity testing and, 459
  stress and, 446
  transmission in foods, 375
  treatment, 472
  treatment regimens, 520–527
Disinfectants
  administration, 467, 775
  amyloodinium disease, 492
  as causes of irritation, 468
  as stress factors, 492
  chlorine-produced oxidants, 469
  copper, 468, 469, 471, 758
  definition, 467
  effect on mycobacteriosis, 765
  efficacy of formulated products, 468, 756
  in treatment regimens, 458
  ozone-produced oxidants, 468, 469
  predisposing factors in fin rot, 488
  toxicity, 472
  use in disease treatments, 472
Disinfecting agents (see Disinfectants)
Disordering effects, 600
Displacements
  as near-field effects, 258
  definition, 257, 681
  detection, 683–685
  far-field effects and, 269
  "fish displacements," 264, 265
  in defining sound, 256
  labyrinth stimulation and, 265, 266
  measurement, 682
  of water particles, 259, 260, 262
Dissecting microscope, 418
Dissimilation
  ammonia formation, 67
  ammonia reduction, 75, 627
  anaerobic conditions and, 72
  definition, 74
  denitrification and, 13, 75
  dissimilatory bacteria, 71, 77, 619
  dissolved organic carbon and, 75, 78
  end products, 74, 75
  factors affecting, 75–78
  in denitrification columns, 95, 627

Dissimilation *(Continued)*
introduction, 54
nitrate reduction, 55, 67, 627
nitrite reduction, 67, 627
nitrogen removal, 54, 627
Dissociation, 2
Dissolution
air, 153
carbonate minerals, 593–595, 599, 600
definition, 2
dolomite, 600
foods, 371
saturated solutions and, 595
Dissolution rate, 17, 22
Dissolved inorganic phosphorus, DIP (see Orthophosphate)
Dissolved organic carbon, DOC (also see Surfactants)
adsorption onto calcium carbonate, 596
age in the oceans, 607
as adsorbate, 100
assimilation by heterotrophic bacteria, 612, 613
breakthrough in columnar denitrification, 95
compared with particulate organic carbon, 606
determination, 95
diffusion, 94
effect of substratum adsorption on mineralization, 612
effect on coloration, 564
effect on light, 535
fin rot and, 488
in aquarium and aquaculture water, 75, 95
in denitrification columns, 95, 627
in dissimilation, 75, 78
in seawater, 58
in wastewater, 75, 95
interference in turbidity determination, 638, 640
labile (nonrefractory) components, 100, 630
light absorption, 638
mineralization, 57, 58, 68, 78, 606
oxidation by ozone, 100, 629
refractory components, 100, 630
release by seaweeds, 58, 78, 97, 99
removal by foam fractionation, 136, 163, 164, 166, 193
removal by granular activated carbon, 99–107
toxicity, 95, 608
uptake by heterotrophic bacteria, 82
Dissolved organic phosphorus, DOP
assimilation by algae, 605
assimilation by seaweeds, 57
determination, 631
effect on calcium carbonate precipitation, 595
excretion by fishes, 57
in feces, 57
in seawater, 56
release by seaweeds, 57
Dolomite
composition, 13, 14
effect of tumbling on solubility, 600
definition, 13, 14, 593
magnesium adsorption, 598
solubility, 600
Dolostones, 593
Dolphin
vibriosis, 771
Dome patch reefs, 332–334
Dominance
as antisocial behavior, 274, 287, 707, 708
definition, 287, 706
fitness and, 298–303
hierarchies, 287–289
shelter spaces and, 353
space-related, 287, 708, 723
types, 287–289
Dormant eggs, 398
Dormitator maculatus (see Fat sleeper)
Dottybacks
protogyny, 712
DPTA (also see Aminocarboxylates, Complexing agents)
as an iron complexing agent, 423, 748
Drag
effect of schooling, 285
from amyloodinium disease, 491
Drinking waters
flocculation, 143
UV irradiation, 755
Drums
sound production, 267
Dry feeds (also see Feeds, Moist feeds)
addition of carotenoids, 733
administration of chemotherapeutic agents in, 459
binders, 389
contamination, 391
flaked, 358, 383, 390, 391, 733
in defining feeds, 358
manufacture, 377
nutrient leaching from, 390
pelleted, 383, 390
stability, 390
storage and handling, 391
water content, 377
"Dry-wet" filters, 53
DS-677 K
efficacy against *Aeromonas* spp., 520, 521
Dual media filters
decision to use, 174, 643, 644
definition, 140
filtrant size selection, 176, 177
support media, 644
Dunaliella spp., 430, 438
Dunaliella tertiolecta
assimilation of urea, 423
effect of precipitates on growth, 746
Dusky damselfish, 291
Dwarf herring
milling behavior, 691
vision in schooling, 694
Dyes, 763
Dyspnea, 477
definition, 477
mycobacteriosis, 477

Eardrum, 263
Ears, 256, 263
Earstones (see Otoliths)
Ecchymosis
vibriosis, 480
Ecotope, 321, 723
Ectocarpus spp., 610
Ectoparasites
removal by cleaners, 309, 310
Ectothermic (see Cold-blooded)
Edema
gas-bubble trauma, 516
EDDHA (also see Aminocarboxylates, Complexing agents)
as an iron complexing agent, 423, 749
EDTA (also see Aminocarboxylates, Complexing agents)
as a copper complexing agent, 750, 777, 778
as an iron complexing agent, 748, 749
complexing of minor ions, 423
photodegradation, 423
Eduction pipes, 159, 161, 163, 188, 189
Eels
vibriosis, 479
Effective depth, 68
Effective size, 175–177, 644
Egg sacs, 513, 514
Eicosatrienoic acid, 732
Elasmobranchs
absence of Bohr and Root effects, 662
ammonia transport, 649
ammonia excretion, 651
branchial ion exchange, 657
definition, 205
effect of oxygen on acid-base balance, 660, 661
electric organs, 688
electroreception, 270, 272
far-field localization, 687
freshwater, 647
hearing, 685
interrenal tissues, 664
ionic and osmotic regulation, 205, 206, 209, 647, 648, 770
labyrinth, 263
lymphocystis disease and, 761
rectal gland ion exchange, 656
resistance to cryptocaryoniasis, 779
sound detection, 258
sound localization, 261, 268, 269
sound production, 267
sounds and, 256
susceptibility to cryptocaryoniasis, 493
swimbladder and, 266, 267
thyroid of, 512
transepithelial potentials, 269, 656
treatment of goiter disease, 519
Elasticity, 256, 259
Electric eel, 688, 689
Electric fishes, 269
Electric organs, 269, 688
Electrode drift, 117
Electrodes
electrolytes and, 590, 591
in ozone generation, 466
specific ion, 111, 634
Electrolytes
activated carbons and, 104
definition, 7
electric currents and, 590, 591
in gel formation, 734, 735

precipitation, 17
Electromagnetic spectrum, 529
Electromagnetic waves, 528, 529
Electron acceptors
in denitrification, 77
in redox reactions, 55
Electron donors
in denitrification, 77
in redox reactions, 55
Electronic strobes, 548–552, 555, 572, 573, 795
Electronic voltmeter (see pH meters)
Electrons, 55, 794
Electrophorus electricus (see Electric eel)
Electroreception, 269, 270, 272, 688, 689
Electrostatic attraction, 5
Elements, 1, 2
Elephantfishes, 689
Emaciation
goiter disease, 518
ichthyophonus disease, 503
mycobacteriosis, 477
tang turbellarian disease, 508
uronema disease, 497
Embolisms, 515, 516
Embryonic cuticle, 411
Emetine, 777
Emperors
protogyny, 712
Emphysemas, 516
Endoblasts, 501, 503
Endocrine systems, 225
Endospores, 501, 503
Energy
acoustic, 258, 259, 684
aeration, 157
capacitors of electronic strobes, 551, 552
change with growth in brine shrimp, 739
chemical, 55
dietary, 371–374, 732
determination, 374
effect of cooking, 375
efficiency and, 283
far-field, 265, 266, 269
fluorescent lamps, 540, 794
from carbohydrates, 365
from glucose, 365, 366
from inorganic nitrogen, 64
from lipids, 365, 366
from organic carbon, 64
from organic nitrogen, 62, 63
from proteins, 360, 365
function in foods, 371
hyposmotic regulation and, 654
in active transport, 205
in brine shrimp, 394
incandescent lamps, 539, 794
in defining intensity, 257
in detritus, 67
in fatty acid conversion, 363
in foraging, 298, 711
in ion exchange, 654
in leafy green vegetables, 375
in particulate organic carbon, 67
in predation, 357
in vision, 239
lipids as, 362
near-field, 265, 266, 269
net, 373
optimal territory size and, 298
partitioning of, 372, 373
physiological fuel values and, 372
proteins as, 385, 387
radiant, 529, 532, 533, 537, 542
requirements, 388
sound, 685
transducers and, 265
transformation from pressure to displacement, 687
wave, 330, 331
Enterobacter, 619
Enteromorpha spp.
in seaweed filters, 621
Entobdella spp., 786
Entomorphthorales, 500
Environmental hypercapnia
as a stress factor, 224, 227, 229
definition, 217
effect on acid-base balance, 230, 659–661
effect on physiological hypercapnia, 217, 218
Environmental hyperoxia
definition, 218
effect of hyperventilation, 221
effect on acid-base balance, 218–221, 661
effect on ventilation rate, 218, 220
in aquariums, 218
in sealed plastic bags, 218
in the oceans, 218
oxygen assimilation and, 219
Environmental hypoxia (also see Physiological hypoxia)
as a stress factor, 224, 227, 229
effect of blood glucose, 673
effect on adrenaline, 230
effect on blood oxygen, 222
effect of corticosteroids, 672
effect on lamellar recruitment, 230
effect on oxygen transfer, 673
effect on ventilation rate, 221
Enzootics
amyloodinium disease, 774
definition, 457
ichthyophonus disease, 503
mycobacteriosis, 476
vibriosis, 769
Enzymes
chitinases, 384
complement, 449
hydrolyzing of carbohydrates, 365
in live foods, 391
lysozyme, 449
proteolytic, 736
thiaminase, 375
Eosin, 763
Epidermis
definition, 447, 448
cryptocaryoniasis, 495
gas-bubble trauma, 516
ichthyophonus disease, 504
of fishes, 447
Epinephelus cruentatus (see Graysby)
Epinephrine
effect of ionic and osmotic regulation, 672
Epipelagic zone, 238
Epiphysis, 247
Epithelium
amyloodinium disease, 490, 491
apical cell surface, 208, 209, 649–651, 656, 671
branchial, 206–209, 649, 650, 653, 656, 657, 660, 671
cells, 447
definition, 203
gill, 230
gut, 480
ion exchange, 214
lymphocystis virus in, 474
pillar cells and, 212
rectal gland, 656
secondary lamellae, 212, 213, 221
serosal cell surface, 208, 209, 649, 656, 671
thyroid follicles, 518
transepithelial potential, 269, 654–656
uronema disease, 498
Epizootics
amyloodinium disease, 775
cryptocaryoniasis, 779
definition, 457
exophiala disease, 785
fin rot, 488
ichthyophonus disease, 784
lymphocystis disease, 474, 762
mycobacteriosis, 476, 764
UV irradiation and, 463, 756
vibriosis, 479, 480, 482, 766–771
Epizootiology
definition, 456
factors affecting, 456, 457
Epoxy coatings, 195
Epoxy grating, 91
Epoxy paints (also see Acrylic paints, Paints)
cleaning, 200
for concrete protection, 170, 171
walls of exhibit aquariums, 564
Equilibrium
definition, 2
expression, 589
heterogeneous, 594
saturation and, 594
solid phases and, 597
Equilibrium constant, 589, 590, 594
Equivalents, 592, 593
Erythema
vibriosis, 480
Erythrocytes
assimilation of oxygen, 212, 213
as units of respiration, 212
hemolytic toxins and, 769, 770
lysing from gas-bubble trauma, 516
organophosphates in, 222
permeability to urea, 647
release of carbon dioxide, 213
Erythromycin
efficacy of formulated products, 755
toxicity to nitrifying bacteria, 72
treatment of mycobacteriosis, 478
Erythropenia
vibriosis, 480, 481
Erythrophores, 247
Erythrosomes, 247

Esophagus
amyloodinium disease, 489
Esox lucius (see Northern pike)
Essential amino acids, EAAs (also see Amino acids, Free amino acids, Nonessential amino acids)
definition, 360
in proteins, 357, 383
leaching from feeds, 383, 384, 390
requirements for, 360
Essential fatty acids, EFAs (also see Fatty acids)
deficiency, 731, 732
definition, 364
effect of carbohydrate, 731, 732
effect on lipid deposition, 733
in brine shrimp nauplii, 738
in lipids, 357
requirements for, 364, 388, 731
Ethanol
use in denitrification, 75
Ethyl cellulose
as a feed encapsulating agent, 390, 391, 736
European eel
hemoglobin oxygen affinity, 662
nitrate toxicity, 610
nitrite toxicity, 610
transepithelial potentials, 655
treatment for monogeneans, 524, 525
vibriosis, 768
Euryhaline (see Brackish water)
Euthynnus affinis (see Kawakawa)
Euthynnus lineatus (see Black skipjack)
Euthynnus pelamis (see Skipjack)
Eutrophic waters, 53, 99, 100
Eutrophication
fin rot and, 488
from seaweed filters, 78
Evaporated sea salts, 48
Evaporation
effect on calcium carbonate, 17
of aquarium seawater, 33, 35
Evaporator coils, 169, 195
Evermannichthys metzelaari, 308
Excess (sound) pressure
definition, 257
detection, 684
measurement, 681, 682
transformation, 687
Excess solid phase, 594, 595
Exercise stress
delayed post-exercise mortality and, 227, 228
effect on acid-base balance, 227, 228, 230, 456, 665, 666
effect on hyperglycemia, 456
effect on tissue oxygen, 665, 667
effect on tissue water balance, 671, 672
Exhibit layouts, 556–559
Exhibit philosophy, 555, 556
Exit coefficient, 641, 642
Exophiala disease
clinical signs and pathological effects, 505
epizootiology, 505
etiology, 505, 785
prophylaxis and treatment, 505, 785
Exophiala spp., 505, 785
Exophthalmia
definition, 477
exophiala disease, 505
gas-bubble trauma, 515, 787, 788
ichthyophonus disease, 504
mycobacteriosis, 477
vibriosis, 480
Expansion valves, 169
Extinction photometer, 638, 639
Extrinsic resources, 351
Eyes
amyloodinium disease, 489
copper deposition, 759
cryptocaryoniasis, 493, 495, 496
description, 232–236
effect of lymphocystis disease, 475
effect of mycobacteriosis, 478
effect of vibriosis, 480
gas-bubble trauma, 515, 516
injury to, 455, 456
lesions, 447
monogenean infestations, 509
pigment deposition in, 368
size, 234
Eyespot, 491

Fairmount Park Aquarium, 476
Falco sparverius (see American kestrel)
"Fancy carp"
effect of astaxanthin on skin coloration, 734
Far-field effects
definition, 258
detection, 258, 265, 686, 687
in aquariums, 682
models, 258, 259
sound localization, 268, 269, 687
swimbladder and, 267, 685, 687
transduction, 265, 266
Farsightedness (see Hyperopic vision)
Fasting
effect on predisposition to disease, 454, 455
Fathead minnow, 636
Fats
adsorption onto calcium carbonate, 596
animal, 362
as lipids, 362
physiological fuel value, 372
storage in tissues, 387
Fat sleeper
immunity to amyloodinium disease, 775
transepithelial potentials, 655
Fatty acids (also see Essential fatty acids)
chain elongation, 364, 731, 732
chemical structures, 263
definition, 362
desaturation, 732
from lipids, 371
in zooplankton, 364
iodine number, 362
metabolism, 730
modification by brine shrimp, 737
of brine shrimp nauplii, 377, 394, 737–739
of oceanic origin, 730
polyunsaturated, 362, 364, 365, 388, 391
requirements for, 363–365
saturated, 362
tissue deposition, 363, 733
unsaturated, 362, 364, 388
Favia fragum, 332
Feces
chitin, 384
energy, 373
fatty acids, 363
fiber, 365
formation, 371
mycobacteriosis transmission, 476
organic carbon, 58
organic phosphorus, 57
Feeding
effect on schooling, 278, 280
Feeding associations, 312, 719
Feeding metabolism, 372
Feeding spaces, 343
Feeding-time maximizers, 298, 711
Feeding-time minimizers, 298, 711
Feeds (also see Dry feeds, Moist feeds)
addition of proteins, 383
alginate-bound moist, 358
binders, 389, 390
carbohydrate addition, 388
carotenoid addition, 388, 389
definition, 357, 358
disease transmission in, 764
effect of temperature, 391
encapsulation, 390, 391, 736
for crustacean larvae, 413
leaching of ascorbic acid, 735, 736
leaching of chemotherapeutic agents, 459
leaching of nutrients, 384, 390, 391
leaching of riboflavin and choline, 736
lipids in, 362
lipid quality, 388
live foods and, 391
microencapsulation, 390
pelleted, 391
pigments in, 368
protein quality, 384, 385
stability, 390, 735
storage and handling, 391
vitamins, 388
Ferntastsinn (also see Lateral line), 263, 683
Fiber
as cellulose, 365
in fish and invertebrate flesh, 375
in foods, 374
in leafy green vegetables, 375
Fiberglass, 580
Fiberglass-reinforced plastic casts, 580, 581, 587
Fiberglass-reinforced plastic decorations
advantages, 574
detailing of, 555
first use, 796
procedure, 574, 576–581
Fiberglass tape, 91
Films (see Biological films, Photographic films)
Filter bed bacteria
activity levels, 82

attachment to detritus, 94
factors affecting, 67–78
in humification, 62
in seawater yellowing, 61
population stability, 82
rate of nitrogen conversion by, 84
removal, 94
surface area and, 68
Filter beds (also see Bacteriological filters)
anaerobic conditions, 620
carrying capacity, 355
copper in, 471
definition, 56
design criteria, 91
design depth, 86–90
detritus, 67
dissimilation, 78, 619
effect of chemotherapeutic agents, 460
fish standing crop density and, 355
flow rate through, 84
mineralization, 55, 58
newly conditioned, 355
oxidation, 67
oxygen, 56, 620
phosphorus precipitation, 57
size, 84
thickness of biological films, 613
Filter plates, 91
Filter sterilization
antibiotic mixtures, 438
GP2 culture solution D, 422, 425, 427
Filtrants
abrasion during backwash, 641
functions, 44
grain size, 84, 626
specific surface area, 87, 89, 90
Filtration mode
definition, 142
filtrant stability and, 175
underdrains and, 145
variables, 142–144
Filtration rate
definition, 143
high rate filters, 140
rapid sand filters, 137
void fraction and, 144
Fin erosion disease (see Fin rot)
Fine sand filters
definition, 137, 140
filtrant loss, 146
support media, 145
Finger corals, 332
Fin rays
sound production by, 267
Fin rot
clinical signs and pathological effects, 487, 488
epizootiology, 486, 487, 772, 773
etiology, 486, 772
prophylaxis and treatment, 488
synonyms, 486
Fins
amyloodinium disease, 489
gas-bubble trauma, 515, 516
ichthyophonus disease, 504
lymphocystis disease, 475
mycobacteriosis, 477
necrosis from fin rot, 487
tang turbellarian disease, 508
vibriosis, 480
Fire corals, 330
Fishes (also see)
acceptance of moist feeds, 399
acid-base balance, 213–221
advanced bony, 201
antibodies, 450
antisocial behavior, 274
as resource generalists, 322, 323, 721–726
as resource specialists, 321–323, 721–726
assemblages, 275–285
biotopes and, 321
benefit from seaweed filters, 78
burrowing and mound-building, 315–318, 720
caloric requirements, 388
carbon excretion, 58
carnivorous, 358, 364–366, 371, 372, 388, 697, 709, 710, 730
carotenoid metabolism, 370, 371, 388, 389
"changeover," 679, 680
chromatic, 246–248
cleaning associations, 309, 310, 312
color vision, 676
crepuscular, 234, 235, 238, 242, 243, 272, 676, 678–680
cryptic coloration, 253–256
deepwater, 675–679
density of, 328
diel effect on coloration and pattern, 250, 251
digestion, 371–374
diurnal, 234, 235, 238, 240, 242–246, 272, 676, 678, 680, 692, 697
diversity, 319, 322, 323, 328, 334, 349
dominance behavior, 285–293, 295, 298–303, 708–712
ecotopes and, 321
effect of corals on diversity and abundance, 334, 341, 349, 351, 728, 729
energy partitioning, 372–374
energy requirements, 373, 374
feeding associations, 312, 719
feeding rate, 85
feeding spaces and, 343
filter bed bacteria and, 67
flesh of, as natural foods, 358, 374, 375
foods in nature, 357
freshwater drinking, 205, 647
growth, 47
habitats and, 319, 321
herbivorous, 280, 304, 332, 335, 358, 365, 371, 686, 709, 730, 731
herbivory in captivity, 730
maintenance in artificial seawaters, 46
milling, 275–277, 285, 690, 691, 697, 720
minor ions and, 47
nitrogen excretion, 64
nocturnal, 676, 678, 680, 697
nomadic, 353
nutrient ingestion, 47
nutrient sources, 421
omnivorous, 304, 358, 365, 371, 731
pelagic, 223, 238, 284, 676, 677
phosphorus excretion, 57
physical barriers to diseases, 447
piscivorous, 284, 304
planktivorous, 280, 284, 295, 347, 397, 411, 646, 696, 697, 703, 704, 708, 709, 716
polyunsaturated fatty acids in tissues, 364
predisposition to disease, 454–456
protective associations, 304, 306
proximate composition, 383
quarantine, 356
refuge associations, 306–309
schooling, 275–277, 285, 312, 353, 689–706, 720
seawater drinking, 47, 228
sensitivity tests and, 458
shallow-water, 676, 679
shelter in vertical zones, 334
shelter on patch reefs, 332
shelter spaces and, 341, 343, 347, 352, 353
shoaling, 275–277, 285, 312, 689–691, 697
silvery, 248–250, 565
social behavior, 274, 275
standing crop density, 349, 351, 355
stress and, 353, 356, 459, 460
stress response, 225–227
superiority of live foods for, 391
surface area, 460
symbiotic associations, 303, 304, 306–310, 312, 712–719
tolerance of deviant major ion ratios, 422
use of coral reefs, 323
variation in nutrient requirements, 357
vision, 233–239
visual pigments, 675, 677
vitamin synthesis, 366
Fish larvae
decapsulated brine shrimp cysts as food, 743
effect of live foods on growth and survival, 391, 736
effect of ozone- and chlorine-produced oxidants, 757
growth, 47
metamorphosis, 47, 723
recruitment, 322, 323, 722–726
Fish louse infestations (see Crustacean infestations)
Fish meal
addition to moist feeds, 403, 406
protein quality, 384
Fish tuberculosis (see Mycobacteriosis)
Fitness
definition, 290, 319
dominance and, 706
effect of mating system, 301
effect of resources, 291
individual dominance and, 298–303
optimal territory size and, 711
sex reversal and, 298, 301
territorial dominance and, 290, 291

Fixed bed configuration
 definition, 142, 143
 in filtration mode, 144
 intermixed filtrant zones, 181
Flagellar canal, 490
Flagellates, 491
Flagellum, 491
Flamefish, 251
Flatworms, 505
Flavobacterium spp.
 fin rot, 486
Flexibacter spp.
 fin rot, 486, 773
Flocculation, 143
Florida pompano
 treatment for monogeneans, 524
Flounders
 lymphocystis disease, 475
 predation by, 272
 resistance to cryptocaryoniasis, 779
Flow meters, 52
Flow rate
 airlift pumps, 136
 bacteriological filters, 84–86, 88, 90
 granular activated carbon contactors, 104, 107
Fluidization
 air scour and, 146
 backwash rate and, 145, 181
 bulk density and, 181
 definition, 144
 effect of filtrant settling velocities, 175
 effect on filtrant grain size, 175
 effect on uniformity coefficients, 175
 surface wash and, 147
Fluorescence, 539
Fluorescent lamps (also see Incandescent lamps, Lamps)
 angled viewing window exhibits, 586
 chromaticity, 538
 color compensating filters and, 546
 daylight, 541
 description, 539–541, 793, 794
 for hatch of brine shrimp cysts, 406
 cool white, 406, 434, 541, 565
 incubation of tertiary phytoplankton cultures, 442
 in exhibits, 539
 in vitro fish photography and, 547
 phytoplankton culture, 434
 warm white, 538, 541
 waste heat, 431
 white, 541
Fluorescent light
 cool white, 98
 effect on brine shrimp cysts, 742
 for seaweed filters, 98
Flux, 154
Foam
 drainability, 164, 166
 formation, 163, 164, 167, 193, 195
 height, 192
 stability, 166, 195
 surface tension, 166
 viscosity, 166
Foam fractionation
 as a process, 53
 definition, 163
 factors afffecting, 164
 removal of organic carbon, 136
Foam fractionators
 concurrent, 193, 194
 contact columns, 192–194
 countercurrent, 193, 194
 design, 192–195, 645, 646
Foam separation (see Foam fractionation)
Focal dermatitis
 tang turbellarian disease, 508
Foods (also see Live foods)
 addition of iodide, 518
 as ecological resources, 291–293, 295, 319, 351, 352, 708–711
 as sources of iodide, 517
 definition, 357, 358
 digestion, 371
 disease transmission, 457, 476, 478, 480, 484, 503–505, 509, 764, 768, 771
 energy in, 372
 freeze-dried, 374, 375, 377, 736, 741
 in nature, 357
 metabolism of, 372, 373
 natural, 358, 374, 375, 377
 nutrient leaching from, 390
 of terrestrial origin, 364, 730
 pigments in, 366, 368
 qualities affecting rotifers, 399
 size, 352
 uptake by rotifers, 740, 741
 vacuum-dried, 377
 vitamins and, 366
Footpiece, 159
Formaldehyde solution
 in species label photography, 567
Formalin
 as a stress factor, 664
 effect on *Amyloodinium ocellatum* development, 777
 efficacy of formulated products, 756
 toxicity to nitrifying bacteria, 616
 treatment of amyloodinium disease, 777, 778
 treatment of cryptocaryoniasis, 782
 treatment of exophiala disease, 785
 treatment of tang turbellarian disease, 509
Formazin turbidity units, FTUs, 639
Formula weight, 589
Free amino acids (also see Amino acids, Essential amino acids, Nonessential amino acids)
 addition to feeds, 383
 assimilation, 733
 leaching from feeds, 383, 384, 390, 735
Free ammonia
 effect of autoclaving seawater, 751
 effect on acid-base balance, 214
 effect on immunity, 637
 excretion, 649–653
 immune suppression and, 637
 lipid solubility, 650
 loss in specific ion electrode determination, 116, 634
 partial pressure, 115
 physiological regulation, 208, 214, 649–653
 proportion of ammonia, 117
 toxicity to a rotifer, 398, 740
 toxicity to nitrifying bacteria, 71, 615
 toxicity to fishes, 117–122, 635–637
Free ammonia nitrogen
 arbitrary limit, 118–121, 636, 637
 ratio to total ammonia nitrogen, 71
 water quality criteria and, 117
Free nitrous acid
 toxicity to nitrifying bacteria, 71
French grunt
 diel movements, 281, 282, 697
Freon, 168
Frequency
 attraction of sharks, 268, 686
 attraction of teleosts, 268, 269, 686, 687
 definition, 257, 529
 effect on shark behavior, 686
 electric stimuli, 270
 in model sound production, 258, 259
 muscle contraction and, 268
 radiant energy and, 529
 swimbladder and, 266
 velocity and, 683
Freshwaters (also see Pure water, Water)
 acid-base regulation, 217
 air bubble formation, 153
 ammonia dissociation, 635
 ammonia toxicity, 635
 biofouling and, 147
 biological film formation, 614
 carbon dioxide, 210
 copper toxicity, 759
 decapsulation of brine shrimp cysts, 744
 differential hyperbaric gas pressure, 198
 effect of pH on ammonia excretion, 652
 effect of pH on blood pH, 659
 effect on development of *Amyloodinium ocellatum*, 776, 777
 effect on development of *Cryptocaryon irritans*, 781
 exophiala disease, 505
 fin rot, 486
 gas-bubble trauma, 515
 humus, 607, 608
 ichthyophonus disease, 500, 503, 784
 inhibition of nitrification, 71
 ions, 1
 lymphocystic disease, 474
 mycobacteriosis, 476
 nitrite toxicity, 609, 610
 opaqueness and transparency to light, 533–535
 oxygen, 210
 ozonation, 468, 758
 physiological solution regulation, 205
 reactions of ozone, 468, 756, 758

rotifers in, 397
sound velocity, 257
treatment of amyloodinium disease, 778
vacuum degassing, 187
vibriosis, 479, 768
Friction, 285
Fringing reefs, 326, 328, 331, 332, 727
Froth flotation, 163
Fucus spp., 610, 620, 621
Fulvic acids
adsorption onto calcium carbonate, 596
age, 607
definition, 607
in seawater, 59
Fumed silica, 578, 579, 580
Fundulus grandis (see Gulf killifish)
Fundulus heteroclitus (see Mummichog)
Fundulus zebrinus (see Plains killifish)
Fungi
as parasites, 500
as primary infectious agents, 459
as secondary infectious agents, 475
effect of cellular immune response, 450
efficacy of formulated products, 469
feed contamination by, 391
multicellular, 447
ozone and, 466
systemic infections, 459
unicellular, 447
Furanace® (see Nifurpirinol)
Furazolidone, 777

Gadus morhua (see Atlantic cod)
Galvanic corrosion, 171–173
Gametes, 301
Gamma rays, 529
Garden eels
substratum for exhibition, 316
Garibaldi
cultivation of algal lawns, 292, 709
territorial defense, 710
Garnet
cost, 174
granular media filters, 137
intermixing with sand, 181
multimedia filters, 140
relative grain size, 176, 644
60% size, 183
specific gravity, 175
support media and, 644
transport to surface, 183
Gas-bubble disease (see Gas-bubble trauma)
Gas embolism (see Gas-bubble trauma)
Gas-bubble trauma
clinical signs and pathological effects, 515, 516, 788
epizootiology, 515
etiology, 515, 787
gas supersaturation and, 788
prophylaxis and treatment, 516
seawater supplies and, 149, 515
synonyms, 515
total gas pressure and, 151
Gas exchange
gills, 201–203, 211, 673
impairment by amyloodinium disease, 491
Gases
aeration and, 148–151, 153
assimilation by secondary lamellae, 211
diffusion rate into water, 154
partial pressures, 149–151, 153, 154, 210, 657
passive transport, 212
refrigerant, 168, 169
supersaturation, 136, 148–151, 153, 185, 787, 788
tension, 150, 151
transfer, 153, 154, 159, 162, 163
undersaturation, 136
Gasping
amyloodinium disease, 491
Gas slugs, 161
Gasterosteus aculeatus (see Threespine stickleback)
Gas transfer
effect of blood pressure, 221
effect of hydrostatic pressure, 642
introduction, 136, 137
Gastrointestinal tract
lymphocystis disease, 762
Gastrula, 736
Gel, 389, 734
Gelatin
as a feed binder, 389
as a feed encapsulating agent, 391
as a suspension, 735
derivation from collagen, 734
Gelatin-bound moist feeds
nutrient composition, 399
procedure, 403, 406
Gelbstoff (see Humus)
Giant blue damselfish
cultivation of algal lawns, 709
Gill arches
definition, 201
in ventilation, 202, 646
thyroid and, 517
Gill filaments, 202
Gill hyperplasia
ammonia and, 488
amyloodinium disease, 491
chemical irritants, 453
fin rot, 488, 772
Gill lamellae (also see Secondary lamellae)
amyloodinium disease, 491
cryptocaryoniasis, 495, 496
gas-bubble trauma, 515, 516
goiter disease, 518
ichthyophonus disease, 504
uronema disease, 498
Gill rakers, 202, 646
Gills
acid-base balance and, 660
adsorption of chemotherapeutic agents, 460
ammonia excretion, 649–654, 657
ammonia transport, 230
amyloodinium disease, 489, 491, 492, 775, 776
assimilation of oxygen, 221, 222
bioelectric fields, 269
blood flow, 212, 213, 222, 230
cryptocaryoniasis, 493, 495
design, 201, 202
diffusion distance, 212
diffusion limitation, 662
effect of ammonia, 609
effect of copper, 759
effect of epinephrine on water transport, 672
effect of zinc displacement by copper, 759
effect of mycobacteriosis, 476, 479
effect of vibriosis, 480
energy release, 373
entry site for *Vibrio* spp., 768
excretion of hydrogen ions, 214
function in acid-base balance, 214
gas-bubble trauma, 516
gas exchange, 201–203, 211, 673
goiter disease, 518
hemoglobin and, 222
ichthyophonus disease, 504
injury and, 455
ion exchange, 205, 207, 208, 648–656
lesions, 447
lymphocystis disease, 762
monogenean infestations, 509
morphology, 646
mucous cells, 447
nitrite toxicity, 609
oxygen transfer, 230, 661, 673
partial pressure of oxygen and, 218
permeability, 205
polyelectrolytes and, 641
release of carbon dioxide, 220
surface area, 230
tang turbellarian disease, 508
trace ions and, 47
transepithelial potentials, 654–656
uronema disease, 497, 498
vascular constriction, 673
vibriosis epizootics and, 483
water flow, 212
water turnover, 648
Gilthead bream
cryptocaryoniasis, 780
immunity to amyloodinium disease, 775
vibriosis, 767
Ginglymostoma cirratum (see Nurse shark)
Girdle, 491
Glacial acetic acid, 778
Glitter, 532
Glomerate corals, 349
Glucose (also see Blood glucose)
as a carbon source in denitrification, 619
assimilation, 365, 731
effect of protein, 732
use in denitrification, 75
vs. "glycose," 731
Glucose bottles
as brine shrimp cyst hatch vessels, 407
Glycine
use by nitrifying bacteria, 612
Glycogen
as a polysaccharide, 365
effect of carbohydrates, 731
energy storage as, 372
glucose and, 365

Glycoproteins
  immunoglobulins as, 450
Glycylglycine
  addition to culture solutions, 747
Goatfishes
  as nocturnal predators, 280
Gobies
  association with crustaceans, 308, 309
  association with sea anemones, 306
  association with sponges, 308
  cleaning, 310
  predation on, 272
  protogyny, 712
  resistance to cryptocaryoniasis, 779
Gobiodon, 289
Gobiosoma spp., 308, 310
Goiter (see Goiter disease)
Goiter disease
  clinical signs and pathological effects, 518
  epizootiology, 517, 518, 789–791
  etiology, 516, 517, 789
  goitrogens, 517, 518, 790
  prophylaxis and treatment, 518, 519
  synonyms, 516
Goldfish
  ammonia excretion, 648
  carbon dioxide excretion, 649
  effect of ammonium ion on sodium uptake, 648
  effect of capture stress, 670
  effect of thermal stress, 672
  goiter disease, 518
  nocturnal disintegration of shoals, 694
  treatment for *Aeromonas* infections, 520, 521
  treatment for vibriosis, 522
Gonads
  definition, 478
  goiter disease, 518
  Mycobacterium tubercles, 478
  pigment deposition in, 368
Gorgonians, 254, 255
GP2 culture solution (also see Artificial seawaters)
  autoclaving, 48, 422, 423, 425–427, 735, 751
  contamination checks of phytoplankton stock cultures, 436–438
  description, 422, 423, 747
  inoculation of phytoplankton carboy cultures, 442
  inoculation of phytoplankton primary stock cultures, 439, 440
  inoculation of phytoplankton secondary stock cultures, 440
  inoculation of phytoplankton tertiary stock cultures, 442
  low-salinity formula, 428, 429, 747, 751, 752
  major ions, 48
  mixing procedures, 424, 425–429
  pH, 605
  phytoplankton culture, 429, 434–440, 442
  transfer of phytoplankton primary stock cultures, 439
Gracilaria tikvahiae
  in seaweed filters, 621
Grammistidae (see Soapfishes)
Gram's stain, 763
Granular activated carbon, GAC
  biological enhancement, 104, 630
  contactors, 105–107
  definition, 102, 629
  exhaustion, 103
  film formation on, 104
  fin rot and, 488
  handling, 106, 107
  reactivation, 107, 630, 631
  replacement, 105, 107
  selection, 104, 106, 107
Granular media filters
  backwash mode variables, 144–147
  capture mechanisms, 640
  classification, 137–140
  comparative performance, 643, 644
  filtration mode variables, 142–144
Granular media filtrants
  backwash and, 145, 176
  capture mechanisms in, 140–142
  clogging, 144
  size, 148
  definition, 137
  density, 179, 181
  depth, 140, 175
  distribution, 140, 144, 181
  during fluidization, 175
  effective size, 175–177
  expansion, 145, 146
  grain sizes, 137, 140, 144, 145, 175, 181
  grain size uniformity, 175, 178
  hydrodynamic shear forces, 145
  in filtration mode, 175
  intermixing, 176, 179, 181
  intermixing with support media, 146
  loss, 176
  placement, 140
  representative sizes, 175
  screen sizes, 178, 179
  settling velocities, 175
  60% size, 176, 177, 181
  size selection, 176, 177
  specific gravity, 137, 140, 175, 181
  uniformity coefficients, 175–177
  void fraction, 143
Granular media filtration, 136, 137
Graphics, 275
Graphite, 102
Gravel
  adsorption of chemotherapeutic agents, 460
  as support media, 173
  attachment of bacteria, 53, 56
  biological films, 68
  depth in bacteriological filters, 90
  for conditioning bacteriological filters, 82, 83
  in filter beds, 56
  linear flow rate through, 90
  phosphorus precipitation onto, 57, 606
  screen sizes, 179
  seawater supplies and, 147
  stirring, 94
Gravity, 264
Gravity filters (see Vacuum filters)
Graysby, 719
"Green water" procedures, 417, 418
Gross energy, 373
Groupers
  attraction by sound, 686
  predation by, 272
  protogyny, 712
  "riding" behavior and, 719
Group spawning, 302
Growth
  amino acid requirements for, 361
  definition, 358
  effect of ammonia, 609, 637
  effect of carbohydrates, 731
  effect of ions, 47
  effect of live foods, 736
  effect of nitrate, 610
  effect of nitrite, 610
  impairment by ichthyophonus disease, 503
  metabolism and, 372, 373
  protein requirements for, 360, 385, 387
Grunts
  as nocturnal predators, 280, 281, 728
  damselfishes and, 710
  nocturnal coloration, 251
  sound attraction, 686
  sound production, 267
Guanine, 248
Guilds
  damselfishes, 723
  definition, 322, 722
  overlap of resource use, 725
  rarefaction and, 726
Gulf killifish
  immunity to amyloodinium disease, 774
Gulf toadfish
  ammonia excretion, 650
  immunity to amyloodinium disease, 774
Gums
  as feed encapsulating agents, 391
  in biological films, 68
  natural, 734
Guppy
  effect of predation on schooling, 696
  ichthyophonus disease, 504
Gut
  amyloodinium disease, 779
  effect of vibriosis, 480
  gas-bubble trauma, 516
  ichthyophonus disease and, 503
  entry of lymphocystis virus, 474
  ionic and osmoregulation in, 205
Gymnarchus niloticus, 688
Gymnotids, 266, 688
Gyrodactylus aculeati
  levamisole hydrochloride treatment, 526, 527
  niclosamide treatment, 526
  praziquantel treatment, 526, 786

Habitats
  captive, 353
  competition, 723
  coral reefs as, 323
  definition, 319, 721

effect of tides, 348
feeding spaces in, 343
fish occupation, 319
partitioning, 347, 348, 722
shelter spaces, 341, 343, 347
species and, 321
Haddock
ichthyophonus disease, 784
Haemulidae (see Grunts)
Haemulon flavolineatum (see French grunt)
Haemulon plumieri (see White grunt)
Hagfish
blood osmolality, 647
Half-life, 468
Halichoeres garnoti, 306
Halimeda spp., 316, 622
Halobates robustus (see Ocean skater)
Halquinol
efficacy against vibriosis, 523
Handling stress
acid-base balance and, 230
as a stress factor, 224, 227, 454, 456, 496
definition, 228
effect on blood glucose, 670, 671
effect on catecholamines, 669, 670, 672
effect on corticosteroids, 667–670
effect on tissue water balance, 671, 672
effect on thyroid hormones, 518, 791
injury and, 456
predisposing factor in cryptocaryoniasis, 496
predisposing factor in mycobacteriosis, 477
predisposing factor in vibriosis, 482, 767, 771
stress responses, 228
Haploid, 397
Harems
individual dominance and, 287, 289
sex reversal and, 303
Harpacticoida, 512
Hawaiian anchovy
individual distance, 692
isolation during attack, 705
survival in schools, 700, 702, 704
Head kidney
amyloodinium disease, 775
Headloss
after backwash, 145, 176
dual *vs.* multimedia, 643, 644
effect of filtrant intermixing, 181
entrapment and, 144
terminal, 144
Hearing
definition, 256, 263, 265, 681, 684, 685
directional, 268, 269
effectiveness, 266
Heart
gas-bubble trauma, 516
ichthyophonus disease, 503
in thyroid function, 517
lymphocystis disease, 762
Mycobacterium tubercles, 478
Heat exchange, 136, 137
Heating requirements, 168, 198, 199
Heat transfer coefficients, 168, 196, 197
Hemacytometer
phytoplankton cell counts, 443–445
Hematocrit
effect of exercise stress, 228, 667
Hematology
effect of stress, 226
Hematopoietic tissue
uronema disease, 498
Hemiglyphidodon plagiometopon, 293
Hemipteronotus novacula, 306
Hemoconcentration, 228
Hemodilution, 228
Hemoglobins
affinity for oxygen, 222, 223, 662
changes in oxygen binding, 226
definition, 213
effect of acidosis, 456
effect of exercise stress, 228, 667
of fishes, 223
saturation, 222, 223
water fleas, 698
Hemorrhagic septicemia
vibriosis, 480
Henry's law, 115
Herrings
as nocturnal predators, 280
Heterodontus francisci (see Horn shark)
Heterotrophic bacteria
anaerobic, 68
as denitrifiers, 75
as nitrifiers, 80–82, 610, 611
as periphytes, 614
assimilation of dissolved organic carbon, 612, 613
competition with phytoplankton, 611
definition, 55
effect of filter bed depth, 626
in biological films, 68
in brine shrimp cultures, 743
in eutrophic waters, 99, 100
inorganic nitrogen conversion, 64
in unconditioned bacteriological filters, 79, 80
mineralization of dissolved organic carbon, 58, 68
mineralization of nitrogenous organics, 62, 63, 67
on conditioned gravel, 83
organic phosphorus and, 57
oxidation by, 64
population growth in filter beds, 623
surface area requirements, 67–69
use of ammonium ions, 611
High rate filters
backwash rate, 181, 183, 184
filtrant depth, 175
filtrant distribution, 144
filtrant size selection, 176, 177
filtrant intermixing, 176, 179
filtrant loss, 146
headloss, 181
streamlines, 137
support media, 145
High rate filtration, 140
Hippocampus erectus (see Lined seahorse)
Hippocampus spp. (see Pipefishes)
Hippoglossus hippoglossus (see Atlantic halibut)
Hitra disease (see Vibriosis)
H^+-selective membranes, 35, 36
Holiday detectors, 172
Holocentridae (see Squirrelfishes)
Home range
damselfishes, 287
definition, 287, 708
optimal size, 295, 298
Horn shark
sound detection, 685
Horse mackerel
individual distance, 692
Hosts (of nonparasitic symbionts)
commensalism and, 304, 719
in cleaning behavior, 309, 310, 719
mutualism and, 304, 310, 312, 713, 719
sea anemones as, 304, 406, 713–716
Hosts (of parasites)
adaptation to parasites, 456, 457
amyloodinium disease and, 490, 492, 774
assimilation of chemotherapeutic agents, 520
cleaning behavior and, 719
crustacean parasites, 513, 514
cryptocaryoniasis and, 493-496
definition, 446
effect of copper treatment, 758
effect of treatments, 472
enzootics and, 457
ichthyophonus disease, 500, 501, 503
immune suppression, 769
infections and infestations, 446, 447, 752
intermediate, 456, 509
Koch's postulates and, 767
lymphocystis disease and, 475
monogeneans, 509, 511
tang turbellarian disease, 507
vibriosis, 766
HPI axis, 227
Hue
chromaticity and, 538
definition, 531
fiberglass-reinforced plastic decorations, 579
paints, 542–544
paint selection and, 563
primary colors and, 545
of fishes, 247
Humic acids
adsorption onto calcium carbonate, 596
as ligands for complexing copper, 760, 761
definition, 607
in seawater, 59
origin, 760
Humic compounds
effect on coloration, 564
effect on light absorption, 535, 542
Humidity
effect on sound velocity, 257
Humification
definition, 59
importance, 607

Humification *(Continued)*
- in aquariums, 61, 62
- toxic processes, 608

Humoral immune response, 450, 451
Humoral immunity (see Immunity)
Humus
- allochthonous 607, 608
- autochthonous, 607, 608
- definition, 59
- description, 606, 607
- formation, 61, 62
- light absorption, 639
- percentage of total organic carbon, 59
- pigmented fraction, 607
- refractory forms, 59, 607
- toxicity, 608

Hydrated aluminum sulfate, 143
Hydrated CO_2 (see Carbonic acid)
Hydration, 2, 10, 16, 17
Hydrochloric acid
- effect on alkalinity, 12
- effect on total CO_2, 12
- in alkalinity determinations, 41–43

Hydrogen
- in carbohydrates, 365
- in protoplasm, 358
- in unsaturated fatty acids, 362

Hydrogen ions
- activity (effective concentration), 35, 36, 41, 42, 602, 603
- effect on alkalinity, 10, 12
- effect on ammonia toxicity, 636
- effect on pH, 17, 19
- excretion, 208, 214
- excretion as ammonia, 214
- formation from carbonic acid, 17
- in acid-base balance, 214, 217
- in defining alkalinity, 658
- in seawater, 5, 594
- in seawater buffering, 594
- in the ion product of pure water, 592
- in water, 1, 2
- penetration of H^+-selective membranes, 36, 38, 603
- pH and, 9
- physiological regulation, 208, 210, 213, 214, 217, 228, 648, 649, 652–654, 656, 657, 659, 665, 666
- production in muscles, 228
- relative pH and, 658
- toxicity as net H^+, 210

Hydrogen peroxide, 742, 777
Hydrometer readings
- correction term, 30, 31, 33, 601
- definition, 9
- error, 26
- expression, 29
- salinity determinations from, 26
- sample temperature and, 8
- specific gravity and, 1, 9, 30

Hydrometers
- accuracy, 26
- calibration, 26, 30
- definition, 7
- for brines, 52
- history, 591, 592
- procedure for use, 30
- reference temperature and, 29
- standard temperature and, 29
- use, 8

Hydrophone, 681
Hydroxyl ions
- as copper complexing agents, 760, 761
- in specific ion ammonia determination, 634
- in the ion product of pure water, 592
- pH and, 9
- physiological regulation, 213, 214, 656, 659
- relative pH and, 658

Hypercapnia (also see Environmental hypercapnia and Physiological hypercapnia), 217
Hyperglycemia (also see Blood glucose)
- definition, 228
- effect of capture stress, 671
- effect of exercise stress, 456
- effect of handling stress, 228
- effect of transport stress, 671

Hyperopic vision, 233, 234, 314, 702
Hyperosmotic solutions, 205
- as physiological environments, 209

Hyperoxia (see Environmental hyperoxia)
Hyperoxia-hypercapnia
- effect on partial pressure of oxygen, 218, 220

Hyperoxia-normcapnia
- effect on partial pressure of oxygen, 218

Hyperplasia (also see Gill hyperplasia), 453
Hyperventilation
- effect on acid-base balance, 221

Hyphae, 500, 503
Hyphal bodies, 500, 503
Hyphessobrycon innesi (see Neon tetra)
Hypobromous acid
- formation during decapsulation of brine shrimp cysts, 744
- formation in ozonated seawater, 757

Hypochlorite ions
- formation in ozonated seawater, 757

Hypochlorous acid
- formation during decapsulation of brine shrimp cysts, 744

Hypophysis
- control of melanin, 247
- function in HPI axis, 227

Hyposmotic solutions, 205, 209
Hypothalamus
- function in HPI axis, 227
- synthesis of melanin aggregating hormone, 248
- thyroid function and, 517, 789, 791

Hypoxanthine, 248
Hypoxia (also see Environmental hypoxia)
- as a stress factor, 456
- definition, 218

Hypsypops rubicundus (see Garibaldi)

Iceland spar, 14, 597
Ichthyophaga spp., 505
Ichthyophonus disease
- clinical signs and pathological effects, 503, 504, 784, 785
- epizootiology, 500–503, 783, 784
- etiology, 500, 783
- prophylaxis and treatment, 504, 505
- synonyms, 498

Ichthyophonus gasterophilum, 500, 783
Ichthyophonus hoferi, 500, 783
Ichthyophonus spp.
- distribution, 500
- life cycle, 500–503, 783, 784
- taxonomic history, 500, 783

Ichthyophthirius marinus, 779
Ichthyophthirius multifiliis, 492, 494
Ichthyosporidiosis (see Ichthyophonus disease)
Ichthyosporidium spp., 500, 783
Ictalurus melas (see Black bullhead)
Ictalurus punctatus (see Channel catfish)
Igneous rocks, 593
Ilmenite
- cost, 174
- granular media filters, 137
- multimedia filters, 140
- relative grain size, 176, 644
- 60% size, 183
- specific gravity, 175
- support media and, 644

Immersion heaters, 198, 199
Immersion treatment
- administration of disinfectants, 467
- amyloodinium disease, 492, 778
- as baths and dips, 754, 755
- copper, 525
- definition, 459
- DS 677 K, 521
- halquinol, 523
- levamisole hydrochloride, 527
- limitations, 459, 460
- mebendazole, 524
- monogenean infestations, 512
- mycobacteriosis, 478
- niclosamide, 526
- oxolinic acid, 524
- praziquantel, 525, 526
- testing of chemotherapeutic agents, 520
- trichlorfon, 524, 525

Immune response
- definition, 450
- effect of stress, 454
- fin rot, 772
- infections, 451
- lymphocystis disease, 475
- resistance, 447
- vibriosis, 768, 769

Immune suppression
- as a predisposing factor in mycobacteriosis, 764
- as a stress factor, 227
- effect of ammonia, 609
- effect of fasting, 455
- effect of stress, 226
- effect of temperature, 764
- free ammonia and, 637

Immunity
- amyloodinium disease, 489, 775
- cryptocaryoniasis, 495, 781

definition, 447
description, 449–451
diseases and, 451
epizootics and, 457
lymphocystis disease, 475
mycobacteriosis, 764
predisposition to disease and, 454
vibriosis, 480, 484
Immunoglobulins, 450, 753
Impervious carbon, 198
Incandescent lamps (also see Fluorescent lamps, Lamps)
chromaticity, 538
color conversion filters and, 546
daylight simulation, 542
description, 539, 541, 793, 794
in dark-field illuminators, 565
in vitro fish photography, 571
paint selection and, 542, 543
Incandescent light
for seaweed filters, 98
Individual distance
definition, 277
lateral line and, 696
measured distances, 692
models, 692, 693
vision and, 693–696, 701
Individual dominance
definition, 287
dominance hierarchies and, 289
fitness and, 298–303
in group spawning, 295
Industrial-grade salts, 48
Inertial impaction, 142
Infections (also see Clinical, Latent, Local, Secondary, Subclinical, Systemic infections)
amyloodinium disease, 489, 491, 492
definition, 447, 752
effect of UV irradiation, 755, 756
epizootiology and, 457
mycobacteriosis, 477, 478
sensitivity testing and, 459
Infestations
definition, 752
epizootiology and, 457
Inflammation
classification, 452
definition, 452
description, 452, 453
ichthyophonus disease and, 504, 785
mycobacteriosis and, 763
uronema disease, 498
tang tubellarian disease, 508
vibriosis, 481
Inflammatory response (see Inflammation)
Infrared
as electromagnetic waves, 529
effect of particulate organic carbon, 535
incandescent lamps, 539, 794
Initial coloration, 298
Injury
as a stress factor, 227
effect on infections, 451
effect on predisposition to disease, 455, 456
immune response and, 451
mycobacteriosis and, 476
inflammation and, 452
necrosis and, 453
predisposing factor in fin rot, 488
Inland silverside
immunity to amyloodinium disease, 775
shoaling behavior, 697
Inner ear (see Labyrinth)
Inoculation
of unconditioned bacteriological filters, 82
Inorganic ions
assimilation and excretion, 201, 205–209
assimilation by the secondary lamellae, 211
effect on brine shrimp cysts, 396
effect on calcium carbonate precipitation, 18
effect on hagfish blood osmolality, 647
effect on optical properties of water, 535
equivalents in seawater, 592
excretion by secondary lamellae, 211
incorporation into cells, 620
ingestion with food, 205
in protoplasm, 359
ion pairing, 592
leaching from concrete, 170
rate of dissolution and precipitation, 590
saturation and, 594
transepithelial potential and, 269
Inorganic nitrogen
conversion, 64, 67
diffusion, 94
excretion by animals, 82
precursors, 62
removal by seaweed filters, 78
Insecticides, 106
Instant Ocean® Synthetic Sea Salts, 604
Instar stage, 513
Interception, 141
Interface, 100, 104
Interferon, 449
Interrenal tissues
function in HPI axis, 227
location, 664
Intestinal mucosa, 447, 455
Intestine
absence of *Mycobacterium* tubercles, 478
amyloodinium disease, 489
effect of vibriosis, 480
ichthyophonus disease, 500, 502
intestinal mucosa and, 447
swimbladder and, 265
Intrinsic resources, 351
Invertebrates
as foods, 358, 374, 375
as refuge hosts, 306
as *Vibrio* commensals, 479
bioelectric potentials, 688
carotenoids in, 370
copper toxicity to, 758, 759
coral boring by, 293
digestibility of, 371
effect of ozone- and chlorine-producted oxidants, 757
on coral reefs, 323
removal by garibaldis, 709, 710
In vitro fish photography
cameras, 544
definition, 544
filters and films, 544–547, 570
procedure, 570–572
Iodate
thyroid function and, 517
Iodide
effect of nitrate thyroid assimilation, 518
in defining salinity, 590, 601
thyroid function and, 517, 789, 790
Iodine
effect on metamorphosis of *Amphiprion ocellaris*, 604
in sediments, 517
loss from aquarium seawater, 790
seawater concentration, 517, 604
thyroid function and, 517
Iodine number, 362, 629
Ion depletion
in closed and open systems, 20, 21
Ion flux models
freshwater teleosts, 207, 208, 210, 648, 649, 652, 653, 657
seawater elasmobranchs, 205, 209, 210, 651, 656, 657
seawater teleosts, 208–210, 649–652, 654–657
Ionic loading
definition, 205
seawater teleosts, 205, 206, 209
Ionic regulation
definition, 203
disruption by amyloodinium disease, 491
introduction, 201
Ionic strength
artificial seawaters, 46
effect on ammonium ion dissociation, 117
effect on formation of toxic oxidants, 757
effect on vibriosis, 771
NBS buffers, 602
pH determination and, 36, 602, 603
seawater, 153, 602
Ion pairing, 5, 592, 757
Ions
as electrolytes, 7
definition, 1
effect on fish growth, 47
effect on fish metamorphosis, 47
flux from carbonate minerals, 17
in seawater, 6
volatile, 6
Ipronidazole, 777
Iridophores, 247
Iridosomes, 247, 249, 250
Iridoviruses, 474
Iron
assimilation by phytoplankton, 423, 748
complexing, 423
in culture solutions, 748
in hemoglobins, 222
loss to culture vessels, 423
seawater chemistry, 747–749
uptake and assimilation by phytoplankton, 748, 749

Irritants
- as stress factors, 454
- disinfectants, 468
- hyperplasia and, 453
- inflammation and, 452
- necrosis and, 453
- predisposing factors in fin rot, 772, 486

ISCC-NBS color system, 543, 563, 564, 794
Isochrysis galbana
- as rotifer food, 741

Isopods, 512
Isopotential point, 39
Isosmotic solutions
- definition, 205, 647
- elasmobranch body fluids, 206

Isotonic solutions, 647
Isothermal point, 39, 40
Ivermectin, 777

Jack mackerel
- as schooling prey, 705
- response time in schools, 692

Jacks
- cooperative hunting, 284

Jackson candle turbidimeter, 638
Jackson turbidity units, JTUs, 639
Japanese eel
- chain elongation of fatty acids, 731
- essential amino acid requirements, 361
- treatment for *Aeromonas* infections, 520, 521
- treatment for vibriosis, 522

Jawfishes
- substratum for exhibition, 310, 317

Jenkinsia lamprotaenia (see Dwarf herring)
Jenkinsia sp., 691
Jenkinsia stolifera (see Shortband herring)
Juvenile coloration, 299

Kawakawa
- effect of lateral line in schooling, 695

Kelps
- as sources of alginic acid, 734

Ketoconazole
- treatment of ichthyophonus disease, 504

Kidney
- amyloodinium disease, 489
- chromaffin tissues, 664
- copper deposition, 759
- copper displacement of zinc, 759
- effect of ammonia, 609
- effect of fin rot, 488
- energy release, 373
- exophiala disease, 505
- ichthyophonus disease, 503
- interrenal tissues, 227, 664
- in thyroid function, 517
- monogenean infestations, 787
- mycobacteriosis, 476
- *Mycobacterium* tubercles, 478
- uronema disease, 497, 498
- vibriosis, 770

Kilocalorie, 372
Kjeldahl method, 730
Koch's postulates, 767
Koopman theory of search, 701
Krill, 734
k selection, 726

Labeo capensis (see Mudfish)
Labile
- complexes as, 747
- copper complexes, 761
- definition, 58
- dissolved organic carbon, 100

Labroides dimidiatus
- occupation of pair territories, 289
- protogyny, 303

Labroides phthirophagus
- as a cleaner, 719

Labrus bergylta, 661
Labyrinth
- as an acoustic organ, 256, 266
- description, 263–265
- displacement sensitivity, 266, 267
- far-field effects and, 269
- near-field detection, 687
- ordinary lateral line organs and, 261
- sharks, 685

Lactate ions
- effect on acid-base balance, 226, 228, 230, 665, 666

Lactate metabolism
- effect of stress, 226

Lactic acid
- effect on acid-base balance, 228, 665, 666
- effect on delayed post-exercise mortality, 228

Lactobacillus spp., 619
Lactose, 365
Lagena, 264
Lagodon rhomboides, 650
Lake trout
- effect of confinement stress, 667, 668
- exophiala disease, 785

Lamellar recruitment
- definition, 212
- effect of adrenaline, 230
- effect of blood pressure, 221

Laminar layer, 153, 154, 641, 642
Laminaria spp., 610
Lamps (also see Fluorescent lamps, Incandescent lamps)
- color temperatures, 538, 541, 542, 568, 571
- spectral distribution, 98, 538, 539

Larger spotted dogfish
- acid-base regulation, 214, 217, 218
- effect of environmental hypercapnia, 659, 660
- effect of exercise stress, 665, 666
- effect of oxygen on acid-base balance, 661
- effect of temperature on blood pH, 659

Latent infections, 451
Lateral line (also see Ordinary lateral line organs)
- as a sound receptor, 256, 282, 283
- as a tactile receptor, 263, 682, 683
- damage by argulids, 514
- damage by gas-bubble trauma, 515
- effect of copper, 759
- electroreception, 269, 270
- embryology and structure, 682
- function in schooling, 277, 695, 696
- mechanoreception, 261–263

Latex molding rubber, 574, 576, 580
Latex molds, 574, 576, 578–580
Laurencia carabica, 622
Law of refraction (see Snell's law)
Leafy green vegetables
- as natural foods, 358
- proximate composition, 374, 375

Leatherjackets
- sound production, 267

Lekking
- definition, 290, 708
- occupation of territories and, 289
- parrotfishes, 295
- wrasses, 295

Lemon shark
- sound detection, 685
- stress-induced vibriosis, 482, 483
- treatment for monogeneans, 525
- vibriosis, 767, 770

Lens
- of fish eyes, 233, 234

Leopold filter bottom, 177, 178, 644
Lepidosirenidae, 688
Lepomis auritus (see Redbreast sunfish)
Leptocottus armatus (see Pacific staghorn sculpin)
Leptotricha spp., 619
Lernaeopodoida, 512
Lesions
- antigen entry through, 450
- argulid infestations, 514
- as stress factors, 454, 455
- capture and, 456
- classification, 452
- definition, 447
- disease transmission through, 457
- entry of fin rot bacteria, 486, 488, 773, 774
- entry of lymphocystis virus, 474
- entry of *Mycobacterium*, 476, 477
- entry of *Vibrio*, 480, 482, 767, 768, 771
- excision of lymphocystis, 475
- exophiala disease, 505
- from tags, 762, 767
- gas-bubble trauma, 515
- humans from *Mycobacterium marinum* infections, 478, 479
- ichthyophonus disease, 503, 504
- inflammation and, 453
- surface, 459
- tang turbellarian disease, 508
- thyroid, 519
- uronema disease, 497

Lethrinidae (see Emperors)
Lettuce coral, 332
Leucophores, 247
Leucosomes, 247
Leukocytes
- lysozyme in, 449
- polymorphonuclear, 451, 456

Leukocytosis
vibriosis, 480
Leukopenia
vibriosis, 480
Levamisole hydrochloride
treatment of monogenean infestations, 512, 526, 527
Lift, 159
Lift pipes (see Education pipes)
Ligands
copper complexes, 750
definition, 747
effect of pH, 747
effect of temperature, 747
effect on copper chemistry, 759, 760
effect on copper toxicity, 750
iron complexes, 748, 749
Light (also see Infrared, Ultraviolet light, Visible spectrum)
absorption, 529, 531–533, 535, 545, 638, 639, 793
attenuation, 529, 533, 535, 640, 675, 676, 793
color, 530, 537, 570
definition, 529
effect in stage plays, 555
effect of mixing, 794, 795
effect on ascorbic acid loss from feeds, 735
effect on brine shrimp cysts, 394, 396
effect on chemotherapeutic agents, 520
effect on complexing agents, 748, 749
effect on dome patch reef formation, 332
effect on DS 677 K, 521
effect on hatching of argulid eggs, 514
electronic strobes, 551
emission from lamps, 794
fish pigments and, 246, 247, 250
focusing in exhibits, 556, 564, 565
gathered on the retina, 233, 234
incident, 530, 532, 562, 675, 677
in exhibit design, 528
monochromatic, 239–241, 675, 676, 792
orientation by schooling fishes, 314, 315, 720
penetration in water, 532–536
rearing brine shrimp nauplii and, 415
reflected from exhibits, 558, 586
reflection, 529, 531, 532, 675, 677–679
refraction, 233, 234, 529, 530, 532, 560–562, 793
scattering, 532, 534, 535, 638, 639, 793
species label photography and, 568
transmission, 530–532, 545, 566, 638–640, 677
wavelengths in underwater vision, 237, 238, 243–246
waves, 529
white, 530, 538, 540, 544, 677, 795
Light intensity
effect of attenuation, 529
effect on brine shrimp cysts, 742
effect on phytoplankton growth, 418, 420, 438
effect on schooling, 692–695
exhibits and, 537, 541, 542
in vitro fish photography and, 570
paint selection and, 542
photon flux density and, 674, 675
phytoplankton culture requirements, 97, 434
seaweed filters, 97, 98
stage plays, 555
undersea photography, 549, 550
Lightness (see Brightness, Value)
Limanda limanda (see Dab)
Limestone, 627
Lined seahorse
ammonia excretion, 650
Lined sole
ammonia excretion, 650
Linolenic acid, 363, 730, 732
Lipids
adsorption onto calcium carbonate, 596
ammonia solubility, 650
as antigens, 450
as energy *vs.* proteins, 385, 387
as nutrients, 366
assimilation, 730
carbohydrates and, 365, 366
deposition, 733
description, 361–365
determination, 374
effect of carbohydrates, 732
effect of stress, 226
effect on feeding, 388
effect on protein use, 388
energy from, 365, 366
energy storage as, 372
fish meal and, 384
in biological membranes, 363
in brine shrimp, 739
in fish and invertebrate flesh, 375
in leafy green vegetables, 375
in protoplasm, 359
melting points, 364
preferential use to carbohydrates, 731, 732
recommended percentage in feeds, 388
reduction to fatty acids, 371
requirements for, 357, 363–365, 388
solvents, 361, 732
Liquid phase, 594
Little skate
ammonia excretion, 651
Live foods (also see Foods)
brine shrimp as, 358
effect on growth and survival, 391, 736
effect on rotifers, 399
effect on vitamin deficiencies, 388
growing, 357
importance, 392
proteolytic enzymes in, 391, 392, 736
rotifers as, 358
superiority, 391
Liver
amyloodinium disease, 489
copper deposition, 759
effect of fin rot, 488
energy storage in, 372
exophiala disease, 505
fatty acid deposition, 732
glycogen deposition, 731
goiter disease, 518
ichthyophonus disease, 503
in thyroid function, 517
Mycobacterium tubercles, 478
pigment deposition, 368
vibriosis, 770
Local infections
fin rot, 488
Loligo vulgaris, 700
Longhorn sculpin
ammonia excretion, 651
Longspine sea urchin, 293
Lugol's iodine
for counting phytoplankton cells, 443
treatment of amyloodinium disease, 777
Lumen, 656
Lungfishes
electroreceptors, 688
thyroids, 517
Lungs
of mammals, 222
Lutein
occurrence in fishes, 370, 371
Lutjanidae (see Snappers)
Lutjanus buccanella (see Blackfin snapper)
Lutjanus mahogoni (see Mahogany snapper)
Lymphocystis (see Lymphocystis disease)
Lymphocystis disease
clinical signs and pathological effects, 475, 762
epizootiology, 474, 475, 762
etiology, 474, 761, 762
immunity, 475
prophylaxis and treatment, 475
synonyms, 474
Lymphocytes, 450, 451
Lyophilized foods (see Foods, freeze-dried)
Lysins, 449
Lysis
ammonia formation and, 62
definition, 57, 63
erythrocytes in gas-bubble trauma, 516
in biological films, 68
of animal cells, 57
of bacteria, 57, 61, 64, 449
of plant cells, 57
T cells and, 450
Lysozyme, 449, 753
Lythrulon flaviguttatum (see Cortez grunt)
Lythrypnus spp.
resistance to cryptocaryoniasis, 779
Lytic substances, 490

Mackerels
as schooling predators, 699
Macroalgae (see Seaweeds)
Macrobrachium rosenbergii, 636
Macrophages, 449, 451
Macula, 264, 685
Magnesite, 14
Magnesium carbonate
dissolution of carbonate minerals and, 600
in dolomite, 14
in magnesian calcite, 593, 594, 597
precipitation, 23

Magnesium ions
  adsorption into magnesian calcite overgrowths, 597–600
  calcium ion ratio in seawater, 596, 597
  coprecipitation with calcium, 20, 21, 605
  coprecipitation with phosphorus, 605
  effect on calcium carbonate precipitation, 596
  effect on copper complexing, 760, 761
  effect on precipitation of carbonate minerals, 18, 22
  effect on solubility of carbonate minerals, 22, 597
  excretion in urine, 205
  in calcites, 14, 20
  in magnesite, 14
  in magnesian calcites, 18–20
  in seawater, 18, 19
  ion pairing, 6, 592, 606
  loss from carbonate minerals, 17, 44
  precipitation from autoclaved seawater, 746, 747
  struvite formation and, 606
Magnesian calcites
  alkalinity and, 23
  biogenic, 594
  composition, 593, 594
  definition, 4, 18
  on new carbonate filtrants, 45
  overgrowths, 18, 20, 21, 24, 597, 599, 600
  precipitation, 20, 21, 45
  solubility, 21–24, 597, 598
Magnesite, 598
Mahogany snapper
  effect on recruitment, 722
  Major ions (elements)
complexing, 747
definition, 2, 3
in artificial seawaters, 46, 601
in culture solutions, 421, 422
in GP2 solutions, 47, 48, 422
in seawater, 5, 6
ratios, 6, 422
salinity and, 6
Maintenance solutions (also see Artificial seawaters)
  culture solutions and, 421
  definition, 46
  description, 46–48
  early formulas, 604
Malacanthidae (see Tilefishes)
Malacanthus plumieri (see Sand tilefish)
Malachite green
  effect on *Amyloodinium ocellatum* development, 777
  toxicity to nitrifying bacteria, 616
  treatment of amyloodinium disease, 777, 778
Malate
  as a carbon source in denitrification, 75, 619
Malathion
  treatment of crustacean infestations, 514
Malnutrition
  effect on infections, 451
  predisposing factor in monogenean infestations, 511
Mammals
  lactate dissociation, 666
  lungs, 222
Manganese sulfate
  primary stock solution, 426, 429
Marcet's principle (see Rule of constant proportions)
Mating systems
  effect on fitness, 301
  monogamous, 301, 302
  parrotfishes, 295
  polygamous, 290
  wrasses, 295
Matrices (see Biological films)
Matter, 1, 528, 529
Mebendazole
  treatment of monogenean infestations, 512, 524, 425
Mechanoreception, 261–263
Meiosis, 397
Melanin, 247, 248, 680, 681
Melanin aggregating hormone (MAH) 248, 680
Melanin dispersing hormone (MDH) 247, 680
Melanogrammus aeglefinus (see Haddock)
Melanophore release inhibiting hormone (MRH), 680
Melanophores, 247, 681
Melanophore stimulating hormone (MSH), 680
Melanosomes, 247
Melatonin, 247, 248
Membranes
  active transport and, 205
  ammonia movement, 650
  Amyloodinium ocellatum trophonts, 492
  branchial cavity, 489
  Cryptocaryon irritans trophonts, 494
  cuticular, 411, 413
  effect of copper, 758
  effect of lipids, 362, 363
  effect of ozone, 466
  effect of UV radiation, 462
  mesenteries, 477, 478
  necrosis, 453
  peristomial, 587
  pH electrodes, 603
  plasmalemma, 620
  semipermeable, 203, 204, 654
  specific ion electrodes, 115, 634
Menidia beryllina (see Inland silverside)
Menidia menidia (see Atlantic silverside)
Menidia sp.
  light threshold for schooling, 693
Merbromin
  efficacy as a formulated product, 755
Merluccius tenuis (see Silver hake)
Mesenteries
  amyloodinium disease, 775
  definition, 477
  effect of mycobacteriosis, 477
  gas-bubble trauma, 516
  liver, 489
Metabolic acidosis
  definition, 228
  effect of ammonia perfusion, 650
Metabolism
  algae, 55
  amino acid requirements for, 361
  animals, 53
  bacteria, 53, 82, 99
  biological films, 68
  carbon dioxide production, 210
  carbohydrate, 365, 366
  carotenoid, 370
  definition, 372
  effect on ammonia toxicity, 636
  fatty acid, 730
  in muscles, 227
  lactate, 226
  lipid, 226
  lipid requirements for, 362
  nitrogen, 230
  of foods, 58
  plants, 53
  protein, 62, 385, 387
  thyroid function and, 517
Metabolizable energy, 373
Metamorphosis
  Amphiprion ocellaris, 604
  effect of ions, 47
Metanauplius, 514
Methanol
  in activated carbon manufacture, 101
  toxicity, 95
  use in denitrification, 75, 77, 95
Methemoglobin
  effect of nitrite toxicity, 609
Methylene blue
  as a dye, 763
  efficacy as a formulated product, 756
  toxicity to nitrifying bacteria, 72
  treatment of amyloodinium disease, 777
Methylene blue number, 629
Methyl ethyl ketone
  polyster resin hardener, 578, 580
Metronidazole, 777
Mexican cavefish
  light threshold for schooling, 693
Microcide®, 778
Micrococcus spp., 619
Microfiltration
  of maintenance solutions, 48
  of stored seawater samples, 633, 634
Microorganisms
  antibacterial compounds, from, 377
  B cells and, 451
  definition, 447
  disinfectants and, 472
  effect of antibiotics, 458
  effect of ozone, 466
  effect of UV radiation, 463, 465
  invasion of hosts, 448
  Koch's postulates and, 767
  natural resistance and, 449
  necrosis and, 453
  on granular activated carbon, 104, 630
  organic phosphorus and, 56
  removal by point contact sterilization, 756
  resistance to chemotherapeutic agents, 460
  resistance transfer factors, 754
  sensitivity tests and, 458, 459

Microspathodon dorsalis (see Giant blue damselfish)
Microspathodon chrysurus (see Yellowtail damselfish)
Mictic egg, 397
Milkfish
  nitrite toxicity, 610
  rotifers as live food, 741
Millimole, 647
Milling
  absence of dominance, 285
  by captive fishes, 720
  definition, 276, 690
  effect of amyloodinium disease, 491
  effect of seasonal changes, 697
  in captivity, 314
  individual distance and, 277
  mills as assemblages, 275, 285
  schooling and, 691
  shoaling and, 691
  swimming precision and, 276
Millipora alcicornis, 332
Millipora spp. (see Fire corals)
Mineralization
  ammonia production, 606
  by heterotrophic bacteria, 611
  definition, 55
  detritus and, 57
  dissolved organic carbon, 57, 58, 68, 78
  dissolved organic phosphorus, 57
  effect of substratum adsorption, 612
  factors affecting, 67–69
  in bacteriological filtration, 64
  in filter beds, 55
  in defining conditioning, 623
  in stored seawater samples, 633
  introduction, 54
  in unconditioned bacteriological filters, 83
  labile compounds, 58
  nitrogenous compounds, 62, 64, 67
  on exhausted granular activated carbon, 630
  oxygen requirements, 55
  particulate organic carbon, 57
  "pseudohumus," 62
  refractory compounds, 59
  seaweed filters and, 78
Minimum inhibitory concentration, MIC
  definition, 458
  formulated antibacterial agents, 755
Minimum lethal concentration, MLC
  definition, 458
  testing of chemotherapeutic agents, 520
Minor ions (elements)
  assimilation by fishes, 47
  complexing, 422, 747, 760, 761
  definition, 2
  in artificial seawaters, 46
  in culture solutions, 421, 422
  rule of constant proportions and, 6
Misaki Aquarium, 624
Mixed media filters (see Multimedia filters)
Mixing containers
  for artificial seawaters, 48, 49
Mogula sp., 689
Moist feeds (also see Dry feeds, Feeds)
  administration of chemotherapeutic agents in, 459
  alginate-bound, 358
  considerations, 383
  gelatin-bound, 358
  in defining feeds, 258
  leaching of free amino acids, 735
  manufacture, 357, 383
  nutrient leaching, 390
  pelleted, 358, 383
  procedures, 399, 400, 403, 406, 741
  proteins in, 385
  stability, 390
  storage and handling, 391
  texture, 383
  vitamin addition, 388
  water content, 377
Molar concentration, 589
Molarity, 589
Molasses
  use in denitrification, 75
Molasses number, 629
Mole, 589, 592
Molecules
  as antigens, 449, 450
  definition, 1
  dyes, 763
  effect on osmotic pressure, 204
  fatty acid, 362
  free ammonia, 214
  gas, 153, 529, 532, 534, 535, 793
  gel permeability to, 390
  hemoglobin, 222
  humic acid, 760
  magnesian calcite, 22
  nonpolar, 629
  osmotic pressure, 647
  oxygen, 213, 756
  ozone, 466, 468
  particles and, 257
  random motion, 203
  semipermeable membranes and, 203, 204
  surfactant, 164, 192
  visual pigment, 675
  water, 7, 534, 671, 793
  waves and, 534
Molybdenum
  requirements for seaweeds, 424
Monacanthus tuckeri (see Slender filefish)
Monandric, 300
Monarchial systems, 287
Monochloramine
  formation during decapsulation of brine shrimp cysts, 744
Monochromatic, 239–241
Monogeneans
  as fish parasites, 509
  as vectors in vibriosis, 767, 770
  chemotherapeutic agents and, 520
  life cycles, 509–512
Monogenetic trematode infestations
  clinical signs and pathological effects, 511
  epizootiology, 509–511, 786
  etiology, 509
  prophylaxis and treatment, 512, 524–527, 786, 787
  synonyms, 509
Monogenetic trematodes (see Monogeneans)
Monosaccharides
  from carbohydrates, 371
  glucose as, 365
Monstrilloida, 512
Montastrea annularis, 332
Montastrea spp. (see Star corals)
Moonlight, 242, 244–246, 680
Moray eels
  protandry, 712
  resistance to cryptocaryoniasis, 779
Mormyridae (see Elephantfishes)
Mouth
  bioelectric fields, 269
  gas-bubble trauma, 516
  monogenean infestations, 509
  vibriosis, 480
Moving water exhibits, 582–586, 796
Mucopolysaccharides
  production by garden eels, 316
Mucosal cell surface (see Epithelium, apical cell surface)
Mucous cells
  amyloodinium disease, 491
  dermis, 447
  effect of fin rot, 488
  gills, 447
  intestinal mucosa, 447
Mucous "cocoons," 246
Mucus (of fishes)
  as a physical barrier, 447, 448
  discoloration from amyloodinium disease, 491
  excessive production during halquinol treatment, 523
  excessive production from cryptocaryoniasis, 495
  gas-bubble trauma, 515
  lysozyme in, 449
  monogenean hatching factor in, 786
  natural resistance factors, 447, 448
  of the secondary lamellae, 213
  protection against sea anemones, 306, 717, 718
  protection from *Amyloodinium ocellatum*, 492
  removal by cleaners, 309, 310
  secretion, 447
Mudfish
  effect of ammonia, 673
  effect of capture stress, 671
  effect of environmental hypoxia, 673
  effect of transport stress, 671
Mugil capito
  effect of epinephrine on drinking rate, 672
Mugil cephalus (see Striped mullet)
Mugil labrosus, 661
Mullidae (see Goatfishes)
Mulloidichthys martinicus (see Yellow goatfish)

Multimedia filters
 decision to use, 174, 643, 644
 definition, 140
 support media, 644
Multiple drug resistance, 754
Mummichog
 cryptocaryoniasis, 781
 effect of ammonia, 674
 fin rot, 774
 hemoglobin oxygen affinity, 662
 individual distance, 692
Munsell color scales, 543
Muscles
 copper deposition, 759
 effect of mycobacteriosis, 477, 478
 effect of uronema disease, 497, 498
 effect of vibriosis, 480
 energy storage in, 372
 goiter disease, 518
 hydrogen ion production, 228
 ichthyophonus disease, 502
 in acid-base balance, 217
 in thyroid function, 517
 metabolism, 227, 228
 pharynx, 489
 pigment deposition in, 368
 production of organic acids, 227, 228
 sound production by, 267, 268
Mussa spp., 332
Mussels, 147
Mustelis canis (see Smooth dogfish)
Mutualism
 anemonefishes and sea anemones, 304, 713
 cleaning behavior, 310, 719
 definition, 304
Mycobacteriosis
 clinical signs and pathological effects, 477, 478, 765
 compared with exophiala disease, 505
 efficacy of disinfectants, 765
 epizootiology, 476, 477, 764
 etiology, 476, 763, 764
 history, 763
 inflammation and, 763
 prophylaxis and treatment, 478, 765
 synonyms, 476
 tubercles, 477
 zoonosis, 478, 479, 754
Mycobacterium chelonae, 763, 764
Mycobacterium chelonae abscessus, 763, 764
Mycobacterium chelonae chelonae, 763
Mycobacterium chelonae piscarius, 763, 764
Mycobacterium fortuitum, 763, 764
Mycobacterium marinum, 478, 764
Mycobacterum salmoniphilum, 764
Mycobacterium spp., 476, 477, 763
Mycropharynx spp., 505
Myocardium
 exophiala disease, 505
Myoxocephalus octodecemspinosus (see Longhorn sculpin)
Mysids, 734
Mystic Marinelife Aquarium, 519, 624, 785
Mytilus edulis (see Blue mussel)

Nanophyetus salmincola
 praziquantel treatment, 787
Nasal passages
 amyloodinium disease, 489
National Aquarium in Baltimore, 519
National Museum of Natural History, 621
Natural immunity (see Natural resistance)
Natural resistance
 amyloodinium disease and, 491
 definition, 447, 753
 description, 448, 449
 immunoglobulins and, 753
 infections and, 451
 lymphocystis disease and, 475
 predisposition to disease and, 454
Natural selection, 706
Nauplius
 argulids, 514
 definition, 392
 parasitic copepods, 513
NBS buffers, 602
Near-field effects
 definition, 258
 detection, 258, 261–264, 683, 684, 687
 effect on schooling, 277
 far-field effects and, 265, 266, 268, 269
 in aquariums, 682
 labyrinth stimulation and, 265–267
 models, 258–260
 schooling and, 695, 696
Necrosis
 amyloodinium disease, 491
 definition, 453
 fin rot, 487, 488
 ichthyophonus disease, 504
 uronema disease, 497
Negaprion brevirostris (see Lemon shark)
Negative feedback, 517, 789
Nematocysts, 713
Németh correlation, 188–190, 192
Neomycin sulfate
 efficacy as a formulated product, 755
Neon tetra
 mycobacteriosis, 477
Neoplasms, 453, 753
Neoprene coatings, 195
Nephelometric turbidity units, NTUs, 639
Nephelometry, 639
Nernst equation
 electrochemical gradients, 654
 in pH determination, 38, 39, 603
 specific ion electrodes and, 634
Nerves, 447
Net energy, 373
Neural canal
 uronema disease, 497
Neuroendocrine responses (also see Primary stress response, Secondary stress responses, Stress response)
 effect of stress factors, 225–227
Neurohypophysis
 storage of melanin aggregating hormone, 248
Neutral carrier, 207 (Fig. 4-7), 208
New England Aquarium, 584, 785
New York Aquarium, 497, 691, 779, 789
Niche
 definition, 319, 721
 ecotope and, 321
 guilds and, 322
 rarefaction and, 726
Niclosamide
 treatment of monogenean infestations, 512, 526
Nifurpirinol
 efficacy as a formulated product, 755
 toxicity to nitrifying bacteria, 616
 treatment of amyloodinium disease, 777
Nitrate ions
 as electron acceptors, 74, 77
 as goitrogens, 518, 790
 as nitrogen sources for phytoplankton, 751
 assimilation by plants, 12
 control by seaweed filters, 99, 621, 622
 diel fluctuation, 95
 effect of uptake and assimilation on alkalinity, 12, 424, 429, 751
 effect of uptake and assimilation on pH, 423, 429, 751
 formation, 64, 67, 71, 610
 in GP2 low-salinity culture solution, 428, 751
 optical density and, 637
 organic precursors, 62
 recommended upper limit for fishes, 610
 reduction, 67, 95, 96
 reduction by denitrification, 75
 removal by assimilation, 74, 75, 77
 removal by seaweed filters, 78
 removal from wastewaters, 75
 toxicity, 62
 toxicity to fishes, 78, 610
 uptake and assimilation by seaweeds, 620, 621
Nitrate nitrogen
 determination of high concentrations, 133–135
 determination of low concentrations, 128–132
Nitrate respiration (see Dissimilation)
Nitric oxide, 74, 75
Nitrification
 ammonia control by, 78
 anaerobic conditions and, 616
 as a measure of conditioning, 79
 by autotrophic bacteria, 64
 chemical attraction and, 68
 definition, 64
 dissimilation and, 77
 effect of aeration, 616
 effect of filter bed depth, 612
 effect of surface area, 67, 612, 613, 626, 627
 effect on alkalinity, 13
 effect on pH, 71
 factors affecting, 67–74, 81
 in bacteriological filtration, 64

incomplete, 71
in defining conditioning, 622
inhibition by toxicity, 69–72, 95, 614–616
inhibition of growth *vs.* activity, 614, 615
introduction, 54
in unconditioned bacteriological filters, 80, 81
in wastewater treatment, 75
lag phases, 623–625
nitrate accumulation, 67
oxygen requirements, 55, 616, 617
pH requirements, 74, 618
reaction products, 64, 95
temperature requirements, 78, 617, 618
Nitrifiers (see Nitrifying bacteria)
Nitrifying bacteria
acclimation, 80
addition to seawater, 81
amino acid assimilation, 612
amino acid synthesis, 612
as facultative autotrophs, 64, 611, 612
assimilation of organic compounds, 611, 612
attachment, 53
factors affecting, 67–74
freeze-dried, 82, 624
from activated sludge, 70
from soils, 70
inhibition of activity and growth, 70, 71, 614, 615
inoculation of unconditioned bacteriological filters, 82
in unconditioned bacteriological filters, 79, 80
laboratory culture, 81
nitrogen conversion, 67
on conditioned gravel, 83
oxygen requirements, 72, 616, 617
pH requirements, 72, 74, 618
population growth in filter beds, 79–81, 623, 624
salinity requirements, 74, 618
sources of inoculants, 82, 624, 625
surface area requirements, 67–69, 612, 613
taxonomy, 64, 611
temperature requirements, 72, 617, 618
toxicity to, 69–72, 614, 615
Nitrite ions
as nitrogen sources for phytoplankton, 751
concentrations in seawater aquarium exhibits, 610
control by seaweed filters, 621, 622
effect of inorganic ions on toxicity, 609, 610
effect of uptake and assimilation on alkalinity and pH, 751
formation from organic nitrogen by heterotrophic bacteria, 611
from dissimilation, 74, 95
from nitrification, 64, 67
interference with ammonia determination, 111, 632, 633
organic precursors, 62
oxidation, 70–72, 80, 83, 612
"peaking" in unconditioned bacteriological filters, 80–83
persistence, 71
production by heterotrophic bacteria, 610
reduction, 67, 75
toxicity, 62
toxicity to nitrifying bacteria, 71, 615
toxicity to fishes, 609, 610
Nitrite nitrogen
determination, 122–128
nitrate nitrogen determination and, 128, 132, 133
Nitrite oxidizers (see Nitrifying bacteria)
Nitrobacter winogradski, 64, 611, 612
Nitrofurazone, 777
Nitrogen
ammonia formation, 230
as protein, 360
assimilation by algae, 55
atmospheric, 210
chitinous, 384, 385, 733
conversion, 54, 55
conversion rate in bacteriological filters, 83
cycling in aquariums, 66, 67
cycling in the oceans, 611
determination in proteins, 730
dietary balance, 388
dietary excess, 385
diffusivity, 154
entry into aquariums, 64–67
excretion as ammonia, 210
excretion rate by animals, 84
equilibration in rising air bubbles, 642, 643
fin rot and, 488
in calculating carrying capacity, 84
in chitin, 384, 385
in embolisms, 515
in eutrophication, 53
in GP2 low-salinity culture solution, 428, 751, 752
in protoplasm, 358
in seawater, 5, 6
partial pressure, 75, 151, 154
percentage in air, 149
percentage of protein, 83
production, 54
removal, 54, 96
solubility, 154
supersaturation in seawater, 515
Nitrogen fixation, 66
Nitrogenous organic compounds
heterotrophic conversion to nitrite, 611
labile, 62
released by algae, 62
released by bacteria, 62, 63
reduction, 55
Nitrosococcus oceanus, 64, 616, 617
Nitrosococcus mobilis, 64
Nitrosomonas europaea, 64, 611, 612, 615, 617
Nitrospina gracilis, 64
Nitrous oxide, 75, 620
Nocardia spp., 763
Nonelectrolytes, 7, 647
Nonessential amino acids (also see Amino acids, Free amino acids, Essential amino acids), 361
Nonspecific immunity (see Natural resistance)
Noradrenaline (also see Catecholamines)
effect of handling stress, 670
primary stress response and, 225
Normality, 603
Normal response, 224
Normcapnia
definition, 218
effect on acid-base balance, 661
Normoxia
assimilation of oxygen and, 219, 220, 222
definition, 218
Normoxia-hypercapnia
effect on partial pressure of oxygen, 219, 220
Normoxia-normcapnia
effect on acid-base balance, 221
effect on partial pressure of oxygen, 219, 220
Northern pike
as a schooling predator, 700
effect of handling stress, 670
Notodelphyoida, 512
Notropis hudsonius (see Spottail shiner)
Nuclei, 500
Nucleic acids, 450, 763
Nurse shark
goiter disease, 791
Nutrient elements
conversion, 94
definition, 6
in biological films, 68, 69
loss from stored seawater samples, 633
metabolism, 82
production, 53
toxicity, 64
Nutrients
classification, 358–366
definition, 358
loss from freezing and freeze-drying, 736
sources for algae, 421
sources for fishes, 358, 421
vitamins as, 366
Nutrition
definition, 358
effect on rotifers, 399
importance of physiology and, 201
Nystatin
treatment of ichthyophonus disease, 504

Occlusion, 606
Ocean skater
dilution effect on predation, 700
Ocean water (see Seawater)
Ocular opacity
vibriosis, 480, 766
Offset adjustment (see Standardization)
Oils
addition to moist feeds, 403, 406
as lipids, 362
fish, 362, 388
vegetable, 362
Oleic acid, 732
Olfaction
function in schooling, 695, 696
Olfactory stimuli
effect on schooling, 277

Onchomiracidia, 509
Oncorhynchus kisutch (see Coho salmon)
Oncorhynchus mykiss (see Rainbow trout)
Oncorhynchus nerka (see Sockeye salmon)
Oncorhynchus tshawytscha (see Chinook salmon)
Oodinium cyprinodontum, 774
Oodiniasis (see Amyloodinium disease)
Oodinium disease (see Amyloodinium disease)
Open systems
 carbonate minerals, 22
 comparison with plug flow systems, 463
 definition, 20
Opercula
 definition, 202
 gas-bubble trauma, 516
 goiter disease, 518
Opercular cavity, 202, 221, 646
Opisthaptor, 510
Opistognathidae (see Jawfishes)
Opistognathus aurifrons (see Yellowhead jawfish)
Opsanus beta (see Gulf toadfish)
Opsanus tau (see Oyster toadfish)
Opsonins, 449
Optical density, 637, 677
Optics
 in exhibit design, 528, 559–563
Optimal visual distance, 702
Oral cavity
 description, 202
 gas-bubble trauma, 515
 per os administration of iodine, 519
Oral valve, 202
Ordinary lateral line organs (also see Lateral line)
 definition, 261
 early descriptions, 682, 683
 evolution, 263
 mechanoreception, 262, 266, 267
 response to near-field displacements, 683, 687
 sharks, 685
Ordinate, 25
Oreochromis mossambica
 effect of stresses on body mass, 671
 nitrate toxicity, 610
Oreochromis spp., 610
Organic acids
 in seawater, 607
 leaked by seaweeds, 97
 production by muscles, 227, 228
 toxicity, 228
Organic carbon, 58, 83
Organic compounds
 carbohydrates, 365
 in protoplasm, 359
 vitamins, 366
Organic matter
 as ligands for complexing copper, 759–761
 decomposition, 6
 effect of ozone on, 100
 labile, 58
 orthophosphate binding, 58
 production, 53
 reaction with chlorine-based oxidants, 744
 refractory, 58, 59
 struvite formation and, 606
Organic molecules
 adsorption by activated carbon, 103, 104
 dissolution of cabonate minerals, 22
 effect on osmotic pressure, 205, 206
 phosphorus binding, 57
 precipitation of carbonate minerals, 18, 22
Organophosphates
 in erythrocytes, 222
O-rings, 553–555
Orion Model 701A Digital Ionalyzer, 40
Orthophosphate, DIP
 adsorption onto air bubbles, 57, 58
 assimilation by algae, 605
 assimilation by seaweeds, 57
 determination, 57, 108–110, 631
 effect on calcium carbonate precipitation, 595
 excretion by fishes, 57
 in seawater, 56
 loss from stored seawater samples, 631
 precipitation from autoclaved seawater, 747
 precipitation on gravel, 606
 release by seaweeds, 57
 removal by aeration, 58, 606
Osmolality, 646
Osmole, 647
Osmoregulation (see Osmotic regulation)
Osmosis, 203
Osmotic loading, 205, 206
Osmotic pressure
 definition, 204
 elasmobranch body fluids, 205
 osmolality and, 646, 647
 teleost body fluids, 205
Osmotic regulation
 definition, 203
 effect of stress, 226
 introduction, 201
Ostariophysans, 266
Otoliths, 264, 265
Ouabain, 655, 656
Ovaries
 copper deposition, 759
 mycobacteriosis, 478
 ichthyophonus disease, 504
 lymphocystis disease, 762
Oviparous, 417
Ovoviviparous, 417, 738
Oxolinic acid
 treatment of vibriosis, 523, 524
Oxygen
 activated carbon and, 104
 aeration and, 153
 assimilation by erythrocytes, 212
 assimilation during respiration, 210, 213, 221, 222
 atmospheric, 210
 biological films and, 68, 69, 613
 concentration in water, 210, 218
 conversion of units, 657
 deficiency as a stress factor, 456
 deficiency in water, 212
 diffusion into water, 155, 641
 diffusivity, 154
 effect of acidosis, 456
 effect of salinity and temperature, 210
 effect on biological enhancement of activated carbon, 630
 effect on blood carbon dioxide, 214
 effect on brine shrimp cysts, 742
 effect on nitrification, 81
 effect on nitrogen cycling, 84
 effect on reproductive mode of brine shrimp, 417
 effect on rotifers, 398
 environmental hyperoxia and, 218
 equilibration in rising air bubbles, 642, 643
 extraction coefficient, 661
 filter bed bacteria and, 67
 hemoglobin affinity, 222, 223
 in carbohydrates, 365
 in denitrification, 77
 in dissimilation, 74, 75, 77, 78, 619, 620
 in filter beds, 56, 620
 in freshwaters, 210
 in oxides, 590
 in ozone generation, 466
 in protoplasm, 358
 in redox reactions, 55
 in seawater, 5, 210
 in sediments, 94
 in water, 1, 2
 nitrification and, 72
 oxidation of sugars and, 366
 partial pressure in blood, 212, 213, 222, 223
 partial pressure in seawater, 642
 partial pressure in water, 151, 154, 210, 218, 219, 220
 percentage in air, 149
 requirements during exercise stress, 227, 228
 requirements for nitrification, 55, 72, 81, 616, 617
 reversible binding, 222, 223
 saturation, 155, 787
 solubility, 154, 661
 transfer in gills, 230
"Oxygen consumed during filtration" (OCF), 84, 85, 626
Oxygen dissociation curves, 222, 223
Oxyhemoglobin, 222, 662
Oyster toadfish
 hemoglobin, 223
Oxygen transfer rate
 definition, 154, 155
 effect of turbulence, 156
 factors affecting, 156, 157
 in airlift pumps, 163
Ozonation
 chlorination and, 469, 757, 758
 contact chambers, 466
 definition, 466
 effectiveness, 467, 756
 of freshwaters, 468, 758
 of seawater, 468, 469, 757, 758
Ozonators, 466
Ozone
 activated carbon and, 104
 as a point contact sterilizing agent, 461

as a sterilizing agent, 466–468
determination in water, 757
dissolved organic carbon and, 100
lethal mechanisms, 466
Ozone-produced oxidants (OPOs)
as disinfectants, 468, 469
determination, 468, 756, 757
formation in seawater, 469, 757, 758
toxicity, 468, 469, 757, 758

Pacific electric ray
monogenean infestations, 786
Pacific sardine
as a schooling predator, 700
Pacific staghorn sculpin, 655
Packed column degassers
design, 185, 644, 645
gas supersaturation and, 149
Paints (also see Acrylic paints, Epoxy paints)
camera lenses, 544, 550
color characteristics, 542–544
color selection, 563
procedure for applying to exhibit aquariums, 564, 565
reflectivity, 563
p-aminobenzoic acid, 741, 742
Pancreas
Mycobacterium tubercles, 478
Pantothenic acid, 742
Paracellular excretion
ammonium ions, 653
definition, 208, 270
free ammonia, 208, 653
inorganic ions, 208, 209
potassium ions, 656
Paracolobactrum spp., 619
Paragobiodon echinocephalus, 309
Paragobiodon lacunicola, 308, 309
Paragobiodon spp., 289
Paranthias furcifer (see Creole-fish)
Parasites (also see Pathogens)
adaptation to hosts, 456, 457
copper and, 469
definition, 446, 447, 753
effect of copper treatment, 758
effect of treatment regimens, 458
modes of transmission, 457
of captive seawater fishes, 471
predisposition to disease and, 454
Parasiticides
effect on nitrifying bacteria, 71
Parasitism
cleaning behavior as, 719
definition, 303, 304
effect on schooling, 283
Paravortex spp. (also see Tang turbellarian)
in tang turbellarian disease, 505
life cycle, 507, 508, 786
Parental care, 289
Parrotfishes
association with sea anemones, 306
daily movements, 280
feeding associations, 719
food competitors of damselfishes, 710
grazing, 292
lekking, 290
mating systems, 295
protogyny, 298, 712
territorial dominance, 289
thyroid, 517
visual pigments, 246
Pars inferior, 264, 265
Pars superior, 264
Parthenogenesis
definition, 397
brine shrimp, 738, 745
rotifers, 397
turbellarians, 507
Partial pressure
definition, 210
dinitrogen, 66
effect of temperature, 150
effect on gas transfer, 154
in gas transfer, 153
Particle
definition in physics, 257
Particle displacement (see Displacement)
Particulate organic carbon (also see Surfactants)
as adsorbate, 100
attachment, 137
capture mechanisms, 137, 140–142
compared with dissolved organic carbon, 606
density, 141, 142, 179
effect in undersea photography, 573, 574
effect on coloration, 564
effect on heterotrophic assimilation of dissolved organic carbon, 613
effect on light absorption, 529, 535
effect on nitrification, 613
effect on turbidity, 638
entrapment on patch reefs, 332
flocculation, 143
foam fractionation and, 164
from freshwater runoff, 147
from plankton blooms, 147
froth flotation and, 163
headloss and, 144
in determination of turbidity, 638, 640
in seawater, 58, 175
in stored seawater samples, 633
mineralization, 57
nutrient adsorption, 67
penetration in granular media filters, 140
polyelectrolyte toxicity and, 641
removal by backwash, 145, 179
removal by foam fractionation, 136
removal by granular media filtration, 137, 142
surface area, 67
suspended, 136
void fraction and, 144
Particulate organic phosphorus, 56
Particle separation
introduction, 136, 137
in granular media filters, 137–147
Parts per thousand, 5
Passive denitrification method (see Anoxic sediment denitrification)
Passive transport (also see Diffusion)
definition, 204
gases, 212
ions, 208
transepithelial transport and, 655
Pasteurella piscicida (see Pseudotuberculosis)
Patch reefs
description, 332–334, 727
fish abundance, 728, 729
fish diversity, 349, 728, 729
recruitment onto, 723, 724
use by fishes, 323
Pathogens (also see Parasites)
as antigens, 447
chemotherapeutic agents and, 519
definition, 447, 753
entry into hosts, 447, 448
gill hyperplasia and, 453
in hosts *vs.* water, 457
in infections and infestations, 446, 447, 752
latent infections and, 451
opportunistic, 455
ozone and, 466
point contact sterilization and, 461, 466
tracing the origin of, 779
UV irradiation and, 463, 472, 755, 756
Pathological effects, 452
Pearl gourami
effect of carotenoids, 733
Pectoral fins
sound production by, 267
Pempheris oualensis
schooling behavior, 280, 697
Pempheris spp. (see Sweepers)
Penaeus sp., 689
Penicillin
efficacy as a formulated product, 755
manufacture, 377
treatment of contaminated phytoplankton stock cultures, 438
Penicillus spp., 622
Pentamidine, 777
Peptides, 66
Perca flavescens (see Yellow perch)
Perca fluviatilis
as a schooling predator, 700
Perfusion limited, 221, 222
Period, 257, 529
Periodic time (see Period)
Periphytes, 614
Peritoneal cavity
gas-bubble trauma, 516
vibriosis, 770
Permanganate
activated carbon and, 104
Per os administration
definition, 459
DS 677 K, 521
halquinol, 523
oxolinic acid, 524
piromidic acid, 522
praziquantel, 512
sodium nifurstyrenate, 521
spiramycin embonate, 522
testing of chemotherapeutic agents, 520
Petechiae
vibriosis, 480, 481
pH
aeration and, 153
alkalinity and, 9
blood, 213–217, 221, 230

pH *(Continued)*
carbon dioxide and, 600
control in phytoplankton cultures, 431
control in the oceans, 593
decline in closed systems, 44
definition, 9, 592
determination, 35–41, 45, 602
during transport, 229
effect of acids, 9
effect of ammonia uptake and assimilation, 424, 751
effect of bases, 9
effect of calcium chloride, 604
effect of carbonate ion, 44
effect of carbonate minerals, 9, 594–596, 600
effect of filtrants, 600
effect of hydrogen ion, 19
effect of lime, 605
effect of nitrate uptake and assimilation, 423, 429, 751
effect of nitrification, 71
effect of nitrite uptake and assimilation, 751
effect of seaweed filters, 97
effect of temperature, 658
effect on activated carbon adsorption efficiency, 104, 629
effect on ammonia toxicity, 635, 636
effect on ammonium ion dissociation, 117, 119, 121, 122, 635
effect on assimilation of chemotherapeutic agents, 460
effect on blood pH, 659–661
effect on brine shrimp cysts, 394, 396
effect on chlorine reactions, 744
effect on copper chemistry, 469, 759–761
effect on copper toxicity, 758, 759
effect on foam stability, 166
effect on free nitrous acid, 71
effect on hemoglobin oxygen affinity, 662
effect on ligands, 747
effect on nitrification, 81
effect on nitrogen cycling, 84
effect on solubility of carbonate minerals, 23
in alkalinity determinations, 42, 43
inorganic carbon and, 58
introduction, 1, 9
"mean pH," 602, 603
NBS buffers, 602
of aquarium water, 45
of GP2 solutions, 48, 605
of seawater, 9, 10, 39, 45
phytoplankton tolerance, 422
requirements for denitrifying bacteria, 75, 78, 620
requirements for nitrifying bacteria, 72, 74, 618
reduction in artificial seawaters, 23
reduction in seawater, 23, 45
scale, 592
stability, 9
tolerance limits of fishes, 23
Phaeophyceae (see Brown seaweeds)
Phaeoptyx xenus, 308
Phagocytes
classification, 451
inflammation and, 452, 453
Phagocytosis, 449, 451, 456
Pharynx
amyloodinium disease, 489, 775
lymphocystis disease, 762
sound production, 267
thyroid and, 517
Phasic electroreceptors, 270, 688
pH buffer standards
in alkalinity determinations, 38, 41, 43
in pH determinations, 37–41, 602, 603
NBS, 41, 43
pH control
adjustment procedure, 45
by anions, 19
by bicarbonate ions, 17, 19
by carbonate ions, 17, 19
by carbonate minerals, 11, 17, 19, 24, 45
with sodium bicarbonate, 45
pH electrode pair
in alkalinity determinations, 41, 43
in pH determinations, 35, 36, 38–40, 602, 603
pH electrodes
double junction, 36
electrode pairs, 35, 36, 38–41, 43, 602
function, 35, 36
glass, 35
ideal and nonideal behavior, 38, 39
single junction, 36
types, 35
use, 38
Phenols
in brown seaweeds, 59
in humus, 607
preservation of seawater samples, 633
release by seaweeds, 97, 608
toxicity, 59
pH meters
calibration, 36–41, 43, 603
carbonate saturometer and, 595
hydrogen ion activity and, 602
in alkalinity determinations, 41
standardization, 36–41, 603
types, 35
with expanded scales, 39
Phosphate (see Orthophosphate)
Phosphate ions
effect on dissolution of carbonate minerals, 22
effect on precipitation of carbonate minerals, 18
Phosphoric acid, 100
Phosphors, 540, 541
Phosphorus
autolysis and release, 56, 57
chemical states, 56
cycling in aquariums, 56–58
excretion by fishes, 56
fin rot and, 488
in eutrophication, 53
in GP2 low-salinity culture solution, 428, 673, 751, 752
in seawater, 6, 56
ion pairing, 605, 606
lysis and release, 57
precipitation on gravel, 57, 605, 606
reaction with ammonium ions, 606
release by seaweeds, 56, 57
release from microfilters, 633
removal by seaweed filters, 78
Photographic films
color temperatures, 546, 555, 571
daylight, 546, 555
effect of photographic filters, 545, 546
photographic filters and, 545, 546, 795
species label photography and, 568, 569
tungsten, 546
type A, 546
undersea photography and, 549, 555, 572
Photographic filters
color compensating, 546, 547
color conversion, 545, 546, 569, 571
density, 545
description, 545
photographic films and, 545, 546, 795
polarizing, 545, 568–570
undersea photography, 545
Photographics, 544, 545
Photon flux density, 674, 675
Photons
cones and, 674, 675
definition, 794
effect on visual pigments, 675
energy, 794
visual acuity and, 236
Photoperiod
effect on melatonin, 247
effect on monogenean life cycles, 511, 512
phytoplankton culture, 434
seaweed filters, 97
Photopic vision
contrast perception and, 678, 679
definition, 235, 246
of crepuscular predators, 243, 246
transition to scotopic vision, 272
Photopositive, 406
Photoreceptor cells (see Retinal cells)
Photosensitivity
contrast perception and, 238
definition, 235
enhancement, 679
limits, 237
matched visual pigments and, 240, 679
offset visual pigments and, 677, 678
visual acuity and, 238
Photosynthesis
carotenoid synthesis and, 370
effect on alkalinity, 12, 593
effect on calcium carbonate, 17
effect on carbon dioxide, 17, 210
production of oxygen, 210
Photosynthetic pigments, 97
Physical adsorption
by activated carbon, 100

definition, 100
location, 99
seaweed filters and, 97
"pH-sensitive" membranes (see H^+-sensitive membranes)
Physiological hypercapnia (also see Respiratory acidosis)
definition, 217
effect of environmental hypercapnia, 217, 218
effect of environmental hyperoxia, 218–221
effect of exercise stress, 227
effect of ventilation rate, 218
Physiological hypoxia
amyloodinium disease, 491
as a cause of vascular constriction, 673
as a stress factor, 227
effect on blood glucose, 670, 671
Phytoplankton (also see Algae, Seaweeds)
as live foods for brine shrimp nauplii, 415, 417
as live foods for rotifers, 418, 741
competition with heterotrophic bacteria, 611
copper requirements, 750
copper toxicity, 424, 750, 758
effect on turbidity, 638
humus production, 608
iron assimilation, 423, 748, 749
lag growth phase, 750
phosphorus cycling and, 56
powdered as foods, 413, 418, 420
tolerance of environmental conditions, 422
vitamin requirements, 421
Phytoplankton culture (also see Carboys)
aeration, 420
cell counting procedure, 443–445
cell density, 418
culture solution, 418–424, 425–429
effect of alkalinity and pH, 429
effect of light, 415
effect of light intensity, 97, 418, 420, 430
effect of nutrient availability, 418
effect of temperature, 418, 420, 430
effect on light absorption and scattering, 535
exponential growth, 415, 417, 442, 445
factors affecting incubation time, 438
freeze-dried, 741
iron as growth limiting, 423
manganese as growth limiting, 423
nitrogen sources, 424
preparation of glassware, 434, 435
preparation of GP2 culture solution, 435
requirements for, 430–432, 434
stationary growth phase, 418, 420
Phytoplankton stock cultures
antibiotic treatment of contaminated cultures, 437, 438, 752
availability, 430
cleaning of contaminated cultures, 436, 437
contamination, 430, 431
contamination check, 436, 439, 440–442
contamination check procedure, 437
incubation procedure for primary stocks, 440
incubation procedure for secondary stocks, 440, 441
inoculation procedure for primary stocks, 439, 440
inoculation procedure for tertiary stocks, 441, 442
maintenance, 437
transfer of primary stocks, 438
transfer procedure for primary stocks, 439
Pigmentation, 246, 247
Pigments
carotenoid, 368, 370, 371
in foods, 366
of fishes, 246, 247
primary colors and, 794, 795
Pillar cells, 212
Pimephales promelas (see Fathead minnow)
Pineal gland (see Epiphysis)
Pinfish
ammonia excretion, 650
Pipefishes
sound production, 267
uronema disease, 497
Pipe lateral underdrains, 177, 178, 644
Piromidic acid
treatment of vibriosis, 522
Pituitary gland (see Hypophysis)
Plaice
chain elongation of fatty acids, 731
hemoglobin oxygen affinity, 662
ichthyophonus disease, 784
production of electric gradients, 270
toxicity of algal exudates, 608
Plains killifish, 655
Plankton nets, 420
Plants
as nutrient sources for fishes, 421
assimilation of ammonium ions, 12
assimilation of carbon dioxide, 210
assimilation of nitrate, 12
assimilation of oxygen, 210
as sources of meal, 384
autochthonous humus and, 607
binders from, 389
carbohydrates in, 365
carbon in, 58
carotenoid synthesis, 370, 371
celluloses in, 365
digestibility of, 371
fatty acids, 730
fiber in, 374
humification and, 59
in biotopes, 334
metabolism, 53
nitrogen release, 66
nutrient sources for, 358
production of oxygen, 210
proteins in, 383
symbiosis and, 303
terrestrial, 364, 730
toxicity of reactivated activated carbon, 631
trace elements and, 6
Plastic packing
ammonia removal, 90
attachment of nitrifiers, 53
depth in bacteriological filters, 90
specific surface area, 87, 90
in packed column degassing, 185
surface area, 185
void fraction, 87, 90
Plastic roofing panels, 91
Platichthys stellatus (see Starry flounder)
Platyhelminths (see Flatworms)
Platymonas sp.
as live food for rotifers, 741
Plecoglossus altivelis (see Ayu)
Pleuronectes platessa (see Plaice)
Plotosus anguillaris, 270, 688
Plug flow systems, 463
Poecilia latipinna (see Sailfin molly)
Poecilia reticulatus (see Guppy)
Point contact sterilization, 461, 756
Polarization
of electrical charges, 2
of schooling fishes, 276
Polarizing screens, 565
Pollachius virens (see Pollock)
Pollock
effect of environmental hypercapnia, 661
effect of the lateral line on schooling, 695
sound attraction, 686
vibriosis, 766
"Pollution load," 85
Polychaetes, 758, 759
Polyelectrolytes, 143, 641
Polyester resin, 576–581
Polyester resin pigments, 577, 580, 581
Polyethylene
as a feed encapsulating agent, 391
Polymerization, 61, 62, 581, 749
Polymers
as feed encapsulating agents, 391
definition, 59
polyelectrolytes, 143
Polymorphonuclear leukocytes (PMNs), 451, 456
Polyodon spathula, 688
Polypropylene coatings, 195
Polypteridae, 688
Polysaccharides
as antigens, 450
definition, 365
in biological films, 68
Polysiphonia spp.
cultivation on algal lawns, 709
proteinaceous exudates, 610
Polyunsaturated fatty acids
chain elongation, 364, 731
definition, 362
effect of carbohydrates, 732
effect on lipid deposition, 733
in dry feeds, 391
in fish oils, 388
in humus formation, 607
of oceanic origin, 730
of terrestrial origin, 364, 730

Polyunsaturated fatty acids *(Continued)*
requirements for, 364, 365
Polyvinyl alcohol
as a feed encapsulating agent, 390
Polyvinyl chloride (PVC) pipe, 49, 91, 105, 155, 170, 171, 178, 186, 460, 474, 585
Pomacanthidae (see Angelfishes)
Pomacentridae (see Damselfishes)
Pomacentrus bankanensis, 293
Pomacentrus lividus
cultivation of algal lawns, 709
Pomatomus saltatrix (see Bluefish)
"Popeye" (see Exophthalmia)
Populations
definition, 319
recruitment and, 723, 725
Porgies
sex reversal, 712
Porites spp. (see Finger corals)
Porkfish
amyloodinium disease, 775
Porosity (see Void fraction)
Postcardinal veins, 664
Post-maturational secondary males, 712
Potamotrygonidae, 647
Potassium alginate, 734
Potassium ions
physiological regulation, 205, 208, 209, 655, 656
Potassium permanganate
efficacy as a formulated product, 756
toxicity to nitrifying bacteria, 72
treatment of amyloodinium disease, 778
Powdered activated carbons (also see Activated, Granular activated carbons), 102, 629
Pranesus insularum
individual distance, 692
Pranesus pinguis
schooling behavior, 280, 697
Praziquantel
treatment of monogenean infestations, 512, 525, 526, 786, 787
Precipitation
definition, 2
calcites, 20
calcium carbonate, 594–596
carbonate minerals, 17, 19
humic acids, 607
humus in seawater, 608
in saturated solutions, 595
magnesian calcite overgrowths, 18, 19, 21, 23, 597–599
phosphorus, 605, 606
Precipitation rate, 17, 22, 590
Precipitins, 449
Predation
attack sequence, 283, 701–703
at twilight, 680
confusion and, 283–285, 700–703, 706
contrast perception and, 677
dilution effect of prey, 283, 700, 701
effect of ammonia, 609
effect of conspicuousness, 698, 699
effect of frequency of encounters, 700, 701
effect of length of the hunt, 700
effect of sound, 686
effect of variable prey behavior, 699
effect of vision, 700–704
effect on schooling, 696
energy use in, 357
isolation of prey, 702, 705, 706
probability of detection, 701
rarefaction and, 727
resource partitioning and, 322
shelter spaces and, 347, 353
shoaling and, 278
substratum and, 728
symbiotic associations, 304
Pre-maturational secondary males, 712
Premnas spp.
as obligate sea anemone symbionts, 713
"feeding" of sea anemones, 715
taxonomy, 712
Preoral sting, 514
Pressure
air diffusers and, 167
atmospheric, 210, 787
dominance and, 353
effect on calcium carbonate solubility, 16
effect on gas-bubble trauma, 515
effect on gas exchange, 642
effect on rate of precipitation, 590
effect on solubility of gases, 151
effect on temperature, 257
hydrostatic, 151, 156, 169
in defining sound, 256
in foam fractionators, 166
in pressure filters, 137
in refrigeration cycling, 168
on the swimbladder, 265, 266, 268
Pressure filters
decision to use, 174
definition, 137
material composition, 137, 171–174
underdrains, 177
Pressure waves
as far-field effects, 258, 259
effect on the swimbladder, 265, 266
sound in air and, 257
Primaquine, 777
Primary consumers, 56
Primary males, 300
Primary producers, 56, 95
Primary stress response (also see Neuroendocrine responses)
catecholamines and, 225, 228
conceptual history, 664
corticosteroids and, 225, 226, 228
definition, 225
effect of captivity, 674
effect of confinement stress, 667–669
effect of environmental stress factors, 229, 230
goiter disease and, 518
Prisms
colors and, 530
in refractometers, 32, 33
prism-shaped aquariums, 556
Pristis sp. (see Sawfish)
Procerodes spp., 505
Process variables, 142
Productive protein value (PPV), 387
Protandry
advantages in monogamous species, 302
definition, 298
random pairing and, 302, 303
Protein efficiency ratio (PER), 387
Protein nitrogen, 83
Protein quality, 384
Proteins (also see Total protein)
addition to feeds, 383–385
ammonia from, 62
as antigens, 450
as binders, 389
as energy sources, 385, 733
as energy *vs.* lipids, 385, 387
as nutrients, 366
collagen as, 734
description, 360, 361
determination, 374
effect of dyes, 763
effect on carbohydrate tolerance, 731, 732
effect on feeding, 385
energy in, 385
essential amino acids in, 383
in biological membranes, 363
in fish and invertebrate flesh, 375
in humification, 59
in leafy green vegetables, 375
in protoplasm, 359
leaching from feeds, 390
metabolism, 385
metabolism by animals, 66
mineralization, 62
nitrogen in, 730
physiological fuel value, 372
protein sparing, 365, 387, 731
recommended percentage in feeds, 385
reduction to amino acids, 371
requirements for, 357, 360, 361, 383–385, 387, 388
tissue deposition, 385, 387
use by fishes, 387
Protein skimming (see Foam fractionation)
Proteus spp., 619
Protogyny
definition, 298
in *Labroides dimidiatus*, 303
in teleosts, 712
Protoplasm, 358, 359
Protopterus dolloi, 688
Protozoans
as contaminants in phytoplankton stock cultures, 430, 437
as microorganisms, 447
as primary infectious agents, 459
effect of cellular immune response, 450
effect of copper, 758
effect of ozone, 466
efficacy of formulated products, 468
Ichthyosporidium as, 783
lesions caused by, 455

testing of chemotherapeutic agents, 520
Proximate analysis, 374
Proximate composition, 374, 375, 383
Pseudochromidae (see Dottybacks)
Pseudodactylogyrus spp., 524, 525
"Pseudohumus," 62
Pseudolabrus celidotus, 723
Pseudomonas aeruginosa, 620
Pseudomonas spp.
dissimilation by, 619
fin rot, 486, 772, 773
Pseudopeneus maculatus (see Spotted goatfish)
Pseudopleuronectes americanus (see Winter flounder)
Pseudotuberculosis
sodium nifurstyrenate treatment, 521
Puffers
sound production, 267
Puissance, 603
Pumps (also see Airlift pumps)
centrifugal, 163
energy, 159
in granular media filtration, 137
leaks in, 151
mechanical, 56, 185
plastic, 52
rotating vane, 187, 188
stainless steel, 52
surface wash, 146
Pure water (also see Freshwaters, Water)
air bubbles in, 167
as a conductor, 7
attenuation of light, 535
definition, 7
density, 7, 26, 27, 591
in defining specific gravity, 601
ion product, 592, 658
light scattering, 793
pH, 213
refractive index, 530
specific gravity, 29
Pycnometer, 591
Pyloric ceca
gas-bubble trauma, 516
Pyramimonas spp., 430, 438
Pyrex®, 591
Pyrolysis, 631

Quarantine, 356, 473, 474
Queen triggerfish, 267
"Quiet period," 242
Quinacrine
treatment of amyloodinium disease, 777
Quinine hydrochloride
treatment of cryptocaryoniasis, 496, 782
Quisquilius hipoliti, 306

Rabbitfish
immunity to amyloodinium disease, 775
Radar, 529
Radiance
definition, 239
submarine light and, 535, 793
Radio waves, 529
Rainbow trout
acid-base regulation, 217
ammonia excretion, 648, 650, 653
ammonia toxicity, 636
chain elongation of fatty acids, 731
effect of capture stress, 669
effect of confinement stress, 667–669
effect of environmental hypercapnia, 659
effect of environmental hypoxia, 662
effect of exercise stress, 665
effect of handling stress, 668–670
effect of temperature on blood pH, 659
effect of transport stress, 669, 791
goiter disease, 790
ichthyophonus disease, 783–785
intracellular water transport, 671
nitrite toxicity, 610
transepithelial potentials, 655
vibriosis, 766
Raja clavata, 270
Raja erinacea (see Little skate)
Raja montagu, 648
Ramose corals, 349
Rank order (see Dominance hierarchy)
Rapid sand filters
decision to use, 174
definition, 137
filtrant distribution, 144
filtration rate, 137
support media, 145
Raptor, 397
Rarefaction, 726, 727
Rays (also see Elasmobranchs)
detection of bioelectric fields, 270
ionic and osmotic regulation, 205
Reactive phosphate (see Orthophosphate)
Rectal gland
ion exchange by, 209, 656
transepithelial potentials, 656
Red algae, 709
Red blood cells (see Erythrocytes)
Red boil (see Vibriosis)
Redbreast sunfish
nocturnal disintegration of schools, 693
Red disease (see Vibriosis)
Red drum
nitrite toxicity, 610
Red hake
fin rot, 773
Redox reaction, 55
Red pest (see Vibriosis)
Red plague (see Vibriosis)
Red seabream
brine shrimp nauplii as early food, 738
carbohydrate tolerance, 731
chain elongation of fatty acids, 731
effect of astaxanthin on coloration, 733, 734
fin rot, 773
Red shift, 678
Reference electrodes, 35, 36
Reference temperature
definition, 8
expression, 29, 30
hydrometer readings and, 29, 30, 52
specific gravity corrected to, 26, 601
Reflecting platelets, 247
Refractive index
acrylic, 561
air, 233
cytoplasm, 248
definition, 6, 792
effect of density, 233
eye, 233, 234
glass, 560
particulate organic carbon, 638
seawater, 562
Snell's law and, 530, 792
water, 233, 234, 560, 561
Refractometers
calibration, 31
definition, 6
effect on dissolution of calcium carbonate, 17
suitability for brines, 52
use, 32, 33
use with artificial seawaters, 601
Refractory
complexes as, 747
copper complexes, 760, 761
definition, 58, 59
dissolved organic carbon, 100
humus, 607
Refrigeration compressors, 168, 169
Refrigeration cycle, 168, 169
Refrigeration requirements, 168, 169, 196–198
Refuge associations, 306–309, 718
Relative pH, 214, 658
Renal tubules
uronema disease, 498
Representative size, 175
Reptiles, 213, 658, 659
Reproductive capacity (see Fitness)
Residue, 164, 166, 192, 195
Resonance, 685
Resource generalist hypothesis, 322, 323, 721–726
Resource partitioning, 319
Resources
categories, 293, 351
competition for, 287, 321–323, 708–711, 725, 726, 729
definition, 291, 319
dominance behavior and, 287
food, 291–293, 295, 298, 319, 351, 708–711
in defining fitness, 291
in defining territory, 287, 708
priority of access, 287, 291, 706
space, 319, 351
Resource specialist hypothesis, 321–323, 721–726
Respiration
aerobic, 55
anaerobic, 55
assimilation of oxygen, 210
bacterial, 62, 64
by anaerobic bacteria, 74
carbon dioxide and, 58
erythrocytes and, 212
introduction, 201

Respiratory acidosis (also see Physiological hypercapnia)
definition, 217, 227
effect of exercise stress, 228, 456, 665, 666
effect of handling stress, 228
Respiratory distress
cryptocaryoniasis, 495
Respiratory pigment (see Hemoglobin)
Resting spore, 500, 502–504
Restraint
as a stress factor, 227
Retina
cone cells, 676
diurnal fishes, 238
light gathering, 233, 234
visual sensations, 531, 793
Retinal cells (see Visual cells)
Rhipocephalus phoenix, 622
Rhipocephalus spp., 622
Rhizoclonium spp.
in seaweed filters, 621
Rhizoids, 490, 491
Rhodopsins, 680
Rhodophyceae (see Red algae)
Rhodotorula sp.
as live food for rotifers, 741
Riboflavin
leaching from feeds, 736
Rice bran
as food for brine shrimp nauplii, 413, 415, 738, 745
Rifampicin
treatment of mycobacteriosis, 478
Rinoptera bonasus (see Cownose ray)
Risor ruber, 308
Rock salts, 48
Rods
definition, 235
diurnal fishes, 235
effect of photons, 675
nocturnal fishes, 236
offset visual pigments, 676, 678
rhodopsins, 680
visual pigments, 237, 238, 243, 246
Root effect, 662
Rotating filters, 53
Rotifer
amino acid composition, 397
as live food, 358
cryopreservation of eggs, 398
effect of chlorinity on reproduction, 740
effect of salinity on reproduction, 398, 740
factors affecting survival and reproduction, 398, 399, 740
length, 418, 745
morphology, 418
reproduction, 397, 398
Rotifer culture
changing tanks procedure, 418, 420, 745
drain-down procedure, 418, 420, 421, 745
effect of food composition, 741
effect of food uptake on culture density, 741
food particle size, 741
inoculation density, 420
inoculation of phytoplankton cultures, 442
live phytoplankton and, 430
mass culture, 745
optimal temperature range, 740, 741
Routine metabolism, 372
Roxanthin® Red 10 Beadlets (also see Canthaxanthin), 400
Rudd
milling, 691
olfaction in schooling, 695
vision in schooling, 693
Rule of constant proportions, 6
Rust disease (see Amyloodinium disease)

Saccharides, 365
Saccharomyces cerevisiae (see Baker's yeast)
Sacculus, 264
Safranin, 763
Sailfin molly
ammonia excretion, 650
immunity to amyloodinium disease, 774
Sakai Aquarium, 624
Salinity
as a stress factor, 227, 229, 454, 456, 492
brine shrimp tolerance to, 392
concentration by evaporation, 780
concentration by sodium chloride addition, 496, 782
conversion from specific gravity, 31
definition, 5, 6, 590
density and, 7
determination, 6, 26, 31–33
effect of major ions, 5
effect of temperature, 6
effect on ammonia toxicity, 635, 636
effect on ammonium ion dissociation, 117, 119, 121, 122, 635
effect on amyloodinium disease, 778
effect on *Amyloodinium ocellatum* life cycle, 491, 492, 496, 776–778
effect on assimilation of chemotherapeutic agents, 460
effect on brine shrimp cysts, 394, 396
effect on calcium carbonate solubility, 16
effect on *Cryptocaryon irritans* life cycle, 495, 496, 780
effect on fin rot, 486
effect on growth of brine shrimp nauplii, 414
effect on molting in brine shrimp, 738, 739
effect on nitrification, 81
effect on nitrogen cycling, 84
effect on refractive index of water, 520
effect on rotifer size and reproduction, 398, 740
effect on sound velocity, 257
effect on survival of brine shrimp nauplii, 739
effect on *Uronema marinum* life cycle, 497
expression, 6, 33
ichthyophonus disease and, 503
in alkalinity determinations, 42, 43
in GP2 low-salinity culture solution, 428
in phytoplankton culture, 434
introduction, 1
manipulation for treatment of cryptocaryoniasis, 496, 781
manipulation with sodium chloride, 496
of brines, 52
of seawater, 5
phytoplankton tolerance, 422, 434
predisposing factor in vibriosis, 771
proper use of the term, 601
range in the oceans, 590
reduction in aquariums, 33-35
requirements of nitrifying bacteria, 74, 618
rule of constant proportions and, 6
specific gravity and, 8
specific gravity equivalent, 34
thyroid hormones and, 517
tolerance by fishes, 496, 509
units, 8
Salinometers (see Conductivity meters)
Salmo clarkii (see Cutthroat trout)
Salmonids
carotenoid deposition, 371
daily ammonia excretion, 83
diets, 358
differences in fatty acid requirements, 731
effect of carotenoids on flesh coloration, 734
effect of mycobacteriosis on coloration, 477
exophiala disease, 785
gas-bubble disease, 788
ichthyophonus disease, 503
iodide balance, 790
mycobacteriosis, 763–765
nitrite toxicity, 609, 610
thyroid hormones and migration, 517
vaccination against vibriosis, 484, 771
vibriosis, 766, 768
Salmo salar (see Atlantic salmon)
Salmo trutta (see Brown trout)
Salts
bagged, 49, 51
bulk, 51
definition, 1
dissociation, 2, 7
evaporated sea salts, 48
in artificial seawaters, 48, 49
industrial-grade, 48
in seawater, 6
reagent-grade, 48
rock, 48
technical-grade, 48
treatment of exophiala disease, 785
Saltwater furunculosis (see Vibriosis)
Saltwater "ich" (see Cryptocaryoniasis)
Salvelinus fontinalis (see Brook trout)
Salvelinus namycush (see Lake trout)
Sample temperature
definition, 8
expression, 29

in hydrometer readings, 29–31, 601
in salinity determinations, 26, 32
Sand
"algal," 316
anoxic sediment denitrification, 95
attachment of nitrifying bacteria, 53
calcareous, 329, 332
depth in bacteriological filters, 90
denitrification columns, 95
dual media filters, 140
effective size, 176, 177
effect on alkalinity, 599, 600
effect on O-rings, 555
effect on pH, 600
granular media filters, 137, 140
intermixing with anthracite, 181
intermixing with garnet, 181
linear flow rate through, 90
multimedia filters, 140
relative grain size, 176, 644
seawater supplies and, 147
selection for burrowing fishes, 316
60% size, 177, 183
specific gravity, 175
support media and, 644
uniformity coefficients, 176, 177
Sandbar shark
vibriosis, 770
Sandpaper disease (see Ichthyophonus disease)
Sand seatrout, 659
Sand tilefish
mound building, 720
substratum for exhibition, 317, 318
Sardinops sagax (see Pacific sardine)
Saturated fatty acids, 362, 364
Sawfish
treatment for monogenean infestations, 525
Scad
as schooling prey, 704, 705
Scales
effect of mycobacteriosis, 477
effect of vibriosis, 480
guanine, 248
hypoxanthine, 248
injury and, 456
origin in dermis, 447
removal by cleaners, 309, 310
vibriosis, 767, 768
Scardinius erythrophthalmus (see Rudd)
Schooling
absence of dominance, 285, 286
amyloodinium disease and, 491
anonymity, 283, 285
aquarium design for, 314, 315
confusion of predators, 700–702
cover seeking, 698
definition, 276, 314, 690
diel rhythms, 278, 696, 697
dilution effect, 283, 700, 701
effect of predation, 696
effect on drag and friction, 285
feeding and, 276, 286
heterotypic and homotypic, 283, 698
hydrodynamic advantages, 285, 706
in captivity, 312, 314, 720
individual distance, 277, 692, 693, 703
lateral line and, 695, 696
mechanisms of cohesion, 276, 277
milling and, 691
models, 692
nocturnal cessation, 692–694
olfaction and, 695, 696
parasitism and, 283
planktivores, 703, 704
position within the school, 703
requirements for, 276, 277
safety in numbers, 699–701
schools as assemblages, 274, 275, 285
seasonal rhythms, 696, 697
spawning and, 276
survival value, 282–285, 689, 697, 699–701, 703, 705, 706
swimming precision and, 276
vision and, 692–696
Sciaenidae (see Drums)
Sciaenops ocellatus (see Red drum)
Scleractinians (see Corals, hard)
Scomber japonicus (see Chub mackerel)
Scomber scombrus (see Atlantic mackerel)
Scophthalmus maximus (see Turbot)
Scorpaenidae (see Scorpionfishes)
Scorpionfishes
cryptocaryoniasis, 782
sound production, 267, 268
Scotopic vision
contrast perception and, 678
crepuscular predators, 680
definition, 235
predation and, 242–246, 272
Screen sizes, 178, 179
Scyliorhinus canicula (see Smaller spotted dogfish)
Scyliorhinus stellaris (see Larger spotted dogfish)
Sea anemones
as anemonefish hosts, 303
as damselfish territories, 716
as food, 292
association with damselfishes, 304
as territories, 304
danger to symbionts, 304, 306
danger to predators of symbionts, 307
"feeding" by anemonefishes, 713–716
stinging cells, 712, 713
Sea basses
cryptocaryoniasis, 782
sound attraction, 686
sound production, 267
Sea catfishes
sound production, 267
Sealed plastic bags
environmental hyperoxia and, 218, 221
Sea urchin bioassay, 586–588
Sea urchin gametes, 587, 588
Sea urchins, 332
Seawater (also see Artificial seawaters)
acid-base balance and, 215, 217, 218, 220
addition of nitrifying bacteria to, 81
addition to gelatin-bound moist feeds, 403, 406
aeration, 58, 153
air bubble formation, 151, 153
alkalinity, 10, 45
alkalinity loss in, 23, 44
as a conductor, 6, 7
as a hyperosmotic environment, 209
as an ionic solution, 592
as base for enrichment additives, 745
buffering, 17, 594
calcium carbonate precipitation, 595–600
calcium carbonate supersaturation, 594–596
chlorination, 468, 469, 756–758
coloration, 535, 563, 564, 608
compared with blood ion concentration, 205
compared with concentrated brines, 52
compared with GP2 culture solution, 422, 423
conduction, 7
copper determination, 758
corrosive action, 171, 173, 178
denitrification, 94, 620
density, 7, 141, 142, 167, 591, 601
distillation, 6
effect of autoclaving, 746, 747, 750, 751
effect on concrete, 170
enrichment additives, 422, 745, 746, 749, 752
equivalents, 592, 593
evaporation, 6, 590
for backwash, 184
gas saturation, 136
gas supersaturation, 515
humus, 59, 607, 608
in closed systems, 21
inert materials, 195, 198
in granular media filters, 142
in open systems, 20
iodine, 517, 604
ionic strength, 153, 602
ions, 1
iron chemistry, 747–749
labile compounds, 59
light penetration, 535, 792, 793
magnesium-calcium ratio, 596
major ions, 5, 601
mass, 7
opaqueness and transparency to light, 533–535
osmotic pressure, 205
ozonation, 468, 469, 472, 756–758
pH, 9, 10, 39, 45, 594, 595, 602, 603
pH control, 10, 17
pH during transport, 229
pH reduction, 23, 44
precipitation of carbonate minerals, 18, 19
refractive index, 562
refractory compounds in, 59
salinity, 5, 7, 392

Seawater *(Continued)*
sample preservation and storage, 631, 633
similarity to artificial seawaters, 46
sodium bicarbonate dissolved in, 45
solubility of carbon dioxide, 210
solubility of oxygen, 210
solute concentration, 5, 52, 205
specific gravity, 29
surface tension, 167
surfactants, 167
turbidity, 136
viscosity, 167
yellowing, 61, 760
Seawater supplies
backwash rate and, 182, 184
biofouling and, 147
coarse sand filtration, 147, 148
gas supersaturation of, 151, 515
particulate organic carbon, 147, 175
rapid-flow systems, 187
subsurface, 147
surface, 147
turbidity, 147, 175, 638
Seawater supply systems, 147, 149, 151
Seaweed filters
columnar denitrification and, 95
design and maintenance, 97–99
effect of cobalt and molybdenum, 423
efficacy, 78, 621
eutrophication and, 78, 97
location, 99
nitrate removal, 78
Seaweeds (also see Algae, Phytoplankton)
amino acid release, 78
ammonia uptake, 78
as algal lawns, 291, 292, 709
as sources of binding agents, 389
attachment, 98, 99
desiccation, 78
humus producton, 608
nitrogen release, 66
nitrogen removal, 54, 67
phosphorus assimilation, 57
phosphorus excretion, 57
powdered as food, 413
proteinaceous exudates, 610
release of dissolved organic carbon, 78, 97
requirements for cobalt and molybdenum, 424
temperature stress, 78
toxic products and exudates, 59, 97, 607, 608, 622
uptake and assimilation of inorganic nitrogen, 620, 621
vitamin release, 78
Secondary consumers, 56
Secondary infections
bacteria in amyloodinium disease, 491
bacteria in argulid infestations, 514
bacteria in fin rot, 486
bacteria in lymphocystis disease, 475
bacteria in monogenean infestations, 511
bacteria in tang turbellarian disease, 508
fungi in lymphocystis disease, 475
injury and, 455, 456
mortality from, 459
Vibrio angullarum, 767
Secondary infestations
by *Ichthyophonus*, 501, 503
Secondary lamellae (also see Gill lamellae)
assimilation of gases, 212, 213
blood flow, 212
effect of blood pressure, 212, 221
epithelium, 212, 213, 646
excretion of gases, 212, 213
gas exchange, 202, 203, 646
inorganic ion exchange, 202
mucus, 213
residence time of water, 212
Secondary males, 300
Secondary stress responses
conceptual history, 664
effect of argulids, 514
effect of crowding, 456
effect of environmental stress factors, 226–230
Sedimentary rocks, 593
Sedimentation, 142, 332
Sediments
calcareous, 332
carbonate minerals in, 15, 58
copper in, 488
in denitrification, 95, 96
in groove and spur regions, 329
iodine in, 517
monogenean development in, 786
oxygen in, 94
silicates in, 593
Semicircular canals, 264
Semipermeable membrane, 203
Sensitivity adjustment (see Calibration)
Sensitivity test, 458–460
Sepia officinalis, 700
Septicemias, 448
Sequential hermaphrodites, 298, 301
Sequestrants, 389
Seriola lalandei
cooperative hunting, 705
Seriola quinqueradiata (see Yellowtail)
Serranidae (see Sea basses)
Serratia spp., 619
Settling velocity, 175
Sex reversal (also see Protandry, Protogyny)
behavioral aspects, 298–303
fish families affected, 712
from ichthyophonus disease, 504
social control, 712
Sexual dichromatism, 299, 300
Sexual dimorphism, 298
Sexual monochromatism, 299
Shallow-water confinement
as a stress factor, 227
Sharks (also see Elasmobranchs)
attraction by acoustic stimuli, 268
far-field effects and, 269
goiter disease, 519, 791
immunoglobulins, 753
ionic and osmotic regulation, 205, 209, 210, 651, 656, 657
larger spotted dogfish, 214, 215
shipping practices, 221
sound detection, 686–687
vibriosis, 766, 767
Sheepshead minnow
immunity to amyloodinium disease, 774
Shelter spaces
as resources, 291
definition, 341, 343
description, 343, 347
fish standing crop density and, 349, 351
in community exhibits, 351–353, 355
in corals, 349
in ramose corals, 349
in sponges, 347
in tubeworm holes, 347
newly acquired fishes and, 356
predation and, 353
requirements in aquariums, 353
stress and, 353
Shoaling
absence of dominance, 285
definition, 276, 689, 690
diel patterns, 697
effect of currents, 278
effect of diel rhythms, 278, 280
effect of tidal flow, 278
heterotypic and homotypic, 278, 280, 281
in captivity, 312, 314
individual distance, 277
milling and, 691
nocturnal cessation, 692
predation and, 696
shoals as assemblages, 275, 285
swimming precision and, 276
vision and, 694
Shore reefs (see Fringing reefs)
Shortband herring
nocturnal disintegration of schools, 693
Shrimps
as carotenoid sources, 733, 734
as sources of meal, 384, 385, 733
bioelectric fields, 689
cleaning fishes, 718
sheltering with fishes, 308
Sibling species, 393
Siderastrea spp. (see Siderastreans)
Siderastreans, 332
Siganus rivulatus (see Rabbitfish)
Silent (ozone) discharge, 466
Silicates, 593
Silicon
addition to culture solutions, 749
in seawater, 6
precipitation from autoclaved seawater, 746
requirements of diatoms, 423–424
Silicone mold release, 574, 578
Silicone sealant, 91
Silt, 94, 147, 326, 638
Silurids
electroreceptors, 688
hearing, 266
Silver hake
fin rot, 773

Silver oxide
efficacy as a formulated product, 756
Silversides
as nocturnal predators, 280
Simple sugars (see Monosaccharides)
Single plasmodial masses, 503
Site attachment
anemonefishes to sea anemones, 304
changeover and, 351
creole wrasse, 729, 730
definition, 708
in captive fishes, 356
in schooling, 690
Size advantage hypothesis, 301, 712
60% size
anthracite, 177
definition, 177
effect on backwash rate, 183
filtrants, 181
sand, 181
Skates (also see Elasmobranchs)
electric organs, 688
ionic and osmotic regulation, 205
Skin
amyloodinium disease, 489, 491
antigen entry and, 450
as a physical barrier, 447, 448
bioelectric fields, 269
chromatophores, 246, 247
cryptocaryoniasis, 493, 495
definition, 448
diminished coloration, 366
effect of carotenoids, 388, 389
effect of fin rot, 488
effect of mycobacteriosis, 476–478
effect of vibriosis, 480, 481
effect on absorption of chemotherapeutic agents, 460
gas-bubble trauma, 515
guanine and hypoxanthine, 248
ichthyophonus disease, 498, 503, 504
injury and, 455
minor ions and, 47
monogenean infestations, 509
mucous layer, 306
necrosis and, 453
ordinary lateral line organs, 261
permeability, 205
pigment deposition, 368
sound production and, 267
structure, 753
tang turbellarian disease, 508
uronema disease, 497
vibriosis and, 483, 770
Skipjack
secondary lamellar epithelium, 646
Slaked lime, 598, 605
Slender filefish
cryptic coloration, 255
Slimes (see Biological films)
Slope (see Calibration)
Slug flow pattern, 161
Smaller spotted dogfish
effect of oxygen on acid-base balance, 660, 661
permeability to water, 648
seawater drinking, 647
sound detection, 685
Smooth dogfish
effect of physiological hypoxia, 670, 671
sound detection, 685
Snappers
as nocturnal predators, 280, 728
sound attraction, 686
Snell's law, 529, 530, 560–562
Snook
vibriosis, 766
Soapfishes
protogyny, 712
Social conflict
as a stress factor, 227
Sockeye salmon
position within the school, 703
Sodium alginate (also see Alginates)
as a feed binding agent, 389
availability, 734
in moist feeds, 400, 403
Sodium bicarbonate
as a suspension, 735
autoclaving, 423, 747, 751
dissolved in artificial seawaters, 45
effect on calcium carbonate precipitation, 595
effect on nitrite toxicity, 609
for alkalinity control, 44, 45
for cleaning, 49
for pH control, 45
in the Solvay process, 605
requirement for brine shrimp cysts, 740
Sodium chloride
addition to brine shrimp rearing solutions, 414
addition to moist feeds, 403, 406
as brine, 51, 52
dissociation, 2
effect on nitrite toxicity, 610
for raising salinity, 496, 782
in brine, 396, 413
in the Solvay process, 605
requirements for brine shrimp cysts, 740
Sodium glycerophosphate
addition to culture solutions, 747
Sodium hydroxide
decapsulation of brine shrimp cysts and, 413
effect on alkalinity, 12
effect on total CO_2, 12
Sodium hypochlorite (also see Clorox®)
decapsulation of brine shrimp cysts, 413
formation in ozonated seawater, 757
use in quarantine procedures, 474
Sodium ions
as electrolytes, 590
concentration in blood, 654
effect on nitrite toxicity, 609
equivalents in seawater, 592
in table salt, 2
ion pairing, 592
physiological regulation, 205–209, 230, 231, 648–657, 659
requirements for brine shrimp cysts, 396
Na^+-K^+-activated ATPase, 655, 656
Sodium metasilicate
addition for diatom cultures, 748
addition to culture solutions for diatoms, 749
Sodium nifurstyrenate
treatment of pseudotuberculosis, 521
Sodium pyrophosphate
addition to alginate-bound moist feeds, 400
as a sequestrant, 389
Sodium sulfamerazine
efficacy as a formulated product, 755
Sodium sulfate
effect on nitrite toxicity, 609
Sodium sulfathiozole, 755
Solea solea (see Common sole)
Solid phase, 594, 597, 599
Solid solutions, 597, 599
Sols
as colloids, 735
colloidal suspensions and, 734
definition, 389
Solubility
calcium carbonate, 16
carbonate minerals, 16–18, 24, 597
carbon dioxide, 210
gases, 151, 154
magnesian calcite overgrowths, 20, 597
oxygen, 210
Solubility product, 594, 595, 598
Solute concentration
in salinity reduction, 34
Solutes
concentration by active transport, 205
definition, 2
effect on osmotic pressure, 204
elimination by active transport, 205
hyperosmotic solutions, 205
hyposmotic solutions, 205
in defining osmole, 647
in defining salinity, 590
in pure water, 7
in seawater, 33
isosmotic solutions, 205
physiological regulation, 204
semipermeable membranes and, 204
Solute throughput, 192
Solutions
definition, 2, 735
hyperosmotic, 205
hyposmotic, 205
isosmotic, 205
solid, 597
Solvay process, 605
Solvents, 2
Sound, 256, 263, 684
Sound intensity
acoustic gradient hypothesis and, 269
attenuation, 686
attraction of sharks, 268
attraction of teleosts, 268
definition, 257
localization, 268, 269, 684, 686, 687
measurement, 681
Sound pressure (see Excess pressure)
Sound production, 267, 268
Sound velocity, 257

Sound waves, 256, 257
Soybeans, 384
Space
  allocation in community exhibits, 351, 352
  as a limiting factor on coral reefs, 725
  as a resource, 319, 351
  dominance and, 723
  exhibit design, 528
  for feeding, 341
  for reproduction, 341
  partitioning, 321–323, 334, 335, 341, 723, 724
  recruitment and, 722–726
  requirements for phytoplankton culture, 430
  sharing, 351, 729
  shelter, 341, 343, 347, 349, 351, 356
Span (see Calibration)
Spanish hogfish
  in feeding associations, 312, 719
Sparidae (see Porgies)
Sparisoma viride (see Stoplight parrotfish)
Sparus aurata (see Gilthead bream)
Specialized lateral line organs (also see Electroreception), 270
Species labels, 544, 545, 566–570
Specific gravity
  accuracy, 26
  brine shrimp rearing solutions, 414
  conversion to salinity, 31
  definition, 7, 8, 601
  density and, 9, 33, 591
  determination in brines, 52
  determination, 30, 31
  distilled water and, 8
  effect of temperature, 9
  effect on molting in brine shrimp, 738, 739
  error, 26
  hydrometer readings and, 1, 9, 30
  introduction, 1
  of air columns, 155, 159
  of brines, 49–52
  of granular media filtrants, 175, 181, 641
  of pure water, 29
  of seawater, 29
  reduction in aquariums, 34, 35
  salinity and, 8
  salinity determination from, 26
  salinity equivalent, 34
  units, 8
Spermaceti, 638
Spinal column
  exhibition of, 565
Spinal curvature
  ichthyophonus disease, 503
Spine
  swimbladder and, 265
Spiny dogfish
  effect of environmental hypercapnia, 660
  rectal gland, 656
  secondary lamellar epithelium, 646
  vibriosis, 770
Spiramycin embonate
  treatment of *Streptococcus* infections, 521
Spirillum spp., 619
Splash towers, 644
Spleen
  effect of exercise stress, 228, 667
  exophiala disease, 505
  ichthyophonus disease, 503
  lymphocystis disease, 762
  Mycobacterium tubercles, 478
  vibriosis, 770
Sponges
  as food, 292
  as refuge hosts, 306, 307
  as shelter spaces, 347, 730
Sporulation, 490, 491
Spottail shiner
  feeding efficiency, 704
Spotted goatfish
  nocturnal coloration, 251
Sprat
  safety in numbers, 699
Sprattus sprattus (see Sprat)
Squalus acanthias (see Spiny dogfish)
Squirrelfishes
  sound production, 267
Stage flats, 555
Staggers (see Ichthyophonus disease)
Stainless steel
  fittings, 173
  immersion heaters, 199
  in surge action exhibits, 583
  pipe, 51
  pumps, 52
Standard additions, 111, 114, 634
Standard International (SI) units, 33
Standardization
  definition, 38
  of pH meters, 36–41, 43
Standard metabolism, 373–374
Standard temperature
  definition, 8
  expression, 29, 30
  in hydrometer calibration, 26
  in hydrometer readings, 27, 30, 52, 601
Standing crop density (fishes), 349, 351, 355, 356
Starches, 365, 374
Star corals, 332, 334, 574
Starksia hassi, 306
Starlight, 242, 244, 245
Starry flounder
  effect of exercise stress, 665
  fin rot, 772
Starvation
  as a stress factor, 227
Steady state
  acid-base balance and, 214
  definition, 59
  gases, 187
  gases in air bubbles, 642
  of conditioned bacteriological filters, 79
  resource specialist view and, 322
Steam
  as an activating agent, 102
  thermometer calibration in, 25
Stearic acid, 596
Steelhead trout
  nitrite toxicity, 610
Stegastes apicalis
  cultivation of algal lawns, 709
Stegastes dorsopunicans (see Dusky damselfish)
Stegastes fasciolatus
  cultivation of algal lawns, 709
Stegastes leucostictus (see Beaugregory)
Stegastes partitus (see Bicolor damselfish)
Stegastes planifrons (see Threespot damselfish)
Steinhart Aquarium, 393
Sterilizing agents
  definition, 461
  disinfectants and, 467
  effect on vibriosis epizootics, 483
  in treatment regimens, 458
  ozone, 466, 467, 472, 756
  ozone- and chlorine-produced oxidants, 468, 469, 756–758
  use in disease treatments, 472
  UV radiation, 461–463, 465, 466, 472
Sterling Brinomat®, 51, 52
Stichodactyla giganteum, 712
Stichodactyla sp., 714, 718
Stilling effect, 156
Stingrays
  freshwater, 647
Stizostedion vitreum (see Walleye)
Stolephorus purpureus (see Hawaiian anchovy)
Stomach
  amyloodinium disease, 775
Stomopode, 490
Stoplight parrotfish
  nocturnal coloration, 251
Storage vats, 48, 49
Straining, 141
Streamlines, 137, 141, 142, 144
Streptococcus sp.
  spiramycin embonate treatment, 521, 522
Streptomycin
  treatment for mycobacteriosis, 478
Streptomycin sulfate
  efficacy as a formulated product, 755
  treatment of contaminated phytoplankton stock cultures, 438
Stress
  as a nonspecific response, 662, 663
  behavioral during treatment, 460
  definition, 224, 663
  diseases and, 446
  effect of copper, 492
  effect of disinfectants, 492
  effect of dominance, 353
  effect of heavy parasitism, 496
  effect of salinity, 492
  effect of temperature, 492
  effect on pathogenicity of *Vibrio*, 480, 483, 484
  introduction, 201
  newly acquired fishes and, 356
  of chemotherapeutic agents, 459
  osmotic, 483
  predisposing factor in amyloodinium disease, 775
  predisposing factor in fin rot, 486
  predisposition to disease and, 454, 456

quarantine and, 473
Stress factors
effect on neuroendocrine responses, 225–227
effect on thyroid hormones, 518
examples, 224
measurement of effect in rotifers, 740
nonspecific responses and, 663
Stressors (see Stress factors)
Stress response (also see Neuroendocrine responses, Primary stress response, Secondary stress responses), 224–231, 664
Stridulation, 267
Strike
in defining predation, 283
Striped bass x white bass hybrids
effect of handling stress, 667
Striped burrfish
ammonia excretion, 650
Striped marlin
hemoglobin, 223
Striped mullet
vision in schooling, 694
Stroke volume, 221
Strongylocentrotus purpuratus, 622
Strontium, 6
Struvite, 606
Stylet, 514
Stypopodium zonale, 622
Subclinical infections
definition, 451
epizootics and, 457
predisposition to disease and, 454
treatment regimens and, 458
Subfluidization, 146
Subgravel filters
design criteria, 91
effectiveness, 53
in exhibits, 315
nitrate and, 96
Sublimation, 377
Submergence, 159
Submergence ratio, 159, 163, 188–192, 645
Sucrose, 365
Sugars, 7, 365, 366
Sulfamerazine
treatment of amyloodinium disease, 777
treatment of exophiala disease, 785
Sulfanilamide
toxicity to nitrifying bacteria, 72
Sulfate ions
effect on nitrite toxicity, 609
excretion in urine, 205
in seawater, 6
Sulfathiazole, 777
Sulfide ions
toxicity to nitrifying bacteria, 70, 71, 615
Suma Aquarium, 782
Supersaturation (also see Undersaturation)
calcium carbonate in artificial seawaters, 18
calcium carbonate in seawater, 16–18, 20, 21, 594, 595
calcium carbonate precipitation and, 18
definition, 16, 595
early use of the term, 787
gases, 136, 148–151, 153, 185, 515
Support media
anoxic conditions, 173
coarse sand filters, 145, 146
definition, 137
depth, 179
disturbance during backwash, 178
function, 145
grain size uniformity, 178
high rate filters, 145
intermixing with filtrants, 146
rapid sand filters, 145
sizes, 179, 644
Suramin, 777
Surface activity, 58
Surface area
activated carbons, 103, 104
aeration tanks, 156
air bubbles, 167
bacteriological filters, 67–69
brine shrimp cyst hatch vessels, 409
coral reefs, 349, 728, 729
determination for activated carbons, 627
detritus, 94
effectiveness of UV irradiation and, 463
effect on nitrification, 67–69, 612, 613
in foam fractionators, 192
ocean surface, 532
of fishes, 460
of gills, 230
plastic packing, 185
Surface oxides, 103, 104
Surface tension
air bubble formation and, 153, 167
effect on laminar layer formation, 153
in packed column degassing, 185
of foam, 166
of seawater, 167
Surface wash, 146, 174, 175
Surfactants
definition, 163
effect on bubble size, 167
effect of concentration on foam stability, 166, 195
mass transfer in foam fractionation, 192, 193, 195
polarity, 164
Surgeonfishes
daily movements, 280
food competitors of damselfishes, 710
grazing, 292
lekking, 290
territorial dominance, 289
Suspension, 735
Swamp-eel, 659
Sweepers
schooling behavior, 280, 697
Swimbladder
absence of, 266, 267
definition, 265
effect of far-field pressure waves, 266, 269
effect of vibriosis, 480
exhibition of, 565
exophiala disease, 505
far-field detection and, 685
gas-bubble trauma, 516
sound localization, 687
sound production, 267, 268
Swinging disease (see Ichthyophonus disease)
Symbiosis
cleaning associations, 309, 310, 312
definition, 303
feeding associations, 312
protective associations, 304, 306
refuge associations, 306–309
Synbranchus marmoratus (see Swamp-eel)
Syndrome, 486
Syngnathidae (see Pipefishes)
Syngnathus louisianae (see Chain pipefish)
Synthroid®, 519
Syringodium filiforme, 332
Systemic infections (also see Septicemias)
assimilation of chemotherapeutic agents and, 755
bacterial infections, 459
definition, 448
efficacy of disinfectants, 472
fin rot, 488
fungal infections, 459
Systemic infestations
Ichthyophonus, 503, 504

Table salt (see Sodium chloride)
Tail rot (see Fin rot)
Tang turbellarian (also see *Paravortex* spp.), 507, 508
Tang turbellarian disease
clinical signs and pathological effects, 508
distribution, 505, 785
epizootiology, 507, 508
etiology, 505
prophylaxis and treatment, 508, 509
synonyms, 505
taxonomic status, 785
Tap water
artificial seawaters and, 48, 49, 605
diluent for brine shrimp hatch solutions, 406
for backwash, 184
in brine making, 52, 396, 413
per os administration of iodine, 519
survival of *Amyloodinium ocellatum*, 776
use in quarantine procedures, 474
use in surge action exhibits, 583
Tars, 101
Taskmaster®, 170, 171
Taste buds, 759
Taumelkrankheit (see Ichthyophonus disease)
Taylor bubbles (see Gas slugs)
Technical-grade salts, 48
Teeth
amyloodinium disease, 489
sound production by, 267
Teflon®, 195, 198, 633, 747
Teleology, 697, 698
Teleosts (also see Fishes)
ammonia excretion, 230, 649–652
definition, 201
effect of oxygen on acid-base balance, 660, 661
electroreception, 270, 689
fitness and, 301, 303
labyrinth, 263
localization, 261, 268, 269
ostariophysans, 266
protogyny, 712

Teleosts *(Continued)*
sound detection, 258
sound localization, 687
sound production, 267, 268
thyroid structure, 789, 791
water turnover, 648
Temperature
absolute, 538
as a stress factor, 229, 454, 456, 492, 672
brine shrimp tolerance to, 392
color and, 538, 539, 541, 542, 555, 568, 571
control, 136, 168, 169, 195–199
correction for specific gravity, 30
determination, 24–26
effect of pressure, 257
effect on acid-base balance, 214–217
effect on activated carbon adsorption, 629
effect on adsorption efficiency, 104
effect on ammonia determination, 111, 115
effect on ammonia toxicity, 635, 636
effect on ammonium ion dissociation, 117, 119, 121, 122, 635
effect on *Amyloodinium ocellatum* life cycle, 491, 492, 776, 777
effect on ascorbic acid loss from feeds, 735
effect on assimilation of chemotherapeutic agents, 460
effect on backwash rate, 183, 184
effect on bacterial growth, 764
effect on blood pH, 213, 214, 658, 659
effect on brine shrimp cysts, 394, 396, 406
effect on calcium carbonate solubility, 16
effect on carbon dioxide, 210
effect on color, 794
effect on copper chemistry, 469
effect on copper toxicity, 758
effect on coral growth, 326
effect on *Cryptocaryon irritans* life cycle, 494–496, 780, 781
effect on dietary protein, 387
effect on diffusion, 203
effect on digestion rate, 371
effect on density, 7
effect on energy requirements, 373
effect on equilibrium constants, 589
effect on feeds, 391
effect on foam stability, 166
effect on hemoglobin oxygen affinity, 662
effect on infections, 451
effect on ligands, 747
effect on lipids, 364
effect on molecular activity, 629
effect on monogenean development, 511
effect on mycobacteriosis, 764
effect on nitrification, 81, 626
effect on nitrogen cycling, 84
effect on nutrient requirements, 357
effect on orthophosphate determination, 110
effect on oxygen, 210
effect on oxygen diffusion into water, 642
effect on partial pressure of gases, 150
effect on pH, 658
effect on pH adjustments, 45
effect on pH determinations, 37–41
effect on phytoplankton growth, 418, 420, 430, 438
effect on rate of precipitation, 590
effect on refractive index of water, 530
effect on rotifer cultures, 740
effect on rotifer size, 398
effect on salinity, 6
effect on salinity determinations, 26
effect on seaweeds, 78
effect on solubility of gases, 151
effect on sound velocity, 257
effect on specific gravity, 9, 52
effect on specific ion electrodes, 117
effect on standard metabolism, 373, 374
effect on survival of brine shrimp nauplii, 739
effect on *Uronema marinum* life cycle, 497
for breeding brine shrimp, 417
for rearing brine shrimp, 414, 415, 417
in activated carbon manufacture, 100–102
in defining calorie, 372
in defining specific gravity, 601
in denitrification, 78
in dissimilation, 75
in feed manufacture, 383
in mixing artificial seawaters, 48, 49
manipulation for treatment of cryptocaryoniasis, 496, 781
predisposing factor in mycobacteriosis, 477
requirements for phytoplankton culture, 430, 431
requirements of filter bed bacteria, 67
requirements for denitrification, 620
requirements for nitrification, 72, 74, 617, 618
Temporary cytopharynx, 490
Tench
effect of environmental hypoxia, 662
effect of exercise stress, 666
Terminal coloration, 298, 300
Terminal headloss (also see Headloss), 144
Terpenoids, 622
Territorial dominance
aggression and, 707
anemonefishes, 304
as antisocial behavior, 274
definition, 287, 706, 707
dominance hierarchies and, 287–289
dominance reversal, 708
fitness and, 290, 291
food supplies and, 291–293, 295, 709, 710
harems and, 287, 295
historical usage, 706–708
individual, 289
pair, 289
reproduction and, 293, 295
shelter space requirements and, 353
Territories
damselfishes, 287, 709, 710
defense, 267, 287, 707–711, 716
definition, 287, 706–708
exclusive use, 707, 708
occupation, 289
optimal size, 295, 298, 711
sea anemones as, 304, 714, 715
site attachment, 708
social dominance, 707, 708
Tertiary stress responses
definition, 227
conceptual history, 664
Testes, 478
Tetracycline, 778
Tetracycline hydrochloride
efficacy of formulated products, 755
Tetrahymena corlissi, 498
Tetraiodothyronine, T_4 (see Thyroxine)
Tetraodontidae (see Puffers)
Tetrapturus audax (see Striped marlin)
Thalassia testidinum, 332
Thalassiosira weissflogii
uptake and assimilation of iron, 748, 749
Thalassoma bifasciatum (see Bluehead wrasse)
Therapeutic concentrations, 459, 755
Thermal stress (shock)
as an environmental factor, 227, 229, 230, 456
effect on corticosteroids, 672
effect on the immune response, 768, 769, 772
in treatment of amyloodinium disease, 492
predisposing factor in fin rot, 486, 772, 773
predisposing factor in vibriosis, 480, 768, 769
predisposition to disease and, 454
Thermometers
calibration, 24–26
in refractometers, 32
mixing artificial seawaters and, 49
specific gravity of brines and, 52
Thiamin
function, 366
in GP2 culture solution, 427
phytoplankton requirements, 421
requirements of algae, 751
Thiaminase, 375
Threespine stickleback
as predators, 698, 700
individual distance, 692
treatment for monogenean infestations, 526, 527
vision in schooling, 693
Threespot damselfish

cultivation of algal lawns, 709
exclusion of food competitors, 293
territorial defense, 709, 710
Threonine, 394, 738
Thunnus thynnus (see Bluefin tuna)
Thymallus arcticus (see Arctic grayling)
Thyroid
function, 517
impairment from goiter disease, 516
location, 517
structure, 789, 791
Thyroid hormones
effect of goiter disease, 517, 518, 789, 790
effect of stress factors, 518, 791
function, 517
synthetic, 519
Thyroid hyperplasia (see Goiter disease)
Thyroid stimulating hormone (TSH)
effect on hypertrophy and hyperplasia, 789, 790
function, 517
stress and, 791
Thyronines (see Thyroid hormones)
Thyroxine, T_4
effect of iodine, 789
effect of stress factors, 518, 791
formation, 517
Tidal flow, 278
Tilefishes
substratum for exhibition, 316
Time lags
unconditioned bacteriological filters, 79, 81
nutrient conversion, 94
Tinca tinca (see Tench)
Titanium, 195, 198, 199
Tomites
Amyloodinium ocellatum, 489
Cryptocaryon irritans, 493–496
Tomonts
Amyloodinium ocellatum, 489–491
Cryptocaryon irritans, 493–495
Torpedo californica (see Pacific electric ray)
Torpedo marmorata
water permeability, 648
Tonic electroreceptors, 270, 688
Total ammonia nitrogen
allowable upper limit, 89, 90, 117–122, 634
composition in seawater, 117, 118
definition, 71
determination by indophenol blue, 110–115
determination by specific ion electrode, 115–117
in the environment, 230
pH effect on oxidation, 74
ratio to free ammonia nitrogen, 71
toxicity, 210, 535, 536
water quality criteria and, 117
Total CO_2, 11, 12
Total gas pressure, 151
Total lift, 159
Total organic carbon (TOC)
humus fraction, 59
in seawater, 58
oxidation by ozone, 628, 629
removal by activated carbon, 100, 104, 630
Total protein (also see Proteins)
chitin and, 384, 385
requirements for, 360
Toxicants
addition to stored seawater samples, 633
as stress factors, 227, 229, 664
secretions of argulids, 514
Toxicity
acid as net H^+, 210
affecting nitrification, 81
ammonia, 54, 62, 71, 117, 118, 210, 230, 398, 424, 428, 604, 609, 635, 636, 673, 674, 740, 751
bioassay and, 586
carbon sources in columnar denitrification, 95
chemotherapeutic agents to hosts, 520
chemotherapeutic agents to pathogenic bacteria, 461
chlorine-produced oxidants, 469, 757, 758
copper, 195, 423, 469, 750, 758, 759
disinfectants, 472
dissolved organic carbon, 608
humus, 608
hydrated aluminum sulfate, 143
nitrate ions, 62, 78
nitrite ions, 62, 609, 610
nitrogen, 54, 71, 95, 615
nutrient elements, 54
methanol, 95
organic acids, 228
ozone-produced oxidants, 468, 469, 757, 758
phenols, 59
polyelectrolytes, 143, 640, 641
polyester resin pigments, 580, 581
reactivated activated carbon, 630, 631
sulfide ions, 70, 71, 615
Trachinotus carolinus (see Florida pompano)
Trachurus mediterraneus ponticus (see Horse mackerel)
Trachurus symmetricus (see Jack mackerel)
Transamination, 62
Transducer, 265, 266
Transepithelial potential (TEP), 269, 654–656
Transmissometers, 639, 640
Transport fluid, 137
Transport stress, 224, 227–229, 791
Trapezia cymodoce, 308, 309
Treatment regimes, 458
Trichlorfon, 512, 514, 524
Trichogaster leeri (see Pearl gourami)
Trickling filters, 53
Trigla lyra, 661
Triiodothyronine (T_3)
effect of stress factors, 518, 791
formation, 517
Trimethylamine oxide, 206
Tris buffer (Trizma®), 747
Trisodium phosphate, 170
Trophonts
Amyloodinium ocellatum, 489–492
Cryptocaryon irritans, 493–496
Trumpetfish
cryptic coloration, 254
feeding associations, 312, 719
"riding" behavior, 719
TSH releasing hormone, 517
Tuberous electroreceptors, 270, 688
Tubeworm holes, 347
Tumors (see Neoplasms)
Tunas
as schooling predators, 699
cooperating hunting, 284
Tunaxanthin, 370
Tungsten lamps, 546, 568, 571
Tunicates, 689
Turbellarians (also see Tang turbellarian), 505
Turbidity (also see Particulate organic carbon)
causes, 44, 638
determination, 638–640
in exhibits, 537
in seawater supplies, 136, 147, 175
removal by granular media filtration, 137
Turbot
chain elongation of fatty acids, 731
treatment for vibriosis, 523, 524
vaccination against vibriosis, 771
Turbulence
air bubbles and, 154
detection by fishes, 695
effect on oxygen transfer, 156
from amyloodinium disease, 491
in airlift pumps, 162
in foam fractionators, 192, 195, 646
Turbulent flow degassing, 185
Twilight
crepuscular predation and, 242–246
definition, 234
fish behavior, 679, 680
in exhibits, 272
light spectrum, 242, 678
scotopic visual pigments and, 242

Udotea spp., 622
Ulcer disease (see Vibriosis)
Ulcers
definition, 453
exophiala disease, 505
ichthyophonus disease, 504
uronema disease, 497
vibriosis, 480, 481
Ultraviolet (UV) irradiation
definition, 461
effectiveness, 463, 755, 756
efficacy against vibriosis, 768
Ultraviolet (UV) lamps
in total ammonia nitrogen determination, 113, 114
in UV sterilizers, 462
ozone generation by, 466

Ultraviolet (UV) light
as magnetic waves, 529
effect of particulate organic carbon, 535
emission by incandescent lamps, 539
fluorescent lamps, 794
in UV sterilizers, 461
opaqueness of water to, 533
Ultraviolet (UV) radiation
as a point contact sterilizing agent, 461, 467
for sterilizing plastic carboys, 425
generation by ozone, 466
Ultraviolet (UV) sterilizers
description, 461, 462
epizootics and, 463
factors affecting efficacy, 463, 465
lethal mechanisms, 462
Ulva spp., 621
Uncharacterized fraction (see Humus)
Underdrains
backwash and, 177, 178
coarse sand filters, 148
definition, 145
for air scour, 146
functions, 145
Leopold filter bottom, 177, 644
pipe lateral, 177, 178, 644
Wheeler filter bottom, 177, 178, 644
Unsaturated fatty acids
chain elongation, 364, 388
definition, 362
in vegetable oils, 388
melting point, 364
Undersaturation (also see Supersaturation)
definition, 16
effect on solubility of carbonate minerals, 598
gases, 136, 151
of calcium carbonate, 16, 17
Undersea photography
cameras, 548–550, 572
electronic strobes, 548–552, 555, 572, 573
photographic filters and, 545
procedure, 572–574
watertight housings, 548, 550, 552–555, 572
Uniformity coefficients, 175–177
Uptake, 620
Urea
as a goitrogen, 518, 790
as a nitrogen source for phytoplankton, 751
as energy, 373
assimilation by phytoplankton, 423, 751
effect on alkalinity and pH, 429, 751
effect on osmotic pressure, 206
from nitrogen metabolism, 67
hydrolyzing by *Vibrio*, 770
in GP2 culture solution, 423, 427
removal by seaweed filters, 78
toxic ammonia reactions, 428
uptake by seaweeds, 621
Uric acid
from nitrogen metabolism, 67
Urinary bladder
uronema disease, 497
Urine
ion excretion, 205, 657
mycobacteriosis transmission, 476
organic carbon in, 58
Urogenital openings
monogenean infestations, 509
Uronema disease (also see *Uronema marinum*)
clinical signs and pathological effects, 497, 498
epizootiology, 497
etiology, 496, 497
prophylaxis and treatment, 498
synonyms, 496
Uronema marinum, 496
Urophycis chuss (see Red hake)
Utricular otolith, 264
Utriculus, 264

Vaccines
disease prevention and, 472
vibriosis, 484, 771
Vacuum
electromagnetic waves in, 528
in incandescent lamps, 539
speed of light, 792
Vacuum degassers
design, 187, 188
gas supersaturation and, 149
Vacuum filters
decision to use, 174
definition, 137
design, 169
underdrains, 177, 178
Value (also see Brightness)
chromaticity and, 538
definition, 531
fiberglass-reinforced plastic decorations and, 579
in vitro fish photography and, 571
paints, 542–544
paint selection and, 563
species label photography and, 568
Valves, 49, 52
van Bergeijk's acoustic modality model, 263, 684, 685
Vancouver Public Aquarium, 582
Vasculitis
vibriosis, 481, 770
Vaterite, 14
Vegetable oils
unsaturated fatty acids in, 388
Velvet disease (see Amyloodinium disease)
Ventilation, 202
Ventilation rate
control, 211
effect of environmental hyperoxia, 218, 220, 221
effect of environmental hypoxia, 221
Ventilatory convection, 661
Vertebrae
copper deposition, 759
Vertebral column
uronema disease, 497
Vertical zonation (see Zonation)
Vibrations
definition, 257
in aquariums, 682
in definition of sound, 256
in model sound production, 259
in sound production, 257, 528
swimbladder and, 265
Vibrio disease (see Vibriosis)
Vibriosis
clinical signs and pathological effects, 480–482, 768–770
epizootiology, 480, 766–769
etiology, 479, 480, 766
handling stress as a predisposing factor, 771
hemolytic toxins, 769
history, 765
prophylaxis and treatment, 482–484, 771
salinity stress as a predisposing factor, 771
synonyms, 479
zoonosis, 484, 486, 766
Vibrio alginolyticus
as a fish pathogen, 480, 767
as a human pathogen, 484
Vibrio anguillarum
as a fish pathogen, 480, 765–771
dissimilation by, 619
exotoxins, 769
halquinol treatment, 523
optimal *in vitro* temperature, 768
oxolinic acid treatment, 523, 524
piromidic acid treatment, 522
vaccines, 484, 771
Vibrio carchariae
as a fish pathogen, 480, 767, 770
hydrolyzing of urea, 770
lemon sharks, 483
vasculitis and, 770
Vibrio cholerae
as a fish pathogen, 480, 766
human cholera, 484
Vibrio damsela
as a fish pathogen, 480, 767
cytotoxins, 770
hemolytic toxins, 770
hydrolyzing of urea, 770
resistance to, 770
Vibrio fluviales
as a human pathogen, 484, 767
Vibrio furnissii
as a fish pathogen, 480, 767
Vibrio harveyi
as a fish pathogen, 480, 766, 767
Vibrio metschnikovii
as a human pathogen, 484
Vibrio ordalii
as a fish pathogen, 480, 767, 770
leukocytolytic factor, 770
Vibrio parahaemolyticus
as a human pathogen, 484, 766, 767
Vibrio salmonicida
history of nomenclature, 767
Vibrio splendidus
as a fish pathogen, 480, 766
Vibrio vulnificus
as a fish pathogen, 480
as a human pathogen, 484
Vibrio spp.
description, 479
erythrocytolytic and leukocytolytic factors, 481
fin rot, 486, 488, 772, 773

fish commensals, 479, 480, 484, 766
host specificity, 479
invertebrate commensals, 479
on commercial brine shrimp cysts, 743
secondary infections in tang turbellarian disease, 508
sharks, 767
taxonomy, 767
toxins, 769, 770
virulence, 766
Vinyl coatings, 195
Virulence, 446
Viruses
as microorganisms, 447
effect of the cellular immune response, 450
effect of the humoral immune response, 450
natural resistance and, 448, 449
Viscosity
backwash water, 183
definition, 735
foam, 166
seawater, 167
water, 629
Visible spectrum (also see Color spectrum)
definition, 529
effect of attenuation, 675
effect of water depth, 533
incandescent lamps, 539, 794
in exhibits, 538
photosynthetic pigments and, 98
Visual acuity
color vision and, 676, 679
definition, 232
effect of visual cells, 236
in fish schools, 694
in the ocean, 236–241
photosensitivity and, 238
predation and, 272, 283
rhodopsins, 680
schooling and, 277
wrasses, 680
Visual cells, 235, 236
Visual pigments
at twilight, 245, 246
effect of photons, 675
in rods and cones, 237, 239, 678
matched, 237, 238, 240, 241, 244, 677, 678
mismatched, 675
offset, 238-241, 676–678
photolabile, 237
spectral characteristics, 237
Visual purple (see Rhodopsins)
Vitamin B_1 (see Thiamin)
Vitamin C (see Ascorbic acid)
Vitamin deficiencies, 288
Vitamins
addition to moist feeds, 388–400, 403
definition, 366
essential, 366, 388
for rearing brine shrimp, 414
in culture solutions, 422
in protoplasm, 359, 360
leaching from feeds, 390
lipid soluble, 366
physiological fuel value, 373
release by seaweeds, 78
requirements of algae, 421
water soluble, 366, 390
Void fraction
backwash rate and, 145
definition, 87, 143, 641
dual *vs.* multimedia, 644
effect of backwash, 181
filtration rate and, 144
fluidization and, 144
in exhibits, 315
in intermixed filtrant zones, 181
of gravel, 90
of plastic packing, 90
of sand, 89
Vitreous humor, 233

Walleye
lymphocystis disease, 762
Wardley's Aqua Tonic, 778
Warm-blooded animals
maintenance of blood pH, 213
maintenance of body temperature, 373
regulation of acid-base balance, 214
Wastewater
activated carbon treatment, 629, 630
biological films, 68, 69
biological enhancement of activated carbons, 620
denitrification, 94, 95, 620
determination of turbidity, 639
dissolved organic carbon, 75
effect of ozonation on total organic carbon, 628, 629
flocculation, 143
granular activated carbon and, 104
nitrate ion removal from, 75
nitrification, 75
steel pressure filters and, 171
treatment by UV irradiation, 755
Wasting disease (see Mycobacteriosis)
Water (also see Freshwaters, Pure water)
ammonium ion dissociation, 117
as an elastic medium, 256, 259
as a solvent, 2
assimilation by secondary lamellae, 211
carbon dioxide, 210
coloration, 541
compressibility, 257–259, 265
denitrification, 619
density, 232–234, 532
depth effect on light absorption, 533, 534, 541
disease transmission, 480, 764, 767, 768
effect of temperature on, 7
excretion by secondary lamellae, 211
excretion of gases to, 213
flow through the gills, 212
gases at equilibrium, 210
in dry feeds, 377
in ionic and osmotic regulation, 205–209
in moist feeds, 377
in protoplasm, 358
in seawater, 2, 590
in the Solvay process, 605
light absorption, 542
molecules of, 7
optical properties, 237
oxygen deficient, 212
physiological permeability to, 228
refractive index, 559–561
residence time between secondary lamellae, 211, 212
sound velocity in, 257
vapor pressure, 150
viscosity, 629
Water changes
for ammonia dilution, 119, 121
of closed systems, 94
Water flea
effect of conspicuousness on predation, 698
location within the school, 703
survival effect of schooling, 700
Water stops, 170
Water traps, 432
Wavelength
absorption and transmission, 531
color and, 530
definition, 529
effect of water depth, 533
energy, 537
radiant energy and, 529
Waves, 528
Waxes
as feed encapsulating agents, 391
as lipids, 362
in bacteria, 763
Weberian ossicles, 266
Well points, 147
Wescodyne®
sterilizing of pipettes, 435
sterilizing of work surfaces, 439
Wheat, 384
Wheeler filter bottom, 177, 178, 644
Whey, 384
Whirling disease (see Ichthyophonus disease)
White blood cells (see Leukocytes)
White grunt
diel movements, 281, 282, 697
White light
iridosomes and, 249
White shark
vibriosis, 767
White-spot disease (see Cryptocaryoniasis)
Winter flounder
effect of environmental hypoxia, 662
vibriosis, 768, 769
Worms, 447, 455
Wrasses
association with sea anemones, 306
lekking, 290
mating systems, 295
predation on, 272
protogyny, 298, 303, 712
substratum for exhibition, 316
visual pigments, 246, 680

Xanthophores, 247
Xanthosomes, 247
Xenon, 552
X-ray diffraction, 606, 746
X-rays, 529

Yeasts
  as microorganisms, 447
  Baker's, 737
  caked, 741
  powdered as foods, 418
Yellow goatfish
  in feeding associations, 312
Yellowhead jawfish
  burrows, 720
  goiter disease, 791
Yellow humus (see Humus)
Yellow perch
  mycobacteriosis, 764
Yellow substance (see Humus)
Yellowtail
  carbohydrate tolerance, 731
  effect of exercise stress, 667, 672
  treatment for pseudotuberculosis, 521
  treatment for *Streptococcus* infections, 521
Yellowtail damselfish, 291
Yellow tang
  tang turbellarian disease, 507, 508

Zeaxanthin
  carotenoid metabolism and, 370
  occurrence in fishes, 370, 371
Zebrasoma flavescens (see Yellow tang)
Zinc
  displacement by copper, 759
  in cathodic protection, 171–174
Zinc chloride
  in activated carbon manufacture, 100
Zonation
  biotopes and, 334, 341, 343
  description, 326, 328–331
  habitats and, 343
  hard corals, 328
  use by fishes, 323, 334
Zooplankton
  as foods, 374, 430, 697
  as prey, 703
  digestibility of, 371
  fatty acids, 364
  inoculation of phytoplankton cultures, 442
  loss of proteolytic enzymes, 738
  phosphorus cycling and, 56

Credits

Chapter 1

Tables: **1-1**—Bidwell J. P., S. Spotte, Artificial seawaters: formulas and methods. Table 1, p. 7, 8. Boston: Jones and Bartlett Publishers, 1985. **1-3**—Auburn University. **1-4, 1-9**—Reprinted by permission of Wiley-Interscience, a division of John Wiley and Sons, Inc. **1-5**—Classification of sedimentary carbonate rocks, H. J. Bissel, G. V. Chilingar *in* Carbonate rocks: origin, occurrence and classification, G. V. Chilingar (ed.). Reprinted by permission of Elsevier Science Publishers Ltd., Copyright 1967. **1-8**—Reprinted from Amer. Lab., 17 (9): 124–133, 1985. Copyright 1985 by International Scientific Communications, Inc. **1-10, 1-11**—Reprinted by permission of Wiley-Liss, a division of John Wiley and Sons, Inc.

Figures: **1-5**—Anikouchine/Sternberg, The world ocean: an introduction to oceanography, 2nd ed., © 1981, pp. 96, 145, 146. Reprinted by permission of Prentice-Hall, Inc., Englewood Cliffs, N.J. **1-6**—Reprinted from C. C. Wescott, pH measurements. Academic Press, Inc., copyright 1978. **1-7**—R. G. C. Bathurst, Carbonate sediments and their diagenesis. Reprinted by permission of Elsevier Science Publishers Ltd., copyright 1971. **1-8, 1-9, 1-10, 1-11, 1-14, 1-30, 1-31**—Reprinted by permission of Wiley-Interscience, a division of John Wiley and Sons, Inc. **1-13**—Reprinted by permission of the Society of Economic Paleontologists and Mineralogists. **1-14**—Reprinted with permission from Geochemica Cosmochimica Acta, Volume 34, R. A. Berner, The role of magnesium in the crystal growth of calcite and aragonite from sea water, copyright 1975, Pergamon Press, Ltd. **1-15, 1-17, 1-29**—American Journal of Science, R. Wollast, R. M. Garrels, F. T. Mackenzie, reprinted by permission of American Journal of Science, 1980. **1-19**—G. Adams, S. Spotte, Aquacult. Eng'g. 4: 305–311. Reprinted by permission of Elsevier Science Publishers Ltd., copyright 1985. **1-20**—C. E. Bower, D. T. Turner, S. Spotte, Aquaculture 23: 211–217, Reprinted by permission of Elsevier Science Publishers Ltd., copyright 1981. **1-27**—Reprinted from Amer. Lab., 17 (9): 124, 1985. Copyright 1985 by International Scientific Communications, Inc.

Chapter 2

Tables: **2-2**—Walter de Gruyter Publishers, Science Division, Genthiner Strasse 13, D-1000 Berlin 30, Federal Republic of Germany. **2-7**—Reprinted by permission of Wiley-Interscience, a division of John Wiley and Sons, Inc. **2-12**—Reprinted from Journal AWWA, Vol. 70, No. 11 (November 1978), by permission. Copyright 1978, American Water Works Association. **2-13, 2-14, 2-15, 2-16**—From C. E. Bower and J. P. Bidwell. 1978. J. Fish. Res. Board Can. 35: 1012–1016, Tables 2-6.

Figures: **2-2, 2-3, 2-4, 2-5, 2-10, 2-15, 2-22, 2-23, 2-27**—Reprinted by permission of Wiley-Interscience, a division of John Wiley and Sons, Inc. **2-8**—Thomas D. Brock, Biology of microorganisms, © 1970, p. 133. Reprinted by permission of Prentice Hall, Inc., Englewood Cliffs, New Jersey. **2-11**—Reprinted from J. Water Pollut. Contr. Fed. 48: 9–24, © 1976 WPCF. **2-12**—Reprinted from J. Water Pollut. Contr. Fed. 45: 2302–2320, © 1973 WPCF. **2-13, 2-17**—Reprinted from J. Water Pollut. Contr. Fed. 48: 835–852, © 1976 WPCF. **2-14**—Reprinted with permission from Water Res. Vol. 18, A. V. Quinlan, Prediction of the optimum pH for ammonia-N oxidation by *Nitrosomonas europaea* in well-aerated natural and domestic-waste waters, copyright 1984, Pergamon Press PLC. **2-18**—C. E. Bower, D. T. Turner, Aquaculture 24: 1-9. Reprinted by permission of Elsevier Applied Science Publishers, Ltd., copyright 1981. **2-25**—Reprinted with permission from p. 103 of Bulletin de l'Institut oceanographique special issue No. 5, 1989. **2-28**—Reprinted with permission from Environ. Sci. Technol. 22: 292–298, D. Grosjean, P. M. Whitmore, G. R. Cass, J. R. Druzik. Copyright 1988 American Chemical Society, 1155 16th St., N.W., Washington, D.C. 20036. **2-33, 2-34, 2-35, 2-36**—S. Spotte, G. Adams, Aquacult. Eng'g. 3: 207–220. Reprinted by permission of Elsevier Applied Science Publishers Ltd., copyright 1984. **2-39, 2-40**—Reprinted from J. Water Pollut. Contr. Fed. 45: 905–912, © 1973 WPCF.

Chapter 3

Tables: **3-7, 3-8, 3-12, 3-13, 3-14**—Reprinted by permission of Wiley-Interscience, a division of John Wiley and Sons, Inc.

Figures: **3-6, 3-7**—Reprinted with permission from J. P. Herzig, M. M. Leclerc, and P. Le Goff (1970). Copyright 1970 American Chemical Society, 1155 16th St., N.W., Washington, D.C. 20036. **3-8, 3-24a, 3-25, 3-32, 3-33, 3-35, 3-48, 3-53**—Reprinted by permission of Wiley-Interscience, a division of John Wiley and Sons, Inc. **3-9**—Reprinted from G. Tchobanoglous, J. Water Pollut. Contr. Fed. 42: 604–623, © 1970 WPCF. **3-11**—G. Tchobanoglous, E. D. Schroeder, © 1985 by Addison-Wesley Publishing Company. Reprinted by permission of Addison-Wesley Publishing Co., Inc. Reading, MA. **3-12**—P. Scholes. 1980. The sea-water well system at the fisheries laboratory, Lowestoft and the methods in use for keeping marine fish. J. Mar. Biol. Assoc. U.K. 60: 215–225. Cambridge University Press, copyright 1980. **3-15**—J. Colt, Aquacult. Eng'g 5: 49–85. Reprinted by permission of Elsevier Science Publishers Ltd., copyright 1986. **3-16**—Reprinted from D. R. Kester *in* Chemical oceanography, Vol. 1, J. P. Riley, G. Skirrow (eds.). Academic Press, Inc., copyright 1975. **3-17**—Environmental systems engineering, L. G. Rich. Reprinted by permission from McGraw-Hill Book Company, copyright 1973. **3-22**—Reprinted from J. Water Pollut. Contr. Fed. 52: 2315–2326, © 1980 WPCF. **3-26, 3-27, 3-28, 3-29**—D. J. Reinemann, M. B. Timmons, Aquacult. Eng'g. 8: 29–46. Reprinted by permission of Elsevier Science Publishers Ltd., copyright 1989. **3-31**—Reproduced from Water & Sewage Works 122(6): 48–55, 1975. **3-41, 3-42**—Reprinted from J. Am. Water Works Assoc., Vol. 67, No. 10 (October 1975), by permission. Copyright 1975, American Water Works Association. **3-45**—G. R. Bouck, R. E. King, G. Bouck-Schmidt, Aquacult. Eng'g 3: 159–176. Reprinted by permission of Elsevier Science Publishers Ltd., copyright 1984. **3-46**—Reprinted with permission from Ocean Eng'g., Vol. 17, A. C. Caolo, S. Spotte. Design of a rapid-flow seawater supply system for the University of Connecticut's marine laboratory at Noank, copyright 1990. **3-4**—J. T. Fuss, Aquacult. Eng'g. 2: 301–307. Reprinted by permission of Elsevier Science Publishers Ltd., copyright 1983. **3-51**—F. Sebba, Ion Flotation. Reprinted by permission of Elsevier Science Publishers Ltd., copyright 1962.

Chapter 4

Figures: **4-3, 4-10**—The Company of Biologists Ltd., Dept. of Zoology, Downing Street, Cambridge CB2 3EJ. **4-4**—From Zoology by E. Lendell Cockrum and William J. McCauley. Copyright © 1965 by W. B. Saunders Co. Reprinted by permission of W. B. Saunders, CBS College Publishing. **4-5**—Thomas D. Brock, Biology of microorganisms. © 1970, p. 151. Reprinted by permission of Prentice-Hall, Inc., Englewood Cliffs, N.J. **4-6**—Adapted from Vertebrate physiology by William J. McCauley. Copyright © 1971 by W. B. Saunders Company. Reprinted by permission of Holt, Rinehart and Winston, CBS College Publishing. **4-7, 4-8**—D. H. Evans, *in* Gills, D. F. Houlihan, J. C. Rankin, T. J. Shuttleworth (eds.). Cambridge University Press, copyright 1982. **4-9**—Am. J. Physiol. Reprinted by permission of the American Physiological Society. **4-12, 4-13, 4-14, 4-15, 4-20**—N. Heisler, Respir. Physiol. 41: 13–18. Reprinted by permission of Plenum Publishing Corp., copyright 1978. **4-16**—J-P. Truchot, A. Toulmond, P. Dejours, Respir. Physiol. 41: 31-28. Reprinted by permission of Elsevier Science Publishers Ltd., copyright 1980. **4-17**—P. Dejours *in* Claude Bernard and the internal environment, E. D. Robin (ed.), Marcel Dekker, Inc., N. Y. Reprinted by courtesy of Marcel Dekker, Inc. **4-18**—Striped marlin curve reprinted with permission from Comp. Biochem. Physiol. 81A, R. M. G. Wells, P. S. Davie, Oxygen binding by the blood and hematological effects of capture stress in two big gamefish: mako shark and striped marlin, copyright 1985, Pergamon Press PLC. **4-21**—K. B. Davis and N. C. Parker, Aquaculture 32: 189–194. Reprinted by permission of Elsevier Science Publishers Ltd., copyright 1983.

Chapter 5

Figures: **5-1**—Courtesy of Oceanus magazine, © 1980 by Woods Hole Oceanographic Institution; Cranbrook Institute of Science. **5-3**—From Biology by Ebert, Loewy, Miller and Scheiderman. Copyright © 1973 by Holt, Rinehart and Winston, Inc. Reprinted by permission of CBS College Publishing. **5-7**—Courtesy of Oceanus magazine, © 1980 by Woods Hole Oceanographic Institution. **5-8**—F. W. Munz and W. N. McFarland *in* Handbook of sensory physiology, Vol. VII/5, F. Crescitelli (ed.). Reprinted by permission of Springer-Verlag, copyright 1977. **5-9, 5-10**—Reprinted with permission from Vis. Res., Vol. 15, W. N. McFarland and F. W. Munz, The evolution of photopic visual pigments in fishes, Part III, copyright 1975, Pergamon Press, Ltd. **5-13**—Reprinted with permission from Vis. Res., Vol. 15, F. W. Munz and W. N. McFarland, The significance of spectral position in the rhodopsins of tropical marine fishes, copyright 1973, Pergamon Press plc. **5-14**—From E. O. Wilson et al., Life on earth (1978). **5-16, 5-19**—From Reflectors in fishes, E. Denton. Copyright © 1971 by Scientific American, Inc. All rights reserved. **5-24, 5-26**—Reprinted from W. A. van Bergeijk *in* Marine bioacoustics, W. N. Tavolga (ed.). Copyright 1975, Pergamon Press, Ltd. Also reprinted from W. A. van Bergeijk *in* Contributions to sensory physiology, Vol. 2, W. D. Neff (ed.). Academic Press, Inc., copyright 1967. **5-28**—Reprinted from W. A. van Bergeijk *in* Contributions to sensory physiology, Vol. 2, W. D. Neff (ed.). Academic Press, Inc., copyright 1967. **5-29**—Reprinted by permission of J. Acoust. Soc. Am.: 53: 1515–1529, copyright 1973. **5-31**—J. T. Corwin *in* Hearing and sound communication in fishes, W. N. Tavolga, A. N. Popper, R. R. Fay (eds.). Reprinted by permission of Springer-Verlag, copyright 1981. **5-32**—K. von Frisch. Z. Vergl. Physiol. 17: 703–747. Reprinted by permission of Springer-Verlag, copyright 1938. **5-33**—T. Szabo in Handbook of sensory physiology, III/3, A. Fessard (ed.). Reprinted by permission of Springer-Verlag, copyright 1974. **5-34**—S. Dijkgraaf, Z. Vergl. Physiol. 47: 438–456. Reprinted by permission of Springer-Verlag, copyright 1963.

Chapter 6

Figures: **6-11**—Reprinted by permission of the Zoological Society of London. **6-21**—B. B. Lassig. Mar. Biol. 42: 82–85. Reprinted by permission of Springer-Verlag, copyright 1977.

Chapter 7

Figures: **7-5**—Figure 6-3 from Invertebrate zoology, fifth edition, by Robert D. Barnes and J & R Technical Services, copyright © 1987 by Saunders College Publishing, a division of Holt, Rinehart and Winston, Inc., reprinted by permission of the publisher. **7-8**—Reprinted by permission of Wiley-Interscience, a division of John Wiley and Sons, Inc. **7-17**—F. H. Talbot, Proc. Zool. Soc. London 145: 431–470. Reprinted by permission, copyright 1965. **7-20**—R. D. Clarke. Mar. Biol. 40: 277–289. Reprinted by permission of Springer-Verlag, copyright 1977. **7-21**—D. A. Thomson and C. E. Lehner. J. Mar. Biol. Ecol. 22: 1-29. Reprinted by permission of Elsevier Science Publishers Ltd., copyright 1976.

Chapter 8

Tables: **8-2**—Reprinted from R. P. Wilson *in* Nutrition and feeding in fish, C. B. Cowey, A. M. Mackie, J. G. Bell (eds.). Academic Press, Inc., copyright 1985. **8-4**—Reprinted from A. Kanazawa *in* Nutrition and feeding in fish, C. B. Cowey, A. M. Mackie, J. G. Bell (eds.). Copyright 1985, Academic Press, Inc. **8-6, 8-22**—Reprinted from J. E. Halver *in* Fish nutrition, 2nd ed., J. E. Halver (ed.). Copyright 1989, Academic Press, Inc. **8-24, 8-28, 8-29, 8-30, 8-31, 8-33, 8-38, 8-39**—Reprinted by permission of Wiley-Liss, a division of John Wiley and Sons, Inc.

Figures: **8-3, 8-4**—Reprinted from R. W. Hardy *in* Fish nutrition, 2nd ed., J. E. Halver (ed.). Academic Press, Inc., copyright 1989. **8-7**—P. B. Weisz, R. N. Keogh, The science of biology, 5th ed. McGraw-Hill Book Company, copyright 1982. **8-6, 8-9a, 8-10, 8-11, 8-12**—Reprinted by permission of Wiley-Interscience, a division of John Wiley and Sons, Inc. **8-17**—J. Fabregas, J. Abalde, B. Cabezas, C. Herrero, Aquacult. Eng'g. 8: 223-239. Reprinted by permission of Elsevier Science Publishers Ltd., copyright 1989.

Chapter 9

Figures: **9-10, 9-11, 9-32, 9-50, 9-51**—Reprinted by permission of Wiley-Interscience, a division of John Wiley and Sons, Inc. **9-14**—H. M. Rosen, J. Water Pollut. Contr. Fed. 45: 2521-2536. Reprinted by permission, copyright 1973. **9–15**—Reprinted from Water & Sewage Works 122(12): 57–60, 1975. **9-16**—Reprinted from J. Am. Water Works Assoc., Vol. 57, No. 9 (September 1965), by permission, copyright © 1965, American Water Works Association. **9-17**—J. L. Symes, D. R. Kester, Mar. Chem. 16: 189-211. Reprinted by permission of Elsevier Science Publishers Ltd., copyright 1985. **9-18, 9-19**—M. L. Franklin, J. W. Morse, Ocean Sci. Eng'g., Vol. 7, Marcel Dekker, Inc., N. Y., 1982. Reprinted by courtesy of Marcel Dekker, Inc. **9–29**—C. E. Bower, D. T. Turner, R. C. Biever, J. Parasitol. 73: 85–88. Reprinted by permission, copyright 1987. **9–38**—P. J. Cheung, R. F. Nigrelli, G. D. Ruggieri, J. Fish. Dis. 3: 295-303. Reprinted by permission by Blackwell Scientific Publications Inc., copyright 1980.

Chapter 10

Tables: **10–3**—Eastman Kodak Company. **10-4**—Reprinted by permission of Wiley-Interscience, a division of John Wiley and Sons, Inc.

Figures: **10-1**—Fig. 19.5 Types of electromagnetic waves (p. 400) in Technical physics, 3rd Edition by Frederick Bueche, copyright © 1985 by Harper & Row, Publishers, Inc. **10-3, 10-14, 10-19**—Reprinted with permission of The encyclopedia Americana, copyright 1984, Grolier Inc. **10-9**—From Oceanus, Vol. 23, No. 3, page 24. **10-12**—Courtesy of GTE Lighting Products, Danvers, Mass. 01923. **10-16, 10-17, 10-18**—Eastman Kodak Company. **10-20**—Photograph courtesy of Nikon Inc. **10-33, 10-40**—Reprinted from Bull. Inst. Oceanogr., Monaco. Copyright 1960. **10-46, 10-47, 10-48, 10-49, 10-50, 10-52**—Reprinted by permission of Wiley-Interscience, a division of John Wiley and Sons, Inc.